THE LAW OF DISABILITY DISCRIMINATION HANDBOOK

THE LAW OF DISABILITY DISCRIMINATION HANDBOOK

EIGHTH EDITION

RUTH COLKER
Distinguished University Professor and
Heck-Faust Memorial Chair in Constitutional Law
Moritz College of Law
The Ohio State University

PAUL D. GROSSMAN
Adjunct Professor
Hastings College of Law, University of California

CAROLINA ACADEMIC PRESS
Durham, North Carolina

ISBN: 978-0-7698-8203-1 (Print)
ISBN: 978-0-7698-8205-5 (eBook)

Carolina Academic Press
700 Kent Street
Durham, North Carolina 27701
Telephone (919) 489-7486
Fax (919) 493-5668
www.caplaw.com

Printed in the United States of America
2019 Printing

PREFACE

This Handbook includes reference material relevant to interpreting federal law prohibiting discrimination on the basis of disability. The Eighth Edition also includes the recently adopted United Nations Convention on the Rights of Individuals with Disabilities.

The Handbook begins by including reference material relevant to interpreting the Americans with Disabilities Act of 1990 ("the ADA"). Chapter One contains a redlined version of the ADA as amended in 2008. Chapter Two contains the EEOC Regulations to Implement the Equal Employment Provisions of the ADA, and Chapter Three contains the EEOC Section by Section Analysis. Chapter Four contains a redlined version of the ADA Title II regulations and Chapter Five contains the DOJ Title II Section by Section Analysis. Chapter Six contains a redlined version of the ADA Title III regulations and Chapter Seven contains the DOJ Title III Section by Section Analysis. These redlined versions should help the reader understand the impact of the 2008 Amendments.

Chapter Eight contains the DOJ 2010 ADA Standards for Accessible Design.

Chapter Nine contains the statutory language of Section 504 of the Rehabilitation Act. Chapter Ten contains some of the regulations and Section by Section Analysis promulgated by the Department of Education to enforce Section 504.

Chapters Eleven and Twelve contain the Fair Housing Act Amendments of 1988 ("FHAA") and the regulations promulgated by the Department of Housing and Urban Development to enforce the FHAA. Chapter Thirteen contains excerpts from the Civil Rights Act of 1991 which relate to the issue of damages in employment discrimination actions.

Chapter Fourteen contains the Individuals with Disabilities Education Act, including the amendments made as part of the reauthorization in late 2004. Excerpts from the regulations promulgated by the United States Department of Education to enforce the IDEA are also included in Chapter Fifteen.

Finally, the Handbook contains the text of the United Nations Convention on the Rights of Individuals with Disabilities in Chapter Sixteen.

A disk version of this volume will be made available upon request to individuals with disabilities who are unable to utilize the written version.

Ruth Colker
Paul Grossman

September 2013

ACKNOWLEDGMENTS

The Eight Edition of this Handbook was made possible, in part, by generous research assistance support at the Ohio State University Moritz College of Law. I appreciate the effort that Adam Milani made in adding the IDEA to the Fifth Edition of this Handbook. I thank Katherine Hall for her help when she was with the Moritz Law Library in updating the prior Edition with the IDEA regulations and the United Nations Convention of the Rights of Individuals with Disabilities.

SUMMARY OF CONTENTS

TABLE OF CONTENTS

TABLE OF CONTENTS

TABLE OF CONTENTS

Chapter 2   **EEOC REGULATIONS TO IMPLEMENT THE EQUAL EMPLOYMENT PROVISIONS OF THE ADA 69**

Chapter 3   **EEOC SECTION BY SECTION ANALYSIS OF REGULATIONS TO IMPLEMENT THE EQUAL EMPLOYMENT PROVISIONS OF THE ADA 89**

TABLE OF CONTENTS

TABLE OF CONTENTS

TABLE OF CONTENTS

TABLE OF CONTENTS

TABLE OF CONTENTS

Chapter 6   DOJ ADA TITLE III REGULATIONS [Redlined Version] **327**

TABLE OF CONTENTS

TABLE OF CONTENTS

TABLE OF CONTENTS

TABLE OF CONTENTS

TABLE OF CONTENTS

TABLE OF CONTENTS

TABLE OF CONTENTS

TABLE OF CONTENTS

TABLE OF CONTENTS

CHAPTER 3: BUILDING BLOCKS

TABLE OF CONTENTS

CHAPTER 4: ACCESSIBLE ROUTES

TABLE OF CONTENTS

TABLE OF CONTENTS

TABLE OF CONTENTS

TABLE OF CONTENTS

TABLE OF CONTENTS

TABLE OF CONTENTS

TABLE OF CONTENTS

CHAPTER 7: COMMUNICATION ELEMENTS AND FEATURES

TABLE OF CONTENTS

TABLE OF CONTENTS

TABLE OF CONTENTS

TABLE OF CONTENTS

TABLE OF CONTENTS

CHAPTER 10: RECREATION FACILITIES

TABLE OF CONTENTS

TABLE OF CONTENTS

TABLE OF CONTENTS

TABLE OF CONTENTS

TABLE OF CONTENTS

TABLE OF CONTENTS

TABLE OF CONTENTS

TABLE OF CONTENTS

TABLE OF CONTENTS

TABLE OF CONTENTS

TABLE OF CONTENTS

TABLE OF CONTENTS

Chapter 1
AMERICANS WITH DISABILITIES ACT

ADA Amendments Act of 2008, 29 USC § 705 note

(a) Findings. Congress finds that —

(1) in enacting the Americans with Disabilities Act of 1990 (ADA) [42 USC §§ 12101 et seq.], Congress intended that the Act 'provide a clear and comprehensive national mandate for the elimination of discrimination against individuals with disabilities' and provide broad coverage;

(2) in enacting the ADA, Congress recognized that physical and mental disabilities in no way diminish a person's right to fully participate in all aspects of society, but that people with physical or mental disabilities are frequently precluded from doing so because of prejudice, antiquated attitudes, or the failure to remove societal and institutional barriers;

(3) while Congress expected that the definition of disability under the ADA would be interpreted consistently with how courts had applied the definition of a handicapped individual under the Rehabilitation Act of 1973 that expectation has not been fulfilled;

(4) the holdings of the Supreme Court in Sutton v. United Air Lines, Inc., 527 U.S. 471 (1999) and its companion cases have narrowed the broad scope of protection intended to be afforded by the ADA, thus eliminating protection for many individuals whom Congress intended to protect;

(5) the holding of the Supreme Court in Toyota Motor Manufacturing, Kentucky, Inc. v. Williams, 534 U.S. 184 (2002) further narrowed the broad scope of protection intended to be afforded by the ADA;

(6) as a result of these Supreme Court cases, lower courts have incorrectly found in individual cases that people with a range of substantially limiting impairments are not people with disabilities;

(7) in particular, the Supreme Court, in the case of Toyota Motor Manufacturing, Kentucky, Inc. v. Williams, 534 U.S. 184 (2002), interpreted the term

'substantially limits' to require a greater degree of limitation than was intended by Congress; and

(8) Congress finds that the current Equal Employment Opportunity Commission ADA regulations defining the term 'substantially limits' as 'significantly restricted' are inconsistent with congressional intent, by expressing too high a standard.

(b)   Purposes. The purposes of this Act are —

(1) to carry out the ADA's objectives of providing 'a clear and comprehensive national mandate for the elimination of discrimination' and 'clear, strong, consistent, enforceable standards addressing discrimination' by reinstating a broad scope of protection to be available under the ADA;

(2) to reject the requirement enunciated by the Supreme Court in Sutton v. United Air Lines, Inc., 527 U.S. 471 (1999) and its companion cases that whether an impairment substantially limits a major life activity is to be determined with reference to the ameliorative effects of mitigating measures;

(3) to reject the Supreme Court's reasoning in Sutton v. United Air Lines, Inc., 527 U.S. 471 (1999) with regard to coverage under the third prong of the definition of disability and to reinstate the reasoning of the Supreme Court in School Board of Nassau County v. Arline, 480 U.S. 273 (1987) which set forth a broad view of the third prong of the definition of handicap under the Rehabilitation Act of 1973;

(4) to reject the standards enunciated by the Supreme Court in Toyota Motor Manufacturing, Kentucky, Inc. v. Williams, 534 U.S. 184 (2002), that the terms 'substantially' and 'major' in the definition of disability under the ADA 'need to be interpreted strictly to create a demanding standard for qualifying as disabled,' and that to be substantially limited in performing a major life activity under the ADA 'an individual must have an impairment that prevents or severely restricts the individual from doing activities that are of central importance to most people's daily lives';

(5) to convey congressional intent that the standard created by the Supreme Court in the case of Toyota Motor Manufacturing, Kentucky, Inc. v. Williams, 534 U.S. 184 (2002) for 'substantially limits', and applied by lower courts in numerous decisions, has created an inappropriately high level of limitation necessary to obtain coverage under the ADA, to convey that it is the intent of Congress that the primary object of attention in cases brought under the ADA should be whether entities covered under the ADA have complied with their obligations, and to convey that the question of whether an individual's impairment is a disability under the ADA should not demand extensive analysis; and

(6) to express Congress' expectation that the Equal Employment Opportunity Commission will revise that portion of its current regulations that defines the term 'substantially limits' as 'significantly restricted' to be consistent with this Act, including the amendments made by this Act.

TITLE 42   THE PUBLIC HEALTH AND WELFARE
CHAPTER 126   EQUAL OPPORTUNITY FOR INDIVIDUALS WITH DISABILITIES [REDLINED VERSION]

Sec. 12101.   Findings and purpose — *ADAA Amendments*

(a)   Findings

The Congress finds that

(1) ~~some 43,000,000 Americans have one or more physical or mental disabilities, and this number is increasing as the population as a whole is growing older;~~ **physical or mental disabilities in no way diminish a person's right to fully participate in all aspects of society, yet many people with physical or mental disabilities have been precluded from doing so because of discrimination; others who have a record of a disability or are regarded as having a disability also have been subjected to discrimination;** *{ New language*

(2) historically, society has tended to isolate and segregate individuals with disabilities, and, despite some improvements, such forms of discrimination against individuals with disabilities continue to be a serious and pervasive social problem;

(3) discrimination against individuals with disabilities persists in such critical areas as employment, housing, public accommodations, education, transportation, communication, recreation, institutionalization, health services, voting, and access to public services;

(4) unlike individuals who have experienced discrimination on the basis of race, color, sex, national origin, religion, or age, individuals who have experienced discrimination on the basis of disability have often had no legal recourse to redress such discrimination;

(5) individuals with disabilities continually encounter various forms of discrimination, including outright intentional exclusion, the discriminatory effects of architectural, transportation, and communication barriers, overprotective rules and policies, failure to make modifications to existing facilities and practices, exclusionary qualification standards and criteria, segregation, and relegation to lesser services, programs, activities, benefits, jobs, or other opportunities;

(6) census data, national polls, and other studies have documented that people with disabilities, as a group, occupy an inferior status in our society, and are severely disadvantaged socially, vocationally, economically, and educationally;

(7) ~~individuals with disabilities are a discrete and insular minority who have been faced with restrictions and limitations, subjected to a history of purposeful unequal treatment, and relegated to a position of political powerlessness in our society, based on characteristics that are beyond the control of such individuals and resulting from stereotypic assumptions not truly indicative of the individual ability of such individuals to participate in, and contribute to, society;~~

(~~8~~ **7**) the Nation's proper goals regarding individuals with disabilities are to assure equality of opportunity, full participation, independent living, and economic self-sufficiency for such individuals; and

(~~9~~ 8) the continuing existence of unfair and unnecessary discrimination and prejudice denies people with disabilities the opportunity to compete on an equal basis and to pursue those opportunities for which our free society is justifiably famous, and costs the United States billions of dollars in unnecessary expenses resulting from dependency and nonproductivity.

(b)   Purpose

It is the purpose of this chapter

(1) to provide a clear and comprehensive national mandate for the elimination of discrimination against individuals with disabilities;

(2) to provide clear, strong, consistent, enforceable standards addressing discrimination against individuals with disabilities;

(3) to ensure that the Federal Government plays a central role in enforcing the standards established in this chapter on behalf of individuals with disabilities; and

(4) to invoke the sweep of congressional authority, including the power to enforce the fourteenth amendment and to regulate commerce, in order to address the major areas of discrimination faced day-to-day by people with disabilities.

— **Sec. 12101   note: Findings and Purposes of ADA Amendments Act of 2008, Pub. L. 110-325, § 2, Sept. 25, 2008, 122 Stat. 3553, provided that:**

(a)   Findings

Congress finds that —

(1) in enacting the Americans with Disabilities Act of 1990 (ADA), Congress intended that the Act "provide a clear and comprehensive national mandate for the elimination of discrimination against individuals with disabilities" and provide broad coverage;

(2) in enacting the ADA, Congress recognized that physical and mental disabilities in no way diminish a person's right to fully participate in all aspects of society, but that people with physical or mental disabilities are frequently precluded from doing so because of prejudice, antiquated attitudes, or the failure to remove societal and institutional barriers;

(3) while Congress expected that the definition of disability under the ADA would be interpreted consistently with how courts had applied the definition of a handicapped individual under the Rehabilitation Act of 1973, that expectation has not been fulfilled;

(4) the holdings of the Supreme Court in 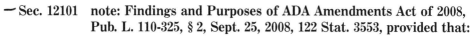Sutton v. United Air Lines, Inc., 527 U.S. 471 (1999) and its companion cases have narrowed the broad scope of protection intended to be afforded by the ADA, thus eliminating protection for many individuals whom Congress intended to protect;

(5) the holding of the Supreme Court in Toyota Motor Manufacturing, Kentucky, Inc. v. Williams, 534 U.S. 184 (2002) further narrowed the broad scope of protection intended to be afforded by the ADA;

(6) as a result of these Supreme Court cases, lower courts have incorrectly found in individual cases that people with a range of substantially limiting impairments are not people with disabilities;

(7) in particular, the Supreme Court, in the case of Toyota Motor Manufacturing, Kentucky, Inc. v. Williams, 534 U.S. 184 (2002), interpreted the term "substantially limits" to require a greater degree of limitation than was intended by Congress; and

(8) Congress finds that the current Equal Employment Opportunity Commission ADA regulations defining the term "substantially limits" as "significantly restricted" are inconsistent with congressional intent, by expressing too high a standard.

(b)   Purposes

The purposes of this Act are —

(1) to carry out the ADA's objectives of providing "a clear and comprehensive national mandate for the elimination of discrimination" and "clear, strong, consistent, enforceable standards addressing discrimination" by reinstating a broad scope of protection to be available under the ADA;

(2) to reject the requirement enunciated by the Supreme Court in Sutton v. United Air Lines, Inc., 527 U.S. 471 (1999) and its companion cases that whether an impairment substantially limits a major life activity is to be determined with reference to the ameliorative effects of mitigating measures;

(3) to reject the Supreme Court's reasoning in Sutton v. United Air Lines, Inc., 527 U.S. 471 (1999) with regard to coverage under the third prong of the definition of disability and to reinstate the reasoning of the Supreme Court in School Board of Nassau County v. Arline, 480 U.S. 273 (1987) which set forth a broad view of the third prong of the definition of handicap under the Rehabilitation Act of 1973;

(4) to reject the standards enunciated by the Supreme Court in Toyota Motor Manufacturing, Kentucky, Inc. v. Williams, 534 U.S. 184 (2002), that the terms "substantially" and "major" in the definition of disability under the ADA "need to be interpreted strictly to create a demanding standard for qualifying as disabled," and that to be substantially limited in performing a major life activity under the ADA "an individual must have an impairment that prevents or severely restricts the individual from doing activities that are of central importance to most people's daily lives";

(5) to convey congressional intent that the standard created by the Supreme Court in the case of Toyota Motor Manufacturing, Kentucky, Inc. v. Williams, 534 U.S. 184 (2002) for "substantially limits", and applied by lower courts in numerous decisions, has created an inappropriately high level of limitation necessary to obtain coverage under the ADA, to convey that it is the intent of Congress that the primary object of attention in cases brought under the ADA should be whether entities covered under the ADA have complied with their obligations, and to convey that the question of

whether an individual's impairment is a disability under the ADA should not demand extensive analysis; and

(6) to express Congress' expectation that the Equal Employment Opportunity Commission will revise that portion of its current regulations that defines the term "substantially limits" as "significantly restricted" to be consistent with this Act, including the amendments made by this Act.

Sec. 12102. ~~Definitions~~ **Definition of disability**

As used in this chapter:

~~(1) Auxiliary aids and services~~

~~The term "auxiliary aids and services" includes~~

~~(A) qualified interpreters or other effective methods of making aurally delivered materials available to individuals with hearing impairments;~~

~~(B) qualified readers, taped texts, or other effective methods of making visually delivered materials available to individuals with visual impairments;~~

~~(C) acquisition or modification of equipment or devices; and~~

~~(D) other similar services and actions.~~

[Note: the definition of "auxiliary aids and services" has been moved to Section 12103.]

(~~2~~ 1) Disability

The term "disability" means, with respect to an individual

(~~i~~ A) a physical or mental impairment that substantially limits one or more major life activities of such individual;

(~~ii~~ B) a record of such an impairment; or

(~~iii~~ C) being regarded as having such an impairment (**as described in paragraph (3)**).

~~(3) State~~

~~The term "State" means each of the several States, the District of Columbia, the Commonwealth of Puerto Rico, Guam, American Samoa, the Virgin Islands, the Trust Territory of the Pacific Islands, and the Commonwealth of the Northern Mariana Islands.~~

[Note: the definition of "state" has been moved to Section 12103.]

(2) **Major Life Activities**

(A) **In general**

For purposes of paragraph (1), major life activities include, but are not limited to, caring for oneself, performing manual tasks, seeing, hearing, eating, sleeping, walking, standing, lifting, bending, speaking, breathing, learning, reading, concentrating, thinking, communicating, and working.

(B) **Major bodily functions**

For purposes of paragraph (1), a major life activity also includes the operation of a major bodily function, including but not limited to, functions of the immune system, normal cell growth, digestive, bowel, bladder, neurological, brain, respiratory, circulatory, endocrine, and reproductive functions.

(3) Regarded as having such an impairment

For purposes of paragraph (1)(C):

(A) An individual meets the requirement of "being regarded as having such an impairment" if the individual establishes that he or she has been subjected to an action prohibited under this chapter because of an actual or perceived physical or mental impairment whether or not the impairment limits or is perceived to limit a major life activity.

(B) Paragraph (1)(C) shall not apply to impairments that are transitory and minor. A transitory impairment is an impairment with an actual or expected duration of 6 months or less.

(4) Rules of construction regarding the definition of disability

The definition of "disability" in paragraph (1) shall be construed in accordance with the following:

(A) The definition of disability in this chapter shall be construed in favor of broad coverage of individuals under this chapter, to the maximum extent permitted by the terms of this chapter.

(B) The term "substantially limits" shall be interpreted consistently with the findings and purposes of the ADA Amendments Act of 2008.

(C) An impairment that substantially limits one major life activity need not limit other major life activities in order to be considered a disability.

(D) An impairment that is episodic or in remission is a disability if it would substantially limit a major life activity when active.

(E) (i) The determination of whether an impairment substantially limits a major life activity shall be made without regard to the ameliorative effects of mitigating measures such as

(I) medication, medical supplies, equipment, or appliances, low-vision devices (which do not include ordinary eyeglasses or contact lenses), prosthetics including limbs and devices, hearing aids and cochlear implants or other implantable hearing devices, mobility devices, or oxygen therapy equipment and supplies;

(II) use of assistive technology;

(III) reasonable accommodations or auxiliary aids or services; or

(IV) learned behavioral or adaptive neurological modifications.

(ii) The ameliorative effects of the mitigating measures of ordinary eyeglasses or contact lenses shall be considered in determining whether an impairment substantially limits a major life activity.

(iii) As used in this subparagraph

(I) the term "ordinary eyeglasses or contact lenses" means lenses that are intended to fully correct visual acuity or eliminate refractive error; and

(II) the term "low-vision devices" means devices that magnify, enhance, or otherwise augment a visual image.

Sec. 12103.   Additional definitions

As used in this chapter

(1)   Auxiliary aids and services

The term "auxiliary aids and services" includes

(A) qualified interpreters or other effective methods of making aurally delivered materials available to individuals with hearing impairments;

(B) qualified readers, taped texts, or other effective methods of making visually delivered materials available to individuals with visual impairments;

(C) acquisition or modification of equipment or devices; and

(D) other similar services and actions.

(2)   State

The term "State" means each of the several States, the District of Columbia, the Commonwealth of Puerto Rico, Guam, American Samoa, the Virgin Islands of the United States, the Trust Territory of the Pacific Islands, and the Commonwealth of the Northern Mariana Islands.

SUBCHAPTER I   EMPLOYMENT

Sec. 12111.   Definitions

As used in this subchapter:

(1)   Commission

The term "Commission" means the Equal Employment Opportunity Commission established by section 2000e-4 of this title.

(2)   Covered entity

The term "covered entity" means an employer, employment agency, labor organization, or joint labor-management committee.

(3)   Direct threat

The term "direct threat" means a significant risk to the health or safety of others that cannot be eliminated by reasonable accommodation.

(4)   Employee

The term "employee" means an individual employed by an employer. With respect to employment in a foreign country, such term includes an individual who is a citizen of the United States.

(5)   Employer

(A)   In general

The term "employer" means a person engaged in an industry affecting commerce who has 15 or more employees for each working day in each of 20 or more calendar weeks in the current or preceding calendar year, and any agent of such person, except that, for two years following the effective date of this subchapter, an employer means a person engaged in an industry affecting commerce who has 25 or more employees for each working day in each of 20 or more calendar weeks in the current or preceding year, and any agent of such person.

(B)   Exceptions

The term "employer" does not include

(i) the United States, a corporation wholly owned by the government of the United States, or an Indian tribe; or

(ii) a bona fide private membership club (other than a labor organization) that is exempt from taxation under section 501(c) of title 26.

(6)   Illegal use of drugs

(A)   In general

The term "illegal use of drugs" means the use of drugs, the possession or distribution of which is unlawful under the Controlled Substances Act [21 U.S.C. 801 et seq.]. Such term does not include the use of a drug taken under supervision by a licensed health care professional, or other uses authorized by the Controlled Substances Act or other provisions of Federal law.

(B)   Drugs

The term "drug" means a controlled substance, as defined in schedules I through V of section 202 of the Controlled Substances Act [21 U.S.C. 812].

(7)   Person, etc.

The terms "person", "labor organization", "employment agency", "commerce", and "industry affecting commerce", shall have the same meaning given such terms in section 2000e of this title.

(8)   Qualified individual ~~with a disability~~

The term "qualified individual ~~with a disability~~" means an individual ~~with a disability~~ who, with or without reasonable accommodation, can perform the essential functions of the employment position that such individual holds or desires. For the purposes of this subchapter, consideration shall be given to the employer's judgment as to what functions of a job are essential, and if an employer has prepared a written description before advertising or interviewing applicants for the job, this description shall be considered evidence of the essential functions of the job.

(9)   Reasonable accommodation

The term "reasonable accommodation" may include

(A) making existing facilities used by employees readily accessible to and usable by individuals with disabilities; and

(B) job restructuring, part-time or modified work schedules, reassignment to a vacant position, acquisition or modification of equipment or devices, appropriate adjustment or modifications of examinations, training materials or policies, the provision of qualified readers or interpreters, and other similar accommodations for individuals with disabilities.

(10)   Undue hardship

(A)   In general

The term "undue hardship" means an action requiring significant difficulty or expense, when considered in light of the factors set forth in subparagraph (B).

(B)   Factors to be considered

In determining whether an accommodation would impose an undue hardship on a covered entity, factors to be considered include

(i) the nature and cost of the accommodation needed under this chapter;

(ii) the overall financial resources of the facility or facilities involved in the provision of the reasonable accommodation; the number of persons employed at such facility; the effect on expenses and resources, or the impact otherwise of such accommodation upon the operation of the facility;

(iii) the overall financial resources of the covered entity; the overall size of the business of a covered entity with respect to the number of its employees; the number, type, and location of its facilities; and

(iv) the type of operation or operations of the covered entity, including the composition, structure, and functions of the workforce of such entity; the geographic separateness, administrative, or fiscal relationship of the facility or facilities in question to the covered entity.

Sec. 12112. Discrimination

(a) General rule

No covered entity shall discriminate against a qualified individual ~~with a disability because of the disability of such individual~~ **on the basis of disability** in regard to job application procedures, the hiring, advancement, or discharge of employees, employee compensation, job training, and other terms, conditions, and privileges of employment.

(b) Construction

As used in subsection (a) of this section, the term ~~"discriminate"~~ **"discriminate against a qualified individual on the basis of disability"** includes

(1) limiting, segregating, or classifying a job applicant or employee in a way that adversely affects the opportunities or status of such applicant or employee because of the disability of such applicant or employee;

(2) participating in a contractual or other arrangement or relationship that has the effect of subjecting a covered entity's qualified applicant or employee with a disability to the discrimination prohibited by this subchapter (such relationship includes a relationship with an employment or referral agency, labor union, an organization providing fringe benefits to an employee of the covered entity, or an organization providing training and apprenticeship programs);

(3) utilizing standards, criteria, or methods of administration

(A) that have the effect of discrimination on the basis of disability;

(B) that perpetuates the discrimination of others who are subject to common administrative control;

(4) excluding or otherwise denying equal jobs or benefits to a qualified individual because of the known disability of an individual with whom the qualified individual is known to have a relationship or association;

(5) (A) not making reasonable accommodations to the known physical or mental limitations of an otherwise qualified individual with a disability who is an applicant or employee, unless such covered entity can demonstrate that the accommodation would impose an undue hardship on the operation of the business of such covered entity; or

(B) denying employment opportunities to a job applicant or employee who is an otherwise qualified individual with a disability, if such denial is based on the need of such covered entity to make reasonable accommodation to the physical or mental impairments of the employee or applicant;

(6) using qualification standards, employment tests or other selection criteria that screen out or tend to screen out an individual with a disability or a class of individuals with disabilities unless the standard, test or other selection criteria, as used by the covered entity, is shown to be job-related for the position in question and is consistent with business necessity; and

(7) failing to select and administer tests concerning employment in the most effective manner to ensure that, when such test is administered to a job applicant or employee who has a disability that impairs sensory, manual, or speaking skills, such test results accurately reflect the skills, aptitude, or whatever other factor of such applicant or employee that such test purports to measure, rather than reflecting the impaired sensory, manual, or speaking skills of such employee or applicant (except where such skills are the factors that the test purports to measure).

(c) Covered entities in foreign countries

(1) In general

It shall not be unlawful under this section for a covered entity to take any action that constitute discrimination under this section with respect to an employee in a workplace in a foreign country if compliance with this section would cause such covered entity to violate the law of the foreign country in which such workplace is located.

(2) Control of corporation

(A) Presumption

If an employer controls a corporation whose place of incorporation is a foreign country, any practice that constitutes discrimination under this section and is engaged in by such corporation shall be presumed to be engaged in by such employer.

(B) Exception

This section shall not apply with respect to the foreign operations of an employer that is a foreign person not controlled by an American employer.

(C) Determination

For purposes of this paragraph, the determination of whether an employer controls a corporation shall be based on

(i) the interrelation of operations;

(ii) the common management;

(iii) the centralized control of labor relations; and

(iv) the common ownership or financial control of the employer and the corporation.

(d) Medical examinations and inquiries

(1) In general

The prohibition against discrimination as referred to in subsection (a) of this section shall include medical examinations and inquiries.

(2) Preemployment

(A) Prohibited examination or inquiry

Except as provided in paragraph (3), a covered entity shall not conduct a medical examination or make inquiries of a job applicant as to whether such applicant is an individual with a disability or as to the nature or severity of such disability.

(B)   Acceptable inquiry

A covered entity may make preemployment inquiries into the ability of an applicant to perform job-related functions.

(3)   Employment entrance examination

A covered entity may require a medical examination after an offer of employment has been made to a job applicant and prior to the commencement of the employment duties of such applicant, and may condition an offer of employment on the results of such examination, if

(A) all entering employees are subjected to such an examination regardless of disability;

(B) information obtained regarding the medical condition or history of the applicant is collected and maintained on separate forms and in separate medical files and is treated as a confidential medical record, except that

(i) supervisors and managers may be informed regarding necessary restrictions on the work or duties of the employee and necessary accommodations;

(ii) first aid and safety personnel may be informed, when appropriate, if the disability might require emergency treatment; and

(iii) government officials investigating compliance with this chapter shall be provided relevant information on request; and

(C) the results of such examination are used only in accordance with this subchapter.

(4) Examination and inquiry

(A)   Prohibited examinations and inquiries

A covered entity shall not require a medical examination and shall not make inquiries of an employee as to whether such employee is an individual with a disability or as to the nature or severity of the disability, unless such examination or inquiry is shown to be job-related and consistent with business necessity.

(B)   Acceptable examinations and inquiries

A covered entity may conduct voluntary medical examinations, including voluntary medical histories, which are part of an employee health program available to employees at that work site. A covered entity may make inquiries into the ability of an employee to perform job-related functions.

(C)   Requirement

Information obtained under subparagraph (B) regarding the medical condition or history of any employee are subject to the requirements of subparagraphs (B) and (C) of paragraph (3).

Sec. 12113.   Defenses

(a)   In general

It may be a defense to a charge of discrimination under this chapter that an alleged application of qualification standards, tests, or selection criteria that screen out or tend to screen out or otherwise deny a job or benefit to an individual with a disability has been shown to be job- related and consistent with business necessity, and such performance cannot be accomplished by reasonable accommodation, as required under this subchapter.

(b) Qualification standards

The term "qualification standards" may include a requirement that an individual shall not pose a direct threat to the health or safety of other individuals in the workplace.

(c) Qualification standards and tests related to uncorrected vision

Notwithstanding section 12102(4)(E)(ii), a covered entity shall not use qualification standards, employment tests, or other selection criteria based on an individual's uncorrected vision unless the standard, test, or other selection criteria, as used by the covered entity, is shown to be job-related for the position in question and consistent with business necessity.

(e d) Religious entities

(1) In general

This subchapter shall not prohibit a religious corporation, association, educational institution, or society from giving preference in employment to individuals of a particular religion to perform work connected with the carrying on by such corporation, association, educational institution, or society of its activities.

(2) Religious tenets requirement

Under this subchapter, a religious organization may require that all applicants and employees conform to the religious tenets of such organization.

(d e) List of infectious and communicable diseases

(1) In general

The Secretary of Health and Human Services, not later than 6 months after July 26, 1990, shall

(A) review all infectious and communicable diseases which may be transmitted through handling the food supply;

(B) publish a list of infectious and communicable diseases which are transmitted through handling the food supply;

(C) publish the methods by which such diseases are transmitted; and

(D) widely disseminate such information regarding the list of diseases and their modes of transmissibility to the general public.

Such list shall be updated annually.

(2) Applications

In any case in which an individual has an infectious or communicable disease that is transmitted to others through the handling of food, that is included on the list developed by the Secretary of Health and Human Services under paragraph (1), and which cannot be eliminated by reasonable accommodation, a covered entity may refuse to assign or continue to assign such individual to a job involving food handling.

(3)   Construction

Nothing in this chapter shall be construed to preempt, modify, or amend any State, county, or local law, ordinance, or regulation applicable to food handling which is designed to protect the public health from individuals who pose a significant risk to the health or safety of others, which cannot be eliminated by reasonable accommodation, pursuant to the list of infectious or communicable diseases and the modes of transmissibility published by the Secretary of Health and Human Services.

Sec. 12114.   Illegal use of drugs and alcohol

(a)   Qualified individual with a disability

For purposes of this subchapter, ~~the term "qualified individual with a disability" shall a~~ **qualified individual with a disability shall** not include any employee or applicant who is currently engaging in the illegal use of drugs, when the covered entity acts on the basis of such use.

(b)   Rules of construction

Nothing in subsection (a) of this section shall be construed to exclude as a qualified individual with a disability an individual who

(1) has successfully completed a supervised drug rehabilitation program and is no longer engaging in the illegal use of drugs, or has otherwise been rehabilitated successfully and is no longer engaging in such use;

(2) is participating in a supervised rehabilitation program and is no longer engaging in such use; or

(3) is erroneously regarded as engaging in such use, but is not engaging in such use;

except that it shall not be a violation of this chapter for a covered entity to adopt or administer reasonable policies or procedures, including but not limited to drug testing, designed to ensure that an individual described in paragraph (1) or (2) is no longer engaging in the illegal use of drugs.

(c)   Authority of covered entity

A covered entity

(1) may prohibit the illegal use of drugs and the use of alcohol at the workplace by all employees;

(2) may require that employees shall not be under the influence of alcohol or be engaging in the illegal use of drugs at the workplace;

(3) may require that employees behave in conformance with the requirements established under the Drug-Free Workplace Act of 1988 (41 U.S.C. 701 et seq.);

(4) may hold an employee who engages in the illegal use of drugs or who is an alcoholic to the same qualification standards for employment or job performance

and behavior that such entity holds other employees, even if any unsatisfactory performance or behavior is related to the drug use or alcoholism of such employee; and

(5) may, with respect to Federal regulations regarding alcohol and the illegal use of drugs, require that

(A) employees comply with the standards established in such regulations of the Department of Defense, if the employees of the covered entity are employed in an industry subject to such regulations, including complying with regulations (if any) that apply to employment in sensitive positions in such an industry, in the case of employees of the covered entity who are employed in such positions (as defined in the regulations of the Department of Defense);

(B) employees comply with the standards established in such regulations of the Nuclear Regulatory Commission, if the employees of the covered entity are employed in an industry subject to such regulations, including complying with regulations (if any) that apply to employment in sensitive positions in such an industry, in the case of employees of the covered entity who are employed in such positions (as defined in the regulations of the Nuclear Regulatory Commission); and

(C) employees comply with the standards established in such regulations of the Department of Transportation, if the employees of the covered entity are employed in a transportation industry subject to such regulations, including complying with such regulations (if any) that apply to employment in sensitive positions in such an industry, in the case of employees of the covered entity who are employed in such positions (as defined in the regulations of the Department of Transportation).

(d) Drug testing

(1)   In general

For purposes of this subchapter, a test to determine the illegal use of drugs shall not be considered a medical examination.

(2)   Construction

Nothing in this subchapter shall be construed to encourage, prohibit, or authorize the conducting of drug testing for the illegal use of drugs by job applicants or employees or making employment decisions based on such test results.

(e)   Transportation employees

Nothing in this subchapter shall be construed to encourage, prohibit, restrict, or authorize the otherwise lawful exercise by entities subject to the jurisdiction of the Department of Transportation of authority to

(1) test employees of such entities in, and applicants for, positions involving safety-sensitive duties for the illegal use of drugs and for on-duty impairment by alcohol; and

(2) remove such persons who test positive for illegal use of drugs and on-duty impairment by alcohol pursuant to paragraph (1) from safety-sensitive duties in implementing subsection (c) of this section.

Sec. 12115.   Posting notices

Every employer, employment agency, labor organization, or joint labor-management committee covered under this subchapter shall post notices in an accessible format to applicants, employees, and members describing the applicable provisions of this chapter, in the manner prescribed by section 2000e-10 of this title.

Sec. 12116. Regulations

Not later than 1 year after July 26, 1990, the Commission shall issue regulations in an accessible format to carry out this subchapter in accordance with subchapter II of chapter 5 of title 5.

Sec. 12117. Enforcement

(a) Powers, remedies, and procedures

The powers, remedies, and procedures set forth in sections 2000e-4, 2000e-5, 2000e-6, 2000e-8, and 2000e-9 of this title shall be the powers, remedies, and procedures this subchapter provides to the Commission, to the Attorney General, or to any person alleging discrimination on the basis of disability in violation of any provision of this chapter, or regulations promulgated under section 12116 of this title, concerning employment.

(b) Coordination

The agencies with enforcement authority for actions which allege employment discrimination under this subchapter and under the Rehabilitation Act of 1973 [29 U.S.C. 701 et seq.] shall develop procedures to ensure that administrative complaints filed under this subchapter and under the Rehabilitation Act of 1973 are dealt with in a manner that avoids duplication of effort and prevents imposition of inconsistent or conflicting standards for the same requirements under this subchapter and the Rehabilitation Act of 1973. The Commission, the Attorney General, and the Office of Federal Contract Compliance Programs shall establish such coordinating mechanisms (similar to provisions contained in the joint regulations promulgated by the Commission and the Attorney General at part 42 of title 28 and part 1691 of title 29, Code of Federal Regulations, and the Memorandum of Understanding between the Commission and the Office of Federal Contract Compliance Programs dated January 16, 1981 (46 Fed. Reg. 7435, January 23, 1981)) in regulations implementing this subchapter and Rehabilitation Act of 1973 not later than 18 months after July 26, 1990.

SUBCHAPTER II PUBLIC SERVICES

Part A Prohibition Against Discrimination and Other Generally Applicable Provisions

Sec. 12131. Definitions

As used in this subchapter:

(1) Public entity

The term "public entity" means

(A) any State or local government;

(B) any department, agency, special purpose district, or other instrumentality of a State or States or local government; and

(C) the National Railroad Passenger Corporation, and any commuter authority (as defined in section 24102(4) of title 49).

(2) Qualified individual with a disability

The term "qualified individual with a disability" means an individual with a disability who, with or without reasonable modifications to rules, policies, or practices, the removal of architectural, communication, or transportation barriers, or the provision of auxiliary aids and services, meets the essential eligibility requirements for the receipt of services or the participation in programs or activities provided by a public entity.

Sec. 12132. Discrimination

Subject to the provisions of this subchapter, no qualified individual with a disability shall, by reason of such disability, be excluded from participation in or be denied the benefits of services, programs, or activities of a public entity, or be subjected to discrimination by any such entity.

Sec. 12133. Enforcement

The remedies, procedures, and rights set forth in section 794a of title 29 shall be the remedies, procedures, and rights this subchapter provides to any person alleging discrimination on the basis of disability in violation of section 12132 of this title.

Sec. 12134. Regulations

(a) In general

Not later than 1 year after July 26, 1990, the Attorney General shall promulgate regulations in an accessible format that implement this part. Such regulations shall not include any matter within the scope of the authority of the Secretary of Transportation under section 12143, 12149, or 12164 of this title.

(b) Relationship to other regulations

Except for "program accessibility, existing facilities", and "communications", regulations under subsection (a) of this section shall be consistent with this chapter and with the coordination regulations under part 41 of title 28, Code of Federal Regulations (as promulgated by the Department of Health, Education, and Welfare on January 13, 1978), applicable to recipients of Federal financial assistance under section 794 of title 29. With respect to "program accessibility, existing facilities", and "communications", such regulations shall be consistent with regulations and analysis as in part 39 of title 28 of the Code of Federal Regulations, applicable to federally conducted activities under section 794 of title 29.

(c) Standards

Regulations under subsection (a) of this section shall include standards applicable to facilities and vehicles covered by this part, other than facilities, stations, rail passenger cars, and vehicles covered by part B of this subchapter. Such standards shall be consistent with the minimum guidelines and requirements issued by the Architectural and Transportation Barriers Compliance Board in accordance with section 12204(a) of this title.

Part B   Actions Applicable to Public Transportation Provided by Public Entities Considered Discriminatory

Subpart I   Public Transportation Other than by Aircraft or Certain Rail Operations

Sec. 12141.   Definitions

As used in this subpart:

(1) Demand responsive system

The term "demand responsive system" means any system of providing designated public transportation which is not a fixed route system.

(2) Designated public transportation

The term "designated public transportation" means transportation (other than public school transportation) by bus, rail, or any other conveyance (other than transportation by aircraft or intercity or commuter rail transportation (as defined in section 12161 of this title)) that provides the general public with general or special service (including charter service) on a regular and continuing basis.

(3) Fixed route system

The term "fixed route system" means a system of providing designated public transportation on which a vehicle is operated along a prescribed route according to a fixed schedule.

(4) Operates

The term "operates", as used with respect to a fixed route system or demand responsive system, includes operation of such system by a person under a contractual or other arrangement or relationship with a public entity.

(5) Public school transportation

The term "public school transportation" means transportation by school bus vehicles of schoolchildren, personnel, and equipment to and from a public elementary or secondary school and school-related activities.

(6) Secretary

The term "Secretary" means the Secretary of Transportation.

Sec. 12142. Public entities operating fixed route systems

(a) Purchase and lease of new vehicles

It shall be considered discrimination for purposes of section which operates a fixed route system to purchase or lease a new bus, a new rapid rail vehicle, a new light rail vehicle, or any other new vehicle to be used on such system, if the solicitation for such purchase or lease is made after the 30th day following July 26, 1990, and if such bus, rail vehicle, or other vehicle is not readily accessible to and usable by individuals with disabilities, including individuals who use wheelchairs.

(b) Purchase and lease of used vehicles

Subject to subsection (c)(1) of this section, it shall be considered discrimination for purposes of section 12132 of this title and section 794 of title 29 for a public entity which operates a fixed route system to purchase or lease, after the 30th day following July 26, 1990, a used vehicle for use on such system unless such entity makes demonstrated good faith efforts to purchase or lease a used vehicle for use on such system that is readily accessible to and usable by individuals with disabilities, including individuals who use wheelchairs.

(c) Remanufactured vehicles

(1) General rule

Except as provided in paragraph (2), it shall be considered discrimination for purposes of section 12132 of this title and section 794 of title 29 for a public entity which operates a fixed route system

(A) to remanufacture a vehicle for use on such system so as to extend its usable life for 5 years or more, which remanufacture begins (or for which the solicitation is made) after the 30th day following July 26, 1990; or

(B) to purchase or lease for use on such system a remanufactured vehicle which has been remanufactured so as to extend its usable life for 5 years or more, which purchase or lease occurs after such 30th day and during the period in which the usable life is extended; unless, after remanufacture, the vehicle is, to the maximum extent feasible, readily accessible to and usable by individuals with disabilities, including individuals who use wheelchairs.

(2) Exception for historic vehicles

(A) General rule

If a public entity operates a fixed route system any segment of which is included on the National Register of Historic Places and if making a vehicle of historic character to be used solely on such segment readily accessible to and usable by individuals with disabilities would significantly alter the historic character of such vehicle, the public entity only has to make (or to purchase or lease a remanufactured vehicle with) those modifications which are necessary to meet the requirements of paragraph (1) and which do not significantly alter the historic character of such vehicle.

(B) Vehicles of historic character defined by regulations

For purposes of this paragraph and section 12148(a) of this title, a vehicle of historic character shall be defined by the regulations issued by the Secretary to carry out this subsection.

Sec. 12143.   Paratransit as a complement to fixed route service

(a)   General rule

It shall be considered discrimination for purposes of section 12132 of this title and section 794 of title 29 for a public entity which operates a fixed route system (other than a system which provides solely commuter bus service) to fail to provide with respect to the operations of its fixed route system, in accordance with this section, paratransit and other special transportation services to individuals with disabilities, including individuals who use wheelchairs that are sufficient to provide to such individuals a level of service

(1) which is comparable to the level of designated public transportation services provided to individuals without disabilities using such system; or

(2) in the case of response time, which is comparable, to the extent practicable, to the level of designated public transportation services provided to individuals without disabilities using such system.

(b)   Issuance of regulations

Not later than 1 year after July 26, 1990, the Secretary shall issue final regulations to carry out this section.

(c) Required contents of regulations

(1)   Eligible recipients of service

The regulations issued under this section shall require each public entity which operates a fixed route system to provide the paratransit and other special transportation services required under this section

(A) (i) to any individual with a disability who is unable, as a result of a physical or mental impairment (including a vision impairment) and without the assistance of another individual (except an operator of a wheelchair lift or other boarding assistance device), to board, ride, or disembark from any vehicle on the system which is readily accessible to and usable by individuals with disabilities;

(ii) to any individual with a disability who needs the assistance of a wheelchair lift or other boarding assistance device (and is able with such assistance) to board, ride, and disembark from any vehicle which is readily accessible to and usable by individuals with disabilities if the individual wants to travel on a route on the system during the hours of operation of the system at a time (or within a reasonable period of such time) when such a vehicle is not being used to provide designated public transportation on the route; and

(iii) to any individual with a disability who has a specific impairment-related condition which prevents such individual from traveling to a boarding location or from a disembarking location on such system;

(B) to one other individual accompanying the individual with the disability; and

(C) to other individuals, in addition to the one individual described in subparagraph (a), accompanying the individual with a disability provided that space for these additional individuals are available on the paratransit vehicle carrying the individual with a disability and that the transportation of such additional individuals will not result in a denial of service to individuals with disabilities.

For purposes of clauses (i) and (ii) of subparagraph (A), boarding or disembarking from a vehicle does not include travel to the boarding location or from the disembarking location.

(2) Service area

The regulations issued under this section shall require the provision of paratransit and special transportation services required under this section in the service area of each public entity which operates a fixed route system, other than any portion of the service area in which the public entity solely provides commuter bus service.

(3) Service criteria

Subject to paragraphs (1) and (2), the regulations issued under this section shall establish minimum service criteria for determining the level of services to be required under this section.

(4) Undue financial burden limitation

The regulations issued under this section shall provide that, if the public entity is able to demonstrate to the satisfaction of the Secretary that the provision of paratransit and other special transportation services otherwise required under this section would impose an undue financial burden on the public entity, the public entity, notwithstanding any other provision of this section (other than paragraph (5)), shall only be required to provide such services to the extent that providing such services would not impose such a burden.

(5) Additional services

The regulations issued under this section shall establish circumstances under which the Secretary may require a public entity to provide, notwithstanding paragraph (4), paratransit and other special transportation services under this section beyond the level of paratransit and other special transportation services which would otherwise be required under paragraph (4).

(6) Public participation

The regulations issued under this section shall require that each public entity which operates a fixed route system hold a public hearing, provide an opportunity for public comment, and consult with individuals with disabilities in preparing its plan under paragraph (7).

(7) Plans

The regulations issued under this section shall require that each public entity which operates a fixed route system

(A) within 18 months after July 26, 1990, submit to the Secretary, and commence implementation of, a plan for providing paratransit and other special transportation services which meets the requirements of this section; and

(B) on an annual basis thereafter, submit to the Secretary, and commence implementation of, a plan for providing such services.

(8)   Provision of services by others

The regulations issued under this section shall

(A) require that a public entity submitting a plan to the Secretary under this section identify in the plan any person or other public entity which is providing a paratransit or other special transportation service for individuals with disabilities in the service area to which the plan applies; and

(B) provide that the public entity submitting the plan does not have to provide under the plan such service for individuals with disabilities.

(9)   Other provisions

The regulations issued under this section shall include such other provisions and requirements as the Secretary determines are necessary to carry out the objectives of this section.

(d)   Review of plan

(1)   General rule

The Secretary shall review a plan submitted under this section for the purpose of determining whether or not such plan meets the requirements of this section, including the regulations issued under this section.

(2)   Disapproval

If the Secretary determines that a plan reviewed under this subsection fails to meet the requirements of this section, the Secretary shall disapprove the plan and notify the public entity which submitted the plan of such disapproval and the reasons therefor.

(3)   Modification of disapproved plan

Not later than 90 days after the date of disapproval of a plan under this subsection, the public entity which submitted the plan shall modify the plan to meet the requirements of this section and shall submit to the Secretary, and commence implementation of, such modified plan.

(e)   "Discrimination" defined

As used in subsection (a) of this section, the term "discrimination" includes

(1) a failure of a public entity to which the regulations issued under this section apply to submit, or commence implementation of, a plan in accordance with subsections (c)(6) and (c)(7) of this section;

(2) a failure of such entity to submit, or commence implementation of, a modified plan in accordance with subsection (d) (3) of this section;

(3) submission to the Secretary of a modified plan under subsection (d)(3) of this section which does not meet the requirements of this section; or

(4) a failure of such entity to provide paratransit or other special transportation services in accordance with the plan or modified plan the public entity submitted to

the Secretary under this section.

(f) Statutory construction

Nothing in this section shall be construed as preventing a public entity

(1) from providing paratransit or other special transportation services at a level which is greater than the level of such services which are required by this section,

(2) from providing paratransit or other special transportation services in addition to those paratransit and special transportation services required by this section, or

(3) from providing such services to individuals in addition to those individuals to whom such services are required to be provided by this section.

Sec. 12144. Public entity operating a demand responsive system

If a public entity operates a demand responsive system, it shall be considered discrimination, for purposes of section 12132 of this title and section 794 of title 29, for such entity to purchase or lease a new vehicle for use on such system, for which a solicitation is made after the 30th day following July 26, 1990, that is not readily accessible to and usable by individuals with disabilities, including individuals who use wheelchairs, unless such system, when viewed in its entirety, provides a level of service to such individuals equivalent to the level of service such system provides to individuals without disabilities.

Sec. 12145. Temporary relief where lifts are unavailable

(a) Granting

With respect to the purchase of new buses, a public entity may apply for, and the Secretary may temporarily relieve such public entity from the obligation under section 12142(a) or 12144 of this title to purchase new buses that are readily accessible to and usable by individuals with disabilities if such public entity demonstrates to the satisfaction of the Secretary

(1) that the initial solicitation for new buses made by the public entity specified that all new buses were to be lift-equipped and were to be otherwise accessible to and usable by individuals with disabilities;

(2) the unavailability from any qualified manufacturer of hydraulic, electromechanical, or other lifts for such new buses;

(3) that the public entity seeking temporary relief has made good faith efforts to locate a qualified manufacturer to supply the lifts to the manufacturer of such buses in sufficient time to comply with such solicitation; and

(4) that any further delay in purchasing new buses necessary to obtain such lifts would significantly impair transportation services in the community served by the public entity.

(b) Duration and notice to Congress

Any relief granted under subsection (a) of this section shall be limited in duration by a specified date, and the appropriate committees of Congress shall be notified of any such relief granted.

(c) Fraudulent application

If, at any time, the Secretary has reasonable cause to believe that any relief granted under subsection (a) of this section was fraudulently applied for, the Secretary shall

(1) cancel such relief if such relief is still in effect; and

(2) take such other action as the Secretary considers appropriate.

Sec. 12146.   New facilities

For purposes of section 12132 of this title and section 794 of title 29, it shall be considered discrimination for a public entity to construct a new facility to be used in the provision of designated public transportation services unless such facility is readily accessible to and usable by individuals with disabilities, including individuals who use wheelchairs.

For purposes of section 12132 of this title and section 794 of title 29, it shall be considered discrimination for a public entity to construct a new facility to be used in the provision of designated public transportation services unless such facility is readily accessible to and usable by individuals with disabilities, including individuals who use wheelchairs.

Sec. 12147.   Alterations of existing facilities

(a) General rule

With respect to alterations of an existing facility or part thereof used in the provision of designated public transportation services that affect or could affect the usability of the facility or part thereof, it shall be considered discrimination, for purposes of section 12132 of this title and section 794 of title 29, for a public entity to fail to make such alterations (or to ensure that the alterations are made) in such a manner that, to the maximum extent feasible, the altered portions of the facility are readily accessible to and usable by individuals with disabilities, including individuals who use wheelchairs, upon the completion of such alterations. Where the public entity is undertaking an alteration that affects or could affect usability of or access to an area of the facility containing a primary function, the entity shall also make the alterations in such a manner that, to the maximum extent feasible, the path of travel to the altered area and the bathrooms, telephones, and drinking fountains serving the altered area, are readily accessible to and usable by individuals with disabilities, including individuals who use wheelchairs, upon completion of such alterations, where such alterations to the path of travel or the bathrooms, telephones, and drinking fountains serving the altered area are not disproportionate to the overall alterations in terms of cost and scope (as determined under criteria established by the Attorney General).

(b) Special rule for stations

(1) General rule

For purposes of section 12132 of this title and section 794 of title 29, it shall be considered discrimination for a public entity that provides designated public transportation to fail, in accordance with the provisions of this subsection, to make key stations (as determined under criteria established by the Secretary by regulation) in rapid rail and light rail systems readily accessible to and usable by individuals with disabilities, including individuals who use wheelchairs.

(2) Rapid rail and light rail key stations

(A) Accessibility

Except as otherwise provided in this paragraph, all key stations (as determined under criteria established by the Secretary by regulation] in rapid rail and light rail systems shall be made readily accessible to and usable by individuals with disabilities, including individuals who use wheelchairs, as soon as practicable but in no event later than the last day of the 3-year period beginning on July 26, 1990.

(B) Extension for extraordinarily expensive structural changes

The Secretary may extend the 3-year period under subparagraph (A) up to a 30-year period for key stations in a rapid rail or light rail system which stations need extraordinarily expensive structural changes to, or replacement of, existing facilities; except that by the last day of the 20th year following July 26, 1990, at least 2/3 of such key stations must be readily accessible to and usable by individuals with disabilities.

(3) Plans and milestones

The Secretary shall require the appropriate public entity to develop and submit to the Secretary a plan for compliance with this subsection

(A) that reflects consultation with individuals with disabilities affected by such plan and the results of a public hearing and public comments on such plan, and

(B) that establishes milestones for achievement of the requirements of this subsection.

Sec. 12148. Public transportation programs and activities in existing facilities and one car per train rule

(a) Public transportation programs and activities in existing facilities

(1) In general

With respect to existing facilities used in the provision of designated public transportation services, it shall be considered discrimination, for purposes of section 12132 of this title and section 794 of title 29, for a public entity to fail to operate a designated public transportation program or activity conducted in such facilities so that, when viewed in the entirety, the program or activity is readily accessible to and usable by individuals with disabilities.

(2) Exception

Paragraph (1) shall not require a public entity to make structural changes to existing facilities in order to make such facilities accessible to individuals who use wheelchairs, unless and to the extent required by section 12147(a) of this title (relating to alterations) or section 12147(a) of this title (relating to key stations).

(3) Utilization

Paragraph (1) shall not require a public entity to which paragraph (2) applies, to provide to individuals who use wheelchairs services made available to the general public at such facilities when such individuals could not utilize or benefit from such services provided at such facilities.

(b) One car per train rule

(1) General rule

Subject to paragraph (2), with respect to 2 or more vehicles operated as a train by a light or rapid rail system, for purposes of section 12132 of this title and section 794 of title 29, it shall be considered discrimination for a public entity to fail to have at least 1 vehicle per train that is accessible to individuals with disabilities, including individuals who use wheelchairs, as soon as practicable but in no event later than the last day of the 5-year period beginning on the effective date of this section.

(2) Historic trains

In order to comply with paragraph (1) with respect to the remanufacture of a vehicle of historic character which is to be used on a segment of a light or rapid rail system which is included on the National Register of Historic Places, if making such vehicle readily accessible to and usable by individuals with disabilities would significantly alter the historic character of such vehicle, the public entity which operates such system only has to make (or to purchase or lease a remanufactured vehicle with) those modifications which are necessary to meet the requirements of section 12142(c)(1) of this title and which do not significantly alter the historic character of such vehicle.

Sec. 12149. Regulations

(a) In general

Not later than 1 year after July 26, 1990, the Secretary of Transportation shall issue regulations, in an accessible format, necessary for carrying out this subpart (other than section 12143 of this title).

(b) Standards

The regulations issued under this section and section 12143 of this title shall include standards applicable to facilities and vehicles covered by this part. The standards shall be consistent with the minimum guidelines and requirements issued by the Architectural and Transportation Barriers Compliance Board in accordance with section 12204 of this title.

Sec. 12150. Interim accessibility requirements

If final regulations have not been issued pursuant to section 12149 of this title, for new construction or alterations for which a valid and appropriate State or local building permit is obtained prior to the issuance of final regulations under such section, and for which the construction or alteration authorized by such permit begins within one year of the receipt of such permit and is completed under the terms of such permit, compliance with the Uniform Federal Accessibility Standards in effect at the time the building permit is issued shall suffice to satisfy the requirement that facilities be readily accessible to and usable by persons with disabilities as required under sections 12146 and 12147 of this title, except that, if such final regulations have not been issued one year after the Architectural and Transportation Barriers Compliance Board has issued the supplemental minimum guidelines required under section 12204(a) of this title, compliance with such supplemental minimum guidelines shall be necessary to satisfy the requirement that facilities be readily accessible to and usable by persons with disabilities prior to issuance of the final regulations.

Subpart II Public Transportation by Intercity and Commuter Rail

Sec. 12161. Definitions

As used in this subpart:

(1) Commuter authority

The term "commuter authority" has the meaning given such term in section 24102(4) of title 49.

(2) Commuter rail transportation

The term "commuter rail transportation" has the meaning given the term "commuter rail passenger transportation" in section 24102(5) of title 49.

(3) Intercity rail transportation

The term "intercity rail transportation" means transportation provided by the National Railroad Passenger Corporation.

(4) Rail passenger car

The term "rail passenger car" means, with respect to intercity rail transportation, single-level and bi-level coach cars, single-level and bi-level dining cars, single-level and bi-level sleeping cars, single-level and bi-level lounge cars, and food service cars.

(5) Responsible person

The term "responsible person" means

(A) in the case of a station more than 50 percent of which is owned by a public entity, such public entity;

(B) in the case of a station more than 50 percent of which is owned by a private party, the persons providing intercity or commuter rail transportation to such station, as allocated on an equitable basis by regulation by the Secretary of Transportation; and

(C) in a case where no party owns more than 50 percent of a station, the persons providing intercity or commuter rail transportation to such station and the owners of the station, other than private party owners, as allocated on an equitable basis by regulation by the Secretary of Transportation.

(6) Station

The term "station" means the portion of a property located appurtenant to a right-of-way on which intercity or commuter rail transportation is operated, where such portion is used by the general public and is related to the provision of such transportation, including passenger platforms, designated waiting areas, ticketing areas, restrooms, and, where a public entity providing rail transportation owns the property, concession areas, to the extent that such public entity exercises control over the selection, design, construction, or alteration of the property, but such term does not include flag stops.

Sec. 12162.   Intercity and commuter rail actions considered discriminatory

(a) Intercity rail transportation

(1)   One car per train rule

It shall be considered discrimination for purposes of section 12132 of this title and section 794 of title 29 for a person who provides intercity rail transportation to fail to have at least one passenger car per train that is readily accessible to and usable by individuals with disabilities, including individuals who use wheelchairs, in accordance with regulations issued under section 12164 of this title, as soon as practicable, but in no event later than 5 years after July 26, 1990.

(2) New intercity cars

(A)   General rule

Except as otherwise provided in this subsection with respect to individuals who use wheelchairs, it shall be considered discrimination for purposes of section 12132 of this title and section 794 of title 29 for a person to purchase or lease any new rail passenger cars for use in intercity rail transportation, and for which a solicitation is made later than 30 days after July 26, 1990, unless all such rail cars are readily accessible to and usable by individuals with disabilities, including individuals who use wheelchairs, as prescribed by the Secretary of Transportation in regulations issued under section 12164 of this title.

(B)   Special rule for single-level passenger coaches for individuals who use wheelchairs

Single-level passenger coaches shall be required to

(i) be able to be entered by an individual who uses a wheelchair;

(ii) have space to park and secure a wheelchair;

(iii) have a seat to which a passenger in a wheelchair can transfer, and a space to fold and store such passenger's wheelchair; and

(iv) have a restroom usable by an individual who uses a wheelchair, only to the extent provided in paragraph (3).

(C) Special rule for single-level dining cars for individuals who use wheelchairs

Single-level dining cars shall not be required to

(i) be able to be entered from the station platform by an individual who uses a wheelchair; or

(ii) have a restroom usable by an individual who uses a wheelchair if no restroom is provided in such car for any passenger.

(D) Special rule for bi-level dining cars for individuals who use wheelchairs

Bi-level dining cars shall not be required to

(i) be able to be entered by an individual who uses a wheelchair;

(ii) have space to park and secure a wheelchair;

(iii) have a seat to which a passenger in a wheelchair can transfer, or a space to fold and store such passenger's wheelchair; or

(iv) have a restroom usable by an individual who uses a wheelchair.

(3) Accessibility of single-level coaches

(A)   General rule

It shall be considered discrimination for purposes of section 12132 of this title and section 794 of title 29 for a person who provides intercity rail transportation to fail to have on each train which includes one or more single-level rail passenger coaches

(i) a number of spaces

(I) to park and secure wheelchairs (to accommodate individuals who wish to remain in their wheelchairs) equal to not less than one-half of the number of single-level rail passenger coaches in such train; and

(II) to fold and store wheelchairs (to accommodate individuals who wish to transfer to coach seats) equal to not less than one-half of the number of single-level rail passenger coaches in such train, as soon as practicable, but in no event later than 5 years after July 26, 1990; and

(B)   Location

Spaces required by subparagraph (A) shall be located in single-level rail passenger coaches or food service cars.

(C)   Limitation

Of the number of spaces required on a train by subparagraph (A), not more than two spaces to park and secure wheelchairs nor more than two spaces to fold and store wheelchairs shall be located in any one coach or food service car.

(D)   Other accessibility features

Single-level rail passenger coaches and food service cars on which the spaces required by subparagraph (a) are located shall have a restroom usable by an individual who uses a wheelchair and shall be able to be entered from the station platform by an individual who uses a wheelchair.

(4) Food service

(A)   Single-level dining cars

On any train in which a single-level dining car is used to provide food service

(i) if such single-level dining car was purchased after July 26, 1990, table service in such car shall be provided to a passenger who uses a wheelchair if

(I) the car adjacent to the end of the dining car through which a wheelchair may enter is itself accessible to a wheelchair;

(II) such passenger can exit to the platform from the car such passenger occupies, move down the platform, and enter the adjacent accessible car described in subclause (I) without the necessity of the train being moved within the station; and

(III) space to park and secure a wheelchair is available in the dining car at the time such passenger wishes to eat (if such passenger wishes to remain in a wheelchair), or space to store and fold a wheelchair is available in the dining car at the time such passenger wishes to eat (if such passenger wishes to transfer to a dining car seat); and

(ii) appropriate auxiliary aids and services, including a hard surface on which to eat, shall be provided to ensure that other equivalent food service is available to individuals with disabilities, including individuals who use wheelchairs, and to passengers traveling with such individuals. Unless not practicable, a person providing intercity rail transportation shall place an accessible car adjacent to the end of a dining car described in clause (I) through which an individual who uses a wheelchair may enter.

(B)　Bi-level dining cars

On any train in which a bi-level dining car is used to provide food service

(i) if such train includes a bi-level lounge car purchased after July 26, 1990, table service in such lounge car shall be provided to individuals who use wheelchairs and to other passengers; and

(ii) appropriate auxiliary aids and services, including a hard surface on which to eat, shall be provided to ensure that other equivalent food service is available to individuals with disabilities, including individuals who use wheelchairs, and to passengers traveling with such individuals.

(b) Commuter rail transportation

(1)　One car per train rule

It shall be considered discrimination for purposes of section 12132 of this title and section 794 of title 29 for a person who provides commuter rail transportation to fail to have at least one passenger car per train that is readily accessible to and usable by individuals with disabilities, including individuals who use wheelchairs, in accordance with regulations issued under section 12164 of this title, as soon as practicable, but in no event later than 5 years after July 26, 1990.

(2) New commuter rail cars

(A)　General rule

It shall be considered discrimination for purposes of section 12132 of this title and section 794 of title 29 for a person to purchase or lease any new rail passenger cars for use in commuter rail transportation, and for which a solicitation is made later than 30 days after July 26, 1990, unless all such rail cars are readily accessible to and usable by individuals with disabilities, including individuals who use wheelchairs, as prescribed by the Secretary of Transportation in regulations issued under section 12164 of this title.

(B)　Accessibility

For purposes of section 12132 of this title and section 794 of title 29, a requirement that a rail passenger car used in commuter rail transportation be accessible to or readily accessible to and usable by individuals with disabilities, including individuals who use wheelchairs, shall not be construed to require

(i) a restroom usable by an individual who uses a wheelchair if no restroom is provided in such car for any passenger;

(ii) space to fold and store a wheelchair; or

(iii) a seat to which a passenger who uses a wheelchair can transfer.

(c)   Used rail cars

It shall be considered discrimination for purposes of section 1132 of this title and section 794 of title 29 for a person to purchase or lease a used rail passenger car for use in intercity or commuter rail transportation, unless such person makes demonstrated good faith efforts to purchase or lease a used rail car that is readily accessible to and usable by individuals with disabilities, including individuals who use wheelchairs, as prescribed by the Secretary of Transportation in regulations issued under section 12164 of this title.

(d) Remanufactured rail cars

(1)   Remanufacturing

It shall be considered discrimination for purposes of section 12132 of this title and section 794 of title 29 for a person to remanufacture a rail passenger car for use in intercity or commuter rail transportation so as to extend its usable life for 10 years or more, unless the rail car, to the maximum extent feasible, is made readily accessible to and usable by individuals with disabilities, including individuals who use wheelchairs, as prescribed by the Secretary of Transportation in regulations issued under section 12164 of this title.

(2)   Purchase or lease

It shall be considered discrimination for purposes of section 12132 of this title and section 794 of title 29 for a person to purchase or lease a remanufactured rail passenger car for use in intercity or commuter rail transportation unless such car was remanufactured in accordance with paragraph (1).

(e) Stations

(1)   New stations

It shall be considered discrimination for purposes of section 12132 of this title and section 794 of title 29 for a person to build a new station for use in intercity or commuter rail transportation that is not readily accessible to and usable by individuals with disabilities, including individuals who use wheelchairs, as prescribed by the Secretary of Transportation in regulations issued under section 12164 of this title.

(2) Existing stations

(A) Failure to make readily accessible

(i)   General rule

It shall be considered discrimination for purposes of section 12132 of this title and section 794 of title 29 for a responsible person to fail to make existing stations in the intercity rail transportation system, and existing key stations in commuter rail transportation systems, readily accessible to and usable by individuals with disabilities, including individuals who use wheelchairs, as prescribed by the

Secretary of Transportation in regulations issued under section 12164 of this title.

(ii) Period for compliance

(I)   Intercity rail

All stations in the intercity rail transportation system shall be made readily accessible to and usable by individuals with disabilities, including individuals who use wheelchairs, as soon as practicable, but in no event later than 20 years after July 26, 1990.

(II)   Commuter rail

Key stations in commuter rail transportation systems shall be made readily accessible to and usable by individuals with disabilities, including individuals who use wheelchairs, as soon as practicable but in no event later than 3 years after July 26, 1990, except that the time limit may be extended by the Secretary of Transportation up to 20 years after July 26, 1990, in a case where the raising of the entire passenger platform is the only means available of attaining accessibility or where other extraordinarily expensive structural changes are necessary to attain accessibility.

(iii)   Designation of key stations

Each commuter authority shall designate the key stations in its commuter rail transportation system, in consultation with individuals with disabilities and organizations representing such individuals, taking into consideration such factors as high ridership and whether such station serves as a transfer or feeder station. Before the final designation of key stations under this clause, a commuter authority shall hold a public hearing.

(iv)   Plans and milestones

The Secretary of Transportation shall require the appropriate person to develop a plan for carrying out this subparagraph that reflects consultation with individuals with disabilities affected by such plan and that establishes milestones for achievement of the requirements of this subparagraph.

(B) Requirement when making alterations

(i)   General rule

It shall be considered discrimination, for purposes of section 12132 of this title and section 794 of title 29, with respect to alterations of an existing station or part thereof in the intercity or commuter rail transportation systems that affect or could affect the usability of the station or part thereof, for the responsible person, owner, or person in control of the station to fail to make the alterations in such a manner that, to the maximum extent feasible, the altered portions of the station are readily accessible to and usable by individuals with disabilities, including individuals who use wheelchairs, upon completion of such alterations.

(ii)   Alterations to a primary function area

It shall be considered discrimination, for purposes of section 12132 of this title and section 794 of title 29, with respect to alterations that affect or could affect the usability of or access to an area of the station containing a primary function, for the responsible person, owner, or person in control of the station to fail to make the alterations in such a manner that, to the maximum extent feasible, the path of travel to the altered area, and the bathrooms, telephones, and drinking fountains serving the altered area, are readily accessible to and usable by individuals with disabilities, including individuals who use wheelchairs, upon completion of such alterations, where such alterations to the path of travel or the bathrooms, telephones, and drinking fountains serving the altered area are not disproportionate to the overall alterations in terms of cost and scope (as determined under criteria established by the Attorney General).

(C) Required cooperation

It shall be considered discrimination for purposes of section 12132 of this title and section 794 of title 29 for an owner, or person in control, of a station governed by subparagraph (a) or (b) to fail to provide reasonable cooperation to a responsible person with respect to such station in that responsible person's efforts to comply with such subparagraph. An owner, or person in control, of a station shall be liable to a responsible person for any failure to provide reasonable cooperation as required by this subparagraph. Failure to receive reasonable cooperation required by this subparagraph shall not be a defense to a claim of discrimination under this chapter.

Sec. 12163. Conformance of accessibility standards

Accessibility standards included in regulations issued under this subpart shall be consistent with the minimum guidelines issued by the Architectural and Transportation Barriers Compliance Board under section 504(a) of this title.

Sec. 12164. Regulations

Not later than 1 year after July 26, 1990, the Secretary of Transportation shall issue regulations, in an accessible format, necessary for carrying out this subpart.

Sec. 12165. Interim accessibility requirements

(a) Stations

If final regulations have not been issued pursuant to section 12164 of this title, for new construction or alterations for which a valid and appropriate State or local building permit is obtained prior to the issuance of final regulations under such section, and for which the construction or alteration authorized by such permit begins within one year of the receipt of such permit and is completed under the terms of such permit, compliance with the Uniform Federal Accessibility Standards in effect at the time the building permit is issued shall suffice to satisfy the requirement that stations be readily accessible to and usable by persons with disabilities as required under section 12162(e) of this title, except that, if such final regulations have not been issued one year after the Architectural and Transportation Barriers Compliance Board has issued the supplemental minimum guidelines required under section 12204(a) of this title, compliance with such supplemental minimum guidelines shall be necessary to satisfy the requirement that stations be readily accessible to and usable by persons with disabilities prior to issuance of the final regulations.

(b) Rail passenger cars

If final regulations have not been issued pursuant to section 12164 of this title, a person shall be considered to have complied with the requirements of section 12162(a) through (d) of this title that a rail passenger car be readily accessible to and usable by individuals with disabilities, if the design for such car complies with the laws and regulations (including the Minimum Guidelines and Requirements for Accessible Design and such supplemental minimum guidelines as are issued under section 12204(a) of this title) governing accessibility of such cars, to the extent that such laws and regulations are not inconsistent with this subpart and are in effect at the time such design is substantially completed.

SUBCHAPTER III PUBLIC ACCOMMODATIONS AND SERVICES OPERATED BY PRIVATE ENTITIES

Sec. 12181. Definitions

As used in this subchapter:

(1) Commerce

The term "commerce" means travel, trade, traffic, commerce, transportation, or communications

(A) among the several States;

(B) between any foreign country or any territory or possession and any State; or

(C) between points in the same State but through another State or foreign country.

(2) Commercial facilities

The term "commercial facilities" means facilities

(A) that are intended for nonresidential use; and

(B) whose operations will affect commerce.

Such term shall not include railroad locomotives, railroad freight cars, railroad cabooses, railroad cars described in section 12162 of this title or covered under this subchapter, railroad rights-of-way, or facilities that are covered or expressly exempted from coverage under the Fair Housing Act of 1968 (42 U.S.C. 3601 et seq.).

(3) Demand responsive system

The term "demand responsive system" means any system of providing transportation of individuals by a vehicle, other than a system which is a fixed route system.

(4) Fixed route system

The term "fixed route system" means a system of providing transportation of individuals (other than by aircraft) on which a vehicle is operated along a prescribed route according to a fixed schedule.

(5) Over-the-road bus

The term "over-the-road bus" means a bus characterized by an elevated passenger deck located over a baggage compartment.

(6) Private entity

The term "private entity" means any entity other than a public entity (as defined in section 12131(1) of this title).

(7) Public accommodation

The following private entities are considered public accommodations for purposes of this subchapter, if the operations of such entities affect commerce

(A) an inn, hotel, motel, or other place of lodging, except for an establishment located within a building that contains not more than five rooms for rent or hire and that is actually occupied by the proprietor of such establishment as the residence of such proprietor;

(B) a restaurant, bar, or other establishment serving food or drink;

(C) a motion picture house, theater, concert hall, stadium, or other place of exhibition entertainment;

(D) an auditorium, convention center, lecture hall, or other place of public gathering;

(E) a bakery, grocery store, clothing store, hardware store, shopping center, or other sales or rental establishment;

(F) a laundromat, dry-cleaner, bank, barber shop, beauty shop, travel service, shoe repair service, funeral parlor, gas station, office of an accountant or lawyer, pharmacy, insurance office, professional office of a health care provider, hospital, or other service establishment;

(G) a terminal, depot, or other station used for specified public transportation;

(H) a museum, library, gallery, or other place of public display or collection;

(I) a park, zoo, amusement park, or other place of recreation;

(J) a nursery, elementary, secondary, undergraduate, or postgraduate private school, or other place of education;

(K) a day care center, senior citizen center, homeless shelter, food bank, adoption agency, or other social service center establishment; and

(L) a gymnasium, health spa, bowling alley, golf course, or other place of exercise or recreation.

(8)   Rail and railroad

The terms "rail" and "railroad" have the meaning given the term "railroad" in section 20102[1] of title 49.

(9)   Readily achievable

The term "readily achievable" means easily accomplishable and able to be carried out without much difficulty or expense. In determining whether an action is readily achievable, factors to be considered include

(A) the nature and cost of the action needed under this chapter;

(B) the overall financial resources of the facility or facilities involved in the action; the number of persons employed at such facility; the effect on expenses and resources, or the impact otherwise of such action upon the operation of the facility;

(C) the overall financial resources of the covered entity; the overall size of the business of a covered entity with respect to the number of its employees; the number, type, and location of its facilities; and

(D) the type of operation or operations of the covered entity, including the composition, structure, and functions of the workforce of such entity; the geographic separateness, administrative or fiscal relationship of the facility or facilities in question to the covered entity.

(10)   Specified public transportation

The term "specified public transportation" means transportation by bus, rail, or any other conveyance (other than by aircraft) that provides the general public with general or special service (including charter service) on a regular and continuing basis.

(11)   Vehicle

The term "vehicle" does not include a rail passenger car, railroad locomotive, railroad freight car, railroad caboose, or a railroad car described in section 12162 of this title or covered under this subchapter.

Sec. 12182.   Prohibition of discrimination by public accommodations

(a)   General rule

No individual shall be discriminated against on the basis of disability in the full and equal enjoyment of the goods, services, facilities, privileges, advantages, or accommodations of any place of public accommodation by any person who owns, leases (or leases to), or operates a place of public accommodation.

(b)   Construction

(1)   General prohibition

(A)   Activities

(i)   Denial of participation

It shall be discriminatory to subject an individual or class of individuals on the basis of a disability or disabilities of such individual or class, directly, or through contractual, licensing, or other arrangements, to a denial of the opportunity of the individual or class to participate in or benefit from the goods, services, facilities, privileges, advantages, or accommodations of an entity.

(ii)   Participation in unequal benefit

It shall be discriminatory to afford an individual or class of individuals, on the basis of a disability or disabilities of such individual or class, directly, or through contractual, licensing, or other arrangements with the opportunity to participate in or benefit from a good, service, facility, privilege, advantage, or accommodation that is not equal to that afforded to other individuals.

(iii)   Separate benefit

It shall be discriminatory to provide an individual or class of individuals, on the basis of a disability or disabilities of such individual or class, directly, or through contractual, licensing, or other arrangements with a good, service, facility, privilege, advantage, or accommodation that is different or separate from that provided to other individuals, unless such action is necessary to provide the individual or class of individuals with a good, service, facility, privilege, advantage, or accommodation, or other opportunity that is as effective as that provided to others.

(iv)   Individual or class of individuals

For purposes of clauses (i) through (iii) of this subparagraph, the term "individual or class of individuals" refers to the clients or customers of the covered public accommodation that enters into the contractual, licensing or other arrangement.

(B)   Integrated settings

Goods, services, facilities, privileges, advantages, and accommodations shall be afforded to an individual with a disability in the most integrated setting appropriate to the needs of the individual.

(C)   Opportunity to participate

Notwithstanding the existence of separate or different programs or activities provided in accordance with this section, an individual with a disability shall not be denied the opportunity to participate in such programs or activities that are not separate or different.

(D)   Administrative methods

An individual or entity shall not, directly or through contractual or other arrangements, utilize standards or criteria or methods of administration

(i) that have the effect of discriminating on the basis of disability; or

(ii) that perpetuate the discrimination of others who are subject to common administrative control.

(E)   Association

It shall be discriminatory to exclude or otherwise deny equal goods, services, facilities, privileges, advantages, accommodations, or other opportunities to an individual or entity because of the known disability of an individual with whom the individual or entity is known to have a relationship or association.

(2)   Specific prohibitions

(A)   Discrimination

For purposes of subsection (a) of this section, discrimination includes

(i) the imposition or application of eligibility criteria that screen out or tend to screen out an individual with a disability or any class of individuals with disabilities from fully and equally enjoying any goods, services, facilities, privileges, advantages, or accommodations, unless such criteria can be shown to be necessary for the provision of the goods, services, facilities, privileges, advantages, or accommodations being offered;

(ii) a failure to make reasonable modifications in policies, practices, or procedures, when such modifications are necessary to afford such goods, services, facilities, privileges, advantages, or accommodations to individuals with disabilities, unless the entity can demonstrate that making such modifications would fundamentally alter the nature of such goods, services, facilities, privileges, advantages, or accommodations;

(iii) a failure to take such steps as may be necessary to ensure that no individual with a disability is excluded, denied services, segregated or otherwise treated differently than other individuals because of the absence of auxiliary aids and services, unless the entity can demonstrate that taking such steps would fundamentally alter the nature of the good, service, facility, privilege, advantage, or accommodation being offered or would result in an undue burden;

(iv) a failure to remove architectural barriers, and communication barriers that are structural in nature, in existing facilities, and transportation barriers in existing vehicles and rail passenger cars used by an establishment for transporting individuals (not including barriers that can only be removed through the retrofitting of vehicles or rail passenger cars by the installation of a hydraulic or other lift), where such removal is readily achievable; and

(v) where an entity can demonstrate that the removal of a barrier under clause (iv) is not readily achievable, a failure to make such goods, services, facilities, privileges, advantages, or accommodations available through alternative methods if such methods are readily achievable.

(B)   Fixed route system

(i)   Accessibility

It shall be considered discrimination for a private entity which operates a fixed route system and which is not subject to section 12184 of this title to purchase or lease a vehicle with a seating capacity in excess of 16 passengers (including the driver) for use on such system, for which a solicitation is made after the 30th day following the effective date of this subparagraph, that is not readily accessible to and usable by individuals with disabilities, including individuals who use wheelchairs.

(ii)   Equivalent service

If a private entity which operates a fixed route system and which is not subject to section 12184 of this title purchases or leases a vehicle with a seating capacity of 16 passengers or less (including the driver) for use on such system after the effective date of this subparagraph that is not readily accessible to or usable by individuals with disabilities, it shall be considered discrimination for such entity to fail to operate such system so that, when viewed in its entirety, such system ensures a level of service to individuals with disabilities, including individuals who use wheelchairs, equivalent to the level of service provided to individuals without disabilities.

(C)   Demand responsive system

For purposes of subsection (a) of this section, discrimination includes

(i) a failure of a private entity which operates a demand responsive system and which is not subject to section 12184 of this title to operate such system so that, when viewed in its entirety, such system ensures a level of service to individuals with disabilities, including individuals who use wheelchairs, equivalent to the level of service provided to individuals without disabilities; and

(ii) the purchase or lease by such entity for use on such system of a vehicle with a seating capacity in excess of 16 passengers (including the driver), for which solicitations are made after the 30th day following the effective date of this subparagraph, that is not readily accessible to and usable by individuals with disabilities (including individuals who use wheelchairs) unless such entity can demonstrate that such system, when viewed in its entirety, provides a level of service to individuals with disabilities equivalent to that provided to individuals without disabilities.

(D) Over-the-road buses

(i)   Limitation on applicability

Subparagraphs (B) and (C) do not apply to over-the-road buses.

(ii)   Accessibility requirements

For purposes of subsection (a) of this section, discrimination includes

(I) the purchase or lease of an over-the-road bus which does not comply with the regulations issued under section 12186(a)(2) of this title by a private entity which provides transportation of individuals and which is not primarily engaged in the business of transporting people, and

(II) any other failure of such entity to comply with such regulations.

(3)   Specific construction

Nothing in this subchapter shall require an entity to permit an individual to participate in or benefit from the goods, services, facilities, privileges, advantages and accommodations of such entity where such individual poses a direct threat to the health or safety of others. The term "direct threat" means a significant risk to the health or safety of others that cannot be eliminated by a modification of policies, practices, or procedures or by the provision of auxiliary aids or services.

Sec. 12183.   New construction and alterations in public accommodations and commercial facilities

(a)   Application of term

Except as provided in subsection (b) of this section, as applied to public accommodations and commercial facilities, discrimination for purposes of section 12182(a) of this title includes

(1) a failure to design and construct facilities for first occupancy later than 30 months after July 26, 1990, that are readily accessible to and usable by individuals with disabilities, except where an entity can demonstrate that it is structurally impracticable to meet the requirements of such subsection in accordance with standards set forth or incorporated by reference in regulations issued under this subchapter; and

(2) with respect to a facility or part thereof that is altered by, on behalf of, or for the use of an establishment in a manner that affects or could affect the usability of the facility or part thereof, a failure to make alterations in such a manner that, to the maximum extent feasible, the altered portions of the facility are readily accessible to and usable by individuals with disabilities, including individuals who use wheelchairs. Where the entity is undertaking an alteration that affects or could affect usability of or access to an area of the facility containing a primary function, the entity shall also make the alterations in such a manner that, to the maximum extent feasible, the path of travel to the altered area and the bathrooms, telephones, and drinking fountains serving the altered area, are readily accessible to and usable by individuals with disabilities where such alterations to the path of travel or the bathrooms, telephones, and drinking fountains serving the altered area are not disproportionate to the overall alterations in terms of cost and scope (as determined under criteria established by the Attorney General).

(b) Elevator

Subsection (a) of this section shall not be construed to require the installation of an elevator for facilities that are less than three stories or have less than 3,000 square feet per story unless the building is a shopping center, a shopping mall, or the professional office of a health care provider or unless the Attorney General determines that a particular category of such facilities requires the installation of elevators based on the usage of such facilities.

Sec. 12184. Prohibition of discrimination in specified public transportation services provided by private entities

(a) General rule

No individual shall be discriminated against on the basis of disability in the full and equal enjoyment of specified public transportation services provided by a private entity that is primarily engaged in the business of transporting people and whose operations affect commerce.

(b) Construction

For purposes of subsection (a) of this section, discrimination includes

(1) the imposition or application by an entity described in subsection (a) of eligibility criteria that screen out or tend to screen out an individual with a disability or any class of individuals with disabilities from fully enjoying the specified public transportation services provided by the entity, unless such criteria can be shown to be necessary for the provision of the services being offered;

(2) the failure of such entity to

(A) make reasonable modifications consistent with those required under section 12182(b)(2)(A)(ii) of this title;

(B) provide auxiliary aids and services consistent with the requirements of section 12182(b)(2)(A)(iii) of this title; and

(C) remove barriers consistent with the requirements of section 12182(b)(2)(A) of this title and with the requirements of section 12183(a)(2) of this title;

(3) the purchase or lease by such entity of a new vehicle (other than an automobile, a van with a seating capacity of less than 8 passengers, including the driver, or an over- the-road bus) which is to be used to provide specified public transportation and for which a solicitation is made after the 30th day following the effective date of this section, that is not readily accessible to and usable by individuals with disabilities, including individuals who use wheelchairs; except that the new vehicle need not be readily accessible to and usable by such individuals if the new vehicle is to be used solely in a demand responsive system and if the entity can demonstrate that such system, when viewed in its entirety, provides a level of service to such individuals equivalent to the level of service provided to the general public;

(4) (A) the purchase or lease by such entity of an over-the-road bus which does not comply with the regulations issued under section 12186(a)(2) of this title; and

(B) any other failure of such entity to comply with such regulations; and

(5) the purchase or lease by such entity of a new van with a seating capacity of less than 8 passengers, including the driver, which is to be used to provide specified public transportation and for which a solicitation is made after the 30th day following the effective date of this section that is not readily accessible to or usable by individuals with disabilities, including individuals who use wheelchairs; except that the new van need not be readily accessible to and usable by such individuals if the entity can demonstrate that the system for which the van is being purchased or leased, when viewed in its entirety, provides a level of service to such individuals equivalent to the level of service provided to the general public;

(6) the purchase or lease by such entity of a new rail passenger car that is to be used to provide specified public transportation, and for which a solicitation is made later than 30 days after the effective date of this paragraph, that is not readily accessible to and usable by individuals with disabilities, including individuals who use wheelchairs; and

(7) the remanufacture by such entity of a rail passenger car that is to be used to provide specified public transportation so as to extend its usable life for 10 years or more, or the purchase or lease by such entity of such a rail car, unless the rail car, to the maximum extent feasible, is made readily accessible to and usable by individuals with disabilities, including individuals who use wheelchairs.

(c) Historical or antiquated cars

(1)   Exception

To the extent that compliance with subsection (a)(2)© or (a)(7)of this section would significantly alter the historic or antiquated character of a historical or antiquated rail passenger car, or a rail station served exclusively by such cars, or would result in violation of any rule, regulation, standard, or order issued by the Secretary of Transportation under the Federal Railroad Safety Act of 1970, such compliance shall not be required.

(2)   Definition

As used in this subsection, the term "historical or antiquated rail passenger car" means a rail passenger car

(A) which is not less than 30 years old at the time of its use for transporting individuals;

(B) the manufacturer of which is no longer in the business of manufacturing rail passenger cars; and

(C) which

(i) has a consequential association with events or persons significant to the past; or

(ii) embodies, or is being restored to embody, the distinctive characteristics of a type of rail passenger car used in the past, or to represent a time period which has passed.

Sec. 12185.   Study

(a)   Purposes

The Office of Technology Assessment shall undertake a study to determine

(1) the access needs of individuals with disabilities to over-the-road buses and over-the- road bus service; and

(2) the most cost-effective methods for providing access to over-the-road buses and over-the-road bus service to individuals with disabilities, particularly individuals who use wheelchairs, through all forms of boarding options.

(b)   Contents

The study shall include, at a minimum, an analysis of the following:

(1) The anticipated demand by individuals with disabilities for accessible over-the-road buses and over-the-road bus service.

(2) The degree to which such buses and service, including any service required under sections 12184(a)(4) and 12186(a)(2) of this title, are readily accessible to and usable by individuals with disabilities.

(3) The effectiveness of various methods of providing accessibility to such buses and service to individuals with disabilities.

(4) The cost of providing accessible over-the-road buses and bus service to individuals with disabilities, including consideration of recent technological and cost saving developments in equipment and devices.

(5) Possible design changes in over-the-road buses that could enhance accessibility, including the installation of accessible restrooms which do not result in a loss of seating capacity.

(6) The impact of accessibility requirements on the continuation of over-the-road bus service, with particular consideration of the impact of such requirements on such service to rural communities.

(c)   Advisory committee

In conducting the study required by subsection (a) of this section, the Office of Technology Assessment shall establish an advisory committee, which shall consist of

(1) members selected from among private operators and manufacturers of over-the-road buses;

(2) members selected from among individuals with disabilities, particularly individuals who use wheelchairs, who are potential riders of such buses; and

(3) members selected for their technical expertise on issues included in the study, including manufacturers of boarding assistance equipment and devices.

The number of members selected under each of paragraphs (1) and (2) shall be equal, and the total number of members selected under paragraphs (1) and (2) shall exceed the number of members selected under paragraph (3).

(d)   Deadline

The study required by subsection (a) of this section, along with recommendations by the Office of Technology Assessment, including any policy options for legislative action, shall be submitted to the President and Congress within 36 months after

July 26, 1990. If the President determines that compliance with the regulations issued pursuant to section 12186(a)(2)(B) of this title on or before the applicable deadlines specified in section 12186(a)(2)(B) of this title will result in a significant reduction in intercity over-the-road bus service, the President shall extend each such deadline by 1 year.

(e)   Review

In developing the study required by subsection (a) of this section, the Office of Technology Assessment shall provide a preliminary draft of such study to the Architectural and Transportation Barriers Compliance Board established under section 792 of title 29. The Board shall have an opportunity to comment on such draft study, and any such comments by the Board made in writing within 120 days after the Board's receipt of the draft study shall be incorporated as part of the final study required to be submitted under subsection (d) of this section.

Sec. 12186.   Regulations

(a)   Transportation provisions

(1)   General rule

Not later than 1 year after July 26, 1990, the Secretary of Transportation shall issue regulations in an accessible format to carry out sections 12182 (a)(2)(a) and (C) of this title and to carry out section 12184 of this title (other than subsection (a)(4)).

(2) Special rules for providing access to over-the-road buses

(A) Interim requirements

(i)   Issuance

Not later than 1 year after July 26, 1990, the Secretary of Transportation shall issue regulations in an accessible format to carry out sections 12184(b)(4) and 12182(b)(2)(D)(ii) of this title that require each private entity which uses an over-the-road bus to provide transportation of individuals to provide accessibility to such bus; except that such regulations shall not require any structural changes in over-the-road buses in order to provide access to individuals who use wheelchairs during the effective period of such regulations and shall not require the purchase of boarding assistance devices to provide access to such individuals.

(ii)   Effective period

The regulations issued pursuant to this subparagraph shall be effective until the effective date of the regulations issued under subparagraph (a).

(B)   Final requirement

(i)   Review of study and interim requirements

The Secretary shall review the study submitted under section 12185 of this title and the regulations issued pursuant to subparagraph (A).

(ii)   Issuance

Not later than 1 year after the date of the submission of the study under section 12185 of this title, the Secretary shall issue in an accessible format new regulations to carry out sections 12184(b)(4) and 12182(b)(2)(D)(ii) of this title that require, taking into account the purposes of the study under section 12185 of this title and any recommendations resulting from such study, each private entity which uses an over-the-road bus to provide transportation to individuals to provide accessibility to such bus to individuals with disabilities, including individuals who use wheelchairs.

(iii)　Effective period

Subject to section 12185(d) of this title, the regulations issued pursuant to this subparagraph shall take effect

(I) with respect to small providers of transportation (as defined by the Secretary), 3 years after the date of issuance of final regulations under clause (ii); and

(II) with respect to other providers of transportation, 2 years after the date of issuance of such final regulations.

(C)　Limitation on requiring installation of accessible restrooms

The regulations issued pursuant to this paragraph shall not require the installation of accessible restrooms in over-the-road buses if such installation would result in a loss of seating capacity.

(3)　Standards

The regulations issued pursuant to this subsection shall include standards applicable to facilities and vehicles covered by sections 12182(b) (2) and 12184 of this title.

(b)　Other provisions

Not later than 1 year after July 26, 1990, the Attorney General shall issue regulations in an accessible format to carry out the provisions of this subchapter not referred to in subsection (a) of this section that include standards applicable to facilities and vehicles covered under section 12182 of this title.

(c)　Consistency with ATBCB guidelines

Standards included in regulations issued under subsections (a) and (b) of this section shall be consistent with the minimum guidelines and requirements issued by the Architectural and Transportation Barriers Compliance Board in accordance with section 12204 of this title.

(d) Interim accessibility standards

(1)　Facilities

If final regulations have not been issued pursuant to this section, for new construction or alterations for which a valid and appropriate State or local building permit is obtained prior to the issuance of final regulations under this section, and for which the construction or alteration authorized by such permit begins within one year of the receipt of such permit and is completed under the terms of such permit, compliance with the Uniform Federal Accessibility Standards in effect at the time the building permit is issued shall suffice to satisfy the requirement that facilities be readily accessible to and usable by persons with disabilities as required under section 12183 of this title, except that, if such final regulations have not been issued one year after the Architectural and Transportation Barriers Compliance Board has issued the supplemental minimum guidelines required under section 12204(a) of this title, compliance with such supplemental minimum guidelines shall be necessary to satisfy the requirement that facilities be readily accessible to and usable by persons with disabilities prior to issuance of the final regulations.

(2)   Vehicles and rail passenger cars

If final regulations have not been issued pursuant to this section, a private entity shall be considered to have complied with the requirements of this subchapter, if any, that a vehicle or rail passenger car be readily accessible to and usable by individuals with disabilities, if the design for such vehicle or car complies with the laws and regulations (including the Minimum Guidelines and Requirements for Accessible Design and such supplemental minimum guidelines as are issued under section 12204(a) of this title) governing accessibility of such vehicles or cars, to the extent that such laws and regulations are not inconsistent with this subchapter and are in effect at the time such design is substantially completed.

Sec. 12187.   Exemptions for private clubs and religious organizations

The provisions of this subchapter shall not apply to private clubs or establishments exempted from coverage under title II of the Civil Rights Act of 1964 (42 U.S.C. 2000-a(e)) or to religious organizations or entities controlled by religious organizations, including places of worship.

Sec. 12188.   Enforcement

(a) In general

(1)   Availability of remedies and procedures

The remedies and procedures set forth in section 2000a-3(a) of this title are the remedies and procedures this subchapter provides to any person who is being subjected to discrimination on the basis of disability in violation of this subchapter or who has reasonable grounds for believing that such person is about to be subjected to discrimination in violation of section 12183 of this title. Nothing in this section shall require a person with a disability to engage in a futile gesture if such person has actual notice that a person or organization covered by this subchapter does not intend to comply with its provisions.

(2)   Injunctive relief

In the case of violations of sections 12182(b)(2)(A)(iv) and Section 12183(a) of this title, injunctive relief shall include an order to alter facilities to make such facilities readily accessible to and usable by individuals with disabilities to the extent required by this subchapter. Where appropriate, injunctive relief shall also include requiring the provision of an auxiliary aid or service, modification of a policy, or provision of alternative methods, to the extent required by this subchapter.

(b) Enforcement by Attorney General

(1) Denial of rights

(A) Duty to investigate

(i)   In general

The Attorney General shall investigate alleged violations of this subchapter, and shall undertake periodic reviews of compliance of covered entities under this subchapter.

(ii)   Attorney General certification

On the application of a State or local government, the Attorney General may, in consultation with the Architectural and Transportation Barriers Compliance Board, and after prior notice and a public hearing at which persons, including individuals with disabilities, are provided an opportunity to testify against such certification, certify that a State law or local building code or similar ordinance that establishes accessibility requirements meets or exceeds the minimum requirements of this chapter for the accessibility and usability of covered facilities under this subchapter. At any enforcement proceeding under this section, such certification by the Attorney General shall be rebuttable evidence that such State law or local ordinance does meet or exceed the minimum requirements of this chapter.

(B)   Potential violation

If the Attorney General has reasonable cause to believe that

(i) any person or group of persons is engaged in a pattern or practice of discrimination under this subchapter; or

(ii) any person or group of persons has been discriminated against under this subchapter and such discrimination raises an issue of general public importance, the Attorney General may commence a civil action in any appropriate United States district court.

(2)   Authority of court

In a civil action under paragraph (1) (B), the court

(A) may grant any equitable relief that such court considers to be appropriate, including, to the extent required by this subchapter

(i) granting temporary, preliminary, or permanent relief;

(ii) providing an auxiliary aid or service, modification of policy, practice, or procedure, or alternative method; and

(iii) making facilities readily accessible to and usable by individuals with disabilities;

(B) may award such other relief as the court considers to be appropriate, including monetary damages to persons aggrieved when requested by the Attorney General; and

(C) may, to vindicate the public interest, assess a civil penalty against the entity in an amount

(i) not exceeding $50,000 for a first violation; and

(ii) not exceeding $100,000 for any subsequent violation.

(3)   Single violation

For purposes of paragraph (2) (C), in determining whether a first or subsequent violation has occurred, a determination in a single action, by judgment or settlement, that the covered entity has engaged in more than one discriminatory act shall be counted as a single violation.

(4)   Punitive damages

For purposes of subsection (b) (2) (B) of this section, the term "monetary damages" and "such other relief" does not include punitive damages.

(5)   Judicial consideration

In a civil action under paragraph (1)(B), the court, when considering what amount of civil penalty, if any, is appropriate, shall give consideration to any good faith effort or attempt to comply with this chapter by the entity. In evaluating good faith, the court shall consider, among other factors it deems relevant, whether the entity could have reasonably anticipated the need for an appropriate type of auxiliary aid needed to accommodate the unique needs of a particular individual with a disability.

Sec. 12189.   Examinations and courses

Any person that offers examinations or courses related to applications, licensing, certification, or credentialing for secondary or postsecondary education, professional, or trade purposes shall offer such examinations or courses in a place and manner accessible to persons with disabilities or offer alternative accessible arrangements for such individuals.

SUBCHAPTER IV   MISCELLANEOUS PROVISIONS

Sec. 12201.   Construction

(a)   In general

Except as otherwise provided in this chapter, nothing in this chapter shall be construed to apply a lesser standard than the standards applied under title V of the Rehabilitation Act of 1973 (29 U.S.C. 790 et seq.) or the regulations issued by Federal agencies pursuant to such title.

(b)   Relationship to other laws

Nothing in this chapter shall be construed to invalidate or limit the remedies, rights, and procedures of any Federal law or law of any State or political subdivision of any State or jurisdiction that provides greater or equal protection for the rights of individuals with disabilities than are afforded by this chapter. Nothing in this chapter shall be construed to preclude the prohibition of, or the imposition of restrictions on, smoking in places of employment covered by subchapter I of this chapter, in transportation covered by subchapter II or III of this chapter, or in places of public accommodation covered by subchapter III of this chapter.

(c)   Insurance

Subchapters I through III of this chapter and title IV of this Act shall not be construed to prohibit or restrict

(1) an insurer, hospital or medical service company, health maintenance organization, or any agent, or entity that administers benefit plans, or similar organizations from underwriting risks, classifying risks, or administering such risks that are based on or not inconsistent with State law; or

(2) a person or organization covered by this chapter from establishing, sponsoring, observing or administering the terms of a bona fide benefit plan that are based on underwriting risks, classifying risks, or administering such risks that are based on or not inconsistent with State law; or

(3) a person or organization covered by this chapter from establishing, sponsoring, observing or administering the terms of a bona fide benefit plan that is not subject to State laws that regulate insurance.

Paragraphs (1), (2), and (3) shall not be used as a subterfuge to evade the purposes of subchapter I and III of this chapter.

(d)   Accommodations and services

Nothing in this chapter shall be construed to require an individual with a disability to accept an accommodation, aid, service, opportunity, or benefit which such individual chooses not to accept.

(e)   Benefits under State worker's compensation laws

Nothing in this chapter alters the standards for determining eligibility for benefits under State worker's compensation laws or under State and Federal disability benefit programs.

(f)   Fundamental alteration

Nothing in this chapter alters the provision of section 12182(b)(2)(A)(ii), specifying that reasonable modifications in policies, practices, or procedures shall be required, unless an entity can demonstrate that making such modifications in policies, practices, or procedures, including academic requirements in postsecondary education, would fundamentally alter the nature of the goods, services, facilities, privileges, advantages, or accommodations involved.

(g) Claims of no disability

Nothing in this chapter shall provide the basis for a claim by an individual without a disability that the individual was subject to discrimination because of the individual's lack of disability.

(h) Reasonable accommodations and modifications

A covered entity under subchapter I, a public entity under subchapter II, and any person who owns, leases (or leases to), or operates a place of public accommodation under subchapter III, need not provide a reasonable accommodation or a reasonable modification to policies, practices, or procedures to an individual who meets the definition of disability in section 12102(1) solely under subparagraph (C) of such section.

Sec. 12202. State immunity

A State shall not be immune under the eleventh amendment to the Constitution of the United States from an action in Federal or State court of competent jurisdiction for a violation of this chapter. In any action against a State for a violation of the requirements of this chapter, remedies (including remedies both at law and in equity) are available for such a violation to the same extent as such remedies are available for such a violation in an action against any public or private entity other than a State.

Sec. 12203. Prohibition against retaliation and coercion

(a) Retaliation

No person shall discriminate against any individual because such individual has opposed any act or practice made unlawful by this chapter or because such individual made a charge, testified, assisted, or participated in any manner in an investigation, proceeding, or hearing under this chapter.

(b) Interference, coercion, or intimidation

It shall be unlawful to coerce, intimidate, threaten, or interfere with any individual in the exercise or enjoyment of, or on account of his or her having exercised or enjoyed, or on account of his or her having aided or encouraged any other individual in the exercise or enjoyment of, any right granted or protected by this chapter.

(c) Remedies and procedures

The remedies and procedures available under sections 12117, 12133, and 12188 of this title shall be available to aggrieved persons for violations of subsections (a) and (b) of this section, with respect to subchapter I, subchapter II and subchapter III of this chapter, respectively.

Sec. 12204. Regulations by Architectural and Transportation Barriers Compliance Board

(a) Issuance of guidelines

Not later than 9 months after July 26, 1990, the Architectural and Transportation Barriers Compliance Board shall issue minimum guidelines that shall supplement the existing Minimum Guidelines and Requirements for Accessible Design for purposes of subchapters II and III of this chapter.

(b) Contents of guidelines

The supplemental guidelines issued under subsection (a) of this section shall establish additional requirements, consistent with this chapter, to ensure that buildings, facilities, rail passenger cars, and vehicles are accessible, in terms of architecture and design, transportation, and communication, to individuals with disabilities.

(c) Qualified historic properties

(1) In general

The supplemental guidelines issued under subsection (a) of this section shall include procedures and requirements for alterations that will threaten or destroy the historic significance of qualified historic buildings and facilities as defined in 4.1.7(1)(a) of the Uniform Federal Accessibility Standards.

(2) Sites eligible for listing in National Register

With respect to alterations of buildings or facilities that are eligible for listing in the National Register of Historic Places under the National Historic Preservation Act (16 U.S.C. 470 et seq.), the guidelines described in paragraph (1) shall, at a minimum, maintain the procedures and requirements established in 4.1.7(1) and (2) of the Uniform Federal Accessibility Standards.

(3) Other sites

With respect to alterations of buildings or facilities designated as historic under State or local law, the guidelines described in paragraph (1) shall establish procedures equivalent to those established by 4.1.7(1)(b) and (c) of the Uniform Federal Accessibility Standards, and shall require, at a minimum, compliance with the requirements established in 4.1.7(2) of such standards.

Sec. 12205. Attorney's fees

In any action or administrative proceeding commenced pursuant to this chapter, the court or agency, in its discretion, may allow the prevailing party, other than the United States, a reasonable attorney's fee, including litigation expenses, and costs, and the United States shall be liable for the foregoing the same as a private individual.

Sec. 12205a. Rule of Construction Regarding Regulatory Authority

The authority to issue regulations granted to the Equal Employment Opportunity Commission, the Attorney General, and the Secretary of Transportation under this chapter includes the authority to issue regulations implementing the definitions of disability in section 12102 (including rules of construction) and the definitions in section 12103, consistent with the ADA Amendments Act of 2008.

Sec. 12206.   Technical assistance

(a) Plan for assistance

(1)   In general

Not later than 180 days after July 26, 1990, the Attorney General, in consultation with the Chair of the Equal Employment Opportunity Commission, the Secretary of Transportation, the Chair of the Architectural and Transportation Barriers Compliance Board, and the Chairman of the Federal Communications Commission, shall develop a plan to assist entities covered under this chapter, and other Federal agencies, in understanding the responsibility of such entities and agencies under this chapter.

(2)   Publication of plan

The Attorney General shall publish the plan referred to in paragraph (1) for public comment in accordance with subchapter II of chapter 5 of title 5 (commonly known as the Administrative Procedure Act).

(b)   Agency and public assistance

The Attorney General may obtain the assistance of other Federal agencies in carrying out subsection (a) of this section, including the National Council on Disability, the President's Committee on Employment of People with Disabilities, the Small Business Administration, and the Department of Commerce.

(c) Implementation

(1)   Rendering assistance

Each Federal agency that has responsibility under paragraph (2) for implementing this chapter may render technical assistance to individuals and institutions that have rights or duties under the respective subchapter or subchapters of this chapter for which such agency has responsibility.

(2) Implementation of subchapters

(A)   Subchapter I

The Equal Employment Opportunity Commission and the Attorney General shall implement the plan for assistance developed under subsection (a) of this section, for subchapter I of this chapter.

(B) Subchapter II

(i)   Part A

The Attorney General shall implement such plan for assistance for part A of subchapter II of this chapter.

(ii)   Part B

The Secretary of Transportation shall implement such plan for assistance for part B of subchapter II of this chapter.

(C)   Subchapter III

The Attorney General, in coordination with the Secretary of Transportation and the Chair of the Architectural Transportation Barriers Compliance Board, shall implement such plan for assistance for subchapter III of this chapter, except for section 12184 of this title, the plan for assistance for which shall be implemented by the Secretary of Transportation.

(D)   Title IV

The Chairman of the Federal Communications Commission, in coordination with the Attorney General, shall implement such plan for assistance for title IV.

(3)   Technical assistance manuals

Each Federal agency that has responsibility under paragraph (2) for implementing this chapter shall, as part of its implementation responsibilities, ensure the availability and provision of appropriate technical assistance manuals to individuals or entities with rights or duties under this chapter no later than six months after applicable final regulations are published under subchapters I, II, and III of this chapter and title IV.

(d) Grants and contracts

(1)   In general

Each Federal agency that has responsibility under subsection (c) (2) of this section for implementing this chapter may make grants or award contracts to effectuate the purposes of this section, subject to the availability of appropriations. Such grants and contracts may be awarded to individuals, institutions not organized for profit and no part of the net earnings of which inures to the benefit of any private shareholder or individual (including educational institutions), and associations representing individuals who have rights or duties under this chapter. Contracts may be awarded to entities organized for profit, but such entities may not be the recipients or grants described in this paragraph.

(2)   Dissemination of information

Such grants and contracts, among other uses, may be designed to ensure wide dissemination of information about the rights and duties established by this chapter and to provide information and technical assistance about techniques for effective compliance with this chapter.

(e)   Failure to receive assistance

An employer, public accommodation, or other entity covered under this chapter shall not be excused from compliance with the requirements of this chapter because of any failure to receive technical assistance under this section, including any failure in the development or dissemination of any technical assistance manual authorized by this section.

Sec. 12207.   Federal wilderness areas

(a)   Study

The National Council on Disability shall conduct a study and report on the effect that wilderness designations and wilderness land management practices have on the ability of individuals with disabilities to use and enjoy the National Wilderness

Preservation System as established under the Wilderness Act (16 U.S.C. 1131 et seq.).

(b)   Submission of report

Not later than 1 year after July 26, 1990, the National Council on Disability shall submit the report required under subsection (a) of this section to Congress.

(c) Specific wilderness access

(1)   In general

Congress reaffirms that nothing in the Wilderness Act (16 U.S.C. 1131 et seq.) is to be construed as prohibiting the use of a wheelchair in a wilderness area by an individual whose disability requires use of a wheelchair, and consistent with the Wilderness Act no agency is required to provide any form of special treatment or accommodation, or to construct any facilities or modify any conditions of lands within a wilderness area in order to facilitate such use.

(2)   "Wheelchair" defined

For purposes of paragraph (1), the term "wheelchair" means a device designed solely for use by a mobility-impaired person for locomotion, that is suitable for use in an indoor pedestrian area.

Sec. 12208.   Transvestites

For the purposes of this chapter, the term "disabled" or "disability" shall not apply to an individual solely because that individual is a transvestite.

Sec. 12209.   Instrumentalities of Congress

The General Accounting Office, the Government Printing Office, and the Library of Congress shall be covered as follows:

(1)   In general

The rights and protections under this chapter shall, subject to paragraph (2), apply with respect to the conduct of each instrumentality of the Congress.

(2)   Establishment of remedies and procedures by instrumentalities

The chief official of each instrumentality of the Congress shall establish remedies and procedures to be utilized with respect to the rights and protections provided pursuant to paragraph (1).

(3)   Report to Congress

The chief official of each instrumentality of the Congress shall, after establishing remedies and procedures for purposes of paragraph (2), submit to the Congress a report describing the remedies and procedures.

(4)   Definition of instrumentalities

For purposes of this section, the term "instrumentality of the Congress" means the following: the General Accounting Office, the Government Printing Office, and the Library of Congress.

(5)   Enforcement of employment rights

The remedies and procedures set forth in section 2000e -16 of this title shall be available to any employee of an instrumentality of the Congress who alleges a violation of the rights and protections under sections 12112 through 12114 of this title that are made applicable by this section, except that the authorities of the Equal Employment Opportunity Commission shall be exercised by the chief official of the instrumentality of the Congress.

(6)   Enforcement of rights to public services and accommodations

The remedies and procedures set forth in section 2000e -16 of this title shall be available to any qualified person with a disability who is a visitor, guest, or patron of an instrumentality of Congress and who alleges a violation of the rights and protections under sections 12131 through 12150 of this title or section 12182 or 12183 of this title that are made applicable by this section, except that the authorities of the Equal Employment Opportunity Commission shall be exercised by the chief official of the instrumentality of the Congress.

(7)   Construction

Nothing in this section shall alter the enforcement procedures for individuals with disabilities provided in the General Accounting Office Personnel Act of 1980 and regulations promulgated pursuant to that Act.

Sec. 12210.   Illegal use of drugs

(a)   In general

For purposes of this chapter, the term "individual with a disability" does not include an individual who is currently engaging in the illegal use of drugs, when the covered entity acts on the basis of such use.

(b)   Rules of construction

Nothing in subsection (a) of this section shall be construed to exclude as an individual with a disability an individual who

(1) has successfully completed a supervised drug rehabilitation program and is no longer engaging in the illegal use of drugs, or has otherwise been rehabilitated successfully and is no longer engaging in such use;

(2) is participating in a supervised rehabilitation program and is no longer engaging in such use; or

(3) is erroneously regarded as engaging in such use, but is not engaging in such use;

except that it shall not be a violation of this chapter for a covered entity to adopt or administer reasonable policies or procedures, including but not limited to drug testing, designed to ensure that an individual described in paragraph (1) or (2) is no longer engaging in the illegal use of drugs; however, nothing in this section shall be construed to encourage, prohibit, restrict, or authorize the conducting of testing for the illegal use of drugs.

(c)   Health and other services

Notwithstanding subsection (a) of this section and section 12211(b)(3) of this subchapter, an individual shall not be denied health services, or services provided in connection with drug rehabilitation, on the basis of the current illegal use of drugs if the individual is otherwise entitled to such services.

(d) "Illegal use of drugs" defined

(1) In general

The term "illegal use of drugs" means the use of drugs, the possession or distribution of which is unlawful under the Controlled Substances Act (21 U.S.C. 801 et seq.). Such term does not include the use of a drug taken under supervision by a licensed health care professional, or other uses authorized by the Controlled Substances Act or other provisions of Federal law.

(2) Drugs

The term "drug" means a controlled substance, as defined in schedules I through V of section 202 of the Controlled Substances Act (21 U.S.C. 812).

Sec. 12211.   Definitions

(a) Homosexuality and bisexuality

For purposes of the definition of "disability" in section 12102(2) of this title, homosexuality and bisexuality are not impairments and as such are not disabilities under this chapter.

(b) Certain conditions

Under this chapter, the term "disability" shall not include

(1) transvestism, transsexualism, pedophilia, exhibitionism, voyeurism, gender identity disorders not resulting from physical impairments, or other sexual behavior disorders;

(2) compulsive gambling, kleptomania, or pyromania; or

(3) psychoactive substance use disorders resulting from current illegal use of drugs.

Sec. 12212.   Alternative means of dispute resolution

Where appropriate and to the extent authorized by law, the use of alternative means of dispute resolution, including settlement negotiations, conciliation, facilitation, mediation, fact-finding, minitrials, and arbitration, is encouraged to resolve disputes arising under this chapter.

Sec. 12213.   Severability

Should any provision in this chapter be found to be unconstitutional by a court of law, such provision shall be severed from the remainder of the chapter, and such action shall not affect the enforceability of the remaining provisions of the chapter.

TITLE 47   TELEGRAPHS, TELEPHONES, AND RADIOTELEGRAPHS
CHAPTER 5   WIRE OR RADIO COMMUNICATION

SUBCHAPTER II   COMMON CARRIERS
Part I   Common Carrier Regulation

Sec. 225.   Telecommunications services for hearing-impaired and speech-impaired individuals

(a)   Definitions

As used in this section

(1)   Common carrier or carrier

The term "common carrier" or "carrier" includes any common carrier engaged in interstate communication by wire or radio as defined in section 153 of this title and any common carrier engaged in intrastate communication by wire or radio, notwithstanding sections 152(a) and 221(a) of this title.

(2)   TDD

The term "TDD" means a Telecommunications Device for the Deaf which is a machine that employs graphic communication in the transmission of coded signals through a wire or radio communication system.

(3)   Telecommunications relay services

The term "telecommunications relay services" means telephone transmission relay services that provide the ability for an individual who has a hearing impairment or speech impairment to engage in communication by wire or radio with a hearing individual in a manner that is functionally equivalent to the ability of an individual who does not have a hearing impairment or speech impairment to communicate using voice communication services by wire or radio. Such term includes services that enable two-way communication between an individual who uses a TDD or other nonvoice terminal device and an individual who does not use such a device.

(b) Availability of telecommunications relay service

(1)   In general

In order to carry out the purposes established under section 151 of this title, to make available to all individuals in the United States a rapid, efficient nationwide communication service, and to increase the utility of the telephone system of the Nation, the Commission shall ensure that interstate and intrastate telecommunications relay services are available, to the extent possible and in the most efficient manner, to hearing-impaired and speech-impaired individuals in the United States.

(2)   Use of general authority and remedies

For the purposes of administering and enforcing the provisions of this section and the regulations prescribed thereunder, the Commission shall have the same authority, power, and functions with respect to common carriers engaged in intrastate communication as the Commission has in administering and enforcing the provisions of this subchapter with respect to any common carrier engaged in interstate communication. Any violation of this section by any common carrier engaged in intrastate communication shall be subject to the same remedies, penalties, and procedures as are applicable to a violation of this chapter by a common carrier engaged in interstate communication.

(c) Provision of services

Each common carrier providing telephone voice transmission services shall, not later than 3 years after July 26, 1990, provide in compliance with the regulations prescribed under this section, throughout the area in which it offers service, telecommunications relay services, individually, through designees, through a competitively selected vendor, or in concert with other carriers. A common carrier shall be considered to be in compliance with such regulations

(1) with respect to intrastate telecommunications relay services in any State that does not have a certified program under subsection (f) of this section and with respect to interstate telecommunications relay services, if such common carrier (or other entity through which the carrier is providing such relay services) is in compliance with the Commission's regulations under subsection (d) of this section; or

(2) with respect to intrastate telecommunications relay services in any State that has a certified program under subsection (f) of this section for such State, if such common carrier (or other entity through which the carrier is providing such relay services) is in compliance with the program certified under subsection (f) of this section for such State.

(d) Regulations

(1) In general

The Commission shall, not later than 1 year after July 26, 1990, prescribe regulations to implement this section, including regulations that

(A) establish functional requirements, guidelines, and operations procedures for telecommunications relay services;

(B) establish minimum standards that shall be met in carrying out subsection (c) of this section;

(C) require that telecommunications relay services operate every day for 24 hours per day;

(D) require that users of telecommunications relay services pay rates no greater than the rates paid for functionally equivalent voice communication services with respect to such factors as the duration of the call, the time of day, and the distance from point of origination to point of termination;

(E) prohibit relay operators from failing to fulfill the obligations of common carriers by refusing calls or limiting the length of calls that use telecommunications relay services;

(F) prohibit relay operators from disclosing the content of any relayed conversation and from keeping records of the content of any such conversation beyond the duration of the call; and

(G) prohibit relay operators from intentionally altering a relayed conversation.

(2) Technology

The Commission shall ensure that regulations prescribed to implement this section encourage, consistent with section 157(a) of this title, the use of existing technology and do not discourage or impair the development of improved technology.

(3) Jurisdictional separation of costs

(A) In general

Consistent with the provisions of section 410 of this title, the Commission shall prescribe regulations governing the jurisdictional separation of costs for the services provided pursuant to this section.

(B) Recovering costs

Such regulations shall generally provide that costs caused by interstate telecommunications relay services shall be recovered from all subscribers for every interstate service and costs caused by intrastate telecommunications relay services shall be recovered from the intrastate jurisdiction. In a State that has a certified program under subsection (f) of this section, a State commission shall permit a common carrier to recover the costs incurred in providing intrastate telecommunications relay services by a method consistent with the requirements of this section.

(e) Enforcement

(1) In general

Subject to subsections (f) and (g) of this section, the Commission shall enforce this section.

(2) Complaint

The Commission shall resolve, by final order, a complaint alleging a violation of this section within 180 days after the date such complaint is filed.

(f) Certification

(1) State documentation

Any State desiring to establish a State program under this section shall submit documentation to the Commission that describes the program of such State for implementing intrastate telecommunications relay services and the procedures and remedies available for enforcing any requirements imposed by the State program.

(2) Requirements for certification

After review of such documentation, the Commission shall certify the State program if the Commission determines that

(A) the program makes available to hearing-impaired and speech-impaired individuals, either directly, through designees, through a competitively selected vendor, or through regulation of intrastate common carriers, intrastate telecommunications relay services in such State in a manner that meets or exceeds the requirements of regulations prescribed by the Commission under subsection (d) of this section; and

(B) the program makes available adequate procedures and remedies for enforcing the requirements of the State program.

(3)   Method of funding

Except as provided in subsection (d) of this section, the Commission shall not refuse to certify a State program based solely on the method such State will implement for funding intrastate telecommunication relay services.

(4)   Suspension or revocation of certification

The Commission may suspend or revoke such certification if, after notice and opportunity for hearing, the Commission determines that such certification is no longer warranted. In a State whose program has been suspended or revoked, the Commission shall take such steps as may be necessary, consistent with this section, to ensure continuity of telecommunications relay services.

(g)   Complaint

(1)   Referral of complaint

If a complaint to the Commission alleges a violation of this section with respect to intrastate telecommunications relay services within a State and certification of the program of such State under subsection (f) of this section is in effect, the Commission shall refer such complaint to such State.

(2)   Jurisdiction of Commission

After referring a complaint to a State under paragraph (1), the Commission shall exercise jurisdiction over such complaint only if

(A) final action under such State program has not been taken on such complaint by such State

(i) within 180 days after the complaint is filed with such State; or

(ii) within a shorter period as prescribed by the regulations of such State; or

(B) the Commission determines that such State program is no longer qualified for certification under subsection (f) of this section.

SUBCHAPTER VI MISCELLANEOUS PROVISIONS

Sec. 611. Closed-captioning of public service announcements

Any television public service announcement that is produced or funded in whole or in part by any agency or instrumentality of Federal Government shall include closed captioning of the verbal content of such announcement. A television broadcast station licensee

(1) shall not be required to supply closed captioning for any such announcement that fails to include it; and

(2) shall not be liable for broadcasting any such announcement without transmitting a closed caption unless the licensee intentionally fails to transmit the closed caption that was included with the announcement.

Chapter 2
EEOC REGULATIONS TO IMPLEMENT THE EQUAL EMPLOYMENT PROVISIONS OF THE ADA

EEOC REGULATIONS

§ 1630.1 Purpose, applicability, and construction.

(a) *Purpose*. The purpose of this part is to implement title I of the Americans with Disabilities Act (ADA), as amended by the ADA Amendments Act of 2008 (ADAAA or Amendments Act), 42 U.S.C. 12101, et seq.) requiring equal employment opportunities for individuals with disabilities. The ADA as amended, and these regulations, are intended to provide a clear and comprehensive national mandate for the elimination of discrimination against individuals with disabilities, and to provide clear, strong, consistent, enforceable standards addressing discrimination.

(b) *Applicability*. This part applies to "covered entities" as defined at § 1630.2(b).

(c) Construction —

(1) In general. Except as otherwise provided in this part, this part does not apply a lesser standard than the standards applied under title V of the Rehabilitation Act of 1973 (29 U.S.C. 790–794a, as amended), or the regulations issued by Federal agencies pursuant to that title.

(2) Relationship to other laws. This part does not invalidate or limit the remedies, rights, and procedures of any Federal law or law of any State or political subdivision of any State or jurisdiction that provides greater or equal

protection for the rights of individuals with disabilities than are afforded by this part.

(3) *State workers' compensation laws and disability benefit programs.* Nothing in this part alters the standards for determining eligibility for benefits under State workers' compensation laws or under State and Federal disability benefit programs.

(4) *Broad coverage.* The primary purpose of the ADAAA is to make it easier for people with disabilities to obtain protection under the ADA. Consistent with the Amendments Act's purpose of reinstating a broad scope of protection under the ADA, the definition of "disability" in this part shall be construed broadly in favor of expansive coverage to the maximum extent permitted by the terms of the ADA. The primary object of attention in cases brought under the ADA should be whether covered entities have complied with their obligations and whether discrimination has occurred, *not* whether the individual meets the definition of disability. The question of whether an individual meets the definition of disability under this part should not demand extensive analysis.

§ 1630.2 Definitions.

(a) Commission means the Equal Employment Opportunity Commission established by section 705 of the Civil Rights Act of 1964 (42 U.S.C. 2000e-4).

(b) Covered Entity means an employer, employment agency, labor organization, or joint labor management committee.

(c) Person, labor organization, employment agency, commerce and industry affecting commerce shall have the same meaning given those terms in section 701 of the Civil Rights Act of 1964 (42 U.S.C. 2000e).

(d) State means each of the several States, the District of Columbia, the Commonwealth of Puerto Rico, Guam, American Samoa, the Virgin Islands, the Trust Territory of the Pacific Islands, and the Commonwealth of the Northern Mariana Islands.

(e) Employer —

(1) In general. The term employer means a person engaged in an industry affecting commerce who has 15 or more employees for each working day in each of 20 or more calendar weeks in the current or preceding calendar year, and any agent of such person, except that, from July 26, 1992 through July 25, 1994, an employer means a person engaged in an industry affecting commerce who has 25 or more employees for each working day in each of 20 or more calendar weeks in the current or preceding year and any agent of such person.

(2) Exceptions. The term employer does not include —

(i) The United States, a corporation wholly owned by the government of the United States, or an Indian tribe; or

(ii) A bona fide private membership club (other than a labor organization) that is exempt from taxation under section 501(c) of the Internal Revenue Code of 1986.

(f) Employee means an individual employed by an employer.

(g) *Definition of "disability."*

(1) In general. Disability means, with respect to an individual —

(i) A physical or mental impairment that substantially limits one or more of the major life activities of such individual;

(ii) A record of such an impairment; or

(iii) being regarded as having such an impairment as described in paragraph (l) of this section. This means that the individual has been subjected to an action prohibited by the ADA as amended because of an actual or perceived impairment that is not both "transitory and minor."

(2) An individual may establish coverage under any one or more of these three prongs of the definition of disability, i.e., paragraphs (g)(1)(i) (the "actual disability" prong), (g)(1)(ii) (the "record of" prong), and/or (g)(1)(iii) (the "regarded as" prong) of this section.

(3) Where an individual is not challenging a covered entity's failure to make reasonable accommodations and does not require a reasonable accommodation, it is generally unnecessary to proceed under the "actual disability" or "record of" prongs, which require a showing of an impairment that substantially limits a major life activity or a record of such an impairment. In these cases, the evaluation of coverage can be made solely under the "regarded as" prong of the definition of disability, which does not require a showing of an impairment that substantially limits a major life activity or a record of such an impairment. An individual may choose, however, to proceed under the "actual disability" and/or "record of" prong regardless of whether the individual is challenging a covered entity's failure to make reasonable accommodations or requires a reasonable accommodation.

(Note to paragraph g: See § 1630.3 for exceptions to this definition).

(h) Physical or mental impairment means: —

(1) Any physiological disorder, or condition, cosmetic disfigurement, or anatomical loss affecting one or more body systems, such as: neurological, musculoskeletal, special sense organs, respiratory (including speech organs), cardiovascular, reproductive, digestive, genitourinary, immune, circulatory, hemic, lymphatic, skin, and endocrine; or

(2) Any mental or psychological disorder, such as an intellectual disability (formerly termed "mental retardation"), organic brain syndrome, emotional or mental illness, and specific learning disabilities.

(i) Major Life Activities

(1) *In general.* Major life activities include, but are not limited to:

(i) Caring for oneself, performing manual tasks, seeing, hearing, eating, sleeping, walking, standing, sitting, reaching, lifting, bending, speaking, breathing, learning, reading, concentrating, thinking, communicating, interacting with others, and working; and

(ii) The operation of a major bodily function, including functions of the immune system, special sense organs and skin; normal cell growth; and digestive, genitourinary, bowel, bladder, neurological, brain, respiratory, circulatory, cardiovascular, endocrine, hemic, lymphatic, musculoskeletal, and reproductive functions. The operation of a major bodily function includes the operation of an individual organ within a body system.

(2) In determining other examples of major life activities, the term "major" shall not be interpreted strictly to create a demanding standard for disability. ADAAA Section 2(b)(4) (Findings and Purposes). Whether an activity is a "major life activity" is not determined by reference to whether it is of "central importance to daily life."

(j) *Substantially limits* —

(1) Rules of construction. The following rules of construction apply when determining whether an impairment substantially limits an individual in a major life activity:

(i) The term "substantially limits" shall be construed broadly in favor of expansive coverage, to the maximum extent permitted by the terms of the ADA. "Substantially limits" is not meant to be a demanding standard.

(ii) An impairment is a disability within the meaning of this section if it substantially limits the ability of an individual to perform a major life activity as compared to most people in the general population. An impairment need not prevent, or significantly or severely restrict, the individual from performing a major life activity in order to be considered substantially limiting. Nonetheless, not every impairment will constitute a disability within the meaning of this section.

(iii) The primary object of attention in cases brought under the ADA should be whether covered entities have complied with their obligations and whether discrimination has occurred, not whether an individual's impairment substantially limits a major life activity. Accordingly, the threshold issue of whether an impairment "substantially limits" a major life activity should not demand extensive analysis.

(iv) The determination of whether an impairment substantially limits a major life activity requires an individualized assessment. However, in making this assessment, the term "substantially limits" shall be interpreted and applied to require a degree of functional limitation that is lower than the standard for "substantially limits" applied prior to the ADAAA.

(v) The comparison of an individual's performance of a major life activity to the performance of the same major life activity by most people in the general population usually will not require scientific, medical, or statistical analysis. Nothing in this paragraph is intended, however, to prohibit the presentation of scientific, medical, or statistical evidence to make such a comparison where appropriate.

(vi) The determination of whether an impairment substantially limits a major life activity shall be made without regard to the ameliorative effects of mitigating measures. However, the ameliorative effects of ordinary eyeglasses or contact lenses shall be considered in determining whether an impairment substantially limits a major life activity.

(vii) An impairment that is episodic or in remission is a disability if it would substantially limit a major life activity when active.

(viii) An impairment that substantially limits one major life activity need not substantially limit other major life activities in order to be considered a substantially limiting impairment.

(ix) The six-month "transitory" part of the "transitory and minor" exception to "regarded as" coverage in § 1630.15(f) does not apply to the definition of "disability" under paragraphs (g)(1)(i) (the "actual disability" prong) or (g)(1)(ii) (the "record of" prong) of this section. The effects of an impairment lasting or expected to last fewer than six months can be substantially limiting within the meaning of this section.

(2) Non-applicability to the "regarded as" prong. Whether an individual's impairment "substantially limits" a major life activity is not relevant to coverage under paragraph (g)(1)(iii) (the "regarded as" prong) of this section.

(3) Predictable assessments —

(i) The principles set forth in paragraphs (j)(1)(i) through (ix) of this section are intended to provide for more generous coverage and application of the ADA's prohibition on discrimination through a framework that is predictable, consistent, and workable for all individuals and entities with rights and responsibilities under the ADA as amended.

(ii) Applying the principles set forth in paragraphs (j)(1)(i) through (ix) of this section, the individualized assessment of some types of impairments will, in virtually all cases, result in a determination of coverage under paragraphs (g)(1)(i) (the "actual disability" prong) or (g)(1)(ii) (the "record of" prong) of this section. Given their inherent nature, these types of impairments will, as a factual matter, virtually always be found to impose a substantial limitation on a major life activity. Therefore, with respect to these types of impairments, the necessary individualized assessment should be particularly simple and straightforward.

(iii) For example, applying the principles set forth in paragraphs (j)(1)(i) through (ix) of this section, it should easily be concluded that the following types of impairments will, at a minimum, substantially limit the major life activities indicated: deafness substantially limits hearing; blindness substantially limits seeing; an intellectual disability (formerly termed mental retardation) substantially limits brain function; partially or completely missing limbs or mobility impairments requiring the use of a wheelchair substantially limit musculoskeletal function; autism substantially limits brain function; cancer substantially limits normal cell growth; cerebral palsy substantially limits brain function; diabetes substantially limits endocrine function; epilepsy substantially limits neurological function; Human Immunodeficiency Virus (HIV) infection substantially limits immune function; multiple sclerosis substantially limits neurological function; muscular dystrophy substantially limits neurological function; and major depressive disorder, bipolar disorder, post-traumatic stress disorder, obsessive compulsive disorder, and schizophrenia substantially limit brain function. The types of impairments described in this section may substantially limit additional major life activities not explicitly listed above.

(4) Condition, manner, or duration —

(i) At all times taking into account the principles in paragraphs (j)(1)(i) through (ix) of this section, in determining whether an individual is substantially limited in a major life activity, it may be useful in appropriate cases to consider, as compared to most people in the general population, the condition under which the individual performs the major life activity; the manner in which the individual performs the major life activity; and/or the duration of time it takes the individual to perform the major life activity, or for which the individual can perform the major life activity.

(ii) Consideration of facts such as condition, manner, or duration may include, among other things, consideration of the difficulty, effort, or time required to perform a major life activity; pain experienced when performing a major life activity; the length of time a major life activity can be performed; and/or the way an impairment affects the operation of a major bodily function. In addition, the non-ameliorative effects of mitigating measures, such as negative side effects of medication or burdens associated with following a particular treatment regimen, may be considered when determining whether an individual's impairment substantially limits a major life activity.

(iii) In determining whether an individual has a disability under the "actual disability" or "record of" prongs of the definition of disability, the focus is on how a major life activity is substantially limited, and not on what outcomes an individual can achieve. For example, someone with a learning disability may achieve a high level of academic success, but may nevertheless be substantially limited in the major life activity of learning because of the additional time or effort he or she must spend to read, write, or learn compared to most people in the general population.

(iv) Given the rules of construction set forth in paragraphs (j)(1)(i) through (ix) of this section, it may often be unnecessary to conduct an analysis involving most or all of these types of facts. This is particularly true with respect to impairments such as those described in paragraph (j)(3)(iii) of this section, which by their inherent nature should be easily found to impose a substantial limitation on a major life activity, and for which the individualized assessment should be particularly simple and straightforward.

(5) Examples of mitigating measures — Mitigating measures include, but are not limited to:

(i) Medication, medical supplies, equipment, or appliances, low-vision devices (defined as devices that magnify, enhance, or otherwise augment a visual

image, but not including ordinary eyeglasses or contact lenses), prosthetics including limbs and devices, hearing aid(s) and cochlear implant(s) or other implantable hearing devices, mobility devices, and oxygen therapy equipment and supplies;

(ii) Use of assistive technology;

(iii) Reasonable accommodations or "auxiliary aids or services" (as defined by 42 U.S.C. 12103(1));

(iv) Learned behavioral or adaptive neurological modifications; or

(v) Psychotherapy, behavioral therapy, or physical therapy.

(6) Ordinary eyeglasses or contact lenses — defined. Ordinary eyeglasses or contact lenses are lenses that are intended to fully correct visual acuity or to eliminate refractive error.

(k) Has a record of such an impairment —

(1) *In general.* An individual has a record of a disability if the individual has a history of, or has been misclassified as having, a mental or physical impairment that substantially limits one or more major life activities.

(2) *Broad construction.* Whether an individual has a record of an impairment that substantially limited a major life activity shall be construed broadly to the maximum extent permitted by the ADA and should not demand extensive analysis. An individual will be considered to have a record of a disability if the individual has a history of an impairment that substantially limited one or more major life activities when compared to most people in the general population, or was misclassified as having had such an impairment. In determining whether an impairment substantially limited a major life activity, the principles articulated in paragraph (j) of this section apply.

(3) *Reasonable accommodation.* An individual with a record of a substantially limiting impairment may be entitled, absent undue hardship, to a reasonable accommodation if needed and related to the past disability. For example, an employee with an impairment that previously limited, but no longer substantially limits, a major life activity may need leave or a schedule change to permit him or her to attend follow-up or "monitoring" appointments with a health care provider.

(l) "Is regarded as having such an impairment." The following principles apply under the "regarded as" prong of the definition of disability (paragraph (g)(1)(iii) of this section) above:

(1) Except as provided in § 1630.15(f), an individual is "regarded as having such an impairment" if the individual is subjected to a prohibited action because of an actual or perceived physical or mental impairment, whether or not that impairment substantially limits, or is perceived to substantially limit, a major life activity. Prohibited actions include but are not limited to refusal to hire, demotion, placement on involuntary leave, termination, exclusion for failure to meet a qualification standard, harassment, or denial of any other term, condition, or privilege of employment

(2) Except as provided in § 1630.15(f), an individual is "regarded as having such an impairment" any time a covered entity takes a prohibited action against the individual because of an actual or perceived impairment, even if the entity asserts, or may or does ultimately establish, a defense to such action.

(3) Establishing that an individual is "regarded as having such an impairment" does not, by itself, establish liability. Liability is established under title I of the ADA only when an individual proves that a covered entity discriminated on the basis of disability within the meaning of section 102 of the ADA, 42 U.S.C. 12112.

(m) The term "*qualified*," with respect to an individual with a disability means that the individual satisfies the requisite skill, experience, education and other job-related requirements of the employment position such individual holds or desires, and who, with or without reasonable accommodation, can perform the essential functions of such position. See § 1630.3 for exceptions to this definition.

(n) Essential functions. —

(1) In general. The term essential functions means the fundamental job duties of the employment position the individual with a disability holds or desires. The term "essential functions" does not include the marginal functions of the position.

(2) A job function may be considered essential for any of several reasons, including but not limited to the following:

(i) The function may be essential because the reason the position exists is to perform that function;

(ii) The function may be essential because of the limited number of employees available among whom the performance of that job function can be distributed; and/or

(iii) The function may be highly specialized so that the incumbent in the position is hired for his or her expertise or ability to perform the particular function.

(3) Evidence of whether a particular function is essential includes, but is not limited to:

(i) The employer's judgment as to which functions are essential;

(ii) Written job descriptions prepared before advertising or interviewing applicants for the job;

(iii) The amount of time spent on the job performing the function;

(iv) The consequences of not requiring the incumbent to perform the function;

(v) The terms of a collective bargaining agreement;

(vi) The work experience of past incumbents in the job; and/or

(vii) The current work experience of incumbents in similar jobs.

(o) Reasonable accommodation.

(1) The term reasonable accommodation means:

(i) Modifications or adjustments to a job application process that enable a qualified applicant with a disability to be considered for the position such qualified applicant desires; or

(ii) Modifications or adjustments to the work environment, or to the manner or circumstances under which the position held or desired is customarily performed, that enable a qualified individual with a disability to perform the essential functions of that position; or

(iii) Modifications or adjustments that enable a covered entity's employee with a disability to enjoy equal benefits and privileges of employment as are enjoyed by its other similarly situated employees without disabilities.

(2) Reasonable accommodation may include but is not limited to:

(i) Making existing facilities used by employees readily accessible to and usable by individuals with disabilities; and

(ii) Job restructuring; part-time or modified work schedules; reassignment to a vacant position; acquisition or modifications of equipment or devices; appropriate adjustment or modifications of examinations, training materials, or policies; the provision of qualified readers or interpreters; and other similar accommodations for individuals with disabilities.

(3) To determine the appropriate reasonable accommodation it may be necessary for the covered entity to initiate an informal, interactive process with the qualified individual with a disability in need of the accommodation. This process should identify the precise limitations resulting from the disability and potential reasonable accommodations that could overcome those limitations.

(4) A covered entity is required, absent undue hardship, to provide a reasonable accommodation to an otherwise qualified individual who meets the definition of disability under the "actual disability" prong (paragraph (g)(1)(i) of this section), or "record of" prong (paragraph (g)(1)(ii) of this section), but is not required to provide a reasonable accommodation to an individual who meets the definition of disability solely under the "regarded as" prong (paragraph (g)(1)(iii) of this section).

(p) Undue hardship —

(1) In general. Undue hardship means, with respect to the provision of an accommodation, significant difficulty or expense incurred by a covered entity, when considered in light of the factors set forth in paragraph (p)(2) of this section.

(2) Factors to be considered. In determining whether an accommodation would impose an undue hardship on a covered entity, factors to be considered include:

(i) The nature and net cost of the accommodation needed under this part, taking into consideration the availability of tax credits and deductions, and/or outside funding;

(ii) The overall financial resources of the facility or facilities involved in the provision of the reasonable accommodation, the number of persons employed at such facility, and the effect on expenses and resources;

(iii) The overall financial resources of the covered entity, the overall size of the business of the covered entity with respect to the number of its employees, and the number, type and location of its facilities;

(iv) The type of operation or operations of the covered entity, including the composition, structure and functions of the work force of such entity, and the geographic separateness and administrative or fiscal relationship of the facility or facilities in question to the covered entity; and

(v) The impact of the accommodation upon the operation of the facility, including the impact on the ability of other employees to perform their duties and the impact on the facility's ability to conduct business.

(q) Qualification standards means the personal and professional attributes including the skill, experience, education, physical, medical, safety and other requirements established by a covered entity as requirements which an individual must meet in order to be eligible for the position held or desired.

(r) Direct Threat means a significant risk of substantial harm to the health or safety of the individual or others that cannot be eliminated or reduced by reasonable accommodation. The determination that an individual poses a "direct threat" shall be based on an individualized assessment of the individual's present ability to safely perform the essential functions of the job. This assessment shall be based on a reasonable medical judgment that relies on the most current medical knowledge and/or on the best available objective evidence. In determining whether an individual would pose a direct threat, the factors to be considered include:

(1) The duration of the risk;

(2) The nature and severity of the potential harm;

(3) The likelihood that the potential harm will occur; and

(4) The imminence of the potential harm.

§ 1630.3 Exceptions to the definitions of "Disability" and "Qualified Individual with a Disability."

(a) The terms disability and qualified individual with a disability do not include individuals currently engaging in the illegal use of drugs, when the covered entity acts on the basis of such use.

(1) Drug means a controlled substance, as defined in schedules I through V of Section 202 of the Controlled Substances Act (21 U.S.C. 812)

(2) Illegal use of drugs means the use of drugs the possession or distribution of which is unlawful under the Controlled Substances Act, as periodically updated by the Food and Drug Administration. This term does not include the use of a drug taken under the supervision of a licensed health care professional, or other uses authorized by the Controlled Substances Act or other provisions of Federal law.

(b) However, the terms disability and qualified individual with a disability may not exclude an individual who:

(1) Has successfully completed a supervised drug rehabilitation program and is no longer engaging in the illegal use of drugs, or has otherwise been rehabilitated successfully and is no longer engaging in the illegal use of drugs; or

(2) Is participating in a supervised rehabilitation program and is no longer engaging in such use; or

(3) Is erroneously regarded as engaging in such use, but is not engaging in such use.

(c) It shall not be a violation of this part for a covered entity to adopt or administer reasonable policies or procedures, including but not limited to drug testing, designed to ensure that an individual described in paragraph (b) (1) or (2) of this section is no longer engaging in the illegal use of drugs. (See § 1630.16(c) Drug testing).

(d) Disability does not include:

(1) Transvestism, transsexualism, pedophilia, exhibitionism, voyeurism, gender identity disorders not resulting from physical impairments, or other sexual behavior disorders;

(2) Compulsive gambling, kleptomania, or pyromania; or

(3) Psychoactive substance use disorders resulting from current illegal use of drugs.

(e) Homosexuality and bisexuality are not impairments and so are not disabilities as defined in this part.

§ 1630.4   Discrimination prohibited.

(a) *In general —*

(1) It is unlawful for a covered entity to discriminate on the basis of disability against a qualified individual in regard to:

(i) Recruitment, advertising, and job application procedures;

(ii) Hiring, upgrading, promotion, award of tenure, demotion, transfer, layoff, termination, right of return from layoff, and rehiring;

(iii) Rates of pay or any other form of compensation and changes in compensation;

(iv) Job assignments, job classifications, organizational structures, position descriptions, lines of progression, and seniority lists;

(v) Leaves of absence, sick leave, or any other leave;

(vi) Fringe benefits available by virtue of employment, whether or not administered by the covered entity;

(vii) Selection and financial support for training, including: apprenticeships, professional meetings, conferences and other related activities, and selection for leaves of absence to pursue training;

(viii) Activities sponsored by a covered entity including social and recreational programs; and

(ix) Any other term, condition, or privilege of employment.

(2) The term discrimination includes, but is not limited to, the acts described in §§ 1630.5 through 1630.13 of this part.

(b) *Claims of no disability.* Nothing in this part shall provide the basis for a claim that an individual without a disability was subject to discrimination because of his lack of disability, including a claim that an individual with a disability was granted an accommodation that was denied to an individual without a disability.

§ 1630.5   Limiting segregating, and classifying.

It is unlawful for a covered entity to limit, segregate, or classify a job applicant or employee in a way that adversely affects his or her employment opportunities or status on the basis of disability.

§ 1630.6   Contractual or other arrangements.

(a)   In general. It is unlawful for a covered entity to participate in a contractual or other arrangement or relationship that has the effect of subjecting the covered entity's own qualified applicant or employee with a disability to the discrimination prohibited by this part.

(b)   Contractual or other arrangement defined. The phrase contractual or other arrangement or relationship includes, but is not limited to, a relationship with an employment or referral agency; labor union, including collective bargaining agreements; an organization providing fringe benefits to an employee of the covered entity; or an organization providing training and apprenticeship programs.

(c)   Application. This section applies to a covered entity, with respect to its own applicants or employees, whether the entity offered the contract or initiated the relationship, or whether the entity accepted the contract or acceded to the relationship. A covered entity is not liable for the actions of the other party or parties to the contract which only affect that other party's employees or applicants.

§ 1630.7   Standards, criteria, or methods of administration.

It is unlawful for a covered entity to use standards, criteria, or methods of administration, which are not job-related and consistent with business necessity, and:

(a) That have the effect of discriminating on the basis of disability; or

(b) That perpetuate the discrimination of others who are subject to common administrative control.

§ 1630.8   Relationship or association with an individual with a disability.

It is unlawful for a covered entity to exclude or deny equal jobs or benefits to, or otherwise discriminate against, a qualified individual because of the known disability of an individual with whom the qualified individual is known to have a family, business, social or other relationship or association.

§ 1630.9   Not making reasonable accommodation.

(a) It is unlawful for a covered entity not to make reasonable accommodation to the known physical or mental limitations of an otherwise qualified applicant or employee with a disability, unless such covered entity can demonstrate that the accommodation would impose an undue hardship on the operation of its business.

(b) It is unlawful for a covered entity to deny employment opportunities to an otherwise qualified job applicant or employee with a disability based on the need of such covered entity to make reasonable accommodation to such individual's physical or mental impairments.

(c) A covered entity shall not be excused from the requirements of this part because of any failure to receive technical assistance authorized by section 507 of the ADA, including any failure in the development or dissemination of any technical assistance manual authorized by that Act.

(d) An individual with a disability is not required to accept an accommodation, aid, service, opportunity or benefit which such qualified individual chooses not to accept. However, if such individual rejects a reasonable accommodation, aid, service, opportunity or benefit that is necessary to enable the individual to perform the essential functions of the position held or desired, and cannot, as a result of that rejection, perform the essential functions of the position, the individual will not be considered qualified.

(e) A covered entity is required, absent undue hardship, to provide a reasonable accommodation to an otherwise qualified individual who meets the definition of disability under the "actual disability" prong (§ 1630.2(g)(1)(i)), or "record of" prong (§ 1630.2(g)(1)(ii)), but is not required to provide a reasonable accommodation to an individual who meets the definition of disability solely under the "regarded as" prong (§ 1630.2(g)(1)(iii)).

§ 1630.10   Qualification standards, tests, and other selection criteria.

(a)   *In general.* It is unlawful for a covered entity to use qualification standards, employment tests or other selection criteria that screen out or tend to screen out an individual with a disability or a class of individuals with disabilities, on the basis of disability, unless the standard, test or other selection criteria, as used by the covered entity, is shown to be job-related for the position in question and is consistent with business necessity.

(b)   *Qualification standards and tests related to uncorrected vision.* Notwithstanding § 1630.2(j)(1)(vi) of this part, a covered entity shall not use qualification standards, employment tests, or other selection criteria based on an individual's uncorrected vision unless the standard, test, or other selection criterion, as used by the covered entity, is shown to be job related for the position in question and is consistent with business necessity. An individual challenging a covered entity's application of a qualification standard, test, or other criterion based on uncorrected vision need not be a person with a disability, but must be adversely affected by the application of the standard, test, or other criterion.

§ 1630.11 Administration of tests.

It is unlawful for a covered entity to fail to select and administer tests concerning employment in the most effective manner to ensure that, when a test is administered to a job applicant or employee who has a disability that impairs sensory, manual or speaking skills, the test results accurately reflect the skills, aptitude, or whatever other factor of the applicant or employee that the test purports to measure, rather than reflecting the impaired sensory, manual, or speaking skills of such employee or applicant (except where such skills are the factors that the test purports to measure).

§ 1630.12 Retaliation and coercion.

(a) Retaliation. It is unlawful to discriminate against any individual because that individual has opposed any act or practice made unlawful by this part or because that individual made a charge, testified, assisted, or participated in any manner in an investigation, proceeding, or hearing to enforce any provision contained in this part.

(b) Coercion, interference or intimidation. It is unlawful to coerce, intimidate, threaten, harass or interfere with any individual in the exercise or enjoyment of, or because that individual aided or encouraged any other individual in the exercise of, any right granted or protected by this part.

§ 1630.13 Prohibited medical examinations and inquiries.

(a) Pre-employment examination or inquiry. Except as permitted by § 1630.14, it is unlawful for a covered entity to conduct a medical examination of an applicant or to make inquiries as to whether an applicant is an individual with a disability or as to the nature or severity of such disability.

(b) Examination or inquiry of employees. Except as permitted by § 1630.14, it is unlawful for a covered entity to require a medical examination of an employee or to make inquiries as to whether an employee is an individual with a disability or as to the nature or severity of such disability.

§ 1630.14 Medical examinations and inquiries specifically permitted.

(a) Acceptable pre-employment inquiry. A covered entity may make pre-employment inquiries into the ability of an applicant to perform job-related functions, and/or may ask an applicant to describe or to demonstrate how, with or without reasonable accommodation, the applicant will be able to perform job-related functions.

(b) Employment entrance examination. A covered entity may require a medical examination (and/or inquiry) after making an offer of employment to a job applicant and before the applicant begins his or her employment duties, and may condition an offer of employment on the results of such examination (and/or inquiry), if all entering employees in the same job category are subjected to such an examination (and/or inquiry) regardless of disability.

(1) Information obtained under paragraph (b) of this section regarding the medical condition or history of the applicant shall be collected and maintained on

separate forms and in separate medical files and be treated as a confidential medical record, except that:

(i) Supervisors and managers may be informed regarding necessary restrictions on the work or duties of the employee and necessary accommodations;

(ii) First aid and safety personnel may be informed, when appropriate, if the disability might require emergency treatment; and

(iii) Government officials investigating compliance with this part shall be provided relevant information on request.

(2) The results of such examination shall not be used for any purpose inconsistent with this part.

(3) Medical examinations conducted in accordance with this section do not have to be job-related and consistent with business necessity. However, if certain criteria are used to screen out an employee or employees with disabilities as a result of such an examination or inquiry, the exclusionary criteria must be job-related and consistent with business necessity, and performance of the essential job functions cannot be accomplished with reasonable accommodation as required in this part. (See § 1630.15(b) Defenses to charges of discriminatory application of selection criteria.)

(c)   Examination of employees. A covered entity may require a medical examination (and/or inquiry) of an employee that is job-related and consistent with business necessity. A covered entity may make inquiries into the ability of an employee to perform job-related functions.

(1) Information obtained under paragraph (c) of this section regarding the medical condition or history of any employee shall be collected and maintained on separate forms and in separate medical files and be treated as a confidential medical record, except that:

(i) Supervisors and managers may be informed regarding necessary restrictions on the work or duties of the employee and necessary accommodations;

(ii) First aid and safety personnel may be informed, when appropriate, if the disability might require emergency treatment; and

(iii) Government officials investigating compliance with this part shall be provided relevant information on request.

(2) Information obtained under paragraph (c) of this section regarding the medical condition or history of any employee shall not be used for any purpose inconsistent with this part.

(d)   Other acceptable examinations and inquiries. A covered entity may conduct voluntary medical examinations and activities, including voluntary medical histories, which are part of an employee health program available to employees at the work site.

(1) Information obtained under paragraph (d) of this section regarding the medical condition or history of any employee shall be collected and maintained on separate forms and in separate medical files and be treated as a confidential

medical record, except that:

(i) Supervisors and managers may be informed regarding necessary restrictions on the work or duties of the employee and necessary accommodations;

(ii) First aid and safety personnel may be informed, when appropriate, if the disability might require emergency treatment; and

(iii) Government officials investigating compliance with this part shall be provided relevant information on request.

(2) Information obtained under paragraph (d) of this section regarding the medical condition or history of any employee shall not be used for any purpose inconsistent with this part.

§ 1630.15   Defenses.

Defenses to an allegation of discrimination under this part may include, but are not limited to, the following:

(a)   Disparate treatment charges. It may be a defense to a charge of disparate treatment brought under §§ 1630.4 through 1630.8 and 1630.11 through 1630.12 that the challenged action is justified by a legitimate, nondiscriminatory reason.

(b) Charges of discriminatory application of selection criteria —

(1)   In general. It may be a defense to a charge of discrimination, as described in § 1630.10, that an alleged application of qualification standards, tests, or selection criteria that screens out or tends to screen out or otherwise denies a job or benefit to an individual with a disability has been shown to be job-related and consistent with business necessity, and such performance cannot be accomplished with reasonable accommodation, as required in this part.

(2)   Direct threat as a qualification standard. The term "qualification standard" may include a requirement that an individual shall not pose a direct threat to the health or safety of the individual or others in the workplace. (See § 1630.2(r) defining direct threat.)

(c)   Other disparate impact charges. It may be a defense to a charge of discrimination brought under this part that a uniformly applied standard, criterion, or policy has a disparate impact on an individual with a disability or a class of individuals with disabilities that the challenged standard, criterion or policy has been shown to be job-related and consistent with business necessity, and such performance cannot be accomplished with reasonable accommodation, as required in this part.

(d)   Charges of not making reasonable accommodation. It may be a defense to a charge of discrimination, as described in § 1630.9, that a requested or necessary accommodation would impose an undue hardship on the operation of the covered entity's business.

(e)   Conflict with other federal laws. It may be a defense to a charge of discrimination under this part that a challenged action is required or necessitated by another Federal law or regulation, or that another Federal law or regulation prohibits an action (including the provision of a particular reasonable accommodation) that would otherwise be required by this part.

(f)　Claims based on transitory and minor impairments under the "regarded as" prong. It may be a defense to a charge of discrimination by an individual claiming coverage under the "regarded as" prong of the definition of disability that the impairment is (in the case of an actual impairment) or would be (in the case of a perceived impairment) "transitory and minor." To establish this defense, a covered entity must demonstrate that the impairment is both "transitory" and "minor." Whether the impairment at issue is or would be "transitory and minor" is to be determined objectively. A covered entity may not defeat "regarded as" coverage of an individual simply by demonstrating that it subjectively believed the impairment was transitory and minor; rather, the covered entity must demonstrate that the impairment is (in the case of an actual impairment) or would be (in the case of a perceived impairment) both transitory and minor. For purposes of this section, "transitory" is defined as lasting or expected to last six months or less.

(g)　Additional defenses. It may be a defense to a charge of discrimination under this part that the alleged discriminatory action is specifically permitted by §§ 1630.14 or 1630.16.

§ 1630.16　Specific activities permitted.

(a)　Religious entities. A religious corporation, association, educational institution, or society is permitted to give preference in employment to individuals of a particular religion to perform work connected with the carrying on by that corporation, association, educational institution, or society of its activities. A religious entity may require that all applicants and employees conform to the religious tenets of such organization. However, a religious entity may not discriminate against a qualified individual, who satisfies the permitted religious criteria, on the basis of his or her disability.

(b)　Regulation of alcohol and drugs. A covered entity:

(1) May prohibit the illegal use of drugs and the use of alcohol at the workplace by all employees;

(2) May require that employees not be under the influence of alcohol or be engaging in the illegal use of drugs at the workplace;

(3) May require that all employees behave in conformance with the requirements established under the Drug-Free Workplace Act of 1988 (41 U.S.C. 701 et seq.);

(4) May hold an employee who engages in the illegal use of drugs or who is an alcoholic to the same qualification standards for employment or job performance and behavior to which the entity holds its other employees, even if any unsatisfactory performance or behavior is related to the employee's drug use or alcoholism;

(5) May require that its employees employed in an industry subject to such regulations comply with the standards established in the regulations (if any) of

the Departments of Defense and Transportation, and of the Nuclear Regulatory Commission, regarding alcohol and the illegal use of drugs; and

(6) May require that employees employed in sensitive positions comply with the regulations (if any) of the Departments of Defense and Transportation and of the Nuclear Regulatory Commission that apply to employment in sensitive positions subject to such regulations.

(c) Drug testing —

(1)　General policy. For purposes of this part, a test to determine the illegal use of drugs is not considered a medical examination. Thus, the administration of such drug tests by a covered entity to its job applicants or employees is not a violation of § 1630.13 of this part. However, this part does not encourage, prohibit, or authorize a covered entity to conduct drug tests of job applicants or employees to determine the illegal use of drugs or to make employment decisions based on such test results.

(2)　Transportation Employees. This part does not encourage, prohibit, or authorize the otherwise lawful exercise by entities subject to the jurisdiction of the Department of Transportation of authority to:

(i) Test employees of entities in, and applicants for, positions involving safety sensitive duties for the illegal use of drugs or for on-duty impairment by alcohol; and

(ii) Remove from safety-sensitive positions persons who test positive for illegal use of drugs or on-duty impairment by alcohol pursuant to paragraph (c)(2)(i) of this section.

(3)　Confidentiality. Any information regarding the medical condition or history of any employee or applicant obtained from a test to determine the illegal use of drugs, except information regarding the illegal use of drugs, is subject to the requirements of § 1630.14(b) (2) and (3) of this part.

(d)　Regulation of smoking. A covered entity may prohibit or impose restrictions on smoking in places of employment. Such restrictions do not violate any provision of this part.

(e) Infectious and communicable diseases; food handling jobs —

(1)　In general. Under title I of the ADA, section 103(d)(1), the Secretary of Health and Human Services is to prepare a list, to be updated annually, of infectious and communicable diseases which are transmitted through the handling of food. (Copies may be obtained from Center for Infectious Diseases, Centers for Disease Control, 1600 Clifton Road, NE., Mailstop C09, Atlanta, GA 30333.) If an individual with a disability is disabled by one of the infectious or communicable diseases included on this list, and if the risk of transmitting the disease associated with the handling of food cannot be eliminated by reasonable accommodation, a covered entity may refuse to assign or continue to assign such individual to a job involving food handling. However, if the individual with a disability is a current employee, the employer must consider whether he or she can be accommodated by reassignment to a vacant position not involving food handling.

(2) Effect on state or other laws. This part does not preempt, modify, or amend any State, county, or local law, ordinance or regulation applicable to food handling which:

(i) Is in accordance with the list, referred to in paragraph (e)(1) of this section, of infectious or communicable diseases and the modes of transmissibility published by the Secretary of Health and Human Services; and

(ii) Is designed to protect the public health from individuals who pose a significant risk to the health or safety of others, where that risk cannot be eliminated by reasonable accommodation.

(f) Health insurance, life insurance, and other benefit plans —

(1) An insurer, hospital, or medical service company, health maintenance organization, or any agent or entity that administers benefit plans, or similar organizations may underwrite risks, classify risks, or administer such risks that are based on or not inconsistent with State law.

(2) A covered entity may establish, sponsor, observe or administer the terms of a bona fide benefit plan that are based on underwriting risks, classifying risks, or administering such risks that are based on or not inconsistent with State law.

(3) A covered entity may establish, sponsor, observe, or administer the terms of a bona fide benefit plan that is not subject to State laws that regulate insurance.

(4) The activities described in paragraphs (f)(1), (2), and (3) of this section are permitted unless these activities are being used as a subterfuge to evade the purposes of this part.

Chapter 3
EEOC SECTION BY SECTION ANALYSIS
OF REGULATIONS TO IMPLEMENT THE
EQUAL EMPLOYMENT PROVISIONS OF THE ADA

29 CFR PART 1630 APPENDIX

APPENDIX TO PART 1630 — INTERPRETIVE GUIDANCE ON TITLE I OF THE AMERICANS WITH DISABILITIES ACT

Introduction

The Americans with Disabilities Act (ADA) is a landmark piece of civil rights legislation signed into law on July 26, 1990, and amended effective January 1, 2009. See 42 U.S.C. 12101 et seq., as amended. In passing the ADA, Congress recognized that "discrimination against individuals with disabilities continues to be a serious and pervasive social problem" and that the "continuing existence of unfair and unnecessary discrimination and prejudice denies people with disabilities the opportunity to compete on an equal basis and to pursue those opportunities for which our free society is justifiably famous, and costs the United States billions of dollars in unnecessary expenses resulting from dependency and nonproductivity." 42 U.S.C. 12101(a)(2), (8). Discrimination on the basis of disability persists in critical areas such as housing, public accommodations, education, transportation, communication, recreation, institutionalization, health services, voting, access to public services, and employment. 42 U.S.C. 12101(a)(3). Accordingly, the ADA prohibits discrimination in a wide range of areas, including employment, public services, and public accommodations.

Title I of the ADA prohibits disability-based discrimination in employment. The Equal Employment Opportunity Commission (the Commission or the EEOC) is responsible for enforcement of title I (and parts of title V) of the ADA. Pursuant to the ADA as amended, the EEOC is expressly granted the authority and is expected to amend these regulations. 42 U.S.C. 12205a. Under title I of the ADA, covered entities may not discriminate against qualified individuals on the basis of disability in regard to job application procedures, the hiring, advancement or discharge of employees, employee compensation, job training, or other terms, conditions, and privileges of employment. 42 U.S.C. 12112(a). For these purposes, "discriminate" includes (1) limiting, segregating, or classifying a job applicant or employee in a way that adversely affects the opportunities or status of the applicant or employee; (2) participating in a contractual or other arrangement or relationship that has the effect of subjecting a covered entity's qualified applicants or employees to discrimination; (3) utilizing standards, criteria, or other methods of administration that have the effect of discrimination on the basis of disability; (4) not making reasonable accommodation to the known physical or mental limitations of an otherwise qualified individual with a disability, unless the covered entity can demonstrate that the accommodation would impose an undue hardship on the operation of the business of the covered entity; (5) denying employment opportunities to a job applicant or employee who is otherwise qualified, if such denial is based on the need to make reasonable accommodation; (6) using qualification standards, employment tests or other selection criteria that screen out or tend to screen out an individual with a disability or a class of individuals with disabilities unless the standard, test or other selection criterion is shown to be job related for the position in question and is consistent with business necessity; and (7) subjecting applicants or employees to prohibited medical inquiries or examinations. See 42 U.S.C. 12112(b), (d).

As with other civil rights laws, individuals seeking protection under these anti-discrimination provisions of the ADA generally must allege and prove that they are members of the "protected class."[1] Under the ADA, this typically means they have to show that they meet the statutory definition of "disability." 2008 House Judiciary Committee Report at 5. However, "Congress did not intend for the threshold question of disability to be used as a means of excluding individuals from coverage." Id.

In the original ADA, Congress defined "disability" as (1) a physical or mental impairment that substantially limits one or more major life activities of an individual; (2) a record of such an impairment; or (3) being regarded as having such an impairment. 42 U.S.C. 12202(2). Congress patterned these three parts of the definition of disability — the "actual," "record of," and "regarded as" prongs — after the definition of "handicap" found in the Rehabilitation Act of 1973. 2008 House Judiciary Committee Report at 6. By doing so, Congress intended that the relevant case law developed under the Rehabilitation Act would be generally applicable to the term "disability" as used in the ADA. H.R. Rep. No. 485 part 3, 101st Cong., 2d Sess. 27 (1990) (1990 House Judiciary Report or House Judiciary Report); See also S. Rep. No. 116, 101st Cong., 1st Sess. 21 (1989) (1989 Senate Report or Senate Report); H.R. Rep. No. 485 part 2, 101st Cong., 2d Sess. 50 (1990) (1990 House Labor Report or House Labor Report). Congress expected that the definition of disability and related terms, such as "substantially limits" and "major life activity," would be interpreted under the ADA "consistently with how courts had applied the definition of a handicapped individual under the Rehabilitation Act" — i.e., expansively and in favor of broad coverage. ADA Amendments Act of 2008 (ADAAA or Amendments Act) at Section 2(a)(1)–(8) and (b)(1)–(6) (Findings and Purposes); see also Senate Statement of the Managers to Accompany S. 3406 (2008 Senate Statement of Managers) at 3 ("When Congress passed the ADA in 1990, it adopted the functional definition of disability from section 504 of the Rehabilitation Act of

---

[1] Claims of improper disability-related inquiries or medical examinations, improper disclosure of confidential medical information, or retaliation may be brought by any applicant or employee, not just individuals with disabilities. See, e.g., Cossette v. Minnesota Power & Light, 188 F.3d 964, 969–70 (8th Cir. 1999); Fredenburg v. Contra Costa County Dep't of Health Servs., 172 F.3d 1176, 1182 (9th Cir. 1999); Griffin v. Steeltek, Inc., 160 F.3d 591, 594 (10th Cir. 1998). Likewise, a nondisabled applicant or employee may challenge an employment action that is based on the disability of an individual with whom the applicant or employee is known to have a relationship or association. See 42 U.S.C. 12112(b)(4).

1973, in part, because after 17 years of development through case law the requirements of the definition were well understood. Within this framework, with its generous and inclusive definition of disability, courts treated the determination of disability as a threshold issue but focused primarily on whether unlawful discrimination had occurred."); 2008 House Judiciary Committee Report at 6 & n.6 (noting that courts had interpreted this Rehabilitation Act definition "broadly to include persons with a wide range of physical and mental impairments").

That expectation was not fulfilled. ADAAA Section 2(a)(3). The holdings of several Supreme Court cases sharply narrowed the broad scope of protection Congress originally intended under the ADA, thus eliminating protection for many individuals whom Congress intended to protect. Id. For example, in Sutton v. United Air Lines, Inc., 527 U.S. 471 (1999), the Court ruled that whether an impairment substantially limits a major life activity is to be determined with reference to the ameliorative effects of mitigating measures. In Sutton, the Court also adopted a restrictive reading of the meaning of being "regarded as" disabled under the ADA's definition of disability. Subsequently, in Toyota Motor Mfg., Ky., Inc. v. Williams, 534 U.S. 184 (2002), the Court held that the terms "substantially" and "major" in the definition of disability "need to be interpreted strictly to create a demanding standard for qualifying as disabled" under the ADA, and that to be substantially limited in performing a major life activity under the ADA, "an individual must have an impairment that prevents or severely restricts the individual from doing activities that are of central importance to most people's daily lives."

As a result of these Supreme Court decisions, lower courts ruled in numerous cases that individuals with a range of substantially limiting impairments were not individuals with disabilities, and thus not protected by the ADA. See 2008 Senate Statement of Managers at 3 ("After the Court's decisions in Sutton that impairments must be considered in their mitigated state and in Toyota that there must be a demanding standard for qualifying as disabled, lower courts more often found that an individual's impairment did not constitute a disability. As a result, in too many cases, courts would never reach the question whether discrimination had occurred."). Congress concluded that these rulings imposed a greater degree of limitation and expressed a higher standard than it had originally intended, and coupled with the EEOC's 1991 ADA regulations which had defined the term "substantially limits" as "significantly restricted," unduly precluded many individuals from being covered under the ADA. Id.]("[t]hus, some 18 years later we are faced with a situation in which physical or mental impairments that would previously have been found to constitute disabilities are not considered disabilities under the Supreme Court's narrower standard" and "[t]he resulting court decisions contribute to a legal environment in which individuals must demonstrate an inappropriately high degree of functional limitation in order to be protected from discrimination under the ADA").

Consequently, Congress amended the ADA with the Americans with Disabilities Act Amendments Act of 2008. The ADAAA was signed into law on September 25, 2008, and became effective on January 1, 2009. This legislation is the product of extensive bipartisan efforts, and the culmination of collaboration and coordination between legislators and stakeholders, including representatives of the disability, business, and education communities. See Statement of Representatives Hoyer and

Sensenbrenner, 154 Cong. Rec. H8294-96 (daily ed. Sept. 17, 2008) (Hoyer-Sensenbrenner Congressional Record Statement); Senate Statement of Managers at 1. The express purposes of the ADAAA are, among other things:

(1) To carry out the ADA's objectives of providing "a clear and comprehensive national mandate for the elimination of discrimination" and "clear, strong, consistent, enforceable standards addressing discrimination" by reinstating a broad scope of protection under the ADA;

(2) To reject the requirement enunciated in Sutton and its companion cases that whether an impairment substantially limits a major life activity is to be determined with reference to the ameliorative effects of mitigating measures;

(3) To reject the Supreme Court's reasoning in Sutton with regard to coverage under the third prong of the definition of disability and to reinstate the reasoning of the Supreme Court in School Board of Nassau County v. Arline, 480 U.S. 273 (1987), which set forth a broad view of the third prong of the definition of handicap under the Rehabilitation Act of 1973;

(4) To reject the standards enunciated by the Supreme Court in Toyota that the terms "substantially" and "major" in the definition of disability under the ADA "need to be interpreted strictly to create a demanding standard for qualifying as disabled," and that to be substantially limited in performing a major life activity under the ADA "an individual must have an impairment that prevents or severely restricts the individual from doing activities that are of central importance to most people's daily lives";

(5) To convey congressional intent that the standard created by the Supreme Court in Toyota for "substantially limits," and applied by lower courts in numerous decisions, has created an inappropriately high level of limitation necessary to obtain coverage under the ADA;

(6) To convey that it is the intent of Congress that the primary object of attention in cases brought under the ADA should be whether entities covered under the ADA have complied with their obligations, and to convey that the question of whether an individual's impairment is a disability under the ADA should not demand extensive analysis; and

(7) To express Congress' expectation that the EEOC will revise that portion of its current regulations that defines the term "substantially limits" as "significantly restricted" to be consistent with the ADA as amended.

ADAAA Section 2(b). The findings and purposes of the ADAAA "give[] clear guidance to the courts and * * * [are] intend[ed] to be applied appropriately and consistently." 2008 Senate Statement of Managers at 5.

The EEOC has amended its regulations to reflect the ADAAA's findings and purposes. The Commission believes that it is essential also to amend its appendix to the original regulations at the same time, and to reissue this interpretive guidance as amended concurrently with the issuance of the amended regulations. This will help to ensure that individuals with disabilities understand their rights, and to facilitate and encourage compliance by covered entities under this part.

Accordingly, this amended appendix addresses the major provisions of this part and explains the major concepts related to disability-based employment discrimination. This appendix represents the Commission's interpretation of the issues addressed within it, and the Commission will be guided by this appendix when resolving charges of employment discrimination.

Note on Certain Terminology Used

The ADA, the EEOC's ADA regulations, and this appendix use the term "disabilities" rather than the term "handicaps" which was originally used in the Rehabilitation Act of 1973, 29 U.S.C. 701–796. Substantively, these terms are equivalent. As originally noted by the House Committee on the Judiciary, "[t]he use of the term disabilities' instead of the term handicaps' reflects the desire of the Committee to use the most current terminology. It reflects the preference of persons with disabilities to use that term rather than handicapped' as used in previous laws, such as the Rehabilitation Act of 1973 * * *." 1990 House Judiciary Report at 26–27; See also 1989 Senate Report at 21; 1990 House Labor Report at 50–51.

In addition, consistent with the Amendments Act, revisions have been made to the regulations and this Appendix to refer to "individual with a disability" and "qualified individual" as separate terms, and to change the prohibition on discrimination to "on the basis of disability" instead of prohibiting discrimination against a qualified individual "with a disability because of the disability of such individual." "This ensures that the emphasis in questions of disability discrimination is properly on the critical inquiry of whether a qualified person has been discriminated against on the basis of disability, and not unduly focused on the preliminary question of whether a particular person is a person with a disability.' " 2008 Senate Statement of Managers at 11.

The use of the term "Americans" in the title of the ADA, in the EEOC's regulations, or in this Appendix as amended is not intended to imply that the ADA only applies to United States citizens. Rather, the ADA protects all qualified individuals with disabilities, regardless of their citizenship status or nationality, from discrimination by a covered entity.

Finally, the terms "employer" and "employer or other covered entity" are used interchangeably throughout this Appendix to refer to all covered entities subject to the employment provisions of the ADA.

Section 1630.1 Purpose, Applicability and Construction

Section 1630.1(a) Purpose

The express purposes of the ADA as amended are to provide a clear and comprehensive national mandate for the elimination of discrimination against individuals with disabilities; to provide clear, strong, consistent, enforceable standards addressing discrimination against individuals with disabilities; to ensure that the Federal Government plays a central role in enforcing the standards articulated in the ADA on behalf of individuals with disabilities; and to invoke the sweep of congressional authority to address the major areas of discrimination faced day-to-day by people with disabilities. 42 U.S.C. 12101(b). The EEOC's ADA regulations are intended to implement these Congressional purposes in simple and straightforward terms.

Section 1630.1(b)   Applicability

The EEOC's ADA regulations as amended apply to all "covered entities" as defined at § 1630.2(b). The ADA defines "covered entities" to mean an employer, employment agency, labor organization, or joint labor-management committee. 42 U.S.C. 12111(2). All covered entities are subject to the ADA's rules prohibiting discrimination. 42 U.S.C. 12112.

Section 1630.1(c)   Construction

The ADA must be construed as amended. The primary purpose of the Amendments Act was to make it easier for people with disabilities to obtain protection under the ADA. See Joint Hoyer-Sensenbrenner Statement on the Origins of the ADA Restoration Act of 2008, H.R. 3195 (reviewing provisions of H.R. 3195 as revised following negotiations between representatives of the disability and business communities) (Joint Hoyer-Sensenbrenner Statement) at 2. Accordingly, under the ADA as amended and the EEOC's regulations, the definition of "disability" "shall be construed in favor of broad coverage of individuals under [the ADA], to the maximum extent permitted by the terms of [the ADA]." 42 U.S.C. 12102(4)(A); See also 2008 Senate Statement of Managers at 3 ("The ADA Amendments Act * * * reiterates that Congress intends that the scope of the [ADA] be broad and inclusive."). This construction is also intended to reinforce the general rule that civil rights statutes must be broadly construed to achieve their remedial purpose. Id. at 2; See also 2008 House Judiciary Committee Report at 19 (this rule of construction "directs courts to construe the definition of disability' broadly to advance the ADA's remedial purposes" and thus "brings treatment of the ADA's definition of disability in line with treatment of other civil rights laws, which should be construed broadly to effectuate their remedial purposes").

The ADAAA and the EEOC's regulations also make clear that the primary object of attention in cases brought under the ADA should be whether entities covered under the ADA have complied with their obligations, not]whether the individual meets the definition of disability. ADAAA Section 2(b)(5). This means, for example, examining whether an employer has discriminated against an employee, including whether an employer has fulfilled its obligations with respect to providing a "reasonable accommodation" to an individual with a disability; or whether an employee has met his or her responsibilities under the ADA with respect to engaging in the reasonable accommodation "interactive process." See also 2008 Senate Statement of Managers at 4 ("[L]ower court cases have too often turned solely on the question of whether the plaintiff is an individual with a disability rather than the merits of discrimination claims, such as whether adverse decisions were impermissibly made by the employer on the basis of disability, reasonable accommodations were denied, or qualification standards were unlawfully discriminatory."); 2008 House Judiciary Committee Report at 6 ("An individual who does not qualify as disabled * * * does not meet th[e] threshold question of coverage in the protected class and is therefore not permitted to attempt to prove his or her claim of discriminatory treatment.").

Further, the question of whether an individual has a disability under this part "should not demand extensive analysis." ADAAA Section 2(b)(5). See also House

Education and Labor Committee Report at 9 ("The Committee intends that the establishment of coverage under the ADA should not be overly complex nor difficult. * * *").

In addition, unless expressly stated otherwise, the standards applied in the ADA are intended to provide at least as much protection as the standards applied under the Rehabilitation Act of 1973.

The ADA does not preempt any Federal law, or any State or local law, that grants to individuals with disabilities protection greater than or equivalent to that provided by the ADA. This means that the existence of a lesser standard of protection to individuals with disabilities under the ADA will not provide a defense to failing to meet a higher standard under another law. Thus, for example, title I of the ADA would not be a defense to failing to prepare and maintain an affirmative action program under section 503 of the Rehabilitation Act. On the other hand, the existence of a lesser standard under another law will not provide a defense to failing to meet a higher standard under the ADA. See 1990 House Labor Report at 135; 1990 House Judiciary Report at 69–70.

This also means that an individual with a disability could choose to pursue claims under a State discrimination or tort law that does not confer greater substantive rights, or even confers fewer substantive rights, if the potential available remedies would be greater than those available under the ADA and this part. The ADA does not restrict an individual with a disability from pursuing such claims in addition to charges brought under this part. 1990 House Judiciary Report at 69–70.

The ADA does not automatically preempt medical standards or safety requirements established by Federal law or regulations. It does not preempt State, county, or local laws, ordinances or regulations that are consistent with this part and designed to protect the public health from individuals who pose a direct threat to the health or safety of others that cannot be eliminated or reduced by reasonable accommodation. However, the ADA does preempt inconsistent requirements established by State or local law for safety or security sensitive positions. See 1989 Senate Report at 27; 1990 House Labor Report at 57.

An employer allegedly in violation of this part cannot successfully defend its actions by relying on the obligation to comply with the requirements of any State or local law that imposes prohibitions or limitations on the eligibility of individuals with disabilities who are qualified to practice any occupation or profession. For example, suppose a municipality has an ordinance that prohibits individuals with tuberculosis from teaching school children. If an individual with dormant tuberculosis challenges a private school's refusal to hire him or her on the basis of the tuberculosis, the private school would not be able to rely on the city ordinance as a defense under the ADA.

Paragraph (c)(3) is consistent with language added to section 501 of the ADA by the ADA Amendments Act. It makes clear that nothing in this part is intended to alter the determination of eligibility for benefits under state workers' compensation laws or Federal and State disability benefit programs. State workers' compensation laws and Federal disability benefit programs, such as programs that provide payments to veterans with service-connected disabilities and the Social Security

Disability Insurance program, have fundamentally different purposes than title I of the ADA.

Section 1630.2   Definitions

Section 1630.2(a)–(f)   Commission, Covered Entity, etc.

The definitions section of part 1630 includes several terms that are identical, or almost identical, to the terms found in title VII of the Civil Rights Act of 1964. Among these terms are "Commission," "Person," "State," and "Employer." These terms are to be given the same meaning under the ADA that they are given under title VII. In general, the term "employee" has the same meaning that it is given under title VII. However, the ADA's definition of "employee" does not contain an exception, as does title VII, for elected officials and their personal staffs. It should further be noted that all State and local governments are covered by title II of the ADA whether or not they are also covered by this part. Title II, which is enforced by the Department of Justice, became effective on January 26, 1992. See 28 CFR part 35.

The term "covered entity" is not found in title VII. However, the title VII definitions of the entities included in the term "covered entity" (e.g., employer, employment agency, labor organization, etc.) are applicable to the ADA.

Section 1630.2(g)   Disability

In addition to the term "covered entity," there are several other terms that are unique to the ADA as amended. The first of these is the term "disability." "This definition is of critical importance because as a threshold issue it determines whether an individual is covered by the ADA." 2008 Senate Statement of Managers at 6.

In the original ADA, "Congress sought to protect anyone who experiences discrimination because of a current, past, or perceived disability." 2008 Senate Statement of Managers at 6. Accordingly, the definition of the term "disability" is divided into three prongs: An individual is considered to have a "disability" if that individual (1) has a physical or mental impairment that substantially limits one or more of that person's major life activities (the "actual disability" prong); (2) has a record of such an impairment (the "record of" prong); or (3) is regarded by the covered entity as an individual with a disability as defined in § 1630.2(l) (the "regarded as" prong). The ADAAA retained the basic structure and terms of the original definition of disability. However, the Amendments Act altered the interpretation and application of this critical statutory term in fundamental ways. See 2008 Senate Statement of Managers at 1 ("The bill maintains the ADA's inherently functional definition of disability" but "clarifies and expands the definition's meaning and application.").

As noted above, the primary purpose of the ADAAA is to make it easier for people with disabilities to obtain protection under the ADA. See Joint Hoyer-Sensenbrenner Statement at 2. Accordingly, the ADAAA provides rules of construction regarding the definition of disability. Consistent with the congressional intent to reinstate a broad scope of protection under the ADA, the ADAAA's rules of construction require that the definition of "disability" "shall be construed in favor of broad coverage of individuals under [the ADA], to the maximum extent permitted by the terms of [the ADA]." 42 U.S.C. 12102(4)(A). The legislative history of the ADAAA is replete with references emphasizing this principle. See Joint Hoyer-Sensenbrenner Statement at 2 ("[The bill] establishes that the definition of disability must be interpreted broadly to achieve the remedial purposes of the ADA"); 2008 Senate Statement of Managers at 1 (the ADAAA's purpose is to "enhance the protections of the [ADA]" by "expanding the definition, and by rejecting several opinions of the United States Supreme Court that have had the effect of restricting the meaning and application of the definition of disability"); id. (stressing the importance of removing barriers "to construing and applying the definition of disability more generously"); id. at 4 ("The managers have introduced the [ADAAA] to restore the proper balance and application of the ADA by clarifying and broadening the definition of disability, and to increase eligibility for the protections of the ADA."); id. ("It is our expectation that because the bill makes the definition of disability more generous, some people who were not covered before will now be covered."); id. (warning that "the definition of disability should not be unduly used as a tool for excluding individuals from the ADA's protections"); id. (this principle "sends a clear signal of our intent that the courts must interpret the definition of disability broadly rather than stringently"); 2008 House Judiciary Committee Report at 5 ("The purpose of the bill is to restore protection for the broad range of individuals with disabilities as originally envisioned by Congress by responding to the Supreme Court's narrow interpretation of the definition of disability.").

Further, as the purposes section of the ADAAA explicitly cautions, the "primary object of attention" in cases brought under the ADA should be whether entities covered under the ADA have complied with their obligations. As noted above, this means, for example, examining whether an employer has discriminated against an employee, including whether an employer has fulfilled its obligations with respect to providing a "reasonable accommodation" to an individual with a disability; or whether an employee has met his or her responsibilities under the ADA with respect to engaging in the reasonable accommodation "interactive process." ADAAA Section 2(b)(5); See also 2008 Senate Statement of Managers at 4 ("[L]ower court cases have too often turned solely on the question of whether the plaintiff is an individual with a disability rather than the merits of discrimination claims, such as whether adverse decisions were impermissibly made by the employer on the basis of disability, reasonable accommodations were denied, or qualification standards were unlawfully discriminatory."); 2008 House Judiciary Committee Report (criticizing pre-ADAAA court decisions which "prevented individuals that Congress unquestionably intended to cover from ever getting a chance to prove their case"). Accordingly, the threshold coverage question of whether an individual's impairment is a disability under the ADA "should not demand extensive analysis." ADAAA Section 2(b)(5).

Section 1630.2(g)(2) provides that an individual may establish coverage under any one or more (or all three) of the prongs in the definition of disability. However, to be an individual with a disability, an individual is only required to satisfy one prong.

As § 1630.2(g)(3) indicates, in many cases it may be unnecessary for an individual to resort to coverage under the "actual disability" or "record of" prongs. Where the need for a reasonable accommodation is not at issue — for example, where there is no question that the individual is "qualified" without a reasonable accommodation and is not seeking or has not sought a reasonable accommodation — it would not be necessary to determine whether the individual is substantially limited in a major life activity (under the actual disability prong) or has a record of a substantially limiting impairment (under the record of prong). Such claims could be evaluated solely under the "regarded as" prong of the definition. In fact, Congress expected the first and second prongs of the definition of disability "to be used only by people who are affirmatively seeking reasonable accommodations * * *" and that "[a]ny individual who has been discriminated against because of an impairment — short of being granted a reasonable accommodation * * * — should be bringing a claim under the third prong of the definition which will require no showing with regard to the severity of his or her impairment." Joint Hoyer-Sensenbrenner Statement at 4. An individual may choose, however, to proceed under the "actual disability" and/or "record of" prong regardless of whether the individual is challenging a covered entity's failure to make reasonable accommodation or requires a reasonable accommodation.

To fully understand the meaning of the term "disability," it is also necessary to understand what is meant by the terms "physical or mental impairment," "major life activity," "substantially limits," "record of," and "regarded as." Each of these terms is discussed below.

Section 1630.2(h)   Physical or Mental Impairment

Neither the original ADA nor the ADAAA provides a definition for the terms "physical or mental impairment." However, the legislative history of the Amendments Act notes that Congress "expect[s] that the current regulatory definition of these terms, as promulgated by agencies such as the U.S. Equal Employment Opportunity Commission (EEOC), the Department of Justice (DOJ) and the Department of Education Office of Civil Rights (DOE OCR) will not change." 2008 Senate Statement of Managers at 6. The definition of "physical or mental impairment" in the EEOC's regulations remains based on the definition of the term "physical or mental impairment" found in the regulations implementing section 504 of the Rehabilitation Act at 34 CFR part 104. However, the definition in EEOC's regulations adds additional body systems to those provided in the section 504 regulations and makes clear that the list is non-exhaustive.

It is important to distinguish between conditions that are impairments and physical, psychological, environmental, cultural, and economic characteristics that are not impairments. The definition of the term "impairment" does not include physical characteristics such as eye color, hair color, left-handedness, or height, weight, or muscle tone that are within "normal" range and are not the result of a physiological disorder. The definition, likewise, does not include characteristic predisposition to illness or disease. Other conditions, such as pregnancy, that are not the result of a physiological disorder are also not impairments. However, a pregnancy-related impairment that substantially limits a major life activity is a disability under the first prong of the definition. Alternatively, a pregnancy-related impairment may constitute a "record of" a substantially limiting impairment," or may be covered under the "regarded as" prong if it is the basis for a prohibited employment action and is not "transitory and minor."

The definition of an impairment also does not include common personality traits such as poor judgment or a quick temper where these are not symptoms of a mental or psychological disorder. Environmental, cultural, or economic disadvantages such as poverty, lack of education, or a prison record are not impairments. Advanced age, in and of itself, is also not an impairment. However, various medical conditions commonly associated with age, such as hearing loss, osteoporosis, or arthritis would constitute impairments within the meaning of this part. See 1989 Senate Report at 22–23; 1990 House Labor Report at 51–52; 1990 House Judiciary Report at 28–29.

Section 1630.2(i)   Major Life Activities

The ADAAA provided significant new guidance and clarification on the subject of "major life activities." As the legislative history of the Amendments Act explains, Congress anticipated that protection under the ADA would now extend to a wider range of cases, in part as a result of the expansion of the category of major life activities. See 2008 Senate Statement of Managers at 8 n.17.

For purposes of clarity, the Amendments Act provides an illustrative list of major life activities, including caring for oneself, performing manual tasks, seeing, hearing, eating, sleeping, walking, standing, lifting, bending, speaking, breathing, learning, reading, concentrating, thinking, communicating, and working. The ADA Amendments expressly made this statutory list of examples of major life activities non-exhaustive, and the regulations include sitting, reaching, and interacting with others as additional examples. Many of these major life activities listed in the ADA Amendments Act and the regulations already had been included in the EEOC's 1991 now-superseded regulations implementing title I of the ADA and in sub-regulatory documents, and already were recognized by the courts.

The ADA as amended also explicitly defines "major life activities" to include the operation of "major bodily functions." This was an important addition to the statute. This clarification was needed to ensure that the impact of an impairment on the operation of a major bodily function would not be overlooked or wrongly dismissed as falling outside the definition of "major life activities" under the ADA. 2008 House Judiciary Committee Report at 16; see also 2008 Senate Statement of Managers at 8 ("for the first time [in the ADAAA], the category of major life activities' is defined to include the operation of major bodily functions, thus better addressing chronic impairments that can be substantially limiting").

The regulations include all of those major bodily functions identified in the ADA Amendments Act's non-exhaustive list of examples and add a number of others that are consistent with the body systems listed in the regulations' definition of "impairment" (at § 1630.2(h)) and with the U.S. Department of Labor's nondiscrimination and equal employment opportunity regulations implementing section 188 of the Workforce Investment Act of 1998, 29 U.S.C. 2801, et seq. Thus, special sense organs, skin, genitourinary, cardiovascular, hemic, lymphatic, and musculoskeletal functions are major bodily functions not included in the statutory list of examples but included in § 1630.2(i)(1)(ii). The Commission has added these examples to further illustrate the non-exhaustive list of major life activities, including major bodily functions, and to emphasize that the concept of major life activities is to be interpreted broadly consistent with the Amendments Act. The regulations also provide that the operation of a major bodily function may include the operation of an individual organ within a body system. This would include, for example, the operation of the kidney, liver, pancreas, or other organs.

The link between particular impairments and various major bodily functions should not be difficult to identify. Because impairments, by definition, affect the functioning of body systems, they will generally affect major bodily functions. For example, cancer affects an individual's normal cell growth; diabetes affects the operation of the pancreas and also the function of the endocrine system; and Human Immunodeficiency Virus (HIV) infection affects the immune system. Likewise, sickle cell disease affects the functions of the hemic system, lymphedema affects lymphatic functions, and rheumatoid arthritis affects musculoskeletal functions.

In the legislative history of the ADAAA, Congress expressed its expectation that the statutory expansion of "major life activities" to include major bodily functions (along with other statutory changes) would lead to more expansive coverage. See 2008 Senate Statement of Managers at 8 n.17 (indicating that these changes will make it easier for individuals to show that they are eligible for the ADA's protections under the first prong of the definition of disability). The House Education and Labor Committee explained that the inclusion of major bodily functions would "affect cases such as U.S. v. Happy Time Day Care Ctr. in which the courts struggled to analyze whether the impact of HIV infection substantially limits various major life activities of a five-year-old child, and recognizing, among other things, that there is something inherently illogical about inquiring whether' a five-year-old's ability to procreate is substantially limited by his HIV infection; Furnish v. SVI Sys., Inc, in which the court found that an individual with cirrhosis of the liver caused by Hepatitis B is not disabled because liver function — unlike eating, working, or reproducing — is not integral to one's daily existence;' and Pimental v. Dartmouth-Hitchcock Clinic, in which the court concluded that the plaintiff's stage three breast cancer did not substantially limit her ability to care for herself, sleep, or concentrate. The Committee expects that the plaintiffs in each of these cases could establish a [substantial limitation] on major bodily functions that would qualify them for protection under the ADA." 2008 House Education and Labor Committee Report at 12.

The examples of major life activities (including major bodily functions) in the ADAAA and the EEOC's regulations are illustrative and non-exhaustive, and the absence of a particular life activity or bodily function from the examples does not create a negative implication as to whether an omitted activity or function constitutes a major life activity under the statute. See 2008 Senate Statement of Managers at 8; See also 2008 House Committee on Educ. and Labor Report at 11; 2008 House Judiciary Committee Report at 17.

The Commission anticipates that courts will recognize other major life activities, consistent with the ADA Amendments Act's mandate to construe the definition of disability broadly. As a result of the ADA Amendments Act's rejection of the holding in Toyota Motor Mfg., Ky., Inc. v. Williams, 534 U.S. 184 (2002), whether an activity is a "major life activity" is not determined by reference to whether it is of "central importance to daily life." See Toyota, 534 U.S. at 197 (defining "major life activities" as activities that are of "central importance to most people's daily lives"). Indeed, this holding was at odds with the earlier Supreme Court decision of Bragdon v. Abbott, 524 U.S. 624 (1998), which held that a major life activity (in that case, reproduction) does not have to have a "public, economic or daily aspect." Id. at 639.

Accordingly, the regulations provide that in determining other examples of major life activities, the term "major" shall not be interpreted strictly to create a demanding standard for disability. Cf. 2008 Senate Statement of Managers at 7 (indicating that a person is considered an individual with a disability for purposes of the first prong when one or more of the individual's "important life activities" are restricted) (citing 1989 Senate Report at 23). The regulations also reject the notion that to be substantially limited in performing a major life activity, an individual must have an impairment that prevents or severely restricts the individual from doing "activities that are of central importance to most people's daily lives." Id.; see also 2008 Senate Statement of Managers at 5 n.12.

Thus, for example, lifting is a major life activity regardless of whether an individual who claims to be substantially limited in lifting actually performs activities of central importance to daily life that require lifting. Similarly, the Commission anticipates that the major life activity of performing manual tasks (which was at issue in Toyota) could have many different manifestations, such as performing tasks involving fine motor coordination, or performing tasks involving grasping, hand strength, or pressure. Such tasks need not constitute activities of central importance to most people's daily lives, nor must an individual show that he or she is substantially limited in performing all manual tasks.

Section 1630.2(j)   Substantially Limits

In any case involving coverage solely under the "regarded as" prong of the definition of "disability" (e.g., cases where reasonable accommodation is not at issue), it is not necessary to determine whether an individual is "substantially limited" in any major life activity. See 2008 Senate Statement of Managers at 10; id. at 13 ("The functional limitation imposed by an impairment is irrelevant to the third regarded as' prong."). Indeed, Congress anticipated that the first and second prongs of the definition of disability would "be used only by people who are affirmatively seeking reasonable accommodations * * *" and that "[a]ny individual who has been discriminated against because of an impairment — short of being granted a reasonable accommodation * * * — should be bringing a claim under the third prong of the definition which will require no showing with regard to the severity of his or her impairment." Joint Hoyer-Sensenbrenner Statement at 4. Of course, an individual may choose, however, to proceed under the "actual disability" and/or "record of" prong regardless of whether the individual is challenging a covered entity's failure to make reasonable accommodations or requires a reasonable accommodation. The concept of "substantially limits" is only relevant in cases involving coverage under the "actual disability" or "record of" prong of the definition of disability. Thus, the information below pertains to these cases only.

Section 1630.2(j)(1)   Rules of Construction

It is clear in the text and legislative history of the ADAAA that Congress concluded the courts had incorrectly construed "substantially limits," and disapproved of the EEOC's now-superseded 1991 regulation defining the term to mean "significantly restricts." See 2008 Senate Statement of Managers at 6 ("We do not believe that the courts have correctly instituted the level of coverage we intended to establish with the term substantially limits' in the ADA" and "we believe that the level of limitation, and the intensity of focus, applied by the Supreme Court in Toyota goes beyond what we believe is the appropriate standard to create coverage under this law."). Congress extensively deliberated over whether a new term other than "substantially limits" should be adopted to denote the appropriate functional limitation necessary under the first and second prongs of the definition of disability. See 2008 Senate Statement of Managers at 6–7. Ultimately, Congress affirmatively opted to retain this term in the Amendments Act, rather than replace it. It concluded that "adopting a new, undefined term that is subject to widely disparate meanings is not the best way to achieve the goal of ensuring consistent and appropriately broad coverage under this Act." Id. Instead, Congress determined "a better way * * * to express [its] disapproval of Sutton and Toyota (along with the current EEOC regulation) is to retain the words substantially limits,' but clarify that it is not meant to be a demanding standard." Id. at 7. To achieve that goal, Congress set forth detailed findings and purposes and "rules of construction" to govern the interpretation and application of this concept going forward. See ADAAA Sections 2–4; 42 U.S.C. 12102(4).

The Commission similarly considered whether to provide a new definition of "substantially limits" in the regulation. Following Congress's lead, however, the Commission ultimately concluded that a new definition would inexorably lead to greater focus and intensity of attention on the threshold issue of coverage than intended by Congress. Therefore, the regulations simply provide rules of construction that must be applied in determining whether an impairment substantially limits (or substantially limited) a major life activity. These are each discussed in greater detail below.

Section 1630.2(j)(1)(i):   Broad Construction; not a Demanding Standard

Section 1630.2(j)(1)(i) states: "The term substantially limits' shall be construed broadly in favor of expansive coverage, to the maximum extent permitted by the terms of the ADA. Substantially limits' is not meant to be a demanding standard."

Congress stated in the ADA Amendments Act that the definition of disability "shall be construed in favor of broad coverage," and that "the term substantially limits' shall be interpreted consistently with the findings and purposes of the ADA Amendments Act of 2008." 42 U.S.C. 12101(4)(A)–(B), as amended. "This is a textual provision that will legally guide the agencies and courts in properly interpreting the term substantially limits.'" Hoyer-Sensenbrenner Congressional Record Statement at H8295. As Congress noted in the legislative history of the ADAAA, "[t]o be clear, the purposes section conveys our intent to clarify not only that substantially limits' should be measured by a lower standard than that used in Toyota, but also that the definition of disability should not be unduly used as a tool for excluding individuals from the ADA's protections." 2008 Senate Statement of Managers at 5 (also stating that "[t]his rule of construction, together with the rule of construction providing that the definition of disability shall be construed in favor of broad coverage of individuals sends a clear signal of our intent that the courts must interpret the definition of disability broadly rather than stringently"). Put most succinctly, "substantially limits" "is not meant to be a demanding standard." 2008 Senate Statement of Managers at 7.

Section 1630.2(j)(1)(ii):   Significant or Severe Restriction Not Required;

Nonetheless, Not Every Impairment Is Substantially Limiting

Section 1630.2(j)(1)(ii) states: "An impairment is a disability within the meaning of this section if it substantially limits the ability of an individual to perform a major life activity as compared to most people in the general population. An impairment need not prevent, or significantly or severely restrict, the individual from performing a major life activity in order to be considered substantially limiting. Nonetheless, not every impairment will constitute a disability' within the meaning of this section."

In keeping with the instruction that the term "substantially limits" is not meant to be a demanding standard, the regulations provide that an impairment is a disability if it substantially limits the ability of an individual to perform a major life activity as compared to most people in the general population. However, to be substantially limited in performing a major life activity an individual need not have an impairment that prevents or significantly or severely restricts the individual from performing a major life activity. See 2008 Senate Statement of Managers at 2, 6–8 & n.14; 2008 House Committee on Educ. and Labor Report at 9–10 ("While the limitation imposed by an impairment must be important, it need not rise to the level of severely restricting or significantly restricting the ability to perform a major life activity to qualify as a disability."); 2008 House Judiciary Committee Report at 16 (similarly requiring an "important" limitation). The level of limitation required is "substantial" as compared to most people in the general population, which does not require a significant or severe restriction. Multiple impairments that combine to substantially limit one or more of an individual's major life activities also constitute a disability. Nonetheless, not every impairment will constitute a "disability" within the meaning of this section. See 2008 Senate Statement of Managers at 4 ("We reaffirm that not every individual with a physical or mental impairment is covered by the first prong of the definition of disability in the ADA.")

Section 1630.2(j)(1)(iii): Substantial Limitation Should Not Be Primary Object of Attention; Extensive Analysis Not Needed

Section 1630.2(j)(1)(iii) states: "The primary object of attention in cases brought under the ADA should be whether covered entities have complied with their obligations, not whether an individual's impairment substantially limits a major life activity. Accordingly, the threshold issue of whether an impairment substantially limits' a major life activity should not demand extensive analysis."

Congress retained the term "substantially limits" in part because it was concerned that adoption of a new phrase — and the resulting need for further judicial scrutiny and construction — would not "help move the focus from the threshold issue of disability to the primary issue of discrimination." 2008 Senate Statement of Managers at 7.

This was the primary problem Congress sought to solve in enacting the ADAAA. It recognized that "clearing the initial [disability] threshold is critical, as individuals who are excluded from the definition never have the opportunity to have their condition evaluated in light of medical evidence and a determination made as to whether they [are] otherwise qualified." "2008 House

Judiciary Committee Report at 7; see also id. (expressing concern that "[a]n individual who does not qualify as disabled does not meet th[e] threshold question of coverage in the protected class and is therefore not permitted to attempt to prove his or her claim of discriminatory treatment"); 2008 Senate Statement of Managers at 4 (criticizing pre-ADAAA lower court cases that "too often turned solely on the question of whether the plaintiff is an individual with a disability rather than the merits of discrimination claims, such as whether adverse decisions were impermissibly made by the employer on the basis of disability, reasonable accommodations were denied, or qualification standards were unlawfully discriminatory").

Accordingly, the Amendments Act and the amended regulations make plain that the emphasis in ADA cases now should be squarely on the merits and not on the initial coverage question. The revised regulations therefore provide that an impairment is a disability if it substantially limits the ability of an individual to perform a major life activity as compared to most people in the general population and deletes the language to which Congress objected. The Commission believes that this provides a useful framework in which to analyze whether an impairment satisfies the definition of disability. Further, this framework better reflects Congress's expressed intent in the ADA Amendments Act that the definition of the term "disability" shall be construed broadly, and is consistent with statements in the Amendments Act's legislative history. See 2008 Senate Statement of Managers at 7 (stating that "adopting a new, undefined term" and the "resulting need for further judicial scrutiny and construction will not help move the focus from the threshold issue of disability to the primary issue of discrimination," and finding that "substantially limits' as construed consistently with the findings and purposes of this legislation establishes an appropriate functionality test of determining whether an individual has a disability" and that "using the correct standard — one that is lower than the strict or demanding standard created by the Supreme Court in Toyota — will make the disability determination an appropriate threshold issue but not an onerous burden for those seeking accommodations or modifications").

Consequently, this rule of construction makes clear that the question of whether an impairment substantially limits a major life activity should not demand extensive analysis. As the legislative history explains, "[w]e expect that courts interpreting [the ADA] will not demand such an extensive analysis over whether a person's physical or mental impairment constitutes a disability." Hoyer-Sensenbrenner Congressional Record Statement at H8295; see id. ("Our goal throughout this process has been to simplify that analysis.")

Section 1630.2(j)(1)(iv): Individualized Assessment Required, But With Lower Standard Than Previously Applied

Section 1630.2(j)(1)(iv) states: "The determination of whether an impairment substantially limits a major life activity requires an individualized assessment. However, in making this assessment, the term substantially limits' shall be interpreted and applied to require a degree of functional limitation that is lower than the standard for substantially limits' applied prior to the ADAAA."

By retaining the essential elements of the definition of disability including the key term "substantially limits," Congress reaffirmed that not every individual with a physical or mental impairment is covered by the first prong of the definition of disability in the ADA. See 2008 Senate Statement of Managers at 4. To be covered under the first prong of the definition, an individual must establish that an impairment substantially limits a major life activity. That has not changed — nor will the necessity of making this determination on an individual basis. Id. However, what the ADAAA changed is the standard required for making this determination. Id. at 4–5.

The Amendments Act and the EEOC's regulations explicitly reject the standard enunciated by the Supreme Court in Toyota Motor Mfg., Ky., Inc. v. Williams, 534 U.S. 184 (2002), and applied in the lower courts in numerous cases. See ADAAA Section 2(b)(4). That previous standard created "an inappropriately high level of limitation necessary to obtain coverage under the ADA." Id. at Section 2(b)(5). The Amendments Act and the EEOC's regulations reject the notion that "substantially limits" should be interpreted strictly to create a demanding standard for qualifying as disabled. Id. at Section 2(b)(4). Instead, the ADAAA and these regulations establish a degree of functional limitation required for an impairment to constitute a disability that is consistent with what Congress originally intended. 2008 Senate Statement of Managers at 7. This will make the disability determination an appropriate threshold issue but not an onerous burden for those seeking to prove discrimination under the ADA. Id.

Section 1630.2(j)(1)(v): Scientific, Medical, or Statistical Analysis Not Required, But Permissible When Appropriate

Section 1630.2(j)(1)(v) states: "The comparison of an individual's performance of a major life activity to the performance of the same major life activity by most people in the general population usually will not require scientific, medical, or statistical analysis. Nothing in this paragraph is intended, however, to prohibit the presentation of scientific, medical, or statistical evidence to make such a comparison where appropriate."

The term "average person in the general population," as the basis of comparison for determining whether an individual's impairment substantially limits a major life activity, has been changed to "most people in the general population." This revision is not a substantive change in the concept, but rather is intended to conform the language to the simpler and more straightforward terminology used in the legislative history to the Amendments Act. The comparison between the individual and "most people" need not be exacting, and usually will not require scientific, medical, or statistical analysis. Nothing in this subparagraph is intended, however, to prohibit the presentation of scientific, medical, or statistical evidence to make such a comparison where appropriate.

The comparison to most people in the general population continues to mean a comparison to other people in the general population, not a comparison to those similarly situated. For example, the ability of an individual with an amputated limb to perform a major life activity is compared to other people in the general population, not to other amputees. This does not mean that disability cannot be shown where an impairment, such as a learning disability, is clinically diagnosed based in part on a disparity between an individual's aptitude and that individual's actual versus expected achievement, taking into account the person's chronological age, measured intelligence, and age-appropriate education. Individuals diagnosed with dyslexia or other learning disabilities will typically be substantially limited in performing activities such as learning, reading, and thinking when compared to most people in the general population, particularly when the ameliorative effects of mitigating measures, including therapies, learned behavioral or adaptive neurological modifications, assistive devices (e.g., audio recordings, screen reading devices, voice activated software), studying longer, or receiving more time to take a test, are disregarded as required under the ADA Amendments Act.

Section 1630.2(j)(1)(vi):   Mitigating Measures

Section 1630.2(j)(1)(vi) states: "The determination of whether an impairment substantially limits a major life activity shall be made without regard to the ameliorative effects of mitigating measures. However, the ameliorative effects of ordinary eyeglasses or contact lenses shall be considered in determining whether an impairment substantially limits a major life activity."

The ameliorative effects of mitigating measures shall not be considered in determining whether an impairment substantially limits a major life activity. Thus, "[w]ith the exception of ordinary eyeglasses and contact lenses, impairments must be examined in their unmitigated state." See 2008 Senate Statement of Managers at 5.

This provision in the ADAAA and the EEOC's regulations "is intended to eliminate the catch-22 that exist[ed] * * * where individuals who are subjected to discrimination on the basis of their disabilities [we]re frequently unable to invoke the ADA's protections because they [we]re not considered people with disabilities when the effects of their medication, medical supplies, behavioral adaptations, or other interventions [we]re considered." Joint Hoyer-Sensenbrenner Statement at 2; see also 2008 Senate Statement of Managers at 9 ("This provision is intended to eliminate the situation created under [prior] law in which impairments that are mitigated [did] not constitute disabilities but [were the basis for discrimination]."). To the extent cases pre-dating the 2008 Amendments Act reasoned otherwise, they are contrary to the law as amended. See 2008 House Judiciary Committee Report at 9 & nn.25, 20–21 (citing, e.g., McClure v. General Motors Corp., 75 F. App'x 983 (5th Cir. 2003) (court held that individual with muscular dystrophy who, with the mitigating measure of "adapting" how he performed manual tasks, had successfully learned to live and work with his disability was therefore not an individual with a disability); Orr v. Wal-Mart Stores, Inc., 297 F.3d 720 (8th Cir. 2002) (court held that Sutton v. United Air Lines, Inc., 527 U.S. 471 (1999), required consideration of the ameliorative effects of plaintiff's careful regimen of medicine, exercise and diet, and declined to consider impact of uncontrolled diabetes on plaintiff's ability to see, speak, read, and walk); Gonzales v. National Bd. of Med. Examiners, 225 F.3d 620 (6th Cir. 2000) (where the court found that an individual with a diagnosed learning disability was not substantially limited after considering the impact of self-accommodations that allowed him to read and achieve academic success); McMullin v. Ashcroft, 337 F. Supp.

2d 1281 (D. Wyo. 2004) (individual fired because of clinical depression not protected because of the successful management of the condition with medication for fifteen years); Eckhaus v. Consol. Rail Corp., 2003 WL 23205042 (D.N.J. Dec. 24, 2003) (individual fired because of a hearing impairment was not protected because a hearing aid helped correct that impairment); Todd v. Academy Corp., 57 F. Supp. 2d 448, 452 (S.D. Tex. 1999) (court held that because medication reduced the frequency and intensity of plaintiff's seizures, he was not disabled)).

An individual who, because of the use of a mitigating measure, has experienced no limitations, or only minor limitations, related to the impairment may still be an individual with a disability, where there is evidence that in the absence of an effective mitigating measure the individual's impairment would be substantially limiting. For example, someone who began taking medication for hypertension before experiencing substantial limitations related to the impairment would still be an individual with a disability if, without the medication, he or she would now be substantially limited in functions of the cardiovascular or circulatory system.

Evidence showing that an impairment would be substantially limiting in the absence of the ameliorative effects of mitigating measures could include evidence of limitations that a person experienced prior to using a mitigating measure, evidence concerning the expected course of a particular disorder absent mitigating measures, or readily available and reliable information of other types. However, we expect that consistent with the Amendments Act's command (and the related rules of construction in the regulations) that the definition of disability "should not demand extensive analysis," covered entities and courts will in many instances be able to conclude that a substantial limitation has been shown without resort to such evidence.

The Amendments Act provides an "illustrative but non-comprehensive list of the types of mitigating measures that are not to be considered." See 2008 Senate Statement of Managers at 9. Section 1630.2(j)(5) of the regulations includes all of those mitigating measures listed in the ADA Amendments Act's illustrative list of mitigating measures, including reasonable accommodations (as applied under title I) or "auxiliary aids or services" (as defined by 42 U.S.C. 12103(1) and applied under titles II and III).

Since it would be impossible to guarantee comprehensiveness in a finite list, the list of examples of mitigating measures provided in the ADA and the regulations is non-exhaustive. See 2008 House Judiciary Committee Report at 20. The absence of any particular mitigating measure from the list in the regulations should not convey a negative implication as to whether the measure is a mitigating measure under the ADA. See 2008 Senate Statement of Managers at 9.

For example, the fact that mitigating measures include "reasonable accommodations" generally makes it unnecessary to mention specific kinds of accommodations. Nevertheless, the use of a service animal, job coach, or personal assistant on the job would certainly be considered types of mitigating measures, as would the use of any device that could be considered assistive technology, and whether individuals who use these measures have disabilities would be determined without reference to their ameliorative effects. See 2008 House Judiciary Committee Report at 20; 2008 House Educ. & Labor Rep. at 15. Similarly, adaptive strategies that might mitigate, or even allow an individual to otherwise avoid performing particular major life activities, are mitigating measures and also would not be considered in determining whether an impairment is substantially limiting. Id.

The determination of whether or not an individual's impairment substantially limits a major life activity is unaffected by whether the individual chooses to forgo mitigating measures. For individuals who do not use a mitigating measure (including for example medication or reasonable accommodation that could alleviate the effects of an impairment), the availability of such measures has no bearing on whether the impairment substantially limits a major life activity. The limitations posed by the impairment on the individual and any negative (non-ameliorative) effects of mitigating measures used determine whether an impairment is substantially limiting. The origin of the impairment, whether its effects can be mitigated, and any ameliorative effects of mitigating measures in fact used may not be considered in determining if the impairment is substantially limiting. However, the use or non-use of mitigating measures, and any consequences thereof, including any ameliorative and non-ameliorative effects, may be relevant in determining whether the individual is qualified or poses a direct threat to safety.

The ADA Amendments Act and the regulations state that "ordinary eyeglasses or contact lenses" shall be considered in determining whether someone has a disability. This is an exception to the rule that the ameliorative effects of mitigating measures are not to be taken into account. "The rationale behind this exclusion is that the use of ordinary eyeglasses or contact lenses, without more, is not significant enough to warrant protection under the ADA." Joint Hoyer-Sensenbrenner Statement at 2. Nevertheless, as discussed in greater detail below at § 1630.10(b), if an applicant or employee is faced with a qualification standard that requires uncorrected vision (as the plaintiffs in the Sutton case were), and the applicant or employee who is adversely affected by the standard brings a challenge under the ADA, an employer will be required to demonstrate that the qualification standard is job related and consistent with business necessity. 2008 Senate Statement of Managers at 9.

The ADAAA and the EEOC's regulations both define the term "ordinary eyeglasses or contact lenses" as lenses that are "intended to fully correct visual acuity or eliminate refractive error." So, if an individual with severe myopia uses eyeglasses or contact lenses that are intended to fully correct visual acuity or eliminate refractive error, they are ordinary eyeglasses or contact lenses, and therefore any inquiry into whether such individual is substantially limited in seeing or reading would be based on how the individual sees or reads with the benefit of the eyeglasses or contact lenses. Likewise, if the only visual loss an individual experiences affects the ability to see well enough to read, and the individual's ordinary reading glasses are intended to completely correct for this visual loss, the ameliorative effects of using the reading glasses must be considered in determining whether the individual is substantially limited in seeing. Additionally, eyeglasses or contact lenses that are the wrong prescription or an outdated prescription may nevertheless be "ordinary" eyeglasses or contact lenses, if a proper prescription would fully correct visual acuity or eliminate refractive error.

Both the statute and the regulations distinguish "ordinary eyeglasses or contact lenses" from "low vision devices," which function by magnifying, enhancing, or otherwise augmenting a visual image, and which are not considered when determining whether someone has a disability. The regulations do not establish a specific level of visual acuity (e.g., 20/20) as the basis for determining whether eyeglasses or contact lenses should be considered "ordinary" eyeglasses or contact lenses. Whether lenses fully correct visual acuity or eliminate refractive error is best determined on a case-by-case basis, in light of current and objective medical evidence. Moreover, someone who uses ordinary eyeglasses or contact lenses is not automatically considered to be outside the ADA's protection. Such an individual may demonstrate that, even with the use of ordinary eyeglasses or contact lenses, his vision is still substantially limited when compared to most people.

Section 1630.2(j)(1)(vii): Impairments That Are Episodic or in Remission

Section 1630.2(j)(1)(vii) states: "An impairment that is episodic or in remission is a disability if it would substantially limit a major life activity when active."

An impairment that is episodic or in remission is a disability if it would substantially limit a major life activity in its active state. "This provision is intended to reject the reasoning of court decisions concluding that certain individuals with certain conditions — such as epilepsy or post traumatic stress disorder — were not protected by the ADA because their conditions were episodic or intermittent." Joint Hoyer-Sensenbrenner Statement at 2–3. The legislative history provides: "This * * * rule of construction thus rejects the reasoning of the courts in cases like Todd v. Academy Corp. [57 F. Supp. 2d 448, 453 (S.D. Tex. 1999)] where the court found that the plaintiff's epilepsy, which resulted in short seizures during which the plaintiff was unable to speak and experienced tremors, was not sufficiently limiting, at least in part because those seizures occurred episodically. It similarly rejects the results reached in cases [such as Pimental v. Dartmouth-Hitchock Clinic, 236 F. Supp. 2d 177, 182–83 (D.N.H. 2002)] where the courts have discounted the impact of an impairment [such as cancer] that may be in remission as too short-lived to be substantially limiting. It is thus expected that individuals with impairments that are episodic or in remission (e.g., epilepsy, multiple sclerosis, cancer) will be able to establish coverage if, when active, the impairment or the manner in which it manifests (e.g., seizures) substantially limits a major life activity." 2008 House Judiciary Committee Report at 19–20.

Other examples of impairments that may be episodic include, but are not limited to, hypertension, diabetes, asthma, major depressive disorder, bipolar disorder, and schizophrenia. See 2008 House Judiciary Committee Report at 19–20. The fact that the periods during which an episodic impairment is active and substantially limits a major life activity may be brief or occur infrequently is no longer relevant to determining whether the impairment substantially limits a major life activity. For example, a person with post-traumatic stress disorder who experiences intermittent flashbacks to traumatic events is substantially limited in brain function and thinking.

Section 1630.2(j)(1)(viii):   Substantial Limitation in Only One Major Life Activity Required

Section 1630.2(j)(1)(viii) states: "An impairment that substantially limits one major life activity need not substantially limit other major life activities in order to be considered a substantially limiting impairment."

The ADAAA explicitly states that an impairment need only substantially limit one major life activity to be considered a disability under the ADA. See ADAAA Section 4(a); 42 U.S.C. 12102(4)(C). "This responds to and corrects those courts that have required individuals to show that an impairment substantially limits more than one life activity." 2008 Senate Statement of Managers at 8. In addition, this rule of construction is "intended to clarify that the ability to perform one or more particular tasks within a broad category of activities does not preclude coverage under the ADA." Id. To the extent cases pre-dating the applicability of the 2008 Amendments Act reasoned otherwise, they are contrary to the law as amended. Id. (citing Holt v. Grand Lake Mental Health Ctr., Inc., 443 F. 3d 762 (10th Cir. 2006) (holding an individual with cerebral palsy who could not independently perform certain specified manual tasks was not substantially limited in her ability to perform a "broad range" of manual tasks)); See also 2008 House Judiciary Committee Report at 19 & n.52 (this legislatively corrects court decisions that, with regard to the major life activity of performing manual tasks, "have offset substantial limitation in the performance of some tasks with the ability to perform others" (citing Holt)).

For example, an individual with diabetes is substantially limited in endocrine function and thus an individual with a disability under the first prong of the definition. He need not also show that he is substantially limited in eating to qualify for coverage under the first prong. An individual whose normal cell growth is substantially limited due to lung cancer need not also show that she is substantially limited in breathing or respiratory function. And an individual with HIV infection is substantially limited in the function of the immune system, and therefore is an individual with a disability without regard to whether his or her HIV infection substantially limits him or her in reproduction.

In addition, an individual whose impairment substantially limits a major life activity need not additionally demonstrate a resulting limitation in the ability to perform activities of central importance to daily life in order to be considered an individual with a disability under § 1630.2(g)(1)(i) or § 1630.2(g)(1)(ii), as cases relying on the Supreme Court's decision in Toyota Motor Mfg., Ky., Inc. v. Williams, 534 U.S. 184 (2002), had held prior to the ADA Amendments Act.

Thus, for example, someone with an impairment resulting in a 20-pound lifting restriction that lasts or is expected to last for several months is substantially limited in the major life activity of lifting, and need not also show that he is unable to perform activities of daily living that require lifting in order to be considered substantially limited in lifting. Similarly, someone with monocular vision whose depth perception or field of vision would be substantially limited, with or without any compensatory strategies the individual may have developed, need not also show that he is unable to perform activities of central importance to daily life that require See ing in order to be substantially limited in seeing.

Section 1630.2(j)(1)(ix):   Effects of an Impairment Lasting Fewer Than Six Months Can Be Substantially Limiting

Section 1630.2(j)(1)(ix) states: "The six-month transitory' part of the transitory and minor' exception to regarded as' coverage in § 1630.2(l) does not apply to the definition of disability' under § 1630.2(g)(1)(i) or § 1630.2(g)(1)(ii). The effects of an impairment lasting or expected to last fewer than six months can be substantially limiting within the meaning of this section."

The regulations include a clear statement that the definition of an impairment as transitory, that is, "lasting or expected to last for six months or less," only applies to the "regarded as" (third) prong of the definition of "disability" as part of the "transitory and minor" defense to "regarded as" coverage. It does not apply to the first or second prong of the definition of disability. See Joint Hoyer-Sensenbrenner Statement at 3 ("[T]here is no need for the transitory and minor exception under the first two prongs because it is clear from the statute and the legislative history that a person can only bring a claim if the impairment substantially limits one or more major life activities or the individual has a record of an impairment that substantially limits one or more major life activities.").

Therefore, an impairment does not have to last for more than six months in order to be considered substantially limiting under the first or the second prong of the definition of disability. For example, as noted above, if an individual has a back impairment that results in a 20-pound lifting restriction that lasts for several months, he is substantially limited in the major life activity of lifting, and therefore covered under the first prong of the definition of disability. At the same time, "[t]he duration of an impairment is one factor that is relevant in determining whether the impairment substantially limits a major life activity. Impairments that last only for a short period of time are typically not covered, although they may be covered if sufficiently severe." Joint Hoyer-Sensenbrenner Statement at 5.

Section 1630.2(j)(3)   Predictable Assessments

As the regulations point out, disability is determined based on an individualized assessment. There is no "per se" disability. However, as recognized in the regulations, the individualized assessment of some kinds of impairments will virtually always result in a determination of disability. The inherent nature of these types of medical conditions will in virtually all cases give rise to a substantial limitation of a major life activity. Cf. Heiko v. Columbo Savings Bank, F.S.B., 434 F.3d 249, 256 (4th Cir. 2006) (stating, even pre-ADAAA, that "certain impairments are by their very nature substantially limiting: the major life activity of seeing, for example, is always substantially limited by blindness"). Therefore, with respect to these types of impairments, the necessary individualized assessment should be particularly simple and straightforward.

This result is the consequence of the combined effect of the statutory changes to the definition of disability contained in the Amendments Act and flows from application of the rules of construction set forth in §§ 1630.2(j)(1)(i)–(ix) (including the lower standard for "substantially limits"; the rule that major life activities include major bodily functions; the principle that impairments that are episodic or in remission are disabilities if they would be substantially limiting when active; and the requirement that the ameliorative effects of mitigating measures (other than ordinary eyeglasses or contact lenses) must be disregarded in assessing whether an individual has a disability).

The regulations at § 1630.2(j)(3)(iii) provide examples of the types of impairments that should easily be found to substantially limit a major life activity. The legislative history states that Congress modeled the ADA definition of disability on the definition contained in the Rehabilitation Act, and said it wished to return courts to the way they had construed that definition. See 2008 House Judiciary Committee Report at 6. Describing this goal, the legislative history states that courts had interpreted the Rehabilitation Act definition "broadly to include persons with a wide range of physical and mental impairments such as epilepsy, diabetes, multiple sclerosis, and intellectual and developmental disabilities * * * even where a mitigating measure — like medication or a hearing aid — might lessen their impact on the individual." Id.; See also id. at 9 (referring to individuals with disabilities that had been covered under the Rehabilitation Act and that Congress intended to include under the ADA — "people with serious health conditions like epilepsy, diabetes, cancer, cerebral palsy, multiple sclerosis, intellectual and developmental disabilities"); id. at n.6 (citing cases also finding that cerebral palsy, hearing impairments, mental retardation, heart disease, and vision in only one eye were disabilities under the Rehabilitation Act); id. at 10 (citing testimony from Rep. Steny H. Hoyer, one of the original lead sponsors of the ADA in 1990, stating that "we could not have fathomed that people with diabetes, epilepsy, heart conditions, cancer, mental illnesses and other disabilities would have their ADA claims denied because they would be considered too functional to meet the definition of disability"); 2008 Senate Statement of Managers at 3 (explaining that "we [we]re faced with a situation in which physical or mental impairments that would previously [under the Rehabilitation Act] have been found to constitute disabilities [we]re not considered disabilities" and citing individuals with impairments such as amputation, intellectual disabilities, epilepsy, multiple sclerosis, diabetes, muscular dystrophy, and cancer as examples).

Of course, the impairments listed in subparagraph 1630.2(j)(3)(iii) may substantially limit a variety of other major life activities in addition to those listed in the regulation. For example, mobility impairments requiring the use of a wheelchair substantially limit the major life activity of walking. Diabetes may substantially limit major life activities such as eating, sleeping, and thinking. Major depressive disorder may substantially limit major life activities such as thinking, concentrating, sleeping, and interacting with others. Multiple sclerosis may substantially limit major life activities such as walking, bending, and lifting.

By using the term "brain function" to describe the system affected by various mental impairments, the Commission is expressing no view on the debate concerning whether mental illnesses are caused by environmental or biological factors, but rather intends the term to capture functions such as the ability of the brain to regulate thought processes and emotions.

Section 1630.2(j)(4)   Condition, Manner, or Duration

The regulations provide that facts such as the "condition, manner, or duration" of an individual's performance of a major life activity may be useful in determining whether an impairment results in a substantial limitation. In the legislative history of the ADAAA, Congress reiterated what it had said at the time of the original ADA: "A person is considered an individual with a disability for purposes of the first prong of the definition when [one or more of] the individual's important life activities are restricted as to the conditions, manner, or duration under which they can be performed in comparison to most people." 2008 Senate Statement of Managers at 7 (citing 1989 Senate Report at 23). According to Congress: "We particularly believe that this test, which articulated an analysis that considered whether a person's activities are limited in condition, duration and manner, is a useful one. We reiterate that using the correct standard — one that is lower than the strict or demanding standard created by the Supreme Court in Toyota — will make the disability determination an appropriate threshold issue but not an onerous burden for those seeking accommodations * * *. At the same time, plaintiffs should not be constrained from offering evidence needed to establish that their impairment is substantially limiting." 2008 Senate Statement of Managers at 7.

Consistent with the legislative history, an impairment may substantially limit the "condition" or "manner" under which a major life activity can be performed in a number of ways. For example, the condition or manner under which a major life activity can be performed may refer to the way an individual performs a major life activity. Thus, the condition or manner under which a person with an amputated hand performs manual tasks will likely be more cumbersome than the way that someone with two hands would perform the same tasks.

Condition or manner may also describe how performance of a major life activity affects the individual with an impairment. For example, an individual whose impairment causes pain or fatigue that most people would not experience when performing that major life activity may be substantially limited. Thus, the condition or manner under which someone with coronary artery disease performs the major life activity of walking would be substantially limiting if the individual experiences shortness of breath and fatigue when walking distances that most people could walk without experiencing such effects. Similarly, condition or manner may refer to the extent to which a major life activity, including a major bodily function, can be performed. For example, the condition or manner under which a major bodily function can be performed may be substantially limited when the impairment "causes the operation [of the bodily function] to over-produce or under-produce in some harmful fashion." See 2008 House Judiciary Committee Report at 17.

"Duration" refers to the length of time an individual can perform a major life activity or the length of time it takes an individual to perform a major life activity, as compared to most people in the general population. For example, a person whose back or leg impairment precludes him or her from standing for more than two hours without significant pain would be substantially limited in standing, since most people can stand for more than two hours without significant pain. However, a person who can walk for ten miles continuously is not substantially limited in walking merely because on the eleventh mile, he or she begins to experience pain because most people would not be able to walk eleven miles without experiencing some discomfort. See 2008 Senate Statement of Managers at 7 (citing 1989 Senate Report at 23).

The regulations provide that in assessing substantial limitation and considering facts such as condition, manner, or duration, the non-ameliorative effects of mitigating measures may be considered. Such "non-ameliorative effects" could include negative side effects of medicine, burdens associated with following a particular treatment regimen, and complications that arise from surgery, among others. Of course, in many instances, it will not be necessary to assess the negative impact of a mitigating measure in determining that a particular impairment substantially limits a major life activity. For example, someone with end-stage renal disease is substantially limited in kidney function, and it thus is not necessary to consider the burdens that dialysis treatment imposes.

Condition, manner, or duration may also suggest the amount of time or effort an individual has to expend when performing a major life activity because of the effects of an impairment, even if the individual is able to achieve the same or similar result as someone without the impairment. For this reason, the regulations include language which says that the outcome an individual with a disability is able to achieve is not determinative of whether he or she is substantially limited in a major life activity.

Thus, someone with a learning disability may achieve a high level of academic success, but may nevertheless be substantially limited in the major life activity of learning because of the additional time or effort he or she must spend to read, write, or learn compared to most people in the general population. As Congress emphasized in passing the Amendments Act, "[w]hen considering the condition, manner, or duration in which an individual with a specific learning disability performs a major life activity, it is critical to reject the assumption that an individual who has performed well academically cannot be substantially limited in activities such as learning, reading, writing, thinking, or speaking." 2008 Senate Statement of Managers at 8. Congress noted that: "In particular, some courts have found that students who have reached a high level of academic achievement are not to be considered individuals with disabilities under the ADA, as such individuals may have difficulty demonstrating substantial limitation in the major life activities of learning or reading relative to most people." When considering the condition, manner or duration in which an individual with a specific learning disability performs a major life activity, it is critical to reject the assumption that an individual who performs well academically or otherwise cannot be substantially limited in activities such as learning, reading, writing, thinking, or speaking. As such, the Committee rejects the findings in Price v. National Board of Medical Examiners, Gonzales v. National Board of Medical Examiners, and Wong v. Regents of University of California. The Committee believes that the comparison of individuals with specific learning disabilities to most people' is not problematic unto itself, but requires a careful analysis of the method and manner in which an individual's impairment limits a major life activity. For the majority of the population, the basic mechanics of reading and writing do not pose extraordinary lifelong challenges; rather, recognizing and forming letters and words are effortless, unconscious, automatic processes. Because specific learning disabilities are neurologically-based impairments, the process of reading for an individual with a reading disability (e.g. dyslexia) is word-by-word, and otherwise cumbersome, painful, deliberate and slow — throughout life. The Committee expects that individuals with specific learning disabilities that substantially limit a major life activity will be better protected under the amended Act." 2008 House Educ. & Labor Rep. at 10–11.

It bears emphasizing that while it may be useful in appropriate cases to consider facts such as condition, manner, or duration, it is always necessary to consider and apply the rules of construction in § 1630.2(j)(1)(i)–(ix) that set forth the elements of broad coverage enacted by Congress. 2008 Senate Statement of Managers at 6. Accordingly, while the Commission's regulations retain the concept of "condition, manner, or duration," they no longer include the additional list of "substantial limitation" factors contained in the previous version of the regulations (i.e., the nature and severity of the impairment, duration or expected duration of the impairment, and actual or expected permanent or long-term impact of or resulting from the impairment).

Finally, "condition, manner, or duration" are not intended to be used as a rigid three-part standard that must be met to establish a substantial limitation. "Condition, manner, or duration" are not required "factors" that must be considered as a talismanic test. Rather, in referring to "condition, manner, or duration," the regulations make clear that these are merely the types of facts that may be considered in appropriate cases. To the extent such aspects of limitation may be useful or relevant to show a substantial limitation in a particular fact pattern, some or all of them (and related facts) may be considered, but evidence relating to each of these facts may not be necessary to establish coverage.

At the same time, individuals seeking coverage under the first or second prong of the definition of disability should not be constrained from offering evidence needed to establish that their impairment is substantially limiting. See 2008 Senate Statement of Managers at 7. Of course, covered entities may defeat a showing of "substantial limitation" by refuting whatever evidence the individual seeking coverage has offered, or by offering evidence that shows an impairment does not impose a substantial limitation on a major life activity. However, a showing of substantial limitation is not defeated by facts related to "condition, manner, or duration" that are not pertinent to the substantial limitation the individual has proffered.

Sections 1630.2(j)(5) and (6)   Examples of Mitigating Measures; Ordinary Eyeglasses or Contact Lenses

These provisions of the regulations provide numerous examples of mitigating measures and the definition of "ordinary eyeglasses or contact lenses." These definitions have been more fully discussed in the portions of this interpretive guidance concerning the rules of construction in § 1630.2(j)(1).

Substantially Limited in Working

The Commission has removed from the text of the regulations a discussion of the major life activity of working. This is consistent with the fact that no other major life activity receives special attention in the regulation, and with the fact that, in light of the expanded definition of disability established by the Amendments Act, this major life activity will be used in only very targeted situations.

In most instances, an individual with a disability will be able to establish coverage by showing substantial limitation of a major life activity other than working; impairments that substantially limit a person's ability to work usually substantially limit one or more other major life activities. This will be particularly true in light of the changes made by the ADA Amendments Act. See, e.g., Corley v. Dep't of Veterans Affairs ex rel Principi, 218 F. App'x. 727, 738 (10th Cir. 2007) (employee with seizure disorder was not substantially limited in working because he was not foreclosed from jobs involving driving, operating machinery, childcare, military service, and other jobs; employee would now be substantially limited in neurological function); Olds v. United Parcel Serv., Inc., 127 F. App'x. 779, 782 (6th Cir. 2005) (employee with bone marrow cancer was not substantially limited in working due to lifting restrictions caused by his cancer; employee would now be substantially limited in normal cell growth); Williams v. Philadelphia Hous. Auth. Police Dep't, 380 F.3d 751, 763–64 (3d Cir. 2004) (issue of material fact concerning whether police officer's major depression substantially limited him in performing a class of jobs due to restrictions on his ability to carry a firearm; officer would now be substantially limited in brain function).[2]

In the rare cases where an individual has a need to demonstrate that an impairment substantially limits him or her in working, the individual can do so by showing that the impairment substantially limits his or her ability to perform a class of jobs or broad range of jobs in various classes as compared to most people having comparable training, skills, and abilities. In keeping with the findings and purposes of the Amendments Act, the determination of coverage under the law should not require extensive and elaborate assessment, and the EEOC and the courts are to apply a lower standard in determining when an impairment substantially limits a major life activity, including the major life activity of working, than they applied prior to the Amendments Act. The Commission believes that the courts, in applying an overly strict standard with regard to "substantially limits" generally, have reached conclusions with regard to what is necessary to demonstrate a substantial limitation in the major life activity of working that would be inconsistent with the changes now made by the Amendments Act. Accordingly, as used in this section the terms "class of jobs" and

---

[2] In addition, many cases previously analyzed in terms of whether the plaintiff was "substantially limited in working" will now be analyzed under the "regarded as" prong of the definition of disability as revised by the Amendments Act. See, e.g., Cannon v. Levi Strauss & Co., 29 F. App'x. 331 (6th Cir. 2002) (factory worker laid off due to her carpal tunnel syndrome not regarded as substantially limited in working because her job of sewing machine operator was not a "broad class of jobs"; she would now be protected under the third prong because she was fired because of her impairment, carpal tunnel syndrome); Bridges v. City of Bossier, 92 F.3d 329 (5th Cir. 1996) (applicant not hired for firefighting job because of his mild hemophilia not regarded as substantially limited in working; applicant would now be protected under the third prong because he was not hired because of his impairment, hemophilia).

"broad range of jobs in various classes" will be applied in a more straightforward and simple manner than they were applied by the courts prior to the Amendments Act.[3]

Demonstrating a substantial limitation in performing the unique aspects of a single specific job is not sufficient to establish that a person is substantially limited in the major life activity of working.

A class of jobs may be determined by reference to the nature of the work that an individual is limited in performing (such as commercial truck driving, assembly line jobs, food service jobs, clerical jobs, or law enforcement jobs) or by reference to job-related requirements that an individual is limited in meeting (for example, jobs requiring repetitive bending, reaching, or manual tasks, jobs requiring repetitive or heavy lifting, prolonged sitting or standing, extensive walking, driving, or working under conditions such as high temperatures or noise levels).

For example, if a person whose job requires heavy lifting develops a disability that prevents him or her from lifting more than fifty pounds and, consequently, from performing not only his or her existing job but also other jobs that would similarly require heavy lifting, that person would be substantially limited in working because he or she is substantially limited in performing the class of jobs that require heavy lifting.

Section 1630.2(k)   Record of a Substantially Limiting Impairment

The second prong of the definition of "disability" provides that an individual with a record of an impairment that substantially limits or limited a major life activity is an individual with a disability. The intent of this provision, in part, is to ensure that people are not discriminated against because of a history of disability. For example, the "record of" provision would protect an individual who was treated for cancer ten years ago but who is now deemed by a doctor to be free of cancer, from discrimination based on that prior medical history. This provision also ensures that individuals are not discriminated against because they have been misclassified as disabled. For example, individuals misclassified as having learning disabilities or intellectual disabilities (formerly termed "mental retardation") are protected from discrimination on the basis of that erroneous classification. Senate Report at 23; House Labor Report at 52–53; House Judiciary Report at 29; 2008 House Judiciary Report at 7–8 & n.14. Similarly, an employee who in the past was misdiagnosed with bipolar disorder and hospitalized as the result of a temporary reaction to medication

---

[3] In analyzing working as a major life activity in the past, some courts have imposed a complex and onerous standard that would be inappropriate under the Amendments Act. See, e.g., Duncan v. WMATA, 240 F.3d 1110, 1115 (DC Cir. 2001) (manual laborer whose back injury prevented him from lifting more than 20 pounds was not substantially limited in working because he did not present evidence of the number and types of jobs available to him in the Washington area; testimony concerning his inquiries and applications for truck driving jobs that all required heavy lifting was insufficient); Taylor v. Federal Express Corp., 429 F.3d 461, 463–64 (4th Cir. 2005) (employee's impairment did not substantially limit him in working because, even though evidence showed that employee's injury disqualified him from working in numerous jobs in his geographic region, it also showed that he remained qualified for many other jobs). Under the Amendments Act, the determination of whether a person is substantially limited in working is more straightforward and simple than it was prior to the Act.

she was taking has a record of a substantially limiting impairment, even though she did not actually have bipolar disorder.

This part of the definition is satisfied where evidence establishes that an individual has had a substantially limiting impairment. The impairment indicated in the record must be an impairment that would substantially limit one or more of the individual's major life activities. There are many types of records that could potentially contain this information, including but not limited to, education, medical, or employment records.

Such evidence that an individual has a past history of an impairment that substantially limited a major life activity is all that is necessary to establish coverage under the second prong. An individual may have a "record of" a substantially limiting impairment — and thus be protected under the "record of" prong of the statute — even if a covered entity does not specifically know about the relevant record. Of course, for the covered entity to be liable for discrimination under title I of the ADA, the individual with a "record of" a substantially limiting impairment must prove that the covered entity discriminated on the basis of the record of the disability.

The terms "substantially limits" and "major life activity" under the second prong of the definition of "disability" are to be construed in accordance with the same principles applicable under the "actual disability" prong, as set forth in § 1630.2(j).

Individuals who are covered under the "record of" prong will often be covered under the first prong of the definition of disability as well. This is a consequence of the rule of construction in the ADAAA and the regulations providing that an individual with an impairment that is episodic or in remission can be protected under the first prong if the impairment would be substantially limiting when active. See 42 U.S.C. 12102(4)(D); § 1630.2(j)(1)(vii). Thus, an individual who has cancer that is currently in remission is an individual with a disability under the "actual disability" prong because he has an impairment that would substantially limit normal cell growth when active. He is also covered by the "record of" prong based on his history of having had an impairment that substantially limited normal cell growth.

Finally, this section of the EEOC's regulations makes it clear that an individual with a record of a disability is entitled to a reasonable accommodation currently needed for limitations resulting from or relating to the past substantially limiting impairment. This conclusion, which has been the Commission's long-standing position, is confirmed by language in the ADA Amendments Act stating that individuals covered only under the "regarded as" prong of the definition of disability are not entitled to reasonable accommodation. See 42 U.S.C. 12201(h). By implication, this means that individuals covered under the first or second prongs are otherwise eligible for reasonable accommodations. See 2008 House Judiciary Committee Report at 22 ("This makes clear that the duty to accommodate . . . arises only when an individual establishes coverage under the first or second prong of the definition."). Thus, as the regulations explain, an employee with an impairment that previously substantially limited but no longer substantially limits, a major life activity may need leave or a schedule change to permit him or her to attend follow-up or "monitoring" appointments from a health care provider.

Section 1630.2(l)   Regarded as Substantially Limited in a Major Life Activity

Coverage under the "regarded as" prong of the definition of disability should not be difficult to establish. See 2008 House Judiciary Committee Report at 17 (explaining that Congress never expected or intended it would be a difficult standard to meet). Under the third prong of the definition of disability, an individual is "regarded as having such an impairment" if the individual is subjected to an action prohibited by the ADA because of an actual or perceived impairment that is not "transitory and minor."

This third prong of the definition of disability was originally intended to express Congress's understanding that "unfounded concerns, mistaken beliefs, fears, myths, or prejudice about disabilities are often just as disabling as actual impairments, and [its] corresponding desire to prohibit discrimination founded on such perceptions." 2008 Senate Statement of Managers at 9; 2008 House Judiciary Committee Report at 17 (same). In passing the original ADA, Congress relied extensively on the reasoning of School Board of Nassau County v. Arline[4] "that the negative reactions of others are just as disabling as the actual impact of an impairment." 2008 Senate Statement of Managers at 9. The ADAAA reiterates Congress's reliance on the broad views enunciated in that decision, and Congress "believe[s] that courts should continue to rely on this standard." Id.

Accordingly, the ADA Amendments Act broadened the application of the "regarded as" prong of the definition of disability. 2008 Senate Statement of Managers at 9–10. In doing so, Congress rejected court decisions that had required an individual to establish that a covered entity perceived him or her to have an impairment that substantially limited a major life activity. This provision is designed to restore Congress's intent to allow individuals to establish coverage under the "regarded as" prong by showing that they were treated adversely because of an impairment, without having to establish the covered entity's beliefs concerning the severity of the impairment. Joint Hoyer-Sensenbrenner Statement at 3.

Thus it is not necessary, as it was prior to the ADA Amendments Act, for an individual to demonstrate that a covered entity perceived him as substantially limited in the ability to perform a major life activity in order for the individual to establish that he or she is covered under the "regarded as" prong. Nor is it necessary to demonstrate that the impairment relied on by a covered entity is (in the case of an actual impairment) or would be (in the case of a perceived impairment) substantially limiting for an individual to be "regarded as having such an impairment." In short, to qualify for coverage under the "regarded as" prong, an individual is not subject to any functional test. See 2008 Senate Statement of Managers at 13 ("The functional limitation imposed by an impairment is irrelevant to the third regarded as' prong."); 2008 House Judiciary Committee Report at 17 (that is, "the individual is not required to show that the perceived impairment limits performance of a major life activity"). The concepts of "major life activities" and "substantial limitation" simply are not relevant in evaluating whether an individual is "regarded as having such an impairment."

---

[4] 480 U.S. at 282–83.

To illustrate how straightforward application of the "regarded as" prong is, if an employer refused to hire an applicant because of skin graft scars, the employer has regarded the applicant as an individual with a disability. Similarly, if an employer terminates an employee because he has cancer, the employer has regarded the employee as an individual with a disability.

A "prohibited action" under the "regarded as" prong refers to an action of the type that would be unlawful under the ADA (but for any defenses to liability). Such prohibited actions include, but are not limited to, refusal to hire, demotion, placement on involuntary leave, termination, exclusion for failure to meet a qualification standard, harassment, or denial of any other term, condition, or privilege of employment.

Where an employer bases a prohibited employment action on an actual or perceived impairment that is not "transitory and minor," the employer regards the individual as disabled, whether or not myths, fears, or stereotypes about disability motivated the employer's decision. Establishing that an individual is "regarded as having such an impairment" does not, by itself, establish liability. Liability is established only if an individual meets the burden of proving that the covered entity discriminated unlawfully within the meaning of section 102 of the ADA, 42 U.S.C. 12112.

Whether a covered entity can ultimately establish a defense to liability is an inquiry separate from, and follows after, a determination that an individual was regarded as having a disability. Thus, for example, an employer who terminates an employee with angina from a manufacturing job that requires the employee to work around machinery, believing that the employee will pose a safety risk to himself or others if he were suddenly to lose consciousness, has regarded the individual as disabled. Whether the employer has a defense (e.g., that the employee posed a direct threat to himself or coworkers) is a separate inquiry.

The fact that the "regarded as" prong requires proof of causation in order to show that a person is covered does not mean that proving a "regarded as" claim is complex. While a person must show, for both coverage under the "regarded as" prong and for ultimate liability, that he or she was subjected to a prohibited action because of an actual or perceived impairment, this showing need only be made once. Thus, evidence that a covered entity took a prohibited action because of an impairment will establish coverage and will be relevant in establishing liability, although liability may ultimately turn on whether the covered entity can establish a defense.

As prescribed in the ADA Amendments Act, the regulations provide an exception to coverage under the "regarded as" prong where the impairment on which a prohibited action is based is both transitory (having an actual or expected duration of six months or less) and minor. The regulations make clear (at § 1630.2(l)(2) and § 1630.15(f)) that this exception is a defense to a claim of discrimination. "Providing this exception responds to concerns raised by employer organizations and is reasonable under the regarded as' prong of the definition because individuals seeking coverage under this prong need not meet the functional limitation requirement contained in the first two prongs of the definition." 2008 Senate Statement of Managers at 10; See also 2008 House Judiciary Committee Report at 18 (explaining that "absent this exception, the third prong of the definition would have covered individuals who are regarded as having common ailments like the cold or flu, and this exception responds to concerns raised by members of the business community regarding potential abuse of this provision and misapplication of resources on individuals with minor ailments that last only a short period of time"). However, as an exception to the general rule for broad coverage under the "regarded as" prong, this limitation on coverage should be construed narrowly. 2008 House Judiciary Committee Report at 18.

The relevant inquiry is whether the actual or perceived impairment on which the employer's action was based is objectively "transitory and minor," not whether the employer claims it subjectively believed the impairment was transitory and minor. For example, an employer who terminates an employee whom it believes has bipolar disorder cannot take advantage of this exception by asserting that it believed the employee's impairment was transitory and minor, since bipolar disorder is not objectively transitory and minor. At the same time, an employer that terminated an employee with an objectively "transitory and minor" hand wound, mistakenly believing it to be symptomatic of HIV infection, will nevertheless have "regarded" the employee as an individual with a disability, since the covered entity took a prohibited employment action based on a perceived impairment (HIV infection) that is not "transitory and minor."

An individual covered only under the "regarded as" prong is not entitled to reasonable accommodation. 42 U.S.C. 12201(h). Thus, in cases where reasonable accommodation is not at issue, the third prong provides a more straightforward framework for analyzing whether discrimination occurred. As Congress observed in enacting the ADAAA: "[W]e expect [the first] prong of the definition to be used only by people who are affirmatively seeking reasonable accommodations or modifications. Any individual who has been discriminated against because of an impairment — short of being granted a reasonable accommodation or modification — should be bringing a claim under the third prong of the definition which will require no showing with regard to the severity of his or her impairment." Joint Hoyer-Sensenbrenner Statement at 6.

Section 1630.2(m)   Qualified Individual

The ADA prohibits discrimination on the basis of disability against a qualified individual. The determination of whether an individual with a disability is "qualified" should be made in two steps. The first step is to determine if the individual satisfies the prerequisites for the position, such as possessing the appropriate educational background, employment experience, skills, licenses, etc. For example, the first step in determining whether an accountant who is paraplegic is qualified for a certified public accountant (CPA) position is to examine the individual's credentials to determine whether the individual is a licensed CPA. This is sometimes referred to in the Rehabilitation Act caselaw as determining whether the individual is "otherwise qualified" for the position. See Senate Report at 33; House Labor Report at 64–65. (See § 1630.9 Not Making Reasonable Accommodation).

The second step is to determine whether or not the individual can perform the essential functions of the position held or desired, with or without reasonable accommodation. The purpose of this second step is to ensure that individuals with disabilities who can perform the essential functions of the position held or desired are not denied employment opportunities because they are not able to perform marginal functions of the position. House Labor Report at 55.

The determination of whether an individual with a disability is qualified is to be made at the time of the employment decision. This determination should be based on the capabilities of the individual with a disability at the time of the employment decision, and should not be based on speculation that the employee may become unable in the future or may cause increased health insurance premiums or workers compensation costs.

Section 1630.2(n)   Essential Functions

The determination of which functions are essential may be critical to the determination of whether or not the individual with a disability is qualified. The essential functions are those functions that the individual who holds the position must be able to perform unaided or with the assistance of a reasonable accommodation.

The inquiry into whether a particular function is essential initially focuses on whether the employer actually requires employees in the position to perform the functions that the employer asserts are essential. For example, an employer may state that typing is an essential function of a position. If, in fact, the employer has never required any employee in that particular position to type, this will be evidence that typing is not actually an essential function of the position.

If the individual who holds the position is actually required to perform the function the employer asserts is an essential function, the inquiry will then center around whether removing the function would fundamentally alter that position. This determination of whether or not a particular function is essential will generally include one or more of the following factors listed in part 1630.

The first factor is whether the position exists to perform a particular function. For example, an individual may be hired to proofread documents. The ability to proofread the documents would then be an essential function, since this is the only reason the position exists.

The second factor in determining whether a function is essential is the number of other employees available to perform that job function or among whom the performance of that job function can be distributed. This may be a factor either because the total number of available employees is low, or because of the fluctuating demands of the business operation. For example, if an employer has a relatively small number of available employees for the volume of work to be performed, it may be necessary that each employee perform a multitude of different functions. Therefore, the performance of those functions by each employee becomes more critical and the options for reorganizing the work become more limited. In such a situation, functions that might not be essential if there were a larger staff may become essential because the staff size is small compared to the volume of work that has to be done. See Treadwell v. Alexander, 707 F.2d 473 (11th Cir. 1983).

A similar situation might occur in a larger work force if the workflow follows a cycle of heavy demand for labor intensive work followed by low demand periods. This type of workflow might also make the performance of each function during the peak periods more critical and might limit the employer's flexibility in reorganizing operating procedures. See Dexler v. Tisch, 660 F. Supp. 1418 (D. Conn. 1987).

The third factor is the degree of expertise or skill required to perform the function. In certain professions and highly skilled positions the employee is hired for his or her expertise or ability to perform the particular function. In such a situation, the performance of that specialized task would be an essential function.

Whether a particular function is essential is a factual determination that must be made on a case by case basis. In determining whether or not a particular function is essential, all relevant evidence should be considered. Part 1630 lists various types of evidence, such as an established job description, that should be considered in determining whether a particular function is essential. Since the list is not exhaustive, other relevant evidence may also be presented. Greater weight will not be granted to the types of evidence included on the list than to the types of evidence not listed.

Although part 1630 does not require employers to develop or maintain job descriptions, written job descriptions prepared before advertising or interviewing applicants for the job, as well as the employer's judgment as to what functions are essential are among the relevant evidence to be considered in determining whether a particular function is essential. The terms of a collective bargaining agreement are also relevant to the determination of whether a particular function is essential. The work experience of past employees in the job or of current employees in similar jobs is likewise relevant to the determination of whether a particular function is essential. See H.R. Conf. Rep. No. 101-596, 101st Cong., 2d Sess. 58 (1990) [hereinafter Conference Report]; House Judiciary Report at 33–34. See also Hall v. U.S. Postal Service, 857 F.2d 1073 (6th Cir. 1988).

The time spent performing the particular function may also be an indicator of whether that function is essential. For example, if an employee spends the vast majority of his or her time working at a cash register, this would be evidence that operating the cash register is an essential function. The consequences of failing to require the employee to perform the function may be another indicator of whether a particular function is essential. For example, although a firefighter may not regularly have to carry an unconscious adult out of a burning building, the consequence of failing to require the firefighter to be able to perform this function would be serious.

It is important to note that the inquiry into essential functions is not intended to second guess an employer's business judgment with regard to production standards, whether qualitative or quantitative, nor to require employers to lower such standards. (See § 1630.10 Qualification Standards, Tests and Other Selection Criteria). If an employer requires its typists to be able to accurately type 75 words per minute, it will not be called upon to explain why an inaccurate work product, or a typing speed of 65 words per minute, would not be adequate. Similarly, if a hotel requires its service workers to thoroughly clean 16 rooms per day, it will not have to explain why it requires thorough cleaning, or why it chose a 16 room rather than a 10 room requirement. However, if an employer does require accurate 75 word per minute typing or the thorough cleaning of 16 rooms, it will have to show that it actually imposes such requirements on its employees in fact, and not simply on paper. It should also be noted that, if it is alleged that the employer intentionally selected the particular level of production to exclude individuals with disabilities, the employer may have to offer a legitimate, nondiscriminatory reason for its selection.

Section 1630.2(o)   Reasonable Accommodation

An individual with a disability is considered "qualified" if the individual can perform the essential functions of the position held or desired with or without reasonable accommodation. A covered entity is required, absent undue hardship, to provide reasonable accommodation to an otherwise qualified individual with a substantially limiting impairment or a "record of" such an impairment. However, a covered entity is not required to provide an accommodation to an individual who meets the definition of disability solely under the "regarded as" prong.

The legislative history of the ADAAA makes clear that Congress included this provision in response to various court decisions that had held (pre-Amendments Act) that individuals who were covered solely under the "regarded as" prong were eligible for reasonable accommodations. In those cases, the plaintiffs had been found not to be covered under the first prong of the definition of disability "because of the overly stringent manner in which the courts had been interpreting that prong." 2008 Senate Statement of Managers at 11. The legislative history goes on to explain that "[b]ecause of [Congress's] strong belief that accommodating individuals with disabilities is a key goal of the ADA, some members [of Congress] continue to have reservations about this provision." Id. However, Congress ultimately concluded that clarifying that individuals covered solely under the "regarded as" prong are not entitled to reasonable accommodations "is an acceptable compromise given our strong expectation that such individuals would now be covered under the first prong of the definition [of disability], properly applied"). Further, individuals covered only under the third prong still may bring discrimination claims (other than failure-to-accommodate claims) under title I of the ADA. 2008 Senate Statement of Managers at 9–10.

In general, an accommodation is any change in the work environment or in the way things are customarily done that enables an individual with a disability to enjoy equal employment opportunities. There are three categories of reasonable accommodation. These are (1) accommodations that are required to ensure equal opportunity in the application process; (2) accommodations that enable the employer's employees with disabilities to perform the essential functions of the position held or desired; and (3) accommodations that enable the employer's employees with disabilities to enjoy equal benefits and privileges of employment as are enjoyed by employees without disabilities. It should be noted that nothing in this part prohibits employers or other covered entities from providing accommodations beyond those required by this part.

Part 1630 lists the examples, specified in title I of the ADA, of the most common types of accommodation that an employer or other covered entity may be required to provide. There are any number of other specific accommodations that may be appropriate for particular situations but are not specifically mentioned in this listing. This listing is not intended to be exhaustive of accommodation possibilities. For example, other accommodations could include permitting the use of accrued paid leave or providing additional unpaid leave for necessary treatment, making employer provided transportation accessible, and providing reserved parking spaces. Providing personal assistants, such as a page turner for an employee with no hands or a travel attendant to act as a sighted guide to assist a blind employee on occasional business trips, may also be a reasonable accommodation. Senate Report at 31; House Labor Report at 62; House Judiciary Report at 39.

It may also be a reasonable accommodation to permit an individual with a disability the opportunity to provide and utilize equipment, aids or services that an employer is not required to provide as a reasonable accommodation. For example, it would be a reasonable accommodation for an employer to permit an individual who is blind to use a guide dog at work, even though the employer would not be required to provide a guide dog for the employee.

The accommodations included on the list of reasonable accommodations are generally self explanatory. However, there are a few that require further explanation. One of these is the accommodation of making existing facilities used by employees readily accessible to, and usable by, individuals with disabilities. This accommodation includes both those areas that must be accessible for the employee to perform essential job functions, as well as non-work areas used by the employer's employees for other purposes. For example, accessible break rooms, lunch rooms, training rooms, restrooms etc., may be required as reasonable accommodations.

Another of the potential accommodations listed is "job restructuring." An employer or other covered entity may restructure a job by reallocating or redistributing nonessential, marginal job functions. For example, an employer may have two jobs, each of which entails the performance of a number of marginal functions. The employer hires an individual with a disability who is able to perform some of the marginal functions of each job but not all of the marginal functions of either job. As an accommodation, the employer may redistribute the marginal functions so that all of the marginal functions that the individual with a disability can perform are made a part of the position to be filled by the individual with a disability. The remaining marginal functions that the individual with a disability cannot perform would then be transferred to the other position. See Senate Report at 31; House Labor Report at 62.

An employer or other covered entity is not required to reallocate essential functions. The essential functions are by definition those that the individual who holds the job would have to perform, with or without reasonable accommodation, in order to be considered qualified for the position. For example, suppose a security guard position requires the individual who holds the job to inspect identification cards. An employer would not have to provide an individual who is legally blind with an assistant to look at the identification cards for the legally blind employee. In this situation the assistant would be performing the job for the individual with a disability rather than assisting the individual to perform the job. See Coleman v. Darden, 595 F.2d 533 (10th Cir. 1979).

An employer or other covered entity may also restructure a job by altering when and/or how an essential function is performed. For example, an essential function customarily performed in the early morning hours may be rescheduled until later in the day as a reasonable accommodation to a disability that precludes performance of the function at the customary hour. Likewise, as a reasonable accommodation, an employee with a disability that inhibits the ability to write, may be permitted to computerize records that were customarily maintained manually.

Reassignment to a vacant position is also listed as a potential reasonable accommodation. In general, reassignment should be considered only when accommodation within the individual's current position would pose an undue hardship. Reassignment is not available to applicants. An applicant for a position must be qualified for, and be able to perform the essential functions of, the position sought with or without reasonable accommodation.

Reassignment may not be used to limit, segregate, or otherwise discriminate against employees with disabilities by forcing reassignments to undesirable positions or to designated offices or facilities. Employers should reassign the individual to an equivalent position, in terms of pay, status, etc., if the individual is qualified, and if the position is vacant within a reasonable amount of time. A "reasonable amount of time" should be determined in light of the totality of the circumstances. As an example, suppose there is no vacant position available at the time that an individual with a disability requests reassignment as a reasonable accommodation. The employer, however, knows that an equivalent position for which the individual is qualified, will become vacant next week. Under these circumstances, the employer should reassign the individual to the position when it becomes available.

An employer may reassign an individual to a lower graded position if there are no accommodations that would enable the employee to remain in the current position and there are no vacant equivalent positions for which the individual is qualified with or without reasonable accommodation. An employer, however, is not required to maintain the reassigned individual with a disability at the salary of the higher graded position if it does not so maintain reassigned employees who are not disabled. It should also be noted that an employer is not required to promote an individual with a disability as an accommodation. See Senate Report at 31–32; House Labor Report at 63.

The determination of which accommodation is appropriate in a particular situation involves a process in which the employer and employee identify the precise limitations imposed by the disability and explore potential accommodations that would overcome those limitations. This process is discussed more fully in § 1630.9 Not Making Reasonable Accommodation.

Section 1630.2(p)   Undue Hardship

An employer or other covered entity is not required to provide an accommodation that will impose an undue hardship on the operation of the employer's or other covered entity's business. The term "undue hardship" means significant difficulty or expense in, or resulting from, the provision of the accommodation. The "undue hardship" provision takes into account the financial realities of the particular employer or other covered entity. However, the concept of undue hardship is not limited to financial difficulty. "Undue hardship" refers to any accommodation that would be unduly costly, extensive, substantial, or disruptive, or that would fundamentally alter the nature or operation of the business. See Senate Report at 35; House Labor Report at 67.

For example, suppose an individual with a disabling visual impairment that makes it extremely difficult to see in dim lighting applies for a position as a waiter in a nightclub and requests that the club be brightly lit as a reasonable accommodation. Although the individual may be able to perform the job in bright lighting, the nightclub will probably be able to demonstrate that that particular accommodation, though inexpensive, would impose an undue hardship if the bright lighting would destroy the ambience of the nightclub and/or make it difficult for the customers to see the stage show. The fact that that particular accommodation poses an undue hardship, however, only means that the employer is not required to provide that accommodation. If there is another accommodation that will not create an undue hardship, the employer would be required to provide the alternative accommodation.

An employer's claim that the cost of a particular accommodation will impose an undue hardship will be analyzed in light of the factors outlined in part 1630. In part, this analysis requires a determination of whose financial resources should be considered in deciding whether the accommodation is unduly costly. In some cases the financial resources of the employer or other covered entity in its entirety should be considered in determining whether the cost of an accommodation poses an undue hardship. In other cases, consideration of the financial resources of the employer or other covered entity as a whole may be inappropriate because it may not give an accurate picture of the financial resources available to the particular facility that will actually be required to provide the accommodation. See House Labor Report at 68–69; House Judiciary Report at 40–41; see also Conference Report at 56–57.

If the employer or other covered entity asserts that only the financial resources of the facility where the individual will be employed should be considered, part 1630 requires a factual determination of the relationship between the employer or other covered entity and the facility that will provide the accommodation. As an example, suppose that an independently owned fast food franchise that receives no money from the franchisor refuses to hire an individual with a hearing impairment because it asserts that it would be an undue hardship to provide an interpreter to enable the individual to participate in monthly staff meetings. Since the financial relationship between the franchisor and the franchise is limited to payment of an annual franchise fee, only the financial resources of the franchise would be considered in determining whether or not providing the accommodation would be an undue hardship. See House Labor Report at 68; House Judiciary Report at 40.

If the employer or other covered entity can show that the cost of the accommodation would impose an undue hardship, it would still be required to provide the accommodation if the funding is available from another source, e.g., a State vocational rehabilitation agency, or if Federal, State or local tax deductions or tax credits are available to offset the cost of the accommodation. If the employer or other covered entity receives, or is eligible to receive, monies from an external source that would pay the entire cost of the accommodation, it cannot claim cost as an undue hardship. In the absence of such funding, the individual with a disability requesting the accommodation should be given the option of providing the accommodation or of paying that portion of the cost which constitutes the undue hardship on the operation of the business. To the extent that such monies pay or would pay for only part of the cost of the accommodation, only that portion of the cost of the accommodation that could not be recovered — the final net cost to the entity — may be considered in determining undue hardship. (See § 1630.9 Not Making Reasonable Accommodation). See Senate Report at 36; House Labor Report at 69.

Section 1630.2(r)   Direct Threat

An employer may require, as a qualification standard, that an individual not pose a direct threat to the health or safety of himself/herself or others. Like any other qualification standard, such a standard must apply to all applicants or employees and not just to individuals with disabilities. If, however, an individual poses a direct threat as a result of a disability, the employer must determine whether a reasonable accommodation would either eliminate the risk or reduce it to an acceptable level. If no accommodation exists that would either eliminate or reduce the risk, the employer may refuse to hire an applicant or may discharge an employee who poses a direct threat.

An employer, however, is not permitted to deny an employment opportunity to an individual with a disability merely because of a slightly increased risk. The risk can only be considered when it poses a significant risk, i.e., high probability, of substantial harm; a speculative or remote risk is insufficient. See Senate Report at 27; House Report Labor Report at 56–57; House Judiciary Report at 45.

Determining whether an individual poses a significant risk of substantial harm to others must be made on a case by case basis. The employer should identify the specific risk posed by the individual. For individuals with mental or emotional disabilities, the employer must identify the specific behavior on the part of the individual that would pose the direct threat. For individuals with physical disabilities, the employer must identify the aspect of the disability that would pose the direct threat. The employer should then consider the four factors listed in part 1630:

(1) The duration of the risk;

(2) The nature and severity of the potential harm;

(3) The likelihood that the potential harm will occur; and

(4) The imminence of the potential harm.

Such consideration must rely on objective, factual evidence — not on subjective perceptions, irrational fears, patronizing attitudes, or stereotypes — about the nature or effect of a particular disability, or of disability generally. See Senate Report at 27; House Labor Report at 56–57; House Judiciary Report at 45–46. See also Strathie v. Department of Transportation, 716 F.2d 227 (3d Cir. 1983). Relevant evidence may include input from the individual with a disability, the experience of the individual with a disability in previous similar positions, and opinions of medical doctors, rehabilitation counselors, or physical therapists who have expertise in the disability involved and/or direct knowledge of the individual with the disability.

An employer is also permitted to require that an individual not pose a direct threat of harm to his or her own safety or health. If performing the particular functions of a job would result in a high probability of substantial harm to the individual, the employer could reject or discharge the individual unless a reasonable accommodation that would not cause an undue hardship would avert the harm. For example, an employer would not be required to hire an individual, disabled by narcolepsy, who frequently and unexpectedly loses consciousness for a carpentry job the essential functions of which require the use of power saws and other dangerous equipment, where no accommodation exists that will reduce or eliminate the risk.

The assessment that there exists a high probability of substantial harm to the individual, like the assessment that there exists a high probability of substantial harm to others, must be strictly based on valid medical analyses and/or on other objective evidence. This determination must be based on individualized factual data, using the factors discussed above, rather than on stereotypic or patronizing assumptions and must consider potential reasonable accommodations. Generalized fears about risks from the employment environment, such as exacerbation of the disability caused by stress, cannot be used by an employer to disqualify an individual with a disability. For example, a law firm could not reject an applicant with a history of disabling mental illness based on a generalized fear that the stress of trying to make partner might trigger a relapse of the individual's mental illness. Nor can generalized fears about risks to individuals with disabilities in the event of an evacuation or other emergency be used by an employer to disqualify an individual with a disability. See Senate Report at 56; House Labor Report at 73–74; House Judiciary Report at 45. See also Mantolete v. Bolger, 767 F.2d 1416 (9th Cir. 1985); Bentivegna v. U.S. Department of Labor, 694 F.2d 619 (9th Cir. 1982).

Section 1630.3   Exceptions to the Definitions of "Disability" and "Qualified Individual with a Disability"

Section 1630.3(a) through (c)   Illegal Use of Drugs

Part 1630 provides that an individual currently engaging in the illegal use of drugs is not an individual with a disability for purposes of this part when the employer or other covered entity acts on the basis of such use. Illegal use of drugs refers both to the use of unlawful drugs, such as cocaine, and to the unlawful use of prescription drugs.

Employers, for example, may discharge or deny employment to persons who illegally use drugs, on the basis of such use, without fear of being held liable for discrimination. The term "currently engaging" is not intended to be limited to the use of drugs on the day of, or within a matter of days or weeks before, the employment action in question. Rather, the provision is intended to apply to the illegal use of drugs that has occurred recently enough to indicate that the individual is actively engaged in such conduct. See Conference Report at 64.

Individuals who are erroneously perceived as engaging in the illegal use of drugs, but are not in fact illegally using drugs are not excluded from the definitions of the terms "disability" and "qualified individual with a disability." Individuals who are no longer illegally using drugs and who have either been rehabilitated successfully or are in the process of completing a rehabilitation program are, likewise, not excluded from the definitions of those terms. The term "rehabilitation program" refers to both in-patient and out-patient programs, as well as to appropriate employee assistance programs, professionally recognized self-help programs, such as Narcotics Anonymous, or other programs that provide professional (not necessarily medical) assistance and counseling for individuals who illegally use drugs. See Conference Report at 64; see also House Labor Report at 77; House Judiciary Report at 47.

It should be noted that this provision simply provides that certain individuals are not excluded from the definitions of "disability" and "qualified individual with a disability." Consequently, such individuals are still required to establish that they satisfy the requirements of these definitions in order to be protected by the ADA and this part. An individual erroneously regarded as illegally using drugs, for example, would have to show that he or she was regarded as a drug addict in order to demonstrate that he or she meets the definition of "disability" as defined in this part.

Employers are entitled to seek reasonable assurances that no illegal use of drugs is occurring or has occurred recently enough so that continuing use is a real and ongoing problem. The reasonable assurances that employers may ask applicants or employees to provide include evidence that the individual is participating in a drug treatment program and/or evidence, such as drug test results, to show that the individual is not currently engaging in the illegal use of drugs. An employer, such as a law enforcement agency, may also be able to impose a qualification standard that excludes individuals with a history of illegal use of drugs if it can show that the standard is job-related and consistent with business necessity. (See § 1630.10 Qualification Standards, Tests and Other Selection Criteria) See Conference Report at 64.

Section 1630.4   Discrimination Prohibited

Paragraph (a) of this provision prohibits discrimination on the basis of disability against a qualified individual in all aspects of the employment relationship. The range of employment decisions covered by this nondiscrimination mandate is to be construed in a manner consistent with the regulations implementing section 504 of the Rehabilitation Act of 1973.

Paragraph (b) makes it clear that the language "on the basis of disability" is not intended to create a cause of action for an individual without a disability who claims that someone with a disability was treated more favorably (disparate treatment), or was provided a reasonable accommodation that an individual without a disability was not provided. See 2008 House Judiciary Committee Report at 21 (this provision "prohibits reverse discrimination claims by disallowing claims based on the lack of disability"). Additionally, the ADA and this part do not affect laws that may require the affirmative recruitment or hiring of individuals with disabilities, or any voluntary affirmative action employers may undertake on behalf of individuals with disabilities. However, part 1630 is not intended to limit the ability of covered entities to choose and maintain a qualified workforce. Employers can continue to use criteria that are job related and consistent with business necessity to select qualified employees, and can continue to hire employees who can perform the essential functions of the job.

The Amendments Act modified title I's nondiscrimination provision to replace the prohibition on discrimination "against a qualified individual with a disability because of the disability of such individual" with a prohibition on discrimination "against a qualified individual on the basis of disability." As the legislative history of the ADAAA explains: "[T]he bill modifies the ADA to conform to the structure of Title VII and other civil rights laws by requiring an individual to demonstrate discrimination on the basis of disability' rather than discrimination against an individual with a disability' because of the individual's disability. We hope this will be an important signal to both lawyers and courts to spend less time and energy on the minutia of an individual's impairment, and more time and energy on the merits of the case — including whether discrimination occurred because of the disability, whether an individual was qualified for a job or eligible for a service, and whether a reasonable accommodation or modification was called for under the law." Joint Hoyer-Sensenbrenner Statement at 4; see also 2008 House Judiciary Report at 21 ("This change harmonizes the ADA with other civil rights laws by focusing on whether a person who has been discriminated against has proven that the discrimination was based on a personal characteristic (disability), not on whether he or she has proven that the characteristic exists.").

Section 1630.5   Limiting, Segregating and Classifying

This provision and the several provisions that follow describe various specific forms of discrimination that are included within the general prohibition of § 1630.4. The capabilities of qualified individuals must be determined on an individualized, case by case basis. Covered entities are also prohibited from segregating qualified employees into separate work areas or into separate lines of advancement on the basis of their disabilities.

Thus, for example, it would be a violation of this part for an employer to limit the duties of an employee with a disability based on a presumption of what is best for an individual with such a disability, or on a presumption about the abilities of an individual with such a disability. It would be a violation of this part for an employer to adopt a separate track of job promotion or progression for employees with disabilities based on a presumption that employees with disabilities are uninter-ested in, or incapable of, performing particular jobs. Similarly, it would be a violation for an employer to assign or reassign (as a reasonable accommodation) employees with disabilities to one particular office or installation, or to require that employees with disabilities only use particular employer provided non-work facili-ties such as segregated break-rooms, lunch rooms, or lounges. It would also be a violation of this part to deny employment to an applicant or employee with a disability based on generalized fears about the safety of an individual with such a disability, or based on generalized assumptions about the absenteeism rate of an individual with such a disability.

In addition, it should also be noted that this part is intended to require that employees with disabilities be accorded equal access to whatever health insurance coverage the employer provides to other employees. This part does not, however, affect pre-existing condition clauses included in health insurance policies offered by employers. Consequently, employers may continue to offer policies that contain such clauses, even if they adversely affect individuals with disabilities, so long as the clauses are not used as a subterfuge to evade the purposes of this part.

So, for example, it would be permissible for an employer to offer an insurance policy that limits coverage for certain procedures or treatments to a specified number per year. Thus, if a health insurance plan provided coverage for five blood transfusions a year to all covered employees, it would not be discriminatory to offer this plan simply because a hemophiliac employee may require more than five blood transfusions annually. However, it would not be permissible to limit or deny the hemophiliac employee coverage for other procedures, such as heart surgery or the setting of a broken leg, even though the plan would not have to provide coverage for the additional blood transfusions that may be involved in these procedures.

Likewise, limits may be placed on reimbursements for certain procedures or on the types of drugs or procedures covered (e.g. limits on the number of permitted X-rays or non-coverage of experimental drugs or procedures), but that limitation must be applied equally to individuals with and without disabilities. See Senate Report at 28–29; House Labor Report at 58–59; House Judiciary Report at 36.

Leave policies or benefit plans that are uniformly applied do not violate this part simply because they do not address the special needs of every individual with a disability. Thus, for example, an employer that reduces the number of paid sick leave days that it will provide to all employees, or reduces the amount of medical insurance coverage that it will provide to all employees, is not in violation of this part, even if the benefits reduction has an impact on employees with disabilities in need of greater sick leave and medical coverage. Benefits reductions adopted for discriminatory reasons are in violation of this part. See Alexander v. Choate, 469 U.S. 287 (1985). See Senate Report at 85; House Labor Report at 137. (See also, the discussion at § 1630.16(f) Health Insurance, Life Insurance, and Other Benefit Plans).

Section 1630.6   Contractual or Other Arrangements

An employer or other covered entity may not do through a contractual or other relationship what it is prohibited from doing directly. This provision does not affect the determination of whether or not one is a "covered entity" or "employer" as defined in § 1630.2.

This provision only applies to situations where an employer or other covered entity has entered into a contractual relationship that has the effect of discriminating against its own employees or applicants with disabilities. Accordingly, it would be a violation for an employer to participate in a contractual relationship that results in discrimination against the employer's employees with disabilities in hiring, training, promotion, or in any other aspect of the employment relationship. This provision applies whether or not the employer or other covered entity intended for the contractual relationship to have the discriminatory effect.

Part 1630 notes that this provision applies to parties on either side of the contractual or other relationship. This is intended to highlight that an employer whose employees provide services to others, like an employer whose employees receive services, must ensure that those employees are not discriminated against on the basis of disability. For example, a copier company whose service representative is a dwarf could be required to provide a stepstool, as a reasonable accommodation, to enable him to perform the necessary repairs. However, the employer would not be required, as a reasonable accommodation, to make structural changes to its customer's inaccessible premises.

The existence of the contractual relationship adds no new obligations under part 1630. The employer, therefore, is not liable through the contractual arrangement for any discrimination by the contractor against the contractors own employees or applicants, although the contractor, as an employer, may be liable for such discrimination.

An employer or other covered entity, on the other hand, cannot evade the obligations imposed by this part by engaging in a contractual or other relationship. For example, an employer cannot avoid its responsibility to make reasonable accommodation subject to the undue hardship limitation through a contractual arrangement. See Conference Report at 59; House Labor Report at 59–61; House Judiciary Report at 36–37.

To illustrate, assume that an employer is seeking to contract with a company to provide training for its employees. Any responsibilities of reasonable accommodation applicable to the employer in providing the training remain with that employer even if it contracts with another company for this service. Thus, if the training company were planning to conduct the training at an inaccessible location, thereby making it impossible for an employee who uses a wheelchair to attend, the employer would have a duty to make reasonable accommodation unless to do so would impose an undue hardship. Under these circumstances, appropriate accommodations might include (1) having the training company identify accessible training sites and relocate the training program; (2) having the training company make the training site accessible; (3) directly making the training site accessible or providing the training company with the means by which to make the site accessible; (4) identifying and contracting with another training company that uses accessible sites; or (5) any other accommodation that would result in making the training available to the employee.

As another illustration, assume that instead of contracting with a training company, the employer contracts with a hotel to host a conference for its employees. The employer will have a duty to ascertain and ensure the accessibility of the hotel and its conference facilities. To fulfill this obligation the employer could, for example, inspect the hotel first-hand or ask a local disability group to inspect the hotel. Alternatively, the employer could ensure that the contract with the hotel specifies it will provide accessible guest rooms for those who need them and that all rooms to be used for the conference, including exhibit and meeting rooms, are accessible. If the hotel breaches this accessibility provision, the hotel may be liable to the employer, under a non-ADA breach of contract theory, for the cost of any accommodation needed to provide access to the hotel and conference, and for any other costs accrued by the employer. (In addition, the hotel may also be independently liable under title III of the ADA). However, this would not relieve the employer of its responsibility under this part nor shield it from charges of discrimination by its own employees. See House Labor Report at 40; House Judiciary Report at 37.

Section 1630.8 Relationship or Association With an Individual With a Disability

This provision is intended to protect any qualified individual, whether or not that individual has a disability, from discrimination because that person is known to have an association or relationship with an individual who has a known disability. This protection is not limited to those who have a familial relationship with an individual with a disability.

To illustrate the scope of this provision, assume that a qualified applicant without a disability applies for a job and discloses to the employer that his or her spouse has a disability. The employer thereupon declines to hire the applicant because the employer believes that the applicant would have to miss work or frequently leave work early in order to care for the spouse. Such a refusal to hire would be prohibited by this provision. Similarly, this provision would prohibit an employer from discharging an employee because the employee does volunteer work with people who have AIDS, and the employer fears that the employee may contract the disease.

This provision also applies to other benefits and privileges of employment. For example, an employer that provides health insurance benefits to its employees for their dependents may not reduce the level of those benefits to an employee simply because that employee has a dependent with a disability. This is true even if the provision of such benefits would result in increased health insurance costs for the employer.

It should be noted, however, that an employer need not provide the applicant or employee without a disability with a reasonable accommodation because that duty only applies to qualified applicants or employees with disabilities. Thus, for example, an employee would not be entitled to a modified work schedule as an accommodation to enable the employee to care for a spouse with a disability. See Senate Report at 30; House Labor Report at 61–62; House Judiciary Report at 38–39.

Section 1630.9   Not Making Reasonable Accommodation

The obligation to make reasonable accommodation is a form of non-discrimination. It applies to all employment decisions and to the job application process. This obligation does not extend to the provision of adjustments or modifications that are primarily for the personal benefit of the individual with a disability. Thus, if an adjustment or modification is job-related, e.g., specifically assists the individual in performing the duties of a particular job, it will be considered a type of reasonable accommodation. On the other hand, if an adjustment or modification assists the individual throughout his or her daily activities, on and off the job, it will be considered a personal item that the employer is not required to provide. Accordingly, an employer would generally not be required to provide an employee with a disability with a prosthetic limb, wheelchair, or eyeglasses. Nor would an employer have to provide as an accommodation any amenity or convenience that is not job-related, such as a private hot plate, hot pot or refrigerator that is not provided to employees without disabilities. See Senate Report at 31; House Labor Report at 62.

It should be noted, however, that the provision of such items may be required as a reasonable accommodation where such items are specifically designed or required to meet job-related rather than personal needs. An employer, for example, may have to provide an individual with a disabling visual impairment with eyeglasses specifically designed to enable the individual to use the office computer monitors, but that are not otherwise needed by the individual outside of the office.

The term "supported employment," which has been applied to a wide variety of programs to assist individuals with severe disabilities in both competitive and non-competitive employment, is not synonymous with reasonable accommodation. Examples of supported employment include modified training materials, restructuring essential functions to enable an individual to perform a job, or hiring an outside professional ("job coach") to assist in job training. Whether a particular form of assistance would be required as a reasonable accommodation must be determined on an individualized, case by case basis without regard to whether that assistance is referred to as "supported employment." For example, an employer, under certain circumstances, may be required to provide modified training materials or a temporary "job coach" to assist in the training of the individual with a disability as a reasonable accommodation. However, an employer would not be required to restructure the essential functions of a position to fit the skills of an individual with a disability who is not otherwise qualified to perform the position, as is done in certain supported employment programs. See 34 CFR part 363. It should be noted that it would not be a violation of this part for an employer to provide any of these personal modifications or adjustments, or to engage in supported employment or similar rehabilitative programs.

The obligation to make reasonable accommodation applies to all services and programs provided in connection with employment, and to all non-work facilities provided or maintained by an employer for use by its employees. Accordingly, the obligation to accommodate is applicable to employer sponsored placement or counseling services, and to employer provided cafeterias, lounges, gymnasiums, auditoriums, transportation and the like.

The reasonable accommodation requirement is best understood as a means by which barriers to the equal employment opportunity of an individual with a disability are removed or alleviated. These barriers may, for example, be physical or structural obstacles that inhibit or prevent the access of an individual with a disability to job sites, facilities or equipment. Or they may be rigid work schedules that permit no flexibility as to when work is performed or when breaks may be taken, or inflexible job procedures that unduly limit the modes of communication that are used on the job, or the way in which particular tasks are accomplished.

The term "otherwise qualified" is intended to make clear that the obligation to make reasonable accommodation is owed only to an individual with a disability who is qualified within the meaning of § 1630.2(m) in that he or she satisfies all the skill, experience, education and other job-related selection criteria. An individual with a disability is "otherwise qualified," in other words, if he or she is qualified for a job, except that, because of the disability, he or she needs a reasonable accommodation to be able to perform the job's essential functions.

For example, if a law firm requires that all incoming lawyers have graduated from an accredited law school and have passed the bar examination, the law firm need not provide an accommodation to an individual with a visual impairment who has not met these selection criteria. That individual is not entitled to a reasonable accommodation because the individual is not "otherwise qualified" for the position.

On the other hand, if the individual has graduated from an accredited law school and passed the bar examination, the individual would be "otherwise qualified." The law firm would thus be required to provide a reasonable accommodation, such as a machine that magnifies print, to enable the individual to perform the essential functions of the attorney position, unless the necessary accommodation would impose an undue hardship on the law firm. See Senate Report at 33–34; House Labor Report at 64–65.

The reasonable accommodation that is required by this part should provide the individual with a disability with an equal employment opportunity. Equal employment opportunity means an opportunity to attain the same level of performance, or to enjoy the same level of benefits and privileges of employment as are available to the average similarly situated employee without a disability. Thus, for example, an accommodation made to assist an employee with a disability in the performance of his or her job must be adequate to enable the individual to perform the essential functions of the relevant position. The accommodation, however, does not have to be the "best" accommodation possible, so long as it is sufficient to meet the job-related needs of the individual being accommodated. Accordingly, an employer would not have to provide an employee disabled by a back impairment with a state-of-the art mechanical lifting device if it provided the employee with a less expensive or more readily available device that enabled the employee to perform the essential functions of the job. See Senate Report at 35; House Labor Report at 66; see also Carter v. Bennett, 840 F.2d 63 (DC Cir. 1988).

Employers are obligated to make reasonable accommodation only to the physical or mental limitations resulting from the disability of the individual with a disability that is known to the employer. Thus, an employer would not be expected to accommodate disabilities of which it is unaware. If an employee with a known disability is having difficulty performing his or her job, an employer may inquire whether the employee is in need of a reasonable accommodation. In general, however, it is the responsibility of the individual with a disability to inform the employer that an accommodation is needed. When the need for an accommodation is not obvious, an employer, before providing a reasonable accommodation, may require that the individual with a disability provide documentation of the need for accommodation.

See Senate Report at 34; House Labor Report at 65.

Process of Determining the Appropriate Reasonable Accommodation

Once the individual with a disability has requested provision of a reasonable accommodation, the employer must make a reasonable effort to determine the appropriate accommodation. The appropriate reasonable accommodation is best determined through a flexible, interactive process that involves both the employer and the individual with a disability. Although this process is described below in terms of accommodations that enable the individual with a disability to perform the essential functions of the position held or desired, it is equally applicable to accommodations involving the job application process, and to accommodations that enable the individual with a disability to enjoy equal benefits and privileges of employment. See Senate Report at 34–35; House Labor Report at 65–67.

When the individual with a disability has requested a reasonable accommodation to assist in the performance of a job, the employer, using a problem solving approach, should:

(1) Analyze the particular job involved and determine its purpose and essential functions;

(2) Consult with the individual with a disability to ascertain the precise job-related limitations imposed by the individual's disability and how those limitations could be overcome with a reasonable accommodation;

(3) In consultation with the individual to be accommodated, identify potential accommodations and assess the effectiveness each would have in enabling the individual to perform the essential functions of the position; and

(4) Consider the preference of the individual to be accommodated and select and implement the accommodation that is most appropriate for both the employee and the employer.

In many instances, the appropriate reasonable accommodation may be so obvious to either or both the employer and the individual with a disability that it may not be necessary to proceed in this step-by-step fashion. For example, if an employee who uses a wheelchair requests that his or her desk be placed on blocks to elevate the desktop above the arms of the wheelchair and the employer complies, an appropriate accommodation has been requested, identified, and provided without either the employee or employer being aware of having engaged in any sort of "reasonable accommodation process."

However, in some instances neither the individual requesting the accommodation nor the employer can readily identify the appropriate accommodation. For example, the individual needing the accommodation may not know enough about the equipment used by the employer or the exact nature of the work site to suggest an appropriate accommodation. Likewise, the employer may not know enough about the individual's disability or the limitations that disability would impose on the performance of the job to suggest an appropriate accommodation. Under such circumstances, it may be necessary for the employer to initiate a more defined problem solving process, such as the step-by-step process described above, as part of its reasonable effort to identify the appropriate reasonable accommodation.

This process requires the individual assessment of both the particular job at issue, and the specific physical or mental limitations of the particular individual in need of reasonable accommodation. With regard to assessment of the job, "individual assessment" means analyzing the actual job duties and determining the true purpose or object of the job. Such an assessment is necessary to ascertain which job functions are the essential functions that an accommodation must enable an individual with a disability to perform.

After assessing the relevant job, the employer, in consultation with the individual requesting the accommodation, should make an assessment of the specific limitations imposed by the disability on the individual's performance of the job's essential functions. This assessment will make it possible to ascertain the precise barrier to the employment opportunity which, in turn, will make it possible to determine the accommodation(s) that could alleviate or remove that barrier.

If consultation with the individual in need of the accommodation still does not reveal potential appropriate accommodations, then the employer, as part of this process, may find that technical assistance is helpful in determining how to accommodate the particular individual in the specific situation. Such assistance could be sought from the Commission, from state or local rehabilitation agencies, or from disability constituent organizations. It should be noted, however, that, as provided in § 1630.9(c) of this part, the failure to obtain or receive technical assistance from the federal agencies that administer the ADA will not excuse the employer from its reasonable accommodation obligation.

Once potential accommodations have been identified, the employer should assess the effectiveness of each potential accommodation in assisting the individual in need of the accommodation in the performance of the essential functions of the position. If more than one of these accommodations will enable the individual to perform the essential functions or if the individual would prefer to provide his or her own accommodation, the preference of the individual with a disability should be given primary consideration. However, the employer providing the accommodation has the ultimate discretion to choose between effective accommodations, and may choose the less expensive accommodation or the accommodation that is easier for it to provide. It should also be noted that the individual's willingness to provide his or her own accommodation does not relieve the employer of the duty to provide the accommodation should the individual for any reason be unable or unwilling to continue to provide the accommodation.

Reasonable Accommodation Process Illustrated

The following example illustrates the informal reasonable accommodation process. Suppose a Sack Handler position requires that the employee pick up fifty pound sacks and carry them from the company loading dock to the storage room, and that a sack handler who is disabled by a back impairment requests a reasonable accommodation. Upon receiving the request, the employer analyzes the Sack Handler job and determines that the essential function and purpose of the job is not the requirement that the job holder physically lift and carry the sacks, but the requirement that the job holder cause the sack to move from the loading dock to the storage room.

The employer then meets with the sack handler to ascertain precisely the barrier posed by the individual's specific disability to the performance of the job's essential function of relocating the sacks. At this meeting the employer learns that the individual can, in fact, lift the sacks to waist level, but is prevented by his or her disability from carrying the sacks from the loading dock to the storage room. The employer and the individual agree that any of a number of potential accommodations, such as the provision of a dolly, hand truck, or cart, could enable the individual to transport the sacks that he or she has lifted.

Upon further consideration, however, it is determined that the provision of a cart is not a feasible effective option. No carts are currently available at the company, and those that can be purchased by the company are the wrong shape to hold many of the bulky and irregularly shaped sacks that must be moved. Both the dolly and the hand truck, on the other hand, appear to be effective options. Both are readily available to the company, and either will enable the individual to relocate the sacks that he or she has lifted. The sack handler indicates his or her preference for the dolly. In consideration of this expressed preference, and because the employer feels that the dolly will allow the individual to move more sacks at a time and so be more efficient than would a hand truck, the employer ultimately provides the sack handler with a dolly in fulfillment of the obligation to make reasonable accommodation.

Section 1630.9(b)

This provision states that an employer or other covered entity cannot prefer or select a qualified individual without a disability over an equally qualified individual with a disability merely because the individual with a disability will require a reasonable accommodation. In other words, an individual's need for an accommodation cannot enter into the employer's or other covered entity's decision regarding hiring, discharge, promotion, or other similar employment decisions, unless the accommodation would impose an undue hardship on the employer. See House Labor Report at 70.

Section 1630.9(d)

The purpose of this provision is to clarify that an employer or other covered entity may not compel the individual with a disability to accept an accommodation, where that accommodation is neither requested nor needed by the individual. However, if a necessary reasonable accommodation is refused, the individual may not be considered qualified. For example, an individual with a visual impairment that restricts his or her field of vision but who is able to read unaided would not be required to accept a reader as an accommodation. However, if the individual were not able to read unaided and reading was an essential function of the job, the individual would not be qualified for the job if he or she refused a reasonable accommodation that would enable him or her to read. See Senate Report at 34; House Labor Report at 65; House Judiciary Report at 71–72.

Section 1630.9(e)

The purpose of this provision is to incorporate the clarification made in the ADA Amendments Act of 2008 that an individual is not entitled to reasonable accommodation under the ADA if the individual is only covered under the "regarded as" prong of the definition of "individual with a disability." However, if the individual is covered under both the "regarded as" prong and one or both of the other two prongs of the definition of disability, the ordinary rules concerning the provision of reasonable accommodation apply.

Section 1630.10   Qualification Standards, Tests, and Other Selection Criteria

Section 1630.10(a)   In General

The purpose of this provision is to ensure that individuals with disabilities are not excluded from job opportunities unless they are actually unable to do the job. It is to ensure that there is a fit between job criteria and an applicant's (or employee's) actual ability to do the job. Accordingly, job criteria that even unintentionally screen out, or tend to screen out, an individual with a disability or a class of individuals with disabilities because of their disability may not be used unless the employer demonstrates that those criteria, as used by the employer, are job related for the position to which they are being applied and are consistent with business necessity. The concept of "business necessity" has the same meaning as the concept of "business necessity" under section 504 of the Rehabilitation Act of 1973.

Selection criteria that exclude, or tend to exclude, an individual with a disability or a class of individuals with disabilities because of their disability but do not concern an essential function of the job would not be consistent with business necessity.

The use of selection criteria that are related to an essential function of the job may be consistent with business necessity. However, selection criteria that are related to an essential function of the job may not be used to exclude an individual with a disability if that individual could satisfy the criteria with the provision of a reasonable accommodation. Experience under a similar provision of the regulations implementing section 504 of the Rehabilitation Act indicates that challenges to selection criteria are, in fact, often resolved by reasonable accommodation.

This provision is applicable to all types of selection criteria, including safety requirements, vision or hearing requirements, walking requirements, lifting requirements, and employment tests. See 1989 Senate Report at 37–39; House Labor Report at 70–72; House Judiciary Report at 42. As previously noted, however, it is not the intent of this part to second guess an employer's business judgment with regard to production standards. See § 1630.2(n) (Essential Functions). Consequently, production standards will generally not be subject to a challenge under this provision.

The Uniform Guidelines on Employee Selection Procedures (UGESP) 29 CFR part 1607 do not apply to the Rehabilitation Act and are similarly inapplicable to this part.

Section 1630.10(b)   Qualification Standards and Tests Related to Uncorrected Vision

This provision allows challenges to qualification standards based on uncorrected vision, even where the person excluded by a standard has fully corrected vision with ordinary eyeglasses or contact lenses. An individual challenging a covered entity's application of a qualification standard, test, or other criterion based on uncorrected vision need not be a person with a disability. In order to have standing to challenge such a standard, test, or criterion, however, a person must be adversely affected by such standard, test or criterion. The Commission also believes that such individuals will usually be covered under the "regarded as" prong of the definition of disability. Someone who wears eyeglasses or contact lenses to correct vision will still have an impairment, and a qualification standard that screens the individual out because of the impairment by requiring a certain level of uncorrected vision to perform a job will amount to an action prohibited by the ADA based on an impairment. (See § 1630.2(l); Appendix to § 1630.2(l).)

In either case, a covered entity may still defend a qualification standard requiring a certain level of uncorrected vision by showing that it is job related and consistent with business necessity. For example, an applicant or employee with uncorrected vision of 20/100 who wears glasses that fully correct his vision may challenge a police department's qualification standard that requires all officers to have uncorrected vision of no less than 20/40 in one eye and 20/100 in the other, and visual acuity of 20/20 in both eyes with correction. The department would then have to establish that the standard is job related and consistent with business necessity.

Section 1630.11   Administration of Tests

The intent of this provision is to further emphasize that individuals with disabilities are not to be excluded from jobs that they can actually perform merely because a disability prevents them from taking a test, or negatively influences the results of a test, that is a prerequisite to the job. Read together with the reasonable accommodation requirement of section 1630.9, this provision requires that employment tests be administered to eligible applicants or employees with disabilities that impair sensory, manual, or speaking skills in formats that do not require the use of the impaired skill.

The employer or other covered entity is, generally, only required to provide such reasonable accommodation if it knows, prior to the administration of the test, that the individual is disabled and that the disability impairs sensory, manual or speaking skills. Thus, for example, it would be unlawful to administer a written employment test to an individual who has informed the employer, prior to the administration of the test, that he is disabled with dyslexia and unable to read. In such a case, as a reasonable accommodation and in accordance with this provision, an alternative oral test should be administered to that individual. By the same token, a written test may need to be substituted for an oral test if the applicant taking the test is an individual with a disability that impairs speaking skills or impairs the processing of auditory information.

Occasionally, an individual with a disability may not realize, prior to the administration of a test, that he or she will need an accommodation to take that particular test. In such a situation, the individual with a disability, upon becoming aware of the need for an accommodation, must so inform the employer or other covered entity. For example, suppose an individual with a disabling visual impairment does not request an accommodation for a written examination because he or she is usually able to take written tests with the aid of his or her own specially designed lens. When the test is distributed, the individual with a disability discovers that the lens is insufficient to distinguish the words of the test because of the unusually low color contrast between the paper and the ink, the individual would be entitled, at that point, to request an accommodation. The employer or other covered entity would, thereupon, have to provide a test with higher contrast, schedule a retest, or provide any other effective accommodation unless to do so would impose an undue hardship.

Other alternative or accessible test modes or formats include the administration of tests in large print or braille, or via a reader or sign interpreter. Where it is not possible to test in an alternative format, the employer may be required, as a reasonable accommodation, to evaluate the skill to be tested in another manner (e.g., through an interview, or through education license, or work experience requirements). An employer may also be required, as a reasonable accommodation, to allow more time to complete the test. In addition, the employer's obligation to make reasonable accommodation extends to ensuring that the test site is accessible. (See § 1630.9 Not Making Reasonable Accommodation) See Senate Report at 37–38; House Labor Report at 70–72; House Judiciary Report at 42; see also Stutts v. Freeman, 694 F.2d 666 (11th Cir. 1983); Crane v. Dole, 617 F. Supp. 156 (D.D.C. 1985).

This provision does not require that an employer offer every applicant his or her choice of test format. Rather, this provision only requires that an employer provide, upon advance request, alternative, accessible tests to individuals with disabilities that impair sensory, manual, or speaking skills needed to take the test.

This provision does not apply to employment tests that require the use of sensory, manual, or speaking skills where the tests are intended to measure those skills.

Thus, an employer could require that an applicant with dyslexia take a written test for a particular position if the ability to read is the skill the test is designed to measure. Similarly, an employer could require that an applicant complete a test within established time frames if speed were one of the skills for which the applicant was being tested. However, the results of such a test could not be used to exclude an individual with a disability unless the skill was necessary to perform an essential function of the position and no reasonable accommodation was available to enable the individual to perform that function, or the necessary accommodation would impose an undue hardship.

Section 1630.13   Prohibited Medical Examinations and Inquiries

Section 1630.13(a)   Pre-employment Examination or Inquiry

This provision makes clear that an employer cannot inquire as to whether an individual has a disability at the pre-offer stage of the selection process. Nor can an employer inquire at the pre-offer stage about an applicant's workers' compensation history.

Employers may ask questions that relate to the applicant's ability to perform job-related functions. However, these questions should not be phrased in terms of disability. An employer, for example, may ask whether the applicant has a driver's license, if driving is a job function, but may not ask whether the applicant has a visual disability. Employers may ask about an applicant's ability to perform both essential and marginal job functions. Employers, though, may not refuse to hire an applicant with a disability because the applicant's disability prevents him or her from performing marginal functions. See Senate Report at 39; House Labor Report at 72–73; House Judiciary Report at 42–43.

Section 1630.13(b)   Examination or Inquiry of Employees

The purpose of this provision is to prevent the administration to employees of medical tests or inquiries that do not serve a legitimate business purpose. For example, if an employee suddenly starts to use increased amounts of sick eave or starts to appear sickly, an employer could not require that employee to be tested for AIDS, HIV infection, or cancer unless the employer can demonstrate that such testing is job-related and consistent with business necessity. See Senate Report at 39; House Labor Report at 75; House Judiciary Report at 44.

Section 1630.14   Medical Examinations and Inquiries Specifically Permitted

Section 1630.14(a)   Pre-employment Inquiry

Employers are permitted to make pre-employment inquiries into the ability of an applicant to perform job-related functions. This inquiry must be narrowly tailored. The employer may describe or demonstrate the job function and inquire whether or not the applicant can perform that function with or without reasonable accommodation. For example, an employer may explain that the job requires assembling small parts and ask if the individual will be able to perform that function, with or without reasonable accommodation. See Senate Report at 39; House Labor Report at 73; House Judiciary Report at 43.

An employer may also ask an applicant to describe or to demonstrate how, with or without reasonable accommodation, the applicant will be able to perform job-related functions. Such a request may be made of all applicants in the same job category regardless of disability. Such a request may also be made of an applicant whose known disability may interfere with or prevent the performance of a job-related function, whether or not the employer routinely makes such a request of all applicants in the job category. For example, an employer may ask an individual with one leg who applies for a position as a home washing machine repairman to demonstrate or to explain how, with or without reasonable accommodation, he would be able to transport himself and his tools down basement stairs. However, the employer may not inquire as to the nature or severity of the disability. Therefore, for example, the employer cannot ask how the individual lost the leg or whether the loss of the leg is indicative of an underlying impairment.

On the other hand, if the known disability of an applicant will not interfere with or prevent the performance of a job-related function, the employer may only request a description or demonstration by the applicant if it routinely makes such a request of all applicants in the same job category. So, for example, it would not be permitted for an employer to request that an applicant with one leg demonstrate his ability to assemble small parts while seated at a table, if the employer does not routinely request that all applicants provide such a demonstration.

An employer that requires an applicant with a disability to demonstrate how he or she will perform a job-related function must either provide the reasonable accommodation the applicant needs to perform the function or permit the applicant to explain how, with the accommodation, he or she will perform the function. If the job-related function is not an essential function, the employer may not exclude the applicant with a disability because of the applicant's inability to perform that function. Rather, the employer must, as a reasonable accommodation, either provide an accommodation that will enable the individual to perform the function, transfer the function to another position, or exchange the function for one the applicant is able to perform.

An employer may not use an application form that lists a number of potentially disabling impairments and ask the applicant to check any of the impairments he or she may have. In addition, as noted above, an employer may not ask how a particular individual became disabled or the prognosis of the individual's disability. The employer is also prohibited from asking how often the individual will require leave for treatment or use leave as a result of incapacitation because of the disability. However, the employer may state the attendance requirements of the job and inquire whether the applicant can meet them.

An employer is permitted to ask, on a test announcement or application form, that individuals with disabilities who will require a reasonable accommodation in order to take the test so inform the employer within a reasonable established time period prior to the administration of the test. The employer may also request that documentation of the need for the accommodation accompany the request. Requested accommodations may include accessible testing sites, modified testing conditions and accessible test formats. (See § 1630.11 Administration of Tests).

Physical agility tests are not medical examinations and so may be given at any point in the application or employment process. Such tests must be given to all similarly situated applicants or employees regardless of disability. If such tests screen out or tend to screen out an individual with a disability or a class of individuals with disabilities, the employer would have to demonstrate that the test is job-related and consistent with business necessity and that performance cannot be achieved with reasonable accommodation. (See § 1630.9 Not Making Reasonable Accommodation: Process of Determining the Appropriate Reasonable Accommodation).

As previously noted, collecting information and inviting individuals to identify themselves as individuals with disabilities as required to satisfy the affirmative action requirements of section 503 of the Rehabilitation Act is not restricted by this part. (See § 1630.1(b) and (c) Applicability and Construction).

Section 1630.14(b)   Employment Entrance Examination

An employer is permitted to require post-offer medical examinations before the employee actually starts working. The employer may condition the offer of employment on the results of the examination, provided that all entering employees in the same job category are subjected to such an examination, regardless of disability, and that the confidentiality requirements specified in this part are met.

This provision recognizes that in many industries, such as air transportation or construction, applicants for certain positions are chosen on the basis of many factors including physical and psychological criteria, some of which may be identified as a result of post-offer medical examinations given prior to entry on duty. Only those employees who meet the employer's physical and psychological criteria for the job, with or without reasonable accommodation, will be qualified to receive confirmed offers of employment and begin working.

Medical examinations permitted by this section are not required to be job-related and consistent with business necessity. However, if an employer withdraws an offer of employment because the medical examination reveals that the employee does not satisfy certain employment criteria, either the exclusionary criteria must not screen out or tend to screen out an individual with a disability or a class of individuals with disabilities, or they must be job-related and consistent with business necessity. As part of the showing that an exclusionary criteria is job-related and consistent with business necessity, the employer must also demonstrate that there is no reasonable accommodation that will enable the individual with a disability to perform the essential functions of the job. See Conference Report at 59–60; Senate Report at 39; House Labor Report at 73–74; House Judiciary Report at 43.

As an example, suppose an employer makes a conditional offer of employment to an applicant, and it is an essential function of the job that the incumbent be available to work every day for the next three months. An employment entrance examination then reveals that the applicant has a disabling impairment that, according to reasonable medical judgment that relies on the most current medical knowledge, will require treatment that will render the applicant unable to work for a portion of the three month period. Under these circumstances, the employer would be able to withdraw the employment offer without violating this part.

The information obtained in the course of a permitted entrance examination or inquiry is to be treated as a confidential medical record and may only be used in a manner not inconsistent with this part. State workers' compensation laws are not preempted by the ADA or this part. These laws require the collection of information from individuals for state administrative purposes that do not conflict with the ADA or this part. Consequently, employers or other covered entities may submit information to state workers' compensation offices or second injury funds in accordance with state workers' compensation laws without violating this part.

Consistent with this section and with § 1630.16(f) of this part, information obtained in the course of a permitted entrance examination or inquiry may be used for insurance purposes described in § 1630.16(f).

Section 1630.14(c) Examination of Employees

This provision permits employers to make inquiries or require medical examinations (fitness for duty exams) when there is a need to determine whether an employee is still able to perform the essential functions of his or her job. The provision permits employers or other covered entities to make inquiries or require medical examinations necessary to the reasonable accommodation process described in this part. This provision also permits periodic physicals to determine fitness for duty or other medical monitoring if such physicals or monitoring are required by medical standards or requirements established by Federal, state, or local law that are consistent with the ADA and this part (or in the case of a federal standard, with section 504 of the Rehabilitation Act) in that they are job-related and consistent with business necessity.

Such standards may include federal safety regulations that regulate bus and truck driver qualifications, as well as laws establishing medical requirements for pilots or other air transportation personnel. These standards also include health standards promulgated pursuant to the Occupational Safety and Health Act of 1970, the Federal Coal Mine Health and Safety Act of 1969, or other similar statutes that require that employees exposed to certain toxic and hazardous substances be medically monitored at specific intervals. See House Labor Report at 74–75.

The information obtained in the course of such examination or inquiries is to be treated as a confidential medical record and may only be used in a manner not inconsistent with this part.

Section 1630.14(d) Other Acceptable Examinations and Inquiries

Part 1630 permits voluntary medical examinations, including voluntary medical histories, as part of employee health programs. These programs often include, for example, medical screening for high blood pressure, weight control counseling, and cancer detection. Voluntary activities, such as blood pressure monitoring and the administering of prescription drugs, such as insulin, are also permitted. It should be noted, however, that the medical records developed in the course of such activities must be maintained in the confidential manner required by this part and must not be used for any purpose in violation of this part, such as limiting health insurance eligibility. House Labor Report at 75; House Judiciary Report at 43–44.

Section 1630.15 Defenses

The section on defenses in part 1630 is not intended to be exhaustive. However, it is intended to inform employers of some of the potential defenses available to a charge of discrimination under the ADA and this part.

Section 1630.15(a) Disparate Treatment Defenses

The "traditional" defense to a charge of disparate treatment under title VII, as expressed in McDonnell Douglas Corp. v. Green, 411 U.S. 792 (1973), Texas Department of Community Affairs v. Burdine, 450 U.S. 248 (1981), and their progeny, may be applicable to charges of disparate treatment brought under the ADA. See Prewitt v. U.S. Postal Service, 662 F.2d 292 (5th Cir. 1981). Disparate treatment means, with respect to title I of the ADA, that an individual was treated differently on the basis of his or her disability. For example, disparate treatment has occurred where an employer excludes an employee with a severe facial disfigurement from staff meetings because the employer does not like to look at the employee. The individual is being treated differently because of the employer's attitude towards his or her perceived disability. Disparate treatment has also occurred where an employer has a policy of not hiring individuals with AIDS regardless of the individuals' qualifications.

The crux of the defense to this type of charge is that the individual was treated differently not because of his or her disability but for a legitimate nondiscriminatory reason such as poor performance unrelated to the individual's disability. The fact that the individual's disability is not covered by the employer's current insurance plan or would cause the employer's insurance premiums or workers' compensation costs to increase, would not be a legitimate nondiscriminatory reason justifying disparate treatment of an individual with a disability. Senate Report at 85; House Labor Report at 136 and House Judiciary Report at 70. The defense of a legitimate nondiscriminatory reason is rebutted if the alleged nondiscriminatory reason is shown to be pretextual.

Section 1630.15(b) and (c)   Disparate Impact Defenses

Disparate impact means, with respect to title I of the ADA and this part, that uniformly applied criteria have an adverse impact on an individual with a disability or a disproportionately negative impact on a class of individuals with disabilities. Section 1630.15(b) clarifies that an employer may use selection criteria that have such a disparate impact, i.e., that screen out or tend to screen out an individual with a disability or a class of individuals with disabilities only when they are job-related and consistent with business necessity.

For example, an employer interviews two candidates for a position, one of whom is blind. Both are equally qualified. The employer decides that while it is not essential to the job it would be convenient to have an employee who has a driver's license and so could occasionally be asked to run errands by car. The employer hires the individual who is sighted because this individual has a driver's license. This is an example of a uniformly applied criterion, having a driver's permit, that screens out an individual who has a disability that makes it impossible to obtain a driver's permit. The employer would, thus, have to show that this criterion is job-related and consistent with business necessity. See House Labor Report at 55.

However, even if the criterion is job-related and consistent with business necessity, an employer could not exclude an individual with a disability if the criterion could be met or job performance accomplished with a reasonable accommodation. For example, suppose an employer requires, as part of its application process, an interview that is job-related and consistent with business necessity. The employer would not be able to refuse to hire a hearing impaired applicant because he or she could not be interviewed. This is so because an interpreter could be provided as a reasonable accommodation that would allow the individual to be interviewed, and thus satisfy the selection criterion.

With regard to safety requirements that screen out or tend to screen out an individual with a disability or a class of individuals with disabilities, an employer must demonstrate that the requirement, as applied to the individual, satisfies the "direct threat" standard in § 1630.2(r) in order to show that the requirement is job-related and consistent with business necessity.

Section 1630.15(c) clarifies that there may be uniformly applied standards, criteria and policies not relating to selection that may also screen out or tend to screen out an individual with a disability or a class of individuals with disabilities. Like selection criteria that have a disparate impact, non-selection criteria having such an impact may also have to be job-related and consistent with business necessity, subject to consideration of reasonable accommodation.

It should be noted, however, that some uniformly applied employment policies or practices, such as leave policies, are not subject to challenge under the adverse impact theory. "No-leave" policies (e.g., no leave during the first six months of employment) are likewise not subject to challenge under the adverse impact theory. However, an employer, in spite of its "no-leave" policy, may, in appropriate circumstances, have to consider the provision of leave to an employee with a disability as a reasonable accommodation, unless the provision of leave would impose an undue hardship. See discussion at § 1630.5 Limiting, Segregating and Classifying, and § 1630.10 Qualification Standards, Tests, and Other Selection Criteria.

Section 1630.15(d)   Defense to Not Making Reasonable Accommodation

An employer or other covered entity alleged to have discriminated because it did not make a reasonable accommodation, as required by this part, may offer as a defense that it would have been an undue hardship to make the accommodation.

It should be noted, however, that an employer cannot simply assert that a needed accommodation will cause it undue hardship, as defined in § 1630.2(p), and thereupon be relieved of the duty to provide accommodation. Rather, an employer will have to present evidence and demonstrate that the accommodation will, in fact, cause it undue hardship. Whether a particular accommodation will impose an undue hardship for a particular employer is determined on a case by case basis. Consequently, an accommodation that poses an undue hardship for one employer at a particular time may not pose an undue hardship for another employer, or even for the same employer at another time. Likewise, an accommodation that poses an undue hardship for one employer in a particular job setting, such as a temporary construction worksite, may not pose an undue hardship for another employer, or even for the same employer at a permanent worksite. See House Judiciary Report at 42.

The concept of undue hardship that has evolved under section 504 of the Rehabilitation Act and is embodied in this part is unlike the "undue hardship" defense associated with the provision of religious accommodation under title VII of the Civil Rights Act of 1964. To demonstrate undue hardship pursuant to the ADA and this part, an employer must show substantially more difficulty or expense than would be needed to satisfy the "de minimis" title VII standard of undue hardship. For example, to demonstrate that the cost of an accommodation poses an undue hardship, an employer would have to show that the cost is undue as compared to the employer's budget. Simply comparing the cost of the accommodation to the salary of the individual with a disability in need of the accommodation will not suffice. Moreover, even if it is determined that the cost of an accommodation would unduly burden an employer, the employer cannot avoid making the accommodation if the individual with a disability can arrange to cover that portion of the cost that rises to the undue hardship level, or can otherwise arrange to provide the accommodation. Under such circumstances, the necessary accommodation would no longer pose an undue hardship. See Senate Report at 36; House Labor Report at 68–69; House Judiciary Report at 40–41.

Excessive cost is only one of several possible bases upon which an employer might be able to demonstrate undue hardship. Alternatively, for example, an employer could demonstrate that the provision of a particular accommodation would be unduly disruptive to its other employees or to the functioning of its business. The terms of a collective bargaining agreement may be relevant to this determination. By way of illustration, an employer would likely be able to show undue hardship if the employer could show that the requested accommodation of the upward adjustment of the business' thermostat would result in it becoming unduly hot for its other employees, or for its patrons or customers. The employer would thus not have to provide this accommodation. However, if there were an alternate accommodation that would not result in undue hardship, the employer would have to provide that accommodation.

It should be noted, moreover, that the employer would not be able to show undue hardship if the disruption to its employees were the result of those employees fears or prejudices toward the individual's disability and not the result of the provision of the accommodation. Nor would the employer be able to demonstrate undue hardship by showing that the provision of the accommodation has a negative impact on the morale of its other employees but not on the ability of these employees to perform their jobs.

Section 1630.15(e)   Defense — Conflicting Federal Laws and Regulations

There are several Federal laws and regulations that address medical standards and safety requirements. If the alleged discriminatory action was taken in compliance with another Federal law or regulation, the employer may offer its obligation to comply with the conflicting standard as a defense. The employer's defense of a conflicting Federal requirement or regulation may be rebutted by a showing of pretext, or by showing that the Federal standard did not require the discriminatory action, or that there was a nonexclusionary means to comply with the standard that would not conflict with this part. See House Labor Report at 74.

Section 1630.15(f)   Claims Based on Transitory and Minor Impairments Under the "Regarded As" Prong

It may be a defense to a charge of discrimination where coverage would be shown solely under the "regarded as" prong of the definition of disability that the impairment is (in the case of an actual impairment) or would be (in the case of a perceived impairment) both transitory and minor. Section 1630.15(f)(1) explains that an individual cannot be "regarded as having such an impairment" if the impairment is both transitory (defined by the ADAAA as lasting or expected to last less than six months) and minor. Section 1630.15(f)(2) explains that the determination of "transitory and minor" is made objectively. For example, an individual who is denied a promotion because he has a minor back injury would be "regarded as" an individual with a disability if the back impairment lasted or was expected to last more than six months. Although minor, the impairment is not transitory. Similarly, if an employer discriminates against an employee based on the employee's bipolar disorder (an impairment that is not transitory and minor), the employee is "regarded as" having a disability even if the employer subjectively believes that the employee's disorder is transitory and minor.

Section 1630.16   Specific Activities Permitted

Section 1630.16(a)   Religious Entities

Religious organizations are not exempt from title I of the ADA or this part. A religious corporation, association, educational institution, or society may give a preference in employment to individuals of the particular religion, and may require that applicants and employees conform to the religious tenets of the organization. However, a religious organization may not discriminate against an individual who satisfies the permitted religious criteria because that individual is disabled. The religious entity, in other words, is required to consider individuals with disabilities who are qualified and who satisfy the permitted religious criteria on an equal basis with qualified individuals without disabilities who similarly satisfy the religious criteria. See Senate Report at 42; House Labor Report at 76–77; House Judiciary Report at 46.

Section 1630.16(b)   Regulation of Alcohol and Drugs

This provision permits employers to establish or comply with certain standards regulating the use of drugs and alcohol in the workplace. It also allows employers to hold alcoholics and persons who engage in the illegal use of drugs to the same performance and conduct standards to which it holds all of its other employees. Individuals disabled by alcoholism are entitled to the same protections accorded other individuals with disabilities under this part. As noted above, individuals currently engaging in the illegal use of drugs are not individuals with disabilities for purposes of part 1630 when the employer acts on the basis of such use.

Section 1630.16(c)   Drug Testing

This provision reflects title I's neutrality toward testing for the illegal use of drugs. Such drug tests are neither encouraged, authorized nor prohibited. The results of such drug tests may be used as a basis for disciplinary action. Tests for the illegal use of drugs are not considered medical examinations for purposes of this part. If the results reveal information about an individual's medical condition beyond whether the individual is currently engaging in the illegal use of drugs, this additional information is to be treated as a confidential medical record. For example, if a test for the illegal use of drugs reveals the presence of a controlled substance that has been lawfully prescribed for a particular medical condition, this information is to be treated as a confidential medical record. See House Labor Report at 79; House Judiciary Report at 47.

Section 1630.16(e)   Infectious and Communicable Diseases; Food Handling Jobs

This provision addressing food handling jobs applies the "direct threat" analysis to the particular situation of accommodating individuals with infectious or communicable diseases that are transmitted through the handling of food. The Department of Health and Human Services is to prepare a list of infectious and communicable diseases that are transmitted through the handling of food. If an individual with a disability has one of the listed diseases and works in or applies for a position in food handling, the employer must determine whether there is a reasonable accommodation that will eliminate the risk of transmitting the disease through the handling of food. If there is an accommodation that will not pose an undue hardship, and that will prevent the transmission of the disease through the handling of food, the employer must provide the accommodation to the individual. The employer, under these circumstances, would not be permitted to discriminate against the individual because of the need to provide the reasonable accommodation and would be required to maintain the individual in the food handling job.

If no such reasonable accommodation is possible, the employer may refuse to assign, or to continue to assign the individual to a position involving food handling. This means that if such an individual is an applicant for a food handling position the employer is not required to hire the individual. However, if the individual is a current employee, the employer would be required to consider the accommodation of reassignment to a vacant position not involving food handling for which the individual is qualified. Conference Report at 61–63. (See § 1630.2(r) Direct Threat).

Section 1630.16(f)   Health Insurance, Life Insurance, and Other Benefit Plans

This provision is a limited exemption that is only applicable to those who establish, sponsor, observe or administer benefit plans, such as health and life insurance plans. It does not apply to those who establish, sponsor, observe or administer plans not involving benefits, such as liability insurance plans.

The purpose of this provision is to permit the development and administration of benefit plans in accordance with accepted principles of risk assessment. This provision is not intended to disrupt the current regulatory structure for self-insured employers. These employers may establish, sponsor, observe, or administer the terms of a bona fide benefit plan not subject to state laws that regulate insurance. This provision is also not intended to disrupt the current nature of insurance underwriting, or current insurance industry practices in sales, underwriting, pricing, administrative and other services, claims and similar insurance related activities based on classification of risks as regulated by the States.

The activities permitted by this provision do not violate part 1630 even if they result in limitations on individuals with disabilities, provided that these activities are not used as a subterfuge to evade the purposes of this part. Whether or not these activities are being used as a subterfuge is to be determined without regard to the date the insurance plan or employee benefit plan was adopted.

However, an employer or other covered entity cannot deny a qualified individual with a disability equal access to insurance or subject an individual with a disability who is qualified to different terms or conditions of insurance based on disability alone, if the disability does not pose increased risks. Part 1630 requires that decisions not based on risk classification be made in conformity with non-discrimination requirements. See Senate Report at 84–86; House Labor Report at 136–138; House Judiciary Report at 70–71. See the discussion of § 1630.5 Limiting, Segregating and Classifying.

HISTORY: [56 FR 35734, July 26, 1991; 65 FR 36327, June 8, 2000; 76 FR 16978, 17003, Mar. 25, 2011]

AUTHORITY: AUTHORITY NOTE APPLICABLE TO ENTIRE PART:

42 U.S.C. 12116 and 12205a of the Americans with Disabilities Act, as amended.

NOTES: [EFFECTIVE DATE NOTE: 76 FR 16978, 17003, Mar. 25, 2011, amended this section, effective May 24, 2011.]

NOTES APPLICABLE TO ENTIRE SUBTITLE:

CROSS REFERENCES: Railroad Retirement Board: See Employees' Benefits, 20 CFR chapter II.

Social Security Administration: See Employees' Benefits, 20 CFR chapter III.

EDITORIAL NOTE: Other regulations issued by the Department of Labor appear in 20 CFR chapters I, IV, V, VI, VII; 30 CFR chapter I; 41 CFR chapters 50, 60, and 61; and 48 CFR chapter 29.

NOTES TO DECISIONS: COURT AND ADMINISTRATIVE DECISIONS SIGNIFICANTLY DISCUSSING SECTION —

Bombard v Fort Wayne Newspapers (1996, CA7 Ind) 92 F3d 560, 18 ADD 286, 5 AD Cas 1283, 44 Fed Rules Evid Serv 1215; EEOC v Exxon Corp. (2000, CA5 Tex) 203 F3d 871, 10 AD Cas 225, magistrate's recommendation (2000, ND Tex) 124 F Supp 2d 987, 11 AD Cas 871, adopted, objection overruled, dismd (2000, ND Tex) 124 F Supp 2d 987, 11 AD Cas 871 and (criticized in Morton v UPS (2001, CA9 Ariz) 272 F3d 1249, 12 AD Cas 897); Harris v H & W Contr. Co. (1996, CA11 Ga) 102 F3d 516, 19 ADD 1, 6 AD Cas 460, 10 FLW Fed C 608, reh, en banc, den (1997, CA11 Ga) 109 F3d 773 and (criticized in Washington v HCA Health Servs. (1998, CA5 Tex) 152 F3d 464, 8 AD Cas 1044); Skerski v Time Warner Cable Co. (2001, CA3 Pa) 257 F3d 273, 11 AD Cas 1665; Bartlett v New York State Bd. of Law Exam'rs (1997, SD NY) 970 F Supp 1094, 24 ADD 1013, 6 AD Cas 1766, affd in part and vacated in part, remanded (1998, CA2 NY) 156 F3d 321, 8 AD Cas 1004, vacated, remanded (1999) 527 US 1031, 119 S Ct 2388, 144 L Ed 2d 790, 99 CDOS 5058, 99 Daily Journal DAR 6552, 9 AD Cas 768 and affd in part and vacated in part, remanded, in part (2000, CA2 NY) 226 F3d 69, 10 AD Cas 1687, findings of fact/oconclusions of law, injunction gr, on remand (2001, SD NY) 2001 US Dist LEXIS 11926; Gustafson v Burlington N. R.R. (1998, DC Neb) 8 AD Cas 871; Johnson v Otter Tail County (2000, DC Minn) 2000 US Dist LEXIS 20671, affd (2001, CA8 Minn) 2001 US App LEXIS 13280; Canteen Corp., Div. of Compass Group v. Pa. Human Rels. Comm'n (2003, Pa Cmwlth) 814 A2d 805, 13 AD Cas 1647.

Chapter 4
DOJ ADA TITLE II
REGULATIONS [Redlined Version]

Subpart A   General

§ 35.101   Purpose.

The purpose of this part is to effectuate subtitle A of title II of the Americans with Disabilities Act of 1990 (42 U.S. C. 12131), which prohibits discrimination on the basis of disability by public entities.

§ 35.102   Application.

(a) Except as provided in paragraph (b) of this section, this part applies to all services, programs, and activities provided or made available by public entities.

(b) To the extent that public transportation services, programs, and activities of public entities are covered by subtitle B of title II of the ADA, they are not subject to the requirements of this part.

§ 35.103   Relationship to other laws.

(a) *Rule of interpretation.* Except as otherwise provided in this part, this part shall not be construed to apply a lesser standard than the standards applied under title V of the Rehabilitation Act of 1973 or the regulations issued by Federal agencies pursuant to that title.

(b) *Other laws.* This part does not invalidate or limit the remedies, rights, and procedures of any other Federal laws, or State or local laws (including State common law) that provide greater or equal protection for the rights of individuals with disabilities or individuals associated with them.

§ 35.104 Definitions.

For purposes of this part, the term —

1991 Standards **means the requirements set forth in the ADA Standards for Accessible Design, originally published on July 26, 1991, and republished as Appendix D to 28 CFR part 36.**

2004 ADAAG **means the requirements set forth in appendices B and D to 36 CFR part 1191 (2009).**

2010 Standards **means the 2010 ADA Standards for Accessible Design, which consist of the 2004 ADAAG and the requirements contained in § 35.151.**

Act means the Americans with Disabilities Act (Pub. L. 101-336, 104 Stat. 327, 42 U.S.C. 12101–12213 and 47 U.S.C. 225 and 611).

Assistant Attorney General means the Assistant Attorney General, Civil Rights Division, United States Department of Justice.

Auxiliary aids and services **includes —**

(1) Qualified interpreters on-site or through video remote interpreting (VRI) services; notetakers; real-time computer-aided transcription services; written materials; exchange of written notes; telephone handset amplifiers; assistive listening devices; assistive listening systems; telephones compatible with hearing aids; closed caption decoders; open and closed captioning, including real-time captioning; voice, text, and video-based telecommunications products and systems, including text telephones (TTYs), videophones, and captioned telephones, or equally effective telecommunications devices; videotext displays; accessible electronic and information technology; or other effective methods of making aurally delivered information available to individuals who are deaf or hard of hearing;

(2) Qualified readers; taped texts; audio recordings; Brailled materials and displays; screen reader software; magnification software; optical readers; secondary auditory programs (SAP); large print materials; accessible electronic and information technology; or other effective methods of making visually delivered materials available to individuals who are blind or have low vision;

(3) Acquisition or modification of equipment or devices; and

(4) Other similar services and actions.

Complete complaint means a written statement that contains the complainant's name and address and describes the public entity's alleged discriminatory action in sufficient detail to inform the agency of the nature and date of the alleged violation of this part. It shall be signed by the complainant or by someone authorized to do so on his or her behalf. Complaints filed on behalf of classes or third parties shall describe or identify (by name, if possible) the alleged victims of discrimination.

Current illegal use of drugs means illegal use of drugs that occurred recently enough to justify a reasonable belief that a person's drug use is current or that continuing use is a real and ongoing problem.

Designated agency means the Federal agency designated under subpart G of this part to oversee compliance activities under this part for particular components of State and local governments.

Direct threat means a significant risk to the health or safety of others that cannot be eliminated by a modification of policies, practices or procedures, or by the provision of auxiliary aids or services as provided in § 35.139.

Disability means, with respect to an individual, a physical or mental impairment that substantially limits one or more of the major life activities of such individual; a record of such an impairment; or being regarded as having such an impairment.

(1) (i) The phrase *physical or mental impairment* means —

(A) Any physiological disorder or condition, cosmetic disfigurement, or anatomical loss affecting one or more of the following body systems: neurological, musculoskeletal, special sense organs, respiratory (including speech organs), cardiovascular, reproductive, digestive, genitourinary, hemic and lymphatic, skin, and endocrine;

(B) Any mental or psychological disorder such as mental retardation, organic brain syndrome, emotional or mental illness, and specific learning disabilities.

(ii) The phrase *physical or mental impairment* includes, but is not limited to, such contagious and noncontagious diseases and conditions as orthopedic, visual, speech and hearing impairments, cerebral palsy, epilepsy, muscular dystrophy, multiple sclerosis, cancer, heart disease, diabetes, mental retardation, emotional illness, specific learning disabilities, HIV disease (whether symptomatic or asymptomatic), tuberculosis, drug addiction, and alcoholism.

(iii) The phrase *physical or mental impairment* does not include homosexuality or bisexuality.

(2) The phrase *major life activities* means functions such as caring for one's self, performing manual tasks, walking, seeing, hearing, speaking, breathing, learning, and working.

(3) The phrase *has a record of such an impairment* means has a history of, or has been misclassified as having, a mental or physical impairment that substantially limits one or more major life activities.

(4) The phrase *is regarded as having an impairment* means —

(i) Has a physical or mental impairment that does not substantially limit major life activities but that is treated by a public entity as constituting such a limitation;

(ii) Has a physical or mental impairment that substantially limits major life activities only as a result of the attitudes of others toward such impairment; or

(iii) Has none of the impairments defined in paragraph (1) of this definition but is treated by a public entity as having such an impairment.

(5) The term *disability* does not include —

(i) Transvestism, transsexualism, pedophilia, exhibitionism, voyeurism, gender identity disorders not resulting from physical impairments, or other sexual behavior disorders;

(ii) Compulsive gambling, kleptomania, or pyromania; or

(iii) Psychoactive substance use disorders resulting from current illegal use of drugs.

Drug means a controlled substance, as defined in schedules I through V of section 202 of the Controlled Substances Act (21 U.S.C. 812).

Existing facility means a facility in existence on any given date, without regard to whether the facility may also be considered newly constructed or altered under this part.

Facility means all or any portion of buildings, structures, sites, complexes, equipment, rolling stock or other conveyances, roads, walks, passageways, parking lots, or other real or personal property, including the site where the building, property, structure, or equipment is located.

Historic preservation programs means programs conducted by a public entity that have preservation of historic properties as a primary purpose.

Historic properties means those properties that are listed or eligible for listing in the National Register of Historic Places or properties designated as historic under State or local law.

Housing at a place of education means housing operated by or on behalf of an elementary, secondary, undergraduate, or postgraduate school, or other place of education, including dormitories, suites, apartments, or other places of residence.

Illegal use of drugs means the use of one or more drugs, the possession or distribution of which is unlawful under the Controlled Substances Act (21 U.S.C. 812). The term illegal use of drugs does not include the use of a drug taken under supervision by a licensed health care professional, or other uses authorized by the Controlled Substances Act or other provisions of Federal law.

Individual with a disability means a person who has a disability. The term individual with a disability does not include an individual who is currently engaging in the illegal use of drugs, when the public entity acts on the basis of such use.

Other power-driven mobility device means any mobility device powered by batteries, fuel, or other engines — whether or not designed primarily for use by individuals with mobility disabilities — that is used by individuals with mobility disabilities for the purpose of locomotion, including golf cars, electronic personal assistance mobility devices (EPAMDs), such as the Segway® PT, or any mobility device designed to operate in areas without defined pedestrian routes, but that is not a wheelchair within the meaning of this section. This definition does not apply to Federal wilderness areas; wheelchairs in such areas are defined in section 508(c)(2) of the ADA, 42 U.S.C. 12207(c)(2).

Public entity means —

(1) Any State or local government;

(2) Any department, agency, special purpose district, or other instrumentality of a State or States or local government; and

(3) The National Railroad Passenger Corporation, and any commuter authority (as defined in section 103(8) of the Rail Passenger Service Act).

Qualified individual with a disability means an individual with a disability who, with or without reasonable modifications to rules, policies, or practices, the removal of architectural, communication, or transportation barriers, or the provision of auxiliary aids and services, meets the essential eligibility requirements for the receipt of services or the participation in programs or activities provided by a public entity.

Qualified interpreter **means an interpreter who, via a video remote interpreting (VRI) service or an on-site appearance, is able to interpret effectively, accurately, and impartially, both receptively and expressively, using any necessary specialized vocabulary. Qualified interpreters include, for example, sign language interpreters, oral transliterators, and cued-language transliterators.**

Qualified reader **means a person who is able to read effectively, accurately, and impartially using any necessary specialized vocabulary.**

Section 504 means section 504 of the Rehabilitation Act of 1973 (Pub. L. 93-112, 87 Stat. 394 (29 U.S.C. 794), as amended.

Service animal **means any dog that is individually trained to do work or perform tasks for the benefit of an individual with a disability, including a physical, sensory, psychiatric, intellectual, or other mental disability. Other species of animals, whether wild or domestic, trained or untrained, are not service animals for the purposes of this definition. The work or tasks performed by a service animal must be directly related to the individual's disability. Examples of work or tasks include, but are not limited to, assisting individuals who are blind or have low vision with navigation and other tasks, alerting individuals who are deaf or hard of hearing to the presence of people or sounds, providing non-violent protection or rescue work, pulling a wheelchair, assisting an individual during a seizure, alerting individuals to the presence of allergens, retrieving items such as medicine or the telephone, providing physical support and assistance with balance and stability to individuals with mobility disabilities, and helping persons with psychiatric and neurological disabilities by preventing or interrupting impulsive or destructive behaviors. The crime deterrent effects of an animal's presence and the provision of emotional support, well-being, comfort, or companionship do not constitute work or tasks for the purposes of this definition.**

State means each of the several States, the District of Columbia, the Commonwealth of Puerto Rico, Guam, American Samoa, the Virgin Islands, the Trust Territory of the Pacific Islands, and the Commonwealth of the Northern Mariana Islands.

Video remote interpreting (VRI) service **means an interpreting service that uses video conference technology over dedicated lines or wireless technology offering high-speed, wide-bandwidth video connection that delivers high-quality video images as provided in § 35.160(d).**

Wheelchair **means a manually-operated or power-driven device designed primarily for use by an individual with a mobility disability for the main purpose of indoor, or of both indoor and outdoor locomotion. This definition does not apply to Federal wilderness areas; wheelchairs in such areas are defined in section 508(c)(2) of the ADA, 42 U.S.C. 12207 (c)(2).**

§ 35.105   Self-evaluation.

(a) A public entity shall, within one year of the effective date of this part, evaluate its current services, policies, and practices, and the effects thereof, that do not or may not meet the requirements of this part and, to the extent modification of any such services, policies, and practices is required, the public entity shall proceed to make the necessary modifications.

(b) A public entity shall provide an opportunity to interested persons, including individuals with disabilities or organizations representing individuals with disabilities, to participate in the self-evaluation process by submitting comments.

(c) A public entity that employs 50 or more persons shall, for at least three years following completion of the self-evaluation, maintain on file and make available for public inspection:

   (1) A list of the interested persons consulted;

   (2) A description of areas examined and any problems identified; and

   (3) A description of any modifications made.

(d) If a public entity has already complied with the self-evaluation requirement of a regulation implementing section 504 of the Rehabilitation Act of 1973, then the requirements of this section shall apply only to those policies and practices that were not included in the previous self-evaluation.

§ 35.106   Notice

A public entity shall make available to applicants, participants, beneficiaries, and other interested persons information regarding the provisions of this part and its applicability to the services, programs, or activities of the public entity, and make such information available to them in such manner as the head of the entity finds necessary to apprise such persons of the protections against discrimination assured them by the Act and this part.

§ 35.107 Designation of responsible employee and adoption of grievance procedures

(a) *Designation of responsible employee.* A public entity that employs 50 or more persons shall designate at least one employee to coordinate its efforts to comply with and carry out its responsibilities under this part, including any investigation of any complaint communicated to it alleging its noncompliance with this part or alleging any actions that would be prohibited by this part. The public entity shall make available to all interested individuals the name, office address, and telephone number of the employee or employees designated pursuant to this paragraph.

(b) *Complaint procedure.* A public entity that employs 50 or more persons shall adopt and publish grievance procedures providing for prompt and equitable resolution of complaints alleging any action that would be prohibited by this part.

§§ 35.108–35.129 [Reserved]

Subpart B   General Requirements

§ 35.130 General prohibitions against discrimination

(a) No qualified individual with a disability shall, on the basis of disability, be excluded from participation in or be denied the benefits of the services, programs, or activities of a public entity, or be subjected to discrimination by any public entity.

(b) (1) A public entity, in providing any aid, benefit, or service, may not, directly or through contractual, licensing, or other arrangements, on the basis of disability —

(i) Deny a qualified individual with a disability the opportunity to participate in or benefit from the aid, benefit, or service;

(ii) Afford a qualified individual with a disability an opportunity to participate in or benefit from the aid, benefit, or service that is not equal to that afforded others;

(iii) Provide a qualified individual with a disability with an aid, benefit, or service that is not as effective in affording equal opportunity to obtain the same result, to gain the same benefit, or to reach the same level of achievement as that provided to others;

(iv) Provide different or separate aids, benefits, or services to individuals with disabilities or to any class of individuals with disabilities than is provided to others unless such action is necessary to provide qualified individuals with disabilities with aids, benefits, or services that are as effective as those provided to others;

(v) Aid or perpetuate discrimination against a qualified individual with a disability by providing significant assistance to an agency, organization, or person that discriminates on the basis of disability in providing any aid, benefit, or service to beneficiaries of the public entity's program;

(vi) Deny a qualified individual with a disability the opportunity to participate as a member of planning or advisory boards;

(vii) Otherwise limit a qualified individual with a disability in the enjoyment of any right, privilege, advantage, or opportunity enjoyed by others receiving the aid, benefit, or service.

(2) A public entity may not deny a qualified individual with a disability the opportunity to participate in services, programs, or activities that are not separate or different, despite the existence of permissibly separate or different programs or activities.

(3) A public entity may not, directly or through contractual or other arrangements, utilize criteria or methods of administration —

(i) That have the effect of subjecting qualified individuals with disabilities to discrimination on the basis of disability;

(ii) That have the purpose or effect of defeating or substantially impairing accomplishment of the objectives of the public entity's program with respect to individuals with disabilities; or

(iii) That perpetuate the discrimination of another public entity if both public entities are subject to common administrative control or are agencies of the same State.

(4) A public entity may not, in determining the site or location of a facility, make selections —

(i) That have the effect of excluding individuals with disabilities from, denying them the benefits of, or otherwise subjecting them to discrimination; or

(ii) That have the purpose or effect of defeating or substantially impairing the accomplishment of the objectives of the service, program, or activity with respect to individuals with disabilities.

(5) A public entity, in the selection of procurement contractors, may not use criteria that subject qualified individuals with disabilities to discrimination on the basis of disability.

(6) A public entity may not administer a licensing or certification program in a manner that subjects qualified individuals with disabilities to discrimination on the basis of disability, nor may a public entity establish requirements for the programs or activities of licensees or certified entities that subject qualified individuals with disabilities to discrimination on the basis of disability. The programs or activities of entities that are licensed or certified by a public entity are not, themselves, covered by this part.

(7) A public entity shall make reasonable modifications in policies, practices, or procedures when the modifications are necessary to avoid discrimination on the basis of disability, unless the public entity can demonstrate that making the modifications would fundamentally alter the nature of the service, program, or activity.

(8) A public entity shall not impose or apply eligibility criteria that screen out or tend to screen out an individual with a disability or any class of individuals with

disabilities from fully and equally enjoying any service, program, or activity, unless such criteria can be shown to be necessary for the provision of the service, program, or activity being offered.

(c) Nothing in this part prohibits a public entity from providing benefits, services, or advantages to individuals with disabilities, or to a particular class of individuals with disabilities beyond those required by this part.

(d) A public entity shall administer services, programs, and activities in the most integrated setting appropriate to the needs of qualified individuals with disabilities.

(e) (1) Nothing in this part shall be construed to require an individual with a disability to accept an accommodation, aid, service, opportunity, or benefit provided under the ADA or this part which such individual chooses not to accept.

(2) Nothing in the Act or this part authorizes the representative or guardian of an individual with a disability to decline food, water, medical treatment, or medical services for that individual.

(f) A public entity may not place a surcharge on a particular individual with a disability or any group of individuals with disabilities to cover the costs of measures, such as the provision of auxiliary aids or program accessibility, that are required to provide that individual or group with the nondiscriminatory treatment required by the Act or this part.

(g) A public entity shall not exclude or otherwise deny equal services, programs, or activities to an individual or entity because of the known disability of an individual with whom the individual or entity is known to have a relationship or association.

(h) A public entity may impose legitimate safety requirements necessary for the safe operation of its services, programs, or activities. However, the public entity must ensure that its safety requirements are based on actual risks, not on mere speculation, stereotypes, or generalizations about individuals with disabilities.

§ 35.131　Illegal use of drugs

(a) *General.*

(1) Except as provided in paragraph (b) of this section, this part does not prohibit discrimination against an individual based on that individual's current illegal use of drugs.

(2) A public entity shall not discriminate on the basis of illegal use of drugs against an individual who is not engaging in current illegal use of drugs and who —

(i) Has successfully completed a supervised drug rehabilitation program or has otherwise been rehabilitated successfully;

(ii) Is participating in a supervised rehabilitation program; or

(iii) Is erroneously regarded as engaging in such use.

(b) *Health and drug rehabilitation services.*

(1) A public entity shall not deny health services, or services provided in connection with drug rehabilitation, to an individual on the basis of that individual's current illegal use of drugs, if the individual is otherwise entitled to such services.

(2) A drug rehabilitation or treatment program may deny participation to individuals who engage in illegal use of drugs while they are in the program.

(c) *Drug testing.*

(1) This part does not prohibit a public entity from adopting or administering reasonable policies or procedures, including but not limited to drug testing, designed to ensure that an individual who formerly engaged in the illegal use of drugs is not now engaging in current illegal use of drugs.

(2) Nothing in paragraph (c) of this section shall be construed to encourage, prohibit, restrict, or authorize the conduct of testing for the illegal use of drugs.

§ 35.132 Smoking

This part does not preclude the prohibition of, or the imposition of restrictions on, smoking in transportation covered by this part.

§ 35.133 Maintenance of accessible features

(a) A public accommodation shall maintain in operable working condition those features of facilities and equipment that are required to be readily accessible to and usable by persons with disabilities by the Act or this part.

(b) This section does not prohibit isolated or temporary interruptions in service or access due to maintenance or repairs.

(c) If the 2010 Standards reduce the technical requirements or the number of required accessible elements below the number required by the 1991 Standards, the technical requirements or the number of accessible elements in a facility subject to this part may be reduced in accordance with the requirements of the 2010 Standards.

§ 35.134 Retaliation or coercion

(a) No private or public entity shall discriminate against any individual because that individual has opposed any act or practice made unlawful by this part, or because that individual made a charge, testified, assisted, or participated in any manner in an investigation, proceeding, or hearing under the Act or this part.

(b) No private or public entity shall coerce, intimidate, threaten, or interfere with any individual in the exercise or enjoyment of, or on account of his or her having exercised or enjoyed, or on account of his or her having aided or encouraged any other individual in the exercise or enjoyment of, any right granted or protected by the Act or this part.

§ 35.135 Personal devices and services

This part does not require a public entity to provide to individuals with disabilities personal devices, such as wheelchairs; individually prescribed devices, such as prescription eyeglasses or hearing aids; readers for personal use or study; or services of a personal nature including assistance in eating, toileting, or dressing.

§ 35.136   Service animals

(a) *General.* Generally, a public entity shall modify its policies, practices, or procedures to permit the use of a service animal by an individual with a disability.

(b) *Exceptions.* A public entity may ask an individual with a disability to remove a service animal from the premises if —

(1) The animal is out of control and the animal's handler does not take effective action to control it; or

(2) The animal is not housebroken.

(c) *If an animal is properly excluded.* If a public entity properly excludes a service animal under § 35.136(b), it shall give the individual with a disability the opportunity to participate in the service, program, or activity without having the service animal on the premises.

(d) *Animal under handler's control.* A service animal shall be under the control of its handler. A service animal shall have a harness, leash, or other tether, unless either the handler is unable because of a disability to use a harness, leash, or other tether, or the use of a harness, leash, or other tether would interfere with the service animal's safe, effective performance of work or tasks, in which case the service animal must be otherwise under the handler's control (*e.g.*, voice control, signals, or other effective means).

(e) *Care or supervision.* A public entity is not responsible for the care or supervision of a service animal.

(f) *Inquiries.* A public entity shall not ask about the nature or extent of a person's disability, but may make two inquiries to determine whether an animal qualifies as a service animal. A public entity may ask if the animal is required because of a disability and what work or task the animal has been trained to perform. A public entity shall not require documentation, such as proof that the animal has been certified, trained, or licensed as a service animal. Generally, a public entity may not make these inquiries about a service animal when it is readily apparent that an animal is trained to do work or perform tasks for an individual with a disability (*e.g.*, the dog is observed guiding an individual who is blind or has low vision, pulling a person's wheelchair, or providing assistance with stability or balance to an individual with an observable mobility disability).

(g) *Access to areas of a public entity.* Individuals with disabilities shall be permitted to be accompanied by their service animals in all areas of a public entity's facilities where members of the public, participants in services, programs or activities, or invitees, as relevant, are allowed to go.

(h) *Surcharges.* A public entity shall not ask or require an individual with a disability to pay a surcharge, even if people accompanied by pets are required to pay fees, or to comply with other requirements generally not applicable to people without pets. If a public entity normally charges individuals for the damage they cause, an individual with a disability may be charged for damage caused by his or her service animal.

(i) *Miniature horses.*

(1) *Reasonable modifications.* A public entity shall make reasonable modifications in policies, practices, or procedures to permit the use of a miniature horse by an individual with a disability if the miniature horse has been individually trained to do work or perform tasks for the benefit of the individual with a disability.

(2) *Assessment factors.* In determining whether reasonable modifications in policies, practices, or procedures can be made to allow a miniature horse into a specific facility, a public entity shall consider —

(i) The type, size, and weight of the miniature horse and whether the facility can accommodate these features;

(ii) Whether the handler has sufficient control of the miniature horse;

(iii) Whether the miniature horse is housebroken; and

(iv) Whether the miniature horse's presence in a specific facility compromises legitimate safety requirements that are necessary for safe operation.

(3) *Other requirements.* Paragraphs 35.136 (c) through (h) of this section, which apply to service animals, shall also apply to miniature horses.

§ 35.137 Mobility devices.

(a) *Use of wheelchairs and manually-powered mobility aids.* A public entity shall permit individuals with mobility disabilities to use wheelchairs and manually-powered mobility aids, such as walkers, crutches, canes, braces, or other similar devices designed for use by individuals with mobility disabilities in any areas open to pedestrian use.

(b) (1) *Use of other power-driven mobility devices.* A public entity shall make reasonable modifications in its policies, practices, or procedures to permit the use of other power-driven mobility devices by individuals with mobility disabilities, unless the public entity can demonstrate that the class of other power-driven mobility devices cannot be operated in accordance with legitimate safety requirements that the public entity has adopted pursuant to § 35.130(h).

(2) *Assessment factors.* In determining whether a particular other power-driven mobility device can be allowed in a specific facility as a reasonable modification under paragraph (b)(1) of this section, a public entity shall consider —

(i) The type, size, weight, dimensions, and speed of the device;

(ii) The facility's volume of pedestrian traffic (which may vary at different times of the day, week, month, or year);

(iii) The facility's design and operational characteristics (*e.g.*, whether its service, program, or activity is conducted indoors, its square footage, the density and placement of stationary devices, and the availability of storage for the device, if requested by the user);

(iv) Whether legitimate safety requirements can be established to permit the safe operation of the other power-driven mobility device in the specific facility; and

(v) Whether the use of the other power-driven mobility device creates a substantial risk of serious harm to the immediate environment or natural or cultural resources, or poses a conflict with Federal land management laws and regulations.

(c) (1) *Inquiry about disability.* A public entity shall not ask an individual using a wheelchair or other power-driven mobility device questions about the nature and extent of the individual's disability.

(2) *Inquiry into use of other power-driven mobility device.* A public entity may ask a person using an other power-driven mobility device to provide a credible assurance that the mobility device is required because of the person's disability. A public entity that permits the use of an other power-driven mobility device by an individual with a mobility disability shall accept the presentation of a valid, State-issued, disability parking placard or card, or other State-issued proof of disability as a credible assurance that the use of the other power-driven mobility device is for the individual's mobility disability. In lieu of a valid, State-issued disability parking placard or card, or State-issued proof of disability, a public entity shall accept as a credible assurance a verbal representation, not contradicted by observable fact, that the other power-driven mobility device is being used for a mobility disability. A "valid" disability placard or card is one that is presented by the individual to whom it was issued and is otherwise in compliance with the State of issuance's requirements for disability placards or cards.

§ 35.138   Ticketing

(a) (1) For the purposes of this section, "accessible seating" is defined as wheelchair spaces and companion seats that comply with sections 221 and 802 of the 2010 Standards along with any other seats required to be offered for sale to the individual with a disability pursuant to paragraph (d) of this section.

(2) *Ticket sales.* A public entity that sells tickets for a single event or series of events shall modify its policies, practices, or procedures to ensure that individuals with disabilities have an equal opportunity to purchase tickets for accessible seating —

(i) During the same hours;

(ii) During the same stages of ticket sales, including, but not limited to, pre-sales, promotions, lotteries, wait-lists, and general sales;

(iii) Through the same methods of distribution;

(iv) In the same types and numbers of ticketing sales outlets, including telephone service, in-person ticket sales at the facility, or third-party ticketing services, as other patrons; and

(v) Under the same terms and conditions as other tickets sold for the same event or series of events.

(b) *Identification of available accessible seating.* A public entity that sells or distributes tickets for a single event or series of events shall, upon inquiry —

(1) Inform individuals with disabilities, their companions, and third parties purchasing tickets for accessible seating on behalf of individuals with disabilities of the locations of all unsold or otherwise available accessible seating for any ticketed event or events at the facility;

(2) Identify and describe the features of available accessible seating in enough detail to reasonably permit an individual with a disability to assess independently whether a given accessible seating location meets his or her accessibility needs; and

(3) Provide materials, such as seating maps, plans, brochures, pricing charts, or other information, that identify accessible seating and information relevant thereto with the same text or visual representations as other seats, if such materials are provided to the general public.

(c) *Ticket prices.* The price of tickets for accessible seating for a single event or series of events shall not be set higher than the price for other tickets in the same seating section for the same event or series of events. Tickets for accessible seating must be made available at all price levels for every event or series of events. If tickets for accessible seating at a particular price level are not available because of inaccessible features, then the percentage of tickets for accessible seating that should have been available at that price level (determined by the ratio of the total number of tickets at that price level to the total number of tickets in the assembly area) shall be offered for purchase, at that price level, in a nearby or similar accessible location.

(d) *Purchasing multiple tickets.*

(1) *General.* For each ticket for a wheelchair space purchased by an individual with a disability or a third-party purchasing such a ticket at his or her request, a public entity shall make available for purchase three additional tickets for seats in the same row that are contiguous with the wheelchair space, provided that at the time of purchase there are three such seats available. A public entity is not required to provide more than three contiguous seats for each wheelchair space. Such seats may include wheelchair spaces.

(2) *Insufficient additional contiguous seats available.* If patrons are allowed to purchase at least four tickets, and there are fewer than three such additional contiguous seat tickets available for purchase, a public entity shall offer the next highest number of such seat tickets available for purchase and shall make up the difference by offering tickets for sale for

seats that are as close as possible to the accessible seats.

(3) *Sales limited to less than four tickets.* If a public entity limits sales of tickets to fewer than four seats per patron, then the public entity is only obligated to offer as many seats to patrons with disabilities, including the ticket for the wheelchair space, as it would offer to patrons without disabilities.

(4) *Maximum number of tickets patrons may purchase exceeds four.* If patrons are allowed to purchase more than four tickets, a public entity shall allow patrons with disabilities to purchase up to the same number of tickets, including the ticket for the wheelchair space.

(5) *Group sales.* If a group includes one or more individuals who need to use accessible seating because of a mobility disability or because their disability requires the use of the accessible features that are provided in accessible seating, the group shall be placed in a seating area with accessible seating so that, if possible, the group can sit together. If it is necessary to divide the group, it should be divided so that the individuals in the group who use wheelchairs are not isolated from their group.

(e) *Hold-and-release of tickets for accessible seating.*

(1) *Tickets for accessible seating may be released for sale in certain limited circumstances.* A public entity may release unsold tickets for accessible seating for sale to individuals without disabilities for their own use for a single event or series of events only under the following circumstances —

(i) When all non-accessible tickets (excluding luxury boxes, club boxes, or suites) have been sold;

(ii) When all non-accessible tickets in a designated seating area have been sold and the tickets for accessible seating are being released in the same designated area; or

(iii) When all non-accessible tickets in a designated price category have been sold and the tickets for accessible seating are being released within the same designated price category.

(2) *No requirement to release accessible tickets.* Nothing in this paragraph requires a facility to release tickets for accessible seating to individuals without disabilities for their own use.

(3) *Release of series-of-events tickets on a series-of-events basis.*

(i) *Series-of-events tickets sell-out when no ownership rights are attached.* When series-of-events tickets are sold out and a public entity releases and sells accessible seating to individuals without disabilities for a series of events, the public entity shall establish a process that prevents the automatic reassignment of the accessible seating to such ticket holders for future seasons, future years, or future series so that individuals with disabilities who require the features of accessible seating and who become newly eligible to purchase tickets when these series-of-events tickets are available for purchase have an opportunity to do so.

(ii) *Series-of-events tickets when ownership rights are attached.* When series-of-events tickets with an ownership right in accessible seating areas are forfeited or otherwise returned to a public entity, the public entity shall make reasonable modifications in its policies, practices, or procedures to afford individuals with mobility disabilities or individuals with disabilities that require the features of accessible seating an opportunity to purchase such tickets in accessible seating areas.

(f) *Ticket transfer.* Individuals with disabilities who hold tickets for accessible seating shall be permitted to transfer tickets to third parties under the same terms and conditions and to the same extent as other spectators holding the same type of tickets, whether they are for a single event or series of events.

(g) *Secondary ticket market.*

(1) A public entity shall modify its policies, practices, or procedures to ensure that an individual with a disability may use a ticket acquired in the secondary ticket market under the same terms and conditions as other individuals who hold a ticket acquired in the secondary ticket market for the same event or series of events.

(2) If an individual with a disability acquires a ticket or series of tickets to an inaccessible seat through the secondary market, a public entity shall make reasonable modifications to its policies, practices, or procedures to allow the individual to exchange his ticket for one to an accessible seat in a comparable location if accessible seating is vacant at the time the individual presents the ticket to the public entity.

(h) *Prevention of fraud in purchase of tickets for accessible seating.* A public entity may not require proof of disability, including, for example, a doctor's note, before selling tickets for accessible seating.

(1) *Single-event tickets.* For the sale of single-event tickets, it is permissible to inquire whether the individual purchasing the tickets for accessible seating has a mobility disability or a disability that requires the use of the accessible features that are provided in accessible seating, or is purchasing the tickets for an individual who has a mobility disability or a disability that requires the use of the accessible features that are provided in the accessible seating.

(2) *Series-of-events tickets.* For series-of-events tickets, it is permissible to ask the individual purchasing the tickets for accessible seating to attest in writing that the accessible seating is for a person who has a mobility disability or a disability that requires the use of the accessible features that are provided in the accessible seating.

(3) *Investigation of fraud.* A public entity may investigate the potential misuse of accessible seating where there is good cause to believe that such seating has been purchased fraudulently.

§ 35.139   Direct threat.

(a) This part does not require a public entity to permit an individual to participate in or benefit from the services, programs, or activities of that public entity when that individual poses a direct threat to the health or safety of others.

(b) In determining whether an individual poses a direct threat to the health or safety of others, a public entity must make an individualized assessment, based on reasonable judgment that relies on current medical knowledge or on the best available objective evidence, to ascertain: the nature, duration, and severity of the risk; the probability that the potential injury will actually occur; and whether reasonable modifications of policies, practices, or procedures or the provision of auxiliary aids or services will mitigate the risk.

Subpart C   Employment

§ 35.140   Employment discrimination prohibited

(a) No qualified individual with a disability shall, on the basis of disability, be subjected to discrimination in employment under any service, program, or activity conducted by a public entity.

(b) (1) For purposes of this part, the requirements of title I of the Act, as established by the regulations of the Equal Employment Opportunity Commission in 29 CFR part 1630, apply to employment in any service, program, or activity conducted by a public entity if that public entity is also subject to the jurisdiction of title I.

(2) For the purposes of this part, the requirements of section 504 of the Rehabilitation Act of 1973, as established by the regulations of the Department of Justice in 28 CFR part 41, as those requirements pertain to employment, apply to employment in any service, program, or activity conducted by a public entity if that public entity is not also subject to the jurisdiction of title I.

§§ 35.141–35.148   [Reserved]

Subpart D   Program Accessibility

§ 35.149   Discrimination prohibited.

Except as otherwise provided in § 35.150, no qualified individual with a disability shall, because a public entity's facilities are inaccessible to or unusable by individuals with disabilities, be excluded from participation in, or be denied the benefits of the services, programs, or activities of a public entity, or be subjected to discrimination by any public entity.

§ 35.150   Existing facilities

(a) *General.* A public entity shall operate each service, program, or activity so that the service, program, or activity, when viewed in its entirety, is readily accessible to and usable by individuals with disabilities. This paragraph does not —

(1) Necessarily require a public entity to make each of its existing facilities accessible to and usable by individuals with disabilities;

(2) Require a public entity to take any action that would threaten or destroy

the historic significance of an historic property; or

(3) Require a public entity to take any action that it can demonstrate would result in a fundamental alteration in the nature of a service, program, or activity or in undue financial and administrative burdens. In those circumstances where personnel of the public entity believe that the proposed action would fundamentally alter the service, program, or activity or would result in undue financial and administrative burdens, a public entity has the burden of proving that compliance with § 35.150(a) of this part would result in such alteration or burdens. The decision that compliance would result in such alteration or burdens must be made by the head of a public entity or his or her designee after considering all resources available for use in the funding and operation of the service, program, or activity, and must be accompanied by a written statement of the reasons for reaching that conclusion. If an action would result in such an alteration or such burdens, a public entity shall take any other action that would not result in such an alteration or such burdens but would nevertheless ensure that individuals with disabilities receive the benefits or services provided by the public entity.

(b) *Methods.*

(1) *General.* A public entity may comply with the requirements of this section through such means as redesign **or acquisition** of equipment, reassignment of services to accessible buildings, assignment of aides to beneficiaries, home visits, delivery of services at alternate accessible sites, alteration of existing facilities and construction of new facilities, use of accessible rolling stock or other conveyances, or any other methods that result in making its services, programs, or activities readily accessible to and usable by individuals with disabilities. A public entity is not required to make structural changes in existing facilities where other methods are effective in achieving compliance with this section. A public entity, in making alterations to existing buildings, shall meet the accessibility requirements of § 35.151. In choosing among available methods for meeting the requirements of this section, a public entity shall give priority to those methods that offer services, programs, and activities to qualified individuals with disabilities in the most integrated setting appropriate.

(2) (i) *Safe harbor.* Elements that have not been altered in existing facilities on or after March 15, 2012, and that comply with the corresponding technical and scoping specifications for those elements in either the 1991 Standards or in the Uniform Federal Accessibility Standards (UFAS), Appendix A to 41 CFR part 101-19.6 (July 1, 2002 ed.), 49 FR 31528, app. A (Aug. 7, 1984) are not required to be modified in order to comply with the requirements set forth in the 2010 Standards.

(ii) The safe harbor provided in § 35.150(b)(2)(i) does not apply to those elements in existing facilities that are subject to supplemental requirements (*i.e.,* elements for which there are neither technical nor scoping specifications in the 1991 Standards). Elements in the 2010 Standards not eligible for the element-by-element safe harbor are identified as follows —

(A) *Residential facilities dwelling units,* sections 233 and 809.

(B) *Amusement rides,* sections 234 and 1002; 206.2.9; 216.12.

(C) *Recreational boating facilities*, sections 235 and 1003; 206.2.10.

(D) *Exercise machines and equipment*, sections 236 and 1004; 206.2.13.

(E) *Fishing piers and platforms*, sections 237 and 1005; 206.2.14.

(F) *Golf facilities*, sections 238 and 1006; 206.2.15.

(G) *Miniature golf facilities*, sections 239 and 1007; 206.2.16.

(H) *Play areas*, sections 240 and 1008; 206.2.17.

(I) *Saunas and steam rooms*, sections 241 and 612.

(J) *Swimming pools, wading pools, and spas*, sections 242 and 1009.

(K) *Shooting facilities with firing positions*, sections 243 and 1010.

(L) *Miscellaneous.*

(1) Team or player seating, section 221.2.1.4.

(2) Accessible route to bowling lanes, section. 206.2.11.

(3) Accessible route in court sports facilities, section 206.2.12.

(3) *Historic preservation programs.* In meeting the requirements of § 35.150(a) in historic preservation programs, a public entity shall give priority to methods that provide physical access to individuals with disabilities. In cases where a physical alteration to an historic property is not required because of paragraph (a)(2) or (a)(3) of this section, alternative methods of achieving program accessibility include —

(i) Using audio-visual materials and devices to depict those portions of an historic property that cannot otherwise be made accessible;

(ii) Assigning persons to guide individuals with handicaps into or through portions of historic properties that cannot otherwise be made accessible; or

(iii) Adopting other innovative methods.

(c) *Time period for compliance.* Where structural changes in facilities are undertaken to comply with the obligations established under this section, such changes shall be made within three years of January 26, 1992, but in any event as expeditiously as possible.

(d) *Transition plan.*

(1) In the event that structural changes to facilities will be undertaken to achieve program accessibility, a public entity that employs 50 or more persons shall develop, within six months of January 26, 1992, a transition plan setting forth the steps necessary to complete such changes. A public entity shall provide an opportunity to interested persons, including individuals with disabilities or organizations representing individuals with disabilities, to participate in the development of the transition plan by submitting comments. A copy of the transition plan shall be made available for public inspection.

(2) If a public entity has responsibility or authority over streets, roads, or

walkways, its transition plan shall include a schedule for providing curb ramps or other sloped areas where pedestrian walks cross curbs, giving priority to walkways serving entities covered by the Act, including State and local government offices and facilities, transportation, places of public accommodation, and employers, followed by walkways serving other areas.

(3) The plan shall, at a minimum —

(i) Identify physical obstacles in the public entity's facilities that limit the accessibility of its programs or activities to individuals with disabilities;

(ii) Describe in detail the methods that will be used to make the facilities accessible;

(iii) Specify the schedule for taking the steps necessary to achieve compliance with this section and, if the time period of the transition plan is longer than one year, identify steps that will be taken during each year of the transition period; and

(iv) Indicate the official responsible for implementation of the plan.

(4) If a public entity has already complied with the transition plan requirement of a Federal agency regulation implementing section 504 of the Rehabilitation Act of 1973, then the requirements of this paragraph (d) shall apply only to those policies and practices that were not included in the previous transition plan.

§ 35.151   New construction and alterations

(a)   *Design and construction.*

(1) Each facility or part of a facility constructed by, on behalf of, or for the use of a public entity shall be designed and constructed in such manner that the facility or part of the facility is readily accessible to and usable by individuals with disabilities, if the construction was commenced after January 26, 1992.

(2)   *Exception for structural impracticability.*

(i) Full compliance with the requirements of this section is not required where a public entity can demonstrate that it is structurally impracticable to meet the requirements. Full compliance will be considered structurally impracticable only in those rare circumstances when the unique characteristics of terrain prevent the incorporation of accessibility features.

(ii) If full compliance with this section would be structurally impracticable, compliance with this section is required to the extent that it is not structurally impracticable. In that case, any portion of the facility that can be made accessible shall be made accessible to the extent that it is not structurally impracticable.

(iii) If providing accessibility in conformance with this section to individuals with certain disabilities (*e.g.*, those who use wheelchairs) would be structurally impracticable, accessibility shall nonetheless be ensured to persons with other types of disabilities, (*e.g.*, those who use crutches or who have sight, hearing, or mental impairments) in accor-

dance with this section.

(b) *Alterations.*

(1) Each facility or part of a facility altered by, on behalf of, or for the use of a public entity in a manner that affects or could affect the usability of the facility or part of the facility shall, to the maximum extent feasible, be altered in such manner that the altered portion of the facility is readily accessible to and usable by individuals with disabilities, if the alteration was commenced after January 26, 1992.

(2) The path of travel requirements of § 35.151(b)(4) shall apply only to alterations undertaken solely for purposes other than to meet the program accessibility requirements of § 35.150.

(3) (i) Alterations to historic properties shall comply, to the maximum extent feasible, with the provisions applicable to historic properties in the design standards specified in § 35.151(c).

(ii) If it is not feasible to provide physical access to an historic property in a manner that will not threaten or destroy the historic significance of the building or facility, alternative methods of access shall be provided pursuant to the requirements of § 35.150.

(4) *Path of travel.* An alteration that affects or could affect the usability of or access to an area of a facility that contains a primary function shall be made so as to ensure that, to the maximum extent feasible, the path of travel to the altered area and the restrooms, telephones, and drinking fountains serving the altered area are readily accessible to and usable by individuals with disabilities, including individuals who use wheelchairs, unless the cost and scope of such alterations is disproportionate to the cost of the overall alteration.

(i) *Primary function.* A "primary function" is a major activity for which the facility is intended. Areas that contain a primary function include, but are not limited to, the dining area of a cafeteria, the meeting rooms in a conference center, as well as offices and other work areas in which the activities of the public entity using the facility are carried out.

(A) Mechanical rooms, boiler rooms, supply storage rooms, employee lounges or locker rooms, janitorial closets, entrances, and corridors are not areas containing a primary function. Restrooms are not areas containing a primary function unless the provision of restrooms is a primary purpose of the area, *e.g.*, in highway rest stops.

(B) For the purposes of this section, alterations to windows, hardware, controls, electrical outlets, and signage shall not be deemed to be alterations that affect the usability of or access to an area containing a primary function.

(ii) A "path of travel" includes a continuous, unobstructed way of pedestrian passage by means of which the altered area may be approached, entered, and exited, and which connects the altered area with

an exterior approach (including sidewalks, streets, and parking areas), an entrance to the facility, and other parts of the facility.

(A) An accessible path of travel may consist of walks and sidewalks, curb ramps and other interior or exterior pedestrian ramps; clear floor paths through lobbies, corridors, rooms, and other improved areas; parking access aisles; elevators and lifts; or a combination of these elements.

(B) For the purposes of this section, the term "path of travel" also includes the restrooms, telephones, and drinking fountains serving the altered area.

(C) *Safe harbor.* If a public entity has constructed or altered required elements of a path of travel in accordance with the specifications in either the 1991 Standards or the Uniform Federal Accessibility Standards before March 15, 2012, the public entity is not required to retrofit such elements to reflect incremental changes in the 2010 Standards solely because of an alteration to a primary function area served by that path of travel.

(iii) *Disproportionality.*

(A) Alterations made to provide an accessible path of travel to the altered area will be deemed disproportionate to the overall alteration when the cost exceeds 20% of the cost of the alteration to the primary function area.

(B) Costs that may be counted as expenditures required to provide an accessible path of travel may include:

(1) Costs associated with providing an accessible entrance and an accessible route to the altered area, for example, the cost of widening doorways or installing ramps;

(2) Costs associated with making restrooms accessible, such as installing grab bars, enlarging toilet stalls, insulating pipes, or installing accessible faucet controls;

(3) Costs associated with providing accessible telephones, such as relocating the telephone to an accessible height, installing amplification devices, or installing a text telephone (TTY); and

(4) Costs associated with relocating an inaccessible drinking fountain.

(iv) *Duty to provide accessible features in the event of disproportionality.*

(A) When the cost of alterations necessary to make the path of travel to the altered area fully accessible is disproportionate to the cost of the overall alteration, the path of travel shall be made accessible to the extent that it can be made accessible without incurring disproportionate costs.

(B) In choosing which accessible elements to provide, priority should be given to those elements that will provide the greatest access, in the following order —

(1) An accessible entrance;

(2) An accessible route to the altered area;

(3) At least one accessible restroom for each sex or a single unisex restroom;

(4) Accessible telephones;

(5) Accessible drinking fountains; and

(6) When possible, additional accessible elements such as parking, storage, and alarms.

(v) *Series of smaller alterations.*

(A) The obligation to provide an accessible path of travel may not be evaded by performing a series of small alterations to the area served by a single path of travel if those alterations could have been performed as a single undertaking.

(B) *(1)* If an area containing a primary function has been altered without providing an accessible path of travel to that area, and subsequent alterations of that area, or a different area on the same path of travel, are undertaken within three years of the original alteration, the total cost of alterations to the primary function areas on that path of travel during the preceding three-year period shall be considered in determining whether the cost of making that path of travel accessible is disproportionate.

(2) Only alterations undertaken on or after March 15, 2011 shall be considered in determining if the cost of providing an accessible path of travel is disproportionate to the overall cost of the alterations.

(c) *Accessibility standards and compliance date.*

(1) If physical construction or alterations commence after July 26, 1992, but prior to September 15, 2010, then new construction and alterations subject to this section must comply with either the UFAS or the 1991 Standards except that the elevator exemption contained at section 4.1.3(5) and section 4.1.6(1)(k) of the 1991 Standards shall not apply. Departures from particular requirements of either standard by the use of other methods shall be permitted when it is clearly evident that equivalent access to the facility or part of the facility is thereby provided.

(2) If physical construction or alterations commence on or after September 15, 2010, and before March 15, 2012, then new construction and alterations subject to this section may comply with one of the following: the 2010 Standards, UFAS, or the 1991 Standards except that the elevator exemption contained at section 4.1.3(5) and section 4.1.6(1)(k) of the 1991 Standards shall not apply. Departures from particular requirements of either standard

by the use of other methods shall be permitted when it is clearly evident that equivalent access to the facility or part of the facility is thereby provided.

(3) If physical construction or alterations commence on or after March 15, 2012, then new construction and alterations subject to this section shall comply with the 2010 Standards.

(4) For the purposes of this section, ceremonial groundbreaking or razing of structures prior to site preparation do not commence physical construction or alterations.

(5) *Noncomplying new construction and alterations.*

(i) Newly constructed or altered facilities or elements covered by §§ 35.151(a) or (b) that were constructed or altered before March 15, 2012, and that do not comply with the 1991 Standards or with UFAS shall before March 15, 2012, be made accessible in accordance with either the 1991 Standards, UFAS, or the 2010 Standards.

(ii) Newly constructed or altered facilities or elements covered by §§ 35.151(a) or (b) that are constructed or altered on or after March 15, 2012, and that do not comply with the 1991 Standards or with UFAS shall, on or after March 15, 2012, be made accessible in accordance with the 2010 Standards.

• Appendix to § 35.151(c)

Compliance Date for New Construction or Alterations	Applicable Standards
Before September 15, 2010	1991 Standards or UFAS
On or after September 15, 2010, and before March 15, 2012	1991 Standards, UFAS, or 2010 Standards
On or after March 15, 2012	2010 Standards

(d) *Scope of coverage.* The 1991 Standards and the 2010 Standards apply to fixed or built-in elements of buildings, structures, site improvements, and pedestrian routes or vehicular ways located on a site. Unless specifically stated otherwise, the advisory notes, appendix notes, and figures contained in the 1991 Standards and the 2010 Standards explain or illustrate the requirements of the rule; they do not establish enforceable requirements.

(e) *Social service center establishments.* Group homes, halfway houses, shelters, or similar social service center establishments that provide either temporary sleeping accommodations or residential dwelling units that are subject to this section shall comply with the provisions of the 2010 Standards applicable to residential facilities, including, but not limited to, the provisions in sections 233 and 809.

(1) In sleeping rooms with more than 25 beds covered by this section, a minimum of 5% of the beds shall have clear floor space complying with section 806.2.3 of the 2010 Standards.

(2) Facilities with more than 50 beds covered by this section that provide common use bathing facilities, shall provide at least one roll-in shower with a seat that complies with the relevant provisions of section 608 of the 2010 Standards. Transfer-type showers are not permitted in lieu of a roll-in shower with a seat, and the exceptions in sections 608.3 and 608.4 for residential dwelling units are not permitted. When separate shower facilities are provided for men and for women, at least one roll-in shower shall be provided for each group.

(f) *Housing at a place of education.* Housing at a place of education that is subject to this section shall comply with the provisions of the 2010 Standards applicable to transient lodging, including, but not limited to, the requirements for transient lodging guest rooms in sections 224 and 806 subject to the following exceptions. For the purposes of the application of this section, the term "sleeping room" is intended to be used interchangeably with the term "guest room" as it is used in the transient lodging standards.

(1) Kitchens within housing units containing accessible sleeping rooms with mobility features (including suites and clustered sleeping rooms) or on floors containing accessible sleeping rooms with mobility features shall provide turning spaces that comply with section 809.2.2 of the 2010 Standards and kitchen work surfaces that comply with section 804.3 of the 2010 Standards.

(2) Multi-bedroom housing units containing accessible sleeping rooms with mobility features shall have an accessible route throughout the unit in accordance with section 809.2 of the 2010 Standards.

(3) Apartments or townhouse facilities that are provided by or on behalf of a place of education, which are leased on a year-round basis exclusively to graduate students or faculty, and do not contain any public use or common use areas available for educational programming, are not subject to the transient lodging standards and shall comply with the requirements for residential facilities in sections 233 and 809 of the 2010 Standards.

(g) *Assembly areas.* Assembly areas subject to this section shall comply with the provisions of the 2010 Standards applicable to assembly areas, including, but not limited to, sections 221 and 802. In addition, assembly areas shall ensure that —

(1) In stadiums, arenas, and grandstands, wheelchair spaces and companion seats are dispersed to all levels that include seating served by an accessible route;

(2) Assembly areas that are required to horizontally disperse wheelchair spaces and companion seats by section 221.2.3.1 of the 2010 Standards and have seating encircling, in whole or in part, a field of play or performance area shall disperse wheelchair spaces and companion seats around that field of play or performance area;

(3) Wheelchair spaces and companion seats are not located on (or obstructed by) temporary platforms or other movable structures, except that

when an entire seating section is placed on temporary platforms or other movable structures in an area where fixed seating is not provided, in order to increase seating for an event, wheelchair spaces and companion seats may be placed in that section. When wheelchair spaces and companion seats are not required to accommodate persons eligible for those spaces and seats, individual, removable seats may be placed in those spaces and seats;

(4) Stadium-style movie theaters shall locate wheelchair spaces and companion seats on a riser or cross-aisle in the stadium section that satisfies at least one of the following criteria —

(i) It is located within the rear 60% of the seats provided in an auditorium; or

(ii) It is located within the area of an auditorium in which the vertical viewing angles (as measured to the top of the screen) are from the 40th to the 100th percentile of vertical viewing angles for all seats as ranked from the seats in the first row (1st percentile) to seats in the back row (100th percentile).

(h) *Medical care facilities.* Medical care facilities that are subject to this section shall comply with the provisions of the 2010 Standards applicable to medical care facilities, including, but not limited to, sections 223 and 805. In addition, medical care facilities that do not specialize in the treatment of conditions that affect mobility shall disperse the accessible patient bedrooms required by section 223.2.1 of the 2010 Standards in a manner that is proportionate by type of medical specialty.

(i) *Curb ramps.*

(1) Newly constructed or altered streets, roads, and highways must contain curb ramps or other sloped areas at any intersection having curbs or other barriers to entry from a street level pedestrian walkway.

(2) Newly constructed or altered street level pedestrian walkways must contain curb ramps or other sloped areas at intersections to streets, roads, or highways.

(j) *Facilities with residential dwelling units for sale to individual owners.*

(1) Residential dwelling units designed and constructed or altered by public entities that will be offered for sale to individuals shall comply with the requirements for residential facilities in the 2010 Standards including sections 233 and 809.

(2) The requirements of paragraph (1) also apply to housing programs that are operated by public entities where design and construction of particular residential dwelling units take place only after a specific buyer has been identified. In such programs, the covered entity must provide the units that comply with the requirements for accessible features to those pre-identified buyers with disabilities who have requested such a unit.

(k) *Detention and correctional facilities.*

(1) New construction of jails, prisons, and other detention and correc-

tional facilities shall comply with the 2010 Standards except that public entities shall provide accessible mobility features complying with section 807.2 of the 2010 Standards for a minimum of 3%, but no fewer than one, of the total number of cells in a facility. Cells with mobility features shall be provided in each classification level.

(2) *Alterations to detention and correctional facilities.* Alterations to jails, prisons, and other detention and correctional facilities shall comply with the 2010 Standards except that public entities shall provide accessible mobility features complying with section 807.2 of the 2010 Standards for a minimum of 3%, but no fewer than one, of the total number of cells being altered until at least 3%, but no fewer than one, of the total number of cells in a facility shall provide mobility features complying with section 807.2. Altered cells with mobility features shall be provided in each classification level. However, when alterations are made to specific cells, detention and correctional facility operators may satisfy their obligation to provide the required number of cells with mobility features by providing the required mobility features in substitute cells (cells other than those where alterations are originally planned), provided that each substitute cell —

(i) Is located within the same prison site;

(ii) Is integrated with other cells to the maximum extent feasible;

(iii) Has, at a minimum, equal physical access as the altered cells to areas used by inmates or detainees for visitation, dining, recreation, educational programs, medical services, work programs, religious services, and participation in other programs that the facility offers to inmates or detainees; and,

(iv) If it is technically infeasible to locate a substitute cell within the same prison site, a substitute cell must be provided at another prison site within the corrections system.

(3) With respect to medical and long-term care facilities in jails, prisons, and other detention and correctional facilities, public entities shall apply the 2010 Standards technical and scoping requirements for those facilities irrespective of whether those facilities are licensed.

§ 35.152   Jails, detention and correctional facilities, and community correctional facilities.

(a) *General.* This section applies to public entities that are responsible for the operation or management of adult and juvenile justice jails, detention and correctional facilities, and community correctional facilities, either directly or through contractual, licensing, or other arrangements with public or private entities, in whole or in part, including private correctional facilities.

(b) *Discrimination prohibited.*

(1) Public entities shall ensure that qualified inmates or detainees with disabilities shall not, because a facility is inaccessible to or unusable by individuals with disabilities, be excluded from participation in, or be denied

the benefits of, the services, programs, or activities of a public entity, or be subjected to discrimination by any public entity.

(2) Public entities shall ensure that inmates or detainees with disabilities are housed in the most integrated setting appropriate to the needs of the individuals. Unless it is appropriate to make an exception, a public entity —

(i) Shall not place inmates or detainees with disabilities in inappropriate security classifications because no accessible cells or beds are available;

(ii) Shall not place inmates or detainees with disabilities in designated medical areas unless they are actually receiving medical care or treatment;

(iii) Shall not place inmates or detainees with disabilities in facilities that do not offer the same programs as the facilities where they would otherwise be housed; and

(iv) Shall not deprive inmates or detainees with disabilities of visitation with family members by placing them in distant facilities where they would not otherwise be housed.

(3) Public entities shall implement reasonable policies, including physical modifications to additional cells in accordance with the 2010 Standards, so as to ensure that each inmate with a disability is housed in a cell with the accessible elements necessary to afford the inmate access to safe, appropriate housing.

§§ 35.153–35.159 [Reserved]

Subpart E Communications

§ 35.160 General.

(a) (1) A public entity shall take appropriate steps to ensure that communications with applicants, participants, members of the public, **and companions with disabilities** are as effective as communications with others.

(2) For purposes of this section, "companion" means a family member, friend, or associate of an individual seeking access to a service, program, or activity of a public entity, who, along with such individual, is an appropriate person with whom the public entity should communicate.

(b) (1) A public entity shall furnish appropriate auxiliary aids and services where necessary to afford qualified individuals with disabilities, **including applicants, participants, companions, and members of the public,** an equal opportunity to participate in, and enjoy the benefits of, a service, program, or activity of a public entity.

(2) The type of auxiliary aid or service necessary to ensure effective communication will vary in accordance with the method of communication used by the individual; the nature, length, and complexity of the communication involved; and the context in which the communication is taking place. In determining what types of auxiliary aids and services are necessary, a public

entity shall give primary consideration to the requests of individuals with disabilities. **In order to be effective, auxiliary aids and services must be provided in accessible formats, in a timely manner, and in such a way as to protect the privacy and independence of the individual with a disability.**

(c) (1) A public entity shall not require an individual with a disability to bring another individual to interpret for him or her.

(2) A public entity shall not rely on an adult accompanying an individual with a disability to interpret or facilitate communication except —

(i) In an emergency involving an imminent threat to the safety or welfare of an individual or the public where there is no interpreter available; or

(ii) Where the individual with a disability specifically requests that the accompanying adult interpret or facilitate communication, the accompanying adult agrees to provide such assistance, and reliance on that adult for such assistance is appropriate under the circumstances.

(3) A public entity shall not rely on a minor child to interpret or facilitate communication, except in an emergency involving an imminent threat to the safety or welfare of an individual or the public where there is no interpreter available.

(d) *Video remote interpreting (VRI) services.* A public entity that chooses to provide qualified interpreters via VRI services shall ensure that it provides —

(1) Real-time, full-motion video and audio over a dedicated high-speed, wide-bandwidth video connection or wireless connection that delivers high-quality video images that do not produce lags, choppy, blurry, or grainy images, or irregular pauses in communication;

(2) A sharply delineated image that is large enough to display the interpreter's face, arms, hands, and fingers, and the participating individual's face, arms, hands, and fingers, regardless of his or her body position;

(3) A clear, audible transmission of voices; and

(4) Adequate training to users of the technology and other involved individuals so that they may quickly and efficiently set up and operate the VRI.

§ 35.161   Telecommunications.

(a) Where a public entity communicates by telephone with applicants and beneficiaries, **text telephones (TTYs)** or equally effective telecommunications systems shall be used to communicate with individuals **who are deaf or hard of hearing or have speech impairments.**

(b) **When a public entity uses an automated-attendant system, including, but not limited to, voice mail and messaging, or an interactive voice response system, for receiving and directing incoming telephone calls, that system must provide effective real-time communication with individuals using auxiliary aids and services, including TTYs and all forms of FCC-approved telecommu-**

nications relay system, including Internet-based relay systems.

(c) A public entity shall respond to telephone calls from a telecommunications relay service established under title IV of the ADA in the same manner that it responds to other telephone calls.

§ 35.162   Telephone emergency services

Telephone emergency services, including 911 services, shall provide direct access to individuals who use TDD's and computer modems.

§ 35.163   Information and signage

(a) A public entity shall ensure that interested persons, including persons with impaired vision or hearing, can obtain information as to the existence and location of accessible services, activities, and facilities.

(b) A public entity shall provide signage at all inaccessible entrances to each of its facilities, directing users to an accessible entrance or to a location at which they can obtain information about accessible facilities. The international symbol for accessibility shall be used at each accessible entrance of a facility.

§ 35.164   Duties

This subpart does not require a public entity to take any action that it can demonstrate would result in a fundamental alteration in the nature of a service, program, or activity or in undue financial and administrative burdens. In those circumstances where personnel of the public entity believe that the proposed action would fundamentally alter the service, program, or activity or would result in undue financial and administrative burdens, a public entity has the burden of proving that compliance with this subpart would result in such alteration or burdens. The decision that compliance would result in such alteration or burdens must be made by the head of the public entity or his or her designee after considering all resources available for use in the funding and operation of the service, program, or activity and must be accompanied by a written statement of the reasons for reaching that conclusion. If an action required to comply with this subpart would result in such an alteration or such burdens, a public entity shall take any other action that would not result in such an alteration or such burdens but would nevertheless ensure that, to the maximum extent possible, individuals with disabilities receive the benefits or services provided by the public entity.

§§ 35.165–35.169   [Reserved]

Subpart F   Compliance Procedures

§ 35.170   Complaints

(a) *Who may file.* An individual who believes that he or she or a specific class of individuals has been subjected to discrimination on the basis of disability by a public entity may, by himself or herself or by an authorized representative, file a complaint under this part.

(b) *Time for filing.* A complaint must be filed not later than 180 days from the date of the alleged discrimination, unless the time for filing is extended by the

designated agency for good cause shown. A complaint is deemed to be filed under this section on the date it is first filed with any Federal agency.

(c) *Where to file.* An individual may file a complaint with any agency that he or she believes to be the appropriate agency designated under subpart G of this part, or with any agency that provides funding to the public entity that is the subject of the complaint, or with the Department of Justice for referral as provided in § 35.171(a)(2).

§ 35.171   Acceptance of complaints

(a) *Receipt of complaints.*

(1) (i) Any Federal agency that receives a complaint of discrimination on the basis of disability by a public entity shall promptly review the complaint to determine whether it has jurisdiction over the complaint under section 504.

(ii) If the agency does not have section 504 jurisdiction, it shall promptly determine whether it is the designated agency under subpart G of this part responsible for complaints filed against that public entity.

(2) (i) If an agency other than the Department of Justice determines that it does not have section 504 jurisdiction and is not the designated agency, it shall promptly refer the complaint **to the appropriate designated agency, the agency that has section 504 jurisdiction, or the Department of Justice, and so notify the complainant.**

(ii) When the Department of Justice receives a complaint for which it does not have jurisdiction under section 504 and is not the designated agency, **it may exercise jurisdiction pursuant to § 35.190(e)** or refer the complaint to an agency that does have jurisdiction under section 504 or to the appropriate agency designated in subpart G of this part or, in the case of an employment complaint that is also subject to title I of the Act, to the Equal Employment Opportunity Commission.

(3) (i) If the agency that receives a complaint has section 504 jurisdiction, it shall process the complaint according to its procedures for enforcing section 504.

(ii) If the agency that receives a complaint does not have section 504 jurisdiction, but is the designated agency, it shall process the complaint according to the procedures established by this subpart.

(b) *Employment complaints.*

(1) If a complaint alleges employment discrimination subject to title I of the Act, and the agency has section 504 jurisdiction, the agency shall follow the procedures issued by the Department of Justice and the Equal Employment Opportunity Commission under section 107(b) of the Act.

(2) If a complaint alleges employment discrimination subject to title I of the Act, and the designated agency does not have section 504 jurisdiction, the agency shall refer the complaint to the Equal Employment Opportunity Commission for processing under title I of the Act.

(3) Complaints alleging employment discrimination subject to this part, but not to title I of the Act shall be processed in accordance with the procedures established by this subpart.

(c) *Complete complaints.*

(1) A designated agency shall accept all complete complaints under this section and shall promptly notify the complainant and the public entity of the receipt and acceptance of the complaint.

(2) If the designated agency receives a complaint that is not complete, it shall notify the complainant and specify the additional information that is needed to make the complaint a complete complaint. If the complainant fails to complete the complaint, the designated agency shall close the complaint without prejudice.

§ 35.172 Investigations and compliance reviews.

(a) **The designated agency shall investigate complaints for which it is responsible under § 35.171.**

(b) **The designated agency may conduct compliance reviews of public entities in order to ascertain whether there has been a failure to comply with the nondiscrimination requirements of this part.**

(c) **Where appropriate, the designated agency shall attempt informal resolution of any matter being investigated under this section, and, if resolution is not achieved and a violation is found, issue to the public entity and the complainant, if any, a Letter of Findings that shall include —**

(1) **Findings of fact and conclusions of law;**

(2) **A description of a remedy for each violation found (including compensatory damages where appropriate); and**

(3) **Notice of the rights and procedures available under paragraph (d) of this section and §§ 35.173 and 35.174.**

(d) **At any time, the complainant may file a private suit pursuant to section 203 of the Act, 42 U.S.C. 12133, whether or not the designated agency finds a violation.**

§ 35.173 Voluntary compliance agreements

(a) When the designated agency issues a noncompliance Letter of Findings, the designated agency shall —

(1) Notify the Assistant Attorney General by forwarding a copy of the Letter of Findings to the Assistant Attorney General; and

(2) Initiate negotiations with the public entity to secure compliance by voluntary means.

(b) Where the designated agency is able to secure voluntary compliance, the voluntary compliance agreement shall —

(1) Be in writing and signed by the parties;

(2) Address each cited violation;

(3) Specify the corrective or remedial action to be taken, within a stated period of time, to come into compliance;

(4) Provide assurance that discrimination will not recur; and

(5) Provide for enforcement by the Attorney General.

§ 35.174   Referral.

If the public entity declines to enter into voluntary compliance negotiations or if negotiations are unsuccessful, the designated agency shall refer the matter to the Attorney General with a recommendation for appropriate action.

§ 35.175   Attorney's fees.

In any action or administrative proceeding commenced pursuant to the Act or this part, the court or agency, in its discretion, may allow the prevailing party, other than the United States, a reasonable attorney's fee, including litigation expenses, and costs, and the United States shall be liable for the foregoing the same as a private individual.

§ 35.176   Alternative means of dispute resolution.

Where appropriate and to the extent authorized by law, the use of alternative means of dispute resolution, including settlement negotiations, conciliation, facilitation, mediation, factfinding, minitrials, and arbitration, is encouraged to resolve disputes arising under the Act and this part.

§ 35.177   Effect of unavailability of technical assistance.

A public entity shall not be excused from compliance with the requirements of this part because of any failure to receive technical assistance, including any failure in the development or dissemination of any technical assistance manual authorized by the Act.

§ 35.178   State immunity.

A State shall not be immune under the eleventh amendment to the Constitution of the United States from an action in Federal or State court of competent jurisdiction for a violation of this Act. In any action against a State for a violation of the requirements of this Act, remedies (including remedies both at law and in equity) are available for such a violation to the same extent as such remedies are available for such a violation in an action against any public or private entity other than a State.

§§ 35.179–35.189   [Reserved]

Subpart G   Designated Agencies

§ 35.190   Designated Agencies.

(a) The Assistant Attorney General shall coordinate the compliance activities of Federal agencies with respect to State and local government components, and shall provide policy guidance and interpretations to designated agencies to ensure the consistent and effective implementation of the requirements of this part.

(b) The Federal agencies listed in paragraph (b)(1)–(8) of this section shall have responsibility for the implementation of subpart F of this part for components of State and local governments that exercise responsibilities, regulate, or administer services, programs, or activities in the following functional areas.

(1) *Department of Agriculture*: All programs, services, and regulatory activities relating to farming and the raising of livestock, including extension services.

(2) *Department of Education*: All programs, services, and regulatory activities relating to the operation of elementary and secondary education systems and institutions, institutions of higher education and vocational education (other than schools of medicine, dentistry, nursing, and other health-related schools), and libraries.

(3) *Department of Health and Human Services*: All programs, services, and regulatory activities relating to the provision of health care and social services, including schools of medicine, dentistry, nursing, and other health-related schools, the operation of health care and social service providers and institutions, including "grass-roots" and community services organizations and programs, and preschool and daycare programs.

(4) *Department of Housing and Urban Development*: All programs, services, and regulatory activities relating to state and local public housing, and housing assistance and referral.

(5) *Department of Interior*: All programs, services, and regulatory activities relating to lands and natural resources, including parks and recreation, water and waste management, environmental protection, energy, historic and cultural preservation, and museums.

(6) *Department of Justice*: All programs, services, and regulatory activities relating to law enforcement, public safety, and the administration of justice, including courts and correctional institutions; commerce and industry, including general economic development, banking and finance, consumer protection, insurance, and small business; planning, development, and regulation (unless assigned to other designated agencies); state and local government support services (*e.g.*, audit, personnel, comptroller, administrative services); all other government functions not assigned to other designated agencies.

(7) *Department of Labor*: All programs, services, and regulatory activities relating to labor and the work force.

(8) *Department of Transportation*: All programs, services, and regulatory activities relating to transportation, including highways, public transportation, traffic management (non-law enforcement), automobile licensing and inspection, and driver licensing.

(c) Responsibility for the implementation of subpart F of this part for components of State or local governments that exercise responsibilities, regulate, or administer services, programs, or activities relating to functions not assigned to specific designated agencies by paragraph (b) of this section may be assigned to other specific agencies by the Department of Justice.

(d) If two or more agencies have apparent responsibility over a complaint, the Assistant Attorney General shall determine which one of the agencies shall be the designated agency for purposes of that complaint.

(e) When the Department receives a complaint directed to the Attorney General alleging a violation of this part that may fall within the jurisdiction of a designated agency or another Federal agency that may have jurisdiction under section 504, the Department may exercise its discretion to retain the complaint for investigation under this part.

§§ 35.191–35.999   [Reserved]

Chapter 5
DOJ TITLE II
SECTION BY SECTION ANALYSIS

28 CFR PART 35 APPENDIX A

Appendix A to Part 35 — Guidance to Revisions to ADA Regulation on Nondiscrimination on the Basis of Disability in State and Local Government Services

[Note: This Appendix contains guidance providing a section-by-section analysis of the revisions to 28 CFR part 35 published on September 15, 2010.]

SECTION-BY-SECTION ANALYSIS AND RESPONSE TO PUBLIC COMMENTS

This section provides a detailed description of the Department's changes to the title II regulation, the reasoning behind those changes, and responses to public comments received on these topics. The Section-by-Section Analysis follows the order of the title II regulation itself, except that, if the Department has not changed a regulatory section, the unchanged section has not been mentioned.

Subpart A — General

Section 35.104 Definitions

"1991 Standards" and "2004 ADAAG"

The Department has included in the final rule new definitions of both the "1991 Standards" and the "2004 ADAAG." The term "1991 Standards" refers to the ADA Standards for Accessible Design, originally published on July 26, 1991, and republished as Appendix D to part 36. The term "2004 ADAAG" refers to ADA Chapter 1, ADA Chapter 2, and Chapters 3 through 10 of the Americans with Disabilities Act and Architectural Barriers Act Accessibility Guidelines, which were issued by the Access Board on July 23, 2004, 36 CFR 1191, app. B and D (2009), and which the Department has adopted in this final rule. These terms are included in the definitions section for ease of reference.

"2010 Standards"

The Department has added to the final rule a definition of the term "2010 Standards." The term "2010 Standards" refers to the 2010 ADA Standards for Accessible Design, which consist of the 2004 ADAAG and the requirements contained in § 35.151.

"Auxiliary Aids and Services"

In the NPRM, the Department proposed revisions to the definition of auxiliary aids and services under § 35.104 to include several additional types of auxiliary aids that have become more readily available since the promulgation of the 1991 title II regulation, and in recognition of new technology and devices available in some places that may provide effective communication in some situations.

The NPRM proposed adding an explicit reference to written notes in the definition of "auxiliary aids." Although this policy was already enunciated in the Department's 1993 Title II Technical Assistance Manual at II — 7.1000, the Department proposed inclusion in the regulation itself because some Title II entities do not understand that exchange of written notes using paper and pencil is an available option in some circumstances. *See* Department of Justice, *The Americans with Disabilities Act, Title II Technical Assistance Manual Covering State and Local Government Programs and Services* (1993), available at http://www.ada.gov/taman2.html. Comments from several disability advocacy organizations and individuals discouraged the Department from including the exchange of written notes in the list of available auxiliary aids in § 35.104. Advocates and persons with disabilities requested explicit limits on the use of written notes as a form of auxiliary aid because, they argue, most exchanges are not simple and are not communicated effectively using handwritten notes. One major advocacy organization, for example, noted that the speed at which individuals communicate orally or use sign language averages about 200 words per minute or more while exchange of notes often leads to truncated or incomplete communication. For persons whose primary language is American Sign Language (ASL), some commenters pointed out, using written English in exchange of notes often is ineffective because ASL syntax and vocabulary is dissimilar from English. By contrast, some commenters from professional medical associations sought more specific guidance on when notes are allowed, especially in the context of medical offices and health care situations.

Exchange of notes likely will be effective in situations that do not involve substantial conversation, for example, blood work for routine lab tests or regular allergy shots. Video Interpreting Services (hereinafter referred to as "video remote interpreting services" or VRI) or an interpreter should be used when the matter involves greater complexity, such as in situations requiring communication of medical history or diagnoses, in conversations about medical procedures and treatment decisions, or when giving instructions for care at home or elsewhere. In the Section-By-Section Analysis of § 35.160 (Communications) below, the Department discusses in greater detail the kinds of situations in which interpreters or captioning would be necessary. Additional guidance on this issue can be found in a number of agreements entered into with health-care providers and hospitals that are available on the Department's Web site at http://www.ada.gov.

In the NPRM, in paragraph (1) of the definition in § 35.104, the Department proposed replacing the term "telecommunications devices for deaf persons (TDD)" with the term "text telephones (TTYs)." TTY has become the commonly accepted term and is consistent with the terminology used by the Access Board in the 2004 ADAAG. Commenters representing advocates and persons with disabilities expressed approval of the substitution of TTY for TDD in the proposed regulation.

Commenters also expressed the view that the Department should expand paragraph (1) of the definition of auxiliary aids to include "TTY's and other voice, text, and video-based telecommunications products and systems such as videophones and captioned telephones." The Department has considered these comments and has revised the definition of "auxiliary aids" to include references to voice, text, and video-based telecommunications products and systems, as well as accessible electronic and information technology.

In the NPRM, the Department also proposed including a reference in paragraph (1) to a new technology, Video Interpreting Services (VIS). The reference remains in the final rule. VIS is discussed in the Section-By- Section Analysis below in reference to § 35.160 (Communications), but is referred to as VRI in both the final rule and Appendix A to more accurately reflect the terminology used in other regulations and among users of the technology.

In the NPRM, the Department noted that technological advances in the 18 years since the ADA's enactment had increased the range of auxiliary aids and services for those who are blind or have low vision. As a result the Department proposed additional examples to paragraph (2) of the definition, including Brailled materials and displays, screen reader software, optical readers, secondary auditory programs (SAP), and accessible electronic and information technology. Some commenters asked for more detailed requirements for auxiliary aids for persons with vision disabilities. The Department has decided it will not make additional changes to that provision at this time.

Several comments suggested expanding the auxiliary aids provision for persons who are both deaf and blind, and in particular, to include in the list of auxiliary aids a new category, "support service providers (SSP)," which was described in comments as a navigator and communication facilitator. The Department believes that services provided by communication facilitators are already encompassed in the requirement to provide qualified interpreters. Moreover, the Department is concerned that as described by the commenters, the category of support service providers would include some services that would be considered personal services and that do not qualify as auxiliary aids. Accordingly, the Department declines to add this new category to the list at this time.

Some commenters representing advocacy organizations and individuals asked the Department to explicitly require title II entities to make any or all of the devices or technology available in all situations upon the request of the person with a disability. The Department recognizes that such devices or technology may provide effective communication and in some circumstances may be effective for some persons, but the Department does not intend to require that every entity covered by title II provide every device or all new technology at all times as long as the communication that is provided is as effective as communication with others. The Department recognized in the preamble to the 1991 title II regulation that the list of auxiliary aids was "not an all-inclusive or exhaustive catalogue of possible or available auxiliary aids or services. It is not possible to provide an exhaustive list, and an attempt to do so would omit the new devices that will become available with emerging technology." 28 CFR part 35, app. A at 560 (2009). The Department continues to endorse that view; thus, the inclusion of a list of examples of possible auxiliary aids in the definition of "auxiliary aids" should not be read as a mandate for a title II entity to offer every possible auxiliary aid listed in the definition in every situation.

"Direct Threat"

In Appendix A of the Department's 1991 title II regulation, the Department included a detailed discussion of "direct threat" that, among other things, explained that "the principles established in § 36.208 of the Department's [title III] regulation" were "applicable" as well to title II, insofar as "questions of safety are involved." 28 CFR part 35, app. A at 565 (2009). In the final rule, the Department has included an explicit definition of "direct threat" that is parallel to the definition in the title III rule and placed it in the definitions section at § 35.104.

"Existing Facility"

The 1991 title II regulation provided definitions for "new construction" at § 35.151(a) and "alterations" at § 35.151(b). In contrast, the term "existing facility" was not explicitly defined, although it is used in the statute and regulations for title II. *See* 42 U.S.C. 12134(b); 28 CFR 35.150. It has been the Department's view that newly constructed or altered facilities are also existing facilities with continuing program access obligations, and that view is made explicit in this rule.

The classification of facilities under the ADA is neither static nor mutually exclusive. Newly constructed or altered facilities are also existing facilities. A newly constructed facility remains subject to the accessibility standards in effect at the time of design and construction, with respect to those elements for which, at that time, there were applicable ADA Standards. And at some point, the facility may undergo alterations, which are subject to the alterations requirements in effect at the time. *See* § 35.151(b)–(c). The fact that the facility is also an existing facility does not relieve the public entity of its obligations under the new construction and alterations requirements in this part.

For example, a facility constructed or altered after the effective date of the original title II regulations but prior to the effective date of the revised title II regulation and Standards, must have been built or altered in compliance with the Standards (or UFAS) in effect at that time, in order to be in compliance with the ADA. In addition, a "newly constructed" facility or "altered" facility is also an "existing facility" for purposes of application of the title II program accessibility requirements. Once the 2010 Standards take effect, they will become the new reference point for determining the program accessibility obligations of all existing facilities. This is because the ADA contemplates that as our knowledge and understanding of accessibility advances and evolves, this knowledge will be incorporated into and result in increased accessibility in the built environment. Under title II, this goal is accomplished through the statute's program access framework. While newly constructed or altered facilities must meet the accessibility standards in effect at the time, the fact that these facilities are also existing facilities ensures that the determination of whether a program is accessible is not frozen at the time of construction or alteration. Program access may require consideration of potential barriers to access that were not recognized as such at the time of construction or alteration, including, but not limited to, the elements that are first covered in the 2010 Standards, as that term is defined in § 35.104. Adoption of the 2010 Standards establishes a new reference point for title II entities that choose to make structural changes to existing facilities to meet their program access requirements.

The NPRM included the following proposed definition of "existing facility." "A facility that has been constructed and remains in existence on any given date." 73 FR 34466, 34504 (June 17, 2008). The Department received a number of comments on this issue. The commenters urged the Department to clarify that all buildings remain subject to the standards in effect at the time of their construction, that is, that a facility designed and constructed for first occupancy between January 26, 1992, and the effective date of the final rule is still considered "new construction" and that alterations occurring between January 26, 1992, and the effective date of the final rule are still considered "alterations."

The final rule includes clarifying language to ensure that the Department's interpretation is accurately reflected. As established by this rule, existing facility means a facility in existence on any given date, without regard to whether the facility may also be considered newly constructed or altered under this part. Thus, this definition reflects the Department's interpretation that public entities have program access requirements that are independent of, but may coexist with, requirements imposed by new construction or alteration requirements in those same facilities.

"Housing at a Place of Education"

The Department has added a new definition to § 35.104, "housing at a place of education," to clarify the types of educational housing programs that are covered by this title. This section defines "housing at a place of education" as "housing operated by or on behalf of an elementary, secondary, undergraduate, or postgraduate school, or other place of education, including dormitories, suites, apartments, or other places of residence." This definition does not apply to social service programs that combine residential housing with social services, such as a residential job training program.

"Other Power-Driven Mobility Device" and "Wheelchair"

Because relatively few individuals with disabilities were using nontraditional mobility devices in 1991, there was no pressing need for the 1991 title II regulation to define the terms "wheelchair" or "other power-driven mobility device," to expound on what would constitute a reasonable modification in policies, practices, or procedures under § 35.130(b)(7), or to set forth within that section specific requirements for the accommodation of mobility devices. Since the issuance of the 1991 title II regulation, however, the choices of mobility devices available to individuals with disabilities have increased dramatically. The Department has received complaints about and has become aware of situations where individuals with mobility disabilities have utilized devices that are not designed primarily for use by an individual with a mobility disability, including the Segway® Personal Transporter (Segway® PT), golf cars, all-terrain vehicles (ATVs), and other locomotion devices.

The Department also has received questions from public entities and individuals with mobility disabilities concerning which mobility devices must be accommodated and under what circumstances. Indeed, there has been litigation concerning the legal obligations of covered entities to accommodate individuals with mobility disabilities who wish to use an electronic personal assistance mobility device (EPAMD), such as the Segway® PT, as a mobility device. The Department has participated in such litigation as amicus curiae. *See Ault* v. *Walt Disney World Co.*, 2009 U.S. Dist. LEXIS 92911 (M.D. Fla. Oct. 6, 2009). Much of the litigation has involved shopping malls where businesses have refused to allow persons with disabilities to use EPAMDs. *See, e.g., McElroy* v. *Simon Property Group*, 2008 U.S. Dist. LEXIS 69622 (D. Kan. Sept. 15, 2008) (enjoining mall from prohibiting the use of a Segway® PT as a mobility device where an individual agrees to all of a mall's policies for use of the device, except indemnification); Shasta Clark, *Local Man Fighting Mall Over Right to Use Segway*, WATE 6 News, July 26, 2005, available at http://www.wate.com/Global/story.asp?s=3643674 (last visited June 24, 2010).

In response to questions and complaints from individuals with disabilities and covered entities concerning which mobility devices must be accommodated and under what circumstances, the Department began developing a framework to address the use of unique mobility devices, concerns about their safety, and the parameters for the circumstances under which these devices must be accommodated. As a result, the Department's NPRM proposed two new approaches to mobility devices. First, the Department proposed a two-tiered mobility device definition that defined the term "wheelchair" separately from "other power-driven mobility device." Second, the Department proposed requirements to allow the use of devices in each definitional category. In § 35.137(a), the NPRM proposed that wheelchairs and manually-powered mobility aids used by individuals with mobility disabilities shall be permitted in any areas open to pedestrian use. Section 35.137(b) of the NPRM provided that a public entity "shall make reasonable modifications in its policies, practices, and procedures to permit the use of other power-driven mobility devices by individuals with disabilities, unless the public entity can demonstrate that the use of the device is not reasonable or that its use will result in a fundamental alteration of the public entity's service, program, or activity." 73 FR 34466, 34504 (June 17, 2008).

The Department sought public comment with regard to whether these steps would, in fact, achieve clarity on these issues. Toward this end, the Department's NPRM asked several questions relating to the definitions of "wheelchair," "other power-driven mobility device," and "manually-powered mobility aids"; the best way to categorize different classes of mobility devices; the types of devices that should be included in each category; and the circumstances under which certain mobility devices must be accommodated or may be excluded pursuant to the policy adopted by the public entity.

Because the questions in the NPRM that concerned mobility devices and their accommodation were interrelated, many of the commenters' responses did not identify the specific question to which they were responding. Instead, the commenters grouped the questions together and provided comments accordingly. Most commenters spoke to the issues addressed in the Department's questions in broad terms and general concepts. As a result, the responses to the questions posed are discussed below in broadly grouped issue categories rather than on a question-by-question basis.

Two-tiered definitional approach. Commenters supported the Department's proposal to use a two-tiered definition of mobility device. Commenters nearly universally said that wheelchairs always should be accommodated and that they should never be subject to an assessment with regard to their admission to a particular public facility. In contrast, the vast majority of commenters indicated they were in favor of allowing public entities to conduct an assessment as to whether, and under which circumstances, other power-driven mobility devices would be allowed on-site.

Many commenters indicated their support for the two-tiered approach in responding to questions concerning the definition of "wheelchair" and "other-powered mobility device." Nearly every disability advocacy group said that the Department's two-tiered approach strikes the proper balance between ensuring access for individuals with disabilities and addressing fundamental alteration and safety concerns held by public entities; however, a minority of disability advocacy groups wanted other power-driven mobility devices to be included in the definition of "wheelchair." Most advocacy, nonprofit, and individual commenters supported the concept of a separate definition for "other power-driven mobility device" because it maintains existing legal protections for wheelchairs while recognizing that some devices that are not designed primarily for individuals with mobility disabilities have beneficial uses for individuals with mobility disabilities. They also favored this concept because it recognizes technological developments and that the innovative uses of varying devices may provide increased access to individuals with mobility disabilities.

Many environmental, transit system, and government commenters indicated they opposed in its entirety the concept of "other power-driven mobility devices" as a separate category. They believe that the creation of a second category of mobility devices will mean that other power-driven mobility devices, specifically ATVs and off-highway vehicles, must be allowed to go anywhere on national park lands, trails, recreational areas, etc.; will conflict with other Federal land management laws and regulations; will harm the environment and natural and cultural resources; will pose safety risks to users of these devices, as well as to pedestrians not expecting to encounter motorized devices in these settings; will interfere with the recreational enjoyment of these areas; and will require too much administrative work to regulate which devices are allowed and under which circumstances. These commenters all advocated a single category of mobility devices that excludes all fuel- powered devices.

Whether or not they were opposed to the two-tier approach in its entirety, virtually every environmental commenter and most government commenters associated with providing public transportation services or protecting land, natural resources, fish and game, etc., said that the definition of "other power-driven mobility device" is too broad. They suggested that they might be able to support the dual category approach if the definition of "other power-driven mobility device" were narrowed. They expressed general and program-specific concerns about permitting the use of other power-driven mobility devices. They noted the same concerns as those who opposed the two- tiered concept — that these devices create a host of environmental, safety, cost, administrative and conflict of law issues. Virtually all of these commenters indicated that their support for the dual approach and the concept of other power-driven mobility devices is, in large measure, due to the other power-driven mobility device assessment factors in § 35.137(c) of the NPRM.

By maintaining the two-tiered approach to mobility devices and defining "wheel-chair" separately from "other power-driven mobility device," the Department is able to preserve the protection users of traditional wheelchairs and other manually powered mobility aids have had since the ADA was enacted, while also recognizing that human ingenuity, personal choice, and new technologies have led to the use of devices that may be more beneficial for individuals with certain mobility disabilities.

Moreover, the Department believes the two-tiered approach gives public entities guidance to follow in assessing whether reasonable modifications can be made to permit the use of other power-driven mobility devices on-site and to aid in the development of policies describing the circumstances under which persons with disabilities may use such devices. The two- tiered approach neither mandates that all other power-driven mobility devices be accommodated in every circumstance, nor excludes these devices. This approach, in conjunction with the factor assessment provisions in § 35.137(b)(2), will serve as a mechanism by which public entities can evaluate their ability to accommodate other power-driven mobility devices. As will be discussed in more detail below, the assessment factors in § 35.137(b)(2) are designed to provide guidance to public entities regarding whether it is appropriate to bar the use of a specific "other power-driven mobility device in a specific facility. In making such a determination, a public entity must consider the device's type, size, weight, dimensions, and speed; the facility's volume of pedestrian traffic; the facility's design and operational characteristics; whether the device conflicts with legitimate safety requirements; and whether the device poses a substantial risk of serious harm to the immediate environment or natural or cultural resources, or conflicts with Federal land management laws or regulations. In addition, if under § 35.130(b)(7), the public entity claims that it cannot make reasonable modifications to its policies, practices, or procedures to permit the use of other power-driven mobility devices by individuals with disabilities, the burden of proof to demonstrate that such devices cannot be operated in accordance with legitimate safety requirements rests upon the public entity.

Categorization of wheelchair versus other power-driven mobility devices. Implicit in the creation of the two-tiered mobility device concept is the question of how to categorize which devices are wheelchairs and which are other power-driven mobility devices. Finding weight and size to be too restrictive, the vast majority of advocacy, nonprofit, and individual commenters opposed using the Department of Transportation's definition of "common wheelchair" to designate the mobility device's appropriate category. Commenters who generally supported using weight and size as the method of categorization did so because of their concerns about potentially detrimental impacts on the environment and cultural and natural resources; on the enjoyment of the facility by other recreational users, as well as their safety; on the administrative components of government agencies required to assess which devices are appropriate on narrow, steeply sloped, or foot-and-hoof only trails; and about the impracticality of accommodating such devices in public transportation settings.

Many environmental, transit system, and government commenters also favored using the device's intended-use to categorize which devices constitute wheelchairs and which are other power-driven mobility devices. Furthermore, the intended-use determinant received a fair amount of support from advocacy, nonprofit, and individual commenters, either because they sought to preserve the broad accommodation of wheelchairs or because they sympathized with concerns about individuals without mobility disabilities fraudulently bringing other power-driven mobility devices into public facilities.

Commenters seeking to have the Segway® PT included in the definition of "wheelchair" objected to classifying mobility devices on the basis of their intended use because they felt that such a classification would be unfair and prejudicial to Segway® PT users and would stifle personal choice, creativity, and innovation. Other advocacy and nonprofit commenters objected to employing an intended-use approach because of concerns that the focus would shift to an assessment of the device, rather than the needs or benefits to the individual with the mobility disability. They were of the view that the mobility-device classification should be based on its function — whether it is used for a mobility disability. A few commenters raised the concern that an intended-use approach might embolden public entities to assess whether an individual with a mobility disability really needs to use the other power-driven mobility device at issue or to question why a wheelchair would not provide sufficient mobility. Those citing objections to the intended use determinant indicated it would be more appropriate to make the categorization determination based on whether the device is being used for a mobility disability in the context of the impact of its use in a specific environment. Some of these commenters preferred this approach because it would allow the Segway® PT to be included in the definition of "wheelchair."

Many environmental and government commenters were inclined to categorize mobility devices by the way in which they are powered, such as battery-powered engines versus fuel or combustion engines. One commenter suggested using exhaust level as the determinant. Although there were only a few commenters who would make the determination based on indoor or outdoor use, there was nearly universal support for banning the indoor use of devices that are powered by fuel or combustion engines.

A few commenters thought it would be appropriate to categorize the devices based on their maximum speed. Others objected to this approach, stating that circumstances should dictate the appropriate speed at which mobility devices should be operated — for example, a faster speed may be safer when crossing streets than it would be for sidewalk use — and merely because a device can go a certain speed does not mean it will be operated at that speed.

The Department has decided to maintain the device's intended use as the appropriate determinant for which devices are categorized as "wheelchairs." However, because wheelchairs may be intended for use by individuals who have temporary conditions affecting mobility, the Department has decided that it is more appropriate to use the phrase "primarily designed" rather than "solely designed" in making such categorizations. The Department will not foreclose any future technological developments by identifying or banning specific devices or setting restrictions on size, weight, or dimensions. Moreover, devices designed primarily for use by individuals with mobility disabilities often are considered to be medical devices and are generally eligible for insurance reimbursement on this basis. Finally, devices designed primarily for use by individuals with mobility disabilities are less subject to fraud concerns because they were not designed to have a recreational component. Consequently, rarely, if ever, is any inquiry or assessment as to their appropriateness for use in a public entity necessary.

Definition of "wheelchair." In seeking public feedback on the NPRM's definition of "wheelchair," the Department explained its concern that the definition of "wheelchair" in section 508(c)(2) of the ADA (formerly section 507(c)(2), July 26, 1990, 104 Stat. 372, 42 U.S.C. 12207, renumbered section 508(c)(2), Public Law 110–325 section 6(a)(2), Sept. 25, 2008, 122 Stat. 3558), which pertains to Federal wilderness areas, is not specific enough to provide clear guidance in the array of settings covered by title II and that the stringent size and weight requirements for the Department of Transportation's definition of "common wheelchair" are not a good fit in the context of most public entities. The Department noted in the NPRM that it sought a definition of "wheelchair" that would include manually-operated and power-driven wheelchairs and mobility scooters (i.e., those that typically are single-user, have three to four wheels, and are appropriate for both indoor and outdoor pedestrian areas), as well as a variety of types of wheelchairs and mobility scooters with individualized or unique features or models with different numbers of wheels. The NPRM defined a wheelchair as "a device designed solely for use by an individual with a mobility impairment for the primary purpose of locomotion in typical indoor and outdoor pedestrian areas. A wheelchair may be manually-operated or power-driven." 73 FR 34466, 34479 (June 17, 2008). Although the NPRM's definition of "wheelchair" excluded mobility devices that are not designed solely for use by individuals with mobility disabilities, the Department, noting that the use of the Segway® PT by individuals with mobility disabilities is on the upswing, inquired as to whether this device should be included in the definition of "wheelchair."

Many environment and Federal government employee commenters objected to the Department's proposed definition of "wheelchair" because it differed from the definition of "wheelchair" found in section 508(c)(2) of the ADA — a definition used in the statute only in connection with a provision relating to the use of a wheelchair in a designated wilderness area. *See* 42 U.S.C. 12207(c)(1). Other government commenters associated with environmental issues wanted the phrase "outdoor pedestrian use" eliminated from the definition of "wheelchair." Some transit system commenters wanted size, weight, and dimensions to be part of the definition because of concerns about costs associated with having to accommodate devices that exceed the dimensions of the "common wheelchair" upon which the 2004 ADAAG was based.

Many advocacy, nonprofit, and individual commenters indicated that as long as the Department intends the scope of the term "mobility impairments" to include other disabilities that cause mobility impairments (e.g., respiratory, circulatory, stamina, etc.), they were in support of the language. Several commenters indicated a preference for the definition of "wheelchair" in section 508(c)(2) of the ADA. One commenter indicated a preference for the term "assistive device," as it is defined in the Rehabilitation Act of 1973, over the term "wheelchair." A few commenters indicated that strollers should be added to the preamble's list of examples of wheelchairs because parents of children with disabilities frequently use strollers as mobility devices until their children get older.

In the final rule, the Department has rearranged some wording and has made some changes in the terminology used in the definition of "wheelchair," but essentially has retained the definition, and therefore the rationale, that was set forth in the NPRM. Again, the text of the ADA makes the definition of "wheelchair" contained in section 508(c)(2) applicable only to the specific context of uses in designated wilderness areas, and therefore does not compel the use of that definition for any other purpose. Moreover, the Department maintains that limiting the definition to devices suitable for use in an "indoor pedestrian area" as provided for in section 508(c)(2) of the ADA, would ignore the technological advances in wheelchair design that have occurred since the ADA went into effect and that the inclusion of the phrase "indoor pedestrian area" in the definition of "wheelchair" would set back progress made by individuals with mobility disabilities who, for many years now, have been using devices designed for locomotion in indoor *and* outdoor settings. The Department has concluded that same rationale applies to placing limits on the size, weight, and dimensions of wheelchairs.

With regard to the term "mobility impairments," the Department intended a broad reading so that a wide range of disabilities, including circulatory and respiratory disabilities, that make walking difficult or impossible, would be included. In response to comments on this issue, the Department has revisited the issue and has concluded that the most apt term to achieve this intent is "mobility disability."

In addition, the Department has decided that it is more appropriate to use the phrase "primarily" designed for use by individuals with disabilities in the final rule, rather than "solely" designed for use by individuals with disabilities — the phrase proposed in the NPRM. The Department believes that this phrase more accurately covers the range of devices the Department intends to fall within the definition of "wheelchair."

After receiving comments that the word "typical" is vague and the phrase "pedestrian areas" is confusing to apply, particularly in the context of similar, but not identical, terms used in the proposed Standards, the Department decided to delete the term "typical indoor and outdoor pedestrian areas" from the final rule. Instead, the final rule references "indoor or of both indoor and outdoor locomotion," to make clear that the devices that fall within the definition of "wheelchair" are those that are used for locomotion on indoor and outdoor pedestrian paths or routes and not those that are intended exclusively for traversing undefined, unprepared, or unimproved paths or routes. Thus, the final rule defines the term "wheelchair" to mean "a manually- operated or power-driven device designed primarily for use by an individual with a mobility disability for the main purpose of indoor or of both indoor and outdoor locomotion."

Whether the definition of "wheelchair" *includes the Segway® PT.* As discussed above, because individuals with mobility disabilities are using the Segway® PT as a mobility device, the Department asked whether it should be included in the definition of "wheelchair." The basic Segway® PT model is a two-wheeled, gyroscopically-stabilized, battery-powered personal transportation device. The user stands on a platform suspended three inches off the ground by wheels on each side, grasps a T-shaped handle, and steers the device similarly to a bicycle. Most Segway® PTs can travel up to 12 ½ miles per hour, compared to the average pedestrian walking speed of three to four miles per hour and the approximate maximum speed for power- operated wheelchairs of six miles per hour. In a study of trail and other non-motorized transportation users including EPAMDs, the Federal Highway Administration (FHWA) found that the eye height of individuals using EPAMDs ranged from approximately 69 to 80 inches. *See* Federal Highway Administration, *Characteristics of Emerging Road and Trail Users and Their Safety* (Oct. 14, 2004), available at http://www.tfhrc.gov/safety/pubs/04103 (last visited June 24, 2010). Thus, the Segway® PT can operate at much greater speeds than wheelchairs, and the average user stands much taller than most wheelchair users.

The Segway® PT has been the subject of debate among users, pedestrians, disability advocates, State and local governments, businesses, and bicyclists. The fact that the Segway® PT is not designed primarily for use by individuals with disabilities, nor used primarily by persons with disabilities, complicates the question of to what extent individuals with disabilities should be allowed to operate them in areas and facilities where other power-driven mobility devices are not allowed. Those who question the use of the Segway® PT in pedestrian areas argue that the speed, size, and operating features of the devices make them too dangerous to operate alongside pedestrians and wheelchair users.

Comments regarding whether to include the Segway® PT in the definition of "wheelchair" were, by far, the most numerous received in the category of comments regarding wheelchairs and other power-driven mobility devices. Significant numbers of veterans with disabilities, individuals with multiple sclerosis, and those advocating on their behalf made concise statements of general support for the inclusion of the Segway® PT in the definition of "wheelchair." Two veterans offered extensive comments on the topic, along with a few advocacy and nonprofit groups and individuals with disabilities for whom sitting is uncomfortable or impossible.

While there may be legitimate safety issues for EPAMD users and bystanders in some circumstances, EPAMDs and other non- traditional mobility devices can deliver real benefits to individuals with disabilities. Among the reasons given by commenters to include the Segway® PT in the definition of "wheelchair" were that the Segway® PT is well-suited for individuals with particular conditions that affect mobility including multiple sclerosis, Parkinson's disease, chronic obstructive pulmonary disease, amputations, spinal cord injuries, and other neurological disabilities, as well as functional limitations, such as gait limitation, inability to sit or discomfort in sitting, and diminished stamina issues. Such individuals often find that EPAMDs are more comfortable and easier to use than more traditional mobility devices and assist with balance, circulation, and digestion in ways that wheelchairs do not. *See* Rachel Metz, *Disabled Embrace Segway*, New York Times, Oct. 14, 2004. Commenters specifically cited pressure relief, reduced spasticity, increased stamina, and improved respiratory, neurologic, and muscular health as secondary medical benefits from being able to stand.

Other arguments for including the Segway® PT in the definition of "wheelchair" were based on commenters' views that the Segway® PT offers benefits not provided by wheelchairs and mobility scooters, including its intuitive response to body movement, ability to operate with less coordination and dexterity than is required for many wheelchairs and mobility scooters, and smaller footprint and turning radius as compared to most wheelchairs and mobility scooters. Several commenters mentioned improved visibility, either due to the Segway® PT's raised platform or simply by virtue of being in a standing position. And finally, some commenters advocated for the inclusion of the Segway® PT simply based on civil rights arguments and the empowerment and self-esteem obtained from having the power to select the mobility device of choice.

Many commenters, regardless of their position on whether to include the Segway® PT in the definition of "wheelchair," noted that the Segway® PT's safety record is as good as, if not better, than the record for wheelchairs and mobility scooters.

Most environmental, transit system, and government commenters were opposed to including the Segway® PT in the definition of "wheelchair" but were supportive of its inclusion as an "other power-driven mobility device." Their concerns about including the Segway® PT in the definition of "wheelchair" had to do with the safety of the operators of these devices (e.g., height clearances on trains and sloping trails in parks) and of pedestrians, particularly in confined and crowded facilities or in settings where motorized devices might be unexpected; the potential harm to the environment; the additional administrative, insurance, liability, and defensive litigation costs; potentially detrimental impacts on the environment and cultural and natural resources; and the impracticality of accommodating such devices in public transportation settings.

Other environmental, transit system, and government commenters would have banned all fuel-powered devices as mobility devices. In addition, these commenters would have classified non-motorized devices as "wheelchairs" and would have categorized motorized devices, such as the Segway® PT, battery-operated wheelchairs, and mobility scooters as "other power-driven mobility devices." In support of this position, some of these commenters argued that because their equipment and facilities have been designed to comply with the dimensions of the "common wheelchair" upon which the ADAAG is based, any device that is larger than the prototype wheelchair would be misplaced in the definition of "wheelchair."

Still others in this group of commenters wished for only a single category of mobility devices and would have included wheelchairs, mobility scooters, and the Segway® PT as "mobility devices" and excluded fuel-powered devices from that definition.

Many disability advocacy and nonprofit commenters did not support the inclusion of the Segway® PT in the definition of "wheelchair." Paramount to these commenters was the maintenance of existing protections for wheelchair users. Because there was unanimous agreement that wheelchair use rarely, if ever, may be restricted, these commenters strongly favored categorizing wheelchairs separately from the Segway® PT and other power-driven mobility devices and applying the intended-use determinant to assign the devices to either category. They indicated that while they support the greatest degree of access in public entities for all persons with disabilities who require the use of mobility devices, they recognize that under certain circumstances, allowing the use of other power-driven mobility devices would result in a fundamental alteration of programs, services, or activities, or run counter to legitimate safety requirements necessary for the safe operation of a public entity. While these groups supported categorizing the Segway® PT as an "other power-driven mobility device," they universally noted that in their view, because the Segway® PT does not present environmental concerns and is as safe to use as, if not safer than, a wheelchair, it should be accommodated in most circumstances.

The Department has considered all the comments and has concluded that it should not include the Segway® PT in the definition of "wheelchair." The final rule provides that the test for categorizing a device as a wheelchair or an other power-driven mobility device is whether the device is designed primarily for use by individuals with mobility disabilities. Mobility scooters are included in the definition of "wheelchair" because they are designed primarily for users with mobility disabilities. However, because the current generation of EPAMDs, including the Segway® PT, was designed for recreational users and not primarily for use by individuals with mobility disabilities, the Department has decided to continue its approach of excluding EPAMDs from the definition of "wheelchair" and including them in the definition of "other power-driven mobility device." Although EPAMDs, such as the Segway® PT, are not included in the definition of a "wheelchair," public entities must assess whether they can make reasonable modifications to permit individuals with mobility disabilities to use such devices on their premises. The Department recognizes that the Segway® PT provides many benefits to those who use them as mobility devices, including a measure of privacy with regard to the nature of one's particular disability, and believes that in the vast majority of circumstances, the application of the factors described in § 35.137 for providing access to other- powered mobility devices will result in the admission of the Segway® PT.

Treatment of "manually-powered *mobility aids.*" The Department's NPRM did not define the term "manually-powered mobility aids." Instead, the NPRM included a non- exhaustive list of examples in § 35.137(a). The NPRM queried whether the Department should maintain this approach to manually- powered mobility aids or whether it should adopt a more formal definition.

Only a few commenters addressed "manually-powered mobility aids." Virtually all commenters were in favor of maintaining a non-exhaustive list of examples of "manually-powered mobility aids" rather than adopting a definition of the term. Of those who commented, a few sought clarification of the term "manually-powered." One commenter suggested that the term be changed to "human-powered." Other commenters requested that the Department include ordinary strollers in the non-exhaustive list of "manually-powered mobility aids." Since strollers are not devices designed primarily for individuals with mobility disabilities, the Department does not consider them to be manually-powered mobility aids; however, strollers used in the context of transporting individuals with disabilities are subject to the same assessment required by the ADA's title II reasonable modification standards at § 35.130(b)(7). The Department believes that because the existing approach is clear and understood easily by the public, no formal definition of the term "manually-powered mobility aids" is required.

Definition of "other *power-driven mobility device.*" The Department's NPRM defined the term "other power-driven mobility device" in § 35.104 as "any of a large range of devices powered by batteries, fuel, or other engines — whether or not designed solely for use by individuals with mobility impairments — that are used by individuals with mobility impairments for the purpose of locomotion, including golf cars, bicycles, electronic personal assistance mobility devices (EPAMDs), or any mobility aid designed to operate in areas without defined pedestrian routes." 73 FR 34466, 34504 (June 17, 2008).

Nearly all environmental, transit systems, and government commenters who supported the two-tiered concept of mobility devices said that the Department's definition of "other power-driven mobility device" is overbroad because it includes fuel-powered devices. These commenters sought a ban on fuel-powered devices in their entirety because they believe they are inherently dangerous and pose environmental and safety concerns. They also argued that permitting the use of many of the contemplated other power-driven mobility devices, fuel-powered ones especially, would fundamentally alter the programs, services, or activities of public entities.

Advocacy, nonprofit, and several individual commenters supported the definition of "other power-driven mobility device" because it allows new technologies to be added in the future, maintains the existing legal protections for wheelchairs, and recognizes that some devices, particularly the Segway® PT, which are not designed primarily for individuals with mobility disabilities, have beneficial uses for individuals with mobility disabilities. Despite support for the definition of "other power-driven mobility device," however, most advocacy and nonprofit commenters expressed at least some hesitation about the inclusion of fuel-powered mobility devices in the definition. While virtually all of these commenters noted that a blanket exclusion of any device that falls under the definition of "other power-driven mobility device" would violate basic civil rights concepts, they also specifically stated that certain devices, particularly, off-highway vehicles, cannot be permitted in certain circumstances. They also made a distinction between the Segway® PT and other power-driven mobility devices, noting that the Segway® PT should be accommodated in most circumstances because it satisfies the safety and environmental elements of the policy analysis. These commenters indicated that they agree that other power-driven mobility devices must be assessed, particularly as to their environmental impact, before they are accommodated.

Although many commenters had reservations about the inclusion of fuel- powered devices in the definition of other power-driven mobility devices, the Department does not want the definition to be so narrow that it would foreclose the inclusion of new technological developments (whether powered by fuel or by some other means). It is for this reason that the Department has maintained the phrase "any mobility device designed to operate in areas without defined pedestrian routes" in the final rule's definition of other power-driven mobility devices. The Department believes that the limitations provided by "fundamental alteration" and the ability to impose legitimate safety requirements will likely prevent the use of fuel and combustion engine-driven devices indoors, as well as in outdoor areas with heavy pedestrian traffic. The Department notes, however, that in the future, technological developments may result in the production of safe fuel-powered mobility devices that do not pose environmental and safety concerns. The final rule allows consideration to be given as to whether the use of a fuel-powered device would create a substantial risk of serious harm to the environment or natural or cultural resources, and to whether the use of such a device conflicts with Federal land management laws or regulations; this aspect of the final rule will further limit the inclusion of fuel-powered devices where they are not appropriate. Consequently, the Department has maintained fuel-powered devices in the definition of "other power-driven mobility device." The Department has also added language to the definition of "other power-driven mobility device" to reiterate that the definition does not apply to Federal wilderness areas, which are not covered by title II of the ADA; the use of wheelchairs in such areas is governed by section 508(c)(2) of the ADA, 42 U.S.C. 12207(c)(2).

"Qualified Interpreter"

In the NPRM, the Department proposed adding language to the definition of "qualified interpreter" to clarify that the term includes, but is not limited to, sign language interpreters, oral interpreters, and cued- speech interpreters. As the Department explained, not all interpreters are qualified for all situations. For example, a qualified interpreter who uses American Sign Language (ASL) is not necessarily qualified to interpret orally. In addition, someone with only a rudimentary familiarity with sign language or finger spelling is not qualified, nor is someone who is fluent in sign language but unable to translate spoken communication into ASL or to translate signed communication into spoken words.

As further explained, different situations will require different types of interpreters. For example, an oral interpreter who has special skill and training to mouth a speaker's words silently for individuals who are deaf or hard of hearing may be necessary for an individual who was raised orally and taught to read lips or was diagnosed with hearing loss later in life and does not know sign language. An individual who is deaf or hard of hearing may need an oral interpreter if the speaker's voice is unclear, if there is a quick-paced exchange of communication (e.g., in a meeting), or when the speaker does not directly face the individual who is deaf or hard of hearing. A cued-speech interpreter functions in the same manner as an oral interpreter except that he or she also uses a hand code or cue to represent each speech sound.

The Department received many comments regarding the proposed modifications to the definition of "interpreter." Many commenters requested that the Department include within the definition a requirement that interpreters be certified, particularly if they reside in a State that licenses or certifies interpreters. Other commenters opposed a certification requirement as unduly limiting, noting that an interpreter may well be qualified even if that same interpreter is not certified. These commenters noted the absence of nationwide standards or universally accepted criteria for certification.

On review of this issue, the Department has decided against imposing a certification requirement under the ADA. It is sufficient under the ADA that the interpreter be qualified. However, as the Department stated in the original preamble, this rule does not invalidate or limit State or local laws that impose standards for interpreters that are equal to or more stringent than those imposed by this definition. *See* 28 CFR part 35, app. A at 566 (2009). For instance, the definition would not supersede any requirement of State law for use of a certified interpreter in court proceedings.

With respect to the proposed additions to the rule, most commenters supported the expansion of the list of qualified interpreters, and some advocated for the inclusion of other types of interpreters on the list as well, such as deaf-blind interpreters, certified deaf interpreters, and speech-to-speech interpreters. As these commenters explained, deaf-blind interpreters are interpreters who have specialized skills and training to interpret for individuals who are deaf and blind; certified deaf interpreters are deaf or hard of hearing interpreters who work with hearing sign language interpreters to meet the specific communication needs of deaf individuals; and speech-to-speech interpreters have special skill and training to interpret for individuals who have speech disabilities.

The list of interpreters in the definition of qualified interpreter is illustrative, and the Department does not believe it necessary or appropriate to attempt to provide an exhaustive list of qualified interpreters. Accordingly, the Department has decided not to expand the proposed list. However, if a deaf and blind individual needs interpreter services, an interpreter who is qualified to handle the needs of that individual may be required. The guiding criterion is that the public entity must provide appropriate auxiliary aids and services to ensure effective communication with the individual. Commenters also suggested various definitions for the term "cued-speech interpreters," and different descriptions of the tasks they performed. After reviewing the various comments, the Department has determined that it is more accurate and appropriate to refer to such individuals as "cued-language transliterators." Likewise, the Department has changed the term "oral interpreters" to "oral transliterators." These two changes have been made to distinguish between sign language interpreters, who translate one language into another language (e.g., ASL to English and English to ASL), from transliterators who interpret within the same language between deaf and hearing individuals. A cued-language transliterator is an interpreter who has special skill and training in the use of the Cued Speech system of handshapes and placements, along with non-manual information, such as facial expression and body language, to show auditory information visually, including speech and environmental sounds. An oral transliterator is an interpreter who has special skill and training to mouth a speaker's words silently for individuals who are deaf or hard of hearing. While the Department included definitions for "cued- speech interpreter" and "oral interpreter" in the regulatory text proposed in the NPRM, the Department has decided that it is unnecessary to include such definitions in the text of the final rule.

Many commenters questioned the proposed deletion of the requirement that a qualified interpreter be able to interpret both receptively and expressively, noting the importance of both these skills. Commenters stated that this phrase was carefully crafted in the original regulation to make certain that interpreters both (1) are capable of understanding what a person with a disability is saying and (2) have the skills needed to convey information back to that individual. These are two very different skill sets and both are equally important to achieve effective communication. For example, in a medical setting, a sign language interpreter must have the necessary skills to understand the grammar and syntax used by an ASL user (receptive skills) and the ability to interpret complicated medical information — presented by medical staff in English — back to that individual in ASL (expressive skills). The Department agrees and has put the phrase "both receptively and expressively" back in the definition.

Several advocacy groups suggested that the Department make clear in the definition of qualified interpreter that the interpreter may appear either on-site or remotely using a video remote interpreting (VRI) service. Given that the Department has included in this rule both a definition of VRI services and standards that such services must satisfy, such an addition to the definition of qualified interpreter is appropriate.

After consideration of all relevant information submitted during the public comment period, the Department has modified the definition from that initially proposed in the NPRM. The final definition now states that "[q]ualified interpreter means an interpreter who, via a video remote interpreting (VRI) service or an on-site appearance, is able to interpret effectively, accurately, and impartially, both receptively and expressively, using any necessary specialized vocabulary. Qualified interpreters include, for example, sign language interpreters, oral transliterators, and cued- language transliterators."

"Qualified Reader"

The 1991 title II regulation identifies a qualified reader as an auxiliary aid, but did not define the term. *See* 28 CFR 35.104(2). Based upon the Department's investigation of complaints alleging that some entities have provided ineffective readers, the Department proposed in the NPRM to define "qualified reader" similarly to "qualified interpreter" to ensure that entities select qualified individuals to read an examination or other written information in an effective, accurate, and impartial manner. This proposal was suggested in order to make clear to public entities that a failure to provide a qualified reader to a person with a disability may constitute a violation of the requirement to provide appropriate auxiliary aids and services.

The Department received comments supporting inclusion in the regulation of a definition of a "qualified reader." Some commenters suggested the Department add to the definition a requirement prohibiting the use of a reader whose accent, diction, or pronunciation makes full comprehension of material being read difficult. Another commenter requested that the Department include a requirement that the reader "will follow the directions of the person for whom he or she is reading." Commenters also requested that the Department define "accurately" and "effectively" as used in this definition.

While the Department believes that its proposed regulatory definition adequately addresses these concerns, the Department emphasizes that a reader, in order to be "qualified," must be skilled in reading the language and subject matter and must be able to be easily understood by the individual with the disability. For example, if a reader is reading aloud the questions for a college microbiology examination, that reader, in order to be qualified, must know the proper pronunciation of scientific terminology used in the text, and must be sufficiently articulate to be easily understood by the individual with a disability for whom he or she is reading. In addition, the terms "effectively" and "accurately" have been successfully used and understood in the Department's existing definition of "qualified interpreter" since 1991 without specific regulatory definitions. Instead, the Department has relied upon the common use and understanding of those terms from standard English dictionaries. Thus, the definition of "qualified reader" has not been changed from that contained in the NPRM. The final rule defines "qualified reader" to mean "a person who is able to read effectively, accurately, and impartially using any necessary specialized vocabulary."

"Service Animal"

Although there is no specific language in the 1991 title II regulation concerning service animals, title II entities have the same legal obligations as title III entities to make reasonable modifications in policies, practices, or procedures to allow service animals when necessary in order to avoid discrimination on the basis of disability, unless the entity can demonstrate that making the modifications would fundamentally alter the nature of the service, program, or activity. *See* 28 CFR 35.130(b)(7). The 1991 title III regulation, 28 CFR 36.104, defines a "service animal" as "any guide dog, signal dog, or other animal individually trained to do work or perform tasks for the benefit of an individual with a disability, including, but not limited to, guiding individuals with impaired vision, alerting individuals with impaired hearing to intruders or sounds, providing minimal protection or rescue work, pulling a wheelchair, or fetching dropped items." Section 36.302(c)(1) of the 1991 title III regulation requires that "[g]enerally, a public accommodation shall modify policies, practices, or procedures to permit the use of a service animal by an individual with a disability." Section 36.302(c)(2) of the 1991 title III regulation states that "a public accommodation [is not required] to supervise or care for a service animal."

The Department has issued guidance and provided technical assistance and publications concerning service animals since the 1991 regulations became effective. In the NPRM, the Department proposed to modify the definition of service animal, added the definition to title II, and asked for public input on several issues related to the service animal provisions of the title II regulation: whether the Department should clarify the phrase "providing minimal protection" in the definition or remove it; whether there are any circumstances where a service animal "providing minimal protection" would be appropriate or expected; whether certain species should be eliminated from the definition of "service animal," and, if so, which types of animals should be excluded; whether "common domestic animal" should be part of the definition; and whether a size or weight limitation should be imposed for common domestic animals even if the animal satisfies the "common domestic animal" part of the NPRM definition.

The Department received extensive comments on these issues, as well as requests to clarify the obligations of State and local government entities to accommodate individuals with disabilities who use service animals, and has modified the final rule in response. In the interests of avoiding unnecessary repetition, the Department has elected to discuss the issues raised in the NPRM questions about service animals and the corresponding public comments in the following discussion of the definition of "service animal."

The Department's final rule defines "service animal" as "any dog that is individually trained to do work or perform tasks for the benefit of an individual with a disability, including a physical, sensory, psychiatric, intellectual, or other mental disability. Other species of animals, whether wild or domestic, trained or untrained, are not service animals for the purposes of this definition. The work or tasks performed by a service animal must be directly related to the handler's disability. Examples of work or tasks include, but are not limited to, assisting individuals who are blind or have low vision with navigation and other tasks, alerting individuals who are deaf or hard of hearing to the presence of people or sounds, providing non-violent protection or rescue work, pulling a wheelchair, assisting an individual during a seizure, alerting individuals to the presence of allergens, retrieving items such as medicine or the telephone, providing physical support and assistance with balance and stability to individuals with mobility disabilities, and helping persons with psychiatric and neurological disabilities by preventing or interrupting impulsive or destructive behaviors. The crime deterrent effects of an animal's presence and the provision of emotional support, well-being, comfort, or companionship do not constitute work or tasks for the purposes of this definition."

This definition has been designed to clarify a key provision of the ADA. Many covered entities indicated that they are confused regarding their obligations under the ADA with regard to individuals with disabilities who use service animals. Individuals with disabilities who use trained guide or service dogs are concerned that if untrained or unusual animals are termed "service animals," their own right to use guide or service dogs may become unnecessarily restricted or questioned. Some individuals who are not individuals with disabilities have claimed, whether fraudulently or sincerely (albeit mistakenly), that their animals are service animals covered by the ADA, in order to gain access to courthouses, city or county administrative offices, and other title II facilities. The increasing use of wild, exotic, or unusual species, many of which are untrained, as service animals has also added to the confusion.

Finally, individuals with disabilities who have the legal right under the Fair Housing Act (FHAct) to use certain animals in their homes as a reasonable accommodation to their disabilities have assumed that their animals also qualify under the ADA. This is not necessarily the case, as discussed below.

The Department recognizes the diverse needs and preferences of individuals with disabilities protected under the ADA, and does not wish to unnecessarily impede individual choice. Service animals play an integral role in the lives of many individuals with disabilities and, with the clarification provided by the final rule, individuals with disabilities will continue to be able to use their service animals as they go about their daily activities and civic interactions. The clarification will also help to ensure that the fraudulent or mistaken use of other animals not qualified as service animals under the ADA will be deterred. A more detailed analysis of the elements of the definition and the comments responsive to the service animal provisions of the NPRM follows.

Providing minimal protection. As previously noted, the 1991 title II regulation does not contain specific language concerning service animals. The 1991 title III regulation included language stating that "minimal protection" was a task that could be performed by an individually trained service animal for the benefit of an individual with a disability. In the Department's "ADA Business Brief on Service Animals" (2002), the Department interpreted the "minimal protection" language within the context of a seizure (i.e., alerting and protecting a person who is having a seizure). The Department received many comments in response to the question of whether the "minimal protection" language should be clarified. Many commenters urged the removal of the "minimal protection" language from the service animal definition for two reasons: (1) The phrase can be interpreted to allow any dog that is trained to be aggressive to qualify as a service animal simply by pairing the animal with a person with a disability; and (2) the phrase can be interpreted to allow any untrained pet dog to qualify as a service animal, since many consider the mere presence of a dog to be a crime deterrent, and thus sufficient to meet the minimal protection standard. These commenters argued, and the Department agrees, that these interpretations were not contemplated under the original title III regulation, and, for the purposes of the final title II regulations, the meaning of "minimal protection" must be made clear.

While many commenters stated that they believe that the "minimal protection" language should be eliminated, other commenters recommended that the language be clarified, but retained. Commenters favoring clarification of the term suggested that the Department explicitly exclude the function of attack or exclude those animals that are trained solely to be aggressive or protective. Other commenters identified non- violent behavioral tasks that could be construed as minimally protective, such as interrupting self-mutilation, providing safety checks and room searches, reminding the handler to take medications, and protecting the handler from injury resulting from seizures or unconsciousness.

Several commenters noted that the existing direct threat defense, which allows the exclusion of a service animal if the animal exhibits unwarranted or unprovoked violent behavior or poses a direct threat, prevents the use of "attack dogs" as service animals. One commenter noted that the use of a service animal trained to provide "minimal protection" may impede access to care in an emergency, for example, where the first responder, usually a title II entity, is unable or reluctant to approach a person with a disability because the individual's service animal is in a protective posture suggestive of aggression.

Many organizations and individuals stated that in the general dog training community, "protection" is code for attack or aggression training and should be removed from the definition. Commenters stated that there appears to be a broadly held misconception that aggression-trained animals are appropriate service animals for persons with post traumatic stress disorder (PTSD). While many individuals with PTSD may benefit by using a service animal, the work or tasks performed appropriately by such an animal would not involve unprovoked aggression but could include actively cuing the handler by nudging or pawing the handler to alert to the onset of an episode and removing the individual from the anxiety-provoking environment.

The Department recognizes that despite its best efforts to provide clarification, the "minimal protection" language appears to have been misinterpreted. While the Department maintains that protection from danger is one of the key functions that service animals perform for the benefit of persons with disabilities, the Department recognizes that an animal individually trained to provide aggressive protection, such as an attack dog, is not appropriately considered a service animal. Therefore, the Department has decided to modify the "minimal protection" language to read "non-violent protection," thereby excluding so- called "attack dogs" or dogs with traditional "protection training" as service animals. The Department believes that this modification to the service animal definition will eliminate confusion, without restricting unnecessarily the type of work or tasks that service animals may perform. The Department's modification also clarifies that the crime-deterrent effect of a dog's presence, by itself, does not qualify as work or tasks for purposes of the service animal definition.

Alerting to intruders. The phrase "alerting to intruders" is related to the issues of minimal protection and the work or tasks an animal may perform to meet the definition of a service animal. In the original 1991 regulatory text, this phrase was intended to identify service animals that alert individuals who are deaf or hard of hearing to the presence of others. This language has been misinterpreted by some to apply to dogs that are trained specifically to provide aggressive protection, resulting in the assertion that such training qualifies a dog as a service animal under the ADA. The Department reiterates that title II entities are not required to admit any animal whose use poses a direct threat under § 35.139. In addition, the Department has decided to remove the word "intruders" from the service animal definition and replace it with the phrase "the presence of people or sounds. The Department believes this clarifies that so-called "attack training" or other aggressive response types of training that cause a dog to provide an aggressive response do not qualify a dog as a service animal under the ADA. Conversely, if an individual uses a breed of dog that is perceived to be aggressive because of breed reputation, stereotype, or the history or experience the observer may have with other dogs, but the dog is under the control of the individual with a disability and does not exhibit aggressive behavior, the title II entity cannot exclude the individual or the animal from a State or local government program, service, or facility. The animal can only be removed if it engages in the behaviors mentioned in § 35.136(b) (as revised in the final rule) or if the presence of the animal constitutes a fundamental alteration to the nature of the service, program, or activity of the title II entity.

Doing "work" *or* "performing *tasks.*" The NPRM proposed that the Department maintain the requirement, first articulated in the 1991 title III regulation, that in order to qualify as a service animal, the animal must "perform tasks" or "do work" for the individual with a disability. The phrases "perform tasks" and "do work" describe what an animal must do for the benefit of an individual with a disability in order to qualify as a service animal.

The Department received a number of comments in response to the NPRM proposal urging the removal of the term "do work" from the definition of a service animal. These commenters argued that the Department should emphasize the performance of tasks instead. The Department disagrees. Although the common definition of work includes the performance of tasks, the definition of work is somewhat broader, encompassing activities that do not appear to involve physical action.

One service dog user stated that in some cases, "critical forms of assistance can't be construed as physical tasks," noting that the manifestations of "brain-based disabilities," such as psychiatric disorders and autism, are as varied as their physical counterparts. The Department agrees with this statement but cautions that unless the animal is individually trained to do something that qualifies as work or a task, the animal is a pet or support animal and does not qualify for coverage as a service animal. A pet or support animal may be able to discern that the handler is in distress, but it is what the animal is trained to do in response to this awareness that distinguishes a service animal from an observant pet or support animal.

The NPRM contained an example of "doing work" that stated "a psychiatric service dog can help some individuals with dissociative identity disorder to remain grounded in time or place." 73 FR 34466, 34504 (June 17, 2008). Several commenters objected to the use of this example, arguing that grounding was not a "task" and therefore, the example inherently contradicted the basic premise that a service animal must perform a task in order to mitigate a disability. Other commenters stated that "grounding" should not be included as an example of "work" because it could lead to some individuals claiming that they should be able to use emotional support animals in public because the dog makes them feel calm or safe. By contrast, one commenter with experience in training service animals explained that grounding is a trained task based upon very specific behavioral indicators that can be observed and measured. These tasks are based upon input from mental health practitioners, dog trainers, and individuals with a history of working with psychiatric service dogs.

It is the Department's view that an animal that is trained to "ground" a person with a psychiatric disorder does work or performs a task that would qualify it as a service animal as compared to an untrained emotional support animal whose presence affects a person's disability. It is the fact that the animal is trained to respond to the individual's needs that distinguishes an animal as a service animal. The process must have two steps: Recognition and response. For example, if a service animal senses that a person is about to have a psychiatric episode and it is trained to respond for example, by nudging, barking, or removing the individual to a safe location until the episode subsides, then the animal has indeed performed a task or done work on behalf of the individual with the disability, as opposed to merely sensing an event.

One commenter suggested defining the term "task," presumably to improve the understanding of the types of services performed by an animal that would be sufficient to qualify the animal for coverage. The Department believes that the common definition of the word "task" is sufficiently clear and that it is not necessary to add to the definitions section. However, the Department has added examples of other kinds of work or tasks to help illustrate and provide clarity to the definition. After careful evaluation of this issue, the Department has concluded that the phrases "do work" and "perform tasks" have been effective during the past two decades to illustrate the varied services provided by service animals for the benefit of individuals with all types of disabilities. Thus, the Department declines to depart from its longstanding approach at this time.

Species limitations. When the Department originally issued its title III regulation in the early 1990s, the Department did not define the parameters of acceptable animal species. At that time, few anticipated the variety of animals that would be promoted as service animals in the years to come, which ranged from pigs and miniature horses to snakes, iguanas, and parrots. The Department has followed this particular issue closely, keeping current with the many unusual species of animals represented to be service animals. Thus, the Department has decided to refine further this aspect of the service animal definition in the final rule.

The Department received many comments from individuals and organizations recommending species limitations. Several of these commenters asserted that limiting the number of allowable species would help stop erosion of the public's trust, which has resulted in reduced access for many individuals with disabilities who use trained service animals that adhere to high behavioral standards. Several commenters suggested that other species would be acceptable if those animals could meet nationally recognized behavioral standards for trained service dogs. Other commenters asserted that certain species of animals (e.g., reptiles) cannot be trained to do work or perform tasks, so these animals would not be covered.

In the NPRM, the Department used the term "common domestic animal" in the service animal definition and excluded reptiles, rabbits, farm animals (including horses, miniature horses, ponies, pigs, and goats), ferrets, amphibians, and rodents from the service animal definition. 73 FR 34466, 34478 (June 17, 2008). However, the term "common domestic animal" is difficult to define with precision due to the increase in the number of domesticated species. Also, several State and local laws define a "domestic" animal as an animal that is not wild. The Department agrees with commenters' views that limiting the number and types of species recognized as service animals will provide greater predictability for State and local government entities as well as added assurance of access for individuals with disabilities who use dogs as service animals. As a consequence, the Department has decided to limit this rule's coverage of service animals to dogs, which are the most common service animals used by individuals with disabilities.

Wild animals, monkeys, and other nonhuman primates. Numerous business entities endorsed a narrow definition of acceptable service animal species, and asserted that there are certain animals (e.g., reptiles) that cannot be trained to do work or perform tasks. Other commenters suggested that the Department should identify excluded animals, such as birds and llamas, in the final rule. Although one commenter noted that wild animals bred in captivity should be permitted to be service animals, the Department has decided to make clear that all wild animals, whether born or bred in captivity or in the wild, are eliminated from coverage as service animals. The Department believes that this approach reduces risks to health or safety attendant with wild animals. Some animals, such as certain nonhuman primates including certain monkeys, pose a direct threat; their behavior can be unpredictably aggressive and violent without notice or provocation. The American Veterinary Medical Association (AVMA) issued a position statement advising against the use of monkeys as service animals, stating that "[t]he AVMA does not support the use of nonhuman primates as assistance animals because of animal welfare concerns, and the potential for serious injury and zoonotic [animal to human disease transmission] risks." AVMA Position Statement, *Nonhuman Primates as Assistance Animals*, (2005) available at http://www.avma.org/issues/policy/ nonhuman_primates.asp (last visited June 24, 2010).

An organization that trains capuchin monkeys to provide in-home services to individuals with paraplegia and quadriplegia was in substantial agreement with the AVMA's views but requested a limited recognition in the service animal definition for the capuchin monkeys it trains to provide assistance for persons with disabilities. The organization commented that its trained capuchin monkeys undergo scrupulous veterinary examinations to ensure that the animals pose no health risks, and are used by individuals with disabilities exclusively in their homes. The organization acknowledged that the capuchin monkeys it trains are not necessarily suitable for use in State or local government facilities. The organization noted that several State and local government entities have local zoning, licensing, health, and safety laws that prohibit nonhuman primates, and that these prohibitions would prevent individuals with disabilities from using these animals even in their homes.

The organization argued that including capuchin monkeys under the service animal umbrella would make it easier for individuals with disabilities to obtain reasonable modifications of State and local licensing, health, and safety laws that would permit the use of these monkeys. The organization argued that this limited modification to the service animal definition was warranted in view of the services these monkeys perform, which enable many individuals with paraplegia and quadriplegia to live and function with increased independence.

The Department has carefully considered the potential risks associated with the use of nonhuman primates as service animals in State and local government facilities, as well as the information provided to the Department about the significant benefits that trained capuchin monkeys provide to certain individuals with disabilities in residential settings. The Department has determined, however, that nonhuman primates, including capuchin monkeys, will not be recognized as service animals for purposes of this rule because of their potential for disease transmission and unpredictable aggressive behavior. The Department believes that these characteristics make nonhuman primates unsuitable for use as service animals in the context of the wide variety of public settings subject to this rule. As the organization advocating the inclusion of capuchin monkeys acknowledges, capuchin monkeys are not suitable for use in public facilities.

The Department emphasizes that it has decided only that capuchin monkeys will not be included in the definition of service animals for purposes of its regulation implementing the ADA. This decision does not have any effect on the extent to which public entities are required to allow the use of such monkeys under other Federal statutes. For example, under the FHAct, an individual with a disability may have the right to have an animal other than a dog in his or her home if the animal qualifies as a "reasonable accommodation" that is necessary to afford the individual equal opportunity to use and enjoy a dwelling, assuming that the use of the animal does not pose a direct threat. In some cases, the right of an individual to have an animal under the FHAct may conflict with State or local laws that prohibit all individuals, with or without disabilities, from owning a particular species. However, in this circumstance, an individual who wishes to request a reasonable modification of the State or local law must do so under the FHAct, not the ADA.

Having considered all of the comments about which species should qualify as service animals under the ADA, the Department has determined the most reasonable approach is to limit acceptable species to dogs.

Size or weight limitations. The vast majority of commenters did not support a size or weight limitation. Commenters were typically opposed to a size or weight limit because many tasks performed by service animals require large, strong dogs. For instance, service animals may perform tasks such as providing balance and support or pulling a wheelchair. Small animals may not be suitable for large adults. The weight of the service animal user is often correlated with the size and weight of the service animal. Others were concerned that adding a size and weight limit would further complicate the difficult process of finding an appropriate service animal. One commenter noted that there is no need for a limit because "if, as a practical matter, the size or weight of an individual's service animal creates a direct threat or fundamental alteration to a particular public entity or accommodation, there are provisions that allow for the animal's exclusion or removal." Some common concerns among commenters in support of a size and weight limit were that a larger animal may be less able to fit in various areas with its handler, such as toilet rooms and public seating areas, and that larger animals are more difficult to control.

Balancing concerns expressed in favor of and against size and weight limitations, the Department has determined that such limitations would not be appropriate. Many individuals of larger stature require larger dogs. The Department believes it would be inappropriate to deprive these individuals of the option of using a service dog of the size required to provide the physical support and stability these individuals may need to function independently. Since large dogs have always served as service animals, continuing their use should not constitute fundamental alterations or impose undue burdens on title II entities.

Breed limitations. A few commenters suggested that certain breeds of dogs should not be allowed to be used as service animals. Some suggested that the Department should defer to local laws restricting the breeds of dogs that individuals who reside in a community may own. Other commenters opposed breed restrictions, stating that the breed of a dog does not determine its propensity for aggression and that aggressive and non-aggressive dogs exist in all breeds.

The Department does not believe that it is either appropriate or consistent with the ADA to defer to local laws that prohibit certain breeds of dogs based on local concerns that these breeds may have a history of unprovoked aggression or attacks. Such deference would have the effect of limiting the rights of persons with disabilities under the ADA who use certain service animals based on where they live rather than on whether the use of a particular animal poses a direct threat to the health and safety of others. Breed restrictions differ significantly from jurisdiction to jurisdiction. Some jurisdictions have no breed restrictions. Others have restrictions that, while well-meaning, have the unintended effect of screening out the very breeds of dogs that have successfully served as service animals for decades without a history of the type of unprovoked aggression or attacks that would pose a direct threat, *e.g.*, German Shepherds. Other jurisdictions prohibit animals over a certain weight, thereby restricting breeds without invoking an express breed ban. In addition, deference to breed restrictions contained in local laws would have the unacceptable consequence of restricting travel by an individual with a disability who uses a breed that is acceptable and poses no safety hazards in the individual's home jurisdiction but is nonetheless banned by other jurisdictions. State and local government entities have the ability to determine, on a case-by-case basis, whether a particular service animal can be excluded based on that particular animal's actual behavior or history — not based on fears or generalizations about how an animal or breed might behave. This ability to exclude an animal whose behavior or history evidences a direct threat is sufficient to protect health and safety.

Recognition of psychiatric service animals but not "emotional *support animals.*" The definition of "service animal" in the NPRM stated the Department's longstanding position that emotional support animals are not included in the definition of "service animal." The proposed text in § 35.104 provided that "[a]nimals whose sole function is to provide emotional support, comfort, therapy, companionship, therapeutic benefits or to promote emotional well-being are not service animals." 73 FR 34466, 34504 (June 17, 2008).

Many advocacy organizations expressed concern and disagreed with the exclusion of comfort and emotional support animals. Others have been more specific, stating that individuals with disabilities may need their emotional support animals in order to have equal access. Some commenters noted that individuals with disabilities use animals that have not been trained to perform tasks directly related to their disability. These animals do not qualify as service animals under the ADA. These are emotional support or comfort animals.

Commenters asserted that excluding categories such as "comfort" and "emotional support" animals recognized by laws such as the FHAct or the Air Carrier Access Act (ACAA) is confusing and burdensome. Other commenters noted that emotional support and comfort animals perform an important function, asserting that animal companionship helps individuals who experience depression resulting from multiple sclerosis.

Some commenters explained the benefits emotional support animals provide, including emotional support, comfort, therapy, companionship, therapeutic benefits, and the promotion of emotional well-being. They contended that without the presence of an emotional support animal in their lives they would be disadvantaged and unable to participate in society. These commenters were concerned that excluding this category of animals will lead to discrimination against, and the excessive questioning of, individuals with non-visible or non-apparent disabilities. Other commenters expressing opposition to the exclusion of individually trained "comfort" or "emotional support" animals asserted that the ability to soothe or de-escalate and control emotion is "work" that benefits the individual with the disability.

Many commenters requested that the Department carve out an exception that permits current or former members of the military to use emotional support animals. They asserted that a significant number of service members returning from active combat duty have adjustment difficulties due to combat, sexual assault, or other traumatic experiences while on active duty. Commenters noted that some current or former members of the military service have been prescribed animals for conditions such as PTSD. One commenter stated that service women who were sexually assaulted while in the military use emotional support animals to help them feel safe enough to step outside their homes. The Department recognizes that many current and former members of the military have disabilities as a result of service-related injuries that may require emotional support and that such individuals can benefit from the use of an emotional support animal and could use such animal in their home under the FHAct. However, having carefully weighed the issues, the Department believes that its final rule appropriately addresses the balance of issues and concerns of both the individual with a disability and the public entity. The Department also notes that nothing in this part prohibits a public entity from allowing current or former military members or anyone else with disabilities to utilize emotional support animals if it wants to do so.

Commenters asserted the view that if an animal's "mere presence" legitimately provides such benefits to an individual with a disability and if those benefits are necessary to provide equal opportunity given the facts of the particular disability, then such an animal should qualify as a "service animal." Commenters noted that the focus should be on the nature of a person's disability, the difficulties the disability may impose and whether the requested accommodation would legitimately address those difficulties, not on evaluating the animal involved. The Department understands this approach has benefitted many individuals under the FHAct and analogous State law provisions, where the presence of animals poses fewer health and safety issues, and where emotional support animals provide assistance that is unique to residential settings. The Department believes, however, that the presence of such animals is not required in the context of title II entities such as courthouses, State and local government administrative buildings, and similar title II facilities.

Under the Department's previous regulatory framework, some individuals and entities assumed that the requirement that service animals must be individually trained to do work or perform tasks excluded all individuals with mental disabilities from having service animals. Others assumed that any person with a psychiatric condition whose pet provided comfort to them was covered by the 1991 title II regulation. The Department reiterates that psychiatric service animals that are trained to do work or perform a task for individuals whose disability is covered by the ADA are protected by the Department's present regulatory approach. Psychiatric service animals can be trained to perform a variety of tasks that assist individuals with disabilities to detect the onset of psychiatric episodes and ameliorate their effects. Tasks performed by psychiatric service animals may include reminding the handler to take medicine, providing safety checks or room searches for persons with PTSD, interrupting self-mutilation, and removing disoriented individuals from dangerous situations.

The difference between an emotional support animal and a psychiatric service animal is the work or tasks that the animal performs. Traditionally, service dogs worked as guides for individuals who were blind or had low vision. Since the original regulation was promulgated, service animals have been trained to assist individuals with many different types of disabilities.

In the final rule, the Department has retained its position on the exclusion of emotional support animals from the definition of "service animal." The definition states that "[t]he provision of emotional support, well-being, comfort, or companionship, * * * do[es] not constitute work or tasks for the purposes of this definition." The Department notes, however, that the exclusion of emotional support animals from coverage in the final rule does not mean that individuals with psychiatric or mental disabilities cannot use service animals that meet the regulatory definition. The final rule defines service animal as follows: "[s]ervice animal means any dog that is individually trained to do work or perform tasks for the benefit of an individual with a disability, including a physical, sensory, psychiatric, intellectual, or other mental disability." This language simply clarifies the Department's longstanding position.

The Department's position is based on the fact that the title II and title III regulations govern a wider range of public settings than the housing and transportation settings for which the Department of Housing and Urban Development (HUD) and DOT regulations allow emotional support animals or comfort animals. The Department recognizes that there are situations not governed by the title II and title III regulations, particularly in the context of residential settings and transportation, where there may be a legal obligation to permit the use of animals that do not qualify as service animals under the ADA, but whose presence nonetheless provides necessary emotional support to persons with disabilities. Accordingly, other Federal agency regulations, case law, and possibly State or local laws governing those situations may provide appropriately for increased access for animals other than service animals as defined under the ADA. Public officials, housing providers, and others who make decisions relating to animals in residential and transportation settings should consult the Federal, State, and local laws that apply in those areas (e.g., the FHAct regulations of HUD and the ACAA) and not rely on the ADA as a basis for reducing those obligations.

Retain term "service *animal.*" Some commenters asserted that the term "assistance animal" is a term of art and should replace the term "service animal." However, the majority of commenters preferred the term "service animal" because it is more specific. The Department has decided to retain the term "service animal" in the final rule. While some agencies, like HUD, use the term "assistance animal," "assistive animal," or "support animal," these terms are used to denote a broader category of animals than is covered by the ADA. The Department has decided that changing the term used in the final rule would create confusion, particularly in view of the broader parameters for coverage under the FHAct, *cf.,* preamble to HUD's Final Rule for Pet Ownership for the Elderly and Persons with Disabilities, 73 FR 63834–38 (Oct. 27, 2008); HUD Handbook No. 4350.3 Rev-1, Chapter 2, Occupancy Requirements of Subsidized Multifamily Housing Programs (June 2007), available at http://www.hud.gov/offices/adm/hudclips/handbooks/hsgh/4350.3 (last visited June 24, 2010). Moreover, as discussed above, the Department's definition of "service animal" in the title II final rule does not affect the rights of individuals with disabilities who use assistance animals in their homes under the FHAct or who use "emotional support animals" that are covered under the ACAA and its implementing regulations. *See* 14 CFR 382.7 *et seq.; see also* Department of Transportation, *Guidance Concerning Service Animals in Air Transportation,* 68 FR 24874, 24877 (May 9, 2003) (discussing accommodation of service animals and emotional support animals on aircraft).

"Video Remote Interpreting" (VRI) Services

In the NPRM, the Department proposed adding Video Interpreting Services (VIS) to the list of auxiliary aids available to provide effective communication described in § 35.104. In the preamble to the NPRM, VIS was defined as "a technology composed of a video phone, video monitors, cameras, a high-speed Internet connection, and an interpreter. The video phone provides video transmission to a video monitor that permits the individual who is deaf or hard of hearing to view and sign to a video interpreter (i.e., a live interpreter in another location), who can see and sign to the individual through a camera located on or near the monitor, while others can communicate by speaking. The video monitor can display a split screen of two live images, with the interpreter in one image and the individual who is deaf or hard of hearing in the other image." 73 FR 34446, 34479 (June 17, 2008). Comments from advocacy organizations and individuals unanimously requested that the Department use the term "video remote interpreting (VRI)," instead of VIS, for consistency with Federal Communications Commission (FCC) regulations. *See* FCC Public Notice, DA- 0502417 (Sept. 7, 2005), and with common usage by consumers. The Department has made that change throughout the regulation to avoid confusion and to make the regulation more consistent with existing regulations.

Many commenters also requested that the Department distinguish between VRI and "video relay service (VRS)." Both VRI and VRS use a remote interpreter who is able to see and communicate with a deaf person and a hearing person, and all three individuals may be connected by a video link. VRI is a fee-based interpreting service conveyed via videoconferencing where at least one person, typically the interpreter, is at a separate location. VRI can be provided as an on-demand service or by appointment. VRI normally involves a contract in advance for the interpreter who is usually paid by the covered entity.

VRS is a telephone service that enables persons with disabilities to use the telephone to communicate using video connections and is a more advanced form of relay service than the traditional voice to text telephones (TTY) relay systems that were recognized in the 1991 title II regulation. More specifically, VRS is a video relay service using interpreters connected to callers by video hook-up and is designed to provide telephone services to persons who are deaf and use American Sign Language that are functionally equivalent to those provided to users who are hearing. VRS is funded through the Interstate Telecommunications Relay Services Fund and overseen by the FCC. *See* 47 CFR 64.601(a)(26). There are no fees for callers to use the VRS interpreters and the video connection, although there may be relatively inexpensive initial costs to the title II entities to purchase the videophone or camera for on-line video connection, or other equipment to connect to the VRS service. The FCC has made clear that VRS functions as a telephone service and is not intended to be used for interpreting services where both parties are in the same room; the latter is reserved for VRI. The Department agrees that VRS cannot be used as a substitute for in-person interpreters or for VRI in situations that would not, absent one party's disability, entail use of the telephone.

Many commenters strongly recommended limiting the use of VRI to circumstances where it will provide effective communication. Commenters from advocacy groups and persons with disabilities expressed concern that VRI may not always be appropriate to provide effective communication, especially in hospitals and emergency rooms. Examples were provided of patients who are unable to see the video monitor because they are semi-conscious or unable to focus on the video screen; other examples were given of cases where the video monitor is out of the sightline of the patient or the image is out of focus; still other examples were given of patients who could not see the image because the signal was interrupted, causing unnatural pauses in the communication, or the image was grainy or otherwise unclear. Many commenters requested more explicit guidelines on the use of VRI, and some recommended requirements for equipment maintenance, high-speed, wide-bandwidth video links using dedicated lines or wireless systems, and training of staff using VRI, especially in hospital and health care situations. Several major organizations requested a requirement to include the interpreter's face, head, arms, hands, and eyes in all transmissions. Finally, one State agency asked for additional guidance, outreach, and mandated advertising about the availability of VRI in title II situations so that local government entities would budget for and facilitate the use of VRI in libraries, schools, and other places.

After consideration of the comments and the Department's own research and experience, the Department has determined that VRI can be an effective method of providing interpreting services in certain circumstances, but not in others. For example, VRI should be effective in many situations involving routine medical care, as well as in the emergency room where urgent care is important, but no in-person interpreter is available; however, VRI may not be effective in situations involving surgery or other medical procedures where the patient is limited in his or her ability to see the video screen. Similarly, VRI may not be effective in situations where there are multiple people in a room and the information exchanged is highly complex and fast-paced. The Department recognizes that in these and other situations, such as where communication is needed for persons who are deaf-blind, it may be necessary to summon an in-person interpreter to assist certain individuals. To ensure that VRI is effective in situations where it is appropriate, the Department has established performance standards in § 35.160(d).

Subpart B — General Requirements

Section 35.130(h)   Safety.

Section 36.301(b) of the 1991 title III regulation provides that a public accommodation "may impose legitimate safety requirements that are necessary for safe operation. Safety requirements must be based on actual risks, and not on mere speculation, stereotypes, or generalizations about individuals with disabilities." 28 CFR 36.301(b). Although the 1991 title II regulation did not include similar language, the Department's 1993 ADA Title II Technical Assistance Manual at II-3.5200 makes clear the Department's view that public entities also have the right to impose legitimate safety requirements necessary for the safe operation of services, programs, or activities. To ensure consistency between the title II and title III regulations, the Department has added a new § 35.130(h) in the final rule incorporating this longstanding position relating to imposition of legitimate safety requirements.

Section 35.133   Maintenance of accessible features.

Section 35.133 in the 1991 title II regulation provides that a public entity must maintain in operable working condition those features of facilities and equipment that are required to be readily accessible to and usable by qualified individuals with disabilities. *See* 28 CFR 35.133(a). In the NPRM, the Department clarified the application of this provision and proposed one change to the section to address the discrete situation in which the scoping requirements provided in the 2010 Standards reduce the number of required elements below the requirements of the 1991 Standards. In that discrete event, a public entity may reduce such accessible features in accordance with the requirements in the 2010 Standards.

The Department received only four comments on this proposed amendment. None of the commenters opposed the change. In the final rule, the Department has revised the section to make it clear that if the 2010 Standards reduce either the technical requirements or the number of required accessible elements below that required by the 1991 Standards, then the public entity may reduce the technical requirements or the number of accessible elements in a covered facility in accordance with the requirements of the 2010 Standards.

One commenter urged the Department to amend § 35.133(b) to expand the language of the section to restocking of shelves as a permissible activity for isolated or temporary interruptions in service or access. It is the Department's position that a temporary interruption that blocks an accessible route, such as restocking of shelves, is already permitted by § 35.133(b), which clarifies that "isolated or temporary interruptions in service or access due to maintenance or repairs" are permitted. Therefore, the Department will not make any additional changes in the final rule to the language of § 35.133(b) other than those discussed in the preceding paragraph.

Section 35.136   *Service animals.*

The 1991 title II regulation states that "[a] public entity shall make reasonable modifications in policies, practices, or procedures when the modifications are necessary to avoid discrimination on the basis of disability, unless the public entity can demonstrate that making the modifications would fundamentally alter the nature of the service, program or activity." 28 CFR 130(b)(7). Unlike the title III regulation, the 1991 title II regulation did not contain a specific provision addressing service animals.

In the NPRM, the Department stated the intention of providing the broadest feasible access to individuals with disabilities and their service animals, unless a public entity can demonstrate that making the modifications to policies excluding animals would fundamentally alter the nature of the public entity's service, program, or activity. The Department proposed creating a new § 35.136 addressing service animals that was intended to retain the scope of the 1991 title III regulation at § 36.302(c), while clarifying the Department's longstanding policies and interpretations, as outlined in published technical assistance, *Commonly Asked Questions About Service Animals in Places of Business* (1996), available at http://www.ada. gov/qasrvc.ftm and *ADA Guide for Small Businesses* (1999), available at http:// www.ada.gov/smbustxt.htm, and to add that a public entity may exclude a service animal in certain circumstances where the service animal fails to meet certain behavioral standards. The Department received extensive comments in response to proposed § 35.136 from individuals, disability advocacy groups, organizations involved in training service animals, and public entities. Those comments and the Department's response are discussed below.

Exclusion of service animals. In the NPRM, the Department proposed incorporating the title III regulatory language of § 36.302(c) into new § 35.136(a), which states that "[g]enerally, a public entity shall modify its policies, practices, or procedures to permit the use of a service animal by an individual with a disability, unless the public entity can demonstrate that the use of a service animal would fundamentally alter the public entity's service, program, or activity." The final rule retains this language with some modifications.

In addition, in the NPRM, the Department proposed clarifying those circumstances where otherwise eligible service animals may be excluded by public entities from their programs or facilities. The Department proposed in § 35.136(b)(1) of the NPRM that a public entity may ask an individual with a disability to remove a service animal from a title II service, program, or activity if: "[t]he animal is out of control and the animal's handler does not take effective action to control it." 73 FR 34466, 34504 (June 17, 2008).

The Department has long held that a service animal must be under the control of the handler at all times. Commenters overwhelmingly were in favor of this language, but noted that there are occasions when service animals are provoked to disruptive or aggressive behavior by agitators or troublemakers, as in the case of a blind individual whose service dog is taunted or pinched. While all service animals are trained to ignore and overcome these types of incidents, misbehavior in response to provocation is not always unreasonable. In circumstances where a service animal misbehaves or responds reasonably to a provocation or injury, the public entity must give the handler a reasonable opportunity to gain control of the animal. Further, if the individual with a disability asserts that the animal was provoked or injured, or if the public entity otherwise has reason to suspect that provocation or injury has occurred, the public entity should seek to determine the facts and, if provocation or injury occurred, the public entity should take effective steps to prevent further provocation or injury, which may include asking the provocateur to leave the public entity. This language is unchanged in the final rule.

The NPRM also proposed language at § 35.136(b)(2) to permit a public entity to exclude a service animal if the animal is not housebroken (i.e., trained so that, absent illness or accident, the animal controls its waste elimination) or the animal's presence or behavior fundamentally alters the nature of the service the public entity provides (e.g., repeated barking during a live performance). Several commenters were supportive of this NPRM language, but cautioned against overreaction by the public entity in these instances. One commenter noted that animals get sick, too, and that accidents occasionally happen. In these circumstances, simple clean up typically addresses the incident. Commenters noted that the public entity must be careful when it excludes a service animal on the basis of "fundamental alteration," asserting for example that a public entity should not exclude a service animal for barking in an environment where other types of noise, such as loud cheering or a child crying, is tolerated. The Department maintains that the appropriateness of an exclusion can be assessed by reviewing how a public entity addresses comparable situations that do not involve a service animal. The Department has retained in § 35.136(b) of the final rule the exception requiring animals to be housebroken. The Department has not retained the specific NPRM language stating that animals can be excluded if their presence or behavior fundamentally alters the nature of the service provided by the public entity, because the Department believes that this exception is covered by the general reasonable modification requirement contained in § 35.130(b)(7).

The NPRM also proposed at § 35.136(b)(3) that a service animal can be excluded where "[t]he animal poses a direct threat to the health or safety of others that cannot be eliminated by reasonable modifications." 73 FR 34466, 34504 (June 17, 2008). Commenters were universally supportive of this provision as it makes express the discretion of a public entity to exclude a service animal that poses a direct threat. Several commenters cautioned against the overuse of this provision and suggested that the Department provide an example of the rule's application. The Department has decided not to include regulatory language specifically stating that a service animal can be excluded if it poses a direct threat. The Department believes that the addition of new § 35.139, which incorporates the language of the title III provisions at § 36.302 relating to the general defense of direct threat, is sufficient to establish the availability of this defense to public entities.

Access to a public entity following the proper exclusion of a service animal. The NPRM proposed that in the event a public entity properly excludes a service animal, the public entity must give the individual with a disability the opportunity to access the programs, services, and facilities of the public entity without the service animal. Most commenters welcomed this provision as a common sense approach. These commenters noted that they do not wish to preclude individuals with disabilities from the full and equal enjoyment of the State or local government's programs, services, or facilities, simply because of an isolated problem with a service animal. The Department has elected to retain this provision in § 35.136(a).

Other requirements. The NPRM also proposed that the regulation include the following requirements: that the work or tasks performed by the service animal must be directly related to the handler's disability; that a service animal must be individually trained to do work or perform a task, be housebroken, and be under the control of the handler; and that a service animal must have a harness, leash, or other tether. Most commenters addressed at least one of these issues in their responses. Most agreed that these provisions are important to clarify further the 1991 service animal regulation. The Department has moved the requirement that the work or tasks performed by the service animal must be related directly to the handler's disability to the definition of "service animal" in § 35.104. In addition, the Department has modified the proposed language in § 35.136(d) relating to the handler's control of the animal with a harness, leash, or other tether to state that "[a] service animal shall have a harness, leash, or other tether, unless either the handler is unable because of a disability to use a harness, leash, or other tether, or the use of a harness, leash, or other tether would interfere with the service animal's safe, effective performance of work or tasks, in which case the service animal must be otherwise under the handler's control (e.g., voice control, signals, or other effective means)." The Department has retained the requirement that the service animal must be individually trained (see Appendix A discussion of § 35.104, definition of "service animal"), as well as the requirement that the service animal be housebroken.

Responsibility for supervision and care of a service animal. The NPRM proposed language at § 35.136(e) stating that "[a] public entity is not responsible for caring for or supervising a service animal." 73 FR 34466, 34504 (June 17, 2008). Most commenters did not address this particular provision. The Department recognizes that there are occasions when a person with a disability is confined to bed in a hospital for a period of time. In such an instance, the individual may not be able to walk or feed the service animal. In such cases, if the individual has a family member, friend, or other person willing to take on these responsibilities in the place of the individual with disabilities, the individual's obligation to be responsible for the care and supervision of the service animal would be satisfied. The language of this section is retained, with minor modifications, in § 35.136(e) of the final rule.

Inquiries about service animals. The NPRM proposed language at § 35.136(f) setting forth parameters about how a public entity may determine whether an animal qualifies as a service animal. The proposed section stated that a public entity may ask if the animal is required because of a disability and what task or work the animal has been trained to do but may not require proof of service animal certification or licensing. Such inquiries are limited to eliciting the information necessary to make a decision without requiring disclosure of confidential disability-related information that a State or local government entity does not need. This language is consistent with the policy guidance outlined in two Department publications, *Commonly Asked Questions about Service Animals in Places of Business* (1996), available at http://www.ada.gov/qasrvc.htm, and *ADA Guide for*

Small Businesses, (1999), available at http://www.ada.gov/smbustxt.htm.

Although some commenters contended that the NPRM service animal provisions leave unaddressed the issue of how a public entity can distinguish between a psychiatric service animal, which is covered under the final rule, and a comfort animal, which is not, other commenters noted that the Department's published guidance has helped public entities to distinguish between service animals and pets on the basis of an individual's response to these questions. Accordingly, the Department has retained the NPRM language incorporating its guidance concerning the permissible questions into the final rule.

Some commenters suggested that a title II entity be allowed to require current documentation, no more than one year old, on letterhead from a mental health professional stating the following: (1) That the individual seeking to use the animal has a mental health-related disability; (2) that having the animal accompany the individual is necessary to the individual's mental health or treatment or to assist the person otherwise; and (3) that the person providing the assessment of the individual is a licensed mental health professional and the individual seeking to use the animal is under that individual's professional care. These commenters asserted that this will prevent abuse and ensure that individuals with legitimate needs for psychiatric service animals may use them. The Department believes that this proposal would treat persons with psychiatric, intellectual, and other mental disabilities less favorably than persons with physical or sensory disabilities. The proposal would also require persons with disabilities to obtain medical documentation and carry it with them any time they seek to engage in ordinary activities of daily life in their communities — something individuals without disabilities have not been required to do. Accordingly, the Department has concluded that a documentation requirement of this kind would be unnecessary, burdensome, and contrary to the spirit, intent, and mandates of the ADA.

Areas of a public entity open to the public, participants in services, programs, or activities, or invitees. The NPRM proposed at § 35.136(g) that an individual with a disability who uses a service animal has the same right of access to areas of a title II entity as members of the public, participants in services, programs, or activities, or invitees. Commenters indicated that allowing individuals with disabilities to go with their service animals into the same areas as members of the public, participants in programs, services, or activities, or invitees is accepted practice by most State and local government entities. The Department has included a slightly modified version of this provision in § 35.136(g) of the final rule.

The Department notes that under the final rule, a healthcare facility must also permit a person with a disability to be accompanied by a service animal in all areas of the facility in which that person would otherwise be allowed. There are some exceptions, however. The Department follows the guidance of the Centers for Disease Control and Prevention (CDC) on the use of service animals in a hospital setting. Zoonotic diseases can be transmitted to humans through bites, scratches, direct contact, arthropod vectors, or aerosols.

Consistent with CDC guidance, it is generally appropriate to exclude a service animal from limited-access areas that employ general infection-control measures, such as operating rooms and burn units. *See* Centers for Disease Control and Prevention, *Guidelines for Environmental Infection Control in Health-Care Fa-*

cilities: Recommendations of CDC and the Healthcare Infection Control Practices Advisory Committee (June 2003), available at http://www.cdc.gov/hicpac/pdf/guidelines/eic_in_HCF_03.pdf (last visited June 24, 2010). A service animal may accompany its handler to such areas as admissions and discharge offices, the emergency room, inpatient and outpatient rooms, examining and diagnostic rooms, clinics, rehabilitation therapy areas, the cafeteria and vending areas, the pharmacy, restrooms, and all other areas of the facility where healthcare personnel, patients, and visitors are permitted without added precaution.

Prohibition against surcharges for use of a service animal. In the NPRM, the Department proposed to incorporate the previously mentioned policy guidance, which prohibits the assessment of a surcharge for the use of a service animal, into proposed § 35.136(h). Several commenters agreed that this provision makes clear the obligation of a public entity to admit an individual with a service animal without surcharges, and that any additional costs imposed should be factored into the overall cost of administering a program, service, or activity, and passed on as a charge to all participants, rather than an individualized surcharge to the service animal user. Commenters also noted that service animal users cannot be required to comply with other requirements that are not generally applicable to other persons. If a public entity normally charges individuals for the damage they cause, an individual with a disability may be charged for damage caused by his or her service animal. The Department has retained this language, with minor modifications, in the final rule at § 35.136(h).

Training requirement. Certain commenters recommended the adoption of formal training requirements for service animals. The Department has rejected this approach and will not impose any type of formal training requirements or certification process, but will continue to require that service animals be individually trained to do work or perform tasks for the benefit of an individual with a disability. While some groups have urged the Department to modify this position, the Department has determined that such a modification would not serve the full array of individuals with disabilities who use service animals, since individuals with disabilities may be capable of training, and some have trained, their service animal to perform tasks or do work to accommodate their disability. A training and certification requirement would increase the expense of acquiring a service animal and might limit access to service animals for individuals with limited financial resources.

Some commenters proposed specific behavior or training standards for service animals, arguing that without such standards, the public has no way to differentiate between untrained pets and service animals. Many of the suggested behavior or training standards were lengthy and detailed. The Department believes that this rule addresses service animal behavior sufficiently by including provisions that address the obligations of the service animal user and the circumstances under which a service animal may be excluded, such as the requirements that an animal be housebroken and under the control of its handler.

Miniature horses. The Department has been persuaded by commenters and the available research to include a provision that would require public entities to make reasonable modifications to policies, practices, or procedures to permit the use of a miniature horse by a person with a disability if the miniature horse has been individually trained to do work or perform tasks for the benefit of the individual with a disability. The traditional service animal is a dog, which has a long history of guiding individuals who are blind or have low vision, and over time dogs have been trained to perform an even wider variety of services for individuals with all types of disabilities. However, an organization that developed a program to train miniature horses, modeled on the program used for guide dogs, began training miniature horses in 1991.

Although commenters generally supported the species limitations proposed in the NPRM, some were opposed to the exclusion of miniature horses from the definition of a service animal. These commenters noted that these animals have been providing assistance to persons with disabilities for many years. Miniature horses were suggested by some commenters as viable alternatives to dogs for individuals with allergies, or for those whose religious beliefs preclude the use of dogs. Another consideration mentioned in favor of the use of miniature horses is the longer life span and strength of miniature horses in comparison to dogs. Specifically, miniature horses can provide service for more than 25 years while dogs can provide service for approximately 7 years, and, because of their strength, miniature horses can provide services that dogs cannot provide. Accordingly, use of miniature horses reduces the cost involved to retire, replace, and train replacement service animals.

The miniature horse is not one specific breed, but may be one of several breeds, with distinct characteristics that produce animals suited to service animal work. The animals generally range in height from 24 inches to 34 inches measured to the withers, or shoulders, and generally weigh between 70 and 100 pounds. These characteristics are similar to those of large breed dogs such as Labrador Retrievers, Great Danes, and Mastiffs. Similar to dogs, miniature horses can be trained through behavioral reinforcement to be "housebroken." Most miniature service horse handlers and organizations recommend that when the animals are not doing work or performing tasks, the miniature horses should be kept outside in a designated area, instead of indoors in a house.

According to information provided by an organization that trains service horses, these miniature horses are trained to provide a wide array of services to their handlers, primarily guiding individuals who are blind or have low vision, pulling wheelchairs, providing stability and balance for individuals with disabilities that impair the ability to walk, and supplying leverage that enables a person with a mobility disability to get up after a fall. According to the commenter, miniature horses are particularly effective for large stature individuals. The animals can be trained to stand (and in some cases, lie down) at the handler's feet in venues where space is at a premium, such as assembly areas or inside some vehicles that provide public transportation. Some individuals with disabilities have traveled by train and have flown commercially with their miniature horses.

The miniature horse is not included in the definition of service animal, which is limited to dogs. However, the Department has added a specific provision at § 35.136(i) of the final rule covering miniature horses. Under this provision, a public entity must make reasonable modifications in policies, practices, or procedures to permit the use of a miniature horse by an individual with a disability if the miniature horse has been individually trained to do work or perform tasks for the benefit of the individual with a disability. The public entity may take into account a series of assessment factors in determining whether to allow a miniature horse into a specific facility. These include the type, size, and weight of the miniature horse; whether the handler has sufficient control of the miniature horse; whether the miniature horse is housebroken; and whether the miniature horse's presence in a specific facility compromises legitimate safety requirements that are necessary for safe operation. In addition, paragraphs (c)–(h) of this section, which are applicable to dogs, also apply to miniature horses.

Ponies and full-size horses are not covered by § 35.136(i). Also, because miniature horses can vary in size and can be larger and less flexible than dogs, covered entities may exclude this type of service animal if the presence of the miniature horse, because of its larger size and lower level of flexibility, results in a fundamental alteration to the nature of the programs activities, or services provided.

Section 35.137   Mobility devices.

Section 35.137 of the NPRM clarified the scope and circumstances under which covered entities are legally obligated to accommodate various "mobility devices." Section 35.137 set forth specific requirements for the accommodation of "mobility devices," including wheelchairs, manually-powered mobility aids, and other power-driven mobility devices. In both the NPRM and the final rule, § 35.137(a) states the general rule that in any areas open to pedestrians, public entities shall permit individuals with mobility disabilities to use wheelchairs and manually- powered mobility aids, including walkers, crutches, canes, braces, or similar devices. Because mobility scooters satisfy the definition of "wheelchair" (i.e., "manually- operated or power-driven device designed primarily for use by an individual with a mobility disability for the main purpose of indoor, or of both indoor and outdoor locomotion"), the reference to them in § 35.137(a) of the final rule has been omitted to avoid redundancy.

Some commenters expressed concern that permitting the use of other power-driven mobility devices by individuals with mobility disabilities would make such devices akin to wheelchairs and would require them to make physical changes to their facilities to accommodate their use. This concern is misplaced. If a facility complies with the applicable design requirements in the 1991 Standards or the 2010 Standards, the public entity will not be required to exceed those standards to accommodate the use of wheelchairs or other power-driven mobility devices that exceed those requirements.

Legal standard for other power-driven mobility devices. The NPRM version of § 35.137(b) provided that "[a] public entity shall make reasonable modifications in its policies, practices, and procedures to permit the use of other power-driven mobility devices by individuals with disabilities, unless the public entity can demonstrate that the use of the device is not reasonable or that its use will result in a fundamental alteration in the public entity's service, program, or activity." 73 FR 34466, 34505 (June 17, 2008). In other words, public entities are by default required to permit the use of other power-driven mobility devices; the burden is on them to prove the existence of a valid exception.

Most commenters supported the notion of assessing whether the use of a particular device is reasonable in the context of a particular venue. Commenters, however, disagreed about the meaning of the word "reasonable" as it is used in § 35.137(b) of the NPRM. Advocacy and nonprofit groups almost universally objected to the use of a general reasonableness standard with regard to the assessment of whether a particular device should be allowed at a particular venue. They argued that the assessment should be based on whether reasonable modifications could be made to allow a particular device at a particular venue, and that the only factors that should be part of the calculus that results in the exclusion of a particular device are undue burden, direct threat, and fundamental alteration.

A few commenters opposed the proposed provision requiring public entities to assess whether reasonable modifications can be made to allow other power-driven mobility devices, preferring instead that the Department issue guidance materials so that public entities would not have to incur the cost of such analyses. Another commenter noted a "fox guarding the hen house"-type of concern with regard to public entities developing and enforcing their own modification policy.

In response to comments received, the Department has revised § 35.137(b) to provide greater clarity regarding the development of legitimate safety requirements regarding other power-driven mobility devices and has added a new § 35.130(h) (Safety) to the title II regulation which specifically permits public entities to impose legitimate safety requirements necessary for the safe operation of their services, programs, and activities. (See discussion below.) The Department has not retained the proposed NPRM language stating that an other power-driven mobility device can be excluded if a public entity can demonstrate that its use is unreasonable or will result in a fundamental alteration of the entity's service, program, or activity, because the Department believes that this exception is covered by the general reasonable modification requirement contained in § 35.130(b)(7).

Assessment factors. Section 35.137(c) of the NPRM required public entities to "establish policies to permit the use of other power-driven mobility devices" and articulated four factors upon which public entities must base decisions as to whether a modification is reasonable to allow the use of a class of other power-driven mobility devices by individuals with disabilities in specific venues (e.g., parks, courthouses, office buildings, etc.). 73 FR 34466, 34504 (June 17, 2008).

The Department has relocated and modified the NPRM text that appeared in § 35.137(c) to new paragraph § 35.137(b)(2) to clarify what factors the public entity shall use in determining whether a particular other power-driven mobility device can be allowed in a specific facility as a reasonable modification. Section 35.137(b)(2) now states that "[i]n determining whether a particular other power-driven mobility device can be allowed in a specific facility as a reasonable modification under (b)(1), a public entity shall consider" certain enumerated factors. The assessment factors are designed to assist public entities in determining whether allowing the use of a particular other power-driven mobility device in a specific facility is reasonable. Thus, the focus of the analysis must be on the appropriateness of the use of the device at a specific facility, rather than whether it is necessary for an individual to use a particular device.

The NPRM proposed the following specific assessment factors: (1) The dimensions, weight, and operating speed of the mobility device in relation to a wheelchair; (2) the potential risk of harm to others by the operation of the mobility device; (3) the risk of harm to the environment or natural or cultural resources or conflict with

Federal land management laws and regulations; and (4) the ability of the public entity to stow the mobility device when not in use, if requested by the user.

Factor 1 was designed to help public entities assess whether a particular device was appropriate, given its particular physical features, for a particular location. Virtually all commenters said the physical features of the device affected their view of whether a particular device was appropriate for a particular location. For example, while many commenters supported the use of another power-driven mobility device if the device were a Segway® PT, because of environmental and health concerns they did not offer the same level of support if the device were an off-highway vehicle, all- terrain vehicle (ATV), golf car, or other device with a fuel-powered or combustion engine. Most commenters noted that indicators such as speed, weight, and dimension really were an assessment of the appropriateness of a particular device in specific venues and suggested that factor 1 say this more specifically.

The term "in relation to a wheelchair" in the NPRM's factor 1 apparently created some concern that the same legal standards that apply to wheelchairs would be applied to other power-driven mobility devices. The Department has omitted the term "in relation to a wheelchair" from § 35.137(b)(2)(i) to clarify that if a facility that is in compliance with the applicable provisions of the 1991 Standards or the 2010 Standards grants permission for an other power-driven mobility device to go on-site, it is not required to exceed those standards to accommodate the use of other power-driven mobility devices.

In response to requests that NPRM factor 1 state more specifically that it requires an assessment of an other power-driven mobility device's appropriateness under particular circumstances or in particular venues, the Department has added several factors and more specific language. In addition, although the NPRM made reference to the operation of other power-driven mobility devices in "specific venues," the Department's intent is captured more clearly by referencing "specific facility" in paragraph (b)(2). The Department also notes that while speed is included in factor 1, public entities should not rely solely on a device's top speed when assessing whether the device can be accommodated; instead, public entities should also consider the minimum speeds at which a device can be operated and whether the development of speed limit policies can be established to address concerns regarding the speed of the device. Finally, since the ability of the public entity to stow the mobility device when not in use is an aspect of its design and operational characteristics, the text proposed as factor 4 in the NPRM has been incorporated in paragraph (b)(2)(iii).

The NPRM's version of factor 2 provided that the "risk of potential harm to others by the operation of the mobility device" is one of the determinants in the assessment of whether other power-driven mobility devices should be excluded from a site. The Department intended this requirement to be consistent with the Department's longstanding interpretation, expressed in § II-3.5200 (Safety) of the 1993 Title II Technical Assistance Manual, which provides that public entities may "impose legitimate safety requirements that are necessary for safe operation." (This language parallels the provision in the title III regulation at § 36.301(b).) However, several commenters indicated that they read this language, particularly the phrase "risk of potential harm," to mean that the Department had adopted a concept of risk analysis different from that which is in the existing standards. The Department did not intend to create a new standard and has changed the language in paragraphs (b)(1) and (b)(2) to clarify the applicable standards, thereby avoiding the introduction of new assessments of risk beyond those necessary for the safe operation of the public entity. In addition, the Department has added a new section, 35.130(h), which incorporates the existing safety standard into the title II regulation.

While all applicable affirmative defenses are available to public entities in the establishment and execution of their policies regarding other power-driven mobility devices, the Department did not explicitly incorporate the direct threat defense into the assessment factors because § 35.130(h) provides public entities the appropriate framework with which to assess whether legitimate safety requirements that may preclude the use of certain other power-driven mobility devices are necessary for the safe operation of the public entities. In order to be legitimate, the safety requirement must be based on actual risks and not mere speculation regarding the device or how it will be operated. Of course, public entities may enforce legitimate safety rules established by the public entity for the operation of other power-driven mobility devices (e.g., reasonable speed restrictions). Finally, NPRM factor 3 concerning environmental resources and conflicts of law has been relocated to § 35.137(b)(2)(v).

As a result of these comments and requests, NPRM factors 1, 2, 3, and 4 have been revised and renumbered within paragraph (b)(2) in the final rule.

Several commenters requested that the Department provide guidance materials or more explicit concepts of which considerations might be appropriate for inclusion in a policy that allows the use of other power-driven mobility devices. A public entity that has determined that reasonable modifications can be made in its policies, practices, or procedures to allow the use of other power-driven mobility devices should develop a policy that clearly states the circumstances under which the use of other power-driven mobility devices by individuals with a mobility disability will be permitted. It also should include clear, concise statements of specific rules governing the operation of such devices. Finally, the public entity should endeavor to provide individuals with disabilities who use other power-driven mobility devices with advanced notice of its policy regarding the use of such devices and what rules apply to the operation of these devices.

For example, the U.S. General Services Administration (GSA) has developed a policy allowing the use of the Segway® PT and other EPAMDs in all Federal buildings under GSA's jurisdiction. *See* General Services Administration, *Interim Segway® Personal Transporter Policy* (Dec. 3, 2007), available at http://www.gsa. gov/graphics/pbs/Interim_Segway_Policy_121007.pdf (last visited June 24, 2010). The GSA policy defines the policy's scope of coverage by setting out what devices are and are not covered by the policy. The policy also sets out requirements for safe operation, such as a speed limit, prohibits the use of EPAMDs on escalators, and provides guidance regarding security screening of these devices and their operators.

A public entity that determines that it can make reasonable modifications to permit the use of an other power-driven mobility device by an individual with a mobility disability might include in its policy the procedure by which claims that the other power-driven mobility device is being used for a mobility disability will be assessed for legitimacy (i.e., a credible assurance that the device is being used for a mobility disability, including a verbal representation by the person with a disability that is not contradicted by observable fact, or the presentation of a disability parking space placard or card, or State-issued proof of disability); the type or classes of other power-driven mobility devices are permitted to be used by individuals with mobility disabilities; the size, weight, and dimensions of the other power-driven mobility devices that are permitted to be used by individuals with mobility disabilities; the speed limit for the other power-driven mobility devices that are permitted to be used by individuals with mobility disabilities; the places, times, or circumstances under which the use of the other power-driven mobility device is or will be restricted or prohibited; safety, pedestrian, and other rules concerning the use of the other power-driven mobility device; whether, and under which circumstances, storage for the other power-driven mobility device will be made available; and how and where individuals with a mobility disability can obtain a copy of the other power-driven mobility device policy.

Public entities also might consider grouping other power-driven mobility devices by type (e.g., EPAMDs, golf cars, gasoline-powered vehicles, and other devices). For example, an amusement park may determine that it is reasonable to allow individuals with disabilities to use EPAMDs in a variety of outdoor programs and activities, but that it would not be reasonable to allow the use of golf cars as mobility devices in similar circumstances. At the same time, the entity may address its concerns about factors such as space limitations by disallowing use of EPAMDs by members of the general public who do not have mobility disabilities.

The Department anticipates that, in many circumstances, public entities will be able to develop policies that will allow the use of other power-driven mobility devices by individuals with mobility disabilities. Consider the following example:

A county courthouse has developed a policy whereby EPAMDs may be operated in the pedestrian areas of the courthouse if the operator of the device agrees not to operate the device faster than pedestrians are walking; to yield to pedestrians; to provide a rack or stand so that the device can stand upright; and to use the device only in courtrooms that are large enough to accommodate such devices. If the individual is selected for jury duty in one of the smaller courtrooms, the county's policy indicates that if it is not possible for the individual with the disability to park the device and walk into the courtroom, the location of the trial will be moved to a larger courtroom.

Inquiry into the use of other power-driven mobility device. The NPRM version of § 35.137(d) provided that "[a] public entity may ask a person using a power-driven mobility device if the mobility device is needed due to the person's disability. A public entity shall not ask a person using a mobility device questions about the nature and extent of the person's disability." 73 FR 34466, 34504 (June 17, 2008).

Many environmental, transit system, and government commenters expressed concern about people feigning mobility disabilities to be able to use other power-driven mobility devices in public entities in which their use is otherwise restricted. These commenters felt that a mere inquiry into whether the device is being used for a mobility disability was an insufficient mechanism by which to detect fraud by other power-driven mobility device users who do not have mobility disabilities. These commenters believed they should be given more latitude to make inquiries of other power-driven mobility device users claiming a mobility disability than they would be given for wheelchair users. They sought the ability to establish a policy or method by which public entities may assess the legitimacy of the mobility disability. They suggested some form of certification, sticker, or other designation. One commenter suggested a requirement that a sticker bearing the international symbol for accessibility be placed on the device or that some other identification be required to signal that the use of the device is for a mobility disability. Other suggestions included displaying a disability parking placard on the device or issuing EPAMDs, like the Segway® PT, a permit that would be similar to permits associated with parking spaces reserved for those with disabilities.

Advocacy, nonprofit, and several individual commenters balked at the notion of allowing any inquiry beyond whether the device is necessary for a mobility disability and encouraged the Department to retain the NPRM's language on this topic. Other commenters, however, were empathetic with commenters who had concerns about fraud. At least one Segway® PT advocate suggested it would be permissible to seek documentation of the mobility disability in the form of a simple sign or permit.

The Department has sought to find common ground by balancing the needs of public entities and individuals with mobility disabilities wishing to use other power-driven mobility devices with the Department's longstanding, well-established policy of not allowing public entities or establishments to require proof of a mobility disability. There is no question that public entities have a legitimate interest in ferreting out fraudulent representations of mobility disabilities, especially given the recreational use of other power-driven mobility devices and the potential safety concerns created by having too many such devices in a specific facility at one time. However, the privacy of individuals with mobility disabilities and respect for those individuals, is also vitally important.

Neither § 35.137(d) of the NPRM nor § 35.137(c) of the final rule permits inquiries into the nature of a person's mobility disability. However, the Department does not believe it is unreasonable or overly intrusive for an individual with a mobility disability seeking to use an other power-driven mobility device to provide a credible assurance to verify that the use of the other power-driven mobility device is for a mobility disability. The Department sought to minimize the amount of discretion and subjectivity exercised by public entities in assessing whether an individual has a mobility disability and to allow public entities to verify the existence of a mobility disability. The solution was derived from comments made by several individuals who said they have been admitted with their Segway® PTs into public entities and public accommodations that ordinarily do not allow these devices on-site when they have presented or displayed State-issued disability parking placards. In the examples provided by commenters, the parking placards were accepted as verification that the Segway® PTs were being used as mobility devices.

Because many individuals with mobility disabilities avail themselves of State programs that issue disability parking placards or cards and because these programs have penalties for fraudulent representations of identity and disability, utilizing the parking placard system as a means to establish the existence of a mobility disability strikes a balance between the need for privacy of the individual and fraud protection for the public entity. Consequently, the Department has decided to include regulatory text in § 35.137(c)(2) of the final rule that requires public entities to accept the presentation of a valid, State- issued disability parking placard or card, or State-issued proof of disability, as verification that an individual uses the other power-driven mobility device for his or her mobility disability. A "valid" disability placard or card is one that is presented by the individual to whom it was issued and is otherwise in compliance with the State of issuance's requirements for disability placards or cards. Public entities are required to accept a valid, State-issued disability parking placard or card, or State-issued proof of disability as a credible assurance, but they cannot demand or require the presentation of a valid disability placard or card, or State- issued proof of disability, as a prerequisite for use of an other power-driven mobility device, because not all persons with mobility disabilities have such means of proof. If an individual with a mobility disability does not have such a placard or card, or State-issued proof of disability, he or she may present other information that would serve as a credible assurance of the existence of a mobility disability.

In lieu of a valid, State-issued disability parking placard or card, or State-issued proof of disability, a verbal representation, not contradicted by observable fact, shall be accepted as a credible assurance that the other power-driven mobility device is being used because of a mobility disability. This does not mean, however, that a mobility disability must be observable as a condition for allowing the use of an other power-driven mobility device by an individual with a mobility disability, but rather that if an individual represents that a device is being used for a mobility disability and that individual is observed thereafter engaging in a physical activity that is contrary to the nature of the represented disability, the assurance given is no longer credible and the individual may be prevented from using the device.

Possession of a valid, State-issued disability parking placard or card or a verbal assurance does not trump a public entity's valid restrictions on the use of other power-driven mobility devices. Accordingly, a credible assurance that the other power-driven mobility device is being used because of a mobility disability is not a guarantee of entry to a public entity because, notwithstanding such credible assurance, use of the device in a particular venue may be at odds with the legal standard in § 35.137(b)(1) or with one or more of the § 35.137(b)(2) factors. Only after an individual with a disability has satisfied all of the public entity's policies regarding the use of other power-driven mobility devices does a credible assurance become a factor in allowing the use of the device. For example, if an individual seeking to use an other power-driven mobility device fails to satisfy any of the public entity's stated policies regarding the use of other power-driven mobility devices, the fact that the individual legitimately possesses and presents a valid, State-issued disability parking placard or card, or State-issued proof of disability, does not trump the policy and require the public entity to allow the use of the device. In fact, in some instances, the presentation of a legitimately held placard or card, or State-issued proof of disability, will have no relevance or bearing at all on whether the other power-driven mobility device may be used, because the public entity's policy does not permit the device in question on-site under any circumstances (e.g., because its use would create a substantial risk of serious harm to the immediate environment or natural or cultural resources). Thus, an individual with a mobility disability who presents a valid disability placard or card, or State-issued proof of disability, will not be able to use an ATV as an other power-driven mobility device in a State park if the State park has adopted a policy banning their use for any or all of the above-mentioned reasons. However, if a public entity permits the use of a particular other power-driven mobility device, it cannot refuse to admit an individual with a disability who uses that device if the individual has provided a credible assurance that the use of the device is for a mobility disability.

Section 35.138   Ticketing.

The 1991 title II regulation did not contain specific regulatory language on ticketing. The ticketing policies and practices of public entities, however, are subject to title II's nondiscrimination provisions. Through the investigation of complaints, enforcement actions, and public comments related to ticketing, the Department became aware that some venue operators, ticket sellers, and distributors were violating title II's nondiscrimination mandate by not providing individuals with disabilities the same opportunities to purchase tickets for accessible seating as they provided to spectators purchasing conventional seats. In the NPRM, the Department proposed § 35.138 to provide explicit direction and guidance on discriminatory practices for entities involved in the sale or distribution of tickets.

The Department received comments from advocacy groups, assembly area trade associations, public entities, and individuals. Many commenters supported the addition of regulatory language pertaining to ticketing and urged the Department to retain it in the final rule. Several commenters, however, questioned why there were inconsistencies between the title II and title III provisions and suggested that the same language be used for both titles. The Department has decided to retain ticketing regulatory language and to ensure consistency between the ticketing provisions in title II and title III.

Because many in the ticketing industry view season tickets and other multi-event packages differently from individual tickets, the Department bifurcated some season ticket provisions from those concerning single- event tickets in the NPRM. This structure, however, resulted in some provisions being repeated for both types of tickets but not for others even though they were intended to apply to both types of tickets. The result was that it was not entirely clear that some of the provisions that were not repeated also were intended to apply to season tickets. The Department is addressing the issues raised by these commenters using a different approach. For the purposes of this section, a *single event* refers to an individual performance for which tickets may be purchased. In contrast, a *series of events* includes, but is not limited to, subscription events, event packages, season tickets, or any other tickets that may be purchased for multiple events of the same type over the course of a specified period of time whose ownership right reverts to the public entity at the end of each season or time period. Series-of-events tickets that give their holders an enhanced ability to purchase such tickets from the public entity in seasons or periods of time that follow, such as a right of first refusal or higher ranking on waiting lists for more desirable seats, are subject to the provisions in this section. In addition, the final rule merges together some NPRM paragraphs that dealt with related topics and has reordered and renamed some of the paragraphs that were in the NPRM.

Ticket sales. In the NPRM, the Department proposed, in § 35.138(a), a general rule that a public entity shall modify its policies, practices, or procedures to ensure that individuals with disabilities can purchase tickets for accessible seating for an event or series of events in the same way as others (i.e., during the same hours and through the same distribution methods as other seating is sold). 73 FR 34466, 34504 (June 17, 2008). "Accessible seating" is defined in§ 35.138(a)(1) of the final rule to mean "wheelchair spaces and companion seats that comply with sections 221 and 802 of the 2010 Standards along with any other seats required to be offered for sale to the individual with a disability pursuant to paragraph (d) of this section." The defined term does not include designated aisle seats. A "wheelchair space" refers to a space for a single wheelchair and its occupant.

The NPRM proposed requiring that accessible seats be sold through the "same methods of distribution" as non-accessible seats. Comments from venue managers and others in the business community, in general, noted that multiple parties are involved in ticketing, and because accessible seats may not be allotted to all parties involved at each stage, such parties should be protected from liability. For example, one commenter noted that a third-party ticket vendor, like Ticketmaster, can only sell the tickets it receives from its client. Because § 35.138(a)(2)(iii) of the final rule requires venue operators to make available accessible seating through the same methods of distribution they use for their regular tickets, venue operators that provide tickets to third- party ticket vendors are required to provide accessible seating to the third-party ticket vendor. This provision will enhance third- party ticket vendors' ability to acquire and sell accessible seating for sale in the future. The Department notes that once third-party ticket vendors acquire accessible tickets, they are obligated to sell them in accordance with these rules.

The Department also has received frequent complaints that individuals with disabilities have not been able to purchase accessible seating over the Internet, and instead have had to engage in a laborious process of calling a customer service line, or sending an e-mail to a customer service representative and waiting for a response. Not only is such a process burdensome, but it puts individuals with disabilities at a disadvantage in purchasing tickets for events that are popular and may sell out in minutes. Because § 35.138(e) of the final rule authorizes venues to release accessible seating in case of a sell- out, individuals with disabilities effectively could be cut off from buying tickets unless they also have the ability to purchase tickets in real time over the Internet. The Department's new regulatory language is designed to address this problem.

Several commenters representing assembly areas raised concerns about offering accessible seating for sale over the Internet. They contended that this approach would increase the incidence of fraud since anyone easily could purchase accessible seating over the Internet. They also asserted that it would be difficult technologically to provide accessible seating for sale in real time over the Internet, or that to do so would require simplifying the rules concerning the purchase of multiple additional accompanying seats. Moreover, these commenters argued that requiring an individual purchasing accessible seating to speak with a customer service representative would allow the venue to meet the patron's needs most appropriately and ensure that wheelchair spaces are reserved for individuals with disabilities who require wheelchair spaces. Finally, these commenters argued that individuals who can transfer effectively and conveniently from a wheelchair to a seat with a movable armrest seat could instead purchase designated aisle seats.

The Department considered these concerns carefully and has decided to continue with the general approach proposed in the NPRM. Although fraud is an important concern, the Department believes that it is best combated by other means that would not have the effect of limiting the ability of individuals with disabilities to purchase tickets, particularly since restricting the purchase of accessible seating over the Internet will, of itself, not curb fraud. In addition, the Department has identified permissible means for covered entities to reduce the incidence of fraudulent accessible seating ticket purchases in § 35.138(h) of the final rule.

Several commenters questioned whether ticket websites themselves must be accessible to individuals who are blind or have low vision, and if so, what that requires. The Department has consistently interpreted the ADA to cover websites that are operated by public entities and stated that such sites must provide their services in an accessible manner or provide an accessible alternative to the website that is available 24 hours a day, seven days a week. The final rule, therefore, does not impose any new obligation in this area. The accessibility of websites is discussed in more detail in the section of Appendix A entitled "Other Issues."

In § 35.138(b) of the NPRM, the Department also proposed requiring public entities to make accessible seating available during all stages of tickets sales including, but not limited to, presales, promotions, lotteries, waitlists, and general sales. For example, if tickets will be presold for an event that is open only to members of a fan club, or to holders of a particular credit card, then tickets for accessible seating must be made available for purchase through those means. This requirement does not mean that any individual with a disability would be able to purchase those seats. Rather, it means that an individual with a disability who meets the requirement for such a sale (e.g., who is a member of the fan club or holds that credit card) will be able to participate in the special promotion and purchase accessible seating. The Department has maintained the substantive provisions of the NPRM's § 35.138(a) and (b) but has combined them in a single paragraph at § 35.138(a)(2) of the final rule so that all of the provisions having to do with the manner in which tickets are sold are located in a single paragraph.

Identification of available accessible seating. In the NPRM, the Department proposed § 35.138(c), which, as modified and renumbered as paragraph (b)(3) in the final rule, requires a facility to identify available accessible seating through seating maps, brochures, or other methods if that information is made available about other seats sold to the general public. This rule requires public entities to provide information about accessible seating to the same degree of specificity that it provides information about general seating. For example, if a seating map displays color- coded blocks pegged to prices for general seating, then accessible seating must be similarly color-coded. Likewise, if covered entities provide detailed maps that show exact seating and pricing for general seating, they must provide the same for accessible seating.

The NPRM did not specify a requirement to identify prices for accessible seating. The final rule requires that if such information is provided for general seating, it must be provided for accessible seating as well.

In the NPRM, the Department proposed in § 35.138(d) that a public entity, upon being asked, must inform persons with disabilities and their companions of the locations of all unsold or otherwise available seating. This provision is intended to prevent the practice of "steering" individuals with disabilities to certain accessible seating so that the facility can maximize potential ticket sales by releasing unsold accessible seating, especially in preferred or desirable locations, for sale to the general public. The Department received no significant comment on this proposal. The Department has retained this provision in the final rule but has added it, with minor modifications, to § 35.138(b) as paragraph (1).

Ticket prices. In the NPRM, the Department proposed § 35.138(e) requiring that ticket prices for accessible seating be set no higher than the prices for other seats in that seating section for that event. The NPRM's provision also required that accessible seating be made available at every price range, and if an existing facility has barriers to accessible seating within a particular price range, a proportionate amount of seating (determined by the ratio of the total number of seats at that price level to the total number of seats in the assembly area) must be offered in an accessible location at that same price. Under this rule, for example, if a public entity has a 20,000- seat facility built in 1980 with inaccessible seating in the $20-price category, which is on the upper deck, and it chooses not to put accessible seating in that section, then it must place a proportionate number of seats in an accessible location for $20. If the upper deck has 2,000 seats, then the facility must place 10 percent of its accessible seating in an accessible location for $20 provided that it is part of a seating section where ticket prices are equal to or more than $20 — a facility may not place the $20-accessible seating in a $10-seating section. The Department received no significant comment on this rule, and it has been retained, as amended, in the final rule in § 35.138(c).

Purchase of multiple tickets. In the NPRM, the Department proposed § 35.138(i) to address one of the most common ticketing complaints raised with the Department: That individuals with disabilities are not able to purchase more than two tickets. The Department proposed this provision to facilitate the ability of individuals with disabilities to attend events with friends, companions, or associates who may or may not have a disability by enabling individuals with disabilities to purchase the maximum number of tickets allowed per transaction to other spectators; by requiring venues to place accompanying individuals in general seating as close as possible to accessible seating (in the event that a group must be divided because of the large size of the group); and by allowing an individual with a disability to purchase up to three additional contiguous seats per wheelchair space if they are available at the time of sale. Section 35.138(i)(2) of the NPRM required that a group containing one or more wheelchair users must be placed together, if possible, and that in the event that the group could not be placed together, the individuals with disabilities may not be isolated from the rest of the group.

The Department asked in the NPRM whether this rule was sufficient to effectuate the integration of individuals with disabilities. Many advocates and individuals praised it as a welcome and much-needed change, stating that the trade-off of being able to sit with their family or friends was worth reducing the number of seats available for individuals with disabilities. Some commenters went one step further and suggested that the number of additional accompanying seats should not be restricted to three.

Although most of the substance of the proposed provision on the purchase of multiple tickets has been maintained in the final rule, it has been renumbered as

§ 35.138(d), reorganized, and supplemented. To preserve the availability of accessible seating for other individuals with disabilities, the Department has not expanded the rule beyond three additional contiguous seats. Section 35.138(d)(1) of the final rule requires public entities to make available for purchase three additional tickets for seats in the same row that are contiguous with the wheelchair space provided that at the time of the purchase there are three such seats available. The requirement that the additional seats be "contiguous with the wheelchair space" does not mean that each of the additional seats must be in actual contact or have a border in common with the wheelchair space; however, at least one of the additional seats should be immediately adjacent to the wheelchair space. The Department recognizes that it will often be necessary to use vacant wheelchair spaces to provide for contiguous seating.

The Department has added paragraphs (d)(2) and (d)(3) to clarify that in situations where there are insufficient unsold seats to provide three additional contiguous seats per wheelchair space or a ticket office restricts sales of tickets to a particular event to less than four tickets per customer, the obligation to make available three additional contiguous seats per wheelchair space would be affected. For example, if at the time of purchase, there are only two additional contiguous seats available for purchase because the third has been sold already, then the ticket purchaser would be entitled to two such seats. In this situation, the public entity would be required to make up the difference by offering one additional ticket for sale that is as close as possible to the accessible seats. Likewise, if ticket purchases for an event are limited to two per customer, a person who uses a wheelchair who seeks to purchase tickets would be entitled to purchase only one additional contiguous seat for the event.

The Department also has added paragraph (d)(4) to clarify that the requirement for three additional contiguous seats is not intended to serve as a cap if the maximum number of tickets that may be purchased by members of the general public exceeds the four tickets an individual with a disability ordinarily would be allowed to purchase (i.e., a wheelchair space and three additional contiguous seats). If the maximum number of tickets that may be purchased by members of the general public exceeds four, an individual with a disability is to be allowed to purchase the maximum number of tickets; however, additional tickets purchased by an individual with a disability beyond the wheelchair space and the three additional contiguous seats provided in § 35.138(d)(1) do not have to be contiguous with the wheelchair space.

The NPRM proposed at § 35.138(i)(2) that for group sales, if a group includes one or more individuals who use a wheelchair, then the group shall be placed in a seating area with accessible seating so that, if possible, the group can sit together. If it is necessary to divide the group, it should be divided so that the individuals in the group who use wheelchairs are not isolated from the rest of the members of their group. The final rule retains the NPRM language in paragraph (d)(5).

Hold-and-release of unsold accessible seating. The Department recognizes that not all accessible seating will be sold in all assembly areas for every event to individuals with disabilities who need such seating and that public entities may have opportunities to sell such seating to the general public. The Department proposed in the NPRM a provision aimed at striking a balance between affording individuals with disabilities adequate time to purchase accessible seating and the entity's desire to maximize ticket sales. In the NPRM, the Department proposed § 35.138(f), which allowed for the release of accessible seating under the following circumstances: (i) When all seating in the facility has been sold, excluding luxury boxes, club boxes, or suites; (ii) when all seating in a designated area has been sold and the accessible seating being released is in the same area; or (iii) when all seating in a designated price range has been sold and the accessible seating being released is within the same price range.

The Department's NPRM asked "whether additional regulatory guidance is required or appropriate in terms of a more detailed or set schedule for the release of tickets in conjunction with the three approaches described above. For example, does the proposed regulation address the variable needs of assembly areas covered by the ADA? Is additional regulatory guidance required to eliminate discriminatory policies, practices and procedures related to the sale, hold, and release of accessible seating? What considerations should appropriately inform the determination of when unsold accessible seating can be released to the general public?" 73 FR 34466, 34484 (June 17, 2008).

The Department received comments both supporting and opposing the inclusion of a hold-and-release provision. One side proposed loosening the restrictions on the release of unsold accessible seating. One commenter from a trade association suggested that tickets should be released regardless of whether there is a sell-out, and that these tickets should be released according to a set schedule. Conversely, numerous individuals, advocacy groups, and at least one public entity urged the Department to tighten the conditions under which unsold tickets for accessible seating may be released. These commenters suggested that venues should not be permitted to release tickets during the first two weeks of sale, or alternatively, that they should not be permitted to be released earlier than 48 hours before a sold-out event. Many of these commenters criticized the release of accessible seating under the second and third prongs of § 35.138(f) in the NPRM (when there is a sell-out in general seating in a designated seating area or in a price range), arguing that it would create situations where general seating would be available for purchase while accessible seating would not be.

Numerous commenters — both from the industry and from advocacy groups — asked for clarification of the term "sell-out." Business groups commented that industry practice is to declare a sell-out when there are only "scattered singles" available — isolated seats that cannot be purchased as a set of adjacent pairs. Many of those same commenters also requested that "sell-out" be qualified with the phrase "of all seating available for sale" since it is industry practice to hold back from release tickets to be used for groups connected with that event (e.g., the promoter, home team, or sports league). They argued that those tickets are not available for sale and any return of these tickets to the general inventory happens close to the event date. Noting the practice of holding back tickets, one advocacy group suggested that covered entities be required to hold back accessible seating in proportion to the number of tickets that are held back for later release.

The Department has concluded that it would be inappropriate to interfere with industry practice by defining what constitutes a "sell-out" and that a public entity should continue to use its own approach to defining a "sell-out." If, however, a public entity declares a sell-out by reference to those seats that are available for sale, but it holds back tickets that it reasonably anticipates will be released later, it must hold back a proportional percentage of accessible seating to be released as well.

Adopting any of the alternatives proposed in the comments summarized above would have upset the balance between protecting the rights of individuals with disabilities and meeting venues' concerns about lost revenue from unsold accessible seating. As a result, the Department has retained § 35.138(f) (renumbered as § 35.138(e)) in the final rule.

The Department has, however, modified the regulation text to specify that accessible seating may be released only when "all non- accessible tickets in a designated seating area have been sold and the tickets for accessible seating are being released in the same designated area." As stated in the NPRM, the Department intended for this provision to allow, for example, the release of accessible seating at the orchestra level when all other seating at the orchestra level is sold. The Department has added this language to the final rule at § 35.138(e)(1)(ii) to clarify that venues cannot designate or redesignate seating areas for the purpose of maximizing the release of unsold accessible seating. So, for example, a venue may not determine on an *ad hoc* basis that a group of seats at the orchestra level is a designated seating area in order to release unsold accessible seating in that area.

The Department also has maintained the hold-and-release provisions that appeared in the NPRM but has added a provision to address the release of accessible seating for series-of-events tickets on a series-of-events basis. Many commenters asked the Department whether unsold accessible seating may be converted to general seating and released to the general public on a season-ticket basis or longer when tickets typically are sold as a season-ticket package or other long-term basis. Several disability rights organizations and individual commenters argued that such a practice should not be permitted, and, if it were, that conditions should be imposed to ensure that individuals with disabilities have future access to those seats.

The Department interprets the fundamental principle of the ADA as a require- ment to give individuals with disabilities equal, not better, access to those opportunities available to the general public. Thus, for example, a public entity that sells out its facility on a season- ticket only basis is not required to leave unsold its accessible seating if no persons with disabilities purchase those season-ticket seats. Of course, public entities may choose to go beyond what is required by reserving accessible seating for individuals with disabilities (or releasing such seats for sale to the general public) on an individual-game basis.

If a covered entity chooses to release unsold accessible seating for sale on a season-ticket or other long-term basis, it must meet at least two conditions. Under § 35.138(g) of the final rule, public entities must leave flexibility for game-day change- outs to accommodate ticket transfers on the secondary market. And public entities must modify their ticketing policies so that, in future years, individuals with disabilities will have the ability to purchase accessible seating on the same basis as other patrons (e.g., as season tickets). Put differently, releasing accessible seating to the general public on a season-ticket or other long-term basis cannot result in that seating being lost to individuals with disabilities in perpetuity. If, in future years, season tickets become available and persons with disabilities have reached the top of the waiting list or have met any other eligibility criteria for season- ticket purchases, public entities must ensure that accessible seating will be made available to the eligible individuals. In order to accomplish this, the Department has added § 35.138(e)(3)(i) to require public entities that release accessible season tickets to individuals who do not have disabilities that require the features of accessible seating to establish a process to prevent the automatic reassignment of such ticket holders to accessible seating. For example, a public entity could have in place a system whereby accessible seating that was released because it was not purchased by individuals with disabilities is not in the pool of tickets available for purchase for the following season unless and until the conditions for ticket release have been satisfied in the following season. Alternatively, a public entity might release tickets for accessible seating only when a purchaser who does not need its features agrees that he or she has no guarantee of or right to the same seats in the following season, or that if season tickets are guaranteed for the following season, the purchaser agrees that the offer to purchase tickets is limited to non-accessible seats having to the extent practicable, comparable price, view, and amenities to the accessible seats such individuals held in the prior year. The Department is aware that this rule may require some administrative changes but believes that this process will not create undue financial and administrative burdens. The Department believes that this approach is balanced and beneficial. It will allow public entities to sell all of their seats and will leave open the possibility, in future seasons or series of events, that persons who need accessible seating may have access to it.

The Department also has added § 35.138(e)(3)(ii) to address how season tickets or series-of-events tickets that have attached ownership rights should be handled if the ownership right returns to the public entity (e.g., when holders forfeit their ownership right by failing to purchase season tickets or sell their ownership right back to a public entity). If the ownership right is for accessible seating, the public entity is required to adopt a process that allows an eligible individual with a disability who requires the features of such seating to purchase the rights and tickets for such seating.

Nothing in the regulatory text prevents a public entity from establishing a process whereby such ticket holders agree to be voluntarily reassigned from accessible seating to another seating area so that individuals with mobility disabilities or disabilities that require the features of accessible seating and who become newly eligible to purchase season tickets have an opportunity to do so. For example, a public entity might seek volunteers to relocate to another location that is at least as good in terms of its location, price, and amenities, or a public entity might use a seat with forfeited ownership rights as an inducement to get a ticket holder to give up accessible seating he or she does not need.

Ticket transfer. The Department received many comments asking whether accessible seating has the same transfer rights as general seats. The proposed regulation at § 35.138(e) required that individuals with disabilities must be allowed to purchase season tickets for accessible seating on the same terms and conditions as individuals purchasing season tickets for general seating, including the right — if it exists for other ticket-holders — to transfer individual tickets to friends or associates. Some commenters pointed out that the NPRM proposed explicitly allowing individuals with disabilities holding season tickets to transfer tickets but did not address the transfer of tickets purchased for individual events. Several commenters representing assembly areas argued that persons with disabilities holding tickets for an individual event should not be allowed to sell or transfer them to third parties because such ticket transfers would increase the risk of fraud or would make unclear the obligation of the entity to accommodate secondary ticket transfers. They argued that individuals holding accessible seating should either be required to transfer their tickets to another individual with a disability or return them to the facility for a refund.

Although the Department is sympathetic to concerns about administrative burden, curtailing transfer rights for accessible seating when other ticket holders are permitted to transfer tickets would be inconsistent with the ADA's guiding principle that individuals with disabilities must have rights equal to others. Thus, the Department has added language in the final rule in § 35.138(f) that requires that individuals with disabilities holding accessible seating for any event have the same transfer rights accorded other ticket holders for that event. Section 35.138(f) also preserves the rights of individuals with disabilities who hold tickets to accessible seats for a series of events to transfer individual tickets to others, regardless of whether the transferee needs accessible seating. This approach recognizes the common practice of individuals splitting season tickets or other multi-event ticket packages with friends, colleagues, or other spectators to make the purchase of season tickets affordable; individuals with disabilities should not be placed in the burdensome position of having to find another individual with a disability with whom to share the package.

This provision, however, does not require public entities to seat an individual who holds a ticket to an accessible seat in such seating if the individual does not need the accessible features of the seat. A public entity may reserve the right to switch these individuals to different seats if they are available, but a public entity is not required to remove a person without a disability who is using accessible seating from that seating, even if a person who uses a wheelchair shows up with a ticket from the secondary market for a non-accessible seat and wants accessible seating.

Secondary ticket market. Section 35.138(g) is a new provision in the final rule that requires a public entity to modify its policies, practices, or procedures to ensure that an individual with a disability, who acquires a ticket in the secondary ticket market, may use that ticket under the same terms and conditions as other ticket holders who acquire a ticket in the secondary market for an event or series of events. This principle was discussed in the NPRM in connection with § 35.138(e), pertaining to season-ticket sales. There, the Department asked for public comment regarding a public entity's proposed obligation to accommodate the transfer of accessible seating tickets on the secondary ticket market to those who do not need accessible seating and vice versa.

The secondary ticket market, for the purposes of this rule, broadly means any transfer of tickets after the public entity's initial sale of tickets to individuals or entities. It thus encompasses a wide variety of transactions, from ticket transfers between friends to transfers using commercial exchange systems. Many commenters noted that the distinction between the primary and secondary ticket market has become blurred as a result of agreements between teams, leagues, and secondary market sellers. These commenters noted that the secondary market may operate independently of the public entity, and parts of the secondary market, such as ticket transfers between friends, undoubtedly are outside the direct jurisdiction of the public entity.

To the extent that venues seat persons who have purchased tickets on the secondary market, they must similarly seat persons with disabilities who have purchased tickets on the secondary market. In addition, some public entities may acquire ADA obligations directly by formally entering the secondary ticket market.

The Department's enforcement experience with assembly areas also has revealed that venues regularly provide for and make last- minute seat transfers. As long as there are vacant wheelchair spaces, requiring venues to provide wheelchair spaces for patrons who acquired inaccessible seats and need wheelchair spaces is an example of a reasonable modification of a policy under title II of the ADA. Similarly, a person who has a ticket for a wheelchair space but who does not require its accessible features could be offered non-accessible seating if such seating is available.

The Department's longstanding position that title II of the ADA requires venues to make reasonable modifications in their policies to allow individuals with disabilities who acquired non-accessible tickets on the secondary ticket market to be seated in accessible seating, where such seating is vacant, is supported by the only Federal court to address this issue. *See Independent Living Resources* v. *Oregon Arena Corp.*, 1 F. Supp. 2d 1159, 1171 (D. Or. 1998). The Department has incorporated this position into the final rule at § 35.138(g)(2).

The NPRM contained two questions aimed at gauging concern with the Department's consideration of secondary ticket market sales. The first question asked whether a secondary purchaser who does not have a disability and who buys an accessible seat should be required to move if the space is needed for someone with a disability.

Many disability rights advocates answered that the individual should move provided that there is a seat of comparable or better quality available for him and his companion. Some venues, however, expressed concerns about this provision, and asked how they are to identify who should be moved and what obligations apply if there are no seats available that are equivalent or better in quality.

The Department's second question asked whether there are particular concerns about the obligation to provide accessible seating, including a wheelchair space, to an individual with a disability who purchases an inaccessible seat through the secondary market.

Industry commenters contended that this requirement would create a "logistical nightmare," with venues scrambling to reseat patrons in the short time between the opening of the venues' doors and the commencement of the event. Furthermore, they argued that they might not be able to reseat all individuals and that even if they were able to do so, patrons might be moved to inferior seats (whether in accessible or non-accessible seating). These commenters also were concerned that they would be sued by patrons moved under such circumstances.

These commenters seem to have misconstrued the rule. Covered entities are not required to seat every person who acquires a ticket for inaccessible seating but needs accessible seating, and are not required to move any individual who acquires a ticket for accessible seating but does not need it. Covered entities that allow patrons to buy and sell tickets on the secondary market must make reasonable modifications to their policies to allow persons with disabilities to participate in secondary ticket transfers. The Department believes that there is no one-size-fits-all rule that will suit all assembly areas. In those circumstances where a venue has accessible seating vacant at the time an individual with a disability who needs accessible seating presents his ticket for inaccessible seating at the box office, the venue must allow the individual to exchange his ticket for an accessible seat in a comparable location if such an accessible seat is vacant. Where, however, a venue has sold all of its accessible seating, the venue has no obligation to provide accessible seating to the person with a disability who purchased an inaccessible seat on the secondary market. Venues may encourage individuals with disabilities who hold tickets for inaccessible seating to contact the box office before the event to notify them of their need for accessible seating, even though they may not require ticketholders to provide such notice.

The Department notes that public entities are permitted, though not required, to adopt policies regarding moving patrons who do not need the features of an accessible seat. If a public entity chooses to do so, it might mitigate administrative concerns by marking tickets for accessible seating as such, and printing on the ticket that individuals who purchase such seats but who do not need accessible seating are subject to being moved to other seats in the facility if the accessible seating is required for an individual with a disability. Such a venue might also develop and publish a ticketing policy to provide transparency to the general public and to put holders of tickets for accessible seating who do not require it on notice that they may be moved.

Prevention of fraud in purchase of accessible seating. Assembly area managers and advocacy groups have informed the Department that the fraudulent purchase of accessible seating is a pressing concern. Curbing fraud is a goal that public entities and individuals with disabilities share. Steps taken to prevent fraud, however, must be balanced carefully against the privacy rights of individuals with disabilities. Such measures also must not impose burdensome requirements upon, nor restrict the rights of, individuals with disabilities.

In the NPRM, the Department struck a balance between these competing concerns by proposing § 35.138(h), which prohibited public entities from asking for proof of disability before the purchase of accessible seating but provided guidance in two paragraphs on appropriate measures for curbing fraud. Paragraph (1) proposed allowing a public entity to ask individuals purchasing single-event tickets for accessible seating whether they are wheelchair users. Paragraph (2) proposed allowing a public entity to require the individuals purchasing accessible seating for season tickets or other multi-event ticket packages to attest in writing that the accessible seating is for a wheelchair user. Additionally, the NPRM proposed to permit venues, when they have good cause to believe that an individual has fraudulently purchased accessible seating, to investigate that individual.

Several commenters objected to this rule on the ground that it would require a wheelchair user to be the purchaser of tickets. The Department has reworded this paragraph to reflect that the individual with a disability does not have to be the ticket purchaser. The final rule allows third parties to purchase accessible tickets at the request of an individual with a disability.

Commenters also argued that other individuals with disabilities who do not use wheelchairs should be permitted to purchase accessible seating. Some individuals with disabilities who do not use wheelchairs urged the Department to change the rule, asserting that they, too, need accessible seating. The Department agrees that such seating, although designed for use by a wheelchair user, may be used by non-wheelchair users, if those persons are persons with a disability who need to use accessible seating because of a mobility disability or because their disability requires the use of the features that accessible seating provides (e.g., individuals who cannot bend their legs because of braces, or individuals who, because of their disability, cannot sit in a straight-back chair).

Some commenters raised concerns that allowing venues to ask questions to determine whether individuals purchasing accessible seating are doing so legitimately would burden individuals with disabilities in the purchase of accessible seating. The Department has retained the substance of this provision in § 35.138(h) of the final rule, but emphasizes that such questions should be asked at the initial time of purchase. For example, if the method of purchase is via the Internet, then the question(s) should be answered by clicking a yes or no box during the transaction. The public entity may warn purchasers that accessible seating is for individuals with disabilities and that individuals purchasing such tickets fraudulently are subject to relocation.

One commenter argued that face-to-face contact between the venue and the ticket holder should be required in order to prevent fraud and suggested that individuals who purchase accessible seating should be required to pick up their tickets at the box office and then enter the venue immediately. The Department has declined to adopt that suggestion. It would be discriminatory to require individuals with disabilities to pick up tickets at the box office when other spectators are not required to do so. If the assembly area wishes to make face-to-face contact with accessible seating ticket holders to curb fraud, it may do so through its ushers and other customer service personnel located within the seating area.

Some commenters asked whether it is permissible for assembly areas to have voluntary clubs where individuals with disabilities self-identify to the public entity in order to become a member of a club that entitles them to purchase accessible seating reserved for club members or otherwise receive priority in purchasing accessible seating. The Department agrees that such clubs are permissible, provided that a reasonable amount of accessible seating remains available at all prices and dispersed at all locations for individuals with disabilities who are non-members.

Section 35.139 *Direct threat.*

In Appendix A of the Department's 1991 title II regulation, the Department included a detailed discussion of "direct threat" that, among other things, explained that "the principles established in § 36.208 of the Department's [title III] regulation" were "applicable" as well to title II, insofar as "questions of safety are involved." 28 CFR part 35, app. A at 565 (2009). In the final rule, the Department has included specific requirements related to "direct threat" that parallel those in the title III rule. These requirements are found in new § 35.139.

Subpart D — Program Accessibility

Section 35.150(b)(2)   Safe harbor.

The "program accessibility" requirement in regulations implementing title II of the Americans with Disabilities Act requires that each service, program, or activity, *when viewed in its entirety,* be readily accessible to and usable by individuals with disabilities. 28 CFR 35.150(a). Because title II evaluates a public entity's programs, services, and activities in their entirety, public entities have flexibility in addressing accessibility issues. Program access does not necessarily require a public entity to make each of its existing facilities accessible to and usable by individuals with disabilities, and public entities are not required to make structural changes to existing facilities where other methods are effective in achieving program access. *See id.* 3 Public entities do, however, have program access considerations that are independent of, but may coexist with, requirements imposed by new construction or alteration requirements in those same facilities.

Where a public entity opts to alter existing facilities to comply with its program access requirements, the entity must meet the accessibility requirements for alterations set out in § 35.151. Under the final rule, these alterations will be subject to the 2010 Standards. The 2010 Standards introduce technical and scoping specifications for many elements not covered by the 1991 Standards. In existing facilities, these supplemental requirements need to be taken into account by a public entity in ensuring program access. Also included in the 2010 Standards are revised technical and scoping requirements for a number of elements that were addressed in the 1991 Standards. These revised requirements reflect incremental changes that were added either because of additional study by the Access Board or in order to harmonize requirements with the model codes.

Although the program accessibility standard offers public entities a level of discretion in determining how to achieve program access, in the NPRM, the Department proposed an addition to § 35.150 at § 35.150(b)(2), denominated "Safe Harbor," to clarify that "[i]f a public entity has constructed or altered elements * * * in accordance with the specifications in either the 1991 Standards or the Uniform Federal Accessibility Standard, such public entity is[3] not, solely because of the Department's adoption of the [2010] Standards, required to retrofit such elements to reflect incremental changes in the proposed standards." 73 FR 34466, 34505 (June 17, 2008). In these circumstances, the public entity would be entitled to a safe harbor for the already compliant elements until those elements are altered. The safe harbor does not negate a public entity's new construction or alteration obligations. A public entity must comply with the new construction or alteration requirements in effect at the time of the construction or alteration. With respect to existing facilities designed and constructed after January 26, 1992, but before the public entities are required to comply with the 2010 Standards, the rule is that any elements in these facilities that were not constructed in conformance with UFAS or the 1991 Standards are in violation of the ADA and must be brought into compliance. If elements in existing facilities were altered after January 26, 1992, and those alterations were not made in conformance with the alteration require-

---

[3] The term "existing facility" is defined in § 35.104 as amended by this rule.

ments in effect at the time, then those alteration violations must be corrected. Section 35.150(b)(2) of the final rule specifies that until the compliance date for the Standards (18 months from the date of publication of the rule), facilities or elements covered by § 35.151(a) or (b) that are noncompliant with either the 1991 Standards or UFAS shall be made accessible in accordance with the 1991 Standards, UFAS, or the 2010 Standards. Once the compliance date is reached, such noncompliant facilities or elements must be made accessible in accordance with the 2010 Standards.

The Department received many comments on the safe harbor during the 60-day public comment period. Advocacy groups were opposed to the safe harbor for compliant elements in existing facilities. These commenters objected to the Department's characterization of revisions between the 1991 and 2010 Standards as incremental changes and assert that these revisions represent important advances in accessibility for individuals with disabilities. Commenters saw no basis for "grandfathering" outdated accessibility standards given the flexibility inherent in the program access standard. Others noted that title II's "undue financial and administrative burdens" and "fundamental alteration" defenses eliminate any need for further exemptions from compliance. Some commenters suggested that entities' past efforts to comply with the program access standard of 28 CFR 35.150(a) might appropriately be a factor in determining what is required in the future.

Many public entities welcomed the Department's proposed safe harbor. These commenters contend that the safe harbor allows public entities needed time to evaluate program access in light of the 2010 Standards, and incorporate structural changes in a careful and thoughtful way toward increasing accessibility entity-wide. Many felt that it would be an ineffective use of public funds to update buildings to retrofit elements that had already been constructed or modified to Department-issued and sanctioned specifications. One entity pointed to the "possibly budget-breaking" nature of forcing compliance with incremental changes.

The Department has reviewed and considered all information received during the 60-day public comment period. Upon review, the Department has decided to retain the title II safe harbor with minor revisions. The Department believes that the safe harbor provides an important measure of clarity and certainty for public entities as to the effect of the final rule with respect to existing facilities. Additionally, by providing a safe harbor for elements already in compliance with the technical and scoping specifications in the 1991 Standards or UFAS, funding that would otherwise be spent on incremental changes and repeated retrofitting is freed up to be used toward increased entity-wide program access. Public entities may thereby make more efficient use of the resources available to them to ensure equal access to their services, programs, or activities for all individuals with disabilities.

The safe harbor adopted with this final rule is a narrow one, as the Department recognizes that this approach may delay, in some cases, the increased accessibility that the revised requirements would provide, and that for some individuals with disabilities the impact may be significant. This safe harbor operates only with respect to elements that are in compliance with the scoping and technical specifications in either the 1991 Standards or UFAS; it does not apply to supplemental requirements, those elements for which scoping and technical specifications are first provided in the 2010 Standards.

Existing Facilities

Existing play areas. The 1991 Standards do not include specific requirements for the design and construction of play areas. To meet program accessibility requirements where structural changes are necessary, public entities have been required to apply the general new construction and alteration standards to the greatest extent possible, including with respect to accessible parking, routes to the playground, playground equipment, and playground amenities (e.g., picnic tables and restrooms). The Access Board published final guidelines for play areas in October 2000. The guidelines extended beyond general playground access to establish specific scoping and technical requirements for ground-level and elevated play components, accessible routes connecting the components, accessible ground surfaces, and maintenance of those surfaces. These guidelines filled a void left by the 1991 Standards. They have been referenced in Federal playground construction and safety guidelines and have been used voluntarily when many play areas across the country have been altered or constructed.

In adopting the 2004 ADAAG (which includes the 2000 play area guidelines), the Department acknowledges both the importance of integrated, full access to play areas for children and parents with disabilities, as well as the need to avoid placing an untenable fiscal burden on public entities. In the NPRM, the Department stated it was proposing two specific provisions to reduce the impact on existing facilities that undertake structural modifications pursuant to the program accessibility requirement. First, the Department proposed in § 35.150(b)(4) that existing play areas that are not being altered would be permitted to meet a reduced scoping requirement with respect to their elevated play components. Elevated play components, which are found on most playgrounds, are the individual components that are linked together to form large-scale composite playground equipment (e.g., the monkey bars attached to the suspension bridge attached to the tube slide, etc.) The 2010 Standards provide that a play area that includes both ground level and elevated play components must ensure that a specified number of the ground-level play components and at least 50 percent of the elevated play components are accessible.

In the NPRM, the Department asked for specific public comment with regard to whether existing play areas should be permitted to substitute additional ground-level play components for the elevated play components they would otherwise have been required to make accessible. The Department also queried if there were other requirements applicable to play areas in the 2004 ADAAG for which the Department should consider exemptions or reduced scoping. Many commenters opposed permitting existing play areas to make such substitutions. Several commenters stated that the Access Board already completed significant negotiation and cost balancing in its rulemaking, so no additional exemptions should be added in either meeting program access requirements or in alterations. Others noted that elevated components are generally viewed as the more challenging and exciting by children, so making more ground than elevated play components accessible would result in discrimination against children with disabilities in general and older children with disabilities in particular. They argued that the ground components would be seen as equipment for younger children and children with disabilities, while elevated components would serve only older children without disabilities. In addition, commenters advised that including additional ground- level play components would require more accessible route and use zone surfacing, which would result in a higher cost burden than making elevated components accessible.

The Department also asked for public comment on whether it would be appropriate for the Access Board to consider issuing guidelines for alterations to play and recreational facilities that would permit reduced scoping of accessible components or substitution of ground-level play components in lieu of elevated play components. Most commenters opposed any additional reductions in scoping and substitutions. These commenters uniformly stated that the Access Board completed sufficient negotiation during its rulemaking on its play area guidelines published in 2000 and that those guidelines consequently should stand as is. One commenter advocated reduced scoping and substitution of ground play components during alterations only for those play areas built prior to the finalization of the guidelines.

The Department has considered the comments it has received and has determined that it is not necessary to provide a specific exemption to the scoping for components for existing play areas or to recommend reduced scoping or additional exemptions for alteration, and has deleted the reduced scoping proposed in NPRM § 35.150(b)(4)(i) from the final rule. The Department believes that it is preferable for public entities to try to achieve compliance with the design standards established in the 2010 Standards. If this is not possible to achieve in an existing setting, the requirements for program accessibility provide enough flexibility to permit the covered entity to pursue alternative approaches to provide accessibility.

Second, in § 35.150(b)(5)(i) of the NPRM, the Department proposed language stating that existing play areas that are less than 1,000 square feet in size and are not otherwise being altered, need not comply with the scoping and technical requirements for play areas in section 240 of the 2004 ADAAG. The Department stated it selected this size based on the provision in section 1008.2.4.1 of the 2004 ADAAG, Exception 1, which permits play areas less than 1,000 square feet in size to provide accessible routes with a reduced clear width (44 inches instead of 60 inches). In its 2000 regulatory assessment for the play area guidelines, the Access Board assumed that such "small" play areas represented only about 20 percent of the play areas located in public schools, and none of the play areas located in city and State parks (which the Board assumed were typically larger than 1,000 square feet).

In the NPRM, the Department asked if existing play areas less than 1,000 square feet should be exempt from the requirements applicable to play areas. The vast majority of commenters objected to such an exemption. One commenter stated that many localities that have parks this size are already making them accessible; many cited concerns that this would leave all or most public playgrounds in small towns inaccessible; and two commenters stated that, since many of New York City's parks are smaller than 1,000 square feet, only scattered larger parks in the various boroughs would be obliged to become accessible. Residents with disabilities would then have to travel substantial distances outside their own neighborhoods to find accessible playgrounds. Some commenters responded that this exemption should not apply in instances where the play area is the only one in the program, while others said that if a play area is exempt for reasons of size, but is the only one in the area, then it should have at least an accessible route and 50 percent of its ground-level play components accessible. One commenter supported the exemption as presented in the question.

The Department is persuaded by these comments that it is inappropriate to exempt public play areas that are less than 1,000 square feet in size. The Department believes that the factors used to determine program accessibility, including the limits established by the undue financial and administrative burdens defense, provide sufficient flexibility to public entities in determining how to make their existing play areas accessible. In those cases where a title II entity believes that present economic concerns make it an undue financial and administrative burden to immediately make its existing playgrounds accessible in order to comply with program accessibility requirements, then it may be reasonable for the entity to develop a multi- year plan to bring its facilities into compliance.

In addition to requesting public comment about the specific sections in the NPRM, the Department also asked for public comment about the appropriateness of a general safe harbor for existing play areas and a safe harbor for public entities that have complied with State or local standards specific to play areas. In the almost 200 comments received on title II play areas, the vast majority of commenters strongly opposed all safe harbors, exemptions, and reductions in scoping. By contrast, one commenter advocated a safe harbor from compliance with the 2004 ADAAG play area requirements along with reduced scoping and exemptions for both program accessibility and alterations; a second commenter advocated only the general safe harbor from compliance with the supplemental requirements.

In response to the question of whether the Department should exempt public entities from specific compliance with the supplemental requirements for play areas, commenters stated that since no specific standards previously existed, play areas are more than a decade behind in providing full access for individuals with disabilities. When accessible play areas were created, public entities, acting in good faith, built them according to the 2004 ADAAG requirements; many equipment manufacturers also developed equipment to meet those guidelines. If existing playgrounds were exempted from compliance with the supplemental guidelines, commenters said, those entities would be held to a lesser standard and left with confusion, a sense of wasted resources, and federally condoned discrimination and segregation. Commenters also cited Federal agency settlement agreements on play areas that required compliance with the guidelines. Finally, several commenters observed that the provision of a safe harbor in this instance was invalid for two reasons: (1) The rationale for other safe harbors — that entities took action to comply with the 1991 Standards and should not be further required to comply with new standards — does not exist; and (2) concerns about financial and administrative burdens are adequately addressed by program access requirements.

The question of whether accessibility of play areas should continue to be assessed on the basis of case-by-case evaluations elicited conflicting responses. One commenter asserted that there is no evidence that the case-by-case approach is not working and so it should continue until found to be inconsistent with the ADA's goals. Another commenter argued that case-by-case evaluations result in unpredictable outcomes which result in costly and long court actions. A third commenter, advocating against case- by-case evaluations, requested instead increased direction and scoping to define what constitutes an accessible play area program.

The Department has considered all of the comments it received in response to its questions and has concluded that there is insufficient basis to establish a safe harbor from compliance with the supplemental guidelines. Thus, the Department has eliminated the proposed exemption contained in § 35.150(b)(5)(i) of the NPRM for existing play areas that are less than 1,000 square feet. The Department believes that the factors used to determine program accessibility, including the limits established by the undue financial and administrative burdens defense, provide sufficient flexibility to public entities in determining how to make their existing play areas accessible.

In the NPRM, the Department also asked whether there are State and local standards addressing play and recreation area accessibility and, to the extent that there are such standards, whether facilities currently governed by, and in compliance with, such State and local standards or codes should be subject to a safe harbor from compliance with applicable requirements in the 2004 ADAAG. The Department also asked whether it would be appropriate for the Access Board to consider the implementation of guidelines that would permit such a safe harbor with respect to play and recreation areas undertaking alterations. In response, commenters stated that few State or local governments have standards that address issues of accessibility in play areas, and one commenter organization said that it was unaware of any State or local standards written specifically for accessible play areas. One commenter observed from experience that most State and local governments were waiting for the Access Board guidelines to become enforceable standards as they had no standards themselves to follow. Another commenter offered that public entities across the United States already include in their playground construction bid specifications language that requires compliance with the Access Board's guidelines. A number of commenters advocated for the Access Board's guidelines to become comprehensive Federal standards that would complement any abbreviated State and local standards. One commenter, however, supported a safe harbor for play areas undergoing alterations if the areas currently comply with State or local standards.

The Department is persuaded by these comments that there is insufficient basis to establish a safe harbor for program access or alterations for play areas built in compliance with State or local laws.

In the NPRM, the Department asked whether "a reasonable number, but at least one" is a workable standard to determine the appropriate number of existing play areas that a public entity must make accessible. Many commenters objected to this standard, expressing concern that the phrase "at least one" would be interpreted as a maximum rather than a minimum requirement. Such commenters feared that this language would allow local governments to claim compliance by making just one public park accessible, regardless of the locality's size, budget, or other factors, and would support segregation, forcing children with disabilities to leave their neighborhoods to enjoy an accessible play area. While some commenters criticized what they viewed as a new analysis of program accessibility, others asserted that the requirements of program accessibility should be changed to address issues related to play areas that are not the main program in a facility but are essential components of a larger program (e.g., drop-in child care for a courthouse).

The Department believes that those commenters who opposed the Department's "reasonable number, but at least one" standard for program accessibility misunderstood the Department's proposal. The Department did not intend any change in its longstanding interpretation of the program accessibility requirement. Program accessibility requires that each service, program, or activity be operated "so that the service, program, or activity, when viewed in its entirety, is readily accessible to and usable by individuals with disabilities," 28 CFR 35.150(a), subject to the undue financial and administrative burdens and fundamental alterations defenses provided in 28 CFR 35.150. In determining how many facilities of a multi-site program must be made accessible in order to make the overall program accessible, the standard has always been an assessment of what is reasonable under the circumstances to make the program readily accessible to and usable by individuals with disabilities, taking into account such factors as the size of the public entity, the particular program features offered at each site, the geographical distance between sites, the travel times to the sites, the number of sites, and availability of public transportation to the sites. In choosing among available methods for meeting this requirement, public entities are required to give priority "to those methods that offer services, programs, and activities * * * in the most integrated setting appropriate." 28 CFR 35.150(b)(1). As a result, in cases where the sites are widely dispersed with difficult travel access and where the program features offered vary widely between sites, program accessibility will require a larger number of facilities to be accessible in order to ensure program accessibility than where multiple sites are located in a concentrated area with easy travel access and uniformity in program offerings.

Commenters responded positively to the Department's question in the NPRM whether the final rule should provide a list of factors that a public entity should use to determine how many of its existing play areas should be made accessible. Commenters also asserted strongly that the number of existing parks in the locality should not be the main factor. In addition to the Department's initial list — including number of play areas in an area, travel times or geographic distances between play areas, and the size of the public entity — commenters recommended such factors as availability of accessible pedestrian routes to the playgrounds, ready availability of accessible transportation, comparable amenities and services in and surrounding the play areas, size of the playgrounds, and sufficient variety in accessible play components within the playgrounds. The Department agrees that these factors should be considered, where appropriate, in any determination of whether program accessibility has been achieved. However, the Department has decided that it need not address these factors in the final rule itself because the range of factors that might need to be considered would vary depending upon the circumstances of particular public entities. The Department does not believe any list would be sufficiently comprehensive to cover every situation.

The Department also requested public comment about whether there was a "tipping point" at which the costs of compliance with the new requirements for existing play areas would be so burdensome that the entity would simply shut down the playground. Commenters generally questioned the feasibility of determining a "tipping point." No commenters offered a recommended "tipping point." Moreover, most commenters stated that a "tipping point" is not a valid consideration for various reasons, including that "tipping points" will vary based upon each entity's budget and other mandates, and costs that are too high will be addressed by the limitations of the undue financial and administrative burdens defense in the program accessibility requirement and that a "tipping point" must be weighed against quality of life issues, which are difficult to quantify. The Department has decided that comments did not establish any clear "tipping point" and therefore provides no regulatory requirement in this area.

Swimming pools. The 1991 Standards do not contain specific scoping or technical requirements for swimming pools. As a result, under the 1991 title II regulation, title II entities that operate programs or activities that include swimming pools have not been required to provide an accessible route into those pools via a ramp or pool lift, although they are required to provide an accessible route to such pools. In addition, these entities continue to be subject to the general title II obligation to make their programs usable and accessible to persons with disabilities.

The 2004 ADAAG includes specific technical and scoping requirements for new and altered swimming pools at sections 242 and 1009. In the NPRM, the Department sought to address the impact of these requirements on existing swimming pools. Section 242.2 of the 2004 ADAAG states that swimming pools must provide two accessible means of entry, except that swimming pools with less than 300 linear feet of swimming pool wall are only required to provide one accessible means of entry, provided that the accessible means of entry is either a swimming pool lift complying with section 1009.2 or a sloped entry complying with section 1009.3.

In the NPRM, the Department proposed, in § 35.150(b)(4)(ii), that for measures taken to comply with title II's program accessibility requirements, existing swimming pools with at least 300 linear feet of swimming pool wall would be required to provide only one accessible means of access that complied with section 1009.2 or section 1009.3 of the 2004 ADAAG.

The Department specifically sought comment from public entities and individuals with disabilities on the question whether the Department should "allow existing public entities to provide only one accessible means of access to swimming pools more than 300 linear feet long?" The Department received significant public comment on this proposal.

Most commenters opposed any reduction in the scoping required in the 2004 ADAAG, citing the fact that swimming is a common therapeutic form of exercise for many individuals with disabilities. Many commenters also stated that the cost of a swimming pool lift, approximately $5,000, or other nonstructural options for pool access such as transfer steps, transfer walls, and transfer platforms, would not be an undue financial and administrative burden for most title II entities. Other commenters pointed out that the undue financial and administrative burdens defense already provided public entities with a means to reduce their scoping requirements. A few commenters cited safety concerns resulting from having just one accessible means of access, and stated that because pools typically have one ladder for every 75 linear feet of pool wall, they should have more than one accessible means of access. One commenter stated that construction costs for a public pool are approximately $4,000– 4,500 per linear foot, making the cost of a pool with 300 linear feet of swimming pool wall approximately $1.2 million, compared to $5,000 for a pool lift. Some commenters did not oppose the one accessible means of access for larger pools so long as a lift was used. A few commenters approved of the one accessible means of access for larger pools. The Department also considered the

American National Standard for Public Swimming Pools, ANSI/NSPI-1 2003, section 23 of which states that all pools should have at least two means of egress.

In the NPRM, the Department also proposed at § 35.150(b)(5)(ii) that existing swimming pools with less than 300 linear feet of swimming pool wall be exempted from having to comply with the provisions of section 242.2. The Department's NPRM requested public comment about the potential effect of this approach, asking whether existing swimming pools with less than 300 linear feet of pool wall should be exempt from the requirements applicable to swimming pools.

Most commenters were opposed to this proposal. A number of commenters stated, based on the Access Board estimates that 90 percent of public high school pools, 40 percent of public park and community center pools, and 30 percent of public college and university pools have less than 300 linear feet of pool wall, that a large number of public swimming pools would fall under this exemption. Other commenters pointed to the existing undue financial and administrative burdens defenses as providing public entities with sufficient protection from excessive compliance costs. Few commenters supported this exemption.

The Department also considered the fact that many existing swimming pools owned or operated by public entities are recipients of Federal financial assistance and therefore, are also subject to the program accessibility requirements of section 504 of the Rehabilitation Act.

The Department has carefully considered all the information available to it including the comments submitted on these two proposed exemptions for swimming pools owned or operated by title II entities. The Department acknowledges that swimming provides important therapeutic, exercise, and social benefits for many individuals with disabilities and is persuaded that exemption of many publicly owned or operated pools from the 2010 Standards is neither appropriate nor necessary. The Department agrees with the commenters that title II already contains sufficient limitations on public entities' obligations to make their programs accessible. In particular, the Department agrees that those public entities that can demonstrate that making particular existing swimming pools accessible in accordance with the 2010 Standards would be an undue financial and administrative burden are sufficiently protected from excessive compliance costs. Thus, the Department has eliminated proposed §§ 35.150(b)(4)(ii) and (b)(5)(ii) from the final rule.

In addition, although the NPRM contained no specific proposed regulatory language on this issue, the NPRM sought comment on what would be a workable standard for determining the appropriate number of existing swimming pools that a public entity must make accessible for its program to be accessible. The Department asked whether a "reasonable number, but at least one" would be a workable standard and, if not, whether there was a more appropriate specific standard. The Department also asked if, in the alternative, the Department should provide "a list of factors that a public entity could use to determine how many of its existing swimming pools to make accessible, e.g., number of swimming pools, travel times or geographic distances between swimming pools, and the size of the public entity?"

A number of commenters expressed concern over the "reasonable number, but at least one" standard and contended that, in reality, public entities would never provide more than one accessible existing pool, thus segregating individuals with disabilities. Other commenters felt that the existing program accessibility standard was sufficient. Still others suggested that one in every three existing pools should be made accessible. One commenter suggested that all public pools should be accessible. Some commenters proposed a list of factors to determine how many existing pools should be accessible. Those factors include the total number of pools, the location, size, and type of pools provided, transportation availability, and lessons and activities available. A number of commenters suggested that the standard should be based on geographic areas, since pools serve specific neighborhoods. One commenter argued that each pool should be examined individually to determine what can be done to improve its accessibility.

The Department did not include any language in the final rule that specifies the "reasonable number, but at least one" standard for program access. However, the Department believes that its proposal was misunderstood by many commenters. Each service, program, or activity conducted by a public entity, when viewed in its entirety, must still be readily accessible to and usable by individuals with disabilities unless doing so would result in a fundamental alteration in the nature of the program or activity or in undue financial and administrative burdens. Determining which pool(s) to make accessible and whether more than one accessible pool is necessary to provide program access requires analysis of a number of factors, including, but not limited to, the size of the public entity, geographical distance between pool sites, whether more than one community is served by particular pools, travel times to the pools, the total number of pools, the availability of lessons and other programs and amenities at each pool, and the availability of public transportation to the pools. In many instances, making one existing swimming pool accessible will not be sufficient to ensure program accessibility. There may, however, be some circumstances where a small public entity can demonstrate that modifying one pool is sufficient to provide access to the public entity's program of providing public swimming pools. In all cases, a public entity must still demonstrate that its programs, including the program of providing public swimming pools, when viewed in their entirety, are accessible.

Wading pools. The 1991 Standards do not address wading pools. Section 242.3 of the 2004 ADAAG requires newly constructed or altered wading pools to provide at least one sloped means of entry to the deepest part of the pool. The Department was concerned about the potential impact of this new requirement on existing wading pools. Therefore, in the NPRM, the Department sought comments on whether existing wading pools that are not being altered should be exempt from this requirement, asking, "[w]hat site constraints exist in existing facilities that could make it difficult or infeasible to install a sloped entry in an existing wading pool? Should existing wading pools that are not being altered be exempt from the requirement to provide a sloped entry?" 73 FR 34466, 34487–88 (June 17, 2008). Most commenters agreed that existing wading pools that are not being altered should be exempt from this requirement. Almost all commenters felt that during alterations a sloped entry should be provided unless it was technically infeasible to do so. Several commenters felt that the required clear deck space surrounding a pool provided sufficient space for a sloped entry during alterations.

The Department also solicited comments on the possibility of exempting existing wading pools from the obligation to provide program accessibility. Most commenters argued that installing a sloped entry in an existing wading pool is not very feasible. Because covered entities are not required to undertake modifications that would be technically infeasible, the Department believes that the rule as drafted provides sufficient protection from unwarranted expense to the operators of small existing wading pools. Other existing wading pools, particularly those larger pools associated with facilities such as aquatic centers or water parks, must be assessed on a case-by- case basis. Therefore, the Department has not included such an exemption for wading pools in its final rule.

Saunas and steam rooms. The 1991 Standards do not address saunas and steam rooms. Section 35.150(b)(5)(iii) of the NPRM exempted existing saunas and steam rooms that seat only two individuals and were not being altered from section 241 of the 2004 ADAAG, which requires an accessible turning space. Two commenters objected to this exemption as unnecessary, and argued that the cost of accessible saunas is not high and public entities still have an undue financial and administrative burdens defense.

The Department considered these comments and has decided to eliminate the exemption for existing saunas and steam rooms that seat only two people. Such an exemption is unnecessary because covered entities will not be subject to program accessibility requirements to make existing saunas and steam rooms accessible if doing so constitutes an undue financial and administrative burden. The Department believes it is likely that because of their pre- fabricated forms, which include built-in seats, it would be either technically infeasible or an undue financial and administrative burden to modify such saunas and steams rooms. Consequently, a separate exemption for saunas and steam rooms would have been superfluous. Finally, employing the program accessibility standard for small saunas and steam rooms is consistent with the Department's decisions regarding the proposed exemptions for play areas and swimming pools.

Several commenters also argued in favor of a specific exemption for existing spas. The Department notes that the technical infeasibility and program accessibility defenses are applicable equally to existing spas and declines to adopt such an exemption.

Other recreational facilities. In the NPRM, the Department asked about a number of issues relating to recreation facilities such as team or player seating areas, areas of sport activity, exercise machines, boating facilities, fishing piers and platforms, and miniature golf courses. The Department's questions addressed the costs and benefits of applying the 2004 ADAAG to these spaces and facilities and the application of the specific technical requirements in the 2004 ADAAG for these spaces and facilities. The discussion of the comments received by the Department on these issues and the Department's response to those comments can be found in either the section of Appendix A to this rule entitled "Other Issues," or in Appendix B to the final title III rule, which will be published today elsewhere in this volume. redesignated as § 35.151(a)(1). The Department has added a new section, designated as § 35.151(a)(2), to provide that full compliance with the requirements of this section is not required where an entity can demonstrate that it is structurally impracticable to meet the requirements. Full compliance will be considered structurally impracticable only in those rare circumstances when the unique characteristics of terrain prevent the incorporation of accessibility features. This exception was contained in the title III regulation and in the 1991 Standards (applicable to both public accommodations and facilities used by public entities), so it has applied to any covered facility that was constructed under the 1991 Standards since the effective date of the ADA. The Department added it to the text of § 35.151 to maintain consistency between the design requirements that apply under title II and those that apply under title III. The Department received no significant comments about this section.

Section 35.151   New construction and alterations.

Section 35.151(a), which provided that those facilities that are constructed or altered by, on behalf of, or for the use of a public entity shall be designed, constructed, or altered to be readily accessible to and usable by individuals with disabilities, is unchanged in the final rule, but has been redesignated as § 35.151(a)(1). The Department has added a new section, designated as § 35.151(a)(2), to provide that full compliance with the requirements of this section is not required where an entity can demonstrate that it is structurally impracticable to meet the requirements. Full compliance will be considered structurally impracticable only in those rare circumstances when the unique characteristics of terrain prevent the incorporation of accessibility features. This exception was contained in the title III regulation and in the 1991 Standards (applicable to both public accommodations and facilities used by public entities), so it has applied to any covered facility that was constructed under the 1991 Standards since the effective date of the ADA. The Department added it to the text of § 35.151 to maintain consistency between the design requirements that apply under title II and those that apply under title III. The Department received no significant comments about this section.

Section 35.151(b)   Alterations

The 1991 title II regulation does not contain any specific regulatory language comparable to the 1991 title III regulation relating to alterations and path of travel for covered entities, although the 1991 Standards describe standards for path of travel during alterations to a primary function. See 28 CFR part 36, app A., section 4.1.6(a) (2009).

The path of travel requirements contained in the title III regulation are based on section 303(a)(2) of the ADA, 42 U.S.C. 12183(a)(2), which provides that when an entity undertakes an alteration to a place of public accommodation or commercial facility that affects or could affect the usability of or access to an area that contains a primary function, the entity shall ensure that, to the maximum extent feasible, the path of travel to the altered area — and the restrooms, telephones, and drinking fountains serving it — is readily accessible to and usable by individuals with disabilities, including individuals who use wheelchairs.

The NPRM proposed amending § 35.151 to add both the path of travel requirements and the exemption relating to barrier removal (as modified to apply to the program accessibility standard in title II) that are contained in the title III regulation to the title II regulation. Proposed § 35.151(b)(4) contained the requirements for path of travel. Proposed § 35.151(b)(2) stated that the path of travel requirements of § 35.151(b)(4) shall not apply to measures taken solely to comply with program accessibility requirements.

Where the specific requirements for path of travel apply under title III, they are limited to the extent that the cost and scope of alterations to the path of travel are disproportionate to the cost of the overall alteration, as determined under criteria established by the Attorney General.

The Access Board included the path of travel requirement for alterations to facilities covered by the standards (other than those subject to the residential facilities standards) in section 202.4 of 2004 ADAAG. Section 35.151(b)(4)(iii) of the final rule establishes the criteria for determining when the cost of alterations to the path of travel is "disproportionate" to the cost of the overall alteration.

The NPRM also provided that areas such as supply storage rooms, employee lounges and locker rooms, janitorial closets, entrances, and corridors are not areas containing a primary function. Nor are restroom areas considered to contain a primary function unless the provision of restrooms is a primary purpose of the facility, such as at a highway rest stop. In that situation, a restroom would be considered to be an "area containing a primary function" of the facility.

The Department is not changing the requirements for program accessibility. As provided in § 35.151(b)(2) of the regulation, the path of travel requirements of § 35.151(b)(4) only apply to alterations undertaken solely for purposes other than to meet the program accessibility requirements. The exemption for the specific path of travel requirement was included in the regulation to ensure that the specific requirements and disproportionality exceptions for path of travel are not applied when areas are being altered to meet the title II program accessibility requirements in § 35.150. In contrast, when areas are being altered to meet program accessibility requirements, they must comply with all of the applicable requirements referenced in section 202 of the 2010 Standards. A covered title II entity must provide accessibility to meet the requirements of § 35.150 unless doing so is an undue financial and administrative burden in accordance with § 35.150(a)(3). A covered title II entity may not use the disproportionality exception contained in the path of travel provisions as a defense to providing an accessible route as part of its obligation to provide program accessibility. The undue financial and administrative burden standard does *not* contain any bright line financial tests.

The Department's proposed § 35.151(b)(4) adopted the language now contained in § 36.403 of the title III regulation, including the disproportionality limitation (i.e., alterations made to provide an accessible path of travel to the altered area would be deemed disproportionate to the overall alteration when the cost exceeds 20 percent of the cost of the alteration to the primary function area). Proposed § 35.151(b)(2) provided that the path of travel requirements do not apply to alterations undertaken solely to comply with program accessibility requirements.

The Department received a substantial number of comments objecting to the Department's adoption of the exemption for the path of travel requirements when alterations are undertaken solely to meet program accessibility requirements. These commenters argued that the Department had no statutory basis for providing this exemption nor does it serve any purpose. In addition, these commenters argued that the path of travel exemption has the effect of placing new limitations on the obligations to provide program access. A number of commenters argued that doing away with the path of travel requirement would render meaningless the concept of program access.

They argued that just as the requirement to provide an accessible path of travel to an altered area (regardless of the reason for the alteration), including making the restrooms, telephones, and drinking fountains that serve the altered area accessible, is a necessary requirement in other alterations, it is equally necessary for alterations made to provide program access. Several commenters expressed concern that a readily accessible path of travel be available to ensure that persons with disabilities can get to the physical location in which programs are held. Otherwise, they will not be able to access the public entity's service, program, or activity. Such access is a cornerstone of the protections provided by the ADA. Another commenter argued that it would be a waste of money to create an accessible facility without having a way to get to the primary area. This commenter also stated that the International Building Code (IBC) requires the path of travel to a primary function area, up to 20 percent of the cost of the project. Another commenter opposed the exemption, stating that the trigger of an alteration is frequently the only time that a facility must update its facilities to comply with evolving accessibility standards.

In the Department's view, the commenters objecting to the path of travel exemption contained in § 35.151(b)(2) did not understand the intention behind the exemption. The exemption was not intended to eliminate any existing requirements related to accessibility for alterations undertaken in order to meet program access obligations under § 35.149 and § 35.150. Rather, it was intended to ensure that covered entities did not apply the path of travel requirements in lieu of the overarching requirements in this Subpart that apply when making a facility accessible in order to comply with program accessibility. The exemption was also intended to make it clear that the disproportionality test contained in the path of travel standards is not applicable in determining whether providing program access results in an undue financial and administration burden within the meaning of § 35.150(a)(3). The exemption was also provided to maintain consistency with the title III path of travel exemption for barrier removal, *see* § 36.304(d), in keeping with the Department's regulatory authority under title II of the ADA. *See* 42 U.S.C. 12134(b); *see also* H. R Rep. No. 101B485, pt. 2, at 84 (1990) ("The committee intends, however, that the forms of discrimination prohibited by section 202 be identical to those set out in the applicable provisions of titles I and III of this legislation.").

For title II entities, the path of travel requirements are of significance in those cases where an alteration is being made solely for reasons other than program accessibility. For example, a public entity might have six courtrooms in two existing buildings and might determine that only three of those courtrooms and the public use and common use areas serving those courtrooms in one building are needed to be made accessible in order to satisfy its program access obligations. When the public entity makes those courtrooms and the public use and common use areas serving them accessible in order to meet its program access obligations, it will have to comply with the 2010 Standards unless the public entity can demonstrate that full compliance would result in undue financial and administrative burdens as described in § 35.150(a)(3). If such action would result in an undue financial or administrative burden, the public entity would nevertheless be required to take some other action that would not result in such an alteration or such burdens but would ensure that the benefits and services provided by the public entity are readily accessible to persons with disabilities. When the public entity is making modifications to meet its program access obligation, it may not rely on the path of travel exception under § 35.151(b)(4), which limits the requirement to those alterations where the cost and scope of the alterations are not disproportionate to the cost and scope of the overall alterations. If the public entity later decides to alter courtrooms in the other building, for purposes of updating the facility (and, as previously stated, has met its program access obligations) then in that case, the public entity would have to comply with the path of travel requirements in the 2010 Standards subject to the disproportionality exception set forth in § 35.151(b)(4).

The Department has slightly revised proposed § 35.151(b)(2) to make it clearer that the path of travel requirements only apply when alterations are undertaken solely for purposes other than program accessibility.

Section 35.151(b)(4)(ii)(C)   Path of travel — safe harbor.

In § 35.151(b)(4)(ii)(C) of the NPRM, the Department included a provision that stated that public entities that have brought required elements of path of travel into compliance with the 1991 Standards are not required to retrofit those elements in order to reflect incremental changes in the 2010 Standards solely because of an alteration to a primary function area that is served by that path of travel. In these circumstances, the public entity is entitled to a safe harbor and is only required to modify elements to comply with the 2010 Standards if the public entity is planning an alteration to the element.

A substantial number of commenters objected to the Department's imposition of a safe harbor for alterations to facilities of public entities that comply with the 1991 Standards. These commenters argued that if a public entity is already in the process of altering its facility, there should be a legal requirement that individuals with disabilities be entitled to increased accessibility by using the 2010 Standards for path of travel work. They also stated that they did not believe there was a statutory basis for "grandfathering" facilities that comply with the 1991 Standards.

The ADA is silent on the issue of "grandfathering" or establishing a safe harbor for measuring compliance in situations where the covered entity is not undertaking a planned alteration to specific building elements. The ADA delegates to the Attorney General the responsibility for issuing regulations that define the parameters of covered entities' obligations when the statute does not directly address an issue. This regulation implements that delegation of authority.

One commenter proposed that a previous record of barrier removal be one of the factors in determining, prospectively, what renders a facility, when viewed in its entirety, usable and accessible to persons with disabilities. Another commenter asked the Department to clarify, at a minimum, that to the extent compliance with the 1991 Standards does not provide program access, particularly with regard to areas not specifically addressed in the 1991 Standards, the safe harbor will not operate to relieve an entity of its obligations to provide program access.

One commenter supported the proposal to add a safe harbor for path of travel. The final rule retains the safe harbor for required elements of a path of travel to altered primary function areas for public entities that have already complied with the 1991 Standards with respect to those required elements. The Department believes that this safe harbor strikes an appropriate balance between ensuring that individuals with disabilities are provided access to buildings and facilities and potential financial burdens on existing public entities that are undertaking alterations subject to the 2010 Standards. This safe harbor is not a blanket exemption for facilities. If a public entity undertakes an alteration to a primary function area, only the required elements of a path of travel to that area that already comply with the 1991 Standards are subject to the safe harbor. If a public entity undertakes an alteration to a primary function area and the required elements of a path of travel to the altered area do not comply with the 1991 Standards, then the public entity must bring those elements into compliance with the 2010 Standards.

Section 35.151(b)(3)   Alterations to historic facilities.

The final rule renumbers the requirements for alterations to historic facilities enumerated in current § 35.151(d)(1) and (2) as § 35.151(b)(3)(i) and (ii). Currently, the regulation provides that alterations to historic facilities shall comply to the maximum extent feasible with section 4.1.7 of UFAS or section 4.1.7 of the 1991 Standards. *See* 28 CFR 35.151(d)(1). Section 35.151(b)(3)(i) of the final rule eliminates the option of using UFAS for alterations that commence on or after March 15, 2012. The substantive requirement in current § 35.151(d)(2) — that alternative methods of access shall be provided pursuant to the requirements of § 35.150 if it is not feasible to provide physical access to an historic property in a manner that will not threaten or destroy the historic significance of the building or facility — is contained in § 35.151(b)(3)(ii).

Section 35.151(c)   Accessibility standards for new construction and alterations.

Section 35.151(c) of the NPRM proposed to adopt ADA Chapter 1, ADA Chapter 2, and Chapters 3 through 10 of the Americans with Disabilities Act and Architectural Barriers Act Guidelines (2004 ADAAG) into the ADA Standards for Accessible Design (2010 Standards). As the Department has noted, the development of these standards represents the culmination of a lengthy effort by the Access Board to update its guidelines, to make the Federal guidelines consistent to the extent permitted by law, and to harmonize the Federal requirements with the private sector model codes that form the basis of many State and local building code requirements. The full text of the 2010 Standards is available for public review on the ADA Home Page (http://www.ada.gov) and on the Access Board's Web site (http://www.access-board.gov/gs.htm) (last visited June 24, 2010). The Access Board site also includes an extensive discussion of the development of the 2004 ADA/ABA Guidelines, and a detailed comparison of the 1991 Standards, the 2004 ADA/ABA Guidelines, and the 2003 International Building Code.

Section 204 of the ADA, 42 U.S.C. 12134, directs the Attorney General to issue regulations to implement title II that are consistent with the minimum guidelines published by the Access Board. The Attorney General (or his designee) is a statutory member of the Access Board (see 29 U.S.C. 792(a)(1)(B(vii)) and was involved in the development of the 2004 ADAAG. Nevertheless, during the process of drafting the NPRM, the Department reviewed the 2004 ADAAG to determine if additional regulatory provisions were necessary. As a result of this review, the Department decided to propose new sections, which were contained in § 35.151(e)–(h) of the NPRM, to clarify how the Department will apply the proposed standards to social service center establishments, housing at places of education, assembly areas, and medical care facilities. Each of these provisions is discussed below.

Congress anticipated that there would be a need for close coordination of the ADA building requirements with State and local building code requirements. Therefore, the ADA authorized the Attorney General to establish an ADA code certification process under title III of the ADA. That process is addressed in 28 CFR part 36, subpart F. Revisions to that process are addressed in the regulation amending the title III regulation published elsewhere in the **Federal Register** today. In addition, the Department operates an extensive technical assistance program. The Department anticipates that once this rule is final, revised technical assistance material will be issued to provide guidance about its implementation.

Section 35.151(c) of the 1991 title II regulation establishes two standards for accessible new construction and alteration. Under paragraph (c), design, construction, or alteration of facilities in conformance with UFAS or with the 1991 Standards (which, at the time of the publication of the rule were also referred to as the Americans with Disabilities Act Accessibility Guidelines for Buildings and Facilities (1991 ADAAG)) is deemed to comply with the requirements of this section with respect to those facilities (except that if the 1991 Standards are chosen, the elevator exemption does not apply). The 1991 Standards were based on the 1991

ADAAG, which was initially developed by the Access Board as guidelines for the accessibility of buildings and facilities that are subject to title III. The Department adopted the 1991 ADAAG as the standards for places of public accommodation and commercial facilities under title III of the ADA and it was published as Appendix A to the Department's regulation implementing title III, 56 FR 35592 (July 26, 1991) as amended, 58 FR 17522 (April 5, 1993), and as further amended, 59 FR 2675 (Jan. 18, 1994), codified at 28 CFR part 36 (2009).

Section 35.151(c) of the final rule adopts the 2010 Standards and establishes the compliance date and triggering events for the application of those standards to both new construction and alterations. Appendix B of the final title III rule (Analysis and Commentary on the 2010 ADA Standards for Accessible Design) (which will be published today elsewhere in this volume and codified as Appendix B to 28 CFR part 36) provides a description of the major changes in the 2010 Standards (as compared to the 1991 ADAAG) and a discussion of the public comments that the Department received on specific sections of the 2004 ADAAG. A number of commenters asked the Department to revise certain provisions in the 2004 ADAAG in a manner that would reduce either the required scoping or specific technical accessibility requirements. As previously stated, although the ADA requires the enforceable standards issued by the Department under title II and title III to be consistent with the minimum guidelines published by the Access Board, it is the sole responsibility of the Attorney General to promulgate standards and to interpret and enforce those standards. The guidelines adopted by the Access Board are "minimum guidelines." 42 U.S.C. 12186(c).

Compliance date. When the ADA was enacted, the effective dates for various provisions were delayed in order to provide time for covered entities to become familiar with their new obligations. Titles II and III of the ADA generally became effective on January 26, 1992, six months after the regulations were published. *See* 42 U.S.C. 12131 note; 42 U.S.C. 12181 note. New construction under title II and alterations under either title II or title III had to comply with the design standards on that date. *See* 42 U.S.C. 12183(a)(1). For new construction under title III, the requirements applied to facilities designed and constructed for first occupancy after January 26, 1993 — 18 months after the 1991 Standards were published by the Department. In the NPRM, the Department proposed to amend § 35.151(c)(1) by revising the current language to limit the application of the 1991 standards to facilities on which construction commences within six months of the final rule adopting revised standards. The NPRM also proposed adding paragraph (c)(2) to § 35.151, which states that facilities on which construction commences on or after the date six months following the effective date of the final rule shall comply with the proposed standards adopted by that rule.

As a result, under the NPRM, for the first six months after the effective date, public entities would have the option to use either UFAS or the 1991 Standards and be in compliance with title II. Six months after the effective date of the rule, the new standards would take effect. At that time, construction in accordance with UFAS would no longer satisfy ADA requirements. The Department stated that in order to avoid placing the burden of complying with both standards on public entities, the Department would coordinate a government-wide effort to revise Federal agencies' section 504 regulations to adopt the 2004 ADAAG as the standard for new construction and alterations.

The purpose of the proposed six-month delay in requiring compliance with the 2010 Standards was to allow covered entities a reasonable grace period to transition between the existing and the proposed standards. For that reason, if a title II entity preferred to use the 2010 Standards as the standard for new construction or alterations commenced within the six-month period after the effective date of the final rule, such entity would be considered in compliance with title II of the ADA.

The Department received a number of comments about the proposed six-month effective date for the title II regulation that were similar in content to those received on this issue for the proposed title III regulation. Several commenters supported the six-month effective date. One commenter stated that any revisions to its State building code becomes effective six months after adoption and that this has worked well. In addition, this commenter stated that since 2004 ADAAG is similar to IBC 2006 and ICC/ANSI A117.1– 2003, the transition should be easy. By contrast, another commenter advocated for a minimum 12-month effective date, arguing that a shorter effective date could cause substantial economic hardships to many cities and towns because of the lengthy lead time necessary for construction projects. This commenter was concerned that a six-month effective date could lead to projects having to be completely redrawn, rebid, and rescheduled to ensure compliance with the new standards. Other commenters advocated that the effective date be extended to at least 18 months after the publication of the rule. One of these commenters expressed concern that the kinds of bureaucratic organizations subject to the title II regulations lack the internal resources to quickly evaluate the regulatory changes, determine whether they are currently compliant with the 1991 standards, and determine what they have to do to comply with the new standards. The other commenter argued that 18 months is the minimum amount of time necessary to ensure that projects that have already been designed and approved do not have to undergo costly design revisions at taxpayer expense.

The Department is persuaded by the concerns raised by commenters for both the title II and III regulations that the six-month compliance date proposed in the NPRM for application of the 2010 Standards may be too short for certain projects that are already in the midst of the design and permitting process. The Department has determined that for new construction and alterations, compliance with the 2010 Standards will not be required until 18 months from the date the final rule is published. Until the time compliance with the 2010 Standards is required, public entities will have the option of complying with the 2010 Standards, the UFAS, or the 1991 Standards. However, public entities that choose to comply with the 2010 Standards in lieu of the 1991 Standards or UFAS prior to the compliance date described in this rule must choose one of the three standards, and may not rely on some of the requirements contained in one standard and some of the requirements contained in the other standards.

Triggering event. In § 35.151(c)(2) of the NPRM, the Department proposed that the commencement of construction serve as the triggering event for applying the proposed standards to new construction and alterations under title II. This language is consistent with the triggering event set forth in § 35.151(a) of the 1991 title II regulation. The Department received only four comments on this section of the title II rule. Three commenters supported the use of "start of construction" as the triggering event. One commenter argued that the Department should use the "last building permit or start of physical construction, whichever comes first," stating that "altering a design after a building permit has been issued can be an undue burden."

After considering these comments, the Department has decided to continue to use the commencement of physical construction as the triggering event for application of the 2010 Standards for entities covered by title II. The Department has also added clarifying language at § 35.151(c)(4) to the regulation to make it clear that the date of ceremonial groundbreaking or the date a structure is razed to make it possible for construction of a facility to take place does not qualify as the commencement of physical construction.

Section 234 of the 2010 Standards provides accessibility guidelines for newly designed and constructed amusement rides. The amusement ride provisions do not provide a "triggering event" for new construction or alteration of an amusement ride. An industry commenter requested that the triggering event of "first use," as noted in the Advisory note to section 234.1 of the 2004 ADAAG, be included in the final rule. The Advisory note provides that "[a] custom designed and constructed ride is new upon its first use, which is the first time amusement park patrons take the ride." The Department declines to treat amusement rides differently than other types of new construction and alterations. Under the final rule, they are subject to § 35.151(c). Thus, newly constructed and altered amusement rides shall comply with the 2010 Standards if the start of physical construction or the alteration is on or after 18 months from the publication date of this rule. The Department also notes that section 234.4.2 of the 2010 Standards only applies where the structural or operational characteristics of an amusement ride are altered. It does not apply in cases where the only change to a ride is the theme.

Noncomplying new construction and alterations. The element-by-element safe harbor referenced in § 35.150(b)(2) has no effect on new or altered elements in existing facilities that were subject to the 1991 Standards or UFAS on the date that they were constructed or altered, but do not comply with the technical and scoping specifications for those elements in the 1991 Standards or UFAS. Section 35.151(c)(5) of the final rule sets forth the rules for noncompliant new construction or alterations in facilities that were subject to the requirements of this part. Under those provisions, noncomplying new construction and alterations constructed or altered after the effective date of the applicable ADA requirements and before March 15, 2012 shall, before March 15, 2012, be made accessible in accordance with either the 1991 Standards, UFAS, or the 2010 Standards. Noncomplying new construction and alterations constructed or altered after the effective date of the applicable ADA requirements and before March 15, 2012, shall, on or after March 15, 2012 be made accessible in accordance with the 2010 Standards.

Section 35.151(d)   Scope of coverage.

In the NPRM, the Department proposed a new provision, § 35.151(d), to clarify that the requirements established by § 35.151, including those contained in the 2004 ADAAG, prescribe what is necessary to ensure that buildings and facilities, including fixed or built-in elements in new or altered facilities, are accessible to individuals with disabilities. Once the construction or alteration of a facility has been completed, all other aspects of programs, services, and activities conducted in that facility are subject to the operational requirements established in this final rule. Although the Department may use the requirements of the 2010 Standards as a guide to determining when and how to make equipment and furnishings accessible, those determinations fall within the discretionary authority of the Department.

The Department also wishes to clarify that the advisory notes, appendix notes, and figures that accompany the 1991 and 2010 Standards do not establish separately enforceable requirements unless specifically stated otherwise in the text of the standards. This clarification has been made to address concerns expressed by ANPRM commenters who mistakenly believed that the advisory notes in the 2004 ADAAG established requirements beyond those established in the text of the guidelines (e.g., Advisory 504.4 suggests, but does not require, that covered entities provide visual contrast on stair tread nosing to make them more visible to individuals with low vision). The Department received no significant comments on this section and it is unchanged in the final rule.

Definitions of residential facilities and transient lodging. The 2010 Standards add a definition of "residential dwelling unit" and modify the current definition of "transient lodging." Under section 106.5 of the 2010 Standards, "residential dwelling unit" is defined as "[a] unit intended to be used as a residence, that is primarily long-term in nature" and does not include transient lodging, inpatient medical care, licensed long-term care, and detention or correctional facilities.

Additionally, section 106.5 of the 2010 Standards changes the definition of "transient lodging" to a building or facility "containing one or more guest room(s) for sleeping that provides accommodations that are primarily short-term in nature." "Transient lodging" does not include residential dwelling units intended to be used as a residence. The references to "dwelling units" and "dormitories" that are in the definition of the 1991 Standards are omitted from the 2010 Standards.

The comments about the application of transient lodging or residential standards to social service center establishments, and housing at a place of education are addressed separately below. The Department received one additional comment on this issue from an organization representing emergency response personnel seeking an exemption from the transient lodging accessibility requirements for crew quarters and common use areas serving those crew quarters (e.g., locker rooms, exercise rooms, day room) that are used exclusively by on-duty emergency response personnel and that are not used for any public purpose. The commenter argued that since emergency response personnel must meet certain physical qualifications that have the effect of exempting persons with mobility disabilities, there is no need to build crew quarters and common use areas serving those crew quarters to meet the 2004 ADAAG. In addition, the commenter argued that applying the transient lodging standards would impose significant costs and create living space that is less usable for most emergency response personnel.

The ADA does not exempt spaces because of a belief or policy that excludes persons with disabilities from certain work. However, the Department believes that crew quarters that are used exclusively as a residence by emergency response personnel and the kitchens and bathrooms exclusively serving those quarters are more like residential dwelling units and are therefore covered by the residential dwelling standards in the 2010 Standards, not the transient lodging standards. The residential dwelling standards address most of the concerns of the commenter. For example, the commenter was concerned that sinks in kitchens and lavatories in bathrooms that are accessible under the transient lodging standards would be too low to be comfortably used by emergency response personnel. The residential dwelling standards allow such features to be adaptable so that they would not have to be lowered until accessibility was needed. Similarly, grab bars and shower seats would not have to be installed at the time of construction provided that reinforcement has been installed in walls and located so as to permit their installation at a later date.

Section 35.151(e)   Social service center establishments.

In the NPRM, the Department proposed a new § 35.151(e) requiring group homes, halfway houses, shelters, or similar social service center establishments that provide temporary sleeping accommodations or residential dwelling units to comply with the provisions of the 2004 ADAAG that apply to residential facilities, including, but not limited to, the provisions in sections 233 and 809.

The NPRM explained that this proposal was based on two important changes in the 2004 ADAAG. First, for the first time, residential dwelling units are explicitly covered in the 2004 ADAAG in section 233. Second, the 2004 ADAAG eliminates the language contained in the 1991 Standards addressing scoping and technical requirements for homeless shelters, group homes, and similar social service center establishments. Currently, such establishments are covered in section 9.5 of the transient lodging section of the 1991 Standards. The deletion of section 9.5 creates an ambiguity of coverage that must be addressed.

The NPRM explained the Department's belief that transferring coverage of social service center establishments from the transient lodging standards to the residential facilities standards would alleviate conflicting requirements for social service center providers. The Department believes that a substantial percentage of social service center establishments are recipients of Federal financial assistance from the Department of Housing and Urban Development (HUD). The Department of Health and Human Services (HHS) also provides financial assistance for the operation of shelters through the Administration for Children and Families programs. As such, these establishments are covered both by the ADA and section 504 of the Rehabilitation Act. UFAS is currently the design standard for new construction and alterations for entities subject to section 504. The two design standards for accessibility — the 1991 Standards and UFAS — have confronted many social service providers with separate, and sometimes conflicting, requirements for design and construction of facilities. To resolve these conflicts, the residential facilities standards in the 2004 ADAAG have been coordinated with the section 504 requirements. The transient lodging standards, however, are not similarly coordinated. The deletion of section 9.5 of the 1991 Standards from the 2004 ADAAG presented two options: (1) Require coverage under the transient lodging standards, and subject such facilities to separate, conflicting requirements for design and construction; or (2) require coverage under the residential facilities standards, which would harmonize the regulatory requirements under the ADA and section 504. The Department chose the option that harmonizes the regulatory requirements: coverage under the residential facilities standards.

In the NPRM, the Department expressed concern that the residential facilities standards do not include a requirement for clear floor space next to beds similar to the requirement in the transient lodging standards and as a result, the Department proposed adding a provision that would require certain social service center establishments that provide sleeping rooms with more than 25 beds to ensure that a minimum of 5 percent of the beds have clear floor space in accordance with section 806.2.3 or 3004 ADAAG.

In the NPRM, the Department requested information from providers who operate homeless shelters, transient group homes, halfway houses, and other social service center establishments, and from the clients of these facilities who would be affected by this proposed change, asking, "[t]o what extent have conflicts between the ADA and section 504 affected these facilities? What would be the effect of applying the residential dwelling unit requirements to these facilities, rather than the requirements for transient lodging guest rooms?" 73 FR 34466, 34491 (June 17, 2008).

Many of the commenters supported applying the residential facilities requirements to social service center establishments, stating that even though the residential facilities requirements are less demanding in some instances, the existence of one clear standard will result in an overall increased level of accessibility by eliminating the confusion and inaction that are sometimes caused by the current existence of multiple requirements. One commenter also stated that "it makes sense to treat social service center establishments like residential facilities because this is how these establishments function in practice."

Two commenters agreed with applying the residential facilities requirements to social service center establishments but recommended adding a requirement for various bathing options, such as a roll-in shower (which is not required under the residential standards).

One commenter objected to the change and asked the Department to require that social service center establishments continue to comply with the transient lodging standards. One commenter stated that it did not agree that the standards for residential coverage would serve persons with disabilities as well as the 1991 transient lodging standards. This commenter expressed concern that the Department had eliminated guidance for social service agencies and that the rule should be put on hold until those safeguards are restored. Another commenter argued that the rule that would provide the greatest access for persons with disabilities should prevail.

Several commenters argued for the application of the transient lodging standards to all social service center establishments except those that were "intended as a person's place of abode," referencing the Department's question related to the definition of "place of lodging" in the title III NPRM. One commenter stated that the International Building Code requires accessible units in all transient facilities. The commenter expressed concern that group homes should be built to be accessible, rather than adaptable.

The Department continues to be concerned about alleviating the challenges for social service providers that are also subject to section 504 and would likely be subject to conflicting requirements if the transient lodging standards were applied. Thus, the Department has retained the requirement that social service center establishments comply with the residential dwelling standards. The Department believes, however, that social service center establishments that provide emergency shelter to large transient populations should be able to provide bathing facilities that are accessible to persons with mobility disabilities who need roll-in showers. Because of the transient nature of the population of these large shelters, it will not be feasible to modify bathing facilities in a timely manner when faced with a need to provide a roll-in shower with a seat when requested by an overnight visitor. As a result, the Department has added a requirement that social service center establishments with sleeping accommodations for more than 50 individuals must provide at least one roll-in shower with a seat that complies with the relevant provisions of section 608 of the 2010 Standards. Transfer-type showers are not permitted in lieu of a roll-in shower with a seat and the exceptions in sections 608.3 and 608.4 for residential dwelling units are not permitted. When separate shower facilities are provided for men and for women, at least one roll-in shower shall be provided for each group. This supplemental requirement to the residential facilities standards is in addition to the supplemental requirement that was proposed in the NPRM for clear floor space in sleeping rooms with more than 25 beds.

The Department also notes that while dwelling units at some social service center establishments are also subject to the Fair Housing Act (FHAct) design and construction requirements that require certain features of adaptable and accessible design, FHAct units do not provide the same level of accessibility that is required for residential facilities under the 2010 Standards. The FHAct requirements, where also applicable, should not be considered a substitute for the 2010 Standards. Rather, the 2010 Standards must be followed in addition to the FHAct requirements.

The Department also notes that whereas the NPRM used the term "social service establishment," the final rule uses the term "social service center establishment." The Department has made this editorial change so that the final rule is consistent with the terminology used in the ADA. *See* 42 U.S.C. 12181(7)(k).

Section 35.151(f) Housing at a place of education.

The Department of Justice and the Department of Education share responsibility for regulation and enforcement of the ADA in postsecondary educational settings, including its requirements for architectural features. In addition, the Department of Housing and Urban Development (HUD) has enforcement responsibility for housing subject to title II of the ADA. Housing facilities in educational settings range from traditional residence halls and dormitories to apartment or townhouse-style residences. In addition to title II of the ADA, public universities and schools that receive Federal financial assistance are also subject to section 504, which contains its own accessibility requirements through the application of UFAS. Residential housing in an educational setting is also covered by the FHAct, which requires newly constructed multifamily housing to include certain features of accessible and adaptable design. Covered entities subject to the ADA must always be aware of, and comply with, any other Federal statutes or regulations that govern the operation of residential properties.

Although the 1991 Standards mention dormitories as a form of transient lodging, they do not specifically address how the ADA applies to dormitories or other types of residential housing provided in an educational setting. The 1991 Standards also do not contain any specific provisions for residential facilities, allowing covered entities to elect to follow the residential standards contained in UFAS. Although the 2004 ADAAG contains provisions for both residential facilities and transient lodging, the guidelines do not indicate which requirements apply to housing provided in an educational setting, leaving it to the adopting agencies to make that choice. After evaluating both sets of standards, the Department concluded that the benefits of applying the transient lodging standards outweighed the benefits of applying the residential facilities standards. Consequently, in the NPRM, the Department proposed a new § 35.151(f) that provided that residence halls or dormitories operated by or on behalf of places of education shall comply with the provisions of the proposed standards for transient lodging, including, but not limited to, the provisions in sections 224 and 806 of the 2004 ADAAG.

Both public and private school housing facilities have varied characteristics. College and university housing facilities typically provide housing for up to one academic year, but may be closed during school vacation periods. In the summer, they are often used for short-term stays of one to three days, a week, or several months. Graduate and faculty housing is often provided year-round in the form of apartments, which may serve individuals or families with children. These housing facilities are diverse in their layout. Some are double-occupancy rooms with a shared toilet and bathing room, which may be inside or outside the unit. Others may contain cluster, suite, or group arrangements where several rooms are located inside a defined unit with bathing, kitchen, and similar common facilities. In some cases, these suites are indistinguishable in features from traditional apartments. Universities may build their own housing facilities or enter into agreements with private developers to build, own, or lease housing to the educational institution or to its students. Academic housing may be located on the campus of the university or may be located in nearby neighborhoods.

Throughout the school year and the summer, academic housing can become program areas in which small groups meet, receptions and educational sessions are held, and social activities occur. The ability to move between rooms — both accessible rooms and standard rooms — in order to socialize, to study, and to use all public use and common use areas is an essential part of having access to these educational programs and activities. Academic housing is also used for short-term transient educational programs during the time students are not in regular residence and may be rented out to transient visitors in a manner similar to a hotel for special university functions.

The Department was concerned that applying the new construction requirements for residential facilities to educational housing facilities could hinder access to educational programs for students with disabilities. Elevators are not generally required under the 2004 ADAAG residential facilities standards unless they are needed to provide an accessible route from accessible units to public use and common use areas, while under the 2004 ADAAG as it applies to other types of facilities, multistory public facilities must have elevators unless they meet very specific exceptions. In addition, the residential facilities standards do not require accessible roll-in showers in bathrooms, while the transient lodging requirements require some of the accessible units to be served by bathrooms with roll-in showers. The transient lodging standards also require that a greater number of units have accessible features for persons with communication disabilities. The transient lodging standards provide for installation of the required accessible features so that they are available immediately, but the residential facilities standards allow for certain features of the unit to be adaptable. For example, only reinforcements for grab bars need to be provided in residential dwellings, but the actual grab bars must be installed under the transient lodging standards. By contrast, the residential facilities standards do require certain features that provide greater accessibility within units, such as more usable kitchens, and an accessible route throughout the dwelling. The residential facilities standards also require 5 percent of the units to be accessible to persons with mobility disabilities, which is a continuation of the same scoping that is currently required under UFAS, and is therefore applicable to any educational institution that is covered by section 504. The transient lodging standards require a lower percentage of accessible sleeping rooms for facilities with large numbers of rooms than is required by UFAS. For example, if a dormitory had 150 rooms, the transient lodging standards would require seven accessible rooms while the residential standards would require eight. In a large dormitory with 500 rooms, the transient lodging standards would require 13 accessible rooms and the residential facilities standards would require 25. There are other differences between the two sets of standards as well with respect to requirements for accessible windows, alterations, kitchens, accessible route throughout a unit, and clear floor space in bathrooms allowing for a side transfer.

In the NPRM, the Department requested public comment on how to scope educational housing facilities, asking, "[w]ould the residential facility requirements or the transient lodging requirements in the 2004 ADAAG be more appropriate for housing at places of education? How would the different requirements affect the cost when building new dormitories and other student housing?" 73 FR 34466, 34492 (June 17, 2008).

The vast majority of the comments received by the Department advocated using the residential facilities standards for housing at a place of education instead of the transient lodging standards, arguing that housing at places of public education are in fact homes for the students who live in them. These commenters argued, however, that the Department should impose a requirement for a variety of options for accessible bathing and should ensure that all floors of dormitories be accessible so that students with disabilities have the same opportunities to participate in the life of the dormitory community that are provided to students without disabilities. Commenters representing persons with disabilities and several individuals argued that, although the transient lodging standards may provide a few more accessible features (such as roll-in showers), the residential facilities standards would ensure that students with disabilities have access to all rooms in their assigned unit, not just to the sleeping room, kitchenette, and wet bar. One commenter stated that, in its view, the residential facilities standards were congruent with overlapping requirements from HUD, and that access provided by the residential facilities requirements within alterations would ensure dispersion of accessible features more effectively. This commenter also argued that while the increased number of required accessible units for residential facilities as compared to transient lodging may increase the cost of construction or alteration, this cost would be offset by a reduced need to adapt rooms later if the demand for accessible rooms exceeds the supply. The commenter also encouraged the Department to impose a visitability (accessible doorways and necessary clear floor space for turning radius) requirement for both the residential facilities and transient lodging requirements to allow students with mobility impairments to interact and socialize in a fully integrated fashion.

Two commenters supported the Department's proposed approach. One commenter argued that the transient lodging requirements in the 2004 ADAAG would provide greater accessibility and increase the opportunity of students with disabilities to participate fully in campus life. A second commenter generally supported the provision of accessible dwelling units at places of education, and pointed out that the relevant scoping in the International Building Code requires accessible units "consistent with hotel accommodations."

The Department has considered the comments recommending the use of the residential facilities standards and acknowledges that they require certain features that are not included in the transient lodging standards and that should be required for housing provided at a place of education. In addition, the Department notes that since educational institutions often use their academic housing facilities as short-term transient lodging in the summers, it is important that accessible features be installed at the outset. It is not realistic to expect that the educational institution will be able to adapt a unit in a timely manner in order to provide accessible accommodations to someone attending a one-week program during the summer.

The Department has determined that the best approach to this type of housing is to continue to require the application of transient lodging standards, but at the same time to add several requirements drawn from the residential facilities standards related to accessible turning spaces and work surfaces in kitchens, and the accessible route throughout the unit. This will ensure the maintenance of the transient lodging standard requirements related to access to all floors of the facility, roll-in showers in facilities with more than 50 sleeping rooms, and other important accessibility features not found in the residential facilities standards, but will also ensure usable kitchens and access to all the rooms in a suite or apartment.

The Department has added a new definition to § 35.104, "Housing at a Place of Education," and has revised § 35.151(f) to reflect the accessible features that now will be required in addition to the requirements set forth under the transient lodging standards. The Department also recognizes that some educational institutions provide some residential housing on a year-round basis to graduate students and staff which is comparable to private rental housing, and which contains no facilities for educational programming. Section 35.151(f)(3) exempts from the transient lodging standards apartments or townhouse facilities provided by or on behalf of a place of education that are leased on a year-round basis exclusively to graduate students or faculty, and do not contain any public use or common use areas available for educational programming; instead, such housing shall comply with the requirements for residential facilities in sections 233 and 809 of the 2010 Standards.

Section 35.151(f) uses the term "sleeping room" in lieu of the term "guest room," which is the term used in the transient lodging standards. The Department is using this term because it believes that, for the most part, it provides a better description of the sleeping facilities used in a place of education than "guest room." The final rule states that the Department intends the terms to be used interchangeably in the application of the transient lodging standards to housing at a place of education.

Section 35.151(g) Assembly areas.

In the NPRM, the Department proposed § 35.151(g) to supplement the assembly area requirements of the 2004 ADAAG, which the Department is adopting as part of the 2010 Standards. The NPRM proposed at § 35.151(g)(1) to require wheelchair spaces and companion seating locations to be dispersed to all levels of the facility and are served by an accessible route. The Department received no significant comments on this paragraph and has decided to adopt the proposed language with minor modifications. The Department has retained the substance of this section in the final rule but has clarified that the requirement applies to stadiums, arenas, and grandstands. In addition, the Department has revised the phrase "wheelchair and companion seating locations" to "wheelchair spaces and companion seats."

Section 35.151(g)(1) ensures that there is greater dispersion of wheelchair spaces and companion seats throughout stadiums, arenas, and grandstands than would otherwise be required by sections 221 and 802 of the 2004 ADAAG. In some cases, the accessible route may not be the same route that other individuals use to reach their seats. For example, if other patrons reach their seats on the field by an inaccessible route (e.g., by stairs), but there is an accessible route that complies with section 206.3 of the 2010 Standards that could be connected to seats on the field, wheelchair spaces and companion seats must be placed on the field even if that route is not generally available to the public.

Regulatory language that was included in the 2004 ADAAG advisory, but that did not appear in the NPRM, has been added by the Department in § 35.151(g)(2). Section 35.151(g)(2) now requires an assembly area that has seating encircling, in whole or in part, a field of play or performance area such as an arena or stadium, to place wheelchair spaces and companion seats around the entire facility. This rule, which is designed to prevent a public entity from placing wheelchair spaces and companion seats on one side of the facility only, is consistent with the Department's enforcement practices and reflects its interpretation of section 4.33.3 of the 1991 Standards.

In the NPRM, the Department proposed § 35.151(g)(2) which prohibits wheelchair spaces and companion seating locations from being "located on, (or obstructed by) temporary platforms or other moveable structures." Through its enforcement actions, the Department discovered that some venues place wheelchair spaces and companion seats on temporary platforms that, when removed, reveal conventional seating underneath, or cover the wheelchair spaces and companion seats with temporary platforms on top of which they place risers of conventional seating. These platforms cover groups of conventional seats and are used to provide groups of wheelchair seats and companion seats.

Several commenters requested an exception to the prohibition of the use of temporary platforms for public entities that sell most of their tickets on a season-ticket or other multi-event basis. Such commenters argued that they should be able to use temporary platforms because they know, in advance, that the patrons sitting in certain areas for the whole season do not need wheelchair spaces and companion seats. The Department declines to adopt such an exception. As it explained in detail in the NPRM, the Department believes that permitting the use of movable platforms that seat four or more wheelchair users and their companions have the potential to reduce the number of available wheelchair seating spaces below the level required, thus reducing the opportunities for persons who need accessible seating to have the same choice of ticket prices and amenities that are available to other patrons in the facility. In addition, use of removable platforms may result in instances where last minute requests for wheelchair and companion seating cannot be met because entire sections of accessible seating will be lost when a platform is removed. *See* 73 FR 34466, 34493 (June 17, 2008). Further, use of temporary platforms allows facilities to limit persons who need accessible seating to certain seating areas, and to relegate accessible seating to less desirable locations. The use of temporary platforms has the effect of neutralizing dispersion and other seating requirements (e.g., line of sight) for wheelchair spaces and companion seats. *Cf. Independent Living Resources* v. *Oregon Arena Corp.*, 1 F. Supp. 2d 1159, 1171 (D. Or. 1998) (holding that while a public accommodation may "infill" wheelchair spaces with removable seats when the wheelchair spaces are not needed to accommodate individuals with disabilities, under certain circumstances "[s]uch a practice might well violate the rule that wheelchair spaces must be dispersed throughout the arena in a manner that is roughly proportionate to the overall distribution of seating"). In addition, using temporary platforms to convert unsold wheelchair spaces to conventional seating undermines the flexibility facilities need to accommodate secondary ticket markets exchanges as required by § 35.138(g) of the final rule.

As the Department explained in the NPRM, however, this provision was not designed to prohibit temporary seating that increases seating for events (e.g., placing temporary seating on the floor of a basketball court for a concert). Consequently, the final rule, at § 35.151(g)(3), has been amended to clarify that if an entire seating section is on a temporary platform for a particular event, then wheelchair spaces and companion seats may be in that seating section. However, adding a temporary platform to create wheelchair spaces and companion seats that are otherwise dissimilar from nearby fixed seating and then simply adding a small number of additional seats to the platform would not qualify as an "entire seating section" on the platform. In addition, § 35.151(g)(3) clarifies that facilities may fill in wheelchair spaces with removable seats when the wheelchair spaces are not needed by persons who use wheelchairs.

The Department has been responsive to assembly areas' concerns about reduced revenues due to unused accessible seating. Accordingly, the Department has reduced scoping requirements significantly — by almost half in large assembly areas — and determined that allowing assembly areas to infill unsold wheelchair spaces with readily removable temporary individual seats appropriately balances their economic concerns with the rights of individuals with disabilities. *See* section 221.2 of the 2010 Standards.

For stadium-style movie theaters, in § 35.151(g)(4) of the NPRM the Department proposed requiring placement of wheelchair seating spaces and companion seats on a riser or cross-aisle in the stadium section of the theater and placement of such seating so that it satisfies at least one of the following criteria: (1) It is located within the rear 60 percent of the seats provided in the auditorium; or (2) it is located within the area of the auditorium where the vertical viewing angles are between the 40th to 100th percentile of vertical viewing angles for all seats in that theater as ranked from the first row (1st percentile) to the back row (100th percentile). The vertical viewing angle is the angle between a horizontal line perpendicular to the seated viewer's eye to the screen and a line from the seated viewer's eye to the top of the screen.

The Department proposed this bright-line rule for two reasons: (1) The movie theater industry petitioned for such a rule; and (2) the Department has acquired expertise on the design of stadium style theaters from litigation against several major movie theater chains. *See U.S.* v. *AMC Entertainment*, 232 F. Supp. 2d 1092 (C.D. Ca. 2002), *rev'd in part*, 549 F. 3d 760 (9th Cir. 2008); *U.S.* v. *Cinemark USA, Inc.*, 348 F. 3d 569 (6th Cir. 2003), *cert. denied*, 542 U.S. 937 (2004). Two industry commenters — at least one of whom otherwise supported this rule — requested that the Department explicitly state that this rule does not apply retroactively to existing theaters. Although this rule on its face applies to new construction and alterations, these commenters were concerned that the rule could be interpreted to apply retroactively because of the Department's statement in the ANPRM that this bright-line rule, although newly-articulated, does not represent a "substantive change from the existing line-of-sight requirements" of section 4.33.3 of the 1991 Standards. *See* 69 FR 58768, 58776 (Sept. 30, 2004).

Although the Department intends for § 35.151(g)(4) of this rule to apply prospectively to new construction and alterations, this rule is not a departure from, and is consistent with, the line-of-sight requirements in the 1991 Standards. The Department has always interpreted the line- of-sight requirements in the 1991 Standards to require viewing angles provided to patrons who use wheelchairs to be comparable to those afforded to other spectators. Section 35.151(g)(4) merely represents the application of these requirements to stadium- style movie theaters.

One commenter from a trade association sought clarification whether § 35.151(g)(4) applies to stadium-style theaters with more than 300 seats, and argued that it should not since dispersion requirements apply in those theaters. The Department declines to limit this rule to stadium-style theaters with 300 or fewer seats; stadium-style theaters of all sizes must comply with this rule. So, for example, stadium-style theaters that must vertically disperse wheelchair and companion seats must do so within the parameters of this rule.

The NPRM included a provision that required assembly areas with more than 5,000 seats to provide at least five wheelchair spaces with at least three companion seats for each of those five wheelchair spaces. The Department agrees with commenters who asserted that group seating is better addressed through ticketing policies rather than design and has deleted that provision from this section of the final rule.

Section 35.151(h)   Medical care facilities.

In the 1991 title II regulation, there was no provision addressing the dispersion of accessible sleeping rooms in medical care facilities. The Department is aware, however, of problems that individuals with disabilities face in receiving full and equal medical care when accessible sleeping rooms are not adequately dispersed. When accessible rooms are not fully dispersed, a person with a disability is often placed in an accessible room in an area that is not medically appropriate for his or her condition, and is thus denied quick access to staff with expertise in that medical specialty and specialized equipment. While the Access Board did not establish specific design requirements for dispersion in the 2004 ADAAG, in response to extensive comments in support of dispersion it added an advisory note, Advisory 223.1 General, encouraging dispersion of accessible rooms within the facility so that accessible rooms are more likely to be proximate to appropriate qualified staff and resources.

In the NPRM, the Department sought additional comment on the issue, asking whether it should require medical care facilities, such as hospitals, to disperse their accessible sleeping rooms, and if so, by what method (by specialty area, floor, or other criteria). All of the comments the Department received on this issue supported dispersing accessible sleeping rooms proportionally by specialty area. These comments, from individuals, organizations, and a building code association, argued that it would not be difficult for hospitals to disperse rooms by specialty area, given the high level of regulation to which hospitals are subject and the planning that hospitals do based on utilization trends. Further, commenters suggested that without a requirement, it is unlikely that hospitals would disperse the rooms. In addition, concentrating accessible rooms in one area perpetuates segregation of individuals with disabilities, which is counter to the purpose of the ADA.

The Department has decided to require medical care facilities to disperse their accessible sleeping rooms in a manner that is proportionate by type of medical specialty. This does not require exact mathematical proportionality, which at times would be impossible. However, it does require that medical care facilities disperse their accessible rooms by medical specialty so that persons with disabilities can, to the extent practical, stay in an accessible room within the wing or ward that is appropriate for their medical needs. The language used in this rule ("in a manner that is proportionate by type of medical specialty") is more specific than that used in the NPRM ("in a manner that enables patients with disabilities to have access to appropriate specialty services") and adopts the concept of proportionality proposed by the commenters. Accessible rooms should be dispersed throughout all medical specialties, such as obstetrics, orthopedics, pediatrics, and cardiac care.

Section 35.151(i)   Curb ramps.

Section 35.151(e) on curb ramps in the 1991 rule has been redesignated as § 35.151(i). In the NPRM, the Department proposed making a minor editorial change to this section, deleting the phrase "other sloped areas" from the two places in which it appears in the 1991 title II regulation. In the NPRM, the Department stated that the phrase "other sloped areas" lacks technical precision. The Department received no significant public comments on this proposal. Upon further consideration, however, the Department has concluded that the regulation should acknowledge that there are times when there are transitions from sidewalk to road surface that do not technically qualify as "curb ramps" (sloped surfaces that have a running slope that exceed 5 percent). Therefore, the Department has decided not to delete the phrase "other sloped areas."

Section 35.151(j)   Residential housing for sale to individual owners.

Although public entities that operate residential housing programs are subject to title II of the ADA, and therefore must provide accessible residential housing, the 1991 Standards did not contain scoping or technical standards that specifically applied to residential housing units. As a result, under the Department's title II regulation, these agencies had the choice of complying with UFAS, which contains specific scoping and technical standards for residential housing units, or applying the ADAAG transient lodging standards to their housing. Neither UFAS nor the 1991 Standards distinguish between residential housing provided for rent and those provided for sale to individual owners. Thus, under the 1991 title II regulation, public entities that construct residential housing units to be sold to individual owners must ensure that some of those units are accessible. This requirement is in addition to any accessibility requirements imposed on housing programs operated by public entities that receive Federal financial assistance from Federal agencies such as HUD.

The 2010 Standards contain scoping and technical standards for residential dwelling units. However, section 233.3.2 of the 2010 Standards specifically defers to the Department and to HUD, the standard-setting agency under the ABA, to decide the appropriate scoping for those residential dwelling units built by or on behalf of public entities with the intent that the finished units will be sold to individual owners. These programs include, for example, HUD's public housing and HOME programs as well as State-funded programs to construct units for sale to individuals. In the NPRM, the Department did not make a specific proposal for this scoping. Instead, the Department stated that after consultation and coordination with HUD, the Department would make a determination in the final rule. The Department also sought public comment on this issue stating that "[t]he Department would welcome recommendations from individuals with disabilities, public housing authorities, and other interested parties that have experience with these programs. Please comment on the appropriate scoping for residential dwelling units built by or on behalf of public entities with the intent that the finished units will be sold to individual owners." 73 FR 34466, 34492 (June 17, 2008).

All of the public comments received by the Department in response to this question were supportive of the Department's ensuring that the residential standards apply to housing built on behalf of public entities with the intent that the finished units would be sold to individual owners. The vast majority of commenters recommended that the Department require that projects consisting of five or more units, whether or not the units are located on one or multiple locations, comply with the 2004 ADAAG requirements for scoping of residential units, which require that 5 percent, and no fewer than one, of the dwelling units provide mobility features, and that 2 percent, and no fewer than one, of the dwelling units provide communication features. *See* 2004 ADAAG Section 233.3. These commenters argued that the Department should not defer to HUD because HUD has not yet adopted the 2004 ADAAG and there is ambiguity on the scope of coverage of pre-built for sale units under HUD's current section 504 regulations. In addition, these commenters expressed concern that HUD's current regulation, 24 CFR 8.29, presumes that a prospective buyer is identified before design and construction begins so that disability features can be incorporated prior to construction. These commenters stated that State and Federally funded homeownership programs typically do not identify prospective buyers before construction has commenced. One commenter stated that, in its experience, when public entities build accessible for-sale units, they often sell these units through a lottery system that does not make any effort to match persons who need the accessible features with the units that have those features. Thus, accessible units are often sold to persons without disabilities. This commenter encouraged the Department to make sure that accessible for-sale units built or funded by public entities are placed in a separate lottery restricted to income-eligible persons with disabilities.

Two commenters recommended that the Department develop rules for four types of for-sale projects: single family pre-built (where buyer selects the unit after construction), single family post-built (where the buyer chooses the model prior to its construction), multi-family pre-built, and multi-family post-built. These commenters recommended that the Department require pre-built units to comply with the 2004 ADAAG 233.1 scoping requirements. For post-built units, the commenters recommended that the Department require all models to have an alternate design with mobility features and an alternate design with communications features in compliance with 2004 ADAAG. Accessible models should be available at no extra cost to the buyer. One commenter recommended that, in addition to required fully accessible units, all ground floor units should be readily convertible for accessibility or for sensory impairments technology enhancements.

The Department believes that consistent with existing requirements under title

II, housing programs operated by public entities that design and construct or alter residential units for sale to individual owners should comply with the 2010 Standards, including the requirements for residential facilities in sections 233 and 809. These requirements will ensure that a minimum of 5 percent of the units, but no fewer than one unit, of the total number of residential dwelling units will be designed and constructed to be accessible for persons with mobility disabilities. At least 2 percent, but no fewer than one unit, of the total number of residential dwelling units shall provide communication features.

The Department recognizes that there are some programs (such as the one identified by the commenter), in which units are not designed and constructed until an individual buyer is identified. In such cases, the public entity is still obligated to comply with the 2010 Standards. In addition, the public entity must ensure that pre-identified buyers with mobility disabilities and visual and hearing disabilities are afforded the opportunity to buy the accessible units. Once the program has identified buyers who need the number of accessible units mandated by the 2010 Standards, it may have to make reasonable modifications to its policies, practices, and procedures in order to provide accessible units to other buyers with disabilities who request such units.

The Department notes that the residential facilities standards allow for construction of units with certain features of adaptability. Public entities that are concerned that fully accessible units are less marketable may choose to build these units to include the allowable adaptable features, and then adapt them at their own expense for buyers with mobility disabilities who need accessible units. For example, features such as grab bars are not required but may be added by the public entity if needed by the buyer at the time of purchase and cabinets under sinks may be designed to be removable to allow access to the required knee space for a forward approach.

The Department agrees with the commenters that covered entities may have to make reasonable modifications to their policies, practices, and procedures in order to ensure that when they offer pre-built accessible residential units for sale, the units are offered in a manner that gives access to those units to persons with disabilities who need the features of the units and who are otherwise eligible for the housing program. This may be accomplished, for example, by adopting preferences for accessible units for persons who need the features of the units, holding separate lotteries for accessible units, or other suitable methods that result in the sale of accessible units to persons who need the features of such units. In addition, the Department believes that units designed and constructed or altered that comply with the requirements for residential facilities and are offered for sale to individuals must be provided at the same price as units without such features.

Section 35.151(k)   *Detention and correctional facilities.*

The 1991 Standards did not contain specific accessibility standards applicable to cells in correctional facilities. However, correctional and detention facilities operated by or on behalf of public entities have always been subject to the nondiscrimination and program accessibility requirements of title II of the ADA. The 2004 ADAAG established specific requirements for the design and construction and alterations of cells in correctional facilities for the first time.

Based on complaints received by the Department, investigations, and compliance reviews of jails, prisons, and other detention and correctional facilities, the Department has determined that many detention and correctional facilities do not have enough accessible cells, toilets, and shower facilities to meet the needs of their inmates with mobility disabilities and some do not have any at all. Inmates are sometimes housed in medical units or infirmaries separate from the general population simply because there are no accessible cells. In addition, some inmates have alleged that they are housed at a more restrictive classification level simply because no accessible housing exists at the appropriate classification level. The Department's compliance reviews and investigations have substantiated certain of these allegations.

The Department believes that the insufficient number of accessible cells is, in part, due to the fact that most jails and prisons were built long before the ADA became law and, since then, have undergone few alterations that would trigger the obligation to provide accessible features in accordance with UFAS or the 1991 Standards. In addition, the Department has found that even some new correctional facilities lack accessible features. The Department believes that the unmet demand for accessible cells is also due to the changing demographics of the inmate population. With thousands of prisoners serving life sentences without eligibility for parole, prisoners are aging, and the prison population of individuals with disabilities and elderly individuals is growing. A Bureau of Justice Statistics study of State and Federal sentenced inmates (those sentenced to more than one year) shows the total estimated count of State and Federal prisoners aged 55 and older grew by 36,000 inmates from 2000 (44,200) to 2006 (80,200). William J. Sabol *et al., Prisoners in 2006*, Bureau of Justice Statistics Bulletin, Dec. 2007, at 23 (app. table 7), available at http://bjs.ojp.usdoj.gov/ index.cfm?ty=pbdetail&iid=908 (last visited July 16, 2008); Allen J. Beck et al., *Prisoners in 2000*, Bureau of Justice Statistics Bulletin, Aug. 2001, at 10 (Aug. 2001) (Table 14), available at *bjs.ojp.usdoj.gov/ index.cfm?ty=pbdetail&iid=927* (last visited July 16, 2008). This jump constitutes an increase of 81 percent in prisoners aged 55 and older during this period.

In the NPRM, the Department proposed a new section, § 35.152, which combined a range of provisions relating to both program accessibility and application of the proposed standards to detention and correctional facilities. In the final rule, the Department is placing those provisions that refer to design, construction, and alteration of detention and correction facilities in a new paragraph (k) of § 35.151, the section of the rule that addresses new construction and alterations for covered entities. Those portions of the final rule that address other issues, such as placement policies and program accessibility, are placed in the new § 35.152.

In the NPRM, the Department also sought input on how best to meet the needs of inmates with mobility disabilities in the design, construction, and alteration of detention and correctional facilities. The Department received a number of comments in response to this question.

New Construction. The NPRM did not expressly propose that new construction of correctional and detention facilities shall comply with the proposed standards because the Department assumed it would be clear that the requirements of § 35.151 would apply to new construction of correctional and detention facilities in the same manner that they apply to other facilities constructed by covered entities.

The Department has decided to create a new section, § 35.151(k)(1), which clarifies that new construction of jails, prisons, and other detention facilities shall comply with the requirements of 2010 Standards. Section 35.151(k)(1) also increases the scoping for accessible cells from the 2 percent specified in the 2004 ADAAG to 3 percent.

Alterations. Although the 2010 Standards contain specifications for alterations in existing detention and correctional facilities, section 232.2 defers to the Attorney General the decision as to the extent these requirements will apply to alterations of cells. The NPRM proposed at § 35.152(c) that "[a]lterations to jails, prisons, and other detention and correctional facilities will comply with the requirements of § 35.151(b)." 73 FR 34466, 34507 (June 17, 2008). The final rule retains that requirement at § 35.151(k)(2), but increases the scoping for accessible cells from the 2 percent specified in the 2004 ADAAG to 3 percent.

Substitute cells. In the ANPRM, the Department sought public comment about the most effective means to ensure that existing correctional facilities are made accessible to prisoners with disabilities and presented three options: (1) Require all altered elements to be accessible, which would maintain the current policy that applies to other ADA alteration requirements; (2) permit substitute cells to be made accessible within the same facility, which would permit correctional authorities to meet their obligation by providing the required accessible features in cells within the same facility, other than those specific cells in which alterations are planned; or (3) permit substitute cells to be made accessible within a prison system, which would focus on ensuring that prisoners with disabilities are housed in facilities that best meet their needs, as alterations within a prison environment often result in piecemeal accessibility.

In § 35.152(c) of the NPRM, the Department proposed language based on Option 2, providing that when cells are altered, a covered entity may satisfy its obligation to provide the required number of cells with mobility features by providing the required mobility features in substitute cells (i.e., cells other than those where alterations are originally planned), provided that each substitute cell is located within the same facility, is integrated with other cells to the maximum extent feasible, and has, at a minimum, physical access equal to that of the original cells to areas used by inmates or detainees for visitation, dining, recreation, educational programs, medical services, work programs, religious services, and participation in other programs that the facility offers to inmates or detainees.

The Department received few comments on this proposal. The majority who chose to comment supported an approach that allowed substitute cells to be made accessible within the same facility. In their view, such an approach balanced administrators' needs, cost considerations, and the needs of inmates with disabilities. One commenter noted, however, that with older facilities, required modifications may be inordinately costly and technically infeasible. A large county jail system supported the proposed approach as the most viable option allowing modification or alteration of existing cells based on need and providing a flexible approach to provide program and mobility accessibility. It noted, as an alternative, that permitting substitute cells to be made accessible within a prison system would also be a viable option since such an approach could create a centralized location for accessibility needs and, because that jail system's facilities were in close proximity, it would have little impact on families for visitation or on accessible programming.

A large State department of corrections objected to the Department's proposal. The commenter stated that some very old prison buildings have thick walls of concrete and reinforced steel that are difficult, if not impossible to retrofit, and to do so would be very expensive. This State system approaches accessibility by looking at its system as a whole and providing access to programs for inmates with disabilities at selected prisons. This commenter explained that not all of its facilities offer the same programs or the same levels of medical or mental health services. An inmate, for example, who needs education, substance abuse treatment, and sex offender counseling may be transferred between facilities in order to meet his needs. The inmate population is always in flux and there are not always beds or program availability for every inmate at his security level. This commenter stated that the Department's proposed language would put the State in the position of choosing between adding accessible cells and modifying paths of travel to programs and services at great expense or not altering old facilities, causing them to become in states of disrepair and obsolescent, which would be fiscally irresponsible.

The Department is persuaded by these comments and has modified the alterations requirement in § 35.151(k)(2)(iv) in the final rule to allow that if it is technically infeasible to provide substitute cells in the same facility, cells can be provided elsewhere within the corrections system.

Number of accessible cells. Section 232.2.1 of the 2004 ADAAG requires at least 2 percent, but no fewer than one, of the cells in newly constructed detention and correctional facilities to have accessibility features for individuals with mobility disabilities. Section 232.3 provides that, where special holding cells or special housing cells are provided, at least one cell serving each purpose shall have mobility features. The Department sought input on whether these 2004 ADAAG requirements are sufficient to meet the needs of inmates with mobility disabilities. A major association representing county jails throughout the country stated that the 2004 ADAAG 2 percent requirement for accessible cells is sufficient to meet the needs of county jails. Similarly, a large county sheriff's department advised that the 2 percent requirement far exceeds the need at its detention facility, where the average age of the population is 32. This commenter stressed that the regulations need to address the differences between a local detention facility with low average lengths of stay as opposed to a State prison housing inmates for lengthy periods. This commenter asserted that more stringent requirements will raise construction costs by requiring modifications that are not needed. If more stringent requirements are adopted, the commenter suggested that they apply only to State and Federal prisons that house prisoners sentenced to long terms. The Department notes that a prisoner with a mobility disability needs a cell with mobility features regardless of the length of incarceration. However, the length of incarceration is most relevant in addressing the needs of an aging population.

The overwhelming majority of commenters responded that the 2 percent ADAAG requirement is inadequate to meet the needs of the incarcerated. Many commenters suggested that the requirement be expanded to apply to each area, type, use, and class of cells in a facility. They asserted that if a facility has separate areas for specific programs, such as a dog training program or a substance abuse unit, each of these areas should also have 2 percent accessible cells but not less than one.

These same commenters suggested that 5–7 percent of cells should be accessible to meet the needs of both an aging population and the larger number of inmates with mobility disabilities. One organization recommended that the requirement be increased to 5 percent overall, and that at least 2 percent of each type and use of cell be accessible. Another commenter recommended that 10 percent of cells be accessible. An organization with extensive corrections experience noted that the integration mandate requires a sufficient number and distribution of accessible cells so as to provide distribution of locations relevant to programs to ensure that persons with disabilities have access to the programs.

Through its investigations and compliance reviews, the Department has found that in most detention and correctional facilities, a 2 percent accessible cell requirement is inadequate to meet the needs of the inmate population with disabilities. That finding is supported by the majority of the commenters that recommended a 5–7 percent requirement. Indeed, the Department itself requires more than 2 percent of the cells to be accessible at its own corrections facilities. The Federal Bureau of Prisons is subject to the requirements of the 2004 ADAAG through the General Services Administration's adoption of the 2004 ADAAG as the enforceable accessibility standard for Federal facilities under the Architectural Barriers Act of 1968. 70 FR 67786, 67846–47 (Nov. 8, 2005). However, in order to meet the needs of inmates with mobility disabilities, the Bureau of Prisons has elected to increase that percentage and require that 3 percent of inmate housing at its facilities be accessible. Bureau of Prisons, Design Construction Branch, Design Guidelines, Attachment A: Accessibility Guidelines for Design, Construction, and Alteration of Federal Bureau of Prisons (Oct. 31, 2006).

The Department believes that a 3 percent accessible requirement is reasonable. Moreover, it does not believe it should impose a higher percentage on detention and corrections facilities than it utilizes for its own facilities. Thus, the Department has adopted a 3 percent requirement in § 35.151(k) for both new construction and alterations. The Department notes that the 3 percent requirement is a minimum. As corrections systems plan for new facilities or alterations, the Department urges planners to include numbers of inmates with disabilities in their population projections in order to take the necessary steps to provide a sufficient number of accessible cells to meet inmate needs.

Dispersion of Cells. The NPRM did not contain express language addressing dispersion of cells in a facility. However, Advisory 232.2 of the 2004 ADAAG recommends that "[a]ccessible cells or rooms should be dispersed among different levels of security, housing categories, and holding classifications (e.g., male/female and adult/ juvenile) to facilitate access." In explaining the basis for recommending, but not requiring, this type of dispersal, the Access Board stated that "[m]any detention and correctional facilities are designed so that certain areas (e.g., 'shift' areas) can be adapted to serve as different types of housing according to need" and that "[p]lacement of accessible cells or rooms in shift areas may allow additional flexibility in meeting requirements for dispersion of accessible cells or rooms."

The Department notes that inmates are typically housed in separate areas of detention and correctional facilities based on a number of factors, including their classification level. In many instances, detention and correctional facilities have housed inmates in inaccessible cells, even though accessible cells were available elsewhere in the facility, because there were no cells in the areas where they needed to be housed, such as in administrative or disciplinary segregation, the women's section of the facility, or in a particular security classification area.

The Department received a number of comments stating that dispersal of accessible cells together with an adequate number of accessible cells is necessary to prevent inmates with disabilities from placement in improper security classification and to ensure integration. Commenters recommended modification of the scoping requirements to require a percentage of accessible cells in each program, classification, use or service area. The Department is persuaded by these comments. Accordingly, § 35.151(k)(1) and (k)(2) of the final rule require accessible cells in each classification area.

Medical facilities. The NPRM also did not propose language addressing the application of the 2004 ADAAG to medical and long-term care facilities in correctional and detention facilities. The provisions of the 2004 ADAAG contain requirements for licensed medical and long-term care facilities, but not those that are unlicensed. A disability advocacy group and a number of other commenters recommended that the Department expand the application of section 232.4 to apply to all such facilities in detention and correctional facilities, regardless of licensure. They recommended that whenever a correctional facility has a program that is addressed specifically in the 2004 ADAAG, such as a long-term care facility, the 2004 ADAAG scoping and design features should apply for those elements. Similarly, a building code organization noted that its percentage requirements for accessible units is based on what occurs in the space, not on the building type.

The Department is persuaded by these comments and has added § 35.151(k)(3), which states that "[w]ith respect to medical and long-term care facilities in jails, prisons, and other detention and correctional facilities, public entities shall apply the 2010 Standards technical and scoping requirements for those facilities irrespective of whether those facilities are licensed."

Section 35.152   Detention and correctional facilities — program requirements.

As noted in the discussion of § 35.151(k), the Department has determined that inmates with mobility and other disabilities in detention and correctional facilities do not have equal access to prison services. The Department's concerns are based not only on complaints it has received, but the Department's substantial experience in investigations and compliance reviews of jails, prisons, and other detention and correctional facilities. Based on that review, the Department has found that many detention and correctional facilities have too few or no accessible cells, toilets, and shower facilities to meet the needs of their inmates with mobility disabilities. These findings, coupled with statistics regarding the current percentage of inmates with mobility disabilities and the changing demographics of the inmate population reflecting thousands of prisoners serving life sentences and increasingly large numbers of aging inmates who are not eligible for parole, led the Department to conclude that a new regulation was necessary to address these concerns.

In the NPRM, the Department proposed a new section, § 35.152, which combined a range of provisions relating to both program accessibility and application of the proposed standards to detention and correctional facilities. As mentioned above, in the final rule, the Department is placing those provisions that refer to design, construction, and alteration of detention and correction facilities in new paragraph (k) in § 35.151 dealing with new construction and alterations for covered entities. Those portions of the final rule that address other program requirements remain in § 35.152.

The Department received many comments in response to the program accessibility requirements in proposed § 35.152. These comments are addressed below.

Facilities operated through contractual, licensing, or other arrangements with other public entities or private entities. The Department is aware that some public entities are confused about the applicability of the title II requirements to correctional facilities built or run by other public entities or private entities. It has consistently been the Department's position that title II requirements apply to correctional facilities used by State or local government entities, irrespective of whether the public entity contracts with another public or private entity to build or run the correctional facility. The power to incarcerate citizens rests with the State or local government, not a private entity. As the Department stated in the preamble to the original title II regulation, "[a]ll governmental activities of public entities are covered, even if they are carried out by contractors." 28 CFR part 35, app. A at 558 (2009). If a prison is occupied by State prisoners and is inaccessible, the State is responsible under title II of the ADA. The same is true for a county or city jail. In essence, the private builder or contractor that operates the correctional facility does so at the direction of the government entity. Moreover, even if the State enters into a contractual, licensing, or other arrangement for correctional services with a public entity that has its own title II obligations, the State is still responsible for ensuring that the other public entity complies with title II in providing these services.

Also, through its experience in investigations and compliance reviews, the Department has noted that public entities contract for a number of services to be run by private or other public entities, for example, medical and mental health services, food services, laundry, prison industries, vocational programs, and drug treatment and substance abuse programs, all of which must be operated in accordance with title II requirements.

Proposed § 35.152(a) in the NPRM was designed to make it clear that title II applies to all State and local detention and correctional facilities, regardless of whether the detention or correctional facility is directly operated by the public entity or operated by a private entity through a contractual, licensing, or other arrangement. Commenters specifically supported the language of this section. One commenter cited Department of Justice statistics stating that of the approximately 1.6 million inmates in State and Federal facilities in December 2006, approximately 114,000 of these inmates were held in private prison facilities. *See* William J. Sabol *et al., Prisoners in 2006*, Bureau of Justice Statistics Bulletin, Dec. 2007, at 1, 4, available at http:// bjs.ojp.usdoj.gov/ index.cfm?ty=pbdetail&iid=908. Some commenters wanted the text "through contracts or other arrangements" changed to read "through contracts or any other arrangements" to make the intent clear. However, a large number of commenters recommended that the text of the rule make explicit that it applies to correctional facilities operated by private contractors. Many commenters also suggested that the text make clear that the rule applies to adult facilities, juvenile justice facilities, and community correctional facilities. In the final rule, the Department is adopting these latter two suggestions in order to make the section's intent explicit.

Section 35.152(a) of the final rule states specifically that the requirements of the section apply to public entities responsible for the operation or management of correctional facilities, "either directly or through contractual, licensing, or other arrangements with public or private entities, in whole or in part, including private correctional facilities." Additionally, the section explicitly provides that it applies to adult and juvenile justice detention and correctional facilities and community correctional facilities.

Discrimination prohibited. In the NPRM, § 35.152(b)(1) proposed language stating that public entities are prohibited from excluding qualified detainees and inmates from participation in, or denying, benefits, services, programs, or activities because a facility is inaccessible to persons with disabilities "unless the public entity can demonstrate that the required actions would result in a fundamental alteration or undue burden." 73 FR 34446, 34507 (June 17, 2008). One large State department of corrections objected to the entire section applicable to detention and correctional facilities, stating that it sets a higher standard for correctional and detention facilities because it does not provide a defense for undue administrative burden. The Department has not retained the proposed NPRM language referring to the defenses of fundamental alteration or undue burden because the Department believes that these exceptions are covered by the general language of 35.150(a)(3), which states that a public entity is not required to take "any action that it can demonstrate would result in a fundamental alteration in the nature of a service, program, or activity, or in undue financial and administrative burdens." The Department has revised the language of § 35.152(b)(1) accordingly.

Integration of inmates and detainees with disabilities. In the NPRM, the Department proposed language in § 35.152(b)(2) specifically applying the ADA's general integration mandate to detention and correctional facilities. The proposed language would have required public entities to ensure that individuals with disabilities are housed in the most integrated setting appropriate to the needs of the individual. It further stated that unless the public entity can demonstrate that it is appropriate to make an exception for a specific individual, a public entity:

(1) Should not place inmates or detainees with disabilities in locations that exceed their security classification because there are no accessible cells or beds in the appropriate classification;

(2) should not place inmates or detainees with disabilities in designated medical areas unless they are actually receiving medical care or treatment;

(3) should not place inmates or detainees with disabilities in facilities that do not offer the same programs as the facilities where they would ordinarily be housed; and

(4) should not place inmates or detainees with disabilities in facilities farther away from their families in order to provide accessible cells or beds, thus diminishing their opportunity for visitation based on their disability. 73 FR 34466, 34507 (June 17, 2008).

In the NPRM, the Department recognized that there are a wide range of considerations that affect decisions to house inmates or detainees and that in specific cases there may be compelling reasons why a placement that does not meet the general requirements of § 35.152(b)(2) may, nevertheless, comply with the ADA. However, the Department noted that it is essential that the planning process initially assume that inmates or detainees with disabilities will be assigned within the system under the same criteria that would be applied to inmates who do not have disabilities. Exceptions may be made on a case-by-case basis if the specific situation warrants different treatment. For example, if an inmate is deaf and communicates only using sign language, a prison may consider whether it is more appropriate to give priority to housing the prisoner in a facility close to his family that houses no other deaf inmates, or if it would be preferable to house the prisoner in a setting where there are sign language interpreters and other sign language users with whom he can communicate.

In general, commenters strongly supported the NPRM's clarification that the title II integration mandate applies to State and local corrections agencies and the facilities in which they house inmates. Commenters pointed out that inmates with disabilities continue to be segregated based on their disabilities and also excluded from participation in programs. An organization actively involved in addressing the needs of prisoners cited a number of recent lawsuits in which prisoners allege such discrimination.

The majority of commenters objected to the language in proposed § 35.152(b)(2) that creates an exception to the integration mandate when the "public entity can demonstrate that it is appropriate to make an exception for a specific individual." 73 FR 34466, 34507 (June 17, 2008). The vast majority of commenters asserted that, given the practice of many public entities to segregate and cluster inmates with disabilities, the exception will be used to justify the status quo. The commenters acknowledged that the intent of the section is to ensure that an individual with a disability who can be better served in a less integrated setting can legally be placed in that setting. They were concerned, however, that the proposed language would allow certain objectionable practices to continue, *e.g.*, automatically placing persons with disabilities in administrative segregation. An advocacy organization with extensive experience working with inmates recommended that the inmate have "input" in the placement decision.

Others commented that the exception does not provide sufficient guidance on when a government entity may make an exception, citing the need for objective standards. Some commenters posited that a prison administration may want to house a deaf inmate at a facility designated and equipped for deaf inmates that is several hundred miles from the inmate's home. Although under the exception language, such a placement may be appropriate, these commenters argued that this outcome appears to contradict the regulation's intent to eliminate or reduce the segregation of inmates with disabilities and prevent them from being placed far from their families. The Department notes that in some jurisdictions, the likelihood of such outcomes is diminished because corrections facilities with different programs and levels of accessibility are clustered in close proximity to one another, so that being far from family is not an issue. The Department also takes note of advancements in technology that will ease the visitation dilemma, such as family visitation through the use of videoconferencing.

Only one commenter, a large State department of corrections, objected to the integration requirement. This commenter stated it houses all maximum security inmates in maximum security facilities. Inmates with lower security levels may or may not be housed in lower security facilities depending on a number of factors, such as availability of a bed, staffing, program availability, medical and mental health needs, and enemy separation. The commenter also objected to the proposal to prohibit housing inmates with disabilities in medical areas unless they are receiving medical care. This commenter stated that such housing may be necessary for several days, for example, at a stopover facility for an inmate with a disability who is being transferred from one facility to another. Also, this commenter stated that inmates with disabilities in disciplinary status may be housed in the infirmary because not every facility has accessible cells in disciplinary housing. Similarly the commenter objected to the prohibition on placing inmates in facilities without the same programs as facilities where they normally would be housed. Finally, the commenter objected to the prohibition on placing an inmate at a facility distant from where the inmate would normally be housed. The commenter stressed that in its system, there are few facilities near most inmates' homes. The commenter noted that most inmates are housed at facilities far from their homes, a fact shared by all inmates, not just inmates with disabilities. Another commenter noted that in some jurisdictions, inmates who need assistance in activities of daily living cannot obtain that assistance in the general population, but only in medical facilities where they must be housed.

The Department has considered the concerns raised by the commenters with respect to this section and recognizes that corrections systems may move inmates routinely and for a variety of reasons, such as crowding, safety, security, classification change, need for specialized programs, or to provide medical care. Sometimes these moves are within the same facility or prison system. On other occasions, inmates may be transferred to facilities in other cities, counties, and States. Given the nature of the prison environment, inmates have little say in their placement and administrators must have flexibility to meet the needs of the inmates and the system. The Department has revised the language of the exception contained in renumbered § 35.152(b)(2) to better accommodate corrections administrators' need for flexibility in making placement decisions based on legitimate, specific reasons. Moreover, the Department believes that temporary, short-term moves that are necessary for security or administrative purposes (e.g., placing an inmate with a disability in a medical area at a stopover facility during a transfer from one facility to another) do not violate the requirements of § 35.152(b)(2).

The Department notes that § 35.150(a)(3) states that a public entity is not required to take "any action that it can demonstrate would result in a fundamental alteration in the nature of a service, program, or activity or in undue financial and administrative burdens." Thus, corrections systems would not have to comply with the requirements of § 35.152(b)(1) in any specific circumstance where these defenses are met.

Several commenters recommended that the word "should" be changed to "shall" in the subparts to § 35.152(b)(2). The Department agrees that because the rule contains a specific exception and because the integration requirement is subject to the defenses provided in paragraph (a) of that section, it is more appropriate to use the word "shall" and the Department accordingly is making that change in the final rule.

Program requirements. In a unanimous decision, the Supreme Court, in *Pennsylvania Department of Corrections* v. *Yeskey*, 524 U.S. 206 (1998), stated explicitly that the ADA covers the operations of State prisons; accordingly, title II's program accessibility requirements apply to State and local correctional and detention facilities. In the NPRM, in addressing the accessibility of existing correctional and detention facilities, the Department considered the challenges of applying the title II program access requirement for existing facilities under § 31.150(a) in light of the realities of many inaccessible correctional facilities and strained budgets.

Correctional and detention facilities commonly provide a variety of different programs for education, training, counseling, or other purposes related to rehabilitation. Some examples of programs generally available to inmates include programs to obtain GEDs, computer training, job skill training and on-the-job training, religious instruction and guidance, alcohol and substance abuse groups, anger management, work assignments, work release, halfway houses, and other programs. Historically, individuals with disabilities have been excluded from such programs because they are not located in accessible locations, or inmates with disabilities have been segregated in units without equivalent programs. In light of the Supreme Court's decision in *Yeskey* and the requirements of title II, however, it is critical that public entities provide these opportunities to inmates with disabilities. In proposed § 35.152, the Department sought to clarify that title II required equal access for inmates with disabilities to participate in programs offered to inmates without disabilities.

The Department wishes to emphasize that detention and correctional facilities are unique facilities under title II. Inmates cannot leave the facilities and must have their needs met by the corrections system, including needs relating to a disability. If the detention and correctional facilities fail to accommodate prisoners with disabilities, these individuals have little recourse, particularly when the need is great (e.g., an accessible toilet; adequate catheters; or a shower chair). It is essential that corrections systems fulfill their nondiscrimination and program access obligations by adequately addressing the needs of prisoners with disabilities, which include, but are not limited to, proper medication and medical treatment, accessible toilet and shower facilities, devices such as a bed transfer or a shower chair, and assistance with hygiene methods for prisoners with physical disabilities.

In the NPRM, the Department also sought input on whether it should establish a program accessibility requirement that public entities modify additional cells at a detention or correctional facility to incorporate the accessibility features needed by specific inmates with mobility disabilities when the number of cells required by sections 232.2 and 232.3 of the 2004 ADAAG are inadequate to meet the needs of their inmate population.

Commenters supported a program accessibility requirement, viewing it as a flexible and practical means of allowing facilities to meet the needs of inmates in a cost effective and expedient manner. One organization supported a requirement to modify additional cells when the existing number of accessible cells is inadequate. It cited the example of a detainee who was held in a hospital because the local jail had no accessible cells. Similarly, a State agency recommended that the number of accessible cells should be sufficient to accommodate the population in need. One group of commenters voiced concern about accessibility being provided in a timely manner and recommended that the rule specify that the program accessibility requirement applies while waiting for the accessibility modifications. A group with experience addressing inmate needs recommended the inmate's input should be required to prevent inappropriate segregation or placement in an inaccessible or inappropriate area.

The Department is persuaded by these comments. Accordingly, § 35.152(b)(3) requires public entities to "implement reasonable policies, including physical modifications to additional cells in accordance with the 2010 Standards, so as to ensure that each inmate with a disability is housed in a cell with the accessible elements necessary to afford the inmate access to safe, appropriate housing."

Communication. Several large disability advocacy organizations commented on the 2004 ADAAG section 232.2.2 requirement that at least 2 percent of the general holding cells and housing cells must be equipped with audible emergency alarm systems. Permanently installed telephones within these cells must have volume control. Commenters said that the communication features in the 2004 ADAAG do not address the most common barriers that deaf and hard- of-hearing inmates face. They asserted that few cells have telephones and the requirements to make them accessible is limited to volume control, and that emergency alarm systems are only a small part of the amplified information that inmates need. One large association commented that it receives many inmate complaints that announcements are made over loudspeakers or public address systems, and that inmates who do not hear announcements for inmate count or other instructions face disciplinary action for failure to comply. They asserted that inmates who miss announcements miss meals, exercise, showers, and recreation. They argued that systems that deliver audible announcements, signals, and emergency alarms must be made accessible and that TTYs must be made available. Commenters also recommended that correctional facilities should provide access to advanced forms of telecommunications. Additional commenters noted that few persons now use TTYs, preferring instead to communicate by email, texting, and videophones.

The Department agrees with the commenters that correctional facilities and jails must ensure that inmates who are deaf or hard of hearing actually receive the same information provided to other inmates. The Department believes, however, that the reasonable modifications, program access, and effective communications requirements of title II are sufficient to address the needs of individual deaf and hard of hearing inmates, and as a result, declines to add specific requirements for communications features in cells for deaf and hard of hearing inmates at this time. The Department notes that as part of its ongoing enforcement of the reasonable modifications, program access, and effective communications requirements of title II, the Department has required correctional facilities and jails to provide communication features in cells serving deaf and hard of hearing inmates.

Subpart E — Communications

Section 35.160 Communications.

Section 35.160 of the 1991 title II regulation requires a public entity to take appropriate steps to ensure that communications with applicants, participants, and members of the public with disabilities are as effective as communications with others. 28 CFR 35.160(a). In addition, a public entity must "furnish appropriate auxiliary aids and services where necessary to afford an individual with a disability an equal opportunity to participate in, and enjoy the benefits of, a service, program, or activity conducted by a public entity." 28 CFR 35.160(b)(1). Moreover, the public entity must give "primary consideration to the requests of the individual with disabilities" in determining what type of auxiliary aid and service is necessary. 28 CFR 35.160(b)(2).

Since promulgation of the 1991 title II regulation, the Department has investigated hundreds of complaints alleging failures by public entities to provide effective communication, and many of these investigations resulted in settlement agreements and consent decrees. From these investigations, the Department has concluded that public entities sometimes misunderstand the scope of their obligations under the statute and the regulation. Section 35.160 in the final rule codifies the Department's longstanding policies in this area and includes provisions that reflect technological advances in the area of auxiliary aids and services.

In the NPRM, the Department proposed adding "companion" to the scope of coverage under § 35.160 to codify the Department's longstanding position that a public entity's obligation to ensure effective communication extends not just to applicants, participants, and members of the public with disabilities, but to *companions* as well, if any of them are individuals with disabilities. The NPRM defined companion as a person who is a family member, friend, or associate of a program participant, who, along with the program participant, is "an appropriate person with whom the public entity should communicate." 73 FR 34466, 34507 (June 17, 2008).

Many commenters supported inclusion of "companions" in the rule, and urged even more specific language about public entities' obligations. Some commenters asked the Department to clarify that a companion with a disability may be entitled to effective communication from a public entity even though the applicants, participants, or members of the general public seeking access to, or participating in, the public entity's services, programs, or activities are not individuals with disabilities. Others requested that the Department explain the circumstances under which auxiliary aids and services should be provided to companions. Still others requested explicit clarification that where the individual seeking access to or participating in the public entity's program, services, or activities requires auxiliary aids and services, but the companion does not, the public entity may not seek out, or limit its communications to, the companion instead of communicating directly with the individual with a disability when it would be appropriate to do so.

Some in the medical community objected to the inclusion of any regulatory language regarding companions, asserting that such language is overbroad, seeks services for individuals whose presence is not required by the public entity, is not necessary for the delivery of the services or participation in the program, and places additional burdens on the medical community. These commenters asked that the Department limit the public entity's obligation to communicate effectively with a companion to situations where such communications are necessary to serve the interests of the person who is receiving the public entity's services.

After consideration of the many comments on this issue, the Department believes that explicit inclusion of "companions" in the final rule is appropriate to ensure that public entities understand the scope of their effective communication obligations.

There are many situations in which the interests of program participants without disabilities require that their companions with disabilities be provided effective communication. In addition, the program participant need not be physically present to trigger the public entity's obligations to a companion. The controlling principle is that auxiliary aids and services must be provided if the companion is an appropriate person with whom the public entity should or would communicate.

Examples of such situations include back- to-school nights or parent-teacher conferences at a public school. If the faculty writes on the board or otherwise displays information in a visual context during a back- to-school night, this information must be communicated effectively to parents or guardians who are blind or have low vision. At a parent-teacher conference, deaf parents or guardians must be provided with appropriate auxiliary aids and services to communicate effectively with the teacher and administrators. It makes no difference that the child who attends the school does not have a disability. Likewise, when a deaf spouse attempts to communicate with public social service agencies about the services necessary for the hearing spouse, appropriate auxiliary aids and services to the deaf spouse must be provided by the public entity to ensure effective communication. Parents or guardians, including foster parents, who are individuals with disabilities, may need to interact with child services agencies on behalf of their children; in such a circumstance, the child services agencies would need to provide appropriate auxiliary aids and services to those parents or guardians.

Effective communication with companions is particularly critical in health care settings where miscommunication may lead to misdiagnosis and improper or delayed medical treatment. The Department has encountered confusion and reluctance by medical care providers regarding the scope of their obligation with respect to such companions. Effective communication with a companion is necessary in a variety of circumstances. For example, a companion may be legally authorized to make health care decisions on behalf of the patient or may need to help the patient with information or instructions given by hospital personnel. A companion may be the patient's next-of-kin or health care surrogate with whom hospital personnel must communicate about the patient's medical condition. A companion could be designated by the patient to communicate with hospital personnel about the patient's symptoms, needs, condition, or medical history. Or the companion could be a family member with whom hospital personnel normally would communicate.

Accordingly, § 35.160(a)(1) in the final rule now reads, "[a] public entity shall take appropriate steps to ensure that communications with applicants, participants, members of the public, and companions with disabilities are as effective as communications with others." Section 35.160(a)(2) further defines "companion" as "a family member, friend, or associate of an individual seeking access to a service, program, or activity of a public entity, who, along with the individual, is an appropriate person with whom the public entity should communicate." Section 35.160(b)(1) clarifies that the obligation to furnish auxiliary aids and services extends to companions who are individuals with disabilities, whether or not the individual accompanied also is an individual with a disability. The provision now states that "[a] public entity shall furnish appropriate auxiliary aids and services where necessary to afford individuals with disabilities, including applicants, participants, companions, and members of the public, an equal opportunity to participate in, and enjoy the benefits of, a service, program, or activity of a public entity."

These provisions make clear that if the companion is someone with whom the public entity normally would or should communicate, then the public entity must provide appropriate auxiliary aids and services to that companion to ensure effective communication with the companion. This common-sense rule provides the guidance necessary to enable public entities to properly implement the nondiscrimination requirements of the ADA.

As set out in the final rule, § 35.160(b)(2) states, in pertinent part, that "[t]he type of auxiliary aid or service necessary to ensure effective communication will vary in accordance with the method of communication used by the individual, the nature, length, and complexity of the communication involved, and the context in which the communication is taking place. In determining what types of auxiliary aids and services are necessary, a public entity shall give primary consideration to the requests of individuals with disabilities."

The second sentence of § 35.160(b)(2) of the final rule restores the "primary consideration" obligation set out at § 35.160(b)(2) in the 1991 title II regulation. This provision was inadvertently omitted from the NPRM, and the Department agrees with the many commenters on this issue that this provision should be retained. As noted in the preamble to the 1991 title II regulation, and reaffirmed here: "The public entity shall honor the choice [of the individual with a disability] unless it can demonstrate that another effective means of communication exists or that use of the means chosen would not be required under § 35.164. Deference to the request of the individual with a disability is desirable because of the range of disabilities, the variety of auxiliary aids and services, and different circumstances requiring effective communication." 28 CFR part 35, app. A at 580 (2009).

The first sentence in § 35.160(b)(2) codifies the axiom that the type of auxiliary aid or service necessary to ensure effective communication will vary with the situation, and provides factors for consideration in making the determination, including the method of communication used by the individual; the nature, length, and complexity of the communication involved; and the context in which the communication is taking place. Inclusion of this language under title II is consistent with longstanding policy in this area. *See, e.g., The Americans with Disabilities Act Title II Technical Assistance Manual Covering State and Local Government Programs and Services*, section II–7.1000, available at www.ada.gov/taman2.html ("The type of auxiliary aid or service necessary to ensure effective communication will vary in accordance with the length and complexity of the communication involved. * * * Sign language or oral interpreters, for example, may be required when the information being communicated in a transaction with a deaf individual is complex, or is exchanged for a lengthy period of time. Factors to be considered in determining whether an interpreter is required include the context in which the communication is taking place, the number of people involved, and the importance of the communication."); *see also* 28 CFR part 35, app. A at 580 (2009). As explained in the NPRM, an individual who is deaf or hard of hearing may need a qualified interpreter to communicate with municipal hospital personnel about diagnoses, procedures, tests, treatment options, surgery, or prescribed medication (e.g., dosage, side effects, drug interactions, etc.), or to explain follow-up treatments, therapies, test results, or recovery. In comparison, in a simpler, shorter interaction, the method to achieve effective communication can be more basic. An individual who is seeking local tax forms may only need an exchange of written notes to achieve effective communication.

Section 35.160(c)(1) has been added to the final rule to make clear that a public entity shall not require an individual with a disability to bring another individual to interpret for him or her. The Department receives many complaints from individuals who are deaf or hard of hearing alleging that public entities expect them to provide their own sign language interpreters. Proposed § 35.160(c)(1) was intended to clarify that when a public entity is interacting with a person with a disability, it is the public entity's responsibility to provide an interpreter to ensure effective communication. It is not appropriate to require the person with a disability to bring another individual to provide such services.

Section 35.160(c)(2) of the NPRM proposed codifying the Department's position that there are certain limited instances when a public entity may rely on an accompanying individual to interpret or facilitate communication: (1) In an emergency involving a threat to the public safety or welfare; or (2) if the individual with a disability specifically requests it, the accompanying individual agrees to provide the assistance, and reliance on that individual for this assistance is appropriate under the circumstances.

Many commenters supported this provision, but sought more specific language to address what they see as a particularly entrenched problem. Some commenters requested that the Department explicitly require the public entity first to notify the individual with a disability that the individual has a right to request and receive appropriate auxiliary aids and services without charge from the public entity before using that person's accompanying individual as a communication facilitator. Advocates stated that an individual who is unaware of his or her rights may decide to use a third party simply because he or she believes that is the only way to communicate with the public entity.

The Department has determined that inclusion of specific language requiring notification is unnecessary. Section 35.160(b)(1) already states that is the responsibility of the public entity to provide auxiliary aids and services. Moreover, § 35.130(f) already prohibits the public entity from imposing a surcharge on a particular individual with a disability or on any group of individuals with disabilities to cover the costs of auxiliary aids. However, the Department strongly advises public entities that they should first inform the individual with a disability that the public entity can and will provide auxiliary aids and services, and that there would be no cost for such aids or services.

Many commenters requested that the Department make clear that the public entity cannot request, rely upon, or coerce an adult accompanying an individual with a disability to provide effective communication for that individual with a disability — that only a voluntary offer is acceptable. The Department states unequivocally that consent of, and for, the adult accompanying the individual with a disability to facilitate communication must be provided freely and voluntarily both by the individual with a disability and the accompanying third party — absent an emergency involving an imminent threat to the safety or welfare of an individual or the public where there is no interpreter available. The public entity may not coerce or attempt to persuade another adult to provide effective communication for the individual with a disability. Some commenters expressed concern that the regulation could be read by public entities, including medical providers, to prevent parents, guardians, or caregivers from providing effective communication for children or that a child, regardless of age, would have to specifically request that his or her caregiver act as interpreter. The Department does not intend § 35.160(c)(2) to prohibit parents, guardians, or caregivers from providing effective communication for children where so doing would be appropriate. Rather, the rule prohibits public entities, including medical providers, from requiring, relying on, or forcing adults accompanying individuals with disabilities, including parents, guardians, or caregivers, to facilitate communication.

Several commenters asked that the Department make absolutely clear that children are not to be used to provide effective communication for family members and friends, and that it is the public entity's responsibility to provide effective communication, stating that often interpreters are needed in settings where it would not be appropriate for children to be interpreting, such as those involving medical issues, domestic violence, or other situations involving the exchange of confidential or adult-related material. Commenters observed that children are often hesitant to turn down requests to provide communication services, and that such requests put them in a very difficult position vis-a-vis family members and friends. The Department agrees. It is the Department's position that a public entity shall not rely on a minor child to facilitate communication with a family member, friend, or other individual, except in an emergency involving imminent threat to the safety or welfare of an individual or the public where there is no interpreter available. Accordingly, the Department has revised the rule to state: "A public entity shall not rely on a minor child to interpret or facilitate communication, except in an emergency involving imminent threat to the safety or welfare of an individual or the public where there is no interpreter available." § 35.160(c)(3). Sections 35.160(c)(2) and (3) have no application in circumstances where an interpreter would not otherwise be required in order to provide effective communication (e.g., in simple transactions such as purchasing movie tickets at a theater). The Department stresses that privacy and confidentiality must be maintained but notes that covered entities, such as hospitals, that are subject to the Health Insurance Portability and Accountability Act of 1996 (HIPAA), Public Law 104–191, Privacy Rules are permitted to disclose to a patient's relative, close friend, or any other person identified by the patient (such as an interpreter) relevant patient information if the patient agrees to such disclosures. *See* 45 CFR parts 160 and 164. The agreement need not be in writing. Covered entities should consult the HIPAA Privacy Rules regarding other ways disclosures might be able to be made to such persons.

With regard to emergency situations, the NPRM proposed permitting reliance on an individual accompanying an individual with a disability to interpret or facilitate communication in an emergency involving a threat to the public safety or welfare. Commenters requested that the Department make clear that often a public entity can obtain appropriate auxiliary aids and services in advance of an emergency by making necessary advance arrangements, particularly in anticipated emergencies such as predicted dangerous weather or certain medical situations such as childbirth. These commenters did not want public entities to be relieved of their responsibilities to provide effective communication in emergency situations, noting that the obligation to provide effective communication may be more critical in such situations. Several commenters requested a separate rule that requires public entities to provide timely and effective communication in the event of an emergency, noting that the need for effective communication escalates in an emergency.

Commenters also expressed concern that public entities, particularly law enforcement authorities and medical personnel, would apply the "emergency situation" provision in inappropriate circumstances and would rely on accompanying individuals without making any effort to seek appropriate auxiliary aids and services. Other commenters asked that the Department narrow this provision so that it would not be available to entities that are responsible for emergency preparedness and response. Some commenters noted that certain exigent circumstances, such as those that exist during and perhaps immediately after, a major hurricane, temporarily may excuse public entities of their responsibilities to provide effective communication. However, they asked that the Department clarify that these obligations are ongoing and that, as soon as such situations begin to abate or stabilize, the public entity must provide effective communication.

The Department recognizes that the need for effective communication is critical in emergency situations. After due consideration of all of these concerns raised by commenters, the Department has revised § 35.160(c) to narrow the exception permitting reliance on individuals accompanying the individual with a disability during an emergency to make it clear that it only applies to emergencies involving an "imminent threat to the safety or welfare of an individual or the public." *See* § 35.160(c)(2)–(3). Arguably, all visits to an emergency room or situations to which emergency workers respond are by definition emergencies. Likewise, an argument can be made that most situations that law enforcement personnel respond to involve, in one way or another, a threat to the safety or welfare of an individual or the public. The imminent threat exception in § 35.160(c)(2)– (3) is not intended to apply to the typical and foreseeable emergency situations that are part of the normal operations of these institutions. As such, a public entity may rely on an accompanying individual to interpret or facilitate communication under the § 35.160(c)(2)–(3) imminent threat exception only where in truly exigent circumstances, i.e., where any delay in providing immediate services to the individual could have life- altering or life-ending consequences.

Many commenters urged the Department to stress the obligation of State and local courts to provide effective communication. The Department has received many complaints that State and local courts often do not provide needed qualified sign language interpreters to witnesses, litigants, jurors, potential jurors, and companions and associates of persons participating in the legal process. The Department cautions public entities that without appropriate auxiliary aids and services, such individuals are denied an opportunity to participate fully in the judicial process, and denied benefits of the judicial system that are available to others.

Another common complaint about access to State and local court systems is the failure to provide effective communication in deferral programs that are intended as an alternative to incarceration, or for other court-ordered treatment programs. These programs must provide effective communication, and courts referring individuals with disabilities to such programs should only refer individuals with disabilities to programs or treatment centers that provide effective communication.

No person with a disability should be denied access to the benefits conferred through participation in a court-ordered referral program on the ground that the program purports to be unable to provide effective communication.

The general nondiscrimination provision in § 35.130(a) provides that no individual with a disability shall, on the basis of disability, be excluded from participation in or be denied the benefits of the services, programs, or activities of a public entity. The Department consistently interprets this provision and § 35.160 to require effective communication in courts, jails, prisons, and with law enforcement officers. Persons with disabilities who are participating in the judicial process as witnesses, jurors, prospective jurors, parties before the court, or companions of persons with business in the court, should be provided auxiliary aids and services as needed for effective communication. The Department has developed a variety of technical assistance and guidance documents on the requirements for title II entities to provide effective communication; those materials are available on the Department Web site at: http://www.ada.gov.

Many advocacy groups urged the Department to add language in the final rule that would require public entities to provide accessible material in a manner that is timely, accurate, and private. The Department has included language in § 35.160(b)(2) stating that "[i]n order to be effective, auxiliary aids and services must be provided in accessible formats, in a timely manner, and in such a way so as to protect the privacy and independence of the individual with a disability."

Because the appropriateness of particular auxiliary aids and services may vary as a situation changes, the Department strongly encourages public entities to do a communication assessment of the individual with a disability when the need for auxiliary aids and services is first identified, and to re- assess communication effectiveness regularly throughout the communication. For example, a deaf individual may go to an emergency department of a public community health center with what is at first believed to be a minor medical emergency, such as a sore knee, and the individual with a disability and the public community health center both believe that exchanging written notes will be effective. However, during that individual's visit, it is determined that the individual is, in fact, suffering from an anterior cruciate ligament tear and must have surgery to repair the torn ligament. As the situation develops and the diagnosis and recommended course of action evolve into surgery, an interpreter most likely will be necessary. A public entity has a continuing obligation to assess the auxiliary aids and services it is providing, and should consult with individuals with disabilities on a continuing basis to assess what measures are required to ensure effective communication. Public entities are further advised to keep individuals with disabilities apprised of the status of the expected arrival of an interpreter or the delivery of other requested or anticipated auxiliary aids and services.

Video remote interpreting (VRI) services. In § 35.160(d) of the NPRM, the Department proposed the inclusion of four performance standards for VRI (which the NPRM termed video interpreting services (VIS)), for effective communication: (1) High-quality, clear, real-time, full-motion video and audio over a dedicated high-speed Internet connection; (2) a clear, sufficiently large, and sharply delineated picture of the participating individual's head, arms, hands, and fingers, regardless of his body position; (3) clear transmission of voices; and (4) persons who are trained to set up and operate the VRI quickly. Commenters generally approved of those performance standards, but recommended that some additional standards be included in the final rule. Some State agencies and advocates for persons with disabilities requested that the Department add more detail in the description of the first standard, including modifying the term "dedicated high-speed Internet connection" to read "dedicated high-speed, wide- bandwidth video connection." These commenters argued that this change was necessary to ensure a high-quality video image that will not produce lags, choppy images, or irregular pauses in communication. The Department agrees with those comments and has amended the provision in the final rule accordingly.

For persons who are deaf with limited vision, commenters requested that the Department include an explicit requirement that interpreters wear high-contrast clothing with no patterns that might distract from their hands as they are interpreting, so that a person with limited vision can see the signs made by the interpreter. While the Department reiterates the importance of such practices in the delivery of effective VRI, as well as in-person interpreting, the Department declines to adopt such performance standards as part of this rule. In general, professional interpreters already follow such practices — the Code of Professional Conduct for interpreters developed by the Registry of Interpreters for the Deaf, Inc. and the National Association of the Deaf incorporates attire considerations into their standards of professionalism and conduct. (This code is available at http://www.vid.org/userfiles/file/pdfs/codeofethics.pdf (Last visited July 18, 2010). Moreover, as a result of this code, many VRI agencies have adopted detailed dress standards that interpreters hired by the agency must follow. In addition, commenters urged that a clear image of the face and eyes of the interpreter and others be explicitly required. Because the face includes the eyes, the Department has amended § 35.160(d)(2) of the final rule to include a requirement that the interpreter's face be displayed.

In response to comments seeking more training for users and non-technicians responsible for VRI in title II facilities, the Department is extending the requirement in § 35.160(d)(4) to require training for "users of the technology" so that staff who would have reason to use the equipment in an emergency room, State or local court, or elsewhere are properly trained. Providing for such training will enhance the success of VRI as means of providing effective communication.

Captioning at sporting venues. In the NPRM at § 35.160(e), the Department proposed that sports stadiums that have a capacity of 25,000 or more shall provide captioning for safety and emergency information on scoreboards and video monitors. In addition, the Department posed four questions about captioning of information, especially safety and emergency information announcements, provided over public address (PA) systems. The Department received many extremely detailed and divergent responses to each of the four questions and the proposed regulatory text. Because comments submitted on the Department's title II and title III proposals were intertwined, because of the similarity of issues involved for title II entities and title III entities, and in recognition of the fact that many large sports stadiums are covered by both title II and title III as joint operations of State or local governments and one or more public accommodations, the Department presents here a single consolidated review and summary of the issues raised in comments.

The Department asked whether requiring captioning of safety and emergency information made over the public address system in stadiums seating fewer than 25,000 would create an undue burden for smaller entities, whether it would be feasible for small stadiums, or whether a larger threshold, such as sports stadiums with a capacity of 50,000 or more, would be appropriate.

There was a consensus among the commenters, including disability advocates as well as venue owners and stadium designers and operators, that using the stadium size or seating capacity as the exclusive deciding factor for any obligation to provide captioning for safety and emergency information broadcast over the PA system is not preferred. Most disability advocacy organizations and individuals with disabilities complained that using size or seating capacity as a threshold for captioning safety and emergency information would undermine the "undue burden" defense found in both titles II and III. Many commenters provided examples of facilities like professional hockey arenas that seat less than 25,000 fans but which, commenters argued, should be able to provide real-time captioning. Other commenters suggested that some high school or college stadiums, for example, may hold 25,000 fans or more and yet lack the resources to provide real-time captioning. Many commenters noted that real-time captioning would require trained stenographers and that most high school and college sports facilities rely upon volunteers to operate scoreboards and PA systems, and they would not be qualified stenographers, especially in case of an emergency. One national association noted that the typical stenographer expense for a professional football game in Washington, DC is about $550 per game. Similarly, one trade association representing venues estimated that the cost for a professional stenographer at a sporting event runs between $500 and $1,000 per game or event, the cost of which, they argued, would be unduly burdensome in many cases. Some commenters posited that schools that do not sell tickets to athletic events would find it difficult to meet such expenses, in contrast to major college athletic programs and professional sports teams, which would be less likely to prevail using an "undue burden" defense.

Some venue owners and operators and other covered entities argued that stadium size should not be the key consideration when requiring scoreboard captioning. Instead, these entities suggested that equipment already installed in the stadium, including necessary electrical equipment and backup power supply, should be the determining factor for whether captioning is mandated. Many commenters argued that the requirement to provide captioning should only apply to stadiums with scoreboards that meet the National Fire Protection Association (NFPA) National Fire Alarm Code (NFPA 72). Commenters reported that NFPA 72 requires at least two independent and reliable power supplies for emergency information systems, including one source that is a generator or battery sufficient to run the system in the event the primary power fails. Alternatively, some stadium designers and title II entities commented that the requirement should apply when the facility has at least one elevator providing firefighter emergency operation, along with approval of authorities with responsibility for fire safety. Other commenters argued for flexibility in the requirements for providing captioning and that any requirement should only apply to stadiums constructed after the effective date of the regulation.

In the NPRM, the Department also asked whether the rule should address the specific means of captioning equipment, whether it should be provided through any effective means (scoreboards, line boards, handheld devices, or other means), or whether some means, such as handheld devices, should be eliminated as options. This question elicited many comments from advocates for persons with disabilities as well as from covered entities. Advocacy organizations and individuals with experience using handheld devices argue that such devices do not provide effective communication. These commenters noted that information is often delayed in the transmission to such devices, making them hard to use when following action on the playing field or in the event of an emergency when the crowd is already reacting to aural information provided over the PA system well before it is received on the handheld device.

Several venue owners and operators and others commented that handheld technology offers advantages of flexibility and portability so that it may be used successfully regardless of where in the facility the user is located, even when not in the line of sight of a scoreboard or other captioning system. Still other commenters urged the Department not to regulate in such a way as to limit innovation and use of such technology now and in the future. Cost considerations were included in some comments from some stadium designers and venue owners and operators, who reported that the cost of providing handheld systems is far less than the cost of real-time captioning on scoreboards, especially in facilities that do not currently have the capacity to provide real-time captions on existing equipment. Others noted that handheld technology is not covered by fire and safety model codes, including the NFPA, and thus would be more easily adapted into existing facilities if captioning were required by the Department.

The Department also asked about providing open captioning of all public address announcements, and not limiting captioning to safety and emergency information. A variety of advocates and persons with disabilities argued that all information broadcast over a PA system should be captioned in real time at all facilities in order to provide effective communication and that a requirement only to provide emergency and safety information would not be sufficient. A few organizations for persons with disabilities commented that installation of new systems should not be required, but that all systems within existing facilities that are capable of providing captioning must be utilized to the maximum extent possible to provide captioning of as much information as possible. Several organizations representing persons with disabilities commented that all facilities must include in safety planning the requirement to caption all aurally-provided information for patrons with communication disabilities. Some advocates suggested that demand for captions will only increase as the number of deaf and hard of hearing persons grows with the aging of the general population and with increasing numbers of veterans returning from war with disabilities. Multiple comments noted that the captioning would benefit others as well as those with communication disabilities.

By contrast, venue owners and operators and others commented that the action on the sports field is self-explanatory and does not require captioning and they objected to an explicit requirement to provide real-time captioning for all information broadcast on the PA system at a sporting event. Other commenters objected to requiring captioning even for emergency and safety information over the scoreboard rather than through some other means. By contrast, venue operators, State government agencies, and some model code groups, including NFPA, commented that emergency and safety information must be provided in an accessible format and that public safety is a paramount concern. Other commenters argued that the best method to deliver safety and emergency information would be television monitors showing local TV broadcasts with captions already mandated by the FCC. Some commenters posited that the most reliable information about a major emergency would be provided on the television news broadcasts. Several commenters argued that television monitors may be located throughout the facility, improving line of sight for patrons, some of whom might not be able to see the scoreboard from their seats or elsewhere in the facility. Some stadium designers, venue operators, and model code groups pointed out that video monitors are not regulated by the NFPA or other agencies, so that such monitors could be more easily provided. Video monitors may receive transmissions from within the facility and could provide real-time captions if there is the necessary software and equipment to feed the captioning signal to a closed video network within the facility. Several comments suggested that using monitors would be preferable to requiring captions on the scoreboard if the regulation mandates real- time captioning. Some venue owners and operators argued that retrofitting existing stadiums with new systems could easily cost hundreds of thousands of dollars per scoreboard or system. Some stadium designers and others argued that captioning should only be required in stadiums built after the effective date of the regulation. For stadiums with existing systems that allow for real-time captioning, one commenter posited that dedicating the system exclusively to real-time captioning would lead to an annual loss of between $2 and $3 million per stadium in revenue from advertising currently running in that space.

After carefully considering the wide range of public comments on this issue, the Department has concluded that the final rule will not provide additional requirements for effective communication or emergency information provided at sports stadiums at this time. The 1991 title II and title III regulations and statutory requirements are not in any way affected by this decision. The decision to postpone rulemaking on this complex issue is based on a number of factors, including the multiple layers of existing regulation by various agencies and levels of government, and the wide array of information, requests, and recommendations related to developing technology offered by the public. In addition, there is a huge variety of covered entities, information and communication systems, and differing characteristics among sports stadiums. The Department has concluded that further consideration and review would be prudent before it issues specific regulatory requirements

Section 35.161   Telecommunications.

The Department proposed to retitle this section "Telecommunications" to reflect situations in which the public entity must provide an effective means to communicate by telephone for individuals with disabilities. First, the NPRM proposed redesignating § 35.161 as § 35.161(a) and replacing the term "Telecommunications devices for the deaf (TDD)" with "Text telephones (TTY)." Public comment was universally supportive of this change in nomenclature to TTY.

In the NPRM, at § 35.161(b), the Department addressed automated-attendant systems that handle telephone calls electronically. Often individuals with disabilities, including persons who are deaf or hard of hearing, are unable to use such automated systems. Some systems are not compatible with TTYs or the telecommunications relay service. Automated systems can and often do disconnect calls from TTYs or relay calls, making it impossible for persons using a TTY or relay system to do business with title II entities in the same manner as others. The Department proposed language that would require a telecommunications service to permit persons using relay or TTYs or other assistive technology to use the automated- attendant system provided by the public entity. The FCC raised this concern with the Department after the 1991 title II regulation went into effect, and the Department acted upon that request in the NPRM. Comments from disability advocates and persons with disabilities consistently requested the provision be amended to cover "voice mail, messaging, auto-attendant, and interactive voice response systems." The Department recognizes that those are important features of widely used telecommunications technology that should be as accessible to persons who are deaf or hard of hearing as they are to others, and has amended the section in the final rule to include the additional features.

Many commenters, including advocates and persons with disabilities, as well as State agencies and national organizations, asked that all automated systems have an option for the caller to bypass the automated system and speak to a live person who could communicate using relay services. The Department understands that automated telecommunications systems typically do not offer the opportunity to avoid or bypass the automated system and speak to a live person. The Department believes that at this time it is inappropriate to add a requirement that all such systems provide an override capacity that permits a TTY or relay caller to speak with a live clerk on a telecommunications relay system. However, if a system already provides an option to speak to a person, that system must accept TTY and relay calls and must not disconnect or refuse to accept such calls.

Other comments from advocacy organizations and individuals urged the Department to require specifications for the operation of such systems that would involve issuing technical requirements for encoding and storage of automated text, as well as controls for speed, pause, rewind, and repeat, and prompts without any background noise. The same comments urged that these requirements should be consistent with a pending advisory committee report to the Access Board, submitted in April 2008. *See* Telecommunications and Electronic Information Technology Advisory Committee, Report to the Access Board Refreshed Accessibility Standards and Guidelines in Telecommunications and Electronic and Information Technology (Apr. 2008) available at http://www.access-board.gov/sec508/refresh/report/. The Department is declining at this time to preempt ongoing consideration of these issues by the Board. Instead, the Department will monitor activity by the Board. The Department is convinced that the general requirement to make such automated systems usable by persons with disabilities is appropriate at this time and title II entities should evaluate their automated systems in light of concerns about providing systems that offer effective communication to persons with disabilities.

Finally, the Department has adopted in § 35.161(c) of the final rule the requirement that all such systems must not disconnect or refuse to take calls from all forms of FCC- approved telecommunications relay systems, including Internet-based relay systems. (Internet-based relay systems refer to the mechanism by which the message is relayed). They do not require a public entity to have specialized computer equipment. Commenters from some State agencies, many advocacy organizations, and individuals strongly urged the Department to mandate such action because of the high proportion of TTY calls and relay service calls that are not completed because the title II entity's phone system or employees do not take the calls. This presents a serious obstacle for persons doing business with State and local government and denies persons with disabilities access to use the telephone for business that is typically handled over the phone for others.

In addition, commenters requested that the Department include "real-time" before any mention of "computer-aided" technology to highlight the value of simultaneous translation of any communication. The Department has added "real-time" before "computer-aided transcription services" in the definition of "auxiliary aids in § 35.104 and before "communication" in § 35.161(b).

Subpart F — Compliance Procedures

Section 35.171 Acceptance of complaints.

In the NPRM, the Department proposed changing the current language in § 35.171(a)(2)(i) regarding misdirected complaints to make it clear that if an agency receives a complaint for which it lacks jurisdiction either under section 504 or as a designated agency under the ADA, the agency may refer the complaint to the appropriate agency with title II or section 504 jurisdiction or to the Department of Justice. The language of the 1991 title II regulation only requires the agency to refer such a complaint to the Department, which in turn refers the complaint to the appropriate designated agency. The proposed revisions to § 35.171 made it clear that an agency can refer a misdirected complaint either directly to the appropriate agency or to the Department. This amendment was intended to protect against the unnecessary backlogging of complaints and to prevent undue delay in an agency taking action on a complaint.

Several commenters supported this amendment as a more efficient means of directing title II complaints to the appropriate enforcing agency. One commenter requested that the Department emphasize the need for timeliness in referring a complaint. The Department does not believe it is appropriate to adopt a specific time frame but will continue to encourage designated agencies to make timely referrals. The final rule retains, with minor modifications, the language in proposed § 35.171(a)(2)(i). The Department has also amended § 35.171(a)(2)(ii) to be consistent with the changes in the rule at § 35.190(e), as discussed below.

Section 35.172 Investigations and compliance reviews.

In the NPRM, the Department proposed a number of changes to language in § 35.172 relating to the resolution of complaints. Subtitle A of title II of the ADA defines the remedies, procedures, and rights provided for qualified individuals with disabilities who are discriminated against on the basis of disability in the services, programs, or activities of State and local governments. 42 U.S.C. 12131–12134. Subpart F of the current regulation establishes administrative procedures for the enforcement of title II of the ADA. 28 CFR 35.170–35.178. Subpart G identifies eight "designated agencies," including the Department, that have responsibility for investigating complaints under title II. *See* 28 CFR 35.190(b).

The Department's 1991 title II regulation is based on the enforcement procedures established in regulations implementing section 504. Thus, the Department's 1991 title II regulation provides that the designated agency "shall investigate each complete complaint" alleging a violation of title II and shall "attempt informal resolution" of such complaint. 28 CFR 35.172(a). The full range of remedies (including compensatory damages) that are available to the Department when it resolves a complaint or resolves issues raised in a compliance review are available to designated agencies when they are engaged in informal complaint resolution or resolution of issues raised in a compliance review under title II.

In the years since the 1991 title II regulation went into effect, the Department has received many more complaints alleging violations of title II than its resources permit it to resolve. The Department has reviewed each complaint that the Department has received and directed its resources to resolving the most critical matters. In the NPRM, the Department proposed deleting the word "each" as it appears before "complaint" in § 35.172(a) of the 1991 title II regulation as a means of clarifying that designated agencies may exercise discretion in selecting title II complaints for resolution.

Many commenters opposed the removal of the term "each," requesting that all title II complaints be investigated. The commenters explained that complaints against title II entities implicate the fundamental right of access to government facilities and programs, making an administrative enforcement mechanism critical. Rather than aligning enforcement discretion of title II complaints with the discretion under the enforcement procedures of title III, the commenters favored obtaining additional resources to address more complaints. The commenters highlighted the advantage afforded by Federal involvement in complaint investigations in securing favorable voluntary resolutions. When Federal involvement results in settlement agreements, commenters believed those agreements are more persuasive to other public entities than private settlements. Private litigation as a viable alternative was rejected by the commenters because of the financial limitations of many complainants, and because in some scenarios legal barriers foreclose private litigation as an option.

Several of those opposing this amendment argued that designated agencies are required to investigate each complaint under section 504, and a departure for title II complaints would be an inconsistency. The Department believes that § 35.171(a) of the final rule is consistent with the obligation to evaluate all complaints. However, there is no statutory requirement that every title II complaint receive a full investigation. Section 203 of the ADA, 42 U.S.C. 12133, adopts the "remedies, procedures, and rights set forth in section 505 of the Rehabilitation Act of 1973" (29 U.S.C. 794a). Section 505 of the Rehabilitation Act, in turn, incorporates the remedies available under title VI of the Civil Rights Act of 1964 into section 504. Under these statutes, agencies may engage in conscientious enforcement without fully investigating each citizen complaint. An agency's decision to conduct a full investigation requires a complicated balancing of a number of factors that are particularly within its expertise. Thus, the agency must not only assess whether a violation may have occurred, but also whether agency resources are best spent on this complaint or another, whether the agency is likely to succeed if it acts, and whether the particular enforcement action requested best fits the agency's overall policies. Availability of resources will always be a factor, and the Department believes discretion to maximize these limited resources will result in the most effective enforcement program. If agencies are bound to investigate each complaint fully, regardless of merit, such a requirement could have a deleterious effect on their overall enforcement efforts. The Department continues to expect that each designated agency will review the complaints the agency receives to determine whether further investigation is appropriate.

The Department also proposed revising § 35.172 to add a new paragraph (b) that provided explicit authority for compliance reviews consistent with the Department's longstanding position that such authority exists. The proposed section stated, "[t]he designated agency may conduct compliance reviews of public entities based on information indicating a possible failure to comply with the nondiscrimination requirements of this part." Several commenters supported this amendment, identifying title III compliance reviews as having been a successful means for the Department and designated agencies to improve accessibility. The Department has retained this section. However, the Department has modified the language of the section to make the authority to conduct compliance reviews consistent with that available under section 504 and title VI. *See, e.g.*, 28 CFR 42.107(a). The new provision reads as follows: "(b) The designated agency may conduct compliance reviews of public entities in order to ascertain whether there has been a failure to comply with the nondiscrimination requirements of this part." The Department has also added a provision to § 35.172(c)(2) clarifying the Department's longstanding view that agencies may obtain compensatory damages on behalf of complainants as the result of a finding of discrimination pursuant to a compliance review or in informal resolution of a complaint.

Finally, in the NPRM, the Department proposed revising the requirements for letters of findings for clarification and to reflect current practice. Section 35.172(a) of the 1991 title II regulation required designated agencies to issue a letter of findings at the conclusion of an investigation if the complaint was not resolved informally, and to attempt to negotiate a voluntary compliance agreement if a violation was found. The Department's proposed changes to the 1991 title II regulation moved the discussion of letters of findings to a new paragraph (c) in the NPRM, and clarified that letters of findings are only required when a violation is found.

One commenter opposed the proposal to eliminate the obligation of the Department and designated agencies to issue letters of finding at the conclusion of every investigation. The commenter argued that it is beneficial for public entities, as well as complainants, for the Department to provide a reasonable explanation of both compliance and noncompliance findings.

The Department has considered this comment but continues to believe that this change will promote the overall effectiveness of its enforcement program. The final rule retains the proposed language.

Subpart G — Designated Agencies

Section 35.190 Designated agencies.

Subpart G of the 1991 title II regulation designates specific Federal agencies to investigate certain title II complaints. Paragraph 35.190(b) specifies these agency designations. Paragraphs 35.190(c) and (d), respectively, grant the Department discretion to designate further oversight responsibilities for matters not specifically assigned or where there are apparent conflicts of jurisdiction. The NPRM proposed adding a new § 35.190(e) further refining procedures for complaints filed with the Department of Justice. Proposed § 35.190(e) provides that when the Department receives a complaint alleging a violation of title II that is directed to the Attorney General but may fall within the jurisdiction of a designated agency or another Federal agency with jurisdiction under section 504, the Department may exercise its discretion to retain the complaint for investigation under this part. The Department would, of course, consult with the designated agency when the Department plans to retain a complaint. In appropriate circumstances, the Department and the designated agency may conduct a joint investigation.

Several commenters supported this amendment as a more efficient means of processing title II complaints. The commenters supported the Department using its discretion to conduct timely investigations of such complaints. The language of the proposed § 35.190(e) remains unchanged in the final rule.

Other Issues

Questions Posed in the NPRM Regarding Costs and Benefits of Complying With the 2010 Standards

In the NPRM, the Department requested comment on various cost and benefit issues related to eight requirements in the Department's Initial Regulatory Impact Analysis (Initial RIA), available at *ada.gov/NPRM2008/ria.htm)*, that were projected to have incremental costs exceeding monetized benefits by more than $100 million when using the 1991 Standards as the comparative baseline, *i.e.*, side reach, water closet clearances in single-user toilet rooms with in- swinging doors, stairs, elevators, location of accessible routes to stages, accessible attorney areas and witness stands, assistive listening systems, and accessible teeing grounds, putting greens, and weather shelters at golf courses. 73 FR 34466, 34469 (June 17, 2008). The Department noted that pursuant to the ADA, the Department does not have statutory authority to modify the 2004 ADAAG and is required instead to issue regulations implementing the ADA that are consistent with the Board's guidelines. In that regard, the Department also requested comment about whether any of these eight elements in the 2010 Standards should be returned to the Access Board for further consideration, in particular as applied to alterations. Many of the comments received by the Department in response to these questions addressed both titles II and III. As a result, the Department's discussion of these comments and its response are collectively presented for both titles.

Side reach. The 1991 Standards at section 4.2.6 establish a maximum side-reach height of 54 inches. The 2010 Standards at section 308.3 reduce that maximum height to 48 inches. The 2010 Standards also add exceptions for certain elements to the scoping requirement for operable parts.

The vast majority of comments the Department received were in support of the lower side-reach maximum of 48 inches in the 2010 Standards. Most of these comments, but not all, were received from individuals of short stature, relatives of individuals of short stature, or organizations representing the interests of persons with disabilities, including individuals of short stature. Comments from individuals with disabilities and disability advocacy groups stated that the 48-inch side reach would permit independence in performing many activities of daily living for individuals with disabilities, including individuals of short stature, persons who use wheelchairs, and persons who have limited upper body strength. In this regard, one commenter who is a business owner pointed out that as a person of short stature there were many occasions when he was unable to exit a public restroom independently because he could not reach the door handle. The commenter said that often elevator control buttons are out of his reach and, if he is alone, he often must wait for someone else to enter the elevator so that he can ask that person to press a floor button for him. Another commenter, who is also a person of short stature, said that he has on several occasions pulled into a gas station only to find that he was unable to reach the credit card reader on the gas pump. Unlike other customers who can reach the card reader, swipe their credit or debit cards, pump their gas and leave the station, he must use another method to pay for his gas. Another comment from a person of short stature pointed out that as more businesses take steps to reduce labor costs — a trend expected to continue — staffed booths are being replaced with automatic machines for the sale, for example, of parking tickets and other products. He observed that the "ability to access and operate these machines becomes ever more critical to function in society," and, on that basis, urged the Department to adopt the 48-inch side-reach requirement. Another individual commented that persons of short stature should not have to carry with them adaptive tools in order to access building or facility elements that are out of their reach, any more than persons in wheelchairs should have to carry ramps with them in order to gain access to facilities.

Many of the commenters who supported the revised side-reach requirement pointed out that lowering the side-reach requirement to 48 inches would avoid a problem sometimes encountered in the built environment when an element was mounted for a parallel approach at 54 inches only to find afterwards that a parallel approach was not possible. Some commenters also suggested that lowering the maximum unobstructed side reach to 48 inches would reduce confusion among design professionals by making the unobstructed forward and side-reach maximums the same (the unobstructed forward reach in both the 1991 and 2010 Standards is 48 inches maximum). These commenters also pointed out that the ICC/ANSI A117.1 Standard, which is a private sector model accessibility standard, has included a 48-inch maximum high side- reach requirement since 1998. Many jurisdictions have already incorporated this requirement into their building codes, which these commenters believed would reduce the cost of compliance with the 2010 Standards. Because numerous jurisdictions have already adopted the 48-inch side-reach requirement, the Department's failure to adopt the 48-inch side-reach requirement in the 2010 Standards, in the view of many commenters, would result in a significant reduction in accessibility, and would frustrate efforts that have been made to harmonize private sector model construction and accessibility codes with Federal accessibility requirements. Given these concerns, they overwhelmingly opposed the idea of returning the revised side-reach requirement to the Access Board for further consideration.

The Department also received comments in support of the 48-inch side-reach requirement from an association of professional commercial property managers and operators and from State governmental entities. The association of property managers pointed out that the revised side- reach requirement provided a reasonable approach to "regulating elevator controls and all other operable parts" in existing facilities in light of the manner in which the safe harbor, barrier removal, and alterations obligations will operate in the 2010 Standards. One governmental entity, while fully supporting the 48-inch side-reach requirement, encouraged the Department to adopt an exception to the lower reach range for existing facilities similar to the exception permitted in the ICC/ANSI A117.1 Standard. In response to this latter concern, the Department notes that under the safe harbor, existing facilities that are in compliance with the 1991 Standards, which require a 54-inch side-reach maximum, would not be required to comply with the lower side-reach requirement, unless there is an alteration. *See* § 35.150(b)(2).

A number of commenters expressed either concern with, or opposition to, the 48-inch side-reach requirement and suggested that it be returned to the Access Board for further consideration. These commenters included trade and business associations, associations of retail stores, associations of restaurant owners, retail and convenience store chains and a model code organization. Several businesses expressed the view that the lower side-reach requirement would discourage the use of their products and equipment by most of the general public. In particular, concerns were expressed by a national association of pay phone service providers regarding the possibility that pay telephones mounted at the lower height would not be used as frequently by the public to place calls, which would result in an economic burden on the pay phone industry. The commenter described the lower height required for side reach as creating a new "barrier" to pay phone use, which would reduce revenues collected from pay phones and, consequently, further discourage the installation of new pay telephones. In addition, the commenter expressed concern that phone service providers would simply decide to remove existing pay phones rather than incur the costs of relocating them at the lower height. With regard to this latter concern, the commenter misunderstood the manner in which the safe harbor obligation will operate in the revised title II regulation for elements that comply with the 1991 Standards. If the pay phones comply with the 1991 Standards or UFAS, the adoption of the 2010 Standards does not require retrofitting of these elements to reflect incremental changes in the 2010 Standards (see § 35.150(b)(2)). However, pay telephones that were required to meet the 1991 Standards as part of new construction or alterations, but do not in fact comply with those standards, will need to be brought into compliance with the 2010 Standards as of 18 months from the publication date of this final rule. *See* § 35.151(c)(5)(ii).

The Department does not agree with the concerns expressed by the commenter about reduced revenues from pay phones mounted at lower heights. The Department believes that, while given the choice some individuals may prefer to use a pay phone that is at a higher height, the availability of some phones at a lower height will not deter individuals from making needed calls.

The 2010 Standards will not require every pay phone to be installed or moved to a lowered height. The table accompanying section 217.2 of the 2010 Standards makes clear that, where one or more telephones are provided on a floor, level, or an exterior site, only one phone per floor, level, or exterior site must be placed at an accessible height. Similarly, where there is one bank of phones per floor, level, or exterior site, only one phone per floor, level, or exterior site must be accessible. And if there are two or more banks of phones per floor, level, or exterior site, only one phone per bank must be placed at an accessible height.

Another comment in opposition to the lower reach range requirement was submitted on behalf of a chain of convenience stores with fuel stops. The commenter expressed the concern that the 48-inch side reach "will make it uncomfortable for the majority of the public," including persons of taller stature who would need to stoop to use equipment such as fuel dispensers mounted at the lower height. The commenter offered no objective support for the observation that a majority of the public would be rendered uncomfortable if, as required in the 2010 Standards, at least one of each type of fuel dispenser at a facility was made accessible in compliance with the lower reach range. Indeed, the Department received no comments from any individuals of tall stature expressing concern about accessible elements or equipment being mounted at the 48-inch height.

Several convenience store, restaurant, and amusement park commenters expressed concern about the burden the lower side-reach requirement would place on their businesses in terms of self-service food stations and vending areas if the 48-inch requirement were applied retroactively. The cost of lowering counter height, in combination with the lack of control businesses exercise over certain prefabricated service or vending fixtures, outweighed, they argued, any benefits to persons with disabilities. For this reason, they suggested the lower side-reach requirement be referred back to the Access Board.

These commenters misunderstood the safe harbor and barrier removal obligations that will be in effect under the 2010 Standards. Those existing self-service food stations and vending areas that already are in compliance with the 1991 Standards will not be required to satisfy the 2010 Standards unless they engage in alterations. With regard to prefabricated vending machines and food service components that will be purchased and installed in businesses after the 2010 Standards become effective, the Department expects that companies will design these machines and fixtures to comply with the 2010 Standards in the future, as many have already done in the 10 years since the 48-inch side-reach requirement has been a part of the model codes and standards used by many jurisdictions as the basis for their construction codes.

A model code organization commented that the lower side-reach requirement would create a significant burden if it required entities to lower the mounting height for light switches, environmental controls, and outlets when an alteration did not include the walls where these elements were located, such as when "an area is altered or as a path of travel obligation." The Department believes that the final rule adequately addresses those situations about which the commenter expressed concern by not requiring the relocation of existing elements, such as light switches, environmental controls, and outlets, unless they are altered. Moreover, under § 35.151(b)(4)(iii) of the final rule, costs for altering the path of travel to an altered area of primary function that exceed 20 percent of the overall costs of the alteration will be deemed disproportionate.

The Department has determined that the revised side-reach requirement should not be returned to the Access Board for further consideration, based in large part on the views expressed by a majority of the commenters regarding the need for, and importance of, the lower side-reach requirement to ensure access for persons with disabilities.

Alterations and Water Closet Clearances in Single-User Toilet Rooms With In-Swinging Doors

The 1991 Standards allow a lavatory to be placed a minimum of 18 inches from the water closet centerline and a minimum of 36 inches from the side wall adjacent to the water closet, which precludes side transfers. The 1991 Standards do not allow an in- swinging door in a toilet or bathing room to overlap the required clear floor space at any accessible fixture. To allow greater transfer options, section 604.3.2 of the 2010 Standards prohibits lavatories from overlapping the clear floor space at water closets, except in residential dwelling units. Section 603.2.3 of the 2010 Standards maintains the prohibition on doors swinging into the clear floor space or clearance required for any fixture, except that they permit the doors of toilet or bathing rooms to swing into the required turning space, provided that there is sufficient clearance space for the wheelchair outside the door swing. In addition, in single-user toilet or bathing rooms, exception 2 of section 603.2.3 of the 2010 Standards permits the door to swing into the clear floor space of an accessible fixture if a clear floor space that measures at least 30 inches by 48 inches is available outside the arc of the door swing.

The majority of commenters believed that this requirement would increase the number of toilet rooms accessible to individuals with disabilities who use wheel-chairs or mobility scooters, and will make it easier for them to transfer. A number of commenters stated that there was no reason to return this provision to the Access Board. Numerous commenters noted that this requirement is already included in other model accessibility standards and many State and local building codes and that the adoption of the 2010 Standards is an important part of harmonization efforts.

Other commenters, mostly trade associations, opposed this requirement, arguing that the added cost to the industry outweighs any increase in accessibility. Two commenters stated that these proposed requirements would add two feet to the width of an accessible single-user toilet room; however, another commenter said the drawings in the proposed regulation demonstrated that there would be no substantial increase in the size of the toilet room. Several commenters stated that this requirement would require moving plumbing fixtures, walls, or doors at significant additional expense. Two commenters wanted the permissible overlap between the door swing and clearance around any fixture eliminated. One com-menter stated that these new requirements will result in fewer alterations to toilet rooms to avoid triggering the requirement for increased clearances, and suggested that the Department specify that repairs, maintenance, or minor alterations would not trigger the need to provide increased clearances. Another commenter requested that the Department exempt existing guest room bathrooms and single- user toilet rooms that comply with the 1991 Standards from complying with the increased clearances in alterations.

After careful consideration of these comments, the Department believes that the revised clearances for single-user toilet rooms will allow safer and easier transfers for individuals with disabilities, and will enable a caregiver, aide, or other person to accompany an individual with a disability into the toilet room to provide assistance.

The illustrations in Appendix B to the final title III rule, "Analysis and Commentary on the 2010 ADA Standards for Accessible Design," published elsewhere in this volume and codified as Appendix B to 28 CFR part 36, describe several ways for public entities and public accommodations to make alterations while minimizing additional costs or loss of space. Further, in any isolated instances where existing structural limitations may entail loss of space, the public entity and public accommodation may have a technical infeasibility defense for that alteration. The Department also recognizes that in attempting to create the required clear floor space pursuant to section 604.3.2, there may be certain specific circumstances where it would be technically infeasible for a covered entity to comply with the clear floor space requirement, such as where an entity must move a plumbing wall in a multistory building where the mechanical chase for plumbing is an integral part of a building's structure or where the relocation of a wall or fixture would violate applicable plumbing codes. In such circumstances, the required clear floor space would not have to be provided although the covered entity would have to provide accessibility to the maximum extent feasible. The Department has, therefore, decided not to return this requirement to the Access Board.

Alterations to stairs. The 1991 Standards only require interior and exterior stairs to be accessible when they provide access to levels that are not connected by an elevator, ramp, or other accessible means of vertical access. In contrast, section 210.1 of the 2010 Standards requires all newly constructed stairs that are part of a means of egress to be accessible. However, exception 2 of section 210.1 of the 2010 Standards provides that in alterations, stairs between levels connected by an accessible route need not be accessible, except that handrails shall be provided. Most commenters were in favor of this requirement for handrails in alterations, and stated that adding handrails to stairs during alterations was not only feasible and not cost- prohibitive, but also provided important safety benefits. One commenter stated that making all points of egress accessible increased the number of people who could use the stairs in an emergency. A majority of the commenters did not want this requirement returned to the Access Board for further consideration.

The International Building Code (IBC), which is a private sector model construction code, contains a similar provision, and most jurisdictions enforce a version of the IBC as their building code, thereby minimizing the impact of this provision on public entities and public accommodations. The Department believes that by requiring only the addition of handrails to altered stairs where levels are connected by an accessible route, the costs of compliance for public entities and public accommodations are minimized, while safe egress for individuals with disabilities is increased. Therefore, the Department has decided not to return this requirement to the Access Board.

Alterations to elevators. Under the 1991 Standards, if an existing elevator is altered, only that altered elevator must comply with the new construction requirements for accessible elevators to the maximum extent feasible. It is therefore possible that a bank of elevators controlled by a single call system may contain just one accessible elevator, leaving an individual with a disability with no way to call an accessible elevator and thus having to wait indefinitely until an accessible elevator happens to respond to the call system. In the 2010 Standards, when an element in one elevator is altered, section 206.6.1 will require the same element to be altered in all elevators that are programmed to respond to the same call button as the altered elevator.

Most commenters favored the proposed requirement. This requirement, according to these commenters, is necessary so a person with a disability need not wait until an accessible elevator responds to his or her call. One commenter suggested that elevator owners could also comply by modifying the call system so the accessible elevator could be summoned independently. One commenter suggested that this requirement would be difficult for small businesses located in older buildings, and one commenter suggested that this requirement be sent back to the Access Board.

After considering the comments, the Department agrees that this requirement is necessary to ensure that when an individual with a disability presses a call button, an accessible elevator will arrive in a timely manner. The IBC contains a similar provision, and most jurisdictions enforce a version of the IBC as their building code, minimizing the impact of this provision on public entities and public accommodations. Public entities and businesses located in older buildings need not comply with this requirement where it is technically infeasible to do so. Further, as pointed out by one commenter, modifying the call system so the accessible elevator can be summoned independently is another means of complying with this requirement in lieu of altering all other elevators programmed to respond to the same call button. Therefore, the Department has decided not to return this requirement to the Access Board.

Location of accessible routes to stages. The 1991 Standards at section 4.33.5 require an accessible route to connect the accessible seating and the stage, as well as other ancillary spaces used by performers. The 2010 Standards at section 206.2.6 provide in addition that where a circulation path directly connects the seating area and the stage, the accessible route must directly connect the accessible seating and the stage, and, like the 1991 Standards, an accessible route must connect the stage with the ancillary spaces used by performers.

In the NPRM, the Department asked operators of auditoria about the extent to which auditoria already provide direct access to stages and whether there were planned alterations over the next 15 years that included accessible direct routes to stages.

The Department also asked how to quantify the benefits of this requirement for persons with disabilities, and invited commenters to provide illustrative anecdotal experiences about the requirement's benefits. The Department received many comments regarding the costs and benefits of this requirement. Although little detail was provided, many industry and governmental entity commenters anticipated that the costs of this requirement would be great and that it would be difficult to implement. They noted that premium seats may have to be removed and that load-bearing walls may have to be relocated. These commenters suggested that the significant costs would deter alterations to the stage area for a great many auditoria. Some commenters suggested that ramps to the front of the stage may interfere with means of egress and emergency exits. Several commenters requested that the requirement apply to new construction only, and one industry commenter requested an exemption for stages used in arenas or amusement parks where there is no audience participation or where the stage is a work area for performers only.

One commenter requested that the requirement not apply to temporary stages.

The final rule does not require a direct accessible route to be constructed where a direct circulation path from the seating area to the stage does not exist. Consequently, those commenters who expressed concern about the burden imposed by the revised requirement (i.e., where the stage is constructed with no direct circulation path connecting the general seating and performing area) should note that the final rule will not require the provision of a direct accessible route under these circumstances. The final rule applies to permanent stages, as well as "temporary stages," if there is a direct circulation path from the seating area to the stage. However, the Department does recognize that in some circumstances, such as an alteration to a primary function area, the ability to provide a direct accessible route to a stage may be costly or technically infeasible, the auditorium owner is not precluded by the revised requirement from asserting defenses available under the regulation. In addition, the Department notes that since section 4.33.5 of the 1991 Standards requires an accessible route to a stage, the safe harbor will apply to existing facilities whose stages comply with the 1991 Standards.

Several governmental entities supported accessible auditoria and the revised requirement. One governmental entity noted that its State building code already required direct access, that it was possible to provide direct access, and that creative solutions had been found to do so.

Many advocacy groups and individual commenters strongly supported the revised requirement, discussing the acute need for direct access to stages as it impacts a great number of people at important life events such as graduations and awards ceremonies, at collegiate and competitive performances and other school events, and at entertainment events that include audience participation. Many commenters expressed the belief that direct access is essential for integration mandates to be satisfied and that separate routes are stigmatizing and unequal. The Department agrees with these concerns.

Commenters described the impact felt by persons in wheelchairs who are unable to access the stage at all when others are able to do so. Some of these commenters also discussed the need for performers and production staff who use wheelchairs to have direct access to the stage and provided a number of examples that illustrated the importance of the rule proposed in the NPRM. Personal anecdotes were provided in comments and at the Department's public hearing on the NPRM. One mother spoke passionately and eloquently about the unequal treatment experienced by her daughter, who uses a wheelchair, at awards ceremonies and band concerts. Her daughter was embarrassed and ashamed to be carried by her father onto a stage at one band concert. When the venue had to be changed for another concert to an accessible auditorium, the band director made sure to comment that he was unhappy with the switch. Rather than endure the embarrassment and indignities, her child dropped out of band the following year. Another father commented about how he was unable to speak from the stage at a PTA meeting at his child's school. Speaking from the floor limited his line of sight and his participation. Several examples were provided of children who could not participate on stage during graduation, awards programs, or special school events, such as plays and festivities. One student did not attend his college graduation because he would not be able to get on stage. Another student was unable to participate in the class Christmas programs or end-of-year parties unless her father could attend and lift her onto the stage. These commenters did not provide a method to quantify the benefits that would accrue by having direct access to stages. One commenter stated, however, that "the cost of dignity and respect is without measure."

Many industry commenters and governmental entities suggested that the requirement be sent back to the Access Board for further consideration. One industry commenter mistakenly noted that some international building codes do not incorporate the requirement and that therefore there is a need for further consideration. However, the Department notes that both the 2003 and 2006 editions of the IBC include scoping provisions that are almost identical to this requirement and that these editions of the model code are the most frequently used. Many individuals and advocacy group commenters requested that the requirement be adopted without further delay. These commenters spoke of the acute need for direct access to stages and the amount of time it would take to resubmit the requirement to the Access Board. Several commenters noted that the 2004 ADAAG tracks recent model codes and thus there is no need for further consideration. The Department agrees that no further delay is necessary and therefore has decided not to return the requirement to the Access Board for further consideration.

Attorney areas and witness stands. The 1991 Standards do not require that public entities meet specific architectural standards with regard to the construction and alteration of courtrooms and judicial facilities. Because it is apparent that the judicial facilities of State and local governments have often been inaccessible to individuals with disabilities, as part of the NPRM, the Department proposed the adoption of sections 206.2.4, 231.2, 808, 304, 305, and 902 of the 2004 ADAAG concerning judicial facilities and courtrooms, including requirements for accessible courtroom stations and accessible jury boxes and witness stands.

Those who commented on access to judicial facilities and courtrooms uniformly favored the adoption of the 2010 Standards. Virtually all of the commenters stated that accessible judicial facilities are crucial to ensuring that individuals with disabilities are afforded due process under law and have an equal opportunity to participate in the judicial process. None of the commenters favored returning this requirement to the Access Board for further consideration.

The majority of commenters, including many disability rights and advocacy organizations, stated that it is crucial for individuals with disabilities to have effective and meaningful access to our judicial system so as to afford them due process under law. They objected to asking the Access Board to reconsider this requirement. In addition to criticizing the initial RIA for virtually ignoring the intangible and non-monetary benefits associated with accessible courtrooms, these commenters frequently cited the Supreme Court's decision in *Tennessee* v. *Lane*, 541 U.S. 509, 531 (2004),[4] as ample justification for the requirement, noting the Court's finding that "[t]he unequal treatment of disabled persons in the administration of judicial services has a long history, and has persisted despite several legislative efforts to remedy the problem of disability discrimination." *Id.* at 531.

---

[4] The Supreme Court in *Tennessee* v. *Lane*, 541 U.S. 509, 533–534 (2004), held that title II of the ADA constitutes a valid exercise of Congress' enforcement power under the Fourteenth Amendment in cases implicating the fundamental right of access to the courts.

These commenters also made a number of observations, including the following: providing effective access to individuals with mobility impairments is not possible when architectural barriers impede their path of travel and negatively emphasize an individual's disability; the perception generated by makeshift accommodations discredits witnesses and attorneys with disabilities, who should not be stigmatized or treated like second-class citizens; the cost of accessibility modifications to existing courthouses can often be significantly decreased by planning ahead, by focusing on low-cost options that provide effective access, and by addressing existing barriers when reasonable modifications to the courtroom can be made; by planning ahead and by following best practices, jurisdictions can avoid those situations where it is apparent that someone's disability is the reason why ad hoc arrangements have to be made prior to the beginning of court proceedings; and accessibility should be a key concern during the planning and construction process so as to ensure that both courtroom grandeur and accessibility are achieved. One commenter stated that, in order for attorneys with disabilities to perform their professional duties to their clients and the court, it is essential that accessible courtrooms, conference rooms, law libraries, judicial chambers, and other areas of a courthouse be made barrier-free by taking accessible design into account prior to construction.

Numerous commenters identified a variety of benefits that would accrue as a result of requiring judicial facilities to be accessible. These included the following: maintaining the decorum of the courtroom and eliminating the disruption of court proceedings when individuals confront physical barriers; providing an accessible route to the witness stand and attorney area and clear floor space to accommodate a wheelchair within the witness area; establishing crucial lines of sight between the judge, jury, witnesses, and attorneys — which commenters described as crucial; ensuring that the judge and the jury will not miss key visual indicators of a witness; maintaining a witness's or attorney's dignity and credibility; shifting the focus from a witness's disability to the substance of that person's testimony; fostering the independence of an individual with disability; allowing persons with mobility impairments to testify as witnesses, including as expert witnesses; ensuring the safety of various participants in a courtroom proceeding; and avoiding unlawful discrimination. One commenter stated that equal access to the well of the courtroom for both attorney and client is important for equal participation and representation in our court system. Other commenters indicated that accessible judicial facilities benefit a wide range of people, including many persons without disabilities, senior citizens, parents using strollers with small children, and attorneys and court personnel wheeling documents into the courtroom. One commenter urged the adoption of the work area provisions because they would result in better workplace accessibility and increased productivity. Several commenters urged the adoption of the rule because it harmonizes the ADAAG with the model IBC, the standards developed by the American National Standards Institute (ANSI), and model codes that have been widely adopted by State and local building departments, thus increasing the prospects for better understanding and compliance with the ADAAG by architects, designers, and builders.

Several commenters mentioned the report "Justice for All: Designing Accessible Courthouses" (Nov. 15, 2006), available at http://www.access-board.gov/caac/report. htm (Nov. 24, 2009) (last visited June 24, 2010). The report, prepared by the

Courthouse Access Advisory Committee for the Access Board, contained recommendations for the Board's use in developing and disseminating guidance on accessible courthouse design under the ADA and the ABA. These commenters identified some of the report's best practices concerning courtroom accessibility for witness stands, jury boxes, and attorney areas; addressed costs and benefits arising from the use of accessible courtrooms; and recommended that the report be incorporated into the Department's final rule. With respect to existing courtrooms, one commenter in this group suggested that consideration be given to ensuring that there are barrier-free emergency evacuation routes for all persons in the courtroom, including different evacuation routes for different classes of individuals given the unique nature of judicial facilities and courtrooms.

The Department declines to incorporate the report into the regulation. However, the Department encourages State and local governments to consult the Committee report as a useful guide on ways to facilitate and increase accessibility of their judicial facilities. The report includes many excellent examples of accessible courtroom design.

One commenter proposed that the regulation also require a sufficient number of accessible benches for judges with disabilities. Under section 206.2.4 of the 2004 ADAAG, raised courtroom stations used by judges and other judicial staff are not required to provide full vertical access when first constructed or altered, as long as the required clear floor space, maneuvering space, and any necessary electrical service for future installation of a means of vertical access, is provided at the time of new construction or can be achieved without substantial reconstruction during alterations. The Department believes that this standard easily allows a courtroom station to be adapted to provide vertical access in the event a judge requires an accessible judge's bench.

The Department received several anecdotal accounts of courtroom experiences of individuals with disabilities. One commenter recalled numerous difficulties that her law partner faced as the result of inaccessible courtrooms, and their concerns that the attention of judge and jury was directed away from the merits of case to the lawyer and his disability. Among other things, the lawyer had to ask the judges on an appellate panel to wait while he maneuvered through insufficient space to the counsel table; ask judges to relocate bench conferences to accessible areas; and make last-minute preparations and rearrangements that his peers without disabilities did not have to make. Another commenter with extensive experience as a lawyer, witness, juror, and consultant observed that it is common practice for a witness who uses mobility devices to sit in front of the witness stand. He described how disconcerting and unsettling it has been for him to testify in front of the witness stand, which allowed individuals in the courtroom to see his hands or legs shaking because of spasticity, making him feel like a second-class citizen.

Two other commenters with mobility disabilities described their experiences testifying in court. One accessibility consultant stated that she was able to represent her clients successfully when she had access to an accessible witness stand because it gave her the ability "to look the judge in the eye, speak comfortably and be heard, hold up visual aids that could be seen by the judge, and perform without an architectural stigma." She did not believe that she was able to achieve a comparable outcome or have meaningful access to the justice system when she testified from an inaccessible location. Similarly, a licensed clinical social worker indicated that she has testified in several cases in accessible courtrooms, and that having full access to the witness stand in the presence of the judge and the jury was important to her effectiveness as an expert witness. She noted that accessible courtrooms often are not available, and that she was aware of instances in which victims, witnesses, and attorneys with disabilities have not been able to obtain needed disability accommodations in order to fulfill their roles at trial.

Two other commenters indicated that they had been chosen for jury duty but that they were effectively denied their right to participate as jurors because the courtrooms were not accessible. Another commenter indicated that he has had to sit apart from the other jurors because the jury box was inaccessible.

A number of commenters expressed approval of actions taken by States to facilitate access in judicial facilities. A member of a State commission on disability noted that the State had been working toward full accessibility since 1997 when the Uniform Building Code required interior accessible routes. This commenter stated that the State's district courts had been renovated to the maximum extent feasible to provide greater access. This commenter also noted that a combination of Community Development Block Grant money and State funds are often awarded for renovations of courtroom areas. One advocacy group that has dealt with court access issues stated that members of the State legal community and disability advocates have long been promoting efforts to ensure that the State courts are accessible to individuals with disabilities. The comment cited a publication distributed to the Washington State courts by the State bar association entitled, "Ensuring Equal Access to the Courts for Persons with Disabilities." (Aug. 2006), available at http://www.wsba.org/ensuringaccessguidebook.pdf (last visited July 20, 2010). In addition, the commenter also indicated that the State supreme court had promulgated a new rule governing how the courts should respond to requests of accommodation based upon disability; the State legislature had created the position of Disability Access Coordinator for Courts to facilitate accessibility in the court system; and the State legislature had passed a law requiring that all planned improvements and alterations to historic courthouses be approved by the ADA State facilities program manager and committee in order to ensure that the alterations will enhance accessibility.

The Department has decided to adopt the requirements in the 2004 ADAAG with respect to judicial facilities and courtrooms and will not ask the Access Board to review these requirements. The final rule is wholly consistent with the objectives of the ADA. It addresses a well-documented history of discrimination with respect to judicial administration and significantly increases accessibility for individuals with disabilities.

It helps ensure that they will have an opportunity to participate equally in the judicial process. As stated, the final rule is consistent with a number of model and local building codes that have been widely adopted by State and local building departments and provides greater uniformity for planners, architects, and builders.

Assistive listening systems. The 1991 Standards at sections 4.33.6 and 4.33.7 require assistive listening systems (ALS) in assembly areas and prescribe general performance standards for ALS systems. In the NPRM, the Department proposed adopting the technical specifications in the 2004 ADAAG for ALS that are intended to ensure better quality and effective delivery of sound and information for persons with hearing impairments, especially those using hearing aids. The Department noted in the NPRM that since 1991, advancements in ALS and the advent of digital technology have made these systems more amenable to uniform standards, which, among other things, should ensure that a certain percentage of required ALS systems are hearing-aid compatible. 73 FR 34466, 34471 (June 17, 2008). The 2010 Standards at section 219 provide scoping requirements and at section 706 address receiver jacks, hearing aid compatibility, sound pressure level, signal-to-noise ratio, and peak clipping level. The Department requested comments specifically from arena and assembly area administrators on the cost and maintenance issues associated with ALS, asked generally about the costs and benefits of ALS, and asked whether, based upon the expected costs of ALS, the issue should be returned to the Access Board for further consideration.

Comments from advocacy organizations noted that persons who develop significant hearing loss often discontinue their normal routines and activities, including meetings, entertainment, and large group events, due to a sense of isolation caused by the hearing loss or embarrassment. Individuals with longstanding hearing loss may never have participated in group activities for many of the same reasons. Requiring ALS may allow individuals with disabilities to contribute to the community by joining in government and public events, and increasing economic activity associated with community activities and entertainment. Making public events and entertainment accessible to persons with hearing loss also brings families and other groups that include persons with hearing loss into more community events and activities, thus exponentially increasing the benefit from ALS.

Many commenters noted that when a person has significant hearing loss, that person may be able to hear and understand information in a quiet situation with the use of hearing aids or cochlear implants; however, as background noise increases and the distance between the source of the sound and the listener grows, and especially where there is distortion in the sound, an ALS becomes essential for basic comprehension and understanding. Commenters noted that among the 31 million Americans with hearing loss, and with a projected increase to over 78 million Americans with hearing loss by 2030, the benefit from ALS is huge and growing. Advocates for persons with disabilities and individuals commented that they appreciated the improvements in the 2004 ADAAG standards for ALS, including specifications for the ALS systems and performance standards. They noted that neckloops that translate the signal from the ALS transmitter to a frequency that can be heard on a hearing aid or cochlear implant are much more effective than separate ALS system headsets, which sometimes create feedback, often malfunction, and may create distractions for others seated nearby. Comments from advocates and users of ALS systems consistently noted that the Department's regulation should, at a minimum, be consistent with the 2004 ADAAG. Although there were requests for adjustments in the scoping requirements from advocates seeking increased scoping requirements, and from large venue operators seeking fewer requirements, there was no significant concern expressed by commenters about the technical specifications for ALS in the 2004 ADAAG.

Some commenters from trade associations and large venue owners criticized the scoping requirements as too onerous and one commenter asked for a remand to the

Access Board for new scoping rules. However, one State agency commented that the 2004 ADAAG largely duplicates the requirements in the 2006 IBC and the 2003 ANSI codes, which means that entities that comply with those standards would not incur additional costs associated with ADA compliance.

According to one State office of the courts, the cost to install either an infrared system or an FM system at average-sized facilities, including most courtrooms covered by title II, would be between $500 and $2,000, which the agency viewed as a small price in comparison to the benefits of inclusion. Advocacy organizations estimated wholesale costs of ALS systems at about $250 each and individual neckloops to link the signal from the ALS transmitter to hearing aids or cochlear implants at less than $50 per unit. Many commenters pointed out that if a facility already is using induction neckloops, it would already be in compliance and would not have any additional installation costs. One major city commented that annual maintenance is about $2,000 for the entire system of performance venues in the city. A trade association representing very large venues estimated annual maintenance and upkeep expenses, including labor and replacement parts, to be at most about $25,000 for a very large professional sports stadium.

One commenter suggested that the scoping requirements for ALS in the 2004 ADAAG were too stringent and that the Department should return them to the Access Board for further review and consideration. Others commented that the requirement for new ALS systems should mandate multichannel receivers capable of receiving audio description for persons who are blind, in addition to a channel for amplification for persons who are hard of hearing. Some comments suggested that the Department should require a set schedule and protocol of mandatory maintenance. Department regulations already require maintenance of accessible features at § 35.133(a) of the title II regulation, which obligates a title II entity to maintain ALS in good working order. The Department recognizes that maintenance of ALS is key to its usability. Necessary maintenance will vary dramatically from venue to venue based upon a variety of factors including frequency of use, number of units, quality of equipment, and others items. Accordingly, the Department has determined that it is not appropriate to mandate details of maintenance, but notes that failure to maintain ALS would violate § 35.133(a) of this rule.

The NPRM asked whether the Department should return the issue of ALS requirements to the Access Board. The Department has received substantial feedback on the technical and scoping requirements for ALS and is convinced that these requirements are reasonable and that the benefits justify the requirements. In addition, the Department believes that the new specifications will make ALS work more effectively for more persons with disabilities, which, together with a growing population of new users, will increase demand for ALS, thus mooting criticism from some large venue operators about insufficient demand. Thus, the Department has determined that it is unnecessary to refer this issue back to the Access Board for reconsideration.

Accessible teeing grounds, putting greens, and weather shelters. In the NPRM, the Department sought public input on the proposed requirements for accessible golf courses. These requirements specifically relate to accessible routes within the boundaries of courses, as well as the accessibility of golfing elements (e.g., teeing grounds, putting greens, weather shelters).

In the NPRM, the Department sought information from the owners and operators of golf courses, both public and private, on the extent to which their courses already have golf car passages, and, if so, whether they intended to avail themselves of the proposed accessible route exception for golf car passages. 73 FR 34466, 34471 (June 17, 2008).

Most commenters expressed support for the adoption of an accessible route requirement that includes an exception permitting golf car passage as all or part of an accessible route. Comments in favor of the proposed standard came from golf course owners and operators, individuals, organizations, and disability rights groups, while comments opposing adoption of the golf course requirements generally came from golf courses and organizations representing the golf course industry.

The majority of commenters expressed the general viewpoint that nearly all golf courses provide golf cars and have either well- defined paths or permit golf cars to drive on the course where paths are not present, thus meeting the accessible route requirement. Several commenters disagreed with the assumption in the initial RIA, that virtually every tee and putting green on an existing course would need to be regraded in order to provide compliant accessible routes. According to one commenter, many golf courses are relatively flat with little slope, especially those heavily used by recreational golfers. This commenter concurred with the Department that it is likely that most existing golf courses have a golf car passage to tees and greens, thereby substantially minimizing the cost of bringing an existing golf course into compliance with the proposed standards. One commenter reported that golf course access audits found that the vast majority of public golf courses would have little difficulty in meeting the proposed golf course requirements. In the view of some commenters, providing access to golf courses would increase golf participation by individuals with disabilities.

The Department also received many comments requesting clarification of the term "golf car passage." For example, one commenter requesting clarification of the term "golf car passage" argued that golf courses typically do not provide golf car paths or pedestrian paths onto the actual teeing grounds or greens, many of which are higher or lower than the car path. This commenter argued that if golf car passages were required to extend onto teeing grounds and greens in order to qualify for an exception, then some golf courses would have to substantially regrade teeing grounds and greens at a high cost.

After careful consideration of the comments, the Department has decided to adopt the 2010 Standards specific to golf facilities. The Department believes that in order for individuals with mobility disabilities to have an opportunity to play golf that is equal to golfers without disabilities, it is essential that golf courses provide an accessible route or accessible golf car passage to connect accessible elements and spaces within the boundary of the golf course, including teeing grounds, putting greens, and weather shelters.

Public Comments on Other NPRM Issues

Equipment and furniture. In the 1991 title II regulation, there are no specific provisions addressing equipment and furniture, although § 35.150(b) states that one means by which a public entity can make its program accessible to individuals with disabilities is "redesign of equipment." In the NPRM, the Department announced its intention not to regulate equipment, proposing instead to continue with the current approach, under which equipment and furniture are covered by other provisions, including those requiring reasonable modifications of policies, practices, or procedures, program accessibility, and effective communication. The Department suggested that entities apply the accessibility standards for fixed equipment in the 2004 ADAAG to analogous free-standing equipment in order to ensure that such equipment is accessible, and that entities consult relevant portions of the 2004 ADAAG and standards from other Federal agencies to make equipment accessible to individuals who are blind or have low vision (e.g., the communication-related standards for ATMs in the 2004 ADAAG).

The Department received numerous comments objecting to this decision and urging the Department to issue equipment and furniture regulations. Based on these comments, the Department has decided that it needs to revisit the issuance of equipment and furniture regulations and it intends to do so in future rulemaking.

Among the commenters' key concerns, many from the disability community and some public entities, were objections to the Department's earlier decision not to issue equipment regulations, especially for medical equipment. These groups recommended that the Department list by name certain types of medical equipment that must be accessible, including exam tables (that lower to 15 inches above floor or lower), scales, medical and dental chairs, and radiologic equipment (including mammography equipment). These commenters emphasized that the provision of medically related equipment and furniture should also be specifically regulated since they are not included in the 2004 ADAAG (while depositories, change machines, fuel dispensers, and ATMs were) and because of their crucial role in the provision of healthcare. Commenters described how the lack of accessible medical equipment negatively affects the health of individuals with disabilities. For example, some individuals with mobility disabilities do not get thorough medical care because their health providers do not have accessible examination tables or scales.

Commenters also said that the Department's stated plan to assess the financial impact of free-standing equipment on businesses was not necessary, as any regulations could include a financial balancing test. Other commenters representing persons who are blind or have low vision urged the Department to mandate accessibility for a wide range of equipment — including household appliances (stoves, washers, microwaves, and coffee makers), audiovisual equipment (stereos and DVD players), exercise machines, vending equipment, ATMs, computers at Internet cafes or hotel business centers, reservations kiosks at hotels, and point-of-sale devices — through speech output and tactile labels and controls. They argued that modern technology allows such equipment to be made accessible at minimal cost. According to these commenters, the lack of such accessibility in point-of-sale devices is particularly problematic because it forces blind individuals to provide personal or sensitive information (such as personal identification numbers) to third parties, which exposes them to identity fraud. Because the ADA does not apply directly to the manufacture of products, the Department lacks the authority to issue design requirements for equipment designed exclusively for use in private homes. *See* Department of Justice, Americans with Disabilities Act, *ADA Title III Technical Assistance Manual Covering Public Accommodations and*

Commercial Facilities, III-4.4200, available at http://www.ada.gov/taman3.

Some commenters urged the Department to require swimming pool operators to provide aquatic wheelchairs for the use of persons with disabilities when the swimming pool has a sloped entry. If there is a sloped entry, a person who uses a wheelchair would require a wheelchair designed for use in the water in order to gain access to the pool because taking a personal wheelchair into water would rust and corrode the metal on the chair and damage any electrical components of a power wheelchair. Providing an aquatic wheelchair made of non-corrosive materials and designed for access into the water will protect the water from contamination and avoid damage to personal wheelchairs or other mobility aids.

Additionally, many commenters urged the Department to regulate the height of beds in accessible hotel guest rooms and to ensure that such beds have clearance at the floor to accommodate a mechanical lift. These commenters noted that in recent years, hotel beds have become higher as hotels use thicker mattresses, thereby making it difficult or impossible for many individuals who use wheelchairs to transfer onto hotel beds. In addition, many hotel beds use a solid-sided platform base with no clearance at the floor, which prevents the use of a portable lift to transfer an individual onto the bed. Consequently, individuals who bring their own lift to transfer onto the bed cannot independently get themselves onto the bed. Some commenters suggested various design options that might avoid these situations.

The Department intends to provide specific guidance relating to both hotel beds and aquatic wheelchairs in a future rulemaking. For the present, the Department reminds covered entities that they have an obligation to undertake reasonable modifications to their current policies and to make their programs accessible to persons with disabilities. In many cases, providing aquatic wheelchairs or adjusting hotel bed heights may be necessary to comply with those requirements.

The Department has decided not to add specific scoping or technical requirements for equipment and furniture in this final rule. Other provisions of the regulation, including those requiring reasonable modifications of policies, practices, or procedures, program accessibility, and effective communication may require the provision of accessible equipment in individual circumstances. The 1991 title II regulation at § 35.150(a) requires that entities operate each service, program, or activity so that, when viewed in its entirety, each is readily accessible to, and usable by, individuals with disabilities, subject to a defense of fundamental alteration or undue financial and administrative burdens. Section 35.150(b) specifies that such entities may meet their program accessibility obligation through the "redesign of equipment." The Department expects to undertake a rulemaking to address these issues in the near future.

Accessible golf cars. An accessible golf car means a device that is designed and manufactured to be driven on all areas of a golf course, is independently usable by individuals with mobility disabilities, has a hand-operated brake and accelerator, carries golf clubs in an accessible location, and has a seat that both swivels and raises to put the golfer in a standing or semi-standing position.

The 1991 title II regulation contained no language specifically referencing accessible golf cars. After considering the comments addressing the ANPRM's proposed requirement that golf courses make at least one specialized golf car available for the use of individuals with disabilities, and the safety of accessible golf cars and their use on golf course greens, the Department stated in the NPRM that it would not issue regulations specific to golf cars.

The Department received many comments in response to its decision to propose no new regulation specific to accessible golf cars. The majority of commenters urged the Department to require golf courses to provide accessible golf cars. These comments came from individuals, disability advocacy and recreation groups, a manufacturer of accessible golf cars, and representatives of local government. Comments supporting the Department's decision not to propose a new regulation came from golf course owners, associations, and individuals.

Many commenters argued that while the existing title II regulation covered the issue, the Department should nonetheless adopt specific regulatory language requiring golf courses to provide accessible golf cars. Some commenters noted that many local governments and park authorities that operate public golf courses have already provided accessible golf cars. Experience indicates that such golf cars may be used without damaging courses. Some argued that having accessible golf cars would increase golf course revenue by enabling more golfers with disabilities to play the game. Several commenters requested that the Department adopt a regulation specifically requiring each golf course to provide one or more accessible golf cars. Other commenters recommended allowing golf courses to make "pooling" arrangements to meet demands for such cars. A few commenters expressed support for using accessible golf cars to accommodate golfers with and without disabilities. Commenters also pointed out that the Departments of the Interior and Defense have already mandated that golf courses under their jurisdictional control must make accessible golf cars available unless it can be demonstrated that doing so would change the fundamental nature of the game.

While an industry association argued that at least two models of accessible golf cars meet the specifications recognized in the field, and that accessible golf cars cause no more damage to greens or other parts of golf courses than players standing or walking across the course, other commenters expressed concerns about the potential for damage associated with the use of accessible golf cars. Citing safety concerns, golf organizations recommended that an industry safety standard be developed.

Although the Department declines to add specific scoping or technical requirements for golf cars to this final rule, the Department expects to address requirements for accessible golf cars in future rulemaking. In the meantime, the Department believes that golfers with disabilities who need accessible golf cars are protected by other existing provisions in the title II regulation, including those requiring reasonable modifications of policies, practices, or procedures, and program accessibility.

Web site accessibility. Many commenters expressed disappointment that the NPRM did not require title II entities to make their Web sites, through which they offer programs and services, accessible to individuals disabilities, including those who are blind or have low vision. Commenters argued that the cost of making Web sites accessible, through Web site design, is minimal, yet critical to enabling individuals with disabilities to benefit from the entity's programs and services.

Internet Web sites, when accessible, provide individuals with disabilities great independence, and have become an essential tool for many Americans. Commenters recommended that the Department require covered entities, at a minimum, to meet the section 508 Standard for Electronic and Information Technology for Internet accessibility. Under section 508 of the Rehabilitation Act of 1973, Federal agencies are required to make their Web sites accessible. 29 U.S.C. 794(d); 36 CFR 1194. The Department agrees that the ability to access, on an equal basis, the programs and activities offered by public entities through Internet-based Web sites is of great importance to individuals with disabilities, particularly those who are blind or who have low vision. When the ADA was enacted in 1990, the Internet was unknown to most Americans. Today, the Internet plays a critical role in daily life for personal, civic, commercial, and business purposes. In a period of shrinking resources, public entities increasingly rely on the web as an efficient and comprehensive way to deliver services and to inform and communicate with their citizens and the general public. In light of the growing importance Web sites play in providing access to public services and to disseminating the information citizens need to participate fully in civic life, accessing the Web sites of public entities can play a significant role in fulfilling the goals of the ADA.

Although the language of the ADA does not explicitly mention the Internet, the Department has taken the position that title II covers Internet Web site access. Public entities that choose to provide services through web-based applications (e.g., renewing library books or driver's licenses) or that communicate with their constituents or provide information through the Internet must ensure that individuals with disabilities have equal access to such services or information, unless doing so would result in an undue financial and administrative burden or a fundamental alteration in the nature of the programs, services, or activities being offered. The Department has issued guidance on the ADA as applied to the Web sites of public entities in a 2003 publication entitled, *Accessibility of State and Local Government Web sites to People with Disabilities*, (June 2003) available at http://www.ada.gov/websites2.htm. As the Department stated in that publication, an agency with an inaccessible Web site may also meet its legal obligations by providing an alternative accessible way for citizens to use the programs or services, such as a staffed telephone information line. However, such an alternative must provide an equal degree of access in terms of hours of operation and the range of options and programs available. For example, if job announcements and application forms are posted on an inaccessible Web site that is available 24 hours a day, seven days a week to individuals without disabilities, then the alternative accessible method must also be available 24 hours a day, 7 days a week. Additional guidance is available in the Web Content Accessibility Guidelines (WCAG), (May 5, 1999) available at http://www.w3.org/TR/WAI-WEBCONTENT (last visited June 24, 2010) which are developed and maintained by the Web Accessibility Initiative, a subgroup of the World Wide Web Consortium (W3C®).

The Department expects to engage in rulemaking relating to website accessibility under the ADA in the near future. The Department has enforced the ADA in the area of website accessibility on a case-by-case basis under existing rules consistent with the guidance noted above, and will continue to do so until the issue is addressed in a final regulation.

Multiple chemical sensitivities. The Department received comments from a number of individuals asking the Department to add specific language to the final rule addressing the needs of individuals with chemical sensitivities. These commenters expressed concern that the presence of chemicals interferes with their ability to participate in a wide range of activities. These commenters also urged the Department to add multiple chemical sensitivities to the definition of a disability.

The Department has determined not to include specific provisions addressing multiple chemical sensitivities in the final rule. In order to be viewed as a disability under the ADA, an impairment must substantially limit one or more major life activities. An individual's major life activities of respiratory or neurological functioning may be substantially limited by allergies or sensitivity to a degree that he or she is a person with a disability. When a person has this type of disability, a covered entity may have to make reasonable modifications in its policies and practices for that person. However, this determination is an individual assessment and must be made on a case-by-case basis.

Examinations and Courses. The Department received one comment requesting that it specifically include language regarding examinations and courses in the title II regulation. Because section 309 of the ADA 42 U.S.C. 12189, reaches "[a]ny person that offers examinations or courses related to applications, licensing, certification, or credentialing for secondary or post secondary education, professional, or trade purposes," public entities also are covered by this section of the ADA. Indeed, the requirements contained in title II (including the general prohibitions against discrimination, the program access requirements, the reasonable modifications requirements, and the communications requirements) apply to courses and examinations administered by public entities that meet the requirements of section 309. While the Department considers these requirements to be sufficient to ensure that examinations and courses administered by public entities meet the section 309 requirements, the Department acknowledges that the title III regulation, because it addresses examinations in some detail, is useful as a guide for determining what constitutes discriminatory conduct by a public entity in testing situations. *See* 28 CFR 36.309.

Hotel Reservations. In the NPRM, at§ 36.302(e), the Department proposed adding specific language to title III addressing the requirements that hotels, timeshare resorts, and other places of lodging make reasonable modifications to their policies, practices, or procedures, when necessary to ensure that individuals with disabilities are able to reserve accessible hotel rooms with the same efficiency, immediacy, and convenience as those who do not need accessible guest rooms. The NPRM did not propose adding comparable language to the title II regulation as the Department believes that the general nondiscrimination, program access, effective communication, and reasonable modifications requirements of title II provide sufficient guidance to public entities that operate places of lodging (i.e., lodges in State parks, hotels on public college campuses). The Department received no public comments suggesting that it add language on hotel reservations comparable to that proposed for the title III regulation. Although the Department continues to believe that it is unnecessary to add specific language to the title II regulation on this issue, the Department acknowledges that the title III regulation, because it addresses hotel reservations in some detail, is useful as a guide for determining what constitutes discriminatory conduct by a public entity that operates a reservation system serving a place of lodging. *See* 28 CFR 36.302(e).

Chapter 6
DOJ ADA TITLE III REGULATIONS
[Redlined Version]

Subpart A   General

§ 36.101   Purpose.

The purpose of this part is to implement title III of the Americans with Disabilities Act of 1990 (42 U.S.C. 12181), which prohibits discrimination on the basis of disability by public accommodations and requires places of public accommodation and commercial facilities to be designed, constructed, and altered in compliance with the accessibility standards established by this part.

§ 36.102   Application.

(a)   *General.* This part applies to any —

(1) Public accommodation;

(2) Commercial facility; or

(3) Private entity that offers examinations or courses related to applications, licensing, certification, or credentialing for secondary or postsecondary education, professional, or trade purposes.

(b)   *Public accommodations.*

(1) The requirements of this part applicable to public accommodations are set forth in subparts B, C, and D of this part.

(2) The requirements of subparts B and C of this part obligate a public accommodation only with respect to the operations of a place of public accommodation.

(3) The requirements of subpart D of this part obligate a public accommodation only with respect to —

(i) A facility used as, or designed or constructed for use as, a place of public accommodation; or

(ii) A facility used as, or designed and constructed for use as, a commercial facility.

(c)   *Commercial facilities.* The requirements of this part applicable to commercial facilities are set forth in subpart D of this part.

(d)   *Examinations and courses.* The requirements of this part applicable to private entities that offer examinations or courses as specified in paragraph (a) of this section are set forth in § 36.309.

(e)   *Exemptions and exclusions.* This part does not apply to any private club (except to the extent that the facilities of the private club are made available to customers or patrons of a place of public accommodation), or to any religious entity or public entity.

§ 36.103   Relationship to other laws.

(a)   *Rule of interpretation.* Except as otherwise provided in this part, this part shall not be construed to apply a lesser standard than the standards applied under title V of the Rehabilitation Act of 1973 (29 U.S.C. 791) or the regulations issued by

Federal agencies pursuant to that title.

(b) *Section 504.* This part does not affect the obligations of a recipient of Federal financial assistance to comply with the requirements of section 504 of the Rehabilitation Act of 1973 (29 U.S.C. 794) and regulations issued by Federal agencies implementing section 504.

(c) *Other laws.* This part does not invalidate or limit the remedies, rights, and procedures of any other Federal laws, or State or local laws (including State common law) that provide greater or equal protection for the rights of individuals with disabilities or individuals associated with them.

§ 36.104   Definitions.

For purposes of this part, the term —

1991 Standards **means requirements set forth in the ADA Standards for Accessible Design, originally published on July 26, 1991, and republished as Appendix D to this part.**

2004 ADAAG **means the requirements set forth in appendices B and D to 36 CFR part 1191 (2009).**

2010 Standards **means the 2010 ADA Standards for Accessible Design, which consist of the 2004 ADAAG and the requirements contained in subpart D of this part.**

Act means the Americans with Disabilities Act of 1990 (Pub. L. 101-336, 104 Stat. 327, 42 U.S.C. 12101–12213 and 47 U.S.C. 225 and 611).

Commerce means travel, trade, traffic, commerce, transportation, or communication —

(1) Among the several States;

(2) Between any foreign country or any territory or possession and any State; or

(3) Between points in the same State but through another State or foreign country.

Commercial facilities means facilities —

(1) Whose operations will affect commerce;

(2) That are intended for nonresidential use by a private entity; and

(3) That are not —

(i) Facilities that are covered or expressly exempted from coverage under the Fair Housing Act of 1968, as amended (42 U.S.C. 3601–3631);

(ii) Aircraft; or

(iii) Railroad locomotives, railroad freight cars, railroad cabooses, commuter or intercity passenger rail cars (including coaches, dining cars, sleeping cars, lounge cars, and food service cars), any other railroad cars described in section 242 of the Act or covered under title II of the Act, or railroad rights-of-way. For purposes of this definition, "rail" and "railroad" have the meaning given the term "railroad" in section 202(e) of the Federal Railroad Safety Act of 1970 (45 U.S.C. 431(e)).

Current illegal use of drugs means illegal use of drugs that occurred recently enough to justify a reasonable belief that a person's drug use is current or that continuing use is a real and ongoing problem.

Direct threat means a significant risk to the health or safety of others that cannot be eliminated by a modification of policies, practices, or procedures, or by the provision of auxiliary aids or services, as provided in § 36.208.

Disability means, with respect to an individual, a physical or mental impairment that substantially limits one or more of the major life activities of such individual; a record of such an impairment; or being regarded as having such an impairment.

(1) The phrase *physical or mental impairment* means —

(i) Any physiological disorder or condition, cosmetic disfigurement, or anatomical loss affecting one or more of the following body systems: neurological; musculoskeletal; special sense organs; respiratory, including speech organs; cardiovascular; reproductive; digestive; genitourinary; hemic and lymphatic; skin; and endocrine;

(ii) Any mental or psychological disorder such as mental retardation, organic brain syndrome, emotional or mental illness, and specific learning disabilities;

(iii) The phrase *physical or mental impairment* includes, but is not limited to, such contagious and noncontagious diseases and conditions as orthopedic, visual, speech, and hearing impairments, cerebral palsy, epilepsy, muscular dystrophy, multiple sclerosis, cancer, heart disease, diabetes, mental retardation, emotional illness, specific learning disabilities, HIV disease (whether symptomatic or asymptomatic), tuberculosis, drug addiction, and alcoholism;

(iv) The phrase *physical or mental impairment* does not include homosexuality or bisexuality.

(2) The phrase *major life activities* means functions such as caring for one's self, performing manual tasks, walking, seeing, hearing, speaking, breathing, learning, and working.

(3) The phrase *has a record of such an impairment* means has a history of, or has been misclassified as having, a mental or physical impairment that substantially limits one or more major life activities.

(4) The phrase *is regarded as having an impairment* means —

(i) Has a physical or mental impairment that does not substantially limit major life activities but that is treated by a private entity as constituting such a limitation;

(ii) Has a physical or mental impairment that substantially limits major life activities only as a result of the attitudes of others toward such impairment; or

(iii) Has none of the impairments defined in paragraph (1) of this definition but is treated by a private entity as having such an impairment.

(5) The term *disability* does not include —

(i) Transvestism, transsexualism, pedophilia, exhibitionism, voyeurism, gender identity disorders not resulting from physical impairments, or other sexual behavior disorders;

(ii) Compulsive gambling, kleptomania, or pyromania; or

(iii) Psychoactive substance use disorders resulting from current illegal use of drugs.

Drug means a controlled substance, as defined in schedules I through V of section 202 of the Controlled Substances Act (21 U.S.C. 812).

Existing facility means a facility in existence on any given date, without regard to whether the facility may also be considered newly constructed or altered under this part.

Facility means all or any portion of buildings, structures, sites, complexes, equipment, rolling stock or other conveyances, roads, walks, passageways, parking lots, or other real or personal property, including the site where the building, property, structure, or equipment is located.

Housing at a place of education means housing operated by or on behalf of an elementary, secondary, undergraduate, or postgraduate school, or other place of education, including dormitories, suites, apartments, or other places of residence.

Illegal use of drugs means the use of one or more drugs, the possession or distribution of which is unlawful under the Controlled Substances Act (21 U.S.C. 812). The term "illegal use of drugs" does not include the use of a drug taken under supervision by a licensed health care professional, or other uses authorized by the Controlled Substances Act or other provisions of Federal law.

Individual with a disability means a person who has a disability. The term "individual with a disability" does not include an individual who is currently engaging in the illegal use of drugs, when the private entity acts on the basis of such use.

Other power-driven mobility device means any mobility device powered by batteries, fuel, or other engines — whether or not designed primarily for use by individuals with mobility disabilities — that is used by individuals with mobility disabilities for the purpose of locomotion, including golf cars, electronic personal assistance mobility devices (EPAMDs), such as the Segway® PT, or any mobility device designed to operate in areas without defined pedestrian routes, but that is not a wheelchair within the meaning of this section. This definition does not apply to Federal wilderness areas; wheelchairs in such areas are defined in section 508(c)(2) of the ADA, 42 U.S.C. 12207(c)(2).

Place of public accommodation means a facility operated by a private entity whose operations affect commerce and fall within at least one of the following categories —

(1) Place of lodging, except for an establishment located within a facility that contains not more than five rooms for rent or hire and that actually is occupied by the proprietor of the establishment as the residence of the

proprietor. For purposes of this part, a facility is a "place of lodging" if it is —

(i) An inn, hotel, or motel; or

(ii) A facility that —

(A) Provides guest rooms for sleeping for stays that primarily are short-term in nature (generally 30 days or less) where the occupant does not have the right to return to a specific room or unit after the conclusion of his or her stay; and

(B) Provides guest rooms under conditions and with amenities similar to a hotel, motel, or inn, including the following —

(*1*) On- or off-site management and reservations service;

(*2*) Rooms available on a walk-up or call-in basis;

(*3*) Availability of housekeeping or linen service; and

(*4*) Acceptance of reservations for a guest room type without guaranteeing a particular unit or room until check-in, and without a prior lease or security deposit.

(2) A restaurant, bar, or other establishment serving food or drink;

(3) A motion picture house, theater, concert hall, stadium, or other place of exhibition or entertainment;

(4) An auditorium, convention center, lecture hall, or other place of public gathering;

(5) A bakery, grocery store, clothing store, hardware store, shopping center, or other sales or rental establishment;

(6) A laundromat, dry-cleaner, bank, barber shop, beauty shop, travel service, shoe repair service, funeral parlor, gas station, office of an accountant or lawyer, pharmacy, insurance office, professional office of a health care provider, hospital, or other service establishment;

(7) A terminal, depot, or other station used for specified public transportation;

(8) A museum, library, gallery, or other place of public display or collection;

(9) A park, zoo, amusement park, or other place of recreation;

(10) A nursery, elementary, secondary, undergraduate, or postgraduate private school, or other place of education;

(11) A day care center, senior citizen center, homeless shelter, food bank, adoption agency, or other social service center establishment; and

(12) A gymnasium, health spa, bowling alley, golf course, or other place of exercise or recreation.

Private club means a private club or establishment exempted from coverage under title II of the Civil Rights Act of 1964 (42 U.S.C. 2000a(e)).

Private entity means a person or entity other than a public entity.

Public accommodation means a private entity that owns, leases (or leases to), or operates a place of public accommodation.

Public entity means —

(1) Any State or local government;

(2) Any department, agency, special purpose district, or other instrumentality of a State or States or local government; and

(3) The National Railroad Passenger Corporation, and any commuter authority (as defined in section 103(8) of the Rail Passenger Service Act). (45 U.S.C. 541)

Qualified interpreter means an interpreter who, **via a video remote interpreting (VRI) service or an on-site appearance,** is able to interpret effectively, accurately, and impartially, both receptively and expressively, using any necessary specialized vocabulary. **Qualified interpreters include, for example, sign language interpreters, oral transliterators, and cued-language transliterators.**

***Qualified reader* means a person who is able to read effectively, accurately, and impartially using any necessary specialized vocabulary.**

Readily achievable means easily accomplishable and able to be carried out without much difficulty or expense. In determining whether an action is readily achievable factors to be considered include —

(1) The nature and cost of the action needed under this part;

(2) The overall financial resources of the site or sites involved in the action; the number of persons employed at the site; the effect on expenses and resources; legitimate safety requirements that are necessary for safe operation, including crime prevention measures; or the impact otherwise of the action upon the operation of the site;

(3) The geographic separateness, and the administrative or fiscal relationship of the site or sites in question to any parent corporation or entity;

(4) If applicable, the overall financial resources of any parent corporation or entity; the overall size of the parent corporation or entity with respect to the number of its employees; the number, type, and location of its facilities; and

(5) If applicable, the type of operation or operations of any parent corporation or entity, including the composition, structure, and functions of the workforce of the parent corporation or entity.

Religious entity means a religious organization, including a place of worship.

***Service animal* means any dog that is individually trained to do work or perform tasks for the benefit of an individual with a disability, including a physical, sensory, psychiatric, intellectual, or other mental disability. Other species of animals, whether wild or domestic, trained or untrained, are not service animals for the purposes of this definition. The work or tasks performed by a service animal must be directly related to the individual's disability. Examples of work or tasks include, but are not limited to, assisting individuals who are blind or have low vision with navigation and other tasks,**

alerting individuals who are deaf or hard of hearing to the presence of people or sounds, providing non-violent protection or rescue work, pulling a wheelchair, assisting an individual during a seizure, alerting individuals to the presence of allergens, retrieving items such as medicine or the telephone, providing physical support and assistance with balance and stability to individuals with mobility disabilities, and helping persons with psychiatric and neurological disabilities by preventing or interrupting impulsive or destructive behaviors. The crime deterrent effects of an animal's presence and the provision of emotional support, well-being, comfort, or companionship do not constitute work or tasks for the purposes of this definition.

Specified public transportation means transportation by bus, rail, or any other conveyance (other than by aircraft) that provides the general public with general or special service (including charter service) on a regular and continuing basis.

State means each of the several States, the District of Columbia, the Commonwealth of Puerto Rico, Guam, American Samoa, the Virgin Islands, the Trust Territory of the Pacific Islands, and the Commonwealth of the Northern Mariana Islands.

Undue burden means significant difficulty or expense. In determining whether an action would result in an undue burden, factors to be considered include —

(1) The nature and cost of the action needed under this part;

(2) The overall financial resources of the site or sites involved in the action; the number of persons employed at the site; the effect on expenses and resources; legitimate safety requirements that are necessary for safe operation, including crime prevention measures; or the impact otherwise of the action upon the operation of the site;

(3) The geographic separateness, and the administrative or fiscal relationship of the site or sites in question to any parent corporation or entity;

(4) If applicable, the overall financial resources of any parent corporation or entity; the overall size of the parent corporation or entity with respect to the number of its employees; the number, type, and location of its facilities; and

(5) If applicable, the type of operation or operations of any parent corporation or entity, including the composition, structure, and functions of the workforce of the parent corporation or entity.

Video remote interpreting (VRI) service means an interpreting service that uses video conference technology over dedicated lines or wireless technology offering high-speed, wide-bandwidth video connection that delivers high-quality video images as provided in § 36.303(f).

Wheelchair means a manually-operated or power-driven device designed primarily for use by an individual with a mobility disability for the main purpose of indoor or of both indoor and outdoor locomotion. This definition does not apply to Federal wilderness areas; wheelchairs in such areas are defined in section 508(c)(2) of the ADA, 42 U.S.C. 12207(c)(2).

§§ 36.105–36.199   [Reserved]

Subpart B   General Requirements

§ 36.201   General.

(a) *Prohibition of discrimination.* No individual shall be discriminated against on the basis of disability in the full and equal enjoyment of the goods, services, facilities, privileges, advantages, or accommodations of any place of public accommodation by any private entity who owns, leases (or leases to), or operates a place of public accommodation.

(b) *Landlord and tenant responsibilities.* Both the landlord who owns the building that houses a place of public accommodation and the tenant who owns or operates the place of public accommodation are public accommodations subject to the requirements of this part. As between the parties, allocation of responsibility for complying with the obligations of this part may be determined by lease or other contract.

§ 36.202   Activities.

(a) *Denial of participation.* A public accommodation shall not subject an individual or class of individuals on the basis of a disability or disabilities of such individual or class, directly, or through contractual, licensing, or other arrangements, to a denial of the opportunity of the individual or class to participate in or benefit from the goods, services, facilities, privileges, advantages, or accommodations of a place of public accommodation.

(b) *Participation in unequal benefit.* A public accommodation shall not afford an individual or class of individuals, on the basis of a disability or disabilities of such individual or class, directly, or through contractual, licensing, or other arrangements, with the opportunity to participate in or benefit from a good, service, facility, privilege, advantage, or accommodation that is not equal to that afforded to other individuals.

(c) *Separate benefit.* A public accommodation shall not provide an individual or class of individuals, on the basis of a disability or disabilities of such individual or class, directly, or through contractual, licensing, or other arrangements with a good, service, facility, privilege, advantage, or accommodation that is different or separate from that provided to other individuals, unless such action is necessary to provide the individual or class of individuals with a good, service, facility, privilege, advantage, or accommodation, or other opportunity that is as effective as that provided to others.

(d) *Individual or class of individuals.* For purposes of paragraphs (a) through (c) of this section, the term "individual or class of individuals" refers to the clients or customers of the public accommodation that enters into the contractual, licensing, or other arrangement.

§ 36.203   Integrated settings.

(a) *General.* A public accommodation shall afford goods, services, facilities, privileges, advantages, and accommodations to an individual with a disability in the most integrated setting appropriate to the needs of the individual.

(b) *Opportunity to participate.* Notwithstanding the existence of separate or different programs or activities provided in accordance with this subpart, a public accommodation shall not deny an individual with a disability an opportunity to participate in such programs or activities that are not separate or different.

(c) *Accommodations and services.*

(1) Nothing in this part shall be construed to require an individual with a disability to accept an accommodation, aid, service, opportunity, or benefit available under this part that such individual chooses not to accept.

(2) Nothing in the Act or this part authorizes the representative or guardian of an individual with a disability to decline food, water, medical treatment, or medical services for that individual.

§ 36.204 Administrative methods.

A public accommodation shall not, directly or through contractual or other arrangements, utilize standards or criteria or methods of administration that have the effect of discriminating on the basis of disability, or that perpetuate the discrimination of others who are subject to common administrative control.

§ 36.205 Association.

A public accommodation shall not exclude or otherwise deny equal goods, services, facilities, privileges, advantages, accommodations, or other opportunities to an individual or entity because of the known disability of an individual with whom the individual or entity is known to have a relationship or association.

§ 36.206 Retaliation or coercion.

(a) No private or public entity shall discriminate against any individual because that individual has opposed any act or practice made unlawful by this part, or because that individual made a charge, testified, assisted, or participated in any manner in an investigation, proceeding, or hearing under the Act or this part.

(b) No private or public entity shall coerce, intimidate, threaten, or interfere with any individual in the exercise or enjoyment of, or on account of his or her having exercised or enjoyed, or on account of his or her having aided or encouraged any other individual in the exercise or enjoyment of, any right granted or protected by the Act or this part.

(c) Illustrations of conduct prohibited by this section include, but are not limited to:

(1) Coercing an individual to deny or limit the benefits, services, or advantages to which he or she is entitled under the Act or this part;

(2) Threatening, intimidating, or interfering with an individual with a disability who is seeking to obtain or use the goods, services, facilities, privileges, advantages, or accommodations of a public accommodation;

(3) Intimidating or threatening any person because that person is assisting or

encouraging an individual or group entitled to claim the rights granted or protected by the Act or this part to exercise those rights; or

(4) Retaliating against any person because that person has participated in any investigation or action to enforce the Act or this part.

§ 36.207　Places of public accommodation located in private residences.

(a) When a place of public accommodation is located in a private residence, the portion of the residence used exclusively as a residence is not covered by this part, but that portion used exclusively in the operation of the place of public accommodation or that portion used both for the place of public accommodation and for residential purposes is covered by this part.

(b) The portion of the residence covered under paragraph (a) of this section extends to those elements used to enter the place of public accommodation, including the homeowner's front sidewalk, if any, the door or entryway, and hallways; and those portions of the residence, interior or exterior, available to or used by customers or clients, including restrooms.

§ 36.208　Direct threat.

(a) This part does not require a public accommodation to permit an individual to participate in or benefit from the goods, services, facilities, privileges, advantages and accommodations of that public accommodation when that individual poses a direct threat to the health or safety of others.

(b) In determining whether an individual poses a direct threat to the health or safety of others, a public accommodation must make an individualized assessment, based on reasonable judgment that relies on current medical knowledge or on the best available objective evidence, to ascertain: The nature, duration, and severity of the risk; the probability that the potential injury will actually occur; and whether reasonable modifications of policies, practices, or procedures **or the provision of auxiliary aids or services** will mitigate the risk.

§ 36.209　Illegal use of drugs.

(a) *General.*

(1) Except as provided in paragraph (b) of this section, this part does not prohibit discrimination against an individual based on that individual's current illegal use of drugs.

(2) A public accommodation shall not discriminate on the basis of illegal use of drugs against an individual who is not engaging in current illegal use of drugs and who —

(i) Has successfully completed a supervised drug rehabilitation program or has otherwise been rehabilitated successfully;

(ii) Is participating in a supervised rehabilitation program; or

(iii) Is erroneously regarded as engaging in such use.

(b) *Health and drug rehabilitation services.*

(1) A public accommodation shall not deny health services, or services provided in connection with drug rehabilitation, to an individual on the basis of that individual's current illegal use of drugs, if the individual is otherwise entitled to such services.

(2) A drug rehabilitation or treatment program may deny participation to individuals who engage in illegal use of drugs while they are in the program.

(c) *Drug testing.*

(1) This part does not prohibit a public accommodation from adopting or administering reasonable policies or procedures, including but not limited to drug testing, designed to ensure that an individual who formerly engaged in the illegal use of drugs is not now engaging in current illegal use of drugs.

(2) Nothing in this paragraph (c) shall be construed to encourage, prohibit, restrict, or authorize the conducting of testing for the illegal use of drugs.

§ 36.210   Smoking.

This part does not preclude the prohibition of, or the imposition of restrictions on, smoking in places of public accommodation.

§ 36.211   Maintenance of accessible features.

(a) A public accommodation shall maintain in operable working condition those features of facilities and equipment that are required to be readily accessible to and usable by persons with disabilities by the Act or this part.

(b) This section does not prohibit isolated or temporary interruptions in service or access due to maintenance or repairs.

(c) If the 2010 Standards reduce the technical requirements or the number of required accessible elements below the number required by the 1991 Standards, the technical requirements or the number of accessible elements in a facility subject to this part may be reduced in accordance with the requirements of the 2010 Standards.

§ 36.212   Insurance.

(a) This part shall not be construed to prohibit or restrict —

(1) An insurer, hospital or medical service company, health maintenance organization, or any agent, or entity that administers benefit plans, or similar organizations from underwriting risks, classifying risks, or administering such risks that are based on or not inconsistent with State law; or

(2) A person or organization covered by this part from establishing, sponsoring, observing or administering the terms of a bona fide benefit plan that are based on underwriting risks, classifying risks, or administering such risks that are based on or not inconsistent with State law; or

(3) A person or organization covered by this part from establishing, sponsoring, observing or administering the terms of a bona fide benefit plan that is not subject to State laws that regulate insurance.

(b) Paragraphs (a) (1), (2), and (3) of this section shall not be used as a subterfuge to evade the purposes of the Act or this part.

(c) A public accommodation shall not refuse to serve an individual with a disability because its insurance company conditions coverage or rates on the absence of individuals with disabilities.

§ 36.213   Relationship of subpart B to subparts C and D of this part.

Subpart B of this part sets forth the general principles of nondiscrimination applicable to all entities subject to this part. Subparts C and D of this part provide guidance on the application of the statute to specific situations. The specific provisions, including the limitations on those provisions, control over the general provisions in circumstances where both specific and general provisions apply.

§§ 36.214–36.299   [Reserved]

Subpart C   Specific Requirements

§ 36.301   Eligibility criteria.

(a) *General.* A public accommodation shall not impose or apply eligibility criteria that screen out or tend to screen out an individual with a disability or any class of individuals with disabilities from fully and equally enjoying any goods, services, facilities, privileges, advantages, or accommodations, unless such criteria can be shown to be necessary for the provision of the goods, services, facilities, privileges, advantages, or accommodations being offered.

(b) *Safety.* A public accommodation may impose legitimate safety requirements that are necessary for safe operation. Safety requirements must be based on actual risks and not on mere speculation, stereotypes, or generalizations about individuals with disabilities.

(c) *Charges.* A public accommodation may not impose a surcharge on a particular individual with a disability or any group of individuals with disabilities to cover the costs of measures, such as the provision of auxiliary aids, barrier removal, alternatives to barrier removal, and reasonable modifications in policies, practices, or procedures, that are required to provide that individual or group with the nondiscriminatory treatment required by the Act or this part.

§ 36.302   Modifications in policies, practices, or procedures.

(a) *General.* A public accommodation shall make reasonable modifications in policies, practices, or procedures, when the modifications are necessary to afford goods, services, facilities, privileges, advantages, or accommodations to individuals with disabilities, unless the public accommodation can demonstrate that making the modifications would fundamentally alter the nature of the goods, services, facilities, privileges, advantages, or accommodations.

(b) *Specialties —*

(1) *General.* A public accommodation may refer an individual with a disability to another public accommodation, if that individual is seeking, or requires, treatment or services outside of the referring public accommodation's area of

specialization, and if, in the normal course of its operations, the referring public accommodation would make a similar referral for an individual without a disability who seeks or requires the same treatment or services.

(2) *Illustration — medical specialties.* A health care provider may refer an individual with a disability to another provider, if that individual is seeking, or requires, treatment or services outside of the referring provider's area of specialization, and if the referring provider would make a similar referral for an individual without a disability who seeks or requires the same treatment or services. A physician who specializes in treating only a particular condition cannot refuse to treat an individual with a disability for that condition, but is not required to treat the individual for a different condition.

(c) *Service animals.*

(1) *General.* Generally, a public accommodation shall modify policies, practices, or procedures to permit the use of a service animal by an individual with a disability.

(2) **Exceptions.** A public accommodation may ask an individual with a disability to remove a service animal from the premises if:

(i) The animal is out of control and the animal's handler does not take effective action to control it; or

(ii) The animal is not housebroken.

(3) **If an animal is properly excluded.** If a public accommodation properly excludes a service animal under § 36.302(c)(2), it shall give the individual with a disability the opportunity to obtain goods, services, and accommodations without having the service animal on the premises.

(4) **Animal under handler's control.** A service animal shall be under the control of its handler. A service animal shall have a harness, leash, or other tether, unless either the handler is unable because of a disability to use a harness, leash, or other tether, or the use of a harness, leash, or other tether would interfere with the service animal's safe, effective performance of work or tasks, in which case the service animal must be otherwise under the handler's control (*e.g.,* voice control, signals, or other effective means).

(5) **Care or supervision.** A public accommodation is not responsible for the care or supervision of a service animal.

(6) **Inquiries.** A public accommodation shall not ask about the nature or extent of a person's disability, but may make two inquiries to determine whether an animal qualifies as a service animal. A public accommodation may ask if the animal is required because of a disability and what work or task the animal has been trained to perform. A public accommodation shall not require documentation, such as proof that the animal has been certified, trained, or licensed as a service animal. Generally, a public accommodation may not make these inquiries about a service animal when it is readily apparent that an animal is trained to do work or perform tasks for an individual with a disability (*e.g.,* the dog is observed guiding an individual

who is blind or has low vision, pulling a person's wheelchair, or providing assistance with stability or balance to an individual with an observable mobility disability).

(7) *Access to areas of a public accommodation.* Individuals with disabilities shall be permitted to be accompanied by their service animals in all areas of a place of public accommodation where members of the public, program participants, clients, customers, patrons, or invitees, as relevant, are allowed to go.

(8) *Surcharges.* A public accommodation shall not ask or require an individual with a disability to pay a surcharge, even if people accompanied by pets are required to pay fees, or to comply with other requirements generally not applicable to people without pets. If a public accommodation normally charges individuals for the damage they cause, an individual with a disability may be charged for damage caused by his or her service animal.

(9) *Miniature horses.*

(i) A public accommodation shall make reasonable modifications in policies, practices, or procedures to permit the use of a miniature horse by an individual with a disability if the miniature horse has been individually trained to do work or perform tasks for the benefit of the individual with a disability.

(ii) *Assessment factors.* In determining whether reasonable modifications in policies, practices, or procedures can be made to allow a miniature horse into a specific facility, a public accommodation shall consider —

(A) The type, size, and weight of the miniature horse and whether the facility can accommodate these features;

(B) Whether the handler has sufficient control of the miniature horse;

(C) Whether the miniature horse is housebroken; and

(D) Whether the miniature horse's presence in a specific facility compromises legitimate safety requirements that are necessary for safe operation.

(iii) *Other requirements.* Sections 36.302(c)(3) through (c)(8), which apply to service animals, shall also apply to miniature horses.

(d) *Check-out aisles.* A store with check-out aisles shall ensure that an adequate number of accessible check-out aisles are kept open during store hours, or shall otherwise modify its policies and practices, in order to ensure that an equivalent level of convenient service is provided to individuals with disabilities as is provided to others. If only one check-out aisle is accessible, and it is generally used for express service, one way of providing equivalent service is to allow persons with mobility impairments to make all their purchases at that aisle.

(e) (1) *Reservations made by places of lodging.* A public accommodation that owns, leases (or leases to), or operates a place of lodging shall, with respect to reservations made by any means, including by telephone, in-person, or through a third party —

(i) Modify its policies, practices, or procedures to ensure that individuals with disabilities can make reservations for accessible guest rooms during the same hours and in the same manner as individuals who do not need accessible rooms;

(ii) Identify and describe accessible features in the hotels and guest rooms offered through its reservations service in enough detail to reasonably permit individuals with disabilities to assess independently whether a given hotel or guest room meets his or her accessibility needs;

(iii) Ensure that accessible guest rooms are held for use by individuals with disabilities until all other guest rooms of that type have been rented and the accessible room requested is the only remaining room of that type;

(iv) Reserve, upon request, accessible guest rooms or specific types of guest rooms and ensure that the guest rooms requested are blocked and removed from all reservations systems; and

(v) Guarantee that the specific accessible guest room reserved through its reservations service is held for the reserving customer, regardless of whether a specific room is held in response to reservations made by others.

(2) *Exception.* The requirements in paragraphs (iii), (iv), and (v) of this section do not apply to reservations for individual guest rooms or other units not owned or substantially controlled by the entity that owns, leases, or operates the overall facility.

(3) *Compliance date.* The requirements in this section will apply to reservations made on or after March 15, 2012.

(f) *Ticketing.*

(1) (i) For the purposes of this section, "accessible seating" is defined as wheelchair spaces and companion seats that comply with sections 221 and 802 of the 2010 Standards along with any other seats required to be offered for sale to the individual with a disability pursuant to paragraph (4) of this section.

(ii) *Ticket sales.* A public accommodation that sells tickets for a single event or series of events shall modify its policies, practices, or procedures to ensure that individuals with disabilities have an equal opportunity to purchase tickets for accessible seating —

(A) During the same hours;

(B) During the same stages of ticket sales, including, but not limited to, pre-sales, promotions, lotteries, wait-lists, and general sales;

(C) Through the same methods of distribution;

(D) In the same types and numbers of ticketing sales outlets, including telephone service, in-person ticket sales at the facility, or third-party ticketing services, as other patrons; and

(E) Under the same terms and conditions as other tickets sold for the same event or series of events.

(2) *Identification of available accessible seating.* A public accommodation that sells or distributes tickets for a single event or series of events shall, upon inquiry —

(i) Inform individuals with disabilities, their companions, and third parties purchasing tickets for accessible seating on behalf of individuals with disabilities of the locations of all unsold or otherwise available accessible seating for any ticketed event or events at the facility;

(ii) Identify and describe the features of available accessible seating in enough detail to reasonably permit an individual with a disability to assess independently whether a given accessible seating location meets his or her accessibility needs; and

(iii) Provide materials, such as seating maps, plans, brochures, pricing charts, or other information, that identify accessible seating and information relevant thereto with the same text or visual representations as other seats, if such materials are provided to the general public.

(3) *Ticket prices.* The price of tickets for accessible seating for a single event or series of events shall not be set higher than the price for other tickets in the same seating section for the same event or series of events. Tickets for accessible seating must be made available at all price levels for every event or series of events. If tickets for accessible seating at a particular price level cannot be provided because barrier removal in an existing facility is not readily achievable, then the percentage of tickets for accessible seating that should have been available at that price level but for the barriers (determined by the ratio of the total number of tickets at that price level to the total number of tickets in the assembly area) shall be offered for purchase, at that price level, in a nearby or similar accessible location.

(4) *Purchasing multiple tickets.*

(i) *General.* For each ticket for a wheelchair space purchased by an individual with a disability or a third-party purchasing such a ticket at his or her request, a public accommodation shall make available for purchase three additional tickets for seats in the same row that are contiguous with the wheelchair space, provided that at the time of purchase there are three such seats available. A public accommodation is not required to provide more than three contiguous seats for each wheelchair space. Such seats may include wheelchair spaces.

(ii) *Insufficient additional contiguous seats available.* If patrons are allowed to purchase at least four tickets, and there are fewer than three such additional contiguous seat tickets available for purchase, a public accommodation shall offer the next highest number of such seat tickets available for purchase and shall make up the difference by offering tickets for sale for seats that are as close as possible to the accessible seats.

(iii) *Sales limited to fewer than four tickets.* If a public accommodation limits sales of tickets to fewer than four seats per patron, then the public accommodation is only obligated to offer as many seats to patrons with disabilities, including the ticket for the wheelchair space, as it would offer to patrons without disabilities.

(iv) *Maximum number of tickets patrons may purchase exceeds four.* If patrons are allowed to purchase more than four tickets, a public accommodation shall allow patrons with disabilities to purchase up to the same number of tickets, including the ticket for the wheelchair space.

(v) *Group sales.* If a group includes one or more individuals who need to use accessible seating because of a mobility disability or because their disability requires the use of the accessible features that are provided in accessible seating, the group shall be placed in a seating area with accessible seating so that, if possible, the group can sit together. If it is necessary to divide the group, it should be divided so that the individuals in the group who use wheelchairs are not isolated from their group.

(5) *Hold and release of tickets for accessible seating.*

(i) *Tickets for accessible seating may be released for sale in certain limited circumstances.* A public accommodation may release unsold tickets for accessible seating for sale to individuals without disabilities for their own use for a single event or series of events only under the following circumstances —

(A) When all non-accessible tickets (excluding luxury boxes, club boxes, or suites) have been sold;

(B) When all non-accessible tickets in a designated seating area have been sold and the tickets for accessible seating are being released in the same designated area; or

(C) When all non-accessible tickets in a designated price category have been sold and the tickets for accessible seating are being released within the same designated price category.

(ii) *No requirement to release accessible tickets.* Nothing in this paragraph requires a facility to release tickets for accessible seating to individuals without disabilities for their own use.

(iii) *Release of series-of-events tickets on a series-of-events basis.*

(A) *Series-of-events tickets sell-out when no ownership rights are attached.* When series-of-events tickets are sold out and a public accommodation releases and sells accessible seating to individuals without disabilities for a series of events, the public accommodation shall establish a process that prevents the automatic reassignment of the accessible seating to such ticket holders for future seasons, future years, or future series, so that individuals with disabilities who require the features of accessible seating and who become newly eligible to purchase tickets when these series-of-events tickets are available for purchase have an opportunity to do so.

(B) *Series-of-events tickets when ownership rights are attached.* When series-of-events tickets with an ownership right in accessible seating areas are forfeited or otherwise returned to a public accommodation, the public accommodation shall make reasonable modifications in its policies, practices, or procedures to afford individuals with mobility disabilities or individuals with disabilities that require the features of accessible seating an opportunity to purchase such tickets in accessible seating areas.

(6) *Ticket transfer.* Individuals with disabilities who hold tickets for accessible seating shall be permitted to transfer tickets to third parties under the same terms and conditions and to the same extent as other spectators holding the same type of tickets, whether they are for a single event or series of events.

(7) *Secondary ticket market.*

(i) A public accommodation shall modify its policies, practices, or procedures to ensure that an individual with a disability may use a ticket acquired in the secondary ticket market under the same terms and conditions as other individuals who hold a ticket acquired in the secondary ticket market for the same event or series of events.

(ii) If an individual with a disability acquires a ticket or series of tickets to an inaccessible seat through the secondary market, a public accommodation shall make reasonable modifications to its policies, practices, or procedures to allow the individual to exchange his ticket for one to an accessible seat in a comparable location if accessible seating is vacant at the time the individual presents the ticket to the public accommodation.

(8) *Prevention of fraud in purchase of tickets for accessible seating.* A public accommodation may not require proof of disability, including, for example, a doctor's note, before selling tickets for accessible seating.

(i) *Single-event tickets.* For the sale of single-event tickets, it is permissible to inquire whether the individual purchasing the tickets for accessible seating has a mobility disability or a disability that requires the use of the accessible features that are provided in accessible seating, or is purchasing the tickets for an individual who has a mobility disability or a disability that requires the use of the accessible features that are provided in the accessible seating.

(ii) *Series-of-events tickets.* For series-of-events tickets, it is permissible to ask the individual purchasing the tickets for accessible seating to attest in writing that the accessible seating is for a person who has a mobility disability or a disability that requires the use of the accessible features that are provided in the accessible seating.

(iii) *Investigation of fraud.* A public accommodation may investigate the potential misuse of accessible seating where there is good cause to believe that such seating has been purchased fraudulently.

§ 36.303 Auxiliary aids and services.

(a) *General.* A public accommodation shall take those steps that may be necessary to ensure that no individual with a disability is excluded, denied services, segregated or otherwise treated differently than other individuals because of the absence of auxiliary aids and services, unless the public accommodation can demonstrate that taking those steps would fundamentally alter the nature of the goods, services, facilities, privileges, advantages, or accommodations being offered or would result in an undue burden, *i.e.*, significant difficulty or expense.

(b) *Examples.* The term "auxiliary aids and services" includes —

(1) Qualified interpreters **on-site or through video remote interpreting (VRI) services;** notetakers; **real-time** computer-aided transcription services; written materials; **exchange of written notes;** telephone handset amplifiers; assistive listening devices; assistive listening systems; telephones compatible with hearing aids; closed caption decoders; open and closed captioning, **including real-time captioning; voice, text, and video-based telecommunications products and systems,** including **text telephones (TTYs), videophones, and captioned telephones, or equally effective telecommunications devices; videotext displays; accessible electronic and information technology;** or other effective methods of making aurally delivered information available to individuals **who are deaf or hard of hearing;**

(2) Qualified readers; taped texts; audio recordings; Brailled materials **and displays; screen reader software; magnification software; optical readers; secondary auditory programs (SAP);** large print materials; **accessible electronic and information technology;** or other effective methods of making visually delivered materials available to individuals who are blind **or have low vision;**

(3) Acquisition or modification of equipment or devices; and

(4) Other similar services and actions.

(c) *Effective communication.*

(1) A public accommodation shall furnish appropriate auxiliary aids and services where necessary to ensure effective communication with individuals with disabilities. **This includes an obligation to provide effective communication to companions who are individuals with disabilities.**

(i) For purposes of this section, "companion" means a family member, friend, or associate of an individual seeking access to, or participating in, the goods, services, facilities, privileges, advantages, or accommodations of a public accommodation, who, along with such individual, is an appropriate person with whom the public accommodation should communicate.

(ii) The type of auxiliary aid or service necessary to ensure effective communication will vary in accordance with the method of communica-

tion used by the individual; the nature, length, and complexity of the communication involved; and the context in which the communication is taking place. A public accommodation should consult with individuals with disabilities whenever possible to determine what type of auxiliary aid is needed to ensure effective communication, but the ultimate decision as to what measures to take rests with the public accommodation, provided that the method chosen results in effective communication. In order to be effective, auxiliary aids and services must be provided in accessible formats, in a timely manner, and in such a way as to protect the privacy and independence of the individual with a disability.

(2) A public accommodation shall not require an individual with a disability to bring another individual to interpret for him or her.

(3) A public accommodation shall not rely on an adult accompanying an individual with a disability to interpret or facilitate communication, except —

    (i) In an emergency involving an imminent threat to the safety or welfare of an individual or the public where there is no interpreter available; or

    (ii) Where the individual with a disability specifically requests that the accompanying adult interpret or facilitate communication, the accompanying adult agrees to provide such assistance, and reliance on that adult for such assistance is appropriate under the circumstances.

(4) A public accommodation shall not rely on a minor child to interpret or facilitate communication, except in an emergency involving an imminent threat to the safety or welfare of an individual or the public where there is no interpreter available.

(d) *Telecommunications.*

(1) When a public accommodation uses an automated-attendant system, including, but not limited to, voicemail and messaging, or an interactive voice response system, for receiving and directing incoming telephone calls, that system must provide effective real-time communication with individuals using auxiliary aids and services, including text telephones (TTYs) and all forms of FCC-approved telecommunications relay systems, including Internet-based relay systems.

(2) A public accommodation that offers a customer, client, patient, or participant the opportunity to make outgoing telephone calls using the public accommodation's equipment on more than an incidental convenience basis shall make available public telephones, TTYs, or other telecommunications products and systems for use by an individual who is deaf or hard of hearing, or has a speech impairment.

(3) A public accommodation may use relay services in place of direct telephone communication for receiving or making telephone calls incident to its operations.

(4) **A public accommodation shall respond to telephone calls from a telecommunications relay service established under title IV of the ADA in the same manner that it responds to other telephone calls.**

(5) This part does not require a public accommodation to use **a TTY** for receiving or making telephone calls incident to its operations.

(e) *Closed caption decoders.* Places of lodging that provide televisions in five or more guest rooms and hospitals that provide televisions for patient use shall provide, upon request, a means for decoding captions for use by an individual with impaired hearing.

(f) *Video remote interpreting (VRI) services.* **A public accommodation that chooses to provide qualified interpreters via VRI service shall ensure that it provides —**

(1) **Real-time, full-motion video and audio over a dedicated high-speed, wide-bandwidth video connection or wireless connection that delivers high-quality video images that do not produce lags, choppy, blurry, or grainy images, or irregular pauses in communication;**

(2) **A sharply delineated image that is large enough to display the interpreter's face, arms, hands, and fingers, and the participating individual's face, arms, hands, and fingers, regardless of his or her body position;**

(3) **A clear, audible transmission of voices; and**

(4) **Adequate training to users of the technology and other involved individuals so that they may quickly and efficiently set up and operate the VRI.**

(g) *Alternatives.* If provision of a particular auxiliary aid or service by a public accommodation would result in a fundamental alteration in the nature of the goods, services, facilities, privileges, advantages, or accommodations being offered or in an undue burden, *i.e.*, significant difficulty or expense, the public accommodation shall provide an alternative auxiliary aid or service, if one exists, that would not result in an alteration or such burden but would nevertheless ensure that, to the maximum extent possible, individuals with disabilities receive the goods, services, facilities, privileges, advantages, or accommodations offered by the public accommodation.

§ 36.304   Removal of barriers.

(a) *General.* A public accommodation shall remove architectural barriers in existing facilities, including communication barriers that are structural in nature, where such removal is readily achievable, *i.e.*, easily accomplishable and able to be carried out without much difficulty or expense.

(b) *Examples.* Examples of steps to remove barriers include, but are not limited to, the following actions —

(1) Installing ramps;

(2) Making curb cuts in sidewalks and entrances;

(3) Repositioning shelves;

(4) Rearranging tables, chairs, vending machines, display racks, and other furniture;

(5) Repositioning telephones;

(6) Adding raised markings on elevator control buttons;

(7) Installing flashing alarm lights;

(8) Widening doors;

(9) Installing offset hinges to widen doorways;

(10) Eliminating a turnstile or providing an alternative accessible path;

(11) Installing accessible door hardware;

(12) Installing grab bars in toilet stalls;

(13) Rearranging toilet partitions to increase maneuvering space;

(14) Insulating lavatory pipes under sinks to prevent burns;

(15) Installing a raised toilet seat;

(16) Installing a full-length bathroom mirror;

(17) Repositioning the paper towel dispenser in a bathroom;

(18) Creating designated accessible parking spaces;

(19) Installing an accessible paper cup dispenser at an existing inaccessible water fountain;

(20) Removing high pile, low density carpeting; or

(21) Installing vehicle hand controls.

(c) *Priorities.* A public accommodation is urged to take measures to comply with the barrier removal requirements of this section in accordance with the following order of priorities.

(1) First, a public accommodation should take measures to provide access to a place of public accommodation from public sidewalks, parking, or public transportation. These measures include, for example, installing an entrance ramp, widening entrances, and providing accessible parking spaces.

(2) Second, a public accommodation should take measures to provide access to those areas of a place of public accommodation where goods and services are made available to the public. These measures include, for example, adjusting the layout of display racks, rearranging tables, providing Brailled and raised character signage, widening doors, providing visual alarms, and installing ramps.

(3) Third, a public accommodation should take measures to provide access to restroom facilities. These measures include, for example, removal of obstructing furniture or vending machines, widening of doors, installation of ramps, providing accessible signage, widening of toilet stalls, and installation of grab bars.

(4) Fourth, a public accommodation should take any other measures necessary

to provide access to the goods, services, facilities, privileges, advantages, or accommodations of a place of public accommodation.

(d) *Relationship to alterations requirements of subpart D of this part.*

(1) Except as provided in paragraph **(d)(3)** of this section, measures taken to comply with the barrier removal requirements of this section shall comply with the applicable requirements for alterations in § 36.402 and §§ 36.404 through36.406 of this part for the element being altered. The path of travel requirements of § 36.403 shall not apply to measures taken solely to comply with the barrier removal requirements of this section.

(2) (i) *Safe harbor.* Elements that have not been altered in existing facilities on or after March 15, 2012, and that comply with the corresponding technical and scoping specifications for those elements in the 1991 Standards are not required to be modified in order to comply with the requirements set forth in the 2010 Standards.

(ii) (A) Before March 15, 2012, elements in existing facilities that do not comply with the corresponding technical and scoping specifications for those elements in the 1991 Standards must be modified to the extent readily achievable to comply with either the 1991 Standards or the 2010 Standards. Noncomplying newly constructed and altered elements may also be subject to the requirements of § 36.406(a)(5).

(B) On or after March 15, 2012, elements in existing facilities that do not comply with the corresponding technical and scoping specifications for those elements in the 1991 Standards must be modified to the extent readily achievable to comply with the requirements set forth in the 2010 Standards. Noncomplying newly constructed and altered elements may also be subject to the requirements of § 36.406(a)(5).

(iii) The safe harbor provided in § 36.304(d)(2)(i) does not apply to those elements in existing facilities that are subject to supplemental requirements (*i.e.*, elements for which there are neither technical nor scoping specifications in the 1991 Standards), and therefore those elements must be modified to the extent readily achievable to comply with the 2010 Standards. Noncomplying newly constructed and altered elements may also be subject to the requirements of § 36.406(a)(5). Elements in the 2010 Standards not eligible for the element-by-element safe harbor are identified as follows —

(A) *Residential facilities and dwelling units,* sections 233 and 809.

(B) *Amusement rides,* sections 234 and 1002; 206.2.9; 216.12.

(C) *Recreational boating facilities,* sections 235 and 1003; 206.2.10.

(D) *Exercise machines and equipment,* sections 236 and 1004; 206.2.13.

(E) *Fishing piers and platforms,* sections 237 and 1005; 206.2.14.

(F) *Golf facilities,* sections 238 and 1006; 206.2.15.

(G) *Miniature golf facilities,* sections 239 and 1007; 206.2.16.

(H) *Play areas*, sections 240 and 1008; 206.2.17.

(I) *Saunas and steam rooms*, sections 241 and 612.

(J) *Swimming pools, wading pools, and spas*, sections 242 and 1009.

(K) *Shooting facilities with firing positions*, sections 243 and 1010.

(L)　*Miscellaneous.*

(1) Team or player seating, section 221.2.1.4.

(2) Accessible route to bowling lanes, section 206.2.11.

(3) Accessible route in court sports facilities, section 206.2.12.

Appendix to § 36.304(d)

Compliance Dates and Applicable Standards for Barrier Removal and Safe Harbor		
Date	Requirement	Applicable Standards
Before March 15, 2012	Elements that do not comply with the requirements for those elements in the 1991 Standards must be modified to the extent readily achievable.	1991 Standards or 2010 Standards
	Note: Noncomplying newly constructed and altered elements may also be subject to the requirements of § 36.406(a)(5).	
On or after March 15, 2012	Elements that do not comply with the requirements for those elements in the 1991 Standards or that do not comply with the supplemental requirements (*i.e.*, elements for which there are neither technical nor scoping specifications in the 1991 Standards) must be modified to the extent readily achievable.	2010 Standards
	Note: Noncomplying newly constructed and altered elements may also be subject to the requirements of § 36.406(a)(5).	
Elements not altered after March 15, 2012	Elements that comply with the requirements for those elements in the 1991 Standards do not need to be modified.	Safe Harbor

(3) If, as a result of compliance with the alterations requirements specified in paragraph (d)(1) **and (d)(2)** of this section, the measures required to remove a barrier would not be readily achievable, a public accommodation may take other readily achievable measures to remove the barrier that do not fully comply with the specified requirements. Such measures include, for example, providing a ramp with a steeper slope or widening a doorway to a narrower width than that mandated by the alterations requirements. No measure shall be taken, however, that poses a significant risk to the health or safety of individuals with disabilities or others.

(e) *Portable ramps.* Portable ramps should be used to comply with this section only when installation of a permanent ramp is not readily achievable. In order to avoid any significant risk to the health or safety of individuals with disabilities or others in using portable ramps, due consideration shall be given to safety features such as nonslip surfaces, railings, anchoring, and strength of materials.

(f) *Selling or serving space.* The rearrangement of temporary or movable structures, such as furniture, equipment, and display racks is not readily achievable to the extent that it results in a significant loss of selling or serving space.

(g) *Limitation on barrier removal obligations.*

(1) The requirements for barrier removal under § 36.304 shall not be interpreted to exceed the standards for alterations in subpart D of this part.

(2) To the extent that relevant standards for alterations are not provided in subpart D of this part, then the requirements of § 36.304 shall not be interpreted to exceed the standards for new construction in subpart D of this part.

(3) This section does not apply to rolling stock and other conveyances to the extent that § 36.310 applies to rolling stock and other conveyances.

(4) This requirement does not apply to guest rooms in existing facilities that are places of lodging where the guest rooms are not owned by the entity that owns, leases, or operates the overall facility and the physical features of the guest room interiors are controlled by their individual owners.

§ 36.305   Alternatives to barrier removal.

(a) *General.* Where a public accommodation can demonstrate that barrier removal is not readily achievable, the public accommodation shall not fail to make its goods, services, facilities, privileges, advantages, or accommodations available through alternative methods, if those methods are readily achievable.

(b) *Examples.* Examples of alternatives to barrier removal include, but are not limited to, the following actions —

(1) Providing curb service or home delivery;

(2) Retrieving merchandise from inaccessible shelves or racks;

(3) Relocating activities to accessible locations;

(c) *Multiscreen cinemas.* If it is not readily achievable to remove barriers to provide access by persons with mobility impairments to all of the theaters of a multiscreen cinema, the cinema shall establish a film rotation schedule that provides reasonable access for individuals who use wheelchairs to all films. Reasonable notice shall be provided to the public as to the location and time of accessible showings.

§ 36.306 Personal devices and services.

This part does not require a public accommodation to provide its customers, clients, or participants with personal devices, such as wheelchairs; individually prescribed devices, such as prescription eyeglasses or hearing aids; or services of a personal nature including assistance in eating, toileting, or dressing.

§ 36.307 Accessible or special goods.

(a) This part does not require a public accommodation to alter its inventory to include accessible or special goods that are designed for, or facilitate use by, individuals with disabilities.

(b) A public accommodation shall order accessible or special goods at the request of an individual with disabilities, if, in the normal course of its operation, it makes special orders on request for unstocked goods, and if the accessible or special goods can be obtained from a supplier with whom the public accommodation customarily does business.

(c) Examples of accessible or special goods include items such as Brailled versions of books, books on audio cassettes, closed-captioned video tapes, special sizes or lines of clothing, and special foods to meet particular dietary needs.

§ 36.308 Seating in assembly areas.

A public accommodation shall ensure that wheelchair spaces and companion seats are provided in each specialty seating area that provides spectators with distinct services or amenities that generally are not available to other spectators. If it is not readily achievable for a public accommodation to place wheelchair spaces and companion seats in each such specialty seating area, it shall provide those services or amenities to individuals with disabilities and their companions at other designated accessible locations at no additional cost. The number of wheelchair spaces and companion seats provided in specialty seating areas shall be included in, rather than in addition to, wheelchair space requirements set forth in table 221.2.1.1 in the 2010 Standards.

§ 36.309 Examinations and courses.

(a) *General.* Any private entity that offers examinations or courses related to applications, licensing, certification, or credentialing for secondary or postsecondary education, professional, or trade purposes shall offer such examinations or courses in a place and manner accessible to persons with disabilities or offer alternative accessible arrangements for such individuals.

(b) *Examinations.*

(1) Any private entity offering an examination covered by this section must assure that —

(i) The examination is selected and administered so as to best ensure that, when the examination is administered to an individual with a disability that impairs sensory, manual, or speaking skills, the examination results accurately reflect the individual's aptitude or achievement level or whatever other factor the examination purports to measure, rather than reflecting the individual's impaired sensory, manual, or speaking skills (except where those skills are the factors that the examination purports to measure);

(ii) An examination that is designed for individuals with impaired sensory, manual, or speaking skills is offered at equally convenient locations, as often, and in as timely a manner as are other examinations; and

(iii) The examination is administered in facilities that are accessible to individuals with disabilities or alternative accessible arrangements are made.

(iv) Any request for documentation, if such documentation is required, is reasonable and limited to the need for the modification, accommodation, or auxiliary aid or service requested.

(v) When considering requests for modifications, accommodations, or auxiliary aids or services, the entity gives considerable weight to documentation of past modifications, accommodations, or auxiliary aids or services received in similar testing situations, as well as such modifications, accommodations, or related aids and services provided in response to an Individualized Education Program (IEP) provided under the Individuals with Disabilities Education Act or a plan describing services provided pursuant to section 504 of the Rehabilitation Act of 1973, as amended (often referred as a Section 504 Plan).

(vi) The entity responds in a timely manner to requests for modifications, accommodations, or aids to ensure equal opportunity for individuals with disabilities.

(2) Required modifications to an examination may include changes in the length of time permitted for completion of the examination and adaptation of the manner in which the examination is given.

(3) A private entity offering an examination covered by this section shall provide appropriate auxiliary aids for persons with impaired sensory, manual, or speaking skills, unless that private entity can demonstrate that offering a particular auxiliary aid would fundamentally alter the measurement of the skills or knowledge the examination is intended to test or would result in an undue burden. Auxiliary aids and services required by this section may include taped examinations, interpreters or other effective methods of making orally delivered materials available to individuals with hearing impairments, Brailled or large print examinations and answer sheets or qualified readers for individuals with visual impairments or learning disabilities, transcribers for individuals with manual impairments, and other similar services and actions.

(4) Alternative accessible arrangements may include, for example, provision of an examination at an individual's home with a proctor if accessible facilities or equipment are unavailable. Alternative arrangements must provide comparable

conditions to those provided for nondisabled individuals.

(c) *Courses.*

(1) Any private entity that offers a course covered by this section must make such modifications to that course as are necessary to ensure that the place and manner in which the course is given are accessible to individuals with disabilities.

(2) Required modifications may include changes in the length of time permitted for the completion of the course, substitution of specific requirements, or adaptation of the manner in which the course is conducted or course materials are distributed.

(3) A private entity that offers a course covered by this section shall provide appropriate auxiliary aids and services for persons with impaired sensory, manual, or speaking skills, unless the private entity can demonstrate that offering a particular auxiliary aid or service would fundamentally alter the course or would result in an undue burden. Auxiliary aids and services required by this section may include taped texts, interpreters or other effective methods of making orally delivered materials available to individuals with hearing impairments, Brailled or large print texts or qualified readers for individuals with visual impairments and learning disabilities, classroom equipment adapted for use by individuals with manual impairments, and other similar services and actions.

(4) Courses must be administered in facilities that are accessible to individuals with disabilities or alternative accessible arrangements must be made.

(5) Alternative accessible arrangements may include, for example, provision of the course through videotape, cassettes, or prepared notes. Alternative arrangements must provide comparable conditions to those provided for nondisabled individuals.

§ 36.310 Transportation provided by public accommodations.

(a) *General.*

(1) A public accommodation that provides transportation services, but that is not primarily engaged in the business of transporting people, is subject to the general and specific provisions in subparts B, C, and D of this part for its transportation operations, except as provided in this section.

(2) *Examples.* Transportation services subject to this section include, but are not limited to, shuttle services operated between transportation terminals and places of public accommodation, customer shuttle bus services operated by private companies and shopping centers, student transportation systems, and transportation provided within recreational facilities such as stadiums, zoos, amusement parks, and ski resorts.

(b) *Barrier removal.* A public accommodation subject to this section shall remove transportation barriers in existing vehicles and rail passenger cars used for transporting individuals (not including barriers that can only be removed through the retrofitting of vehicles or rail passenger cars by the installation of a hydraulic or other lift) where such removal is readily achievable.

(c) *Requirements for vehicles and systems.* A public accommodation subject to this section shall comply with the requirements pertaining to vehicles and transportation systems in the regulations issued by the Secretary of Transportation pursuant to section 306 of the Act.

§ 36.311 Mobility devices.

(a) *Use of wheelchairs and manually-powered mobility aids.* A public accommodation shall permit individuals with mobility disabilities to use wheelchairs and manually-powered mobility aids, such as walkers, crutches, canes, braces, or other similar devices designed for use by individuals with mobility disabilities in any areas open to pedestrian use.

(b) (1) *Use of other power-driven mobility devices.* A public accommodation shall make reasonable modifications in its policies, practices, or procedures to permit the use of other power-driven mobility devices by individuals with mobility disabilities, unless the public accommodation can demonstrate that the class of other power-driven mobility devices cannot be operated in accordance with legitimate safety requirements that the public accommodation has adopted pursuant to § 36.301(b).

(2) *Assessment factors.* In determining whether a particular other power-driven mobility device can be allowed in a specific facility as a reasonable modification under paragraph (b)(1) of this section, a public accommodation shall consider —

(i) The type, size, weight, dimensions, and speed of the device;

(ii) The facility's volume of pedestrian traffic (which may vary at different times of the day, week, month, or year);

(iii) The facility's design and operational characteristics (*e.g.*, whether its business is conducted indoors, its square footage, the density and placement of stationary devices, and the availability of storage for the device, if requested by the user);

(iv) Whether legitimate safety requirements can be established to permit the safe operation of the other power-driven mobility device in the specific facility; and

(v) Whether the use of the other power-driven mobility device creates a substantial risk of serious harm to the immediate environment or natural or cultural resources, or poses a conflict with Federal land management laws and regulations.

(c)

(1) *Inquiry about disability.* A public accommodation shall not ask an individual using a wheelchair or other power-driven mobility device questions about the nature and extent of the individual's disability.

(2) *Inquiry into use of other power-driven mobility device.* A public accommodation may ask a person using an other power-driven mobility device to provide a credible assurance that the mobility device is required

because of the person's disability. A public accommodation that permits the use of an other power-driven mobility device by an individual with a mobility disability shall accept the presentation of a valid, State-issued disability parking placard or card, or State-issued proof of disability, as a credible assurance that the use of the other power-driven mobility device is for the individual's mobility disability. In lieu of a valid, State-issued disability parking placard or card, or State-issued proof of disability, a public accommodation shall accept as a credible assurance a verbal representation, not contradicted by observable fact, that the other power-driven mobility device is being used for a mobility disability. A "valid" disability placard or card is one that is presented by the individual to whom it was issued and is otherwise in compliance with the State of issuance's requirements for disability placards or cards.

§§ 36.312–36.399 [Reserved]

Subpart D New Construction and Alterations

§ 36.401 New construction.

(a) *General.*

(1) Except as provided in paragraphs (b) and (c) of this section, discrimination for purposes of this part includes a failure to design and construct facilities for first occupancy after January 26, 1993, that are readily accessible to and usable by individuals with disabilities.

(2) For purposes of this section, a facility is designed and constructed for first occupancy after January 26, 1993, only —

(i) If the last application for a building permit or permit extension for the facility is certified to be complete, by a State, County, or local government after January 26, 1992 (or, in those jurisdictions where the government does not certify completion of applications, if the last application for a building permit or permit extension for the facility is received by the State, County, or local government after January 26, 1992); and

(ii) If the first certificate of occupancy for the facility is issued after January 26, 1993.

(b) *Commercial facilities located in private residences.*

(1) When a commercial facility is located in a private residence, the portion of the residence used exclusively as a residence is not covered by this subpart, but that portion used exclusively in the operation of the commercial facility or that portion used both for the commercial facility and for residential purposes is covered by the new construction and alterations requirements of this subpart.

(2) The portion of the residence covered under paragraph (b)(1) of this section extends to those elements used to enter the commercial facility, including the homeowner's front sidewalk, if any, the door or entryway, and hallways; and those portions of the residence, interior or exterior, available to or used by employees or visitors of the commercial facility, including restrooms.

(c) *Exception for structural impracticability.*

(1) Full compliance with the requirements of this section is not required where an entity can demonstrate that it is structurally impracticable to meet the requirements. Full compliance will be considered structurally impracticable only in those rare circumstances when the unique characteristics of terrain prevent the incorporation of accessibility features.

(2) If full compliance with this section would be structurally impracticable, compliance with this section is required to the extent that it is not structurally impracticable. In that case, any portion of the facility that can be made accessible shall be made accessible to the extent that it is not structurally impracticable.

(3) If providing accessibility in conformance with this section to individuals with certain disabilities (*e.g.*, those who use wheelchairs) would be structurally impracticable, accessibility shall nonetheless be ensured to persons with other types of disabilities (*e.g.*, those who use crutches or who have sight, hearing, or mental impairments) in accordance with this section.

(d) *Elevator exemption.*

(1) For purposes of this paragraph (d) —

(i) Professional office of a health care provider means a location where a person or entity regulated by a State to provide professional services related to the physical or mental health of an individual makes such services available to the public. The facility housing the "professional office of a health care provider" only includes floor levels housing at least one health care provider, or any floor level designed or intended for use by at least one health care provider.

(ii) Shopping center or shopping mall means —

(A) A building housing five or more sales or rental establishments; or

(B) A series of buildings on a common site, either under common ownership or common control or developed either as one project or as a series of related projects, housing five or more sales or rental establishments. For purposes of this section, places of public accommodation of the types listed in paragraph (5) of the definition of "place of public accommodation" in section § 36.104 are considered sales or rental establishments. The facility housing a "shopping center or shopping mall" only includes floor levels housing at least one sales or rental establishment, or any floor level designed or intended for use by at least one sales or rental establishment.

(2) This section does not require the installation of an elevator in a facility that is less than three stories or has less than 3000 square feet per story, except with respect to any facility that houses one or more of the following:

(i) A shopping center or shopping mall, or a professional office of a health care provider.

(ii) A terminal, depot, or other station used for specified public transportation, or an airport passenger terminal. In such a facility, any area housing passenger services, including boarding and debarking, loading and unloading, baggage claim, dining facilities, and other common areas open to the public, must be on an accessible route from an accessible entrance.

(3) The elevator exemption set forth in this paragraph (d) does not obviate or limit, in any way the obligation to comply with the other accessibility requirements established in paragraph (a) of this section. For example, in a facility that houses a shopping center or shopping mall, or a professional office of a health care provider, the floors that are above or below an accessible ground floor and that do not house sales or rental establishments or a professional office of a health care provider, must meet the requirements of this section but for the elevator.

§ 36.402   Alterations.

(a) *General.*

(1) Any alteration to a place of public accommodation or a commercial facility, after January 26, 1992, shall be made so as to ensure that, to the maximum extent feasible, the altered portions of the facility are readily accessible to and usable by individuals with disabilities, including individuals who use wheelchairs.

(2) An alteration is deemed to be undertaken after January 26, 1992, if the physical alteration of the property begins after that date.

(b) *Alteration.* For the purposes of this part, an alteration is a change to a place of public accommodation or a commercial facility that affects or could affect the usability of the building or facility or any part thereof.

(1) Alterations include, but are not limited to, remodeling, renovation, rehabilitation, reconstruction, historic restoration, changes or rearrangement in structural parts or elements, and changes or rearrangement in the plan configuration of walls and full-height partitions. Normal maintenance, reroofing, painting or wallpapering, asbestos removal, or changes to mechanical and electrical systems are not alterations unless they affect the usability of the building or facility.

(2) If existing elements, spaces, or common areas are altered, then each such altered element, space, or area shall comply with the applicable provisions of appendix A to this part.

(c) *To the maximum extent feasible.* The phrase "to the maximum extent feasible," as used in this section, applies to the occasional case where the nature of an existing facility makes it virtually impossible to comply fully with applicable accessibility standards through a planned alteration. In these circumstances, the alteration shall provide the maximum physical accessibility feasible. Any altered features of the facility that can be made accessible shall be made accessible. If providing accessibility in conformance with this section to individuals with certain disabilities (*e.g.*, those who use wheelchairs) would not be feasible, the facility shall be made accessible to persons with other types of disabilities (*e.g.*, those who use crutches, those who have impaired vision or hearing, or those who have other impairments).

§ 36.403 Alterations: Path of travel.

(a) *General.*

(1) An alteration that affects or could affect the usability of or access to an area of a facility that contains a primary function shall be made so as to ensure that, to the maximum extent feasible, the path of travel to the altered area and the restrooms, telephones, and drinking fountains serving the altered area, are readily accessible to and usable by individuals with disabilities, including individuals who use wheelchairs, unless the cost and scope of such alterations is disproportionate to the cost of the overall alteration.

(2) If a private entity has constructed or altered required elements of a path of travel at a place of public accommodation or commercial facility in accordance with the specifications in the 1991 Standards, the private entity is not required to retrofit such elements to reflect the incremental changes in the 2010 Standards solely because of an alteration to a primary function area served by that path of travel.

(b) *Primary function.* A "primary function" is a major activity for which the facility is intended. Areas that contain a primary function include, but are not limited to, the customer services lobby of a bank, the dining area of a cafeteria, the meeting rooms in a conference center, as well as offices and other work areas in which the activities of the public accommodation or other private entity using the facility are carried out. Mechanical rooms, boiler rooms, supply storage rooms, employee lounges or locker rooms, janitorial closets, entrances, corridors, and restrooms are not areas containing a primary function.

(c) Alterations to an area containing a primary function.

(1) Alterations that affect the usability of or access to an area containing a primary function include, but are not limited to —

(i) Remodeling merchandise display areas or employee work areas in a department store;

(ii) Replacing an inaccessible floor surface in the customer service or employee work areas of a bank;

(iii) Redesigning the assembly line area of a factory; or

(iv) Installing a computer center in an accounting firm.

(2) For the purposes of this section, alterations to windows, hardware, controls, electrical outlets, and signage shall not be deemed to be alterations that affect the usability of or access to an area containing a primary function.

(d) *Landlord/tenant:* If a tenant is making alterations as defined in § 36.402 that would trigger the requirements of this section, those alterations by the tenant in areas that only the tenant occupies do not trigger a path of travel obligation upon the landlord with respect to areas of the facility under the landlord's authority, if those areas are not otherwise being altered.

(e) *Path of travel.*

(1) A "path of travel" includes a continuous, unobstructed way of pedestrian passage by means of which the altered area may be approached, entered, and exited, and which connects the altered area with an exterior approach (including sidewalks, streets, and parking areas), an entrance to the facility, and other parts of the facility.

(2) An accessible path of travel may consist of walks and sidewalks, curb ramps and other interior or exterior pedestrian ramps; clear floor paths through lobbies, corridors, rooms, and other improved areas; parking access aisles; elevators and lifts; or a combination of these elements.

(3) For the purposes of this part, the term "path of travel" also includes the restrooms, telephones, and drinking fountains serving the altered area.

(f) *Disproportionality.*

(1) Alterations made to provide an accessible path of travel to the altered area will be deemed disproportionate to the overall alteration when the cost exceeds 20% of the cost of the alteration to the primary function area.

(2) Costs that may be counted as expenditures required to provide an accessible path of travel may include:

(i) Costs associated with providing an accessible entrance and an accessible route to the altered area, for example, the cost of widening doorways or installing ramps;

(ii) Costs associated with making restrooms accessible, such as installing grab bars, enlarging toilet stalls, insulating pipes, or installing accessible faucet controls;

(iii) Costs associated with providing accessible telephones, such as relocating the telephone to an accessible height, installing amplification devices, **or installing a text telephone (TTY);**

(iv) Costs associated with relocating an inaccessible drinking fountain.

(g) Duty to provide accessible features in the event of disproportionality.

(1) When the cost of alterations necessary to make the path of travel to the altered area fully accessible is disproportionate to the cost of the overall alteration, the path of travel shall be made accessible to the extent that it can be made accessible without incurring disproportionate costs.

(2) In choosing which accessible elements to provide, priority should be given to those elements that will provide the greatest access, in the following order:

(i) An accessible entrance;

(ii) An accessible route to the altered area;

(iii) At least one accessible restroom for each sex or a single unisex restroom;

(iv) Accessible telephones;

(v) Accessible drinking fountains; and

(vi) When possible, additional accessible elements such as parking, storage, and alarms.

(h) Series of smaller alterations.

(1) The obligation to provide an accessible path of travel may not be evaded by performing a series of small alterations to the area served by a single path of travel if those alterations could have been performed as a single undertaking.

(2) (i) If an area containing a primary function has been altered without providing an accessible path of travel to that area, and subsequent alterations of that area, or a different area on the same path of travel, are undertaken within three years of the original alteration, the total cost of alterations to the primary function areas on that path of travel during the preceding three year period shall be considered in determining whether the cost of making that path of travel accessible is disproportionate.

(ii) Only alterations undertaken after January 26, 1992, shall be considered in determining if the cost of providing an accessible path of travel is disproportionate to the overall cost of the alterations.

§ 36.404 Alterations: Elevator exemption.

(a) This section does not require the installation of an elevator in an altered facility that is less than three stories or has less than 3,000 square feet per story, except with respect to any facility that houses a shopping center, a shopping mall, the professional office of a health care provider, a terminal, depot, or other station used for specified public transportation, or an airport passenger terminal.

(1) For the purposes of this section, "professional office of a health care provider" means a location where a person or entity regulated by a State to provide professional services related to the physical or mental health of an individual makes such services available to the public. The facility that houses a "professional office of a health care provider" only includes floor levels housing by at least one health care provider, or any floor level designed or intended for use by at least one health care provider.

(2) For the purposes of this section, shopping center or shopping mall means —

(i) A building housing five or more sales or rental establishments; or

(ii) A series of buildings on a common site, connected by a common pedestrian access route above or below the ground floor, that is either under common ownership or common control or developed either as one project or as a series of related projects, housing five or more sales or rental establishments. For purposes of this section, places of public accommodation of the types listed in paragraph (5) of the definition of "place of public accommodation" in § 36.104 are considered sales or rental establishments. The facility housing a "shopping center or shopping mall" only includes floor levels housing at least one sales or rental establishment, or any floor level designed or intended for use by at least one sales or rental establishment.

(b) The exemption provided in paragraph (a) of this section does not obviate or limit in any way the obligation to comply with the other accessibility requirements established in this subpart. For example, alterations to floors above or below the accessible ground floor must be accessible regardless of whether the altered facility has an elevator.

§ 36.405   Alterations: Historic preservation.

(a) Alterations to buildings or facilities that are eligible for listing in the National Register of Historic Places under the National Historic Preservation Act (16 U.S.C. 470 *et seq.*) or are designated as historic under State or local law, shall comply to the maximum extent feasible with **this part**.

(b) **If it is determined that it is not feasible to provide physical access to an historic property that is a place of public accommodation in a manner that will not threaten or destroy the historic significance of the building or the facility, alternative methods of access shall be provided pursuant to the requirements of subpart C of this part.**

§ 36.406   Standards for new construction and alterations.

(a) *Accessibility standards and compliance date.*

(1) **New construction and alterations subject to §§ 36.401 or 36.402 shall comply with the 1991 Standards if the date when the last application for a building permit or permit extension is certified to be complete by a State, county, or local government (or, in those jurisdictions where the government does not certify completion of applications, if the date when the last application for a building permit or permit extension is received by the State, county, or local government) is before September 15, 2010, or if no permit is required, if the start of physical construction or alterations occurs before September 15, 2010.**

(2) **New construction and alterations subject to §§ 36.401 or 36.402 shall comply either with the 1991 Standards or with the 2010 Standards if the date when the last application for a building permit or permit extension is certified to be complete by a State, county, or local government (or, in those jurisdictions where the government does not certify completion of applications, if the date when the last application for a building permit or permit extension is received by the State, county, or local government) is on or after September 15, 2010, and before March 15, 2012, or if no permit is required, if the start of physical construction or alterations occurs on or after September 15, 2010, and before March 15, 2012.**

(3) **New construction and alterations subject to §§ 36.401 or 36.402 shall comply with the 2010 Standards if the date when the last application for a building permit or permit extension is certified to be complete by a State, county, or local government (or, in those jurisdictions where the government does not certify completion of applications, if the date when the last application for a building permit or permit extension is received by the State, county, or local government) is on or after March 15, 2012, or if no permit is required, if the start of physical construction or alterations occurs on or after March 15, 2012.**

(4) For the purposes of this section, "start of physical construction or alterations" does not mean ceremonial groundbreaking or razing of structures prior to site preparation.

(5) *Noncomplying new construction and alterations.*

(i) Newly constructed or altered facilities or elements covered by §§ 36.401 or 36.402 that were constructed or altered before March 15, 2012, and that do not comply with the 1991 Standards shall, before March 15, 2012, be made accessible in accordance with either the 1991 Standards or the 2010 Standards.

(ii) Newly constructed or altered facilities or elements covered by §§ 36.401 or 36.402 that are constructed or altered on or after March 15, 2012, that do not comply with the 1991 Standards shall, on or after March 15, 2012, be made accessible in accordance with the 2010 Standards.

Appendix to § 36.406(a)

Compliance Dates for New Construction and Alterations	Applicable Standards
On or after January 26, 1993 and before September 15, 2010	1991 Standards
On or after September 15, 2010, and before March 15, 2012	1991 Standards or 2010 Standards
On or after March 15, 2012	2010 Standards

(b) *Scope of coverage.* The 1991 Standards and the 2010 Standards apply to fixed or built-in elements of buildings, structures, site improvements, and pedestrian routes or vehicular ways located on a site. Unless specifically stated otherwise, advisory notes, appendix notes, and figures contained in the 1991 Standards and 2010 Standards explain or illustrate the requirements of the rule; they do not establish enforceable requirements.

(c) *Places of lodging.* Places of lodging subject to this part shall comply with the provisions of the 2010 Standards applicable to transient lodging, including, but not limited to, the requirements for transient lodging guest rooms in sections 224 and 806 of the 2010 Standards.

(1) *Guest rooms.* Guest rooms with mobility features in places of lodging subject to the transient lodging requirements of 2010 Standards shall be provided as follows —

(i) Facilities that are subject to the same permit application on a common site that each have 50 or fewer guest rooms may be combined for the purposes of determining the required number of accessible rooms and type of accessible bathing facility in accordance with table 224.2 to section 224.2 of the 2010 Standards.

(ii) Facilities with more than 50 guest rooms shall be treated separately for the purposes of determining the required number of accessible rooms and type of accessible bathing facility in accordance with table 224.2 to section 224.2 of the 2010 Standards.

(2) *Exception.* Alterations to guest rooms in places of lodging where the guest rooms are not owned or substantially controlled by the entity that owns, leases, or operates the overall facility and the physical features of the guest room interiors are controlled by their individual owners are not required to comply with § 36.402 or the alterations requirements in section 224.1.1 of the 2010 Standards.

(3) *Facilities with residential units and transient lodging units.* Residential dwelling units that are designed and constructed for residential use exclusively are not subject to the transient lodging standards.

(d) *Social service center establishments.* Group homes, halfway houses, shelters, or similar social service center establishments that provide either temporary sleeping accommodations or residential dwelling units that are subject to this part shall comply with the provisions of the 2010 Standards applicable to residential facilities, including, but not limited to, the provisions in sections 233 and 809.

(1) In sleeping rooms with more than 25 beds covered by this part, a minimum of 5% of the beds shall have clear floor space complying with section 806.2.3 of the 2010 Standards.

(2) Facilities with more than 50 beds covered by this part that provide common use bathing facilities shall provide at least one roll-in shower with a seat that complies with the relevant provisions of section 608 of the 2010 Standards. Transfer-type showers are not permitted in lieu of a roll-in shower with a seat, and the exceptions in sections 608.3 and 608.4 for residential dwelling units are not permitted. When separate shower facilities are provided for men and for women, at least one roll-in shower shall be provided for each group.

(e) *Housing at a place of education.* Housing at a place of education that is subject to this part shall comply with the provisions of the 2010 Standards applicable to transient lodging, including, but not limited to, the requirements for transient lodging guest rooms in sections 224 and 806, subject to the following exceptions. For the purposes of the application of this section, the term "sleeping room" is intended to be used interchangeably with the term "guest room" as it is used in the transient lodging standards.

(1) Kitchens within housing units containing accessible sleeping rooms with mobility features (including suites and clustered sleeping rooms) or on floors containing accessible sleeping rooms with mobility features shall provide turning spaces that comply with section 809.2.2 of the 2010 Standards and kitchen work surfaces that comply with section 804.3 of the 2010 Standards.

(2) Multi-bedroom housing units containing accessible sleeping rooms with mobility features shall have an accessible route throughout the unit in accordance with section 809.2 of the 2010 Standards.

(3) Apartments or townhouse facilities that are provided by or on behalf of a place of education, which are leased on a year-round basis exclusively to

graduate students or faculty and do not contain any public use or common use areas available for educational programming, are not subject to the transient lodging standards and shall comply with the requirements for residential facilities in sections 233 and 809 of the 2010 Standards.

(f) *Assembly areas.* Assembly areas that are subject to this part shall comply with the provisions of the 2010 Standards applicable to assembly areas, including, but not limited to, sections 221 and 802. In addition, assembly areas shall ensure that —

(1) In stadiums, arenas, and grandstands, wheelchair spaces and companion seats are dispersed to all levels that include seating served by an accessible route;

(2) In assembly areas that are required to horizontally disperse wheelchair spaces and companion seats by section 221.2.3.1 of the 2010 Standards and that have seating encircling, in whole or in part, a field of play or performance, wheelchair spaces and companion seats are dispersed around that field of play or performance area;

(3) Wheelchair spaces and companion seats are not located on (or obstructed by) temporary platforms or other movable structures, except that when an entire seating section is placed on temporary platforms or other movable structures in an area where fixed seating is not provided, in order to increase seating for an event, wheelchair spaces and companion seats may be placed in that section. When wheelchair spaces and companion seats are not required to accommodate persons eligible for those spaces and seats, individual, removable seats may be placed in those spaces and seats;

(4) In stadium-style movie theaters, wheelchair spaces and companion seats are located on a riser or cross-aisle in the stadium section that satisfies at least one of the following criteria —

(i) It is located within the rear 60% of the seats provided in an auditorium; or

(ii) It is located within the area of an auditorium in which the vertical viewing angles (as measured to the top of the screen) are from the 40th to the 100th percentile of vertical viewing angles for all seats as ranked from the seats in the first row (1st percentile) to seats in the back row (100th percentile).

(g) *Medical care facilities.* Medical care facilities that are subject to this part shall comply with the provisions of the 2010 Standards applicable to medical care facilities, including, but not limited to, sections 223 and 805. In addition, medical care facilities that do not specialize in the treatment of conditions that affect mobility shall disperse the accessible patient bedrooms required by section 223.2.1 of the 2010 Standards in a manner that is proportionate by type of medical specialty.

§§ 36.407–36.499   [Reserved]

Subpart E   Enforcement

§ 36.501   Private suits.

(a) *General.* Any person who is being subjected to discrimination on the basis of disability in violation of the Act or this part or who has reasonable grounds for believing that such person is about to be subjected to discrimination in violation of section 303 of the Act or subpart D of this part may institute a civil action for preventive relief, including an application for a permanent or temporary injunction, restraining order, or other order. Upon timely application, the court may, in its discretion, permit the Attorney General to intervene in the civil action if the Attorney General or his or her designee certifies that the case is of general public importance. Upon application by the complainant and in such circumstances as the court may deem just, the court may appoint an attorney for such complainant and may authorize the commencement of the civil action without the payment of fees, costs, or security. Nothing in this section shall require a person with a disability to engage in a futile gesture if the person has actual notice that a person or organization covered by title III of the Act or this part does not intend to comply with its provisions.

(b) *Injunctive relief.* In the case of violations of § 36.304, §§ 36.308, 36.310(b), 36.401, 36.402, 36.403, and 36.405 of this part, injunctive relief shall include an order to alter facilities to make such facilities readily accessible to and usable by individuals with disabilities to the extent required by the Act or this part. Where appropriate, injunctive relief shall also include requiring the provision of an auxiliary aid or service, modification of a policy, or provision of alternative methods, to the extent required by the Act or this part.

§ 36.502   Investigations and compliance reviews.

(a) The Attorney General shall investigate alleged violations of the Act or this part.

(b) Any individual who believes that he or she or a specific class of persons has been subjected to discrimination prohibited by the Act or this part may request the Department to institute an investigation.

(c) Where the Attorney General has reason to believe that there may be a violation of this part, he or she may initiate a compliance review.

§ 36.503   Suit by the Attorney General.

Following a compliance review or investigation under § 36.502, or at any other time in his or her discretion, the Attorney General may commence a civil action in any appropriate United States district court if the Attorney General has reasonable cause to believe that —

(a) Any person or group of persons is engaged in a pattern or practice of discrimination in violation of the Act or this part; or

(b) Any person or group of persons has been discriminated against in violation of the Act or this part and the discrimination raises an issue of general public importance.

§ 36.504 Relief.

(a) *Authority of court.* In a civil action under § 36.503, the court —

(1) May grant any equitable relief that such court considers to be appropriate, including, to the extent required by the Act or this part —

(i) Granting temporary, preliminary, or permanent relief;

(ii) Providing an auxiliary aid or service, modification of policy, practice, or procedure, or alternative method; and

(iii) Making facilities readily accessible to and usable by individuals with disabilities;

(2) May award other relief as the court considers to be appropriate, including monetary damages to persons aggrieved when requested by the Attorney General; and

(3) May, to vindicate the public interest, assess a civil penalty against the entity in an amount

(i) Not exceeding $50,000 for a first violation occurring before September 29, 1999, and not exceeding $55,000 for a first violation occurring on or after September 29, 1999; and

(ii) Not exceeding $100,000 for any subsequent violation occurring before September 29, 1999, and not exceeding $110,000 for any subsequent violation occurring on or after September 29, 1999.

(b) *Single violation.* For purposes of paragraph (a) (3) of this section, in determining whether a first or subsequent violation has occurred, a determination in a single action, by judgment or settlement, that the covered entity has engaged in more than one discriminatory act shall be counted as a single violation.

(c) *Punitive damages.* For purposes of paragraph (a)(2) of this section, the terms "monetary damages" and "such other relief" do not include punitive damages.

(d) *Judicial consideration.* In a civil action under § 36.503, the court, when considering what amount of civil penalty, if any, is appropriate, shall give consideration to any good faith effort or attempt to comply with this part by the entity. In evaluating good faith, the court shall consider, among other factors it deems relevant, whether the entity could have reasonably anticipated the need for an appropriate type of auxiliary aid needed to accommodate the unique needs of a particular individual with a disability.

§ 36.505 Attorneys fees.

In any action or administrative proceeding commenced pursuant to the Act or this part, the court or agency, in its discretion, may allow the prevailing party, other than the United States, a reasonable attorney's fee, including litigation expenses, and costs, and the United States shall be liable for the foregoing the same as a private individual.

§ 36.506   Alternative means of dispute resolution.

Where appropriate and to the extent authorized by law, the use of alternative means of dispute resolution, including settlement negotiations, conciliation, facilitation, mediation, factfinding, minitrials, and arbitration, is encouraged to resolve disputes arising under the Act and this part.

§ 36.507   Effect of unavailability of technical assistance.

A public accommodation or other private entity shall not be excused from compliance with the requirements of this part because of any failure to receive technical assistance, including any failure in the development or dissemination of any technical assistance manual authorized by the Act.

§ 36.508   Effective date.

(a)   *General.* Except as otherwise provided in this section and in this part, this part shall become effective on January 26, 1992.

(b)   *Civil actions.* Except for any civil action brought for a violation of section 303 of the Act, no civil action shall be brought for any act or omission described in section 302 of the Act that occurs —

(1) Before July 26, 1992, against businesses with 25 or fewer employees and gross receipts of $1,000,000 or less.

(2) Before January 26, 1993, against businesses with 10 or fewer employees and gross receipts of $500,000 or less.

(c)   Transportation services provided by public accommodations. Newly purchased or leased vehicles required to be accessible by § 36.310 must be readily accessible to and usable by individuals with disabilities, including individuals who use wheelchairs, if the solicitation for the vehicle is made after August 25, 1990.

§§ 36.509–36.599   [Reserved]

Subpart F   Certification of State Laws or Local Building Codes

§ 36.601   Definitions.

Assistant Attorney General means the Assistant Attorney General for Civil Rights or his or her designee.

Certification of equivalency means a final certification that a code meets or exceeds the minimum requirements of title III of the Act for accessibility and usability of facilities covered by that title.

Code means a State law or local building code or similar ordinance, or part thereof, that establishes accessibility requirements.

Model code means a nationally recognized document developed by a private entity for use by State or local jurisdictions in developing codes as defined in this section. A model code is intended for incorporation by reference or adoption in whole or in part, with or without amendment, by State or local jurisdictions.

Preliminary determination of equivalency means a preliminary determination that a code appears to meet or exceed the minimum requirements of title III of the Act for accessibility and usability of facilities covered by that title.

Submitting official means the State or local official who —

(1) Has principal responsibility for administration of a code, or is authorized to submit a code on behalf of a jurisdiction; and

(2) Files a request for certification under this subpart.

§ 36.602 General rule.

On the application of a State or local government, the Assistant Attorney General may certify that a code meets or exceeds the minimum requirements of the Act for the accessibility and usability of places of public accommodation and commercial facilities under this part by issuing a certification of equivalency. At any enforcement proceeding under title III of the Act, such certification shall be rebuttable evidence that such State law or local ordinance does meet or exceed the minimum requirements of title III.

§ 36.603 Preliminary determination. *(Redesignated from Section 36.604)*

Upon receipt and review of all information relevant to a request filed by a submitting official for certification of a code, and after consultation with the Architectural and Transportation Barriers Compliance Board, the Assistant Attorney General shall make a preliminary determination of equivalency or a preliminary determination to deny certification.

§ 36.604 Procedure following preliminary determination of equivalency. *(Redesignated from Section 36.605)*

(a) If the Assistant Attorney General makes a preliminary determination of equivalency under § 36.603, he or she shall inform the submitting official, in writing, of that preliminary determination. The Assistant Attorney General also shall —

(1) Publish a notice in the Federal Register that advises the public of the preliminary determination of equivalency with respect to the particular code, and invite interested persons and organizations, including individuals with disabilities, during a period of at least 60 days following publication of the notice, to file written comments relevant to whether a final certification of equivalency should be issued;

(2) After considering the information received in response to the notice described in paragraph (a) of this section, and after publishing a separate notice in the *Federal Register*, hold an informal hearing, **in the State or local jurisdiction charged with administration and enforcement of the code, at which interested individuals,** including individuals with disabilities, are provided an opportunity to express their views with respect to the preliminary determination of equivalency; and

(b) The Assistant Attorney General, after consultation with the Architectural and Transportation Barriers Compliance Board **and consideration of the materials and information submitted pursuant to this section, as well as information**

provided previously by the submitting official, shall issue either a certification of equivalency or a final determination to deny the request for certification. **The Assistant Attorney General** shall publish notice of the certification of equivalency or denial of certification in the *Federal Register.*

§ 36.605   Procedure following preliminary denial of certification. *(Redesignated from Section 36.606)*

(a) If the Assistant Attorney General makes a preliminary determination to deny certification of a code under § 36.603, he or she shall notify the submitting official of the determination.

(b) The Assistant Attorney General shall allow the submitting official not less than 15 days to submit data, views, and arguments in opposition to the preliminary determination to deny certification. If the submitting official does not submit materials, the Assistant Attorney General shall not be required to take any further action. If the submitting official submits materials, the Assistant Attorney General shall evaluate those materials and any other relevant information. After evaluation of any newly submitted materials, the Assistant Attorney General shall make either a final denial of certification or a preliminary determination of equivalency.

§ 36.606   Effect of certification. *(Redesignated from Section 36.607)*

(a) (1) A certification shall be considered a certification of equivalency only with respect to those features or elements that are both covered by the certified code and addressed by the standards against which equivalency is measured.

(2) For example, if certain equipment is not covered by the code, the determination of equivalency cannot be used as evidence with respect to the question of whether equipment in a building built according to the code satisfies the Act's requirements with respect to such equipment. By the same token, certification would not be relevant to construction of a facility for children, if the regulations against which equivalency is measured do not address children's facilities.

(b) A certification of equivalency is effective only with respect to the particular edition of the code for which certification is granted. Any amendments or other changes to the code after the date of the certified edition are not considered part of the certification.

(c) A submitting official may reapply for certification of amendments or other changes to a code that has already received certification.

(d) When the standards of the Act against which a code is deemed equivalent are revised or amended substantially, a certification of equivalency issued under the preexisting standards is no longer effective, as of the date the revised standards take effect. However, construction in compliance with a certified code during the period when a certification of equivalency was effective shall be considered rebuttable evidence of compliance with the Standards then in effect as to those elements of buildings and facilities that comply with the certified code. A submitting official may reapply for certification pursuant to the Act's revised standards, and, to the extent possible, priority will be afforded

the request in the review process.

§ 36.607 Guidance concerning model codes. *(Redesignated from Section 36.608)*

Upon application by an authorized representative of a private entity responsible for developing a model code, the Assistant Attorney General may review the relevant model code and issue guidance concerning whether and in what respects the model code is consistent with the minimum requirements of the Act for the accessibility and usability of places of public accommodation and commercial facilities under this part.

Chapter 7
DOJ ADA TITLE III
SECTION BY SECTION ANALYSIS

28 CFR PART 36 APPENDIX B

Appendix A to Part 36 — Guidance on Revisions to ADA Regulation on Nondiscrimination on the Basis of Disability by Public Accommodations and Commercial Facilities

This revised title III regulation integrates the Department's new regulatory provisions with the text of the existing title III regulation that was unchanged by the 2010 revisions.

[**Note:** This Appendix contains guidance providing a section-by-section analysis of the revisions to 28 CFR part 36 published on September 15, 2010.]

SECTION-BY-SECTION ANALYSIS AND RESPONSE TO PUBLIC COMMENTS

This section provides a detailed description of the Department's changes to the title III regulation, the reasoning behind those changes, and responses to public comments received on these topics. The Section-by-Section Analysis follows the order of the title III regulation itself, except that if the Department has not changed a regulatory section, the unchanged section has not been mentioned.

Subpart A — General

Section 36.104 Definitions.

"1991 Standards" and "2004 ADAAG"

The Department has included in the final rule new definitions of both the "1991 Standards" and the "2004 ADAAG." The term "1991 Standards" refers to the ADA Standards for Accessible Design, originally published on July 26, 1991, and republished as Appendix D to 28 CFR part 36. The term "2004 ADAAG" refers to ADA Chapter 1, ADA Chapter 2, and Chapters 3 through 10 of the Americans with Disabilities Act and the Architectural Barriers Act Accessibility Guidelines, which were issued by the Access Board on July 23, 2004, codified at 36 CFR 1191, app. B and D (2009), and which the Department has adopted in this final rule. These terms are included in the definitions section for ease of reference.

"2010 Standards"

The Department has added to the final rule a definition of the term "2010 Standards." The term "2010 Standards" refers to the 2010 ADA Standards for Accessible Design, which consist of the 2004 ADAAG and the requirements contained in subpart D of 28 CFR part 36.

"Direct Threat"

The final rule moves the definition of direct threat from § 36.208(b) to the definitions section at § 36.104. This is an editorial change. Consequently, § 36.208(c) becomes § 36.208(b) in the final rule.

"Existing Facility"

The 1991 title III regulation provided definitions for "new construction" at § 36.401(a) and "alterations" at § 36.402(b). In contrast, the term "existing facility" was not explicitly defined, although it is used in the statute and regulations for titles II and III. *See, e.g.*, 42 U.S.C. 12182(b)(2)(A)(iv); 28 CFR 35.150. It has been the Department's view that newly constructed or altered facilities are also existing facilities subject to title III's continuing barrier removal obligation, and that view is made explicit in this rule.

The classification of facilities under the ADA is neither static nor mutually exclusive. Newly constructed or altered facilities are also existing facilities. A newly constructed facility remains subject to the accessibility standards in effect at the time of design and construction, with respect to those elements for which, at that time, there were applicable ADA Standards. That same facility, however, after construction, is also an existing facility, and subject to the public accommodation's continuing obligation to remove barriers where it is readily achievable to do so. The fact that the facility is also an existing facility does not relieve the public accommodation of its obligations under the new construction requirements of this part. Rather, it means that in addition to the new construction requirements, the public accommodation has a continuing obligation to remove barriers that arise, or are deemed barriers, only after construction. Such barriers include but are not limited to the elements that are first covered in the 2010 Standards, as that term is defined in § 36.104.

At some point, the same facility may undergo alterations, which are subject to the alterations requirements in effect at that time. This facility remains subject to its original new construction standards for elements and spaces not affected by the alterations; the facility is subject to the alterations requirements and standards in effect at the time of the alteration for the elements and spaces affected by the alteration; and, throughout, the facility remains subject to the continuing barrier removal obligation.

The Department's enforcement of the ADA is premised on a broad understanding of "existing facility." The ADA contemplates that as the Department's knowledge and understanding of accessibility advances and evolves, this knowledge will be incorporated into and result in increased accessibility in the built environment. Title III's barrier removal provisions strike the appropriate balance between ensuring that accessibility advances are reflected in the built environment and mitigating the costs of those advances to public accommodations. With adoption of the final rule, public accommodations engaged in barrier removal measures will now be guided by the 2010 Standards, defined in § 36.104, and the safe harbor in § 36.304(d)(2).

The NPRM included the following proposed definition of "existing facility": "[A] facility that has been constructed and remains in existence on any given date." 73 FR 34508, 34552 (June 17, 2008). While the Department intended the proposed definition to provide clarity with respect to public accommodations' continuing obligation to remove barriers where it is readily achievable to do so, some commenters pointed out arguable ambiguity in the language and the potential for misapplication of the rule in practice.

The Department received a number of comments on this issue. The commenters urged the Department to clarify that all buildings remain subject to the standards in effect at the time of their construction, that is, that a facility designed and constructed for first occupancy between January 26, 1993, and the effective date of the final rule is still considered "new construction" and that alterations occurring between January 26, 1993, and the effective date of the final rule are still considered "alterations."

The final rule includes clarifying language to ensure that the Department's interpretation is accurately reflected. As established by this rule, existing facility means a facility in existence on any given date, without regard to whether the facility may also be considered newly constructed or altered under this part. Thus, this definition reflects the Department's longstanding interpretation that public accommodations have obligations in existing facilities that are independent of but may coexist with requirements imposed by new construction or alteration requirements in those same facilities.

"Housing at a Place of Education"

The Department has added a new definition to § 36.104, "housing at a place of education," to clarify the types of educational housing programs that are covered by this title. This section defines "housing at a place of education" as "housing operated by or on behalf of an elementary, secondary, undergraduate, or postgraduate school, or other place of education, including dormitories, suites, apartments, or other places of residence." This definition does not apply to social service programs that combine residential housing with social services, such as a residential job training program.

"Other Power-Driven Mobility Device" and "Wheelchair"

Because relatively few individuals with disabilities were using nontraditional mobility devices in 1991, there was no pressing need for the 1991 title III regulation to define the terms "wheelchair" or "other power-driven mobility device," to expound on what would constitute a reasonable modification in policies, practices, or procedures under § 36.302, or to set forth within that section specific requirements for the accommodation of mobility devices. Since the issuance of the 1991 title III regulation, however, the choices of mobility devices available to individuals with disabilities have increased dramatically. The Department has received complaints about and has become aware of situations where individuals with mobility disabilities have utilized devices that are not designed primarily for use by an individual with a mobility disability, including the Segway® Personal Transporter (Segway® PT), golf cars, all-terrain vehicles (ATVs), and other locomotion devices.

The Department also has received questions from public accommodations and individuals with mobility disabilities concerning which mobility devices must be accommodated and under what circumstances. Indeed, there has been litigation concerning the legal obligations of covered entities to accommodate individuals with mobility disabilities who wish to use an electronic personal assistance mobility device (EPAMD), such as the Segway® PT, as a mobility device. The Department has participated in such litigation as amicus curiae. See Ault v. Walt Disney World Co., 2009 U.S. Dist. LEXIS 92911 (M.D. Fla. Oct. 6, 2009). Much of the litigation has involved shopping malls where businesses have refused to allow persons with disabilities to use EPAMDs. See, e.g., McElroy v. Simon Property Group, 2008 U.S. Dist. LEXIS 69622 (D. Kan. Sept. 15, 2008) (enjoining mall from prohibiting the use of a Segway® PT as a mobility device where an individual agrees to all of a mall's policies for use of the device, except indemnification); Shasta Clark, Local Man Fighting Mall Over Right to Use Segway, WATE 6 News, July 26, 2005, available at http://www.wate.com/ Global/story.asp?s=3643674 (last visited June 24, 2010).

In response to questions and complaints from individuals with disabilities and covered entities concerning which mobility devices must be accommodated and under what circumstances, the Department began developing a framework to address the use of unique mobility devices, concerns about their safety, and the parameters for the circumstances under which these devices must be accommodated. As a result, the Department's NPRM proposed two new approaches to mobility devices. First, the Department proposed a two-tiered mobility device definition that defined the term "wheelchair" separately from "other power-driven mobility device." Second, the Department proposed requirements to allow the use of devices in each definitional category. In § 36.311(a), the NPRM proposed that wheelchairs and manually-powered mobility aids used by individuals with mobility disabilities shall be permitted in any areas open to pedestrian use. Section 36.311(b) of the NPRM proposed that a public accommodation "shall make reasonable modifications in its policies, practices, and procedures to permit the use of other power-driven mobility devices by individuals with disabilities, unless the public accommodation can demonstrate that the use of the device is not reasonable or that its use will result in a fundamental alteration in the nature of the public accommodation's goods, services, facilities, privileges, advantages, or accommodations." 73 FR 34508, 34556 (June 17, 2008).

The Department sought public comment with regard to whether these steps would, in fact, achieve clarity on these issues. Toward this end, the Department's NPRM asked several questions relating to the definitions of "wheelchair," "other power-driven mobility device," and "manually-powered mobility aids"; the best way to categorize different classes of mobility devices, the types of devices that should be included in each category; and the circumstances under which certain types of mobility devices must be accommodated or may be excluded pursuant to the policy adopted by the public accommodation.

Because the questions in the NPRM that concerned mobility devices and their accommodation were interrelated, many of the commenters' responses did not identify the specific question to which they were responding. Instead, commenters grouped the questions together and provided comments accordingly. Most commenters spoke to the issues addressed in the Department's questions in broad terms and using general concepts. As a result, the responses to the questions posed are discussed below in broadly grouped issue categories rather than on a question-by-question basis.

Two-tiered definitional approach. Commenters supported the Department's proposal to use a two-tiered definition of mobility device. Commenters nearly universally said that wheelchairs always should be accommodated and that they should never be subject to an assessment with regard to their admission to a particular public accommodation. In contrast, the vast majority of commenters indicated they were in favor of allowing public accommodations to conduct an assessment as to whether, and under which circumstances, other power-driven mobility devices will be allowed onsite.

Many commenters also indicated their support for the two-tiered approach in responding to questions concerning the definition of "wheelchair" and "other power-driven mobility device." Nearly every disability advocacy group said that the Department's two-tiered approach strikes the proper balance between ensuring access for individuals with disabilities and addressing fundamental alteration and safety concerns held by public accommodations; however, a minority of disability advocacy groups wanted other power-driven mobility devices to be included in the definition of "wheelchair." Most advocacy, nonprofit, and individual commenters supported the concept of a separate definition for "other power-driven mobility device" because a separate definition would maintain existing legal protections for wheelchairs while recognizing that some devices that are not designed primarily for individuals with mobility disabilities have beneficial uses for individuals with mobility disabilities. They also favored this concept because it recognizes technological developments and that innovative uses of varying devices may provide increased access to individuals with mobility disabilities.

While two business associations indicated that they opposed the concept of "other power-driven mobility device" in its entirety, other business commenters expressed general and industry specific concerns about permitting their use. They indicated that such devices create a host of safety, cost, and fraud issues that do not exist with wheel-chairs. On balance, however, business commenters indicated that they support the establishment of a two-tiered regulatory approach because defining "other power-driven mobility device" separately from "wheelchair" means that businesses will be able to maintain some measure of control over the admission of the former. Virtually all of these commenters indicated that their support for the dual approach and the concept of other power-driven mobility devices was, in large measure, due to the other power-driven mobility device assessment factors in § 36.311(c) of the NPRM.

By maintaining the two-tiered approach to mobility devices and defining "wheelchair" separately from "other power-driven mobility device," the Department is able to preserve the protection users of traditional wheelchairs and other manually-powered mobility aids have had since the ADA was enacted, while also recognizing that human ingenuity, personal choice, and new technologies have led to the use of devices that may be more beneficial for individuals with certain mobility disabilities.

Moreover, the Department believes the two-tiered approach gives public accommodations guidance to follow in assessing whether reasonable modifications can be made to permit the use of other power-driven mobility devices on-site and to aid in the development of policies describing the circumstances under which persons with disabilities may use such devices. The two-tiered approach neither mandates that all other power-driven mobility devices be accommodated in every circumstance, nor excludes these devices from all protection. This approach, in conjunction with the factor assessment provisions in § 36.311(b) (2), will serve as a mechanism by which public accommodations can evaluate their ability to accommodate other power-driven mobility devices. As will be discussed in more detail below, the assessment factors in § 36.311(b)(2) are specifically designed to provide guidance to public accommodations regarding whether it is permissible to bar the use of a specific other power-driven mobility device in a specific facility. In making such a determination, a public accommodation must consider the device's type, size, weight dimensions, and speed; the facility's volume of pedestrian traffic; the facility's design and operational characteristics; whether the device conflicts with legitimate safety requirements; and whether the device poses a substantial risk of serious harm to the immediate environment or natural or cultural resources, or conflicts with Federal land management laws or regulations. In addition, under § 36.311(b)(i) if the public accommodation claims that it cannot make reasonable modifications to its policies, practices, or procedures to permit the use of other power-driven mobility devices by individuals with disabilities, the burden of proof to demonstrate that such devices cannot be operated in accordance with legitimate safety requirements rests upon the public accommodation.

Categorization of wheelchair versus other power-driven mobility devices. Implicit in the creation of the two-tiered mobility device concept is the question of how to categorize which devices are wheelchairs and which are other power-driven mobility devices. Finding weight and size to be too restrictive, the vast majority of advocacy, non-profit, and individual commenters opposed using the Department of Transportation's definition of "common wheelchair" to designate the mobility device's appropriate category. Business commenters who generally supported using weight and size as the method of categorization did so because of their concerns about having to make physical changes to their facilities to accommodate over-sized devices. The vast majority of business commenters also favored using the device's intended use to categorize which devices constitute wheel-chairs and which are other power-driven mobility devices. Furthermore, the intended-use determinant received a fair amount of support from advocacy, nonprofit, and individual com-menters, either because they sought to preserve the broad accommodation of wheelchairs or because they sympathized with concerns about individuals without mobility disabilities fraudulently bringing other power-driven mobility devices into places of public accommodation.

Commenters seeking to have the Segway® PT included in the definition of "wheelchair" objected to classifying mobility devices on the basis of their intended use because they felt that such a classification would be unfair and prejudicial to Segway® PT users and would stifle personal choice, creativity, and innovation. Other advocacy and nonprofit commenters objected to employing an intended-use approach because of concerns that the focus would shift to an assessment of the device, rather than the needs or benefits to the individual with the mobility disability. They were of the view that the mobility-device classification should be based on its function — whether it is used to address a mobility disability. A few commenters raised the concern that an intended-use approach might embolden public accommodations to assess whether an individual with a mobility disability really needs to use the other power-driven mobility device at issue or to question why a wheelchair would not provide sufficient mobility. Those citing objections to the intended-use determinant indicated it would be more appropriate to make the categorization determination based on whether the device is being used for a mobility disability in the context of the impact of its use in a specific environment. Some of these commenters preferred this approach because it would allow the Segway® PT to be included in the definition of "wheelchair."

Some commenters were inclined to categorize mobility devices by the way in which they are powered, such as battery-powered engines versus fuel or combustion engines. One commenter suggested using exhaust level as the determinant. Although there were only a few commenters who would make the determination based on indoor or outdoor use, there was nearly universal support for banning from indoor use devices that are powered by fuel or combustion engines.

A few commenters thought it would be appropriate to categorize the devices based on their maximum speed. Others objected to this approach, stating that circumstances should dictate the appropriate speed at which mobility devices should be operated — for example, a faster speed may be safer when crossing streets than it would be for sidewalk use — and merely because a device can go a certain speed does not mean it will be operated at that speed.

The Department has decided to maintain the device's intended use as the appropriate determinant for which devices are categorized as "wheelchairs." However, because wheelchairs may be intended for use by individuals who have temporary conditions affecting mobility, the Department has decided that it is more appropriate to use the phrase "primarily designed" rather than "solely designed" in making such categorizations. The Department will not foreclose any future technological developments by identifying or banning specific devices or setting restrictions on size, weight, or dimensions. Moreover, devices designed primarily for use by individuals with mobility disabilities often are considered to be medical devices and are generally eligible for insurance reimbursement on this basis. Finally, devices designed primarily for use by individuals with mobility disabilities are less subject to fraud concerns because they were not designed to have a recreational component. Consequently, rarely, if ever, is any inquiry or assessment as to their appropriateness for use in a public accommodation necessary.

Definition of "wheelchair." In seeking public feedback on the NPRM's definition of "wheel-chair," the Department explained its concern that the definition of "wheelchair" in section 508(c) (2) of the ADA (formerly section 507(c)(2), July 26, 1990, 104 Stat. 372, 42 U.S.C. 12207, renumbered section 508(c)(2), Public Law 110–325 section 6(a)(2), Sept. 25, 2008, 122 Stat. 3558), which pertains to Federal wilderness areas, is not specific enough to provide clear guidance in the array of settings covered by title III and that the stringent size and weight requirements for the Department of Transportation's definition of "common wheelchair" are not a good fit in the context of most public accommodations. The Department noted in the NPRM that it sought a definition of "wheelchair" that would include manually-operated and power-driven wheelchairs and mobility scooters (i.e., those that typically are single-user, have three to four wheels, and are appropriate for both indoor and outdoor pedestrian areas), as well as a variety of types of wheelchairs and mobility scooters with individualized or unique features or models with different numbers of wheels. The NPRM defined a wheelchair as "a device designed solely for use by an individual with a mobility impairment for the primary purpose of locomotion in typical indoor and outdoor pedestrian areas. A wheelchair may be manually-operated or power-driven." 73 FR 34508, 34553 (June 17, 2008).

Although the NPRM's definition of "wheel-chair" excluded mobility devices that are not designed solely for use by individuals with mobility disabilities, the Department, noting that the use of the Segway® PT by individuals with mobility disabilities is on the upswing, inquired as to whether this device should be included in the definition of "wheelchair."

Most business commenters wished the definition of "wheelchair" had included size, weight, and dimension maximums. Ultimately, however, they supported the definition because it excludes other power-driven mobility devices and enables them to engage in an assessment to determine whether a particular device can be allowed as a reasonable modification. These commenters felt this approach gave them some measure of control over whether, and under what circumstances, other power-driven mobility devices may be used in their facilities by individuals with mobility disabilities. Two commenters noted that because many mobility scooters are oversized, they are misplaced in the definition of "wheelchair" and belong with other power-driven mobility devices. Another commenter suggested using maximum size and weight requirements to allocate which mobility scooters should be categorized as wheel-chairs, and which should be categorized as other power-driven mobility devices.

Many advocacy, nonprofit, and individual commenters indicated that as long as the Department intends the scope of the term "mobility impairments" to include other disabilities that cause mobility impairments (e.g., respiratory, circulatory, stamina, etc.), they were in support of the language. Several commenters indicated a preference for the definition of "wheelchair" in section 508(c)(2) of the ADA. One commenter indicated a preference for the term "assistive device," as it is defined in the Rehabilitation Act of 1973, over the term "wheelchair." A few commenters indicated that strollers should be added to the preamble's list of examples of wheelchairs because parents of children with disabilities frequently use strollers as mobility devices until their children get older.

In the final rule, the Department has rearranged some wording and has made some changes in the terminology used in the definition of "wheel-chair," but essentially has retained the definition, and therefore the rationale, that was set forth in the NPRM. Again, the text of the ADA makes the definition of "wheelchair" contained in section 508(c)(2) applicable only to the specific context of uses in designated wilderness areas, and therefore does not compel the use of that definition for any other purpose. Moreover, the Department maintains that limiting the definition to devices suitable for use in an "indoor pedestrian area" as provided for in section 508(c)(2) of the ADA would ignore the technological advances in wheelchair design that have occurred since the ADA went into effect and that the inclusion of the phrase "indoor pedestrian area" in the definition of "wheelchair" would set back progress made by individuals with mobility disabilities who, for many years now, have been using devices designed for locomotion in indoor and outdoor settings. The Department has concluded that same rationale applies to placing limits on the size, weight, and dimensions of wheelchairs.

With regard to the term "mobility impairments," the Department intended a broad reading so that a wide range of disabilities, including circulatory and respiratory disabilities, that make walking difficult or impossible, would be included. In response to comments on this issue, the Department has revisited the issue and has concluded that the most apt term to achieve this intent is "mobility disability."

In addition, the Department has decided that it is more appropriate to use the phrase, "primarily" designed for use by individuals with disabilities in the final rule, rather than, "solely" designed for use by individuals with disabilities — the phrase, proposed in the NPRM. The Department believes that this phrase more accurately covers the range of devices the Department intends to fall within the definition of "wheelchair."

After receiving comments that the word "typical" is vague and the phrase "pedestrian areas" is confusing to apply, particularly in the context of similar, but not identical, terms used in the proposed Standards, the Department decided to delete the term "typical indoor and outdoor pedestrian areas" from the final rule. Instead, the final rule references "indoor or * * * both indoor and out-door locomotion," to make clear that the devices that fall within the definition of "wheelchair" are those that are used for locomotion on indoor and outdoor pedestrian paths or routes and not those that are intended exclusively for traversing undefined, unprepared, or unimproved paths or routes. Thus, the final rule defines the term "wheelchair" to mean "a manually operated or power-driven device designed primarily for use by an individual with a mobility disability for the main purpose of indoor or of both indoor and outdoor locomotion."

Whether the definition of "wheelchair" includes the Segway® PT. As discussed above, because individuals with mobility disabilities are using the Segway® PT as a mobility device, the Department asked whether it should be included in the definition of "wheelchair." The basic Segway® PT model is a two-wheeled, gyroscopically-stabilized, battery-powered personal transportation device. The user stands on a platform suspended three inches off the ground by wheels on each side, grasps a T-shaped handle, and steers the device similarly to a bicycle. Most Segway® PTs can travel up to 12½ miles per hour, compared to the average pedestrian walking speed of 3 to 4 miles per hour and the approximate maximum speed for power-operated wheelchairs of 6 miles per hour. In a study of trail and other non-motorized transportation users including EPAMDs, the Federal Highway Administration (FHWA) found that the eye height of individuals using EPAMDs ranged from approximately 69 to 80 inches. *See* Federal Highway Administration, *Characteristics of Emerging Road and Trail Users and Their Safety* (Oct. 14, 2004), available at http://www.tfhrc.gov/safety/pubs/04103 (last visited June 24, 2010). Thus, the Segway® PT can operate at much greater speeds than wheelchairs, and the average user stands much taller than most wheelchair users.

The Segway® PT has been the subject of debate among users, pedestrians, disability advocates, State and local governments, businesses, and bicyclists. The fact that the Segway® PT is not designed primarily for use by individuals with disabilities, nor used primarily by persons with disabilities, complicates the question of to what extent individuals with disabilities should be allowed to operate them in areas and facilities where other power-driven mobility devices are not allowed. Those who question the use of the Segway® PT in pedestrian areas argue that the speed, size, and operating features of the devices make them too dangerous to operate alongside pedestrians and wheelchair users.

Comments regarding whether to include the Segway® PT in the definition of "wheelchair" were, by far, the most numerous received in the category of comments regarding wheelchairs and other power-driven mobility devices. Significant numbers of veterans with disabilities, individuals with multiple sclerosis, and those advocating on their behalf made concise statements of general support for the inclusion of the Segway® PT in the definition of "wheelchair." Two veterans offered extensive comments on the topic, along with a few advocacy and nonprofit groups and individuals with disabilities for whom sitting is uncomfortable or impossible.

While there may be legitimate safety issues for EPAMD users and bystanders in some circumstances, EPAMDs and other nontraditional mobility devices can deliver real benefits to individuals with disabilities. Among the reasons given by commenters to include the Segway® PT in the definition of "wheelchair" were that the Segway® PT is well-suited for individuals with particular conditions that affect mobility including multiple sclerosis, Parkinson's disease, chronic obstructive pulmonary disease, amputations, spinal cord injuries, and other neurological disabilities, as well as functional limitations, such as gait limitation, inability to sit or discomfort in sitting, and diminished stamina issues. Such individuals often find that EPAMDs are more comfortable and easier to use than more traditional mobility devices and assist with balance, circulation, and digestion in ways that wheelchairs do not. *See* Rachel Metz, *Disabled Embrace Segway*, New York Times, Oct. 14, 2004. Commenters specifically cited pressure relief, reduced spasticity, increased stamina, and improved respiratory, neurologic, and muscular health as secondary medical benefits from being able to stand.

Other arguments for including the Segway® PT in the definition of "wheelchair" were based on commenters' views that the Segway® PT offers benefits not provided by wheelchairs and mobility scooters, including its intuitive response to body movement, ability to operate with less coordination and dexterity than is required for many wheelchairs and mobility scooters, and smaller footprint and turning radius as compared to most wheelchairs and mobility scooters. Several commenters mentioned improved visibility, either due to the Segway® PT's raised platform or simply by virtue of being in a standing position. And finally, some commenters advocated for the inclusion of the Segway® PT simply based on civil rights arguments and the empowerment and self-esteem obtained from having the power to select the mobility device of choice.

Many commenters, regardless of their position on whether to include the Segway® PT in the definition of "wheelchair," noted that the Segway® PT's safety record is as good as, if not better, than the record for wheelchairs and mobility scooters.

Most business commenters were opposed to the inclusion of the Segway® PT in the definition of "wheelchair" but were supportive of its inclusion as an "other power-driven mobility device." They raised industry- or venue-specific concerns about including the Segway® PT in the definition of "wheelchair." For example, civic centers, arenas, and theaters were concerned about the impact on sight-line requirements if Segway® PT users remain on their devices in a designated wheelchair seating area; amusement parks expressed concern that rides have been designed, purchased, and installed to enable wheelchair users to transfer easily or to accommodate wheelchairs on the ride itself; and retail stores mentioned size constraints in some stores. Nearly all business commenters expressed concern — and perceived liability issues — related to having to store or stow the Segway® PT, particularly if it could not be stored in an upright position. These commenters cited concerns about possible damage to the device, injury to customers who may trip over it, and theft of the device as a result of not being able to stow the Segway® PT securely.

Virtually every business commenter mentioned concerns about rider safety, as well as concerns for pedestrians unexpectedly encountering these devices or being hit or run over by these devices in crowded venues where maneuvering space is limited. Their main safety objection to the inclusion of the Segway® PT in the definition of "wheelchair" was that the maximum speed at which the Segway® PT can operate is far faster than that of motorized wheelchairs. There was a universal unease among these commenters with regard to relying on the judgment of the Segway® PT user to exercise caution because its top speed is far in excess of a wheelchair's top speed. Many other safety concerns were industry-specific. For example, amusement parks were concerned that the Segway® PT is much taller than children; that it is too quiet to warn pedestrians, particularly those with low vision or who are blind, of their presence; that it may keep moving after a rider has fallen off or power system fails; and that it has a full-power override which automatically engages when an obstacle is encountered. Hotels and retail stores mentioned that maneuvering the Segway® PT through their tight quarters would create safety hazards.

Business commenters also expressed concern that if the Segway® PT were included in the definition of "wheelchair" they would have to make physical changes to their facilities to accommodate Segway® PT riders who stand much taller in these devices than do users of wheelchairs. They also were concerned that if the Segway® 7 PT was included in the definition of "wheelchair," they would have no ability to assess whether it is appropriate to allow the entry of the Segway® PT into their facilities the way they would have if the device is categorized as an "other power-driven mobility device."

Many disability advocacy and nonprofit commenters did not support the inclusion of the Segway® PT in the definition of "wheelchair." Paramount to these comment-ers was the maintenance of existing protections for wheelchair users. Because there was unanimous agreement that wheelchair use rarely, if ever, may be restricted, these commenters strongly favored categorizing wheelchairs separately from the Segway® PT and other power-driven mobility devices and applying the intended-use determinant to assign the devices to either category. They indicated that while they support the greatest degree of access in public accommodations for all persons with disabilities who require the use of mobility devices, they recognize that under certain circumstances allowing the use of other power-driven mobility devices would result in a fundamental alteration or run counter to legitimate safety requirements necessary for the safe operation of a public accommodation. While these groups supported categorizing the Segway® PT as an "other power-driven mobility device," they universally noted that because the Segway® PT does not present environmental concerns and is as safe to use as, if not safer than, a wheelchair, it should be accommodated in most circumstances.

The Department has considered all the comments and has concluded that it should not include the Segway® PT in the definition of "wheelchair." The final rule provides that the test for categorizing a device as a wheelchair or an other power-driven mobility device is whether the device is designed primarily for use by individuals with mobility disabilities. Mobility scooters are included in the definition of "wheelchair" because they are designed primarily for users with mobility disabilities. However, because the current generation of EPAMDs, including the Segway® PT, was designed for recreational users and not primarily for use by individuals with mobility disabilities, the Department has decided to continue its approach of excluding EPAMDs from the definition of "wheelchair" and including them in the definition of "other power-driven mobility device." Although EPAMDs, such as the Segway® PT, are not included in the definition of a "wheelchair," public accommodations must assess whether they can make reasonable modifications to permit individuals with mobility disabilities to use such devices on their premises. The Department recognizes that the Segway® PT provides many benefits to those who use them as mobility devices, including a measure of privacy with regard to the nature of one's particular disability, and believes that in the vast majority of circumstances, the application of the factors described in § 36.311 for providing access to other powered mobility devices will result in the admission of the Segway® PT.

Treatment of "manually-powered mobility aids." The Department's NPRM did not define the term "manually-powered mobility aids." Instead, the NPRM included a non-exhaustive list of examples in § 36.311(a). The NPRM queried whether the Department should maintain this approach to manually-powered mobility aids or whether it should adopt a more formal definition.

Only a few commenters addressed "manually- powered mobility aids." Virtually all commenters were in favor of maintaining a non-exhaustive list of examples of "manually-powered mobility aids" rather than adopting a definition of the term. Of those who commented, a couple sought clarification of the term "manually-powered." One commenter suggested that the term be changed to "human-powered." Other commenters requested that the Department include ordinary strollers in the non-exhaustive list of manually-powered mobility aids. Since strollers are not devices designed primarily for individuals with mobility disabilities, the Department does not consider them to be manually-powered mobility aids; however, strollers used in the context of transporting individuals with disabilities are subject to the same assessment required by the ADA's reasonable modification standards at § 36.302. The Department believes that because the existing approach is clear and understood easily by the public, no formal definition of the term "manually-powered mobility aids" is required.

Definition of "other power-driven mobility device." The Department's NPRM defined the term "other power-driven mobility device" in § 36.104 as "any of a large range of devices powered by batteries, fuel, or other engines — whether or not designed solely for use by individuals with mobility impairments — that are used by individuals with mobility impairments for the purpose of locomotion, including golf cars, bicycles, electronic personal assistance mobility devices (EPAMDs), or any mobility aid designed to operate in areas without defined pedestrian routes." 73 FR 34508, 34552 (June 17, 2008).

Business commenters mostly were supportive of the definition of "other power-driven mobility device" because it gave them the ability to develop policies pertaining to the admission of these devices, but they expressed concern that individuals will feign mobility disabilities so that they can use devices that are otherwise banned in public accommodations. Advocacy, nonprofit, and several individual commenters supported the definition of "other power-driven mobility device" because it allows new technologies to be added in the future, maintains the existing legal protections for wheel-chairs, and recognizes that some devices, particularly the Segway® PT, which are not designed primarily for individuals with mobility disabilities, have beneficial uses for individuals with mobility disabilities.

Despite support for the definition of "other power-driven mobility device," however, most advocacy and nonprofit commenters expressed at least some hesitation about the inclusion of fuel-powered mobility devices in the definition. While virtually all of these commenters noted that a blanket exclusion of any device that falls under the definition of "other power-driven mobility device" would violate basic civil rights concepts, they also specifically stated that certain devices, particularly off-highway vehicles, cannot be permitted in certain circumstances. They also made a distinction between the Segway® PT and other power-driven mobility devices, noting that the Segway® PT should be accommodated in most circumstances because it satisfies the safety and environmental elements of the policy analysis. These commenters indicated that they agree that other power-driven mobility devices must be assessed, particularly as to their environmental impact, before they are accommodated.

Business commenters were even less supportive of the inclusion of fuel-powered devices in the other power-driven mobility devices category. They sought a complete ban on fuel-powered devices because they believe they are inherently dangerous and pose environmental and safety concerns.

Although many commenters had reservations about the inclusion of fuel-powered devices in the definition of other power-driven mobility devices, the Department does not want the definition to be so narrow that it would foreclose the inclusion of new technological developments, whether powered by fuel or by some other means. It is for this reason that the Department has maintained the phrase "any mobility device designed to operate in areas without defined pedestrian routes" in the final rule's definition of other power-driven mobility devices. The Department believes that the limitations provided by "fundamental alteration" and the ability to impose legitimate safety requirements will likely prevent the use of fuel and combustion engine-driven devices indoors, as well as in outdoor areas with heavy pedestrian traffic. The Department notes, however, that in the future technological developments may result in the production of safe fuel-powered mobility devices that do not pose environmental and safety concerns. The final rule allows consideration to be given as to whether the use of a fuel-powered device would create a substantial risk of serious harm to the environment or natural or cultural resources, and to whether the use of such a device conflicts with Federal land management laws or regulations; this aspect of the final rule will further limit the inclusion of fuel-powered devices where they are not appropriate. Consequently, the Department has maintained fuel-powered devices in the definition of "other power-driven mobility devices." The Department has also added language to the definition of "other power-driven mobility device" to reiterate that the definition does not apply to Federal wilderness areas, which are not covered by title II of the ADA; the use of wheelchairs in such areas is governed by section 508(c)(2) of the ADA, 42 U.S.C. 12207(c)(2).

"Place of Public Accommodation"

Definition of "place of lodging." The NPRM stated that a covered "place of lodging" is a facility that provides guest rooms for sleeping for stays that are primarily short-term in nature (generally two weeks or less), to which the occupant does not have the right or intent to return to a specific room or unit after the conclusion of his or her stay, and which operates under conditions and with amenities similar to a hotel, motel, or inn, particularly including factors such as: (1) An on-site proprietor and reservations desk; (2) rooms available on a walk-up basis; (3) linen service; and (4) a policy of accepting reservations for a room type without guaranteeing a particular unit or room until check- in, without a prior lease or security deposit. The NPRM stated that timeshares and condominiums or corporate hotels that did not meet this definition would not be covered by § 36.406(c) of the proposed regulation, but may be covered by the requirements of the Fair Housing Act (FHAct).

In the NPRM, the Department sought comment on its definition of "place of lodging," specifically seeking public input on whether the most appropriate time period for identifying facilities used for stays that primarily are short-term in nature should be set at 2 weeks or 30 days.

The vast majority of the comments received by the Department supported the use of a 30-day limitation on places of lodging as more consistent with building codes, local laws, and common real estate practices that treat stays of 30 days or less as transient rather than residential use. One commenter recommended using the phrase "fourteen days or less." Another commenter objected to any bright line standard, stating that the difference between two weeks and 30 days for purposes of title III is arbitrary, viewed in light of conflicting regulations by the States. This commenter argued the Department should continue its existing practice under title III of looking to State law as one factor in determining whether a facility is used for stays that primarily are short-term in nature.

The Department is persuaded by the majority of commenters to adopt a 30-day guideline for the purposes of identifying facilities that primarily are short-term in nature and has modified the section accordingly. The 30-day guideline is intended only to determine when the final rule's transient lodging provisions apply to a facility. It does not alter an entity's obligations under any other applicable statute. For example, the Department recognizes that the FHAct does not employ a bright line standard for determining which facilities qualify as residential facilities under that Act and that there are circumstances where units in facilities that meet the definition of places of lodging will be covered under both the ADA and the FHAct and will have to comply with the requirements of both laws.

The Department also received comments about the factors used in the NPRM's definition of "place of lodging." One commenter proposed modifications to the definition as follows: changing the words "guest rooms" to "accommodations for sleeping"; and adding a fifth factor that states that "the in-room decor, furnishings and equipment being specified by the owner or operator of the lodging operation rather than generally being determined by the owner of the individual unit or room." The Department does not believe that "guest room" should be changed to "accommodations for sleeping." Such a change would create confusion because the transient lodging provisions in the 2004 ADAAG use the term "guest rooms" and not "accommodations for sleeping." In addition, the Department believes that it would be confusing to add a factor relating to who dictates the in-room decor and furnishings in a unit or room, because there may be circumstances where particular rental programs require individual owners to use certain decor and furnishings as a condition of participating in that program.

One commenter stated that the factors the Department has included for determining whether a rental unit is a place of lodging for the purposes of title III, and therefore a "place of public accommodation" under the ADA, address only the way an establishment appears to the public. This commenter recommended that the Department also consider the economic relationships among the unit owners, rental managers, and homeowners' associations, noting that where revenues are not pooled (as they are in a hotel), the economic relationships do not make it possible to spread the cost of providing accessibility features over the entire business enterprise. Another commenter argued that private ownership of sleeping accommodations sets certain facilities apart from traditional hotels, motels, and inns, and that the Department should revise the definition of places of lodging to exempt existing places of lodging that have sleeping accommodations separately owned by individual owners (e.g., condominiums) from the accessible transient lodging guest room requirements in sections 224 and 806 of the 2004 ADAAG, although the commenter agreed that newly constructed places of lodging should meet those standards.

One commenter argued that the Department's proposed definition of place of lodging does not reflect fully the nature of a timeshare facility and one single definition does not fit timeshares, condo hotels, and other types of rental accommodations. This commenter proposed that the Department adopt a separate definition for timeshare resorts as a subcategory of place of lodging. The commenter proposed defining timeshare resorts as facilities that provide the recurring right to occupancy for overnight accommodations for the owners of the accommodations, and other occupancy rights for owners exchanging their interests or members of the public for stays that primarily are short-term in nature (generally 30 consecutive days or less), where neither the owner nor any other occupant has the right or intent to use the unit or room on other than a temporary basis for vacation or leisure purposes. This proposed definition also would describe factors for determining when a timeshare resort is operating in a manner similar to a hotel, motel, or inn, including some or all of the following: rooms being available on a walk-in or call-in basis; housekeeping or linen services being available; on-site management; and reservations being accepted for a room type without guaranteeing any guest or owner use of a particular unit or room until check-in, without a prior lease or security deposit. Timeshares that do not meet this definition would not be subject to the transient lodging standards.

The Department has considered these comments and has revised the definition of "place of accommodation" in § 36.104 to include a revised subcategory (B), which more clearly defines the factors that must be present for a facility that is not an inn, motel, or hotel to qualify as a place of lodging. These factors include conditions and amenities similar to an inn, motel, or hotel, including on- or off-site management and reservations service, rooms available on a walk-up or call-in basis, availability of housekeeping or linen service, and accepting reservations for a room type without guaranteeing a particular unit or room until check-in without a prior lease or security deposit.

Although the Department understands some of the concerns about the application of the ADA requirements to places of lodging that have ownership structures that involve individually owned units, the Department does not believe that the definitional section of the regulation is the place to address these concerns and has addressed them in § 36.406(c)(2) and the accompanying discussion in Appendix A.

"Qualified Interpreter"

In the NPRM, the Department proposed adding language to the definition of "qualified interpreter" to clarify that the term includes, but is not limited to, sign language interpreters, oral interpreters, and cued-speech interpreters. As the

Department explained, not all interpreters are qualified for all situations. For example, a qualified interpreter who uses American Sign Language (ASL) is not necessarily qualified to interpret orally. In addition, someone with only a rudimentary familiarity with sign language or finger spelling is not qualified, nor is someone who is fluent in sign language but unable to translate spoken communication into ASL or to translate signed communication into spoken words.

As further explained, different situations will require different types of interpreters. For example, an oral interpreter who has special skill and training to mouth a speaker's words silently for individuals who are deaf or hard of hearing may be necessary for an individual who was raised orally and taught to read lips or was diagnosed with hearing loss later in life and does not know sign language. An individual who is deaf or hard of hearing may need an oral interpreter if the speaker's voice is unclear, if there is a quick-paced exchange of communication (*e.g.*, in a meeting), or when the speaker does not directly face the individual who is deaf or hard of hearing. A cued- speech interpreter functions in the same manner as an oral interpreter except that he or she also uses a hand code or cue to represent each speech sound.

The Department received many comments regarding the proposed modifications to the definition of "qualified interpreter." Many commenters requested that the Department include within the definition a requirement that interpreters be certified, particularly if they reside in a State that licenses or certifies interpreters. Other commenters opposed a certification requirement as unduly limiting, noting that an interpreter may well be qualified even if that same interpreter is not certified. These commenters noted the absence of nationwide standards or universally accepted criteria for certification.

On review of this issue, the Department has decided against imposing a certification requirement under the ADA. It is sufficient under the ADA that the interpreter be qualified. With respect to the proposed additions to the rule, most commenters supported the expansion of the list of qualified interpreters, and some advocated for the inclusion of other types of interpreters on the list as well, such as deaf-blind interpreters, certified deaf interpreters, and speech-to-speech interpreters. As these commenters explained, deaf-blind interpreters are interpreters who have specialized skills and training to interpret for individuals who are deaf and blind. Certified deaf interpreters are deaf or hard of hearing interpreters who work with hearing sign language interpreters to meet the specific communication needs of deaf individuals. Speech- to-speech interpreters have special skill and training to interpret for individuals who have speech disabilities.

The list of interpreters in the definition of "qualified interpreter" is illustrative, and the Department does not believe it is necessary or appropriate to attempt to provide an exhaustive list of qualified interpreters. Accordingly, the Department has decided not to expand the proposed list. However, if a deaf and blind individual needs interpreting services, an interpreter who is qualified to handle the interpreting needs of that individual may be required. The guiding criterion is that the public accommodation must provide appropriate auxiliary aids and services to ensure effective communication with the individual.

Commenters also suggested various definitions for the term "cued-speech interpreters," and different descriptions of the tasks they performed. After reviewing the various comments, the Department has determined that it is more accurate and appropriate to refer to such individuals as "cued-language transliterators." Likewise, the Department has changed the term "oral interpreters" to "oral transliterators." These two changes have been made to distinguish between sign language interpreters, who translate one language into another language (e.g., ASL to English and English to ASL), from transliterators, who interpret within the same language between deaf and hearing individuals. A cued-language transliterator is an interpreter who has special skill and training in the use of the Cued Speech system of handshapes and placements, along with non-manual information, such as facial expression and body language, to show auditory information visually, including speech and environmental sounds. An oral transliterator is an interpreter who has special skill and training to mouth a speaker's words silently for individuals who are deaf or hard of hearing. While the Department included definitions for "cued speech interpreter" and "oral interpreter" in the regulatory text proposed in the NPRM, the Department has decided that it is unnecessary to include such definitions in the text of the final rule.

Many commenters questioned the proposed deletion of the requirement that a qualified interpreter be able to interpret both receptively and expressively, noting the importance of both these skills. Commenters noted that this phrase was carefully crafted in the original regulation to make certain that interpreters both (1) are capable of understanding what a person with a disability is saying and (2) have the skills needed to convey information back to that individual. These are two very different skill sets and both are equally important to achieve effective communication. For example, in a medical setting, a sign language interpreter must have the necessary skills to understand the grammar and syntax used by an ASL user (receptive skills) and the ability to interpret complicated medical information — presented by medical staff in English — back to that individual in ASL (expressive skills). The Department agrees and has put the phrase "both receptively and expressively" back in the definition.

Several advocacy groups suggested that the Department make clear in the definition of qualified interpreter that the interpreter may appear either on-site or remotely using a video remote interpreting (VRI) service. Given that the Department has included in this rule both a definition of VRI services and standards that such services must satisfy, such an addition to the definition of qualified interpreter is appropriate.

After consideration of all relevant information submitted during the public comment period, the Department has modified the definition from that initially proposed in the NPRM. The final definition now states that "[q]ualified interpreter means an interpreter who, via a video remote interpreting (VRI) service or an on-site appearance, is able to interpret effectively, accurately, and impartially, both receptively and expressively, using any necessary specialized vocabulary. Qualified interpreters include, for example, sign language interpreters, oral transliterators, and cued-language transliterators."

"Qualified Reader"

The 1991 title III regulation identified a qualified reader as an auxiliary aid, but did not define the term. Based upon the Department's investigation of complaints alleging that some entities have provided ineffective readers, the Department proposed in the NPRM to define "qualified reader" similarly to "qualified interpreter" to ensure that public accommodations select qualified individuals to read an examination or other written information in an effective, accurate, and impartial manner. This proposal was suggested in order to make clear to public accommodations that a failure to provide a qualified reader to a person with a disability may constitute a violation of the requirement to provide appropriate auxiliary aids and services.

The Department received comments supporting the inclusion in the regulation of a definition of a "qualified reader." Some commenters suggested the Department add to the definition a requirement prohibiting the use of a reader whose accent, diction, or pronunciation makes full comprehension of material being read difficult. Another commenter requested that the Department include a requirement that the reader "will follow the directions of the person for whom he or she is reading." Commenters also requested that the Department define "accurately" and "effectively" as used in this definition.

While the Department believes that the regulatory definition proposed in the NPRM adequately addresses these concerns, the Department emphasizes that a reader, in order to be "qualified," must be skilled in reading the language and subject matter and must be able to be easily understood by the individual with the disability. For example, if a reader is reading aloud the questions for a bar examination, that reader, in order to be qualified, must know the proper pronunciation of all legal terminology used and must be sufficiently articulate to be easily understood by the individual with a disability for whom he or she is reading. In addition, the terms "effectively" and "accurately" have been successfully used and understood in the Department's existing definition of "qualified interpreter" since 1991 without specific regulatory definitions. Instead, the Department has relied upon the common use and understanding of those terms from standard English dictionaries. Thus, the definition of "qualified reader" has not been changed from that contained in the NPRM. The final rule defines a "qualified reader" to mean "a person who is able to read effectively, accurately, and impartially using any necessary specialized vocabulary."

"Service Animal" Section 36.104 of the 1991 title III regulation defines a "service animal" as "any guide dog, signal dog, or other animal individually trained to do work or perform tasks for the benefit of an individual with a disability, including, but not limited to, guiding individuals with impaired vision, alerting individuals with impaired hearing to intruders or sounds, providing minimal protection or rescue work, pulling a wheelchair, or fetching dropped items." Section 36.302(c)(1) of the 1991 title III regulation requires that "[g]enerally, a public accommodation shall modify policies, practices, or procedures to permit the use of a service animal by an individual with a disability." Section 36.302(c)(2) of the 1991 title III regulation states that "a public accommodation [is not required] to supervise or care for a service animal."

The Department has issued guidance and provided technical assistance and publications concerning service animals since the 1991 regulations became effective. In the NPRM, the Department proposed to modify the definition of service animal and asked for public input on several issues related to the service animal provisions of the 1991 title III regulation: whether the Department should clarify the phrase "providing minimal protection" in the definition or remove it; whether there are any circumstances where a service animal "providing minimal protection" would be appropriate or expected; whether certain species should be eliminated from the definition of "service animal," and, if so, which types of animals should be excluded; whether "common domestic animal" should be part of the definition; and whether a size or weight limitation should be imposed for common domestic animals, even if the animal satisfies the "common domestic animal" part of the NPRM definition.

The Department received extensive comments on these issues, as well as requests to clarify the obligations of public accommodations to accommodate individuals with disabilities who use service animals, and has modified the final rule in response. In the interests of avoiding unnecessary repetition, the Department has elected to discuss the issues raised in the NPRM questions about service animals and the corresponding public comments in the following discussion of the definition of "service animal." The Department's final rule defines "service animal" as "any dog that is individually trained to do work or perform tasks for the benefit of an individual with a disability, including a physical, sensory, psychiatric, intellectual, or other mental disability. Other species of animals, whether wild or domestic, trained or untrained, are not service animals for the purposes of this definition. The work or tasks performed by a service animal must be directly related to the individual's disability. Examples of work or tasks include, but are not limited to, assisting individuals who are blind or have low vision with navigation and other tasks, alerting individuals who are deaf or hard of hearing to the presence of people or sounds, providing non-violent protection or rescue work, pulling a wheelchair, assisting an individual during a seizure, alerting individuals to the presence of allergens, retrieving items such as medicine or the telephone, providing physical support and assistance with balance and stability to individuals with mobility disabilities, and helping persons with psychiatric and neurological disabilities by preventing or interrupting impulsive or destructive behaviors. The crime deterrent effects of an animal's presence and the provision of emotional support, well-being, comfort, or companionship do not constitute work or tasks for the purposes of this definition."

This definition has been designed to clarify a key provision of the ADA. Many covered entities indicated that they are confused regarding their obligations under the ADA with regard to individuals with disabilities who use service animals. Individuals with disabilities who use trained guide or service dogs are concerned that if untrained or unusual animals are termed "service animals," their own right to use guide or service dogs may become unnecessarily restricted or questioned. Some individuals who are not individuals with disabilities have claimed, whether fraudulently or sincerely (albeit mistakenly), that their animals are service animals covered by the ADA, in order to gain access to hotels, restaurants, and other places of public accommodation. The increasing use of wild, exotic, or unusual species, many of which are untrained, as service animals has also added to the confusion.

Finally, individuals with disabilities who have the legal right under the Fair Housing Act (FHAct) to use certain animals in their homes as a reasonable accommodation to their disabilities have assumed that their animals also qualify under the ADA. This is not necessarily the case, as discussed below.

The Department recognizes the diverse needs and preferences of individuals with disabilities protected under the ADA, and does not wish to unnecessarily impede individual choice. Service animals play an integral role in the lives of many individuals with disabilities, and with the clarification provided by the final rule, individuals with disabilities will continue to be able to use their service animals as they go about their daily activities. The clarification will also help to ensure that the fraudulent or mistaken use of other animals not qualified as service animals under the ADA will be deterred. A more detailed analysis of the elements of the definition and the comments responsive to the service animal provisions of the NPRM follows.

Providing minimal protection. The 1991 title III regulation included language stating that "minimal protection" was a task that could be performed by an individually trained service animal for the benefit of an individual with a disability. In the Department's "ADA Business Brief on Service Animals" (2002), the Department interpreted the "minimal protection" language within the context of a seizure (i.e., alerting and protecting a person who is having a seizure). The Department received many comments in response to the question of whether the "minimal protection" language should be clarified. Many commenters urged the removal of the "minimal protection" language from the service animal definition for two reasons: (1) The phrase can be interpreted to allow any dog that is trained to be aggressive to qualify as a service animal simply by pairing the animal with a person with a disability; and (2) The phrase can be interpreted to allow any untrained pet dog to qualify as a service animal, since many consider the mere presence of a dog to be a crime deterrent, and thus sufficient to meet the minimal protection standard. These commenters argued, and the Department agrees, that these interpretations were not contemplated under the original title III regulation.

While many commenters stated that they believe that the "minimal protection" language should be eliminated, other commenters recommended that the language be clarified, but retained. Commenters favoring clarification of the term suggested that the Department explicitly exclude the function of attack or exclude those animals that are trained solely to be aggressive or protective. Other commenters identified non- violent behavioral tasks that could be construed as minimally protective, such as interrupting self-mutilation, providing safety checks and room searches, reminding the individual to take medications, and protecting the individual from injury resulting from seizures or unconsciousness.

Several commenters noted that the existing direct threat defense, which allows the exclusion of a service animal if the animal exhibits unwarranted or unprovoked violent behavior or poses a direct threat, prevents the use of "attack dogs" as service animals. One commenter noted that the use of a service animal trained to provide "minimal protection" may impede access to care in an emergency, for example, where the first responder is unable or reluctant to approach a person with a disability because the individual's service animal is in a protective posture suggestive of aggression.

Many organizations and individuals stated that in the general dog training community, "protection" is code for attack or aggression training and should be removed from the definition. Commenters stated that there appears to be a broadly held misconception that aggression-trained animals are appropriate service animals for persons with post traumatic stress disorder (PTSD). While many individuals with PTSD may benefit by using a service animal, the work or tasks performed appropriately by such an animal would not involve unprovoked aggression, but could include actively cuing the individual by nudging or pawing the individual to alert to the onset of an episode and removing the individual from the anxiety-provoking environment.

The Department recognizes that despite its best efforts to provide clarification, the "minimal protection" language appears to have been misinterpreted. While the Department maintains that protection from danger is one of the key functions that service animals perform for the benefit of persons with disabilities, the Department recognizes that an animal individually trained to provide aggressive protection, such as an attack dog, is not appropriately considered a service animal. Therefore, the Department has decided to modify the "minimal protection" language to read "non-violent protection," thereby excluding so-called 'attack dogs" or dogs with traditional "protection training" as service animals. The Department believes that this modification to the service animal definition will eliminate confusion, without restricting unnecessarily the type of work or tasks that service animals may perform. The Department's modification also clarifies that the crime- deterrent effect of a dog's presence, by itself, does not qualify as work or tasks for purposes of the service animal definition.

Alerting to intruders. The phrase "alerting to intruders" is related to the issues of minimal protection and the work or tasks an animal may perform to meet the definition of a service animal. In the original 1991 regulatory text, this phrase was intended to identify service animals that alert individuals who are deaf or hard of hearing to the presence of others. This language has been misinterpreted by some to apply to dogs that are trained specifically to provide aggressive protection, resulting in the assertion that such training qualifies a dog as a service animal under the ADA. The Department reiterates that public accommodations are not required to admit any animal whose use poses a direct threat. In addition, the Department has decided to remove the word "intruders" from the service animal definition and replace it with the phrase "the presence of people or sounds." The Department believes this clarifies that so-called "attack training" or other aggressive response types of training that cause a dog to provide an aggressive response do not qualify a dog as a service animal under the ADA.

Conversely, if an individual uses a breed of dog that is perceived to be aggressive because of breed reputation, stereotype, or the history or experience the observer may have with other dogs, but the dog is under the control of the individual with a disability and does not exhibit aggressive behavior, the public accommodation cannot exclude the individual or the animal from the place of public accommodation. The animal can only be removed if it engages in the behaviors mentioned in § 36.302(c) (as revised in the final rule) or if the presence of the animal constitutes a fundamental alteration to the nature of the goods, services, facilities, and activities of the place of public accommodation.

"Doing work" or "performing tasks." The NPRM proposed that the Department maintain the requirement first articulated in the 1991 title III regulation that in order to qualify as a service animal, the animal must "perform tasks" or "do work" for the individual with a disability. The phrases "perform tasks" and "do work"

describe what an animal must do for the benefit of an individual with a disability in order to qualify as a service animal.

The Department received a number of comments in response to the NPRM proposal urging the removal of the term "do work" from the definition of a service animal. These commenters argued that the Department should emphasize the performance of tasks instead. The Department disagrees. Although the common definition of work includes the performance of tasks, the definition of work is somewhat broader, encompassing activities that do not appear to involve physical action.

One service dog user stated that, in some cases, "critical forms of assistance can't be construed as physical tasks," noting that the manifestations of "brain-based disabilities," such as psychiatric disorders and autism, are as varied as their physical counterparts. The Department agrees with this statement but cautions that unless the animal is individually trained to do something that qualifies as work or a task, the animal is a pet or support animal and does not qualify for coverage as a service animal. A pet or support animal may be able to discern that the individual is in distress, but it is what the animal is trained to do in response to this awareness that distinguishes a service animal from an observant pet or support animal.

The NPRM contained an example of "doing work" that stated "a psychiatric service dog can help some individuals with dissociative identity disorder to remain grounded in time or place." 73 FR 34508, 34521 (June 17, 2008). Several commenters objected to the use of this example, arguing that grounding was not a "task" and therefore the example inherently contradicted the basic premise that a service animal must perform a task in order to mitigate a disability. Other commenters stated that "grounding" should not be included as an example of "work" because it could lead to some individuals claiming that they should be able to use emotional support animals in public because the dog makes them feel calm or safe. By contrast, one commenter with experience in training service animals explained that grounding is a trained task based upon very specific behavioral indicators that can be observed and measured. These tasks are based upon input from mental health practitioners, dog trainers, and individuals with a history of working with psychiatric service dogs.

It is the Department's view that an animal that is trained to "ground" a person with a psychiatric disorder does work or performs a task that would qualify it as a service animal as compared to an untrained emotional support animal whose presence affects a person's disability. It is the fact that the animal is trained to respond to the individual's needs that distinguishes an animal as a service animal. The process must have two steps: Recognition and response. For example, if a service animal senses that a person is about to have a psychiatric episode and it is trained to respond, for example, by nudging, barking, or removing the individual to a safe location until the episode subsides, then the animal has indeed performed a task or done work on behalf of the individual with the disability, as opposed to merely sensing an event.

One commenter suggested defining the term "task," presumably to improve the understanding of the types of services performed by an animal that would be sufficient to qualify the animal for coverage. The Department believes that the common definition of the word "task" is sufficiently clear and that it is not necessary to add to the definitions section. However, the Department has added examples of other kinds of work or tasks to help illustrate and provide clarity to the definition. After careful evaluation of this issue, the Department has concluded that the phrases "do work" and "perform tasks" have been effective during the past two decades to illustrate the varied services provided by service animals for the benefit of individuals with all types of disabilities. Thus, the Department declines to depart from its longstanding approach at this time.

Species limitations. When the Department originally issued its title III regulation in the early 1990s, the Department did not define the parameters of acceptable animal species. At that time, few anticipated the variety of animals that would be promoted as service animals in the years to come, which ranged from pigs and miniature horses to snakes, iguanas, and parrots. The Department has followed this particular issue closely, keeping current with the many unusual species of animals represented to be service animals. Thus, the Department has decided to refine further this aspect of the service animal definition in the final rule. The Department received many comments from individuals and organizations recommending species limitations. Several of these commenters asserted that limiting the number of allowable species would help stop erosion of the public's trust, which has resulted in reduced access for many individuals with disabilities who use trained service animals that adhere to high behavioral standards. Several commenters suggested that other species would be acceptable if those animals could meet nationally recognized behavioral standards for trained service dogs. Other commenters asserted that certain species of animals *(e.g.,* reptiles) cannot be trained to do work or perform tasks, so these animals would not be covered.

In the NPRM, the Department used the term "common domestic animal" in the service animal definition and excluded reptiles, rabbits, farm animals (including horses, miniature horses, ponies, pigs, and goats), ferrets, amphibians, and rodents from the service animal definition. 73 FR 34508, 34553 (June 17, 2008). However, the term "common domestic animal" is difficult to define with precision due to the increase in the number of domesticated species. Also, several State and local laws define a "domestic" animal as an animal that is not wild. The Department is compelled to take into account the practical considerations of certain animals and to contemplate their suitability in a variety of public contexts, such as restaurants, grocery stores, hospitals, and performing arts venues, as well as suitability for urban environments. The Department agrees with commenters' views that limiting the number and types of species recognized as service animals will provide greater predictability for public accommodations as well as added assurance of access for individuals with disabilities who use dogs as service animals. As a consequence, the Department has decided to limit this rule's coverage of service animals to dogs, which are the most common service animals used by individuals with disabilities.

Wild animals, monkeys, and other nonhuman primates. Numerous business entities endorsed a narrow definition of acceptable service animal species, and asserted that there are certain animals *(e.g.,* reptiles) that cannot be trained to do work or perform tasks. Other commenters suggested that the Department should identify excluded animals, such as birds and llamas, in the final rule. Although one commenter noted that wild animals bred in captivity should be permitted to be service animals, the Department has decided to make clear that all wild animals, whether born or bred in captivity or in the wild, are eliminated from coverage as service animals. The Department believes that this approach reduces risks to health or safety attendant with wild animals. Some animals, such as certain nonhuman primates, including certain monkeys, pose a direct threat; their behavior can be unpredictably aggressive and violent without notice or provocation. The American Veterinary Medical Association (AVMA) issued a position statement advising against the use of monkeys as service animals, stating that "[t]he AVMA does not support the use of nonhuman primates as assistance animals because of animal welfare concerns, and the potential for serious injury and zoonotic [animal to human disease transmission] risks." AVMA Position Statement, *Nonhuman Primates as Assistance Animals* (2005), available at http://www.avma.org/issues/policy/nonhuman_primates.asp (last visited June 24, 2010).

An organization that trains capuchin monkeys to provide in-home services to individuals with paraplegia and quadriplegia was in substantial agreement with the AVMA's views but requested a limited recognition in the service animal definition for the capuchin monkeys it trains to provide assistance for persons with disabilities. The organization commented that its trained capuchin monkeys undergo scrupulous veterinary examinations to ensure that the animals pose no health risks, and are used by individuals with disabilities exclusively in their homes. The organization acknowledged that the capuchin monkeys it trains are not necessarily suitable for use in a place of public accommodation but noted that the monkeys may need to be used in circumstances that implicate title III coverage, *e.g.*, in the event the handler had to leave home due to an emergency, to visit a veterinarian, or for the initial delivery of the monkey to the individual with a disability. The organization noted that several State and local government entities have local zoning, licensing, health, and safety laws that prohibit non-human primates, and that these prohibitions would prevent individuals with disabilities from using these animals even in their homes.

The organization argued that including capuchin monkeys under the service animal umbrella would make it easier for individuals with disabilities to obtain reasonable modifications of State and local licensing, health, and safety laws that would permit the use of these monkeys. The organization argued that this limited modification to the service animal definition was warranted in view of the services these monkeys perform, which enable many individuals with paraplegia and quadriplegia to live and function with increased independence.

The Department has carefully considered the potential risks associated with the use of nonhuman primates as service animals in places of public accommodation, as well as the information provided to the Department about the significant benefits that trained capuchin monkeys provide to certain individuals with disabilities in residential settings. The Department has determined, however, that nonhuman primates, including capuchin monkeys, will not be recognized as service animals for purposes of this rule because of their potential for disease transmission and unpredictable aggressive behavior. The Department believes that these characteristics make nonhuman primates unsuitable for use as service animals in the context of the wide variety of public settings subject to this rule. As the organization advocating the inclusion of capuchin monkeys acknowledges, capuchin monkeys are not suitable for use in public facilities.

The Department emphasizes that it has decided only that capuchin monkeys will not be included in the definition of service animals for purposes of its regulation implementing the ADA. This decision does not have any effect on the extent to which public accommodations are required to allow the use of such monkeys under other Federal statutes, like the FHAct or the Air Carrier Access Act (ACAA). For example, a public accommodation that also is considered to be a "dwelling" may be covered under both the ADA and the FHAct. While the ADA does not require such a public accommodation to admit people with service monkeys, the FHAct may. Under the FHAct an individual with a disability may have the right to have an animal other than a dog in his or her home if the animal qualifies as a "reasonable accommodation" that is necessary to afford the individual equal opportunity to use and enjoy a dwelling, assuming that the use of the animal does not pose a direct threat. In some cases, the right of an individual to have an animal under the FHAct may conflict with State or local laws that prohibit all individuals, with or without disabilities, from owning a particular species. However, in this circumstance, an individual who wishes to request a reasonable modification of the State or local law must do so under the FHAct, not the ADA.

Having considered all of the comments about which species should qualify as service animals under the ADA, the Department has determined the most reasonable approach is to limit acceptable species to dogs.

Size or weight limitations. The vast majority of commenters did not support a size or weight limitation. Commenters were typically opposed to a size or weight limit because many tasks performed by service animals require large, strong dogs. For instance, service animals may perform tasks such as providing balance and support or pulling a wheelchair. Small animals may not be suitable for large adults. The weight of the service animal user is often correlated with the size and weight of the service animal.

Others were concerned that adding a size and weight limit would further complicate the difficult process of finding an appropriate service animal. One commenter noted that there is no need for a limit because "if, as a practical matter, the size or weight of an individual's service animal creates a direct threat or fundamental alteration to a particular public entity or accommodation, there are provisions that allow for the animal's exclusion or removal." Some common concerns among commenters in support of a size and weight limit were that a larger animal may be less able to fit in various areas with its handler, such as toilet rooms and public seating areas, and that larger animals are more difficult to control.

Balancing concerns expressed in favor of and against size and weight limitations, the Department has determined that such limitations would not be appropriate. Many individuals of larger stature require larger dogs. The Department believes it would be inappropriate to deprive these individuals of the option of using a service dog of the size required to provide the physical support and stability these individuals may need to function independently. Since large dogs have always served as service animals, continuing their use should not constitute fundamental alterations or impose undue burdens on public accommodations.

Breed limitations. A few commenters suggested that certain breeds of dogs should not be allowed to be used as service animals. Some suggested that the Department should defer to local laws restricting the breeds of dogs that individuals who reside in a community may own. Other commenters opposed breed restrictions, stating that the breed of a dog does not determine its propensity for aggression and that aggressive and non-aggressive dogs exist in all breeds.

The Department does not believe that it is either appropriate or consistent with the ADA to defer to local laws that prohibit certain breeds of dogs based on local concerns that these breeds may have a history of unprovoked aggression or attacks. Such deference would have the effect of limiting the rights of persons with disabilities under the ADA who use certain service animals based on where they live rather than on whether the use of a particular animal poses a direct threat to the health and safety of others. Breed restrictions differ significantly from jurisdiction to jurisdiction. Some jurisdictions have no breed restrictions. Others have restrictions that, while well-meaning, have the unintended effect of screening out the very breeds of dogs that have successfully served as service animals for decades without a history of the type of unprovoked aggression or attacks that would pose a direct threat, *e.g.*, German Shepherds. Other jurisdictions prohibit animals over a certain weight, thereby restricting breeds without invoking an express breed ban. In addition, deference to breed restrictions contained in local laws would have the unacceptable consequence of restricting travel by an individual with a disability who uses a breed that is acceptable and poses no safety hazards in the individual's home jurisdiction but is nonetheless banned by other jurisdictions. Public accommodations have the ability to determine, on a case-by-case basis, whether a particular service animal can be excluded based on that particular animal's actual behavior or history — not based on fears or generalizations about how an animal or breed might behave. This ability to exclude an animal whose behavior or history evidences a direct threat is sufficient to protect health and safety.

Recognition of psychiatric service animals, but not "emotional support animals." The definition of "service animal" in the NPRM stated the Department's longstanding position that emotional support animals are not included in the definition of "service animal." The proposed text provided that "[a]nimals whose sole function is to provide emotional support, comfort, therapy, companionship, therapeutic benefits, or to promote emotional well-being are not service animals." 73 FR 34508, 34553 (June 17, 2008).

Many advocacy organizations expressed concern and disagreed with the exclusion of comfort and emotional support animals. Others have been more specific, stating that individuals with disabilities may need their emotional support animals in order to have equal access. Some commenters noted that individuals with disabilities use animals that have not been trained to perform tasks directly related to their disability. These animals do not qualify as service animals under the ADA. These are emotional support or comfort animals.

Commenters asserted that excluding categories such as "comfort" and "emotional support" animals recognized by laws such as the FHAct or the ACAA is confusing and burdensome. Other commenters noted that emotional support and comfort animals perform an important function, asserting that animal companionship helps individuals who experience depression resulting from multiple sclerosis.

Some commenters explained the benefits emotional support animals provide, including emotional support, comfort, therapy, companionship, therapeutic benefits, and the promotion of emotional well-being. They contended that without the presence of an emotional support animal in their lives they would be disadvantaged and unable to participate in society. These commenters were concerned that excluding this category of animals will lead to discrimination against and excessive questioning of individuals with nonvisible or non-apparent disabilities. Other commenters expressing opposition to the exclusion of individually trained "comfort" or "emotional support" animals asserted that the ability to soothe or de-escalate and control emotion is "work" that benefits the individual with the disability.

Many commenters requested that the Department carve out an exception that permits current or former members of the military to use emotional support animals. They asserted that a significant number of service members returning from active combat duty have adjustment difficulties due to combat, sexual assault, or other traumatic experiences while on active duty. Commenters noted that some current or former members of the military service have been prescribed animals for conditions such as PTSD. One commenter stated that service women who were sexually assaulted while in the military use emotional support animals to help them feel safe enough to step outside their homes. The Department recognizes that many current and former members of the military have disabilities as a result of service-related injuries that may require emotional support and that such individuals can benefit from the use of an emotional support animal and could use such animal in their home under the FHAct. However, having carefully weighed the issues, the Department believes that its final rule appropriately addresses the balance of issues and concerns of both the individual with a disability and the public accommodation. The Department also notes that nothing in this part prohibits a public entity from allowing current or former military members or anyone else with disabilities to utilize emotional support animals if it wants to do so.

Commenters asserted the view that if an animal's "mere presence" legitimately provides such benefits to an individual with a disability and if those benefits are necessary to provide equal opportunity given the facts of the particular disability, then such an animal should qualify as a "service animal." Commenters noted that the focus should be on the nature of a person's disability, the difficulties the disability may impose and whether the requested accommodation would legitimately address those difficulties, not on evaluating the animal involved. The Department understands this approach has benefitted many individuals under the FHAct and analogous State law provisions, where the presence of animals poses fewer health and safety issues and where emotional support animals provide assistance that is unique to residential settings. The Department believes, however, that the presence of such animals is not required in the context of public accommodations, such as restaurants, hospitals, hotels, retail establishments, and assembly areas.

Under the Department's previous regulatory framework, some individuals and entities assumed that the requirement that service animals must be individually trained to do work or perform tasks excluded all individuals with mental disabilities from having service animals. Others assumed that any person with a psychiatric condition whose pet provided comfort to them was covered by the 1991 title III regulation. The Department reiterates that psychiatric service animals that are trained to do work or perform a task for individuals whose disability is covered by the ADA are protected by the Department's present regulatory approach. Psychiatric service animals can be trained to perform a variety of tasks that assist individuals with disabilities to detect the onset of psychiatric episodes and ameliorate their effects. Tasks performed by psychiatric service animals may include reminding the individual to take medicine, providing safety checks or room searches for individuals with PTSD, interrupting self-mutilation, and removing disoriented individuals from dangerous situations.

The difference between an emotional support animal and a psychiatric service animal is the work or tasks that the animal performs. Traditionally, service dogs worked as guides for individuals who were blind or had low vision. Since the original regulation was promulgated, service animals have been trained to assist individuals with many different types of disabilities.

In the final rule, the Department has retained its position on the exclusion of emotional support animals from the definition of "service animal." The definition states that "[t]he provision of emotional support, well-being, comfort, or companionship * * * do[es] not constitute work or tasks for the purposes of this definition." The Department notes, however, that the exclusion of emotional support animals from coverage in the final rule does not mean that individuals with psychiatric or mental disabilities cannot use service animals that meet the regulatory definition. The final rule defines service animal as follows: "Service animal means any dog that is individually trained to do work or perform tasks for the benefit of an individual with a disability, including a physical, sensory, psychiatric, intellectual, or other mental disability." This language simply clarifies the Department's long- standing position.

The Department's position is based on the fact that the title II and title III regulations govern a wider range of public settings than the housing and transportation settings for which the Department of Housing and Urban Development (HUD) and the DOT regulations allow emotional support animals or comfort animals. The Department recognizes that there are situations not governed by the title II and title III regulations, particularly in the context of residential settings and transportation, where there may be a legal obligation to permit the use of animals that do not qualify as service animals under the ADA, but whose presence nonetheless provides necessary emotional support to persons with disabilities. Accordingly, other Federal agency regulations, case law, and possibly State or local laws governing those situations may provide appropriately for increased access for animals other than service animals as defined under the ADA. Public officials, housing providers, and others who make decisions relating to animals in residential and transportation settings should consult the Federal, State, and local laws that apply in those areas (e.g., the FHAct regulations of HUD and the ACAA) and not rely on the ADA as a basis for reducing those obligations.

Retain term "service animal." Some commenters asserted that the term "assistance animal" is a term of art and should replace the term "service animal"; however, the majority of commenters preferred the term "service animal" because it is more specific. The Department has decided to retain the term "service animal" in the final rule. While some agencies, like HUD, use the terms "assistance animal," "assistive animal," or "support animal," these terms are used to denote a broader category of animals than is covered by the ADA. The Department has decided that changing the term used in the final rule would create confusion, particularly in view of the broader parameters for coverage under the FHAct, *cf.* Preamble to HUD's Final Rule for Pet Ownership for the Elderly and Persons with Disabilities, 73 FR 63834– 38 (Oct. 27, 2008); HUD Handbook No. 4350.3 Rev-1, Chapter 2, *Occupancy Requirements of Subsidized Multifamily Housing Programs* (June 2007), available at http://www.hud.gov/offices/adm/hudclips/handbooks/hsgh/4350.3 (last visited June 24, 2010). Moreover, as discussed above, the Department's definition of "service animal" in the final rule does not affect the rights of individuals with disabilities who use assistance animals in their homes under the FHAct or who use "emotional support animals" that are covered under the ACAA and its implementing regulations. *See* 14 CFR 382.7 *et seq.; see also* Department of Transportation, *Guidance Concerning Service Animals in Air Transportation*, 68 FR 24874, 24877 (May 9, 2003) (discussing accommodation of service animals and emotional support animals on aircraft).

"Video Remote Interpreting (VRI) Services" In the NPRM, the Department proposed adding "Video Interpreting Services (VIS)" to the list of auxiliary aids available to provide effective communication. In the preamble to the NPRM, VIS was defined as "a technology composed of a video phone, video monitors, cameras, a high- speed Internet connection, and an interpreter. The video phone provides video transmission to a video monitor that permits the individual who is deaf or hard of hearing to view and sign to a video interpreter (i.e., a live interpreter in another location), who can see and sign to the individual through a camera located on or near the monitor, while others can communicate by speaking. The video monitor can display a split screen of two live images, with the interpreter in one image and the individual who is deaf or hard of hearing in the other image." 73 FR 34508, 34522 (June 17, 2008). Comments from advocacy organizations and individuals unanimously requested that the Department use the term "video remote interpreting (VRI)," instead of VIS, for consistency with Federal Communications Commission (FCC) regulations, FCC Public Notice, DA-0502417 (Sept. 7, 2005), and with common usage by consumers. The Department has made that change throughout the regulation to avoid confusion and to make the regulation more consistent with existing regulations.

Many commenters also requested that the Department distinguish between VRI and "video relay service (VRS)." Both VRI and VRS use a remote interpreter who is able to see and communicate with a deaf person and a hearing person, and all three individuals may be connected by a video link. VRI is a fee-based interpreting service conveyed via videoconferencing where at least one person, typically the interpreter, is at a separate location. VRI can be provided as an on-demand service or by appointment. VRI normally involves a contract in advance for the interpreter who is usually paid by the covered entity.

VRS is a telephone service that enables persons with disabilities to use the telephone to communicate using video connections and is a more advanced form of relay service than the traditional voice to text telephones (TTY) relay systems that were recognized in the 1991 title III regulation. More specifically, VRS is a video relay service using interpreters connected to callers by video hook-up and is designed to provide telephone services to persons who are deaf and use American Sign Language that are functionally equivalent to those services provided to users who are hearing. VRS is funded through the Interstate Telecommunications Relay

Services Fund and overseen by the FCC. *See* 47 CFR 64.601(a)(26). There are no fees for callers to use the VRS interpreters and the video connection, although there may be relatively inexpensive initial costs to the title III entities to purchase the videophone or camera for on-line video connection, or other equipment to connect to the VRS service. The FCC has made clear that VRS functions as a telephone service and is not intended to be used for interpreting services where both parties are in the same room; the latter is reserved for VRI. The Department agrees that VRS cannot be used as a substitute for in-person interpreters or for VRI in situations that would not, absent one party's disability, entail use of the telephone.

Many commenters strongly recommended limiting the use of VRI to circumstances where it will provide effective communication. Commenters from advocacy groups and persons with disabilities expressed concern that VRI may not always be appropriate to provide effective communication, especially in hospitals and emergency rooms. Examples were provided of patients who are unable to see the video monitor because they are semi-conscious or unable to focus on the video screen; other examples were given of cases where the video monitor is out of the sightline of the patient or the image is out of focus; still other examples were given of patients who could not see the image because the signal was interrupted, causing unnatural pauses in the communication, or the image was grainy or otherwise unclear. Many commenters requested more explicit guidelines on the use of VRI and some recommended requirements for equipment maintenance, high-speed, wide-bandwidth video links using dedicated lines or wireless systems, and training of staff using VRI, especially in hospital and health care situations. Several major organizations requested a requirement to include the interpreter's face, head, arms, hands, and eyes in all transmissions.

After consideration of the comments and the Department's own research and experience, the Department has determined that VRI can be an effective method of providing interpreting services in certain circumstances, but not in others. For example, VRI should be effective in many situations involving routine medical care, as well as in the emergency room where urgent care is important, but no in-person interpreter is available; however, VRI may not be effective in situations involving surgery or other medical procedures where the patient is limited in his or her ability to see the video screen. Similarly, VRI may not be effective in situations where there are multiple people in a room and the information exchanged is highly complex and fast paced. The Department recognizes that in these and other situations, such as where communication is needed for persons who are deaf-blind, it may be necessary to summon an in-person interpreter to assist certain individuals. To ensure that VRI is effective in situations where it is appropriate, the Department has established performance standards in § 36.303(f).

Subpart B — General Requirements

Section 36.208(b)   Direct Threat.

The Department has revised the language of § 36.208(b) (formerly § 36.208(c) in the 1991 title III regulation) to include consideration of whether the provision of auxiliary aids or services will mitigate the risk that an individual will pose a direct threat to the health or safety of others. Originally, the reference to auxiliary aids or services as a mitigating factor was part of § 36.208. However, that reference was removed from the section when, for editorial purposes, the Department removed the definition of "direct threat" from § 36.208 and placed it in § 36.104. The Department has put the reference to auxiliary aids or services as a mitigating factor back into § 36.208(b) in order to maintain consistency with the current regulation.

Section 36.211   Maintenance of Accessible Features.

Section 36.211 of the 1991 title III regulation provides that a public accommodation must maintain in operable working condition those features of facilities and equipment that are required to be readily accessible to and usable by individuals with disabilities. 28 CFR 36.211. In the NPRM, the Department clarified the application of this provision and proposed one change to the section to address the discrete situation in which the scoping requirements provided in the 2010 Standards reduce the number of required elements below the requirements of the 1991 Standards. In that discrete event, a public accommodation may reduce such accessible features in accordance with the requirements in the 2010 Standards.

The Department received only four comments on this proposed amendment. None of the commenters opposed the change. In the final rule, the Department has revised the section to make it clear that if the 2010 Standards reduce either the technical requirements or the number of required accessible elements below that required by the 1991 Standards, then the public accommodation may reduce the technical requirements or the number of accessible elements in a covered facility in accordance with the requirements of the 2010 Standards. One commenter, an association of convenience stores, urged the Department to expand the language of the section to include restocking of shelves as a permissible activity for isolated or temporary interruptions in service or access. It is the Department's position that a temporary interruption that blocks an accessible route, such as restocking of shelves, is already permitted by existing § 36.211(b), which clarifies that "isolated or temporary interruptions in service or access due to maintenance or repairs" are permitted. Therefore, the Department will not make any additional changes in the language of § 36.211 other than those discussed in the preceding paragraph.

Subpart C   — Specific Requirements

Section 36.302   Modifications in Policies, Practices, or Procedures.

Section 36.302(c) Service Animals Section 36.302(c)(1) of the 1991 title III regulation states that "[g]enerally, a public accommodation shall modify [its] policies, practices, or procedures to permit the use of service animals by an individual with a disability." Section 36.302(c)(2) of the 1991 title III regulation states that "[n]othing in this part requires a public accommodation to supervise or care for a service animal." The Department has decided to retain the scope of the 1991 title III regulation while clarifying the Department's longstanding policies and interpretations. Toward that end, the final rule has been revised to include the Department's policy interpretations as outlined in published technical assistance, *Commonly Asked Questions about Service Animals in Places of Business* (1996), available at http://www.ada.gov/qasrvc.htm, *and ADA Guide for Small Businesses* (1999), available at http://www.ada.gov/smbustxt.htm, and to add that a public accommodation may exclude a service animal in certain circumstances where the service animal fails to meet certain behavioral standards. The Department received extensive comments in response to proposed § 36.302(c) from individuals, disability advocacy groups, organizations involved in training service animals, and public accommodations. Those comments and the Department's response are discussed below.

Exclusion of service animals. The 1991 regulatory provision in § 36.302(c) addresses reasonable modification and remains unchanged in the final rule. However, based on comments received and the Department's analysis, the Department has decided to clarify those circumstances where otherwise eligible service animals may be excluded by public accommodations.

In the NPRM, in § 36.302(c)(2)(i), the Department proposed that a public accommodation may ask an individual with a disability to remove a service animal from the place of public accommodation if "[t]he animal is out of control and the animal's handler does not take effective action to control it." 73 FR 34508, 34553 (June 17, 2008). The Department has long held that a service animal must be under the control of the handler at all times. Commenters overwhelmingly were in favor of this language, but noted that there are occasions when service animals are provoked to disruptive or aggressive behavior by agitators or trouble-makers, as in the case of a blind individual whose service dog is taunted or pinched. While all service animals are trained to ignore and overcome these types of incidents, misbehavior in response to provocation is not always unreasonable. In circumstances where a service animal misbehaves or responds reasonably to a provocation or injury, the public accommodation must give the handler a reasonable opportunity to gain control of the animal. Further, if the individual with a disability asserts that the animal was provoked or injured, or if the public accommodation otherwise has reason to suspect that provocation or injury has occurred, the public accommodation should seek to determine the facts and, if provocation or injury occurred, the public accommodation should take effective steps to prevent further provocation or injury, which may include asking the provocateur to leave the place of public accommodation. This language is unchanged in the final rule.

The NPRM also proposed language at § 36.302(c)(2)(ii) to permit a public accommodation to exclude a service animal if the animal is not housebroken (i.e., trained so that, absent illness or accident, the animal controls its waste elimination) or the animal's presence or behavior fundamentally alters the nature of the service the public accommodation provides (e.g., repeated barking during a live performance). Several commenters were supportive of this NPRM language, but cautioned against overreaction by the public accommodation in these instances. One commenter noted that animals get sick, too, and that accidents occasionally happen. In these circumstances, simple clean up typically addresses the incident. Commenters noted that the public accommodation must be careful when it excludes a service animal on the basis of "fundamental alteration," asserting for example, that a public accommodation should not exclude a service animal for barking in an environment where other types of noise, such as loud cheering or a child crying, is tolerated. The Department maintains that the appropriateness of an exclusion can be assessed by reviewing how a public accommodation addresses comparable situations that do not involve a service animal. The Department has retained in § 36.302(c)(2) of the final rule the exception requiring animals to be housebroken. The Department has not retained the specific NPRM language stating that animals can be excluded if their presence or behavior fundamentally alters the nature of the service provided by the public accommodation, because the Department believes that this exception is covered by the general reasonable modification requirement contained in § 36.302(c)(1).

The NPRM also proposed in § 36.302(c)(2) (iii) that a service animal can be excluded where "[t]he animal poses a direct threat to the health or safety of others that cannot be eliminated by reasonable modifications." 73 FR 34508, 34553 (June 17, 2008). Commenters were universally supportive of this provision as it makes express the discretion of a public accommodation to exclude a service animal that poses a direct threat. Several commenters cautioned against the overuse of this provision and suggested that the Department provide an example of the rule's application. The Department has decided not to include regulatory language specifically stating that a service animal can be excluded if it poses a direct threat. The Department believes that the direct threat provision in § 36.208 already provides this exception to public accommodations.

Access to a public accommodation following the proper exclusion of a service animal. The NPRM proposed that in the event a public accommodation properly excludes a service animal, the public accommodation must give the individual with a disability the opportunity to obtain the goods and services of the public accommodation without having the service animal on the premises. Most commenters welcomed this provision as a common sense approach. These commenters noted that they do not wish to preclude individuals with disabilities from the full and equal enjoyment of the goods and services simply because of an isolated problem with a service animal. The Department has elected to retain this provision in § 36.302(c)(2).

Other requirements. The NPRM also proposed that the regulation include the following requirements: that the work or tasks performed by the service animal must be directly related to the handler's disability; that a service animal must be individually trained to do work or perform a task, be housebroken, and be under the control of the handler; and that a service animal must have a harness, leash, or other tether. Most commenters addressed at least one of these issues in their responses. Most agreed that these provisions are important to clarify further the 1991 service animal regulation. The Department has moved the requirement that the work or tasks performed by the service animal must be related directly to the individual's disability to the definition of "service animal" in § 36.104. In addition, the Department has modified the proposed language relating to the handler's control of the animal with a harness, leash, or other tether to state that "[a] service animal shall have a harness, leash, or other tether, unless either the handler is unable because of a disability to use a harness, leash, or other tether, or the use of a harness, leash, or other tether would interfere with the service animal's safe, effective performance of work or tasks, in which case the service animal must be otherwise under the handler's control (e.g., voice control, signals, or other effective means)." The Department has retained the requirement that the service animal must be individually trained, as well as the requirement that the service animal be housebroken.

Responsibility for supervision and care of a service animal. The 1991 title III regulation, in § 36.302(c)(2), states that "[n]othing in this part requires a public accommodation to supervise or care for a service animal." The NPRM modified this language to state that "[a] public accommodation is not responsible for caring for or supervising a service animal." 73 FR 34508, 34553 (June 17, 2008). Most commenters did not address this particular provision. The Department notes that there are occasions when a person with a disability is confined to bed in a hospital for a period of time. In such an instance, the individual may not be able to walk or feed the service animal. In such cases, if the individual has a family member, friend, or other person willing to take on these responsibilities in the place of the individual with a disability, the individual's obligation to be responsible for the care and supervision of the service animal would be satisfied. The language of this section is retained, with minor modifications, in § 36.302(c) (5) of the final rule.

Inquiries about service animals. The NPRM proposed language at § 36.302(c)(6) setting forth parameters about how a public accommodation may determine whether an animal qualifies as a service animal. The proposed section stated that a public accommodation may ask if the animal is required because of a disability and what task or work the animal has been trained to do but may not require proof of service animal certification or licensing. Such inquiries are limited to eliciting the information necessary to make a decision without requiring disclosure of confidential disability-related information that a public accommodation does not need.

This language is consistent with the policy guidance outlined in two Department publications, *Commonly Asked Questions about Service Animals in Places of Business* (1996), available at http://www.ada.gov/qasrvc.htm, and *ADA Guide for Small Businesses* (1999), available at http://www.ada.gov/smbustxt.htm.

Although some commenters contended that the NPRM service animal provisions leave unaddressed the issue of how a public accommodation can distinguish between a psychiatric service animal, which is covered under the final rule, and a comfort animal, which is not, other commenters noted that the Department's published guidance has helped public accommodations to distinguish between service animals and pets on the basis of an individual's response to these questions. Accordingly, the Department has retained the NPRM language incorporating its guidance concerning the permissible questions into the final rule.

Some commenters suggested that a title III entity be allowed to require current documentation, no more than one year old, on letterhead from a mental health professional stating the following: (1) That the individual seeking to use the animal has a mental health-related disability; (2) that having the animal accompany the individual is necessary to the individual's mental health or treatment or to assist the person otherwise; and (3) that the person providing the assessment of the individual is a licensed mental health professional and the individual seeking to use the animal is under that individual's professional care. These commenters asserted that this will prevent abuse and ensure that individuals with legitimate needs for psychiatric service animals may use them. The Department believes that this proposal would treat persons with psychiatric, intellectual, and other mental disabilities less favorably than persons with physical or sensory disabilities. The proposal would also require persons with disabilities to obtain medical documentation and carry it with them any time they seek to engage in ordinary activities of daily life in their communities — something individuals without disabilities have not been required to do. Accordingly, the Department has concluded that a documentation requirement of this kind would be unnecessary, burdensome, and contrary to the spirit, intent, and mandates of the ADA.

Service animal access to areas of a public accommodation. The NPRM proposed at § 36.302(c) (7) that an individual with a disability who uses a service animal has the same right of access to areas of a public accommodation as members of the public, program participants, and invitees. Commenters indicated that allowing individuals with disabilities to go with their service animals into the same areas as members of the public, program participants, clients, customers, patrons, or invitees is accepted practice by most places of public accommodation. The Department has included a slightly modified version of this provision in § 36.302(c)(7) of the final rule. The Department notes that under the final rule, a healthcare facility must also permit a person with a disability to be accompanied by a service animal in all areas of the facility in which that person would otherwise be allowed. There are some exceptions, however. The Department follows the guidance of the Centers for Disease Control and Prevention (CDC) on the use of service animals in a hospital setting. Zoonotic diseases can be transmitted to humans through bites, scratches, direct contact, arthropod vectors, or aerosols.

Consistent with CDC guidance, it is generally appropriate to exclude a service animal from limited-access areas that employ general infection- control measures, such as operating rooms and burn units. *See* Centers for Disease Control and Prevention, *Guidelines for Environmental Infection Control in Health-Care Facilities: Recommendations of CDC and the Healthcare Infection Control Practices Advisory Committee* (June 2003), available at http://www.cdc.gov/hicpac/pdf/guidelines/eic_in_HCF_03.pdf (last visited June 24, 2010). A service animal may accompany its handler to such areas as admissions and discharge offices, the emergency room, inpatient and out- patient rooms, examining and diagnostic rooms, clinics, rehabilitation therapy areas, the cafeteria and vending areas, the pharmacy, restrooms, and all other areas of the facility where healthcare personnel, patients, and visitors are permitted without taking added precautions.

Prohibition against surcharges for use of a service animal. In the NPRM, the Department proposed to incorporate the previously mentioned policy guidance, which prohibits the assessment of a surcharge for the use of a service animal, into proposed § 36.302(c)(8). Several commenters agreed that this provision makes clear the obligation of a place of public accommodation to admit an individual with a service animal without surcharges, and that any additional costs imposed should be factored into the overall cost of doing business and passed on as a charge to all participants, rather than an individualized surcharge to the service animal user. Commenters also noted that service animal users cannot be required to comply with other requirements that are not generally applicable to other persons. If a public accommodation normally charges individuals for the damage they cause, an individual with a disability may be charged for damage caused by his or her service animals. The Department has retained this language, with minor modifications, in the final rule at § 36.302(c)(8).

Training requirement. Certain commenters recommended the adoption of formal training requirements for service animals. The Department has rejected this approach and will not impose any type of formal training requirements or certification process, but will continue to require that service animals be individually trained to do work or perform tasks for the benefit of an individual with a disability. While some groups have urged the Department to modify this position, the

Department has determined that such a modification would not serve the full array of individuals with disabilities who use service animals, since individuals with disabilities may be capable of training, and some have trained, their service animal to perform tasks or do work to accommodate their disability. A training and certification requirement would increase the expense of acquiring a service animal and might limit access to service animals for individuals with limited financial resources.

Some commenters proposed specific behavior or training standards for service animals, arguing that without such standards, the public has no way to differentiate between untrained pets and service animals. Many of the suggested behavior or training standards were lengthy and detailed. The Department believes that this rule addresses service animal behavior sufficiently by including provisions that address the obligations of the service animal user and the circumstances under which a service animal may be excluded, such as the requirements that an animal be housebroken and under the control of its handler.

Miniature horses. The Department has been persuaded by commenters and the available research to include a provision that would require public accommodations to make reasonable modifications to policies, practices, or procedures to permit the use of a miniature horse by a person with a disability if the miniature horse has been individually trained to do work or perform tasks for the benefit of the individual with a disability. The traditional service animal is a dog, which has a long history of guiding individuals who are blind or have low vision, and over time dogs have been trained to perform an even wider variety of services for individuals with all types of disabilities. However, an organization that developed a program to train miniature horses, modeled on the program used for guide dogs, began training miniature horses in 1991.

Although commenters generally supported the species limitations proposed in the NPRM, some were opposed to the exclusion of miniature horses from the definition of a service animal. These commenters noted that these animals have been providing assistance to persons with disabilities for many years. Miniature horses were suggested by some commenters as viable alternatives to dogs for individuals with allergies, or for those whose religious beliefs preclude the use of dogs. Another consideration mentioned in favor of the use of miniature horses is the longer life span and strength of miniature horses in comparison to dogs. Specifically, miniature horses can provide service for more than 25 years while dogs can provide service for approximately seven years, and, because of their strength, miniature horses can provide services that dogs cannot provide. Accordingly, use of miniature horses reduces the cost involved to retire, replace, and train replacement service animals.

The miniature horse is not one specific breed, but may be one of several breeds, with distinct characteristics that produce animals suited to service animal work. These animals generally range in height from 24 inches to 34 inches measured to the withers, or shoulders, and generally weigh between 70 and 100 pounds. These characteristics are similar to those of large breed dogs, such as Labrador Retrievers, Great Danes, and Mastiffs. Similar to dogs, miniature horses can be trained through behavioral reinforcement to be "house-broken." Most miniature service horse handlers and organizations recommend that when the animals are not doing work or performing tasks, the miniature horses should be kept outside in a designated area instead of indoors in a house.

According to information provided by an organization that trains service horses, these miniature horses are trained to provide a wide array of services to their handlers, primarily guiding individuals who are blind or have low vision, pulling wheelchairs, providing stability and balance for individuals with disabilities that impair the ability to walk, and supplying leverage that enables a person with a mobility disability to get up after a fall. According to the commenter, miniature horses are particularly effective for large stature individuals. The animal can be trained to stand (and in some cases, lie down) at the handler's feet in venues where space is at a premium, such as assembly areas or inside some vehicles that provide public transportation. Some individuals with disabilities have traveled by train and have flown commercially with their miniature horses.

The miniature horse is not included in the definition of service animal, which is limited to dogs. However, the Department has added a specific provision at § 36.302(c)(9) of the final rule covering miniature horses. Under this provision, public accommodations must make reasonable modifications in policies, practices, or procedures to permit the use of a miniature horse by an individual with a disability if the miniature horse has been individually trained to do work or perform tasks for the benefit of the individual with a disability. The public accommodation may take into account a series of assessment factors in determining whether to allow a miniature horse into a specific facility. These include the type, size, and weight of the miniature horse, whether the handler has sufficient control of the miniature horse, whether the miniature horse is housebroken, and whether the miniature horse's presence in a specific facility compromises legitimate safety requirements that are necessary for safe operation. In addition, paragraphs (c)(3)B–(8) of this section, which are applicable to dogs, also apply to miniature horses.

Ponies and full-size horses are not covered by § 36.302(c)(9). Also, because miniature horses can vary in size and can be larger and less flexible than dogs, covered entities may exclude this type of service animal if the presence of the miniature horse, because of its larger size and lower level of flexibility, results in a fundamental alteration to the nature of the services provided.

Section 36.302(e)   Hotel Reservations.

Section 36.302 of the 1991 title III regulation requires public accommodations to make reasonable modifications in policies, practices, or procedures when such modifications are necessary to afford access to any goods, services, facilities, privileges, advantages, or accommodations, unless the entity can demonstrate that making such modifications would fundamentally alter the nature of such goods, services, facilities, privileges, advantages, or accommodations. Hotels, timeshare resorts, and other places of lodging are subject to this requirement and must make reasonable modifications to reservations policies, practices, or procedures when necessary to ensure that individuals with disabilities are able to reserve accessible hotel rooms with the same efficiency, immediacy, and convenience as those who do not need accessible guest rooms.

Each year the Department receives many complaints concerning failed reservations. Most of these complaints involve individuals who have reserved an accessible hotel room only to discover upon arrival that the room they reserved is either not available or not accessible. Although problems with reservations services were not addressed in the ANPRM, commenters independently noted an ongoing problem with hotel reservations and urged the Department to provide regulatory guidance. In response, the Department proposed specific language in the NPRM to address hotel reservations. In addition, the Department posed several questions regarding the current practices of hotels and other reservations services including questions about room guarantees and the holding and release of accessible rooms. The Department also questioned whether public accommodations that provide reservations services for a place or places of lodging but do not own, lease (or lease to), or operate a place of lodging — referred to in this discussion as "third-party reservations services" — should also be subject to the NPRM's proposals concerning hotel reservations.

Although reservations issues were discussed primarily in the context of traditional hotels, the new rule modifies the definition of "places of lodging" to clarify the scope of the rule's coverage of rental accommodations in timeshare properties, condominium hotels, and mixed-use and corporate hotel facilities that operate as places of public accommodation (as that term is now defined in § 36.104), and the Department received detailed comments, discussed below, regarding the application of reservations requirements to this category of rental accommodations.

General rule on reservations. Section 36.302(e) (1) of the NPRM required a public accommodation that owns, leases (or leases to), or operates a place of lodging to:

Modify its policies, practices, or procedures to ensure that individuals with disabilities can make reservations, including reservations made by telephone, in-person, or through a third party, for accessible guest rooms during the same hours and in the same manner as individuals who do not need accessible rooms. 73 FR 34508, 34553 (June 17, 2008).

Most individual commenters and organizations that represent individuals with disabilities strongly supported the requirement that individuals with disabilities should be able to make reservations for accessible guest rooms during the same hours and in the same manner as individuals who do not need accessible rooms. In many cases individuals with disabilities expressed frustration because, while they are aware of improvements in architectural access brought about as a result of the ADA, they are unable to take advantage of these improvements because of shortcomings in current hotel reservations systems. A number of these commenters pointed out that it can be difficult or impossible to obtain information about accessible rooms and hotel features and that even when information is provided it often is found to be incorrect upon arrival. They also noted difficulty reserving accessible rooms and the inability to guarantee or otherwise ensure that the appropriate accessible room is available when the guest arrives. The ability to obtain information about accessible guest rooms, to make reservations for accessible guest rooms in the same manner as other guests, and to be assured of an accessible room upon arrival was of critical importance to these commenters.

Other commenters, primarily hotels, resort developers, travel agencies, and organizations commenting on their behalf, did not oppose the general rule on reservations, but recommended that the language requiring that reservations be made "in the same manner" be changed to require that reservations be made "in a substantially similar manner." These commenters argued that hotel reservations are made in many different ways and through a variety of systems. In general, they argued that current reservations database systems may not contain s guests, travel agents, or other third-party reservations services to select the most appropriate room without consulting directly with the hotel, and that updating these systems might be expensive and time consuming. They also noted that in some cases, hotels do not always automatically book accessible rooms when requested to do so. Instead, guests may select from a menu of accessibility and other room options when making reservations. This information is transmitted to the hotel's reservations staff, who then contact the individual to verify the guest's accessibility needs. Only when such verification occurs will the accessible room be booked.

The Department is not persuaded that individuals who need to reserve accessible rooms cannot be served in the same manner as those who do not, and it appears that there are hotels of all types and sizes that already meet this requirement. Further, the Department has been able to accomplish this goal in settlement agreements resolving complaints about this issue. As stated in the preamble to the NPRM, basic nondiscrimination principles mandate that individuals with disabilities should be able to reserve hotel rooms with the same efficiency, immediacy, and convenience as those who do not need accessible guest rooms. The regulation does not require reservations services to create new methods for reserving hotel rooms or available timeshare units; instead, covered entities must make the modifications needed to ensure that individuals who need accessible rooms are able to reserve them in the same manner as other guests. If, for example, hotel reservations are not final until all hotel guests have been contacted by the hotel to discuss the guest's needs, a hotel may follow the same process when reserving accessible rooms. Therefore, the Department declines to change this language, which has been moved to § 36.302(e)(1)(i). However, in response to the commenters who recommended a transition period that would allow reservations services time to modify existing reservations systems to meet the requirements of this rule, § 36.302(e)(3) now provides a 18-month transition period before the requirements of § 36.302(e)(1) will be enforced.

Hotels and organizations commenting on their behalf also requested that the language be changed to eliminate any liability for reservations made through third parties, arguing that they are unable to control the actions of unrelated parties. The rule, both as proposed and as adopted, requires covered public accommodations to ensure that reservations made on their behalf by third parties are made in a manner that results in parity between those who need accessible rooms and those who do not.

Hotels and other places of lodging that use third-party reservations services must make reasonable efforts to make accessible rooms available through at least some of these services and must provide these third-party services with information concerning the accessible features of the hotel and the accessible rooms. To the extent a hotel or other place of lodging makes available such rooms and information to a third-party reservation provider, but the third party fails to provide the information or rooms to people with disabilities in accordance with this section, the hotel or other place of lodging will not be responsible.

Identification of accessible features in hotels and guest rooms. NPRM § 36.302(e)(2) required public accommodations that provide hotel reservations services to identify and describe the accessible features in the hotels and guest rooms offered through that service. This requirement is essential to ensure that individuals with disabilities receive the information they need to benefit from the services offered by the place of lodging. As a practical matter, a public accommodation's designation of a guest room as "accessible" will not ensure necessarily that the room complies with all of the 1991 Standards. In older facilities subject to barrier removal requirements, strict compliance with the 1991 Standards is not required. Instead, public accommodations must remove barriers to the extent that it is readily achievable to do so.

Further, hotel rooms that are in full compliance with current standards may differ, and individuals with disabilities must be able to ascertain which features — in new and existing facilities — are included in the hotel's accessible guest rooms. For example, under certain circumstances, an accessible hotel bathroom may meet accessibility requirements with either a bathtub or a roll-in shower. The presence or absence of particular accessible features such as these may be the difference between a room that is usable by a particular person with a disability and one that is not.

Individuals with disabilities strongly supported this requirement. In addition to the importance of information about specific access features, several commenters pointed out the importance of knowing the size and number of beds in a room. Many individuals with disabilities travel with family members, personal care assistants, or other companions and require rooms with at least two beds. Although most hotels provide this information when generally categorizing the type or class of room (e.g., deluxe suite with king bed), as described below, all hotels should consider the size and number of beds to be part of the basic information they are required to provide.

Comments made on behalf of reservations services expressed concern that unless the word "hotels" is stricken from the text, § 36.302(e)(2) of the NPRM essentially would require reservations systems to include a full accessibility report on each hotel or resort property in its system. Along these lines, commenters also suggested that the Department identify the specific accessible features of hotel rooms that must be described in the reservations system. For example, commenters suggested limiting features that must be included to bathroom type (tub or roll-in shower) and communications features.

The Department recognizes that a reservations system is not intended to be an accessibility survey. However, specific information concerning accessibility features is essential to travelers with disabilities. Because of the wide variations in the level of accessibility that travelers will encounter, the Department cannot specify what information must be included in every instance. For hotels that were built in compliance with the 1991 Standards, it may be sufficient to specify that the hotel is accessible and, for each accessible room, to describe the general type of room (e.g., deluxe executive suite), the size and number of beds (e.g., two queen beds), the type of accessible bathing facility (e.g., roll-in shower), and communications features available in the room (e.g., alarms and visual notification devices). Based on that information, many individuals with disabilities will be comfortable making reservations.

For older hotels with limited accessibility features, information about the hotel should include, at a minimum, information about accessible entrances to the hotel, the path of travel to guest check-in and other essential services, and the accessible route to the accessible room or rooms. In addition to the room information described above, these hotels should provide information about important features that do not comply with the 1991 Standards. For example, if the door to the "accessible" room or bathroom is narrower than required, this information should be included (e.g., door to guest room measures 30 inches clear). This width may not meet current standards but may be adequate for some wheelchair users who use narrower chairs. In many cases, older hotels provide services through alternatives to barrier removal, for example, by providing check- in or concierge services at a different, accessible location. Reservations services for these entities should include this information and provide a way for guests to contact the appropriate hotel employee for additional information. To recognize that the information and level of detail needed will vary based on the nature and age of the facility, § 36.302(e)(2) has been moved to § 36.302(e)(1)(ii) in the final rule and modified to require reservations services to:

Identify and describe accessible features in the hotels and guest rooms offered through its reservations service *in enough detail to reasonably permit individuals with disabilities to assess independently whether a given hotel or guest room meets his or her accessibility needs.* [Emphasis added]

As commenters representing hotels have described, once reservations are made, some hotels may wish to contact the guest to offer additional information and services. Or, many individuals with disabilities may wish to contact the hotel or reservations service for more detailed information. At that point, trained staff (including staff located on-site at the hotel and staff located off-site at a reservations center) should be available to provide additional information such as the specific layout of the room and bathroom, shower design, grab- bar locations, and other amenities available (e.g., bathtub bench).

In the NPRM, the Department sought guidance concerning whether this requirement should be applied to third-party reservations services. Comments made by or on behalf of hotels, resort managers, and other members of the lodging and resort industry pointed out that, in most cases, these third parties do not have direct access to this information and must obtain it from the hotel or other place of lodging. Because third-party reservations services must rely on the place of lodging to provide the requisite information and to ensure that it is accurate and timely, the Department has declined to extend this requirement directly to third-party reservations services.

Hold and release of accessible guest rooms. The Department has addressed the hold and release of accessible guest rooms in settlement agreements and recognizes that current practices vary widely. The Department is concerned about current practices by which accessible guest rooms are released to the general public even though the hotel is not sold out. In such instances, individuals with disabilities may be denied an equal opportunity to benefit from the services offered by the public accommodation, *i.e.*, a hotel guest room.

In the NPRM, the Department requested information concerning the current practices of hotels and third-party reservations services with respect to (1) holding accessible rooms for individuals with disabilities and (2) releasing accessible rooms to individuals without disabilities.

Individuals with disabilities and organizations commenting on their behalf strongly supported requiring accessible rooms to be held back for rental by individuals with disabilities. In some cases commenters supported holding back all accessible rooms until all non-accessible rooms were rented. Others supported holding back accessible rooms in each category of rooms until all other rooms of that type were reserved. This latter position was also supported in comments received on behalf of the lodging industry; commenters also noted that this is the current practice of many hotels. In general, holding accessible rooms until requested by an individual who needs a room with accessible features or until it is the only available room of its type was viewed widely as a sensible approach to allocating scarce accessible rooms without imposing unnecessary costs on hotels.

The Department agrees with this latter approach and has added § 36.302(e)(1)(iii), which requires covered entities to hold accessible rooms for use by individuals with disabilities until all other guest rooms of that type have been rented and the accessible room requested is the only remaining room of that type. For example, if there are 25 rooms of a given type and two of these rooms are accessible, the reservations service is required to rent all 23 non-accessible rooms before it is permitted to rent these two accessible rooms to individuals without disabilities. If a one-of-a-kind room is accessible, that room is available to the first party to request it. The Department believes that this is the fairest approach available since it reserves accessible rooms for individuals who require them until all non-accessible rooms of that type have been reserved, and then provides equal access to any remaining rooms. It is also fair to hotels because it does not require them to forego renting a room that actually has been requested in favor of the possibility that an individual with a disability may want to reserve it at a later date.

Requirement to block accessible guest room reservations. NPRM § 36.302(e)(3) required a public accommodation that owns, leases (or leases to), or operates a place of lodging to guarantee accessible guest rooms that are reserved through a reservations service to the same extent that it guarantees rooms that are not accessible. In the NPRM, the Department sought comment on the current practices of hotels and third party reservations services with respect to "guaranteed" hotel reservations and on the impact of requiring a public accommodation to guarantee accessible rooms to the extent it guarantees other rooms.

Comments received by the Department by and on behalf of both individuals with disabilities and public accommodations that provide reservations services made clear that, in many cases, when speaking of room guarantees, parties who are not familiar with hotel terminology actually mean to refer to policies for blocking and holding specific hotel rooms. Several commenters explained that, in most cases, when an individual makes "reservations," hotels do not reserve specific rooms; rather the individual is reserving a room with certain features at a given price. When the hotel guest arrives, he or she is provided with a room that has those features.

In most cases, this does not pose a problem because there are many available rooms of a given type. However, in comparison, accessible rooms are much more limited in availability and there may be only one room in a given hotel that meets a guest's needs. As described in the discussion on the identification of accessible features in hotels and guest rooms, the presence or absence of particular accessible features may be the difference between a room that is usable by a particular person with a disability and one that is not.

For that reason, the Department has added § 36.302(e)(1)(iv) to the final rule. Section 36.302(e)(1)(iv) requires covered entities to reserve, upon request, accessible guest rooms or specific types of guest rooms and ensure that the guest rooms requested are blocked and removed from all reservations systems (to eliminate double- booking, which is a common problem that arises when rooms are made available to be reserved through more than one reservations service). Of course, if a public accommodation typically requires a payment or deposit from its patrons in order to reserve a room, it may require the same payment or deposit from individuals with disabilities before it reserves an accessible room and removes it from all its reservations systems. These requirements should alleviate the widely-reported problem of arriving at a hotel only to discover that, although an accessible room was reserved, the room available is not accessible or does not have the specific accessible features needed. Many hotels already have a similar process in place for other guest rooms that are unique or one-of-a-kind, such as "Presidential" suites. The Department has declined to extend this requirement directly to third-party reservations services. Comments the Department received in response to the NPRM indicate that most of the actions required to implement these requirements primarily are within the control of the entities that own the place of lodging or that manage it on behalf of its owners.

Guarantees of reservations for accessible guest rooms. The Department recognizes that not all reservations are guaranteed, and the rule does not impose an affirmative duty to guarantee reservations. When a public accommodation does guarantee hotel or other room reservations, it must provide the same guarantee for accessible guest rooms as it makes for other rooms, except that it must apply that guarantee to the specific room reserved and blocked, even if in other situations, its guarantee policy only guarantees that a room of a specific type will be available at the guaranteed price. Without this reasonable modification to its guarantee policy, any guarantee for accessible rooms would be meaningless. If, for example, a hotel makes reservations for an accessible "Executive Suite" but, upon arrival, offers its guest an inaccessible Executive Suite that the guest is unable to enter, it would be meaningless to consider the hotel's guarantee fulfilled. As with the requirements for identifying, holding, and blocking accessible rooms, the Department has declined to extend this requirement directly to third-party reservations services because the fulfillment of guarantees largely is beyond their power to control.

Application to rental units in timeshare, vacation communities, and condo-hotels. Because the Department has revised the definition of "Places of Lodging" in the final rule, the reservations requirements now apply to guest rooms and other rental units in timeshares, vacation communities, and condo-hotels where some or all of the units are owned and controlled by individual owners and rented out some portion of time to the public, as compared to traditional hotels and motels that are owned, controlled, and rented to the public by one entity. If a reservations service owns and controls one or more of the guest rooms or other units in the rental property (e.g., a developer who retains and rents out unsold inventory), it is subject to the requirements set forth in § 36.302(e).

Several commenters expressed concern about any rule that would require accessible units that are owned individually to be removed from the rental pool and rented last. Commenters pointed out that this would be a disadvantage to the owners of accessible units because they would be rented last, if at all. Further, certain vacation property managers consider holding specific units back to be a violation of their ethical responsibility to present all properties they manage at an equal advantage. To address these concerns, the Department has added § 36.302(e)(2), which exempts reservations for individual guest rooms and other units that are not owned or substantially controlled by the entity that owns, leases, or operates the overall facility from the requirement that accessible guest rooms be held back from rental until all other guest rooms of that type have been rented. Section 36.302(e)(2) also exempts such rooms from requirements for blocking and guaranteeing reserved rooms. In resort developments with mixed ownership structures, such as a resort where some units are operated as hotel rooms and others are owned and controlled individually, a reservations service operated by the owner of the hotel portion may apply the exemption only to the rooms that are not owned or substantially controlled by the entity that owns, manages, or otherwise controls the overall facility.

Other reservations-related comments made on behalf of these entities reflected concerns similar to the general concerns expressed with respect to traditional hotel properties. For example, commenters noted that because of the unique nature of the timeshare industry, additional flexibility is needed when making reservations for accessible units. One commenter explained that reservations are sometimes made through unusual entities such as exchange companies, which are not public accommodations and which operate to trade ownership interests of millions of individual owners. The commenter expressed concern that developers or resort owners would be held responsible for the actions of these exchange entities. If, as described, the choice to list a unit with an exchange company is made by the individual owner of the property and the exchange company does not operate on behalf of the reservations service, the reservations service is not liable for the exchange company's actions.

As with hotels, the Department believes that within the 18-month transition period these reservations services should be able to modify their systems to ensure that potential guests with disabilities who need accessible rooms can make reservations during the same hours and in the same manner as those who do not need accessible rooms.

Section 36.302(f) Ticketing.

The 1991 title III regulation did not contain specific regulatory language on ticketing. The ticketing policies and practices of public accommodations, however, are subject to title III's non- discrimination provisions. Through the investigation of complaints, enforcement actions, and public comments related to ticketing, the Department became aware that some venue operators, ticket sellers, and distributors were violating title III's nondiscrimination mandate by not providing individuals with disabilities the same opportunities to purchase tickets for accessible seating as provided to spectators purchasing conventional seats. In the NPRM, the Department proposed § 36.302(f) to provide explicit direction and guidance on discriminatory practices for entities involved in the sale or distribution of tickets.

The Department received comments from advocacy groups, assembly area trade associations, public accommodations, and individuals. Many commenters supported the addition of regulatory language pertaining to ticketing and urged the Department to retain it in the final rule. Several commenters, however, questioned why there were inconsistencies between the title II and title III provisions and suggested that the same language be used for both titles. The Department has decided to retain ticketing regulatory language and to ensure consistency between the ticketing provisions in title II and title III.

Because many in the ticketing industry view season tickets and other multi-event packages differently from individual tickets, the Department bifurcated some season ticket provisions from those concerning single-event tickets in the NPRM. This structure, however, resulted in some provisions being repeated for both types of tickets but not for others even though they were intended to apply to both types of tickets. The result was that it was not entirely clear that some of the provisions that were not repeated also were intended to apply to season tickets. The Department is addressing the issues raised by these commenters using a different approach. For the purposes of this section, a single event refers to an individual performance for which tickets may be purchased. In contrast, a series of events includes, but is not limited to, subscription events, event packages, season tickets, or any other tickets that may be purchased for multiple events of the same type over the course of a specified period of time whose ownership right reverts to the public accommodation at the end of each season or time period. Series-of-events tickets that give their holders an enhanced ability to purchase such tickets from the public accommodation in seasons or periods of time that follow, such as a right of first refusal or higher ranking on waiting lists for more desirable seats, are subject to the provisions in this section. In addition, the final rule merges together some NPRM paragraphs that dealt with related topics and has reordered and renamed some of the paragraphs that were in the NPRM.

Ticket sales. In the NPRM, the Department proposed, in § 36.302(f)(1), a general rule that a public accommodation shall modify its policies, practices, or procedures to ensure that individuals with disabilities can purchase tickets for accessible seating for an event or series of events in the same way as others (i.e., during the same hours and through the same distribution methods as other seating is sold). "Accessible seating" is defined in § 36.302(f)(1)(i) of the final rule to mean "wheelchair spaces and companion seats that comply with sections 221 and 802 of the 2010 Standards along with any other seats required to be offered for sale to the individual with a disability pursuant to paragraph (4) of this section." The defined term does not include designated aisle seats. A "wheelchair space" refers to a space for a single wheelchair and its occupant.

The NPRM proposed requiring that accessible seats be sold through the "same methods of distribution" as non-accessible seats. 73 FR 34508, 34554 (June 17, 2008). Comments from venue managers and others in the business community, in general, noted that multiple parties are involved in ticketing, and because accessible seats may not be allotted to all parties involved at each stage, such parties should be protected from liability. For example, one commenter noted that a third-party ticket vendor, like Ticketmaster, can only sell the tickets it receives from its client. Because § 36.302(f)(1) of the final rule requires venue operators to make available accessible seating through the same methods of distribution they use for their regular tickets, venue operators that provide tickets to third-party ticket vendors are required to provide accessible seating to the third-party ticket vendor. This provision will enhance third-party ticket vendors' ability to acquire and sell accessible seating for sale in the future. The Department notes that once third-party ticket vendors acquire accessible tickets, they are obligated to sell them in accordance with these rules.

The Department also has received frequent complaints that individuals with disabilities have not been able to purchase accessible seating over the Internet, and instead have had to engage in a laborious process of calling a customer service line, or sending an email to a customer service representative and waiting for a response. Not only is such a process burdensome, but it puts individuals with disabilities at a disadvantage in purchasing tickets for events that are popular and may sell out in minutes. Because § 36.302(f)(5) of the final rule authorizes venues to release accessible seating in case of a sell-out, individuals with disabilities effectively could be cut off from buying tickets unless they also have the ability to purchase tickets in real time over the Internet. The Department's new regulatory language is designed to address this problem.

Several commenters representing assembly areas raised concerns about offering accessible seating for sale over the Internet. They contended that this approach would increase the incidence of fraud since anyone easily could purchase accessible seating over the Internet. They also asserted that it would be difficult technologically to provide accessible seating for sale in real time over the Internet, or that to do so would require simplifying the rules concerning the purchase of multiple additional accompanying seats. More- over, these commenters argued that requiring an individual purchasing accessible seating to speak with a customer service representative would allow the venue to meet the patron's needs most appropriately and ensure that wheelchair spaces are reserved for individuals with disabilities who require wheelchair spaces. Finally, these commenters argued that individuals who can transfer effectively and conveniently from a wheelchair to a seat with a movable armrest seat could instead purchase designated aisle seats.

The Department considered these concerns carefully and has decided to continue with the general approach proposed in the NPRM. Although fraud is an important concern, the Department believes that it is best combated by other means that would not have the effect of limiting the ability of individuals with disabilities to purchase tickets, particularly since restricting the purchase of accessible seating over the Internet will, of itself, not curb fraud. In addition, the Department has identified permissible means for covered entities to reduce the incidence of fraudulent accessible seating ticket purchases in § 36.302(f)(8) of the final rule.

Several commenters questioned whether ticket Web sites themselves must be accessible to individuals who are blind or have low vision, and if so, what that requires. The Department has consistently interpreted the ADA to cover Web sites that are operated by public accommodations and stated that such sites must provide their services in an accessible manner or provide an accessible alternative to the Web site that is available 24 hours a day, seven days a week. The final rule, therefore, does not impose any new obligation in this area. The accessibility of Web sites is discussed in more detail in the section entitled "Other Issues."

In § 36.302(f)(2) of the NPRM, the Department also proposed requiring public accommodations to make accessible seating available during all stages of tickets sales including, but not limited to, pre-sales, promotions, lotteries, waitlists, and general sales. For example, if tickets will be presold or an event that is open only to members of a fan club, or to holders of a particular credit card, then tickets for accessible seating must be made available for purchase through those means. This requirement does not mean that any individual with a disability would be able to purchase those seats. Rather, it means that an individual with a disability who meets the requirement for such a sale (e.g., who is a member of the fan club or holds that credit card) will be able to participate in the special promotion and purchase accessible seating. The Department has maintained the substantive provisions of the NPRM's §§ 36.302(f)(1) and (f)(2) but has combined them in a single paragraph at § 36.302(f)(1)(ii) of the final rule so that all of the provisions having to do with the manner in which tickets are sold are located in a single paragraph.

Identification of available accessible seating. In the NPRM, the Department proposed § 36.302(f)(3), which, as modified and renumbered § 36.302(f)(2)(iii) in the final rule, requires a facility to identify available accessible seating through seating maps, brochures, or other methods if that information is made available about other seats sold to the general public. This rule requires public accommodations to provide information about accessible seating to the same degree of specificity that it provides information about general seating. For example, if a seating map displays color-coded blocks pegged to prices for general seating, then accessible seating must be similarly color-coded. Likewise, if covered entities provide detailed maps that show exact seating and pricing for general seating, they must provide the same for accessible seating.

The NPRM did not specify a requirement to identify prices for accessible seating. The final rule requires that if such information is provided for general seating, it must be provided for accessible seating as well.

In the NPRM, the Department proposed in § 36.302(f)(4) that a public accommodation, upon being asked, must inform persons with disabilities and their companions of the locations of all un- sold or otherwise available seating. This provision is intended to prevent the practice of "steering" individuals with disabilities to certain accessible seating so that the facility can maximize potential ticket sales by releasing unsold accessible seating, especially in preferred or desirable locations, for sale to the general public. The Department received no significant comment on this proposal. The Department has retained this provision in the final rule but has added it, with minor modifications, to § 36.302(f)(2) as paragraph (i).

Ticket prices. In the NPRM, the Department proposed § 36.302(f)(7) requiring that ticket prices for accessible seating be set no higher than the prices for other seats in that seating section for that event. The NPRM's provision also required that accessible seating be made available at every price range, and if an existing facility has barriers to accessible seating within a particular price range, a proportionate amount of seating (determined by the ratio of the total number of seats at that price level to the total number of seats in the assembly area) must be offered in an accessible location at that same price. Under this rule, for example, if it is not readily achievable for a 20,000 seat facility built in 1980 to place accessible seating in the $20-price category, which is on the upper deck, it must place a proportionate number of seats in an accessible location for $20. If the upper deck has 2,000 seats, then the facility must place 10 percent of its accessible seating in an accessible location for $20 provided that it is part of a seating section where ticket prices are equal to or more than $20 — a facility may not place the $20-accessible seating in a $10-seating section. The Department received no significant comment on this rule, and it has been retained, as amended, in the final rule in § 36.302(f)(3).

Purchase of multiple tickets. In the NPRM, the Department proposed § 36.302(f)(9) to address one of the most common ticketing complaints raised with the Department: that individuals with disabilities are not able to purchase more than two tickets. The Department proposed this provision to facilitate the ability of individuals with disabilities to attend events with friends, companions, or associates who may or may not have a disability by enabling individuals with disabilities to purchase the maximum number of tickets allowed per transaction to other spectators; by requiring venues to place accompanying individuals in general seating as close as possible to accessible seating (in the event that a group must be divided because of the large size of the group); and by allowing an individual with a disability to purchase up to three additional contiguous seats per wheelchair space if they are available at the time of sale. Section 36.302(f)(9)(ii) of the NPRM required that a group containing one or more wheelchair users must be placed together, if possible, and that in the event that the group could not be placed together, the individuals with disabilities may not be isolated from the rest of the group.

The Department asked in the NPRM whether this rule was sufficient to effectuate the integration of individuals with disabilities. Many advocates and individuals praised it as a welcome and much needed change, stating that the trade-off of being able to sit with their family or friends was worth reducing the number of seats available for individuals with disabilities. Some commenters went one step further and suggested that the number of additional accompanying seats should not be restricted to three.

Although most of the substance of the proposed provision on the purchase of multiple tickets has been maintained in the final rule, it has been renumbered as § 36.302(f)(4), reorganized, and supplemented. To preserve the availability of accessible seating for other individuals with disabilities, the Department has not expanded the rule beyond three additional contiguous seats. Section 36.302(f)(4)(i) of the final rule requires public accommodations to make available for purchase three additional tickets for seats in the same row that are contiguous with the wheelchair space, provided that at the time of purchase there are three such seats available. The requirement that the additional seats be "contiguous with the wheelchair space" does not mean that each of the additional seats must be in actual contact or have a border in common with the wheelchair space; however, at least one of the additional seats should be immediately adjacent to the wheelchair space. The Department recognizes that it will often be necessary to use vacant wheelchair spaces to provide for contiguous seating.

The Department has added paragraphs (4)(ii) and (4)(iii) to clarify that in situations where there are insufficient unsold seats to provide three additional contiguous seats per wheelchair space or a ticket office restricts sales of tickets to a particular event to less than four tickets per customer, the obligation to make available three additional contiguous seats per wheelchair space would be affected. For example, if at the time of purchase, there are only two additional contiguous seats available for purchase because the third has been sold already, then the ticket purchaser would be entitled to two such seats. In this situation, the public entity would be required to make up the difference by offering one additional ticket for sale that is as close as possible to the accessible seats. Likewise, if ticket purchases for an event are limited to two per customer, a person who uses a wheelchair who seeks to purchase tickets would be entitled to purchase only one additional contiguous seat for the event.

The Department has also added paragraph (4) (iv) to clarify that the requirement for three additional contiguous seats is not intended to serve as a cap if the maximum number of tickets that may be purchased by members of the general public exceeds the four tickets an individual with a disability ordinarily would be allowed to purchase (i.e., a wheelchair space and three additional contiguous seats). If the maximum number of tickets that may be purchased by members of the general public exceeds four, an individual with a disability is to be allowed to purchase the maximum number of tickets; however, additional tickets purchased by an individual with a disability beyond the wheelchair space and the three additional contiguous seats provided in § 36.302(f)(4)(i) do not have to be contiguous with the wheelchair space.

The NPRM proposed at § 36.302(f)(9)(ii) that for group sales, if a group includes one or more individuals who use a wheelchair, then the group shall be placed in a seating area with accessible seating so that, if possible, the group can sit together. If it is necessary to divide the group, it should be divided so that the individuals in the group who use wheelchairs are not isolated from the rest of the members of their group. The final rule retains the NPRM language in paragraph (4) (v).

Hold and release of unsold accessible seating.

The Department recognizes that not all accessible seating will be sold in all assembly areas for every event to individuals with disabilities who need such seating and that public accommodations may have opportunities to sell such seating to the general public. The Department proposed in the NPRM a provision aimed at striking a balance between affording individuals with disabilities adequate time to purchase accessible seating and the entity's desire to maximize ticket sales. In the NPRM, the Department proposed § 36.302(f)(6), which allowed for the release of accessible seating under the following circumstances: (i) When all seating in the facility has been sold, excluding luxury boxes, club boxes, or suites; (ii) when all seating in a designated area has been sold and the accessible seating being released is in the same area; or (iii) when all seating in a designated price range has been sold and the accessible seating being released is within the same price range.

The Department's NPRM asked "whether additional regulatory guidance is required or appropriate in terms of a more detailed or set schedule for the release of tickets in conjunction with the three approaches described above. For example, does the proposed regulation address the variable needs of assembly areas covered by the ADA? Is additional regulatory guidance required to eliminate discriminatory policies, practices and procedures related to the sale, hold, and release of accessible seating? What considerations should appropriately inform the determination of when unsold accessible seating can be released to the general public?" 73 FR 34508, 34527 (June 17, 2008).

The Department received comments both supporting and opposing the inclusion of a hold-and- release provision. One side proposed loosening the restrictions on the release of unsold accessible seating. One commenter from a trade association suggested that tickets should be released regardless of whether there is a sell-out, and that these tickets should be released according to a set schedule. Conversely, numerous individuals, advocacy groups, and at least one public entity urged the Department to tighten the conditions under which unsold tickets for accessible seating may be released. These commenters suggested that venues should not be permitted to release tickets during the first two weeks of sale, or alternatively, that they should not be permitted to be released earlier than 48 hours before a sold-out event. Many of these commenters criticized the release of accessible seating under the second and third prongs of § 36.302(f)(6) in the NPRM (when there is a sell- out in general seating in a designated seating area or in a price range), arguing that it would create situations where general seating would be available for purchase while accessible seating would not be.

Numerous commenters — both from the industry and from advocacy groups — asked for clarification of the term "sell-out." Business groups commented that industry practice is to declare a sell-out when there are only "scattered singles" available — isolated seats that cannot be purchased as a set of adjacent pairs. Many of those same commenters also requested that "sell-out" be qualified with the phrase "of all seating available for sale" since it is industry practice to hold back from release tickets to be used for groups connected with that event (e.g., the promoter, home team, or sports league). They argued that those tickets are not available for sale and any return of these tickets to the general inventory happens close to the event date. Noting the practice of holding back tickets, one advocacy group suggested that covered entities be required to hold back accessible seating in proportion to the number of tickets that are held back for later release.

The Department has concluded that it would be inappropriate to interfere with industry practice by defining what constitutes a "sell-out" and that a public accommodation should continue to use its own approach to defining a "sell-out." If, however, a public accommodation declares a sell-out by reference to those seats that are available for sale, but it holds back tickets that it reasonably anticipates will be released later, it must hold back a proportional percentage of accessible seating to be released as well.

Adopting any of the alternatives proposed n the comments summarized above would have upset the balance between protecting the rights of individuals with disabilities and meeting venues' concerns about lost revenue from unsold accessible seating. As a result, the Department has retained § 36.302(f)(6) renumbered as § 36.302(f) (5) in the final rule. The Department has, however, modified the regulation text to specify that accessible seating may be released only when "all non- accessible tickets in a designated seating area have been sold and the tickets for accessible seating are being released in the same designated area." As stated in the NPRM, the Department intended for this provision to allow, for example, the release of accessible seating at the orchestra level when all other seating at the orchestra level is sold. The Department has added this language to the final rule at § 36.302(f)(5)(B) to clarify that venues cannot designate or redesignate seating areas for the purpose of maximizing the release of unsold accessible seating. So, for example, a venue may not determine on an ad hoc basis that a group of seats at the orchestra level is a designated seating area in order to release unsold accessible seating in that area.

The Department also has maintained the hold-and-release provisions that appeared in the NPRM, but has added a provision to address the release of accessible seating for series-of-events tickets on a series-of-events basis. Many commenters asked the Department whether unsold accessible seating may be converted to general seating and released to the general public on a season- ticket basis or longer when tickets typically are sold as a season-ticket package or other long-term basis. Several disability rights organizations and individual commenters argued that such a practice should not be permitted, and, if it were, that conditions should be imposed to ensure that individuals with disabilities have future access to those seats.

The Department interprets the fundamental principle of the ADA as a require- ment to give individuals with disabilities equal, not better, access to those opportunities available to the general public. Thus, for example, a public accommo- dation that sells out its facility on a season-ticket only basis is not required to leave unsold its accessible seating if no persons with disabilities purchase those season- ticket seats. Of course, public accommodations may choose to go beyond what is required by reserving accessible seating for individuals with disabilities (or releasing such seats for sale to the general public) on an individual- game basis.

If a covered entity chooses to release unsold accessible seating for sale on a season-ticket or other long-term basis, it must meet at least two conditions. Under § 36.302(f)(5)(iii) of the final rule, public accommodations must leave flexibility for game-day change-outs to accommodate ticket transfers on the secondary market. And public accommodations must modify their ticketing policies so that, in future years, individuals with disabilities will have the ability to purchase accessible seating on the same basis as other patrons (e.g., as season tickets). Put differently, releasing accessible seating to the general public on a season-ticket or other long-term basis cannot result in that seating being lost to individuals with disabilities in perpetuity. If, in future years, season tickets become available and persons with disabilities have reached the top of the waiting list or have met any other eligibility criteria for season ticket purchases, public accommodations must ensure that accessible seating will be made available to the eligible individuals. In order to accomplish this, the Department has added § 36.302(f)(5)(iii) (A) to require public accommodations that release accessible season tickets to individuals who do not have disabilities that require the features of accessible seating to establish a process to prevent the automatic reassignment of such ticket holders to accessible seating. For example, a public accommodation could have in place a system whereby accessible seating that was released because it was not purchased by individuals with disabilities is not in the pool of tickets available for purchase for the following season unless and until the conditions for ticket release have been satisfied in the following season. Alternatively, a public accommodation might release tickets for accessible seating only when a purchaser who does not need its features agrees that he or she has no guarantee of or right to the same seats in the following season, or that if season tickets are guaranteed for the following season, the purchaser agrees that the offer to purchase tickets is limited to non-accessible seats with, to the extent practicable, comparable price, view, and amenities to the accessible seats such individuals held in the prior year. The Department is aware that this rule may require some administrative changes but believes that this process will not create undue financial and administrative burdens. The Department believes that this approach is balanced and beneficial. It will allow public accommodations to sell all of their seats and will leave open the possibility, in future seasons or series of events, that persons who need accessible seating may have access to it.

The Department also has added § 36.302(f)(5) (iii)(B) to address how season tickets or series-of- events tickets that have attached ownership rights should be handled if the ownership right returns to the public accommodation (e.g., when holders forfeit their ownership right by failing to purchase season tickets or sell their ownership right back to a public accommodation). If the ownership right is for accessible seating, the public accommodation is required to adopt a process that allows an eligible individual with a disability who requires the features of such seating to purchase the rights and tickets for such seating.

Nothing in the regulatory text prevents a public accommodation from establishing a process whereby such ticket holders agree to be voluntarily reassigned from accessible seating to another seating area so that individuals with mobility disabilities or disabilities that require the features of accessible seating and who become newly eligible to purchase season tickets have an opportunity to do so. For example, a public accommodation might seek volunteers to relocate to another location that is at least as good in terms of its location, price, and amenities or a public accommodation might use a seat with forfeited ownership rights as an inducement to get a ticket holder to give up accessible seating he or she does not need.

Ticket transfer. The Department received many comments asking whether accessible seating has the same transfer rights as general seats. The proposed regulation at § 36.302(f)(5) required that individuals with disabilities must be allowed to purchase season tickets for accessible seating on the same terms and conditions as individuals purchasing season tickets for general seating, including the right — if it exists for other ticket- holders — to transfer individual tickets to friends or associates. Some commenters pointed out that the NPRM proposed explicitly allowing individuals with disabilities holding season tickets to transfer tickets but did not address the transfer of tickets purchased for individual events. Several commenters representing assembly areas argued that persons with disabilities holding tickets for an individual event should not be allowed to sell or transfer them to third parties because such ticket transfers would increase the risk of fraud or would make unclear the obligation of the entity to accommodate secondary ticket transfers. They argued that individuals holding accessible seating should either be required to transfer their tickets to another individual with a disability or return them to the facility for a refund.

Although the Department is sympathetic to concerns about administrative burden, curtailing transfer rights for accessible seating when other ticket holders are permitted to transfer tickets would be inconsistent with the ADA's guiding principle that individuals with disabilities must have rights equal to others. Thus, the Department has added language in the final rule in § 36.302(f) (6) that requires that individuals with disabilities holding accessible seating for any event have the same transfer rights accorded other ticket holders for that event. Section 36.302(f)(6) also preserves the rights of individuals with disabilities who hold tickets to accessible seats for a series of events to transfer individual tickets to others, regardless of whether the transferee needs accessible seating. This approach recognizes the common practice of individuals splitting season tickets or other multi- event ticket packages with friends, colleagues, or other spectators to make the purchase of season tickets affordable; individuals with disabilities should not be placed in the burdensome position of having to find another individual with a disability with whom to share the package.

This provision, however, does not require public accommodations to seat an individual who holds a ticket to an accessible seat in such seating if the individual does not need the accessible features of the seat. A public accommodation may reserve the right to switch these individuals to different seats if they are available, but a public accommodation is not required to remove a person without a disability who is using accessible seating from that seating, even if a person who uses a wheelchair shows up with a ticket from the secondary market for a non-accessible seat and wants accessible seating.

Secondary ticket market. Section 36.302(f)(7) is a new provision in the final rule that requires a public accommodation to modify its policies, practices, or procedures to ensure that an individual with a disability, who acquires a ticket in the secondary ticket market, may use that ticket under the same terms and conditions as other ticket holders who acquire a ticket in the secondary market for an event or series of events. This principle was discussed in the NPRM in connection with § 36.302(f)(5), pertaining to season-ticket sales. There, the Department asked for public comment regarding a public accommodation's proposed obligation to accommodate the transfer of accessible seating tickets on the secondary ticket market to those who do not need accessible seating and vice versa.

The secondary ticket market, for the purposes of this rule, broadly means any transfer of tickets after the public accommodation's initial sale of tickets to individuals or entities. It thus encompasses a wide variety of transactions, from ticket transfers between friends to transfers using commercial exchange systems. Many commenters noted that the distinction between the primary and secondary ticket market has become blurred as a result of agreements between teams, leagues, and secondary market sellers. These commenters noted that the secondary market may operate independently of the public accommodation, and parts of the secondary market, such as ticket transfers between friends, undoubtedly are outside the direct jurisdiction of the public accommodation. To the extent that venues seat persons who have purchased tickets on the secondary market, they must similarly seat persons with disabilities who have purchased tickets on the secondary market. In addition, some public accommodations may acquire ADA obligations directly by formally entering the secondary ticket market.

The Department's enforcement experience with assembly areas also has revealed that venues regularly provide for and make last-minute seat transfers. As long as there are vacant wheelchair spaces, requiring venues to provide wheelchair spaces for patrons who acquired inaccessible seats and need wheelchair spaces is an example of a reasonable modification of a policy under title III of the ADA. Similarly, a person who has a ticket for a wheelchair space but who does not require its accessible features could be offered non-accessible seating if such seating is available.

The Department's longstanding position that title III of the ADA requires venues to make reasonable modifications in their policies to allow individuals with disabilities who acquired nonaccessible tickets on the secondary ticket market to be seated in accessible seating, where such seating is vacant, is supported by the only Federal court to address this issue. *See* Independent *Living Resources v. Oregon Arena Corp.*, 1 F. Supp. 2d 1159, 1171 (D. Or. 1998). The Department has incorporated this position into the final rule at § 36.302(f)(7)(ii).

The NPRM contained two questions aimed at gauging concern with the Department's consideration of secondary ticket market sales. The first question asked whether a secondary purchaser who does not have a disability and who buys an accessible seat should be required to move if the space is needed for someone with a disability.

Many disability rights advocates answered that the individual should move provided that there is a seat of comparable or better quality available for him and his companion. Some venues, however, expressed concerns about this provision, and asked how they are to identify who should be moved and what obligations apply if there are no seats available that are equivalent or better in quality.

The Department's second question asked whether there are particular concerns about the obligation to provide accessible seating, including a wheelchair space, to an individual with a disability who purchases an inaccessible seat through the secondary market.

Industry commenters contended that this requirement would create a "logistical nightmare," with venues scrambling to reseat patrons in the short time between the opening of the venues' doors and the commencement of the event. Furthermore, they argued that they might not be able to reseat all individuals and that even if they were able to do so, patrons might be moved to inferior seats (whether in accessible or non-accessible seating). These commenters also were concerned that they would be sued by patrons moved under such circumstances.

These commenters seem to have misconstrued the rule. Covered entities are not required to seat every person who acquires a ticket for inaccessible seating but needs accessible seating, and are not required to move any individual who acquires a ticket for accessible seating but does not need it. Covered entities that allow patrons to buy and sell tickets on the secondary market must make reasonable modifications to their policies to allow persons with disabilities to participate in secondary ticket transfers. The Department believes that there is no one-size-fits-all rule that will suit all assembly areas. In those circumstances where a venue has accessible seating vacant at the time an individual with a disability who needs accessible seating presents his ticket for inaccessible seating at the box office, the venue must allow the individual to exchange his ticket for an accessible seat in a comparable location if such an accessible seat is vacant. Where, however, a venue has sold all of its accessible seating, the venue has no obligation to provide accessible seating to the person with a disability who purchased an inaccessible seat on the secondary market. Venues may encourage individuals with disabilities who hold tickets for inaccessible seating to contact the box office before the event to notify them of their need for accessible seating, even though they may not require ticketholders to provide such notice.

The Department notes that public accommodations are permitted, though not required, to adopt policies regarding moving patrons who do not need the features of an accessible seat. If a public accommodation chooses to do so, it might mitigate administrative concerns by marking tickets for accessible seating as such, and printing on the ticket that individuals who purchase such seats but who do not need accessible seating are subject to being moved to other seats in the facility if the accessible seating is required for an individual with a disability. Such a venue might also develop and publish a ticketing policy to provide transparency to the general public and to put holders of tickets for accessible seating who do not require it on notice that they may be moved.

Prevention of fraud in purchase of accessible seating. Assembly area managers and advocacy groups have informed the Department that the fraudulent purchase of accessible seating is a pressing concern. Curbing fraud is a goal that public accommodations and individuals with disabilities share. Steps taken to prevent fraud, however, must be balanced carefully against the privacy rights of individuals with disabilities. Such measures also must not impose burdensome requirements upon, nor restrict the rights of, individuals with disabilities.

In the NPRM, the Department struck a balance between these competing concerns by proposing § 36.302(f)(8), which prohibited public accommodations from asking for proof of disability before the purchase of accessible seating but provided guidance in two paragraphs on appropriate measures for curbing fraud. Paragraph (i) proposed allowing a public accommodation to ask individuals purchasing single-event tickets for accessible seating whether they are wheelchair users. Paragraph (ii) proposed allowing a public accommodation to require individuals purchasing accessible seating for season tickets or other multi-event ticket packages to attest in writing that the accessible seating is for a wheelchair user. Additionally, the NPRM proposed to permit venues, when they have good cause to believe that an individual has fraudulently purchased accessible seating, to investigate that individual.

Several commenters objected to this rule on the ground that it would require a wheelchair user to be the purchaser of tickets. The Department has reworded this paragraph to reflect that the individual with a disability does not have to be the ticket purchaser. The final rule allows third parties to purchase accessible tickets at the request of an individual with a disability.

Commenters also argued that other individuals with disabilities who do not use wheelchairs should be permitted to purchase accessible seating. Some individuals with disabilities who do not use wheelchairs urged the Department to change the rule, asserting that they, too, need accessible seating. The Department agrees that such seating, although designed for use by a wheelchair user, may be used by non-wheelchair users, if those persons are persons with a disability who need to use accessible seating because of a mobility disability or because their disability requires the use of the features that accessible seating provides (e.g., individuals who cannot bend their legs because of braces, or individuals who, because of their disability, cannot sit in a straight-back chair).

Some commenters raised concerns that allowing venues to ask questions to determine whether individuals purchasing accessible seating are doing so legitimately would burden individuals with disabilities in the purchase of accessible seating. The Department has retained the substance of this provision in § 36.302(f)(8) of the final rule, but emphasizes that such questions should be asked at the initial time of purchase. For example, if the method of purchase is via the Internet, then the question(s) should be answered by clicking a yes or no box during the transaction. The public accommodation may warn purchasers that accessible seating is for individuals with disabilities and that individuals purchasing such tickets fraudulently are subject to relocation.

One commenter argued that face-to-face contact between the venue and the ticket holder should be required in order to prevent fraud and suggested that individuals who purchase accessible seating should be required to pick up their tickets at the box office and then enter the venue immediately. The Department has declined to adopt that suggestion. It would be discriminatory to require individuals with disabilities to pick up tickets at the box office when other spectators are not required to do so. If the assembly area wishes to make face-to- face contact with accessible seating ticket holders to curb fraud, it may do so through its ushers and other customer service personnel located within the seating area.

Some commenters asked whether it is permissible for assembly areas to have voluntary clubs where individuals with disabilities self-identify to the public accommodation in order to become a member of a club that entitles them to purchase accessible seating reserved for club members or otherwise receive priority in purchasing accessible seating. The Department agrees that such clubs are permissible, provided that a reasonable amount of accessible seating remains available at all prices and dispersed at all locations for individuals with disabilities who are non-members.

Section 36.303   Auxiliary Aids and Services.

Section 36.303(a) of the 1991 title III regulation requires a public accommodation to take such steps as may be necessary to ensure that no individual with a disability is excluded, denied services, segregated, or otherwise treated differently than other individuals because of the absence of auxiliary aids and services, unless the public accommodation can demonstrate that taking such steps would fundamentally alter the nature of the goods, services, facilities, advantages, or accommodations being offered or would result in an undue burden. Implicit in this duty to provide auxiliary aids and services is the underlying obligation of a public accommodation to communicate effectively with customers, clients, patients, companions, or participants who have disabilities affecting hearing, vision, or speech. The Department notes that § 36.303(a) does not require public accommodations to provide assistance to individuals with disabilities that is unrelated to effective communication, although requests for such assistance may be otherwise subject to the reasonable modifications or barrier removal requirements.

The Department has investigated hundreds of complaints alleging that public accommodations have failed to provide effective communication, and many of these investigations have resulted in settlement agreements and consent decrees. During the course of these investigations, the Department has determined that public accommodations sometimes misunderstand the scope of their obligations under the statute and the regulation. Section 36.303 in the final rule codifies the Department's longstanding policies in this area, and includes provisions based on technological advances and breakthroughs in the area of auxiliary aids and services that have occurred since the 1991 title III regulation was published.

Video remote interpreting (VRI). Section 36.303(b)(1) sets out examples of auxiliary aids and services. In the NPRM, the Department proposed adding video remote services (hereafter referred to as "video remote interpreting" or "VRI") and the exchange of written notes among the examples. The Department also proposed amending the provision to reflect technological advances, such as the wide availability of realtime capability in transcription services and captioning.

VRI is defined in the final rule at § 36.104 as "an interpreting service that uses video conference technology over dedicated lines or wireless technology offering high-speed, wide-bandwidth video connection or wireless connection that delivers high-quality video images as provided in § 36.303(f)." The Department notes that VRI generally consists of a videophone, monitors, cameras, a high-speed video connection, and an interpreter provided by the public accommodation pursuant to a contract for services. The term's inclusion within the definition of "qualified interpreter" makes clear that a public accommodation's use of VRI satisfies its title III obligations only where VRI affords effective communication. Comments from advocates and persons with disabilities expressed concern that VRI may not always provide effective communication, especially in hospitals and emergency rooms. Examples were provided of patients who are unable to see the video monitor because they are semi-conscious or unable to focus on the video screen; other examples were given of cases where the video monitor is out of the sightline of the patient or the image is out of focus; still other examples were given of patients who cannot see the screen because the signal is interrupted, causing unnatural pauses in communication, or the image is grainy or otherwise unclear. Many commenters requested more explicit guidelines on the use of VRI, and some recommended requirements for equipment maintenance, dedicated high-speed, wide-bandwidth video connections, and training of staff using VRI, especially in hospital and health care situations. Several major organizations requested a requirement to include the interpreter's face, head, arms, hands, and eyes in all transmissions.

The Department has determined that VRI can be an effective method of providing interpreting service in certain situations, particularly when a live interpreter cannot be immediately on the scene. To ensure that VRI is effective, the Department has established performance standards for VRI in § 36.303(f).The Department recognizes that reliance on VRI may not be effective in certain situations, such as those involving the exchange of complex information or involving multiple parties, and for some individuals, such as for persons who are deaf-blind, and using VRI in those circumstances would not satisfy a public accommodation's obligation to provide effective communication.

Comments from several disability advocacy organizations and individuals discouraged the Department from adding the exchange of written notes to the list of available auxiliary aids in § 36.303(b). The Department consistently has recognized that the exchange of written notes may provide effective communication in certain contexts. The NPRM proposed adding an explicit reference to written notes because some title III entities do not understand that exchange of written notes using paper and pencil may be an available option in some circumstances. Advocates and persons with disabilities requested explicit limits on the use of written notes as a form of auxiliary aid because, they argued, most exchanges are not simple, and handwritten notes do not afford effective communication. One major advocacy organization, for example, noted that the speed at which individuals communicate orally or use sign language averages about 200 words per minute or more, and thus, the exchange of notes may provide only truncated or incomplete communication. For persons whose primary language is American Sign Language (ASL), some commenters pointed out, using written English in exchange of notes often is ineffective because ASL syntax and vocabulary is dissimilar from English. By contrast, some commenters from professional medical associations sought more specific guidance on when notes are allowed, especially in the context of medical offices and health care situations.

Exchange of notes likely will be effective in situations that do not involve substantial conversation, for example, when blood is drawn for routine lab tests or regular allergy shots are administered. However, interpreters should be used when the matter involves more complexity, such as in communication of medical history or diagnoses, in conversations about medical procedures and treatment decisions, or in communication of instructions for care at home or elsewhere. The Department discussed in the NPRM the kinds of situations in which use of interpreters or captioning is necessary. Additional guidance on this issue can be found in a number of agreements entered into with health care providers and hospitals that are available on the Department's Web site at http://www.ada.gov.

In addition, commenters requested that the Department include "real-time" before any mention of "computer-aided" or "captioning" technology to highlight the value of simultaneous translation of any communication. The Department has added to the final rule appropriate references to "real-time" to recognize this aspect of effective communication. Lastly, in this provision and elsewhere in the title III regulation, the Department has replaced the term "telecommunications devices for deaf persons (TDD)" with "text telephones (TTYs)." As noted in the NPRM, TTY has become the commonly accepted term and is consistent with the terminology used by the Access Board in the 2004 ADAAG. Comments from advocates and persons with disabilities expressed approval of the substitution of TTY for TDD in the proposed regulation, but expressed the view that the Department should expand the definition to "voice, text, and video-based telecommunications products and systems, including TTY's, videophones, and captioned telephones, or equally effective telecommunications systems." The Department has expanded its definition of 'auxiliary aids and services" in § 36.303 to include those examples in the final rule. Other additions proposed in the NPRM, and retained in the final rule, include Brailled materials and displays, screen reader software, magnification software, optical readers, secondary auditory programs (SAP), and accessible electronic and information technology.

As the Department noted in the preamble to the NPRM, the list of auxiliary aids in § 36.303(b) is merely illustrative. The Department does not intend that every public accommodation covered by title III must have access to every device or all new technology at all times, as long as the communication provided is effective.

Companions who are individuals with disabilities. The Department has added several new provisions to § 36.303(c), but these provisions do not impose new obligations on places of public accommodation. Rather, these provisions simply codify the Department's longstanding positions. Section 36.303(c)(1) now states that "[a] public accommodation shall furnish appropriate auxiliary aids and services where necessary to ensure effective communication with individuals with disabilities. This includes an obligation to provide effective communication to companions who are individuals with disabilities." Section 36.303(c)(1)(i) defines "companion" as "a family member, friend, or associate of an individual seeking access to, or participating in, the goods, services, facilities, privileges, advantages, or accommodations of a public accommodation, who, along with such individual, is an appropriate person with whom the public accommodation should communicate."

This provision makes clear that if the companion is someone with whom the public accommodation normally would or should communicate, then the public accommodation must provide appropriate auxiliary aids and services to that companion to ensure effective communication with the companion. This commonsense rule provides the necessary guidance to public accommodations to implement properly the nondiscrimination requirements of the ADA. Commenters also questioned why, in the NPRM, the Department defined companion as "a family member, friend, or associate of a program participant * * *," noting that the scope of a public accommodation's obligation is not limited to "program participants" but rather includes all individuals seeking access to, or participating in, the goods, services, facilities, privileges, advantages, or accommodations of the public accommodation. 73 FR 34508, 34554 (June 17, 2008). The Department agrees and has amended the regulatory language accordingly. Many commenters supported inclusion of companions in the rule and requested that the Department clarify that a companion with a disability may be entitled to effective communication from the public accommodation, even though the individual seeking access to, or participating in, the goods, services, facilities, privileges, advantages, or accommodations of the public accommodation is not an individual with a disability. Some commenters asked the Department to make clear that if the individual seeking access to or participating in the public accommodation's program or services is an individual with a disability and the companion is not, the public accommodation may not limit its communication to the companion, instead of communicating directly with the individual with a disability, when it would otherwise be appropriate to communicate with the individual with the disability.

Most entities and individuals from the medical field objected to the Department's proposal, suggesting that medical and health care providers, and they alone, should determine to whom medical information should be communicated and when auxiliary aids and services should be provided to companions. Others asked that the Department limit the public accommodation's obligation to communicate effectively with a companion to situations where such communication is necessary to serve the interests of the person who is receiving the public accommodation's services. It also was suggested that companions should receive auxiliary aids and services only when necessary to ensure effective communication with the person receiving the public accommodation's services, with an emphasis on the particular needs of the patient requiring assistance, not the patient's family or guardian. Some in the medical community objected to the inclusion of any regulatory language regarding companions, asserting that such language is overbroad, seeks services for individuals whose presence is neither required by the public accommodation nor necessary for the delivery of the services or good, places additional burdens on the medical community, and represents an uncompensated mandate. One medical association commenter stated that such a mandate was particularly burdensome in situations where a patient is fully and legally capable of participating in the decision-making process and needs little or no assistance in obtaining care and following through on physician's instructions.

The final rule codifies the Department's longstanding interpretation of the ADA, and clarifies that public accommodations have effective communication obligations with respect to companions who are individuals with disabilities even where the individual seeking to participate in or benefit from what a public accommodation offers does not have a disability. There are many instances in which such an individual may not be an individual with a disability but his or her companion is an individual with a disability. The effective communication requirement applies equally to that companion.

Effective communication with companions is particularly critical in health care settings where miscommunication may lead to misdiagnosis and improper or delayed medical treatment. The Department has encountered confusion and reluctance by medical care providers regarding the scope of their obligation with respect to such companions. Effective communication with a companion is necessary in a variety of circumstances. For example, a companion may be legally authorized to make health care decisions on behalf of the patient or may need to help the patient with information or instructions given by hospital personnel. In addition, a companion may be the patient's next of kin or health care surrogate with whom hospital personnel need to communicate concerning the patient's medical condition. Moreover, a companion could be designated by the patient to communicate with hospital personnel about the patient's symptoms, needs, condition, or medical history. Furthermore, the companion could be a family member with whom hospital personnel normally would communicate. It has been the Department's longstanding position that public accommodations are required to provide effective communication to companions when they accompany patients to medical care providers for treatment.

The individual with a disability does not need to be present physically to trigger the public accommodation's obligation to provide effective communication to a companion. The controlling principle regarding whether appropriate auxiliary aids and services should be provided is whether the companion is an appropriate person with whom the public accommodation should communicate. Examples of such situations include back-to-school night or parent-teacher conferences at a private school. If the faculty writes on the board or otherwise displays information in a visual context during back-to-school night, this information must be communicated effectively to parents or guardians who are blind or have low vision. At a parent-teacher conference, deaf parents or guardians are to be provided with appropriate auxiliary aids and service to communicate effectively with the teacher and administrators. Likewise, when a deaf spouse attempts to communicate with private social service agencies about the services necessary for the hearing spouse, appropriate auxiliary aids and services must be provided to the deaf spouse by the public accommodation to ensure effective communication.

One medical association sought approval to impose a charge against an individual with a disability, either the patient or the companion, where that person had stated he or she needed an interpreter for a scheduled appointment, the medical provider had arranged for an interpreter to appear, and then the individual requiring the interpreter did not show up for the scheduled appointment. Section 36.301(c) of the 1991 title III regulation prohibits the imposition of surcharges to cover the costs of necessary auxiliary aids and services. As such, medical providers cannot pass along to their patients with disabilities the cost of obtaining an interpreter, even in situations where the individual cancels his or her appointment at the last minute or is a "no-show" for the scheduled appointment. The medical provider, however, may charge for the missed appointment if all other patients are subject to such a charge in the same circumstances.

Determining appropriate auxiliary aids. The type of auxiliary aid the public accommodation provides is dependent on which auxiliary aid is appropriate under the particular circumstances. Section 36.303(c)(1)(ii) codifies the Department's longstanding interpretation that the type of auxiliary aid or service necessary to ensure effective communication will vary in accordance with the method of communication used by the individual; the nature, length, and complexity of the communication involved; and the context in which the communication is taking place. As the Department explained in the NPRM, this provision lists factors the public accommodation should consider in determining which type of auxiliary aids and services are necessary. For example, an individual with a disability who is deaf or hard of hearing may need a qualified interpreter to discuss with hospital personnel a diagnosis, procedures, tests, treatment options, surgery, or prescribed medication (e.g., dosage, side effects, drug interactions, etc.). In comparison, an individual who is deaf or hard of hearing who purchases an item in the hospital gift shop may need only an exchange of written notes to achieve effective communication.

The language in the first sentence of § 36.303(c)(1)(ii) is derived from the Department's Technical Assistance Manual. *See* Department of Justice, Americans with Disabilities Act, *ADA Title III Technical Assistance Manual Covering Public Accommodations and Commercial Facilities*, III-4.3200, available at http://www.ada.gov/taman3.html. There were few comments regarding inclusion of this policy in the regulation itself, and those received were positive.

Many advocacy groups, particularly those representing blind individuals and those with low vision, urged the Department to add language in the final rule requiring the provision of accessible material in a manner that is timely, accurate, and private. This, they argued, would be especially important with regard to billing information, other time-sensitive material, or confidential information. The Department has added a provision in § 36.303(c)(1)(ii) stating that in "order to be effective, auxiliary aids and services must be provided in accessible formats, in a timely manner, and in such a way so as to protect the privacy and independence of the individual with a disability."

The second sentence of § 36.303(c)(1)(ii) states that "[a] public accommodation should consult with individuals with disabilities whenever possible to determine what type of auxiliary aid is needed to ensure effective communication, but the ultimate decision as to what measures to take rests with the public accommodation, provided that the method chosen results in effective communication." Many commenters urged the Department to amend this provision to require public accommodations to give primary consideration to the expressed choice of an individual with a disability. However, as the Department explained when it initially promulgated the 1991 title III regulation, the Department believes that Congress did not intend under title III to impose upon a public accommodation the requirement that it give primary consideration to the request of the individual with a disability. *See* 28 CFR part 36, app. B at 726 (2009). The legislative history does, however, demonstrate congressional intent to strongly encourage consulting with persons with disabilities. *Id.* As the Department explained in the 1991 preamble, "the House Education and Labor Committee stated that it 'expects' that 'public accommodation(s) will consult with the individual with a disability before providing a particular auxiliary aid or service.' (Education and Labor report at 107)." *Id.*

The commenters who urged that primary consideration be given to the individual with a disability noted, for example, that a public accommodation would not provide effective communication by using written notes where the individual requiring an auxiliary aid is in severe pain, or by providing a qualified ASL interpreter when an individual needs an oral interpreter instead. Both examples illustrate the importance of consulting with the individual with a disability in order to ensure that the communication provided is effective. When a public accommodation ignores the communication needs of the individual requiring an auxiliary aid or service, it does so at its peril, for if the communication provided is not effective, the public accommodation will have violated title III of the ADA.

Consequently, the regulation strongly encourages the public accommodation to engage in a dialogue with the individual with a disability to determine what auxiliary aids and services are appropriate under the circumstances. This dialogue should include a communication assessment of the individual with a disability initially, regularly, and as needed, because the auxiliary aids and services necessary to provide effective communication to the individual may fluctuate. For example, a deaf individual may go to a private community health center with what is at first believed to be a minor medical emergency, such as a sore knee, and the individual with a disability and the community health center both may believe that exchanging written notes will be effective; however, during that individual's visit, it may be determined that the individual is, in fact, suffering from an anterior cruciate ligament tear and must have surgery to repair the torn ligament. As the situation develops and the diagnosis and recommended course of action evolve into surgery, an interpreter likely will be necessary. The community health center has a continuing obligation to assess the auxiliary aids and services it is providing, and should consult with individuals with disabilities on a continuing basis to assess what measures are required to ensure effective communication.

Similarly, the Department strongly encourages public accommodations to keep individuals with disabilities apprised of the status of the expected arrival of an interpreter or the delivery of other requested or anticipated auxiliary aids and services. Also, when the public accommodation decides not to provide the auxiliary aids and services requested by an individual with a disability, the public accommodation should provide that individual with the reason for its decision.

Family members and friends as interpreters.

Section 36.303(c)(2), which was proposed in the NPRM, has been included in the final rule to make clear that a public accommodation shall not require an individual with a disability to bring another individual to interpret for him or her. The Department has added this regulatory requirement to emphasize that when a public accommodation is interacting with a person with a disability, it is the public accommodation's responsibility to provide an interpreter to ensure effective communication. It is not appropriate to require the person with a disability to bring another individual to provide such services. any commenters supported inclusion of this language in the new rule. A representative from a cruise line association opined, however, that if a guest chose to cruise without an interpreter or companion, the ship would not be compelled to provide an interpreter for the medical facility. On the contrary, when an individual with a disability goes on a cruise, the cruise ship has an obligation to provide effective communication, including, if necessary, a qualified interpreter as defined in the rule.

Some representatives of pediatricians objected to this provision, stating that parents of children with disabilities often know best how to interpret their children's needs and health status and relay that information to the child's physician, and to remove that parent, or add a stranger into the examining room, may frighten children. These commenters requested clarification in the regulation that public accommodations should permit parents, guardians, or caregivers of children with disabilities to accompany them in medical settings to ensure effective communication. The regulation does not prohibit parents, guardians, or caregivers from being present or providing effective communication for children. Rather, it prohibits medical professionals (and other public accommodations) from requiring or forcing individuals with disabilities to bring other individuals with them to facilitate communication so that the public accommodation will not have to provide appropriate auxiliary aids and services. The public accommodation cannot avoid its obligation to provide an interpreter except under the circumstances described in § 36.303(c)(3)–(4).

A State medical association also objected to this provision, opining that medical providers should have the authority to ask patients to bring someone with them to provide interpreting services if the medical provider determines that such a practice would result in effective communication and that patient privacy and confidentiality would be maintained. While the public accommodation has the obligation to determine what type of auxiliary aids and services are necessary to ensure effective communication, it cannot unilaterally determine whether the patient's privacy and confidentiality would be maintained.

Section 36.303(c)(3) of the final rule codifies the Department's position that there are certain limited instances when a public accommodation may rely on an accompanying adult to interpret or facilitate communication: (1) In an emergency involving an imminent threat to the safety or welfare of an individual or the public; or (2) If the individual with a disability specifically requests it, the accompanying adult agrees to provide the assistance, and reliance on that adult for this assistance is appropriate under the circumstances. In such instances, the public accommodation should first offer to provide appropriate auxiliary aids and services free of charge.

Commenters requested that the Department make clear that the public accommodation cannot request, rely on, or coerce an accompanying adult to provide effective communication for an individual with a disability, and that only a voluntary offer of assistance is acceptable. The Department states unequivocally that consent of, and for, the accompanying adult to facilitate communication must be provided freely and voluntarily both by the individual with a disability and the accompanying adult — absent an emergency involving an imminent threat to the safety or welfare of an individual or the public. The public accommodation cannot coerce or attempt to persuade another adult to provide effective communication for the individual with a disability.

Several commenters asked that the Department make clear that children are not to be used to provide effective communication for family members and friends and that it is the responsibility of the public accommodation to provide effective communication, stating that interpreters often are needed in settings where it would not be appropriate for children to be interpreting, such as those involving medical issues, domestic violence, or other situations involving the exchange of confidential or adult-related material. Children often are hesitant to decline requests to provide communication services, which puts them in a very difficult position vis-a-vis family members and friends. The Department agrees. It is the Department's position that a public accommodation shall not rely on a minor child to facilitate communication with a family member, friend, or other individual except in an emergency involving an imminent threat to the safety or welfare of an individual or the public where no interpreter is available. Accordingly, the Department has revised the rule to state that "[a] public accommodation shall not rely on a minor child to interpret or facilitate communication, except in an emergency involving an imminent threat to the safety or welfare of an individual or the public where there is no interpreter available." § 36.303(c)(4). Sections 36.303(c)(3) and (c)(4) have no application in circumstances where an interpreter would not otherwise be required in order to provide effective communication (e.g., in simple transactions such as purchasing movie tickets at a theater).

The Department stresses that privacy and confidentiality must be maintained but notes that covered entities, such as hospitals, that are subject to the Privacy Rules, 45 CFR parts 160 and 164, of the Health Insurance Portability and Accountability Act of 1996 (HIPAA), Public Law 104–191, are permitted to disclose to a patient's relative, close friend, or any other person identified by the patient (such as an interpreter) relevant patient information if the patient agrees to such disclosures. *See* 45 CFR parts 160 and 164. The agreement need not be in writing. Covered entities should consult the HIPAA Privacy Rules regarding other ways disclosures may be made to such persons.

With regard to emergency situations, proposed § 36.303(c)(3) permitted reliance on an individual accompanying an individual with a disability to interpret or facilitate communication in an emergency involving a threat to the safety or welfare of an individual or the public. Commenters requested that the Department make clear that often a public accommodation can obtain appropriate auxiliary aids and services in advance of an emergency, particularly in anticipated emergencies, such as predicted dangerous weather, or in certain medical situations, such as pending childbirth, by making necessary pre-arrangements. These commenters did not want public accommodations to be relieved of their responsibilities to provide effective communication in emergency situations noting that the need for effective communication in emergencies is heightened. For the same reason, several commenters requested a separate rule that requires public accommodations to provide timely and effective communication in the event of an emergency.

One group of commenters asked that the Department narrow the regulation permitting reliance on a companion to interpret or facilitate communication in emergency situations so that it is not available to entities with responsibilities for emergency preparedness and response. Some commenters noted that certain exigent circumstances, such as those that exist during and, perhaps, immediately after a major hurricane, temporarily may excuse public accommodations of their responsibilities to provide effective communication. However, they asked that the Department clarify that these obligations are ongoing, and that as soon as such situations begin to abate or become stabilized, the public accommodation must provide effective communication.

The Department recognizes the need for effective communication is critical in emergency situations. After due consideration of all of these concerns raised by commenters, the Department has revised § 36.303(c) to narrow the exception-permitting reliance on individuals accompanying the individual with a disability during an emergency to make it clear that it applies only to emergencies involving an "imminent threat to the safety or welfare of an individual or the public * * *." § 36.303(c)(3)–(4). The Department wishes to emphasize, however, that application of this exception is narrowly tailored to emergencies involving an imminent threat to the safety or welfare of individuals or the public. Arguably, all visits to an emergency room are by definition emergencies.

Likewise, an argument can be made that most situations to which emergency workers respond involve, in one way or another, a threat to the safety or welfare of an individual or the public. The imminent threat exception in § 36.303(c)(3)– (4) is not intended to apply to typical and foreseeable emergency situations that are part of the normal operations of these institutions. As such, a public accommodation may rely on an accompanying individual to interpret or facilitate communication under the § 36.303(c)(3)–(4) imminent threat exception only where there is a true emergency, *i.e.*, where any delay in providing immediate services to the individual could have life-altering or life- ending consequences.

Telecommunications. In addition to the changes discussed in § 36.303(b) regarding telecommunications, telephones, and text telephones, the Department has adopted provisions in § 36.303(d) of the final rule (which also were included in the NPRM) requiring that public accommodations must not disconnect or refuse to take calls from FCC-approved telecommunications relay systems, including

Internet-based relay systems. Commenters from some State agencies, many advocacy organizations, and individuals strongly urged the Department to mandate such action because of the high proportion of TTY calls and relay service calls to title III entities that are not completed because of phone systems or employees not taking the calls. This refusal presents a significant obstacle for persons using TTYs who do business with public accommodations and denies persons with disabilities telephone access for business that typically is handled over the telephone.

Section 36.303(d)(1)(ii) of the NPRM added public telephones equipped with volume control mechanisms and hearing aid compatible telephones to the examples of types of telephone equipment to be provided. Commenters from the disability community and from telecommunications relay service providers argued that requirements for these particular features on telephones are obsolete not only because the deaf and hard of hearing community uses video technology more frequently than other types of telecommunication, but also because all public coin phones have been hearing-aid compatible since 1983, pursuant to the Telecommunications for the Disabled Act of 1982, 47 U.S.C. 610. The Hearing Aid Compatibility Act of 1988, 47 U.S.C. 610, extended this requirement to all wireline telephones imported into or manufactured in the United States since 1989. In 1997, the FCC further required that all such phones also be equipped with volume control. *See* 47 CFR 68.6. Given these existing statutory obligations, the proposed language is unnecessary. Accordingly, the Department has deleted that language from the final rule.

The Department understands that there are many new devices and advances in technology that should be included in the definition of available auxiliary aids and is including many of the telecommunications devices and some new technology. While much of this technology is not expensive and should be available to most title III entities, there may be legitimate reasons why in a particular situation some of these new and developing auxiliary aids may not be available, may be prohibitively costly (thus supporting an undue burden defense), or may otherwise not be suitable given other circumstances related to the particular terrain, situation, or functionality in specialized areas where security, among other things, may be a factor limiting the appropriateness of the use of a particular technology or device. The Department recognizes that the available new technology may provide more effective communication than existing technology and that providing effective communication often will include use of new technology and video relay services, as well as interpreters. However, the Department has not mandated that title III entities make all technology or services available upon demand in all situations. When a public accommodation provides the opportunity to make outgoing phone calls on more than an incidental-convenience basis, it shall make available accessible public telephones, TTYs, or other telecommunications products and systems for use by an individual who is deaf or hard of hearing, or has a speech impairment.

Video remote interpreting (VRI) services. In § 36.303(f) of the NPRM, the Department proposed the inclusion of four performance standards for VRI (which the NPRM termed video interpreting services (VIS)), for effective communication: (1) High-quality, clear, real-time, full-motion video, and audio over a dedicated high-speed Internet connection; (2) a clear, sufficiently large, and sharply delineated picture of the participants' heads, arms, hands, and fingers, regardless of their body position; (3) clear transmission of voices; and (4) persons who are trained to set up and operate the VIS quickly and efficiently.

Commenters generally approved of these proposed performance standards, but recommended that some additional standards be included in the final rule. For persons who are deaf with limited vision, commenters requested that the Department include an explicit requirement that interpreters wear high-contrast clothing with no patterns that might distract from their hands as they are interpreting, so that a person with limited vision could still see the signs made by the interpreter. While the Department reiterates the importance of such practices in the delivery of effective VRI as well as in-person interpreting, the Department declines to adopt such performance standards as part of this rule. In general, professional interpreters already follow such practices, as the Code of Professional Conduct for interpreters the Deaf and the National Association of the Deaf incorporates attire considerations into their standards of professionalism and conduct. Moreover, as a result of this code, many VRI agencies have adopted detailed dress standards that interpreters hired by the agency must follow. Commenters also urged explicit requirement of a clear image of the face and eyes of the interpreter and others. Because the face includes the eyes, the Department has amended § 36.303(f)(2) of the final rule to include a requirement that the interpreter's face be displayed. Other commenters requested requirement of a wide- bandwidth video connection for the VRI system, and the Department has included this requirement in § 36.303(f)(1) of the final rule.

ATMs. The 2010 Standards set out detailed requirements for ATMs, including communication- related requirements to make ATMs usable by individuals who are blind or have low vision. In the NPRM, the Department discussed the application of a safe harbor to the communication-related elements of ATMs. The NPRM explained that the Department considers the communication-related elements of ATMs to be auxiliary aids and services, to which the safe harbor for elements built in compliance with the 1991 standards does not apply.

The Department received several comments regarding this issue. Several commenters representing banks objected to the exclusion of communication-related aspects of ATMs from the safe harbor provision. They explained that the useful life of ATMs — on average 10 years — was longer than the Department noted; thus, without the safe harbor, banks would be forced to retrofit many ATMs in order to comply with the proposed regulation. Such retrofitting, they noted, would be costly to the industry. A few representatives of the disability community commented that communication- related aspects of ATMs should be excluded from the safe harbor.

The Department consistently has taken the position that the communication-related elements of ATMs are auxiliary aids and services, rather than structural elements. *See* 28 CFR part 36, app. B at 728 (2009). Thus, the safe harbor provision does not apply to these elements. The Department believes that the limitations on the effective communication requirements, which provide that a covered entity does not have to take measures that would result in a fundamental alteration of its program or would cause undue burdens, provide adequate protection to covered entities that operate ATMs.

Captioning at sporting venues. In § 36.303(g) of the NPRM, the Department proposed that sports stadiums that have a capacity of 25,000 or more shall provide captioning for safety and emergency information on scoreboards and video monitors. In addition, the Department posed four questions about captioning of information, especially safety and emergency information announcements, provided over public address (PA) systems. The Department received many detailed and divergent responses to each of the four questions and the proposed regulatory text. Because comments submitted on the Department's title II and title III proposals were intertwined, because of the similarity of issues involved for title II entities and title III entities, and in recognition of the fact that many large sports stadiums are covered by both title II and title III as joint operations of State or local government and one or more public accommodations, the Department presents here a single consolidated review and summary of the issues raised in comments.

The Department asked whether requiring captioning of safety and emergency information made over the public address system in stadiums seating fewer than 25,000 would create an undue burden for smaller entities, and whether it would be feasible for small stadiums to provide such captioning, or whether a larger threshold, such as sports stadiums with a capacity of 50,000 or more, would be appropriate.

There was a consensus among the commenters, including disability advocates as well as venue owners and stadium designers and operators, that using the stadium size or seating capacity should not be the exclusive deciding factor for any obligation to provide captioning for safety and emergency information broadcast over the PA system. Most disability advocacy organizations and individuals with disabilities complained that using size or seating capacity as a threshold for captioning safety and emergency information would undermine the "undue burden" defense found in both titles II and III. Many commenters provided examples of facilities such as professional hockey arenas that seat less than 25,000 fans but that, commenters argued, should be able to provide real-time captioning. Other commenters suggested that some high school or college stadiums, for example, may hold 25,000 fans or more and yet lack the resources to provide real-time captioning. Many commenters noted that real-time captioning would require use of trained stenographers, and that most high school and college sports facilities rely upon volunteers to operate scoreboards and PA systems and they would not be qualified stenographers, especially in case of an emergency. One national association noted that the typical stenographer expense for a professional football game in Washington, DC, is about $550 per game. Similarly, one trade association representing venues estimated that the cost for a professional stenographer at a sporting event runs between $500 and $1,000 per game or event, the cost of which, they argued, would be unduly burdensome in many cases. Some commenters posited that schools that do not sell tickets to athletic events would be challenged to meet such expenses, in contrast to major college athletic programs and professional sports teams, which would be less likely to prevail using an "undue burden" defense.

Some venue owners and operators and other covered entities also argued that stadium size should not be the key consideration for whether scoreboard captioning will be required. Instead, these entities suggested that equipment already installed in the stadium, including necessary electrical equipment and backup power supply, should be the determining factor for whether captioning is mandated. Many commenters argued that the requirement to provide captioning should apply only to stadiums with scoreboards that meet the National Fire Protection Association (NFPA) National Fire Alarm Code. Commenters reported that NFPA 72 requires at least two independent and reliable power supplies for emergency information systems, including one source that is a generator or a battery sufficient to run the system in the event the primary power fails. Alternatively, some stadium designers and title II entities commented that the requirement should arise when the facility has at least one elevator providing firefighter emergency operation, along with approval of authorities with responsibility for fire safety. An organization concerned with fire safety codes commented that the Department lacks the expertise to regulate on this topic. Other commenters argued for flexibility in the requirements for providing captioning and contended that any requirement should apply only to stadiums constructed after the effective date of the regulation.

In the NPRM, the Department also asked whether the rule should address the specific means of captioning equipment, whether captioning should be provided through any effective means (e.g., scoreboards, line boards, handheld devices, or other means), or whether some means, such as handheld devices, should be eliminated as options. This question elicited many comments from advocates for persons with disabilities as well as from covered entities. Advocacy organizations and individuals with experience using handheld devices argued that such devices do not provide effective communication. These commenters noted that information is often delayed in the transmission to such devices, making them hard to use when following action on the playing field or in the event of an emergency when the crowd is already reacting to aural information provided over the PA system well before it is received on the handheld device.

Several venue owners and operators and others commented that handheld technology offers advantages of flexibility and portability so that it may be used successfully regardless of where in the facility the user is located, even when not in the line of sight of a scoreboard or other captioning system. Still other commenters urged the Department not to regulate in such a way as to limit innovation and use of such technology now and in the future. Cost considerations were included in comments from some stadium designers and venue owners and operators who reported that the cost of providing handheld systems is far less than the cost of providing real-time captioning on scoreboards, especially in facilities that do not currently have the capacity to provide real-time captions on existing equipment. Others noted that handheld technology is not covered by fire and safety model codes, including the NFPA, and thus would be more easily adapted into existing facilities if captioning were required by the Department.

The Department also asked about requiring open captioning of all public address announcements, rather than limiting the captioning requirement to safety and emergency information. A variety of advocates and persons with disabilities argued that all information broadcast over a PA system should be captioned in real time at all facilities in order to provide effective communication, and that a requirement only to provide emergency and safety information would not be sufficient. A few organizations representing persons with disabilities commented that installation of new systems should not be required, but that all systems within existing facilities that are capable of providing captioning should provide captioning of information to the maximum extent possible. Several organizations for persons with disabilities commented that all facilities should include in their safety planning measures a requirement that all aurally provided information for patrons with communication disabilities be captioned. Some advocates suggested that demand for captions will only increase as the number of deaf and hard of hearing persons grows with the aging of the general population and with increasing numbers of veterans returning from war with disabilities. Multiple commenters noted that the captioning would benefit others as well as those with communication disabilities.

By contrast, venue owners and operators and others commented that the action on the sports field is self-explanatory and does not require captioning. These commenters objected to an explicit requirement to provide real-time captioning for all information broadcast on the PA system at a sporting event. Other commenters objected to requiring captioning even for emergency and safety information over the scoreboard rather than through some other means. By contrast, venue operators, State government agencies, and some model code groups, including the NFPA, commented that emergency and safety information must be provided in an accessible format and that public safety is a paramount concern. Other commenters argued that the best method to deliver safety and emergency information would be television monitors showing local TV broadcasts with captions already mandated by the FCC. Some commenters posited that the most reliable information about a major emergency would be provided on the television news broadcasts. They argued that television monitors may be located throughout the facility, improving line of sight for patrons, some of whom might not be able to see the scoreboard from their seats or elsewhere in the facility. Some stadium designers, venue operators, and model code groups pointed out that video monitors are not regulated by the NFPA or other agencies, so that such monitors could be more easily provided. Video monitors may receive transmissions from within the facility and could provide real-time captions if there is the necessary software and equipment to feed the captioning signal to a closed video network within the facility. Several commenters suggested that using monitors would be preferable to requiring captions on the scoreboard if the regulation mandates real-time captioning. Some venue owners and operators argued that retrofitting existing stadiums with new systems could easily cost in the hundreds of thousands of dollars per scoreboard or system. Some stadium designers and others argued that captioning should be required only in stadiums built after the effective date of the regulation. For stadiums with existing systems that allow for real-time captioning, one commenter posited that dedicating the system exclusively to real-time captioning would lead to an annual loss of between two and three million dollars per stadium in revenue from advertising currently running in that space.

After carefully considering the wide range of public comments on this issue, the Department has concluded that the final rule will not provide additional require-ments for effective communication or emergency information provided at sports stadiums at this time. The 1991 title II and title III regulations and statutory requirements are not in any way affected by this decision. The decision to postpone rulemaking on this complex issue is based on a number of factors, including the multiple layers of existing regulations by various agencies and levels of government, and the wide array of information, requests, and recommendations related to developing technology offered by the public. The diversity of existing information and communication systems and other characteristics among sports stadiums also complicates the regulation of captioning. The Department has concluded that further consideration and review is prudent before it issues specific regulatory requirements.

Movie captioning. In the NPRM, the Department stated that options were being considered to require movie theater owners and operators to exhibit movies that are captioned for patrons who are deaf or hard of hearing. Captioning makes films accessible to individuals whose hearing is too limited to benefit from assistive listening devices. Both open and closed captioning are examples of auxiliary aids and services required under the Department's 1991 title III regulation. *See* 28 CFR 36.303(b)(1). Open captions are similar to subtitles in that the text is visible to everyone in the theater, while closed captioning displays the written text of the audio only to those individuals who request it.

In the NPRM, the Department also stated that options were being considered to require movie theater owners and operators to exhibit movies with video description,[3] a technology that enables individuals who are blind or have low vision to enjoy movies by providing a spoken interpretation of key visual elements of a movie, such as actions, settings, facial expressions, costumes, and scene changes. The descriptions are narrated and recorded onto an audiotape or disk that can be synchronized with the film as it is projected. An audio recording is an example of an auxiliary aid and service required under the Department's 1991 title III regulation. *See* 28 CFR 36.303(b)(2).

The NPRM stated that technological advances since the early 1990s have made open and closed captioning and video description for movies more readily available and effective and noted that the Department was considering options to require captioning and video description for movies exhibited by public accommodations. The NPRM also noted that the Department is aware that the movie industry is transitioning, in whole or in part, to movies in digital format and that movie theater owners and operators are beginning to purchase digital projectors. The Department noted in the NPRM that movie theater owners and operators with digital projectors may have available to them different capabilities than those without digital projectors. The Department sought comment regarding whether and how to require captioning and video description while the film industry makes this transition. In addition, the NPRM stated the Department's concern about the potential cost to exhibit captioned movies, noting that cost may vary depending upon whether open or closed captioning is used and whether or not digital projectors are used, and stated that the cost of captioning must stay within the parameters of the undue burden requirement in 28 CFR 36.303(a). The Department further noted that it understands the cost of video description equipment to be less than that for closed captioning. The Department then stated that it was considering the possibility of requiring public accommodations to exhibit all new movies in captioned format and with video description at every showing. The NPRM stated that the Department would not specify the types of captioning required, leaving such decisions to the discretion of the movie theater owners and operators.

---

[3] In the NPRM, the Department referred to this technology as "narrative description." 73 FR 34508, 34531 (June 17, 2008). Several commenters informed the Department that the more accurate and commonly understood term is "videodescription," even though the subject is movies, not video, and so the Department decided to employ that term.

In the NPRM, the Department requested public comment as to whether public accommodations should be required to exhibit all new movies in captioned format at every showing, whether it would be more appropriate to require captioning less frequently, and, if so, with what frequency captioning should be provided. The Department also inquired as to whether the requirement for captioning should be tied to the conversion of movies from film to the use of a digital format. The Department also asked for public comment regarding the exhibition of all new movies with narrative description, whether it would it be more appropriate to require narrative description less frequently, and whether narrative description of movies should be tied to the use of a digital format.

Representatives from the movie industry, a commenter from a non-profit organization, and a disability rights advocacy group provided information in their comments on the status of captioning and video description technology today as well as an update on the transition to digital cinema in the industry. A representative of major movie producers and distributors commented that traditionally open captions were created by "burning" the captions onto a special print of a selected movie, which the studios would make available to the exhibitors (movie theater owners and operators). Releases with open captions typically would be presented at special screenings. More recently, according to this commenter, alternative methods have been developed for presenting movies with open captions, but their common feature is that the captions are visible to all theater-goers. Closed captioning is an innovation in technology that was first made available in a feature film presentation in late 1997. Closed captioning technology currently in use allows viewers to see captions using a clear panel that is mounted in front of the viewer's seat.[4] According to commenters from the industry, the panel reflects captions that are shown in reverse on an LED display in the back of the theater, with captions appearing on or near the movie image. Moviegoers may use this technology at any showing at a theater that has been equipped with the technology, so that the theater does not have to arrange limited special screenings.

Video description technology also has existed since 1997, according to a commenter who works with the captioning and video description industry. According to a movie industry commenter, video description requires the creation of a separate script written by specially trained writers called "describers." As the commenter explained, a describer initially listens to the movie without watching it in order to approximate the experience of an audience member who is blind or has low vision. Using software to map out the pauses in the soundtrack, the describer writes a description in the space available. After an initial script is written for video description, it is edited and checked for timing, continuity, accuracy, and a natural flow. A narrator then records the new script to match the corresponding movie. This same industry commenter said that video description currently is provided in theaters through screens equipped with the same type of technology as that used for closed captioning. As commenters explained, technologies in use today deliver video descriptions via infrared or FM listening systems to headsets worn by

---

[4] Other closed captioning technologies for movies that have been developed but are not in use at this time include hand-held displays similar to a PDA (personal digital assistant); eyeglasses fitted with a prism over one lens; and projected bitmap captions. The PDA and eyeglass systems use a wireless transmitter to send the captions to the display device.

individuals who are blind or have low vision.

According to the commenter representing major movie producers and distributors, the percentage of motion pictures produced with closed captioning by its member studios had grown to 88 percent of total releases by 2007; the percentage of motion pictures produced with open captioning by its member studios had grown to 78 percent of total releases by 2007; and the percentage of motion pictures provided with video description has ranged consistently between 50 percent and 60 percent of total releases. It is the movie producers and distributors, not the movie theater owners and operators, who determine what to caption and describe, the type of captioning to use, and the content of the captions and video description script. These same producers and distributors also assume the costs of captioning and describing movies. Movie theater owners and operators simply purchase the equipment to display the captions and play the video description in their auditoria.

The transition to digital cinema, considered by the industry to be one of the most profound advancements in motion picture production and technology of the last 100 years, will provide numerous advantages both for the industry and the audience. According to one commenter, currently there are sufficient standards and interim solutions to support captioning and video description now in digital format. Additionally, movie studios are supporting those efforts by providing accessibility tracks (captioning and video description) in many digital cinema content packages. Moreover, a group of industry commenters composed in pertinent part of members of the motion picture industry, the central standards organizations for this industry, and key digital equipment vendors, noted that they are participating in a joint venture to establish the remaining accessibility specifications and standards for access audio tracks. Access audio tracks are supplemental sound audio tracks for the hard of hearing and narrative audio tracks for individuals who have vision disabilities. According to a commenter and to industry documents, these standards were expected to be in place by spring 2009. According to a commenter, at that time, all of the major digital cinema equipment vendors were expected to have support for a variety of closed caption display and video description products. This same commenter stated that these technologies will be supported by the studios that produce and distribute feature films, by the theaters that show these films to the public, and by the full complement of equipment in the production, distribution, and display chain.

The initial investment for movie theater owners and operators to convert to digital cinema is expensive. One industry commenter estimated that converting theaters to digital projection costs between $70,000 and $100,000 per screen and that maintenance costs for digital projectors are estimated to run between $5,000 and $10,000 a year — approximately five times as expensive as the maintenance costs for film projectors. According to this same commenter, while there has been progress in making the conversion, only approximately 5,000 screens out of 38,794 nationwide have been converted, and the cost to make the remaining conversions involves a total investment of several billion dollars. According to another commenter, predictions as to when more than half of all screens will have been converted to digital projection are 10 years or more, depending on the finances of the movie theater owners and operators, the state of the economy, and the incentives supporting conversion. That said, according to one commenter who represents movie theater owners and operators, the majority of screens in the United States were expected to enter into agreements by the end of 2008 to convert to digital cinema. Most importantly, however, according to a few commenters, the systems in place today for captioning and video description will not become obsolete once a theater has converted to digital cinema but still can be used by the movie theater owner and operator to exhibit captions and description. The only difference for a movie theater owner or operator will be the way the data is delivered to the captioning and video description equipment in place in an auditorium. Despite the current availability of movies that are captioned and provide video description, movie theater owners and operators rarely exhibit the captions or descriptions. According to several commenters, less than 1 percent of all movies being exhibited in theaters are shown with captions.

Individuals with disabilities, advocacy groups, the representative from a non-profit, and representatives of State governments, including 11 State attorneys general, overwhelmingly supported issuance of a regulation requiring movie theater owners and operators to exhibit captioned and video described movies at all showings unless doing so would result in an undue burden or fundamental alteration of the goods and services offered by the public accommodation. In addition, this same group of commenters urged that any such regulation should be made effective now, and should not be tied to the conversion to digital cinema by the movie theater owners and operators. In support of such arguments, these commenters stated that the technology exists now to display movies with captions and video descriptions, regardless of whether the movie is exhibited on film or using digital cinema. Moreover, since the technology in use for displaying captions and video descriptions on film will be compatible with digital projection systems, they argued, there is no need to postpone implementation of a captioning or video description regulation until the conversion to digital has been made. Furthermore, since the conversion to digital may take years, commenters urged the Department to issue a regulation requiring captioning and video description now, rather than several years from now.

Advocacy groups and the 11 State attorneys general also requested that any regulation include factors describing what constitutes effective captioning and video description. Recommendations included requiring that captioning be within the same line of sight to the screen as the movie so that individuals who are deaf or hard of hearing can watch the movie and read the captions at the same time; that the captioning be accessible from each seat; that the captions be of sufficient size and contrast to the background so as to be readable easily; and that the recent recommendations of the Telecommunications and Electronics and Information Technology Advisory Committee Report to the Access Board that captions be "timely, accurate, complete, and efficient"[5] also be included.

The State attorneys general supported the Department's statement in the NPRM that the Department did not anticipate specifying which type of captioning to provide or what type of technology to use to provide video description, but would instead leave that to the discretion of the movie theater owners and operators.

---

[5] *Refreshed Accessibility Standards and Guidelines in Telecommunications and Electronic and Information Technology* (April 2008), available at http://www.access-board.gov/sec508/refresh/report/ (last visited June 24, 2010).

These State attorneys general opined that such discretion in the selection of the type of technology was consistent with the statutory and regulatory scheme of the ADA and would permit any new regulation to keep pace with future advancements in captioning and video description technology. These same commenters stated that such discretion may result in a mixed use of both closed captioning and open captioning, affording more choices both for the movie theater owners and operators and for individuals who are deaf or hard of hearing.

The representatives from the movie theater industry strongly urged the Department against issuing a regulation requiring captioning or video description. These commenters argued that the legislative history of the ADA expressly precluded regulating in the area of captioning. (These same commenters were silent with regard to video description on this issue.) The industry commenters also argued that to require movie theater owners and operators to exhibit captioned and video described movies would constitute a fundamental alteration in the nature of the goods and services offered by the movie theater owners and operators. In addition, some industry commenters argued that any such regulation by the Department would be inconsistent with the Access Board's guidelines. Also, these commenters noted the progress that has been made in the industry in making cinema more accessible even though there is no mandate to caption or describe movies, and they questioned whether any mandate is necessary. Finally, all the industry commenters argued that to require captioning or video description in 100 percent of movie theater screens for all showings would constitute an undue burden.

The comments have provided the Department with significant information on the state of the movie industry with regard to the availability of captioning and video description, the status of closed captioning technology, and the status of the transition to digital cinema. The Department also has given due consideration to the comments it has received from individuals, advocacy groups, governmental entities, and representatives of the movie industry. Recently, the United States Court of Appeals for the Ninth Circuit held that the ADA requires a chain of movie theaters to exhibit movies with closed captioning and video description unless the theaters can show that to do so would amount to a fundamental alteration or undue burden. *Arizona ex rel. Goddard v. Harkins Amusement Enterprises, Inc.*, 603 F.3d 666 (9th Cir. 2010). However, rather than issue specific regulatory text at this time, the Department has determined that it should obtain additional information regarding issues raised by commenters that were not contemplated at the time of the 2008 NPRM, supplemental technical information, and updated information regarding the current and future status of the conversion to digital cinema by movie theater owners and operators. To this end, the Department is planning to engage in rulemaking relating specifically to movie captioning under the ADA in the near future.

Section 36.304 Removal of Barriers.

With the adoption of the 2010 Standards, an important issue that the Department must address is the effect that the new (referred to as "supplemental") and revised ADA Standards will have on the continuing obligation of public accommodations to remove architectural, transportation, and communication barriers in existing facilities to the extent that it is readily achievable to do so. *See* 42 U.S.C. 12182(b)(2)(A)(iv). This issue was not addressed in the 2004 ADAAG because it was outside the scope of the Access Board's statutory authority under the ADA and section 502 of the Rehabilitation Act of 1973. *See* 29 U.S.C. 792(b)(3)(A)–(B) (authorizing the Access Board to establish and maintain minimum guidelines for the standards issued pursuant to the Architectural Barriers Act of 1968 and titles II and III of the ADA). Responsibility for implementing title III's requirement that public accommodations eliminate barriers in existing facilities where such removal is readily achievable rests solely with the Department. The term "existing facility" is defined in § 36.104 of the final rule. This definition is discussed in more detail above. *See* Appendix A discussion of definitions (§ 36.104).

The requirements for barrier removal by public accommodations are established in the Department's title III regulation. 28 CFR 36.304. Under this regulation, the Department used the 1991 Standards as a guide to identify what constitutes an architectural barrier, as well as the specifications that covered entities must follow in making architectural changes to remove the barrier to the extent that such removal is readily achievable. 28 CFR 36.304(d); 28 CFR part 36, app. A (2009). With adoption of the final rule, public accommodations will now be guided by the 2010 Standards, defined in § 36.104 as the 2004 ADAAG and the requirements contained in subpart D of 28 CFR part 36.

The 2010 Standards include technical and scoping specifications for a number of elements that were not addressed specifically in the 1991 Standards; these new requirements were identified as "supplemental requirements" in the NPRM. The 2010 Standards also include revisions to technical or scoping specifications for certain elements that were addressed in the 1991 Standards, *i.e.*, elements for which there already were technical and scoping specifications. Requirements for which there are revised technical or scoping specifications in the 2010 Standards are referred to in the NPRM as "incremental changes."

The Department expressed concern that requiring barrier removal for incremental changes might place unnecessary cost burdens on businesses that already had removed barriers in existing facilities in compliance with the 1991 Standards. With this rulemaking, the Department sought to strike an appropriate balance between ensuring that individuals with disabilities are provided access to facilities and mitigating potential financial burdens from barrier removal on existing places of public accommodation that satisfied their obligations under the 1991 Standards.

In the NPRM, the Department proposed several potential additions to § 36.304(d) that might reduce such financial burdens. First, the Department proposed a safe harbor for elements in existing facilities that were compliant with the 1991 Standards. Under this approach, an element that is not altered after the effective date of the 2010 Standards and that complies with the scoping and technical requirements for that element in the 1991 Standards would not be required to undergo modification to comply with the 2010 Standards to satisfy the ADA's barrier removal obligations. The public accommodation would thus be deemed to have met its barrier removal obligation with respect to that element.

The Department received many comments on this issue during the 60-day public comment period. After consideration of all relevant information presented on the issue, it is the Department's view that this element-by-element safe harbor provision should be retained in the final rule. This issue is discussed further below.

Second, the NPRM proposed several exceptions and exemptions from certain supplemental requirements to mitigate the barrier removal obligations of existing play areas and recreation facilities under the 2004 ADAAG. These proposals elicited many comments from both the business and disability communities. After consideration of all relevant information presented on the issue, it is the Department's view that these exceptions and exemptions should not be retained in the final rule. The specific proposals and comments, and the Department's conclusions, are discussed below.

Third, the NPRM proposed a new safe harbor approach to readily achievable barrier removal as applied to qualified small businesses. This proposed small business safe harbor was based on suggestions from small business advocacy groups that requested clearer guidance on the barrier removal obligations for small businesses. According to these groups, the Department's traditional approach to barrier removal disproportionately affects small businesses. They argued that most small businesses owners neither are equipped to understand the ADA Standards nor can they afford the architects, consultants, and attorneys that might provide some level of assurance of compliance with the ADA. For these same reasons, these commenters contended, small business owners are vulnerable to litigation, particularly lawsuits arising under title III, and often are forced to settle because the ADA Standards' complexity makes inadvertent noncompliance likely, even when a small business owner is acting in good faith, or because the business cannot afford the costs of litigation.

To address these and similar concerns, the NPRM proposed a level of barrier removal expenditures at which qualified small businesses would be deemed to have met their readily achievable barrier removal obligations for certain tax years. This safe harbor would have provided some protection from litigation because compliance could be assessed easily. Such a rule, the Department believed, also could further accessibility, because qualified small businesses would have an incentive to incorporate barrier removal into short- and long-term planning. The Department recognized that a qualified small business safe harbor would be a significant change to the Department's title III enforcement scheme. Accordingly, the Department sought comment on whether such an approach would further the aims underlying the statute's barrier removal provisions, and, if so, the appropriate parameters of the provision.

After consideration of the many comments received on this issue, the Department has decided not to include a qualified small business safe harbor in the final rule. This decision is discussed more fully below.

Element-by-element safe harbor for public accommodations. Public accommodations have a continuing obligation to remove certain architectural, communications, and transportation barriers in existing facilities to the extent readily achievable. 42 U.S.C. 12182(b)(2)(A)(iv). Because the Department uses the ADA Standards as a guide to identifying what constitutes an architectural barrier, the 2010 Standards, once they become effective, will provide a new reference point for assessing an entity's barrier removal obligations. The 2010 Standards introduce technical and scoping specifications for many elements that were not included in the 1991 Standards. Accordingly, public accommodations will have to consider these supplemental requirements when evaluating whether there are covered barriers in existing facilities, and, if so, remove them to the extent readily achievable. Also included in the 2010 Standards are revised technical and scoping requirements for elements that were addressed in the 1991 Standards. These incremental changes were made to address technological changes that have occurred since the promulgation of the 1991 Standards, to reflect additional study by the Access Board, and to harmonize ADAAG requirements with the model codes.

In the NPRM, the Department sought input on a safe harbor in proposed § 36.304(d)(2) intended to address concerns about the practical effects of the incremental changes on public accommodations' readily achievable barrier removal obligations. The proposed element-by-element safe harbor provided that in existing facilities elements that are, as of the effective date of the 2010 Standards, fully compliant with the applicable technical and scoping requirements in the 1991 Standards, need not be modified or retrofitted to meet the 2010 Standards, until and unless those elements are altered. The Department posited that it would be an inefficient use of resources to require covered entities that have complied with the 1991 Standards to retrofit already compliant elements when the change might only provide a minimal improvement in accessibility. In addition, the Department was concerned that covered entities would have a strong disincentive for voluntary compliance if every time the applicable standards were revised covered entities would be required once again to modify elements to keep pace with new requirements. The Department recognized that revisions to some elements might confer a significant benefit on some individuals with disabilities and because of the safe harbor these benefits would be unavailable until the facility undergoes alterations.

The Department received many comments on this issue from the business and disability communities. Business owners and operators, industry groups and trade associations, and business advocacy organizations strongly supported the element-by-element safe harbor. By contrast, disability advocacy organizations and individuals commenting on behalf of the disability community were opposed to this safe harbor with near unanimity. Businesses and business groups agreed with the concerns outlined by the Department in the NPRM, and asserted that the element-by-element safe harbor is integral to ensuring continued good faith compliance efforts by covered entities. These commenters argued that the financial cost and business disruption resulting from retrofitting elements constructed or previously modified to comply with 1991 Standards would be detrimental to nearly all businesses and not readily achievable for most. They contended that it would be fundamentally unfair to place these entities in a position where, despite full compliance with the 1991 Standards, the entities would now, overnight, be vulnerable to barrier removal litigation. They further contended that public accommodations will have little incentive to undertake large barrier removal projects or incorporate barrier removal into long-term planning if there is no assurance that the actions taken and money spent for barrier removal would offer some protection from litigation. One commenter also pointed out that the proposed safe harbor would be consistent with practices under other Federal accessibility standards, including the Uniform Federal Accessibility Standards (UFAS) and the ADAAG.

Some business commenters urged the Department to expand the element-by-element safe harbor to include supplemental requirements. These commenters argued that imposing the 2010 Standards on existing facilities will provide a strong incentive for such facilities to eliminate some elements entirely, particularly where the element is not critical to the public accommodation's business or operations (e.g., play areas in fast food restaurants) or the cost of retrofitting is significant. Some of these same commenters urged the Department to include within the safe harbor those elements not covered by the 1991 Standards, but which an entity had built in compliance with State or local accessibility laws. Other commenters requested safe harbor protection where a business had attempted barrier removal prior to the establishment of technical and scoping requirements for a particular element (e.g., play area equipment) if the business could show that the element now covered by the 2010 Standards was functionally accessible.

Other commenters noted ambiguity in the NPRM as to whether the element-by-element safe harbor applies only to elements that comply fully with the 1991 Standards, or also encompasses elements that comply with the 1991 Standards to the extent readily achievable. Some commenters proposed that the safe harbor should exist in perpetuity — that an element subject to a safe harbor at one point in time also should be afforded the same protection with respect to all future revisions to the ADA Standards (as with many building codes). These groups contended that allowing permanent compliance with the 1991 Standards will ensure readily accessible and usable facilities while also mitigating the need for expensive and time-consuming documentation of changes and maintenance.

A number of commenters inquired about the effect of the element-by-element safe harbor on elements that are not in strict compliance with the 1991 Standards, but conform to the terms of settlement agreements or consent decrees resulting from private litigation or Federal enforcement actions. These commenters noted that litigation or threatened litigation often has resulted in compromise among parties as to what is readily achievable. Business groups argued that facilities that have made modifications subject to those negotiated agreements should not be subject to the risk of further litigation as a result of the 2010 Standards.

Lastly, some business groups that supported the element-by-element safe harbor nevertheless contended that a better approach would be to separate barrier removal altogether from the 2010 Standards, such that the 2010 Standards would not be used to determine whether access to an existing facility is impeded by architectural barriers. These commenters argued that application of the 2010 Standards to barrier removal obligations is contrary to the ADA's directive that barrier removal is required only where "easily accomplishable and able to be carried out without much difficulty or expense," 42 U.S.C. 12181(9).

Nearly all commenters from the disability community objected to the proposed element-by- element safe harbor. These commenters asserted that the adoption of this safe harbor would permit and sanction the retention of outdated access standards even in cases where retrofitting to the 2010 Standards would be readily achievable. They argued that title III's readily achievable defense is adequate to address businesses' cost concerns, and rejected the premise that requiring businesses to retrofit currently compliant elements would be an inefficient use of resources where readily achievable to do so. The proposed regulations, these commenters asserted, incorporate advances in technology, design, and construction, and reflect congressional and societal understanding that accessibility is not a static concept and that the ADA is a civil rights law intended to maximize accessibility.

Additionally, these commenters noted that since the 2004 revision of the ADAAG will not be the last, setting a precedent of safe harbors for compliant elements will have the effect of preserving and protecting layers of increasingly outdated accessibility standards.

Many commenters objected to the Department's characterization of the requirements subject to the safe harbor as reflecting only incremental changes and asserted that many of these incremental changes will result in significantly enhanced accessibility at little cost. The requirement concerning side-reach ranges was highlighted as an example of such requirements. Commenters from the disability community argued that the revised maximum side-reach range (from 54 inches to 48 inches) will result in a substantial increase in accessibility for many persons with disabilities — particularly individuals of short stature, for whom the revised reach range represents the difference between independent access to many features and dependence — and that the revisions should be made where readily achievable to do so. Business commenters, on the other hand, contended that application of the safe harbor to this requirement is critical because retrofitting items, such as light switches and thermostats often requires work (e.g., rewiring, patching, painting, and re-wallpapering), that would be extremely burdensome for entities to undertake. These commenters argued that such a burden is not justified where many of the affected entities already have retrofitted to meet the 1991 Standards.

Some commenters that were opposed to the element-by-element safe harbor proposed that an entity's past efforts to comply with the 1991 Standards might appropriately be a factor in the readily achievable analysis. Several commenters proposed a temporary 5- year safe harbor that would provide reassurance and stability to covered entities that have recently taken proactive steps for barrier removal, but would also avoid the problems of preserving access deficits in perpetuity and creating multiple standards as subsequent updates are adopted.

After consideration of all relevant information presented on this issue during the comment period, the Department has decided to retain the proposed element-by-element safe harbor. Title III's architectural barrier provisions place the most significant requirements of accessibility on new construction and alterations. The aim is to require businesses to make their facilities fully accessible at the time they are first constructing or altering those facilities, when burdens are less and many design elements will necessarily be in flux, and to impose a correspondingly lesser duty on businesses that are not changing their facilities. The Department believes that it would be consistent with this statutory structure not to change the requirements for design elements that were specifically addressed in our prior standards for those facilities that were built or altered in full compliance with those standards. The Department similarly believes it would be consistent with the statutory scheme not to change the requirements for elements that were specifically addressed in our prior standards for those existing facilities that came into full compliance with those standards. Accordingly, the final rule at § 36.304(d)(2)(i) provides that elements that have not been altered in existing facilities on or after March 15, 2012 and that comply with the corresponding technical and scoping specifications for those elements in the 1991 Standards are not required to be modified in order to comply with the requirements set forth in the 2010 Standards.

The safe harbor adopted is consistent in principle with the proposed provision in the NPRM, and reflects the Department's determination that this approach furthers the statute's barrier removal provisions and promotes continued good-faith compliance by public accommodations.

The element-by-element safe harbor adopted in this final rule is a narrow one. The Department recognizes that this safe harbor will delay, in some cases, the increased accessibility that the incremental changes would provide and that for some individuals with disabilities the impact may be significant. This safe harbor, however, is not a blanket exemption for every element in existing facilities. Compliance with the 1991 Standards is determined on an element-by-element basis in each existing facility.

Section 36.304(d)(2)(ii)(A) provides that prior to the compliance date of the rule March 15, 2012, noncompliant elements that have not been altered are obligated to be modified to the extent readily achievable to comply with the requirements set forth in the 1991 Standards or the 2010 Standards. Section 36.304(d)(2)(ii)(B) provides that after the date the 2010 Standards take effect (18 months after publication of the rule), noncompliant elements that have not been altered must be modified to the extent readily achievable to comply with the requirements set forth in the 2010 Standards. Noncomplying newly constructed and altered elements may also be subject to the requirements of § 36.406(a)(5).

The Department has not expanded the scope of the element-by-element safe harbor beyond those elements subject to the incremental changes. The Department has added § 36.304(d)(2)(iii), explicitly clarifying that existing elements subject to supplemental requirements for which scoping and technical specifications are provided for the first time in the 2010 Standards (e.g., play area requirements) are not covered by the safe harbor and, therefore, must be modified to comply with the 2010 Standards to the extent readily achievable. Section 36.304(d)(2)(iii) also identifies the elements in the 2010 Standards that are not eligible for the element-by-element safe harbor. The safe harbor also does not apply to the accessible routes not previously scoped in the 1991 standards, such as those required to connect the boundary of each area of sport activity, including soccer fields, basketball courts, baseball fields, running tracks, skating rinks, and areas surrounding a piece of gymnastic equipment. *See* Advisory note to section F206.2.2 of the 2010 Standards. The resource and fairness concerns underlying the element-by- element safe harbor are not implicated by barrier removal involving supplemental requirements. Public accommodations have not been subject previously to technical and scoping specifications for these supplemental requirements. Thus, with respect to supplemental requirements, the existing readily achievable standard best maximizes accessibility in the built environment without imposing unnecessary burdens on public accommodations.

The Department also has declined to expand the element-by-element safe harbor to cover existing elements subject to supplemental requirements that also may have been built in compliance with State or local accessibility laws. Measures taken to remove barriers under a Federal accessibility provision logically must be considered in regard to Federal standards, in this case the 2010 Standards. This approach is based on the Department's determination that reference to ADA Standards for barrier removal will promote certainty, safety, and good design while still permitting slight deviations through readily achievable alternative methods. The Department continues to believe that this approach provides an appropriate and workable framework for implementation of title III's barrier removal provisions. Because compliance with State or local accessibility codes is not a reliable indicator of effective access for purposes of the ADA Standards, the Department has decided not to include reliance on such codes as part of the safe harbor provision.

Only elements compliant with the 1991 Standards are eligible for the safe harbor. Thus, where a public accommodation attempted barrier removal but full compliance with the 1991 Standards was not readily achievable, the modified element does not fall within the scope of the safe harbor provision. A public accommodation at any point in time must remove barriers to the extent readily achievable. For existing elements, for which removal is not readily achievable at any given time, the public accommodation must provide its goods, services, facilities, privileges, advantages, or accommodations through alternative methods that are readily achievable. *See* 42 U.S.C. 12182(b)(2) (A)(iv), (v).

One-time evaluation and implementation of the readily achievable standard is not the end of the public accommodation's barrier-removal obligation. Public accommodations have a continuing obligation to reevaluate barrier removal on a regular basis. For example, if a public accommodation identified barriers under the 1991 Standards but did not remove them because removal was not readily achievable based on cost considerations, it has a continuing obligation to remove these barriers if the economic considerations for the public accommodation change. The fact that the public accommodation has been providing its goods or services through alternative methods does not negate the continuing obligation to assess whether removal of the barrier at issue has become readily achievable. Public accommodations should incorporate consideration of their continuing barrier removal obligations in both short-term and long- term business planning.

The Department notes that commenters across the board expressed concern with recordkeeping burdens implicated by the element-by-element safe harbor. Businesses noted the additional costs and administrative burdens associated with identifying elements that fall within the element- by-element safe harbor, as well as tracking, documenting, and maintaining data on installation dates. Disability advocates expressed concern that varying compliance standards will make enforcement efforts more difficult, and urged the Department to clarify that title III entities bear the burden of proof regarding entitlement to safe harbor protection. The Department emphasizes that public accommodations wishing to benefit from the element-by-element safe harbor must demonstrate their safe harbor eligibility. The Department encourages public accommodations to take appropriate steps to confirm and document the compliance of existing elements with the 1991 Standards. Finally, while the Department has decided not to adopt in this rulemaking the suggestion by some commenters to make the protection afforded by the element-by-element safe harbor temporary, the Department believes this proposal merits further consideration. The Department, therefore, will continue to evaluate the efficacy and appropriateness of a safe harbor expiration or sunset provision.

Application to specific scenarios raised in comments. In response to the NPRM, the Department received a number of comments that raised issues regarding application of the element-by-element safe harbor to particular situations. Business commenters requested guidance on whether the replacement for a broken or malfunctioning element that is covered by the 1991 Standards would have to comply with the 2010 Standards. These commenters expressed concern that in some cases replacement of a broken fixture might necessitate moving a number of other accessible fixtures (such as in a bathroom) in order to comply with the fixture and space requirements of the 2010 Standards. Others questioned the effect of the new standards where an entity replaces an existing element currently protected by the safe harbor provision for water or energy conservation reasons. The Department intends to address these types of scenarios in technical guidance.

Effective date for barrier removal. Several commenters expressed concern that the NPRM did not propose a transition period for applying the 2004 ADAAG to barrier removal in existing facilities in cases where the safe harbors do not apply. These commenters argued that for newly covered elements, they needed time to hire attorneys and consultants to assess the impact of the new requirements, determine whether they need to make additional retrofits, price those retrofits, assess whether the change actually is "readily achievable," obtain approval for the removal from owners who must pay for the changes, obtain permits, and then do the actual work. The commenters recognized that there may be some barrier removal actions that require little planning, but stated that other actions cost significantly more and require more budgeting, planning, and construction time.

Barrier removal has been an ongoing requirement that has applied to public accommodations since the original regulation took effect on January 26, 1992. The final rule maintains the existing regulatory provision that barrier removal does not have to be undertaken unless it is "readily achievable." The Department has provided in § 36.304(d)(2)(ii)(B) that public accommodations are not required to apply the 2010 Standards to barrier removal until 18 months after the publication date of this rule. It is the Department's view that 18 months is a sufficient amount of time for application of the 2010 Standards to barrier removal for those elements not subject to the safe harbor. This is also consistent with the compliance date the Department has specified for applying the 2010 Standards to new construction and alterations.

Reduced scoping for play areas and other recreation facilities.

Play areas. The Access Board published final guidelines for play areas in October 2000. 65 FR 62498 (Oct. 18, 2000). The guidelines include requirements for ground-level and elevated play components, accessible routes connecting the components, accessible ground surfaces, and maintenance of those surfaces. They have been referenced in Federal playground construction and safety guidelines and in some State and local codes and have been used voluntarily when many play areas across the country have been altered or constructed.

In adopting the 2004 ADAAG (which includes the play area guidelines published in 2000), the Department acknowledges both the importance of integrated, full access to play areas for children and parents with disabilities as well as the need to avoid placing an untenable fiscal burden on businesses. Consequently, the Department asked seven questions in the NPRM related to existing play areas. Two questions related to safe harbors: one on the appropriateness of a general safe harbor for existing play areas and another on public accommodations that have complied with State or local standards specific to play areas. The others related to reduced scoping, limited exemptions, and whether there is a "tipping point" at which the costs of compliance with supplemental requirements would be so burdensome that a public accommodation would shut down a program rather than comply with the new requirements. In the nearly 100 comments received on title III play areas, the majority of commenters strongly opposed all safe harbors, exemptions, and reductions in scoping, and questioned the feasibility of determining a tipping point. A smaller number of commenters advocated for a safe harbor from compliance with the 2004 ADAAG play area requirements along with reduced scoping and exemptions for both readily achievable barrier removal and alterations.

Commenters were split as to whether the Department should exempt owners and operators of public accommodations from compliance with the supplemental requirements for play areas and recreation facilities and instead continue to determine accessibility in these facilities on a case-by-case basis under existing law. Many commenters were of the view that the exemption was not necessary because concerns of financial burden are addressed adequately by the defenses inherent in the standard for what constitutes readily achievable barrier removal. A number of commenters found the exemption inappropriate because no standards for play areas previously existed. Commenters also were concerned that a safe harbor applicable only to play areas and recreation facilities (but not to other facilities operated by a public accommodation) would create confusion, significantly limit access for children and parents with disabilities, and perpetuate the discrimination and segregation individuals with disabilities face in the important social arenas of play and recreation — areas where little access has been provided in the absence of specific standards. Many commenters suggested that instead of an exemption, the Department should provide guidance on barrier removal with respect to play areas and other recreation facilities.

Several commenters supported the exemption, mainly on the basis of the cost of barrier removal. More than one commenter noted that the most expensive aspect of barrier removal on existing play areas is the surfaces for the accessible routes and use zones. Several commenters expressed the view that where a play area is ancillary to a public accommodation (e.g., in quick service restaurants or shopping centers), the play area should be exempt from compliance with the supplemental requirements because barrier removal would be too costly, and as a result, the public accommodation might eliminate the area.

The Department has been persuaded that the ADA's approach to barrier removal, the readily achievable standard, provides the appropriate balance for the application of the 2010 Standards to existing play areas. Thus, in existing playgrounds, public accommodations will be required to remove barriers to access where these barriers can be removed without much difficulty or expense.

The NPRM asked if there are State and local standards specifically regarding play and recreation area accessibility and whether facilities currently governed by, and in compliance with, such State and local standards or codes should be subject to a safe harbor from compliance with similar applicable requirements in the 2004 ADAAG. The Department also requested comments on whether it would be appropriate for the Access Board to consider the implementation of guidelines that would extend such a safe harbor to play and recreation areas undertaking alterations. In response, no comprehensive State or local codes were identified, and commenters generally noted that because the 2004 ADAAG contained comprehensive accessibility requirements for these unique areas, public accommodations should not be afforded a safe harbor from compliance with them when altering play and recreation areas. The Department is persuaded by these comments that there is insufficient basis to apply a safe harbor for readily achievable barrier removal or alterations for play areas built in compliance with State or local laws.

In the NPRM, the Department requested that public accommodations identify a "tipping point" at which the costs of compliance with the supplemental requirements for existing play areas would be so burdensome that the entity simply would shut down the playground. In response, no tipping point was identified. Some commenters noted, however, that the scope of the requirements may create the choice between wholesale replacement of play areas and discontinuance of some play areas, while others speculated that some public accommodations may remove play areas that are merely ancillary amenities rather than incur the cost of barrier removal under the 2010 Standards. The Department has decided that the comments did not establish any clear tipping point and therefore that no regulatory response is appropriate in this area.

The NPRM also asked for comment about the potential effect of exempting existing play areas of less than 1,000 square feet in size from the requirements applicable to play areas. Many trade and business associations favored exempting these small play areas, with some arguing that where the play areas are only ancillary amenities, the cost of barrier removal may dictate that they be closed down. Some commenters sought guidance on the definition of a 1,000-square-foot play area, seeking clarification that seating and bathroom spaces associated with a play area are not included in the size definition. Disability rights advocates, by contrast, overwhelmingly opposed this exemption, arguing that these play areas may be some of the few available in a community; that restaurants and day care facilities are important places for socialization between children with disabilities and those without disabilities; that integrated play is important to the mission of day care centers and that many day care centers and play areas in large cities, such as New York City, have play areas that are less than 1,000 square feet in size; and that 1,000 square feet was an arbitrary size requirement.

The Department agrees that children with disabilities are entitled to access to integrated play opportunities. However, the Department is aware that small public accommodations are concerned about the costs and efforts associated with barrier removal. The Department has given careful consideration as to how best to insulate small entities from overly burdensome costs and undertakings and has concluded that the existing readily achievable standard, not a separate exemption, is an effective and employable method by which to protect these entities. Under the existing readily achievable standard, small public accommodations would be required to comply only with the scoping and technical requirements of the 2010 Standards that are easily accomplishable and able to be carried out without much difficulty or expense. Thus, concerns about prohibitive costs and efforts clearly are addressed by the existing readily achievable standard. Moreover, as evidenced by comments inquiring as to how 1,000- square- foot play areas are to be measured and complaining that the 1,000-square-foot cutoff is arbitrary, the exemption posited in the NPRM would have been difficult to apply. Finally, a separate exemption would have created confusion as to whether, or when, to apply the exemption or the readily achievable standard. Consequently, the Department has decided that an exemption, separate and apart from the readily achievable standard, is not appropriate or necessary for small private play areas.

In the NPRM, the Department requested public comment as to whether existing play areas should be permitted to substitute additional ground-level play components for the elevated play components that they otherwise would have been required to make accessible. Most commenters opposed this substitution because the guidelines as well as considerations of "readily achievable barrier removal" inherently contain the flexibility necessary for a variety of situations. Such commenters also noted that the Access Board adopted extensive guidelines with ample public input, including significant negotiation and balancing of costs. In addition, commenters advised that including additional ground level play components might result in higher costs because more accessible route surfaces might be required. A limited number of commenters favored substitution. The Department is persuaded by these comments that the proposed substitution of elements may not be beneficial. The current rules applicable to readily achievable barrier removal will be used to determine the number and type of accessible elements appropriate for a specific facility.

In the NPRM, the Department requested public comment on whether it would be appropriate for the Access Board to consider issuing guidelines for alterations to play and recreation facilities that would permit reduced scoping of accessible components or substitution of ground level play components in lieu of elevated play components. The Department received little input on this issue, and most commenters disfavored the suggestion. One commenter that supported this approach conjectured that it would encourage public accommodations to maintain and improve their playgrounds as well as provide more accessibility. The Department is persuaded that it is not necessary to ask the Access Board to revisit this issue.

The NPRM also asked whether only one play area of each type should be required to comply at existing sites with multiple play areas and whether there are other select requirements applicable to play areas in the 2004 ADAAG for which the Department should consider exemptions or reduced scoping. Some commenters were opposed to the concept of requiring compliance at one play area of each type at a site with multiple play areas, citing lack of choice and ongoing segregation of children and adults with disabilities. Other commenters who supported an exemption and reduced scoping for alterations noted that the play equipment industry has adjusted to, and does not take issue with, the provisions of the 2004 ADAAG; however, they asked for some flexibility in the barrier removal requirements as applied to play equipment, arguing that augmentation of the existing equipment and installation of accessible play surfacing equates to wholesale replacement of the play equipment. The Department is persuaded that the current rules applicable to readily achievable barrier removal should be used to decide which play areas must comply with the supplemental requirements presented in the 2010 Standards.

Swimming pools, wading pools, saunas, and steam rooms. Section 36.304(d)(3)(ii) in the NPRM specified that for measures taken to comply with the barrier removal requirements, existing swimming pools with at least 300 linear feet of swimming pool wall would need to provide only one accessible means of entry that complies with section 1009.2 or section 1009.3 of the 2004 ADAAG, instead of the two means required for new construction. Commenters opposed the Department's reducing the scoping from that required in the 2004 ADAAG. The following were among the factors cited in comments: that swimming is a common therapeutic form of exercise for many individuals with disabilities; that the cost of a swimming pool lift or other options for pool access is readily achievable and can be accomplished without much difficulty or expense; and that the readily achievable standard already provides public accommodations with a means to reduce their scoping requirements. A few commenters cited safety concerns resulting from having just one accessible means of access, and stated that because pools typically have one ladder for every 75 linear feet of pool wall, they should have more than one accessible means of egress. Other commenters either approved or did not oppose providing one accessible means of access for larger pools so long as a lift was used.

Section 36.304(d)(4)(ii) of the NPRM proposed to exempt existing swimming pools with fewer than 300 linear feet of swimming pool wall from the obligation to provide an accessible means of entry. Most commenters strongly opposed this provision, arguing that aquatic activity is a safe and beneficial form of exercise that is particularly appropriate for individuals with disabilities. Many argued that the readily achievable standard for barrier removal is available as a defense and is preferable to creating an exemption for pool operators for whom providing an accessible means of entry would be readily achievable. Commenters who supported this provision apparently assumed that providing an accessible means of entry would be readily achievable and that therefore the exemption is needed so that small pool operators do not have to provide an accessible means of entry.

The Department has carefully considered all the information available to it as well as the comments submitted on these two proposed exemptions for swimming pools owned or operated by title III entities. The Department acknowledges that swimming provides important therapeutic, exercise, and social benefits for many individuals with disabilities and is persuaded that exemption of the vast majority of privately owned or operated pools from the 2010 Standards is neither appropriate nor necessary. The Department agrees with the commenters that title III already contains sufficient limitations on private entities' obligations to remove barriers. In particular, the Department agrees that those public accommodations that can demonstrate that making particular existing swimming pools accessible in accordance with the 2010 Standards is not readily achievable are sufficiently protected from excessive compliance costs. Thus, the Department has eliminated proposed § 36.304(d)(3)(ii) and (d)(4)(ii) from the final rule.

Proposed § 36.304(d)(4)(iii) would have exempted existing saunas and steam rooms that seat only two individuals from the obligation to remove barriers. This provision generated far fewer comments than the provisions for swimming pools. People who commented were split fairly evenly between those who argued that the readily achievable standard for barrier removal should be applied to all existing saunas and steam rooms and those who argued that all existing saunas and steam rooms, regardless of size, should be exempt from any barrier removal obligations. The Department considered these comments and has decided to eliminate the exemption for existing saunas and steam rooms that seat only two people. Such an exemption for saunas and steam rooms that seat only two people is unnecessary because the readily achievable standard provides sufficient protection against barrier removal that is overly expensive or too difficult. Moreover, the Department believes barrier removal likely will not be readily achievable for most of these small saunas because the nature of their prefabricated forms, which include built-in seats, make it either technically infeasible or too difficult or expensive to remove barriers. Consequently a separate exemption for saunas and steam rooms would have been superfluous. Finally, employing the readily achievable standard for small saunas and steam rooms is consistent with the Department's decisions regarding the proposed exemptions for play areas and swimming pools.

Several commenters also argued in favor of a specific exemption for existing spas. The Department notes that the technically infeasible and readily achievable defenses are applicable equally to existing spas and declines to adopt such an exemption.

The Department also solicited comment on the possibility of exempting existing wading pools from the obligation to remove barriers where readily achievable. Most commenters stated that installing a sloped entry in an existing wading pool is not likely to be feasible. Because covered entities are not required to undertake modifications that are not readily achievable or that would be technically infeasible, the Department believes that the rule as drafted provides sufficient protection from unwarranted expense to the operators of small existing wading pools. Other existing wading pools, particularly those large wading pools found in facilities such as water parks, must be assessed on a case-by-case basis. Therefore, the Department has not included an exemption for wading pools in its final rule.

The Department received several comments recommending that existing wave pools be exempt from barrier removal requirements. The commenters pointed out that existing wave pools often have a sloped entry, but do not have the handrails, level landings, or edge protection required for accessible entry. Because pool bottom slabs are structural, they could be subject to catastrophic failure if the soil pressure stability or the under slab de- watering are not maintained during the installation of these accessibility features in an already constructed pool. They also argue that the only safe design scenario is to design the wheelchair ramp, pool lift, or transfer access in a side cove where the mean water level largely is unaffected by the wave action, and that this additional construction to an existing wave pool is not readily achievable. If located in the main pool area, the handrails, stanchions, and edge protection for sloped entry will become underwater hazards when the wave action is pushing onto pool users, and the use of a pool lift will not be safe without a means of stabilizing the person against the forces of the waves while using the lift. They also pointed out that a wheelchair would pose a hazard to all wave pool users, in that the wave action might push other pool users into the wheelchair or push the wheelchair into other pool users. The wheelchair would have to be removed from the pool after the user has entered (and has transferred to a flotation device if needed). The commenters did not specify if these two latter concerns are applicable to all wave pools or only to those with more aggressive wave action. The Department has decided that the issue of modifications to wave pools is best addressed on a case-by-case basis, and therefore, this rule does not contain barrier removal exemptions applicable to wave pools.

The Department also received comments suggesting that it is not appropriate to require two accessible means of entry to wave pools, lazy rivers, sand bottom pools, and other water amusements that have only one point of entry. The Department agrees. The 2010 Standards (at section 242.2, Exception 2) provide that only one means of entry is required for wave pools, lazy rivers, sand bottom pools, and other water amusement where user access is limited to one area.

Other recreation facilities. In the NPRM, the Department asked about a number of issues relating to recreation facilities, such as team or player seating areas, areas of sport activity, exercise machines, boating facilities, fishing piers and platforms, golf courses, and miniature golf courses. The Department asked for public comment on the costs and benefits of applying the 2004 ADAAG to these spaces and facilities. The discussion of the comments received by the Department on these issues and the Department's response to those comments can be found in either the section entitled "Other Issues" of Appendix A to this final rule.

Safe harbor for qualified small businesses.

Section 36.304(d)(5) of the NPRM would have provided that a qualified small business would meet its obligation to remove architectural barriers where readily achievable for a given year if, during that tax year, the entity spent at least 1 percent of its gross revenue in the preceding tax year on measures undertaken in compliance with barrier removal requirements. Proposed § 36.304(d)(5) has been omitted from the final rule. The qualified small business safe harbor was proposed in response to small business advocates' requests for clearer guidance on when barrier removal is, and is not, readily achievable. According to these groups, the Department's approach to readily achievable barrier removal disproportionately affects small business for the following reasons: (1) Small businesses are more likely to operate in older buildings and facilities; (2) the 1991 Standards are too numerous and technical for most small business owners to understand and determine how they relate to State and local building or accessibility codes; and (3) small businesses are vulnerable to title III litigation and often are compelled to settle because they cannot afford the litigation costs involved in proving that an action is not readily achievable.

The 2010 Standards go a long way toward meeting the concern of small businesses with regard to achieving compliance with both Federal and State accessibility requirements, because the Access Board harmonized the 2004 ADAAG with the model codes that form the basis of most State and local accessibility codes. Moreover, the element-by-element safe harbor will ensure that unless and until a small business engages in alteration of affected elements, the small business will not have to retrofit elements that were constructed in compliance with the 1991 Standards or, with respect to elements in an existing facility, that were retrofitted to the 1991 Standards in conjunction with the business's barrier removal obligation prior to the rule's compliance date.

In proposing an additional safe harbor for small businesses, the Department had sought to promulgate a rule that would provide small businesses a level of certainty in short-term and long-term planning with respect to barrier removal. This in turn would benefit individuals with disabilities in that it would encourage small businesses to consider and incorporate barrier removal in their yearly budgets. Such a rule also would provide some protection, through diminished litigation risks, to small businesses that undertake significant barrier removal projects.

As proposed in the NPRM, the qualified small business safe harbor would provide that a qualified small business has met its readily achievable barrier removal obligations for a given year if, during that tax year, the entity has spent at least 1 percent of its gross revenue in the preceding tax year on measures undertaken to comply with title III barrier removal requirements. (Several small business advocacy organizations pointed out an inconsistency between the Department's description of the small business safe harbor in the Section-by-Section Analysis for § 36.304 and the proposed regulatory text for that provision. The proposed regulatory text sets out the correct parameters of the proposed rule. The Department does not believe that the error substantively affected the comments on this issue. Some commenters noted the discrepancy and commented on both; others commented more generally on the proposal, so the discrepancy was not relevant.) The Department noted that the efficacy of any proposal for a small business safe harbor would turn on the following two determinations: (1) The definition of a qualified small business, and (2) the formula for calculating what percentage of revenue is sufficient to satisfy the readily achievable presumption.

As proposed in § 36.104 in the NPRM, a "qualified small business" is a business entity defined as a small business concern under the regulations promulgated by the Small Business Administration (SBA) pursuant to the Small Business Act. *See* 15 U.S.C. 632; 13 CFR part 121. The Department noted that under section 3(a)(2)(C) of the Small Business Act, Federal departments and agencies are prohibited from prescribing a size standard for categorizing a business concern as a small business unless the department or agency has been authorized specifically to do so or has proposed a size standard in compliance with the criteria set forth in the SBA regulations, has provided an opportunity for public notice and comment on the proposed standard, and has received approval from the Administrator of the SBA to use the standard. *See* 15 U.S.C. 632(a)(2)(C). The Department further noted that Federal agencies or departments promulgating regulations relating to small businesses usually use SBA size criteria, and they otherwise must be prepared to justify how they arrived at a different standard and why the SBA's regulations do not satisfy the agency's program requirements. *See* 13 CFR 121.903. The ADA does not define "small business" or specifically authorize the Department to prescribe size standards.

In the NPRM, the Department indicated its belief that the size standards developed by the SBA are appropriate for determining which businesses subject to the ADA should be eligible for the small business safe harbor provisions, and proposed to adopt the SBA's size standards to define small businesses for purposes of the qualified small business safe harbor. The SBA's small business size standards define the maximum size that a concern, together with all of its affiliates, may be if it is to be eligible for Federal small business programs or to be considered a small business for the purpose of other Federal agency programs. Concerns primarily engaged in the same kind of economic activity are classified in the same industry regardless of their types of ownership (such as sole proprietorship, partnership, or corporation). Approximately 1200 industries are described in detail in the North American Industry Classification System — United States, 2007. For most businesses, the SBA has established a size standard based on average annual receipts.

The majority of places of public accommodation will be classified as small businesses if their average annual receipts are less than $6.5 million. However, some will qualify with higher annual receipts. The SBA small business size standards should be familiar to many if not most small businesses, and using these standards in the ADA regulation would provide some certainty to owners, operators, and individuals because the SBA's current size standards can be changed only after notice and comment rulemaking.

The Department explained in the NPRM that the choice of gross revenue as the basis for calculating the safe harbor threshold was intended to avoid the effect of differences in bookkeeping practices and to maximize accessibility consistent with congressional intent. The Department recognized, however, that entities with similar gross revenue could have very different net revenue, and that this difference might affect what is readily achievable for a particular entity. The Department also recognized that adopting a small business safe harbor would effect a marked change to the Department's current position on barrier removal. Accordingly, the Department sought public comment on whether a presumption should be adopted whereby qualifying small businesses are presumed to have done what is readily achievable for a given year if, during that tax year, the entity spent at least 1 percent of its gross revenue in the preceding tax year on barrier removal, and on whether 1 percent is an appropriate amount or whether gross revenue would be the appropriate measure.

The Department received many comments on the proposed qualified small business safe harbor. From the business community, comments were received from individual business owners and operators, industry and trade groups, and advocacy organizations for business and industry. From the disability community, comments were received from individuals, disability advocacy groups, and nonprofit organizations involved in providing services for persons with disabilities or involved in disability-related fields. The Department has considered all relevant matter submitted on this issue during the 60-day public comment period.

Small businesses and industry groups strongly supported a qualified small business safe harbor of some sort, but none supported the structure proposed by the Department in the NPRM. All felt strongly that clarifications and modifications were needed to strengthen the provision and to provide adequate protection from litigation.

Business commenters' objections to the proposed qualified small business safe harbor fell generally into three categories: (1) That gross revenue is an inappropriate and inaccurate basis for determining what is readily achievable by a small business since it does not take into account expenses that may result in a small business operating at a loss; (2) that courts will interpret the regulation to mean that a small business must spend 1 percent of gross revenue each year on barrier removal, i.e., that expenditure of 1 percent of gross revenue on barrier removal is always "readily achievable"; and (3) that a similar misinterpretation of the 1 percent gross revenue concept, i.e., that 1 percent of gross revenue is always "readily achievable," will be applied to public accommodations that are not small businesses and that have substantially larger gross revenue. Business groups also expressed significant concern about the recordkeeping burdens they viewed as inherent in the Department's proposal.

Across the board, business commenters objected to the Department's proposed use of gross revenue as the basis for calculating whether the small business safe harbor has been met. All contended that 1 percent of gross revenue is too substantial a trigger for safe harbor protection and would result in barrier removal burdens far exceeding what is readily achievable or "easily accomplishable and able to be carried out without much difficulty or expense." 42U.S.C. 12181(9). These commenters further pointed out that gross revenue and receipts vary considerably from industry to industry depending on the outputs sold in each industry, and that the use of gross revenue or receipts would therefore result in arbitrary and inequitable burdens on those subject to the rule. These commenters stated that the readily achievable analysis, and thus the safe harbor threshold, should be premised on a business's net revenue so that operating expenses are offset before determining what amount might be available for barrier removal. Many business commenters contended that barrier removal is not readily achievable if an entity is operating at a loss, and that a spending formula premised on net revenue can reflect more accurately businesses' ability to engage in barrier removal.

There was no consensus among the business commenters as to a formula that would reflect more accurately what is readily achievable for small businesses with respect to barrier removal. Those that proposed alternative formulas offered little in the way of substantive support for their proposals. One advocacy organization representing a large cross-section of small businesses provided some detail on the gross and net revenue of various industry types and sizes in support of its position that for nearly all small businesses, net revenue is a better indicator of a business's financial ability to spend money on barrier removal. The data also incidentally highlighted the importance and complexity of ensuring that each component in a safe harbor formula accurately informs and contributes to the ultimate question of what is and is not readily achievable for a small business.

Several business groups proposed that a threshold of 0.5 percent (or one-half of 1 percent) of gross revenue, or 2.5 percent of net revenue, spent on ADA compliance might be a workable measure of what is "readily achievable" for small businesses. Other groups proposed 3 to 5 percent of net revenue as a possible measure. Several commenters proposed affording small businesses an option of using gross or net revenue to determine safe harbor eligibility. Another commenter proposed premising the safe harbor threshold on a designated percentage of the amount spent on renovation in a given year. Others proposed averaging gross or net revenue over a number of years to account for cyclical changes in economic and business environments. Additionally, many proposed that an entity should be able to roll over expenditures in excess of the safe harbor for inclusion in safe harbor analysis in subsequent years, to facilitate barrier removal planning and encourage large-scale barrier removal measures.

Another primary concern of many businesses and business groups is that the 1 percent threshold for safe harbor protection would become a de facto "floor" for what is readily achievable for any small business entity. These commenters urged the Department to clarify that readily achievable barrier removal remains the standard, and that in any given case, an entity retains the right to assert that barrier removal expenditures below the 1 percent threshold are not readily achievable. Other business groups worried that courts would apply the 1 percent calculus to questions of barrier removal by businesses too large to qualify for the small business safe harbor. These commenters requested clarification that the rationale underlying the Department's determination that a percentage of gross revenue can appropriately approximate readily achievable barrier removal for small businesses does not apply outside the small business context.

Small businesses and business groups uniformly requested guidance as to what expenses would be included in barrier removal costs for purposes of determining whether the safe harbor threshold has been met. These commenters contended that any and all expenses associated with ADA compliance — e.g., consultants, architects, engineers, staff training, and recordkeeping — should be included in the calculation. Some proposed that litigation-related expenses, including defensive litigation costs, also should be accounted for in a small business safe harbor. Additionally, several commenters urged the Department to issue a small business compliance guide with detailed guidance and examples regarding application of the readily achievable barrier removal standard and the safe harbor. Some commenters felt that the Department's regulatory efforts should be focused on clarifying the readily achievable standard rather than on introducing a safe harbor based on a set spending level.

Businesses and business groups expressed concern that the Department's proposed small business safe harbor would not alleviate small business vulnerability to litigation. Individuals and advocacy groups were equally concerned that the practical effect of the Department's proposal likely would be to accelerate or advance the initiation of litigation. These commenters pointed out that an individual encountering barriers in small business facilities will not know whether the entity is noncompliant or entitled to safe harbor protection. Safe harbor eligibility can be evaluated only after review of the small business's barrier removal records and financial records. Individuals and advocacy groups argued that the Department should not promulgate a rule by which individuals must file suit to obtain the information needed to determine whether a lawsuit is appropriate in a particular case, and that, therefore, the rule should clarify that small businesses are required to produce such documentation to any individual upon request.

Several commenters noted that a small business safe harbor based on net, rather than gross, revenue would complicate exponentially its efficacy as an affirmative defense, because accounting practices and asserted expenses would be subject to discovery and dispute. One business advocacy group representing a large cross-section of small businesses noted that some small business owners and operators likely would be uncomfortable with producing detailed financial information, or could be prevented from using the safe harbor because of inadvertent recordkeeping deficiencies.

Individuals, advocacy groups, and nonprofit organizations commenting on behalf of the disability community uniformly and strongly opposed a safe harbor for qualified small businesses, saying it is fundamentally at odds with the intent of Congress and the plain language of the ADA. These commenters contended that the case-specific factors underlying the statute's readily achievable standard cannot be reconciled with a formulaic accounting approach, and that a blanket formula inherently is less fair, less flexible, and less effective than the current case-by-case determination for whether an action is readily achievable. Moreover, they argued, a small business safe harbor for readily achievable barrier removal is unnecessary because the statutory standard explicitly provides that a business need only spend what is readily achievable — an amount that may be more or less than 1 percent of revenue in any given year.

Several commenters opined that the formulaic approach proposed by the Department overlooks the factors that often prove most conducive and integral to readily achievable barrier removal — planning and prioritization. Many commenters expressed concern that the safe harbor creates an incentive for business entities to forego large-scale barrier removal in favor of smaller, less costly removal projects, regardless of the relative access the measures might provide. Others commented that an emphasis on a formulaic amount rather than readily achievable barrier removal might result in competition among types of disabilities as to which barriers get removed first, or discrimination against particular types of disabilities if barrier removal for those groups is more expensive.

Many commenters opposed to the small business safe harbor proposed clarifications and limiting rules. A substantial number of commenters were strongly opposed to what they perceived as a vastly overbroad and overly complicated definition of "qualified small business" for purposes of eligibility for the safe harbor, and urged the Department to limit the qualified small business safe harbor to those businesses eligible for the ADA small business tax credit under section 44 of the Tax Code. Some commenters from the disability community contended that the spending level that triggers the safe harbor should be cumulative, to reflect the continuing nature of the readily achievable barrier obligation and to preclude a business from erasing years of unjustifiable inaction or insufficient action by spending up to the safe harbor threshold for one year. These commenters also sought explicit clarification that the small business safe harbor is an affirmative defense.

A number of commenters proposed that a business seeking to use the qualified small business safe harbor should be required to have a written barrier removal plan that contains a prioritized list of significant access barriers, a schedule for removal, and a description of the methods used to identify and prioritize barriers. These commenters argued that only spending consistent with the plan should count toward the qualified small business threshold.

After consideration of all relevant matter presented, the Department has concluded that neither the qualified small business safe harbor proposed in the NPRM nor any of the alternatives proposed by commenters will achieve the Department's intended results. Business and industry commenters uniformly objected to a safe harbor based on gross revenue, argued that 1 percent of gross revenue was out of reach for most, if not all, small businesses, and asserted that a safe harbor based on net revenue would better capture whether and to what extent barrier removal is readily achievable for small businesses. Individuals and disability advocacy groups rejected a set formula as fundamentally inconsistent with the case-specific approach reflected in the statute.

Commenters on both sides noted ambiguity as to which ADA-related costs appropriately should be included in the calculation of the safe harbor threshold, and expressed concern about the practical effect of the proposed safe harbor on litigation. Disability organizations expressed concern that the proposal might increase litigation because individuals with disabilities confronted with barriers in places of public accommodation would not be able to independently assess whether an entity is noncompliant or is, in fact, protected by the small business safe harbor. The Department notes that the concerns about enforcement-related complexity and expense likely would increase exponentially with a small business safe harbor based on net revenue.

The Department continues to believe that promulgation of a small business safe harbor would be within the scope of the Attorney General's mandate under 42 U.S.C. 12186(b) to issue regulations to carry out the provisions of title III. Title III defines "readily achievable" to mean "easily accomplishable and able to be carried out without much difficulty or expense," 42 U.S.C. 12181(9), and sets out factors to consider in determining whether an action is readily achievable. While the statutory factors reflect that whether an action is readily achievable is a fact-based determination, there is no inherent inconsistency with the Department's proposition that a formula based on revenue and barrier removal expenditure could accurately approximate the high end of the level of expenditure that can be considered readily achievable for a circumscribed subset of title III entities defined, in part, by their maximum annual average receipts. Moreover, the Department's obligation under the SBREFA to consider alternative means of compliance for small businesses, *see* 5 U.S.C. 603(c), further supports the Department's conclusion that a well-targeted formula is a reasonable approach to implementation of the statute's readily achievable standard. While the Department ultimately has concluded that a small business safe harbor should not be included in the final rule, the Department continues to believe that it is within the Department's authority to develop and implement such a safe harbor.

As noted above, the business community strongly objected to a safe harbor premised on gross revenue, on the ground that gross revenue is an unreliable indicator of an entity's ability to remove barriers, and urged the Department to formulate a safe harbor based on net revenue. The Department's proposed use of gross revenue was intended to offer a measure of certainty for qualified small businesses while ensuring that those businesses continue to meet their ongoing obligation to remove architectural barriers where doing so is readily achievable.

The Department believes that a qualified small business safe harbor based on net revenue would be an unreliable indicator of what is readily achievable and would be unworkable in practice. Evaluation of what is readily achievable for a small business cannot rest solely on a business's net revenue because many decisions about expenses are inherently subjective, and in some cases a net loss may be more beneficial (in terms of taxes, for example) than a small net profit. The Department does not read the ADA's readily achievable standard to mean necessarily that architectural barrier removal is to be, or should be, a business's last concern, or that a business can claim that every barrier removal obligation is not readily achievable. Therefore, if a qualified small business safe harbor were to be premised on net revenue, assertion of the affirmative defense would trigger discovery and examination of the business's accounting methods and the validity or necessity of offsetting expenses. The practical benefits and legal certainty intended by the NPRM would be lost.

Because there was little to no support for the Department's proposed use of gross revenue and no workable alternatives are available at this time, the Department will not adopt a small business safe harbor in this final rule. Small business public accommodations are subject to the barrier removal requirements set out in § 36.304 of the final rule. In addition, the Department plans to provide small businesses with more detailed guidance on assessing and meeting their barrier removal obligations in a small business compliance guide.

Section 36.308 Seating in Assembly Areas.

In the 1991 rule, § 36.308 covered seating obligations for public accommodations in assembly areas. It was bifurcated into (a) existing facilities and (b) new construction and alterations. The new construction and alterations provision, § 36.308(b), merely stated that assembly areas should be built or altered in accordance with the applicable provisions in the 1991 Standards. Section 36.308(a), by contrast, provided detailed guidelines on what barrier removal was required.

The Department explained in the preamble to the 1991 rule that § 36.308 provided specific rules on assembly areas to ensure that wheelchair users, who typically were relegated to inferior seating in the back of assembly areas separate from their friends and family, would be provided access to seats that were integrated and equal in quality to those provided to the general public. Specific guidance on assembly areas was desirable because they are found in many different types of places of public accommodation, ranging from opera houses (places of exhibition or entertainment) to private university lecture halls (places of education), and include assembly areas that range in size from small movie theaters of 100 or fewer seats to 100,000-seat sports stadiums.

In the NPRM, the Department proposed to update § 36.308(a) by incorporating some of the applicable assembly area provisions from the 2010 Standards. Upon further review, however, the Department has determined that the need to provide special guidance for assembly areas in a separate section no longer exists, except for specialty seating areas, as discussed below. Since enactment of the ADA, the Department has interpreted the 1991 Standards as a guide for determining the existence of barriers. Courts have affirmed this interpretation. *See, e.g., Colorado Cross Disability Coalition v. Too, Inc.*, 344 F. Supp. 2d 707 (D. Colo. 2004); *Access Now, Inc. v. AMH CGH, Inc.*, 2001 U.S. Dist. LEXIS 12876 (S.D. Fla. May 8, 2001); *Pascuiti v. New York Yankees*, 87 F. Supp. 2d 221 (S.D.N.Y. 1999).

The 2010 Standards now establish detailed guidance for newly constructed and altered assembly areas, which is provided in § 36.406(f), and these Standards will serve as a new guide for barrier removal. Accordingly, the former § 36.308(a) has been replaced in the final rule. Assembly areas will benefit from the same safe harbor provisions applicable to barrier removal in all places of public accommodations as provided in § 36.304(d)(2) of the final rule.

The Department has also decided to remove proposed § 36.308(c)(2) from the final rule. This provision would have required assembly areas with more than 5,000 seats to provide five wheelchair spaces with at least three designated companion seats for each of those five wheelchair spaces. The Department agrees with commenters who asserted that group seating already is addressed more appropriately in ticketing under § 36.302(f).

The Department has determined that proposed § 36.308(c)(1), addressing specialty seating in assembly areas, should remain as § 36.308 in the final rule with additional language. This paragraph is designed to ensure that individuals with disabilities have an opportunity to access specialty seating areas that entitle spectators to distinct services or amenities not generally available to others. This provision is not, as several commenters mistakenly thought, designed to cover luxury boxes and suites. Those areas have separate requirements outlined in section 221 of the 2010 Standards.

Section 36.308 requires only that accessible seating be provided in each area with distinct services or amenities. To the extent a covered entity provides multiple seating areas with the same services and amenities, each of those areas would not be distinct and thus all of them would not be required to be accessible. For example, if a facility has similar dining service in two areas, both areas would not need to be made accessible; however, if one dining service area is open to families, while the other is open only to individuals over the age of 21, both areas would need to be made accessible. Factors distinguishing specialty seating areas generally are dictated by the type of facility or event, but may include, for example, such distinct services and amenities as access to wait staff for in-seat food or beverage service; availability of catered food or beverages for pre-game, intermission, or post-game events; restricted access to lounges with special amenities, such as couches or flat-screen televisions; or access to team personnel or facilities for team-sponsored events (e.g., autograph sessions, sideline passes, or facility tours) not otherwise available to other spectators.

The NPRM required public accommodations to locate wheelchair seating spaces and companion seats in each specialty seating area within the assembly area. The Department has added language in the final rule stating that public accommodations that cannot place wheelchair seating spaces and companion seats in each specialty area because it is not readily achievable to do so may meet their obligation by providing specialty services or amenities to individuals with disabilities and their companions at other designated accessible locations at no additional cost. For example, if a theater that only has barrier removal obligations provides wait service to spectators in the mezzanine, and it is not readily achievable to place accessible seating there, it may meet its obligation by providing wait service to patrons with disabilities who use wheelchairs and their companions at other designated accessible locations at no additional cost. This provision does not obviate the obligation to comply with applicable requirements for new construction and alterations, including dispersion of accessible seating.

Section 36.309 Examinations and Courses.

Section 36.309(a) sets forth the general rule that any private entity that offers examinations or courses relating to applications, licensing, certification, or credentialing for secondary or postsecondary education, professional, or trade purposes shall offer such examinations or courses in a place and manner accessible to persons with disabilities or offer alternative accessible arrangements for such individuals. In the NPRM preamble and proposed regulatory amendment and in this final rule, the Department relied on its history of enforcement efforts, research, and body of knowledge of testing and modifications, accommodations, and aids in detailing steps testing entities should take to ensure that persons with disabilities receive appropriate modifications, accommodations, or auxiliary aids in examination and course settings as required by the ADA. The Department received comments from disability rights groups, organizations that administer tests, State governments, professional associations, and individuals on the language appearing in the NPRM preamble and amended regulation and has carefully considered these comments.

The Department initially set out the parameters of appropriate documentation requests relating to examinations and courses covered by this section in the 1991 preamble at 28 CFR part 36, stating that "requests for documentation must be reasonable and must be limited to the need for the modification or aid requested." *See* 28 CFR part 36, app. B at 735 (2009). Since that time, the Department, through its enforcement efforts pursuant to section 309, has addressed concerns that requests by testing entities for documentation regarding the existence of an individual's disability and need for a modification or auxiliary aid or service were often inappropriate and burdensome. The Department proposed language stating that while it may be appropriate for a testing entity to request that an applicant provide documentation supporting the existence of a disability and the need for a modification, accommodation, or auxiliary aid or service, the request by the testing entity for such documentation must be reasonable and limited. The NPRM proposed that testing entities should narrowly tailor requests for documentation, limiting those requests to materials that will allow the testing entities to ascertain the nature of the disability and the individual's need for the requested modification, accommodation, or auxiliary aid or service. This proposal codified the 1991 rule's preamble language regarding testing entities' requests for information supporting applicants' requests for testing modifications or accommodations.

Overall, most commenters supported this addition to the regulation. These commenters generally agreed that documentation sought by testing entities to support requests for modifications and testing accommodations should be reasonable and tailored. Commenters noted, for example, that the proposal to require reasonable and tailored documentation requests "is not objectionable. Indeed, it largely tracks DOJ's long-standing informal guidance that 'requests for documentation must be reasonable and limited to the need for the modification or aid requested.'" Commenters including disability rights groups, State governments, professional associations, and individuals made it clear that, in addition to the proposed regulatory change, other significant problems remain for individuals with disabilities who seek necessary modifications to examinations and courses. These problems include detailed questions about the nature of documentation materials submitted by candidates, testing entities' questioning of documentation provided by qualified professionals with expertise in the particular disability at issue, and lack of timeliness in determining whether to provide requested accommodations or modifications. Several commenters expressed enthusiasm for the preamble language addressing some of these issues, and some of these commenters recommended the incorporation of portions of this preamble language into the regulatory text. Some testing entities expressed concerns and uncertainty about the language in the preamble and sought clarifications about its meaning. These commenters focused most of their attention on the following language from the NPRM preamble:

Generally, a testing entity should accept without further inquiry documentation provided by a qualified professional who has made an individualized assessment of the applicant. Appropriate documentation may include a letter from a qualified professional or evidence of a prior diagnosis, or accommodation, or classification, such as eligibility for a special education program. When an applicant's documentation is recent and demonstrates a consistent history of a diagnosis, there is no need for further inquiry into the nature of the disability. A testing entity should consider an applicant's past use of a particular auxiliary aid or service. 73 FR 34508, 34539 (June 17, 2008).

Professional organizations, State governments, individuals, and disability rights groups fully supported the Department's preamble language and recommended further modification of the regulations to encompass the issues raised in the preamble. A disability rights group recommended that the Department incorporate the preamble language into the regulations to ensure that "documentation demands are strictly limited in scope and met per se when documentation of previously provided accommodations or aids is provided." One professional education organization noted that many testing corporations disregard the documented diagnoses of qualified professionals, and instead substitute their own, often unqualified diagnoses of individuals with disabilities. Commenters confirmed that testing entities sometimes ask for unreasonable information that is either impossible, or extremely onerous, to provide. A disability rights organization supported the Department's proposals and noted that private testing companies impose burdensome documentation requirements upon applicants with disabilities seeking accommodations and that complying with the documentation requests is frequently so difficult, and negotiations over the requests so prolonged, that test applicants ultimately forgo taking the test. Another disability rights group urged the Department to "expand the final regulatory language to ensure that regulations accurately provide guidance and support the comments made about reducing the burden of documenting the diagnosis and existence of a disability."

Testing entities, although generally supportive of the proposed regulatory amendment, expressed concern regarding the Department's proposed pre- amble language. The testing entities provided the Department with lengthy comments in which they suggested that the Department's rationale delineated in the preamble potentially could limit them from gathering meaningful and necessary documentation to determine whether, in any given circumstance, a disability is presented, whether modifications are warranted, and which modifications would be most appropriate. Some testing entities raised concerns about individuals skewing testing results by falsely claiming or feigning disabilities as an improper means of seeking advantage on an examination. Several testing entities raised concerns about and sought clarification regarding the Department's use of certain terms and concepts in the preamble, including "without further inquiry," "appropriate documentation," "qualified professional," "individualized assessment," and "consider." These entities discussed the preamble language at length, noting that testing entities need to be able to question some aspects of testing applicants' documentation or to request further documentation from some candidates when the initial documentation is unclear or incomplete. One testing entity expressed concern that the Department's preamble language would require the acceptance of a brief note on a doctor's prescription pad as adequate documentation of a disability and the need for an accommodation. One medical examination organization stated that the Department's preamble language would result in persons without disabilities receiving accommodations and passing examinations as part of a broad expansion of unwarranted accommodations, potentially endangering the health and welfare of the general public. Another medical board "strenuously objected" to the "without further inquiry" language. Several of the testing entities expressed concern that the Department's preamble language might require testing companies to accept documentation from persons with temporary or questionable disabilities, making test scores less reliable, harming persons with legitimate entitlements, and resulting in additional expense for testing companies to accommodate more test takers.

It remains the Department's view that, when testing entities receive documentation provided by a qualified professional who has made an individualized assessment of an applicant that supports the need for the modification, accommodation, or aid requested, they shall generally accept such documentation and provide the accommodation.

Several commenters sought clarifications on what types of documentation are acceptable to demonstrate the existence of a disability and the need for a requested modification, accommodation, or aid. The Department believes that appropriate documentation may vary depending on the nature of the disability and the specific modification or aid requested, and accordingly, testing entities should consider a variety of types of information submitted. Examples of types of information to consider include recommendations of qualified professionals familiar with the individual, results of psycho-educational or other professional evaluations, an applicant's history of diagnosis, participation in a special education program, observations by educators, or the applicant's past use of testing accommodations. If an applicant has been granted accommodations post-high school by a standardized testing agency, there is no need for reassessment for a subsequent examination.

Some commenters expressed concern regarding the use of the term "letter" in the proposed preamble sentence regarding appropriate documentation. The NPRM preamble language stated that "[a]ppropriate documentation may include a letter from a qualified professional or evidence of a prior diagnosis, accommodation, or classification, such as eligibility for a special education program." 73 FR 34508, 34539 (June 17, 2008). Some testing entities posited that the preamble language would require them to accept a brief letter from a doctor or even a doctor's note on a prescription pad indicating "I've been treating (student) for ADHD and he/she is entitled to extend time on the ACT." The Department's reference in the NPRM preamble to letters from physicians or other professionals was provided in order to offer examples of some types of acceptable documentation that may be considered by testing entities in evaluating the existence of an applicant's disability and the need for a certain modification, accommodation, or aid. No one piece of evidence may be dispositive in make a testing accommodation determination. The significance of a letter or other communication from a doctor or other qualified professional would depend on the professional's relationship with the candidate and the specific content of the communication, as well as how the letter fits in with the totality of the other factors used to determine testing accommodations under this rule. Similarly, an applicant's failure to provide results from a specific test or evaluation instrument should not of itself preclude approval of requests for modifications, accommodations, or aids if the documentation provided by the applicant, in its entirety, is sufficient to demonstrate that the individual has a disability and requires a requested modification, accommodation, or aid on the relevant examination. This issue is discussed in more detail below.

One disability rights organization noted that requiring a 25-year old who was diagnosed in junior high school with a learning disability and accommodated ever since "to produce elementary school report cards to demonstrate symptomology before the age of seven is unduly burdensome." The same organization commented that requiring an individual with a long and early history of disability to be assessed within three years of taking the test in question is similarly burdensome, stating that "[t]here is no scientific evidence that learning disabilities abate with time, nor that Attention Deficits abate with time * * *." This organization noted that there is no justification for repeatedly subjecting people to expensive testing regimens simply to satisfy a disbelieving industry. This is particularly true for adults with, for example, learning disabilities such as dyslexia, a persistent condition without the need for retesting once the diagnosis has been established and accepted by a standardized testing agency.

Some commenters from testing entities sought clarification regarding who may be considered a "qualified professional." Qualified professionals are licensed or otherwise properly credentialed and possess expertise in the disability for which modifications or accommodations are sought. For example, a podiatrist would not be considered to be a qualified professional to diagnose a learning disability or support a request for testing accommodations on that basis. Types of professionals who might possess the appropriate credentials and expertise are doctors (including psychiatrists), psychologists, nurses, physical therapists, occupational therapists, speech therapists, vocational rehabilitation specialists, school counselors, and licensed mental health professionals. Additionally, while testing applicants should present documentation from qualified professionals with expertise in the pertinent field, it also is critical that testing entities that review documentation submitted by prospective examinees in support of requests for testing modifications or accommodations ensure that their own reviews are conducted by qualified professionals with similarly relevant expertise.

Commenters also sought clarification of the term individualized assessment. The Department's intention in using this term is to ensure that documentation provided on behalf of a testing candidate is not only provided by a qualified professional, but also reflects that the qualified professional has individually and personally evaluated the candidate as opposed to simply considering scores from a review of documents. This is particularly important in the learning disabilities context, where proper diagnosis requires face-to- face evaluation. Reports from experts who have personal familiarity with the candidate should take precedence over those from, for example, reviewers for testing agencies, who have never personally met the candidate or conducted the requisite assessments for diagnosis and treatment.

Some testing entities objected to the NPRM preamble's use of the phrase "without further inquiry." The Department's intention here is to address the extent to which testing entities should accept documentation provided by an applicant when the testing entity is determining the need for modifications, accommodations, or auxiliary aids or services. The Department's view is that applicants who submit appropriate documentation, *e.g.*, documentation that is based on the careful individual consideration of the candidate by a professional with expertise relating to the disability in question, should not be subjected to unreasonably burdensome requests for additional documentation. While some testing commenters objected to this standard, it reflects the Department's long- standing position. When an applicant's documentation demonstrates a consistent history of a diagnosis of a disability, and is prepared by a qualified professional who has made an individualized evaluation of the applicant, there is little need for further inquiry into the nature of the disability and generally testing entities should grant the requested modification, accommodation, or aid.

After a careful review of the comments, the Department has decided to maintain the proposed regulatory language on the scope of appropriate documentation in § 36.309(b)(1)(iv). The Department has also added new regulatory language at § 36.309(b)(1)(v) that provides that testing entities shall give considerable weight to documentation of past modifications, accommodations, or auxiliary aids or services received in similar testing situations as well as such modifications, accommodations, or related aids and services provided in response to an Individualized Education Program (IEP) provided under the Individuals with Disabilities Education Act (IDEA) or a plan providing services pursuant to section 504 of the Rehabilitation Act of 1973, as amended (often referred to as a Section 504 Plan). These additions to the regulation are necessary because the Department's position on the bounds of appropriate documentation contained in Appendix B, 28 CFR part 36, app. B (2009), has not been implemented consistently and fully by organizations that administer tests.

The new regulatory language clarifies that an applicant's past use of a particular modification, accommodation, or auxiliary aid or service in a similar testing setting or pursuant to an IEP or Section 504 Plan provides critical information in determining those examination modifications that would be applicable in a given circumstance. The addition of this language and the appropriate weight to be accorded it is seen as important by the Department because the types of accommodations provided in both these circumstances are typically granted in the context of individual consideration of a student's needs by a team of qualified and experienced professionals. Even though these accommodations decisions form a common sense and logical basis for testing entities to rely upon, they are often discounted and ignored by testing entities.

For example, considerable weight is warranted when a student with a Section 504 Plan in place since middle school that includes the accommodations of extra time and a quiet room for testing is seeking these same accommodations from a testing entity covered by section 309 of the Act. In this example, a testing entity receiving such documentation should clearly grant the request for accommodations. A history of test accommodations in secondary schools or in post-secondary institutions, particularly when determined through the rigors of a process required and detailed by Federal law, is as useful and instructive for determining whether a specific accommodation is required as accommodations provided in standardized testing situations.

It is important to note, however, that the inclusion of this weight does not suggest that individuals without IEPs or Section 504 Plans are not also entitled to receive testing accommodations. Indeed, it is recommended that testing entities must consider the entirety of an applicant's history to determine whether that history, even without the context of a IEP or Section 504 Plan, indicates a need for accommodations. In addition, many students with learning disabilities have made use of informal, but effective accommodations. For example, such students often receive undocumented accommodations such as time to complete tests after school or at lunchtime, or being graded on content and not form or spelling of written work. Finally, testing entities shall also consider that because private schools are not subject to the IDEA, students at private schools may have a history of receiving accommodations in similar settings that are not pursuant to an IEP or Section 504 Plan. Some testing entities sought clarification that they should only be required to consider particular use of past modifications, accommodations, auxiliary aids or services received by testing candidates for prior testing and examination settings. These commenters noted that it would be unhelpful to consider the classroom accommodations for a testing candidate, as those accommodations would not typically apply in a standardized test setting. The Department's history of enforcement in this area has demonstrated that a recent history of past accommodations is critical to an understanding of the applicant's disability and the appropriateness of testing accommodations.

The Department also incorporates the NPRM preamble's "timely manner" concept into the new regulatory language at § 36.309(b)(1)(vi). Under this provision, testing entities are required to respond in a timely manner to requests for testing accommodations in order to ensure equal opportunity for persons with disabilities. Testing entities are to ensure that their established process for securing testing accommodations provides applicants with a reasonable opportunity to supplement the testing entities' requests for additional information, if necessary, and still be able to take the test in the same testing cycle. A disability rights organization commented that testing entities should not subject applicants to unreasonable and intrusive requests for information in a process that should provide persons with disabilities effective modifications in a timely manner, fulfilling the core objective of title III to provide equal access. Echoing this perspective, several disability rights organizations and a State government commenter urged that testing entities should not make unreasonably burdensome demands for documentation, particularly where those demands create impediments to receiving accommodations in a timely manner. Access to examinations should be offered to persons with disabilities in as timely a manner as it is offered to persons without disabilities. Failure by a testing entity to act in a timely manner, coupled with seeking unnecessary documentation, could result in such an extended delay that it constitutes a denial of equal opportunity or equal treatment in an examination setting for persons with disabilities.

Section 36.311 Mobility Devices.

Section 36.311 of the NPRM clarified the scope and circumstances under which covered entities are legally obligated to accommodate various "mobility devices." Section 36.311 set forth specific requirements for the accommodation of mobility devices, including wheelchairs, manually-powered mobility aids, and other power-driven mobility devices.

In both the NPRM and the final rule, § 36.311(a) states the general rule that in any areas open to pedestrians, public accommodations shall permit individuals with mobility disabilities to use wheelchairs and manually-powered mobility aids, including walkers, crutches, canes, braces, or similar devices. Because mobility scooters satisfy the definition of "wheelchair" (i.e., "a manually-operated or power-driven device designed primarily for use by an individual with a mobility disability for the main purpose of indoor, or of both indoor and outdoor locomotion"), the reference to them in § 36.311(a) of the final rule has been omitted to avoid redundancy.

Most business commenters expressed concern that permitting the use of other power-driven mobility devices by individuals with mobility disabilities would make such devices akin to wheelchairs and would require them to make physical changes to their facilities to accommodate their use. This concern is misplaced. If a facility complies with the applicable design requirements in the 1991 Standards or the 2010 Standards, the public accommodation will not be required to exceed those standards to accommodate the use of wheelchairs or other power-driven mobility devices that exceed those requirements.

Legal standard for other power-driven mobility devices. The NPRM version of § 36.311(b) provided that a public accommodation "shall make reasonable modifi-  cations in its policies, practices, and procedures to permit the use of other power-driven mobility devices by individuals with disabilities, unless the public accommodation can demonstrate that the use of the device is not reasonable or that its use will result in a fundamental alteration in the nature of the public accommodation's goods, services, facilities, privileges, advantages, or accommoda- tions." 73 FR 34508, 34556 (June 17, 2008). In other words, public accommodations are by default required to permit the use of other power-driven mobility devices; the burden is on them to prove the existence of a valid exception. Most commenters supported the notion of assessing whether the use of a particular device is reasonable in the context of a particular venue. Commenters, however, disagreed about the meaning of the word "reasonable" as it is used in § 36.311(b) of the NPRM. Virtually every business and industry commenter took the use of the word "reasonable" to mean that a general reasonableness standard would be applied in making such an assessment. Advocacy and nonprofit groups almost universally objected to the use of a general reasonableness standard with regard to the assessment of whether a particular device should be allowed at a particular venue. They argued that the assessment should be based on whether reasonable modifi- cations could be made to allow a particular device at a particular venue, and that the only factors that should be part of the calculus that results in the exclusion of a particular device are undue burden, direct threat, and fundamental alteration.

A few commenters opposed the proposed provision requiring public accommoda- tions to assess whether reasonable modifications can be made to allow other power-driven mobility devices, preferring instead that the Department issue guidance materials so that public accommodations would not have to incur the cost of such analyses. Another commenter noted a "fox guarding the hen house"-type of concern with regard to public accommodations developing and enforcing their own modification policy. In response to comments received, the Department has revised § 36.311(b) to provide greater clarity regarding the development of legitimate safety requirements regarding other power-driven mobility devices. The Depart- ment has not retained the proposed NPRM language stating that an other power-driven mobility device can be excluded if a public accommodation can demonstrate that the use of the device is not reasonable or that its use fundamentally alters the nature of the goods, services, facilities, privileges, advantages, or accommodations offered by the public accommodation because the Department believes that these exceptions are covered by the general reasonable modification requirement contained in § 36.302.

Assessment factors. Section 36.311(c) of the NPRM required public accommodations to "establish policies to permit the use of other power-driven mobility devices" and articulated four factors upon which public accommodations must base decisions as to whether a modification is reasonable to allow the use of a class of other power-driven mobility devices by individuals with disabilities in specific venues (e.g., doctors' offices, parks, commercial buildings, etc.). 73 FR 34508, 34556 (June 17, 2008).

The Department has relocated and modified the NPRM text that appeared in § 36.311(c) to new paragraph § 36.311(b)(2) to clarify what factors the public accommodation shall use in determining whether a particular other power-driven mobility device can be allowed in a specific facility as a reasonable modification. Section 36.311(b) (2) now states that "[i]n determining whether a particular other power-driven mobility device can be allowed in a specific facility as a reasonable modification under (b)(1), a public accommodation shall consider" certain enumerated factors. The assessment factors are designed to assist public accommodations in determining whether allowing the use of a particular other power-driven mobility device in a specific facility is reasonable. Thus, the focus of the analysis must be on the appropriateness of the use of the device at a specific facility, rather than whether it is necessary for an individual to use a particular device.

The NPRM proposed the following specific assessment factors: (1) The dimensions, weight, and operating speed of the mobility device in relation to a wheelchair; (2) the potential risk of harm to others by the operation of the mobility device; (3) the risk of harm to the environment or natural or cultural resources or conflict with Federal land management laws and regulations; and (4) the ability of the public accommodation to stow the mobility device when not in use, if requested by the user.

Factor 1 was designed to help public accommodations assess whether a particular device was appropriate, given its particular physical features, for a particular location. Virtually all commenters said the physical features of the device affected their view of whether a particular device was appropriate for a particular location. For example, while many commenters supported the use of an other power-driven mobility device if the device were a Segway® PT, because of environmental and health concerns they did not offer the same level of support if the device were an off-highway vehicle, all-terrain vehicle (ATV), golf car, or other device with a fuel-powered or combustion engine. Most commenters noted that indicators such as speed, weight, and dimension really were an assessment of the appropriateness of a particular device in specific venues and suggested that factor 1 say this more specifically.

The term "in relation to a wheelchair" in the NPRM's factor 1 apparently created some concern that the same legal standards that apply to wheel-chairs would be applied to other power-driven mobility devices. The Department has omitted the term "in relation to a wheelchair" from § 36.311(b)(2)(i) to clarify that if a facility that is in compliance with the applicable provisions of the 1991 Standards or the 2010 Standards grants permission for an other power-driven mobility device to go on-site, it is not required to exceed those standards to accommodate the use of other power-driven mobility devices. In response to requests that NPRM factor 1 state more specifically that it requires an assessment of an other power-driven mobility device's appropriateness under particular circumstances or in particular venues, the Department has added several factors and more specific language. In addition, although the NPRM made reference to the operation of other power-driven mobility devices in "specific venues," the Department's intent is captured more clearly by referencing "specific facility" in paragraph (b)(2). The Department also notes that while speed is included in factor 1, public accommodations should not rely solely on a device's top speed when assessing whether the device can be accommodated; instead, public accommodations should also consider the minimum speeds at which a device can be operated and whether the development of speed limit policies can be established to address concerns regarding the speed of the device. Finally, since the ability of the public accommodation to stow the mobility device when not in use is an aspect of its design and operational characteristics, the text proposed as factor 4 in the NPRM has been incorporated in paragraph (b)(2)(iii).

The NPRM's version of factor 2 provided that the "potential risk of harm to others by the operation of the mobility device" is one of the determinants in the assessment of whether other power-driven mobility devices should be excluded from a site. With this language, the Department intended to incorporate the safety standard found in § 36.301(b), which provides that public accommodations may "impose legitimate safety requirements that are necessary for safe operation" into the assessment. However, several commenters indicated that they read this language, particularly the phrase 'potential risk of harm" to mean that the Department had adopted a concept of risk analysis different from that which is in the existing standards. The Department did not intend to create a new standard and has changed the language in paragraphs (b)(1) and (b)(2) to clarify the applicable standards, thereby avoiding the introduction of new assessments of risk beyond those necessary for the safe operation of the public accommodation.

While all applicable affirmative defenses are available to public accommodations in the establishment and execution of their policies regarding other power-driven mobility devices, the Department did not explicitly incorporate the direct threat defense into the assessment factors because § 36.301(b) provides public accommodations the appropriate framework with which to assess whether legitimate safety requirements that may preclude the use of certain other power-driven mobility devices are necessary for the safe operation of the public accommodation. In order to be legitimate, the safety requirement must be based on actual risks and not mere speculation regarding the device or how it will be operated. Of course, public accommodations may enforce legitimate safety rules established for the operation of other- power driven mobility devices (e.g., reasonable speed restrictions). Finally, NPRM factor 3 concerning environmental resources and conflicts of law has been relocated to paragraph (b)(2)(v).

As a result of these comments and requests, NPRM factors 1, 2, 3, and 4 have been revised and renumbered within paragraph 36.311(b)(2) in the final rule.

Several commenters requested that the Department provide guidance materials or more explicit concepts of which considerations might be appropriate for inclusion in a policy that allows the use of other power-driven mobility devices. A public accommodation that has determined that reasonable modifications can be made in its policies, practices, or procedures to allow the use of other power-driven mobility devices should develop a policy that clearly states the circumstances under which the use of other power-driven mobility devices by individuals with a mobility disability will be permitted. It also should include clear, statements of specific rules governing the operation of such devices. Finally, the public accommodation should endeavor to provide individuals with disabilities who use other power-driven mobility devices with advanced notice of its policy regarding the use of such devices and what rules apply to the operation of these devices.

For example, the U.S. General Services Administration (GSA) has developed a policy allowing the use of the Segway® PT and other EPAMDs in all Federal buildings under GSA's jurisdiction. *See* General Services Administration, *Interim Segway® Personal Transporter Policy* (Dec. 3, 2007), available at http://www.gsa.gov/graphics/pbs/Inter-im_Segway_Policy_121007.pdf (last visited June 24, 2010). The GSA policy defines the policy's scope of coverage by setting out what devices are and are not covered by the policy. The policy also sets out requirements for safe operation, such as a speed limit, prohibits the use of EPAMDs on escalators, and provides guidance regarding security screening of these devices and their operators.

A public accommodation that determines that it can make reasonable modifications to permit the use of an other power-driven mobility device by an individual with a mobility disability might include in its policy the procedure by which claims that the other power-driven mobility device is being used for a mobility disability will be assessed for legitimacy (i.e., a credible assurance that the device is being used for a mobility disability, including a verbal representation by the person with a disability that is not contradicted by observable fact, or the presentation of a disability parking space placard or card, or State-issued proof of disability); the type or classes of other power-driven mobility devices are permitted to be used by individuals with mobility disabilities; the size, weight, and dimensions of the other power-driven mobility devices that are permitted to be used by individuals with mobility disabilities; the speed limit for the other power-driven mobility devices that are permitted to be used by individuals with mobility disabilities; the places, times, or circumstances under which the use of the other power-driven mobility devices is or will be restricted or prohibited; safety, pedestrian, and other rules concerning the use of the other power-driven mobility devices; whether, and under which circumstances, storage for the other power-driven mobility devices will be made available; and how and where individuals with a mobility disability can obtain a copy of the other power-driven mobility device policy.

Public accommodations also might consider grouping other power-driven mobility devices by type (e.g., EPAMDs, golf cars, gasoline-powered vehicles, and other devices). For example, an amusement park may determine that it is reasonable to allow individuals with disabilities to use EPAMDs in a variety of outdoor programs and activities, but that it would not be reasonable to allow the use of golf cars as mobility devices in similar circumstances. At the same time, the entity may address its concerns about factors such as space limitations by disallowing use of EPAMDs by members of the general public who do not have mobility disabilities.

The Department anticipates that in many circumstances, public accommodations will be able to develop policies that will allow the use of other power-driven mobility devices by individuals with mobility disabilities without resulting in a fundamental alteration of a public accommodation's goods, services, facilities, privileges, advantages, or accommodations. Consider the following examples:

Example 1: Although individuals who do not have mobility disabilities are prohibited from operating EPAMDs at a theme park, the park has developed a policy allowing individuals with mobility disabilities to use EPAMDs as their mobility device at the park. The policy states that EPAMDs are allowed in all areas of the theme park that are open to pedestrians as a reasonable modification to its general policy on EPAMDs. The public accommodation has determined that the facility provides adequate space for a taller device, such as an EPAMD, and that it does not fundamentally alter the nature of the theme park's goods and services. The theme park's policies do, however, require that EPAMDs be operated at a safe speed limit. A theme park employee may inquire at the ticket gate whether the device is needed due to the user's disability or may request the presentation of a valid, State-issued, disability parking placard (though presentation of such a placard is not necessary), or other State-issued proof of disability or a credible assurance that the use of the EPAMD is for the individual's mobility disability. The park employee also may inform an individual with a disability using an EPAMD that the theme park's policy requires that it be operated at or below the park's designated speed limit.

Example 2: A shopping mall has developed a policy whereby EPAMDs may be operated by individuals with mobility disabilities in the common pedestrian areas of the mall if the operator of the device agrees to the following: to operate the device no faster than the speed limit set by the policy; to use the elevator, not the escalator, to transport the EPAMD to different levels; to yield to pedestrian traffic; not to leave the device unattended unless it can stand upright and has a locking system; to refrain from using the device temporarily if the mall manager determines that the volume of pedestrian traffic is such that the operation of the device would interfere with legitimate safety requirements; and to present the mall management office with a valid, State-issued, disability parking placard (though presentation of such a placard is not necessary), or State-issued proof of disability, as a credible assurance that the use of the EPAMD is for the individual's mobility disability, upon entry to the mall.

Inquiry into the use of other power-driven mobility device. Section 36.311(d) of the NPRM provided that a "public accommodation may ask a person using a power-driven mobility device if the mobility device is required because of the person's disability. A public accommodation shall not ask a person using a mobility device questions about the nature and extent of the person's disability." 73 FR 34508, 34556 (June 17, 2008).

While business commenters did not take issue with applying this standard to individuals who use wheelchairs, they were not satisfied with the application of this standard to other power-driven mobility devices. Business commenters expressed concern about people feigning mobility disabilities to be able to use other power-driven mobility devices in public accommodations in which their use is otherwise restricted. These commenters felt that a mere inquiry into whether the device is being used for a mobility disability was an insufficient mechanism by which to detect fraud by other power-driven mobility device users who do not have mobility disabilities. These commenters believed they should be given more latitude to make inquiries of other power-driven mobility device users claiming a mobility disability than they would be given for wheelchair users. They sought the ability to establish a policy or method by which public accommodations may assess the legitimacy of the mobility disability. They suggested some form of certification, sticker, or other designation. One commenter suggested a requirement that a sticker bearing the international symbol for accessibility be placed on the device or that some other identification be required to signal that the use of the device is for a mobility disability. Other suggestions included displaying a disability parking placard on the device or issuing EPAMDs, like the Segway® PT, a permit that would be similar to permits associated with parking spaces reserved for those with disabilities.

Advocacy, nonprofit, and several individual commenters balked at the notion of allowing any inquiry beyond whether the device is necessary for a mobility disability and encouraged the Department to retain the NPRM's language on this topic. Other commenters, however, were empathetic with commenters who had concerns about fraud. At least one Segway® PT advocate suggested it would be permissible to seek documentation of the mobility disability in the form of a simple sign or permit.

The Department has sought to find common ground by balancing the needs of businesses and individuals with mobility disabilities wishing to use other power-driven mobility devices with the Department's longstanding, well-established policy of not allowing public accommodations or establishments to require proof of a mobility disability. There is no question that public accommodations have a legitimate interest in ferreting out fraudulent representations of mobility disabilities, especially given the recreational use of other power-driven mobility devices and the potential safety concerns created by having too many such devices in a specific facility at one time. However, the privacy of individuals with mobility disabilities and respect for those individuals are also vitally important.

Neither § 36.311(d) of the NPRM nor § 36.311(c) of the final rule permits inquiries into the nature of a person's mobility disability. However, the Department does not believe it is unreasonable or overly intrusive for an individual with a mobility disability seeking to use an other power-driven mobility device to provide a credible assurance to verify that the use of the other power-driven mobility device is for a mobility disability. The Department sought to minimize the amount of discretion and subjectivity exercised by public accommodations in assessing whether an individual has a mobility disability and to allow public accommodations to verify the existence of a mobility disability. The solution was derived from comments made by several individuals who said they have been admitted with their Segway® PTs into public entities and public accommodations that ordinarily do not allow these devices onsite when they have presented or displayed State-issued disability parking placards. In the examples provided by commenters, the parking placards were accepted as verification that the Segway® PTs were being used as mobility devices.

Because many individuals with mobility disabilities avail themselves of State programs that issue disability parking placards or cards and be- cause these programs have penalties for fraudulent representations of identity and disability, utilizing the parking placard system as a means to establish the existence of a mobility disability strikes a balance between the need for privacy of the individual and fraud protection for the public accommodation. Consequently, the Department has decided to include regulatory text in § 36.311(c)(2) of the final rule that requires public accommodations to accept the presentation of a valid, State-issued disability parking placard or card, or State-issued proof of disability, as verification that an individual uses the other power-driven mobility device for his or her mobility disability. A "valid" disability placard or card is one that is presented by the individual to whom it was issued and is otherwise in compliance with the State of issuance's requirements for disability placards or cards. Public accommodations are required to accept a valid, State-issued disability parking placard or card, or State-issued proof of disability, as a credible assurance, but they cannot demand or require the presentation of a valid disability placard or card, or State-issued proof of disability, as a prerequisite for use of an other power-driven mobility device, because not all persons with mobility disabilities have such means of proof. If an individual with a mobility disability does not have such a placard or card, or State-issued proof of disability, he or she may present other information that would serve as a credible assurance of the existence of a mobility disability.

In lieu of a valid, State-issued disability parking placard or card, or State-issued proof of disability, a verbal representation, not contradicted by observable fact, shall be accepted as a credible assurance that the other power-driven mobility device is being used because of a mobility disability. This does not mean, however, that a mobility disability must be observable as a condition for allowing the use of an other power-driven mobility device by an individual with a mobility disability, but rather that if an individual represents that a device is being used for a mobility disability and that individual is observed thereafter engaging in a physical activity that is contrary to the nature of the represented disability, the assurance given is no longer credible and the individual may be prevented from using the device.

Possession of a valid, State-issued disability parking placard or card or a verbal assurance does not trump a public accommodation's valid restrictions on the use of other power-driven mobility devices. Accordingly, a credible assurance that the other power-driven mobility device is being used because of a mobility disability is not a guarantee of entry to a public accommodation because notwithstanding such a credible assurance, use of the device in a particular venue may be at odds with the legal standard in § 36.311(b)(1) or with one or more of the § 36.311(b)(2) factors. Only after an individual with a disability has satisfied all of the public accommoda- tion's policies regarding the use of other power-driven mobility devices does a credible assurance become a factor in allowing the use of the device. For example, if an individual seeking to use an other power-driven mobility device fails to satisfy any of the public accommodation's stated policies regarding the use of other power-driven mobility devices, the fact that the individual legitimately possesses and presents a valid, State-issued disability parking placard or card, or State-issued proof of disability, does not trump the policy and require the public accommodation to allow the use of the device. In fact, in some instances, the presentation of a legitimately held placard or card, or State-issued proof of disability, will have no relevance or bearing at all on whether the other power-driven mobility device may be used, because the public accommodation's policy does not permit the device in question on- site under any circumstances (e.g., because its use would create a substantial risk of serious harm to the immediate environment or natural or cultural resources). Thus, an individual with a mobility disability who presents a valid disability placard or card, or State-issued proof of disability, will not be able to use an ATV as an other power-driven mobility device in a mall or a restaurant if the mall or restaurant has adopted a policy banning their use for any or all of the above-mentioned reasons.

However, an individual with a mobility disability who has complied with a public accommodation's stated policies cannot be refused use of the other power-driven mobility device if he or she has provided a credible assurance that the use of the device is for a mobility disability.

Subpart D   — New Construction and Alterations

Subpart D establishes the title I requirements applicable to new construction and alterations. The Department has amended this subpart to adopt the 2004 ADAAG, set forth the effective dates for implementation of the 2010 Standards, and make related revisions as described below.

Section 36.403   Alterations: Path of Travel.

In the NPRM, the Department proposed one change to Sec. 36.403 on alterations and path of travel by adding a path of travel safe harbor. Proposed Sec. 36.403(a)(1) stated that if a private entity has constructed or altered required elements of a path of travel in accordance with the 1991 Standards, the private entity is not required to retrofit such elements to reflect incremental changes in the 2010 Standards solely because of an alteration to a primary function area served by that path of travel.

A substantial number of commenters objected to the Department's creation of a safe harbor for alterations to required elements of a path of travel that comply with the current 1991 Standards. These commenters argued that if a public accommodation already is in the process of altering its facility, there should be a legal requirement that individuals with disabilities are entitled to increased accessibility provided by the 2004 ADAAG for path of travel work. These commenters also stated that they did not believe there was a statutory basis for "grandfathering" facilities that comply with the 1991 Standards. Another commenter argued that the updates incorporated into the 2004 ADAAG provide very substantial improvements for access, and that since there already is a 20 percent cost limit on the amount that can be expended on path of travel alterations, there is no need for a further limitation.

Some commenters supported the safe harbor as lessening the economic costs of implementing the 2004 ADAAG for existing facilities. One commenter also stated that without the safe harbor, entities that already have complied with the 1991 Standards will have to make and pay for compliance twice, as compared to those entities that made no effort to comply in the first place. Another commenter asked that the safe harbor be revised to include pre-ADA facilities that have been made compliant with the 1991 Standards to the extent "readily achievable" or, in the case of alterations, "to the maximum extent feasible," but that are not in full compliance with the 1991 Standards.

The final rule retains the safe harbor for required elements of a path of travel to altered primary function areas for private entities that already have complied with the 1991 Standards with respect to those required elements. As discussed with respect to Sec. 36.304, the Department believes that this safe harbor strikes an appropriate balance between ensuring that individuals with disabilities are provided access to buildings and facilities and mitigating potential financial burdens on existing places of public accommodation that are undertaking alterations subject to the 2010 Standards. This safe harbor is not a blanket exemption for facilities. If a private entity undertakes an alteration to a primary function area, only the required elements of a path of travel to that area that already comply with the 1991 Standards are subject to the safe harbor. If a private entity undertakes an alteration to a primary function area and the required elements of a path of travel to the altered area do not comply with the 1991 Standards, then the private entity must bring those elements into compliance with the 2010 Standards.

Section 36.405   Alterations: Historic Preservation.

In the 1991 rule, the Department provided guidance on making alterations to buildings or facilities that are eligible for listing in the National Register of Historic Places under the National Historic Preservation Act or that are designated as historic under State or local law. That provision referenced the 1991 Standards. Because those cross-references to the 1991 Standards are no longer applicable, it is necessary in this final rule to provide new regulatory text. No substantive change in the Department's approach in this area is intended by this revision.

Section 36.406   Standards for New Construction and Alterations.

Applicable standards. Section 306 of the ADA, 42 U.S.C. 12186, directs the Attorney General to issue regulations to implement title III that are consistent with the guidelines published by the Access Board. As described in greater detail elsewhere in this Appendix, the Department is a statutory member of the Access Board and was involved significantly in the development of the 2004 ADAAG. Nonetheless, the Department has reviewed the standards and has determined that additional regulatory provisions are necessary to clarify how the Department will apply the 2010 Standards to places of lodging, social service center establishments, housing at a place of education, assembly areas, and medical care facilities. Those provisions are contained in Sec. 36.406(c)- (g). Each of these provisions is discussed below.

Section 36.406(a) adopts the 2004 ADAAG as part of the 2010 Standards and establishes the compliance date and triggering events for the application of those standards to both new construction and alterations. Appendix B of this final rule (Analysis and Commentary on the 2010 ADA Standards for Accessible Design) provides a description of the major changes in the 2010 Standards (as compared to the 1991 ADAAG) and a discussion of the public comments that the Department received on specific sections of the 2004 ADAAG. A number of commenters asked the Department to revise certain provisions in the 2004 ADAAG in a manner that would reduce either the required scoping or specific technical accessibility requirements. As previously stated, the ADA requires the Department to adopt standards consistent with the guidelines adopted by the Access Board. The Department will not adopt any standards that provide less accessibility than is provided under the guidelines contained in the 2004 ADAAG because the guidelines adopted by the Access Board are "minimum guidelines." 42 U.S.C. 12186(c).

In the NPRM, the Department specifically proposed amending Sec. 36.406(a) by dividing it into two sections. Proposed Sec. 36.406(a)(1) specified that new construction and alterations subject to this part shall comply with the 1991 Standards if physical construction of the property commences less than six months after the effective date of the rule. Proposed Sec. 36.406(a)(2) specified that new construction and alterations subject to this part shall comply with the proposed standards if physical construction of the property commences six months or more after the effective date of the rule. The Department also proposed deleting the advisory information now published in a table at Sec. 36.406(b).

Compliance date. When the ADA was enacted, the compliance dates for various provisions were delayed in order to provide time for covered entities to become familiar with their new obligations. Titles II and III of the ADA generally became effective on January 26, 1992, six months after the regulations were published. *See* 42 U.S.C. 12131 note; 42 U.S.C. 12181 note. New construction under title II and alterations under either title II or title III had to comply with the design standards on that date. *See* 42 U.S.C. 12131 note; 42 U.S.C. 12183(a)(2). For new construction under title III, the requirements applied to facilities designed and constructed for first occupancy after January 26, 1993 — 18 months after the 1991 Standards were published by the Department. *See* 42 U.S.C. 12183(a)(1).

The Department received numerous comments on the issue of effective date, many of them similar to those received in response to the ANPRM. A substantial number of commenters advocated a minimum of 18 months from publication of the final rule to the effective date for application of the standards to new construction, consistent with the time period used for implementation of the 1991 Standards. Many of these commenters argued that the 18-month period was necessary to minimize the likelihood of having to redesign projects already in the design and permitting stages at the time that the final rule is published. According to these commenters, large projects take several years from design to occupancy, and can be subject to delays from obtaining zoning, site approval, third-party design approval (i.e., architectural review), and governmental permits. To the extent the new standards necessitate changes in any previous submissions or permits already issued, businesses might have to expend significant funds and incur delays due to redesign and resubmission.

Some commenters also expressed concern that a six-month period would be hard to implement given that many renovations are planned around retail selling periods, holidays, and other seasonal concerns. For example, hotels plan renovations during their slow periods, retail establishments avoid renovations during the major holiday selling periods, and businesses in certain parts of the country cannot do any major construction during parts of the winter.

Some commenters argued that chain establishments need additional time to redesign their "master facility" designs for replication at multiple locations, taking into account both the new standards and applicable State and local accessibility requirements.

Other commenters argued for extending the effective date from six months to a minimum of 12 months for many of the same reasons, and one commenter argued that there should be a tolling of the effective date for those businesses that are in the midst of the permitting process if the necessary permits are delayed due to legal challenges or other circumstances outside the business's control.

Several commenters took issue with the Department's characterization of the 2004 ADAAG and the 1991 Standards as two similar rules. These commenters argued that many provisions in the 2004 ADAAG represent a "substantial and significant" departure from the 1991 Standards and that it will take a great deal of time and money to identify all the changes and implement them. In particular, they were concerned that small businesses lacked the internal resources to respond quickly to the new changes and that they would have to hire outside experts to assist them. One commenter expressed concern that regardless of familiarity with the 2004 ADAAG, since the 2004 ADAAG standards are organized in an entirely different manner from the 1991 Standards, and contain, in the commenter's view, extensive changes, it will make the shift from the old to the new standards quite complicated.

Several commenters also took issue with the Department's proffered rationale that by adopting a six-month effective date, the Department was following the precedent of other Federal agencies that have adopted the 2004 ADAAG for facilities whose accessibility they regulate. These commenters argued that the Department's title III regulation applies to a much broader range and number of facilities and programs than the other Federal agencies (i.e., Department of Transportation and the General Services Administration) and that those agencies regulate accessibility primarily in either governmental facilities or facilities operated by quasi-governmental authorities.

Several commenters representing the travel, vacation, and golf industries argued that the Department should adopt a two-year effective date for new construction. In addition to many of the arguments made by commenters in support of an 18-month effective date, these commenters also argued that a two-year time frame would allow States with DOJ-certified building codes to have the time to amend their codes to meet the 2004 ADAAG so that design professionals can work from compatible codes and standards.

Several commenters recommended treating alterations differently than new construction, arguing for a one-year effective date for alterations. Another commenter representing building officials argued that a minimum of a six-month phase-in for alterations was sufficient, since a very large percentage of alteration projects "are of a scale that they should be able to accommodate the phase-in."

In contrast, many commenters argued that the proposed six-month effective date should be retained in the final rule.

The Department has been persuaded by concerns raised by some of the commenters that the six month compliance date proposed in the NPRM for application of the 2010 Standards may be too short for certain projects that are already in the midst of the design and permitting process. The Department has determined that for new construction and alterations, compliance with the 2010 Standards will not be required until 18 months from the date the final rule is published. This is consistent with the amount of time given when the 1991 regulation was published. Since many State and local building codes contain provisions that are consistent with 2004 ADAAG, the Department has decided that public accommodations that choose to comply with the 2010 Standards as defined in Sec. 36.104 before the compliance date will still be considered in compliance with the ADA. However, public accommodations that choose to comply with the 2010 Standards in lieu of the 1991 Standards prior to the compliance date described in this rule must choose one or the other standard, and may not rely on some of the requirements contained in one standard and some of the requirements contained in the other standard.

Triggering event. In the NPRM, the Department proposed using the start of physical construction as the triggering event for applying the proposed standards to new construction under title III. This triggering event parallels that for the alterations provisions (i.e., the date on which construction begins), and would apply clearly across all types of covered public accommodations. The Department also proposed that for prefabricated elements, such as modular buildings and amusement park rides and attractions, or installed equipment, such as ATMs, the start of construction means the date on which the site preparation begins. Site preparation includes providing an accessible route to the element.

The Department's NPRM sought public comment on how to define the start of construction and the practicality of applying commencement of construction as a triggering event. The Department also requested input on whether the proposed definition of the start of construction was sufficiently clear and inclusive of different types of facilities. The Department also sought input about facilities subject to title III for which commencement of construction would be ambiguous or problematic.

The Department received numerous comments recommending that the Department adopt a two- pronged approach to defining the triggering event. In those cases where permits are required, the Department should use "date of permit application" as the effective date triggering event, and if no permit is required, the Department should use "start of construction." A number of these commenters argued that the date of permit application is appropriate because the applicant would have to consider the applicable State and Federal accessibility standards in order to submit the designs usually required with the application. Moreover, the date of permit application is a typical triggering event in other code contexts, such as when jurisdictions introduce an updated building code. Some commenters expressed concern that using the date of "start of construction" was problematic because the date can be affected by factors that are outside the control of the owner. For example, an owner can plan construction to start before the new standards take effect and therefore use the 1991 Standards in the design. If permits are not issued in a timely manner, then the construction could be delayed until after the effective date, and then the project would have to be redesigned. This problem would be avoided if the permit application date was the triggering event. Two commenters expressed concern that the term "start of construction" is ambiguous, because it is unclear whether start of construction means the razing of structures on the site to make way for a new facility or means site preparation, such as re-grading or laying the foundation.

One commenter recommended using the "signing date of a construction contract," and an additional commenter recommended that the new standards apply only to "buildings permitted after the effective date of the regulations."

One commenter stated that for facilities that fall outside the building permit requirements (ATMs, prefabricated saunas, small sheds), the triggering event should be the date of installation, rather than the date the space for the facility is constructed.

The Department is persuaded by the comments to adopt a two-pronged approach to defining the triggering event for new construction and alterations. The final rule states that in those cases where permits are required, the triggering event shall be the date when the last application for a building permit application or permit extension is certified to be complete by a State, county, or local government, or in those jurisdictions where the government does not certify completion of applications, the date when the last application for a building permit or permit extension is received by the State, county, or local government. If no permits are required, then the triggering event shall be the "start of physical construction or alterations." The Department has also added clarifying language related to the term "start of physical construction or alterations" to make it clear that "start of physical construction or alterations" is not intended to mean the date of ceremonial groundbreaking or the date a structure is razed to make it possible for construction of a facility to take place.

Amusement rides. Section 234 of the 2010 Standards provides accessibility guidelines for newly designed and constructed amusement rides. The amusement ride provisions do not provide a "triggering event" for new construction or alteration of an amusement ride. An industry commenter requested that the triggering event of "first use" as noted in the Advisory note to section 234.1 of the 2004 ADAAG be included in the final rule. The Advisory note provides that "[a] custom designed and constructed ride is new upon its first use, which is the first time amusement park patrons take the ride." The Department declines to treat amusement rides differently than other types of new construction and alterations and under the final rule, they are subject to Sec. 36.406(a)(3). Thus, newly constructed and altered amusement rides shall comply with the 2010 Standards if the start of physical construction or the alteration is on or after 18 months from the publication date of this rule. The Department also notes that section 234.4.2 of the 2010 Standards only applies where the structural or operational characteristics of an amusement ride are altered. It does not apply in cases where the only change to a ride is the theme.

Noncomplying new construction and alterations. The element-by-element safe harbor referenced in Sec. 36.304(d)(2) has no effect on new or altered elements in existing facilities that were subject to the 1991 Standards on the date that they were constructed or altered, but do not comply with the technical and scoping specifications for those elements in the 1991 Standards. Section 36.406(a)(5) of the final rule sets forth the rules for noncompliant new construction or alterations in facilities that were subject to the requirements of this part. Under those provisions, noncomplying new construction and alterations constructed or altered after the effective date of the applicable ADA requirements and before March 15, 2012 shall, before March 15, 2012, be made accessible in accordance with either the 1991 Standards or the 2010 Standards. Noncomplying new construction and alterations constructed or altered after the effective date of the applicable ADA requirements and before March 15, 2012, shall, on or after March 15, 2012, be made accessible in accordance with the 2010 Standards.

Section 36.406(b)   Application of Standards to Fixed Elements.

The final rule contains a new Sec. 36.406(b) that clarifies that the requirements established by this section, including those contained in the 2004 ADAAG, prescribe the requirements necessary to ensure that fixed or built-in elements in new or altered facilities are accessible to individuals with disabilities. Once the construction or alteration of a facility has been completed, all other aspects of programs, services, and activities conducted in that facility are subject to the operational requirements established elsewhere in this final rule. Although the Department has often chosen to use the requirements of the 1991 Standards as a guide to determining when and how to make equipment and furnishings accessible, those coverage determinations fall within the discretionary authority of the Department.

The Department is also clarifying that the advisory notes, appendix notes, and figures that accompany the 1991 and 2010 Standards do not establish separately enforceable requirements unless otherwise specified in the text of the standards. This clarification has been made to address concerns expressed by ANPRM commenters who mistakenly believed that the advisory notes in the 2004 ADAAG established requirements beyond those established in the text of the guidelines (e.g., Advisory 504.4 suggests, but does not require, that covered entities provide visual contrast on stair tread nosings to make them more visible to individuals with low vision). The Department received no comments on this provision in the NPRM.

Section 36.406(c)   Places of Lodging.

In the NPRM, the Department proposed a new definition for public accommodations that are "places of lodging" and a new Sec. 36.406(c) to clarify the scope of coverage for places of public accommodation that meet this definition. For many years the Department has received inquiries from members of the public seeking clarification of ADA coverage of rental accommodations in timeshares, condominium hotels, and mixed-use and corporate hotel facilities that operate as places of public accommodation (as that term is now defined in Sec. 36.104). These facilities, which have attributes of both residential dwellings and transient lodging facilities, have become increasingly popular since the ADA's enactment in 1990 and make up the majority of new hotel construction in some vacation destinations. The hybrid residential and lodging characteristics of these new types of facilities, as well as their ownership characteristics, complicate determinations of ADA coverage, prompting questions from both industry and individuals with disabilities. While the Department has interpreted the ADA to encompass these hotel-like facilities when they are used to provide transient lodging, the regulation previously has specifically not addressed them. In the NPRM, the Department proposed a new Sec. 36.406(c), entitled "Places of Lodging," which was intended to clarify that places of lodging, including certain timeshares, condominium hotels, and mixed-use and corporate hotel facilities, shall comply with the provisions of the proposed standards, including, but not limited to, the requirements for transient lodging in sections 224 and 806 of the 2004 ADAAG.

The Department's NPRM sought public input on this proposal. The Department received a substantial number of comments on these issues from industry representatives, advocates for persons with disabilities, and individuals. A significant focus of these comments was on how the Department should define and regulate vacation rental units in timeshares, vacation communities, and condo-hotels where the units are owned and controlled by individual owners and rented out some portion of time to the public, as compared to traditional hotels and motels that are owned, controlled, and rented to the public by one entity.

Scoping and technical requirements applicable to "places of lodging." In the NPRM, the Department asked for public comment on its proposal in Sec. 36.406(c) to apply to places of lodging the scoping and technical requirements for transient lodging, rather than the scoping and technical requirements for residential dwelling units.

Commenters generally agreed that the transient lodging requirements should apply to places of lodging. Several commenters stated that the determination as to which requirements apply should be made based on the intention for use at the time of design and construction. According to these commenters, if units are intended for transient rentals, then the transient lodging standards should apply, and if they are intended to be used for residential purposes, the residential standards should apply. Some commenters agreed with the application of transient lodging standards to places of lodging in general, but disagreed about the characterization of certain types of facilities as covered places of lodging.

The Department agrees that the scoping and technical standards applicable to transient lodging should apply to facilities that contain units that meet the definition of "places of lodging."

Scoping for timeshare or condominium hotels. In the NPRM, the Department sought comment on the appropriate basis for determining scoping for a timeshare or condominium-hotel. A number of commenters indicated that scoping should be based on the usage of the facility. Only those units used for short-term stays should be counted for application of the transient lodging standards, while units sold as residential properties should be treated as residential units not subject to the ADA. One commenter stated that scoping should be based on the maximum number of sleeping units available for public rental. Another commenter pointed out that unlike traditional hotels and motels, the number of units available for rental in a facility or development containing individually owned units is not fixed over time. Owners have the right to participate in a public rental program some, all, or none of the time, and individual owner participation changes from year to year.

The Department believes that the determination for scoping should be based on the number of units in the project that are designed and constructed with the intention that their owners may participate in a transient lodging rental program. The Department cautions that it is not the number of owners that actually exercise their right to participate in the program that determines the scoping. Rather it is the units that could be placed into an on-site or off-site transient lodging rental program. In the final rule, the Department has added a provision to Sec. 36.406(c)(3), which states that units intended to be used exclusively for residential purposes that are contained in facilities that also meet the definition of place of lodging are not covered by the transient lodging standards. Title III of the ADA does not apply to units designed and constructed with the intention that they be rented or sold as exclusively residential units. Such units are covered by the Fair Housing Act (FHAct), which contains requirements for certain features of accessible and adaptable design both for units and for public and common use areas. All units designed and constructed with the intention that they may be used for both residential and transient lodging purposes are covered by the ADA and must be counted for determining the required number of units that must meet the transient lodging standards in the 2010 Standards. Public use and common use areas in facilities containing units subject to the ADA also must meet the 2010 Standards. In some developments, units that may serve as residential units some of the time and rental units some of the time will have to meet both the FHAct and the ADA requirements. For example, all of the units in a vacation condominium facility whose owners choose to rent to the public when they are not using the units themselves would be counted for the purposes of determining the appropriate number of units that must comply with the 2010 Standards. In a newly constructed condominium that has three floors with units dedicated to be sold solely as residential housing and three floors with units that may be used as residences or hotel units, only the units on the three latter floors would be counted for applying the 2010 Standards. In a newly constructed timeshare development containing 100 units, all of which may be made available to the public through an exchange or rental program, all 100 units would be counted for purposes of applying the 2010 Standards.

One commenter also asked the Department for clarification of how to count individually owned "lock-off units." Lock-off units are units that are multi-bedroom but can be "locked off" into two separate units, each having individual external access. This commenter requested that the Department state in the final rule that individually owned lock-off units do not constitute multiple guest rooms for purposes of calculating compliance with the scoping requirements for accessible units, since for the most part the lock-off units are used as part of a larger accessible unit, and portions of a unit not locked off would constitute both an accessible one-bedroom unit or an accessible two- bedroom unit with the lock-off unit.

It is the Department's view that lock-off units that are individually owned that can be temporarily converted into two units do not constitute two separate guest rooms for purposes of calculating compliance with the scoping requirements.

One commenter asked the Department how developers should scope units where buildings are constructed in phases over a span of years, recommending that the scoping be based on the total number of units expected to be constructed at the project and not on a building-by-building basis or on a phase-by-phase basis. The Department does not think scoping should be based on planned number of units, which may or may not be actually constructed over a period of years. However, the Department recognizes that resort developments may contain buildings and facilities that are of all sizes from single-unit cottages to facilities with hundreds of units. The Department believes it would be appropriate to allow designers, builders, and developers to aggregate the units in facilities with 50 or fewer units that are subject to a single permit application and that are on a common site or that are constructed at the same time for the purposes of applying the scoping requirements in table 224.2. Facilities with more than 50 units should be scoped individually in accordance with the table. The regulation has been revised to reflect this application of the scoping requirements.

One commenter also asked the Department to use the title III regulation to declare that time- shares subject to the transient lodging standards are exempt from the design and construction requirements of the FHAct. The coverage of the FHAct is set by Congress and interpreted by regulations issued by the Department of Housing and Urban Development. The Department has no authority to exempt anyone from coverage of the FHAct.

Application of ADA to places of lodging that contain individually owned units. The Department believes that regardless of ownership structure for individual units, rental programs (whether they are on- or off-site) that make transient lodging guest rooms available to the public must comply with the general nondiscrimination requirements of the ADA. In addition, as provided in Sec. 36.406(c), newly constructed facilities that contain accommodations intended to be used for transient lodging purposes must comply with the 2010 Standards.

In the NPRM, the Department asked for public comment on several issues related to ensuring the availability of accessible units in a rental program operated by a place of lodging. The Department sought input on how it could address a situation in which a new or converted facility constructs the required number of accessible units, but the owners of those units choose not to participate in the rental program; whether the facility has an obligation to encourage or require owners of accessible units to participate in the rental program; and whether the facility developer, the condominium association, or the hotel operator has an obligation to retain ownership or control over a certain number of accessible units to avoid this problem.

In the NPRM, the Department sought public input on how to regulate scoping for a timeshare or condominium-rental facility that decides, after the sale of units to individual owners, to begin a rental program that qualifies the facility as a place of lodging, and how the condominium association, operator, or developer should determine which units to make accessible.

A number of commenters expressed concerns about the ability of the Department to require owners of accessible units to participate in the rental program, to require developers, condo associations, or homeowners associations to retain ownership of accessible units, and to impose accessibility requirements on individual owners who choose to place inaccessible units into a rental program after purchase. These commenters stated that individuals who purchase accessible vacation units in condominiums, individual vacation homes, and timeshares have ownership rights in their units and may choose lawfully to make their units available to the public some, all, or none of the time. Commenters advised the Department that the Securities and Exchange Commission takes the position that if condominium units are offered in connection with participation in a required rental program for any part of the year, require the use of an exclusive rental agent, or impose conditions otherwise restricting the occupancy or rental of the unit, then that offering will be viewed as an offering of securities in the form of an investment (rather than a real estate offering). SEC Release No. 33-5347, Guidelines as to the Applicability of the Federal Securities Laws to Offers and Sales of Condominiums or Units in a Real Estate Development (Jan. 4, 1973). Consequently, most condominium developers do not impose such restrictions at the time of sale. Moreover, owners who choose to rent their units as a short-term vacation rental can select any rental or management company to lease and manage their unit, or they may rent them out on their own. They also may choose never to lease those units. Thus, there are no guarantees that at any particular time, accessible units will be available for rental by the public. According to this commenter, providing incentives for owners of accessible units to place their units in the rental program will not work, because it does not guarantee the availability of the requisite number of rooms dispersed across the development, and there is not any reasonable, identifiable source of funds to cover the costs of such incentives.

A number of commenters also indicated that it potentially is discriminatory as well as economically infeasible to require that a developer hold back the accessible units so that the units can be maintained in the rental program year-round. One commenter pointed out that if a developer did not sell the accessible condominiums or timeshares in the building inventory, the developer would be subject to a potential ADA or FHAct complaint because persons with disabilities who wanted to buy accessible units rather than rent them each year would not have the option to purchase them. In addition, if a developer held back accessible units, the cost of those units would have to be spread across all the buyers of the inaccessible units, and in many cases would make the project financially infeasible. This would be especially true for smaller projects. Finally, this commenter argued that requiring units to be part of the common elements that are owned by all of the individual unit owners is infeasible because the common ownership would result in pooled rental income, which would transform the owners into participants in a rental pool, and thus turn the sale of the condominiums into the sale of securities under SEC Release 33-5347.

Several commenters noted that requiring the operator of the rental program to own the accessible units is not feasible either because the operator of the rental program would have to have the funds to invest in the purchase of all of the accessible units, and it would not have a means of recouping its investment. One commenter stated that in Texas, it is illegal for on-site rental programs to own condominium units. Another commenter noted that such a requirement might lead to the loss of on-site rental programs, leaving owners to use individual third-party brokers, or rent the units privately. One commenter acknowledged that individual owners cannot be required to place their units in a rental pool simply to offer an accessible unit to the public, since the owners may be purchasing units for their own use. However, this commenter recommended that owners who choose to place their units in a rental pool be required to contribute to a fund that would be used to renovate units that are placed in the rental pool to increase the availability of accessible units. One commenter argued that the legal entity running the place of lodging has an obligation to retain control over the required number of accessible units to ensure that they are available in accordance with title III.

A number of commenters also argued that the Department has no legal authority to require individual owners to engage in barrier removal where an existing development adds a rental program. One commenter stated that Texas law prohibits the operator of on-site rental program from demanding that alterations be made to a particular unit. In addition, under Texas law, condominium declarations may not require some units and not others to make changes, because that would lead to unequal treatment of units and owners, which is not permissible.

One commenter stated that since it was not possible for operators of rental programs offering privately owned condominiums to comply with accessible scoping, the Department should create exemptions from the accessible scoping, especially for existing facilities. In addition, this commenter stated that if an operator of an on-site rental program were to require renovations as a condition of participation in the rental program, unit owners might just rent their units through a different broker or on their own, in which case such requirements would not apply.

A number of commenters argued that if a development decides to create a rental program, it must provide accessible units. Otherwise the development would have to ensure that units are retrofitted. A commenter argued that if an existing building is being converted, the Department should require that if alterations of the units are performed by an owner or developer prior to sale of the units, then the alterations requirements should apply, in order to ensure that there are some accessible units in the rental pool. This commenter stated that because of the proliferation of these type of developments in Hawaii, mandatory alteration is the only way to guarantee the availability of accessible units in the long run. In this commenter's view, since conversions almost always require makeover of existing buildings, this will not lead to a significant expense.

The Department agrees with the commenters that it would not be feasible to require developers to hold back or purchase accessible units for the purposes of making them available to the public in a transient lodging rental program, nor would it be feasible to require individual owners of accessible units to participate in transient lodging rental programs.

The Department recognizes that places of lodging are developed and financed under myriad ownership and management structures and agrees that there will be circumstances where there are legal barriers to requiring compliance with either the alterations requirements or the requirements related to barrier removal. The Department has added an exception to Sec. 36.406(c), providing that in existing facilities that meet the definition of places of lodging, where the guest rooms are not owned or substantially controlled by the entity that owns, leases, or operates the overall facility and the physical features of the guest room interiors are controlled by their individual owners, the units are not subject to the alterations requirement, even where the owner rents the unit out to the public through a transient lodging rental program. In addition, the Department has added an exception to the barrier removal requirements at Sec. 36.304(g) providing that in existing facilities that meet the definition of places of lodging, where the guest rooms are not owned or substantially controlled by the entity that owns, leases, or operates the overall facility and the physical features of the guest room interiors are controlled by their individual owners, the units are not subject to the barrier removal requirement. The Department notes, however, that there are legal relationships for some timeshares and cooperatives where the ownership interests do not convey control over the physical features of units. In those cases, it may be the case that the facility has an obligation to meet the alterations or barrier removal requirements or to maintain accessible features.

Section 36.406(d)   Social Service Center Establishments.

In the NPRM, the Department proposed a new Sec. 36.406(d) requiring group homes, halfway houses, shelters, or similar social service center establishments that provide temporary sleeping accommodations or residential dwelling units to comply with the provisions of the 2004 ADAAG that apply to residential facilities, including, but not limited to, the provisions in sections 233 and 809.

The NPRM explained that this proposal was based on two important changes in the 2004 ADAAG. First, for the first time, residential dwelling units are explicitly covered in the 2004 ADAAG in section 233. Second, the 2004 ADAAG eliminates the language contained in the 1991 Standards addressing scoping and technical requirements for homeless shelters, group homes, and similar social service center establishments. Currently, such establishments are covered in section 9.5 of the transient lodging section of the 1991 Standards. The deletion of section 9.5 creates an ambiguity of coverage that must be addressed.

The NPRM explained the Department's belief that transferring coverage of social service center establishments from the transient lodging standards to the residential facilities standards would alleviate conflicting requirements for social service providers. The Department believes that a substantial percentage of social service providers are recipients of Federal financial assistance from the Department of Housing and Urban Development (HUD). The Department of Health and Human Services (HHS) also provides financial assistance for the operation of shelters through the Administration for Children and Families programs. As such, they are covered both by the ADA and section 504. UFAS is currently the design standard for new construction and alterations for entities subject to section 504. The two design standards for accessibility — the 1991 Standards and UFAS — have confronted many social service providers with separate, and sometimes conflicting, requirements for design and construction of facilities. To resolve these conflicts, the residential facilities standards in the 2004 ADAAG have been coordinated with the section 504 requirements. The transient lodging standards, however, are not similarly coordinated. The deletion of section 9.5 of the 1991 Standards from the 2004 ADAAG presented two options: (1) Require coverage under the transient lodging standards, and subject such facilities to separate, conflicting requirements for design and construction; or (2) require coverage under the residential facilities standards, which would harmonizes the regulatory requirements under the ADA and section 504. The Department chose the option that harmonizes the regulatory requirements: coverage under the residential facilities standards.

In the NPRM, the Department expressed concern that the residential facilities standards do not include a requirement for clear floor space next to beds similar to the requirement in the transient lodging standards; as a result, the Department proposed adding a provision that would require certain social service center establishments that provide sleeping rooms with more than 25 beds to ensure that a minimum of 5 percent of the beds have clear floor space in accordance with section 806.2.3 of the 2004 ADAAG.

The Department requested information from providers who operate homeless shelters, transient group homes, halfway houses, and other social service center establishments, and from the clients of these facilities who would be affected by this proposed change. In the NPRM, the Department asked to what extent conflicts between the ADA and section 504 have affected these facilities and what the effect would be of applying the residential dwelling unit requirements to these facilities, rather than the requirements for transient lodging guest rooms.

Many of the commenters supported applying the residential facilities requirements to social service center establishments stating that even though the residential facilities requirements are less demanding, in some instances, the existence of one clear standard will result in an overall increased level of accessibility by eliminating the confusion and inaction that are sometimes caused by the current existence of multiple requirements. One commenter stated that the residential facilities guidelines were more appropriate because individuals housed in social service center establishments typically stay for a prolonged period of time, and guests of a transient lodging facility typically are not housed to participate in a program or receive services.

One commenter opposed to the proposed section argued for the application of the transient lodging standards to all social service center establishments except those that were "intended as a person's place of abode," referencing the Department's question related to the definition of place of lodging in the title III NPRM. A second commenter stated that the use of transient lodging guidelines would lead to greater accessibility.

The Department continues to be concerned about alleviating the challenges for social service providers that are also subject to section 504 and that would likely be subject to conflicting requirements if the transient lodging standard were applied. Thus, the Department has retained the requirement that social service center establishments comply with the residential dwelling standards. The Department did not receive comments regarding adding a requirement for bathing options, such as a roll-in shower, in social service center establishments operated by public accommodations. The Department did, however, receive comments in support of adding such a requirement regarding public entities under title II. The Department believes that social service center establishments that provide emergency shelter to large transient populations should be able to provide bathing facilities that are accessible to persons with mobility disabilities who need roll-in showers. Because of the transient nature of the population of these large shelters, it will not be feasible to modify bathing facilities in a timely manner when faced with a need to provide a roll-in shower with a seat when requested by an overnight visitor. As a result, the Department has added a requirement that social service center establishments with sleeping accommodations for more than 50 individuals must provide at least one roll-in shower with a seat that complies with the relevant provisions of section 608 of the 2010 Standards. Transfer-type showers are not permitted in lieu of a roll-in shower with a seat, and the exceptions in sections 608.3 and 608.4 for residential dwelling units are not permitted. When separate shower facilities are provided for men and for women, at least one roll-in shower must be provided for each group. This supplemental requirement to the residential facilities standards is in addition to the supplemental requirement that was proposed in the NPRM for clear floor space in sleeping rooms with more than 25 beds.

The Department also notes that while dwelling units at some social service center establishments are also subject to FHAct design and construction requirements that require certain features of adaptable and accessible design, FHAct units do not provide the same level of accessibility that is required for residential facilities under the 2010 Standards. The FHAct requirements, where also applicable, should not be considered a substitute for the 2010 Standards. Rather, the 2010 Standards must be followed in addition to the FHAct requirements.

The Department also notes that while in the NPRM the Department used the term "social service establishment," the final rule uses the term "social service center establishment." The Department has made this editorial change so that the final rule is consistent with the terminology used in the ADA. *See* 42 U.S.C. 12181(7)(K).

Section 36.406(e) Housing at a Place of Education.

The Department of Justice and the Department of Education share responsibility for regulation and enforcement of the ADA in postsecondary educational settings, including architectural features. Housing types in educational settings range from traditional residence halls and dormitories to apartment or townhouse-style residences. In addition to title III of the ADA, universities and schools that are recipients of Federal financial assistance also are subject to section 504, which contains its own accessibility requirements currently through the application of UFAS. Residential housing, including housing in an educational setting, is also covered by the FHAct, which requires newly constructed multifamily housing to include certain features of accessible and adaptable design. Covered entities subject to the ADA must always be aware of, and comply with, any other Federal statutes or regulations that govern the operation of residential properties.

Although the 1991 Standards mention dormitories as a form of transient lodging, they do not specifically address how the ADA applies to dormitories and other types of residential housing provided in an educational setting. The 1991 Standards also do not contain any specific provisions for residential facilities, allowing covered entities to elect to follow the residential standards contained in UFAS. Although the 2004 ADAAG contains provisions for both residential facilities and transient lodging, the guidelines do not indicate which requirements apply to housing provided in an educational setting, leaving it to the adopting agencies to make that choice. After evaluating both sets of standards, the Department concluded that the benefits of applying the transient lodging standards outweighed the benefits of applying the residential facilities standards. Consequently, in the NPRM, the Department proposed a new Sec. 36.406(e) that provided that residence halls or dormitories operated by or on behalf of places of education shall comply with the provisions of the proposed standards for transient lodging, including, but not limited to, the provisions in sections 224 and 806 of the 2004 ADAAG.

Private universities and schools covered by title III as public accommodations are required to make their programs and activities accessible to persons with disabilities. The housing facilities that they provide have varied characteristics. College and university housing facilities typically provide housing for up to one academic year, but may be closed during school vacation periods. In the summer, they often are used for short-term stays of one to three days, a week, or several months. Graduate and faculty housing often is provided year-round in the form of apartments, which may serve individuals or families with children. These housing facilities are diverse in their layout. Some are double-occupancy rooms with a shared toilet and bathing room, which may be inside or outside the unit. Others may contain cluster, suite, or group arrangements where several rooms are located inside a defined unit with bathing, kitchen, and similar common facilities. In some cases, these suites are indistinguishable in features from traditional apartments. Universities may build their own housing facilities or enter into agreements with private developers to build, own, or lease housing to the educational institution or to its students. Academic housing may be located on the campus of the university or may be located in nearby neighborhoods.

Throughout the school year and the summer, academic housing can become program areas in which small groups meet, receptions and educational sessions are held, and social activities occur. The ability to move between rooms — both accessible rooms and standard rooms — in order to socialize, to study, and to use all public use and common use areas is an essential part of having access to these educational programs and activities. Academic housing also is used for short-term transient educational programs during the time students are not in regular residence and may be rented out to transient visitors in a manner similar to a hotel for special university functions.

The Department was concerned that applying the new construction requirements for residential facilities to educational housing facilities could hinder access to educational programs for students with disabilities. Elevators generally are not required under the 2004 ADAAG residential facilities standards unless they are needed to provide an accessible route from accessible units to public use and common use areas, while under the 2004 ADAAG as it applies to other types of facilities, multistory private facilities must have elevators unless they meet very specific exceptions. In addition, the residential facilities standards do not require accessible roll-in showers in bathrooms, while the transient lodging requirements require some of the accessible units to be served by bathrooms with roll-in showers. The transient lodging standards also require that a greater number of units have accessible features for persons with communication disabilities. The transient lodging standards provide for installation of the required accessible features so that they are available immediately, but the residential facilities standards allow for certain features of the unit to be adaptable. For example, only reinforcements for grab bars need to be provided in residential dwellings, but the actual grab bars must be installed under the transient lodging standards. By contrast, the residential facilities standards do require certain features that provide greater accessibility within units, such as usable kitchens and an accessible route throughout the dwelling. The residential facilities standards also require 5 percent of the units to be accessible to persons with mobility disabilities, which is a continuation of the same scoping that is currently required under UFAS and is therefore applicable to any educational institution that is covered by section 504. The transient lodging standards require a lower percentage of accessible sleeping rooms for facilities with large numbers of rooms than is required by UFAS. For example, if a dormitory has 150 rooms, the transient lodging standards would require 7 accessible rooms, while the residential standards would require 8. In a large dormitory with 500 rooms, the transient lodging standards would require 13 accessible rooms, and the residential facilities standards would require 25. There are other differences between the two sets of standards, including requirements for accessible windows, alterations, kitchens, an accessible route throughout a unit, and clear floor space in bathrooms allowing for a side transfer.

In the NPRM, the Department requested public comment on how to scope educational housing facilities, and it asked whether the residential facilities requirements or the transient lodging requirements in the 2004 ADAAG would be more appropriate for housing at places of education and asked how the different requirements would affect the cost of building new dormitories and other student housing. *See* 73 FR 34508, 34545 (June 17, 2008).

The Department received several comments on this issue under title III. One commenter stated that the Department should adopt the residential facilities standards for housing at a place of education. In the commenter's view, the residential facilities standards are congruent with overlapping requirements imposed by HUD, and the residential facilities requirements would ensure dispersion of accessible features more effectively. This commenter also argued that while the increased number of required accessible units for residential facilities as compared to transient lodging may increase the cost of construction or alteration, this cost would be offset by a reduced need later to adapt rooms if the demand for accessible rooms exceeds the supply. The commenter also encouraged the Department to impose a visitability (accessible doorways and necessary clear floor space for turning radius) requirement for both the residential facilities and transient lodging requirements to allow students with mobility impairments to interact and socialize in a fully integrated fashion. Another commenter stated that while dormitories should be treated like residences as opposed to transient lodging, the Department should ensure that "all floors are accessible," thus ensuring community integration and visitability. Another commenter argued that housing at a place of education is comparable to residential housing, and that most of the housing types used by schools do not have the same amenities and services or function like transient lodging and should not be treated as such.

Several commenters focused on the length of stay at this type of housing and suggested that if the facilities are subject to occupancy for greater than 30 days, the residential standards should apply. Another commenter supported the Department's adoption of the transient lodging standards, arguing this will provide greater accessibility and therefore increase opportunities for students with disabilities to participate. One commenter, while supporting the use of transient lodging standards in this area, argued that the Department also should develop regulations relating to the usability of equipment in housing facilities by persons who are blind or visually impaired. Another commenter argued that the Department should not impose the transient lodging requirements on K-12 schools because the cost of adding elevators can be prohibitive, and because there are safety concerns related to evacuating students in wheelchairs living on floors above the ground floor in emergencies causing elevator failures.

The Department has considered the comments recommending the use of the residential facilities standards and acknowledges that they require certain features that are not included in the transient lodging standards and that should be required for housing provided at a place of education. In addition, the Department notes that since educational institutions often use their academic housing facilities as short-term transient lodging in the summers, it is important that accessible features be installed at the outset. It is not realistic to expect that the educational institution will be able to adapt a unit in a timely manner in order to provide accessible accommodations to someone attending a one-week program during the summer.

The Department has determined that the best approach to this type of housing is to continue to require the application of transient lodging standards but, at the same time, to add several requirements drawn from the residential facilities standards related to accessible turning spaces and work surfaces in kitchens, and the accessible route throughout the unit. This will ensure the maintenance of the transient lodging standard requirements related to access to all floors of the facility, roll-in showers in facilities with more than 50 sleeping rooms, and other important accessibility features not found in the residential facilities standards, but also will ensure usable kitchens and access to all the rooms in a suite or apartment.

The Department has added a new definition to Sec. 36.104, "Housing at a Place of Education," and has revised Sec. 36.406(e) to reflect the accessible features that now will be required in addition to the requirements set forth under the transient lodging standards. The Department also recognizes that some educational institutions provide some residential housing on a year-round basis to graduate students and staff that is comparable to private rental housing but contains no facilities for educational programming. Section 36.406(e)(3) exempts from the transient lodging standards apartments or townhouse facilities that are provided with a lease on a year-round basis exclusively to graduate students or faculty and that do not contain any public use or common use areas available for educational programming; instead, such housing must comply with the requirements for residential facilities in sections 233 and 809 of the 2010 Standards.

The regulatory text uses the term "sleeping room" in lieu of the term "guest room," which is the term used in the transient lodging standards. The Department is using this term because it believes that for the most part, it provides a better description of the sleeping facilities used in a place of education than "guest room." The final rule states in Sec. 36.406(e) that the Department intends the terms to be used interchangeably in the application of the transient lodging standards to housing at a place of education.

Section 36.406(f) Assembly Areas.

In the NPRM, the Department proposed Sec. 36.406(f) to supplement the assembly area requirements of the 2004 ADAAG, which the Department is adopting as part of the 2010 Standards. The NPRM proposed at Sec. 36.406(f)(1) to require wheelchair spaces and companion seating locations to be dispersed to all levels of the facility that are served by an accessible route. The Department received no significant comments on this paragraph and has decided to adopt the proposed language with minor modifications.

Section 36.406(f)(1) ensures that there is greater dispersion of wheelchair spaces and companion seats throughout stadiums, arenas, and grandstands than would otherwise be required by sections 221 and 802 of the 2004 ADAAG. In some cases, the accessible route may not be the same route that other individuals use to reach their seats. For example, if other patrons reach their seats on the field by an inaccessible route (e.g., by stairs), but there is an accessible route that complies with section 206.3 of the 2004 ADAAG that could be connected to seats on the field, wheelchair spaces and companion seats must be placed on the field even if that route is not generally available to the public.

Regulatory language that was included in the 2004 ADAAG advisory, but that did not appear in the NPRM, has been added by the Department in Sec. 36.406(f)(2). Section 36.406(f)(2) now requires an assembly area that has seating encircling, in whole or in part, a field of play or performance area, such as an arena or stadium, to place wheelchair spaces and companion seats around the entire facility. This rule, which is designed to prevent a public accommodation from placing wheelchair spaces and companion seats on one side of the facility only, is consistent with the Department's enforcement practices and reflects its interpretation of section 4.33.3 of the 1991 Standards.

In the NPRM, the Department proposed Sec. 36.406(f)(2), which prohibits wheelchair spaces and companion seating locations from being "located on (or obstructed by) temporary platforms * * *." 73 FR 34508, 34557 (June 17, 2008). Through its enforcement actions, the Department discovered that some venues place wheelchair spaces and companion seats on temporary platforms that, when removed, reveal conventional seating underneath, or cover the wheelchair spaces and companion seats with temporary platforms on top of which they place risers of conventional seating. These platforms cover groups of conventional seats and are used to provide groups of wheelchair seats and companion seats.

Several commenters requested an exception to the prohibition of the use of temporary platforms for public accommodations that sell most of their tickets on a season-ticket or other multi- event basis. Such commenters argued that they should be able to use temporary platforms because they know, in advance, that the patrons sitting in certain areas for the whole season do not need wheelchair spaces and companion seats. The Department declines to adopt such an exception. As it explained in detail in the NPRM, the Department believes that permitting the use of movable platforms that seat four or more wheelchair users and their companions have the potential to reduce the number of available wheelchair seating spaces below the level required, thus reducing the opportunities for persons who need accessible seating to have the same choice of ticket prices and amenities that are available to other patrons in the facility. In addition, use of removable platforms may result in instances where last minute requests for wheelchair and companion seating cannot be met because entire sections of accessible seating will be lost when a platform is removed. *See* 73 FR 34508, 34546 (June 17, 2008). Further, use of temporary platforms allows facilities to limit persons who need accessible seating to certain seating areas, and to relegate accessible seating to less desirable locations. The use of temporary platforms has the effect of neutralizing dispersion and other seating requirements (e.g., line of sight) for wheelchair spaces and companion seats. *Cf. Independent Living Resources v. Oregon Arena Corp.*, 1 F. Supp. 2d 1159, 1171 (D. Or. 1998) (holding that while a public accommodation may "infill" wheelchair spaces with removable seats when the wheelchair spaces are not needed to accommodate individuals with disabilities, under certain circumstances "[s]uch a practice might well violate the rule that wheelchair spaces must be dispersed throughout the arena in a manner that is roughly proportionate to the overall distribution of seating"). In addition, using temporary platforms to convert unsold wheelchair spaces to conventional seating undermines the flexibility facilities need to accommodate secondary ticket market exchanges as required by Sec. 36.302(f)(7) of the final rule.

As the Department explained in the NPRM, however, this provision was not designed to prohibit temporary seating that increases seating for events (e.g., placing temporary seating on the floor of a basketball court for a concert). Consequently, the final rule, at Sec. 36.406(f)(3), has been amended to clarify that if an entire seating section is on a temporary platform for a particular event, then wheelchair spaces and companion seats may also be in that seating section. However, adding a temporary platform to create wheelchair spaces and companion seats that are otherwise dissimilar from nearby fixed seating and then simply adding a small number of additional seats to the platform would not qualify as an "entire seating section" on the platform. In addition, Sec. 36.406(f)(3) clarifies that facilities may fill in wheelchair spaces with removable seats when the wheelchair spaces are not needed by persons who use wheelchairs.

The Department has been responsive to assembly areas' concerns about reduced revenues due to unused accessible seating. Accordingly, the Department has reduced scoping requirements significantly — by almost half in large assembly areas — and determined that allowing assembly areas to in-fill unsold wheelchair spaces with readily removable temporary individual seats appropriately balances their economic concerns with the rights of individuals with disabilities. *See* section 221.1 of the 2010 Standards.

For stadium-style movie theaters, in Sec. 36.406(f)(4) of the NPRM the Department proposed requiring placement of wheelchair seating spaces and companion seats on a riser or cross-aisle in the stadium section of the theater that satisfies at least one of the following criteria: (1) It is located within the rear 60 percent of the seats provided in the auditorium; or (2) It is located within the area of the auditorium where the vertical viewing angles are between the 40th and 100th percentile of vertical viewing angles for all seats in that theater as ranked from the first row (1st percentile) to the back row (100th percentile). The vertical viewing angle is the angle between a horizontal line perpendicular to the seated viewer's eye to the screen and a line from the seated viewer's eye to the top of the screen.

The Department proposed this bright-line rule for two reasons: (1) the movie theater industry petitioned for such a rule; and (2) the Department has acquired expertise in the design of stadium-style theaters during its litigation with several major movie theater chains. *See United States. v. AMC Entertainment, Inc.*, 232 F. Supp.2d 1092 (C.D. Cal. 2002), *rev'd in part*, 549 F.3d 760 (9th Cir. 2008); *United States v. Cinemark USA, Inc.*, 348 F.3d 569 (6th Cir. 2003). Two industry commenters — at least one of whom otherwise supported this rule — requested that the Department explicitly state that this rule does not apply retroactively to existing theaters. Although this provision on its face applies to new construction and alterations, these commenters were concerned that the rule could be interpreted to apply retroactively because of the Department's statements in the NPRM and ANPRM that this bright line rule, although newly articulated, is not a new standard but "merely codifi[es] longstanding Department requirement[s]," 73 FR 34508, 34534 (June 17, 2008), and does not represent a "substantive change from the existing line-of-sight requirements" of section 4.33.3 of the 1991 Standards, 69 FR 58768, 58776 (Sept. 30, 2004).

Although the Department intends for Sec. 36.406(f)(4) of this rule to apply prospectively to new construction and alterations, this rule is not a departure from, and is consistent with, the line-of-sight requirements in the 1991 Standards. The Department has always interpreted the line- of-sight requirements in the 1991 Standards to require viewing angles provided to patrons who use wheelchairs to be comparable to those afforded to other spectators. Section 36.406(f)(4) merely represents the application of these requirements to stadium-style movie theaters.

One commenter from a trade association sought clarification whether Sec. 36.406(f)(4) applies to stadium-style theaters with more than 300 seats, and argued that it should not since dispersion requirements apply in those theaters. The Department declines to limit this rule to stadium- style theaters with 300 or fewer seats; stadium- style theaters of all sizes must comply with this rule. So, for example, stadium-style theaters that must vertically disperse wheelchair spaces and companion seats must do so within the parameters of this rule.

The NPRM included a provision that required assembly areas with more than 5,000 seats to provide at least five wheelchair spaces with at least three companion seats for each of those five wheelchair spaces. The Department agrees with commenters who asserted that group seating is better addressed through ticketing policies rather than design and has deleted that provision from this section of the final rule.

Section 36.406(g)   Medical Care Facilities.

In the 1991 title III regulation, there was no provision addressing the dispersion of accessible sleeping rooms in medical care facilities. The Department is aware, however, of problems that individuals with disabilities face in receiving full and equal medical care when accessible sleeping rooms are not adequately dispersed. When accessible rooms are not fully dispersed, a person with a disability is often placed in an accessible room in an area that is not medically appropriate for his or her condition, and is thus denied quick access to staff with expertise in that medical specialty and specialized equipment. While the Access Board did not establish specific design requirements for dispersion in the 2004 ADAAG, in response to extensive comments in support of dispersion it added an advisory note, Advisory 223.1 General, encouraging dispersion of accessible rooms within the facility so that accessible rooms are more likely to be proximate to appropriate qualified staff and resources.

In the NPRM, the Department sought additional comment on the issue, asking whether it should require medical care facilities, such as hospitals, to disperse their accessible sleeping rooms, and if so, by what method (by specialty area, floor, or other criteria). All of the comments the Department received on this issue supported dispersing accessible sleeping rooms proportionally by specialty area. These comments from individuals, organizations, and a building code association, argued that it would not be difficult for hospitals to disperse rooms by specialty area, given the high level of regulation to which hospitals are subject and the planning that hospitals do based on utilization trends. Further, comments suggest that without a requirement, it is unlikely that hospitals would disperse the rooms. In addition, concentrating accessible rooms in one area perpetuates segregation of individuals with disabilities, which is counter to the purpose of the ADA.

The Department has decided to require medical care facilities to disperse their accessible sleeping rooms in a manner that is proportionate by type of medical specialty. This does not require exact mathematical proportionality, which at times would be impossible. However, it does require that medical care facilities disperse their accessible rooms by medical specialty so that persons with disabilities can, to the extent practical, stay in an accessible room within the wing or ward that is appropriate for their medical needs. The language used in this rule ("in a manner that is proportionate by type of medical specialty") is more specific than that used in the NPRM ("in a manner that enables patients with disabilities to have access to appropriate specialty services") and adopts the concept of proportionality proposed by the commenters. Accessible rooms should be dispersed throughout all medical specialties, such as obstetrics, orthopedics, pediatrics, and cardiac care.

Subpart F — Certification of State Laws or Local Building Codes

Subpart F contains procedures implementing section 308(b)(1)(A)(ii) of the ADA, which provides that on the application of a State or local jurisdiction, the Attorney General may certify that a State or local building code or similar ordinance meets or exceeds the minimum accessibility requirements of the Act. In enforcement proceedings, this certification will constitute rebuttable evidence that the law or code meets or exceeds the ADA's requirements. In its NPRM, the Department proposed three changes in subpart F that would streamline the process for public entities seeking certification, all of which are adopted in this final rule.

First, the Department proposed deleting the existing § 36.603, which establishes the obligations of a submitting authority that is seeking certification of its code, and issue in its place informal regulatory guidance regarding certification submission requirements. Due to the deletion of § 36.603, §§ 36.604 through 36.608 are renumbered, and § 36.603 in the final rule is modified to indicate that the Assistant Attorney General for the Civil Rights Division (Assistant Attorney General) shall make a preliminary determination of equivalency after "receipt and review of all information relevant to a request filed by a submitting official for certification of a code." Second, the Department proposed that the requirement in renumbered § 36.604 (previously § 36.605) that an informal hearing be held in Washington, DC, if the Assistant Attorney General makes a preliminary determination of equivalency be changed to a requirement that the hearing be held in the State or local jurisdiction charged with administration and enforcement of the code. Third, the Department proposed adding language to renumbered § 36.606 (previously § 36.607) to explain the effect of the 2010 Standards on the codes of State or local jurisdictions that were determined in the past to meet or exceed the 1991 Standards. Once the 2010 Standards take effect, certifications issued under the 1991 Standards would not have any future effect, and States and local jurisdictions with codes certified under the 1991 Standards would need to reapply for certification under the 2010 Standards. With regard to elements of existing buildings and facilities constructed in compliance with a code when a certification of equivalency was in effect, the final rule requires that in any enforcement action this compliance would be treated as rebuttable evidence of compliance with the standards then in effect. The new provision added to § 36.606 may also have implications in determining an entity's eligibility for the element-by-element safe harbor.

No substantive comments were received regarding the Department's proposed changes in subpart F, and no other changes have been made to this subpart in the final rule. The Department did receive several comments addressing other issues raised in the NPRM that are related to subpart F. Because the 2010 Standards include specific design requirements for recreation facilities and play areas that may be new to many title III facilities, the Department sought comments in the NPRM about how the certification review process would be affected if the State or local jurisdiction allocates the authority to implement the new requirements to State or local agencies that are not ordinarily involved in administering building codes. One commenter, an association of building owners and managers, suggested that because of the increased scope of the 2010 Standards, it is likely that parts of covered elements in the new standards will be under the jurisdiction of multiple State or local agencies. In light of these circumstances, the commenter recommended that the Department allow State or local agencies to seek certification even if only one State or local regulatory agency requests certification. For example, if a State agency that regulates buildings seeks certification of its building code, it should be able to do so, even if another State agency that regulates amusement rides and miniature golf courses does not seek certification.

The Department's discussion of this issue in the NPRM contemplated that all of a State or local government's accessibility requirements for title III facilities would be the subject of a request for certification. Any other approach would require the Department to certify only part of a State or local government's accessibility requirements as compared to the entirety of the revised ADA standards. As noted earlier, the Attorney General is authorized by section 308(b)(1)(A)(ii) of the ADA to certify that a State or local building code meets or exceeds the ADA's minimum accessibility requirements, which are contained in this regulation. The Department has concluded that this is a decision that must be made on a case-by-case basis because of the wide variety of enforcement schemes adopted by the States. Piecemeal certification of laws or codes that do not contain all of the minimum accessibility requirements could fail to satisfy the Attorney General's responsibility to ensure that a State or local building code meets or exceeds the minimum accessibility requirements of the Act before granting certification. However, the Department wants to permit State and local code administrators to have maximum flexibility, so the Department will leave open the possibility for case-by-case review to determine if a State has successfully met the burden of demonstrating that its accessibility codes or other laws meet or exceed the ADA requirements.

The commenter representing building owners and managers also urged the Department to extend the proposed effective date for the final rule. The commenter explained that a six-month phase-in period is inadequate for States to begin and complete a code amendment process. The commenter asserted that the inadequate phase-in period will place entities undertaking new construction and alterations, particularly in those States with certified codes, in a difficult position because State officials will continue to enforce previously certified State or local accessibility requirements that may be in conflict with the new 2010 Standards. The Department received numerous comments on the issue of the effective date, many of them similar to the concerns expressed above, in response to both the NPRM and the ANPRM. *See* Appendix A discussion of compliance dates for new construction and alterations (§ 36.406). The Department has been persuaded by the concerns raised by many commenters addressing the time and costs related to the design process for both new construction and alterations, and has determined that for new construction and alterations, compliance with the 2010 Standards will not be required until 18 months from the date the final rule is published. For more information on the issue of the compliance date, refer to subpart D — New Construction and Alterations.

One commenter, an association of theater owners, recommended that the Department establish a training program for State building inspectors for those States that receive certification to ensure more consistent ADA compliance and to facilitate the review of builders' architectural plans. The commenter also recommended that State building inspectors, once trained, review architectural plans, and after completion and inspection of facilities, be authorized to certify that the inspected building or facility meets both the certified State and the Federal accessibility requirements. Although supportive of the idea of additional training for State and local building code officials regarding ADA compliance, the Department believes that the approach suggested by the commenter of allowing State and local code officials to determine if a covered facility is in compliance with Federal accessibility requirements is not consistent with or permissible under the statutory enforcement scheme established by the ADA. As the Department stated in the NPRM, certification of State and local codes serves, to some extent, to mitigate the absence of a Federal mechanism for conducting at the national level a review of all architectural plans and inspecting all covered buildings under construction to ensure compliance with the ADA. In this regard, certification operates as a bridge between the obligation to comply with the 1991 Standards in new construction and alterations, and the administrative schemes of State and local governments that regulate the design and construction process. By ensuring consistency between State or local codes and Federal accessibility standards, certification has the additional benefit of streamlining the regulatory process, thereby making it easier for those in the design and construction industry to satisfy both State and Federal requirements. The Department notes, however, that although certification has the potential to increase compliance with the ADA, this result, however desirable, is not guaranteed. The ADA contemplated that there could be enforcement actions brought even in States with certified codes, and it provided some protection in litigation to builders who adhered to the provisions of the code certified to be ADA-equivalent. The Department's certification determinations make it clear that to get the benefit of certification, a facility must comply with the applicable code requirements — without relying on waivers or variances. The certified code, however, remains within the authority of the adopting State or local jurisdiction to interpret and enforce: Certification does not transform a State's building code into Federal law. Nor can certification alone authorize State and local building code officials implementing a certified code to do more than they are authorized to do under State or local law, and these officials cannot acquire authority through certification to render binding interpretations of Federal law. Therefore, the Department, while understanding the interest in obtaining greater assurance of compliance with the ADA through the interpretation and enforcement of a certified code by local code officials, declined in the NPRM to confer on local officials the authority not granted to them under the ADA to certify the compliance of individual facilities. The Department in the final rule finds no reason to alter its position on this issue in response to the comments that were received. The commenter representing theater owners also urged the Department to provide a safe harbor to facilities constructed in compliance with State or local building codes certified under the 1991 Standards. With regard to elements of facilities constructed in compliance with a certified code prior to the effective date of the 2010 Standards, and during the period when a certification of equivalency was in effect, the Department noted in the NPRM that its approach would be consistent with the approach to the safe harbor discussed in subpart C, § 36.304 of the NPRM, with respect to elements in existing facilities constructed in compliance with the 1991 Standards. For example, elements in existing facilities in States with codes certified under the 1991 Standards would be eligible for a safe harbor if they were constructed in compliance with an ADA-certified code. In this scenario, compliance with the certified code would be treated as evidence of compliance with the 1991 Standards for purposes of determining the application of the safe harbor provision to those elements. For more information on safe harbor, refer to subpart C, § 36.304 of the final rule.

One commenter, an advocacy group for the blind, suggested that, similar to the procedures for certifying a State or local building code, the Department should establish a program to certify an entity's obligation to make its goods and services accessible to persons with sensory disabilities. The Department believes that this commenter was suggesting that covered entities should be able to request that the Department review their business operations to determine if they have met their ADA obligations. As noted earlier, subpart F contains procedures implementing section 308(b) (1)(A)(ii) of the ADA, which provides that on the application of a State or local jurisdiction, the Attorney General may certify that a State or local building code or similar ordinance meets or exceeds the minimum accessibility requirements of the ADA. The only mechanism through which the Department is authorized to ensure a covered entity's compliance with the ADA is the enforcement scheme established under section 308(b)(1)(A)(i) of the ADA. The Department notes, however, that title III of the ADA and its implementing regulation, which includes the standards for accessible design, already require existing, altered, and newly constructed places of public accommodation, such as retail stores, hotels, restaurants, movie theaters, and stadiums, to make their facilities readily accessible to and usable by individuals with disabilities, which includes individuals with sensory disabilities, so that individuals with disabilities have a full and equal opportunity to enjoy the benefits of a public accommodation's goods, services, facilities, privileges and advantages.

Other Issues

Questions Posed in the NPRM Regarding Costs and Benefits of Complying With the 2010 Standards.

In the NPRM, the Department requested comments on various cost and benefit issues related to eight requirements in the Department's Initial RIA, that were projected to have incremental costs that exceeded monetized benefits by more than $100 million when using the 1991 Standards as a comparative baseline, *i.e.*, side reach, water closet clearances in single-user toilet rooms with in-swinging doors, stairs, elevators, location of accessible routes to stages, accessible attorney areas and witness stands, assistive listening systems, and accessible teeing grounds, putting greens, and weather shelters at golf courses. 73 FR 34508, 34512 (June 17, 2008). The Department was particularly concerned about how these costs applied to alterations. The Department noted that pursuant to the ADA, the Department does not have statutory authority to modify the 2004 ADAAG and is required instead to issue regulations implementing the ADA that are consistent with the Board's guidelines. In that regard, the Department also requested comment about whether any of these eight elements in the 2010 Standards should be returned to the Access Board for further consideration, in particular as applied to alterations. Many of the comments received by the Department in response to these questions addressed both titles II and III. As a result, the Department's discussion of these comments and its response are collectively presented for both titles.

Side reach. The 1991 Standards at section 4.2.6 establish a maximum side-reach height of 54 inches. The 2010 Standards at section 308.3.1 reduce that maximum height to 48 inches. The 2010 Standards also add exceptions for certain elements to the scoping requirement for operable parts. The vast majority of comments the Department received were in support of the lower side-reach maximum of 48 inches in the 2010 Standards. Most of these comments, but not all, were received from individuals of short stature, relatives of individuals of short stature, or organizations representing the interests of persons with disabilities, including individuals of short stature. Comments from individuals with disabilities and disability advocacy groups stated that the 48-inch side reach would permit independence in performing many activities of daily living for individuals with disabilities, including individuals of short stature, persons who use wheelchairs, and persons who have limited upper body strength. In this regard, one commenter who is a business owner pointed out that as a person of short stature there were many occasions when he was unable to exit a public restroom independently because he could not reach the door handle. The commenter said that often elevator control buttons are out of his reach, and, if he is alone, he often must wait for someone else to enter the elevator so that he can ask that person to press a floor button for him. Another commenter, who is also a person of short stature, said that he has on several occasions pulled into a gas station only to find that he was unable to reach the credit card reader on the gas pump. Unlike other customers who can reach the card reader, swipe their credit or debit cards, pump their gas, and leave the station, he must use another method to pay for his gas. Another comment from a person of short stature pointed out that as more businesses take steps to reduce labor costs — a trend expected to continue — staffed booths are being replaced with automatic machines for the sale, for example, of parking tickets and other products. He observed that the "ability to access and operate these machines becomes ever more critical to function in society," and, on that basis, urged the Department to adopt the 48-inch side-reach requirement. Another individual commented that persons of short stature should not have to carry with them adaptive tools in order to access building or facility elements that are out of their reach, any more than persons in wheelchairs should have to carry ramps with them in order to gain access to facilities.

Many of the commenters who supported the revised side-reach requirement pointed out that lowering the side-reach requirement to 48 inches would avoid a problem sometimes encountered in the built environment when an element was mounted for a parallel approach at 54 inches, only to find afterwards that a parallel approach was not possible. Some commenters also suggested that lowering the maximum unobstructed side-reach to 48 inches would reduce confusion among design professionals by making the unobstructed forward and side-reach maximums the same (the unobstructed forward reach in both the 1991 and 2010 Standards is 48 inches maximum). These commenters also pointed out that the

ICC/ANSI A117.1 Standard, which is a private sector model accessibility standard, has included a 48-inch maximum high side-reach requirement since 1998. Many jurisdictions have already incorporated this requirement into their building codes, which these commenters believed would reduce the cost of compliance with the 2010 Standards. Because numerous jurisdictions have already adopted the 48-inch side-reach requirement, the Department's failure to adopt the 48-inch side-reach requirement in the 2010 Standards, in the view of many commenters, would result in a significant reduction in accessibility, and would frustrate efforts that have been made to harmonize private sector model construction and accessibility codes with Federal accessibility requirements. Given these concerns, they overwhelmingly opposed the idea of returning the revised side-reach requirement to the Access Board for further consideration.

The Department also received comments in support of the 48-inch side-reach requirement from an association of professional commercial property managers and operators and from State governmental entities. The association of property managers pointed out that the revised side-reach requirement provided a reasonable approach to "regulating elevator controls and all other operable parts" in existing facilities in light of the manner in which the safe harbor, barrier removal, and alterations obligations will operate in the 2010 Standards. One governmental entity, while fully supporting the 48-inch side-reach requirement, encouraged the Department to adopt an exception to the lower reach range for existing facilities similar to the exception permitted in the ICC/ANSI A117.1 Standard. In response to this latter concern, the Department notes that under the safe harbor, existing facilities that are in compliance with the 1991 Standards, which required a 54-inch side-reach maximum, would not be required to comply with the lower side-reach requirement, unless there is an alteration. *See* § 36.304(d)(2)(i).

A number of commenters expressed either concern with, or opposition to, the 48-inch side-reach requirement and suggested that it be returned to the Access Board for further consideration. These commenters included trade and business associations, associations of retail stores, associations of restaurant owners, retail and convenience store chains, and a model code organization. Several businesses expressed the view that the lower side-reach requirement would discourage the use of their products and equipment by most of the general public. In particular, concerns were expressed by a national association of pay phone service providers regarding the possibility that pay telephones mounted at the lower height would not be used as frequently by the public to place calls, which would result in an economic burden on the- pay phone industry. The commenter described the lower height required for side reach as creating a new "barrier" to pay phone use, which would reduce revenues collected from pay phones and, consequently, further discourage the installation of new pay telephones. In addition, the commenter expressed concern that phone service providers would simply decide to remove existing pay phones rather than incur the costs of relocating them at the lower height. With regard to this latter concern, the commenter misunderstood the manner in which the safe harbor and barrier removal obligations under § 36.304 will operate in the revised title III regulation for elements that comply with the 1991 Standards.

The Department does not anticipate that wholesale relocation of pay telephones in existing facilities will be required under the final rule where the telephones in existing facilities already are in compliance with the 1991 Standards. If the pay phones comply with the 1991 Standards, the adoption of the 2010 Standards does not require retrofitting of these elements to reflect incremental changes in the 2010 Standards. *See* § 36.304(d) (2). However, pay telephones that were required to meet the 1991 Standards as part of new construction or alterations, but do not in fact comply with those standards, will need to be brought into compliance with the 2010 Standards as of 18 months from the publication date of this final rule. *See* § 36.406(a)(5).

The Department does not agree with the concerns expressed by the commenter about reduced revenues from pay phones mounted at lower heights. The Department believes that while given the choice some individuals may prefer to use a pay phone that is at a higher height, the availability of some phones at a lower height will not deter individuals from making needed calls.

The 2010 Standards will not require every pay phone to be installed or moved to a lowered height. The table accompanying section 217.2 of the 2010 Standards makes clear that where one or more telephones are provided on a floor, level, or an exterior site, only one phone per floor, level, or exterior site must be placed at an accessible height. Similarly, where there is one bank of phones per floor, level, or exterior site, only one phone per floor, level, or exterior site must be accessible. And if there are two or more banks of phones per floor, level, or exterior site, only one phone per bank must be placed at an accessible height.

Another comment in opposition to the lower reach range requirement was submitted on behalf of a chain of convenience stores with fuel stops. The commenter expressed the concern that the 48-inch side reach "will make it uncomfortable for the majority of the public," including persons of taller stature who would need to stoop to use equipment such as fuel dispensers mounted at the lower height. The commenter offered no objective support for the observation that a majority of the public would be rendered uncomfortable if, as required in the 2010 Standards, at least one of each type of fuel dispenser at a facility was made accessible in compliance with the lower reach range. Indeed, the Department received no comments from any individuals of tall stature expressing concern about accessible elements or equipment being mounted at the 48-inch height.

Several retail, convenience store, restaurant, and amusement park commenters expressed concern about the burden the lower side-reach requirement would place on their businesses in terms of self- service food stations and vending areas if the 48- inch requirement were applied retroactively. The cost of lowering counter height, in combination with the lack of control businesses exercise over certain prefabricated service or vending fixtures, outweighed, they argued, any benefits to persons with disabilities. For this reason, they suggested the lower side-reach requirement be referred back to the Access Board.

These commenters misunderstood the safe harbor and barrier removal obligations that will be in effect under the 2010 Standards. Those existing self-service food stations and vending areas that already are in compliance with the 1991 Standards will not be required to satisfy the 2010 Standards unless they engage in alterations. With regard to prefabricated vending machines and food service components that will be purchased and installed in businesses after the 2010 Standards become effective, the Department expects that companies will design these machines and fixtures to comply with the 2010 Standards in the future, as many have already done in the 10 years since the 48- inch side- reach requirement has been a part of the model codes and standards used by many jurisdictions as the basis for their construction codes.

A model code organization commented that the lower side-reach requirement would create a significant burden if it required entities to lower the mounting height for light switches, environmental controls, and outlets when an alteration did not include the walls where these elements were located, such as when "an area is altered or as a path of travel obligation." The Department believes that the final rule adequately addresses those situations about which the commenter expressed concern by not requiring the relocation of existing elements, such as light switches, environmental controls, and outlets, unless they are altered. Moreover, under § 36.403 of the 1991 rule, costs for altering the path of travel to an altered area of primary function that exceed 20 percent of the overall costs of the alteration will continue to be deemed disproportionate.

The Department has determined that the revised side-reach requirement should not be returned to the Access Board for further consideration based in large part on the views expressed by a majority of the commenters regarding the need for, and importance of, the lower side-reach requirement to ensure access for persons with disabilities.

Alterations and water closet clearances in single-user toilet rooms with in-swinging doors. The 1991 Standards allow a lavatory to be placed a minimum of 18 inches from the water closet centerline and a minimum of 36 inches from the side wall adjacent to the water closet, which precludes side transfers. The 1991 Standards do not allow an in-swinging door in a toilet or bathing room to overlap the required clear floor space at any accessible fixture. To allow greater transfer options, section 604.3.2 of the 2010 Standards prohibits lavatories from overlapping the clear floor space at water closets, except in certain residential dwelling units. Section 603.2.3 of the 2010 Standards maintains the prohibition on doors swinging into the clear floor space or clearance required for any fixture, except that they permit the doors of toilet or bathing rooms to swing into the required turning space, provided that there is sufficient clearance space for the wheelchair outside the door swing. In addition, in single-user toilet or bathing rooms, exception 2 of section 603.2.3 of the 2010 Standards permits the door to swing into the clear floor space of an accessible fixture if a clear floor space that measures at least 30 inches by 48 inches is available outside the arc of the door swing.

The majority of commenters believed that this requirement would increase the number of toilet rooms accessible to individuals with disabilities who use wheel-chairs or mobility scooters, and will make it easier for them to transfer. A number of commenters stated that there was no reason to return this provision to the Access Board. Numerous commenters noted that this requirement is already included in other model accessibility standards and many State and local building codes and that the adoption of the 2010 Standards is an important part of harmonization efforts.

Other commenters, mostly trade associations, opposed this requirement, arguing that the added cost to the industry outweighs any increase in accessibility. Two commenters stated that these proposed requirements would add two feet to the width of an accessible single-user toilet room; however, another commenter said the drawings in the proposed regulation demonstrated that there would be no substantial increase in the size of the toilet room. Several commenters stated that this requirement would require moving plumbing fixtures, walls, or doors at significant additional expense. Two commenters wanted the permissible overlap between the door swing and clearance around any fixture eliminated. One commenter stated that these new requirements will result in fewer alterations to toilet rooms to avoid triggering the requirement for increased clearances, and suggested that the Department specify that repairs, maintenance, or minor alterations would not trigger the need to provide increased clearances. Another commenter requested that the Department exempt existing guest room bathrooms and single-user toilet rooms that comply with the 1991Standards from complying with the increased clearances in alterations.

After careful consideration of these comments, the Department believes that the revised clearances for single-user toilet rooms will allow safer and easier transfers for individuals with disabilities, and will enable a caregiver, aide, or other person to accompany an individual with a disability into the toilet room to provide assistance. The illustrations in Appendix B to this final rule, "Analysis and Commentary on the 2010 ADA Standards for Accessible Design," describe several ways for public entities and public accommodations to make alterations while minimizing additional costs or loss of space. Further, in any isolated instances where existing structural limitations may entail loss of space, the public entity and public accommodation may have a technical infeasibility defense for that alteration. The Department has, therefore, decided not to return this requirement to the Access Board.

Alterations to stairs. The 1991 Standards only require interior and exterior stairs to be accessible when they provide access to levels that are not connected by an elevator, ramp, or other accessible means of vertical access. In contrast, section 210.1 of the 2010 Standards requires all newly constructed stairs that are part of a means of egress to be accessible. However, exception 2 of section 210.1 of the 2010 Standards provides that in alterations, stairs between levels connected by an accessible route need not be accessible, except that handrails shall be provided. Most commenters were in favor of this requirement for handrails in alterations, and stated that adding handrails to stairs during alterations was not only feasible and not cost prohibitive, but also provided important safety benefits. One commenter stated that making all points of egress accessible increased the number of people who could use the stairs in an emergency. A majority of the commenters did not want this requirement returned to the Access Board for further consideration. The International Building Code (IBC), which is a private sector model construction code, contains a similar provision, and most jurisdictions enforce a version of the IBC as their building code, thereby minimizing the impact of this provision on public entities and public accommodations. The Department believes that by requiring only the addition of handrails to altered stairs where levels are connected by an accessible route, the costs of compliance for public entities and public accommodations are minimized, while safe egress for individuals with disabilities is increased. Therefore, the Department has decided not to return this requirement to the Access Board.

Alterations to elevators. Under the 1991 Standards, if an existing elevator is altered, only that altered elevator must comply with the new construction requirements for accessible elevators to the maximum extent feasible. It is therefore possible that a bank of elevators controlled by a single call system may contain just one accessible elevator, leaving an individual with a disability with no way to call an accessible elevator and thus having to wait indefinitely until an accessible elevator happens to respond to the call system. In the 2010 Standards, when an element in one elevator is altered, section 206.6.1 will require the same element to be altered in all elevators that are programmed to respond to the same call button as the altered elevator. Almost all commenters favored the proposed requirement. This requirement, according to these commenters, is necessary so a person with a disability need not wait until an accessible elevator responds to his or her call. One commenter suggested that elevator owners also could comply by modifying the call system so the accessible elevator could be summoned independently. One commenter suggested that this requirement would be difficult for small businesses located in older buildings, and one commenter suggested that this requirement be sent back to the Access Board.

After considering the comments, the Department agrees that this requirement is necessary to ensure that when an individual with a disability presses a call button, an accessible elevator will arrive. The IBC contains a similar provision, and most jurisdictions enforce a version of the IBC as their building code, minimizing the impact of this provision on public entities and public accommodations. Public entities and small businesses located in older buildings need not comply with this requirement where it is technically infeasible to do so. Further, as pointed out by one commenter, modifying the call system so the accessible elevator can be summoned independently is another means of complying with this requirement in lieu of altering all other elevators programmed to respond to the same call button. Therefore, the Department has decided not to return this requirement to the Access Board.

Location of accessible routes to stages. The 1991 Standards, at section 4.33.5, require an accessible route to connect the accessible seating and the stage, as well as other ancillary spaces used by performers. The 2010 Standards, at section 206.2.6, provide in addition that where a circulation path directly connects the seating area and the stage, the accessible route must connect directly the accessible seating and the stage, and, like the 1991 Standards, an accessible route must connect the stage with the ancillary spaces used by performers.

In the NPRM, the Department asked operators of auditoria about the extent to which auditoria already provide direct access to stages and whether there were planned alterations over the next 15 years that included accessible direct routes to stages. The Department also asked how to quantify the benefits of this requirement for persons with disabilities, and invited commenters to provide illustrative anecdotal experiences about the requirement's benefits.

The Department received many comments regarding the costs and benefits of this requirement. Although little detail was provided, many industry and governmental entity commenters anticipated that the costs of this requirement would be great and that it would be difficult to implement. They noted that premium seats may have to be removed and that load-bearing walls may have to be relocated. These commenters suggested that the significant costs would deter alterations to the stage area for a great many auditoria. Some commenters suggested that ramps to the front of the stage may interfere with means of egress and emergency exits. Several commenters requested that the requirement apply to new construction only, and one industry commenter requested an exemption for stages used in arenas or amusement parks where there is no audience participation or where the stage is a work area for performers only. One commenter requested that the requirement not apply to temporary stages.

The final rule does not require a direct accessible route to be constructed where a direct circulation path from the seating area to the stage does not exist. Consequently, those commenters who expressed concern about the burden imposed by the revised requirement (i.e., where the stage is constructed with no direct circulation path connecting the general seating and performing area) should note that the final rule will not require the provision of a direct accessible route under these circumstances. The final rule applies to permanent stages, as well as "temporary stages," if there is a direct circulation path from the seating area to the stage. However, the Department recognizes that in some circumstances, such as an alteration to a primary function area, the ability to provide a direct accessible route to a stage may be costly or technically infeasible, and the auditorium owner is not precluded by the revised requirement from asserting defenses available under the regulation. In addition, the Department notes that since section 4.33.5 of the 1991 Standards requires an accessible route to a stage, the safe harbor will apply to existing facilities whose stages comply with the 1991 Standards.

Several governmental entities supported accessible auditoria and the revised requirement. One governmental entity noted that its State building code already required direct access, that it was possible to provide direct access, and that creative solutions had been found to do so.

Many advocacy groups and individual commenters strongly supported the revised requirement, discussing the acute need for direct access to stages, as such access has an impact on a great number of people at important life events, such as graduations and awards ceremonies, at collegiate and competitive performances and other school events, and at entertainment events that include audience participation. Many commenters expressed the belief that direct access is essential for integration mandates to be satisfied, and that separate routes are stigmatizing and unequal. The Department agrees with these concerns.

Commenters described the impact felt by persons in wheelchairs who are unable to access the stage at all when others are able to do so. Some of these commenters also discussed the need for the performers and production staff who use wheelchairs to have direct access to the stage, and they provided a number of examples that illustrated the importance of the rule proposed in the NPRM. Personal anecdotes were provided in comments and at the Department's public hearing on the NPRM. One mother spoke passionately and eloquently about the unequal treatment experienced by her daughter, who uses a wheelchair, at awards ceremonies and band concerts. Her daughter was embarrassed and ashamed to be carried by her father onto a stage at one band concert. When the venue had to be changed for another concert to an accessible auditorium, the band director made sure to comment that he was unhappy with the switch. Rather than endure the embarrassment and indignities, her child dropped out of band the following year.

Another father commented about how he was unable to speak from the stage at a PTA meeting at his child's school. Speaking from the floor limited his line of sight and his participation. Several examples were provided of children who could not participate on stage during graduation, awards programs, or special school events, such as plays and festivities. One student did not attend his college graduation because he would not be able to get on stage. Another student was unable to participate in the class Christmas programs or end-of-year parties unless her father could attend and lift her onto the stage. These commenters did not provide a method to quantify the benefits that would accrue by having direct access to stages. One commenter stated, however, that "the cost of dignity and respect is without measure."

Many industry commenters and governmental entities suggested that the requirement be sent back to the Access Board for further consideration. One industry commenter mistakenly noted that some international building codes do not incorporate the requirement and that, therefore, there is a need for further consideration. However, the Department notes that both the 2003 and 2006 editions of the IBC include scoping provisions that are almost identical to this requirement and that these editions of the model code are the most frequently used. Many individuals and advocacy group commenters requested that the requirement be adopted without further delay. These commenters spoke of the acute need for direct access to stages and the amount of time it would take to resubmit the requirement to the Access Board. Several commenters noted that the 2004 ADAAG tracks recent model codes, and that there is thus no need for further consideration. The Department agrees that no further delay is necessary and therefore has decided it will not return the requirement to the Access Board for further consideration.

Assistive listening systems. The 1991 Standards at sections 4.33.6 and 4.33.7 require assistive listening systems (ALS) in assembly areas and prescribe general performance standards for ALS systems. In the NPRM, the Department proposed adopting the technical specifications in the 2004 ADAAG for ALS that are intended to ensure better quality and effective delivery of sound and information for persons with hearing impairments, especially those using hearing aids. The Department noted in the NPRM that since 1991, advancements in ALS and the advent of digital technology have made these systems more amenable to uniform standards, which, among other things, should ensure that a certain percentage of required ALS systems are hearing-aid compatible. 73 FR 34508, 34513 (June 17, 2008). The 2010 Standards at section 219 provide scoping requirements and at section 706 address receiver jacks, hearing aid compatibility, sound pressure level, signal-to-noise ratio, and peak clipping level. The Department requested comments specifically from arena and assembly area administrators on the cost and maintenance issues associated with ALS, and asked generally about the costs and benefits of ALS, and asked whether, based upon the expected costs of ALS, the issue should be returned to the Access Board for further consideration.

Commenters from advocacy organizations noted that persons who develop significant hearing loss often discontinue their normal routines and activities, including meetings, entertainment, and large group events, due to a sense of isolation caused by the hearing loss or embarrassment. Individuals with longstanding hearing loss may never have participated in group activities for many of the same reasons. Requiring ALS may allow individuals with disabilities to contribute to the community by joining in government and public events, and through increased economic activity associated with community activities and entertainment. Making public events and entertainment accessible to persons with hearing loss also brings families and other groups that include persons with hearing loss into more community events and activities, thus exponentially increasing the benefit from ALS.

Many commenters noted that when a person has significant hearing loss, that person may be able to hear and understand information in a quiet situation with the use of hearing aids or cochlear implants; however, as background noise increases and the distance between the source of the sound and the listener grows, and especially where there is distortion in the sound, an ALS becomes essential for basic comprehension and understanding. Commenters noted that among the 31 million Americans with hearing loss, and with a projected increase to over 78 million Americans with hearing loss by 2030, the benefit from ALS is huge and growing. Advocates for persons with disabilities and individuals commented that they appreciated the improvements in the 2004 ADAAG standards for ALS, including specifications for the ALS systems and performance standards. They noted that providing neckloops that translate the signal from the ALS transmitter to a frequency that can be heard on a hearing aid or cochlear implant are much more effective than separate ALS system headsets, which sometimes create feedback, often malfunction, and may create distractions for others seated nearby. Comments from advocates and users of ALS systems consistently noted that the Department's regulation should, at a minimum, be consistent with the 2004 ADAAG. Although there were requests for adjustments in the scoping requirements from advocates seeking increased scoping requirements, and from large venue operators seeking fewer requirements, there was no significant concern expressed by commenters about the technical specifications for ALS in the 2004 ADAAG.

Some commenters from trade associations and large venue owners criticized the scoping requirements as too onerous, and one commenter asked for a remand to the Access Board for new scoping rules. However, one State agency commented that the 2004 ADAAG largely duplicates the requirements in the 2006 IBC and the 2003 ANSI codes, which means that entities that comply with those standards would not incur additional costs associated with ADA compliance.

According to one State office of the courts, the costs to install either an infrared system or an FM system at average-sized facilities, including most courtrooms covered by title II, would be between $500 and $2,000, which the agency viewed as a small price in comparison to the benefits of inclusion. Advocacy organizations estimated wholesale costs of ALS systems at about $250 each, and individual neckloops to link the signal from the ALS transmitter to hearing aids or cochlear implants at less than $50 per unit. Many commenters pointed out that if a facility already is using induction neckloops, it would already be in compliance already and would not have any additional installation costs. One major city commented that annual maintenance is about $2,000 for the entire system of performance venues in the city. A trade association representing very large venues estimated annual maintenance and upkeep expenses, including labor and replacement parts, to be at most about $25,000 for a very large professional sports stadium.

One commenter suggested that the scoping requirements for ALS in the 2004 ADAAG were too stringent and that the Department should refer them back to the Access Board for further review and consideration. Others commented that the requirement for new ALS systems should mandate multichannel receivers capable of receiving audio description for persons who are blind, in addition to a channel for amplification for persons who are hard of hearing. Some commenters suggested that the Department should require a set schedule and protocol of mandatory maintenance. Department regulations already require maintenance of accessible features at § 36.211(a) of the title III regulation, which obligates a title III entity to maintain ALS in good working order. The Department recognizes that maintenance of ALS is key to its usability. Necessary maintenance will vary dramatically from venue to venue based upon a variety of factors including frequency of use, number of units, quality of equipment, and other items. Accordingly, the Department has determined that it is not appropriate to mandate details of maintenance, but notes that failure to maintain ALS would violate § 36.211(a) of this rule.

The NPRM asked whether the Department should return the issue of ALS requirements to the Access Board for further review. The Department has received substantial feedback on the technical and scoping requirements for ALS and is convinced that these requirements are reasonable — especially in light of the fact that the requirements largely duplicate those in the 2006 IBC and the 2003 ANSI codes already adopted in many States — and that the benefits justify the requirements. In addition, the Department believes that the new specifications will make ALS work more effectively for more persons with disabilities, which, together with a growing population of new users, will increase demand for ALS, thus mooting criticism from some large venue operators about insufficient demand. Thus, the Department has determined that it is unnecessary to refer this issue back to the Access Board for reconsideration.

Accessible teeing grounds, putting greens, and weather shelters. The Department's NPRM sought public input on the proposed requirements for accessible golf courses. These requirements specifically relate to accessible routes within the boundaries of the courses, as well as the accessibility of golfing elements (e.g., teeing grounds, putting greens, weather shelters).

In the NPRM, the Department sought information from the owners and operators of golf courses, both public and private, on the extent to which their courses already have golf car passages, and, if so, whether they intended to avail themselves of the proposed accessible route exception for golf car passages. 73 FR 34508, 34513 (June 17, 2008).

Most commenters expressed support for the adoption of an accessible route requirement that includes an exception permitting golf car passage as all or part of an accessible route. Comments in favor of the proposed standard came from golf course owners and operators, individuals, organizations, and disability rights groups, golf course requirements generally came from golf courses and organizations representing the golf course industry.

The majority of commenters expressed the general viewpoint that nearly all golf courses provide golf cars and have either well-defined paths or permit golf cars to drive on the course where paths are not present — and thus meet the accessible route requirement. Several commenters disagreed with the assumption in the

Initial RIA that virtually every tee and putting green on an existing course would need to be regraded in order to provide compliant accessible routes. According to one commenter, many golf courses are relatively flat with little slope, especially those heavily used by recreational golfers. This commenter concurred with the Department that it is likely that most existing golf courses have a golf car passage to tees and greens, thereby substantially minimizing the cost of bringing an existing golf course into compliance with the proposed standards. One commenter reported that golf course access audits found that the vast majority of public golf courses would have little difficulty in meeting the proposed golf course requirements. In the view of some commenters, providing access to golf courses would increase golf participation by individuals with disabilities.

The Department also received many comments requesting clarification of the term "golf car passage." For example, one commenter requesting clarification of the term "golf car passage" argued that golf courses typically do not provide golf car paths or pedestrian paths onto the actual teeing grounds or greens, many of which are higher or lower than the car path. This commenter argued that if golf car passages were required to extend onto teeing grounds and greens in order to qualify for an exception, then some golf courses would have to substantially regrade teeing grounds and greens at a high cost.

After careful consideration of the comments, the Department has decided to adopt the 2010 Standards specific to golf facilities. The Department believes that in order for individuals with mobility disabilities to have an opportunity to play golf that is equal to golfers without disabilities, it is essential that golf courses provide an accessible route or accessible golf car passage to connect accessible elements and spaces within the boundary of the golf course, including teeing grounds, putting greens, and weather shelters.

Public Comments on Other NPRM Issues

Equipment and furniture. Equipment and furniture are covered under the Department's ADA regulations, including under the provision requiring modifications in policies, practices, and procedures and the provision requiring barrier removal. *See* 28 CFR 36.302,36.304. The Department has not issued specific regulatory guidance on equipment and furniture, but proposed such regulations in 1991. The Department decided not to establish specific equipment requirements at that time because the requirements could be addressed under other sections of the regulation and because there were no appropriate accessibility standards applicable to many types of equipment at that time. *See* 28 CFR part 36, app. B (2009) ("Proposed Section 36.309 Purchase of Furniture and Equipment").

In the NPRM, the Department announced its intention not to regulate equipment, proposing instead to continue with the current approach. The Department received numerous comments objecting to this decision and urging the Department to issue equipment and furniture regulations. Based on these comments, the Department has decided that it needs to revisit the issuance of equipment and furniture regulations, and it intends to do so in future rulemaking.

Among the commenters' key concerns, many from the disability community objected to the Department's earlier decision not to issue equipment regulations, especially for medical equipment. These groups recommended that the Department list by name certain types of medical equipment that must be accessible, including exam tables (that lower to 15 inches above the floor or lower), scales, medical and dental chairs, and radiologic equipment (including mammography equipment). These commenters emphasized that the provision of medically-related equipment and furniture also should be specifically regulated since they are not included in the 2004 ADAAG (while depositories, change machines, fuel dispensers, and ATMs are) and because of their crucial role in the provision of healthcare. Commenters described how the lack of accessible medical equipment negatively affects the health of individuals with disabilities. For example, some individuals with mobility disabilities do not get thorough medical care because their health providers do not have accessible examination tables or scales.

Commenters also said that the Department's stated plan to assess the financial impact of free-standing equipment on businesses was not necessary, as any regulations could include a financial balancing test. Other commenters representing persons who are blind or have low vision urged the Department to mandate accessibility for a wide range of equipment — including household appliances (stoves, washers, microwaves, and coffee makers), audiovisual equipment (stereos and DVD players), exercise machines, vending equipment, ATMs, computers at Internet cafes or hotel business centers, reservations kiosks at hotels, and point-of-sale devices — through speech output and tactile labels and controls. They argued that modern technology allows such equipment to be made accessible at minimal cost. According to these commenters, the lack of such accessibility in point-of-sale devices is particularly problematic because it forces blind individuals to provide personal or sensitive information (such as personal identification numbers) to third parties, which exposes them to identity fraud. Because the ADA does not apply directly to the manufacture of products, the Department lacks the authority to issue design requirements for equipment designed exclusively for use in private homes. *See* Department of Justice, Americans with Disabilities Act, *ADA Title III Technical Assistance Manual Covering Public Accommodations and Commercial Facilities*, III-4.4200, available at http://www.ada.gov/taman3.html. To the extent that equipment intended for such use is used by a covered entity to facilitate a covered service or activity, that covered entity must make the equipment accessible to the extent that it can. *See id.:* 28 CFR part 36, app. B (2009) ("Proposed Section 36.309 Purchase of Furniture and Equipment").

Some commenters urged the Department to require swimming pool operators to provide aquatic wheelchairs for the use of persons with disabilities when the swimming pool has a sloped entry. If there is a sloped entry, a person who uses a wheelchair would require a wheelchair designed for use in the water in order to gain access to the pool since taking a personal wheelchair into water would rust and corrode the metal on the chair and damage any electrical components of a power wheelchair. Providing an aquatic wheelchair made of non-corrosive materials and designed for access into the water will protect the water from contamination and avoid damage to personal wheelchairs or other mobility aids.

Additionally, many commenters urged the Department to regulate the height of beds in accessible hotel guest rooms and to ensure that such beds have clearance at the floor to accommodate a mechanical lift. These commenters noted that in recent years, hotel beds have become higher as hotels use thicker mattresses, thereby making it difficult or impossible for many individuals who use wheelchairs to transfer onto hotel beds. In addition, many hotel beds use a solid-sided platform base with no clearance at the floor, which prevents the use of a portable lift to transfer an individual onto the bed. Consequently, individuals who bring their own lift to transfer onto the bed cannot independently get themselves onto the bed. Some commenters suggested various design options that might avoid these situations.

The Department intends to provide specific guidance relating to both hotel beds and aquatic wheelchairs in a future rulemaking. For the present, the Department reminds covered entities that they have the obligation to undertake reasonable modifications to their current policies and procedures and to undertake barrier removal or provide alternatives to barrier removal to make their facilities accessible to persons with disabilities. In many cases, providing aquatic wheelchairs or adjusting hotel bed heights may be necessary to comply with those requirements.

Commenters from the business community objected to the lack of clarity from the NPRM as to which equipment must be accessible and how to make it accessible. Several commenters urged the Department to clarify that equipment located in a public accommodation need not meet the technical specifications of ADAAG so long as the service provided by the equipment can be provided by alternative means, such as an employee. For example, the commenters suggested that a self-service check-in kiosk in a hotel need not comply with the reach range requirement so long as a guest can check in at the front desk nearby. Several commenters argued that the Department should not require that point-of-sale devices be accessible to individuals who are blind or have low vision (although complying with accessible route and reach range was acceptable), especially until the Department adopts specific standards governing such access.

The Department has decided not to add specific scoping or technical requirements for equipment and furniture in this final rule. Other provisions of the regulation, including those requiring reasonable modifications of policies, practices, or procedures, readily achievable barrier removal, and effective communication will require the provision of accessible equipment in appropriate circumstances. Because it is clear that many commenters want the Department to provide additional specific requirements for accessible equipment, the Department plans to initiate a rulemaking to address these issues in the near future.

Accessible golf cars. An accessible golf car means a device that is designed and manufactured to be driven on all areas of a golf course, is independently usable by individuals with mobility disabilities, has a hand-operated brake and accelerator, carries golf clubs in an accessible location, and has a seat that both swivels and raises to put the golfer in a standing or semi-standing position. The 1991 regulation contained no language specifically referencing accessible golf cars. After considering the comments addressing the ANPRM's proposed requirement that golf courses make at least one specialized golf car available for the use of individuals with disabilities, and the safety of accessible golf cars and their use on golf course greens, the Department stated in the NPRM that it would not issue regulations specific to golf cars.

The Department received many comments in response to its decision to propose no new regulation specific to accessible golf cars. The majority of commenters urged the Department to require golf courses to provide accessible golf cars. These comments came from individuals, disability advocacy and recreation groups, a manufacturer of accessible golf cars, and representatives of local government. Comments supporting the Department's decision not to propose a new regulation came from golf course owners, associations, and individuals.

Many commenters argued that while the existing title III regulation covered the issue, the Department should nonetheless adopt specific regulatory language requiring golf courses to provide accessible golf cars. Some commenters noted that many local governments and park authorities that operate public golf courses have already provided accessible golf cars. Experience indicates that such golf cars may be used without damaging courses. Some argued that having accessible golf cars would increase golf course revenue by enabling more golfers with disabilities to play the game. Several commenters requested that the Department adopt a regulation specifically requiring each golf course to provide one or more accessible golf cars. Other commenters recommended allowing golf courses to make "pooling" arrangements to meet demands for such cars. A few commenters expressed support for using accessible golf cars to accommodate golfers with and without disabilities. Commenters also pointed out that the Departments of the Interior and Defense have already mandated that golf courses under their jurisdictional control must make accessible golf cars available unless it can be demonstrated that doing so would change the fundamental nature of the game.

While an industry association argued that at least two models of accessible golf cars meet the specifications recognized in the field, and that accessible golf cars cause no more damage to greens or other parts of golf courses than players standing or walking across the course, other commenters expressed concerns about the potential for damage associated with the use of accessible golf cars. Citing safety concerns, golf organizations recommended that an industry safety standard be developed.

Although the Department declines to add specific scoping or technical requirements for golf cars to this final rule, the Department expects to address requirements for accessible golf cars in future rulemaking. In the meantime, the Department believes that golfers with disabilities who need accessible golf cars are protected by other existing provisions in the title III regulation, including those requiring reasonable modifications of policies, practices, or procedures, and readily achievable barrier removal.

Web site accessibility. Many commenters expressed disappointment that the NPRM did not specifically require title III-covered entities to make their Web sites, through which they offer goods and services, accessible to individuals with disabilities. Commenters urged the Department to require specifically that entities that provide goods or services on the Internet make their Web- sites accessible, regardless of whether or not these entities also have a "bricks and mortar' location. The commenters explained that such clarification was needed because of the current ambiguity caused by court decisions as to whether web-only businesses are covered under title III. Commenters argued that the cost of making Web sites accessible through Web site design is minimal, yet critical, to enabling individuals with disabilities to benefit from the goods and services an entity offers through its Web site. The Internet has become an essential tool for many Americans and, when accessible, provides individuals with disabilities great independence. Commenters recommended that, at a minimum, the Department require covered entities to meet the Electronic and Information Technology Accessibility Standards issued pursuant to section 508. Under section 508 of the Rehabilitation Act of 1973, Federal agencies are required to make their Web sites accessible. 29 U.S.C. 794(d); 36 CFR Part 1194.

The Department agrees that the ability to access the goods and services offered on the Internet through the Web sites of public accommodations is of great importance to individuals with disabilities, particularly those who are blind or who have low vision. When the ADA was enacted in 1990, the Internet was unknown to most of the public. Today, the Internet plays a critical role in daily life for personal, civic, commercial, and business purposes. In light of the growing importance of e-commerce, ensuring nondiscriminatory access to the goods and services offered through the Web sites of covered entities can play a significant role in fulfilling the goals of the ADA.

Although the language of the ADA does not explicitly mention the Internet, the Department has taken the position that title III covers access to Web sites of public accommodations. The Department has issued guidance on the ADA as applied to the Web sites of public entities, which includes the availability of standards for Web site accessibility. *See Accessibility of State and Local Government Websites to People with Disabilities* (June 2003), available at www.ada.gov/websites2. htm. As the Department stated in that publication, an agency (and similarly a public accommodation) with an inaccessible Web site also may meet its legal obligations by providing an accessible alternative for individuals to enjoy its goods or services, such as a staffed telephone information line. However, such an alternative must provide an equal degree of access in terms of hours of operation and range of options and programs available. For example, if retail goods or bank services are posted on an inaccessible Web site that is available 24 hours a day, 7 days a week to individuals without disabilities, then the alternative accessible method must also be available 24 hours a day, 7 days a week. Additional guidance is available in the Web Content Accessibility Guidelines (WCAG), available at http://www.w3.org/TR/WAIWEBCONTENT (last visited June 24, 2010), which are developed and maintained by the Web Accessibility Initiative, a subgroup of the World Wide Web Consortium (W3C®).

The Department did not issue proposed regulations as part of its NPRM, and thus is unable to issue specific regulatory language on Web site accessibility at this time. However, the Department expects to engage in rulemaking relating to Web site accessibility under the ADA in the near future.

Multiple chemical sensitivities. The Department received comments from a number of individuals asking the Department to add specific language to the final rule addressing the needs of individuals with chemical sensitivities. These commenters expressed concern that the presence of chemicals interferes with their ability to participate in a wide range of activities. These commenters also urged the Department to add multiple chemical sensitivities to the definition of a disability.

The Department has determined not to include specific provisions addressing multiple chemical sensitivities in the final rule. In order to be viewed as a disability under the ADA, an impairment must substantially limit one or more major life activities. An individual's major life activities of respiratory or neurological functioning may be substantially limited by allergies or sensitivity to a degree that he or she is a person with a disability. When a person has this type of disability, a covered entity may have to make reasonable modifications in its policies and practices for that person. However, this determination is an individual assessment and must be made on a case-by-case basis.

Chapter 8
DOJ 2010 ADA STANDARDS FOR ACCESSIBLE DESIGN

State and local government facilities must follow the requirements of the 2010 Standards, including both the Title II regulations at 28 CFR 35.151; and the 2004 ADAAG at 36 CFR part 1191, appendices B and D.

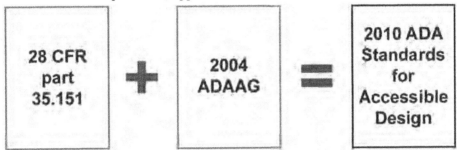

In the few places where requirements between the two differ, the requirements of 28 CFR 35.151 prevail.

Compliance Date for Title II

If the start date for construction is on or after March 15, 2012, all newly constructed or altered State and local government facilities must comply with the 2010 Standards. Before that date, the 1991 Standards (without the elevator exemption), the UFAS, or the 2010 Standards may be used for such projects when the start of construction commences on or after September 15, 2010.

CONTENTS

CONTENTS

Chapter 10: Recreation Facilities

28 CFR 35.151   New construction and alterations

(a)   Design and construction.

(1) Each facility or part of a facility constructed by, on behalf of, or for the use of a public entity shall be designed and constructed in such manner that the facility or part of the facility is readily accessible to and usable by individuals with disabilities, if the construction was commenced after January 26, 1992.

(2) Exception for structural impracticability.

(i) Full compliance with the requirements of this section is not required where a public entity can demonstrate that it is structurally impracticable to meet the requirements. Full compliance will be considered structurally impracticable only in those rare circumstances when the unique characteristics of terrain prevent the incorporation of accessibility features.

(ii) If full compliance with this section would be structurally impracticable, compliance with this section is required to the extent that it is not structurally impracticable. In that case, any portion of the facility that can be made accessible shall be made accessible to the extent that it is not structurally impracticable.

(iii) If providing accessibility in conformance with this section to individuals with certain disabilities (e.g., those who use wheelchairs) would be structurally impracticable, accessibility shall nonetheless be ensured to persons with other types of disabilities, (e.g., those who use crutches or who have sight, hearing, or mental impairments) in accordance with this section.

(b)   Alterations.

(1) Each facility or part of a facility altered by, on behalf of, or for the use of a public entity in a manner that affects or could affect the usability of the facility or part of the facility shall, to the maximum extent feasible, be altered in such manner that the altered portion of the facility is readily accessible to and usable by individuals with disabilities, if the alteration was commenced after January 26, 1992.

(2) The path of travel requirements of § 35.151(b)(4) shall apply only to alterations undertaken solely for purposes other than to meet the program accessibility requirements of § 35.150.

(3)

(i) Alterations to historic properties shall comply, to the maximum extent feasible, with the provisions applicable to historic properties in the design standards specified in § 35.151(c).

(ii) If it is not feasible to provide physical access to an historic property in a manner that will not threaten or destroy the historic significance of the building or facility, alternative methods of access shall be provided pursuant to the requirements of § 35.150.

(4) Path of travel. An alteration that affects or could affect the usability of or access to an area of a facility that contains a primary function shall be made so as to ensure that, to the maximum extent feasible, the path of travel to the altered area and the restrooms, telephones, and drinking fountains serving the altered area are readily accessible to and usable by individuals with disabilities, including individuals who use wheelchairs, unless the cost and scope of such alterations is disproportionate to the cost of the overall alteration.

(i) Primary function. A "primary function" is a major activity for which the facility is intended. Areas that contain a primary function include, but are not limited to, the dining area of a cafeteria, the meeting rooms in a conference center, as well as offices and other work areas in which the activities of the public entity using the facility are carried out.

(A) Mechanical rooms, boiler rooms, supply storage rooms, employee lounges or locker rooms, janitorial closets, entrances, and corridors are not areas containing a primary function. Restrooms are not areas containing a primary function unless the provision of restrooms is a primary purpose of the area, e.g., in highway rest stops.

(B) For the purposes of this section, alterations to windows, hardware, controls, electrical outlets, and signage shall not be deemed to be alterations that affect the usability of or access to an area containing a primary function.

(ii) A "path of travel" includes a continuous, unobstructed way of pedestrian passage by means of which the altered area may be approached, entered, and exited, and which connects the altered area with an exterior approach (including sidewalks, streets, and parking areas), an entrance to the facility, and other parts of the facility.

(A) An accessible path of travel may consist of walks and sidewalks, curb ramps and other interior or exterior pedestrian ramps; clear floor paths through lobbies, corridors, rooms, and other improved areas; parking access aisles; elevators and lifts; or a combination of these elements.

(B) For the purposes of this section, the term "path of travel" also includes the restrooms, telephones, and drinking fountains serving the altered area.

(C) Safe harbor. If a public entity has constructed or altered required elements of a path of travel in accordance with the specifications in either the 1991 Standards or the Uniform Federal Accessibility Standards before March 15, 2012, the public entity is not required to retrofit such elements to reflect incremental changes in the 2010 Standards solely because of an alteration to a primary function area served by that path of travel.

(iii)   Disproportionality

(A) Alterations made to provide an accessible path of travel to the altered area will be deemed disproportionate to the overall alteration when the cost exceeds 20 % of the cost of the alteration to the primary function area.

(B) Costs that may be counted as expenditures required to provide an accessible path of travel may include:

(1) Costs associated with providing an accessible entrance and an accessible route to the altered area, for example, the cost of widening doorways or installing ramps;

(2) Costs associated with making restrooms accessible, such as installing grab bars, enlarging toilet stalls, insulating pipes, or installing accessible faucet controls;

(3) Costs associated with providing accessible telephones, such as relocating the telephone to an accessible height, installing amplification devices, or installing a text telephone (TTY); and

(4) Costs associated with relocating an inaccessible drinking fountain.

(iv) Duty to provide accessible features in the event of disproportionality.

(A) When the cost of alterations necessary to make the path of travel to the altered area fully accessible is disproportionate to the cost of the overall alteration, the path of travel shall be made accessible to the extent that it can be made accessible without incurring disproportionate costs.

(B) In choosing which accessible elements to provide, priority should be given to those elements that will provide the greatest access, in the following order—

(1) An accessible entrance;

(2) An accessible route to the altered area;

(3) At least one accessible restroom for each sex or a single unisex restroom;

(4) Accessible telephones;

(5) Accessible drinking fountains; and

(6) When possible, additional accessible elements such as parking, storage, and alarms.

(v) Series of smaller alterations.

(A) The obligation to provide an accessible path of travel may not be evaded by performing a series of small alterations to the area served by a single path of travel if those alterations could have been performed as a single undertaking.

(B)

(1) If an area containing a primary function has been altered without providing an accessible path of travel to that area, and subsequent alterations of that area, or a different area on the same path of travel, are undertaken within three years of the original alteration, the total cost of

alterations to the primary function areas on that path of travel during the preceding three-year period shall be considered in determining whether the cost of making that path of travel accessible is disproportionate.

(2) Only alterations undertaken on or after March 15, 2011, shall be considered in determining if the cost of providing an accessible path of travel is disproportionate to the overall cost of the alterations.

(c)   Accessibility standards and compliance date.

(1) If physical construction or alterations commence after July 26, 1992, but prior to the September 15, 2010, then new construction and alterations subject to this section must comply with either the UFAS or the 1991 Standards except that the elevator exemption contained at section 4.1.3(5) and section 4.1.6(1)(k) of the 1991 Standards shall not apply. Departures from particular requirements of either standard by the use of other methods shall be permitted when it is clearly evident that equivalent access to the facility or part of the facility is thereby provided.

(2) If physical construction or alterations commence on or after September 15, 2010, and before March 15, 2012, then new construction and alterations subject to this section may comply with one of the following: the 2010 Standards, UFAS, or the 1991 Standards except that the elevator exemption contained at section 4.1.3(5) and section 4.1.6(1)(k) of the 1991 Standards shall not apply. Departures from particular requirements of either standard by the use of other methods shall be permitted when it is clearly evident that equivalent access to the facility or part of the facility is thereby provided.

(3) If physical construction or alterations commence on or after March 15, 2012, then new construction and alterations subject to this section shall comply with the 2010 Standards.

(4) For the purposes of this section, ceremonial groundbreaking or razing of structures prior to site preparation do not commence physical construction or alterations.

(5) Noncomplying new construction and alterations.

(i) Newly constructed or altered facilities or elements covered by §§ 35.151(a) or (b) that were constructed or altered before March 15, 2012, and that do not comply with the 1991 Standards or with UFAS shall before March 15, 2012, be made accessible in accordance with either the 1991 Standards, UFAS, or the 2010 Standards.

(ii) Newly constructed or altered facilities or elements covered by §§ 35.151(a) or (b) that were constructed or altered before March 15, 2012 and that do not comply with the 1991 Standards or with UFAS shall, on or after March 15, 2012, be made accessible in accordance with the 2010 Standards.

Appendix to 35.151(c)

Compliance Date for New Construction or Alterations	Applicable Standards
Before September 15, 2010	1991 Standards or UFAS
On or after September 15, 2010, and before March 15, 2012	1991 Standards, UFAS, or 2010 Standards
On or after March 15, 2012	2010 Standards

(d) Scope of coverage. The 1991 Standards and the 2010 Standards apply to fixed or built-in elements of buildings, structures, site improvements, and pedestrian routes or vehicular ways located on a site. Unless specifically stated otherwise, the advisory notes, appendix notes, and figures contained in the 1991 Standards and the 2010 Standards explain or illustrate the requirements of the rule; they do not establish enforceable requirements.

(e) Social service center establishments. Group homes, halfway houses, shelters, or similar social service center establishments that provide either temporary sleeping accommodations or residential dwelling units that are subject to this section shall comply with the provisions of the 2010 Standards applicable to residential facilities, including, but not limited to, the provisions in sections 233 and 809.

(1) In sleeping rooms with more than 25 beds covered by this section, a minimum of 5% of the beds shall have clear floor space complying with section 806.2.3 of the 2010 Standards.

(2) Facilities with more than 50 beds covered by this section that provide common use bathing facilities, shall provide at least one roll-in shower with a seat that complies with the relevant provisions of section 608 of the 2010 Standards. Transfer-type showers are not permitted in lieu of a roll-in shower with a seat, and the exceptions in sections 608.3 and 608.4 for residential dwelling units are not permitted. When separate shower facilities are provided for men and for women, at least one roll-in shower shall be provided for each group.

(f) Housing at a place of education. Housing at a place of education that is subject to this section shall comply with the provisions of the 2010 Standards applicable to transient lodging, including, but not limited to, the requirements for transient lodging guest rooms in sections 224 and 806 subject to the following exceptions. For the purposes of the application of this section, the term "sleeping room" is intended to be used interchangeably with the term "guest room" as it is used in the transient lodging standards.

(1) Kitchens within housing units containing accessible sleeping rooms with mobility features (including suites and clustered sleeping rooms) or on floors containing accessible sleeping rooms with mobility features shall provide turning spaces that comply with section 809.2.2 of the 2010 Standards and kitchen work surfaces that comply with section 804.3 of the 2010 Standards.

(2) Multi-bedroom housing units containing accessible sleeping rooms with mobility features shall have an accessible route throughout the unit in accordance

with section 809.2 of the 2010 Standards.

(3) Apartments or townhouse facilities that are provided by or on behalf of a place of education, which are leased on a year-round basis exclusively to graduate students or faculty, and do not contain any public use or common use areas available for educational programming, are not subject to the transient lodging standards and shall comply with the requirements for residential facilities in sections 233 and 809 of the 2010 Standards.

(g) Assembly areas. Assembly areas subject to this section shall comply with the provisions of the 2010 Standards applicable to assembly areas, including, but not limited to, sections 221 and 802. In addition, assembly areas shall ensure that—

(1) In stadiums, arenas, and grandstands, wheelchair spaces and companion seats are dispersed to all levels that include seating served by an accessible route;

(2) Assembly areas that are required to horizontally disperse wheelchair spaces and companion seats by section 221.2.3.1 of the 2010 Standards and have seating encircling, in whole or in part, a field of play or performance area shall disperse wheelchair spaces and companion seats around that field of play or performance area;

(3) Wheelchair spaces and companion seats are not located on (or obstructed by) temporary platforms or other movable structures, except that when an entire seating section is placed on temporary platforms or other movable structures in an area where fixed seating is not provided, in order to increase seating for an event, wheelchair spaces and companion seats may be placed in that section. When wheelchair spaces and companion seats are not required to accommodate persons eligible for those spaces and seats, individual, removable seats may be placed in those spaces and seats;

(4) Stadium-style movie theaters shall locate wheelchair spaces and companion seats on a riser or cross-aisle in the stadium section that satisfies at least one of the following criteria—

(i) It is located within the rear 60% of the seats provided in an auditorium; or

(ii) It is located within the area of an auditorium in which the vertical viewing angles (as measured to the top of the screen) are from the 40th to the 100th percentile of vertical viewing angles for all seats as ranked from the seats in the first row (1st percentile) to seats in the back row (100th percentile).

(h)   Medical care facilities. Medical care facilities that are subject to this section shall comply with the provisions of the 2010 Standards applicable to medical care facilities, including, but not limited to, sections 223 and 805. In addition, medical care facilities that do not specialize in the treatment of conditions that affect mobility shall disperse the accessible patient bedrooms required by section 223.2.1 of the 2010 Standards in a manner that is proportionate by type of medical specialty.

(i) Curb ramps.

(1) Newly constructed or altered streets, roads, and highways must contain curb ramps or other sloped areas at any intersection having curbs or other

barriers to entry from a street level pedestrian walkway.

(2) Newly constructed or altered street level pedestrian walkways must contain curb ramps or other sloped areas at intersections to streets, roads, or highways.

(j) Facilities with residential dwelling units for sale to individual owners.

(1) Residential dwelling units designed and constructed or altered by public entities that will be offered for sale to individuals shall comply with the requirements for residential facilities in the 2010 Standards including sections 233 and 809.

(2) The requirements of paragraph (1) also apply to housing programs that are operated by public entities where design and construction of particular residential dwelling units take place only after a specific buyer has been identified. In such programs, the covered entity must provide the units that comply with the requirements for accessible features to those pre-identified buyers with disabilities who have requested such a unit.

(k) Detention and correctional facilities.

(1) New construction of jails, prisons, and other detention and correctional facilities shall comply with the 2010 Standards except that public entities shall provide accessible mobility features complying with section 807.2 of the 2010 Standards for a minimum of 3%, but no fewer than one, of the total number of cells in a facility. Cells with mobility features shall be provided in each classification level.

(2) Alterations to detention and correctional facilities. Alterations to jails, prisons, and other detention and correctional facilities shall comply with the 2010 Standards except that public entities shall provide accessible mobility features complying with section 807.2 of the 2010 Standards for a minimum of 3%, but no fewer than one, of the total number of cells being altered until at least 3%, but no fewer than one, of the total number of cells in a facility shall provide mobility features complying with section 807.2. Altered cells with mobility features shall be provided in each classification level. However, when alterations are made to specific cells, detention and correctional facility operators may satisfy their obligation to provide the required number of cells with mobility features by providing the required mobility features in substitute cells (cells other than those where alterations are originally planned), provided that each substitute cell—

(i) Is located within the same prison site;

(ii) Is integrated with other cells to the maximum extent feasible;

(iii) Has, at a minimum, equal physical access as the altered cells to areas used by inmates or detainees for visitation, dining, recreation, educational programs, medical services, work programs, religious services, and participation in other programs that the facility offers to inmates or detainees; and,

(iv) If it is technically infeasible to locate a substitute cell within the same prison site, a substitute cell must be provided at another prison site within the corrections system.

(3) With respect to medical and long-term care facilities in jails, prisons, and other detention and correctional facilities, public entities shall apply the 2010 Standards technical and scoping requirements for those facilities irrespective of whether those facilities are licensed.

2010 STANDARDS FOR PUBLIC ACCOMMODATIONS AND COMMERCIAL FACILITIES: TITLE III

Public accommodations and commercial facilities must follow the requirements of the 2010 Standards, including both the Title III regulations at 28 CFR part 36, subpart D; and the 2004 ADAAG at 36 CFR part 1191, appendices B and D.

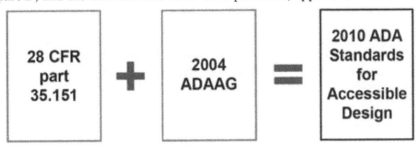

In the few places where requirements between the two differ, the requirements of 28 CFR part 36, subpart D prevail.

Compliance Date for Title III

The compliance date for the 2010 Standards for new construction and alterations is determined by:

- the date the last application for a building permit or permit extension is certified to be complete by a State, county, or local government;
- the date the last application for a building permit or permit extension is received by a State, county, or local government, where the government does not certify the completion of applications; or
- the start of physical construction or alteration, if no permit is required.

If that date is on or after March 15, 2012, then new construction and alterations must comply with the 2010 Standards. If that date is on or after September 15, 2010, and before March 15, 2012, then new construction and alterations must comply with either the 1991 or the 2010 Standards.

28 CFR part 36, subpart D – New Construction and Alterations

§ 36.401   New construction.

(a)   General.

(1) Except as provided in paragraphs (b) and (c) of this section, discrimination for purposes of this part includes a failure to design and construct facilities for first occupancy after January 26, 1993, that are readily accessible to and usable by individuals with disabilities.

(2) For purposes of this section, a facility is designed and constructed for first occupancy after January 26, 1993, only —

(i) If the last application for a building permit or permit extension for the facility is certified to be complete, by a State, County, or local government after January 26, 1992 (or, in those jurisdictions where the government does not certify completion of applications, if the last application for a building permit or permit extension for the facility is received by the State, County, or local government after January 26, 1992); and

(ii) If the first certificate of occupancy for the facility is issued after January 26, 1993.

(b)   Commercial facilities located in private residences.

(1) When a commercial facility is located in a private residence, the portion of the residence used exclusively as a residence is not covered by this subpart, but that portion used exclusively in the operation of the commercial facility or that portion used both for the commercial facility and for residential purposes is covered by the new construction and alterations requirements of this subpart.

(2) The portion of the residence covered under paragraph (b)(1) of this section extends to those elements used to enter the commercial facility, including the homeowner's front sidewalk, if any, the door or entryway, and hallways; and those portions of the residence, interior or exterior, available to or used by employees or visitors of the commercial facility, including restrooms.

(c)   Exception for structural impracticability.

(1) Full compliance with the requirements of this section is not required where an entity can demonstrate that it is structurally impracticable to meet the requirements. Full compliance will be considered structurally impracticable only in those rare circumstances when the unique characteristics of terrain prevent the incorporation of accessibility features.

(2) If full compliance with this section would be structurally impracticable, compliance with this section is required to the extent that it is not structurally impracticable. In that case, any portion of the facility that can be made accessible shall be made accessible to the extent that it is not structurally impracticable.

(3) If providing accessibility in conformance with this section to individuals with certain disabilities (e.g., those who use wheelchairs) would be structurally impracticable, accessibility shall nonetheless be ensured to persons with other types of disabilities (e.g., those who use crutches or who have sight, hearing, or mental impairments) in accordance with this section.

(d)   Elevator exemption.

(1) For purposes of this paragraph (d) —

(i) Professional office of a health care provider means a location where a person or entity regulated by a State to provide professional services related to the physical or mental health of an individual makes such services available to the public. The facility housing the "professional office of a health care provider" only includes floor levels housing at least one health care provider, or any floor level designed or intended for use by at least one health care provider.

(ii) Shopping center or shopping mall means —

(A) A building housing five or more sales or rental establishments; or

(B) A series of buildings on a common site, either under common ownership or common control or developed either as one project or as a series of related projects, housing five or more sales or rental establishments. For purposes of this section, places of public accommodation of the types listed in paragraph (5) of the definition of "place of public accommodation" in section § 36.104 are considered sales or rental establishments. The facility housing a "shopping center or shopping mall" only includes floor levels housing at least one sales or rental establishment, or any floor level designed or intended for use by at least one sales or rental establishment.

(2) This section does not require the installation of an elevator in a facility that is less than three stories or has less than 3000 square feet per story, except with respect to any facility that houses one or more of the following:

(i) A shopping center or shopping mall, or a professional office of a health care provider.

(ii) A terminal, depot, or other station used for specified public transportation, or an airport passenger terminal. In such a facility, any area housing passenger services, including boarding and debarking, loading and unloading, baggage claim, dining facilities, and other common areas open to the public, must be on an accessible route from an accessible entrance.

(3) The elevator exemption set forth in this paragraph (d) does not obviate or limit, in any way the obligation to comply with the other accessibility requirements established in paragraph (a) of this section. For example, in a facility that houses a shopping center or shopping mall, or a professional office of a health care provider, the floors that are above or below an accessible ground floor and that do not house sales or rental establishments or a professional office of a health care provider, must meet the requirements of this section but for the elevator.

§ 36.402 Alterations.

(a) General.

(1) Any alteration to a place of public accommodation or a commercial facility, after January 26, 1992, shall be made so as to ensure that, to the maximum extent feasible, the altered portions of the facility are readily accessible to and usable by individuals with disabilities, including individuals who use wheelchairs.

(2) An alteration is deemed to be undertaken after January 26, 1992, if the physical alteration of the property begins after that date.

(b) Alteration. For the purposes of this part, an alteration is a change to a place of public accommodation or a commercial facility that affects or could affect the usability of the building or facility or any part thereof.

(1) Alterations include, but are not limited to, remodeling, renovation, rehabilitation, reconstruction, historic restoration, changes or rearrangement in structural parts or elements, and changes or rearrangement in the plan configuration of walls and full-height partitions. Normal maintenance, reroofing, painting or wallpapering, asbestos removal, or changes to mechanical and electrical systems are not alterations unless they affect the usability of the building or facility.

(2) If existing elements, spaces, or common areas are altered, then each such altered element, space, or area shall comply with the applicable provisions of appendix A to this part.

(c) To the maximum extent feasible. The phrase "to the maximum extent feasible," as used in this section, applies to the occasional case where the nature of an existing facility makes it virtually impossible to comply fully with applicable accessibility standards through a planned alteration. In these circumstances, the alteration shall provide the maximum physical accessibility feasible. Any altered features of the facility that can be made accessible shall be made accessible. If providing accessibility in conformance with this section to individuals with certain disabilities (e.g., those who use wheelchairs) would not be feasible, the facility shall be made accessible to persons with other types of disabilities (e.g., those who use crutches, those who have impaired vision or hearing, or those who have other impairments).

§ 36.403   Alterations: Path of travel.

(a) General.

(1) An alteration that affects or could affect the usability of or access to an area of a facility that contains a primary function shall be made so as to ensure that, to the maximum extent feasible, the path of travel to the altered area and the restrooms, telephones, and drinking fountains serving the altered area, are readily accessible to and usable by individuals with disabilities, including individuals who use wheelchairs, unless the cost and scope of such alterations is disproportionate to the cost of the overall alteration.

(2) If a private entity has constructed or altered required elements of a path of travel at a place of public accommodation or commercial facility in accordance with the specifications in the 1991 Standards, the private entity is not required to retrofit such elements to reflect the incremental changes in the 2010 Standards solely because of an alteration to a primary function area served by that path of travel.

(b) Primary function. A "primary function" is a major activity for which the facility is intended. Areas that contain a primary function include, but are not limited to, the customer services lobby of a bank, the dining area of a cafeteria, the meeting rooms in a conference center, as well as offices and other work areas in which the activities of the public accommodation or other private entity using the facility are carried out. Mechanical rooms, boiler rooms, supply storage rooms, employee lounges or locker rooms, janitorial closets, entrances, corridors, and restrooms are not areas containing a primary function.

(c)   Alterations to an area containing a primary function.

(1) Alterations that affect the usability of or access to an area containing a primary function include, but are not limited to —

(i) Remodeling merchandise display areas or employee work areas in a department store;

(ii) Replacing an inaccessible floor surface in the customer service or employee work areas of a bank;

(iii) Redesigning the assembly line area of a factory; or

(iv) Installing a computer center in an accounting firm.

(2) For the purposes of this section, alterations to windows, hardware, controls, electrical outlets, and signage shall not be deemed to be alterations that affect the usability of or access to an area containing a primary function.

(d)   Landlord/tenant: If a tenant is making alterations as defined in § 36.402 that would trigger the requirements of this section, those alterations by the tenant in areas that only the tenant occupies do not trigger a path of travel obligation upon the landlord with respect to areas of the facility under the landlord's authority, if those areas are not otherwise being altered.

(e)   Path of travel.

(1) A "path of travel" includes a continuous, unobstructed way of pedestrian passage by means of which the altered area may be approached, entered, and exited, and which connects the altered area with an exterior approach (including sidewalks, streets, and parking areas), an entrance to the facility, and other parts of the facility.

(2) An accessible path of travel may consist of walks and sidewalks, curb ramps and other interior or exterior pedestrian ramps; clear floor paths through lobbies, corridors, rooms, and other improved areas; parking access aisles; elevators and lifts; or a combination of these elements.

(3) For the purposes of this part, the term "path of travel" also includes the restrooms, telephones, and drinking fountains serving the altered area.

(f)   Disproportionality.

(1) Alterations made to provide an accessible path of travel to the altered area will be deemed disproportionate to the overall alteration when the cost exceeds 20% of the cost of the alteration to the primary function area.

(2) Costs that may be counted as expenditures required to provide an accessible path of travel may include:

(i) Costs associated with providing an accessible entrance and an accessible route to the altered area, for example, the cost of widening doorways or installing ramps;

(ii) Costs associated with making restrooms accessible, such as installing grab bars, enlarging toilet stalls, insulating pipes, or installing accessible faucet controls;

(iii) Costs associated with providing accessible telephones, such as relocating the telephone to an accessible height, installing amplification devices, or installing a text telephone (TTY);

(iv) Costs associated with relocating an inaccessible drinking fountain.

(g) Duty to provide accessible features in the event of disproportionality.

(1) When the cost of alterations necessary to make the path of travel to the altered area fully accessible is disproportionate to the cost of the overall alteration, the path of travel shall be made accessible to the extent that it can be made accessible without incurring disproportionate costs.

(2) In choosing which accessible elements to provide, priority should be given to those elements that will provide the greatest access, in the following order:

(i) An accessible entrance;

(ii) An accessible route to the altered area;

(iii) At least one accessible restroom for each sex or a single unisex restroom;

(iv) Accessible telephones;

(v) Accessible drinking fountains; and

(vi) When possible, additional accessible elements such as parking, storage, and alarms.

(h) Series of smaller alterations.

(1) The obligation to provide an accessible path of travel may not be evaded by performing a series of small alterations to the area served by a single path of travel if those alterations could have been performed as a single undertaking.

(2)

(i) If an area containing a primary function has been altered without providing an accessible path of travel to that area, and subsequent alterations of that area, or a different area on the same path of travel, are undertaken within three years of the original alteration, the total cost of alterations to the primary function areas on that path of travel during the preceding three year period shall be considered in determining whether the cost of making that path of travel accessible is disproportionate.

(ii) Only alterations undertaken after January 26, 1992, shall be considered in determining if the cost of providing an accessible path of travel is disproportionate to the overall cost of the alterations.

§ 36.404   Alterations: Elevator exemption.

(a) This section does not require the installation of an elevator in an altered facility that is less than three stories or has less than 3,000 square feet per story, except with respect to any facility that houses a shopping center, a shopping mall, the professional office of a health care provider, a terminal, depot, or other station used for specified public transportation, or an airport passenger terminal.

(1) For the purposes of this section, professional office of a health care provider means a location where a person or entity regulated by a State to provide professional services related to the physical or mental health of an individual makes such services available to the public. The facility that houses a professional office of a health care provider only includes floor levels housing by at least one health care provider, or any floor level designed or intended for use by at least one health care provider.

(2) For the purposes of this section, shopping center or shopping mall means —

(i) A building housing five or more sales or rental establishments; or

(ii) A series of buildings on a common site, connected by a common pedestrian access route above or below the ground floor, that is either under common ownership or common control or developed either as one project or as a series of related projects, housing five or more sales or rental establishments. For purposes of this section, places of public accommodation of the types listed in paragraph (5) of the definition of place of public accommodation in § 36.104 are considered sales or rental establishments. The facility housing a "shopping center or shopping mall" only includes floor levels housing at least one sales or rental establishment, or any floor level designed or intended for use by at least one sales or rental establishment.

(b) The exemption provided in paragraph (a) of this section does not obviate or limit in any way the obligation to comply with the other accessibility requirements established in this subpart. For example, alterations to floors above or below the accessible ground floor must be accessible regardless of whether the altered facility has an elevator.

§ 36.405   Alterations: Historic preservation.

(a) Alterations to buildings or facilities that are eligible for listing in the National Register of Historic Places under the National Historic Preservation Act (16 U.S.C. 470 et seq.) or are designated as historic under State or local law, shall comply to the maximum extent feasible with this part.

(b) If it is determined that it is not feasible to provide physical access to an historic property that is a place of public accommodation in a manner that will not threaten or destroy the historic significance of the building or the facility, alternative methods of access shall be provided pursuant to the requirements of subpart C of this part.

§ 36.406   Standards for new construction and alterations.

(a)   Accessibility standards and compliance date.

(1) New construction and alterations subject to §§ 36.401 or 36.402 shall comply with the 1991 Standards if the date when the last application for a building permit

or permit extension is certified to be complete by a State, county, or local government (or, in those jurisdictions where the government does not certify completion of applications, if the date when the last application for a building permit or permit extension is received by the State, county, or local government) is before September 15, 2010, or if no permit is required, if the start of physical construction or alterations occurs before September 15, 2010.

(2) New construction and alterations subject to §§ 36.401 or 36.402 shall comply either with the 1991 Standards or with the 2010 Standards if the date when the last application for a building permit or permit extension is certified to be complete by a State, county, or local government (or, in those jurisdictions where the government does not certify completion of applications, if the date when the last application for a building permit or permit extension is received by the State, county, or local government) is on or after September 15, 2010, and before March 15, 2012, or if no permit is required, if the start of physical construction or alterations occurs on or after September 15, 2010, and before March 15, 2012.

(3) New construction and alterations subject to §§ 36.401 or 36.402 shall comply with the 2010 Standards if the date when the last application for a building permit or permit extension is certified to be complete by a State, county, or local government (or, in those jurisdictions where the government does not certify completion of applications, if the date when the last application for a building permit or permit extension is received by the State, county, or local government) is on or after March 15, 2012, or if no permit is required, if the start of physical construction or alterations occurs on or after March 15, 2012.

(4) For the purposes of this section, "start of physical construction or alterations" does not mean ceremonial groundbreaking or razing of structures prior to site preparation.

(5) Noncomplying new construction and alterations.

(i) Newly constructed or altered facilities or elements covered by §§ 36.401 or 36.402 that were constructed or altered before March 15, 2012 and that do not comply with the 1991 Standards shall, before March 15, 2012, be made accessible in accordance with either the 1991 Standards or the 2010 Standards.

(ii) Newly constructed or altered facilities or elements covered by §§ 36.401 or 36.402 that were constructed or altered before March 15, 2012 and that do not comply with the 1991 Standards shall, on or after March 15, 2012, be made accessible in accordance with the 2010 Standards.

Appendix to 36.406(a)

Compliance Dates for New Construction and Alterations	Applicable Standards
On or after January 26, 1993 and before September 15, 2010	1991 Standards
On or after September 15, 2010, and before March 15, 2012	1991 Standards or 2010 Standards
On or after March 15, 2012	2010 Standards

(b)   Scope of coverage. The 1991 Standards and the 2010 Standards apply to fixed or built-in elements of buildings, structures, site improvements, and pedestrian routes or vehicular ways located on a site. Unless specifically stated otherwise, advisory notes, appendix notes, and figures contained in the 1991 Standards and 2010 Standards explain or illustrate the requirements of the rule; they do not establish enforceable requirements.

(c)   Places of lodging. Places of lodging subject to this part shall comply with the provisions of the 2010 Standards applicable to transient lodging, including, but not limited to, the requirements for transient lodging guest rooms in sections 224 and 806 of the 2010 Standards.

(1)   Guest rooms. Guest rooms with mobility features in places of lodging subject to the transient lodging requirements of 2010 Standards shall be provided as follows —

(i) Facilities that are subject to the same permit application on a common site that each have 50 or fewer guest rooms may be combined for the purposes of determining the required number of accessible rooms and type of accessible bathing facility in accordance with table 224.2 to section 224.2 of the 2010 Standards.

(ii) Facilities with more than 50 guest rooms shall be treated separately for the purposes of determining the required number of accessible rooms and type of accessible bathing facility in accordance with table 224.2 to section 224.2 of the 2010 Standards.

(2)   Exception. Alterations to guest rooms in places of lodging where the guest rooms are not owned or substantially controlled by the entity that owns, leases, or operates the overall facility and the physical features of the guest room interiors are controlled by their individual owners are not required to comply with § 36.402 or the alterations requirements in section 224.1.1 of the 2010 Standards.

(3) Facilities with residential units and transient lodging units. Residential dwelling units that are designed and constructed for residential use exclusively are not subject to the transient lodging standards.

(d)   Social service center establishments. Group homes, halfway houses, shelters, or similar social service center establishments that provide either temporary sleeping accommodations or residential dwelling units that are subject to this part shall comply with the provisions of the 2010 Standards applicable to residential facilities, including, but not limited to, the provisions in sections 233 and 809.

(1) In sleeping rooms with more than 25 beds covered by this part, a minimum of 5% of the beds shall have clear floor space complying with section 806.2.3 of the 2010 Standards.

(2) Facilities with more than 50 beds covered by this part that provide common use bathing facilities shall provide at least one roll-in shower with a seat that complies with the relevant provisions of section 608 of the 2010 Standards. Transfer-type showers are not permitted in lieu of a roll-in shower with a seat, and the exceptions in sections 608.3 and 608.4 for residential dwelling units are

not permitted. When separate shower facilities are provided for men and for women, at least one roll-in shower shall be provided for each group.

(e) Housing at a place of education. Housing at a place of education that is subject to this part shall comply with the provisions of the 2010 Standards applicable to transient lodging, including, but not limited to, the requirements for transient lodging guest rooms in sections 224 and 806, subject to the following exceptions. For the purposes of the application of this section, the term "sleeping room" is intended to be used interchangeably with the term "guest room" as it is used in the transient lodging standards.

(1) Kitchens within housing units containing accessible sleeping rooms with mobility features (including suites and clustered sleeping rooms) or on floors containing accessible sleeping rooms with mobility features shall provide turning spaces that comply with section 809.2.2 of the 2010 Standards and kitchen work surfaces that comply with section 804.3 of the 2010 Standards.

(2) Multi-bedroom housing units containing accessible sleeping rooms with mobility features shall have an accessible route throughout the unit in accordance with section 809.2 of the 2010 Standards.

(3) Apartments or townhouse facilities that are provided by or on behalf of a place of education, which are leased on a year-round basis exclusively to graduate students or faculty and do not contain any public use or common use areas available for educational programming, are not subject to the transient lodging standards and shall comply with the requirements for residential facilities in sections 233 and 809 of the 2010 Standards.

(f) Assembly areas. Assembly areas that are subject to this part shall comply with the provisions of the 2010 Standards applicable to assembly areas, including, but not limited to, sections 221 and 802. In addition, assembly areas shall ensure that —

(1) In stadiums, arenas, and grandstands, wheelchair spaces and companion seats are dispersed to all levels that include seating served by an accessible route;

(2) In assembly areas that are required to horizontally disperse wheelchair spaces and companion seats by section 221.2.3.1 of the 2010 Standards and that have seating encircling, in whole or in part, a field of play or performance, wheelchair spaces and companion seats are dispersed around that field of play or performance area;

(3) Wheelchair spaces and companion seats are not located on (or obstructed by) temporary platforms or other movable structures, except that when an entire seating section is placed on temporary platforms or other movable structures in an area where fixed seating is not provided, in order to increase seating for an event, wheelchair spaces and companion seats may be placed in that section. When wheelchair spaces and companion seats are not required to accommodate persons eligible for those spaces and seats, individual, removable seats may be placed in those spaces and seats;

(4) In stadium-style movie theaters, wheelchair spaces and companion seats are located on a riser or cross-aisle in the stadium section that satisfies at least

one of the following criteria —

(i) It is located within the rear 60% of the seats provided in an auditorium; or

(ii) It is located within the area of an auditorium in which the vertical viewing angles (as measured to the top of the screen) are from the 40th to the 100th percentile of vertical viewing angles for all seats as ranked from the seats in the first row (1st percentile) to seats in the back row (100th percentile).

(g) Medical care facilities. Medical care facilities that are subject to this part shall comply with the provisions of the 2010 Standards applicable to medical care facilities, including, but not limited to, sections 223 and 805. In addition, medical care facilities that do not specialize in the treatment of conditions that affect mobility shall disperse the accessible patient bedrooms required by section 223.2.1 of the 2010 Standards in a manner that is proportionate by type of medical specialty.

§ 36.407–36.499   [Reserved]

2010 STANDARDS FOR TITLES II AND III FACILITIES: 2004 ADAAG

The following section applies to **both** State and local government facilities (Title II) and public accommodations and commercial facilities (Title III). The section consists of (ADA) Chapters 1 and 2 and Chapters 3 through 10, of the 2004 ADAAG (36 CFR part 1191, appendices B and D, adopted as part of both the Title II and Title III 2010 Standards).

State and local government facilities must follow the requirements of the 2010 Standards, including both the Title II regulations at 28 CFR 35.151; and the 2004 ADAAG at 36 CFR part 1191, appendices B and D.

Public accommodations and commercial facilities must follow the requirements of the 2010 Standards, including both the Title III regulations at 28 CFR part 36, subpart D; and the 2004 ADAAG at 36 CFR part 1191, appendices B and D.

In the few places where requirements between the regulation and the 2004 ADAAG differ, the requirements of 28 CFR 35.151 or 28 CFR part 36, subpart D, prevail.

CHAPTER 1: APPLICATION AND ADMINISTRATION

101 Purpose

101.1 General. This document contains scoping and technical requirements for accessibility to sites, facilities, buildings, and elements by individuals with disabilities. The requirements are to be applied during the design, construction, additions to, and alteration of sites, facilities, buildings, and elements to the extent required by regulations issued by Federal agencies under the Americans with Disabilities Act of 1990 (ADA).

Advisory 101.1 General.

In addition to these requirements, covered entities must comply with the regulations issued by the Department of Justice and the Department of Transportation under the Americans with Disabilities Act. There are issues affecting individuals with disabilities which are not addressed by these requirements, but which are covered by the Department of Justice and the Department of Transportation regulations.

101.2 Effect on Removal of Barriers in Existing Facilities. This document does not address existing facilities unless altered at the discretion of a covered entity. The Department of Justice has authority over existing facilities that are subject to the requirement for removal of barriers under Title III of the ADA. Any determination that this document applies to existing facilities subject to the barrier removal requirement is solely within the discretion of the Department of Justice and is effective only to the extent required by regulations issued by the Department of Justice.

102 Dimensions for Adults and Children

The technical requirements are based on adult dimensions and anthropometrics. In addition, this document includes technical requirements based on children's dimensions and anthropometrics for drinking fountains, water closets, toilet compartments, lavatories and sinks, dining surfaces, and work surfaces.

103 Equivalent Facilitation

Nothing in these requirements prevents the use of designs, products, or technologies as alternatives to those prescribed, provided they result in substantially equivalent or greater accessibility and usability.

Advisory 103 Equivalent Facilitation.

The responsibility for demonstrating equivalent facilitation in the event of a challenge rests with the covered entity. With the exception of transit facilities, which are covered by regulations issued by the Department of Transportation, there is no process for certifying that an alternative design provides equivalent facilitation.

104 Conventions

104.1 Dimensions. Dimensions that are not stated as "maximum" or "minimum" are absolute.

104.1.1 Construction and Manufacturing Tolerances. All dimensions are subject to conventional industry tolerances except where the requirement is stated as a range with specific minimum and maximum end points.

Advisory 104.1.1 Construction and Manufacturing Tolerances.

Conventional industry tolerances recognized by this provision include those for field conditions and those that may be a necessary consequence of a particular manufacturing process. Recognized tolerances are not intended to apply to design work.

It is good practice when specifying dimensions to avoid specifying a tolerance where dimensions are absolute. For example, if this document requires "1 inches," avoid specifying "1 inches plus or minus X inches."

Where the requirement states a specified range, such as in Section 609.4 where grab bars must be installed between 33 inches and 36 inches above the floor, the range provides an adequate tolerance and therefore no tolerance outside of the range at either end point is permitted.

Where a requirement is a minimum or a maximum dimension that does not have two specific minimum and maximum end points, tolerances may apply. Where an element is to be installed at the minimum or maximum permitted dimension, such as "15 inches minimum" or "5 pounds maximum", it would not be good practice to specify "5 pounds (plus X pounds) or 15 inches (minus X inches)." Rather, it would be good practice to specify a dimension less than the required maximum (or more than the required minimum) by the amount of the expected field or manufacturing tolerance and not to state any tolerance in conjunction with the specified dimension.

Specifying dimensions in design in the manner described above will better ensure that facilities and elements accomplish the level of accessibility intended by these requirements. It will also more often produce an end result of strict and literal compliance with the stated requirements and eliminate enforcement difficulties and issues that might otherwise arise. Information on specific tolerances may be available from industry or trade organizations, code groups and building officials, and published references.

104.2 Calculation of Percentages. Where the required number of elements or facilities to be provided is determined by calculations of ratios or percentages and remainders or fractions result, the next greater whole number of such elements or facilities shall be provided. Where the determination of the required size or dimension of an element or facility involves ratios or percentages, rounding down for values less than one half shall be permitted.

104.3 Figures. Unless specifically stated otherwise, figures are provided for informational purposes only.

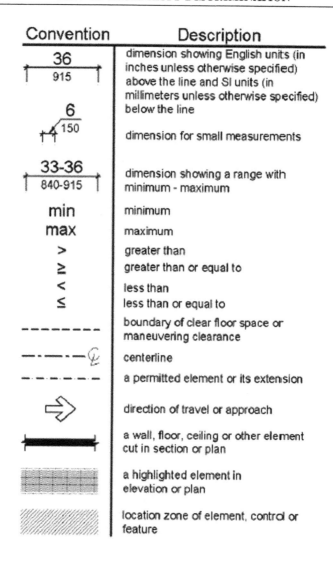

Convention	Description
36 / 915	dimension showing English units (in inches unless otherwise specified) above the line and SI units (in millimeters unless otherwise specified) below the line
6 / 150	dimension for small measurements
33-36 / 840-915	dimension showing a range with minimum - maximum
min	minimum
max	maximum
>	greater than
≥	greater than or equal to
<	less than
≤	less than or equal to
	boundary of clear floor space or maneuvering clearance
	centerline
	a permitted element or its extension
	direction of travel or approach
	a wall, floor, ceiling or other element cut in section or plan
	a highlighted element in elevation or plan
	location zone of element, control or feature

Figure 104

Graphic Convention for Figures

105   Referenced Standards

105.1   General. The standards listed in 105.2 are incorporated by reference in this document and are part of the requirements to the prescribed extent of each such reference. The Director of the Federal Register has approved these standards for incorporation by reference in accordance with 5 U.S.C. 552(a) and 1 CFR part 51. Copies of the referenced standards may be inspected at the Architectural and Transportation Barriers Compliance Board, 1331 F Street, NW, Suite 1000, Washington, DC 20004; at the Department of Justice, Civil Rights Division,

Disability Rights Section, 1425 New York Avenue, NW, Washington, DC; at the Department of Transportation, 400 Seventh Street, SW, Room 10424, Washington DC; or at the National Archives and Records Administration (NARA). For information on the availability of this material at NARA, call (202) 741-6030, or go to http://www.archives.gov/federal_register/code_of_federal_regulations/ibr_locations.html.

105.2 Referenced Standards. The specific edition of the standards listed below are referenced in this document. Where differences occur between this document and the referenced standards, this document applies.

105.2.1 ANSI/BHMA. Copies of the referenced standards may be obtained from the Builders Hardware Manufacturers Association, 355 Lexington Avenue, 17th floor, New York, NY 10017 (http://www.buildershardware.com).

ANSI/BHMA A156.10-1999 American National Standard for Power Operated Pedestrian Doors (see 404.3).

ANSI/BHMA A156.19-1997 American National Standard for Power Assist and Low Energy Power Operated Doors (see 404.3, 408.3.2.1, and 409.3.1).

ANSI/BHMA A156.19-2002 American National Standard for Power Assist and Low Energy Power Operated Doors (see 404.3, 408.3.2.1, and 409.3.1).

Advisory 105.2.1 ANSI/BHMA.

ANSI/BHMA A156.10-1999 applies to power operated doors for pedestrian use which open automatically when approached by pedestrians. Included are provisions intended to reduce the chance of user injury or entrapment.

ANSI/BHMA A156.19-1997 and A156.19-2002 applies to power assist doors, low energy power operated doors or low energy power open doors for pedestrian use not provided for in ANSI/BHMA A156.10 for Power Operated Pedestrian Doors. Included are provisions intended to reduce the chance of user injury or entrapment.

105.2.2 ASME. Copies of the referenced standards may be obtained from the American Society of Mechanical Engineers, Three Park Avenue, New York, New York 10016 (http://www.asme.org).

ASME A17.1- 2000 Safety Code for Elevators and Escalators, including ASME A17.1a-2002 Addenda and ASME A17.1b-2003 Addenda (see 407.1, 408.1, 409.1, and 810.9).

ASME A18.1-1999 Safety Standard for Platform Lifts and Stairway Chairlifts, including ASME A18.1a-2001 Addenda and ASME A18.1b-2001 Addenda (see 410.1).

ASME A18.1-2003 Safety Standard for Platform Lifts and Stairway Chairlifts, (see 410.1).

Advisory 105.2.2 ASME.

ASME A17.1-2000 is used by local jurisdictions throughout the United States for the design, construction, installation, operation, inspection, testing, maintenance, alteration, and repair of elevators and escalators. The majority of the requirements apply to the operational machinery not seen or used by elevator passengers. ASME A17.1 requires a two-way means of emergency communications in passenger elevators. This means of communication must connect with emergency or authorized personnel and not an automated answering system. The communication system must be push button activated. The activation button must be permanently identified with the word "HELP." A visual indication acknowledging the establishment of a communications link to authorized personnel must be provided. The visual indication must remain on until the call is terminated by authorized personnel. The building location, the elevator car number, and the need for assistance must be provided to authorized personnel answering the emergency call. The use of a handset by the communications system is prohibited. Only the authorized personnel answering the call can terminate the call. Operating instructions for the communications system must be provided in the elevator car.

The provisions for escalators require that at least two flat steps be provided at the entrance and exit of every escalator and that steps on escalators be demarcated by yellow lines 2 inches wide maximum along the back and sides of steps.

ASME A18.1-1999 and ASME A18.1-2003 address the design, construction, installation, operation, inspection, testing, maintenance and repair of lifts that are intended for transportation of persons with disabilities. Lifts are classified as: vertical platform lifts, inclined platform lifts, inclined stairway chairlifts, private residence vertical platform lifts, private residence inclined platform lifts, and private residence inclined stairway chairlifts.

This document does not permit the use of inclined stairway chairlifts which do not provide platforms because such lifts require the user to transfer to a seat.

ASME A18.1 contains requirements for runways, which are the spaces in which platforms or seats move. The standard includes additional provisions for runway enclosures, electrical equipment and wiring, structural support, headroom clearance (which is 80 inches minimum), lower level access ramps and pits. The enclosure walls not used for entry or exit are required to have a grab bar the full length of the wall on platform lifts. Access ramps are required to meet requirements similar to those for ramps in Chapter 4 of this document.

Each of the lift types addressed in ASME A18.1 must meet requirements for capacity, load, speed, travel, operating devices, and control equipment. The maximum permitted height for operable parts is consistent with Section 308 of this document. The standard also addresses attendant operation. However, Section 410.1 of this document does not permit attendant operation.

105.2.3 ASTM. Copies of the referenced standards may be obtained from the American Society for Testing and Materials, 100 Bar Harbor Drive, West Conshohocken, Pennsylvania 19428 (http://www.astm.org).

ASTM F 1292-99 Standard Specification for Impact Attenuation of Surface Systems Under and Around Playground Equipment (see 1008.2.6.2).

ASTM F 1292-04 Standard Specification for Impact Attenuation of Surfacing

Materials Within the Use Zone of Playground Equipment (see 1008.2.6.2).

ASTM F 1487-01 Standard Consumer Safety Performance Specification for Playground Equipment for Public Use (see 106.5).

ASTM F 1951-99 Standard Specification for Determination of Accessibility of Surface Systems Under and Around Playground Equipment (see 1008.2.6.1).

Advisory 105.2.3 ASTM.

ASTM F 1292-99 and ASTM F 1292-04 establish a uniform means to measure and compare characteristics of surfacing materials to determine whether materials provide a safe surface under and around playground equipment. These standards are referenced in the play areas requirements of this document when an accessible surface is required inside a play area use zone where a fall attenuating surface is also required. The standards cover the minimum impact attenuation requirements, when tested in accordance with Test Method F 355, for surface systems to be used under and around any piece of playground equipment from which a person may fall.

ASTM F 1487-01 establishes a nationally recognized safety standard for public playground equipment to address injuries identified by the U.S. Consumer Product Safety Commission. It defines the use zone, which is the ground area beneath and immediately adjacent to a play structure or play equipment designed for unrestricted circulation around the equipment and on whose surface it is predicted that a user would land when falling from or exiting a play structure or equipment. The play areas requirements in this document reference the ASTM F 1487 standard when defining accessible routes that overlap use zones requiring fall attenuating surfaces. If the use zone of a playground is not entirely surfaced with an accessible material, at least one accessible route within the use zone must be provided from the perimeter to all accessible play structures or components within the playground.

ASTM F 1951-99 establishes a uniform means to measure the characteristics of surface systems in order to provide performance specifications to select materials for use as an accessible surface under and around playground equipment. Surface materials that comply with this standard and are located in the use zone must also comply with ASTM F 1292. The test methods in this standard address access for children and adults who may traverse the surfacing to aid children who are playing. When a surface is tested it must have an average work per foot value for straight propulsion and for turning less than the average work per foot values for straight propulsion and for turning, respectively, on a hard, smooth surface with a grade of 7% (1:14).

105.2.4 ICC/IBC. Copies of the referenced standard may be obtained from the International Code Council, 5203 Leesburg Pike, Suite 600, Falls Church, Virginia 22041 (www.iccsafe.org).

International Building Code, 2000 Edition (see 207.1, 207.2, 216.4.2, 216.4.3, and 1005.2.1).

International Building Code, 2001 Supplement (see 207.1 and 207.2).

International Building Code, 2003 Edition (see 207.1, 207.2, 216.4.2, 216.4.3, and 1005.2.1).

Advisory 105.2.4 ICC/IBC.

International Building Code (IBC)-2000 (including 2001 Supplement to the International Codes) and IBC-2003 are referenced for means of egress, areas of refuge, and railings provided on fishing piers and platforms. At least one accessible means of egress is required for every accessible space and at least two accessible means of egress are required where more than one means of egress is required. The technical criteria for accessible means of egress allow the use of exit stairways and evacuation elevators when provided in conjunction with horizontal exits or areas of refuge. While typical elevators are not designed to be used during an emergency evacuation, evacuation elevators are designed with standby power and other features according to the elevator safety standard and can be used for the evacuation of individuals with disabilities. The IBC also provides requirements for areas of refuge, which are fire-rated spaces on levels above or below the exit discharge levels where people unable to use stairs can go to register a call for assistance and wait for evacuation.

The recreation facilities requirements of this document references two sections in the IBC for fishing piers and platforms. An exception addresses the height of the railings, guards, or handrails where a fishing pier or platform is required to include a guard, railing, or handrail higher than 34 inches (865 mm) above the ground or deck surface.

105.2.5 NFPA. Copies of the referenced standards may be obtained from the National Fire Protection Association, 1 Batterymarch Park, Quincy, Massachusetts 02169-7471, (http://www.nfpa.org).

NFPA 72 National Fire Alarm Code, 1999 Edition (see 702.1 and 809.5.2).

NFPA 72 National Fire Alarm Code, 2002 Edition (see 702.1 and 809.5.2).

Advisory 105.2.5 NFPA.

NFPA 72-1999 and NFPA 72-2002 address the application, installation, performance, and maintenance of protective signaling systems and their components. The NFPA 72 incorporates Underwriters Laboratory (UL) 1971 by reference. The standard specifies the characteristics of audible alarms, such as placement and sound levels. However, Section 702 of these requirements limits the volume of an audible alarm to 110 dBA, rather than the maximum 120 dBA permitted by NFPA 72-1999.

NFPA 72 specifies characteristics for visible alarms, such as flash frequency, color, intensity, placement, and synchronization. However, Section 702 of this document requires that visual alarm appliances be permanently installed. UL 1971 specifies intensity dispersion requirements for visible alarms. In particular, NFPA 72 requires visible alarms to have a light source that is clear or white and has polar dispersion complying with UL 1971.

106   Definitions

106.1   General. For the purpose of this document, the terms defined in 106.5 have the indicated meaning.

Advisory 106.1 General.

Terms defined in Section 106.5 are italicized in the text of this document.

106.2   Terms Defined in Referenced Standards. Terms not defined in 106.5 or in regulations issued by the Department of Justice and the Department of Transportation to implement the Americans with Disabilities Act, but specifically defined in a referenced standard, shall have the specified meaning from the referenced standard unless otherwise stated.

106.3   Undefined Terms. The meaning of terms not specifically defined in 106.5 or in regulations issued by the Department of Justice and the Department of Transportation to implement the Americans with Disabilities Act or in referenced standards shall be as defined by collegiate dictionaries in the sense that the context implies.

106.4   Interchangeability. Words, terms and phrases used in the singular include the plural and those used in the plural include the singular.

106.5   Defined Terms. Accessible. A site, building, facility, or portion thereof that complies with this part.

Accessible Means of Egress. A continuous and unobstructed way of egress travel from any point in a building or facility that provides an accessible route to an area of refuge, a horizontal exit, or a public way.

Addition. An expansion, extension, or increase in the gross floor area or height of a building or facility.

Administrative Authority. A governmental agency that adopts or enforces regulations and guidelines for the design, construction, or alteration of buildings and facilities.

Alteration. A change to a building or facility that affects or could affect the usability of the building or facility or portion thereof. Alterations include, but are not limited to, remodeling, renovation, rehabilitation, reconstruction, historic restoration, resurfacing of circulation paths or vehicular ways, changes or rearrangement of the structural parts or elements, and changes or rearrangement in the plan configuration of walls and full-height partitions. Normal maintenance, reroofing, painting or wallpapering, or changes to mechanical and electrical systems are not alterations unless they affect the usability of the building or facility.

Amusement Attraction. Any facility, or portion of a facility, located within an amusement park or theme park which provides amusement without the use of an amusement device. Amusement attractions include, but are not limited to, fun houses, barrels, and other attractions without seats.

Amusement Ride. A system that moves persons through a fixed course within a defined area for the purpose of amusement.

Amusement Ride Seat. A seat that is built-in or mechanically fastened to an amusement ride intended to be occupied by one or more passengers.

Area of Sport Activity. That portion of a room or space where the play or practice of a sport occurs.

Assembly Area. A building or facility, or portion thereof, used for the purpose of entertainment, educational or civic gatherings, or similar purposes. For the purposes of these requirements, assembly areas include, but are not limited to, classrooms, lecture halls, courtrooms, public meeting rooms, public hearing rooms, legislative chambers, motion picture houses, auditoria, theaters, playhouses, dinner theaters, concert halls, centers for the performing arts, amphitheaters, arenas, stadiums, grandstands, or convention centers.

Assistive Listening System (ALS). An amplification system utilizing transmitters, receivers, and coupling devices to bypass the acoustical space between a sound source and a listener by means of induction loop, radio frequency, infrared, or direct-wired equipment.

Boarding Pier. A portion of a pier where a boat is temporarily secured for the purpose of embarking or disembarking.

Boat Launch Ramp. A sloped surface designed for launching and retrieving trailered boats and other water craft to and from a body of water.

Boat Slip. That portion of a pier, main pier, finger pier, or float where a boat is moored for the purpose of berthing, embarking, or disembarking.

Building. Any structure used or intended for supporting or sheltering any use or occupancy.

Catch Pool. A pool or designated section of a pool used as a terminus for water slide flumes.

Characters. Letters, numbers, punctuation marks and typographic symbols.

Children's Use. Describes spaces and elements specifically designed for use primarily by people 12 years old and younger.

Circulation Path. An exterior or interior way of passage provided for pedestrian travel, including but not limited to, walks, hallways, courtyards, elevators, platform lifts, ramps, stairways, and landings.

Closed-Circuit Telephone. A telephone with a dedicated line such as a house phone, courtesy phone or phone that must be used to gain entry to a facility.

Common Use. Interior or exterior circulation paths, rooms, spaces, or elements that are not for public use and are made available for the shared use of two or more people.

Cross Slope. The slope that is perpendicular to the direction of travel (see running slope).

Curb Ramp. A short ramp cutting through a curb or built up to it.

Detectable Warning. A standardized surface feature built in or applied to walking surfaces or other elements to warn of hazards on a circulation path.

Element. An architectural or mechanical component of a building, facility, space, or site.

Elevated Play Component. A play component that is approached above or below grade and that is part of a composite play structure consisting of two or more play components attached or functionally linked to create an integrated unit providing more than one play activity.

Employee Work Area. All or any portion of a space used only by employees and used only for work. Corridors, toilet rooms, kitchenettes and break rooms are not employee work areas.

Entrance. Any access point to a building or portion of a building or facility used for the purpose of entering. An entrance includes the approach walk, the vertical access leading to the entrance platform, the entrance platform itself, vestibule if provided, the entry door or gate, and the hardware of the entry door or gate.

Facility. All or any portion of buildings, structures, site improvements, elements, and pedestrian routes or vehicular ways located on a site.

Gangway. A variable-sloped pedestrian walkway that links a fixed structure or land with a floating structure. Gangways that connect to vessels are not addressed by this document.

Golf Car Passage. A continuous passage on which a motorized golf car can operate.

Ground Level Play Component. A play component that is approached and exited at the ground level.

Key Station. Rapid and light rail stations, and commuter rail stations, as defined under criteria established by the Department of Transportation in 49 CFR 37.47 and 49 CFR 37.51, respectively.

Mail Boxes. Receptacles for the receipt of documents, packages, or other deliverable matter. Mail boxes include, but are not limited to, post office boxes and receptacles provided by commercial mail-receiving agencies, apartment facilities, or schools.

Marked Crossing. A crosswalk or other identified path intended for pedestrian use in crossing a vehicular way.

Mezzanine. An intermediate level or levels between the floor and ceiling of any story with an aggregate floor area of not more than one-third of the area of the room or space in which the level or levels are located. Mezzanines have sufficient elevation that space for human occupancy can be provided on the floor below.

Occupant Load. The number of persons for which the means of egress of a building or portion of a building is designed.

Operable Part. A component of an element used to insert or withdraw objects, or to activate, deactivate, or adjust the element.

Pictogram. A pictorial symbol that represents activities, facilities, or concepts.

Play Area. A portion of a site containing play components designed and constructed for children.

Play Component. An element intended to generate specific opportunities for play, socialization, or learning. Play components are manufactured or natural; and are stand-alone or part of a composite play structure.

Private Building or Facility. A place of public accommodation or a commercial building or facility subject to Title III of the ADA and 28 CFR part 36 or a transportation building or facility subject to Title III of the ADA and 49 CFR 37.45.

Public Building or Facility. A building or facility or portion of a building or facility designed, constructed, or altered by, on behalf of, or for the use of a public entity subject to Title II of the ADA and 28 CFR part 35 or to Title II of the ADA and 49 CFR 37.41 or 37.43.

Public Entrance. An entrance that is not a service entrance or a restricted entrance.

Public Use. Interior or exterior rooms, spaces, or elements that are made available to the public. Public use may be provided at a building or facility that is privately or publicly owned.

Public Way. Any street, alley or other parcel of land open to the outside air leading to a public street, which has been deeded, dedicated or otherwise permanently appropriated to the public for public use and which has a clear width and height of not less than 10 feet (3050 mm).

Qualified Historic Building or Facility. A building or facility that is listed in or eligible for listing in the National Register of Historic Places, or designated as historic under an appropriate State or local law.

Ramp. A walking surface that has a running slope steeper than 1:20.

Residential Dwelling Unit. A unit intended to be used as a residence, that is primarily long-term in nature. Residential dwelling units do not include transient lodging, inpatient medical care, licensed long-term care, and detention or correctional facilities.

Restricted Entrance. An entrance that is made available for common use on a controlled basis but not public use and that is not a service entrance.

Running Slope. The slope that is parallel to the direction of travel (see cross slope).

Self-Service Storage. Building or facility designed and used for the purpose of renting or leasing individual storage spaces to customers for the purpose of storing and removing personal property on a self-service basis.

Service Entrance. An entrance intended primarily for delivery of goods or services.

Site. A parcel of land bounded by a property line or a designated portion of a public right-of-way.

Soft Contained Play Structure. A play structure made up of one or more play components where the user enters a fully enclosed play environment that utilizes pliable materials, such as plastic, netting, or fabric.

Space. A definable area, such as a room, toilet room, hall, assembly area, entrance, storage room, alcove, courtyard, or lobby.

Story. That portion of a building or facility designed for human occupancy included between the upper surface of a floor and upper surface of the floor or roof next above. A story containing one or more mezzanines has more than one floor level.

Structural Frame. The columns and the girders, beams, and trusses having direct connections to the columns and all other members that are essential to the stability of the building or facility as a whole.

Tactile. An object that can be perceived using the sense of touch.

Technically Infeasible. With respect to an alteration of a building or a facility, something that has little likelihood of being accomplished because existing structural conditions would require removing or altering a load-bearing member that is an essential part of the structural frame; or because other existing physical or site constraints prohibit modification or addition of elements, spaces, or features that are in full and strict compliance with the minimum requirements.

Teeing Ground. In golf, the starting place for the hole to be played.

Transfer Device. Equipment designed to facilitate the transfer of a person from a wheelchair or other mobility aid to and from an amusement ride seat.

Transient Lodging. A building or facility containing one or more guest room(s) for sleeping that provides accommodations that are primarily short-term in nature. Transient lodging does not include residential dwelling units intended to be used as a residence, inpatient medical care facilities, licensed long-term care facilities, detention or correctional facilities, or private buildings or facilities that contain not more than five rooms for rent or hire and that are actually occupied by the proprietor as the residence of such proprietor.

Transition Plate. A sloping pedestrian walking surface located at the end(s) of a gangway.

TTY. An abbreviation for teletypewriter. Machinery that employs interactive text-based communication through the transmission of coded signals across the telephone network. TTYs may include, for example, devices known as TDDs (telecommunication display devices or telecommunication devices for deaf persons) or computers with special modems. TTYs are also called text telephones.

Use Zone. The ground level area beneath and immediately adjacent to a play structure or play equipment that is designated by ASTM F 1487 (incorporated by reference, see "Referenced Standards" in Chapter 1) for unrestricted circulation around the play equipment and where it is predicted that a user would land when falling from or exiting the play equipment.

Vehicular Way. A route provided for vehicular traffic, such as in a street, driveway, or parking facility.

Walk. An exterior prepared surface for pedestrian use, including pedestrian areas such as plazas and courts.

Wheelchair Space. Space for a single wheelchair and its occupant.

Work Area Equipment. Any machine, instrument, engine, motor, pump, conveyor, or other apparatus used to perform work. As used in this document, this term shall apply only to equipment that is permanently installed or built-in in employee work areas. Work area equipment does not include passenger elevators and other accessible means of vertical transportation.

ADA CHAPTER 2: SCOPING REQUIREMENTS

201 Application

201.1 Scope. All areas of newly designed and newly constructed buildings and facilities and altered portions of existing buildings and facilities shall comply with these requirements.

Advisory 201.1 Scope.

These requirements are to be applied to all areas of a facility unless exempted, or where scoping limits the number of multiple elements required to be accessible. For example, not all medical care patient rooms are required to be accessible; those that are not required to be accessible are not required to comply with these requirements. However, common use and public use spaces such as recovery rooms, examination rooms, and cafeterias are not exempt from these requirements and must be accessible.

201.2 Application Based on Building or Facility Use. Where a site, building, facility, room, or space contains more than one use, each portion shall comply with the applicable requirements for that use.

201.3 Temporary and Permanent Structures. These requirements shall apply to temporary and permanent buildings and facilities.

Advisory 201.3 Temporary and Permanent Structures.

Temporary buildings or facilities covered by these requirements include, but are not limited to, reviewing stands, temporary classrooms, bleacher areas, stages, platforms and daises, fixed furniture systems, wall systems, and exhibit areas, temporary banking facilities, and temporary health screening facilities. Structures and equipment directly associated with the actual processes of construction are not required to be accessible as permitted in 203.2.

202 Existing Buildings and Facilities

202.1 General. Additions and alterations to existing buildings or facilities shall comply with 202.

202.2 Additions. Each addition to an existing building or facility shall comply with the requirements for new construction. Each addition that affects or could affect the usability of or access to an area containing a primary function shall comply with 202.4.

202.3 Alterations. Where existing elements or spaces are altered, each altered element or space shall comply with the applicable requirements of Chapter 2.

EXCEPTIONS:

1. Unless required by 202.4, where elements or spaces are altered and the circulation path to the altered element or space is not altered, an accessible route shall not be required.

2. In alterations, where compliance with applicable requirements is technically infeasible, the alteration shall comply with the requirements to the maximum extent feasible.

3. Residential dwelling units not required to be accessible in compliance with a standard issued pursuant to the Americans with Disabilities Act or Section 504 of the Rehabilitation Act of 1973, as amended, shall not be required to comply with 202.3.

Advisory 202.3 Alterations.

Although covered entities are permitted to limit the scope of an alteration to individual elements, the alteration of multiple elements within a room or space may provide a cost-effective opportunity to make the entire room or space accessible. Any elements or spaces of the building or facility that are required to comply with these requirements must be made accessible within the scope of the alteration, to the maximum extent feasible. If providing accessibility in compliance with these requirements for people with one type of disability (e.g., people who use wheelchairs) is not feasible, accessibility must still be provided in compliance with the requirements for people with other types of disabilities (e.g., people who have hearing impairments or who have vision impairments) to the extent that such accessibility is feasible.

202.3.1 Prohibited Reduction in Access. An alteration that decreases or has the effect of decreasing the accessibility of a building or facility below the requirements for new construction at the time of the alteration is prohibited.

202.3.2 Extent of Application. An alteration of an existing element, space, or area of a building or facility shall not impose a requirement for accessibility greater than required for new construction.

202.4 Alterations Affecting Primary Function Areas. In addition to the requirements of 202.3, an alteration that affects or could affect the usability of or access to an area containing a primary function shall be made so as to ensure that, to the maximum extent feasible, the path of travel to the altered area, including the rest rooms, telephones, and drinking fountains serving the altered area, are readily accessible to and usable by individuals with disabilities, unless such alterations are disproportionate to the overall alterations in terms of cost and scope as determined under criteria established by the Attorney General. In existing transportation facilities, an area of primary function shall be as defined under regulations published by the Secretary of the Department of Transportation or the Attorney General.

EXCEPTION: Residential dwelling units shall not be required to comply with 202.4.

Advisory 202.4 Alterations Affecting Primary Function Areas.

An area of a building or facility containing a major activity for which the building or facility is intended is a primary function area. Department of Justice ADA regulations state, "Alterations made to provide an accessible path of travel to the altered area will be deemed disproportionate to the overall alteration when the cost exceeds 20% of the cost of the alteration to the primary function area." (28 CFR 36.403 (f)(1)). See also Department of Transportation ADA regulations, which use similar concepts in the context of public sector transportation facilities (49 CFR 37.43 (e)(1)).

There can be multiple areas containing a primary function in a single building. Primary function areas are not limited to public use areas. For example, both a bank lobby and the bank's employee areas such as the teller areas and walk-in safe are primary function areas.

Also, mixed use facilities may include numerous primary function areas for each use. Areas containing a primary function do not include: mechanical rooms, boiler rooms, supply storage rooms, employee lounges or locker rooms, janitorial closets, entrances, corridors, or restrooms.

202.5 Alterations to Qualified Historic Buildings and Facilities. Alterations to a qualified historic building or facility shall comply with 202.3 and 202.4.

EXCEPTION: Where the State Historic Preservation Officer or Advisory Council on Historic Preservation determines that compliance with the requirements for accessible routes, entrances, or toilet facilities would threaten or destroy the historic significance of the building or facility, the exceptions for alterations to qualified historic buildings or facilities for that element shall be permitted to apply.

Advisory 202.5 Alterations to Qualified Historic Buildings and Facilities Exception.

State Historic Preservation Officers are State appointed officials who carry out certain responsibilities under the National Historic Preservation Act. State Historic Preservation Officers consult with Federal and State agencies, local governments, and private entities on providing access and protecting significant elements of qualified historic buildings and facilities. There are exceptions for alterations to qualified historic buildings and facilities for accessible routes (206.2.1 Exception 1 and 206.2.3 Exception 7); entrances (206.4 Exception 2); and toilet facilities (213.2 Exception 2). When an entity believes that compliance with the requirements for any of these elements would threaten or destroy the historic significance of the building or facility, the entity should consult with the State Historic Preservation Officer. If the State Historic Preservation Officer agrees that compliance with the requirements for a specific element would threaten or destroy the historic significance of the building or facility, use of the exception is permitted. Public entities have an additional obligation to achieve program accessibility under the Department of Justice ADA regulations. See 28 CFR 35.150. These regulations require public entities that operate historic preservation programs to give priority to methods that provide physical access to individuals with disabilities. If alterations to a qualified historic building or facility to achieve program accessibility would threaten or destroy the historic significance of the building or facility, fundamentally alter the program, or result in undue financial or administrative burdens, the Department of Justice ADA regulations allow alternative methods to be used to achieve program accessibility. In the case of historic preservation programs, such as an historic house museum, alternative methods include using audio-visual materials to depict portions of the house that cannot otherwise be made accessible. In the case of other qualified historic properties, such as an historic government office building, alternative methods include relocating programs and services to accessible locations. The

Department of Justice ADA regulations also allow public entities to use alternative methods when altering qualified historic buildings or facilities in the rare situations where the State Historic Preservation Officer determines that it is not feasible to provide physical access using the exceptions permitted in Section 202.5 without threatening or destroying the historic significance of the building or facility. See 28 CFR 35.151(d).

The AccessAbility Office at the National Endowment for the Arts (NEA) provides a variety of resources for museum operators and historic properties including: the Design for Accessibility Guide and the Disability Symbols. Contact NEA about these and other resources at (202) 682-5532 or www.arts.gov.

203 General Exceptions

203.1 General. Sites, buildings, facilities, and elements are exempt from these requirements to the extent specified by 203.

203.2 Construction Sites. Structures and sites directly associated with the actual processes of construction, including but not limited to, scaffolding, bridging, materials hoists, materials storage, and construction trailers shall not be required to comply with these requirements or to be on an accessible route. Portable toilet units provided for use exclusively by construction personnel on a construction site shall not be required to comply with 213 or to be on an accessible route.

203.3 Raised Areas. Areas raised primarily for purposes of security, life safety, or fire safety, including but not limited to, observation or lookout galleries, prison guard towers, fire towers, or life guard stands shall not be required to comply with these requirements or to be on an accessible route.

203.4 Limited Access Spaces. Spaces accessed only by ladders, catwalks, crawl spaces, or very narrow passageways shall not be required to comply with these requirements or to be on an accessible route.

203.5 Machinery Spaces. Spaces frequented only by service personnel for maintenance, repair, or occasional monitoring of equipment shall not be required to comply with these requirements or to be on an accessible route. Machinery spaces include, but are not limited to, elevator pits or elevator penthouses; mechanical, electrical or communications equipment rooms; piping or equipment catwalks; water or sewage treatment pump rooms and stations; electric substations and transformer vaults; and highway and tunnel utility facilities.

203.6 Single Occupant Structures. Single occupant structures accessed only by passageways below grade or elevated above standard curb height, including but not limited to, toll booths that are accessed only by underground tunnels, shall not be required to comply with these requirements or to be on an accessible route.

203.7 Detention and Correctional Facilities. In detention and correctional facilities, common use areas that are used only by inmates or detainees and security personnel and that do not serve holding cells or housing cells required to comply with 232, shall not be required to comply with these requirements or to be on an accessible route.

203.8 Residential Facilities. In residential facilities, common use areas that do not serve residential dwelling units required to provide mobility features complying with 809.2 through 809.4 shall not be required to comply with these requirements or to be on an accessible route.

203.9 Employee Work Areas. Spaces and elements within employee work areas shall only be required to comply with 206.2.8, 207.1, and 215.3 and shall be designed and constructed so that individuals with disabilities can approach, enter, and exit the employee work area. Employee work areas, or portions of employee work areas, other than raised courtroom stations, that are less than 300 square feet (28 m2) and elevated 7 inches (180 mm) or more above the finish floor or ground where the elevation is essential to the function of the space shall not be required to comply with these requirements or to be on an accessible route.

Advisory 203.9 Employee Work Areas.

Although areas used exclusively by employees for work are not required to be fully accessible, consider designing such areas to include non-required turning spaces, and provide accessible elements whenever possible. Under the ADA, employees with disabilities are entitled to reasonable accommodations in the workplace; accommodations can include alterations to spaces within the facility. Designing employee work areas to be more accessible at the outset will avoid more costly retrofits when current employees become temporarily or permanently disabled, or when new employees with disabilities are hired. Contact the Equal Employment Opportunity Commission (EEOC) at www.eeoc.gov for information about title I of the ADA prohibiting discrimination against people with disabilities in the workplace.

203.10 Raised Refereeing, Judging, and Scoring Areas. Raised structures used solely for refereeing, judging, or scoring a sport shall not be required to comply with these requirements or to be on an accessible route.

203.11 Water Slides. Water slides shall not be required to comply with these requirements or to be on an accessible route.

203.12 Animal Containment Areas. Animal containment areas that are not for public use shall not be required to comply with these requirements or to be on an accessible route.

Advisory 203.12 Animal Containment Areas.

Public circulation routes where animals may travel, such as in petting zoos and passageways alongside animal pens in State fairs, are not eligible for the exception.

203.13 Raised Boxing or Wrestling Rings. Raised boxing or wrestling rings shall not be required to comply with these requirements or to be on an accessible route.

203.14 Raised Diving Boards and Diving Platforms. Raised diving boards and diving platforms shall not be required to comply with these requirements or to be on an accessible route.

204 Protruding Objects

204.1   General. Protruding objects on circulation paths shall comply with 307.

EXCEPTIONS:

1. Within areas of sport activity, protruding objects on circulation paths shall not be required to comply with 307.

2. Within play areas, protruding objects on circulation paths shall not be required to comply with 307 provided that ground level accessible routes provide vertical clearance in compliance with 1008.2.

205   Operable Parts

205.1   General. Operable parts on accessible elements, accessible routes, and in accessible rooms and spaces shall comply with 309.

EXCEPTIONS:

1. Operable parts that are intended for use only by service or maintenance personnel shall not be required to comply with 309.

2. Electrical or communication receptacles serving a dedicated use shall not be required to comply with 309.

3. Where two or more outlets are provided in a kitchen above a length of counter top that is uninterrupted by a sink or appliance, one outlet shall not be required to comply with 309.

4. Floor electrical receptacles shall not be required to comply with 309.

5. HVAC diffusers shall not be required to comply with 309.

6. Except for light switches, where redundant controls are provided for a single element, one control in each space shall not be required to comply with 309.

7. Cleats and other boat securement devices shall not be required to comply with 309.3.

8. Exercise machines and exercise equipment shall not be required to comply with 309.

Advisory 205.1 General.

Controls covered by 205.1 include, but are not limited to, light switches, circuit breakers, duplexes and other convenience receptacles, environmental and appliance controls, plumbing fixture controls, and security and intercom systems.

206   Accessible Routes

206.1   General. Accessible routes shall be provided in accordance with 206 and shall comply with Chapter 4.

206.2   Where Required. Accessible routes shall be provided where required by 206.2.

206.2.1   Site Arrival Points. At least one accessible route shall be provided within the site from accessible parking spaces and accessible passenger loading zones; public streets and sidewalks; and public transportation stops to the accessible building or facility entrance they serve.

EXCEPTIONS:

1. Where exceptions for alterations to qualified historic buildings or facilities are permitted by 202.5, no more than one accessible route from a site arrival point to an accessible entrance shall be required.

2. An accessible route shall not be required between site arrival points and the building or facility entrance if the only means of access between them is a vehicular way not providing pedestrian access.

Advisory 206.2.1 Site Arrival Points.

Each site arrival point must be connected by an accessible route to the accessible building entrance or entrances served. Where two or more similar site arrival points, such as bus stops, serve the same accessible entrance or entrances, both bus stops must be on accessible routes. In addition, the accessible routes must serve all of the accessible entrances on the site.

Advisory 206.2.1 Site Arrival Points Exception 2. Access from site arrival points may include vehicular ways. Where a vehicular way, or a portion of a vehicular way, is provided for pedestrian trvel, such as within a shopping center or shopping mall parking lot, this exception does not apply.

206.2.2   Within a Site. At least one accessible route shall connect accessible buildings, accessible facilities, accessible elements, and accessible spaces that are on the same site.

EXCEPTION: An accessible route shall not be required between accessible buildings, accessible facilities, accessible elements, and accessible spaces if the only means of access between them is a vehicular way not providing pedestrian access.

Advisory 206.2.2 Within a Site.

An accessible route is required to connect to the boundary of each area of sport activity. Examples of areas of sport activity include: soccer fields, basketball courts, baseball fields, running tracks, skating rinks, and the area surrounding a piece of gymnastic equipment. While the size of an area of sport activity may vary from sport to sport, each includes only the space needed to play. Where multiple sports fields or courts are provided, an accessible route is required to each field or area of sport activity.

206.2.3   Multi-Story Buildings and Facilities. At least one accessible route shall connect each story and mezzanine in multi-story buildings and facilities.

EXCEPTIONS:

1. In private buildings or facilities that are less than three stories or that have less than 3000 square feet (279 m2) per story, an accessible route shall not be required to connect stories provided that the building or facility is not a shopping center, a shopping mall, the professional office of a health care provider, a terminal, depot or other station used for specified public transportation, an airport passenger terminal, or another type of facility as determined by the Attorney General.

2. Where a two story public building or facility has one story with an occupant load of five or fewer persons that does not contain public use space, that story shall not be required to be connected to the story above or below.

3. In detention and correctional facilities, an accessible route shall not be required to connect stories where cells with mobility features required to comply with 807.2, all common use areas serving cells with mobility features required to comply with 807.2, and all public use areas are on an accessible route.

4. In residential facilities, an accessible route shall not be required to connect stories where residential dwelling units with mobility features required to comply with 809.2 through 809.4, all common use areas serving residential dwelling units with mobility features required to comply with 809.2 through 809.4, and public use areas serving residential dwelling units are on an accessible route.

5. Within multi-story transient lodging guest rooms with mobility features required to comply with 806.2, an accessible route shall not be required to connect stories provided that spaces complying with 806.2 are on an accessible route and sleeping accommodations for two persons minimum are provided on a story served by an accessible route.

6. In air traffic control towers, an accessible route shall not be required to serve the cab and the floor immediately below the cab.

7. Where exceptions for alterations to qualified historic buildings or facilities are permitted by 202.5, an accessible route shall not be required to stories located above or below the accessible story.

Advisory 206.2.3 Multi-Story Buildings and Facilities.

Spaces and elements located on a level not required to be served by an accessible route must fully comply with this document. While a mezzanine may be a change in level, it is not a story. If an accessible route is required to connect stories within a building or facility, the accessible route must serve all mezzanines.

Advisory 206.2.3 Multi-Story Buildings and Facilities Exception 4. Where common use areas are provided for the use of residents, it is presumed that all such common use areas "serve" accessible dwelling units unless use is restricted to residents occupying certain dwelling units. For example, if all residents are permitted to use all laundry rooms, then all laundry rooms "serve" accessible dwelling units. However, if the laundry room on the first floor is restricted to use by residents on the first floor, and the second floor laundry room is for use by occupants of the second floor, then first floor accessible units are "served" only by laundry rooms on the first floor. In this example, an accessible route is not required to the second floor provided that all accessible units and all common use areas serving them are on the first floor.

206.2.3.1 Stairs and Escalators in Existing Buildings. In alterations and additions, where an escalator or stair is provided where none existed previously and major structural modifications are necessary for the installation, an accessible route shall be provided between the levels served by the escalator or stair unless exempted by 206.2.3 Exceptions 1 through 7.

206.2.4 Spaces and Elements. At least one accessible route shall connect accessible building or facility entrances with all accessible spaces and elements within the building or facility which are otherwise connected by a circulation path unless exempted by 206.2.3 Exceptions 1 through 7.

EXCEPTIONS:

1. Raised courtroom stations, including judges' benches, clerks' stations, bailiffs' stations, deputy clerks' stations, and court reporters' stations shall not be required to provide vertical access provided that the required clear floor space, maneuvering space, and, if appropriate, electrical service are installed at the time of initial construction to allow future installation of a means of vertical access complying with 405, 407, 408, or 410 without requiring substantial reconstruction of the space.

2. In assembly areas with fixed seating required to comply with 221, an accessible route shall not be required to serve fixed seating where wheelchair spaces required to be on an accessible route are not provided.

3. Accessible routes shall not be required to connect mezzanines where buildings or facilities have no more than one story. In addition, accessible routes shall not be required to connect stories or mezzanines where multi-story buildings or facilities are exempted by 206.2.3 Exceptions 1 through 7.

Advisory 206.2.4 Spaces and Elements.

Accessible routes must connect all spaces and elements required to be accessible including, but not limited to, raised areas and speaker platforms.

Advisory 206.2.4 Spaces and Elements Exception 1. The exception does not apply to areas that are likely to be used by members of the public who are not employees of the court such as jury areas, attorney areas, or witness stands.

206.2.5 Restaurants and Cafeterias. In restaurants and cafeterias, an accessible route shall be provided to all dining areas, including raised or sunken dining areas, and outdoor dining areas.

EXCEPTIONS:

1. In buildings or facilities not required to provide an accessible route between stories, an accessible route shall not be required to a mezzanine dining area where the mezzanine contains less than 25 percent of the total combined area for seating and dining and where the same decor and services are provided in the accessible area.

2. In alterations, an accessible route shall not be required to existing raised or sunken dining areas, or to all parts of existing outdoor dining areas where the same services and decor are provided in an accessible space usable by the public and not restricted to use by people with disabilities.

3. In sports facilities, tiered dining areas providing seating required to comply with 221 shall be required to have accessible routes serving at least 25 percent of the dining area provided that accessible routes serve seating complying with 221 and each tier is provided with the same services.

Advisory 206.2.5 Restaurants and Cafeterias Exception 2.

Examples of "same services" include, but are not limited to, bar service, rooms having smoking and non-smoking sections, lotto and other table games, carry-out, and buffet service. Examples of "same decor" include, but are not limited to, seating at or near windows and railings with views, areas designed with a certain theme, party and banquet rooms, and rooms where entertainment is provided.

206.2.6   Performance Areas. Where a circulation path directly connects a performance area to an assembly seating area, an accessible route shall directly connect the assembly seating area with the performance area. An accessible route shall be provided from performance areas to ancillary areas or facilities used by performers unless exempted by 206.2.3 Exceptions 1 through 7.

206.2.7   Press Boxes. Press boxes in assembly areas shall be on an accessible route.

EXCEPTIONS:

1. An accessible route shall not be required to press boxes in bleachers that have points of entry at only one level provided that the aggregate area of all press boxes is 500 square feet (46 m2) maximum.

2. An accessible route shall not be required to free-standing press boxes that are elevated above grade 12 feet (3660 mm) minimum provided that the aggregate area of all press boxes is 500 square feet (46 m2) maximum.

Advisory 206.2.7 Press Boxes Exception 2.

Where a facility contains multiple assembly areas, the aggregate area of the press boxes in each assembly area is to be calculated separately. For example, if a university has a soccer stadium with three press boxes elevated 12 feet (3660 mm) or more above grade and each press box is 150 square feet (14 m2), then the aggregate area of the soccer stadium press boxes is less than 500 square feet (46 m2) and Exception 2 applies to the soccer stadium. If that same university also has a football stadium with two press boxes elevated 12 feet (3660 mm) or more above grade and one press box is 250 square feet (23 m2), and the second is 275 square feet (26 m2), then the aggregate area of the football stadium press boxes is more than 500 square feet (46 m2) and Exception 2 does not apply to the football stadium.

206.2.8   Employee Work Areas. Common use circulation paths within employee work areas shall comply with 402.

EXCEPTIONS:

1. Common use circulation paths located within employee work areas that are less than 1000 square feet (93 m2) and defined by permanently installed partitions, counters, casework, or furnishings shall not be required to comply with 402.

2. Common use circulation paths located within employee work areas that are an integral component of work area equipment shall not be required to comply with 402.

3. Common use circulation paths located within exterior employee work areas that are fully exposed to the weather shall not be required to comply with 402.

Advisory 206.2.8 Employee Work Areas Exception 1.

Modular furniture that is not permanently installed is not directly subject to these requirements. The Department of Justice ADA regulations provide additional guidance regarding the relationship between these requirements and elements that are not part of the built environment. Additionally, the Equal Employment Opportunity Commission (EEOC) implements title I of the ADA which requires non-discrimination in the workplace. EEOC can provide guidance regarding employers' obligations to provide reasonable accommodations for employees with disabilities.

Advisory 206.2.8 Employee Work Areas Exception 2. Large pieces of equipment, such as electric turbines or water pumping apparatus, may have stairs and elevated walkways used for overseeing or monitoring purposes which are physically part of the turbine or pump. However, passenger elevators used for vertical transportation between stories are not considered "work area equipment" as defined in Section 106.5.

206.2.9   Amusement Rides. Amusement rides required to comply with 234 shall provide accessible routes in accordance with 206.2.9. Accessible routes serving amusement rides shall comply with Chapter 4 except as modified by 1002.2.

206.2.9.1   Load and Unload Areas. Load and unload areas shall be on an accessible route. Where load and unload areas have more than one loading or unloading position, at least one loading and unloading position shall be on an accessible route.

206.2.9.2   Wheelchair Spaces, Ride Seats Designed for Transfer, and Transfer Devices. When amusement rides are in the load and unload position, wheelchair spaces complying with 1002.4, amusement ride seats designed for transfer complying with 1002.5, and transfer devices complying with 1002.6 shall be on an accessible route.

206.2.10   Recreational Boating Facilities. Boat slips required to comply with 235.2 and boarding piers at boat launch ramps required to comply with 235.3 shall be on an accessible route. Accessible routes serving recreational boating facilities shall comply with Chapter 4, except as modified by 1003.2.

206.2.11   Bowling Lanes. Where bowling lanes are provided, at least 5 percent, but no fewer than one of each type of bowling lane, shall be on an accessible route.

206.2.12   Court Sports. In court sports, at least one accessible route shall directly connect both sides of the court.

206.2.13 Exercise Machines and Equipment. Exercise machines and equipment required to comply with 236 shall be on an accessible route.

206.2.14 Fishing Piers and Platforms. Fishing piers and platforms shall be on an accessible route. Accessible routes serving fishing piers and platforms shall comply with Chapter 4 except as modified by 1005.1.

206.2.15 Golf Facilities. At least one accessible route shall connect accessible elements and spaces within the boundary of the golf course. In addition, accessible routes serving golf car rental areas; bag drop areas; course weather shelters complying with 238.2.3; course toilet rooms; and practice putting greens, practice teeing grounds, and teeing stations at driving ranges complying with 238.3 shall comply with Chapter 4 except as modified by 1006.2.

EXCEPTION: Golf car passages complying with 1006.3 shall be permitted to be used for all or part of accessible routes required by 206.2.15.

206.2.16 Miniature Golf Facilities. Holes required to comply with 239.2, including the start of play, shall be on an accessible route. Accessible routes serving miniature golf facilities shall comply with Chapter 4 except as modified by 1007.2.

206.2.17 Play Areas. Play areas shall provide accessible routes in accordance with 206.2.17. Accessible routes serving play areas shall comply with Chapter 4 except as modified by 1008.2.

206.2.17.1 Ground Level and Elevated Play Components. At least one accessible route shall be provided within the play area. The accessible route shall connect ground level play components required to comply with 240.2.1 and elevated play components required to comply with 240.2.2, including entry and exit points of the play components.

206.2.17.2 Soft Contained Play Structures. Where three or fewer entry points are provided for soft contained play structures, at least one entry point shall be on an accessible route. Where four or more entry points are provided for soft contained play structures, at least two entry points shall be on an accessible route.

206.3 Location. Accessible routes shall coincide with or be located in the same area as general circulation paths. Where circulation paths are interior, required accessible routes shall also be interior.

Advisory 206.3 Location.

The accessible route must be in the same area as the general circulation path. This means that circulation paths, such as vehicular ways designed for pedestrian traffic, walks, and unpaved paths that are designed to be routinely used by pedestrians must be accessible or have an accessible route nearby. Additionally, accessible vertical interior circulation must be in the same area as stairs and escalators, not isolated in the back of the facility.

206.4 Entrances. Entrances shall be provided in accordance with 206.4. Entrance doors, doorways, and gates shall comply with 404 and shall be on an accessible route complying with 402.

EXCEPTIONS:

1. Where an alteration includes alterations to an entrance, and the building or facility has another entrance complying with 404 that is on an accessible route, the altered entrance shall not be required to comply with 206.4 unless required by 202.4.

2. Where exceptions for alterations to qualified historic buildings or facilities are permitted by 202.5, no more than one public entrance shall be required to comply with 206.4. Where no public entrance can comply with 206.4 under criteria established in 202.5 Exception, then either an unlocked entrance not used by the public shall comply with 206.4; or a locked entrance complying with 206.4 with a notification system or remote monitoring shall be provided.

206.4.1   Public Entrances. In addition to entrances required by 206.4.2 through 206.4.9, at least 60 percent of all public entrances shall comply with 404.

206.4.2   Parking Structure Entrances. Where direct access is provided for pedestrians from a parking structure to a building or facility entrance, each direct access to the building or facility entrance shall comply with 404.

206.4.3   Entrances from Tunnels or Elevated Walkways. Where direct access is provided for pedestrians from a pedestrian tunnel or elevated walkway to a building or facility, at least one direct entrance to the building or facility from each tunnel or walkway shall comply with 404.

206.4.4   Transportation Facilities. In addition to the requirements of 206.4.2, 206.4.3, and 206.4.5 through 206.4.9, transportation facilities shall provide entrances in accordance with 206.4.4.

206.4.4.1   Location. In transportation facilities, where different entrances serve different transportation fixed routes or groups of fixed routes, at least one public entrance serving each fixed route or group of fixed routes shall comply with 404.

EXCEPTION: Entrances to key stations and existing intercity rail stations retrofitted in accordance with 49 CFR 37.49 or 49 CFR 37.51 shall not be required to comply with 206.4.4.1.

206.4.4.2   Direct Connections. Direct connections to other facilities shall provide an accessible route complying with 404 from the point of connection to boarding platforms and all transportation system elements required to be accessible. Any elements provided to facilitate future direct connections shall be on an accessible route connecting boarding platforms and all transportation system elements required to be accessible.

EXCEPTION: In key stations and existing intercity rail stations, existing direct connections shall not be required to comply with 404.

206.4.4.3   Key Stations and Intercity Rail Stations. Key stations and existing intercity rail stations required by Subpart C of 49 CFR part 37 to be altered, shall have at least one entrance complying with 404.

206.4.5   Tenant Spaces. At least one accessible entrance to each tenancy in a facility shall comply with 404.

EXCEPTION: Self-service storage facilities not required to comply with 225.3 shall not be required to be on an accessible route.

206.4.6   Residential Dwelling Unit Primary Entrance. In residential dwelling units, at least one primary entrance shall comply with 404. The primary entrance to a residential dwelling unit shall not be to a bedroom.

206.4.7   Restricted Entrances. Where restricted entrances are provided to a building or facility, at least one restricted entrance to the building or facility shall comply with 404.

206.4.8   Service Entrances. If a service entrance is the only entrance to a building or to a tenancy in a facility, that entrance shall comply with 404.

206.4.9   Entrances for Inmates or Detainees. Where entrances used only by inmates or detainees and security personnel are provided at judicial facilities, detention facilities, or correctional facilities, at least one such entrance shall comply with 404.

206.5   Doors, Doorways, and Gates. Doors, doorways, and gates providing user passage shall be provided in accordance with 206.5.

206.5.1   Entrances Each entrance to a building or facility required to comply with 206.4 shall have at least one door, doorway, or gate complying with 404.

206.5.2   Rooms and Spaces. Within a building or facility, at least one door, doorway, or gate serving each room or space complying with these requirements shall comply with 404.

206.5.3   Transient Lodging Facilities. In transient lodging facilities, entrances, doors, and doorways providing user passage into and within guest rooms that are not required to provide mobility features complying with 806.2 shall comply with 404.2.3.

EXCEPTION: Shower and sauna doors in guest rooms that are not required to provide mobility features complying with 806.2 shall not be required to comply with 404.2.3.

206.5.4   Residential Dwelling Units. In residential dwelling units required to provide mobility features complying with 809.2 through 809.4, all doors and doorways providing user passage shall comply with 404.

206.6   Elevators. Elevators provided for passengers shall comply with 407. Where multiple elevators are provided, each elevator shall comply with 407.

EXCEPTIONS:

   1. In a building or facility permitted to use the exceptions to 206.2.3 or permitted by 206.7 to use a platform lift, elevators complying with 408 shall be permitted.

   2. Elevators complying with 408 or 409 shall be permitted in multi-story residential dwelling units.

206.6.1   Existing Elevators. Where elements of existing elevators are altered, the same element shall also be altered in all elevators that are programmed to respond to the same hall call control as the altered elevator and shall comply with the requirements of 407 for the altered element.

206.7 Platform Lifts. Platform lifts shall comply with 410. Platform lifts shall be permitted as a component of an accessible route in new construction in accordance with 206.7. Platform lifts shall be permitted as a component of an accessible route in an existing building or facility.

206.7.1 Performance Areas and Speakers' Platforms. Platform lifts shall be permitted to provide accessible routes to performance areas and speakers' platforms.

206.7.2 Wheelchair Spaces. Platform lifts shall be permitted to provide an accessible route to comply with the wheelchair space dispersion and line-of-sight requirements of 221 and 802.

206.7.3 Incidental Spaces. Platform lifts shall be permitted to provide an accessible route to incidental spaces which are not public use spaces and which are occupied by five persons maximum.

206.7.4 Judicial Spaces. Platform lifts shall be permitted to provide an accessible route to: jury boxes and witness stands; raised courtroom stations including, judges' benches, clerks' stations, bailiffs' stations, deputy clerks' stations, and court reporters' stations; and to depressed areas such as the well of a court.

206.7.5 Existing Site Constraints. Platform lifts shall be permitted where existing exterior site constraints make use of a ramp or elevator infeasible.

Advisory 206.7.5 Existing Site Constraints.

This exception applies where topography or other similar existing site constraints necessitate the use of a platform lift as the only feasible alternative. While the site constraint must reflect exterior conditions, the lift can be installed in the interior of a building. For example, a new building constructed between and connected to two existing buildings may have insufficient space to coordinate floor levels and also to provide ramped entry from the public way. In this example, an exterior or interior platform lift could be used to provide an accessible entrance or to coordinate one or more interior floor levels.

206.7.6 Guest Rooms and Residential Dwelling Units. Platform lifts shall be permitted to connect levels within transient lodging guest rooms required to provide mobility features complying with 806.2 or residential dwelling units required to provide mobility features complying with 809.2 through 809.4.

206.7.7 Amusement Rides. Platform lifts shall be permitted to provide accessible routes to load and unload areas serving amusement rides.

206.7.8 Play Areas. Platform lifts shall be permitted to provide accessible routes to play components or soft contained play structures.

206.7.9 Team or Player Seating. Platform lifts shall be permitted to provide accessible routes to team or player seating areas serving areas of sport activity.

Advisory 206.7.9 Team or Player Seating.

While the use of platform lifts is allowed, ramps are recommended to provide access to player seating areas serving an area of sport activity.

206.7.10   Recreational Boating Facilities and Fishing Piers and Platforms. Platform lifts shall be permitted to be used instead of gangways that are part of accessible routes serving recreational boating facilities and fishing piers and platforms.

206.8   Security Barriers. Security barriers, including but not limited to, security bollards and security check points, shall not obstruct a required accessible route or accessible means of egress.

EXCEPTION: Where security barriers incorporate elements that cannot comply with these requirements such as certain metal detectors, fluoroscopes, or other similar devices, the accessible route shall be permitted to be located adjacent to security screening devices. The accessible route shall permit persons with disabilities passing around security barriers to maintain visual contact with their personal items to the same extent provided others passing through the security barrier.

207   Accessible Means of Egress

207.1   General. Means of egress shall comply with section 1003.2.13 of the International Building Code (2000 edition and 2001 Supplement) or section 1007 of the International Building Code (2003 edition) (incorporated by reference, see "Referenced Standards" in Chapter 1).

EXCEPTIONS:

1. Where means of egress are permitted by local building or life safety codes to share a common path of egress travel, accessible means of egress shall be permitted to share a common path of egress travel.

2. Areas of refuge shall not be required in detention and correctional facilities.

207.2   Platform Lifts. Standby power shall be provided for platform lifts permitted by section 1003.2.13.4 of the International Building Code (2000 edition and 2001 Supplement) or section 1007.5 of the International Building Code (2003 edition) (incorporated by reference, see "Referenced Standards" in Chapter 1) to serve as a part of an accessible means of egress.

208   Parking Spaces

208.1   General. Where parking spaces are provided, parking spaces shall be provided in accordance with 208.

EXCEPTION: Parking spaces used exclusively for buses, trucks, other delivery vehicles, law enforcement vehicles, or vehicular impound shall not be required to comply with 208 provided that lots accessed by the public are provided with a passenger loading zone complying with 503.

208.2   Minimum Number. Parking spaces complying with 502 shall be provided in accordance with Table 208.2 except as required by 208.2.1, 208.2.2, and 208.2.3. Where more than one parking facility is provided on a site, the number of accessible spaces provided on the site shall be calculated according to the number of spaces required for each parking facility.

Table 208.2 Parking Spaces	
Total Number of Parking Spaces Provided in Parking Facility	Minimum Number of Required Accessible Parking Spaces
1 to 25	1
26 to 50	2
51 to 75	3
76 to 100	4
101 to 150	5
151 to 200	6
201 to 300	7
301 to 400	8
401 to 500	9
501 to 1000	2 percent of total
1001 and over	20, plus 1 for each 100, or fraction thereof, over 1000

Advisory 208.2 Minimum Number.

The term "parking facility" is used Section 208.2 instead of the term "parking lot" so that it is clear that both parking lots and parking structures are required to comply with this section. The number of parking spaces required to be accessible is to be calculated separately for each parking facility; the required number is not to be based on the total number of parking spaces provided in all of the parking facilities provided on the site.

208.2.1 Hospital Outpatient Facilities. Ten percent of patient and visitor parking spaces provided to serve hospital outpatient facilities shall comply with 502.

Advisory 208.2.1 Hospital Outpatient Facilities.

The term "outpatient facility" is not defined in this document but is intended to cover facilities or units that are located in hospitals and that provide regular and continuing medical treatment without an overnight stay. Doctors' offices, independent clinics, or other facilities not located in hospitals are not considered hospital outpatient facilities for purposes of this document.

208.2.2 Rehabilitation Facilities and Outpatient Physical Therapy Facilities. Twenty percent of patient and visitor parking spaces provided to serve rehabilitation facilities specializing in treating conditions that affect mobility and outpatient physical therapy facilities shall comply with 502.

Advisory 208.2.2 Rehabilitation Facilities and Outpatient Physical Therapy Facilities.

Conditions that affect mobility include conditions requiring the use or assistance of a brace, cane, crutch, prosthetic device, wheelchair, or powered mobility aid; arthritic, neurological, or orthopedic conditions that severely limit one's ability to walk; respiratory diseases and other conditions which may require the use of portable oxygen; and cardiac conditions that impose significant functional limitations.

208.2.3 Residential Facilities. Parking spaces provided to serve residential facilities shall comply with 208.2.3.

208.2.3.1 Parking for Residents. Where at least one parking space is provided for each residential dwelling unit, at least one parking space complying with 502 shall be provided for each residential dwelling unit required to provide mobility features complying with 809.2 through 809.4.

208.2.3.2 Additional Parking Spaces for Residents. Where the total number of parking spaces provided for each residential dwelling unit exceeds one parking space per residential dwelling unit, 2 percent, but no fewer than one space, of all the parking spaces not covered by 208.2.3.1 shall comply with 502.

208.2.3.3 Parking for Guests, Employees, and Other Non-Residents. Where parking spaces are provided for persons other than residents, parking shall be provided in accordance with Table 208.2.

208.2.4 Van Parking Spaces. For every six or fraction of six parking spaces required by 208.2 to comply with 502, at least one shall be a van parking space complying with 502.

208.3 Location. Parking facilities shall comply with 208.3

208.3.1 General Parking spaces complying with 502 that serve a particular building or facility shall be located on the shortest accessible route from parking to an entrance complying with 206.4. Where parking serves more than one accessible entrance, parking spaces complying with 502 shall be dispersed and located on the shortest accessible route to the accessible entrances. In parking facilities that do not serve a particular building or facility, parking spaces complying with 502 shall be located on the shortest accessible route to an accessible pedestrian entrance of the parking facility.

EXCEPTIONS:

1. All van parking spaces shall be permitted to be grouped on one level within a multi-story parking facility.

2. Parking spaces shall be permitted to be located in different parking facilities if substantially equivalent or greater accessibility is provided in terms of distance from an accessible entrance or entrances, parking fee, and user convenience.

Advisory 208.3.1 General Exception 2.

Factors that could affect "user convenience" include, but are not limited to, protection from the weather, security, lighting, and comparative maintenance of the alternative parking site.

208.3.2 Residential Facilities. In residential facilities containing residential dwelling units required to provide mobility features complying with 809.2 through 809.4, parking spaces provided in accordance with 208.2.3.1 shall be located on the shortest accessible route to the residential dwelling unit entrance they serve. Spaces provided in accordance with 208.2.3.2 shall be dispersed throughout all types of parking provided for the residential dwelling units.

EXCEPTION: Parking spaces provided in accordance with 208.2.3.2 shall not be required to be dispersed throughout all types of parking if substantially equivalent or greater accessibility is provided in terms of distance from an accessible entrance, parking fee, and user convenience.

Advisory 208.3.2 Residential Facilities Exception.

Factors that could affect "user convenience" include, but are not limited to, protection from the weather, security, lighting, and comparative maintenance of the alternative parking site.

209 Passenger Loading Zones and Bus Stops

209.1 General. Passenger loading zones shall be provided in accordance with 209.

209.2 Type. Where provided, passenger loading zones shall comply with 209.2.

209.2.1 Passenger Loading Zones. Passenger loading zones, except those required to comply with 209.2.2 and 209.2.3, shall provide at least one passenger loading zone complying with 503 in every continuous 100 linear feet (30 m) of loading zone space, or fraction thereof.

209.2.2 Bus Loading Zones. In bus loading zones restricted to use by designated or specified public transportation vehicles, each bus bay, bus stop, or other area designated for lift or ramp deployment shall comply with 810.2.

Advisory 209.2.2 Bus Loading Zones.

The terms "designated public transportation" and "specified public transportation" are defined by the Department of Transportation at 49 CFR 37.3 in regulations implementing the Americans with Disabilities Act. These terms refer to public transportation services provided by public or private entities, respectively. For example, designated public transportation vehicles include buses and vans operated by public transit agencies, while specified public transportation vehicles include tour and charter buses, taxis and limousines, and hotel shuttles operated by private entities.

209.2.3 On-Street Bus Stops. On-street bus stops shall comply with 810.2 to the maximum extent practicable.

209.3 Medical Care and Long-Term Care Facilities. At least one passenger loading zone complying with 503 shall be provided at an accessible entrance to licensed medical care and licensed long-term care facilities where the period of stay exceeds twenty-four hours.

209.4 Valet Parking. Parking facilities that provide valet parking services shall provide at least one passenger loading zone complying with 503.

209.5 Mechanical Access Parking Garages. Mechanical access parking garages shall provide at least one passenger loading zone complying with 503 at vehicle drop-off and vehicle pick-up areas.

210   Stairways

210.1 General. Interior and exterior stairs that are part of a means of egress shall comply with 504.

EXCEPTIONS:

1. In detention and correctional facilities, stairs that are not located in public use areas shall not be required to comply with 504.

2. In alterations, stairs between levels that are connected by an accessible route shall not be required to comply with 504, except that handrails complying with 505 shall be provided when the stairs are altered.

3. In assembly areas, aisle stairs shall not be required to comply with 504.

4. Stairs that connect play components shall not be required to comply with 504.

Advisory 210.1 General.

Although these requirements do not mandate handrails on stairs that are not part of a means of egress, State or local building codes may require handrails or guards.

211   Drinking Fountains

211.1 General. Where drinking fountains are provided on an exterior site, on a floor, or within a secured area they shall be provided in accordance with 211.

EXCEPTION: In detention or correctional facilities, drinking fountains only serving holding or housing cells not required to comply with 232 shall not be required to comply with 211.

211.2 Minimum Number. No fewer than two drinking fountains shall be provided. One drinking fountain shall comply with 602.1 through 602.6 and one drinking fountain shall comply with 602.7.

EXCEPTION: Where a single drinking fountain complies with 602.1 through 602.6 and 602.7, it shall be permitted to be substituted for two separate drinking fountains.

211.3 More Than Minimum Number. Where more than the minimum number of drinking fountains specified in 211.2 are provided, 50 percent of the total number of drinking fountains provided shall comply with 602.1 through 602.6, and 50 percent of the total number of drinking fountains provided shall comply with 602.7.

EXCEPTION: Where 50 percent of the drinking fountains yields a fraction, 50 percent shall be permitted to be rounded up or down provided that the total number of drinking fountains complying with 211 equals 100 percent of drinking fountains.

212   Kitchens, Kitchenettes, and Sinks

212.1 General. Where provided, kitchens, kitchenettes, and sinks shall comply with 212.

212.2 Kitchens and Kitchenettes. Kitchens and kitchenettes shall comply with 804.

212.3 Sinks. Where sinks are provided, at least 5 percent, but no fewer than one, of each type provided in each accessible room or space shall comply with 606.

EXCEPTION: Mop or service sinks shall not be required to comply with 212.3.

213 Toilet Facilities and Bathing Facilities

213.1 General. Where toilet facilities and bathing facilities are provided, they shall comply with 213. Where toilet facilities and bathing facilities are provided in facilities permitted by 206.2.3 Exceptions 1 and 2 not to connect stories by an accessible route, toilet facilities and bathing facilities shall be provided on a story connected by an accessible route to an accessible entrance.

213.2 Toilet Rooms and Bathing Rooms. Where toilet rooms are provided, each toilet room shall comply with 603. Where bathing rooms are provided, each bathing room shall comply with 603.

EXCEPTIONS:

1. In alterations where it is technically infeasible to comply with 603, altering existing toilet or bathing rooms shall not be required where a single unisex toilet room or bathing room complying with 213.2.1 is provided and located in the same area and on the same floor as existing inaccessible toilet or bathing rooms.

2. Where exceptions for alterations to qualified historic buildings or facilities are permitted by 202.5, no fewer than one toilet room for each sex complying with 603 or one unisex toilet room complying with 213.2.1 shall be provided.

3. Where multiple single user portable toilet or bathing units are clustered at a single location, no more than 5 percent of the toilet units and bathing units at each cluster shall be required to comply with 603. Portable toilet units and bathing units complying with 603 shall be identified by the International Symbol of Accessibility complying with 703.7.2.1.

4. Where multiple single user toilet rooms are clustered at a single location, no more than 50 percent of the single user toilet rooms for each use at each cluster shall be required to comply with 603.

Advisory 213.2 Toilet Rooms and Bathing Rooms.

These requirements allow the use of unisex (or single-user) toilet rooms in alterations when technical infeasibility can be demonstrated. Unisex toilet rooms benefit people who use opposite sex personal care assistants. For this reason, it is advantageous to install unisex toilet rooms in addition to accessible single-sex toilet rooms in new facilities.

Advisory 213.2 Toilet Rooms and Bathing Rooms Exceptions 3 and 4. A "cluster" is a group of toilet rooms proximate to one another. Generally, toilet rooms in a cluster are within sight of, or adjacent to, one another.

213.2.1 Unisex (Single-Use or Family) Toilet and Unisex Bathing Rooms. Unisex toilet rooms shall contain not more than one lavatory, and two water closets without urinals or one water closet and one urinal. Unisex bathing rooms shall contain one shower or one shower and one bathtub, one lavatory, and one water closet. Doors to unisex toilet rooms and unisex bathing rooms shall have privacy latches.

213.3 Plumbing Fixtures and Accessories. Plumbing fixtures and accessories provided in a toilet room or bathing room required to comply with 213.2 shall comply with 213.3.

213.3.1 Toilet Compartments. Where toilet compartments are provided, at least one toilet compartment shall comply with 604.8.1. In addition to the compartment required to comply with 604.8.1, at least one compartment shall comply with 604.8.2 where six or more toilet compartments are provided, or where the combination of urinals and water closets totals six or more fixtures.

Advisory 213.3.1 Toilet Compartments.

A toilet compartment is a partitioned space that is located within a toilet room, and that normally contains no more than one water closet. A toilet compartment may also contain a lavatory. A lavatory is a sink provided for hand washing. Full-height partitions and door assemblies can comprise toilet compartments where the minimum required spaces are provided within the compartment.

213.3.2 Water Closets. Where water closets are provided, at least one shall comply with 604.

213.3.3 Urinals Where more than one urinal is provided, at least one shall comply with 605.

213.3.4 Lavatories Where lavatories are provided, at least one shall comply with 606 and shall not be located in a toilet compartment.

213.3.5 Mirrors Where mirrors are provided, at least one shall comply with 603.3.

213.3.6 Bathing Facilities. Where bathtubs or showers are provided, at least one bathtub complying with 607 or at least one shower complying with 608 shall be provided.

213.3.7 Coat Hooks and Shelves. Where coat hooks or shelves are provided in toilet rooms without toilet compartments, at least one of each type shall comply with 603.4. Where coat hooks or shelves are provided in toilet compartments, at least one of each type complying with 604.8.3 shall be provided in toilet compartments required to comply with 213.3.1. Where coat hooks or shelves are provided in bathing facilities, at least one of each type complying with 603.4 shall serve fixtures required to comply with 213.3.6.

214 Washing Machines and Clothes Dryers

214.1 General. Where provided, washing machines and clothes dryers shall comply with 214.

214.2 Washing Machines. Where three or fewer washing machines are provided, at least one shall comply with 611. Where more than three washing machines are provided, at least two shall comply with 611.

214.3 Clothes Dryers. Where three or fewer clothes dryers are provided, at least one shall comply with 611. Where more than three clothes dryers are provided, at least two shall comply with 611.

215 Fire Alarm Systems

215.1 General. Where fire alarm systems provide audible alarm coverage, alarms shall comply with 215.

EXCEPTION: In existing facilities, visible alarms shall not be required except where an existing fire alarm system is upgraded or replaced, or a new fire alarm system is installed.

Advisory 215.1 General.

Unlike audible alarms, visible alarms must be located within the space they serve so that the signal is visible. Facility alarm systems (other than fire alarm systems) such as those used for tornado warnings and other emergencies are not required to comply with the technical criteria for alarms in Section 702. Every effort should be made to ensure that such alarms can be differentiated in their signal from fire alarms systems and that people who need to be notified of emergencies are adequately safeguarded. Consult local fire departments and prepare evacuation plans taking into consideration the needs of every building occupant, including people with disabilities.

215.2 Public and Common Use Areas. Alarms in public use areas and common use areas shall comply with 702.

215.3 Employee Work Areas. Where employee work areas have audible alarm coverage, the wiring system shall be designed so that visible alarms complying with 702 can be integrated into the alarm system.

215.4 Transient Lodging. Guest rooms required to comply with 224.4 shall provide alarms complying with 702.

215.5 Residential Facilities. Where provided in residential dwelling units required to comply with 809.5, alarms shall comply with 702.

216 Signs

216.1 General. Signs shall be provided in accordance with 216 and shall comply with 703.

EXCEPTIONS:

1. Building directories, menus, seat and row designations in assembly areas, occupant names, building addresses, and company names and logos shall not be required to comply with 216.

2. In parking facilities, signs shall not be required to comply with 216.2, 216.3, and 216.6 through 216.12.

3. Temporary, 7 days or less, signs shall not be required to comply with 216.

4. In detention and correctional facilities, signs not located in public use areas shall not be required to comply with 216.

216.2 Designations. Interior and exterior signs identifying permanent rooms and spaces shall comply with 703.1, 703.2, and 703.5. Where pictograms are provided as designations of permanent interior rooms and spaces, the pictograms shall comply with 703.6 and shall have text descriptors complying with 703.2 and 703.5.

EXCEPTION: Exterior signs that are not located at the door to the space they serve shall not be required to comply with 703.2.

Advisory 216.2 Designations.

Section 216.2 applies to signs that provide designations, labels, or names for interior rooms or spaces where the sign is not likely to change over time. Examples include interior signs labeling restrooms, room and floor numbers or letters, and room names. Tactile text descriptors are required for pictograms that are provided to label or identify a permanent room or space. Pictograms that provide information about a room or space, such as "no smoking," occupant logos, and the International Symbol of Accessibility, are not required to have text descriptors.

216.3 Directional and Informational Signs. Signs that provide direction to or information about interior spaces and facilities of the site shall comply with 703.5.

Advisory 216.3 Directional and Informational Signs.

Information about interior spaces and facilities includes rules of conduct, occupant load, and similar signs. Signs providing direction to rooms or spaces include those that identify egress routes.

216.4 Means of Egress. Signs for means of egress shall comply with 216.4.

216.4.1 Exit Doors. Doors at exit passageways, exit discharge, and exit stairways shall be identified by tactile signs complying with 703.1, 703.2, and 703.5.

Advisory 216.4.1 Exit Doors.

An exit passageway is a horizontal exit component that is separated from the interior spaces of the building by fire-resistance-rated construction and that leads to the exit discharge or public way. The exit discharge is that portion of an egress system between the termination of an exit and a public way.

216.4.2 Areas of Refuge. Signs required by section 1003.2.13.5.4 of the International Building Code (2000 edition) or section 1007.6.4 of the International Building Code (2003 edition) (incorporated by reference, see "Referenced Standards" in Chapter 1) to provide instructions in areas of refuge shall comply with

703.5.

216.4.3 Directional Signs. Signs required by section 1003.2.13.6 of the International Building Code (2000 edition) or section 1007.7 of the International Building Code (2003 edition) (incorporated by reference, see "Referenced Standards" in Chapter 1) to provide directions to accessible means of egress shall comply with 703.5.

216.5 Parking. Parking spaces complying with 502 shall be identified by signs complying with 502.6.

EXCEPTIONS:

1. Where a total of four or fewer parking spaces, including accessible parking spaces, are provided on a site, identification of accessible parking spaces shall not be required.

2. In residential facilities, where parking spaces are assigned to specific residential dwelling units, identification of accessible parking spaces shall not be required.

216.6 Entrances. Where not all entrances comply with 404, entrances complying with 404 shall be identified by the International Symbol of Accessibility complying with 703.7.2.1. Directional signs complying with 703.5 that indicate the location of the nearest entrance complying with 404 shall be provided at entrances that do not comply with 404.

Advisory 216.6 Entrances.

Where a directional sign is required, it should be located to minimize backtracking. In some cases, this could mean locating a sign at the beginning of a route, not just at the inaccessible entrances to a building.

216.7 Elevators. Where existing elevators do not comply with 407, elevators complying with 407 shall be clearly identified with the International Symbol of Accessibility complying with 703.7.2.1.

216.8 Toilet Rooms and Bathing Rooms. Where existing toilet rooms or bathing rooms do not comply with 603, directional signs indicating the location of the nearest toilet room or bathing room complying with 603 within the facility shall be provided. Signs shall comply with 703.5 and shall include the International Symbol of Accessibility complying with 703.7.2.1. Where existing toilet rooms or bathing rooms do not comply with 603, the toilet rooms or bathing rooms complying with 603 shall be identified by the International Symbol of Accessibility complying with 703.7.2.1. Where clustered single user toilet rooms or bathing facilities are permitted to use exceptions to 213.2, toilet rooms or bathing facilities complying with 603 shall be identified by the International Symbol of Accessibility complying with 703.7.2.1 unless all toilet rooms and bathing facilities comply with 603.

216.9 TTYs. Identification and directional signs for public TTYs shall be provided in accordance with 216.9.

216.9.1 Identification Signs. Public TTYs shall be identified by the International Symbol of TTY complying with 703.7.2.2.

216.9.2 Directional Signs. Directional signs indicating the location of the nearest public TTY shall be provided at all banks of public pay telephones not containing a public TTY. In addition, where signs provide direction to public pay telephones, they shall also provide direction to public TTYs. Directional signs shall comply with 703.5 and shall include the International Symbol of TTY complying with 703.7.2.2.

216.10 Assistive Listening Systems. Each assembly area required by 219 to provide assistive listening systems shall provide signs informing patrons of the availability of the assistive listening system. Assistive listening signs shall comply with 703.5 and shall include the International Symbol of Access for Hearing Loss complying with 703.7.2.4.

EXCEPTION: Where ticket offices or windows are provided, signs shall not be required at each assembly area provided that signs are displayed at each ticket office or window informing patrons of the availability of assistive listening systems.

216.11 Check-Out Aisles. Where more than one check-out aisle is provided, check-out aisles complying with 904.3 shall be identified by the International Symbol of Accessibility complying with 703.7.2.1. Where check-out aisles are identified by numbers, letters, or functions, signs identifying check-out aisles complying with 904.3 shall be located in the same location as the check-out aisle identification.

EXCEPTION: Where all check-out aisles serving a single function comply with 904.3, signs complying with 703.7.2.1 shall not be required.

216.12 Amusement Rides. Signs identifying the type of access provided on amusement rides shall be provided at entries to queues and waiting lines. In addition, where accessible unload areas also serve as accessible load areas, signs indicating the location of the accessible load and unload areas shall be provided at entries to queues and waiting lines.

Advisory 216.12 Amusement Rides.

Amusement rides designed primarily for children, amusement rides that are controlled or operated by the rider, and amusement rides without seats, are not required to provide wheelchair spaces, transfer seats, or transfer systems, and need not meet the sign requirements in 216.12. The load and unload areas of these rides must, however, be on an accessible route and must provide turning space.

217 Telephones

217.1 General. Where coin-operated public pay telephones, coinless public pay telephones, public closed-circuit telephones, public courtesy phones, or other types of public telephones are provided, public telephones shall be provided in accordance with 217 for each type of public telephone provided. For purposes of this section, a bank of telephones shall be considered to be two or more adjacent telephones.

Advisory 217.1 General.

These requirements apply to all types of public telephones including courtesy phones at airports and rail stations that provide a free direct connection to hotels, transportation services, and tourist attractions.

217.2 Wheelchair Accessible Telephones. Where public telephones are provided, wheelchair accessible telephones complying with 704.2 shall be provided in accordance with Table 217.2.

EXCEPTION: Drive-up only public telephones shall not be required to comply with 217.2.

Table 217.2 Wheelchair Accessible Telephones	
Number of Telephones Provided on a Floor, Level, or Exterior Site	Minimum Number of Required Wheelchair Accessible Telephones
1 or more single units	1 per floor, level, and exterior site
1 bank	1 per floor, level, and exterior site
2 or more banks	1 per bank

217.3 Volume Controls. All public telephones shall have volume controls complying with 704.3.

217.4 TTYs. TTYs complying with 704.4 shall be provided in accordance with 217.4.

Advisory 217.4 TTYs.

Separate requirements are provided based on the number of public pay telephones provided at a bank of telephones, within a floor, a building, or on a site. In some instances one TTY can be used to satisfy more than one of these requirements. For example, a TTY required for a bank can satisfy the requirements for a building. However, the requirement for at least one TTY on an exterior site cannot be met by installing a TTY in a bank inside a building. Consideration should be given to phone systems that can accommodate both digital and analog transmissions for compatibility with digital and analog TTYs.

217.4.1 Bank Requirement. Where four or more public pay telephones are provided at a bank of telephones, at least one public TTY complying with 704.4 shall be provided at that bank.

EXCEPTION: TTYs shall not be required at banks of telephones located within 200 feet (61 m) of, and on the same floor as, a bank containing a public TTY.

217.4.2 Floor Requirement. TTYs in public buildings shall be provided in accordance with 217.4.2.1. TTYs in private buildings shall be provided in accordance with 217.4.2.2.

217.4.2.1 Public Buildings. Where at least one public pay telephone is provided on a floor of a public building, at least one public TTY shall be provided on that floor.

217.4.2.2 Private Buildings. Where four or more public pay telephones are provided on a floor of a private building, at least one public TTY shall be provided on that floor.

217.4.3 Building Requirement. TTYs in public buildings shall be provided in accordance with 217.4.3.1. TTYs in private buildings shall be provided in accordance with 217.4.3.2.

217.4.3.1   Public Buildings. Where at least one public pay telephone is provided in a public building, at least one public TTY shall be provided in the building. Where at least one public pay telephone is provided in a public use area of a public building, at least one public TTY shall be provided in the public building in a public use area.

217.4.3.2   Private Buildings. Where four or more public pay telephones are provided in a private building, at least one public TTY shall be provided in the building.

217.4.4   Exterior Site Requirement. Where four or more public pay telephones are provided on an exterior site, at least one public TTY shall be provided on the site.

217.4.5   Rest Stops, Emergency Roadside Stops, and Service Plazas. Where at least one public pay telephone is provided at a public rest stop, emergency roadside stop, or service plaza, at least one public TTY shall be provided.

217.4.6   Hospitals. Where at least one public pay telephone is provided serving a hospital emergency room, hospital recovery room, or hospital waiting room, at least one public TTY shall be provided at each location.

217.4.7   Transportation Facilities. In transportation facilities, in addition to the requirements of 217.4.1 through 217.4.4, where at least one public pay telephone serves a particular entrance to a bus or rail facility, at least one public TTY shall be provided to serve that entrance. In airports, in addition to the requirements of 217.4.1 through 217.4.4, where four or more public pay telephones are located in a terminal outside the security areas, a concourse within the security areas, or a baggage claim area in a terminal, at least one public TTY shall be provided in each location.

217.4.8   Detention and Correctional Facilities. In detention and correctional facilities, where at least one pay telephone is provided in a secured area used only by detainees or inmates and security personnel, at least one TTY shall be provided in at least one secured area.

217.5   Shelves for Portable TTYs. Where a bank of telephones in the interior of a building consists of three or more public pay telephones, at least one public pay telephone at the bank shall be provided with a shelf and an electrical outlet in accordance with 704.5.

EXCEPTIONS:

1. Secured areas of detention and correctional facilities where shelves and outlets are prohibited for purposes of security or safety shall not be required to comply with 217.5.

2. The shelf and electrical outlet shall not be required at a bank of telephones with a TTY.

218   Transportation Facilities

218.1   General. Transportation facilities shall comply with 218.

218.2 New and Altered Fixed Guideway Stations. New and altered stations in rapid rail, light rail, commuter rail, intercity rail, high speed rail, and other fixed guideway systems shall comply with 810.5 through 810.10.

218.3 Key Stations and Existing Intercity Rail Stations. Key stations and existing intercity rail stations shall comply with 810.5 through 810.10.

218.4 Bus Shelters. Where provided, bus shelters shall comply with 810.3.

218.5 Other Transportation Facilities. In other transportation facilities, public address systems shall comply with 810.7 and clocks shall comply with 810.8.

219 Assistive Listening Systems

219.1 General. Assistive listening systems shall be provided in accordance with 219 and shall comply with 706.

219.2 Required Systems. In each assembly area where audible communication is integral to the use of the space, an assistive listening system shall be provided.

EXCEPTION: Other than in courtrooms, assistive listening systems shall not be required where audio amplification is not provided.

219.3 Receivers. Receivers complying with 706.2 shall be provided for assistive listening systems in each assembly area in accordance with Table 219.3. Twenty-five percent minimum of receivers provided, but no fewer than two, shall be hearing-aid compatible in accordance with 706.3.

EXCEPTIONS:

1. Where a building contains more than one assembly area and the assembly areas required to provide assistive listening systems are under one management, the total number of required receivers shall be permitted to be calculated according to the total number of seats in the assembly areas in the building provided that all receivers are usable with all systems.

2. Where all seats in an assembly area are served by an induction loop assistive listening system, the minimum number of receivers required by Table 219.3 to be hearing-aid compatible shall not be required to be provided.

Table 219.3 Receivers for Assistive Listening Systems (text version)		
Capacity of Seating in Assembly Area	Minimum Number of Required Receivers	Minimum Number of Required Receivers Required to be Hearing-aid Compatible
50 or less	2	2
51 to 200	2, plus 1 per 25 seats over 50 seats[1]	2
201 to 500	2, plus 1 per 25 seats over 50 seats[1]	1 per 4 receivers[1]
501 to 1000	20, plus 1 per 33 seats over 500 seats[1]	1 per 4 receivers[1]
1001 to 2000	35, plus 1 per 50 seats over 1000 seats[1]	1 per 4 receivers[1]

Table 219.3 Receivers for Assistive Listening Systems (text version)		
Capacity of Seating in Assembly Area	Minimum Number of Required Receivers	Minimum Number of Required Receivers Required to be Hearing-aid Compatible
2001 and over	55 plus 1 per 100 seats over 2000 seats[1]	1 per 4 receivers[1]

[1] Or fraction thereof.

220   Automatic Teller Machines and Fare Machines

220.1   General. Where automatic teller machines or self-service fare vending, collection, or adjustment machines are provided, at least one of each type provided at each location shall comply with 707. Where bins are provided for envelopes, waste paper, or other purposes, at least one of each type shall comply with 811.

Advisory 220.1 General.

If a bank provides both interior and exterior ATMs, each such installation is considered a separate location. Accessible ATMs, including those with speech and those that are within reach of people who use wheelchairs, must provide all the functions provided to customers at that location at all times. For example, it is unacceptable for the accessible ATM only to provide cash withdrawals while inaccessible ATMs also sell theater tickets.

221   Assembly Areas

221.1   General. Assembly areas shall provide wheelchair spaces, companion seats, and designated aisle seats complying with 221 and 802. In addition, lawn seating shall comply with 221.5. **[See additional requirements at 28 CFR 35.151(g) and 28 CFR 36.406(f).]**

221.2   Wheelchair Spaces. Wheelchair spaces complying with 221.2 shall be provided in assembly areas with fixed seating.

221.2.1   Number and Location. Wheelchair spaces shall be provided complying with 221.2.1.

221.2.1.1   General Seating. Wheelchair spaces complying with 802.1 shall be provided in accordance with Table 221.2.1.1.

Table 221.2.1. Number of Wheelchair Spaces in Assembly Areas	
Number of Seats	Minimum Number of Required Wheelchair Spaces
4 to 25	1
26 to 50	2
51 to 150	4
151 to 300	5
301 to 500	6
501 to 5000	6, plus 1 for each 150, or fraction thereof, between 501 through 5000

Table 221.2.1. Number of Wheelchair Spaces in Assembly Areas	
Number of Seats	Minimum Number of Required Wheelchair Spaces
5001 and over	36, plus 1 for each 200, or fraction thereof, over 5000

221.2.1.2 Luxury Boxes, Club Boxes, and Suites in Arenas, Stadiums, and Grandstands. In each luxury box, club box, and suite within arenas, stadiums, and grandstands, wheelchair spaces complying with 802.1 shall be provided in accordance with Table 221.2.1.1.

Advisory 221.2.1.2 Luxury Boxes, Club Boxes, and Suites in Arenas, Stadiums, and Grandstands.

The number of wheelchair spaces required in luxury boxes, club boxes, and suites within an arena, stadium, or grandstand is to be calculated box by box and suite by suite.

221.2.1.3 Other Boxes. In boxes other than those required to comply with 221.2.1.2, the total number of wheelchair spaces required shall be determined in accordance with Table 221.2.1.1. Wheelchair spaces shall be located in not less than 20 percent of all boxes provided. Wheelchair spaces shall comply with 802.1.

Advisory 221.2.1.3 Other Boxes.

The provision for seating in "other boxes" includes box seating provided in facilities such as performing arts auditoria where tiered boxes are designed for spatial and acoustical purposes. The number of wheelchair spaces required in boxes covered by 221.2.1.3 is calculated based on the total number of seats provided in these other boxes. The resulting number of wheelchair spaces must be located in no fewer than 20% of the boxes covered by this section. For example, a concert hall has 20 boxes, each of which contains 10 seats, totaling 200 seats. In this example, 5 wheelchair spaces would be required, and they must be placed in at least 4 of the boxes. Additionally, because the wheelchair spaces must also meet the dispersion requirements of 221.2.3, the boxes containing these wheelchair spaces cannot all be located in one area unless an exception to the dispersion requirements applies.

221.2.1.4 Team or Player Seating. At least one wheelchair space complying with 802.1 shall be provided in team or player seating areas serving areas of sport activity.

EXCEPTION: Wheelchair spaces shall not be required in team or player seating areas serving bowling lanes not required to comply with 206.2.11.

221.2.2 Integration. Wheelchair spaces shall be an integral part of the seating plan.

Advisory 221.2.2 Integration.

The requirement that wheelchair spaces be an "integral part of the seating plan" means that wheelchair spaces must be placed within the footprint of the seating area. Wheelchair spaces cannot be segregated from seating areas. For example, it would be unacceptable to place only the wheelchair spaces, or only the wheelchair spaces and their associated companion seats, outside the seating areas defined by risers in an assembly area.

221.2.3 Lines of Sight and Dispersion. Wheelchair spaces shall provide lines of sight complying with 802.2 and shall comply with 221.2.3. In providing lines of sight, wheelchair spaces shall be dispersed. Wheelchair spaces shall provide spectators with choices of seating locations and viewing angles that are substantially equivalent to, or better than, the choices of seating locations and viewing angles available to all other spectators. When the number of wheelchair spaces required by 221.2.1 has been met, further dispersion shall not be required.

EXCEPTION: Wheelchair spaces in team or player seating areas serving areas of sport activity shall not be required to comply with 221.2.3.

Advisory 221.2.3 Lines of Sight and Dispersion.

Consistent with the overall intent of the ADA, individuals who use wheelchairs must be provided equal access so that their experience is substantially equivalent to that of other members of the audience. Thus, while individuals who use wheelchairs need not be provided with the best seats in the house, neither may they be relegated to the worst.

221.2.3.1 Horizontal Dispersion. Wheelchair spaces shall be dispersed horizontally.

EXCEPTIONS:

1. Horizontal dispersion shall not be required in assembly areas with 300 or fewer seats if the companion seats required by 221.3 and wheelchair spaces are located within the 2nd or 3rd quartile of the total row length. Intermediate aisles shall be included in determining the total row length. If the row length in the 2nd and 3rd quartile of a row is insufficient to accommodate the required number of companion seats and wheelchair spaces, the additional companion seats and wheelchair spaces shall be permitted to be located in the 1st and 4th quartile of the row.

2. In row seating, two wheelchair spaces shall be permitted to be located side-by-side.

Advisory 221.2.3.1 Horizontal Dispersion.

Horizontal dispersion of wheelchair spaces is the placement of spaces in an assembly facility seating area from side-to-side or, in the case of an arena or stadium, around the field of play or performance area.

221.2.3.2 Vertical Dispersion. Wheelchair spaces shall be dispersed vertically at varying distances from the screen, performance area, or playing field. In addition, wheelchair spaces shall be located in each balcony or mezzanine that is located on an accessible route.

EXCEPTIONS:

1. Vertical dispersion shall not be required in assembly areas with 300 or fewer seats if the wheelchair spaces provide viewing angles that are equivalent to, or better than, the average viewing angle provided in the facility.

2. In bleachers, wheelchair spaces shall not be required to be provided in rows other than rows at points of entry to bleacher seating.

Advisory 221.2.3.2 Vertical Dispersion.

When wheelchair spaces are dispersed vertically in an assembly facility they are placed at different locations within the seating area from front-to-back so that the distance from the screen, stage, playing field, area of sports activity, or other focal point is varied among wheelchair spaces.

Advisory 221.2.3.2 Vertical Dispersion Exception 2. Points of entry to bleacher seating may include, but are not limited to, cross aisles, concourses, vomitories, and entrance ramps and stairs. Vertical, center, or side aisles adjoining bleacher seating that are stepped or tiered are not considered entry points.

221.3 Companion Seats. At least one companion seat complying with 802.3 shall be provided for each wheelchair space required by 221.2.1.

221.4 Designated Aisle Seats. At least 5 percent of the total number of aisle seats provided shall comply with 802.4 and shall be the aisle seats located closest to accessible routes.

EXCEPTION: Team or player seating areas serving areas of sport activity shall not be required to comply with 221.4.

Advisory 221.4 Designated Aisle Seats.

When selecting which aisle seats will meet the requirements of 802.4, those aisle seats which are closest to, not necessarily on, accessible routes must be selected first. For example, an assembly area has two aisles (A and B) serving seating areas with an accessible route connecting to the top and bottom of Aisle A only. The aisle seats chosen to meet 802.4 must be those at the top and bottom of Aisle A, working toward the middle. Only when all seats on Aisle A would not meet the five percent minimum would seats on Aisle B be designated.

221.5 Lawn Seating. Lawn seating areas and exterior overflow seating areas, where fixed seats are not provided, shall connect to an accessible route.

222   Dressing, Fitting, and Locker Rooms

222.1 General. Where dressing rooms, fitting rooms, or locker rooms are provided, at least 5 percent, but no fewer than one, of each type of use in each cluster provided shall comply with 803.

EXCEPTION: In alterations, where it is technically infeasible to provide rooms in accordance with 222.1, one room for each sex on each level shall comply with 803. Where only unisex rooms are provided, unisex rooms shall be permitted.

Advisory 222.1 General.

A "cluster" is a group of rooms proximate to one another. Generally, rooms in a cluster are within sight of, or adjacent to, one another. Different styles of design provide users varying levels of privacy and convenience. Some designs include private changing facilities that are close to core areas of the facility, while other designs use space more economically and provide only group dressing facilities. Regardless of the type of facility, dressing, fitting, and locker rooms should provide people with disabilities rooms that are equally private and convenient to those provided others. For example, in a physician's office, if people without disabilities must traverse the full length of the office suite in clothing other than their street clothes, it is acceptable for people with disabilities to be asked to do the same.

222.2   Coat Hooks and Shelves. Where coat hooks or shelves are provided in dressing, fitting or locker rooms without individual compartments, at least one of each type shall comply with 803.5. Where coat hooks or shelves are provided in individual compartments at least one of each type complying with 803.5 shall be provided in individual compartments in dressing, fitting, or locker rooms required to comply with 222.1.

223   Medical Care and Long-Term Care Facilities

223.1   General. In licensed medical care facilities and licensed long-term care facilities where the period of stay exceeds twenty-four hours, patient or resident sleeping rooms shall be provided in accordance with 223. **[See additional requirements at 28 CFR 35.151(h) and 28 CFR 36.406(g).]**

EXCEPTION: Toilet rooms that are part of critical or intensive care patient sleeping rooms shall not be required to comply with 603.

Advisory 223.1 General.

Because medical facilities frequently reconfigure spaces to reflect changes in medical specialties, Section 223.1 does not include a provision for dispersion of accessible patient or resident sleeping rooms. The lack of a design requirement does not mean that covered entities are not required to provide services to people with disabilities where accessible rooms are not dispersed in specialty areas. Locate accessible rooms near core areas that are less likely to change over time. While dispersion is not required, the flexibility it provides can be a critical factor in ensuring cost effective compliance with applicable civil rights laws, including titles II and III of the ADA and Section 504 of the Rehabilitation Act of 1973, as amended. Additionally, all types of features and amenities should be dispersed among accessible sleeping rooms to ensure equal access to and a variety of choices for all patients and residents.

223.1.1   Alterations Where sleeping rooms are altered or added, the requirements of 223 shall apply only to the sleeping rooms being altered or added until the number of sleeping rooms complies with the minimum number required for new construction.

Advisory 223.1.1 Alterations.

In alterations and additions, the minimum required number is based on the total number of sleeping rooms altered or added instead of on the total number of sleeping rooms provided in a facility. As a facility is altered over time, every effort should be made to disperse accessible sleeping rooms among patient care areas such as pediatrics, cardiac care, maternity, and other units. In this way, people with disabilities can have access to the full-range of services provided by a medical care facility.

223.2 Hospitals, Rehabilitation Facilities, Psychiatric Facilities and Detoxification Facilities. Hospitals, rehabilitation facilities, psychiatric facilities and detoxification facilities shall comply with 223.2.

223.2.1 Facilities Not Specializing in Treating Conditions That Affect Mobility. In facilities not specializing in treating conditions that affect mobility, at least 10 percent, but no fewer than one, of the patient sleeping rooms shall provide mobility features complying with 805.

223.2.2 Facilities Specializing in Treating Conditions That Affect Mobility. In facilities specializing in treating conditions that affect mobility, 100 percent of the patient sleeping rooms shall provide mobility features complying with 805.

Advisory 223.2.2 Facilities Specializing in Treating Conditions That Affect Mobility.

Conditions that affect mobility include conditions requiring the use or assistance of a brace, cane, crutch, prosthetic device, wheelchair, or powered mobility aid; arthritic, neurological, or orthopedic conditions that severely limit one's ability to walk; respiratory diseases and other conditions which may require the use of portable oxygen; and cardiac conditions that impose significant functional limitations. Facilities that may provide treatment for, but that do not specialize in treatment of such conditions, such as general rehabilitation hospitals, are not subject to this requirement but are subject to Section 223.2.1.

223.3 Long-Term Care Facilities. In licensed long-term care facilities, at least 50 percent, but no fewer than one, of each type of resident sleeping room shall provide mobility features complying with 805.

224 Transient Lodging Guest Rooms

224.1 General. Transient lodging facilities shall provide guest rooms in accordance with 224. [**See additional requirements for places of lodging at 28 CFR 36.406(c) and for housing at a place of education at 28 CFR 35.151(f) and 28 CFR 36.406(e).**]

Advisory 224.1 General.

Certain facilities used for transient lodging, including time shares, dormitories, and town homes may be covered by both these requirements and the Fair Housing Amendments Act. The Fair Housing Amendments Act requires that certain residential structures having four or more multi-family dwelling units, regardless of whether they are privately owned or federally assisted, include certain features of accessible and adaptable design according to guidelines established by the U.S. Department of Housing and Urban Development (HUD). This law and the appropriate regulations should be consulted before proceeding with the design and construction of residential housing.

224.1.1   Alterations Where guest rooms are altered or added, the requirements of 224 shall apply only to the guest rooms being altered or added until the number of guest rooms complies with the minimum number required for new construction.

Advisory 224.1.1 Alterations.

In alterations and additions, the minimum required number of accessible guest rooms is based on the total number of guest rooms altered or added instead of the total number of guest rooms provided in a facility. Typically, each alteration of a facility is limited to a particular portion of the facility. When accessible guest rooms are added as a result of subsequent alterations, compliance with 224.5 (Dispersion) is more likely to be achieved if all of the accessible guest rooms are not provided in the same area of the facility.

224.1.2   Guest Room Doors and Doorways. Entrances, doors, and doorways providing user passage into and within guest rooms that are not required to provide mobility features complying with 806.2 shall comply with 404.2.3.

EXCEPTION: Shower and sauna doors in guest rooms that are not required to provide mobility features complying with 806.2 shall not be required to comply with 404.2.3.

Advisory 224.1.2 Guest Room Doors and Doorways.

Because of the social interaction that often occurs in lodging facilities, an accessible clear opening width is required for doors and doorways to and within all guest rooms, including those not required to be accessible. This applies to all doors, including bathroom doors, that allow full user passage. Other requirements for doors and doorways in Section 404 do not apply to guest rooms not required to provide mobility features.

224.2   Guest Rooms with Mobility Features. In transient lodging facilities, guest rooms with mobility features complying with 806.2 shall be provided in accordance with Table 224.2.

Table 224.2 Guest Rooms with Mobility Features (text version)			
Total Number of Guest Rooms Provided	Minimum Number of Required Rooms Without Roll-in Showers	Minimum Number of Required Rooms With Roll-in Showers	Total Number of Required Rooms
1 to 25	1	0	1
26 to 50	2	0	2
51 to 75	3	1	4
76 to 100	4	1	5
101 to 150	5	2	7
151 to 200	6	2	8

Table 224.2 Guest Rooms with Mobility Features (text version)			
Total Number of Guest Rooms Provided	Minimum Number of Required Rooms Without Roll-in Showers	Minimum Number of Required Rooms With Roll-in Showers	Total Number of Required Rooms
201 to 300	7	3	10
301 to 400	8	4	12
401 to 500	9	4	13
501 to 1000	2 percent of total	1 percent of total	3 percent of total
1001 and over	20, plus 1 for each 100, or fraction thereof, over 1000	10, plus 1 for each 100, or fraction thereof, over 1000	30, plus 2 for each 100, or fraction thereof, over 1000

224.3   Beds. In guest rooms having more than 25 beds, 5 percent minimum of the beds shall have clear floor space complying with 806.2.3.

224.4   Guest Rooms with Communication Features. In transient lodging facilities, guest rooms with communication features complying with 806.3 shall be provided in accordance with Table 224.4.

Table 224.4 Guest Rooms with Communication Features	
Total Number of Guest Rooms Provided	Minimum Number of Required Guest Rooms With Communication Features
2 to 25	2
26 to 50	4
51 to 75	7
76 to 100	9
101 to 150	12
151 to 200	14
201 to 300	17
301 to 400	20
401 to 500	22
501 to 1000	5 percent of total
1001 and over	50, plus 3 for each 100 over 1000

224.5   Dispersion. Guest rooms required to provide mobility features complying with 806.2 and guest rooms required to provide communication features complying with 806.3 shall be dispersed among the various classes of guest rooms, and shall provide choices of types of guest rooms, number of beds, and other amenities comparable to the choices provided to other guests. Where the minimum number of guest rooms required to comply with 806 is not sufficient to allow for complete dispersion, guest rooms shall be dispersed in the following priority: guest room type, number of beds, and amenities. At least one guest room required to provide mobility features complying with 806.2 shall also provide communication features complying with 806.3. Not more than 10 percent of guest rooms required to provide mobility features complying with 806.2 shall be used to satisfy the minimum number of guest rooms required to provide communication features complying with 806.3.

Advisory 224.5 Dispersion.

Factors to be considered in providing an equivalent range of options may include, but are not limited to, room size, bed size, cost, view, bathroom fixtures such as hot tubs and spas, smoking and nonsmoking, and the number of rooms provided.

225 Storage

225.1 General. Storage facilities shall comply with 225.

225.2 Storage. Where storage is provided in accessible spaces, at least one of each type shall comply with 811.

Advisory 225.2 Storage.

Types of storage include, but are not limited to, closets, cabinets, shelves, clothes rods, hooks, and drawers. Where provided, at least one of each type of storage must be within the reach ranges specified in 308; however, it is permissible to install additional storage outside the reach ranges.

225.2.1 Lockers Where lockers are provided, at least 5 percent, but no fewer than one of each type, shall comply with 811.

Advisory 225.2.1 Lockers.

Different types of lockers may include full-size and half-size lockers, as well as those specifically designed for storage of various sports equipment.

225.2.2 Self-Service Shelving. Self-service shelves shall be located on an accessible route complying with 402. Self-service shelving shall not be required to comply with 308.

Advisory 225.2.2 Self-Service Shelving.

Self-service shelves include, but are not limited to, library, store, or post office shelves.

225.3 Self-Service Storage Facilities. Self-service storage facilities shall provide individual self-service storage spaces complying with these requirements in accordance with Table 225.3.

Table 225.3 Self-Service Storage Facilities	
Total Spaces in Facility	Minimum Number of Spaces Required to be Accessible
1 to 200	5 percent, but no fewer than 1
201 and over	10, plus 2 percent of total number of units over 200

Advisory 225.3 Self-Service Storage Facilities.

Although there are no technical requirements that are unique to self-service storage facilities, elements and spaces provided in facilities containing self-service storage spaces required to comply with these requirements must comply with this document where applicable. For example: the number of storage spaces required to comply with these requirements must provide Accessible Routes complying with Section 206; Accessible Means of Egress complying with Section 207; Parking Spaces complying with Section 208; and, where provided, other public use or common use elements and facilities such as toilet rooms, drinking fountains, and telephones must comply with the applicable requirements of this document.

225.3.1 Dispersion Individual self-service storage spaces shall be dispersed throughout the various classes of spaces provided. Where more classes of spaces are provided than the number required to be accessible, the number of spaces shall not be required to exceed that required by Table 225.3. Self-service storage spaces complying with Table 225.3 shall not be required to be dispersed among buildings in a multi-building facility.

226 Dining Surfaces and Work Surfaces

226.1 General. Where dining surfaces are provided for the consumption of food or drink, at least 5 percent of the seating spaces and standing spaces at the dining surfaces shall comply with 902. In addition, where work surfaces are provided for use by other than employees, at least 5 percent shall comply with 902.

EXCEPTIONS:

1. Sales counters and service counters shall not be required to comply with 902.

2. Check writing surfaces provided at check-out aisles not required to comply with 904.3 shall not be required to comply with 902.

Advisory 226.1 General.

In facilities covered by the ADA, this requirement does not apply to work surfaces used only by employees. However, the ADA and, where applicable, Section 504 of the Rehabilitation Act of 1973, as amended, provide that employees are entitled to "reasonable accommodations." With respect to work surfaces, this means that employers may need to procure or adjust work stations such as desks, laboratory and work benches, fume hoods, reception counters, teller windows, study carrels, commercial kitchen counters, and conference tables to accommodate the individual needs of employees with disabilities on an "as needed" basis. Consider work surfaces that are flexible and permit installation at variable heights and clearances.

226.2 Dispersion. Dining surfaces and work surfaces required to comply with 902 shall be dispersed throughout the space or facility containing dining surfaces and work surfaces.

227 Sales and Service

227.1 General. Where provided, check-out aisles, sales counters, service counters, food service lines, queues, and waiting lines shall comply with 227 and 904.

227.2 Check-Out Aisles. Where check-out aisles are provided, check-out aisles complying with 904.3 shall be provided in accordance with Table 227.2. Where check-out aisles serve different functions, check-out aisles complying with 904.3 shall be provided in accordance with Table 227.2 for each function. Where check-out aisles are dispersed throughout the building or facility, check-out aisles complying with 904.3 shall be dispersed.

EXCEPTION: Where the selling space is under 5000 square feet (465 m2) no more than one check-out aisle complying with 904.3 shall be required.

Table 227.2 Check-Out Aisles	
Number of Check-Out Aisles of Each Function	Minimum Number of Check-Out Aisles of Each Function Required to Comply with 904.3
1 to 4	1
5 to 8	2
9 to 15	3
16 and over	3, plus 20 percent of additional aisles

227.2.1 Altered Check-Out Aisles. Where check-out aisles are altered, at least one of each check-out aisle serving each function shall comply with 904.3 until the number of check-out aisles complies with 227.2.

227.3 Counters. Where provided, at least one of each type of sales counter and service counter shall comply with 904.4. Where counters are dispersed throughout the building or facility, counters complying with 904.4 also shall be dispersed.

Advisory 227.3 Counters.

Types of counters that provide different services in the same facility include, but are not limited to, order, pick-up, express, and returns. One continuous counter can be used to provide different types of service. For example, order and pick-up are different services. It would not be acceptable to provide access only to the part of the counter where orders are taken when orders are picked-up at a different location on the same counter. Both the order and pick-up section of the counter must be accessible.

227.4 Food Service Lines. Food service lines shall comply with 904.5. Where self-service shelves are provided, at least 50 percent, but no fewer than one, of each type provided shall comply with 308.

227.5 Queues and Waiting Lines. Queues and waiting lines servicing counters or check-out aisles required to comply with 904.3 or 904.4 shall comply with 403.

228 Depositories, Vending Machines, Change Machines, Mail Boxes, and Fuel Dispensers

228.1 General. Where provided, at least one of each type of depository, vending machine, change machine, and fuel dispenser shall comply with 309.

EXCEPTION: Drive-up only depositories shall not be required to comply with 309.

Advisory 228.1 General.

Depositories include, but are not limited to, night receptacles in banks, post offices, video stores, and libraries.

228.2 Mail Boxes. Where mail boxes are provided in an interior location, at least 5 percent, but no fewer than one, of each type shall comply with 309. In residential facilities, where mail boxes are provided for each residential dwelling unit, mail boxes complying with 309 shall be provided for each residential dwelling unit required to provide mobility features complying with 809.2 through 809.4.

229 Windows

229.1 General. Where glazed openings are provided in accessible rooms or spaces for operation by occupants, at least one opening shall comply with 309. Each glazed opening required by an administrative authority to be operable shall comply with 309.

EXCEPTION:

1. Glazed openings in residential dwelling units required to comply with 809 shall not be required to comply with 229.

2. Glazed openings in guest rooms required to provide communication features and in guest rooms required to comply with 206.5.3 shall not be required to comply with 229.

230 Two-Way Communication Systems

230.1 General. Where a two-way communication system is provided to gain admittance to a building or facility or to restricted areas within a building or facility, the system shall comply with 708.

Advisory 230.1 General.

This requirement applies to facilities such as office buildings, courthouses, and other facilities where admittance to the building or restricted spaces is dependent on two-way communication systems.

231 Judicial Facilities

231.1 General. Judicial facilities shall comply with 231.

231.2 Courtrooms. Each courtroom shall comply with 808.

231.3 Holding Cells. Where provided, central holding cells and court-floor holding cells shall comply with 231.3.

231.3.1 Central Holding Cells. Where separate central holding cells are provided for adult male, juvenile male, adult female, or juvenile female, one of each type shall comply with 807.2. Where central holding cells are provided and are not separated by age or sex, at least one cell complying with 807.2 shall be provided.

231.3.2 Court-Floor Holding Cells. Where separate court-floor holding cells are provided for adult male, juvenile male, adult female, or juvenile female, each courtroom shall be served by one cell of each type complying with 807.2. Where court-floor holding cells are provided and are not separated by age or sex, courtrooms shall be served by at least one cell complying with 807.2. Cells may serve more than one courtroom.

231.4   Visiting Areas. Visiting areas shall comply with 231.4.

231.4.1   Cubicles and Counters. At least 5 percent, but no fewer than one, of cubicles shall comply with 902 on both the visitor and detainee sides. Where counters are provided, at least one shall comply with 904.4.2 on both the visitor and detainee sides.

EXCEPTION: The detainee side of cubicles or counters at non-contact visiting areas not serving holding cells required to comply with 231 shall not be required to comply with 902 or 904.4.2.

231.4.2   Partitions Where solid partitions or security glazing separate visitors from detainees at least one of each type of cubicle or counter partition shall comply with 904.6.

232   Detention Facilities and Correctional Facilities

232.1   General. Buildings, facilities, or portions thereof, in which people are detained for penal or correction purposes, or in which the liberty of the inmates is restricted for security reasons shall comply with 232. **[See additional requirements at 28 CFR 35.151(k).]**

Advisory 232.1 General.

Detention facilities include, but are not limited to, jails, detention centers, and holding cells in police stations. Correctional facilities include, but are not limited to, prisons, reformatories, and correctional centers.

232.2   General Holding Cells and General Housing Cells. General holding cells and general housing cells shall be provided in accordance with 232.2.

EXCEPTION: Alterations to cells shall not be required to comply except to the extent determined by the Attorney General.

Advisory 232.2 General Holding Cells and General Housing Cells.

Accessible cells or rooms should be dispersed among different levels of security, housing categories, and holding classifications (e.g., male/female and adult/juvenile) to facilitate access. Many detention and correctional facilities are designed so that certain areas (e.g., "shift" areas) can be adapted to serve as different types of housing according to need. For example, a shift area serving as a medium-security housing unit might be redesignated for a period of time as a high-security housing unit to meet capacity needs. Placement of accessible cells or rooms in shift areas may allow additional flexibility in meeting requirements for dispersion of accessible cells or rooms.

Advisory 232.2 General Holding Cells and General Housing Cells Exception. Although these requirements do not specify that cells be accessible as a consequence of an alteration, Title II of the ADA requires that each service, program, or activity conducted by a public entity, when viewed in its entirety, be readily accessible to and usable by individuals with disabilities. This requirement must be met unless doing so would fundamentally alter the nature of a service, program, or activity or would result in undue financial and administrative burdens.

232.2.1 Cells with Mobility Features. At least 2 percent, but no fewer than one, of the total number of cells in a facility shall provide mobility features complying with 807.2.

232.2.1.1 Beds. In cells having more than 25 beds, at least 5 percent of the beds shall have clear floor space complying with 807.2.3.

232.2.2 Cells with Communication Features. At least 2 percent, but no fewer than one, of the total number of general holding cells and general housing cells equipped with audible emergency alarm systems and permanently installed telephones within the cell shall provide communication features complying with 807.3.

232.3 Special Holding Cells and Special Housing Cells. Where special holding cells or special housing cells are provided, at least one cell serving each purpose shall provide mobility features complying with 807.2. Cells subject to this requirement include, but are not limited to, those used for purposes of orientation, protective custody, administrative or disciplinary detention or segregation, detoxification, and medical isolation.

EXCEPTION: Alterations to cells shall not be required to comply except to the extent determined by the Attorney General.

232.4 Medical Care Facilities. Patient bedrooms or cells required to comply with 223 shall be provided in addition to any medical isolation cells required to comply with 232.3.

232.5 Visiting Areas. Visiting areas shall comply with 232.5.

232.5.1 Cubicles and Counters. At least 5 percent, but no fewer than one, of cubicles shall comply with 902 on both the visitor and detainee sides. Where counters are provided, at least one shall comply with 904.4.2 on both the visitor and detainee or inmate sides.

EXCEPTION: The inmate or detainee side of cubicles or counters at non-contact visiting areas not serving holding cells or housing cells required to comply with 232 shall not be required to comply with 902 or 904.4.2.

232.5.2 Partitions. Where solid partitions or security glazing separate visitors from detainees or inmates at least one of each type of cubicle or counter partition shall comply with 904.6.

233 Residential Facilities

233.1 General. Facilities with residential dwelling units shall comply with 233. **[See additional requirements at 28 CFR 35.151(e) and 28 CFR 35.151(f) and 28 CFR 36.406(d) and 28 CFR 36.406(e).]**

Advisory 233.1 General.

Section 233 outlines the requirements for residential facilities subject to the

Americans with Disabilities Act of 1990. The facilities covered by Section 233, as well as other facilities not covered by this section, may still be subject to other Federal laws such as the Fair Housing Act and Section 504 of the Rehabilitation Act of 1973, as amended. For example, the Fair Housing Act requires that certain residential structures having four or more multi-family dwelling units, regardless of whether they are privately owned or federally assisted, include certain features of accessible and adaptable design according to guidelines established by the U.S. Department of Housing and Urban Development (HUD). These laws and the appropriate regulations should be consulted before proceeding with the design and construction of residential facilities.

Residential facilities containing residential dwelling units provided by entities subject to HUD's Section 504 regulations and residential dwelling units covered by Section 233.3 must comply with the technical and scoping requirements in Chapters 1 through 10 included this document. Section 233 is not a stand-alone section; this section only addresses the minimum number of residential dwelling units within a facility required to comply with Chapter 8. However, residential facilities must also comply with the requirements of this document. For example: Section 206.5.4 requires all doors and doorways providing user passage in residential dwelling units providing mobility features to comply with Section 404; Section 206.7.6 permits platform lifts to be used to connect levels within residential dwelling units providing mobility features; Section 208 provides general scoping for accessible parking and Section 208.2.3.1 specifies the required number of accessible parking spaces for each residential dwelling unit providing mobility features; Section 228.2 requires mail boxes to be within reach ranges when they serve residential dwelling units providing mobility features; play areas are addressed in Section 240; and swimming pools are addressed in Section 242. There are special provisions applicable to facilities containing residential dwelling units at: Exception 3 to 202.3; Exception to 202.4; 203.8; and Exception 4 to 206.2.3.

233.2 Residential Dwelling Units Provided by Entities Subject to HUD Section 504 Regulations. Where facilities with residential dwelling units are provided by entities subject to regulations issued by the Department of Housing and Urban Development (HUD) under Section 504 of the Rehabilitation Act of 1973, as amended, such entities shall provide residential dwelling units with mobility features complying with 809.2 through 809.4 in a number required by the applicable HUD regulations. Residential dwelling units required to provide mobility features complying with 809.2 through 809.4 shall be on an accessible route as required by 206. In addition, such entities shall provide residential dwelling units with communication features complying with 809.5 in a number required by the applicable HUD regulations. Entities subject to 233.2 shall not be required to comply with 233.3.

Advisory 233.2 Residential Dwelling Units Provided by Entities Subject to HUD Section 504 Regulations.

Section 233.2 requires that entities subject to HUD's regulations implementing Section 504 of the Rehabilitation Act of 1973, as amended, provide residential dwelling units containing mobility features and residential dwelling units containing communication features complying with these regulations in a number specified in HUD's Section 504 regulations. Further, the residential dwelling units provided must be dispersed according to HUD's Section 504 criteria. In addition, Section 233.2 defers to HUD the specification of criteria by which the technical requirements of this document will apply to alterations of existing facilities subject to HUD's Section 504 regulations.

233.3   Residential Dwelling Units Provided by Entities Not Subject to HUD Section 504 Regulations. Facilities with residential dwelling units provided by entities not subject to regulations issued by the Department of Housing and Urban Development (HUD) under Section 504 of the Rehabilitation Act of 1973, as amended, shall comply with 233.3.

233.3.1   Minimum Number: New Construction. Newly constructed facilities with residential dwelling units shall comply with 233.3.1.

EXCEPTION: Where facilities contain 15 or fewer residential dwelling units, the requirements of 233.3.1.1 and 233.3.1.2 shall apply to the total number of residential dwelling units that are constructed under a single contract, or are developed as a whole, whether or not located on a common site.

233.3.1.1   Residential Dwelling Units with Mobility Features. In facilities with residential dwelling units, at least 5 percent, but no fewer than one unit, of the total number of residential dwelling units shall provide mobility features complying with 809.2 through 809.4 and shall be on an accessible route as required by 206.

233.3.1.2   Residential Dwelling Units with Communication Features. In facilities with residential dwelling units, at least 2 percent, but no fewer than one unit, of the total number of residential dwelling units shall provide communication features complying with 809.5.

233.3.2   Residential Dwelling Units for Sale. Residential dwelling units offered for sale shall provide accessible features to the extent required by regulations issued by Federal agencies under the Americans with Disabilities Act or Section 504 of the Rehabilitation Act of 1973, as amended. [**See additional requirements at 28 CFR 35.151(j).**]

Advisory 233.3.2 Residential Dwelling Units for Sale.

A public entity that conducts a program to build housing for purchase by individual home buyers must provide access according to the requirements of the ADA regulations and a program receiving Federal financial assistance must comply with the applicable Section 504 regulation.

233.3.3   Additions Where an addition to an existing building results in an increase in the number of residential dwelling units, the requirements of 233.3.1 shall apply only to the residential dwelling units that are added until the total number of residential dwelling units complies with the minimum number required by 233.3.1. Residential dwelling units required to comply with 233.3.1.1 shall be on an accessible route as required by 206.

233.3.4   Alterations. Alterations shall comply with 233.3.4.

EXCEPTION: Where compliance with 809.2, 809.3, or 809.4 is technically infeasible, or where it is technically infeasible to provide an accessible route to a residential dwelling unit, the entity shall be permitted to alter or construct a comparable residential dwelling unit to comply with 809.2 through 809.4 provided that the minimum number of residential dwelling units required by 233.3.1.1 and 233.3.1.2, as applicable, is satisfied.

Advisory 233.3.4 Alterations Exception.

A substituted dwelling unit must be comparable to the dwelling unit that is not made accessible. Factors to be considered in comparing one dwelling unit to another should include the number of bedrooms; amenities provided within the dwelling unit; types of common spaces provided within the facility; and location with respect to community resources and services, such as public transportation and civic, recreational, and mercantile facilities.

233.3.4.1   Alterations to Vacated Buildings. Where a building is vacated for the purposes of alteration, and the altered building contains more than 15 residential dwelling units, at least 5 percent of the residential dwelling units shall comply with 809.2 through 809.4 and shall be on an accessible route as required by 206. In addition, at least 2 percent of the residential dwelling units shall comply with 809.5.

Advisory 233.3.4.1 Alterations to Vacated Buildings.

This provision is intended to apply where a building is vacated with the intent to alter the building. Buildings that are vacated solely for pest control or asbestos removal are not subject to the requirements to provide residential dwelling units with mobility features or communication features.

233.3.4.2   Alterations to Individual Residential Dwelling Units. In individual residential dwelling units, where a bathroom or a kitchen is substantially altered, and at least one other room is altered, the requirements of 233.3.1 shall apply to the altered residential dwelling units until the total number of residential dwelling units complies with the minimum number required by 233.3.1.1 and 233.3.1.2. Residential dwelling units required to comply with 233.3.1.1 shall be on an accessible route as required by 206.

EXCEPTION: Where facilities contain 15 or fewer residential dwelling units, the requirements of 233.3.1.1 and 233.3.1.2 shall apply to the total number of residential dwelling units that are altered under a single contract, or are developed as a whole, whether or not located on a common site.

Advisory 233.3.4.2 Alterations to Individual Residential Dwelling Units.

Section 233.3.4.2 uses the terms "substantially altered" and "altered." A substantial alteration to a kitchen or bathroom includes, but is not limited to, alterations that are changes to or rearrangements in the plan configuration, or replacement of cabinetry. Substantial alterations do not include normal maintenance or appliance and fixture replacement, unless such maintenance or replacement requires changes to or rearrangements in the plan configuration, or replacement of cabinetry. The term "alteration" is defined both in Section 106 of these requirements and in the Department of Justice ADA regulations.

233.3.5   Dispersion. Residential dwelling units required to provide mobility features complying with 809.2 through 809.4 and residential dwelling units required to provide communication features complying with 809.5 shall be dispersed among the various types of residential dwelling units in the facility and shall provide choices of residential dwelling units comparable to, and integrated with, those available to other residents.

EXCEPTION: Where multi-story residential dwelling units are one of the types of residential dwelling units provided, one-story residential dwelling units shall be permitted as a substitute for multi-story residential dwelling units where equivalent spaces and amenities are provided in the one-story residential dwelling unit.

234   Amusement Rides

234.1   General. Amusement rides shall comply with 234.

EXCEPTION: Mobile or portable amusement rides shall not be required to comply with 234.

Advisory 234.1 General.

These requirements apply generally to newly designed and constructed amusement rides and attractions. A custom designed and constructed ride is new upon its first use, which is the first time amusement park patrons take the ride. With respect to amusement rides purchased from other entities, new refers to the first permanent installation of the ride, whether it is used off the shelf or modified before it is installed. Where amusement rides are moved after several seasons to another area of the park or to another park, the ride would not be considered newly designed or newly constructed.

Some amusement rides and attractions that have unique designs and features are not addressed by these requirements. In those situations, these requirements are to be applied to the extent possible. An example of an amusement ride not specifically addressed by these requirements includes "virtual reality" rides where the device does not move through a fixed course within a defined area. An accessible route must be provided to these rides. Where an attraction or ride has unique features for which there are no applicable scoping provisions, then a reasonable number, but at least one, of the features must be located on an accessible route. Where there are appropriate technical provisions, they must be applied to the elements that are covered by the scoping provisions.

Advisory 234.1 General Exception. Mobile or temporary rides are those set up for short periods of time such as traveling carnivals, State and county fairs, and festivals. The amusement rides that are covered by 234.1 are ones that are not regularly assembled and disassembled.

234.2   Load and Unload Areas. Load and unload areas serving amusement rides shall comply with 1002.3.

234.3   Minimum Number. Amusement rides shall provide at least one wheelchair space complying with 1002.4, or at least one amusement ride seat designed for transfer complying with 1002.5, or at least one transfer device complying with 1002.6.

EXCEPTIONS:

1. Amusement rides that are controlled or operated by the rider shall not be required to comply with 234.3.

2. Amusement rides designed primarily for children, where children are assisted on and off the ride by an adult, shall not be required to comply with 234.3.

3. Amusement rides that do not provide amusement ride seats shall not be required to comply with 234.3.

Advisory 234.3 Minimum Number Exceptions 1 through 3.

Amusement rides controlled or operated by the rider, designed for children, or rides without ride seats are not required to comply with 234.3. These rides are not exempt from the other provisions in 234 requiring an accessible route to the load and unload areas and to the ride. The exception does not apply to those rides where patrons may cause the ride to make incidental movements, but where the patron otherwise has no control over the ride.

Advisory 234.3 Minimum Number Exception 2. The exception is limited to those rides designed "primarily" for children, where children are assisted on and off the ride by an adult. This exception is limited to those rides designed for children and not for the occasional adult user. An accessible route to and turning space in the load and unload area will provide access for adults and family members assisting children on and off these rides.

234.4   Existing Amusement Rides. Where existing amusement rides are altered, the alteration shall comply with 234.4.

Advisory 234.4 Existing Amusement Rides.

Routine maintenance, painting, and changing of theme boards are examples of activities that do not constitute an alteration subject to this section.

234.4.1   Load and Unload Areas. Where load and unload areas serving existing amusement rides are newly designed and constructed, the load and unload areas shall comply with 1002.3.

234.4.2   Minimum Number. Where the structural or operational characteristics of an amusement ride are altered to the extent that the amusement ride's performance differs from that specified by the manufacturer or the original design, the amusement ride shall comply with 234.3.

235   Recreational Boating Facilities

235.1   General. Recreational boating facilities shall comply with 235.

235.2   Boat Slips. Boat slips complying with 1003.3.1 shall be provided in accordance with Table 235.2. Where the number of boat slips is not identified, each 40 feet (12 m) of boat slip edge provided along the perimeter of the pier shall be counted as one boat slip for the purpose of this section.

Table 235.2 Boat Slips	
Total Number of Boat Slips Provided in Facility	Minimum Number of Required Accessible Boat Slips
1 to 25	1
26 to 50	2
51 to 100	3
101 to 150	4
151 to 300	5
301 to 400	6
401 to 500	7
501 to 600	8
601 to 700	9
701 to 800	10
801 to 900	11
901 to 1000	12
1001 and over	12, plus 1 for every 100, or fraction thereof, over 1000

Advisory 235.2 Boat Slips.

The requirement for boat slips also applies to piers where boat slips are not demarcated. For example, a single pier 25 feet (7620 mm) long and 5 feet (1525 mm) wide (the minimum width specified by Section 1003.3) allows boats to moor on three sides. Because the number of boat slips is not demarcated, the total length of boat slip edge (55 feet, 17 m) must be used to determine the number of boat slips provided (two). This number is based on the specification in Section 235.2 that each 40 feet (12 m) of boat slip edge, or fraction thereof, counts as one boat slip. In this example, Table 235.2 would require one boat slip to be accessible.

235.2.1 Dispersion Boat slips complying with 1003.3.1 shall be dispersed throughout the various types of boat slips provided. Where the minimum number of boat slips required to comply with 1003.3.1 has been met, no further dispersion shall be required.

Advisory 235.2.1 Dispersion.

Types of boat slips are based on the size of the boat slips; whether single berths or double berths, shallow water or deep water, transient or longer-term lease, covered or uncovered; and whether slips are equipped with features such as telephone, water, electricity or cable connections. The term "boat slip" is intended to cover any pier area other than launch ramp boarding piers where recreational boats are moored for purposes of berthing, embarking, or disembarking. For example, a fuel pier may contain boat slips, and this type of short term slip would be included in determining compliance with 235.2.

235.3 Boarding Piers at Boat Launch Ramps. Where boarding piers are provided at boat launch ramps, at least 5 percent, but no fewer than one, of the boarding piers shall comply with 1003.3.2.

236   Exercise Machines and Equipment

236.1   General. At least one of each type of exercise machine and equipment shall comply with 1004.

Advisory 236.1 General.

Most strength training equipment and machines are considered different types. Where operators provide a biceps curl machine and cable-cross-over machine, both machines are required to meet the provisions in this section, even though an individual may be able to work on their biceps through both types of equipment.

Similarly, there are many types of cardiovascular exercise machines, such as stationary bicycles, rowing machines, stair climbers, and treadmills. Each machine provides a cardiovascular exercise and is considered a different type for purposes of these requirements.

237   Fishing Piers and Platforms

237.1   General. Fishing piers and platforms shall comply with 1005.

238   Golf Facilities

238.1   General. Golf facilities shall comply with 238.

238.2   Golf Courses. Golf courses shall comply with 238.2.

238.2.1   Teeing Grounds. Where one teeing ground is provided for a hole, the teeing ground shall be designed and constructed so that a golf car can enter and exit the teeing ground. Where two teeing grounds are provided for a hole, the forward teeing ground shall be designed and constructed so that a golf car can enter and exit the teeing ground. Where three or more teeing grounds are provided for a hole, at least two teeing grounds, including the forward teeing ground, shall be designed and constructed so that a golf car can enter and exit each teeing ground.

EXCEPTION: In existing golf courses, the forward teeing ground shall not be required to be one of the teeing grounds on a hole designed and constructed so that a golf car can enter and exit the teeing ground where compliance is not feasible due to terrain.

238.2.2   Putting Greens. Putting greens shall be designed and constructed so that a golf car can enter and exit the putting green.

238.2.3   Weather Shelters. Where provided, weather shelters shall be designed and constructed so that a golf car can enter and exit the weather shelter and shall comply with 1006.4.

238.3   Practice Putting Greens, Practice Teeing Grounds, and Teeing Stations at Driving Ranges. At least 5 percent, but no fewer than one, of practice putting greens, practice teeing grounds, and teeing stations at driving ranges shall be designed and constructed so that a golf car can enter and exit the practice putting greens, practice teeing grounds, and teeing stations at driving ranges.

239   Miniature Golf Facilities

239.1   General. Miniature golf facilities shall comply with 239.

239.2   Minimum Number. At least 50 percent of holes on miniature golf courses shall comply with 1007.3.

Advisory 239.2 Minimum Number.

Where possible, providing access to all holes on a miniature golf course is recommended. If a course is designed with the minimum 50 percent accessible holes, designers or operators are encouraged to select holes which provide for an equivalent experience to the maximum extent possible.

239.3   Miniature Golf Course Configuration. Miniature golf courses shall be configured so that the holes complying with 1007.3 are consecutive. Miniature golf courses shall provide an accessible route from the last hole complying with 1007.3 to the course entrance or exit without requiring travel through any other holes on the course.

EXCEPTION: One break in the sequence of consecutive holes shall be permitted provided that the last hole on the miniature golf course is the last hole in the sequence.

Advisory 239.3 Miniature Golf Course Configuration.

Where only the minimum 50 percent of the holes are accessible, an accessible route from the last accessible hole to the course exit or entrance must not require travel back through other holes. In some cases, this may require an additional accessible route. Other options include increasing the number of accessible holes in a way that limits the distance needed to connect the last accessible hole with the course exit or entrance.

240   Play Areas

240.1   General. Play areas for children ages 2 and over shall comply with 240. Where separate play areas are provided within a site for specific age groups, each play area shall comply with 240.

EXCEPTIONS:

1. Play areas located in family child care facilities where the proprietor actually resides shall not be required to comply with 240.

2. In existing play areas, where play components are relocated for the purposes of creating safe use zones and the ground surface is not altered or extended for more than one use zone, the play area shall not be required to comply with 240.

3. Amusement attractions shall not be required to comply with 240.

4. Where play components are altered and the ground surface is not altered, the ground surface shall not be required to comply with 1008.2.6 unless required by 202.4.

Advisory 240.1 General.

Play areas may be located on exterior sites or within a building. Where separate play areas are provided within a site for children in specified age groups (e.g., preschool (ages 2 to 5) and school age (ages 5 to 12)), each play area must comply with this section. Where play areas are provided for the same age group on a site but are geographically separated (e.g., one is located next to a picnic area and another is located next to a softball field), they are considered separate play areas and each play area must comply with this section.

240.1.1 Additions. Where play areas are designed and constructed in phases, the requirements of 240 shall apply to each successive addition so that when the addition is completed, the entire play area complies with all the applicable requirements of 240.

Advisory 240.1.1 Additions.

These requirements are to be applied so that when each successive addition is completed, the entire play area complies with all applicable provisions. For example, a play area is built in two phases. In the first phase, there are 10 elevated play components and 10 elevated play components are added in the second phase for a total of 20 elevated play components in the play area. When the first phase was completed, at least 5 elevated play components, including at least 3 different types, were to be provided on an accessible route. When the second phase is completed, at least 10 elevated play components must be located on an accessible route, and at least 7 ground level play components, including 4 different types, must be provided on an accessible route. At the time the second phase is complete, ramps must be used to connect at least 5 of the elevated play components and transfer systems are permitted to be used to connect the rest of the elevated play components required to be located on an accessible route.

240.2 Play Components. Where provided, play components shall comply with 240.2.

240.2.1 Ground Level Play Components. Ground level play components shall be provided in the number and types required by 240.2.1. Ground level play components that are provided to comply with 240.2.1.1 shall be permitted to satisfy the additional number required by 240.2.1.2 if the minimum required types of play components are satisfied. Where two or more required ground level play components are provided, they shall be dispersed throughout the play area and integrated with other play components.

Advisory 240.2.1 Ground Level Play Components.

Examples of ground level play components may include spring rockers, swings, diggers, and stand-alone slides. When distinguishing between the different types of ground level play components, consider the general experience provided by the play component. Examples of different types of experiences include, but are not limited to, rocking, swinging, climbing, spinning, and sliding. A spiral slide may provide a slightly different experience from a straight slide, but sliding is the general experience and therefore a spiral slide is not considered a different type of play component from a straight slide.

Ground level play components accessed by children with disabilities must be integrated into the play area. Designers should consider the optimal layout of ground level play components accessed by children with disabilities to foster interaction and socialization among all children. Grouping all ground level play components accessed by children with disabilities in one location is not considered integrated.

Where a stand-alone slide is provided, an accessible route must connect the base of the stairs at the entry point to the exit point of the slide. A ramp or transfer system to the top of the slide is not required. Where a sand box is provided, an accessible route must connect to the border of the sand box. Accessibility to the sand box would be enhanced by providing a transfer system into the sand or by providing a raised sand table with knee clearance complying with 1008.4.3.

Ramps are preferred over transfer systems since not all children who use wheelchairs or other mobility devices may be able to use, or may choose not to use, transfer systems. Where ramps connect elevated play components, the maximum rise of any ramp run is limited to 12 inches (305 mm). Where possible, designers and operators are encouraged to provide ramps with a slope less than the 1:12 maximum. Berms or sculpted dirt may be used to provide elevation and may be part of an accessible route to composite play structures.

Platform lifts are permitted as a part of an accessible route. Because lifts must be independently operable, operators should carefully consider the appropriateness of their use in unsupervised settings.

240.2.1.1 Minimum Number and Types. Where ground level play components are provided, at least one of each type shall be on an accessible route and shall comply with 1008.4.

240.2.1.2 Additional Number and Types. Where elevated play components are provided, ground level play components shall be provided in accordance with Table 240.2.1.2 and shall comply with 1008.4.

EXCEPTION: If at least 50 percent of the elevated play components are connected by a ramp and at least 3 of the elevated play components connected by the ramp are different types of play components, the play area shall not be required to comply with 240.2.1.2.

Table 240.2.1.2 Number and Types of Ground Level Play Components Required to be on Accessible Routes (text version)		
Number of Elevated Play Components Provided	Minimum Number of Ground Level Play Components Required to be on an Accessible Route	Minimum Number of Different Types of Ground Level Play Components Required to be on an Accessible Route
1	Not applicable	Not applicable
2 to 4	1	1
5 to 7	2	2
8 to 10	3	3
11 to 13	4	3
14 to 16	5	3

Table 240.2.1.2 Number and Types of Ground Level Play Components Required to be on Accessible Routes (text version)		
Number of Elevated Play Components Provided	Minimum Number of Ground Level Play Components Required to be on an Accessible Route	Minimum Number of Different Types of Ground Level Play Components Required to be on an Accessible Route
17 to 19	6	3
20 to 22	7	4
23 to 25	8	4
26 and over	8, plus 1 for each additional 3,or fraction thereof, over 25	5

Advisory 240.2.1.2 Additional Number and Types.

Where a large play area includes two or more composite play structures designed for the same age group, the total number of elevated play components on all the composite play structures must be added to determine the additional number and types of ground level play components that must be provided on an accessible route.

240.2.2 Elevated Play Components. Where elevated play components are provided, at least 50 percent shall be on an accessible route and shall comply with 1008.4.

Advisory 240.2.2 Elevated Play Components.

A double or triple slide that is part of a composite play structure is one elevated play component. For purposes of this section, ramps, transfer systems, steps, decks, and roofs are not considered elevated play components. Although socialization and pretend play can occur on these elements, they are not primarily intended for play.

Some play components that are attached to a composite play structure can be approached or exited at the ground level or above grade from a platform or deck. For example, a climber attached to a composite play structure can be approached or exited at the ground level or above grade from a platform or deck on a composite play structure. Play components that are attached to a composite play structure and can be approached from a platform or deck (e.g., climbers and overhead play components) are considered elevated play components. These play components are not considered ground level play components and do not count toward the requirements in 240.2.1.2 regarding the number of ground level play components that must be located on an accessible route.

241 Saunas and Steam Rooms

241 General. Where provided, saunas and steam rooms shall comply with 612.

EXCEPTION: Where saunas or steam rooms are clustered at a single location, no more than 5 percent of the saunas and steam rooms, but no fewer than one, of each type in each cluster shall be required to comply with 612.

242   Swimming Pools, Wading Pools, and Spas

242.1   General. Swimming pools, wading pools, and spas shall comply with 242.

242.2   Swimming Pools. At least two accessible means of entry shall be provided for swimming pools. Accessible means of entry shall be swimming pool lifts complying with 1009.2; sloped entries complying with 1009.3; transfer walls complying with 1009.4; transfer systems complying with 1009.5; and pool stairs complying with 1009.6. At least one accessible means of entry provided shall comply with 1009.2 or 1009.3.

EXCEPTIONS:

1. Where a swimming pool has less than 300 linear feet (91 m) of swimming pool wall, no more than one accessible means of entry shall be required provided that the accessible means of entry is a swimming pool lift complying with 1009.2 or sloped entry complying with 1009.3.

2. Wave action pools, leisure rivers, sand bottom pools, and other pools where user access is limited to one area shall not be required to provide more than one accessible means of entry provided that the accessible means of entry is a swimming pool lift complying with 1009.2, a sloped entry complying with 1009.3, or a transfer system complying with 1009.5.

3. Catch pools shall not be required to provide an accessible means of entry provided that the catch pool edge is on an accessible route.

Advisory 242.2 Swimming Pools.

Where more than one means of access is provided into the water, it is recommended that the means be different. Providing different means of access will better serve the varying needs of people with disabilities in getting into and out of a swimming pool. It is also recommended that where two or more means of access are provided, they not be provided in the same location in the pool. Different locations will provide increased options for entry and exit, especially in larger pools.

Advisory 242.2 Swimming Pools Exception 1. Pool walls at diving areas and areas along pool walls where there is no pool entry because of landscaping or adjacent structures are to be counted when determining the number of accessible means of entry required.

242.3   Wading Pools. At least one accessible means of entry shall be provided for wading pools. Accessible means of entry shall comply with sloped entries complying with 1009.3.

242.4   Spas. At least one accessible means of entry shall be provided for spas. Accessible means of entry shall comply with swimming pool lifts complying with1009.2; transfer walls complying with 1009.4; or transfer systems complying with 1009.5.

EXCEPTION: Where spas are provided in a cluster, no more than 5 percent, but no fewer than one, spa in each cluster shall be required to comply with 242.4.

243   Shooting Facilities with Firing Positions

243.1   General. Where shooting facilities with firing positions are designed and constructed at a site, at least 5 percent, but no fewer than one, of each type of firing position shall comply with 1010.

CHAPTER 3: BUILDING BLOCKS

301 General

301.1 Scope. The provisions of Chapter 3 shall apply where required by Chapter 2 or where referenced by a requirement in this document.

302 Floor or Ground Surfaces

302.1 General. Floor and ground surfaces shall be stable, firm, and slip resistant and shall comply with 302.

EXCEPTIONS:

1. Within animal containment areas, floor and ground surfaces shall not be required to be stable, firm, and slip resistant.

2. Areas of sport activity shall not be required to comply with 302.

Advisory 302.1 General.

A stable surface is one that remains unchanged by contaminants or applied force, so that when the contaminant or force is removed, the surface returns to its original condition. A firm surface resists deformation by either indentations or particles moving on its surface. A slip-resistant surface provides sufficient frictional counterforce to the forces exerted in walking to permit safe ambulation.

302.2 Carpet. Carpet or carpet tile shall be securely attached and shall have a firm cushion, pad, or backing or no cushion or pad. Carpet or carpet tile shall have a level loop, textured loop, level cut pile, or level cut/uncut pile texture. Pile height shall be 1/2 inch (13 mm) maximum. Exposed edges of carpet shall be fastened to floor surfaces and shall have trim on the entire length of the exposed edge. Carpet edge trim shall comply with 303.

Advisory 302.2 Carpet.

Carpets and permanently affixed mats can significantly increase the amount of force (roll resistance) needed to propel a wheelchair over a surface. The firmer the carpeting and backing, the lower the roll resistance. A pile thickness up to 1/2 inch (13 mm) (measured to the backing, cushion, or pad) is allowed, although a lower pile provides easier wheelchair maneuvering. If a backing, cushion or pad is used, it must be firm. Preferably, carpet pad should not be used because the soft padding increases roll resistance.

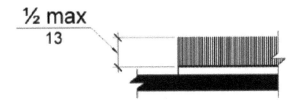

Figure 302.2 Carpet Pile Height

Figure 302.2 Carpet Pile Height 302.3 Openings. Openings in floor or ground surfaces shall not allow passage of a sphere more than 1/2 inch (13 mm) diameter except as allowed in 407.4.3, 409.4.3, 410.4, 810.5.3 and 810.10. Elongated openings shall be placed so that the long dimension is perpendicular to the dominant direction of travel.

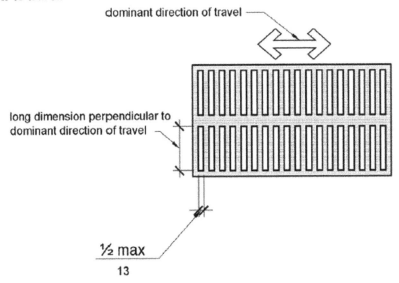

Figure 302.3 Elongated Openings in Floor or Ground Surfaces

303   Changes in Level

303.1   General. Where changes in level are permitted in floor or ground surfaces, they shall comply with 303.

EXCEPTIONS:

1. Animal containment areas shall not be required to comply with 303.

2. Areas of sport activity shall not be required to comply with 303.

303.2   Vertical. Changes in level of 1/4 inch (6.4 mm) high maximum shall be permitted to be vertical.

Figure 303.2 Vertical Change in Level

303.3 Beveled. Changes in level between 1/4 inch (6.4 mm) high minimum and 1/2 inch (13 mm) high maximum shall be beveled with a slope not steeper than 1:2.

Advisory 303.3 Beveled.

A change in level of 1/2 inch (13 mm) is permitted to be 1/4 inch (6.4 mm) vertical plus 1/4 inch (6.4 mm) beveled. However, in no case may the combined change in level exceed 1/2 inch (13 mm). Changes in level exceeding 1/2 inch (13 mm) must comply with 405 (Ramps) or 406 (Curb Ramps).

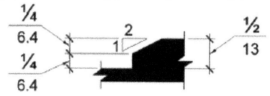

Figure 303.3 Beveled Change in Level

303.4 Ramps. Changes in level greater than 1/2 inch (13 mm) high shall be ramped, and shall comply with 405 or 406.

304   Turning Space

304.1   General. Turning space shall comply with 304.

304.2   Floor or Ground Surfaces. Floor or ground surfaces of a turning space shall comply with 302. Changes in level are not permitted.

EXCEPTION: Slopes not steeper than 1:48 shall be permitted.

Advisory 304.2 Floor or Ground Surface Exception.

As used in this section, the phrase "changes in level" refers to surfaces with slopes and to surfaces with abrupt rise exceeding that permitted in Section 303.3. Such changes in level are prohibited in required clear floor and ground spaces, turning spaces, and in similar spaces where people using wheelchairs and other mobility devices must park their mobility aids such as in wheelchair spaces, or maneuver to use elements such as at doors, fixtures, and telephones. The exception permits slopes not steeper than 1:48.

304.3   Size. Turning space shall comply with 304.3.1 or 304.3.2.

304.3.1   Circular Space. The turning space shall be a space of 60 inches (1525 mm) diameter minimum. The space shall be permitted to include knee and toe clearance complying with 306.

304.3.2   T-Shaped Space. The turning space shall be a T-shaped space within a 60 inch (1525 mm) square minimum with arms and base 36 inches (915 mm) wide minimum. Each arm of the T shall be clear of obstructions 12 inches (305 mm) minimum in each direction and the base shall be clear of obstructions 24 inches (610 mm) minimum. The space shall be permitted to include knee and toe clearance complying with 306 only at the end of either the base or one arm.

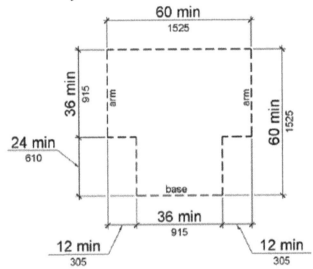

Figure 304.3.2 T-Shaped Turning Space

304.4 Door Swing. Doors shall be permitted to swing into turning spaces.

305   Clear Floor or Ground Space

305.1   General. Clear floor or ground space shall comply with 305.

305.2   Floor or Ground Surfaces. Floor or ground surfaces of a clear floor or ground space shall comply with 302. Changes in level are not permitted.

EXCEPTION: Slopes not steeper than 1:48 shall be permitted.

305.3   Size. The clear floor or ground space shall be 30 inches (760 mm) minimum by 48 inches (1220 mm) minimum.

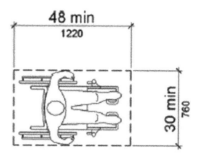

Figure 305.3 Clear Floor or Ground Space

305.4 Knee and Toe Clearance. Unless otherwise specified, clear floor or ground space shall be permitted to include knee and toe clearance complying with 306.

305.5   Position. Unless otherwise specified, clear floor or ground space shall be positioned for either forward or parallel approach to an element.

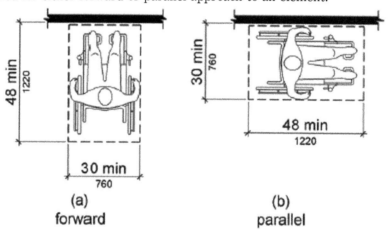

Figure 305.5 Position of Clear Floor or Ground Space

305.6 Approach. One full unobstructed side of the clear floor or ground space shall adjoin an accessible route or adjoin another clear floor or ground space.

305.7   Maneuvering Clearance. Where a clear floor or ground space is located in an alcove or otherwise confined on all or part of three sides, additional maneuvering clearance shall be provided in accordance with 305.7.1 and 305.7.2.

305.7.1   Forward Approach. Alcoves shall be 36 inches (915 mm)wide minimum where the depth exceeds 24 inches (610 mm).

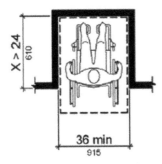

Figure 305.7.1 Maneuvering Clearance in an Alcove, Forward Approach

305.7.2 Parallel Approach. Alcoves shall be 60 inches (1525 mm) wide minimum where the depth exceeds 15 inches (380 mm).

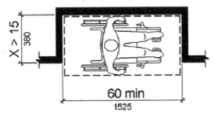

Figure 305.7.2 Maneuvering Clearance in an Alcove, Parallel Approach

306 Knee and Toe Clearance

306.1 General. Where space beneath an element is included as part of clear floor or ground space or turning space, the space shall comply with 306. Additional space shall not be prohibited beneath an element but shall not be considered as part of the clear floor or ground space or turning space.

Advisory 306.1 General.

Clearances are measured in relation to the usable clear floor space, not necessarily to the vertical support for an element. When determining clearance under an object for required turning or maneuvering space, care should be taken to ensure the space is clear of any obstructions.

306.2 Toe Clearance.

306.2.1 General Space under an element between the finish floor or ground and 9 inches (230 mm) above the finish floor or ground shall be considered toe clearance and shall comply with 306.2.

306.2.2 Maximum Depth. Toe clearance shall extend 25 inches (635 mm) maximum under an element.

306.2.3 Minimum Required Depth. Where toe clearance is required at an element as part of a clear floor space, the toe clearance shall extend 17 inches (430 mm) minimum under the element.

306.2.4 Additional Clearance. Space extending greater than 6 inches (150 mm) beyond the available knee clearance at 9 inches (230 mm) above the finish floor or ground shall not be considered toe clearance.

306.2.5 Width Toe clearance shall be 30 inches (760 mm) wide minimum.

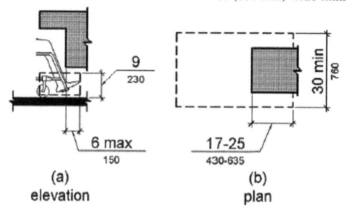

Figure 306.2 Toe Clearance

306.3 Knee Clearance.

306.3.1 General Space under an element between 9 inches (230 mm) and 27 inches (685 mm) above the finish floor or ground shall be considered knee clearance and shall comply with 306.3.

306.3.2 Maximum Depth. Knee clearance shall extend 25 inches (635 mm) maximum under an element at 9 inches (230 mm) above the finish floor or ground.

306.3.3 Minimum Required Depth. Where knee clearance is required under an element as part of a clear floor space, the knee clearance shall be 11 inches (280 mm) deep minimum at 9 inches (230 mm) above the finish floor or ground, and 8 inches (205 mm) deep minimum at 27 inches (685 mm) above the finish floor or ground.

306.3.4 Clearance Reduction. Between 9 inches (230 mm) and 27 inches (685 mm) above the finish floor or ground, the knee clearance shall be permitted to reduce at a rate of 1 inch (25 mm) in depth for each 6 inches (150 mm) in height.

306.3.5 Width Knee clearance shall be 30 inches (760 mm) wide minimum.

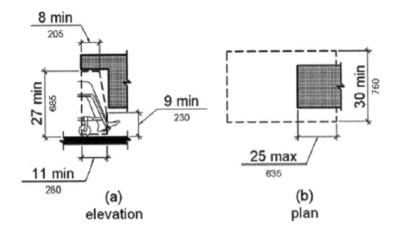

Figure 306.3 Knee Clearance

307 Protruding Objects

307.1 General. Protruding objects shall comply with 307.

307.2 Protrusion Limits. Objects with leading edges more than 27 inches (685 mm) and not more than 80 inches (2030 mm) above the finish floor or ground shall protrude 4 inches (100 mm) maximum horizontally into the circulation path.

EXCEPTION: Handrails shall be permitted to protrude 4 1/2 inches (115 mm) maximum.

Advisory 307.2 Protrusion Limits.

When a cane is used and the element is in the detectable range, it gives a person sufficient time to detect the element with the cane before there is body contact. Elements located on circulation paths, including operable elements, must comply with requirements for protruding objects. For example, awnings and their supporting structures cannot reduce the minimum required vertical clearance. Similarly, casement windows, when open, cannot encroach more than 4 inches (100 mm) into circulation paths above 27 inches (685 mm).

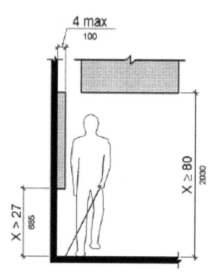

Figure 307.2 Limits of Protruding Objects

307.3 Post-Mounted Objects. Free-standing objects mounted on posts or pylons shall overhang circulation paths 12 inches (305 mm) maximum when located 27 inches (685 mm) minimum and 80 inches (2030 mm) maximum above the finish floor or ground. Where a sign or other obstruction is mounted between posts or pylons and the clear distance between the posts or pylons is greater than 12 inches (305 mm), the lowest edge of such sign or obstruction shall be 27 inches (685 mm) maximum or 80 inches (2030 mm) minimum above the finish floor or ground.

EXCEPTION: The sloping portions of handrails serving stairs and ramps shall not be required to comply with 307.3.

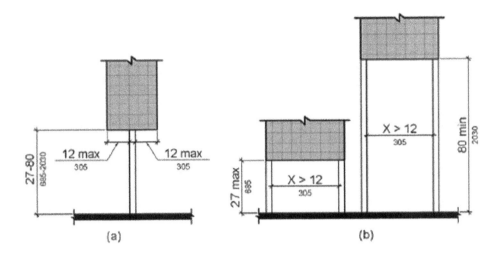

Figure 307.3 Post-Mounted Protruding Objects

307.4 Vertical Clearance. Vertical clearance shall be 80 inches (2030 mm) high minimum. Guardrails or other barriers shall be provided where the vertical clearance is less than 80 inches (2030 mm) high. The leading edge of such guardrail or barrier shall be located 27 inches (685 mm) maximum above the finish floor or ground.

EXCEPTION: Door closers and door stops shall be permitted to be 78 inches (1980 mm) minimum above the finish floor or ground.

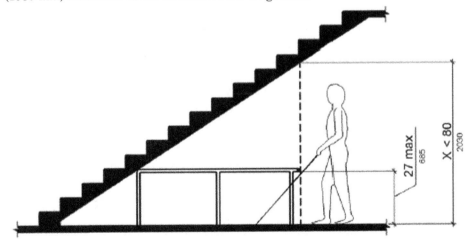

Figure 307.4 Vertical Clearance

307.5 Required Clear Width. Protruding objects shall not reduce the clear width required for accessible routes.

308   Reach Ranges

308.1   **General.** Reach ranges shall comply with 308.

Advisory 308.1 General.

The following table provides guidance on reach ranges for children according to age where building elements such as coat hooks, lockers, or operable parts are designed for use primarily by children. These dimensions apply to either forward or side reaches. Accessible elements and operable parts designed for adult use or children over age 12 can be located outside these ranges but must be within the adult reach ranges required by 308.

Children's Reach Ranges			
Forward or Side Reach	**Ages 3 and 4**	**Ages 5 through 8**	**Ages 9 through 12**
High (maximum)	36 in (915 mm)	40 in (1015 mm)	44 in (1120 mm)
Low (minimum)	20 in (510 mm)	18 in (455 mm)	16 in (405 mm)

308.2   **Forward Reach.**

308.2.1   **Unobstructed** Where a forward reach is unobstructed, the high forward reach shall be 48 inches (1220 mm) maximum and the low forward reach shall be 15 inches (380 mm) minimum above the finish floor or ground.

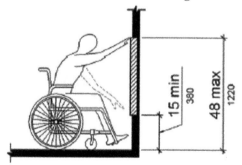

Figure 308.2.1 Unobstructed Forward Reach

308.2.2   **Obstructed High Reach.** Where a high forward reach is over an obstruction, the clear floor space shall extend beneath the element for a distance not less than the required reach depth over the obstruction. The high forward reach shall be 48 inches (1220 mm) maximum where the reach depth is 20 inches (510 mm) maximum. Where the reach depth exceeds 20 inches (510 mm), the high forward reach shall be 44 inches (1120 mm) maximum and the reach depth shall be 25 inches

(635 mm) maximum.

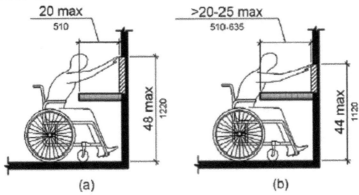

Figure 308.2.2 Obstructed High Forward Reach

308.3 Side Reach.

308.3.1 Unobstructed Where a clear floor or ground space allows a parallel approach to an element and the side reach is unobstructed, the high side reach shall be 48 inches (1220 mm) maximum and the low side reach shall be 15 inches (380 mm) minimum above the finish floor or ground.

EXCEPTIONS:

1. An obstruction shall be permitted between the clear floor or ground space and the element where the depth of the obstruction is 10 inches (255 mm) maximum.

2. Operable parts of fuel dispensers shall be permitted to be 54 inches (1370 mm) maximum measured from the surface of the vehicular way where fuel dispensers are installed on existing curbs.

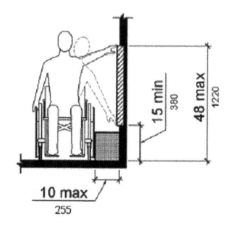

Figure 308.3.1 Unobstructed Side Reach

308.3.2 Obstructed High Reach. Where a clear floor or ground space allows a parallel approach to an element and the high side reach is over an obstruction, the height of the obstruction shall be 34 inches (865 mm) maximum and the depth of the obstruction shall be 24 inches (610 mm) maximum. The high side reach shall be 48 inches (1220 mm) maximum for a reach depth of 10 inches (255 mm) maximum. Where the reach depth exceeds 10 inches (255 mm), the high side reach shall be 46 inches (1170 mm) maximum for a reach depth of 24 inches (610 mm) maximum.

EXCEPTIONS:

1. The top of washing machines and clothes dryers shall be permitted to be 36 inches (915 mm) maximum above the finish floor.

2. Operable parts of fuel dispensers shall be permitted to be 54 inches (1370 mm) maximum measured from the surface of the vehicular way where fuel dispensers are installed on existing curbs.

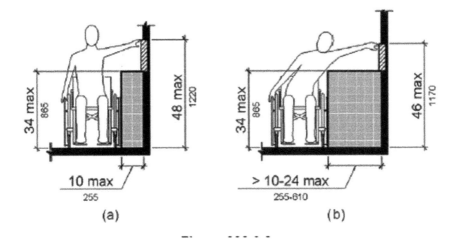

Figure 308.3.2 Obstructed High Side Reach

309 Operable Parts

309.1 General. Operable parts shall comply with 309.

309.2 Clear Floor Space. A clear floor or ground space complying with 305 shall be provided.

309.3 Height. Operable parts shall be placed within one or more of the reach ranges specified in 308.

309.4 Operation. Operable parts shall be operable with one hand and shall not require tight grasping, pinching, or twisting of the wrist. The force required to activate operable parts shall be 5 pounds (22.2 N) maximum.

EXCEPTION: Gas pump nozzles shall not be required to provide operable parts that have an activating force of 5 pounds (22.2 N) maximum.

CHAPTER 4: ACCESSIBLE ROUTES

401 General

401.1 Scope. The provisions of Chapter 4 shall apply where required by Chapter 2 or where referenced by a requirement in this document.

402 Accessible Routes

402.1 General. Accessible routes shall comply with 402.

402.2 Components. Accessible routes shall consist of one or more of the following components: walking surfaces with a running slope not steeper than 1:20, doorways, ramps, curb ramps excluding the flared sides, elevators, and platform lifts. All components of an accessible route shall comply with the applicable requirements of Chapter 4.

Advisory 402.2 Components.

Walking surfaces must have running slopes not steeper than 1:20, see 403.3. Other components of accessible routes, such as ramps (405) and curb ramps (406), are permitted to be more steeply sloped.

403 Walking Surfaces

403.1 General. Walking surfaces that are a part of an accessible route shall comply with 403.

403.2 Floor or Ground Surface. Floor or ground surfaces shall comply with 302.

403.3 Slope. The running slope of walking surfaces shall not be steeper than 1:20. The cross slope of walking surfaces shall not be steeper than 1:48.

403.4 Changes in Level. Changes in level shall comply with 303.

403.5 Clearances. Walking surfaces shall provide clearances complying with 403.5.

EXCEPTION: Within employee work areas, clearances on common use circulation paths shall be permitted to be decreased by work area equipment provided that the decrease is essential to the function of the work being performed.

403.5.1 Clear Width. Except as provided in 403.5.2 and 403.5.3, the clear width of walking surfaces shall be 36 inches (915 mm) minimum.

EXCEPTION: The clear width shall be permitted to be reduced to 32 inches (815 mm) minimum for a length of 24 inches (610 mm) maximum provided that reduced width segments are separated by segments that are 48 inches (1220 mm) long minimum and 36 inches (915 mm) wide minimum.

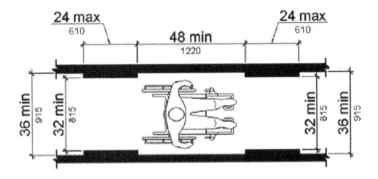

Figure 403.5.1 Clear Width of an Accessible Route

403.5.2 Clear Width at Turn. Where the accessible route makes a 180 degree turn around an element which is less than 48 inches (1220 mm) wide, clear width shall be 42 inches (1065 mm) minimum approaching the turn, 48 inches (1220 mm) minimum at the turn and 42 inches (1065 mm) minimum leaving the turn.

EXCEPTION: Where the clear width at the turn is 60 inches (1525 mm) minimum compliance with 403.5.2 shall not be required.

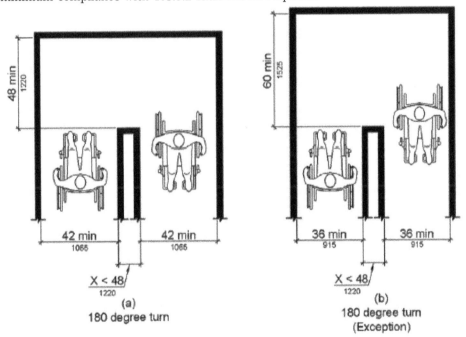

Figure 403.5.2 Clear Width at Turn

403.5.3 Passing Spaces. An accessible route with a clear width less than 60 inches (1525 mm) shall provide passing spaces at intervals of 200 feet (61 m) maximum. Passing spaces shall be either: a space 60 inches (1525 mm) minimum by 60 inches (1525 mm) minimum; or, an intersection of two walking surfaces providing a T-shaped space complying with 304.3.2 where the base and arms of the T-shaped space extend 48 inches (1220 mm) minimum beyond the intersection.

403.6 Handrails. Where handrails are provided along walking surfaces with running slopes not steeper than 1:20 they shall comply with 505.

Advisory 403.6 Handrails.

Handrails provided in elevator cabs and platform lifts are not required to comply with the requirements for handrails on walking surfaces.

404 Doors, Doorways, and Gates

404.1 General. Doors, doorways, and gates that are part of an accessible route shall comply with 404.

EXCEPTION: Doors, doorways, and gates designed to be operated only by security personnel shall not be required to comply with 404.2.7, 404.2.8, 404.2.9, 404.3.2 and 404.3.4 through 404.3.7.

Advisory 404.1 General Exception.

Security personnel must have sole control of doors that are eligible for the Exception at 404.1. It would not be acceptable for security personnel to operate the doors for people with disabilities while allowing others to have independent access.

404.2 Manual Doors, Doorways, and Manual Gates. Manual doors and doorways and manual gates intended for user passage shall comply with 404.2.

404.2.1 Revolving Doors, Gates, and Turnstiles. Revolving doors, revolving gates, and turnstiles shall not be part of an accessible route.

404.2.2 Double-Leaf Doors and Gates. At least one of the active leaves of doorways with two leaves shall comply with 404.2.3 and 404.2.4.

404.2.3 Clear Width. Door openings shall provide a clear width of 32 inches (815 mm) minimum. Clear openings of doorways with swinging doors shall be measured between the face of the door and the stop, with the door open 90 degrees. Openings more than 24 inches (610 mm) deep shall provide a clear opening of 36 inches (915 mm) minimum. There shall be no projections into the required clear opening width lower than 34 inches (865 mm) above the finish floor or ground. Projections into the clear opening width between 34 inches (865 mm) and 80 inches (2030 mm) above the finish floor or ground shall not exceed 4 inches (100 mm).

EXCEPTIONS:

1. In alterations, a projection of 5/8 inch (16 mm) maximum into the required clear width shall be permitted for the latch side stop.

2. Door closers and door stops shall be permitted to be 78 inches (1980 mm) minimum above the finish floor or ground.

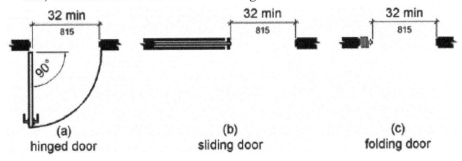

Figure 404.2.3 Clear Width of Doorways

404.2.4 Maneuvering Clearances. Minimum maneuvering clearances at doors and gates shall comply with 404.2.4. Maneuvering clearances shall extend the full width of the doorway and the required latch side or hinge side clearance.

EXCEPTION: Entry doors to hospital patient rooms shall not be required to provide the clearance beyond the latch side of the door.

404.2.4.1 Swinging Doors and Gates. Swinging doors and gates shall have maneuvering clearances complying with Table 404.2.4.1.

Table 404.2.4.1 Maneuvering Clearances at Manual Swinging Doors and Gates (text version)			
Type of Use		**Minimum Maneuvering Clearance**	
Approach Direction	**Door or Gate Side**	**Perpendicular to Doorway**	**Parallel to Doorway (beyond latch side unless noted)**
From front	Pull	60 inches (1525 mm)	18 inches (455 mm)
From front	Push	48 inches (1220 mm)	0 inches (0 mm)[1]
From hinge side	Pull	60 inches (1525 mm)	36 inches (915 mm)
From hinge side	Pull	54 inches (1370 mm)	42 inches (1065 mm)
From hinge side	Push	42 inches (1065 mm)[2]	22 inches (560 mm)[3]
From latch side	Pull	48 inches (1220 mm)[4]	24 inches (610 mm)
From latch side	Push	42 inches (1065 mm)[4]	24 inches (610 mm)
[1] Add 12 inches (305 mm) if closer and latch are provided.			

Table 404.2.4.1 Maneuvering Clearances at Manual Swinging Doors and Gates (text version)			
Type of Use		**Minimum Maneuvering Clearance**	
Approach Direction	**Door or Gate Side**	**Perpendicular to Doorway**	**Parallel to Doorway (beyond latch side unless noted)**
[2.] Add 6 inches (150 mm) if closer and latch are provided.			
[3.] Beyond hinge side.			
[4.] Add 6 inches (150 mm) if closer is provided.			

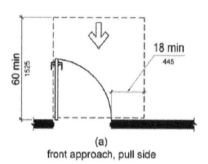

(a)
front approach, pull side

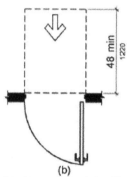

(b)
front approach, push side

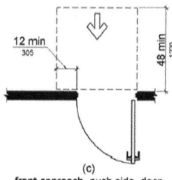

(c)
front approach, push side, door
provided with both closer and latch

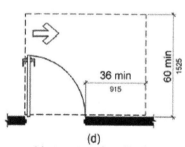

(d)
hinge approach, pull side

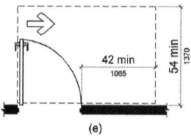

(e)
hinge approach, pull side

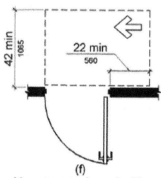

(f)
hinge approach, push side

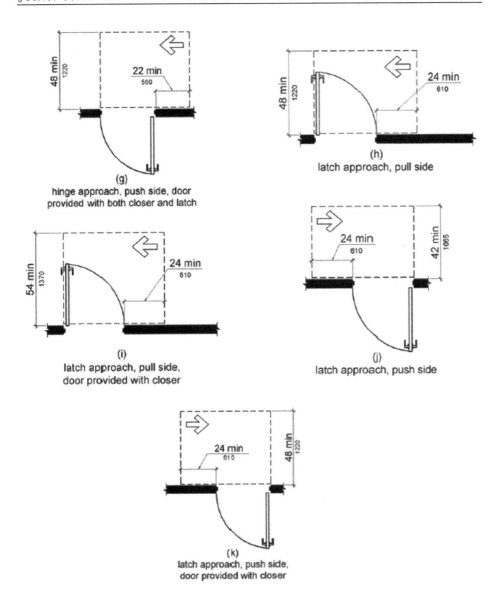

(g)
hinge approach, push side, door
provided with both closer and latch

(h)
latch approach, pull side

(i)
latch approach, pull side,
door provided with closer

(j)
latch approach, push side

(k)
latch approach, push side,
door provided with closer

404.2.4.2 Doorways without Doors or Gates, Sliding Doors, and Folding Doors. Doorways less than 36 inches (915 mm) wide without doors or gates, sliding doors, or folding doors shall have maneuvering clearances complying with Table 404.2.4.2.

Table 404.2.4.2 Maneuvering Clearances at Doorways without Doors or Gates, Manual Sliding Doors, and Manual Folding Doors		
	Minimum Maneuvering Clearance	
Approach Direction	**Perpendicular to Doorway**	**Parallel to Doorway (beyond stop/latch side unless noted)**
From Front	48 inches (1220 mm)	0 inches (0 mm)

Table 404.2.4.2 Maneuvering Clearances at Doorways without Doors or Gates, Manual Sliding Doors, and Manual Folding Doors		
	Minimum Maneuvering Clearance	
Approach Direction	**Perpendicular to Doorway**	**Parallel to Doorway (beyond stop/latch side unless noted)**
From side[1]	42 inches (1065 mm)	0 inches (0 mm)
From pocket/hinge side	42 inches (1065 mm)	22 inches (560 mm)[2]
From stop/latch side	42 inches (1065 mm)	24 inches (610 mm)

1. Doorway with no door only.
2. Beyond pocket/hinge side.

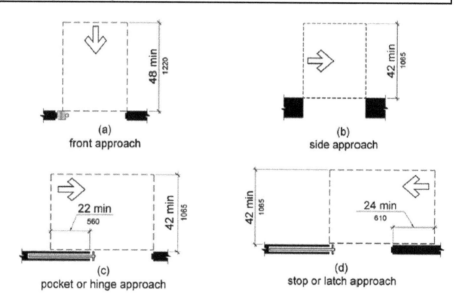

Figure 404.2.4.2 Maneuvering Clearances at Doorways without Doors, Sliding Doors, Gates, and Folding Doors

404.2.4.3 Recessed Doors and Gates. Maneuvering clearances for forward approach shall be provided when any obstruction within 18 inches (455 mm) of the latch side of a doorway projects more than 8 inches (205 mm) beyond the face of the door, measured perpendicular to the face of the door or gate.

Advisory 404.2.4.3 Recessed Doors and Gates.

A door can be recessed due to wall thickness or because of the placement of casework and other fixed elements adjacent to the doorway. This provision must be applied wherever doors are recessed.

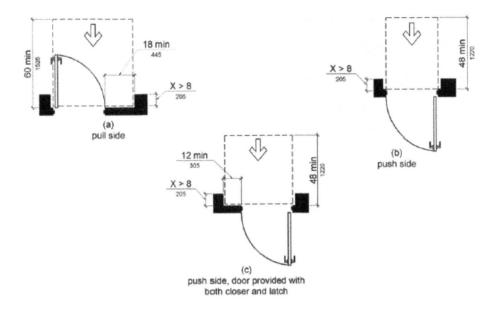

Figure 404.2.4.3 Maneuvering Clearances at Recessed Doors and Gates

404.2.4.4 Floor or Ground Surface. Floor or ground surface within required maneuvering clearances shall comply with 302. Changes in level are not permitted.

EXCEPTIONS:

1. Slopes not steeper than 1:48 shall be permitted.

2. Changes in level at thresholds complying with 404.2.5 shall be permitted.

404.2.5 Thresholds Thresholds, if provided at doorways, shall be 1/2 inch (13 mm) high maximum. Raised thresholds and changes in level at doorways shall comply with 302 and 303.

EXCEPTION: Existing or altered thresholds 3/4 inch (19 mm) high maximum that have a beveled edge on each side with a slope not steeper than 1:2 shall not be required to comply with 404.2.5.

404.2.6 Doors in Series and Gates in Series. The distance between two hinged or pivoted doors in series and gates in series shall be 48 inches (1220 mm) minimum plus the width of doors or gates swinging into the space.

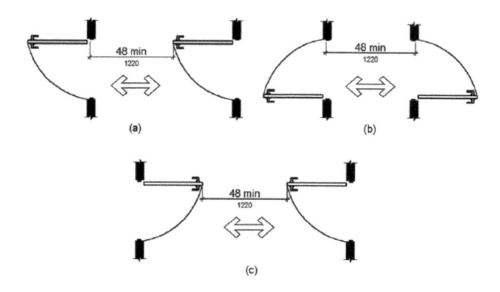

Figure 404.2.6 Doors in Series and Gates in Series

404.2.7 Door and Gate Hardware. Handles, pulls, latches, locks, and other operable parts on doors and gates shall comply with 309.4. Operable parts of such hardware shall be 34 inches (865 mm) minimum and 48 inches (1220 mm) maximum above the finish floor or ground. Where sliding doors are in the fully open position, operating hardware shall be exposed and usable from both sides.

EXCEPTIONS:

1. Existing locks shall be permitted in any location at existing glazed doors without stiles, existing overhead rolling doors or grilles, and similar existing doors or grilles that are designed with locks that are activated only at the top or bottom rail.

2. Access gates in barrier walls and fences protecting pools, spas, and hot tubs shall be permitted to have operable parts of the release of latch on self-latching devices at 54 inches (1370 mm) maximum above the finish floor or ground provided the self-latching devices are not also self-locking devices and operated by means of a key, electronic opener, or integral combination lock.

Advisory 404.2.7 Door and Gate Hardware.

Door hardware that can be operated with a closed fist or a loose grip accommodates the greatest range of users. Hardware that requires simultaneous hand and finger movements require greater dexterity and coordination, and is not recommended.

404.2.8 Closing Speed. Door and gate closing speed shall comply with 404.2.8.

404.2.8.1 Door Closers and Gate Closers. Door closers and gate closers shall be adjusted so that from an open position of 90 degrees, the time required to move the door to a position of 12 degrees from the latch is 5 seconds minimum.

404.2.8.2 Spring Hinges. Door and gate spring hinges shall be adjusted so that from the open position of 70 degrees, the door or gate shall move to the closed position in 1.5 seconds minimum.

404.2.9 Door and Gate Opening Force. Fire doors shall have a minimum opening force allowable by the appropriate administrative authority. The force for pushing or pulling open a door or gate other than fire doors shall be as follows:

1. Interior hinged doors and gates: 5 pounds (22.2 N) maximum.

2. Sliding or folding doors: 5 pounds (22.2 N) maximum.

These forces do not apply to the force required to retract latch bolts or disengage other devices that hold the door or gate in a closed position.

Advisory 404.2.9 Door and Gate Opening Force.

The maximum force pertains to the continuous application of force necessary to fully open a door, not the initial force needed to overcome the inertia of the door. It does not apply to the force required to retract bolts or to disengage other devices used to keep the door in a closed position.

404.2.10 Door and Gate Surfaces. Swinging door and gate surfaces within 10 inches (255 mm) of the finish floor or ground measured vertically shall have a smooth surface on the push side extending the full width of the door or gate. Parts creating horizontal or vertical joints in these surfaces shall be within 1/16 inch (1.6 mm) of the same plane as the other. Cavities created by added kick plates shall be capped.

EXCEPTIONS:

1. Sliding doors shall not be required to comply with 404.2.10.

2. Tempered glass doors without stiles and having a bottom rail or shoe with the top leading edge tapered at 60 degrees minimum from the horizontal shall not be required to meet the 10 inch (255 mm) bottom smooth surface height requirement.

3. Doors and gates that do not extend to within 10 inches (255 mm) of the finish floor or ground shall not be required to comply with 404.2.10.

4. Existing doors and gates without smooth surfaces within 10 inches (255 mm) of the finish floor or ground shall not be required to provide smooth surfaces complying with 404.2.10 provided that if added kick plates are installed, cavities created by such kick plates are capped

404.2.11 Vision Lights. Doors, gates, and side lights adjacent to doors or gates, containing one or more glazing panels that permit viewing through the panels shall have the bottom of at least one glazed panel located 43 inches (1090 mm) maximum above the finish floor.

EXCEPTION: Vision lights with the lowest part more than 66 inches (1675 mm)

from the finish floor or ground shall not be required to comply with 404.2.11.

404.3 Automatic and Power-Assisted Doors and Gates. Automatic doors and automatic gates shall comply with 404.3. Full-powered automatic doors shall comply with ANSI/BHMA A156.10 (incorporated by reference, see "Referenced Standards" in Chapter 1). Low-energy and power-assisted doors shall comply with ANSI/BHMA A156.19 (1997 or 2002 edition) (incorporated by reference, see "Referenced Standards" in Chapter 1).

404.3.1 Clear Width. Doorways shall provide a clear opening of 32 inches (815 mm) minimum in power-on and power-off mode. The minimum clear width for automatic door systems in a doorway shall be based on the clear opening provided by all leaves in the open position.

404.3.2 Maneuvering Clearance. Clearances at power-assisted doors and gates shall comply with 404.2.4. Clearances at automatic doors and gates without standby power and serving an accessible means of egress shall comply with 404.2.4.

EXCEPTION: Where automatic doors and gates remain open in the power-off condition, compliance with 404.2.4 shall not be required.

404.3.3 Thresholds. Thresholds and changes in level at doorways shall comply with 404.2.5.

404.3.4 Doors in Series and Gates in Series. Doors in series and gates in series shall comply with 404.2.6.

404.3.5 Controls. Manually operated controls shall comply with 309. The clear floor space adjacent to the control shall be located beyond the arc of the door swing.

404.3.6 Break Out Opening. Where doors and gates without standby power are a part of a means of egress, the clear break out opening at swinging or sliding doors and gates shall be 32 inches (815 mm) minimum when operated in emergency mode.

EXCEPTION: Where manual swinging doors and gates comply with 404.2 and serve the same means of egress compliance with 404.3.6 shall not be required.

404.3.7 Revolving Doors, Revolving Gates, and Turnstiles. Revolving doors, revolving gates, and turnstiles shall not be part of an accessible route.

405 Ramps

405.1 General. Ramps on accessible routes shall comply with 405.

EXCEPTION: In assembly areas, aisle ramps adjacent to seating and not serving elements required to be on an accessible route shall not be required to comply with 405.

405.2 Slope. Ramp runs shall have a running slope not steeper than 1:12.

EXCEPTION: In existing sites, buildings, and facilities, ramps shall be permitted to have running slopes steeper than 1:12 complying with Table 405.2 where such slopes are necessary due to space limitations.

Table 405.2 Maximum Ramp Slope and Rise for Existing Sites, Buildings, and Facilities	
Slope[1]	**Maximum Rise**
Steeper than 1:10 but not steeper than 1:8	3 inches (75 mm)
Steeper than 1:12 but not steeper than 1:10	6 inches (150 mm)
[1.] A slope steeper than 1:8 is prohibited.	

Advisory 405.2 Slope.

To accommodate the widest range of users, provide ramps with the least possible running slope and, wherever possible, accompany ramps with stairs for use by those individuals for whom distance presents a greater barrier than steps, e.g., people with heart disease or limited stamina.

405.3   Cross Slope. Cross slope of ramp runs shall not be steeper than 1:48.

Advisory 405.3 Cross Slope.

Cross slope is the slope of the surface perpendicular to the direction of travel. Cross slope is measured the same way as slope is measured (i.e., the rise over the run).

405.4   Floor or Ground Surfaces. Floor or ground surfaces of ramp runs shall comply with 302. Changes in level other than the running slope and cross slope are not permitted on ramp runs.

405.5   Clear Width. The clear width of a ramp run and, where handrails are provided, the clear width between handrails shall be 36 inches (915 mm) minimum.

EXCEPTION: Within employee work areas, the required clear width of ramps that are a part of common use circulation paths shall be permitted to be decreased by work area equipment provided that the decrease is essential to the function of the work being performed.

405.6   Rise. The rise for any ramp run shall be 30 inches (760 mm) maximum.

405.7   Landings. Ramps shall have landings at the top and the bottom of each ramp run. Landings shall comply with 405.7.

Advisory 405.7 Landings.

Ramps that do not have level landings at changes in direction can create a compound slope that will not meet the requirements of this document. Circular or curved ramps continually change direction. Curvilinear ramps with small radii also can create compound cross slopes and cannot, by their nature, meet the requirements for accessible routes. A level landing is needed at the accessible door to permit maneuvering and simultaneously door operation.

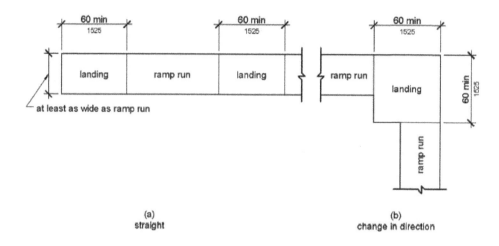

Figure 405.7 Ramp Landings

405.7.1 Slope. Landings shall comply with 302. Changes in level are not permitted.

EXCEPTION: Slopes not steeper than 1:48 shall be permitted.

405.7.2 Width. The landing clear width shall be at least as wide as the widest ramp run leading to the landing.

405.7.3 Length. The landing clear length shall be 60 inches (1525 mm) long minimum.

405.7.4 Change in Direction. Ramps that change direction between runs at landings shall have a clear landing 60 inches (1525 mm) minimum by 60 inches (1525 mm) minimum.

405.7.5 Doorways. Where doorways are located adjacent to a ramp landing, maneuvering clearances required by 404.2.4 and 404.3.2 shall be permitted to overlap the required landing area.

405.8 Handrails. Ramp runs with a rise greater than 6 inches (150 mm) shall have handrails complying with 505.

EXCEPTION: Within employee work areas, handrails shall not be required where ramps that are part of common use circulation paths are designed to permit the installation of handrails complying with 505. Ramps not subject to the exception to 405.5 shall be designed to maintain a 36 inch (915 mm) minimum clear width when handrails are installed.

405.9 Edge Protection. Edge protection complying with 405.9.1 or 405.9.2 shall be provided on each side of ramp runs and at each side of ramp landings.

EXCEPTIONS:

1. Edge protection shall not be required on ramps that are not required to have handrails and have sides complying with 406.3.

2. Edge protection shall not be required on the sides of ramp landings serving an adjoining ramp run or stairway.

3. Edge protection shall not be required on the sides of ramp landings having a vertical drop-off of 1/2 inch (13 mm) maximum within 10 inches (255 mm) horizontally of the minimum landing area specified in 405.7.

405.9.1   Extended Floor or Ground Surface. The floor or ground surface of the ramp run or landing shall extend 12 inches (305 mm) minimum beyond the inside face of a handrail complying with 505.

Advisory 405.9.1 Extended Floor or Ground Surface.

The extended surface prevents wheelchair casters and crutch tips from slipping off the ramp surface.

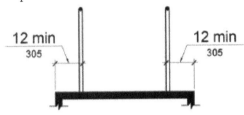

Figure 405.9.1 Extended Floor or Ground Surface Edge Protection

405.9.2   Curb or Barrier. A curb or barrier shall be provided that prevents the passage of a 4 inch (100 mm) diameter sphere, where any portion of the sphere is within 4 inches (100 mm) of the finish floor or ground surface.

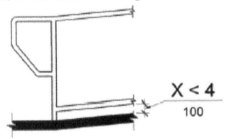

Figure 405.9.2 Curb or Barrier Edge Protection

405.10   Wet Conditions. Landings subject to wet conditions shall be designed to prevent the accumulation of water.

406   Curb Ramps

406.1   General. Curb ramps on accessible routes shall comply with 406, 405.2

through 405.5, and 405.10.

406.2 Counter Slope. Counter slopes of adjoining gutters and road surfaces immediately adjacent to the curb ramp shall not be steeper than 1:20. The adjacent surfaces at transitions at curb ramps to walks, gutters, and streets shall be at the same level.

Figure 406.2 Counter Slope of Surfaces Adjacent to Curb Ramps

406.3 Sides of Curb Ramps. Where provided, curb ramp flares shall not be steeper than 1:10.

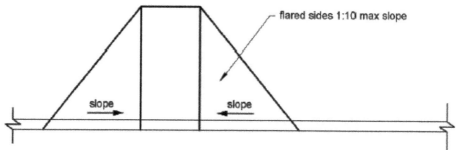

Figure 406.3 Sides of Curb Ramps

406.4 Landings. Landings shall be provided at the tops of curb ramps. The landing clear length shall be 36 inches (915 mm) minimum. The landing clear width shall be at least as wide as the curb ramp, excluding flared sides, leading to the landing.

EXCEPTION: In alterations, where there is no landing at the top of curb ramps, curb ramp flares shall be provided and shall not be steeper than 1:12.

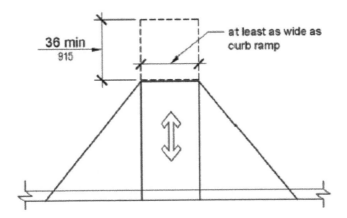

Figure 406.4 Landings at the Top of Curb Ramps

406.5 Location. Curb ramps and the flared sides of curb ramps shall be located so that they do not project into vehicular traffic lanes, parking spaces, or parking access aisles. Curb ramps at marked crossings shall be wholly contained within the markings, excluding any flared sides.

406.6 Diagonal Curb Ramps. Diagonal or corner type curb ramps with returned curbs or other well-defined edges shall have the edges parallel to the direction of pedestrian flow. The bottom of diagonal curb ramps shall have a clear space 48 inches (1220 mm) minimum outside active traffic lanes of the roadway. Diagonal curb ramps provided at marked crossings shall provide the 48 inches (1220 mm) minimum clear space within the markings. Diagonal curb ramps with flared sides shall have a segment of curb 24 inches (610 mm) long minimum located on each side of the curb ramp and within the marked crossing.

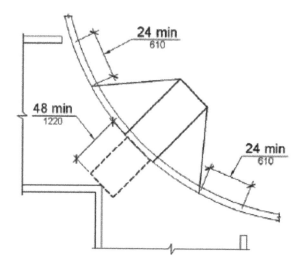

Figure 406.6 Diagonal or Corner Type Curb Ramps

406.7 Islands. Raised islands in crossings shall be cut through level with the street or have curb ramps at both sides. Each curb ramp shall have a level area 48 inches (1220 mm) long minimum by 36 inches (915 mm) wide minimum at the top of the curb ramp in the part of the island intersected by the crossings. Each 48 inch (1220 mm) minimum by 36 inch (915 mm) minimum area shall be oriented so that the 48 inch (1220 mm) minimum length is in the direction of the running slope of the curb ramp it serves. The 48 inch (1220 mm) minimum by 36 inch (915 mm) minimum areas and the accessible route shall be permitted to overlap.

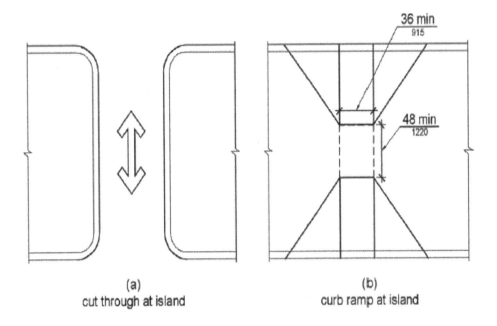

(a)
cut through at island

(b)
curb ramp at island

Figure 406.7 Islands in Crossings

407   Elevators

407.1   General. Elevators shall comply with 407 and with ASME A17.1 (incorporated by reference, see "Referenced Standards" in Chapter 1). They shall be passenger elevators as classified by ASME A17.1. Elevator operation shall be automatic.

Advisory 407.1 General.

The ADA and other Federal civil rights laws require that accessible features be maintained in working order so that they are accessible to and usable by those people they are intended to benefit. Building owners should note that the ASME Safety Code for Elevators and Escalators requires routine maintenance and inspections. Isolated or temporary interruptions in service due to maintenance or repairs may be unavoidable; however, failure to take prompt action to effect repairs could constitute a violation of Federal laws and these requirements.

407.2   Elevator Landing Requirements. Elevator landings shall comply with 407.2.

407.2.1   Call Controls. Where elevator call buttons or keypads are provided, they shall comply with 407.2.1 and 309.4. Call buttons shall be raised or flush.

EXCEPTION: Existing elevators shall be permitted to have recessed call buttons.

407.2.1.1 Height. Call buttons and keypads shall be located within one of the reach ranges specified in 308, measured to the centerline of the highest operable part.

EXCEPTION: Existing call buttons and existing keypads shall be permitted to be located at 54 inches (1370 mm) maximum above the finish floor, measured to the centerline of the highest operable part.

407.2.1.2 Size. Call buttons shall be 3/4 inch (19 mm) minimum in the smallest dimension.

EXCEPTION: Existing elevator call buttons shall not be required to comply with 407.2.1.2.

407.2.1.3 Clear Floor or Ground Space. A clear floor or ground space complying with 305 shall be provided at call controls.

Advisory 407.2.1.3 Clear Floor or Ground Space.

The clear floor or ground space required at elevator call buttons must remain free of obstructions including ashtrays, plants, and other decorative elements that prevent wheelchair users and others from reaching the call buttons. The height of the clear floor or ground space is considered to be a volume from the floor to 80 inches (2030 mm) above the floor. Recessed ashtrays should not be placed near elevator call buttons so that persons who are blind or visually impaired do not inadvertently contact them or their contents as they reach for the call buttons.

407.2.1.4 Location. The call button that designates the up direction shall be located above the call button that designates the down direction.

EXCEPTION: Destination-oriented elevators shall not be required to comply with 407.2.1.4.

Advisory 407.2.1.4 Location Exception.

A destination-oriented elevator system provides lobby controls enabling passengers to select floor stops, lobby indicators designating which elevator to use, and a car indicator designating the floors at which the car will stop. Responding cars are programmed for maximum efficiency by reducing the number of stops any passenger experiences.

407.2.1.5 Signals. Call buttons shall have visible signals to indicate when each call is registered and when each call is answered.

EXCEPTIONS:

1. Destination-oriented elevators shall not be required to comply with 407.2.1.5 provided that visible and audible signals complying with 407.2.2 indicating which elevator car to enter are provided.

2. Existing elevators shall not be required to comply with 407.2.1.5.

407.2.1.6 Keypads. Where keypads are provided, keypads shall be in a standard telephone keypad arrangement and shall comply with 407.4.7.2.

407.2.2   Hall Signals. Hall signals, including in-car signals, shall comply with 407.2.2.

407.2.2.1   Visible and Audible Signals. A visible and audible signal shall be provided at each hoistway entrance to indicate which car is answering a call and the car's direction of travel. Where in-car signals are provided, they shall be visible from the floor area adjacent to the hall call buttons.

EXCEPTIONS:

1. Visible and audible signals shall not be required at each destination-oriented elevator where a visible and audible signal complying with 407.2.2 is provided indicating the elevator car designation information.

2. In existing elevators, a signal indicating the direction of car travel shall not be required.

407.2.2.2   Visible Signals. Visible signal fixtures shall be centered at 72 inches (1830 mm) minimum above the finish floor or ground. The visible signal elements shall be 2 1/2 inches (64 mm) minimum measured along the vertical centerline of the element. Signals shall be visible from the floor area adjacent to the hall call button.

EXCEPTIONS:

1. Destination-oriented elevators shall be permitted to have signals visible from the floor area adjacent to the hoistway entrance.

2. Existing elevators shall not be required to comply with 407.2.2.2.

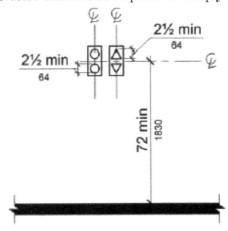

Figure 407.2.2.2 Visible Hall Signals

407.2.2.3   Audible Signals. Audible signals shall sound once for the up direction and twice for the down direction, or shall have verbal annunciators that indicate the direction of elevator car travel. Audible signals shall have a frequency of 1500 Hz maximum. Verbal annunciators shall have a frequency of 300 Hz minimum and 3000 Hz maximum. The audible signal and verbal annunciator shall be 10 dB minimum above ambient, but shall not exceed 80 dB, measured at the hall call button.

EXCEPTIONS:

1. Destination-oriented elevators shall not be required to comply with 407.2.2.3 provided that the audible tone and verbal announcement is the same as those given at the call button or call button keypad.

2. Existing elevators shall not be required to comply with the requirements for frequency and dB range of audible signals.

407.2.2.4   Differentiation. Each destination-oriented elevator in a bank of elevators shall have audible and visible means for differentiation.

407.2.3   Hoistway Signs. Signs at elevator hoistways shall comply with 407.2.3.

407.2.3.1   Floor Designation. Floor designations complying with 703.2 and 703.4.1 shall be provided on both jambs of elevator hoistway entrances. Floor designations shall be provided in both tactile characters and braille. Tactile characters shall be 2 inches (51 mm) high minimum. A tactile star shall be provided on both jambs at the main entry level.

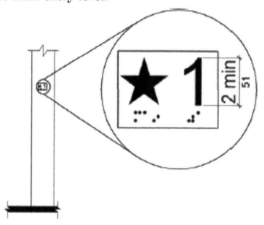

Figure 407.2.3.1 Floor Designations on Jambs of Elevator Hoistway Entrances

407.2.3.2   Car Designations. Destination-oriented elevators shall provide tactile car identification complying with 703.2 on both jambs of the hoistway immediately below the floor designation. Car designations shall be provided in both tactile characters and braille. Tactile characters shall be 2 inches (51 mm) high minimum.

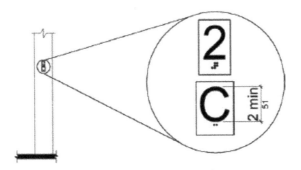

Figure 407.2.3.2 Car Designations on Jambs of Destination-Oriented Elevator Hoistway Entrances

407.3 Elevator Door Requirements. Hoistway and car doors shall comply with 407.3.

407.3.1   Type Elevator doors shall be the horizontal sliding type. Car gates shall be prohibited.

407.3.2   Operation Elevator hoistway and car doors shall open and close automatically.

EXCEPTION: Existing manually operated hoistway swing doors shall be permitted provided that they comply with 404.2.3 and 404.2.9. Car door closing shall not be initiated until the hoistway door is closed.

407.3.3   Reopening Device. Elevator doors shall be provided with a reopening device complying with 407.3.3 that shall stop and reopen a car door and hoistway door automatically if the door becomes obstructed by an object or person.

EXCEPTION: Existing elevators with manually operated doors shall not be required to comply with 407.3.3.

407.3.3.1   Height. The device shall be activated by sensing an obstruction passing through the opening at 5 inches (125 mm) nominal and 29 inches (735 mm) nominal above the finish floor.

407.3.3.2   Contact. The device shall not require physical contact to be activated, although contact is permitted to occur before the door reverses.

407.3.3.3   Duration. Door reopening devices shall remain effective for 20 seconds minimum.

407.3.4   Door and Signal Timing. The minimum acceptable time from notification that a car is answering a call or notification of the car assigned at the means for the entry of destination information until the doors of that car start to close shall be calculated from the following equation:

T = D/(1.5 ft/s) or T = D/(455 mm/s) = 5 seconds minimum where T equals the total time in seconds and D equals the distance (in feet or millimeters) from the point in the lobby or corridor 60 inches (1525 mm) directly in front of the farthest call button controlling that car to the centerline of its hoistway door.

EXCEPTIONS:

1. For cars with in-car lanterns, T shall be permitted to begin when the signal is visible from the point 60 inches (1525 mm) directly in front of the farthest hall call button and the audible signal is sounded.

2. Destination-oriented elevators shall not be required to comply with 407.3.4.

407.3.5 Door Delay. Elevator doors shall remain fully open in response to a car call for 3 seconds minimum.

407.3.6 Width The width of elevator doors shall comply with Table 407.4.1.

EXCEPTION: In existing elevators, a power-operated car door complying with 404.2.3 shall be permitted.

407.4 Elevator Car Requirements. Elevator cars shall comply with 407.4.

407.4.1 Car Dimensions. Inside dimensions of elevator cars and clear width of elevator doors shall comply with Table 407.4.1.

EXCEPTION: Existing elevator car configurations that provide a clear floor area of 16 square feet (1.5 m2) minimum and also provide an inside clear depth 54 inches (1370 mm) minimum and a clear width 36 inches (915 mm) minimum shall be permitted.

Table 407.4.1 Elevator Car Dimensions (text version)				
	Minimum Dimensions			
Door Location	**Door Clear Width**	**Inside Car, Side to Side**	**Inside Car, Back Wall to Front Return**	**Inside Car, Back Wall to Inside Face of Door**
Centered	42 inches (1065 mm)	80 inches (2030 mm)	51 inches (1295 mm)	54 inches (1370 mm)
Side(off-centered)	36 inches (915 mm)[1]	68 inches (1725 mm)	51 inches (1295 mm)	54 inches (1370 mm)
Any	36 inches (915 mm)[2]	54 inches (1370 mm)	80 inches (2030 mm)	80 inches (2030 mm)
Any	36 inches (915 mm)[1]	60 inches (1525 mm)[2]	60 inches (1525 mm)[2]	60 inches (1525 mm)[2]
1. A tolerance of minus 5/8 inch (16 mm) is permitted. 2. Other car configurations that provide a turning space complying with 304 with the door closed shall be permitted.				

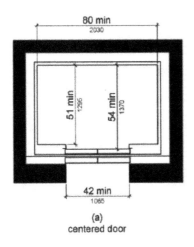

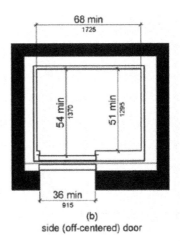

(a)
centered door

(b)
side (off-centered) door

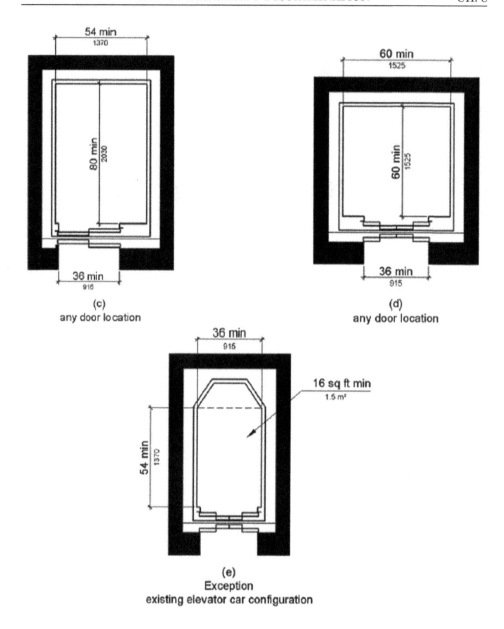

Figure 407.4.1 Elevator Car Dimensions

407.4.2   Floor Surfaces. Floor surfaces in elevator cars shall comply with 302 and 303.

407.4.3   Platform to Hoistway Clearance. The clearance between the car platform sill and the edge of any hoistway landing shall be 1 1/4 inch (32 mm) maximum.

407.4.4   Leveling. Each car shall be equipped with a self-leveling feature that will automatically bring and maintain the car at floor landings within a tolerance of 1/2 inch (13 mm) under rated loading to zero loading conditions.

407.4.5 Illumination. The level of illumination at the car controls, platform, car threshold and car landing sill shall be 5 foot candles (54 lux) minimum.

407.4.6 Elevator Car Controls. Where provided, elevator car controls shall comply with 407.4.6 and 309.4.

EXCEPTION: In existing elevators, where a new car operating panel complying with 407.4.6 is provided, existing car operating panels shall not be required to comply with 407.4.6.

407.4.6.1 Location. Controls shall be located within one of the reach ranges specified in 308.

EXCEPTIONS:

1. Where the elevator panel serves more than 16 openings and a parallel approach is provided, buttons with floor designations shall be permitted to be 54 inches (1370 mm) maximum above the finish floor.

2. In existing elevators, car control buttons with floor designations shall be permitted to be located 54 inches (1370 mm) maximum above the finish floor where a parallel approach is provided.

407.4.6.2 Buttons. Car control buttons with floor designations shall comply with 407.4.6.2 and shall be raised or flush.

EXCEPTION: In existing elevators, buttons shall be permitted to be recessed.

407.4.6.2.1 Size. Buttons shall be 3/4 inch (19 mm) minimum in their smallest dimension.

407.4.6.2.2 Arrangement. Buttons shall be arranged with numbers in ascending order. When two or more columns of buttons are provided they shall read from left to right.

407.4.6.3 Keypads. Car control keypads shall be in a standard telephone keypad arrangement and shall comply with 407.4.7.2.

407.4.6.4 Emergency Controls. Emergency controls shall comply with 407.4.6.4.

407.4.6.4.1 Height. Emergency control buttons shall have their centerlines 35 inches (890 mm) minimum above the finish floor.

407.4.6.4.2 Location. Emergency controls, including the emergency alarm, shall be grouped at the bottom of the panel.

407.4.7 Designations and Indicators of Car Controls. Designations and indicators of car controls shall comply with 407.4.7.

EXCEPTION: In existing elevators, where a new car operating panel complying with 407.4.7 is provided, existing car operating panels shall not be required to comply with 407.4.7.

407.4.7.1 Buttons. Car control buttons shall comply with 407.4.7.1.

407.4.7.1.1 Type. Control buttons shall be identified by tactile characters complying with 703.2.

407.4.7.1.2 Location. Raised character and braille designations shall be placed immediately to the left of the control button to which the designations apply.

EXCEPTION: Where space on an existing car operating panel precludes tactile markings to the left of the controls, markings shall be placed as near to the control as possible.

407.4.7.1.3 Symbols. The control button for the emergency stop, alarm, door open, door close, main entry floor, and phone, shall be identified with tactile symbols as shown in Table 407.4.7.1.3.

Table 407.4.7.1.3 Elevator Control Button Identification		
Control Button	**Tactile Symbol**	**Braille Message**
Emergency Stop	⊗	"ST"OP Three cells
Alarm	🔔	AL"AR"M Four cells
Door Open	◀❙▶	OP"EN" Three cells
Door Close	▶❙◀	CLOSE Five cells
Main Entry Floor	★	MA"IN" Three cells
Phone	☏	PH"ONE" Four cells

407.4.7.1.4 Visible Indicators. Buttons with floor designations shall be provided with visible indicators to show that a call has been registered. The visible indication shall extinguish when the car arrives at the designated floor.

407.4.7.2 Keypads. Keypads shall be identified by characters complying with 703.5 and shall be centered on the corresponding keypad button. The number five key shall have a single raised dot. The dot shall be 0.118 inch (3 mm) to 0.120 inch (3.05 mm) base diameter and in other aspects comply with Table 703.3.1.

407.4.8 Car Position Indicators. Audible and visible car position indicators shall be provided in elevator cars.

407.4.8.1 Visible Indicators. Visible indicators shall comply with 407.4.8.1.

407.4.8.1.1 Size. Characters shall be 1/2 inch (13 mm) high minimum.

407.4.8.1.2 Location. Indicators shall be located above the car control panel or above the door.

407.4.8.1.3 Floor Arrival. As the car passes a floor and when a car stops at a floor served by the elevator, the corresponding character shall illuminate.

EXCEPTION: Destination-oriented elevators shall not be required to comply with 407.4.8.1.3 provided that the visible indicators extinguish when the call has been answered.

407.4.8.1.4 Destination Indicator. In destination-oriented elevators, a display shall be provided in the car with visible indicators to show car destinations.

407.4.8.2 Audible Indicators. Audible indicators shall comply with 407.4.8.2.

407.4.8.2.1 Signal Type. The signal shall be an automatic verbal annunciator which announces the floor at which the car is about to stop.

EXCEPTION: For elevators other than destination-oriented elevators that have a rated speed of 200 feet per minute (1 m/s) or less, a non-verbal audible signal with a frequency of 1500 Hz maximum which sounds as the car passes or is about to stop at a floor served by the elevator shall be permitted.

407.4.8.2.2 Signal Level. The verbal annunciator shall be 10 dB minimum above ambient, but shall not exceed 80 dB, measured at the annunciator.

407.4.8.2.3 Frequency. The verbal annunciator shall have a frequency of 300 Hz minimum to 3000 Hz maximum.

407.4.9 Emergency Communication. Emergency two-way communication systems shall comply with 308. Tactile symbols and characters shall be provided adjacent to the device and shall comply with 703.2.

408 Limited-Use/Limited-Application Elevators

408.1 General. Limited-use/limited-application elevators shall comply with 408 and with ASME A17.1 (incorporated by reference, see "Referenced Standards" in Chapter 1). They shall be passenger elevators as classified by ASME A17.1. Elevator operation shall be automatic.

408.2 Elevator Landings. Landings serving limited-use/limited-application elevators shall comply with 408.2.

408.2.1 Call Buttons. Elevator call buttons and keypads shall comply with 407.2.1.

408.2.2 Hall Signals. Hall signals shall comply with 407.2.2.

408.2.3 Hoistway Signs. Signs at elevator hoistways shall comply with 407.2.3.1.

408.3 Elevator Doors. Elevator hoistway doors shall comply with 408.3.

408.3.1 Sliding Doors. Sliding hoistway and car doors shall comply with 407.3.1 through 407.3.3 and 408.4.1.

408.3.2 Swinging Doors. Swinging hoistway doors shall open and close automatically and shall comply with 404, 407.3.2 and 408.3.2.

408.3.2.1 Power Operation. Swinging doors shall be power-operated and shall comply with ANSI/BHMA A156.19 (1997 or 2002 edition) (incorporated by reference, see "Referenced Standards" in Chapter 1).

408.3.2.2 Duration. Power-operated swinging doors shall remain open for 20 seconds minimum when activated.

408.4 Elevator Cars. Elevator cars shall comply with 408.4.

408.4.1 Car Dimensions and Doors. Elevator cars shall provide a clear width 42 inches (1065 mm) minimum and a clear depth 54 inches (1370 mm) minimum. Car doors shall be positioned at the narrow ends of cars and shall provide 32 inches (815 mm) minimum clear width.

EXCEPTIONS:

1. Cars that provide a clear width 51 inches (1295 mm) minimum shall be permitted to provide a clear depth 51 inches (1295 mm) minimum provided that car doors provide a clear opening 36 inches (915 mm) wide minimum.

2. Existing elevator cars shall be permitted to provide a clear width 36 inches (915 mm) minimum, clear depth 54 inches (1370 mm) minimum, and a net clear platform area 15 square feet (1.4 m2) minimum.

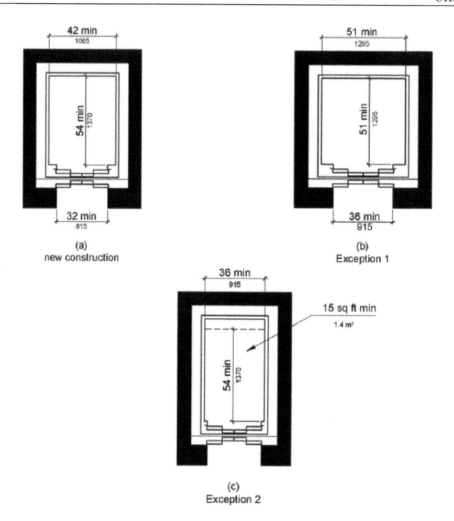

Figure 408.4.1 Limited-Use/Limited-Application (LULA) Elevator Car Dimensions

408.4.2 Floor Surfaces. Floor surfaces in elevator cars shall comply with 302 and 303.

408.4.3 Platform to Hoistway Clearance. The platform to hoistway clearance shall comply with 407.4.3.

408.4.4 Leveling. Elevator car leveling shall comply with 407.4.4.

408.4.5 Illumination. Elevator car illumination shall comply with 407.4.5.

408.4.6 Car Controls. Elevator car controls shall comply with 407.4.6. Control panels shall be centered on a side wall.

408.4.7 Designations and Indicators of Car Controls. Designations and indicators of car controls shall comply with 407.4.7.

408.4.8   Emergency Communications. Car emergency signaling devices complying with 407.4.9 shall be provided.

409   Private Residence Elevators

409.1   General. Private residence elevators that are provided within a residential dwelling unit required to provide mobility features complying with <u>809.2</u> through 809.4 shall comply with 409 and with ASME A17.1 (incorporated by reference, see "Referenced Standards" in Chapter 1). They shall be passenger elevators as classified by ASME A17.1. Elevator operation shall be automatic.

409.2   Call Buttons. Call buttons shall be 3/4 inch (19 mm) minimum in the smallest dimension and shall comply with 309.

409.3   Elevator Doors. Hoistway doors, car doors, and car gates shall comply with 409.3 and 404.

EXCEPTION: Doors shall not be required to comply with the maneuvering clearance requirements in 404.2.4.1 for approaches to the push side of swinging doors.

409.3.1   Power Operation. Elevator car and hoistway doors and gates shall be power operated and shall comply with ANSI/BHMA A156.19 (1997 or 2002 edition) (incorporated by reference, see "Referenced Standards" in Chapter 1). Power operated doors and gates shall remain open for 20 seconds minimum when activated.

EXCEPTION: In elevator cars with more than one opening, hoistway doors and gates shall be permitted to be of the manual-open, self-close type.

409.3.2   Location. Elevator car doors or gates shall be positioned at the narrow end of the clear floor spaces required by 409.4.1.

409.4   Elevator Cars. Private residence elevator cars shall comply with 409.4.

409.4.1   Inside Dimensions of Elevator Cars. Elevator cars shall provide a clear floor space of 36 inches (915 mm) minimum by 48 inches (1220 mm) minimum and shall comply with 305.

409.4.2   Floor Surfaces. Floor surfaces in elevator cars shall comply with 302 and 303.

409.4.3   Platform to Hoistway Clearance. The clearance between the car platform and the edge of any landing sill shall be 1 1/2 inch (38 mm) maximum.

409.4.4   Leveling. Each car shall automatically stop at a floor landing within a tolerance of 1/2 inch (13 mm) under rated loading to zero loading conditions.

409.4.5   Illumination Levels. Elevator car illumination shall comply with 407.4.5.

409.4.6   Car Controls. Elevator car control buttons shall comply with 409.4.6, 309.3, 309.4, and shall be raised or flush.

409.4.6.1   Size. Control buttons shall be 3/4 inch (19 mm) minimum in their smallest dimension.

409.4.6.2 **Location.** Control panels shall be on a side wall, 12 inches (305 mm) minimum from any adjacent wall.

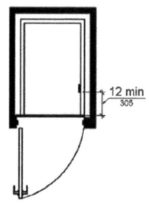

Figure 409.4.6.2 Location of Private Residence Elevator Control Panel

409.4.7 **Emergency Communications.** Emergency two-way communication systems shall comply with 409.4.7.

409.4.7.1 **Type.** A telephone and emergency signal device shall be provided in the car.

409.4.7.2 **Operable Parts.** The telephone and emergency signaling device shall comply with 309.3 and 309.4.

409.4.7.3 **Compartment.** If the telephone or device is in a closed compartment, the compartment door hardware shall comply with 309.

409.4.7.4 **Cord.** The telephone cord shall be 29 inches (735 mm) long minimum.

410   Platform Lifts

410.1 **General.** Platform lifts shall comply with ASME A18.1 (1999 edition or 2003 edition) (incorporated by reference, see "Referenced Standards" in Chapter 1). Platform lifts shall not be attendant-operated and shall provide unassisted entry and exit from the lift.

Advisory 410.1 General.

Inclined stairway chairlifts and inclined and vertical platform lifts are available for short-distance vertical transportation. Because an accessible route requires an 80 inch (2030 mm) vertical clearance, care should be taken in selecting lifts as they may not be equally suitable for use by people using wheelchairs and people standing. If a lift does not provide 80 inch (2030 mm) vertical clearance, it cannot be considered part of an accessible route in new construction.

The ADA and other Federal civil rights laws require that accessible features be maintained in working order so that they are accessible to and usable by those people they are intended to benefit. Building owners are reminded that the

ASME A18 Safety Standard for Platform Lifts and Stairway Chairlifts requires routine maintenance and inspections. Isolated or temporary interruptions in service due to maintenance or repairs may be unavoidable; however, failure to take prompt action to effect repairs could constitute a violation of Federal laws and these requirements.

410.2   Floor Surfaces. Floor surfaces in platform lifts shall comply with 302 and 303.

410.3   Clear Floor Space. Clear floor space in platform lifts shall comply with 305.

410.4   Platform to Runway Clearance. The clearance between the platform sill and the edge of any runway landing shall be 1 inch (32 mm) maximum.

410.5   Operable Parts. Controls for platform lifts shall comply with 309.

410.6   Doors and Gates. Platform lifts shall have low-energy power-operated doors or gates complying with 404.3. Doors shall remain open for 20 seconds minimum. End doors and gates shall provide a clear width 32 inches (815 mm) minimum. Side doors and gates shall provide a clear width 42 inches (1065 mm) minimum.

EXCEPTION: Platform lifts serving two landings maximum and having doors or gates on opposite sides shall be permitted to have self-closing manual doors or gates.

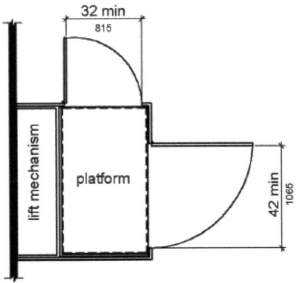

Figure 410.6 Platform Lift Doors and Gates

CHAPTER 5: GENERAL SITE AND BUILDING ELEMENTS

501   General

501.1   Scope. The provisions of Chapter 5 shall apply where required by Chapter 2 or where referenced by a requirement in this document.

502   Parking Spaces

502.1   General. Car and van parking spaces shall comply with 502. Where parking spaces are marked with lines, width measurements of parking spaces and access aisles shall be made from the centerline of the markings.

EXCEPTION: Where parking spaces or access aisles are not adjacent to another parking space or access aisle, measurements shall be permitted to include the full width of the line defining the parking space or access aisle.

502.2   Vehicle Spaces. Car parking spaces shall be 96 inches (2440 mm) wide minimum and van parking spaces shall be 132 inches (3350 mm) wide minimum, shall be marked to define the width, and shall have an adjacent access aisle complying with 502.3.

EXCEPTION: Van parking spaces shall be permitted to be 96 inches (2440 mm) wide minimum where the access aisle is 96 inches (2440 mm) wide minimum.

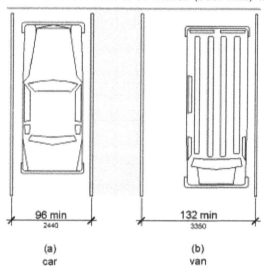

96 min
2440

132 min
3350

(a)
car

(b)
van

Figure 502.2 Vehicle Parking Spaces

502.3 Access Aisle. Access aisles serving parking spaces shall comply with 502.3. Access aisles shall adjoin an accessible route. Two parking spaces shall be permitted to share a common access aisle.

Advisory 502.3 Access Aisle.

Accessible routes must connect parking spaces to accessible entrances. In parking facilities where the accessible route must cross vehicular traffic lanes, marked crossings enhance pedestrian safety, particularly for people using wheelchairs and other mobility aids. Where possible, it is preferable that the accessible route not pass behind parked vehicles.

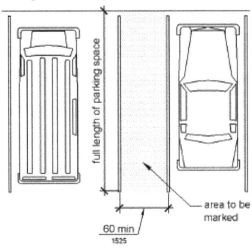

Figure 502.3 Parking Space Access Aisle

502.3.1   Width. Access aisles serving car and van parking spaces shall be 60 inches (1525 mm) wide minimum.

502.3.2   Length. Access aisles shall extend the full length of the parking spaces they serve.

502.3.3   Marking. Access aisles shall be marked so as to discourage parking in them.

Advisory 502.3.3 Marking.

The method and color of marking are not specified by these requirements but may be addressed by State or local laws or regulations. Because these requirements permit the van access aisle to be as wide as a parking space, it is important that the aisle be clearly marked.

502.3.4   Location. Access aisles shall not overlap the vehicular way. Access aisles shall be permitted to be placed on either side of the parking space except for angled van parking spaces which shall have access aisles located on the passenger side of the parking spaces.

Advisory 502.3.4 Location.

Wheelchair lifts typically are installed on the passenger side of vans. Many drivers, especially those who operate vans, find it more difficult to back into parking spaces than to back out into comparatively unrestricted vehicular lanes. For this reason, where a van and car share an access aisle, consider locating the van space so that the access aisle is on the passenger side of the van space.

502.4 Floor or Ground Surfaces. Parking spaces and access aisles serving them shall comply with 302. Access aisles shall be at the same level as the parking spaces they serve. Changes in level are not permitted.

EXCEPTION: Slopes not steeper than 1:48 shall be permitted.

Advisory 502.4 Floor or Ground Surfaces.

Access aisles are required to be nearly level in all directions to provide a surface for wheelchair transfer to and from vehicles. The exception allows sufficient slope for drainage. Built-up curb ramps are not permitted to project into access aisles and parking spaces because they would create slopes greater than 1:48.

502.5 Vertical Clearance. Parking spaces for vans and access aisles and vehicular routes serving them shall provide a vertical clearance of 98 inches (2490 mm) minimum.

Advisory 502.5 Vertical Clearance.

Signs provided at entrances to parking facilities informing drivers of clearances and the location of van accessible parking spaces can provide useful customer assistance.

502.6 Identification. Parking space identification signs shall include the International Symbol of Accessibility complying with 703.7.2.1. Signs identifying van parking spaces shall contain the designation "van accessible." Signs shall be 60 inches (1525 mm) minimum above the finish floor or ground surface measured to the bottom of the sign.

Advisory 502.6 Identification.

The required "van accessible" designation is intended to be informative, not restrictive, in identifying those spaces that are better suited for van use. Enforcement of motor vehicle laws, including parking privileges, is a local matter.

502.7 Relationship to Accessible Routes. Parking spaces and access aisles shall be designed so that cars and vans, when parked, cannot obstruct the required clear width of adjacent accessible routes.

Advisory 502.7 Relationship to Accessible Routes.

Wheel stops are an effective way to prevent vehicle overhangs from reducing the clear width of accessible routes.

503 Passenger Loading Zones

503.1 General. Passenger loading zones shall comply with 503.

503.2   Vehicle Pull-Up Space. Passenger loading zones shall provide a vehicular pull-up space 96 inches (2440 mm) wide minimum and 20 feet (6100 mm) long minimum.

503.3   Access Aisle. Passenger loading zones shall provide access aisles complying with 503 adjacent to the vehicle pull-up space. Access aisles shall adjoin an accessible route and shall not overlap the vehicular way.

503.3.1   Width. Access aisles serving vehicle pull-up spaces shall be 60 inches (1525 mm) wide minimum.

503.3.2   Length. Access aisles shall extend the full length of the vehicle pull-up spaces they serve.

503.3.3   Marking. Access aisles shall be marked so as to discourage parking in them.

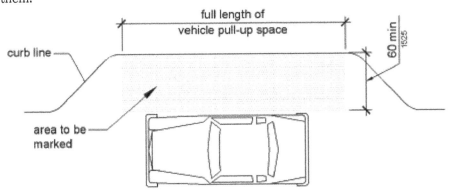

Figure 503.3 Passenger Loading Zone Access Aisle

503.4   Floor and Ground Surfaces. Vehicle pull-up spaces and access aisles serving them shall comply with 302. Access aisles shall be at the same level as the vehicle pull-up space they serve. Changes in level are not permitted.

EXCEPTION: Slopes not steeper than 1:48 shall be permitted.

503.5   Vertical Clearance. Vehicle pull-up spaces, access aisles serving them, and a vehicular route from an entrance to the passenger loading zone, and from the passenger loading zone to a vehicular exit shall provide a vertical clearance of 114 inches (2895 mm) minimum.

504   Stairways

504.1   General. Stairs shall comply with 504.

504.2   Treads and Risers. All steps on a flight of stairs shall have uniform riser heights and uniform tread depths. Risers shall be 4 inches (100 mm) high minimum and 7 inches (180 mm) high maximum. Treads shall be 11 inches (280 mm) deep minimum.

504.3   Open Risers. Open risers are not permitted.

504.4   Tread Surface. Stair treads shall comply with 302. Changes in level are not permitted.

EXCEPTION: Treads shall be permitted to have a slope not steeper than 1:48.

Advisory 504.4 Tread Surface.

   Consider providing visual contrast on tread nosings, or at the leading edges of treads without nosings, so that stair treads are more visible for people with low vision.

504.5   Nosings. The radius of curvature at the leading edge of the tread shall be 1/2 inch (13 mm) maximum. Nosings that project beyond risers shall have the underside of the leading edge curved or beveled. Risers shall be permitted to slope under the tread at an angle of 30 degrees maximum from vertical. The permitted projection of the nosing shall extend 1 1/2 inches (38 mm) maximum over the tread below.

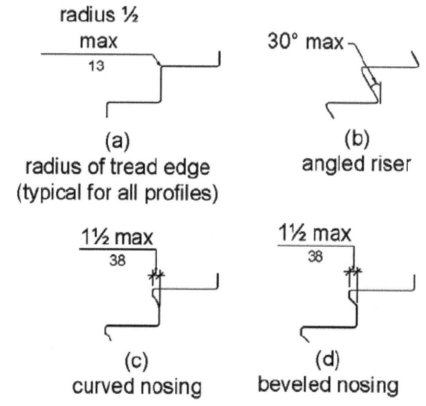

Figure 504.5 Stair Nosings

504.6 Handrails. Stairs shall have handrails complying with 505.

504.7   Wet Conditions. Stair treads and landings subject to wet conditions shall be designed to prevent the accumulation of water.

505   Handrails

505.1   General. Handrails provided along walking surfaces complying with 403, required at ramps complying with 405, and required at stairs complying with 504 shall comply with 505.

Advisory 505.1 General.

Handrails are required on ramp runs with a rise greater than 6 inches (150 mm) (see 405.8) and on certain stairways (see 504). Handrails are not required on walking surfaces with running slopes less than 1:20. However, handrails are required to comply with 505 when they are provided on walking surfaces with running slopes less than 1:20 (see 403.6). Sections 505.2, 505.3, and 505.10 do not apply to handrails provided on walking surfaces with running slopes less than 1:20 as these sections only reference requirements for ramps and stairs.

505.2   Where Required. Handrails shall be provided on both sides of stairs and ramps.

EXCEPTION: In assembly areas, handrails shall not be required on both sides of aisle ramps where a handrail is provided at either side or within the aisle width.

505.3   Continuity. Handrails shall be continuous within the full length of each stair flight or ramp run. Inside handrails on switchback or dogleg stairs and ramps shall be continuous between flights or runs.

EXCEPTION: In assembly areas, handrails on ramps shall not be required to be continuous in aisles serving seating.

505.4   Height. Top of gripping surfaces of handrails shall be 34 inches (865 mm) minimum and 38 inches (965 mm) maximum vertically above walking surfaces, stair nosings, and ramp surfaces. Handrails shall be at a consistent height above walking surfaces, stair nosings, and ramp surfaces.

Advisory 505.4 Height.

The requirements for stair and ramp handrails in this document are for adults. When children are the principal users in a building or facility (e.g., elementary schools), a second set of handrails at an appropriate height can assist them and aid in preventing accidents. A maximum height of 28 inches (710 mm) measured to the top of the gripping surface from the ramp surface or stair nosing is recommended for handrails designed for children. Sufficient vertical clearance between upper and lower handrails, 9 inches (230 mm) minimum, should be provided to help prevent entrapment.

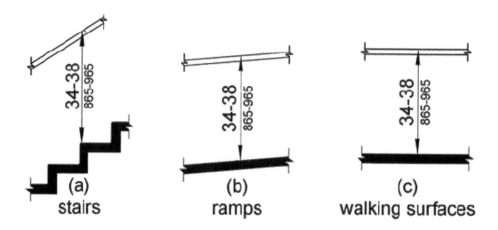

Figure 505.4 Handrail Height

505.5   Clearance. Clearance between handrail gripping surfaces and adjacent surfaces shall be 1 1/2 inches (38 mm) minimum.

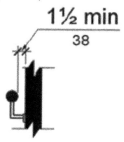

Figure 505.5 Handrail Clearance

505.6   Gripping Surface. Handrail gripping surfaces shall be continuous along their length and shall not be obstructed along their tops or sides. The bottoms of handrail gripping surfaces shall not be obstructed for more than 20 percent of their length. Where provided, horizontal projections shall occur 1 1/2 inches (38 mm) minimum below the bottom of the handrail gripping surface.

EXCEPTIONS:

1. Where handrails are provided along walking surfaces with slopes not steeper than 1:20, the bottoms of handrail gripping surfaces shall be permitted to be obstructed along their entire length where they are integral to crash rails or bumper guards.

2. The distance between horizontal projections and the bottom of the gripping surface shall be permitted to be reduced by 1/8 inch (3.2 mm) for each 1/2 inch (13 mm) of additional handrail perimeter dimension that exceeds 4 inches (100 mm).

Advisory 505.6 Gripping Surface.

People with disabilities, older people, and others benefit from continuous gripping surfaces that permit users to reach the fingers outward or downward to grasp the handrail, particularly as the user senses a loss of equilibrium or begins to fall.

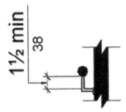

Figure 505.6 Horizontal Projections Below Gripping Surface

505.7 Cross Section. Handrail gripping surfaces shall have a cross section complying with 505.7.1 or 505.7.2.

505.7.1 Circular Cross Section. Handrail gripping surfaces with a circular cross section shall have an outside diameter of 1 1/4 inches (32 mm) minimum and 2 inches (51 mm) maximum.

505.7.2 Non-Circular Cross Sections. Handrail gripping surfaces with a non-circular cross section shall have a perimeter dimension of 4 inches (100 mm) minimum and 6 1/4 inches (160 mm) maximum, and a cross-section dimension of 2 1/4 inches (57 mm) maximum.

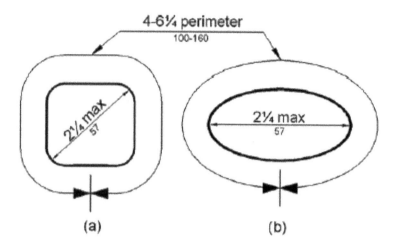

Figure 505.7.2 Handrail Non-Circular Cross Section

505.8 **Surfaces.** Handrail gripping surfaces and any surfaces adjacent to them shall be free of sharp or abrasive elements and shall have rounded edges.

505.9 **Fittings.** Handrails shall not rotate within their fittings.

505.10 **Handrail Extensions.** Handrail gripping surfaces shall extend beyond and in the same direction of stair flights and ramp runs in accordance with 505.10.

EXCEPTIONS:

1. Extensions shall not be required for continuous handrails at the inside turn of switchback or dogleg stairs and ramps.

2. In assembly areas, extensions shall not be required for ramp handrails in aisles serving seating where the handrails are discontinuous to provide access to seating and to permit crossovers within aisles.

3. In alterations, full extensions of handrails shall not be required where such extensions would be hazardous due to plan configuration.

505.10.1 **Top and Bottom Extension at Ramps.** Ramp handrails shall extend horizontally above the landing for 12 inches (305 mm) minimum beyond the top and bottom of ramp runs. Extensions shall return to a wall, guard, or the landing surface, or shall be continuous to the handrail of an adjacent ramp run.

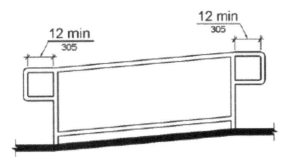

Figure 505.10.1 Top and Bottom Handrail Extension at Ramps

505.10.2 Top Extension at Stairs. At the top of a stair flight, handrails shall extend horizontally above the landing for 12 inches (305 mm) minimum beginning directly above the first riser nosing. Extensions shall return to a wall, guard, or the landing surface, or shall be continuous to the handrail of an adjacent stair flight.

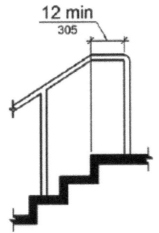

Figure 505.10.2 Top Handrail Extension at Stairs

505.10.3 Bottom Extension at Stairs. At the bottom of a stair flight, handrails shall extend at the slope of the stair flight for a horizontal distance at least equal to one tread depth beyond the last riser nosing. Extension shall return to a wall, guard, or the landing surface, or shall be continuous to the handrail of an adjacent stair flight.

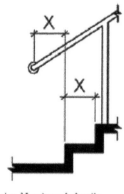

Note: X = tread depth

Figure 505.10.3 Bottom Handrail Extension at Stairs

CHAPTER 6:   PLUMBING ELEMENTS AND FACILITIES

601   General

601.1   Scope. The provisions of Chapter 6 shall apply where required by Chapter 2 or where referenced by a requirement in this document.

602   Drinking Fountains

602.1   General. Drinking fountains shall comply with 307 and 602.

602.2   Clear Floor Space. Units shall have a clear floor or ground space complying with 305 positioned for a forward approach and centered on the unit. Knee and toe clearance complying with 306 shall be provided.

EXCEPTION: A parallel approach complying with 305 shall be permitted at units for children's use where the spout is 30 inches (760 mm) maximum above the finish floor or ground and is 3 1/2 inches (90 mm) maximum from the front edge of the unit, including bumpers.

602.3   Operable Parts. Operable parts shall comply with 309.

602.4   Spout Height. Spout outlets shall be 36 inches (915 mm) maximum above the finish floor or ground.

602.5   Spout Location. The spout shall be located 15 inches (380 mm) minimum from the vertical support and 5 inches (125 mm) maximum from the front edge of the unit, including bumpers.

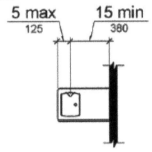

Figure 602.5 Drinking Fountain Spout Location

602.6   Water Flow. The spout shall provide a flow of water 4 inches (100 mm) high minimum and shall be located 5 inches (125 mm) maximum from the front of the unit. The angle of the water stream shall be measured horizontally relative to the front face of the unit. Where spouts are located less than 3 inches (75 mm) of the front of the unit, the angle of the water stream shall be 30 degrees maximum. Where spouts are located between 3 inches (75 mm) and 5 inches (125 mm) maximum from the front of the unit, the angle of the water stream shall be 15 degrees maximum.

Advisory 602.6 Water Flow.

The purpose of requiring the drinking fountain spout to produce a flow of water 4 inches (100 mm) high minimum is so that a cup can be inserted under the flow of water to provide a drink of water for an individual who, because of a disability, would otherwise be incapable of using the drinking fountain.

602.7 Drinking Fountains for Standing Persons. Spout outlets of drinking fountains for standing persons shall be 38 inches (965 mm) minimum and 43 inches (1090 mm) maximum above the finish floor or ground.

603 Toilet and Bathing Rooms

603.1 General. Toilet and bathing rooms shall comply with 603.

603.2 Clearances. Clearances shall comply with 603.2.

603.2.1 Turning Space. Turning space complying with 304 shall be provided within the room.

603.2.2 Overlap Required clear floor spaces, clearance at fixtures, and turning space shall be permitted to overlap.

603.2.3 Door Swing. Doors shall not swing into the clear floor space or clearance required for any fixture. Doors shall be permitted to swing into the required turning space.

EXCEPTIONS:

1. Doors to a toilet room or bathing room for a single occupant accessed only through a private office and not for common use or public use shall be permitted to swing into the clear floor space or clearance provided the swing of the door can be reversed to comply with 603.2.3.

2. Where the toilet room or bathing room is for individual use and a clear floor space complying with 305.3 is provided within the room beyond the arc of the door swing, doors shall be permitted to swing into the clear floor space or clearance required for any fixture.

Advisory 603.2.3 Door Swing Exception 1.

At the time the door is installed, and if the door swing is reversed in the future, the door must meet all the requirements specified in 404. Additionally, the door swing cannot reduce the required width of an accessible route. Also, avoid violating other building or life safety codes when the door swing is reversed.

603.3 Mirrors. Mirrors located above lavatories or countertops shall be installed with the bottom edge of the reflecting surface 40 inches (1015 mm) maximum above the finish floor or ground. Mirrors not located above lavatories or countertops shall be installed with the bottom edge of the reflecting surface 35 inches (890 mm) maximum above the finish floor or ground.

Advisory 603.3 Mirrors.

A single full-length mirror can accommodate a greater number of people, including children. In order for mirrors to be usable by people who are ambulatory and people who use wheelchairs, the top edge of mirrors should be 74 inches (1880 mm) minimum from the floor or ground.

603.4 Coat Hooks and Shelves. Coat hooks shall be located within one of the reach ranges specified in 308. Shelves shall be located 40 inches (1015 mm) minimum and 48 inches (1220 mm) maximum above the finish floor.

604   Water Closets and Toilet Compartments

604.1 General. Water closets and toilet compartments shall comply with 604.2 through 604.8.

EXCEPTION: Water closets and toilet compartments for children's use shall be permitted to comply with 604.9.

604.2   Location. The water closet shall be positioned with a wall or partition to the rear and to one side. The centerline of the water closet shall be 16 inches (405 mm) minimum to 18 inches (455 mm) maximum from the side wall or partition, except that the water closet shall be 17 inches (430 mm) minimum and 19 inches (485 mm) maximum from the side wall or partition in the ambulatory accessible toilet compartment specified in 604.8.2. Water closets shall be arranged for a left-hand or right-hand approach.

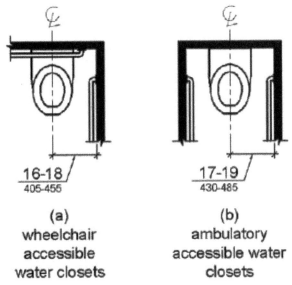

Figure 604.2 Water Closet Location

604.3   Clearance. Clearances around water closets and in toilet compartments shall comply with 604.3.

604.3.1 Size. Clearance around a water closet shall be 60 inches (1525 mm) minimum measured perpendicular from the side wall and 56 inches (1420 mm) minimum measured perpendicular from the rear wall.

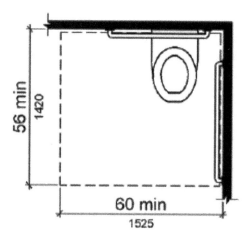

Figure 604.3.1 Size of Clearance at Water Closets

604.3.2 Overlap. The required clearance around the water closet shall be permitted to overlap the water closet, associated grab bars, dispensers, sanitary napkin disposal units, coat hooks, shelves, accessible routes, clear floor space and clearances required at other fixtures, and the turning space. No other fixtures or obstructions shall be located within the required water closet clearance.

EXCEPTION: In residential dwelling units, a lavatory complying with 606 shall be permitted on the rear wall 18 inches (455 mm) minimum from the water closet centerline where the clearance at the water closet is 66 inches (1675 mm) minimum measured perpendicular from the rear wall.

Advisory 604.3.2 Overlap.

When the door to the toilet room is placed directly in front of the water closet, the water closet cannot overlap the required maneuvering clearance for the door inside the room.

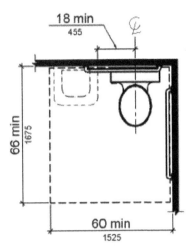

Figure 604.3.2 (Exception) Overlap of Water Closet Clearance in Residential Dwelling Units

604.4 Seats. The seat height of a water closet above the finish floor shall be 17 inches (430 mm) minimum and 19 inches (485 mm) maximum measured to the top of the seat. Seats shall not be sprung to return to a lifted position.

EXCEPTIONS:

1. A water closet in a toilet room for a single occupant accessed only through a private office and not for common use or public use shall not be required to comply with 604.4.

2. In residential dwelling units, the height of water closets shall be permitted to be 15 inches (380 mm) minimum and 19 inches (485 mm) maximum above the finish floor measured to the top of the seat.

604.5   Grab Bars. Grab bars for water closets shall comply with 609. Grab bars shall be provided on the side wall closest to the water closet and on the rear wall.

EXCEPTIONS:

1. Grab bars shall not be required to be installed in a toilet room for a single occupant accessed only through a private office and not for common use or public use provided that reinforcement has been installed in walls and located so as to permit the installation of grab bars complying with 604.5.

2. In residential dwelling units, grab bars shall not be required to be installed in toilet or bathrooms provided that reinforcement has been installed in walls and located so as to permit the installation of grab bars complying with 604.5.

3. In detention or correction facilities, grab bars shall not be required to be installed in housing or holding cells that are specially designed without protrusions for purposes of suicide prevention.

Advisory 604.5 Grab Bars Exception 2.

Reinforcement must be sufficient to permit the installation of rear and side wall grab bars that fully meet all accessibility requirements including, but not limited to, required length, installation height, and structural strength.

604.5.1   Side Wall. The side wall grab bar shall be 42 inches (1065 mm) long minimum, located 12 inches (305 mm) maximum from the rear wall and extending 54 inches (1370 mm) minimum from the rear wall.

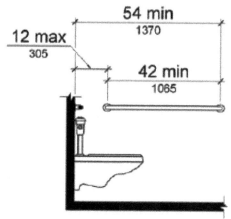

Figure 604.5.1 Side Wall Grab Bar at Water Closets

604.5.2   Rear Wall. The rear wall grab bar shall be 36 inches (915 mm) long minimum and extend from the centerline of the water closet 12 inches (305 mm) minimum on one side and 24 inches (610 mm) minimum on the other side.

EXCEPTIONS:

1. The rear grab bar shall be permitted to be 24 inches (610 mm) long minimum, centered on the water closet, where wall space does not permit a length of 36 inches (915 mm) minimum due to the location of a recessed fixture adjacent to the water closet.

2. Where an administrative authority requires flush controls for flush valves to be located in a position that conflicts with the location of the rear grab bar, then the rear grab bar shall be permitted to be split or shifted to the open side of the toilet area.

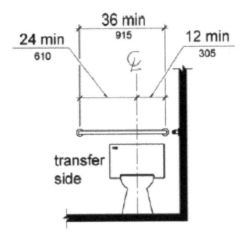

Figure 604.5.2 Rear Wall Grab Bar at Water Closets

604.6   Flush Controls. Flush controls shall be hand operated or automatic. Hand operated flush controls shall comply with 309. Flush controls shall be located on the open side of the water closet except in ambulatory accessible compartments complying with 604.8.2.

Advisory 604.6 Flush Controls.

If plumbing valves are located directly behind the toilet seat, flush valves and related plumbing can cause injury or imbalance when a person leans back against them. To prevent causing injury or imbalance, the plumbing can be located behind walls or to the side of the toilet; or if approved by the local authority having jurisdiction, provide a toilet seat lid.

604.7   Dispensers. Toilet paper dispensers shall comply with 309.4 and shall be 7 inches (180 mm) minimum and 9 inches (230 mm) maximum in front of the water closet measured to the centerline of the dispenser. The outlet of the dispenser shall be 15 inches (380 mm) minimum and 48 inches (1220 mm) maximum above the finish floor and shall not be located behind grab bars. Dispensers shall not be of a type that controls delivery or that does not allow continuous paper flow.

Advisory 604.7 Dispensers.

If toilet paper dispensers are installed above the side wall grab bar, the outlet of the toilet paper dispenser must be 48 inches (1220 mm) maximum above the finish floor and the top of the gripping surface of the grab bar must be 33 inches (840 mm) minimum and 36 inches (915 mm) maximum above the finish floor.

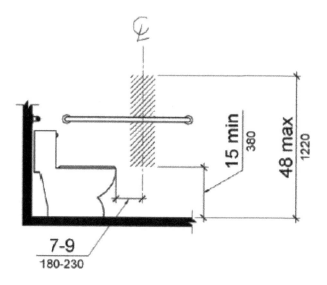

Figure 604.7 Dispenser Outlet Location

604.8 Toilet Compartments. Wheelchair accessible toilet compartments shall meet the requirements of 604.8.1 and 604.8.3. Compartments containing more than one plumbing fixture shall comply with 603. Ambulatory accessible compartments shall comply with 604.8.2 and 604.8.3.

604.8.1 Wheelchair Accessible Compartments. Wheelchair accessible compartments shall comply with 604.8.1.

604.8.1.1 Size. Wheelchair accessible compartments shall be 60 inches (1525 mm) wide minimum measured perpendicular to the side wall, and 56 inches (1420 mm) deep minimum for wall hung water closets and 59 inches (1500 mm) deep minimum for floor mounted water closets measured perpendicular to the rear wall. Wheelchair accessible compartments for children's use shall be 60 inches (1525 mm) wide minimum measured perpendicular to the side wall, and 59 inches (1500 mm) deep minimum for wall hung and floor mounted water closets measured perpendicular to the rear wall.

Advisory 604.8.1.1 Size.

The minimum space required in toilet compartments is provided so that a person using a wheelchair can maneuver into position at the water closet. This space cannot be obstructed by baby changing tables or other fixtures or conveniences, except as specified at 604.3.2 (Overlap). If toilet compartments are to be used to house fixtures other than those associated with the water closet, they must be designed to exceed the minimum space requirements. Convenience fixtures such as baby changing tables must also be accessible to people with disabilities as well as to other users. Toilet compartments that are designed to meet, and not exceed, the minimum space requirements may not provide adequate space for maneuvering into position at a baby changing table.

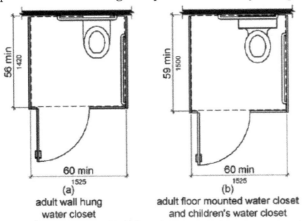

Figure 604.8.1.1 Size of Wheelchair Accessible Toilet Compartment

604.8.1.2 Doors. Toilet compartment doors, including door hardware, shall comply with 404 except that if the approach is to the latch side of the compartment door, clearance between the door side of the compartment and any obstruction shall be 42 inches (1065 mm) minimum. Doors shall be located in the front partition or in the side wall or partition farthest from the water closet. Where located in the front partition, the door opening shall be 4 inches (100 mm) maximum from the side wall or partition farthest from the water closet. Where located in the side wall or partition, the door opening shall be 4 inches (100 mm) maximum from the front partition. The door shall be self-closing. A door pull complying with 404.2.7 shall be placed on both sides of the door near the latch. Toilet compartment doors shall not swing into the minimum required compartment area.

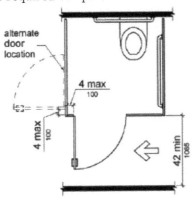

Figure 604.8.1.2 Wheelchair Accessible Toilet Compartment Doors

604.8.1.3 Approach. Compartments shall be arranged for left-hand or right-hand approach to the water closet.

604.8.1.4 Toe Clearance. The front partition and at least one side partition shall provide a toe clearance of 9 inches (230 mm) minimum above the finish floor and 6 inches (150 mm) deep minimum beyond the compartment-side face of the partition, exclusive of partition support members. Compartments for children's use shall provide a toe clearance of 12 inches (305 mm) minimum above the finish floor.

EXCEPTION: Toe clearance at the front partition is not required in a compartment greater than 62 inches (1575 mm) deep with a wall-hung water closet or 65 inches (1650 mm) deep with a floor-mounted water closet. Toe clearance at the side partition is not required in a compartment greater than 66 inches (1675 mm) wide. Toe clearance at the front partition is not required in a compartment for children's use that is greater than 65 inches (1650 mm) deep.

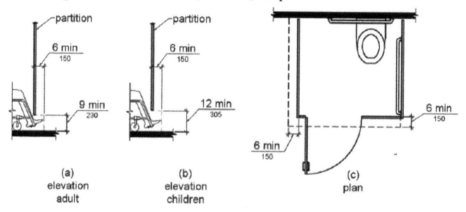

(a)
elevation
adult

(b)
elevation
children

(c)
plan

Figure 604.8.1.4 Wheelchair Accessible Toilet Compartment Toe Clearance

604.8.1.5 Grab Bars. Grab bars shall comply with 609. A side-wall grab bar complying with 604.5.1 shall be provided and shall be located on the wall closest to the water closet. In addition, a rear-wall grab bar complying with 604.5.2 shall be provided.

604.8.2 Ambulatory Accessible Compartments. Ambulatory accessible compartments shall comply with 604.8.2.

604.8.2.1 Size. Ambulatory accessible compartments shall have a depth of 60 inches (1525 mm) minimum and a width of 35 inches (890 mm) minimum and 37 inches (940 mm) maximum.

604.8.2.2 Doors. Toilet compartment doors, including door hardware, shall comply with 404, except that if the approach is to the latch side of the compartment door, clearance between the door side of the compartment and any obstruction shall be 42 inches (1065 mm) minimum. The door shall be self-closing. A door pull complying with 404.2.7 shall be placed on both sides of the door near the latch. Toilet compartment doors shall not swing into the minimum required compartment area.

604.8.2.3   Grab Bars. Grab bars shall comply with 609. A side-wall grab bar complying with 604.5.1 shall be provided on both sides of the compartment.

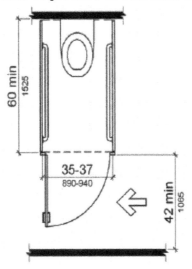

Figure 604.8.2 Ambulatory Accessible Toilet Compartment

604.8.3   Coat Hooks and Shelves. Coat hooks shall be located within one of the reach ranges specified in 308. Shelves shall be located 40 inches (1015 mm) minimum and 48 inches (1220 mm) maximum above the finish floor.

604.9   Water Closets and Toilet Compartments for Children's Use. Water closets and toilet compartments for children's use shall comply with 604.9.

Advisory 604.9 Water Closets and Toilet Compartments for Children's Use.

The requirements in 604.9 are to be followed where the exception for children's water closets in 604.1 is used. The following table provides additional guidance in applying the specifications for water closets for children according to the age group served and reflects the differences in the size, stature, and reach ranges of children ages 3 through 12. The specifications chosen should correspond to the age of the primary user group. The specifications of one age group should be applied consistently in the installation of a water closet and related elements.

Advisory Specifications for Water Closets Serving Children Ages 3 through 12			
	Ages 3 and 4	**Ages 5 through 8**	**Ages 9 through 12**
Water Closet Centerline	12 inches (305 mm)	12 to 15 inches (305 to 380 mm)	15 to 18 inches (380 to 455 mm)

Advisory Specifications for Water Closets Serving Children Ages 3 through 12		
Toilet Seat Height	11 to 12 inches (280 to 305 mm)	12 to 15 inches (305 to 380 mm)	15 to 17 inches (380 to 430 mm)
Grab Bar Height	18 to 20 inches (455 to 510 mm)	20 to 25 inches (510 to 635 mm)	25 to 27 inches (635 to 685 mm)
Dispenser Height	14 inches (355 mm)	14 to 17 inches (355 to 430 mm)	17 to 19 inches (430 to 485 mm)

604.9.1   Location. The water closet shall be located with a wall or partition to the rear and to one side. The centerline of the water closet shall be 12 inches (305 mm) minimum and 18 inches (455 mm) maximum from the side wall or partition, except that the water closet shall be 17 inches (430 mm) minimum and 19 inches (485 mm) maximum from the side wall or partition in the ambulatory accessible toilet compartment specified in 604.8.2. Compartments shall be arranged for left-hand or right-hand approach to the water closet.

604.9.2   Clearance. Clearance around a water closet shall comply with 604.3.

604.9.3   Height. The height of water closets shall be 11 inches (280 mm) minimum and 17 inches (430 mm) maximum measured to the top of the seat. Seats shall not be sprung to return to a lifted position.

604.9.4   Grab Bars. Grab bars for water closets shall comply with 604.5.

604.9.5   Flush Controls. Flush controls shall be hand operated or automatic. Hand operated flush controls shall comply with 309.2 and 309.4 and shall be installed 36 inches (915 mm) maximum above the finish floor. Flush controls shall be located on the open side of the water closet except in ambulatory accessible compartments complying with 604.8.2.

604.9.6   Dispensers. Toilet paper dispensers shall comply with 309.4 and shall be 7 inches (180 mm) minimum and 9 inches (230 mm) maximum in front of the water closet measured to the centerline of the dispenser. The outlet of the dispenser shall be 14 inches (355 mm) minimum and 19 inches (485 mm) maximum above the finish floor. There shall be a clearance of 1 1/2 inches (38 mm) minimum below the grab bar. Dispensers shall not be of a type that controls delivery or that does not allow continuous paper flow.

604.9.7   Toilet Compartments. Toilet compartments shall comply with 604.8.

605   Urinals

605.1   General. Urinals shall comply with 605.

Advisory 605.1 General.

Stall-type urinals provide greater accessibility for a broader range of persons, including people of short stature.

605.2   Height and Depth. Urinals shall be the stall-type or the wall-hung type with the rim 17 inches (430 mm) maximum above the finish floor or ground. Urinals shall be 13 1/2 inches (345 mm) deep minimum measured from the outer face of the urinal rim to the back of the fixture.

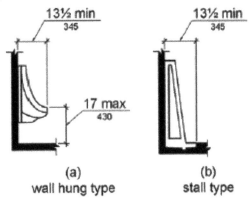

Figure 605.2 Height and Depth of Urinals

605.3   Clear Floor Space. A clear floor or ground space complying with 305 positioned for forward approach shall be provided.

605.4   Flush Controls. Flush controls shall be hand operated or automatic. Hand operated flush controls shall comply with 309.

606   Lavatories and Sinks

606.1   General. Lavatories and sinks shall comply with 606.

Advisory 606.1 General.

If soap and towel dispensers are provided, they must be located within the reach ranges specified in 308. Locate soap and towel dispensers so that they are conveniently usable by a person at the accessible lavatory.

606.2   Clear Floor Space. A clear floor space complying with 305, positioned for a forward approach, and knee and toe clearance complying with 306 shall be provided.

EXCEPTIONS:

1. A parallel approach complying with 305 shall be permitted to a kitchen sink in a space where a cook top or conventional range is not provided and to wet bars.

2. A lavatory in a toilet room or bathing facility for a single occupant accessed only through a private office and not for common use or public use shall not be required to provide knee and toe clearance complying with 306.

3. In residential dwelling units, cabinetry shall be permitted under lavatories and kitchen sinks provided that all of the following conditions are met:

(a) the cabinetry can be removed without removal or replacement of the fixture;

(b) the finish floor extends under the cabinetry; and

(c) the walls behind and surrounding the cabinetry are finished.

4. A knee clearance of 24 inches (610 mm) minimum above the finish floor or ground shall be permitted at lavatories and sinks used primarily by children 6 through 12 years where the rim or counter surface is 31 inches (785 mm) maximum above the finish floor or ground.

5. A parallel approach complying with 305 shall be permitted to lavatories and sinks used primarily by children 5 years and younger.

6. The dip of the overflow shall not be considered in determining knee and toe clearances.

7. No more than one bowl of a multi-bowl sink shall be required to provide knee and toe clearance complying with 306.

606.3 Height. Lavatories and sinks shall be installed with the front of the higher of the rim or counter surface 34 inches (865 mm) maximum above the finish floor or ground.

EXCEPTIONS:

1. A lavatory in a toilet or bathing facility for a single occupant accessed only through a private office and not for common use or public use shall not be required to comply with 606.3.

2. In residential dwelling unit kitchens, sinks that are adjustable to variable heights, 29 inches (735 mm) minimum and 36 inches (915 mm) maximum, shall be permitted where rough-in plumbing permits connections of supply and drain pipes for sinks mounted at the height of 29 inches (735 mm).

606.4 Faucets. Controls for faucets shall comply with 309. Hand-operated metering faucets shall remain open for 10 seconds minimum.

606.5 Exposed Pipes and Surfaces. Water supply and drain pipes under lavatories and sinks shall be insulated or otherwise configured to protect against contact. There shall be no sharp or abrasive surfaces under lavatories and sinks.

607 Bathtubs

607.1 General. Bathtubs shall comply with 607.

607.2 Clearance. Clearance in front of bathtubs shall extend the length of the bathtub and shall be 30 inches (760 mm) wide minimum. A lavatory complying with 606 shall be permitted at the control end of the clearance. Where a permanent seat is provided at the head end of the bathtub, the clearance shall extend 12 inches (305 mm) minimum beyond the wall at the head end of the bathtub.

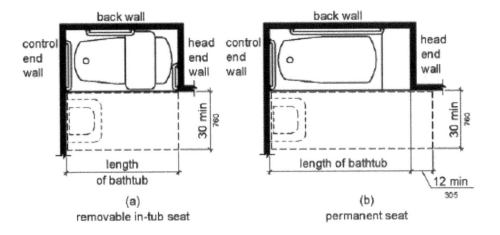

Figure 607.2 Clearance for Bathtubs

607.3 Seat. A permanent seat at the head end of the bathtub or a removable in-tub seat shall be provided. Seats shall comply with 610.

607.4 Grab Bars. Grab bars for bathtubs shall comply with 609 and shall be provided in accordance with 607.4.1 or 607.4.2.

EXCEPTIONS:

1. Grab bars shall not be required to be installed in a bathtub located in a bathing facility for a single occupant accessed only through a private office and not for common use or public use provided that reinforcement has been installed in walls and located so as to permit the installation of grab bars complying with 607.4.

2. In residential dwelling units, grab bars shall not be required to be installed in bathtubs located in bathing facilities provided that reinforcement has been installed in walls and located so as to permit the installation of grab bars complying with 607.4.

607.4.1 Bathtubs With Permanent Seats. For bathtubs with permanent seats, grab bars shall be provided in accordance with 607.4.1.

607.4.1.1 Back Wall. Two grab bars shall be installed on the back wall, one located in accordance with 609.4 and the other located 8 inches (205 mm) minimum and 10 inches (255 mm) maximum above the rim of the bathtub. Each grab bar shall be installed 15 inches (380 mm) maximum from the head end wall and 12 inches (305 mm) maximum from the control end wall.

607.4.1.2 Control End Wall. A grab bar 24 inches (610 mm) long minimum shall be installed on the control end wall at the front edge of the bathtub.

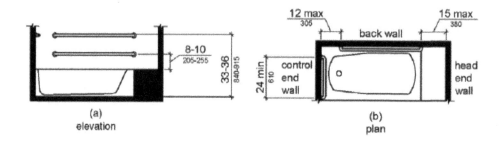

Figure 607.4.1 Grab Bars for Bathtubs with Permanent Seats

607.4.2   Bathtubs Without Permanent Seats. For bathtubs without permanent seats, grab bars shall comply with 607.4.2.

607.4.2.1   Back Wall. Two grab bars shall be installed on the back wall, one located in accordance with 609.4 and other located 8 inches (205 mm) minimum and 10 inches (255 mm) maximum above the rim of the bathtub. Each grab bar shall be 24 inches (610 mm) long minimum and shall be installed 24 inches (610 mm) maximum from the head end wall and 12 inches (305 mm) maximum from the control end wall.

607.4.2.2   Control End Wall. A grab bar 24 inches (610 mm) long minimum shall be installed on the control end wall at the front edge of the bathtub.

607.4.2.3   Head End Wall. A grab bar 12 inches (305 mm) long minimum shall be installed on the head end wall at the front edge of the bathtub.

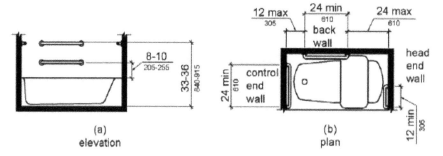

Figure 607.4.2 Grab Bars for Bathtubs with Removable In-Tub Seats

607.5   Controls. Controls, other than drain stoppers, shall be located on an end wall. Controls shall be between the bathtub rim and grab bar, and between the open side of the bathtub and the centerline of the width of the bathtub. Controls shall comply with 309.4.

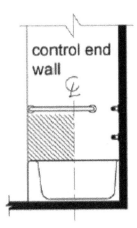

Figure 607.5 Bathtub Control Location

607.6   Shower Spray Unit and Water. A shower spray unit with a hose 59 inches (1500 mm) long minimum that can be used both as a fixed-position shower head and as a hand-held shower shall be provided. The shower spray unit shall have an on/off control with a non-positive shut-off. If an adjustable-height shower head on a vertical bar is used, the bar shall be installed so as not to obstruct the use of grab bars. Bathtub shower spray units shall deliver water that is 120F (49C) maximum.

Advisory 607.6 Shower Spray Unit and Water.

Ensure that hand-held shower spray units are capable of delivering water pressure substantially equivalent to fixed shower heads.

607.7   Bathtub Enclosures. Enclosures for bathtubs shall not obstruct controls, faucets, shower and spray units or obstruct transfer from wheelchairs onto bathtub seats or into bathtubs. Enclosures on bathtubs shall not have tracks installed on the rim of the open face of the bathtub.

608   Shower Compartments

608.1   General. Shower compartments shall comply with 608.

Advisory 608.1 General.

Shower stalls that are 60 inches (1525 mm) wide and have no curb may increase the usability of a bathroom because the shower area provides additional maneuvering space.

608.2   Size and Clearances for Shower Compartments. Shower compartments shall have sizes and clearances complying with 608.2.

608.2.1   Transfer Type Shower Compartments. Transfer type shower compartments shall be 36 inches (915 mm) by 36 inches (915 mm) clear inside dimensions measured at the center points of opposing sides and shall have a 36 inch (915 mm) wide minimum entry on the face of the shower compartment. Clearance of 36 inches (915 mm) wide minimum by 48 inches (1220 mm) long minimum measured from the control wall shall be provided.

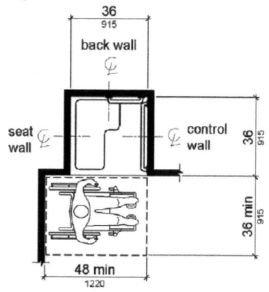

Note: inside finished dimensions measured at the center points of opposing sides

Figure 608.2.1 Transfer Type Shower Compartment Size and Clearance

608.2.2 Standard Roll-In Type Shower Compartments. Standard roll-in type shower compartments shall be 30 inches (760 mm) wide minimum by 60 inches (1525 mm) deep minimum clear inside dimensions measured at center points of opposing sides and shall have a 60 inches (1525 mm) wide minimum entry on the face of the shower compartment.

608.2.2.1 Clearance. A 30 inch (760 mm) wide minimum by 60 inch (1525 mm) long minimum clearance shall be provided adjacent to the open face of the shower compartment.

EXCEPTION: A lavatory complying with 606 shall be permitted on one 30 inch (760 mm) wide minimum side of the clearance provided that it is not on the side of the clearance adjacent to the controls or, where provided, not on the side of the clearance adjacent to the shower seat.

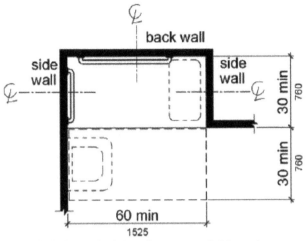

Note: inside finished dimensions measured at the center points of opposing sides

Figure 608.2.2 Standard Roll-In Type Shower Compartment Size and Clearance

608.2.3 Alternate Roll-In Type Shower Compartments. Alternate roll-in type shower compartments shall be 36 inches (915 mm) wide and 60 inches (1525 mm) deep minimum clear inside dimensions measured at center points of opposing sides. A 36 inch (915 mm) wide minimum entry shall be provided at one end of the long side of the compartment.

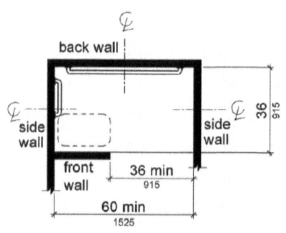

Figure 608.2.3 Alternate Roll-In Type Shower Compartment Size and Clearance

608.3 Grab Bars. Grab bars shall comply with 609 and shall be provided in accordance with 608.3. Where multiple grab bars are used, required horizontal grab bars shall be installed at the same height above the finish floor.

EXCEPTIONS:

1. Grab bars shall not be required to be installed in a shower located in a bathing facility for a single occupant accessed only through a private office, and not for common use or public use provided that reinforcement has been installed in walls and located so as to permit the installation of grab bars complying with 608.3.

2. In residential dwelling units, grab bars shall not be required to be installed in showers located in bathing facilities provided that reinforcement has been installed in walls and located so as to permit the installation of grab bars complying with 608.3.

608.3.1 Transfer Type Shower Compartments. In transfer type compartments, grab bars shall be provided across the control wall and back wall to a point 18 inches (455 mm) from the control wall.

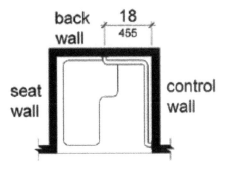

Figure 608.3.1 Grab Bars for Transfer Type Showers

608.3.2 Standard Roll-In Type Shower Compartments. Where a seat is provided in standard roll-in type shower compartments, grab bars shall be provided on the back wall and the side wall opposite the seat. Grab bars shall not be provided above the seat. Where a seat is not provided in standard roll-in type shower compartments, grab bars shall be provided on three walls. Grab bars shall be installed 6 inches (150 mm) maximum from adjacent walls.

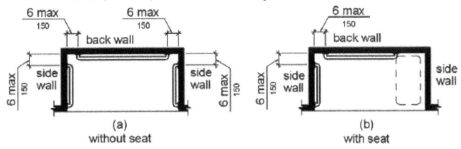

Figure 608.3.2 Grab Bars for Standard Roll-In Type Showers

608.3.3 Alternate Roll-In Type Shower Compartments. In alternate roll-in type shower compartments, grab bars shall be provided on the back wall and the side wall farthest from the compartment entry. Grab bars shall not be provided above the seat. Grab bars shall be installed 6 inches (150 mm) maximum from adjacent walls.

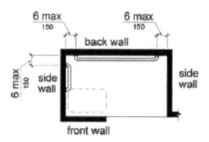

Figure 608.3.3 Grab Bars for Alternate Roll-In Type Showers

608.4   Seats. A folding or non-folding seat shall be provided in transfer type shower compartments. A folding seat shall be provided in roll-in type showers required in transient lodging guest rooms with mobility features complying with 806.2. Seats shall comply with 610.

EXCEPTION: In residential dwelling units, seats shall not be required in transfer type shower compartments provided that reinforcement has been installed in walls so as to permit the installation of seats complying with 608.4.

608.5   Controls. Controls, faucets, and shower spray units shall comply with 309.4.

608.5.1   Transfer Type Shower Compartments. In transfer type shower compartments, the controls, faucets, and shower spray unit shall be installed on the side wall opposite the seat 38 inches (965 mm) minimum and 48 inches (1220 mm) maximum above the shower floor and shall be located on the control wall 15 inches (380 mm) maximum from the centerline of the seat toward the shower opening.

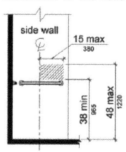

Figure 608.5.1 Transfer Type Shower Compartment Control Location

608.5.2   Standard Roll-In Type Shower Compartments. In standard roll-in type shower compartments, the controls, faucets, and shower spray unit shall be located above the grab bar, but no higher than 48 inches (1220 mm) above the shower floor. Where a seat is provided, the controls, faucets, and shower spray unit shall be installed on the back wall adjacent to the seat wall and shall be located 27 inches (685 mm) maximum from the seat wall.

Advisory 608.5.2 Standard Roll-in Type Shower Compartments.

In standard roll-in type showers without seats, the shower head and operable parts can be located on any of the three walls of the shower without adversely affecting accessibility.

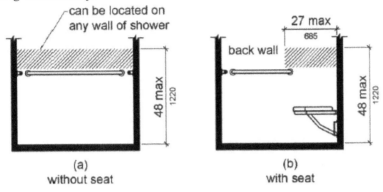

(a) without seat

(b) with seat

Figure 608.5.2 Standard Roll-In Type Shower Compartment Control Location

608.5.3   Alternate Roll-In Type Shower Compartments. In alternate roll-in type shower compartments, the controls, faucets, and shower spray unit shall be located above the grab bar, but no higher than 48 inches (1220 mm) above the shower floor. Where a seat is provided, the controls, faucets, and shower spray unit shall be located on the side wall adjacent to the seat 27 inches (685 mm) maximum from the side wall behind the seat or shall be located on the back wall opposite the seat 15 inches (380 mm) maximum, left or right, of the centerline of the seat. Where a seat is not provided, the controls, faucets, and shower spray unit shall be installed on the side wall farthest from the compartment entry.

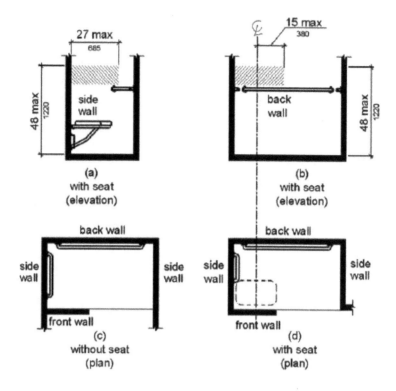

Figure 608.5.3 Alternate Roll-In Type Shower Compartment Control Location

608.6   **Shower Spray Unit and Water.** A shower spray unit with a hose 59 inches (1500 mm) long minimum that can be used both as a fixed-position shower head and as a hand-held shower shall be provided. The shower spray unit shall have an on/off control with a non-positive shut-off. If an adjustable-height shower head on a vertical bar is used, the bar shall be installed so as not to obstruct the use of grab bars. Shower spray units shall deliver water that is 120F (49C) maximum.

EXCEPTION: A fixed shower head located at 48 inches (1220 mm) maximum above the shower finish floor shall be permitted instead of a hand-held spray unit in facilities that are not medical care facilities, long-term care facilities, transient lodging guest rooms, or residential dwelling units.

Advisory 608.6 Shower Spray Unit and Water.

Ensure that hand-held shower spray units are capable of delivering water pressure substantially equivalent to fixed shower heads.

608.7 **Thresholds**. Thresholds in roll-in type shower compartments shall be 1/2 inch (13 mm) high maximum in accordance with 303. In transfer type shower compartments, thresholds 1/2 inch (13 mm) high maximum shall be beveled, rounded, or vertical.

EXCEPTION: A threshold 2 inches (51 mm) high maximum shall be permitted in transfer type shower compartments in existing facilities where provision of a 1/2 inch (13 mm) high threshold would disturb the structural reinforcement of the floor slab.

608.8   Shower Enclosures. Enclosures for shower compartments shall not obstruct controls, faucets, and shower spray units or obstruct transfer from wheelchairs onto shower seats.

609   Grab Bars

609.1   General. Grab bars in toilet facilities and bathing facilities shall comply with 609.

609.2   Cross Section. Grab bars shall have a cross section complying with 609.2.1 or 609.2.2.

609.2.1   Circular Cross Section. Grab bars with circular cross sections shall have an outside diameter of 1 1/4 inches (32 mm) minimum and 2 inches (51 mm) maximum.

609.2.2   Non-Circular Cross Section. Grab bars with non-circular cross sections shall have a cross-section dimension of 2 inches (51 mm) maximum and a perimeter dimension of 4 inches (100 mm) minimum and 4.8 inches (120 mm) maximum.

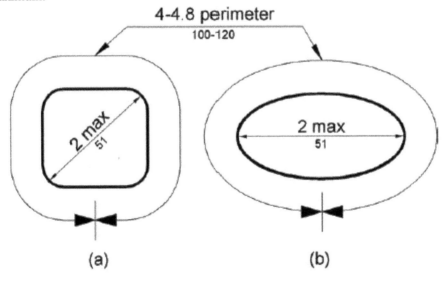

Figure 609.2.2 Grab Bar Non-Circular Cross Section

609.3   Spacing. The space between the wall and the grab bar shall be 1 1/2 inches (38 mm). The space between the grab bar and projecting objects below and at the ends shall be 1 1/2 inches (38 mm) minimum. The space between the grab bar and projecting objects above shall be 12 inches (305 mm) minimum.

EXCEPTION: The space between the grab bars and shower controls, shower fittings, and other grab bars above shall be permitted to be 1 1/2 inches (38 mm) minimum.

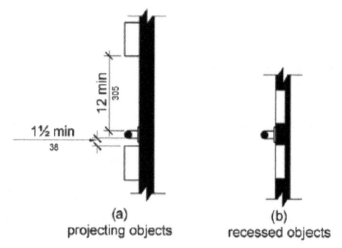

(a)
projecting objects

(b)
recessed objects

Figure 609.3 Spacing of Grab Bars

609.4   Position of Grab Bars. Grab bars shall be installed in a horizontal position, 33 inches (840 mm) minimum and 36 inches (915 mm) maximum above the finish floor measured to the top of the gripping surface, except that at water closets for children's use complying with 604.9, grab bars shall be installed in a horizontal position 18 inches (455 mm) minimum and 27 inches (685 mm) maximum above the finish floor measured to the top of the gripping surface. The height of the lower grab bar on the back wall of a bathtub shall comply with 607.4.1.1 or 607.4.2.1.

609.5   Surface Hazards. Grab bars and any wall or other surfaces adjacent to grab bars shall be free of sharp or abrasive elements and shall have rounded edges.

609.6   Fittings. Grab bars shall not rotate within their fittings.

609.7   Installation. Grab bars shall be installed in any manner that provides a gripping surface at the specified locations and that does not obstruct the required clear floor space.

609.8   Structural Strength. Allowable stresses shall not be exceeded for materials used when a vertical or horizontal force of 250 pounds (1112 N) is applied at any point on the grab bar, fastener, mounting device, or supporting structure.

610   Seats

610.1   General. Seats in bathtubs and shower compartments shall comply with 610.

610.2   Bathtub Seats. The top of bathtub seats shall be 17 inches (430 mm) minimum and 19 inches (485 mm) maximum above the bathroom finish floor. The depth of a removable in-tub seat shall be 15 inches (380 mm) minimum and 16 inches (405 mm) maximum. The seat shall be capable of secure placement. Permanent seats at the head end of the bathtub shall be 15 inches (380 mm) deep minimum and shall extend from the back wall to or beyond the outer edge of the bathtub.

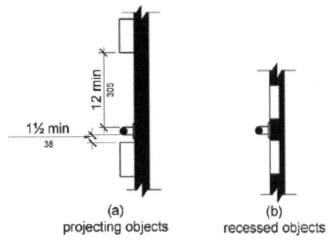

(a)
projecting objects

(b)
recessed objects

Figure 609.3 Spacing of Grab Bars

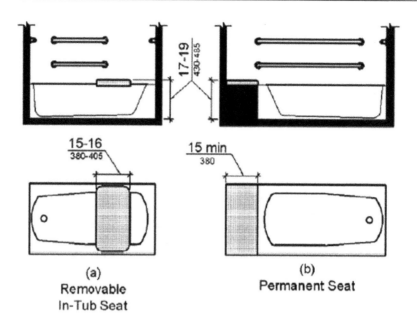

Figure 610.2 Bathtub Seats

610.3 Shower Compartment Seats. Where a seat is provided in a standard roll-in shower compartment, it shall be a folding type, shall be installed on the side wall adjacent to the controls, and shall extend from the back wall to a point within 3 inches (75 mm) of the compartment entry. Where a seat is provided in an alternate roll-in type shower compartment, it shall be a folding type, shall be installed on the front wall opposite the back wall, and shall extend from the adjacent side wall to a point within 3 inches (75 mm) of the compartment entry. In transfer-type showers, the seat shall extend from the back wall to a point within 3 inches (75 mm) of the compartment entry. The top of the seat shall be 17 inches (430 mm) minimum and 19 inches (485 mm) maximum above the bathroom finish floor. Seats shall comply with 610.3.1 or 610.3.2.

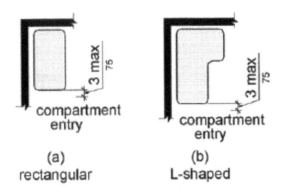

Figure 610.3 Extent of Seat

610.3.1 Rectangular Seats. The rear edge of a rectangular seat shall be 2 1/2 inches (64 mm) maximum and the front edge 15 inches (380 mm) minimum and 16 inches (405 mm) maximum from the seat wall. The side edge of the seat shall be 1 1/2 inches (38 mm) maximum from the adjacent wall.

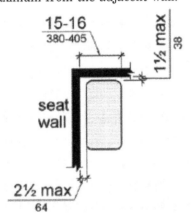

Figure 610.3.1 Rectangular Shower Seat

610.3.2 L-Shaped Seats. The rear edge of an L-shaped seat shall be 2 1/2 inches (64 mm) maximum and the front edge 15 inches (380 mm) minimum and 16 inches (405 mm) maximum from the seat wall. The rear edge of the "L" portion of the seat shall be 1 1/2 inches (38 mm) maximum from the wall and the front edge shall be 14 inches (355 mm) minimum and 15 inches (380 mm) maximum from the wall. The end of the "L" shall be 22 inches (560 mm) minimum and 23 inches maximum (585 mm) from the main seat wall.

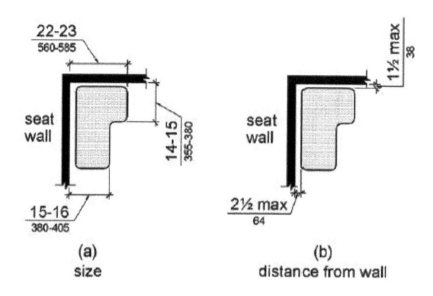

Figure 610.3.2 L-Shaped Shower Seat

610.4 Structural Strength. Allowable stresses shall not be exceeded for materials used when a vertical or horizontal force of 250 pounds (1112 N) is applied at any point on the seat, fastener, mounting device, or supporting structure.

611   Washing Machines and Clothes Dryers

611.1 General. Washing machines and clothes dryers shall comply with 611.

611.2 Clear Floor Space. A clear floor or ground space complying with 305 positioned for parallel approach shall be provided. The clear floor or ground space shall be centered on the appliance.

611.3 Operable Parts. Operable parts, including doors, lint screens, and detergent and bleach compartments shall comply with 309.

611.4 Height. Top loading machines shall have the door to the laundry compartment located 36 inches (915 mm) maximum above the finish floor. Front loading machines shall have the bottom of the opening to the laundry compartment located 15 inches (380 mm) minimum and 36 inches (915 mm) maximum above the finish floor.

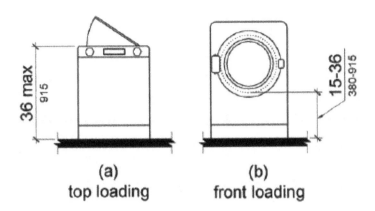

(a)
top loading

(b)
front loading

Figure 611.4 Height of Laundry Compartment Opening

612   Saunas and Steam Rooms

612.1   General. Saunas and steam rooms shall comply with 612.

612.2   Bench. Where seating is provided in saunas and steam rooms, at least one bench shall comply with 903. Doors shall not swing into the clear floor space required by 903.2.

EXCEPTION: A readily removable bench shall be permitted to obstruct the turning space required by 612.3 and the clear floor or ground space required by 903.2.

612.3   Turning Space. A turning space complying with 304 shall be provided within saunas and steam rooms.

CHAPTER 7:   COMMUNICATION ELEMENTS AND FEATURES

701   General

701.1   Scope. The provisions of Chapter 7 shall apply where required by Chapter 2 or where referenced by a requirement in this document.

702   Fire Alarm Systems

702.1   General. Fire alarm systems shall have permanently installed audible and visible alarms complying with NFPA 72 (1999 or 2002 edition) (incorporated by reference, see "Referenced Standards" in Chapter 1), except that the maximum allowable sound level of audible notification appliances complying with section 4-3.2.1 of NFPA 72 (1999 edition) shall have a sound level no more than 110 dB at the minimum hearing distance from the audible appliance. In addition, alarms in guest rooms required to provide communication features shall comply with sections 4-3 and 4-4 of NFPA 72 (1999 edition) or sections 7.4 and 7.5 of NFPA 72 (2002 edition).

EXCEPTION: Fire alarm systems in medical care facilities shall be permitted to be provided in accordance with industry practice.

703   Signs

703.1   General. Signs shall comply with 703. Where both visual and tactile characters are required, either one sign with both visual and tactile characters, or two separate signs, one with visual, and one with tactile characters, shall be provided.

703.2   Raised Characters. Raised characters shall comply with 703.2 and shall be duplicated in braille complying with 703.3. Raised characters shall be installed in accordance with 703.4.

Advisory 703.2 Raised Characters.

Signs that are designed to be read by touch should not have sharp or abrasive edges.

703.2.1   Depth. Raised characters shall be 1/32 inch (0.8 mm) minimum above their background.

703.2.2   Case. Characters shall be uppercase.

703.2.3   Style. Characters shall be sans serif. Characters shall not be italic, oblique, script, highly decorative, or of other unusual forms.

703.2.4   Character Proportions. Characters shall be selected from fonts where the width of the uppercase letter "O" is 55 percent minimum and 110 percent maximum of the height of the uppercase letter "I".

703.2.5   Character Height. Character height measured vertically from the baseline of the character shall be 5/8 inch (16 mm) minimum and 2 inches (51 mm) maximum based on the height of the uppercase letter "I".

EXCEPTION: Where separate raised and visual characters with the same information are provided, raised character height shall be permitted to be 1/2 inch (13 mm) minimum.

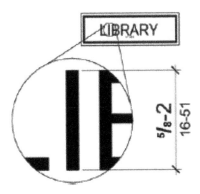

Figure 703.2.5 Height of Raised Characters

703.2.6   Stroke Thickness. Stroke thickness of the uppercase letter "I" shall be 15 percent maximum of the height of the character.

703.2.7   Character Spacing. Character spacing shall be measured between the two closest points of adjacent raised characters within a message, excluding word spaces. Where characters have rectangular cross sections, spacing between individual raised characters shall be 1/8 inch (3.2 mm) minimum and 4 times the raised character stroke width maximum. Where characters have other cross sections, spacing between individual raised characters shall be 1/16 inch (1.6 mm) minimum and 4 times the raised character stroke width maximum at the base of the cross sections, and 1/8 inch (3.2 mm) minimum and 4 times the raised character stroke width maximum at the top of the cross sections. Characters shall be separated from raised borders and decorative elements 3/8 inch (9.5 mm) minimum.

703.2.8   Line Spacing. Spacing between the baselines of separate lines of raised characters within a message shall be 135 percent minimum and 170 percent maximum of the raised character height.

703.3   Braille. Braille shall be contracted (Grade 2) and shall comply with 703.3 and 703.4.

703.3.1   Dimensions and Capitalization. Braille dots shall have a domed or rounded shape and shall comply with Table 703.3.1. The indication of an uppercase letter or letters shall only be used before the first word of sentences, proper nouns and names, individual letters of the alphabet, initials, and acronyms.

Table 703.3.1 Braille Dimensions	
Measurement Range	**Minimum in Inches Maximum in Inches**
Dot base diameter	0.059 (1.5 mm) to 0.063 (1.6 mm)
Distance between two dots in the same cell[1]	0.090 (2.3 mm) to 0.100 (2.5 mm)

Table 703.3.1 Braille Dimensions	
Measurement Range	**Minimum in Inches Maximum in Inches**
Distance between corresponding dots in adjacent cells[1]	0.241 (6.1 mm) to 0.300 (7.6 mm)
Dot height	0.025 (0.6 mm) to 0.037 (0.9 mm)
Distance between corresponding dotsfrom one cell directly below[1]	0.395 (10 mm) to 0.400 (10.2 mm)
1. Measured center to center.	

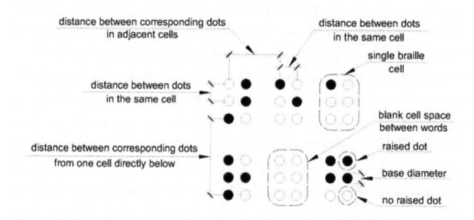

Figure 703.3.1 Braille Measurement

703.3.2 Position Braille shall be positioned below the corresponding text. If text is multi-lined, braille shall be placed below the entire text. Braille shall be separated 3/8 inch (9.5 mm) minimum from any other tactile characters and 3/8 inch (9.5 mm) minimum from raised borders and decorative elements.

EXCEPTION: Braille provided on elevator car controls shall be separated 3/16 inch (4.8 mm) minimum and shall be located either directly below or adjacent to the corresponding raised characters or symbols.

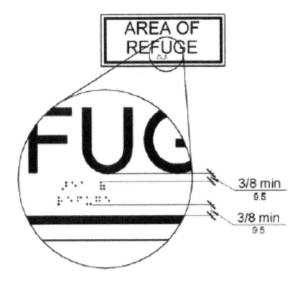

Figure 703.3.2 Position of Braille

703.4 Installation Height and Location. Signs with tactile characters shall comply with 703.4.

703.4.1 Height Above Finish Floor or Ground. Tactile characters on signs shall be located 48 inches (1220 mm) minimum above the finish floor or ground surface, measured from the baseline of the lowest tactile character and 60 inches (1525 mm) maximum above the finish floor or ground surface, measured from the baseline of the highest tactile character.

EXCEPTION: Tactile characters for elevator car controls shall not be required to comply with 703.4.1.

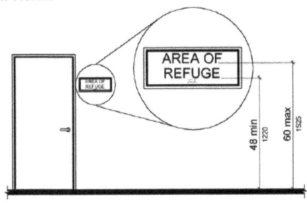

Figure 703.4.1 Height of Tactile Characters Above Finish Floor or Ground

703.4.2 Location. Where a tactile sign is provided at a door, the sign shall be located alongside the door at the latch side. Where a tactile sign is provided at double doors with one active leaf, the sign shall be located on the inactive leaf. Where a tactile sign is provided at double doors with two active leafs, the sign shall be located to the right of the right hand door. Where there is no wall space at the latch side of a single door or at the right side of double doors, signs shall be located on the nearest adjacent wall. Signs containing tactile characters shall be located so that a clear floor space of 18 inches (455 mm) minimum by 18 inches (455 mm) minimum, centered on the tactile characters, is provided beyond the arc of any door swing between the closed position and 45 degree open position.

EXCEPTION: Signs with tactile characters shall be permitted on the push side of doors with closers and without hold-open devices.

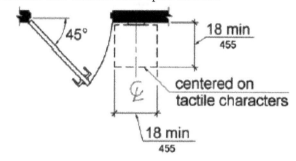

Figure 703.4.2 Location of Tactile Signs at Doors

703.5   Visual Characters. Visual characters shall comply with 703.5.

EXCEPTION: Where visual characters comply with 703.2 and are accompanied by braille complying with 703.3, they shall not be required to comply with 703.5.2 through 703.5.9.

703.5.1   Finish and Contrast. Characters and their background shall have a non-glare finish. Characters shall contrast with their background with either light characters on a dark background or dark characters on a light background.

Advisory 703.5.1 Finish and Contrast.

    Signs are more legible for persons with low vision when characters contrast as much as possible with their background. Additional factors affecting the ease with which the text can be distinguished from its background include shadows cast by lighting sources, surface glare, and the uniformity of the text and its background colors and textures.

703.5.2   Case. Characters shall be uppercase or lowercase or a combination of both.

703.5.3   Style. Characters shall be conventional in form. Characters shall not be italic, oblique, script, highly decorative, or of other unusual forms.

703.5.4   Character Proportions. Characters shall be selected from fonts where the width of the uppercase letter "O" is 55 percent minimum and 110 percent maximum of the height of the uppercase letter "I".

703.5.5   Character Height. Minimum character height shall comply with Table 703.5.5. Viewing distance shall be measured as the horizontal distance between the character and an obstruction preventing further approach towards the sign. Character height shall be based on the uppercase letter "I".

Table 703.5.5 Visual Character Height (text version)		
Height to Finish Floor or Ground From Baseline of Character	**Horizontal Viewing Distance**	**Minimum Character Height**
40 inches (1015 mm) to less than or equal to 70 inches (1780 mm)	less than 72 inches (1830 mm)	5/8 inch (16 mm)
	72 inches (1830 mm) and greater	5/8 inch (16 mm), plus 1/8 inch (3.2 mm) per foot (305 mm) of viewing distance above 72 inches (1830 mm)
Greater than 70 inches (1780 mm) to less than or equal to 120 inches (3050 mm)	less than 180 inches (4570 mm)	2 inches (51 mm)
	180 inches (4570 mm) and greater	2 inches (51 mm), plus 1/8 inch (3.2 mm) per foot (305 mm) of viewing distance above 180 inches (4570 mm)
greater than 120 inches(3050 mm)	less than 21 feet (6400 mm)	3 inches (75 mm)
	21 feet (6400 mm) and greater	3 inches (75 mm), plus 1/8 inch (3.2 mm) per foot (305 mm) of viewing distance above 21 feet (6400 mm)

703.5.6   Height From Finish Floor or Ground. Visual characters shall be 40 inches (1015 mm) minimum above the finish floor or ground.

EXCEPTION: Visual characters indicating elevator car controls shall not be required to comply with 703.5.6.

703.5.7   Stroke Thickness. Stroke thickness of the uppercase letter "I" shall be 10 percent minimum and 30 percent maximum of the height of the character.

703.5.8   Character Spacing. Character spacing shall be measured between the two closest points of adjacent characters, excluding word spaces. Spacing between individual characters shall be 10 percent minimum and 35 percent maximum of character height.

703.5.9   Line Spacing. Spacing between the baselines of separate lines of characters within a message shall be 135 percent minimum and 170 percent maximum of the character height.

703.6   Pictograms. Pictograms shall comply with 703.6.

703.6.1   Pictogram Field. Pictograms shall have a field height of 6 inches (150 mm) minimum. Characters and braille shall not be located in the pictogram field.

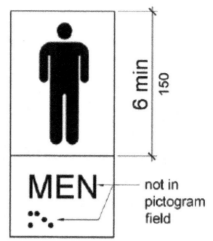

Figure 703.6.1 Pictogram Field

703.6.2   Finish and Contrast. Pictograms and their field shall have a non-glare finish. Pictograms shall contrast with their field with either a light pictogram on a dark field or a dark pictogram on a light field.

Advisory 703.6.2 Finish and Contrast.

Signs are more legible for persons with low vision when characters contrast as much as possible with their background. Additional factors affecting the ease with which the text can be distinguished from its background include shadows cast by lighting sources, surface glare, and the uniformity of the text and background colors and textures.

703.6.3   Text Descriptors. Pictograms shall have text descriptors located directly below the pictogram field. Text descriptors shall comply with 703.2, 703.3 and 703.4.

703.7   Symbols of Accessibility. Symbols of accessibility shall comply with 703.7.

703.7.1   Finish and Contrast. Symbols of accessibility and their background shall have a non-glare finish. Symbols of accessibility shall contrast with their background with either a light symbol on a dark background or a dark symbol on a light background.

Advisory 703.7.1 Finish and Contrast.

Signs are more legible for persons with low vision when characters contrast as much as possible with their background. Additional factors affecting the ease with which the text can be distinguished from its background include shadows cast by lighting sources, surface glare, and the uniformity of the text and background colors and textures.

703.7.2 Symbols.

703.7.2.1 International Symbol of Accessibility. The International Symbol of Accessibility shall comply with Figure 703.7.2.1.

Figure 703.7.2.1 International Symbol of Accessibility

703.7.2.2 International Symbol of TTY. The International Symbol of TTY shall comply with Figure 703.7.2.2.

Figure 703.7.2.2 International Symbol of TTY

703.7.2.3 Volume Control Telephones. Telephones with a volume control shall be identified by a pictogram of a telephone handset with radiating sound waves on a square field such as shown in Figure 703.7.2.3.

Figure 703.7.2.3 Volume Control Telephone

703.7.2.4 Assistive Listening Systems. Assistive listening systems shall be identified by the International Symbol of Access for Hearing Loss complying with Figure 703.7.2.4.

Figure 703.7.2.4 International Symbol of Access for Hearing Loss

704   Telephones

704.1   General. Public telephones shall comply with 704.

704.2   Wheelchair Accessible Telephones. Wheelchair accessible telephones shall comply with 704.2.

704.2.1   Clear Floor or Ground Space. A clear floor or ground space complying with 305 shall be provided. The clear floor or ground space shall not be obstructed by bases, enclosures, or seats.

Advisory 704.2.1 Clear Floor or Ground Space.

Because clear floor and ground space is required to be unobstructed, telephones, enclosures and related telephone book storage cannot encroach on the required clear floor or ground space and must comply with the provisions for protruding objects. (See Section 307).

704.2.1.1 Parallel Approach. Where a parallel approach is provided, the distance from the edge of the telephone enclosure to the face of the telephone unit shall be 10 inches (255 mm) maximum.

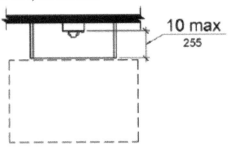

Figure 704.2.1.1 Parallel Approach to Telephone

704.2.1.2 Forward Approach. Where a forward approach is provided, the distance from the front edge of a counter within the telephone enclosure to the face of the telephone unit shall be 20 inches (510 mm) maximum.

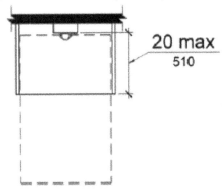

Figure 704.2.1.2 Forward Approach to Telephone

704.2.2 Operable Parts. Operable parts shall comply with 309. Telephones shall have push-button controls where such service is available.

704.2.3 Telephone Directories. Telephone directories, where provided, shall be located in accordance with 309.

704.2.4 Cord Length. The cord from the telephone to the handset shall be 29 inches (735 mm) long minimum.

704.3 Volume Control Telephones. Public telephones required to have volume controls shall be equipped with a receive volume control that provides a gain adjustable up to 20 dB minimum. For incremental volume control, provide at least one intermediate step of 12 dB of gain minimum. An automatic reset shall be provided.

Advisory 704.3 Volume Control Telephones.

Amplifiers on pay phones are located in the base or the handset or are built into the telephone. Most are operated by pressing a button or key. If the microphone in the handset is not being used, a mute button that temporarily turns off the microphone can also reduce the amount of background noise which the person hears in the earpiece. If a volume adjustment is provided that allows the user to set the level anywhere from the base volume to the upper requirement of 20 dB, there is no need to specify a lower limit. If a stepped volume control is provided, one of the intermediate levels must provide 12 dB of gain. Consider compatibility issues when matching an amplified handset with a phone or phone system. Amplified handsets that can be switched with pay telephone handsets are available. Portable and in-line amplifiers can be used with some phones but are not practical at most public phones covered by these requirements.

704.4 TTYs. TTYs required at a public pay telephone shall be permanently affixed within, or adjacent to, the telephone enclosure. Where an acoustic coupler is used, the telephone cord shall be sufficiently long to allow connection of the TTY and the telephone receiver.

Advisory 704.4 TTYs.

Ensure that sufficient electrical service is available where TTYs are to be installed.

704.4.1 Height When in use, the touch surface of TTY keypads shall be 34 inches (865 mm) minimum above the finish floor.

EXCEPTION: Where seats are provided, TTYs shall not be required to comply with 704.4.1.

Advisory 704.4.1 Height.

A telephone with a TTY installed underneath cannot also be a wheelchair accessible telephone because the required 34 inches (865 mm) minimum keypad height can causes the highest operable part of the telephone, usually the coin slot, to exceed the maximum permitted side and forward reach ranges. (See Section 308).

Advisory 704.4.1 Height Exception. While seats are not required at TTYs, reading and typing at a TTY is more suited to sitting than standing. Facilities that often provide seats at TTY's include, but are not limited to, airports and other passenger terminals or stations, courts, art galleries, and convention centers.

704.5 TTY Shelf. Public pay telephones required to accommodate portable TTYs shall be equipped with a shelf and an electrical outlet within or adjacent to the telephone enclosure. The telephone handset shall be capable of being placed flush on the surface of the shelf. The shelf shall be capable of accommodating a TTY and shall have 6 inches (150 mm) minimum vertical clearance above the area where the TTY is to be placed.

705 Detectable Warnings

705.1 General. Detectable warnings shall consist of a surface of truncated domes and shall comply with 705.

705.1.1 Dome Size. Truncated domes in a detectable warning surface shall have a base diameter of 0.9 inch (23 mm) minimum and 1.4 inches (36 mm) maximum, a top diameter of 50 percent of the base diameter minimum to 65 percent of the base diameter maximum, and a height of 0.2 inch (5.1 mm).

705.1.2 Dome Spacing. Truncated domes in a detectable warning surface shall have a center-to-center spacing of 1.6 inches (41 mm) minimum and 2.4 inches (61 mm) maximum, and a base-to-base spacing of 0.65 inch (17 mm) minimum, measured between the most adjacent domes on a square grid.

705.1.3 Contrast. Detectable warning surfaces shall contrast visually with adjacent walking surfaces either light-on-dark, or dark-on-light.

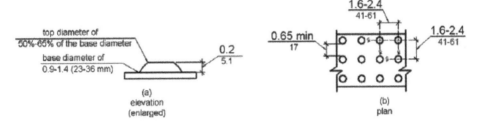

Figure 705.1 Size and Spacing of Truncated Domes

705.2 Platform Edges. Detectable warning surfaces at platform boarding edges shall be 24 inches (610 mm) wide and shall extend the full length of the public use areas of the platform.

706 Assistive Listening Systems

706.1 General. Assistive listening systems required in assembly areas shall comply with 706.

Advisory 706.1 General.

Assistive listening systems are generally categorized by their mode of transmission. There are hard-wired systems and three types of wireless systems: induction loop, infrared, and FM radio transmission. Each has different advantages and disadvantages that can help determine which system is best for a given application. For example, an FM system may be better than an infrared system in some open-air assemblies since infrared signals are less effective in sunlight. On the other hand, an infrared system is typically a better choice than an FM system where confidential transmission is important because it will be contained within a given space.

The technical standards for assistive listening systems describe minimum performance levels for volume, interference, and distortion. Sound pressure levels (SPL), expressed in decibels, measure output sound volume. Signal-to-noise ratio (SNR or S/N), also expressed in decibels, represents the relationship between the loudness of a desired sound (the signal) and the background noise in a space or piece of equipment. The higher the SNR, the more intelligible the signal. The peak clipping level limits the distortion in signal output produced when high-volume sound waves are manipulated to serve assistive listening devices.

Selecting or specifying an effective assistive listening system for a large or complex venue requires assistance from a professional sound engineer. The Access Board has published technical assistance on assistive listening devices and systems.

706.2 Receiver Jacks. Receivers required for use with an assistive listening system shall include a 1/8 inch (3.2 mm) standard mono jack.

706.3 Receiver Hearing-Aid Compatibility. Receivers required to be hearing-aid compatible shall interface with telecoils in hearing aids through the provision of neckloops.

Advisory 706.3 Receiver Hearing-Aid Compatibility.

Neckloops and headsets that can be worn as neckloops are compatible with hearing aids. Receivers that are not compatible include earbuds, which may require removal of hearing aids, earphones, and headsets that must be worn over the ear, which can create disruptive interference in the transmission and can be uncomfortable for people wearing hearing aids.

706.4 Sound Pressure Level. Assistive listening systems shall be capable of providing a sound pressure level of 110 dB minimum and 118 dB maximum with a dynamic range on the volume control of 50 dB.

706.5 Signal-to-Noise Ratio. The signal-to-noise ratio for internally generated noise in assistive listening systems shall be 18 dB minimum.

706.6 Peak Clipping Level. Peak clipping shall not exceed 18 dB of clipping relative to the peaks of speech.

707 Automatic Teller Machines and Fare Machines

Advisory 707 Automatic Teller Machines and Fare Machines.

Interactive transaction machines (ITMs), other than ATMs, are not covered by Section 707. However, for entities covered by the ADA, the Department of Justice regulations that implement the ADA provide additional guidance regarding the relationship between these requirements and elements that are not directly addressed by these requirements. Federal procurement law requires that ITMs purchased by the Federal government comply with standards issued by the

Access Board under Section 508 of the Rehabilitation Act of 1973, as amended. This law covers a variety of products, including computer hardware and software, websites, phone systems, fax machines, copiers, and similar technologies. For more information on Section 508 consult the Access Board's website at **www.access-board.gov**.

707.1 General. Automatic teller machines and fare machines shall comply with 707.

Advisory 707.1 General.

If farecards have one tactually distinctive corner they can be inserted with greater accuracy. Token collection devices that are designed to accommodate tokens which are perforated can allow a person to distinguish more readily between tokens and common coins. Place accessible gates and fare vending machines in close proximity to other accessible elements when feasible so the facility is easier to use.

707.2 Clear Floor or Ground Space. A clear floor or ground space complying with 305 shall be provided.

EXCEPTION: Clear floor or ground space shall not be required at drive-up only automatic teller machines and fare machines.

707.3 Operable Parts. Operable parts shall comply with 309. Unless a clear or correct key is provided, each operable part shall be able to be differentiated by sound or touch, without activation.

EXCEPTION: Drive-up only automatic teller machines and fare machines shall not be required to comply with 309.2 and 309.3.

707.4 Privacy. Automatic teller machines shall provide the opportunity for the same degree of privacy of input and output available to all individuals.

Advisory 707.4 Privacy.

In addition to people who are blind or visually impaired, people with limited reach who use wheelchairs or have short stature, who cannot effectively block the ATM screen with their bodies, may prefer to use speech output. Speech output users can benefit from an option to render the visible screen blank, thereby affording them greater personal security and privacy.

707.5 Speech Output. Machines shall be speech enabled. Operating instructions and orientation, visible transaction prompts, user input verification, error messages, and all displayed information for full use shall be accessible to and independently usable by individuals with vision impairments. Speech shall be delivered through a mechanism that is readily available to all users, including but not limited to, an industry standard connector or a telephone handset. Speech shall be recorded or digitized human, or synthesized.

EXCEPTIONS:

1. Audible tones shall be permitted instead of speech for visible output that is not displayed for security purposes, including but not limited to, asterisks representing personal identification numbers.

2. Advertisements and other similar information shall not be required to be audible unless they convey information that can be used in the transaction being conducted.

3. Where speech synthesis cannot be supported, dynamic alphabetic output shall not be required to be audible.

Advisory 707.5 Speech Output.

If an ATM provides additional functions such as dispensing coupons, selling theater tickets, or providing copies of monthly statements, all such functions must be available to customers using speech output. To avoid confusion at the ATM, the method of initiating the speech mode should be easily discoverable and should not require specialized training. For example, if a telephone handset is provided, lifting the handset can initiate the speech mode.

707.5.1 User Control. Speech shall be capable of being repeated or interrupted. Volume control shall be provided for the speech function.

EXCEPTION: Speech output for any single function shall be permitted to be automatically interrupted when a transaction is selected.

707.5.2 Receipts Where receipts are provided, speech output devices shall provide audible balance inquiry information, error messages, and all other information on the printed receipt necessary to complete or verify the transaction.

EXCEPTIONS:

1. Machine location, date and time of transaction, customer account number, and the machine identifier shall not be required to be audible.

2. Information on printed receipts that duplicates information available on-screen shall not be required to be presented in the form of an audible receipt.

3. Printed copies of bank statements and checks shall not be required to be audible.

707.6 Input. Input devices shall comply with 707.6.

707.6.1 Input Controls. At least one tactilely discernible input control shall be provided for each function. Where provided, key surfaces not on active areas of display screens, shall be raised above surrounding surfaces. Where membrane keys are the only method of input, each shall be tactilely discernable from surrounding surfaces and adjacent keys.

707.6.2 Numeric Keys. Numeric keys shall be arranged in a 12-key ascending or descending telephone keypad layout. The number five key shall be tactilely distinct from the other keys.

Advisory 707.6.2 Numeric Keys.

Telephone keypads and computer keyboards differ in one significant feature, ascending versus descending numerical order. Both types of keypads are acceptable, provided the computer-style keypad is organized similarly to the number pad located at the right on most computer keyboards, and does not resemble the line of numbers located above the computer keys.

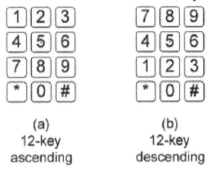

(a)
12-key
ascending

(b)
12-key
descending

Figure 707.6.2 Numeric Key Layout

707.6.3   Function Keys. Function keys shall comply with 707.6.3.

707.6.3.1   Contrast. Function keys shall contrast visually from background surfaces. Characters and symbols on key surfaces shall contrast visually from key surfaces. Visual contrast shall be either light-on-dark or dark-on-light.

EXCEPTION: Tactile symbols required by 707.6.3.2 shall not be required to comply with 707.6.3.1.

707.6.3.2   Tactile Symbols. Function key surfaces shall have tactile symbols as follows: Enter or Proceed key: raised circle; Clear or Correct key: raised left arrow; Cancel key: raised letter ex; Add Value key: raised plus sign; Decrease Value key: raised minus sign.

707.7   Display Screen. The display screen shall comply with 707.7.

EXCEPTION: Drive-up only automatic teller machines and fare machines shall not be required to comply with 707.7.1.

707.7.1   Visibility The display screen shall be visible from a point located 40 inches (1015 mm) above the center of the clear floor space in front of the machine.

707.7.2   Characters Characters displayed on the screen shall be in a sans serif font. Characters shall be 3/16 inch (4.8 mm) high minimum based on the uppercase letter "I". Characters shall contrast with their background with either light characters on a dark background or dark characters on a light background.

707.8   Braille Instructions. Braille instructions for initiating the speech mode shall be provided. Braille shall comply with 703.3.

708   Two-Way Communication Systems

708.1   General. Two-way communication systems shall comply with 708.

Advisory 708.1 General.

Devices that do not require handsets are easier to use by people who have a limited reach.

708.2 Audible and Visual Indicators. The system shall provide both audible and visual signals.

Advisory 708.2 Audible and Visual Indicators.

A light can be used to indicate visually that assistance is on the way. Signs indicating the meaning of visual signals should be provided.

708.3 Handsets. Handset cords, if provided, shall be 29 inches (735 mm) long minimum.

708.4 Residential Dwelling Unit Communication Systems. Communications systems between a residential dwelling unit and a site, building, or floor entrance shall comply with 708.4.

708.4.1 Common Use or Public Use System Interface. The common use or public use system interface shall include the capability of supporting voice and TTY communication with the residential dwelling unit interface.

708.4.2 Residential Dwelling Unit Interface. The residential dwelling unit system interface shall include a telephone jack capable of supporting voice and TTY communication with the common use or public use system interface.

CHAPTER 8:   SPECIAL ROOMS, SPACES AND ELEMENTS

801   General

801.1   Scope. The provisions of Chapter 8 shall apply where required by Chapter 2 or where referenced by a requirement in this document.

Advisory 801.1 Scope.

Facilities covered by these requirements are also subject to the requirements of the other chapters. For example, 806 addresses guest rooms in transient lodging facilities while 902 contains the technical specifications for dining surfaces. If a transient lodging facility contains a restaurant, the restaurant must comply with requirements in other chapters such as those applicable to certain dining surfaces.

802   Wheelchair Spaces, Companion Seats, and Designated Aisle Seats

802.1   Wheelchair Spaces. Wheelchair spaces shall comply with 802.1.

802.1.1   Floor or Ground Surface. The floor or ground surface of wheelchair spaces shall comply with 302. Changes in level are not permitted.

EXCEPTION: Slopes not steeper than 1:48 shall be permitted.

802.1.2   Width. A single wheelchair space shall be 36 inches (915 mm) wide minimum Where two adjacent wheelchair spaces are provided, each wheelchair space shall be 33 inches (840 mm) wide minimum.

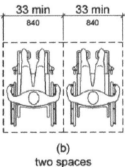

(a)
single space

(b)
two spaces

Figure 802.1.2 Width of Wheelchair Spaces in Assembly Areas

802.1.3   Depth. Where a wheelchair space can be entered from the front or rear, the wheelchair space shall be 48 inches (1220 mm) deep minimum. Where a wheelchair space can be entered only from the side, the wheelchair space shall be 60 inches (1525 mm) deep minimum.

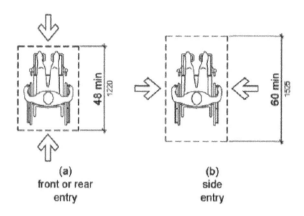

(a)
front or rear
entry

(b)
side
entry

Figure 802.1.3 Depth of Wheelchair Spaces in Assembly Areas

802.1.4 Approach. Wheelchair spaces shall adjoin accessible routes. Accessible routes shall not overlap wheelchair spaces.

Advisory 802.1.4 Approach.

Because accessible routes serving wheelchair spaces are not permitted to overlap the clear floor space at wheelchair spaces, access to any wheelchair space cannot be through another wheelchair space.

802.1.5 Overlap. Wheelchair spaces shall not overlap circulation paths.

Advisory 802.1.5 Overlap.

The term "circulation paths" used in Section 802.1.5 means aisle width required by applicable building or life safety codes for the specific assembly occupancy. Where the circulation path provided is wider than the required aisle width, the wheelchair space may intrude into that portion of the circulation path that is provided in excess of the required aisle width.

802.2 Lines of Sight. Lines of sight to the screen, performance area, or playing field for spectators in wheelchair spaces shall comply with 802.2.

802.2.1 Lines of Sight Over Seated Spectators. Where spectators are expected to remain seated during events, spectators in wheelchair spaces shall be afforded lines of sight complying with 802.2.1.

802.2.1.1 Lines of Sight Over Heads. Where spectators are provided lines of sight over the heads of spectators seated in the first row in front of their seats, spectators seated in wheelchair spaces shall be afforded lines of sight over the heads of seated spectators in the first row in front of wheelchair spaces.

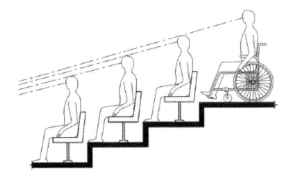

Figure 802.2.1.1 Lines of Sight Over the Heads of Seated Spectators

802.2.1.2   Lines of Sight Between Heads. Where spectators are provided lines of sight over the shoulders and between the heads of spectators seated in the first row in front of their seats, spectators seated in wheelchair spaces shall be afforded lines of sight over the shoulders and between the heads of seated spectators in the first row in front of wheelchair spaces.

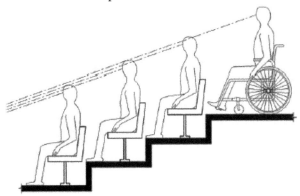

Figure 802.2.1.2 Lines of Sight Between the Heads of Seated Spectators

802.2.2   Lines of Sight Over Standing Spectators. Where spectators are expected to stand during events, spectators in wheelchair spaces shall be afforded lines of sight complying with 802.2.2.

802.2.2.1   Lines of Sight Over Heads. Where standing spectators are provided lines of sight over the heads of spectators standing in the first row in front of their seats, spectators seated in wheelchair spaces shall be afforded lines of sight over the heads of standing spectators in the first row in front of wheelchair spaces.

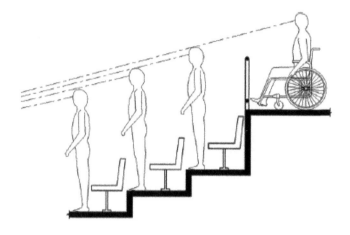

Figure 802.2.2.1 Lines of Sight Over the Heads of Standing Spectators

802.2.2.2 Lines of Sight Between Heads. Where standing spectators are provided lines of sight over the shoulders and between the heads of spectators standing in the first row in front of their seats, spectators seated in wheelchair spaces shall be afforded lines of sight over the shoulders and between the heads of standing spectators in the first row in front of wheelchair spaces.

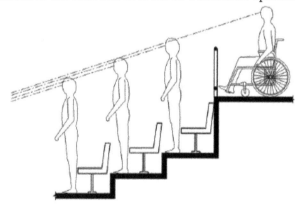

Figure 802.2.2.2 Lines of Sight Between the Heads of Standing Spectators

802.3 Companion Seats. Companion seats shall comply with 802.3.

802.3.1 Alignment. In row seating, companion seats shall be located to provide shoulder alignment with adjacent wheelchair spaces. The shoulder alignment point of the wheelchair space shall be measured 36 inches (915 mm) from the front of the wheelchair space. The floor surface of the companion seat shall be at the same elevation as the floor surface of the wheelchair space.

802.3.2 Type. Companion seats shall be equivalent in size, quality, comfort, and amenities to the seating in the immediate area. Companion seats shall be permitted to be movable.

802.4 Designated Aisle Seats. Designated aisle seats shall comply with 802.4.

802.4.1 Armrests. Where armrests are provided on the seating in the immediate area, folding or retractable armrests shall be provided on the aisle side of the seat.

802.4.2 Identification. Each designated aisle seat shall be identified by a sign or marker.

Advisory 802.4.2 Identification.

Seats with folding or retractable armrests are intended for use by individuals who have difficulty walking. Consider identifying such seats with signs that contrast (light-on-dark or dark-on-light) and that are also photo luminescent.

803   Dressing, Fitting, and Locker Rooms

803.1 General. Dressing, fitting, and locker rooms shall comply with 803.

Advisory 803.1 General.

Partitions and doors should be designed to ensure people using accessible dressing and fitting rooms privacy equivalent to that afforded other users of the facility. Section 903.5 requires dressing room bench seats to be installed so that they are at the same height as a typical wheelchair seat, 17 inches (430 mm) to 19 inches (485 mm). However, wheelchair seats can be lower than dressing room benches for people of short stature or children using wheelchairs.

803.2 Turning Space. Turning space complying with 304 shall be provided within the room.

803.3 Door Swing. Doors shall not swing into the room unless a clear floor or ground space complying with 305.3 is provided beyond the arc of the door swing.

803.4 Benches. A bench complying with 903 shall be provided within the room.

803.5 Coat Hooks and Shelves. Coat hooks provided within the room shall be located within one of the reach ranges specified in 308. Shelves shall be 40 inches (1015 mm) minimum and 48 inches (1220 mm) maximum above the finish floor or ground.

804   Kitchens and Kitchenettes

804.1 General. Kitchens and kitchenettes shall comply with 804.

804.2 Clearance. Where a pass through kitchen is provided, clearances shall comply with 804.2.1. Where a U-shaped kitchen is provided, clearances shall comply with 804.2.2.

EXCEPTION: Spaces that do not provide a cooktop or conventional range shall not be required to comply with 804.2.

Advisory 804.2 Clearance.

Clearances are measured from the furthest projecting face of all opposing base cabinets, counter tops, appliances, or walls, excluding hardware.

804.2.1 Pass Through Kitchen. In pass through kitchens where counters, appliances or cabinets are on two opposing sides, or where counters, appliances or cabinets are opposite a parallel wall, clearance between all opposing base cabinets, counter tops, appliances, or walls within kitchen work areas shall be 40 inches (1015 mm) minimum. Pass through kitchens shall have two entries.

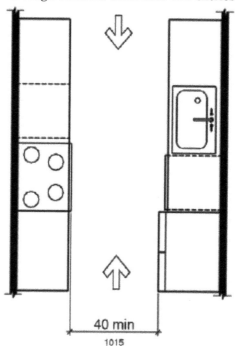

Figure 804.2.1 Pass Through Kitchens

804.2.2 U-Shaped. In U-shaped kitchens enclosed on three contiguous sides, clearance between all opposing base cabinets, counter tops, appliances, or walls within kitchen work areas shall be 60 inches (1525 mm) minimum.

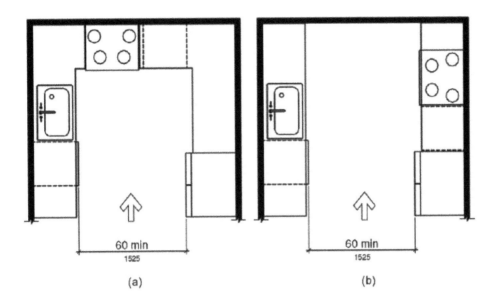

Figure 804.2.2 U-Shaped Kitchens

804.3   Kitchen Work Surface. In residential dwelling units required to comply with 809, at least one 30 inches (760 mm) wide minimum section of counter shall provide a kitchen work surface that complies with 804.3.

804.3.1   Clear Floor or Ground Space. A clear floor space complying with 305 positioned for a forward approach shall be provided. The clear floor or ground space shall be centered on the kitchen work surface and shall provide knee and toe clearance complying with 306.

EXCEPTION: Cabinetry shall be permitted under the kitchen work surface provided that all of the following conditions are met:

(a) the cabinetry can be removed without removal or replacement of the kitchen work surface;

(b) the finish floor extends under the cabinetry; and

(c) the walls behind and surrounding the cabinetry are finished.

804.3.2   Height. The kitchen work surface shall be 34 inches (865 mm) maximum above the finish floor or ground.

EXCEPTION: A counter that is adjustable to provide a kitchen work surface at variable heights, 29 inches (735 mm) minimum and 36 inches (915 mm) maximum, shall be permitted.

804.3.3   Exposed Surfaces. There shall be no sharp or abrasive surfaces under the work surface counters.

804.4   Sinks. Sinks shall comply with 606.

804.5 Storage. At least 50 percent of shelf space in storage facilities shall comply with 811.

804.6 Appliances. Where provided, kitchen appliances shall comply with 804.6.

804.6.1 Clear Floor or Ground Space. A clear floor or ground space complying with 305 shall be provided at each kitchen appliance. Clear floor or ground spaces shall be permitted to overlap.

804.6.2 Operable Parts. All appliance controls shall comply with 309.

EXCEPTIONS:

1. Appliance doors and door latching devices shall not be required to comply with 309.4.

2. Bottom-hinged appliance doors, when in the open position, shall not be required to comply with 309.3.

804.6.3 Dishwasher. Clear floor or ground space shall be positioned adjacent to the dishwasher door. The dishwasher door, in the open position, shall not obstruct the clear floor or ground space for the dishwasher or the sink.

804.6.4 Range or Cooktop. Where a forward approach is provided, the clear floor or ground space shall provide knee and toe clearance complying with 306. Where knee and toe space is provided, the underside of the range or cooktop shall be insulated or otherwise configured to prevent burns, abrasions, or electrical shock. The location of controls shall not require reaching across burners.

804.6.5 Oven. Ovens shall comply with 804.6.5.

804.6.5.1 Side-Hinged Door Ovens. Side-hinged door ovens shall have the work surface required by 804.3 positioned adjacent to the latch side of the oven door.

804.6.5.2 Bottom-Hinged Door Ovens. Bottom-hinged door ovens shall have the work surface required by 804.3 positioned adjacent to one side of the door.

804.6.5.3 Controls. Ovens shall have controls on front panels.

804.6.6 Refrigerator/Freezer. Combination refrigerators and freezers shall have at least 50 percent of the freezer space 54 inches (1370 mm) maximum above the finish floor or ground. The clear floor or ground space shall be positioned for a parallel approach to the space dedicated to a refrigerator/freezer with the center-line of the clear floor or ground space offset 24 inches (610 mm) maximum from the centerline of the dedicated space.

805 Medical Care and Long-Term Care Facilities

805.1 General. Medical care facility and long-term care facility patient or resident sleeping rooms required to provide mobility features shall comply with 805.

805.2 Turning Space. Turning space complying with 304 shall be provided within the room.

805.3 Clear Floor or Ground Space. A clear floor space complying with 305 shall be provided on each side of the bed. The clear floor space shall be positioned for parallel approach to the side of the bed.

805.4 Toilet and Bathing Rooms. Toilet and bathing rooms that are provided as part of a patient or resident sleeping room shall comply with 603. Where provided, no fewer than one water closet, one lavatory, and one bathtub or shower shall comply with the applicable requirements of 603 through 610.

806   Transient Lodging Guest Rooms

806.1   General. Transient lodging guest rooms shall comply with 806. Guest rooms required to provide mobility features shall comply with 806.2. Guest rooms required to provide communication features shall comply with 806.3.

806.2   Guest Rooms with Mobility Features. Guest rooms required to provide mobility features shall comply with 806.2.

Advisory 806.2 Guest Rooms.

The requirements in Section 806.2 do not include requirements that are common to all accessible spaces. For example, closets in guest rooms must comply with the applicable provisions for storage specified in scoping.

806.2.1   Living and Dining Areas. Living and dining areas shall be accessible.

806.2.2   Exterior Spaces. Exterior spaces, including patios, terraces and balconies, that serve the guest room shall be accessible.

806.2.3   Sleeping Areas. At least one sleeping area shall provide a clear floor space complying with 305 on both sides of a bed. The clear floor space shall be positioned for parallel approach to the side of the bed.

EXCEPTION: Where a single clear floor space complying with 305 positioned for parallel approach is provided between two beds, a clear floor or ground space shall not be required on both sides of a bed.

806.2.4   Toilet and Bathing Facilities. At least one bathroom that is provided as part of a guest room shall comply with 603. No fewer than one water closet, one lavatory, and one bathtub or shower shall comply with applicable requirements of 603 through 610. In addition, required roll-in shower compartments shall comply with 608.2.2 or 608.2.3. Toilet and bathing fixtures required to comply with 603 through 610 shall be permitted to be located in more than one toilet or bathing area, provided that travel between fixtures does not require travel between other parts of the guest room.

806.2.4.1   Vanity Counter Top Space. If vanity counter top space is provided in non-accessible guest toilet or bathing rooms, comparable vanity counter top space, in terms of size and proximity to the lavatory, shall also be provided in accessible guest toilet or bathing rooms.

Advisory 806.2.4.1 Vanity Counter Top Space.

This provision is intended to ensure that accessible guest rooms are provided with comparable vanity counter top space.

806.2.5   Kitchens and Kitchenettes. Kitchens and kitchenettes shall comply with 804.

806.2.6 Turning Space. Turning space complying with 304 shall be provided within the guest room.

806.3 Guest Rooms with Communication Features. Guest rooms required to provide communication features shall comply with 806.3.

Advisory 806.3 Guest Rooms with Communication Features.

In guest rooms required to have accessible communication features, consider ensuring compatibility with adaptive equipment used by people with hearing impairments. To ensure communication within the facility, as well as on commercial lines, provide telephone interface jacks that are compatible with both digital and analog signal use. If an audio headphone jack is provided on a speaker phone, a cutoff switch can be included in the jack so that insertion of the jack cuts off the speaker. If a telephone-like handset is used, the external speakers can be turned off when the handset is removed from the cradle. For headset or external amplification system compatibility, a standard subminiature jack installed in the telephone will provide the most flexibility.

806.3.1 Alarms Where emergency warning systems are provided, alarms complying with 702 shall be provided.

806.3.2 Notification Devices. Visible notification devices shall be provided to alert room occupants of incoming telephone calls and a door knock or bell. Notification devices shall not be connected to visible alarm signal appliances. Telephones shall have volume controls compatible with the telephone system and shall comply with 704.3. Telephones shall be served by an electrical outlet complying with 309 located within 48 inches (1220 mm) of the telephone to facilitate the use of a TTY.

807 Holding Cells and Housing Cells

807.1 General. Holding cells and housing cells shall comply with 807.

807.2 Cells with Mobility Features. Cells required to provide mobility features shall comply with 807.2.

807.2.1 Turning Space. Turning space complying with 304 shall be provided within the cell.

807.2.2 Benches. Where benches are provided, at least one bench shall comply with 903.

807.2.3 Beds. Where beds are provided, clear floor space complying with 305 shall be provided on at least one side of the bed. The clear floor space shall be positioned for parallel approach to the side of the bed.

807.2.4 Toilet and Bathing Facilities. Toilet facilities or bathing facilities that are provided as part of a cell shall comply with 603. Where provided, no fewer than one water closet, one lavatory, and one bathtub or shower shall comply with the applicable requirements of 603 through 610.

Advisory 807.2.4 Toilet and Bathing Facilities.

In holding cells, housing cells, or rooms required to be accessible, these requirements do not require a separate toilet room.

807.3 Cells with Communication Features. Cells required to provide communication features shall comply with 807.3.

807.3.1 Alarms Where audible emergency alarm systems are provided to serve the occupants of cells, visible alarms complying with 702 shall be provided.

EXCEPTION: Visible alarms shall not be required where inmates or detainees are not allowed independent means of egress.

807.3.2 Telephones Telephones, where provided within cells, shall have volume controls complying with 704.3.

808 Courtrooms

808.1 General. Courtrooms shall comply with 808.

808.2 Turning Space. Where provided, areas that are raised or depressed and accessed by ramps or platform lifts with entry ramps shall provide unobstructed turning space complying with 304.

808.3 Clear Floor Space. Each jury box and witness stand shall have, within its defined area, clear floor space complying with 305.

EXCEPTION: In alterations, wheelchair spaces are not required to be located within the defined area of raised jury boxes or witness stands and shall be permitted to be located outside these spaces where ramp or platform lift access poses a hazard by restricting or projecting into a means of egress required by the appropriate administrative authority.

808.4 Judges' Benches and Courtroom Stations. Judges' benches, clerks' stations, bailiffs' stations, deputy clerks' stations, court reporters' stations and litigants' and counsel stations shall comply with 902.

809 Residential Dwelling Units

809.1 General. Residential dwelling units shall comply with 809. Residential dwelling units required to provide mobility features shall comply with 809.2 through 809.4. Residential dwelling units required to provide communication features shall comply with 809.5.

809.2 Accessible Routes. Accessible routes complying with Chapter 4 shall be provided within residential dwelling units in accordance with 809.2.

EXCEPTION: Accessible routes shall not be required to or within unfinished attics or unfinished basements.

809.2.1 Location. At least one accessible route shall connect all spaces and elements which are a part of the residential dwelling unit. Where only one accessible route is provided, it shall not pass through bathrooms, closets, or similar spaces.

809.2.2 Turning Space. All rooms served by an accessible route shall provide a turning space complying with 304.

EXCEPTION: Turning space shall not be required in exterior spaces 30 inches (760 mm) maximum in depth or width.

Advisory 809.2.2 Turning Space.

It is generally acceptable to use required clearances to provide wheelchair turning space. For example, in kitchens, 804.3.1 requires at least one work surface with clear floor space complying with 306 to be centered beneath. If designers elect to provide clear floor space that is at least 36 inches (915 mm) wide, as opposed to the required 30 inches (760 mm) wide, that clearance can be part of a T-turn, thereby maximizing efficient use of the kitchen area. However, the overlap of turning space must be limited to one segment of the T-turn so that back-up maneuvering is not restricted. It would, therefore, be unacceptable to use both the clearances under the work surface and the sink as part of a T-turn. See Section 304.3.2 regarding T-turns.

809.3 Kitchen. Where a kitchen is provided, it shall comply with 804.

809.4 Toilet Facilities and Bathing Facilities. At least one bathroom shall comply with 603. No fewer than one of each type of fixture provided shall comply with applicable requirements of 603 through 610. Toilet and bathing fixtures required to comply with 603 through 610 shall be located in the same toilet and bathing area, such that travel between fixtures does not require travel between other parts of the residential dwelling unit.

Advisory 809.4 Toilet Facilities and Bathing Facilities.

In an effort to promote space efficiency, vanity counter top space in accessible residential dwelling units is often omitted. This omission does not promote equal access or equal enjoyment of the unit. Where comparable units have vanity counter tops, accessible units should also have vanity counter tops located as close as possible to the lavatory for convenient access to toiletries.

809.5 Residential Dwelling Units with Communication Features. Residential dwelling units required to provide communication features shall comply with 809.5.

809.5.1 Building Fire Alarm System. Where a building fire alarm system is provided, the system wiring shall be extended to a point within the residential dwelling unit in the vicinity of the residential dwelling unit smoke detection system.

809.5.1.1 Alarm Appliances. Where alarm appliances are provided within a residential dwelling unit as part of the building fire alarm system, they shall comply with 702.

809.5.1.2 Activation. All visible alarm appliances provided within the residential dwelling unit for building fire alarm notification shall be activated upon activation of the building fire alarm in the portion of the building containing the residential dwelling unit.

809.5.2 Residential Dwelling Unit Smoke Detection System. Residential dwelling unit smoke detection systems shall comply with NFPA 72 (1999 or 2002 edition) (incorporated by reference, see "Referenced Standards" in Chapter 1).

809.5.2.1 Activation. All visible alarm appliances provided within the residential dwelling unit for smoke detection notification shall be activated upon smoke detection.

809.5.3 Interconnection. The same visible alarm appliances shall be permitted to provide notification of residential dwelling unit smoke detection and building fire alarm activation.

809.5.4 Prohibited Use. Visible alarm appliances used to indicate residential dwelling unit smoke detection or building fire alarm activation shall not be used for any other purpose within the residential dwelling unit.

809.5.5 Residential Dwelling Unit Primary Entrance. Communication features shall be provided at the residential dwelling unit primary entrance complying with 809.5.5.

809.5.5.1 Notification. A hard-wired electric doorbell shall be provided. A button or switch shall be provided outside the residential dwelling unit primary entrance. Activation of the button or switch shall initiate an audible tone and visible signal within the residential dwelling unit. Where visible doorbell signals are located in sleeping areas, they shall have controls to deactivate the signal.

809.5.5.2 Identification. A means for visually identifying a visitor without opening the residential dwelling unit entry door shall be provided and shall allow for a minimum 180 degree range of view.

Advisory 809.5.5.2 Identification.

In doors, peepholes that include prisms clarify the image and should offer a wide-angle view of the hallway or exterior for both standing persons and wheelchair users. Such peepholes can be placed at a standard height and permit a view from several feet from the door.

809.5.6 Site, Building, or Floor Entrance. Where a system, including a closed-circuit system, permitting voice communication between a visitor and the occupant of the residential dwelling unit is provided, the system shall comply with 708.4.

810 Transportation Facilities

810.1 General. Transportation facilities shall comply with 810.

810.2 Bus Boarding and Alighting Areas. Bus boarding and alighting areas shall comply with 810.2.

Advisory 810.2 Bus Boarding and Alighting Areas.

At bus stops where a shelter is provided, the bus stop pad can be located either within or outside of the shelter.

810.2.1 Surface. Bus stop boarding and alighting areas shall have a firm, stable surface.

810.2.2 Dimensions. Bus stop boarding and alighting areas shall provide a clear length of 96 inches (2440 mm) minimum, measured perpendicular to the curb or vehicle roadway edge, and a clear width of 60 inches (1525 mm) minimum, measured parallel to the vehicle roadway.

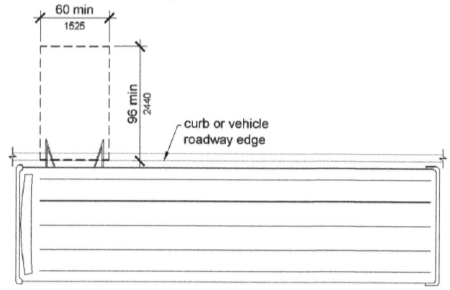

Figure 810.2.2 Dimensions of Bus Boarding and Alighting Areas

810.2.3 Connection. Bus stop boarding and alighting areas shall be connected to streets, sidewalks, or pedestrian paths by an accessible route complying with 402.

810.2.4 Slope. Parallel to the roadway, the slope of the bus stop boarding and alighting area shall be the same as the roadway, to the maximum extent practicable. Perpendicular to the roadway, the slope of the bus stop boarding and alighting area shall not be steeper than1:48.

810.3 Bus Shelters. Bus shelters shall provide a minimum clear floor or ground space complying with 305 entirely within the shelter. Bus shelters shall be connected by an accessible route complying with 402 to a boarding and alighting area complying with 810.2.

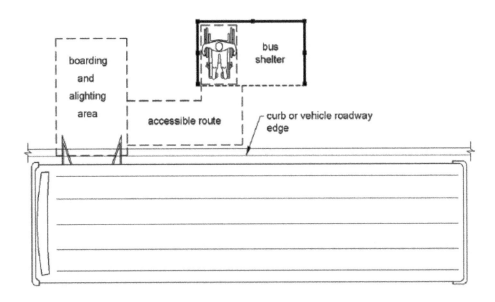

Figure 810.3 Bus Shelters

810.4   Bus Signs. Bus route identification signs shall comply with 703.5.1 through 703.5.4, and 703.5.7 and 703.5.8. In addition, to the maximum extent practicable, bus route identification signs shall comply with 703.5.5.

EXCEPTION: Bus schedules, timetables and maps that are posted at the bus stop or bus bay shall not be required to comply.

810.5   Rail Platforms. Rail platforms shall comply with 810.5.

810.5.1   Slope. Rail platforms shall not exceed a slope of 1:48 in all directions.

EXCEPTION: Where platforms serve vehicles operating on existing track or track laid in existing roadway, the slope of the platform parallel to the track shall be permitted to be equal to the slope (grade) of the roadway or existing track.

810.5.2   Detectable Warnings. Platform boarding edges not protected by platform screens or guards shall have detectable warnings complying with 705 along the full length of the public use area of the platform.

810.5.3   Platform and Vehicle Floor Coordination. Station platforms shall be positioned to coordinate with vehicles in accordance with the applicable requirements of 36 CFR Part 1192. Low-level platforms shall be 8 inches (205 mm) minimum above top of rail.

EXCEPTION: Where vehicles are boarded from sidewalks or street-level, low-level platforms shall be permitted to be less than 8 inches (205 mm).

Advisory 810.5.3 Platform and Vehicle Floor Coordination.

The height and position of a platform must be coordinated with the floor of the vehicles it serves to minimize the vertical and horizontal gaps, in accordance with the ADA Accessibility Guidelines for Transportation Vehicles (36 CFR Part 1192). The vehicle guidelines, divided by bus, van, light rail, rapid rail, commuter rail, intercity rail, are available at **http://www.access-board.gov/**. The preferred alignment is a high platform, level with the vehicle floor. In some cases, the vehicle guidelines permit use of a low platform in conjunction with a lift or ramp. Most such low platforms must have a minimum height of eight inches above the top of the rail. Some vehicles are designed to be boarded from a street or the sidewalk along the street and the exception permits such boarding areas to be less than eight inches high.

810.6 Rail Station Signs. Rail station signs shall comply with 810.6.

EXCEPTION. Signs shall not be required to comply with 810.6.1 and 810.6.2 where audible signs are remotely transmitted to hand-held receivers, or are user- or proximity-actuated.

Advisory 810.6 Rail Station Signs Exception.

Emerging technologies such as an audible sign systems using infrared transmitters and receivers may provide greater accessibility in the transit environment than traditional Braille and raised letter signs. The transmitters are placed on or next to print signs and transmit their information to an infrared receiver that is held by a person. By scanning an area, the person will hear the sign. This means that signs can be placed well out of reach of Braille readers, even on parapet walls and on walls beyond barriers. Additionally, such signs can be used to provide wayfinding information that cannot be efficiently conveyed on Braille signs.

810.6.1 Entrances Where signs identify a station or its entrance, at least one sign at each entrance shall comply with 703.2 and shall be placed in uniform locations to the maximum extent practicable. Where signs identify a station that has no defined entrance, at least one sign shall comply with 703.2 and shall be placed in a central location.

810.6.2 Routes and Destinations. Lists of stations, routes and destinations served by the station which are located on boarding areas, platforms, or mezzanines shall comply with 703.5. At least one tactile sign identifying the specific station and complying with 703.2 shall be provided on each platform or boarding area. Signs covered by this requirement shall, to the maximum extent practicable, be placed in uniform locations within the system.

EXCEPTION: Where sign space is limited, characters shall not be required to exceed 3 inches (75 mm).

Advisory 810.6.2 Routes and Destinations.

Route maps are not required to comply with the informational sign requirements in this document.

810.6.3 Station Names. Stations covered by this section shall have identification signs complying with 703.5. Signs shall be clearly visible and within the sight lines of standing and sitting passengers from within the vehicle on both sides when not obstructed by another vehicle.

Advisory 810.6.3 Station Names.

It is also important to place signs at intervals in the station where passengers in the vehicle will be able to see a sign when the vehicle is either stopped at the station or about to come to a stop in the station. The number of signs necessary may be directly related to the size of the lettering displayed on the sign.

810.7   Public Address Systems. Where public address systems convey audible information to the public, the same or equivalent information shall be provided in a visual format.

810.8   Clocks. Where clocks are provided for use by the public, the clock face shall be uncluttered so that its elements are clearly visible. Hands, numerals and digits shall contrast with the background either light-on-dark or dark-on-light. Where clocks are installed overhead, numerals and digits shall comply with 703.5.

810.9   Escalators. Where provided, escalators shall comply with the sections 6.1.3.5.6 and 6.1.3.6.5 of ASME A17.1 (incorporated by reference, see "Referenced Standards" in Chapter 1) and shall have a clear width of 32 inches (815 mm) minimum.

EXCEPTION: Existing escalators in key stations shall not be required to comply with 810.9.

810.10   Track Crossings. Where a circulation path serving boarding platforms crosses tracks, it shall comply with 402.

EXCEPTION: Openings for wheel flanges shall be permitted to be 2 1/2 inches (64 mm) maximum.

Figure 810.10 (Exception) Track Crossings

811   Storage

811.1   General. Storage shall comply with 811.

811.2   Clear Floor or Ground Space. A clear floor or ground space complying with 305 shall be provided.

811.3   Height. Storage elements shall comply with at least one of the reach ranges specified in 308.

811.4   Operable Parts. Operable parts shall comply with 309.

CHAPTER 9: BUILT-IN ELEMENTS

901 General

901.1 Scope. The provisions of Chapter 9 shall apply where required by Chapter 2 or where referenced by a requirement in this document.

902 Dining Surfaces and Work Surfaces

902.1 General. Dining surfaces and work surfaces shall comply with 902.2 and 902.3.

EXCEPTION: Dining surfaces and work surfaces for children's use shall be permitted to comply with 902.4.

Advisory 902.1 General.

Dining surfaces include, but are not limited to, bars, tables, lunch counters, and booths. Examples of work surfaces include writing surfaces, study carrels, student laboratory stations, baby changing and other tables or fixtures for personal grooming, coupon counters, and where covered by the ABA scoping provisions, employee work stations.

902.2 Clear Floor or Ground Space. A clear floor space complying with 305 positioned for a forward approach shall be provided. Knee and toe clearance complying with 306 shall be provided.

902.3 Height. The tops of dining surfaces and work surfaces shall be 28 inches (710 mm) minimum and 34 inches (865 mm) maximum above the finish floor or ground.

902.4 Dining Surfaces and Work Surfaces for Children's Use. Accessible dining surfaces and work surfaces for children's use shall comply with 902.4.

EXCEPTION: Dining surfaces and work surfaces that are used primarily by children 5 years and younger shall not be required to comply with 902.4 where a clear floor or ground space complying with 305 positioned for a parallel approach is provided.

902.4.1 Clear Floor or Ground Space. A clear floor space complying with 305 positioned for forward approach shall be provided. Knee and toe clearance complying with 306 shall be provided, except that knee clearance 24 inches (610 mm) minimum above the finish floor or ground shall be permitted.

902.4.2 Height The tops of tables and counters shall be 26 inches (660 mm) minimum and 30 inches (760 mm) maximum above the finish floor or ground.

903 Benches

903.1 General. Benches shall comply with 903.

903.2 Clear Floor or Ground Space. Clear floor or ground space complying with 305 shall be provided and shall be positioned at the end of the bench seat and parallel to the short axis of the bench.

903.3 Size. Benches shall have seats that are 42 inches (1065 mm) long minimum and 20 inches (510 mm) deep minimum and 24 inches (610 mm) deep maximum.

903.4   Back Support. The bench shall provide for back support or shall be affixed to a wall. Back support shall be 42 inches (1065 mm) long minimum and shall extend from a point 2 inches (51 mm) maximum above the seat surface to a point 18 inches (455 mm) minimum above the seat surface. Back support shall be 2 1/2 inches (64 mm) maximum from the rear edge of the seat measured horizontally.

Advisory 903.4 Back Support.

To assist in transferring to the bench, consider providing grab bars on a wall adjacent to the bench, but not on the seat back. If provided, grab bars cannot obstruct transfer to the bench.

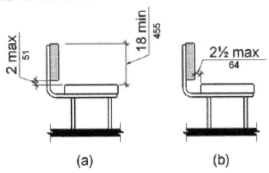

Figure 903.4 Bench Back Support

903.5   Height. The top of the bench seat surface shall be 17 inches (430 mm) minimum and 19 inches (485 mm) maximum above the finish floor or ground.

903.6   Structural Strength. Allowable stresses shall not be exceeded for materials used when a vertical or horizontal force of 250 pounds (1112 N) is applied at any point on the seat, fastener, mounting device, or supporting structure.

903.7   Wet Locations. Where installed in wet locations, the surface of the seat shall be slip resistant and shall not accumulate water.

904   Check-Out Aisles and Sales and Service Counters

904.1   General. Check-out aisles and sales and service counters shall comply with the applicable requirements of 904.

904.2   Approach. All portions of counters required to comply with 904 shall be located adjacent to a walking surface complying with 403.

Advisory 904.2 Approach.

If a cash register is provided at the sales or service counter, locate the accessible counter close to the cash register so that a person using a wheelchair is visible to sales or service personnel and to minimize the reach for a person with a disability.

904.3 Check-Out Aisles. Check-out aisles shall comply with 904.3.

904.3.1 Aisle. Aisles shall comply with 403.

904.3.2 Counter. The counter surface height shall be 38 inches (965 mm) maximum above the finish floor or ground. The top of the counter edge protection shall be 2 inches (51 mm) maximum above the top of the counter surface on the aisle side of the check-out counter.

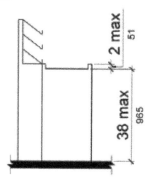

Figure 904.3.2 Check-Out Aisle Counters

904.3.3 Check Writing Surfaces. Where provided, check writing surfaces shall comply with 902.3.

904.4 Sales and Service Counters. Sales counters and service counters shall comply with 904.4.1 or 904.4.2. The accessible portion of the counter top shall extend the same depth as the sales or service counter top.

EXCEPTION: In alterations, when the provision of a counter complying with 904.4 would result in a reduction of the number of existing counters at work stations or a reduction of the number of existing mail boxes, the counter shall be permitted to have a portion which is 24 inches (610 mm) long minimum complying with 904.4.1 provided that the required clear floor or ground space is centered on the accessible length of the counter.

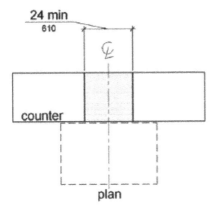

Figure 904.4 (Exception) Alteration of Sales and Service Counters

904.4.1 Parallel Approach. A portion of the counter surface that is 36 inches (915 mm) long minimum and 36 inches (915 mm) high maximum above the finish floor shall be provided. A clear floor or ground space complying with 305 shall be positioned for a parallel approach adjacent to the 36 inch (915 mm) minimum length of counter.

EXCEPTION: Where the provided counter surface is less than 36 inches (915 mm) long, the entire counter surface shall be 36 inches (915 mm) high maximum above the finish floor.

904.4.2 Forward Approach. A portion of the counter surface that is 30 inches (760 mm) long minimum and 36 inches (915 mm) high maximum shall be provided. Knee and toe space complying with 306 shall be provided under the counter. A clear floor or ground space complying with 305 shall be positioned for a forward approach to the counter.

904.5 Food Service Lines. Counters in food service lines shall comply with 904.5.

904.5.1 Self-Service Shelves and Dispensing Devices. Self-service shelves and dispensing devices for tableware, dishware, condiments, food and beverages shall comply with 308.

904.5.2 Tray Slides. The tops of tray slides shall be 28 inches (710 mm) minimum and 34 inches (865 mm) maximum above the finish floor or ground.

904.6 Security Glazing. Where counters or teller windows have security glazing to separate personnel from the public, a method to facilitate voice communication shall be provided. Telephone handset devices, if provided, shall comply with 704.3.

Advisory 904.6 Security Glazing.

Assistive listening devices complying with 706 can facilitate voice communication at counters or teller windows where there is security glazing which promotes distortion in audible information. Where assistive listening devices are installed, place signs complying with 703.7.2.4 to identify those facilities which are so equipped. Other voice communication methods include, but are not limited to, grilles, slats, talk-through baffles, intercoms, or telephone handset devices.

CHAPTER 10: RECREATION FACILITIES

1001 General

1001.1 Scope. The provisions of Chapter 10 shall apply where required by Chapter 2 or where referenced by a requirement in this document.

Advisory 1001.1 Scope.

Unless otherwise modified or specifically addressed in Chapter 10, all other ADAAG provisions apply to the design and construction of recreation facilities and elements. The provisions in Section 1001.1 apply wherever these elements are provided. For example, office buildings may contain a room with exercise equipment to which these sections would apply.

1002 Amusement Rides

1002.1 General. Amusement rides shall comply with 1002.

1002.2 Accessible Routes. Accessible routes serving amusement rides shall comply with Chapter 4.

EXCEPTIONS:

1. In load or unload areas and on amusement rides, where compliance with 405.2 is not structurally or operationally feasible, ramp slope shall be permitted to be 1:8 maximum.

2. In load or unload areas and on amusement rides, handrails provided along walking surfaces complying with 403 and required on ramps complying with 405 shall not be required to comply with 505 where compliance is not structurally or operationally feasible.

Advisory 1002.2 Accessible Routes Exception 1.

Steeper slopes are permitted on accessible routes connecting the amusement ride in the load and unload position where it is "structurally or operationally infeasible." In most cases, this will be limited to areas where the accessible route leads directly to the amusement ride and where there are space limitations on the ride, not the queue line. Where possible, the least possible slope should be used on the accessible route that serves the amusement ride.

1002.3 Load and Unload Areas. A turning space complying with 304.2 and 304.3 shall be provided in load and unload areas.

1002.4 Wheelchair Spaces in Amusement Rides. Wheelchair spaces in amusement rides shall comply with 1002.4.

1002.4.1 Floor or Ground Surface. The floor or ground surface of wheelchair spaces shall be stable and firm.

1002.4.2 Slope. The floor or ground surface of wheelchair spaces shall have a slope not steeper than 1:48 when in the load and unload position.

1002.4.3 Gaps. Floors of amusement rides with wheelchair spaces and floors of load and unload areas shall be coordinated so that, when amusement rides are at rest in the load and unload position, the vertical difference between the floors shall be within plus or minus 5/8 inches (16 mm) and the horizontal gap shall be 3 inches (75 mm) maximum under normal passenger load conditions.

EXCEPTION: Where compliance is not operationally or structurally feasible, ramps, bridge plates, or similar devices complying with the applicable requirements of 36 CFR 1192.83(c) shall be provided.

Advisory 1002.4.3 Gaps Exception.

36 CFR 1192.83(c) ADA Accessibility Guidelines for Transportation Vehicles - Light Rail Vehicles and Systems - Mobility Aid Accessibility is available at **www.access-board.gov**. It includes provisions for bridge plates and ramps that can be used at gaps between wheelchair spaces and floors of load and unload areas.

1002.4.4   Clearances. Clearances for wheelchair spaces shall comply with 1002.4.4.

EXCEPTIONS:

1. Where provided, securement devices shall be permitted to overlap required clearances.

2. Wheelchair spaces shall be permitted to be mechanically or manually repositioned.

3. Wheelchair spaces shall not be required to comply with 307.4.

Advisory 1002.4.4 Clearances Exception 3.

This exception for protruding objects applies to the ride devices, not to circulation areas or accessible routes in the queue lines or the load and unload areas.

1002.4.4.1   Width and Length. Wheelchair spaces shall provide a clear width of 30 inches (760 mm) minimum and a clear length of 48 inches (1220 mm) minimum measured to 9 inches (230 mm) minimum above the floor surface.

1002.4.4.2   Side Entry. Where wheelchair spaces are entered only from the side, amusement rides shall be designed to permit sufficient maneuvering clearance for individuals using a wheelchair or mobility aid to enter and exit the ride.

Advisory 1002.4.4.2 Side Entry.

The amount of clear space needed within the ride, and the size and position of the opening are interrelated. A 32 inch (815 mm) clear opening will not provide sufficient width when entered through a turn into an amusement ride. Additional space for maneuvering and a wider door will be needed where a side opening is centered on the ride. For example, where a 42 inch (1065 mm) opening is provided, a minimum clear space of 60 inches (1525 mm) in length and 36 inches (915mm) in depth is needed to ensure adequate space for maneuvering.

1002.4.4.3 Permitted Protrusions in Wheelchair Spaces. Objects are permitted to protrude a distance of 6 inches (150 mm) maximum along the front of the wheelchair space, where located 9 inches (230 mm) minimum and 27 inches (685 mm) maximum above the floor or ground surface of the wheelchair space. Objects are permitted to protrude a distance of 25 inches (635 mm) maximum along the front of the wheelchair space, where located more than 27 inches (685 mm) above the floor or ground surface of the wheelchair space.

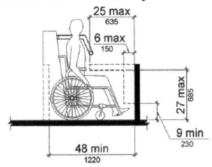

Figure 1002.4.4.3 Protrusions in Wheelchair Spaces in Amusement Rides

1002.4.5   Ride Entry. Openings providing entry to wheelchair spaces on amusement rides shall be 32 inches (815 mm) minimum clear.

1002.4.6   Approach One side of the wheelchair space shall adjoin an accessible route when in the load and unload position.

1002.4.7   Companion Seats. Where the interior width of the amusement ride is greater than 53 inches (1345 mm), seating is provided for more than one rider, and the wheelchair is not required to be centered within the amusement ride, a companion seat shall be provided for each wheelchair space.

1002.4.7.1   Shoulder-to-Shoulder Seating. Where an amusement ride provides shoulder-to-shoulder seating, companion seats shall be shoulder-to-shoulder with the adjacent wheelchair space.

EXCEPTION: Where shoulder-to-shoulder companion seating is not operationally or structurally feasible, compliance with this requirement shall be required to the maximum extent practicable.

1002.5   Amusement Ride Seats Designed for Transfer. Amusement ride seats designed for transfer shall comply with 1002.5 when positioned for loading and unloading.

Advisory 1002.5 Amusement Ride Seats Designed for Transfer.

The proximity of the clear floor or ground space next to an element and the height of the element one is transferring to are both critical for a safe and independent transfer. Providing additional clear floor or ground space both in front of and diagonal to the element will provide flexibility and will increase usability for a more diverse population of individuals with disabilities. Ride seats designed for transfer should involve only one transfer. Where possible, designers are encouraged to locate the ride seat no higher than 17 to 19 inches (430 to 485 mm) above the load and unload surface. Where greater distances are required for transfers, providing gripping surfaces, seat padding, and avoiding sharp objects in the path of transfer will facilitate the transfer.

1002.5.1 Clear Floor or Ground Space. A clear floor or ground space complying with 305 shall be provided in the load and unload area adjacent to the amusement ride seats designed for transfer.

1002.5.2 Transfer Height. The height of amusement ride seats designed for transfer shall be 14 inches (355 mm) minimum and 24 inches (610 mm) maximum measured from the surface of the load and unload area.

1002.5.3 Transfer Entry. Where openings are provided for transfer to amusement ride seats, the openings shall provide clearance for transfer from a wheelchair or mobility aid to the amusement ride seat.

1002.5.4 Wheelchair Storage Space. Wheelchair storage spaces complying with 305 shall be provided in or adjacent to unload areas for each required amusement ride seat designed for transfer and shall not overlap any required means of egress or accessible route.

1002.6 Transfer Devices for Use with Amusement Rides. Transfer devices for use with amusement rides shall comply with 1002.6 when positioned for loading and unloading.

Advisory 1002.6 Transfer Devices for Use with Amusement Rides.

Transfer devices for use with amusement rides should permit individuals to make independent transfers to and from their wheelchairs or mobility devices. There are a variety of transfer devices available that could be adapted to provide access onto an amusement ride. Examples of devices that may provide for transfers include, but are not limited to, transfer systems, lifts, mechanized seats, and custom designed systems. Operators and designers have flexibility in developing designs that will facilitate individuals to transfer onto amusement rides. These systems or devices should be designed to be reliable and sturdy.

Designs that limit the number of transfers required from a wheelchair or mobility device to the ride seat are encouraged. When using a transfer device to access an amusement ride, the least number of transfers and the shortest distance is most usable. Where possible, designers are encouraged to locate the transfer device seat no higher than 17 to 19 inches (430 to 485 mm) above the load and unload surface. Where greater distances are required for transfers, providing gripping surfaces, seat padding, and avoiding sharp objects in the path of transfer will facilitate the transfer. Where a series of transfers are required to reach the amusement ride seat, each vertical transfer should not exceed 8 inches (205 mm).

1002.6.1 Clear Floor or Ground Space. A clear floor or ground space complying with 305 shall be provided in the load and unload area adjacent to the transfer device.

1002.6.2 Transfer Height. The height of transfer device seats shall be 14 inches

(355 mm) minimum and 24 inches (610 mm) maximum measured from the load and unload surface.

1002.6.3 Wheelchair Storage Space. Wheelchair storage spaces complying with 305 shall be provided in or adjacent to unload areas for each required transfer device and shall not overlap any required means of egress or accessible route.

1003   Recreational Boating Facilities

1003.1   General. Recreational boating facilities shall comply with 1003.

1003.2   Accessible Routes. Accessible routes serving recreational boating facilities, including gangways and floating piers, shall comply with Chapter 4 except as modified by the exceptions in 1003.2.

1003.2.1   Boat Slips. Accessible routes serving boat slips shall be permitted to use the exceptions in 1003.2.1.

EXCEPTIONS:

1. Where an existing gangway or series of gangways is replaced or altered, an increase in the length of the gangway shall not be required to comply with 1003.2 unless required by 202.4.

2. Gangways shall not be required to comply with the maximum rise specified in 405.6.

3. Where the total length of a gangway or series of gangways serving as part of a required accessible route is 80 feet (24 m) minimum, gangways shall not be required to comply with 405.2.

4. Where facilities contain fewer than 25 boat slips and the total length of the gangway or series of gangways serving as part of a required accessible route is 30 feet (9145 mm) minimum, gangways shall not be required to comply with 405.2.

5. Where gangways connect to transition plates, landings specified by 405.7 shall not be required.

6. Where gangways and transition plates connect and are required to have handrails, handrail extensions shall not be required. Where handrail extensions are provided on gangways or transition plates, the handrail extensions shall not be required to be parallel with the ground or floor surface.

7. The cross slope specified in 403.3 and 405.3 for gangways, transition plates, and floating piers that are part of accessible routes shall be measured in the static position.

8. Changes in level complying with 303.3 and 303.4 shall be permitted on the surfaces of gangways and boat launch ramps.

Advisory 1003.2.1 Boat Slips Exception 3.

The following example shows how exception 3 would be applied: A gangway is provided to a floating pier which is required to be on an accessible route. The vertical distance is 10 feet (3050 mm) between the elevation where the gangway departs the landside connection and the elevation of the pier surface at the lowest water level. Exception 3 permits the gangway to be 80 feet (24 m) long. Another design solution would be to have two 40 foot (12 m) plus continuous gangways joined together at a float, where the float (as the water level falls) will stop dropping at an elevation five feet below the landside connection. The length of transition plates would not be included in determining if the gangway(s) meet the requirements of the exception.

1003.2.2 Boarding Piers at Boat Launch Ramps. Accessible routes serving boarding piers at boat launch ramps shall be permitted to use the exceptions in 1003.2.2.

EXCEPTIONS:

1. Accessible routes serving floating boarding piers shall be permitted to use Exceptions 1, 2, 5, 6, 7 and 8 in 1003.2.1.

2. Where the total length of the gangway or series of gangways serving as part of a required accessible route is 30 feet (9145 mm) minimum, gangways shall not be required to comply with 405.2.

3. Where the accessible route serving a floating boarding pier or skid pier is located within a boat launch ramp, the portion of the accessible route located within the boat launch ramp shall not be required to comply with 405.

1003.3 Clearances. Clearances at boat slips and on boarding piers at boat launch ramps shall comply with 1003.3.

Advisory 1003.3 Clearances.

Although the minimum width of the clear pier space is 60 inches (1525 mm), it is recommended that piers be wider than 60 inches (1525 mm) to improve the safety for persons with disabilities, particularly on floating piers.

1003.3.1 Boat Slip Clearance. Boat slips shall provide clear pier space 60 inches (1525 mm) wide minimum and at least as long as the boat slips. Each 10 feet (3050 mm) maximum of linear pier edge serving boat slips shall contain at least one continuous clear opening 60 inches (1525 mm) wide minimum.

EXCEPTIONS:

1. Clear pier space shall be permitted to be 36 inches (915 mm) wide minimum for a length of 24 inches (610 mm) maximum, provided that multiple 36 inch (915 mm) wide segments are separated by segments that are 60 inches (1525 mm) wide minimum and 60 inches (1525 mm) long minimum.

2. Edge protection shall be permitted at the continuous clear openings, provided that it is 4 inches (100 mm) high maximum and 2 inches (51 mm) wide maximum.

3. In existing piers, clear pier space shall be permitted to be located perpendicular to the boat slip and shall extend the width of the boat slip, where the facility has at least one boat slip complying with 1003.3, and further compliance with 1003.3 would result in a reduction in the number of boat slips available or result in a reduction of the widths of existing slips.

Advisory 1003.3.1 Boat Slip Clearance Exception 3.

Where the conditions in exception 3 are satisfied, existing facilities are only required to have one accessible boat slip with a pier clearance which runs the length of the slip. All other accessible slips are allowed to have the required pier clearance at the head of the slip. Under this exception, at piers with perpendicular boat slips, the width of most "finger piers" will remain unchanged. However, where mooring systems for floating piers are replaced as part of pier alteration projects, an opportunity may exist for increasing accessibility. Piers may be reconfigured to allow an increase in the number of wider finger piers, and serve as accessible boat slips.

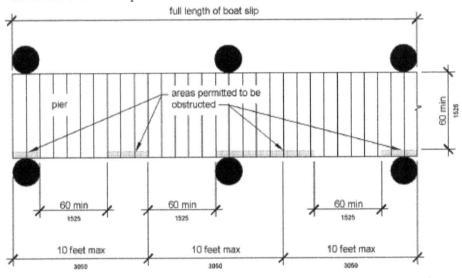

Figure 1003.3.1 Boat Slip Clearance

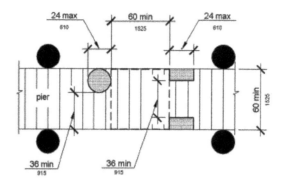

Figure 1003.3.1 (Exception 1) Clear Pier Space Reduction at Boat Slips

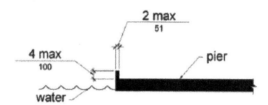

Figure 1003.3.1 (Exception 2) Edge Protection at Boat Slips

1003.3.2   Boarding Pier Clearances. Boarding piers at boat launch ramps shall provide clear pier space 60 inches (1525 mm) wide minimum and shall extend the full length of the boarding pier. Every 10 feet (3050 mm) maximum of linear pier edge shall contain at least one continuous clear opening 60 inches (1525 mm) wide minimum.

EXCEPTIONS:

1. The clear pier space shall be permitted to be 36 inches (915 mm) wide minimum for a length of 24 inches (610 mm) maximum provided that multiple 36 inch (915 mm) wide segments are separated by segments that are 60 inches (1525 mm) wide minimum and 60 inches (1525 mm) long minimum.

2. Edge protection shall be permitted at the continuous clear openings provided that it is 4 inches (100 mm) high maximum and 2 inches (51 mm) wide maximum.

Advisory 1003.3.2 Boarding Pier Clearances.

These requirements do not establish a minimum length for accessible boarding piers at boat launch ramps. The accessible boarding pier should have a length at least equal to that of other boarding piers provided at the facility. If no other boarding pier is provided, the pier would have a length equal to what would have been provided if no access requirements applied. The entire length of accessible boarding piers would be required to comply with the same technical provisions that apply to accessible boat slips. For example, at a launch ramp, if a 20 foot (6100 mm) long accessible boarding pier is provided, the entire 20 feet (6100 mm) must comply with the pier clearance requirements in 1003.3. Likewise, if a 60 foot (18 m) long accessible boarding pier is provided, the pier clearance requirements in 1003.3 would apply to the entire 60 feet (18 m).

The following example applies to a boat launch ramp boarding pier: A chain of floats is provided on a launch ramp to be used as a boarding pier which is required to be accessible by 1003.3.2. At high water, the entire chain is floating and a transition plate connects the first float to the surface of the launch ramp. As the water level decreases, segments of the chain end up resting on the launch ramp surface, matching the slope of the launch ramp.

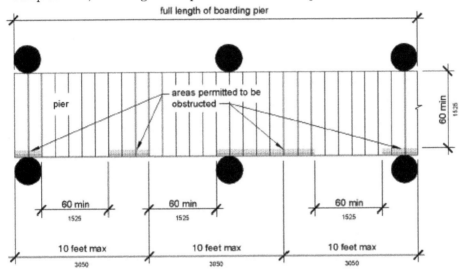

Figure 1003.3.2 Boarding Pier Clearance

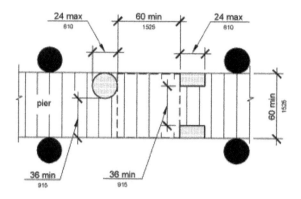

Figure 1003.3.2 (Exception 1) Clear Pier Space Reduction at Boarding Piers

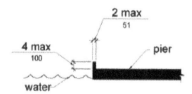

Figure 1003.3.2 (Exception 2) Edge Protection at Boarding Piers

1004   Exercise Machines and Equipment

1004.1   Clear Floor Space. Exercise machines and equipment shall have a clear floor space complying with 305 positioned for transfer or for use by an individual seated in a wheelchair. Clear floor or ground spaces required at exercise machines and equipment shall be permitted to overlap.

Advisory 1004.1 Clear Floor Space.

One clear floor or ground space is permitted to be shared between two pieces of exercise equipment. To optimize space use, designers should carefully consider layout options such as connecting ends of the row and center aisle spaces. The position of the clear floor space may vary greatly depending on the use of the equipment or machine. For example, to provide access to a shoulder press machine, clear floor space next to the seat would be appropriate to allow for transfer. Clear floor space for a bench press machine designed for use by an individual seated in a wheelchair, however, will most likely be centered on the operating mechanisms.

1005   Fishing Piers and Platforms

1005.1   Accessible Routes. Accessible routes serving fishing piers and platforms, including gangways and floating piers, shall comply with Chapter 4.

EXCEPTIONS:

1. Accessible routes serving floating fishing piers and platforms shall be permitted to use Exceptions 1, 2, 5, 6, 7 and 8 in 1003.2.1.

2. Where the total length of the gangway or series of gangways serving as part of a required accessible route is 30 feet (9145 mm) minimum, gangways shall not be required to comply with 405.2.

1005.2 Railings. Where provided, railings, guards, or handrails shall comply with 1005.2.

1005.2.1 Height. At least 25 percent of the railings, guards, or handrails shall be 34 inches (865 mm) maximum above the ground or deck surface.

EXCEPTION: Where a guard complying with sections 1003.2.12.1 and 1003.2.12.2 of the International Building Code (2000 edition) or sections 1012.2 and 1012.3 of the International Building Code (2003 edition) (incorporated by reference, see "Referenced Standards" in Chapter 1) is provided, the guard shall not be required to comply with 1005.2.1.

1005.2.1.1 Dispersion. Railings, guards, or handrails required to comply with 1005.2.1 shall be dispersed throughout the fishing pier or platform.

Advisory 1005.2.1.1 Dispersion.

Portions of the railings that are lowered to provide fishing opportunities for persons with disabilities must be located in a variety of locations on the fishing pier or platform to give people a variety of locations to fish. Different fishing locations may provide varying water depths, shade (at certain times of the day), vegetation, and proximity to the shoreline or bank.

1005.3 Edge Protection. Where railings, guards, or handrails complying with 1005.2 are provided, edge protection complying with 1005.3.1 or 1005.3.2 shall be provided.

Advisory 1005.3 Edge Protection.

Edge protection is required only where railings, guards, or handrails are provided on a fishing pier or platform. Edge protection will prevent wheelchairs or other mobility devices from slipping off the fishing pier or platform. Extending the deck of the fishing pier or platform 12 inches (305 mm) where the 34 inch (865 mm) high railing is provided is an alternative design, permitting individuals using wheelchairs or other mobility devices to pull into a clear space and move beyond the face of the railing. In such a design, curbs or barriers are not required.

1005.3.1 Curb or Barrier. Curbs or barriers shall extend 2 inches (51 mm) minimum above the surface of the fishing pier or platform.

1005.3.2 Extended Ground or Deck Surface. The ground or deck surface shall extend 12 inches (305 mm) minimum beyond the inside face of the railing. Toe clearance shall be provided and shall be 30 inches (760 mm) wide minimum and 9 inches (230 mm) minimum above the ground or deck surface beyond the railing.

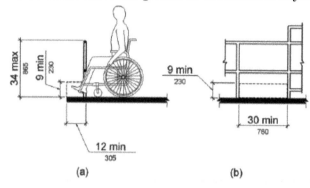

(a)   (b)

Figure 1005.3.2 Extended Ground or Deck Surface at Fishing Piers and Platforms

1005.4   Clear Floor or Ground Space. At each location where there are railings, guards, or handrails complying with 1005.2.1, a clear floor or ground space complying with 305 shall be provided. Where there are no railings, guards, or handrails, at least one clear floor or ground space complying with 305 shall be provided on the fishing pier or platform.

1005.5   Turning Space. At least one turning space complying with 304.3 shall be provided on fishing piers and platforms.

1006   Golf Facilities

1006.1   General. Golf facilities shall comply with 1006.

1006.2   Accessible Routes. Accessible routes serving teeing grounds, practice teeing grounds, putting greens, practice putting greens, teeing stations at driving ranges, course weather shelters, golf car rental areas, bag drop areas, and course toilet rooms shall comply with Chapter 4 and shall be 48 inches (1220 mm) wide minimum. Where handrails are provided, accessible routes shall be 60 inches (1525 mm) wide minimum.

EXCEPTION: Handrails shall not be required on golf courses. Where handrails are provided on golf courses, the handrails shall not be required to comply with 505.

Advisory 1006.2 Accessible Routes.

The 48 inch (1220 mm) minimum width for the accessible route is necessary to ensure passage of a golf car on either the accessible route or the golf car passage. This is important where the accessible route is used to connect the golf car rental area, bag drop areas, practice putting greens, practice teeing grounds, course toilet rooms, and course weather shelters. These are areas outside the boundary of the golf course, but are areas where an individual using an adapted golf car may travel. A golf car passage may not be substituted for other accessible routes to be located outside the boundary of the course. For example, an accessible route connecting an accessible parking space to the entrance of a golf course clubhouse is not covered by this provision.

Providing a golf car passage will permit a person that uses a golf car to practice driving a golf ball from the same position and stance used when playing the game. Additionally, the space required for a person using a golf car to enter and maneuver within the teeing stations required to be accessible should be considered.

1006.3   Golf Car Passages. Golf car passages shall comply with 1006.3.

1006.3.1   Clear Width. The clear width of golf car passages shall be 48 inches (1220 mm) minimum.

1006.3.2   Barriers. Where curbs or other constructed barriers prevent golf cars from entering a fairway, openings 60 inches (1525 mm) wide minimum shall be provided at intervals not to exceed 75 yards (69 m).

1006.4   Weather Shelters. A clear floor or ground space 60 inches (1525 mm) minimum by 96 inches (2440 mm) minimum shall be provided within weather shelters.

1007   Miniature Golf Facilities

1007.1   General. Miniature golf facilities shall comply with 1007.

1007.2   Accessible Routes. Accessible routes serving holes on miniature golf courses shall comply with Chapter 4. Accessible routes located on playing surfaces of miniature golf holes shall be permitted to use the exceptions in 1007.2.

EXCEPTIONS:

1. Playing surfaces shall not be required to comply with 302.2.

2. Where accessible routes intersect playing surfaces of holes, a 1 inch (25 mm) maximum curb shall be permitted for a width of 32 inches (815 mm) minimum.

3. A slope not steeper than 1:4 for a 4 inch (100 mm) maximum rise shall be permitted.

4. Ramp landing slopes specified by 405.7.1 shall be permitted to be 1:20 maximum.

5. Ramp landing length specified by 405.7.3 shall be permitted to be 48 inches (1220 mm) long minimum.

6. Ramp landing size specified by 405.7.4 shall be permitted to be 48 inches (1220 mm) minimum by 60 inches (1525 mm) minimum.

7. Handrails shall not be required on holes. Where handrails are provided on holes, the handrails shall not be required to comply with 505.

1007.3   Miniature Golf Holes. Miniature golf holes shall comply with 1007.3.

1007.3.1   Start of Play. A clear floor or ground space 48 inches (1220 mm) minimum by 60 inches (1525 mm) minimum with slopes not steeper than 1:48 shall be provided at the start of play.

1007.3.2 Golf Club Reach Range Area. All areas within holes where golf balls rest shall be within 36 inches (915 mm) maximum of a clear floor or ground space 36 inches (915 mm) wide minimum and 48 inches (1220 mm) long minimum having a running slope not steeper than 1:20. The clear floor or ground space shall be served by an accessible route.

Advisory 1007.3.2 Golf Club Reach Range Area.

The golf club reach range applies to all holes required to be accessible. This includes accessible routes provided adjacent to or, where provided, on the playing surface of the hole.

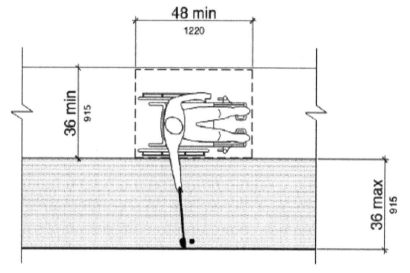

Note: Running Slope of Clear Floor or Ground Space Not Steeper Than 1:20

Figure 1007.3.2 Golf Club Reach Range Area

1008   Play Areas

1008.1   General. Play areas shall comply with 1008.

1008.2   Accessible Routes. Accessible routes serving play areas shall comply with Chapter 4 and 1008.2 and shall be permitted to use the exceptions in 1008.2.1 through 1008.2.3. Where accessible routes serve ground level play components, the vertical clearance shall be 80 inches high (2030 mm) minimum.

1008.2.1   Ground Level and Elevated Play Components. Accessible routes serving ground level play components and elevated play components shall be permitted to use the exceptions in 1008.2.1.

EXCEPTIONS:

1. Transfer systems complying with 1008.3 shall be permitted to connect elevated play components except where 20 or more elevated play components are provided no more than 25 percent of the elevated play components shall be permitted to be connected by transfer systems.

2. Where transfer systems are provided, an elevated play component shall be permitted to connect to another elevated play component as part of an accessible route.

1008.2.2 Soft Contained Play Structures. Accessible routes serving soft contained play structures shall be permitted to use the exception in 1008.2.2.

EXCEPTION: Transfer systems complying with 1008.3 shall be permitted to be used as part of an accessible route.

1008.2.3 Water Play Components. Accessible routes serving water play components shall be permitted to use the exceptions in 1008.2.3.

EXCEPTIONS:

1. Where the surface of the accessible route, clear floor or ground spaces, or turning spaces serving water play components is submerged, compliance with 302, 403.3, 405.2, 405.3, and 1008.2.6 shall not be required.

2. Transfer systems complying with 1008.3 shall be permitted to connect elevated play components in water.

Advisory 1008.2.3 Water Play Components.

Personal wheelchairs and mobility devices may not be appropriate for submerging in water when using play components in water. Some may have batteries, motors, and electrical systems that when submerged in water may cause damage to the personal mobility device or wheelchair or may contaminate the water. Providing an aquatic wheelchair made of non-corrosive materials and designed for access into the water will protect the water from contamination and avoid damage to personal wheelchairs.

1008.2.4 Clear Width. Accessible routes connecting play components shall provide a clear width complying with 1008.2.4.

1008.2.4.1 Ground Level. At ground level, the clear width of accessible routes shall be 60 inches (1525 mm) minimum.

EXCEPTIONS:

1. In play areas less than 1000 square feet (93 m2), the clear width of accessible routes shall be permitted to be 44 inches (1120 mm) minimum, if at least one turning space complying with 304.3 is provided where the restricted accessible route exceeds 30 feet (9145 mm) in length.

2. The clear width of accessible routes shall be permitted to be 36 inches (915 mm) minimum for a distance of 60 inches (1525 mm) maximum provided that multiple reduced width segments are separated by segments that are 60 inches (1525 mm) wide minimum and 60 inches (1525 mm) long minimum.

1008.2.4.2 Elevated. The clear width of accessible routes connecting elevated play components shall be 36 inches (915 mm) minimum.

EXCEPTIONS:

1. The clear width of accessible routes connecting elevated play components shall be permitted to be reduced to 32 inches (815 mm) minimum for a distance of 24 inches (610 mm) maximum provided that reduced width segments are separated by segments that are 48 inches (1220 mm) long minimum and 36 inches (915 mm) wide minimum.

2. The clear width of transfer systems connecting elevated play components shall be permitted to be 24 inches (610 mm) minimum.

1008.2.5 Ramps. Within play areas, ramps connecting ground level play components and ramps connecting elevated play components shall comply with 1008.2.5.

1008.2.5.1 Ground Level. Ramp runs connecting ground level play components shall have a running slope not steeper than 1:16.

1008.2.5.2 Elevated. The rise for any ramp run connecting elevated play components shall be 12 inches (305 mm) maximum.

1008.2.5.3 Handrails. Where required on ramps serving play components, the handrails shall comply with 505 except as modified by 1008.2.5.3.

EXCEPTIONS:

1. Handrails shall not be required on ramps located within ground level use zones.

2. Handrail extensions shall not be required.

1008.2.5.3.1 Handrail Gripping Surfaces. Handrail gripping surfaces with a circular cross section shall have an outside diameter of 0.95 inch (24 mm) minimum and 1.55 inches (39 mm) maximum. Where the shape of the gripping surface is non-circular, the handrail shall provide an equivalent gripping surface.

1008.2.5.3.2 Handrail Height. The top of handrail gripping surfaces shall be 20 inches (510 mm) minimum and 28 inches (710 mm) maximum above the ramp surface.

1008.2.6 Ground Surfaces. Ground surfaces on accessible routes, clear floor or ground spaces, and turning spaces shall comply with 1008.2.6.

Advisory 1008.2.6 Ground Surfaces.

Ground surfaces must be inspected and maintained regularly to ensure continued compliance with the ASTM F 1951 standard. The type of surface material selected and play area use levels will determine the frequency of inspection and maintenance activities.

1008.2.6.1 Accessibility. Ground surfaces shall comply with ASTM F 1951 (incorporated by reference, see "Referenced Standards" in Chapter 1). Ground surfaces shall be inspected and maintained regularly and frequently to ensure continued compliance with ASTM F 1951.

1008.2.6.2 Use Zones. Ground surfaces located within use zones shall comply with ASTM F 1292 (1999 edition or 2004 edition) (incorporated by reference, see "Referenced Standards" in Chapter 1).

1008.3 Transfer Systems. Where transfer systems are provided to connect to elevated play components, transfer systems shall comply with 1008.3.

Advisory 1008.3 Transfer Systems.

Where transfer systems are provided, consideration should be given to the distance between the transfer system and the elevated play components. Moving between a transfer platform and a series of transfer steps requires extensive exertion for some children. Designers should minimize the distance between the points where a child transfers from a wheelchair or mobility device and where the elevated play components are located. Where elevated play components are used to connect to another elevated play component instead of an accessible route, careful consideration should be used in the selection of the play components used for this purpose.

1008.3.1 Transfer Platforms. Transfer platforms shall be provided where transfer is intended from wheelchairs or other mobility aids. Transfer platforms shall comply with 1008.3.1.

1008.3.1.1 Size. Transfer platforms shall have level surfaces 14 inches (355 mm) deep minimum and 24 inches (610 mm) wide minimum.

1008.3.1.2 Height. The height of transfer platforms shall be 11 inches (280 mm) minimum and 18 inches (455 mm) maximum measured to the top of the surface from the ground or floor surface.

1008.3.1.3 Transfer Space. A transfer space complying with 305.2 and 305.3 shall be provided adjacent to the transfer platform. The 48 inch (1220 mm) long minimum dimension of the transfer space shall be centered on and parallel to the 24 inch (610 mm) long minimum side of the transfer platform. The side of the transfer platform serving the transfer space shall be unobstructed.

1008.3.1.4 Transfer Supports. At least one means of support for transferring shall be provided.

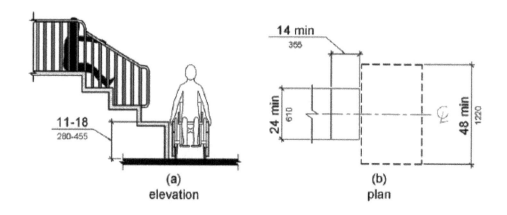

Figure 1008.3.1 Transfer Platforms

1008.3.2 Transfer Steps. Transfer steps shall be provided where movement is intended from transfer platforms to levels with elevated play components required to be on accessible routes. Transfer steps shall comply with 1008.3.2.

1008.3.2.1 Size. Transfer steps shall have level surfaces 14 inches (355 mm) deep minimum and 24 inches (610 mm) wide minimum.

1008.3.2.2 Height. Each transfer step shall be 8 inches (205 mm) high maximum.

1008.3.2.3 Transfer Supports. At least one means of support for transferring shall be provided.

Advisory 1008.3.2.3 Transfer Supports.

Transfer supports are required on transfer platforms and transfer steps to assist children when transferring. Some examples of supports include a rope loop, a loop type handle, a slot in the edge of a flat horizontal or vertical member, poles or bars, or D rings on the corner posts.

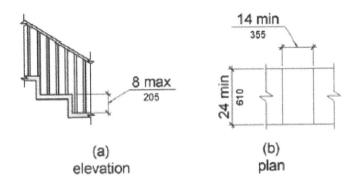

(a)
elevation

(b)
plan

Figure 1008.3.2 Transfer Steps

1008.4   Play Components. Ground level play components on accessible routes and elevated play components connected by ramps shall comply with 1008.4.

1008.4.1   Turning Space. At least one turning space complying with 304 shall be provided on the same level as play components. Where swings are provided, the turning space shall be located immediately adjacent to the swing.

1008.4.2   Clear Floor or Ground Space. Clear floor or ground space complying with 305.2 and 305.3 shall be provided at play components.

Advisory 1008.4.2 Clear Floor or Ground Space.

Clear floor or ground spaces, turning spaces, and accessible routes are permitted to overlap within play areas. A specific location has not been designated for the clear floor or ground spaces or turning spaces, except swings, because each play component may require that the spaces be placed in a unique location. Where play components include a seat or entry point, designs that provide for an unobstructed transfer from a wheelchair or other mobility device are recommended. This will enhance the ability of children with disabilities to independently use the play component.

When designing play components with manipulative or interactive features, consider appropriate reach ranges for children seated in wheelchairs. The following table provides guidance on reach ranges for children seated in wheelchairs. These dimensions apply to either forward or side reaches. The reach ranges are appropriate for use with those play components that children seated in wheelchairs may access and reach. Where transfer systems provide access to elevated play components, the reach ranges are not appropriate.

Children's Reach Ranges			
Forward or Side Reach	Ages 3 and 4	Ages 5 through 8	Ages 9 through 12
High (maximum)	36 in (915 mm)	40 in (1015 mm)	44 in (1120 mm)

Children's Reach Ranges			
Forward or Side Reach	Ages 3 and 4	Ages 5 through 8	Ages 9 through 12
Low (minimum)	20 in (510 mm)	18 in (455 mm)	16 in (405 mm)

1008.4.3 Play Tables. Where play tables are provided, knee clearance 24 inches (610 mm) high minimum, 17 inches deep (430 mm) minimum, and 30 inches (760 mm) wide minimum shall be provided. The tops of rims, curbs, or other obstructions shall be 31 inches (785 mm) high maximum.

EXCEPTION: Play tables designed and constructed primarily for children 5 years and younger shall not be required to provide knee clearance where the clear floor or ground space required by 1008.4.2 is arranged for a parallel approach.

1008.4.4 Entry Points and Seats. Where play components require transfer to entry points or seats, the entry points or seats shall be 11 inches (280 mm) minimum and 24 inches (610 mm) maximum from the clear floor or ground space.

EXCEPTION: Entry points of slides shall not be required to comply with 1008.4.4.

1008.4.5 Transfer Supports. Where play components require transfer to entry points or seats, at least one means of support for transferring shall be provided.

1009   Swimming Pools, Wading Pools, and Spas

1009.1 General. Where provided, pool lifts, sloped entries, transfer walls, transfer systems, and pool stairs shall comply with 1009.

1009.2 Pool Lifts. Pool lifts shall comply with 1009.2.

Advisory 1009.2 Pool Lifts.

There are a variety of seats available on pool lifts ranging from sling seats to those that are preformed or molded. Pool lift seats with backs will enable a larger population of persons with disabilities to use the lift. Pool lift seats that consist of materials that resist corrosion and provide a firm base to transfer will be usable by a wider range of people with disabilities. Additional options such as armrests, head rests, seat belts, and leg support will enhance accessibility and better accommodate people with a wide range of disabilities.

1009.2.1 Pool Lift Location. Pool lifts shall be located where the water level does not exceed 48 inches (1220 mm).

EXCEPTIONS:

1. Where the entire pool depth is greater than 48 inches (1220 mm), compliance with 1009.2.1 shall not be required.

2. Where multiple pool lift locations are provided, no more than one pool lift shall be required to be located in an area where the water level is 48 inches (1220 mm) maximum.

1009.2.2 Seat Location. In the raised position, the centerline of the seat shall be located over the deck and 16 inches (405 mm) minimum from the edge of the pool.

The deck surface between the centerline of the seat and the pool edge shall have a slope not steeper than 1:48.

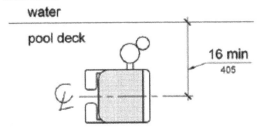

Figure 1009.2.2 Pool Lift Seat Location

1009.2.3 Clear Deck Space. On the side of the seat opposite the water, a clear deck space shall be provided parallel with the seat. The space shall be 36 inches (915 mm) wide minimum and shall extend forward 48 inches (1220 mm) minimum from a line located 12 inches (305 mm) behind the rear edge of the seat. The clear deck space shall have a slope not steeper than 1:48.

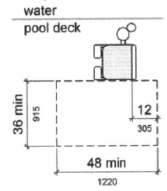

Figure 1009.2.3 Clear Deck Space at Pool Lifts

1009.2.4 Seat Height. The height of the lift seat shall be designed to allow a stop at 16 inches (405 mm) minimum to 19 inches (485 mm) maximum measured from the deck to the top of the seat surface when in the raised (load) position.

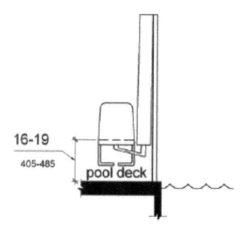

Figure 1009.2.4 Pool Lift Seat Height

1009.2.5   Seat Width. The seat shall be 16 inches (405 mm) wide minimum.

1009.2.6   Footrests and Armrests. Footrests shall be provided and shall move with the seat. If provided, the armrest positioned opposite the water shall be removable or shall fold clear of the seat when the seat is in the raised (load) position.

EXCEPTION: Footrests shall not be required on pool lifts provided in spas.

1009.2.7   Operation. The lift shall be capable of unassisted operation from both the deck and water levels. Controls and operating mechanisms shall be unobstructed when the lift is in use and shall comply with 309.4.

Advisory 1009.2.7 Operation.

Pool lifts must be capable of unassisted operation from both the deck and water levels. This will permit a person to call the pool lift when the pool lift is in the opposite position. It is extremely important for a person who is swimming alone to be able to call the pool lift when it is in the up position so he or she will not be stranded in the water for extended periods of time awaiting assistance. The requirement for a pool lift to be independently operable does not preclude assistance from being provided.

1009.2.8   Submerged Depth. The lift shall be designed so that the seat will submerge to a water depth of 18 inches (455 mm) minimum below the stationary water level.

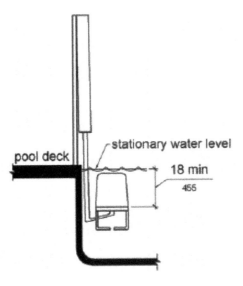

Figure 1009.2.8 Pool Lift Submerged Depth

1009.2.9   Lifting Capacity. Single person pool lifts shall have a weight capacity of 300 pounds. (136 kg) minimum and be capable of sustaining a static load of at least one and a half times the rated load.

Advisory 1009.2.9 Lifting Capacity.

Single person pool lifts must be capable of supporting a minimum weight of 300 pounds (136 kg) and sustaining a static load of at least one and a half times the rated load. Pool lifts should be provided that meet the needs of the population they serve. Providing a pool lift with a weight capacity greater than 300 pounds (136 kg) may be advisable.

1009.3   Sloped Entries. Sloped entries shall comply with 1009.3.

Advisory 1009.3 Sloped Entries.

Personal wheelchairs and mobility devices may not be appropriate for submerging in water. Some may have batteries, motors, and electrical systems that when submerged in water may cause damage to the personal mobility device or wheelchair or may contaminate the pool water. Providing an aquatic wheelchair made of non-corrosive materials and designed for access into the water will protect the water from contamination and avoid damage to personal wheelchairs or other mobility aids.

1009.3.1   Sloped Entries. Sloped entries shall comply with Chapter 4 except as modified in 1109.3.1 through 1109.3.3.

EXCEPTION: Where sloped entries are provided, the surfaces shall not be required to be slip resistant.

1009.3.2 Submerged Depth. Sloped entries shall extend to a depth of 24 inches (610 mm) minimum and 30 inches (760 mm) maximum below the stationary water level. Where landings are required by 405.7, at least one landing shall be located 24 inches (610 mm) minimum and 30 inches (760 mm) maximum below the stationary water level.

EXCEPTION: In wading pools, the sloped entry and landings, if provided, shall extend to the deepest part of the wading pool.

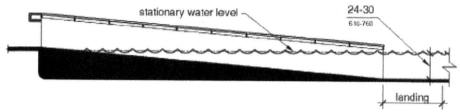

Figure 1009.3.2 Sloped Entry Submerged Depth

1009.3.3 Handrails. At least two handrails complying with 505 shall be provided on the sloped entry. The clear width between required handrails shall be 33 inches (840 mm) minimum and 38 inches (965 mm) maximum.

EXCEPTIONS:

1. Handrail extensions specified by 505.10.1 shall not be required at the bottom landing serving a sloped entry.

2. Where a sloped entry is provided for wave action pools, leisure rivers, sand bottom pools, and other pools where user access is limited to one area, the handrails shall not be required to comply with the clear width requirements of 1009.3.3.

3. Sloped entries in wading pools shall not be required to provide handrails complying with 1009.3.3. If provided, handrails on sloped entries in wading pools shall not be required to comply with 505.

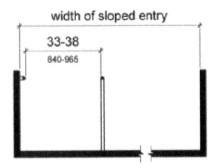

Figure 1009.3.3 Handrails for Sloped Entry

1009.4   Transfer Walls. Transfer walls shall comply with 1009.4.

1009.4.1   Clear Deck Space. A clear deck space of 60 inches (1525 mm) minimum by 60 inches (1525 mm) minimum with a slope not steeper than 1:48 shall be provided at the base of the transfer wall. Where one grab bar is provided, the clear deck space shall be centered on the grab bar. Where two grab bars are provided, the clear deck space shall be centered on the clearance between the grab bars.

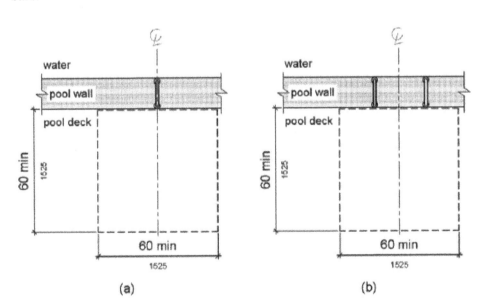

Figure 1009.4.1 Clear Deck Space at Transfer Walls

1009.4.2   Height. The height of the transfer wall shall be 16 inches (405 mm) minimum and 19 inches (485 mm) maximum measured from the deck.

Figure 1009.4.2 Transfer Wall Height

1009.4.3 Wall Depth and Length. The depth of the transfer wall shall be 12 inches (305 mm) minimum and 16 inches (405 mm) maximum. The length of the transfer wall shall be 60 inches (1525 mm) minimum and shall be centered on the clear deck space.

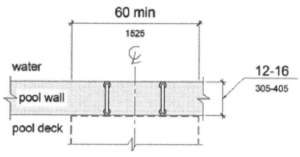

Figure 1009.4.3 Depth and Length of Transfer Walls

1009.4.4 Surface. Surfaces of transfer walls shall not be sharp and shall have rounded edges.

1009.4.5 Grab Bars. At least one grab bar complying with 609 shall be provided on the transfer wall. Grab bars shall be perpendicular to the pool wall and shall extend the full depth of the transfer wall. The top of the gripping surface shall be 4 inches (100 mm) minimum and 6 inches (150 mm) maximum above transfer walls. Where one grab bar is provided, clearance shall be 24 inches (610 mm) minimum on both sides of the grab bar. Where two grab bars are provided, clearance between grab bars shall be 24 inches (610 mm) minimum.

EXCEPTION: Grab bars on transfer walls shall not be required to comply with 609.4.

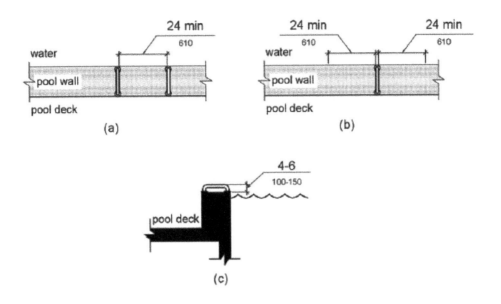

Figure 1009.4.5 Grab Bars for Transfer Walls

1009.5   Transfer Systems. Transfer systems shall comply with 1009.5.

1009.5.1   Transfer Platform. A transfer platform shall be provided at the head of each transfer system. Transfer platforms shall provide 19 inches (485 mm) minimum clear depth and 24 inches (610 mm) minimum clear width.

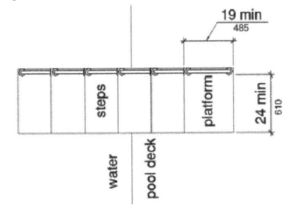

Figure 1009.5.1 Size of Transfer Platform

1009.5.2   Transfer Space. A transfer space of 60 inches (1525 mm) minimum by 60 inches (1525 mm) minimum with a slope not steeper than 1:48 shall be provided at the base of the transfer platform surface and shall be centered along a 24 inch (610 mm) minimum side of the transfer platform. The side of the transfer platform serving the transfer space shall be unobstructed.

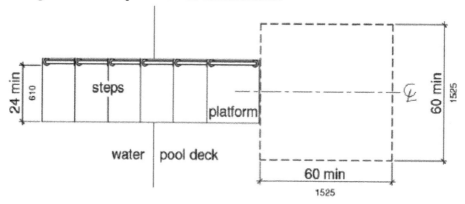

Figure 1009.5.2 Clear Deck Space at Transfer Platform

1009.5.3 Height. The height of the transfer platform shall comply with 1009.4.2.

1009.5.4 Transfer Steps. Transfer step height shall be 8 inches (205 mm) maximum. The surface of the bottom tread shall extend to a water depth of 18 inches (455 mm) minimum below the stationary water level.

Advisory 1009.5.4 Transfer Steps.

Where possible, the height of the transfer step should be minimized to decrease the distance an individual is required to lift up or move down to reach the next step to gain access.

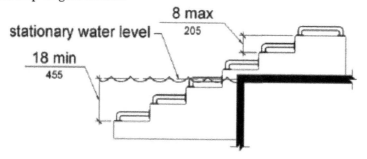

Figure 1009.5.4 Transfer Steps

1009.5.5 Surface. The surface of the transfer system shall not be sharp and shall have rounded edges.

1009.5.6 Size. Each transfer step shall have a tread clear depth of 14 inches (355 mm) minimum and 17 inches (430 mm) maximum and shall have a tread clear width of 24 inches (610 mm) minimum.

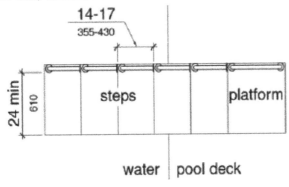

Figure 1009.5.6 Size of Transfer Steps

1009.5.7 Grab Bars. At least one grab bar on each transfer step and the transfer platform or a continuous grab bar serving each transfer step and the transfer platform shall be provided. Where a grab bar is provided on each step, the tops of gripping surfaces shall be 4 inches (100 mm) minimum and 6 inches (150 mm) maximum above each step and transfer platform. Where a continuous grab bar is provided, the top of the gripping surface shall be 4 inches (100 mm) minimum and 6 inches (150 mm) maximum above the step nosing and transfer platform. Grab bars shall comply with 609 and be located on at least one side of the transfer system. The grab bar located at the transfer platform shall not obstruct transfer.

EXCEPTION: Grab bars on transfer systems shall not be required to comply with 609.4.

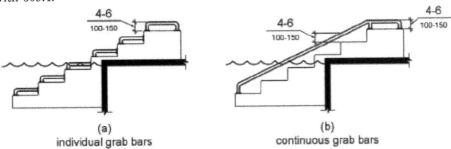

(a)
individual grab bars

(b)
continuous grab bars

Figure 1009.5.7 Grab Bars

1009.6 Pool Stairs. Pool stairs shall comply with 1009.6.

1009.6.1 Pool Stairs. Pool stairs shall comply with 504.

EXCEPTION: Pool step riser heights shall not be required to be 4 inches (100 mm) high minimum and 7 inches (180 mm) high maximum provided that riser heights are uniform.

1009.6.2   Handrails The width between handrails shall be 20 inches (510 mm) minimum and 24 inches (610 mm) maximum. Handrail extensions required by 505.10.3 shall not be required on pool stairs.

1010   Shooting Facilities with Firing Positions

1010.1   Turning Space. A circular turning space 60 inches (1525 mm) diameter minimum with slopes not steeper than 1:48 shall be provided at shooting facilities with firing positions.

Chapter 9
SECTIONS 501, 503, AND 504 OF THE REHABILITATION ACT OF 1973

SECTION 504 OF THE REHABILITATION ACT OF 1973
GENERAL PROVISIONS

§ 705. Definitions

For the purposes of this chapter [29 USCS §§ 701 et seq.]:

(1) Administrative costs

The term "administrative costs" means expenditures incurred in the performance of administrative functions under the vocational rehabilitation program carried out under subchapter I of this chapter [29 USCS § 720 et seq.], including expenses related to program planning, development, monitoring, and evaluation, including expenses for —

(A) quality assurance;

(B) budgeting, accounting, financial management, information systems, and related data processing;

(C) providing information about the program to the public;

(D) technical assistance and support services to other State agencies, private nonprofit organizations, and businesses and industries, except for technical assistance and support services described in section 723(b)(5) of this title;

(E) the State Rehabilitation Council and other advisory committees;

(F) professional organization membership dues for designated State unit employees;

(G) the removal of architectural barriers in State vocational rehabilitation agency offices and State operated rehabilitation facilities;

(H) operating and maintaining designated State unit facilities, equipment, and grounds;

(I) supplies;

(J) administration of the comprehensive system of personnel development described in section 721(a)(7) of this title, including personnel administration, administration of affirmative action plans, and training and staff development;

(K) administrative salaries, including clerical and other support staff salaries, in support of these administrative functions;

(L) travel costs related to carrying out the program, other than travel costs related to the provision of services;

(M) costs incurred in conducting reviews of rehabilitation counselor or coordinator determinations under section 722(c) of this title; and

(N) legal expenses required in the administration of the program.

(2) Assessment for determining eligibility and vocational rehabilitation needs

The term "assessment for determining eligibility and vocational rehabilitation needs" means, as appropriate in each case —

(A) (i) a review of existing data —

(I) to determine whether an individual is eligible for vocational rehabilitation services; and

(II) to assign priority for an order of selection described in section 721(a)(5)(A) of this title in the States that use an order of selection pursuant to section 721(a)(5)(A) of this title; and

(ii) to the extent necessary, the provision of appropriate assessment activities to obtain necessary additional data to make such determination and assignment;

(B) to the extent additional data is necessary to make a determination of the employment outcomes, and the nature and scope of vocational rehabilitation services, to be included in the individualized plan for employment of an eligible individual, a comprehensive assessment to determine the unique strengths, resources, priorities, concerns, abilities, capabilities, interests, and informed choice, including the need for supported employment, of the eligible individual, which comprehensive assessment —

(i) is limited to information that is necessary to identify the rehabilitation needs of the individual and to develop the individualized plan for employment of the eligible individual;

(ii) uses, as a primary source of such information, to the maximum extent possible and appropriate and in accordance with confidentiality requirements —

(I) existing information obtained for the purposes of determining the eligibility of the individual and assigning priority for an order of selection described in section 721(a)(5)(A) of this title for the individual; and

(II) such information as can be provided by the individual and, where appropriate, by the family of the individual;

(iii) may include, to the degree needed to make such a determination, an assessment of the personality, interests, interpersonal skills, intelligence and related functional capacities, educational achievements, work experience, vocational aptitudes, personal and social adjustments, and employment opportunities of the individual, and the medical, psychiatric, psychological, and other pertinent vocational, educational, cultural, social, recreational, and environmental factors, that affect the employment and rehabilitation needs of the individual; and

(iv) may include, to the degree needed, an appraisal of the patterns of work behavior of the individual and services needed for the individual to acquire occupational skills, and to develop work attitudes, work habits, work tolerance, and social and behavior patterns necessary for successful job performance, including the utilization of work in real job situations to assess and develop the capacities of the individual to perform adequately in a work environment;

(C) referral, for the provision of rehabilitation technology services to the individual, to assess and develop the capacities of the individual to perform in a work environment; and

(D) an exploration of the individual's abilities, capabilities, and capacity to perform in work situations, which shall be assessed periodically during trial work experiences, including experiences in which the individual is provided appropriate supports and training.

(3)　Assistive technology device

The term "assistive technology device" has the meaning given such term in section 3002 of this title, except that the reference in such section to the term "individuals with disabilities" shall be deemed to mean more than one individual with a disability as defined in paragraph (20)(A).

(4)　Assistive technology service

The term "assistive technology service" has the meaning given such term in section 3002 of this title, except that the reference in such section —

(A) to the term "individual with a disability" shall be deemed to mean an individual with a disability, as defined in paragraph (20)(A); and

(B) to the term "individuals with disabilities" shall be deemed to mean more than one such individual.

(5)　Community rehabilitation program

The term "community rehabilitation program" means a program that provides directly or facilitates the provision of vocational rehabilitation services to individuals with disabilities, and that provides, singly or in combination, for an individual with a disability to enable the individual to maximize opportunities for employment, including career advancement —

(A) medical, psychiatric, psychological, social, and vocational services that are provided under one management;

(B) testing, fitting, or training in the use of prosthetic and orthotic devices;

(C) recreational therapy;

(D) physical and occupational therapy;

(E) speech, language, and hearing therapy;

(F) psychiatric, psychological, and social services, including positive behavior management;

(G) assessment for determining eligibility and vocational rehabilitation needs;

(H) rehabilitation technology;

(I) job development, placement, and retention services;

(J) evaluation or control of specific disabilities;

(K) orientation and mobility services for individuals who are blind;

(L) extended employment;

(M) psychosocial rehabilitation services;

(N) supported employment services and extended services;

(O) services to family members when necessary to the vocational rehabilitation of the individual;

(P) personal assistance services; or

(Q) services similar to the services described in one of subparagraphs (A) through (P).

(6)   Construction; cost of construction —

(A)   Construction

The term "construction" means —

(i) the construction of new buildings;

(ii) the acquisition, expansion, remodeling, alteration, and renovation of existing buildings; and

(iii) initial equipment of buildings described in clauses (i) and (ii).

(B)   Cost of construction

The term "cost of construction" includes architects' fees and the cost of acquisition of land in connection with construction but does not include the cost of offsite improvements.

(7) Repealed. 105-277, Div. A, § 101(f) [Title VIII, § 402(c)(1)(B)], Oct. 21, 1998, 112 Stat. 2681-415

(8) Designated State agency; designated State unit —

(A)   Designated State agency

The term "designated State agency" means an agency designated under section 721(a)(2)(A) of this title.

(B)   Designated State unit

The term "designated State unit" means —

(i) any State agency unit required under section 721(a)(2)(B)(ii) of this title; or

(ii) in cases in which no such unit is so required, the State agency described in section 721(a)(2)(B)(i) of this title.

(9) Disability

The term "disability" means —

(A) except as otherwise provided in subparagraph (B), a physical or mental impairment that constitutes or results in a substantial impediment to employment; or

(B) for purposes of sections 701, 711, and 712 of this title and subchapters II, IV, V, and VII of this chapter [29 USCS §§ 760 et seq., 780 et seq., 790 et seq., and 796 et seq.], the meaning given it in section 3 of the Americans with Disabilities Act of 1990 (42 U.S.C. 12102, as amended).

(10) Drug and illegal use of drugs

(A) Drug

The term "drug" means a controlled substance, as defined in schedules I through V of section 202 of the Controlled Substances Act (21 U.S.C. 812).

(B) Illegal use of drugs

The term "illegal use of drugs" means the use of drugs, the possession or distribution of which is unlawful under the Controlled Substances Act. Such term does not include the use of a drug taken under supervision by a licensed health care professional, or other uses authorized by the Controlled Substances Act or other provisions of Federal law.

(11) Employment outcome

The term "employment outcome" means, with respect to an individual —

(A) entering or retaining full-time or, if appropriate, part-time competitive employment in the integrated labor market;

(B) satisfying the vocational outcome of supported employment; or

(C) satisfying any other vocational outcome the Secretary may determine to be appropriate (including satisfying the vocational outcome of self-employment, telecommuting, or business ownership), in a manner consistent with this chapter [29 USCS § 701 et seq.].

(12) Establishment of a community rehabilitation program

The term "establishment of a community rehabilitation program" includes the acquisition, expansion, remodeling, or alteration of existing buildings necessary to adapt them to community rehabilitation program purposes or to increase their effectiveness for such purposes (subject, however, to such limitations as the Secretary may determine, in accordance with regulations the Secretary shall prescribe, in order to prevent impairment of the objectives of, or duplication of, other Federal laws providing Federal assistance in the construction of facilities for community rehabilitation programs), and may include such additional equipment and staffing as the Commissioner considers appropriate.

(13)   Extended services

The term "extended services" means ongoing support services and other appropriate services, needed to support and maintain an individual with a most significant disability in supported employment, that —

(A) are provided singly or in combination and are organized and made available in such a way as to assist an eligible individual in maintaining supported employment;

(B) are based on a determination of the needs of an eligible individual, as specified in an individualized plan for employment; and

(C) are provided by a State agency, a nonprofit private organization, employer, or any other appropriate resource, after an individual has made the transition from support provided by the designated State unit.

(14)   Federal share

(A)   In general

Subject to subparagraph (B), the term "Federal share" means 78.7 percent.

(B)   Exception

The term "Federal share" means the share specifically set forth in section 731(a)(3) of this title, except that with respect to payments pursuant to part B of subchapter I of this chapter [29 USCS § 730 et seq.] to any State that are used to meet the costs of construction of those rehabilitation facilities identified in section 723(b)(2) of this title in such State, the Federal share shall be the percentages determined in accordance with the provisions of section 731(a)(3) of this title applicable with respect to the State.

(C)   Relationship to expenditures by a political subdivision

For the purpose of determining the non-Federal share with respect to a State, expenditures by a political subdivision thereof or by a local agency shall be regarded as expenditures by such State, subject to such limitations and conditions as the Secretary shall by regulation prescribe.

(15)   Governor

The term "Governor" means a chief executive officer of a State.

(16)   Impartial hearing officer

(A)   In general

The term "impartial hearing officer" means an individual —

(i) who is not an employee of a public agency (other than an administrative law judge, hearing examiner, or employee of an institution of higher education);

(ii) who is not a member of the State Rehabilitation Council described in section 725 of this title;

(iii) who has not been involved previously in the vocational rehabilitation of the applicant or eligible individual;

(iv) who has knowledge of the delivery of vocational rehabilitation services, the State plan under section 721 of this title, and the Federal and State rules governing the provision of such services and training with respect to the performance of official duties; and

(v) who has no personal or financial interest that would be in conflict with the objectivity of the individual.

(B) Construction

An individual shall not be considered to be an employee of a public agency for purposes of subparagraph (A)(i) solely because the individual is paid by the agency to serve as a hearing officer.

(17) Independent living core services

The term "independent living core services" means —

(A) information and referral services;

(B) independent living skills training;

(C) peer counseling (including cross-disability peer counseling); and

(D) individual and systems advocacy.

(18) Independent living services

The term "independent living services" includes —

(A) independent living core services; and

(B) (i) counseling services, including psychological, psychotherapeutic, and related services;

(ii) services related to securing housing or shelter, including services related to community group living, and supportive of the purposes of this chapter [29 USCS § 701 et seq.] and of the subchapters of this chapter, and adaptive housing services (including appropriate accommodations to and modifications of any space used to serve, or occupied by, individuals with disabilities);

(iii) rehabilitation technology;

(iv) mobility training;

(v) services and training for individuals with cognitive and sensory disabilities, including life skills training, and interpreter and reader services;

(vi) personal assistance services, including attendant care and the training of personnel providing such services;

(vii) surveys, directories, and other activities to identify appropriate housing, recreation opportunities, and accessible transportation, and other support services;

(viii) consumer information programs on rehabilitation and independent living services available under this chapter [29 USCS § 701 et seq.], especially for minorities and other individuals with disabilities who have traditionally been unserved or underserved by programs under this chapter;

(ix) education and training necessary for living in a community and participating in community activities;

(x) supported living;

(xi) transportation, including referral and assistance for such transportation and training in the use of public transportation vehicles and systems;

(xii) physical rehabilitation;

(xiii) therapeutic treatment;

(xiv) provision of needed prostheses and other appliances and devices;

(xv) individual and group social and recreational services;

(xvi) training to develop skills specifically designed for youths who are individuals with disabilities to promote self-awareness and esteem, develop advocacy and self-empowerment skills, and explore career options;

(xvii) services for children;

(xviii) services under other Federal, State, or local programs designed to provide resources, training, counseling, or other assistance, of substantial benefit in enhancing the independence, productivity, and quality of life of individuals with disabilities;

(xix) appropriate preventive services to decrease the need of individuals assisted under this chapter for similar services in the future;

(xx) community awareness programs to enhance the understanding and integration into society of individuals with disabilities; and

(xxi) such other services as may be necessary and not inconsistent with the provisions of this chapter.

(19) Indian; American Indian; Indian American; Indian tribe —

(A)   In general

The terms "Indian", "American Indian", and "Indian American" mean an individual who is a member of an Indian tribe.

(B)   Indian tribe

The term "Indian tribe" means any Federal or State Indian tribe, band, rancheria, pueblo, colony, or community, including any Alaskan native village or regional village corporation (as defined in or established pursuant to the Alaska Native Claims Settlement Act).

(20)   Individual with a disability

(A)   In general

Except as otherwise provided in subparagraph (B), the term "individual with a disability" means any individual who —

(i) has a physical or mental impairment which for such individual constitutes or results in a substantial impediment to employment; and

(ii) can benefit in terms of an employment outcome from vocational rehabilitation services provided pursuant to subchapter I, III, or VI of this chapter [29 USCS § 720 et seq., 771 et seq., or 795 et seq.].

(B) Certain programs; limitations on major life activities

Subject to subparagraphs (C), (D), (E), and (F), the term "individual with a disability" means, for purposes of sections 701, 711, and 712 of this title and subchapters II, IV, V, and VII of this chapter [29 USCS §§ 760 et seq., 780 et seq., 790 et seq., and 796 et seq.], any person who has a disability as defined in section 3 of the Americans with Disabilities Act of 1990 (42 U.S.C. 12102, as amended).

(C) Rights and advocacy provision.

(i) In general; exclusion of individuals engaging in drug use

For purposes of subchapter V of this chapter [29 USCS § 790 et seq.], the term "individual with a disability" does not include an individual who is currently engaging in the illegal use of drugs, when a covered entity acts on the basis of such use.

(ii) Exception for individuals no longer engaging in drug use

Nothing in clause (i) shall be construed to exclude as an individual with a disability an individual who —

(I) has successfully completed a supervised drug rehabilitation program and is no longer engaging in the illegal use of drugs, or has otherwise been rehabilitated successfully and is no longer engaging in such use;

(II) is participating in a supervised rehabilitation program and is no longer engaging in such use; or

(III) is erroneously regarded as engaging in such use, but is not engaging in such use; except that it shall not be a violation of this chapter [29 USCS § 701 et seq.] for a covered entity to adopt or administer reasonable policies or procedures, including but not limited to drug testing, designed to ensure that an individual described in subclause (I) or (II) is no longer engaging in the illegal use of drugs.

(iii) Exclusion for certain services

Notwithstanding clause (i), for purposes of programs and activities providing health services and services provided under subchapters I, II, and III of this chapter [29 USCS §§ 720 et seq., 760 et seq., and 771 et seq.], an individual shall not be excluded from the benefits of such programs or activities on the basis of his or her current illegal use of drugs if he or she is otherwise entitled to such services.

(iv) Disciplinary action

For purposes of programs and activities providing educational services, local educational agencies may take disciplinary action pertaining to the use or possession of illegal drugs or alcohol against any student who is an individual with a disability and who currently is engaging in the illegal use of drugs or in the use of alcohol to the same extent that such disciplinary action is taken against students who are not individuals with disabilities. Furthermore, the due process procedures at section 104.36 of title 34, Code of Federal Regulations (or any corresponding similar regulation or ruling) shall not apply to such disciplinary actions.

(v)   Employment; exclusion of alcoholics

For purposes of sections 793 and 794 of this title as such sections relate to employment, the term "individual with a disability" does not include any individual who is an alcoholic whose current use of alcohol prevents such individual from performing the duties of the job in question or whose employment, by reason of such current alcohol abuse, would constitute a direct threat to property or the safety of others.

(D)   Employment; exclusion of individuals with certain diseases or infections

For the purposes of sections 793 and 794 of this title, as such sections relate to employment, such term does not include an individual who has a currently contagious disease or infection and who, by reason of such disease or infection, would constitute a direct threat to the health or safety of other individuals or who, by reason of the currently contagious disease or infection, is unable to perform the duties of the job.

(E) Rights provisions; exclusion of individuals on basis of homosexuality or bisexuality

For the purposes of sections 791, 793, and 794 of this title —

(i) for purposes of the application of subparagraph (B) to such sections, the term "impairment" does not include homosexuality or bisexuality; and

(ii) therefore the term "individual with a disability" does not include an individual on the basis of homosexuality or bisexuality.

(F) Rights provisions; exclusion of individuals on basis of certain disorders

For the purposes of sections 791, 793, and 794 of this title, the term "individual with a disability" does not include an individual on the basis of —

(i) transvestism, transsexualism, pedophilia, exhibitionism, voyeurism, gender identity disorders not resulting from physical impairments, or other sexual behavior disorders;

(ii) compulsive gambling, kleptomania, or pyromania; or

(iii) psychoactive substance use disorders resulting from current illegal use of drugs.

(G)   Individuals with disabilities

The term "individuals with disabilities" means more than one individual with a disability.

(21) Individual with a significant disability

(A) In general

Except as provided in subparagraph (B) or (C), the term "individual with a significant disability" means an individual with a disability —

(i) who has a severe physical or mental impairment which seriously limits one or more functional capacities (such as mobility, communication, self-care, self-direction, interpersonal skills, work tolerance, or work skills) in terms of an employment outcome;

(ii) whose vocational rehabilitation can be expected to require multiple vocational rehabilitation services over an extended period of time; and

(iii) who has one or more physical or mental disabilities resulting from amputation, arthritis, autism, blindness, burn injury, cancer, cerebral palsy, cystic fibrosis, deafness, head injury, heart disease, hemiplegia, hemophilia, respiratory or pulmonary dysfunction, mental retardation, mental illness, multiple sclerosis, muscular dystrophy, musculo-skeletal disorders, neurological disorders (including stroke and epilepsy), paraplegia, quadriplegia, and other spinal cord conditions, sickle cell anemia, specific learning disability, end-stage renal disease, or another disability or combination of disabilities determined on the basis of an assessment for determining eligibility and vocational rehabilitation needs described in subparagraphs (A) and (B) of paragraph (2) to cause comparable substantial functional limitation.

(B) Independent living services and centers for independent living

For purposes of subchapter VII of this chapter [29 USCS § 796 et seq.], the term "individual with a significant disability" means an individual with a severe physical or mental impairment whose ability to function independently in the family or community or whose ability to obtain, maintain, or advance in employment is substantially limited and for whom the delivery of independent living services will improve the ability to function, continue functioning, or move toward functioning independently in the family or community or to continue in employment, respectively.

(C) Research and training

For purposes of subchapter II of this chapter [29 USCS § 760 et seq.], the term "individual with a significant disability" includes an individual described in subparagraph (A) or (B).

(D) Individuals with significant disabilities

The term "individuals with significant disabilities" means more than one individual with a significant disability.

(E) Individual with a most significant disability

(i) In general

The term "individual with a most significant disability", used with respect to an individual in a State, means an individual with a significant disability who meets criteria established by the State under section 721(a)(5)(C) of this title.

(ii)   Individuals with the most significant disabilities

The term "individuals with the most significant disabilities" means more than one individual with a most significant disability.

(22)   Individual's representative; applicant's representative

The terms "individual's representative" and "applicant's representative" mean a parent, a family member, a guardian, an advocate, or an authorized representative of an individual or applicant, respectively.

(23)   Institution of higher education

The term "institution of higher education" has the meaning given the term in section 1.01 of this title.

(24)   Local agency

The term "local agency" means an agency of a unit of general local government or of an Indian tribe (or combination of such units or tribes) which has an agreement with the designated State agency to conduct a vocational rehabilitation program under the supervision of such State agency in accordance with the State plan approved under section 721 of this title. Nothing in the preceding sentence of this paragraph or in section 721 of this title shall be construed to prevent the local agency from arranging to utilize another local public or nonprofit agency to provide vocational rehabilitation services if such an arrangement is made part of the agreement specified in this paragraph.

(25)   Local workforce investment board

The term "local workforce investment board" means a local workforce investment board established under section 117 of the Workforce Investment Act of 1998 [29 USCS § 2832].

(26)   Nonprofit

The term "nonprofit', when used with respect to a community rehabilitation program, means a community rehabilitation program carried out by a corporation or association, no part of the net earnings of which inures, or may lawfully inure, to the benefit of any private shareholder or individual and the income of which is exempt from taxation under section 501(c)(3) of Title 26.

(27)   Ongoing support services

The term "ongoing support services" means services —

(A) provided to individuals with the most significant disabilities;

(B) provided, at a minimum, twice monthly —

(i) to make an assessment, regarding the employment situation, at the worksite of each such individual in supported employment, or, under special circumstances, especially at the request of the client, off site; and

(ii) based on the assessment, to provide for the coordination or provision of specific intensive services, at or away from the worksite, that are needed to maintain employment stability; and

(C) consisting of —

(i) a particularized assessment supplementary to the comprehensive assessment described in paragraph (2)(B);

(ii) the provision of skilled job trainers who accompany the individual for intensive job skill training at the worksite;

(iii) job development, job retention, and placement services;

(iv) social skills training;

(v) regular observation or supervision of the individual;

(vi) followup services such as regular contact with the employers, the individuals, the individuals' representatives, and other appropriate individuals, in order to reinforce and stabilize the job placement;

(vii) facilitation of natural supports at the worksite;

(viii) any other service identified in section 723 of this title; or

(ix) a service similar to another service described in this subparagraph.

(28)   Personal assistance services

The term "personal assistance services" means a range of services, provided by one or more persons, designed to assist an individual with a disability to perform daily living activities on or off the job that the individual would typically perform if the individual did not have a disability. Such services shall be designed to increase the individual's control in life and ability to perform everyday activities on or off the job.

(29)   Public or nonprofit

The term "public or nonprofit", used with respect to an agency or organization, includes an Indian tribe.

(30)   Rehabilitation technology

The term "rehabilitation technology" means the systematic application of technologies, engineering methodologies, or scientific principles to meet the needs of and address the barriers confronted by individuals with disabilities in areas which include education, rehabilitation, employment, transportation, independent living, and recreation. The term includes rehabilitation engineering, assistive technology devices, and assistive technology services.

(31)   Secretary

The term "Secretary", except when the context otherwise requires, means the Secretary of Education.

(32)   State

The term "State" includes, in addition to each of the several States of the United States, the District of Columbia, the Commonwealth of Puerto Rico, the

United States Virgin Islands, Guam, American Samoa, and the Commonwealth of the Northern Mariana Islands.

(33) State workforce investment board

The term "State workforce investment board" means a State workforce investment board established under section 111 of the Workforce Investment Act of 1998 [29 USCS § 2821].

(34) Statewide workforce investment system

The term "statewide workforce investment system" means a system described in section 111(d)(2) of the Workforce Investment Act of 1998 [29 USCS § 2821(d)(2)].

(35) Supported employment

(A) In general

The term "supported employment" means competitive work in integrated work settings, or employment in integrated work settings in which individuals are working toward competitive work, consistent with the strengths, resources, priorities, concerns, abilities, capabilities, interests, and informed choice of the individuals, for individuals with the most significant disabilities —

(i) (I) for whom competitive employment has not traditionally occurred; or

(II) for whom competitive employment has been interrupted or intermittent as a result of a significant disability; and

(ii) who, because of the nature and severity of their disability, need intensive supported employment services for the period, and any extension, described in paragraph (36)(C) and extended services after the transition described in paragraph (13)(C) in order to perform such work.

(B) Certain transitional employment

Such term includes transitional employment for persons who are individuals with the most significant disabilities due to mental illness.

(36) Supported employment services

The term "supported employment services" means ongoing support services and other appropriate services needed to support and maintain an individual with a most significant disability in supported employment, that —

(A) are provided singly or in combination and are organized and made available in such a way as to assist an eligible individual to achieve competitive employment;

(B) are based on a determination of the needs of an eligible individual, as specified in an individualized plan for employment; and

(C) are provided by the designated State unit for a period of time not to extend beyond 18 months, unless under special circumstances the eligible individual and the rehabilitation counselor or coordinator involved jointly agree to extend the time in order to achieve the employment outcome identified in the individualized plan for employment.

(37)   Transition services

The term "transition services" means a coordinated set of activities for a student, designed within an outcome-oriented process, that promotes movement from school to post school activities, including postsecondary education, vocational training, integrated employment (including supported employment), continuing and adult education, adult services, independent living, or community participation. The coordinated set of activities shall be based upon the individual student's needs, taking into account the student's preferences and interests, and shall include instruction, community experiences, the development of employment and other post school adult living objectives, and, when appropriate, acquisition of daily living skills and functional vocational evaluation.

(38)   Vocational rehabilitation services

The term "vocational rehabilitation services" means those services identified in section 723 of this title which are provided to individuals with disabilities under this chapter [29 USCS § 701 et seq.].

(39)   Workforce investment activities

The term "workforce investment activities" means workforce investment activities, as defined in section 101 of the Workforce Investment Act of 1998, that are carried out under that Act.

§ 791.   Employment of individuals with disabilities

(a) Interagency Committee on Employees who are Individuals with Disabilities; establishment; membership; co-chairmen; availability of other Committee resources; purpose and functions

There is established within the Federal Government an Interagency Committee on Employees who are Individuals with Disabilities (hereinafter in this section referred to as the "Committee"), comprised of such members as the President may select, including the following (or their designees whose positions are Executive Level IV or higher): the Chairman of the Equal Employment Opportunity Commission (hereafter in this section referred to as the "Commission"), the Director of the Office of Personnel Management, the Secretary of Veterans Affairs, the Secretary of Labor, the Secretary of Education, and the Secretary of Health and Human Services. Either the Director of the Office of Personnel Management and the Chairman of the Commission shall serve as co-chairpersons of the Committee or the Director or Chairman shall serve as the sole chairperson of the Committee, as the Director and Chairman jointly determine, from time to time, to be appropriate. The resources of the President's Committees on Employment of People With Disabilities and on Mental Retardation shall be made fully available to the Committee. It shall be the purpose and function of the Committee (1) to provide a focus for Federal and other employment of individuals with disabilities, and to review, on a periodic basis, in cooperation with the Commission, the adequacy of hiring, placement, and advancement practices with respect to individuals with disabilities, by each department, agency, and instrumentality in the executive branch of Government and the Smithsonian Institution, and to insure that the special needs of such individuals are being met; and (2) to consult with the Commission to assist the Commission to carry out its responsibilities under subsections (b), (c), and (d) of this section. On the basis of such review and consultation, the Committee shall periodically make to the Commission such recommendations for legislative and administrative changes as it deems necessary or desirable. The Commission shall timely transmit to the appropriate committees of Congress any such recommendations.

(b)   Federal agencies; affirmative action program plans

Each department, agency, and instrumentality (including the United States Postal Service and the Postal Regulatory Commission) in the executive branch and the Smithsonian Institution shall, within one hundred and eighty days after September 26, 1973, submit to the Commission and to the Committee an affirmative action program plan for the hiring, placement, and advancement of individuals with disabilities in such department, agency, instrumentality, or Institution. Such plan shall include a description of the extent to which and methods whereby the special needs of employees who are individuals with disabilities are being met. Such plan shall be updated annually, and shall be reviewed annually and approved by the Commission, if the Commission determines, after consultation with the Committee, that such plan provides sufficient assurances, procedures and commitments to provide adequate hiring, placement, and advancement opportunities for individuals with disabilities.

(c)   State agencies; rehabilitated individuals, employment

The Commission, after consultation with the Committee, shall develop and recommend to the Secretary for referral to the appropriate State agencies, policies and procedures which will facilitate the hiring, placement, and advancement in employment of individuals who have received rehabilitation services under State vocational rehabilitation programs, veterans' programs, or any other program for individuals with disabilities, including the promotion of job opportunities for such individuals. The Secretary shall encourage such State agencies to adopt and implement such policies and procedures.

(d)   Report to Congressional committees

The Commission, after consultation with the Committee, shall, on June 30, 1974, and at the end of each subsequent fiscal year, make a complete report to the appropriate committees of the Congress with respect to the practices of and achievements in hiring, placement, and advancement of individuals with disabilities by each department, agency, and instrumentality and the Smithsonian Institution and the effectiveness of the affirmative action programs required by subsection (b) of this section, together with recommendations as to legislation which have been submitted to the Commission under subsection (a) of this section, or other appropriate action to insure the adequacy of such practices. Such report shall also include an evaluation by the Committee of the effectiveness of the activities of the Commission under subsections (b) and (c) of this section.

(e)   Federal work experience without pay; non-Federal status

An individual who, as a part of an individualized plan for employment under a State plan approved under this chapter, participates in a program of unpaid work experience in a Federal agency, shall not, by reason thereof, be considered to be a Federal employee or to be subject to the provisions of law relating to Federal employment, including those relating to hours of work, rates of compensation, leave, unemployment compensation, and Federal employee benefits.

(f) Federal agency cooperation; special consideration for positions on President's Committee on Employment of People With Disabilities

(1) The Secretary of Labor and the Secretary of Education are authorized and directed to cooperate with the President's Committee on Employment of People With Disabilities in carrying out its functions.

(2) In selecting personnel to fill all positions on the President's Committee on Employment of People With Disabilities, special consideration shall be given to qualified individuals with disabilities.

(g)   Standards used in determining violation of section

The standards used to determine whether this section has been violated in a complaint alleging nonaffirmative action employment discrimination under this section shall be the standards applied under title I of the Americans with Disabilities Act of 1990 (42 U.S.C. 12111 et seq.) and the provisions of sections 501 through 504, and 510, of the Americans with Disabilities Act of 1990 (42 U.S.C. 12201–12204 and 12210), as such sections relate to employment.

§ 793.   Employment under Federal contracts

(a)   Amount of contracts or subcontracts; provision for employment and advancement of qualified individuals with disabilities; regulations

Any contract in excess of $10,000 entered into by any Federal department or agency for the procurement of personal property and nonpersonal services (including construction) for the United States shall contain a provision requiring that the party contracting with the United States shall take affirmative action to employ and advance in employment qualified individuals with disabilities. The provisions of this section shall apply to any subcontract in excess of $10,000 entered into by a prime contractor in carrying out any contract for the procurement of personal property and nonpersonal services (including construction) for the United States. The President shall implement the provisions of this section by promulgating regulations within ninety days after September 26, 1973.

(b)   Administrative enforcement; complaints; investigations; departmental action

If any individual with a disability believes any contractor has failed or refused to comply with the provisions of a contract with the United States, relating to employment of individuals with disabilities, such individual may file a complaint with the Department of Labor. The Department shall promptly investigate such complaint and shall take such action thereon as the facts and circumstances warrant, consistent with the terms of such contract and the laws and regulations applicable thereto.

(c) Waiver by President; national interest special circumstances for waiver of particular agreements; waiver by Secretary of Labor of affirmative action requirements

(1) The requirements of this section may be waived, in whole or in part, by the President with respect to a particular contract or subcontract, in accordance with guidelines set forth in regulations which the President shall prescribe, when the President determines that special circumstances in the national interest so require and states in writing the reasons for such determination.

(2) (A) The Secretary of Labor may waive the requirements of the affirmative action clause required by regulations promulgated under subsection (a) of this section with respect to any of a prime contractor's or subcontractor's facilities that are found to be in all respects separate and distinct from activities of the prime contractor or subcontractor related to the performance of the contract or subcontract, if the Secretary of Labor also finds that such a waiver will not interfere with or impede the effectuation of this chapter.

(B) Such waivers shall be considered only upon the request of the contractor or subcontractor. The Secretary of Labor shall promulgate regulations that set forth the standards used for granting such a waiver.

(d)   Standards used in determining violation of section

The standards used to determine whether this section has been violated in a complaint alleging nonaffirmative action employment discrimination under this section shall be the standards applied under title I of the Americans with Disabilities Act of 1990 (42 U.S.C. 12111 et seq.) and the provisions of sections 501 through 504, and 510, of the Americans with Disabilities Act of 1990 (42 U.S.C. 12201–12204 and 12210), as such sections relate to employment.

(e)   Avoidance of duplicative efforts and inconsistencies

The Secretary shall develop procedures to ensure that administrative complaints filed under this section and under the Americans with Disabilities Act of 1990 [42 U.S.C.A. § 12101 et seq.] are dealt with in a manner that avoids duplication of effort and prevents imposition of inconsistent or conflicting standards for the same requirements under this section and the Americans with Disabilities Act of 1990 [42 U.S.C.A. § 12101 et seq.].

§ 794.   Nondiscrimination under federal grants and programs

(a)   Promulgation of rules and regulations

No otherwise qualified individual with a disability in the United States, as defined in section 705(20) of this title, shall, solely by reason of her or his disability, be excluded from the participation in, be denied the benefits of, or be subjected to discrimination under any program or activity receiving Federal financial assistance or under any program or activity conducted by any Executive agency or by the United States Postal Service. The head of each such agency shall promulgate such regulations as may be necessary to carry out the amendments to this section made by the Rehabilitation, Comprehensive Services, and Developmental Disabilities Act of 1978. Copies of any proposed regulation shall be submitted to appropriate authorizing committees of the Congress, and such regulation may take effect no earlier than the thirtieth day after the date on which such regulation is so submitted to such committees.

(b)   "Program or activity" defined

For the purposes of this section, the term "program or activity" means all of the operations of —

(1) (A) a department, agency, special purpose district, or other instrumentality of a State or of a local government; or

(B) the entity of such State or local government that distributes such assistance and each such department or agency (and each other State or local government entity) to which the assistance is extended, in the case of assistance to a State or local government;

(2) (A) a college, university, or other post-secondary institution, or a public system of higher education; or

(B) a local educational agency (as defined in section 7801 of Title 20) system of vocational education, or other school system;

(3) (A) an entire corporation, partnership, or other private organization, or an entire sole proprietorship —

(i) if assistance is extended to such corporation, partnership, private organization, or sole proprietorship as a whole; or

(ii) which is principally engaged in the business of providing education, health care, housing, social services, or parks and recreation; or

(B) the entire plant or other comparable, geographically separate facility to which Federal financial assistance is extended, in the case of any other corporation, partnership, private organization, or sole proprietorship; or

(4) any other entity which is established by two or more of the entities described in paragraph (1), (2), or (3); any part of which is extended Federal financial assistance.

(c)   Significant structural alterations by small providers; exception

Small providers are not required by subsection (a) of this section to make significant structural alterations to their existing facilities for the purpose of assuring program accessibility, if alternative means of providing the services are available. The terms used in this subsection shall be construed with reference to the regulations existing on March 22, 1988.

(d)   Standards used in determining violation of section

The standards used to determine whether this section has been violated in a complaint alleging employment discrimination under this section shall be the standards applied under title I of the Americans with Disabilities Act of 1990 (42 U.S.C. 12111 et seq.) and the provisions of sections 501 through 504, and 510, of the Americans with Disabilities Act of 1990 (42 U.S.C. 12201–12204 and 12210), as such sections relate to employment.

§ 794a.   Remedies and attorney fees

(a) (1) The remedies, procedures, and rights set forth in section 717 of the Civil Rights Act of 1964 (42 U.S.C. 2000e-16), including the application of sections

706(f) through 706(k) (42 U.S.C. 2000e-5(f) through (k)), shall be available, with respect to any complaint under section 791 of this title, to any employee or applicant for employment aggrieved by the final disposition of such complaint, or by the failure to take final action on such complaint. In fashioning an equitable or affirmative action remedy under such section, a court may take into account the reasonableness of the cost of any necessary work place accommodation, and the availability of alternatives therefor or other appropriate relief in order to achieve an equitable and appropriate remedy.

(2) The remedies, procedures, and rights set forth in title VI of the Civil Rights Act of 1964 [42 U.S.C.A. § 2000d et seq.] shall be available to any person aggrieved by any act or failure to act by any recipient of Federal assistance or Federal provider of such assistance under section 794 of this title.

(b) In any action or proceeding to enforce or charge a violation of a provision of this subchapter, the court, in its discretion, may allow the prevailing party, other than the United States, a reasonable attorney's fee as part of the costs.

Chapter 10
DEPARTMENT OF EDUCATION SECTION 504 REGULATIONS AND ANALYSIS

DOE SECTION 504 REGULATIONS AND ANALYSIS

§ 104.1 Purpose.

The purpose of this part is to effectuate section 504 of the Rehabilitation Act of 1973, which is designed to eliminate discrimination on the basis of handicap in any program or activity receiving Federal financial assistance.

§ 104.2 Application.

This part applies to each recipient of Federal financial assistance from the Department of Education and to the program or activity that receives such assistance.

§ 104.3 Definitions.

As used in this part, the term:

(a) The Act means the Rehabilitation Act of 1973, Pub. L. 93-112, as amended by the Rehabilitation Act Amendments of 1974, Pub. L. 93-516, 29 U.S.C. 794.

(b) Section 504 means section 504 of the Act.

(c) Education of the Handicapped Act means that statute as amended by the Education for all Handicapped Children Act of 1975, Pub. L. 94-142, 20 U.S.C. 1401 et seq.

(d) Department means the Department of Education.

(e) Assistant Secretary means the Assistant Secretary for Civil Rights of the Department of Education.

(f) Recipient means any state or its political subdivision, any instrumentality of a state or its political subdivision, any public or private agency, institution, organization, or other entity, or any person to which Federal financial assistance is extended directly or through another recipient, including any successor, assignee, or transferee of a recipient, but excluding the ultimate beneficiary of the assistance.

(g) Applicant for assistance means one who submits an application, request, or plan required to be approved by a Department official or by a recipient as a condition to becoming a recipient.

(h) Federal financial assistance means any grant, loan, contract (other than a procurement contract or a contract of insurance or guaranty), or any other arrangement by which the Department provides or otherwise makes available assistance in the form of:

(1) Funds;

(2) Services of Federal personnel; or

(3) Real and personal property or any interest in or use of such property, including:

(i) Transfers or leases of such property for less than fair market value or for reduced consideration; and

(ii) Proceeds from a subsequent transfer or lease of such property if the Federal share of its fair market value is not returned to the Federal Government.

(i) Facility means all or any portion of buildings, structures, equipment, roads, walks, parking lots, or other real or personal property or interest in such property.

(j) Handicapped person —

(1) Handicapped persons means any person who (i) has a physical or mental impairment which substantially limits one or more major life activities, (ii) has a record of such an impairment, or (iii) is regarded as having such an impairment.

(2) As used in paragraph (j)(1) of this section, the phrase:

(i) Physical or mental impairment means (A) any physiological disorder or condition, cosmetic disfigurement, or anatomical loss affecting one or more of the following body systems: neurological; musculoskeletal; special sense organs; respiratory, including speech organs; cardiovascular; reproductive, digestive, genito-urinary; hemic and lymphatic; skin; and endocrine; or (B) any mental or psychological disorder, such as mental retardation, organic brain syndrome, emotional or mental illness, and specific learning disabilities.

(ii) Major life activities means functions such as caring for one's self, performing manual tasks, walking, seeing, hearing, speaking, breathing, learning, and working.

(iii) Has a record of such an impairment means has a history of, or has been misclassified as having, a mental or physical impairment that substantially limits one or more major life activities.

(iv) Is regarded as having an impairment means (A) has a physical or mental impairment that does not substantially limit major life activities but that is treated by a recipient as constituting such a limitation; (B) has a physical or mental impairment that substantially limits major life activities only as a result of the attitudes of others toward such impairment; or (C) has none of the impairments defined in paragraph (j)(2)(i) of this section but is treated by a recipient as having such an impairment.

(k) Program or activity means all of the operations of —

(1) (i) A department, agency, special purpose district, or other instrumentality of a State or of a local government; or

(ii) The entity of such State or local government that distributes such assistance and each such department or agency (and each other State or local government entity) to which the assistance is extended, in the case of assistance to a State or local government;

(2) (i) A college, university, or other postsecondary institution, or a public system of higher education; or

(ii) A local educational agency (as defined in 20 U.S.C. 8801), system of vocational education, or other school system;

(3) (i) An entire corporation, partnership, or other private organization, or an entire sole proprietorship —

(A) If assistance is extended to such corporation, partnership, private organization, or sole proprietorship as a whole; or

(B) Which is principally engaged in the business of providing education, health care, housing, social services, or parks and recreation; or

(ii) The entire plant or other comparable, geographically separate facility to which Federal financial assistance is extended, in the case of any other corporation, partnership, private organization, or sole proprietorship; or

(4) Any other entity which is established by two or more of the entities described in paragraph (k)(1), (2), or (3) of this section; any part of which is extended Federal financial assistance.

(Authority: 29 U.S.C. 794(b))

(l) Qualified handicapped person means:

(1) With respect to employment, a handicapped person who, with reasonable accommodation, can perform the essential functions of the job in question;

(2) With respect to public preschool elementary, secondary, or adult educational services, a handicappped person (i) of an age during which nonhandicapped persons are provided such services, (ii) of any age during which it is mandatory under state law to provide such services to handicapped persons, or (iii) to whom a state is required to provide a free appropriate public education under section 612 of the Education of the Handicapped Act; and

(3) With respect to postsecondary and vocational education services, a handicapped person who meets the academic and technical standards requisite to admission or participation in the recipient's education program or activity;

(4) With respect to other services, a handicapped person who meets the essential eligibility requirements for the receipt of such services.

(m) Handicap means any condition or characteristic that renders a person a handicapped person as defined in paragraph (j) of this section.

§ 104.4 Discrimination prohibited.

(a) General. No qualified handicapped person shall, on the basis of handicap, be excluded from participation in, be denied the benefits of, or otherwise be subjected to discrimination under any program or activitiy which receives Federal financial assistance.

(b) Discriminatory actions prohibited.

(1) A recipient, in providing any aid, benefit, or service, may not, directly or through contractual, licensing, or other arrangements, on the basis of handicap:

(i) Deny a qualified handicapped person the opportunity to participate in or benefit from the aid, benefit, or service;

(ii) Afford a qualified handicapped person an opportunity to participate in or benefit from the aid, benefit, or service that is not equal to that afforded others;

(iii) Provide a qualified handicapped person with an aid, benefit, or service that is not as effective as that provided to others;

(iv) Provide different or separate aid, benefits, or services to handicapped persons or to any class of handicapped persons unless such action is necessary to provide qualified handicapped persons with aid, benefits, or services that are as effective as those provided to others;

(v) Aid or perpetuate discrimination against a qualified handicapped person by providing significant assistance to an agency, organization, or person that discriminates on the basis of handicap in providing any aid, benefit, or service to beneficiaries of the recipients program or activity;

(vi) Deny a qualified handicapped person the opportunity to participate as a member of planning or advisory boards; or

(vii) Otherwise limit a qualified handicapped person in the enjoyment of any right, privilege, advantage, or opportunity enjoyed by others receiving an aid, benefit, or service.

(2) For purposes of this part, aids, benefits, and services, to be equally effective, are not required to produce the identical result or level of achievement for handicapped and nonhandicapped persons, but must afford handicapped persons equal opportunity to obtain the same result, to gain the same benefit, or to reach the same level of achievement, in the most integrated setting appropriate to the person's needs.

(3) Despite the existence of separate or different aid, benefits, or services provided in accordance with this part, a recipient may not deny a qualified handicapped person the opportunity to participate in such aid, benefits, or services that are not separate or different.

(4) A recipient may not, directly or through contractual or other arrangements, utilize criteria or methods of administration (i) that have the effect of subjecting qualified handicapped persons to discrimination on the basis of handicap, (ii) that have the purpose or effect of defeating or substantially impairing accomplishment of the objectives of the recipient's program or activity with respect to handicapped persons, or (iii) that perpetuate the discrimination of another recipient if both recipients are subject to common administrative control or are agencies of the same State.

(5) In determining the site or location of a facility, an applicant for assistance or a recipient may not make selections (i) that have the effect of excluding handicapped persons from, denying them the benefits of, or otherwise subjecting them to discrimination under any program or activity that receives Federal financial assistance or (ii) that have the purpose or effect of defeating or substantially impairing the accomplishment of the objectives of the program or activity with respect to handicapped persons.

(6) As used in this section, the aid, benefit, or service provided under a program or activity receiving Federal financial assistance includes any aid, benefit, or service provided in or through a facility that has been constructed, expanded, altered, leased or rented, or otherwise acquired, in whole or in part, with Federal financial assistance.

(c) Aid, benefits, or services limited by Federal law. The exclusion of nonhandicapped persons from aid, benefits, or services limited by Federal statute or executive order to handicapped persons or the exclusion of a specific class of handicapped persons from aid, benefits, or services limited by Federal statute or executive order to a different class of handicapped persons is not prohibited by this part.

§ 104.5 Assurances required.

(a) Assurances. An applicant for Federal financial assistance to which this part applies shall submit an assurance, on a form specified by the Assistant Secretary, that the program or activity will be operated in compliance with this part. An applicant may incorporate these assurances by reference in subsequent applications to the Department.

(b) Duration of obligation.

(1) In the case of Federal financial assistance extended in the form of real property or to provide real property or structures on the property, the assurance will obligate the recipient or, in the case of a subsequent transfer, the transferee, for the period during which the real property or structures are used for the purpose for which Federal financial assistance is extended or for another purpose involving the provision of similar services or benefits.

(2) In the case of Federal financial assistance extended to provide personal property, the assurance will obligate the recipient for the period during which it retains ownership or possession of the property.

(3) In all other cases the assurance will obligate the recipient for the period during which Federal financial assistance is extended.

(c) Covenants.

(1) Where Federal financial assistance is provided in the form of real property or interest in the property from the Department, the instrument effecting or recording this transfer shall contain a covenant running with the land to assure nondiscrimination for the period during which the real property is used for a purpose for which the Federal financial assistance is extended or for another purpose involving the provision of similar services or benefits.

(2) Where no transfer of property is involved but property is purchased or improved with Federal financial assistance, the recipient shall agree to include the covenant described in paragraph (b)(2) of this section in the instrument effecting or recording any subsequent transfer of the property.

(3) Where Federal financial assistance is provided in the form of real property or interest in the property from the Department, the covenant shall also include a condition coupled with a right to be reserved by the Department to revert title

to the property in the event of a breach of the covenant. If a transferee of real property proposes to mortgage or otherwise encumber the real property as security for financing construction of new, or improvement of existing, facilities on the property for the purposes for which the property was transferred, the Assistant Secretary may, upon request of the transferee and if necessary to accomplish such financing and upon such conditions as he or she deems appropriate, agree to forbear the exercise of such right to revert title for so long as the lien of such mortgage or other encumbrance remains effective.

§ 104.6   Remedial action, voluntary action, and self-evaluation.

(a) Remedial action.

(1) If the Assistant Secretary finds that a recipient has discriminated against persons on the basis of handicap in violation of section 504 or this part, the recipient shall take such remedial action as the Assistant Secretary deems necessary to overcome the effects of the discrimination.

(2) Where a recipient is found to have discriminated against persons on the basis of handicap in violation of section 504 or this part and where another recipient exercises control over the recipient that has discriminated, the Assistant Secretary, where appropriate, may require either or both recipients to take remedial action.

(3) The Assistant Secretary may, where necessary to overcome the effects of discrimination in violation of section 504 or this part, require a recipient to take remedial action (i) with respect to handicapped persons who are no longer participants in the recipient's program or activity but who were participants in the program or activity when such discrimination occurred or (ii) with respect to handicapped persons who would have been participants in the program or activity had the discrimination not occurred.

(b) Voluntary action. A recipient may take steps, in addition to any action that is required by this part, to overcome the effects of conditions that resulted in limited participation in the recipient's program or activity by qualified handicapped persons.

(c) Self-evaluation.

(1) A recipient shall, within one year of the effective date of this part:

(i) Evaluate, with the assistance of interested persons, including handicapped persons or organizations representing handicapped persons, its current policies and practices and the effects thereof that do not or may not meet the requirements of this part;

(ii) Modify, after consultation with interested persons, including handicapped persons or organizations representing handicapped persons, any policies and practices that do not meet the requirements of this part; and

(iii) Take, after consultation with interested persons, including handicapped persons or organizations representing handicapped persons, appropriate remedial steps to eliminate the effects of any discrimination that resulted from adherence to these policies and practices.

(2) A recipient that employs fifteen or more persons shall, for at least three years following completion of the evaluation required under paragraph (c)(1) of this section, maintain on file, make available for public inspection, and provide to the Assistant Secretary upon request:

(i) A list of the interested persons consulted,

(ii) A description of areas examined and any problems identified, and

(iii) A description of any modifications made and of any remedial steps taken.

§ 104.7   Designation of responsible employee and adoption of grievance procedures.

(a) Designation of responsible employee. A recipient that employs fifteen or more persons shall designate at least one person to coordinate its efforts to comply with this part.

(b) Adoption of grievance procedures. A recipient that employs fifteen or more persons shall adopt grievance procedures that incorporate appropriate due process standards and that provide for the prompt and equitable resolution of complaints alleging any action prohibited by this part. Such procedures need not be established with respect to complaints from applicants for employment or from applicants for admission to postsecondary educational institutions.

§ 104.8   Notice.

(a) A recipient that employs fifteen or more persons shall take appropriate initial and continuing steps to notify participants, beneficiaries, applicants, and employees, including those with impaired vision or hearing, and unions or professional organizations holding collective bargaining or professional agreements with the recipient that it does not discriminate on the basis of handicap in violation of section 504 and this part. The notification shall state, where appropriate, that the recipient does not discriminate in admission or access to, or treatment or employment in, its program or activity. The notification shall also include an identification of the responsible employee designated pursuant to § 104.7(a). A recipient shall make the initial notification required by this paragraph within 90 days of the effective date of this part. Methods of initial and continuing notification may include the posting of notices, publication in newspapers and magazines, placement of notices in recipients' publication, and distribution of memoranda or other written communications.

(b) If a recipient publishes or uses recruitment materials or publications containing general information that it makes available to participants, beneficiaries, applicants, or employees, it shall include in those materials or publications a statement of the policy described in paragraph (a) of this section. A recipient may meet the requirement of this paragraph either by including appropriate inserts in existing materials and publications or by revising and reprinting the materials and publications.

§ 104.9   Administrative requirements for small recipients.

The Assistant Secretary may require any recipient with fewer than fifteen employees, or any class of such recipients, to comply with §§ 104.7 and 104.8, in whole or in part, when the Assistant Secretary finds a violation of this part or finds that such compliance will not significantly impair the ability of the recipient or class of recipients to provide benefits or services.

§ 104.10   Effect of state or local law or other requirements and effect of employment opportunities.

(a) The obligation to comply with this part is not obviated or alleviated by the existence of any state or local law or other requirement that, on the basis of handicap, imposes prohibitions or limits upon the eligibility of qualified handicapped persons to receive services or to practice any occupation or profession.

(b) The obligation to comply with this part is not obviated or alleviated because employment opportunities in any occupation or profession are or may be more limited for handicapped persons than for nonhandicapped persons.

§ 104.11   Discrimination prohibited.

(a) General.

(1) No qualified handicapped person shall, on the basis of handicap, be subjected to discrimination in employment under any program or activity to which this part applies.

(2) A recipient that receives assistance under the Education of the Handicapped Act shall take positive steps to employ and advance in employment qualified handicapped persons in programs or activities assisted under that Act.

(3) A recipient shall make all decisions concerning employment under any program or activity to which this part applies in a manner which ensures that discrimination on the basis of handicap does not occur and may not limit, segregate, or classify applicants or employees in any way that adversely affects their opportunities or status because of handicap.

(4) A recipient may not participate in a contractual or other relationship that has the effect of subjecting qualified handicapped applicants or employees to discrimination prohibited by this subpart. The relationships referred to in this paragraph include relationships with employment and referral agencies, with labor unions, with organizations providing or administering fringe benefits to employees of the recipient, and with organizations providing training and apprenticeships.

(b) Specific activities. The provisions of this subpart apply to:

(1) Recruitment, advertising, and the processing of applications for employment;

(2) Hiring, upgrading, promotion, award of tenure, demotion, transfer, layoff, termination, right of return from layoff and rehiring;

(3) Rates of pay or any other form of compensation and changes in compensation;

(4) Job assignments, job classifications, organizational structures, position descriptions, lines of progression, and seniority lists;

(5) Leaves of absense, sick leave, or any other leave;

(6) Fringe benefits available by virtue of employment, whether or not administered by the recipient;

(7) Selection and financial support for training, including apprenticeship, professional meetings, conferences, and other related activities, and selection for leaves of absence to pursue training;

(8) Employer sponsored activities, including those that are social or recreational; and

(9) Any other term, condition, or privilege of employment.

(c) A recipient's obligation to comply with this subpart is not affected by any inconsistent term of any collective bargaining agreement to which it is a party.

§ 104.12 Reasonable accommodation.

(a) A recipient shall make reasonable accommodation to the known physical or mental limitations of an otherwise qualified handicapped applicant or employee unless the recipient can demonstrate that the accommodation would impose an undue hardship on the operation of its program or activity.

(b) Reasonable accommodation may include:

(1) Making facilities used by employees readily accessible to and usable by handicapped persons, and

(2) Job restructuring, part-time or modified work schedules, acquisition or modification of equipment or devices, the provision of readers or interpreters, and other similar actions.

(c) In determining pursuant to paragraph (a) of this section whether an accommodation would impose an undue hardship on the operation of a recipient's program or activity, factors to be considered include:

(1) The overall size of the recipient's program or activity with respect to number of employees, number and type of facilities, and size of budget;

(2) The type of the recipient's operation, including the composition and structure of the recipient's workforce; and

(3) The nature and cost of the accommodation needed.

(d) A recipient may not deny any employment opportunity to a qualified handicapped employee or applicant if the basis for the denial is the need to make reasonable accommodation to the physical or mental limitations of the employee or applicant.

§ 104.13 Employment criteria.

(a) A recipient may not make use of any employment test or other selection criterion that screens out or tends to screen out handicapped persons or any class of handicapped persons unless:

(1) The test score or other selection criterion, as used by the recipient, is shown

to be job-related for the position in question, and

(2) Alternative job-related tests or criteria that do not screen out or tend to screen out as many handicapped persons are not shown by the Director to be available.

(b) A recipient shall select and administer tests concerning employment so as best to ensure that, when administered to an applicant or employee who has a handicap that impairs sensory, manual, or speaking skills, the test results accurately reflect the applicant's or employee's job skills, aptitude, or whatever other factor the test purports to measure, rather than reflecting the applicant's or employee's impaired sensory, manual, or speaking skills (except where those skills are the factors that the test purports to measure).

§ 104.14   Preemployment inquiries.

(a) Except as provided in paragraphs (b) and (c) of this section, a recipient may not conduct a preemployment medical examination or may not make preemployment inquiry of an applicant as to whether the applicant is a handicapped person or as to the nature or severity of a handicap. A recipient may, however, make preemployment inquiry into an applicant's ability to perform job-related functions.

(b) When a recipient is taking remedial action to correct the effects of past discrimination pursuant to § 104.6 (a), when a recipient is taking voluntary action to overcome the effects of conditions that resulted in limited participation in its federally assisted program or activity pursuant to § 104.6(b), or when a recipient is taking affirmative action pursuant to section 503 of the Act, the recipient may invite applicants for employment to indicate whether and to what extent they are handicapped, Provided, That:

(1) The recipient states clearly on any written questionnaire used for this purpose or makes clear orally if no written questionnaire is used that the information requested is intended for use solely in connection with its remedial action obligations or its voluntary or affirmative action efforts; and

(2) The recipient states clearly that the information is being requested on a voluntary basis, that it will be kept confidential as provided in paragraph (d) of this section, that refusal to provide it will not subject the applicant or employee to any adverse treatment, and that it will be used only in accordance with this part.

(c) Nothing in this section shall prohibit a recipient from conditioning an offer of employment on the results of a medical examination conducted prior to the employee's entrance on duty, Provided, That:

(1) All entering employees are subjected to such an examination regardless of handicap, and

(2) The results of such an examination are used only in accordance with the requirements of this part.

(d) Information obtained in accordance with this section as to the medical condition or history of the applicant shall be collected and maintained on separate forms that shall be accorded confidentiality as medical records, except that:

(1) Supervisors and managers may be informed regarding restrictions on the work or duties of handicapped persons and regarding necessary accommodations;

(2) First aid and safety personnel may be informed, where appropriate, if the condition might require emergency treatment; and

(3) Government officials investigating compliance with the Act shall be provided relevant information upon request.

§ 104.21 Discrimination prohibited.

No qualified handicapped person shall, because a recipient's facilities are inaccessible to or unusable by handicapped persons, be denied the benefits of, be excluded from participation in, or otherwise be subjected to discrimination under any program or activity to which this part applies.

§ 104.22 Existing facilities.

(a) Accessibility. A recipient shall operate its program or activity so that when each part is viewed in its entirety, it is readily accessible to handicapped persons. This paragraph does not require a recipient to make each of its existing facilities or every part of a facility accessible to and usable by handicapped persons.

(b) Methods. A recipient may comply with the requirements of paragraph (a) of this section through such means as redesign of equipment, reassignment of classes or other services to accessible buildings, assignment of aides to beneficiaries, home visits, delivery of health, welfare, or other social services at alternate accessible sites, alteration of existing facilities and construction of new facilities in conformance with the requirements of § 104.23, or any other methods that result in making its program or activity accessible to handicapped persons. A recipient is not required to make structural changes in existing facilities where other methods are effective in achieving compliance with paragraph (a) of this section. In choosing among available methods for meeting the requirement of paragraph (a) of this section, a recipient shall give priority to those methods that serve handicapped persons in the most integrated setting appropriate.

(c) Small health, welfare, or other social service providers. If a recipient with fewer than fifteen employees that provides health, welfare, or other social services finds, after consultation with a handicapped person seeking its services, that there is no method of complying with paragraph (a) of this section other than making a significant alteration in its existing facilities, the recipient may, as an alternative, refer the handicapped person to other providers of those services that are accessible.

(d) Time period. A recipient shall comply with the requirement of paragraph (a) of this section within sixty days of the effective date of this part except that where structural changes in facilities are necessary, such changes shall be made within three years of the effective date of this part, but in any event as expeditiously as possible.

(e) Transition plan. In the event that structural changes to facilities are necessary to meet the requirement of paragraph (a) of this section, a recipient shall develop, within six months of the effective date of this part, a transition plan setting forth the steps necessary to complete such changes. The plan shall be developed with the assistance of interested persons, including handicapped persons or organizations representing handicapped persons. A copy of the transition plan shall be made available for public inspection. The plan shall, at a minimum:

(1) Identify physical obstacles in the recipient's facilities that limit the accessibility of its program or activity to handicappped persons;

(2) Describe in detail the methods that will be used to make the facilities accessible;

(3) Specify the schedule for taking the steps necessary to achieve full accessibility in order to comply with paragraph (a) of this section and, if the time period of the transition plan is longer than one year, identify the steps of that will be taken during each year of the transition period; and

(4) Indicate the person responsible for implementation of the plan.

(f) Notice. The recipient shall adopt and implement procedures to ensure that interested persons, including persons with impaired vision or hearing, can obtain information as to the existence and location of services, activities, and facilities that are accessible to and usuable by handicapped persons.

§ 104.23   New construction.

(a) Design and construction. Each facility or part of a facility constructed by, on behalf of, or for the use of a recipient shall be designed and constructed in such manner that the facility or part of the facility is readily accessible to and usable by handicapped persons, if the construction was commenced after the effective date of this part.

(b) Alteration. Each facility or part of a facility which is altered by, on behalf of, or for the use of a recipient after the effective date of this part in a manner that affects or could affect the usability of the facility or part of the facility shall, to the maximum extent feasible, be altered in such manner that the altered portion of the facility is readily accessible to and usable by handicapped persons.

(c) Conformance with Uniform Federal Accessibility Standards.

(1) Effective as of January 18, 1991, design, construction, or alteration of buildings in conformance with sections 3-8 of the Uniform Federal Accessibility Standards (UFAS) (Appendix A to 41 CFR subpart 101-19.6) shall be deemed to comply with the requirements of this section with respect to those buildings. Departures from particular technical and scoping requirements of UFAS by the use of other methods are permitted where substantially equivalent or greater access to and usability of the building is provided.

(2) For purposes of this section, section 4.1.6(1)(g) of UFAS shall be interpreted to exempt from the requirements of UFAS onlu mechanical rooms and other spaces that, because of their intended use, will not require accessibility to the public or beneficiaries or result in the employment or residence therein of persons with phusical handicaps.

(3) This section does not require recipients to make building alterations that have little likelihood of being accomplished without removing or altering a load-bearing structural member.

§ 104.31   Application of this subpart.

Subpart D applies to preschool, elementary, secondary, and adult education programs or activities that receive Federal financial assistance and to recipients that operate, or that receive Federal financial assistance for the operation of, such programs or activities.

§ 104.32   Location and notification.

A recipient that operates a public elementary or secondary education program or activity shall annually:

(a) Undertake to identify and locate every qualified handicapped person residing in the recipient's jurisdiction who is not receiving a public education; and

(b) Take appropriate steps to notify handicapped persons and their parents or guardians of the recipient's duty under this subpart.

§ 104.33   Free appropriate public education.

(a) General. A recipient that operates a public elementary or secondary education program or activity shall provide a free appropriate public education to each qualified handicapped person who is in the recipient's jurisdiction, regardless of the nature or severity of the person's handicap.

(b) Appropriate education.

(1) For the purpose of this subpart, the provision of an appropriate education is the provision of regular or special education and related aids and services that (i) are designed to meet individual educational needs of handicapped persons as adequately as the needs of nonhandicapped persons are met and (ii) are based upon adherence to procedures that satisfy the requirements of §§ 104.34, 104.35, and 104.36.

(2) Implementation of an Individualized Education Program developed in accordance with the Education of the Handicapped Act is one means of meeting the standard established in paragraph (b)(1)(i) of this section.

(3) A recipient may place a handicapped person or refer such a person for aid, benefits, or services other than those that it operates or provides as its means of carrying out the requirements of this subpart. If so, the recipient remains responsible for ensuring that the requirements of this subpart are met with respect to any handicapped person so placed or referred.

(c) Free education —

(1) General. For the purpose of this section, the provision of a free education is the provision of educational and related services without cost to the handicapped person or to his or her parents or guardian, except for those fees that are imposed on non-handicapped persons or their parents or guardian. It may consist either of the provision of free services or, if a recipient places a handicapped

person or refers such person for aid, benefits, or services not operated or provided by the recipient as its means of carrying out the requirements of this subpart, of payment for the costs of the aid, benefits, or services. Funds available from any public or private agency may be used to meet the requirements of this subpart. Nothing in this section shall be construed to relieve an insurer or similar third party from an otherwise valid obligation to provide or pay for services provided to a handicapped person.

(2) *Transportation.* If a recipient places a handicapped person or refers such person for aid, benefits, or services not operated or provided by the recipient as its means of carrying out the requirements of this subpart, the recipient shall ensure that adequate transportation to and from the aid, benefits, or services is provided at no greater cost than would be incurred by the person or his or her parents or guardian if the person were placed in the aid, benefits, or services operated by the recipient.

(3) *Residential placement.* If a public or private residential placement is necessary to provide a free appropriate public education to a handicapped person because of his or her handicap, the placement, including non-medical care and room and board, shall be provided at no cost to the person or his or her parents or guardian.

(4) *Placement of handicapped persons by parents.* If a recipient has made available, in conformance with the requirements of this section and § 104.34, a free appropriate public education to a handicapped person and the person's parents or guardian choose to place the person in a private school, the recipient is not required to pay for the person's education in the private school. Disagreements between a parent or guardian and a recipient regarding whether the recipient has made a free appropriate public education available or otherwise regarding the question of financial responsibility are subject to the due process procedures of § 104.36.

(d) *Compliance.* A recipient may not exclude any qualified handicapped person from a public elementary or secondary education after the effective date of this part. A recipient that is not, on the effective date of this regulation, in full compliance with the other requirements of the preceding paragraphs of this section shall meet such requirements at the earliest practicable time and in no event later than September 1, 1978.

§ 104.34   Educational setting.

(a) *Academic setting.* A recipient to which this subpart applies shall educate, or shall provide for the education of, each qualified handicapped person in its jurisdiction with persons who are not handicapped to the maximum extent appropriate to the needs of the handicapped person. A recipient shall place a handicapped person in the regular educational environment operated by the recipient unless it is demonstrated by the recipient that the education of the person in the regular environment with the use of supplementary aids and services cannot be achieved satisfactorily. Whenever a recipient places a person in a setting other than the regular educational environment pursuant to this paragraph, it shall take into account the proximity of the alternate setting to the person's home.

(b) Nonacademic settings. In providing or arranging for the provision of nonacademic and extracurricular services and activities, including meals, recess periods, and the services and activities set forth in § 104.37(a)(2), a recipient shall ensure that handicapped persons participate with nonhandicapped persons in such activities and services to the maximum extent appropriate to the needs of the handicapped person in question.

(c) Comparable facilities. If a recipient, in compliance with paragraph (a) of this section, operates a facility that is identifiable as being for handicapped persons, the recipient shall ensure that the facility and the services and activities provided therein are comparable to the other facilities, services, and activities of the recipient.

§ 104.35   Evaluation and placement.

(a) Preplacement evaluation. A recipient that operates a public elementary or secondary education program or activity shall shall conduct an evaluation in accordance with the requirements of paragraph (b) of this section of any person who, because of handicap, needs or is belived to need special education or related services before taking any action with respect to the initial placement of the person in regular or special education and any subsequent significant change in placement.

(b) Evaluation procedures. A recipient to which this subpart applies shall establish standards and procedures for the evaluation and placement of persons who, because of handicap, need or are believed to need special education or related services which ensure that:

(1) Tests and other evaluation materials have been validated for the specific purpose for which they are used and are administered by trained personnel in conformance with the instructions provided by their producer;

(2) Tests and other evaluation materials include those tailored to assess specific areas of educational need and not merely those which are designed to provide a single general intelligence quotient; and

(3) Tests are selected and administered so as best to ensure that, when a test is administered to a student with impaired sensory, manual, or speaking skills, the test results accurately reflect the student's aptitude or achievement level or whatever other factor the test purports to measure, rather than reflecting the student's impaired sensory, manual, or speaking skills (except where those skills are the factors that the test purports to measure).

(c) Placement procedures. In interpreting evaluation data and in making placement decisions, a recipient shall (1) draw upon information from a variety of sources, including aptitude and achievement tests, teacher recommendations, physical condition, social or cultural background, and adaptive behavior, (2) establish procedures to ensure that information obtained from all such sources is documented and carefully considered, (3) ensure that the placement decision is made by a group of persons, including persons knowledgeable about the child, the meaning of the evaluation data, and the placement options, and (4) ensure that the placement decision is made in conformity with § 104.34.

(d) Reevaluation. A recipient to which this section applies shall establish procedures, in accordance with paragraph (b) of this section, for periodic reevaluation of students who have been provided special education and related services. A reevaluation procedure consistent with the Education for the Handicapped Act is one means of meeting this requirement.

§ 104.36   Procedural safeguards.

A recipient that operates a public elementary or secondary education program or activity shall establish and implement, with respect to actions regarding the identification, evaluation, or educational placement of persons who, because of handicap, need or are believed to need special instruction or related services, a system of procedural safeguards that includes notice, an opportunity for the parents or guardian of the person to examine relevant records, an impartial hearing with opportunity for participation by the person's parents or guardian and representation by counsel, and a review procedure. Compliance with the procedural safeguards of section 615 of the Education of the Handicapped Act is one means of meeting this requirement.

§ 104.37   Nonacademic services.

(a) General.

(1) A recipient to which this subpart applies shall provide non-academic and extracurricular services and activities in such manner as is necessary to afford handicapped students an equal opportunity for participation in such services and activities.

(2) Nonacademic and extracurricular services and activities may include counseling services, physical recreational athletics, transportation, health services, recreational activities, special interest groups or clubs sponsored by the recipients, referrals to agencies which provide assistance to handicapped persons, and employment of students, including both employment by the recipient and assistance in making available outside employment.

(b) Counseling services. A recipient to which this subpart applies that provides personal, academic, or vocational counseling, guidance, or placement services to its students shall provide these services without discrimination on the basis of handicap. The recipient shall ensure that qualified handicapped students are not counseled toward more restrictive career objectives than are nonhandicapped students with similar interests and abilities.

(c) Physical education and athletics.

(1) In providing physical education courses and athletics and similar aid, benefits, or services to any of its students, a recipient to which this subpart applies may not discriminate on the basis of handicap. A recipient that offers physical education courses or that operates or sponsors interscholastic, club, or intramural athletics shall provide to qualified handicapped students an equal opportunity for participation.

(2) A recipient may offer to handicapped students physical education and athletic activities that are separate or different from those offered to nonhandicapped students only if separation or differentiation is consistent with the

requirements of § 104.34 and only if no qualified handicapped student is denied the opportunity to compete for teams or to participate in courses that are not separate or different.

§ 104.38 Preschool and adult education.

A recipient to which this subpart applies that provides preschool education or day care or adult education may not, on the basis of handicap, exclude qualified handicapped persons and shall take into account the needs of such persons in determining the aid, benefits or services to be provided.

§ 104.39 Private education.

(a) A recipient that provides private elementary or secondary education may not, on the basis of handicap, exclude a qualified handicapped person if the person can, with minor adjustments, be provided an appropriate education, as defined in § 104.33(b)(1), within that recipient's program or activity.

(b) A recipient to which this section applies may not charge more for the provision of an appropriate education to handicapped persons than to nonhandicapped persons except to the extent that any additional charge is justified by a substantial increase in cost to the recipient.

(c) A recipient to which this section applies that provides special education shall do so in accordance with the provisions of §§ 104.35 and 104.36. Each recipient to which this section applies is subject to the provisions of §§ 104.34, 104.37, and 104.38.

§ 104.41 Application of this subpart.

Subpart E applies to postsecondary education programs or activities, including postsecondary vocational education programs or activities, that receive Federal financial assistance and to recipients that operate, or that receive Federal financial assistance for the operation of, such programs or activities.

§ 104.42 Admissions and recruitment.

(a) General. Qualified handicapped persons may not, on the basis of handicap, be denied admission or be subjected to discrimination in admission or recruitment by a recipient to which this subpart applies.

(b) Admissions. In administering its admission policies, a recipient to which this subpart applies:

(1) May not apply limitations upon the number or proportion of handicapped persons who may be admitted;

(2) May not make use of any test or criterion for admission that has a disproportionate, adverse effect on handicapped persons or any class of handicapped persons unless (i) the test or criterion, as used by the recipient, has been validated as a predictor of success in the education program or activity in question and (ii) alternate tests or criteria that have a less disproportionate, adverse effect are not shown by the Assistant Secretary to be available.

(3) Shall assure itself that (i) admissions tests are selected and administered so

as best to ensure that, when a test is administered to an applicant who has a handicap that impairs sensory, manual, or speaking skills, the test results accurately reflect the applicant's aptitude or achievement level or whatever other factor the test purports to measure, rather than reflecting the applicant's impaired sensory, manual, or speaking skills (except where those skills are the factors that the test purports to measure); (ii) admissions tests that are designed for persons with impaired sensory, manual, or speaking skills are offered as often and in as timely a manner as are other admissions tests; and (iii) admissions tests are administered in facilities that, on the whole, are accessible to handicapped persons; and

(4) Except as provided in paragraph (c) of this section, may not make preadmission inquiry as to whether an applicant for admission is a handicapped person but, after admission, may make inquiries on a confidential basis as to handicaps that may require accommodation.

(c) Preadmission inquiry exception. When a recipient is taking remedial action to correct the effects of past discrimination pursuant to § 104.6(a) or when a recipient is taking voluntary action to overcome the effects of conditions that resulted in limited participation in its federally assisted program or activity pursuant to § 104.6(b), the recipient may invite applicants for admission to indicate whether and to what extent they are handicapped, Provided, That:

(1) The recipient states clearly on any written questionnaire used for this purpose or makes clear orally if no written questionnaire is used that the information requested is intended for use solely in connection with its remedial action obligations or its voluntary action efforts; and

(2) The recipient states clearly that the information is being requested on a voluntary basis, that it will be kept confidential, that refusal to provide it will not subject the applicant to any adverse treatment, and that it will be used only in accordance with this part.

(d) Validity studies. For the purpose of paragraph (b)(2) of this section, a recipient may base prediction equations on first year grades, but shall conduct periodic validity studies against the criterion of overall success in the education program or activity in question in order to monitor the general validity of the test scores.

§ 104.43   Treatment of students; general.

(a) No qualified handicapped student shall, on the basis of handicap, be excluded from participation in, be denied the benefits of, or otherwise be subjected to discrimination under any academic, research, occupational training, housing, health insurance, counseling, financial aid, physical education, athletics, recreation, transportation, other extracurricular, or other postsecondary education aid, benefits, or services to which this subpart applies.

(b) A recipient to which this subpart applies that considers participation by students in education programs or activities not operated wholly by the recipient as part of, or equivalent to, and education program or activity operated by the recipient shall assure itself that the other education program or activity, as a whole, provides an equal opportunity for the participation of qualified handicapped persons.

(c) A recipient to which this subpart applies may not, on the basis of handicap, exclude any qualified handicapped student from any course, course of study, or other part of its education program or activity.

(d) A recipient to which this subpart applies shall operate its program or activity in the most integrated setting appropriate.

§ 104.44   Academic adjustments.

(a) Academic requirements. A recipient to which this subpart applies shall make such modifications to its academic requirements as are necessary to ensure that such requirements do not discriminate or have the effect of discriminating, on the basis of handicap, against a qualified handicapped applicant or student. Academic requirements that the recipient can demonstrate are essential to the instruction being pursued by such student or to any directly related licensing requirement will not be regarded as discriminatory within the meaning of this section. Modifications may include changes in the length of time permitted for the completion of degree requirements, substitution of specific courses required for the completion of degree requirements, and adaptation of the manner in which specific courses are conducted.

(b) Other rules. A recipient to which this subpart applies may not impose upon handicapped students other rules, such as the prohibition of tape recorders in classrooms or of dog guides in campus buildings, that have the effect of limiting the participation of handicapped students in the recipient's education program or activity.

(c) Course examinations. In its course examinations or other procedures for evaluating students' academic achievement, a recipient to which this subpart applies shall provide such methods for evaluating the achievement of students who have a handicap that impairs sensory, manual, or speaking skills as will best ensure that the results of the evaluation represents the student's achievement in the course, rather than reflecting the student's impaired sensory, manual, or speaking skills (except where such skills are the factors that the test purports to measure).

(d) Auxiliary aids.

(1) A recipient to which this subpart applies shall take such steps as are necessary to ensure that no handicapped student is denied the benefits of, excluded from participation in, or otherwise subjected to discrimination because of the absence of educational auxiliary aids for students with impaired sensory, manual, or speaking skills.

(2) Auxiliary aids may include taped texts, interpreters or other effective methods of making orally delivered materials available to students with hearing impairments, readers in libraries for students with visual impairments, classroom equipment adapted for use by students with manual impairments, and other similar services and actions. Recipients need not provide attendants, individually prescribed devices, readers for personal use or study, or other devices or services of a personal nature.

§ 104.45   Housing.

(a) Housing provided by the recipient. A recipient that provides housing to its nonhandicapped students shall provide comparable, convenient, and accessible housing to handicapped students at the same cost as to others. At the end of the transition period provided for in Subpart C, such housing shall be available in sufficient quantity and variety so that the scope of handicapped students' choice of living accommodations is, as a whole, comparable to that of nonhandicapped students.

(b) Other housing. A recipient that assists any agency, organization, or person in making housing available to any of its students shall take such action as may be necessary to assure itself that such housing is, as a whole, made available in a manner that does not result in discrimination on the basis of handicap.

§ 104.46   Financial and employment assistance to students.

(a) Provision of financial assistance.

(1) In providing financial assistance to qualified handicapped persons, a recipient to which this subpart applies may not,

(i) On the basis of handicap, provide less assistance than is provided to nonhandicapped persons, limit eligibility for assistance, or otherwise discriminate or

(ii) Assist any entity or person that provides assistance to any of the recipient's students in a manner that discriminates against qualified handicapped persons on the basis of handicap.

(2) A recipient may administer or assist in the administration of scholarships, fellowships, or other forms of financial assistance established under wills, trusts, bequests, or similar legal instruments that require awards to be made on the basis of factors that discriminate or have the effect of discriminating on the basis of handicap only if the overall effect of the award of scholarships, fellowships, and other forms of financial assistance is not discriminatory on the basis of handicap.

(b) Assistance in making available outside employment. A recipient that assists any agency, organization, or person in providing employment opportunities to any of its students shall assure itself that such employment opportunities, as a whole, are made available in a manner that would not violate subpart B if they were provided by the recipient.

(c) Employment of students by recipients. A recipient that employs any of its students may not do so in a manner that violates subpart B.

§ 104.47   Nonacademic services.

(a) Physical education and athletics.

(1) In providing physical education courses and athletics and similar aid, benefits, or services to any of its students, a recipient to which this subpart applies may not discriminate on the basis of handicap. A recipient that offers physical education courses or that operates or sponsors intercollegiate, club, or

intramural athletics shall provide to qualified handicapped students an equal opportunity for participation in these activities.

(2) A recipient may offer to handicapped students physical education and athletic activities that are separate or different only if separation or differentiation is consistent with the requirements of § 104.43(d) and only if no qualified handicapped student is denied the opportunity to compete for teams or to participate in courses that are not separate or different.

(b) Counseling and placement services. A recipient to which this subpart applies that provides personal, academic, or vocational counseling, guidance, or placement services to its students shall provide these services without discrimination on the basis of handicap. The recipient shall ensure that qualified handicapped students are not counseled toward more restrictive career objectives than are nonhandicapped students with similar interests and abilities. This requirement does not preclude a recipient from providing factual information about licensing and certification requirements that may present obstacles to handicapped persons in their pursuit of particular careers.

(c) Social organizations. A recipient that provides significant assistance to fraternities, sororities, or similar organizations shall assure itself that the membership practices of such organizations do not permit discrimination otherwise prohibited by this subpart.

§ 104.51 Application of this subpart.

Subpart F applies to health, welfare, and other social service programs or activities that receive Federal financial assistance and to recipients that operate, or that receive Federal financial assistance for the operation of, such programs or activities.

§ 104.52 Health, welfare, and other social services.

(a) General. In providing health, welfare, or other social services or benefits, a recipient may not, on the basis of handicap:

(1) Deny a qualified handicapped person these benefits or services;

(2) Afford a qualified handicapped person an opportunity to receive benefits or services that is not equal to that offered nonhandicapped persons;

(3) Provide a qualified handicapped person with benefits or services that are not as effective (as defined in § 104.4(b)) as the benefits or services provided to others;

(4) Provide benefits or services in a manner that limits or has the effect of limiting the participation of qualified handicapped persons; or

(5) Provide different or separate benefits or services to handicapped persons except where necessary to provide qualified handicapped persons with benefits and services that are as effective as those provided to others.

(b) Notice. A recipient that provides notice concerning benefits or services or written material concerning waivers of rights or consent to treatment shall take such steps as are necessary to ensure that qualified handicapped persons, including those with impaired sensory or speaking skills, are not denied effective notice because of their handicap.

(c) Emergency treatment for the hearing impaired. A recipient hospital that provides health services or benefits shall establish a procedure for effective communication with persons with impaired hearing for the purpose of providing emergency health care.

(d) Auxiliary aids.

(1) A recipient to which this subpart applies that employs fifteen or more persons shall provide appropriate auxiliary aids to persons with impaired sensory, manual, or speaking skills, where necessary to afford such persons an equal opportunity to benefit from the service in question.

(2) The Assistant Secretary may require recipients with fewer than fifteen employees to provide auxiliary aids where the provision of aids would not significantly impair the ability of the recipient to provide its benefits or services.

(3) For the purpose of this paragraph, auxiliary aids may include brailled and taped material, interpreters, and other aids for persons with impaired hearing or vision.

§ 104.53 Drug and alcohol addicts.

A recipient to which this subpart applies that operates a general hospital or outpatient facility may not discriminate in admission or treatment against a drug or alcohol abuser or alcoholic who is suffering from a medical condition, because of the person's drug or alcohol abuse or alcoholism.

§ 104.54 Education of institutionalized persons.

A recipient to which this subpart applies and that operates or supervises a program or activity that provides aid, benefits or services for persons who are institutionalized because of handicap shall ensure that each qualified handicapped person, as defined in § 104.3(k)(2), in its program or activity is provided an appropriate education, as defined in § 104.33(b). Nothing in this section shall be interpreted as altering in any way the obligations of recipients under subpart D.

§ 104.61 Procedures.

The procedural provisions applicable to title VI of the Civil Rights Act of 1964 apply to this part. These procedures are found in §§ 100.6-100.10 and part 101 of this title.

34 CFR PART 104 APPENDIX A

APPENDIX A TO PART 104 — ANALYSIS OF FINAL REGULATION

SUBPART A — GENERAL PROVISIONS

Definitions —

1. Recipient. Section 104.23 contains definitions used throughout the regulation.

One comment requested that the regulation specify that nonpublic elementary and secondary schools that are not otherwise recipients do not become recipients by virtue of the fact their students participate in certain federally funded programs. The Secretary believes it unnecessary to amend the regulation in this regard, because almost identical language in the Department's regulations implementing title VI and title IX of the Education Amendments of 1972 has consistently been interpreted so as not to render such schools recipients. These schools, however, are indirectly subject to the substantive requirements of this regulation through the application of § 104.4(b)(iv), which prohibits recipients from assisting agencies that discriminate on the basis of handicap in providing services to beneficiaries of the recipients' programs.

2. Federal financial assistance. In § 104.3(h), defining federal financial assistance, a clarifying change has been made: procurement contracts are specifically excluded. They are covered, however, by the Department of Labor's regulation under section 503. The Department has never considered such contracts to be contracts of assistance; the explicit exemption has been added only to avoid possible confusion.

The proposed regulation's exemption of contracts of insurance or guaranty has been retained. A number of comments argued for its deletion on the ground that section 504, unlike title VI and title IX, contains no statutory exemption for such contracts. There is no indication, however, in the legislative history of the Rehabilitation Act of 1973 or of the amendments to that Act in 1974, that Congress intended section 504 to have a broader application, in terms of federal financial assistance, than other civil rights statutes. Indeed, Congress directed that section 504 be implemented in the same manner as titles VI and IX. In view of the long established exemption of contracts of insurance or guaranty under title VI, we think it unlikely that Congress intended section 504 to apply to such contracts.

3. Handicapped person. Section 104.3(j), which defines the class of persons protected under the regulation, has not been substantially changed. The definition of handicapped person in paragraph (j)(1) conforms to the statutory definition of handicapped person that is applicable to section 504, as set forth in section 111(a) of the Rehabilitation Act Amendments of 1974, Pub. L. 93-516.

The first of the three parts of the statutory and regulatory definition includes any person who has a physical or mental impairment that substantially limits one or more major life activities. Paragraph (j)(2)(i) further defines physical or mental impairments. The definition does not set forth a list of specific diseases and conditions that constitute physical or mental impairments because of the difficulty of ensuring the comprehensiveness of any such list. The term includes, however, such diseases and conditions as orthopedic, visual, speech, and hearing impairments, cerebral palsy, epilepsy, muscular dystrophy, multiple sclerosis, cancer, heart disease, diabetes, mental retardation, emotional illness, and, as discussed below, drug addiction and alcoholism.

It should be emphasized that a physical or mental impairment does not constitute a handicap for purposes of section 504 unless its severity is such that it results in a substantial limitation of one or more major life activities. Several comments observed the lack of any definition in the proposed regulation of the phrase "substantially limits." The Department does not believe that a definition of this term is possible at this time.

A related issue raised by several comments is whether the definition of handicapped person is unreasonably broad. Comments suggested narrowing the definition in various ways. The most common recommendation was that only "traditional" handicaps be covered. The Department continues to believe, however, that it has no flexibility within the statutory definition to limit the term to persons who have those severe, permanent, or progressive conditions that are most commonly regarded as handicaps. The Department intends, however, to give particular attention in its enforcement of section 504 to eliminating discrimination against persons with the severe handicaps that were the focus of concern in the Rehabilitation Act of 1973.

The definition of handicapped person also includes specific limitations on what persons are classified as handicapped under the regulation. The first of the three parts of the definition specifies that only physical and mental handicaps are included. Thus, environmental, cultural, and economic disadvantage are not in themselves covered; nor are prison records, age, or homosexuality. Of course, if a person who has any of these characteristics also has a physical or mental handicap, the person is included within the definition of handicapped person.

In paragraph (j)(2)(i), physical or mental impairment is defined to include, among other impairments, specific learning disabilities. The Department will interpret the term as it is used in section 602 of the Education of the Handicapped Act, as amended. Paragraph (15) of section 602 uses the term "specific learning disabilities" to describe such conditions as perceptual handicaps, brain injury, minimal brain dysfunction, dyslexia, and developmental aphasia.

Paragraph (j)(2)(i) has been shortened, but not substantively changed, by the deletion of clause (C), which made explicit the inclusion of any condition which is mental or physical but whose precise nature is not at present known. Clauses (A) and (B) clearly comprehend such conditions.

The second part of the statutory and regulatory definition of handicapped person includes any person who has a record of a physical or mental impairment that substantially limits a major life activity. Under the definition of "record" in paragraph (j)(2)(iii), persons who have a history of a handicapping condition but no longer have the condition, as well as persons who have been incorrectly classified as having such a condition, are protected from discrimination under section 504. Frequently occurring examples of the first group are persons with histories of mental or emotional illness, heart disease, or cancer; of the second group, persons who have been misclassified as mentally retarded.

The third part of the statutory and regulatory definition of handicapped person includes any person who is regarded as having a physical or mental impairment that substantially limits one or more major life activities. It includes many persons who are ordinarily considered to be handicapped but who do not technically fall within the first two parts of the statutory definition, such as persons with a limp. This part of the definition also includes some persons who might not ordinarily be considered handicapped, such as persons with disfiguring scars, as well as persons who have no physical or mental impairment but are treated by a recipient as if they were handicapped.

    4. Drug addicts and alcoholics. As was the case during the first comment period,

the issue of whether to include drug addicts and alcoholics within the definition of handicapped person was of major concern to many commenters. The arguments presented on each side of the issue were similar during the two comment periods, as was the preference of commenters for exclusion of this group of persons. While some comments reflected misconceptions about the implications of including alcoholics and drug addicts within the scope of the regulation, the Secretary understands the concerns that underlie the comments on this question and recognizes that application of section 504 to active alcoholics and drug addicts presents sensitive and difficult questions that must be taken into account in interpretation and enforcement.

The Secretary has carefully examined the issue and has obtained a legal opinion from the Attorney General. That opinion concludes that drug addiction and alcoholism are "physical or mental impairments" within the meaning of section 7(6) of the Rehabilitation Act of 1973, as amended, and that drug addicts and alcoholics are therefore handicapped for purposes of section 504 if their impairment substantially limits one of their major life activities. The Secretary therefore believes that he is without authority to exclude these conditions from the definition. There is a medical and legal consensus that alcoholism and drug addiction are diseases, although there is disagreement as to whether they are primarily mental or physical. In addition, while Congress did not focus specifically on the problems of drug addiction and alcoholism in enacting section 504, the committees that considered the Rehabilitation Act of 1973 were made aware of the Department's long-standing practice of treating addicts and alcoholics as handicapped individuals eligible for rehabilitation services under the Vocational Rehabilitation Act.

The Secretary wishes to reassure recipients that inclusion of addicts and alcoholics within the scope of the regulation will not lead to the consequences feared by many commenters. It cannot be emphasized too strongly that the statute and the regulation apply only to discrimination against qualified handicapped persons solely by reason of their handicap. The fact that drug addiction and alcoholism may be handicaps does not mean that these conditions must be ignored in determining whether an individual is qualified for services or employment opportunities. On the contrary, a recipient may hold a drug addict or alcoholic to the same standard of performance and behavoir to which it holds others, even if any unsatisfactory performance or behavior is related to the person's drug addiction or alcoholism. In other words, while an alcoholic or drug addict may not be denied services or disqualified from employment solely because of his or her condition, the behavioral manifestations of the condition may be taken into account in determining whether he or she is qualified.

With respect to the employment of a drug addict or alcoholic, if it can be shown that the addiction or alcoholism prevents sucessful performance of the job, the person need not be provided the employment opportunity in question. For example, in making employment decisions, a recipient may judge addicts and alcoholics on the same basis it judges all other applicants and employees. Thus, a recipient may consider — for all applicants including drug addicts and alcoholics — past personnel records, absenteeism, disruptive, abusive, or dangerous behavior, violations of rules and unsatisfactory work performance. Moreover, employers may enforce rules prohibiting the possession or use of alcohol or drugs in the work-place, provided that such rules are enforced against all employees.

With respect to other services, the implications of coverage, of alcoholics and drug addicts are two-fold: first, no person may be excluded from services solely by reason of the presence or history of these conditions; second, to the extent that the manifestations of the condition prevent the person from meeting the basic eligibility requirements of the program or cause substantial interference with the operation of the program, the condition may be taken into consideration. Thus, a college may not exclude an addict or alcoholic as a student, on the basis of addiction or alcoholism, if the person can successfully participate in the education program and complies with the rules of the college and if his or her behavior does not impede the performance of other students.

Of great concern to many commenters was the question of what effect the inclusion of drug addicts and alcoholics as handicapped persons would have on school disciplinary rules prohibiting the use or possession of drugs or alcohol by students. Neither such rules nor their application to drug addicts or alcoholics is prohibited by this regulation, provided that the rules are enforced evenly with respect to all students.

5. Qualified handicapped person. Paragraph (k) of § 104.3 defines the term "qualified handicapped person." Throughout the regulation, this term is used instead of the statutory term "otherwise qualified handicapped person." The Department believes that the omission of the word "otherwise" is necessary in order to comport with the intent of the statute because, read literally, "otherwise" qualified handicapped persons include persons who are qualified except for their handicap, rather than in spite of their handicap. Under such a literal reading, a blind person possessing all the qualifications for driving a bus except sight could be said to be "otherwise qualified" for the job of driving. Clearly, such a result was not intended by Congress. In all other respects, the terms "qualified" and "otherwise qualified" are intended to be interchangeable.

Section 104.3(k)(1) defines a qualified handicapped person with respect to employment as a handicapped person who can, with reasonable accommodation, perform the essential functions of the job in question. The term "essential functions" does not appear in the corresponding provision of the Department of Labor's section 503 regulation, and a few commenters objected to its inclusion on the ground that a handicapped person should be able to perform all job tasks. However, the Department believes that inclusion of the phrase is useful in emphasizing that handicapped persons should not be disqualified simply because they may have difficulty in performing tasks that bear only a marginal relationship to a particular job. Further, we are convinced that inclusion of the phrase is not inconsistent with the Department of Labor's application of its definition.

Certain commenters urged that the definition of qualified handicapped person be amended so as explicitly to place upon the employer the burden of showing that a particular mental or physical characteristic is essential. Because the same result is achieved by the requirement contained in paragraph (a) of § 104.13, which requires an employer to establish that any selection criterion that tends to screen out handicapped persons is job-related, that recommendation has not been followed.

Section 104.3(k)(2) defines qualified handicapped person, with respect to preschool, elementary, and secondary programs, in terms of age. Several commenters recommended that eligibility for the services be based upon the standard of substantial benefit, rather than age, because of the need of many handicapped children for early or extended services if they are to have an equal opportunity to benefit from education programs. No change has been made in this provision, again because of the extreme difficulties in administration that would result from the choice of the former standard. Under the remedial action provisions of § 104.6(a)(3), however, persons beyond the age limits prescribed in § 104.3(k)(2) may in appropriate cases be required to be provided services that they were formerly denied because of a recipient's violation of section 504.

Section 104.3(k)(2) states that a handicapped person is qualified for preschool, elementary, or secondary services if the person is of an age at which nonhandicapped persons are eligible for such services or at which State law mandates the provision of educational services to handicapped persons. In addition, the extended age ranges for which recipients must provide full educational opportunity to all handicapped persons in order to be eligible for assistance under the Education of the Handicapped Act — generally, 3-18 as of September 1978, and 3-21 as of September 1980 are incorporated by reference in this paragraph.

Section 104.3(k)(3) defines qualified handicapped person with respect to postsecondary educational programs. As revised, the paragraph means that both academic and technical standards must be met by applicants to these programs. The term technical standards refers to all nonacademic admissions criteria that are essential to participation in the program in question.

6. General prohibitions against discrimination. Section 104.4 contains general prohibitions against discrimination applicable to all recipients of assistance from this Department.

Paragraph (b)(1)(i) Prohibits the exclusion of qualified handicapped persons from aids, benefits, or services, and paragraph (ii) requires that equal opportunity to participate or benefit be provided. Paragraph (iii) requires that services provided to handicapped persons be as effective as those provided to the nonhandicapped. In paragraph (iv), different or separate services are prohibited except when necessary to provide equally effective benefits.

In this context, the term "equally effective," defined in paragraph (b)(2), is intended to encompass the concept of equivalent, as opposed to identical, services and to acknowledge the fact that in order to meet the individual needs of handicapped persons to the same extent that the corresponding needs of nonhandicapped persons are met, adjustments to regular programs or the provisions of different programs may sometimes be necessary. This standard parallels the one established under title VI of Civil Rights Act of 1964 with respect to the provision of educational services to students whose primary language is not English. See Lau v. Nichols, 414 U.S. 563 (1974).To be equally effective, however, an aid, benefit, or service need not produce equal results; it merely must afford an equal opportunity to achieve equal results.

It must be emphasized that, although separate services must be required in some instances, the provision of unnecessarily separate or different services is discriminatory. The addition to paragraph (b)(2) of the phrase "in the most integrated setting appropriated to the person's needs" in intended to reinforce this general concept. A new paragraph (b)(3) has also been added to § 104.4, requiring recipients to give qualified handicapped persons the option of participating in regular programs despite the existence of permissibly separate or different programs. The requirement has been reiterated in §§ 104.38 and 104.47 in connection with physical education and athletics programs.

Section 104.4(b)(1)(v) prohibits a recipient from supporting another entity or person that subjects participants or employees in the recipient's program to discrimination on the basis of handicap. This section would, for example, prohibit financial support by a recipient to a community recreational group or to a professional or social organization that discriminates against handicapped persons. Among the criteria to be considered in each case are the substantiality of the relationship between the recipient and the other entity, including financial support by the recipient, and whether the other entity's activities relate so closely to the recipient's program or activity that they fairly should be considered activities of the recipient itself. Paragraph (b)(1)(vi) was added in response to comment in order to make explicit the prohibition against denying qualified handicapped persons the opportunity to serve on planning and advisory boards responsible for guiding federally assisted programs or activities.

Several comments appeared to interpret § 104.4(b)(5), which proscribes discriminatory site selection, to prohibit a recipient that is located on hilly terrain from erecting any new buildings at its present site. That, of course, is not the case. This paragraph is not intended to apply to construction of additional buildings at an existing site. Of course, any such facilities must be made accessible in accordance with the requirements of § 104.23.

7. Assurances of compliance. Section 104.5(a) requires a recipient to submit to the Assistant Secretary an assurance that each of its programs and activities receiving or benefiting from Federal financial assistance from this Department will be conducted in compliance with this regulation. Many commenters also sought relief from the paperwork requirements imposed by the Department's enforcement of its various civil rights responsibilities by requesting the Department to issue one form incorporating title VI, title IX, and section 504 assurances. The Secretary is sympathetic to this request. While it is not feasible to adopt a single civil rights assurance form at this time, the Office for Civil Rights will work toward that goal.

8. Private rights of action. Several comments urged that the regulation incorporate provision granting beneficiaries a private right of action against recipients under section 504. To confer such a right is beyond the authority of the executive branch of Government. There is, however, case law holding that such a right exists. Lloyd v. Regional Transportation Authority, 548 F. 2d 1277 (7th Cir. 1977); see Hairston v. Drosick, Civil No. 75-0691 (S.D. W. Va., Jan. 14, 1976); Gurmankin v. Castanzo, 411 F. Supp. 982 (E.D. Pa. 1976); cf. Lau v. Nichols, supra.

9. Remedial action. Where there has been a finding of discrimination, § 104.6 requires a recipient to take remedial action to overcome the effects of the discrimination. Actions that might be required under paragraph (a)(1) include provision of services to persons previously discriminated against, reinstatement of employees and development of a remedial action plan. Should a recipient fail to take required remedial action, the ultimate sanctions of court action or termination of

Federal financial assistance may be imposed.

Paragraph (a)(2) extends the responsibility for taking remedial action to a recipient that exercises control over a noncomplying recipient. Paragraph (a)(3) also makes clear that handicapped persons who are not in the program at the time that remedial action is required to be taken may also be the subject of such remedial action. This paragraph has been revised in response to comments in order to include persons who would have been in the program if discriminatory practices had not existed. Paragraphs (a) (1), (2), and (3) have also been amended in response to comments to make plain that, in appropriate cases, remedial action might be required to redress clear violations of the statute itself that occurred before the effective date of this regulation.

10. Voluntary action. In § 104.6(b), the term "voluntary action" has been substituted for the term "affirmative action" because the use of the latter term led to some confusion. We believe the term "voluntary action" more accurately reflects the purpose of the paragraph. This provision allows action, beyond that required by the regulation, to overcome conditions that led to limited participation by handicapped persons, whether or not the limited participation was caused by any discriminatory actions on the part of the recipient. Several commenters urged that paragraphs (a) and (b) be revised to require remedial action to overcome effects of prior discriminatory practices regardless of whether there has been an express finding of discrimination. The self-evaluation requirement in paragraph (c) accomplishes must the same purpose.

11. Self-evaluation. Paragraph (c) requires recipients to conduct a self-evaluation in order to determine whether their policies or practices may discriminate against handicapped persons and to take steps to modify and discriminatory policies and practices and their effects. The Department received many comments approving of the addition to paragraph (c) of a requirement that recipients seek the assistance of handicapped persons in the self-evaluation process. This paragraph has been further amended to require consultation with handicapped persons or organizations representing them before recipients undertake the policy modifications and remedial steps prescribed in paragraphs (c) (ii) and (iii).

Paragraph (c)(2), which sets forth the recordkeeping requirements concerning self-evaluation, now applies only to recipients with fifteen or more employees. This change was made as part of an effort to reduce unnecessary or counterproductive administrative obligations on small recipients. For those recipients required to keep records, the requirements have been made more specific; records must include a list of persons consulted and a description of areas examined, problems identified, and corrective steps taken. Moreover, the records must be made available for public inspection.

12. Grievance procedure. Section 104.7 requires recipients with fifteen or more employees to designate an individual responsible for coordinating its compliance efforts and to adopt a grievance procedure. Two changes were made in the section in response to comment. A general requirement that appropriate due process procedures be followed has been added. It was decided that the details of such procedures could not at this time be specified because of the varied nature of the persons and entities who must establish the procedures and of the programs to which they apply. A sentence was also added to make clear that grievance

procedures are not required to be made available to unsuccessful applicants for employment or to applicants for admission to colleges and universities.

The regulation does not require that grievance procedures be exhausted before recourse is sought from the Department. However, the Secretary believes that it is desirable and efficient in many cases for complainants to seek resolution of their complaints and disputes at the local level and therefore encourages them to use available grievance procedures.

A number of comments asked whether compliance with this section or the notice requirements of § 104.8 could be coordinated with comparable action required by the title IX regulation. The Department encourages such efforts.

13. *Notice.* Section 104.8 (formerly § 84.9) sets forth requirements for dissemination of statements of nondicrimination policy by recipients.

It is important that both handicapped persons and the public at large be aware of the obligations of recipients under section 504. Both the Department and recipients have responsibilities in this regard. Indeed the Department intends to undertake a major public information effort to inform persons of their rights under section 504 and this regulation. In § 104.8 the Department has sought to impose a clear obligation on major recipients to notify beneficiaries and employees of the requirements of section 504, without dictating the precise way in which this notice must be given. At the same time, we have avoided imposing requirements on small recipients (those with fewer than fifteen employees) that would create unnecessary and counterproductive paper work burdens on them and unduly stretch the enforcement resources of the Department.

Section 104.8(a), as simplified, requires recipients with fifteen or more employees to take appropriate steps to notify beneficiaries and employees of the recipient's obligations under section 504. The last sentence of § 104.8(a) has been revised to list possible, rather than required, means of notification. Section 104.8(b) requires recipients to include a notification of their policy of nondiscrimination in recruitment and other general information materials.

In response to a number of comments, § 104.8 has been revised to delete the requirements of publication in local newspapers, which has proved to be both troublesome and ineffective. Several commenters suggested that notification on separate forms be allowed until present stocks of publications and forms are depleted. The final regulation explicitly allows this method of compliance. The separate form should, however, be included with each significant publication or form that is distributed.

Section 104 which prohibited the use of materials that might give the impression that a recipient excludes qualified handicapped persons from its program, has been deleted. The Department is convinced by the comments that this provision is unnecessary and difficult to apply. The Department encourages recipients, however, to include in their recruitment and other general information materials photographs of handicapped persons and ramps and other features of accessible buildings.

Under new § 104.9 the Assistant Secretary may, under certain circumstances, require recipients with fewer than fifteen employees to comply with one or more of these requirements. Thus, if experience shows a need for imposing notice or other requirements on particular recipients or classes of small recipients, the Department is prepared to expand the coverage of these sections.

14. Inconsistent State laws. Section 104.10(a) states that compliance with the regulation is not excused by State or local laws limiting the eligibility of qualified handicapped persons to receive services or to practice an occupation. The provision thus applies only with respect to state or local laws that unjustifiably differentiate on the basis of handicap.

Paragraph (b) further points out that the presence of limited employment opportunities in a particular profession, does not excuse a recipient from complying with the regulation. Thus, a law school could not deny admission to a blind applicant because blind laywers may find it more difficult to find jobs than do nonhandicapped lawyers.

SUBPART B — EMPLOYMENT PRACTICES

Subpart B prescribes requirements for nondiscrimination in the employment practices of recipients of Federal financial assistance administered by the Department. This subpart is consistent with the employment provisions of the Department's regulation implementing title IX of the Education Amendments of 1972 (34 CFR, Part 106) and the regulation of the Department of Labor under section 503 of the Rehabilitation Act, which requires certain Federal contractors to take affirmative action in the employment and advancement of qualified handicapped persons. All recipients subject to title IX are also subject to this regulation. In addition, many recipients subject to this regulation receive Federal procurement contracts in excess of $2,500 and are therefore also subject to section 503.

15. Discriminatory practices. Section 104.11 sets forth general provisions with respect to discrimination in employment. A new paragraph (a)(2) has been added to clarify the employment obligations of recipients that receive Federal funds under Part B of the Education of the Handicapped Act, as amended (EHA). Section 606 of the EHA obligates elementary or secondary school systems that receive EHA funds to take positive steps to employ and advance in employment qualified handicapped persons. This obligation is similar to the nondiscrimination requirement of section 504 but requires recipients to take additional steps to hire and promote handicapped persons. In enacting section 606 Congress chose the words "positive steps" instead of "affirmative action" advisedly and did not intend section 606 to incorporate the types of activities required under Executive Order 11246 (affirmative action on the basis of race, color, sex, or national origin) or under sections 501 and 503 of the Rehabilitation Act of 1973.

Paragraph (b) of § 104.11 sets forth the specific aspects of employment covered by the regulation. Paragraph (c) provides that inconsistent provisions of collective bargaining agreements do not excuse noncompliance.

16. Reasonable accommodation. The reasonable accommodation requirement of § 104.12 generated a substantial number of comments. The Department remains convinced that its approach is both fair and effective. Moreover, the Department of Labor reports that it has experienced little difficulty in administering the requirements of reasonable accommodation. The provision therefore remains basically

unchanged from the proposed regulation.

Section 104.12 requires a recipient to make reasonable accommodation to the known physical or mental limitations of a handicapped applicant or employee unless the recipient can demonstrate that the accommodation would impose an under hardship on the operation of its program. Where a handicapped person is not qualified to perform a particular job, where reasonable accommodation does not overcome the effects of a person's handicap, or where reasonable accommodation causes undue hardship to the employer, failure to hire or promote the handicapped person will not be considered discrimination.

Section 104.12(b) lists some of the actions that constitute reasonable accommodation. The list is neither all-inclusive nor meant to suggest that employers must follow all of the actions listed.

Reasonable accommodation includes modification of work schedules, including part-time employment, and job restructuring. Job restructuring may entail shifting nonessential duties to other employees. In other cases, reasonable accommodation may include physical modifications or relocation of particular offices or jobs so that they are in facilities or parts of facilities that are accessible to and usable by handicapped persons. If such accommodations would cause undue hardship to the employer, they need not be made.

Paragraph (c) of this section sets forth the factors that the Office for Civil Rights will consider in determining whether an accommodation necessary to enable an applicant or employee to perform the duties of a job would impose an undue hardship. The weight given to each of these factors in making the determination as to whether an accommodation constitutes undue hardship will vary depending on the facts of a particular situation. Thus, a small day-care center might not be required to expend more than a nominal sum, such as that necessary to equip a telephone for use by a secretary with impaired hearing, but a large school district might be required to make available a teacher's aide to a blind applicant for a teaching job. The reasonable accommodation standard in § 104.12 is similar to the obligation imposed upon Federal contractors in the regulation implementing section 503 of the Rehabilitation Act of 1973, administered by the Department of Labor. Although the wording of the reasonable accommodation provisions of the two regulations is not identical, the obligation that the two regulations impose is the same, and the Federal Government's policy in implementing the two sections will be uniform. The Department adopted the factors listed in paragraph (c) instead of the "business necessity" standard of the Labor regulation because that erm seemed inappropriate to the nature of the programs operated by the majority of institutions subject to this regulation, e.g., public school systems, colleges and universities. The factors listed in paragraph (c) are intended to make the rationale underlying the business necessity standard applicable to an understandable by recipients of ED funds.

17. Tests and selection criteria. Revised § 104.13(a) prohibits employers from using test or other selection criteria that screen out or tend to screen out handicapped persons unless the test or criterion is shown to be job-related and alternative tests or criteria that do not screen out or tend to screen out as many handicapped persons are not shown by the Assistant Secretary to be available. This paragraph is an application of the principle established under title VII of the Civil

Rights Act of 1964 in Griggs v. Duke Power Company, 401 U.S. 424 (1971).

Under the proposed section, a statistical showing of adverse impact on handicapped persons was required to trigger an employer's obligation to show that employment criteria and qualifications relating to handicap were necessary. This requirement was changed because the small number of handicapped persons taking tests would make statistical showings of "disproportionate, adverse effect" difficult and burdensome. Under the altered, more workable provision, once it is shown that an employment test substantially limits the opportunities of handicapped persons, the employer must show the test to be job-related. A recipient is no longer limited to using predictive validity studies as the method for demonstrating that a test or other selection criterion is in fact job-related. Nor, in all cases, are predictive validity studies sufficient to demonstrate that a test or criterion is jobrelated. In addition, § 104.13(a) has been revised to place the burden on the Assistant Secretary, rather than the recipient, to identify alternate tests.

Section 104.13(b) requires that a recipient take into account that some tests and criteria depend upon sensory, manual, or speaking skills that may not themselves be necessary to the job in question but that may make the handicapped person unable to pass the test. The recipient must select and administer tests so as best to ensure that the test will meure the handicapped person's ability to perform on the job rather than the person's ability to see, hear, speak, or perform manual tasks, except, of cource, where such skills are the factor that the test purports to measure. For example, a person with a speech impediment may be perfectly qualified for jobs that do not or need not, with reasonable accommodation, require ability to speak clearly. Yet, if given an oral test, the person will be unable to perform in a satisfactory manner. The test results will not, therefore, predict job performance but instead will reflect impaired speech.

18. Preemployment inquiries. Section 104.14, concerning preemployment inquiries, generated a large number of comments. Commenters representing handicapped persons strongly favored a ban on preemployment inquiries on the ground that such inquiries are often used to discriminate against handicapped persons and are not necessary to serve any legitimate interests of employers. Some recipients, on the other hand, argued that preemployment inquiries are necessary to determine qualifications of the applicant, safety hazards caused by a particular handicapping condition, and accommodations that might be required.

The Secretary has concluded that a general prohibition of preemployment inquiries is appropriate. However, a sentence has been added to paragraph (a) to make clear that an employer may inquire into an applicant's ability to perform job-related tasks but may not ask if the person has a handicap. For example, an employer may not ask on an employment form if an applicant is visually impaired but may ask if the person has a current driver's license (if that is a necessary qualification for the position in question). Similarly, employers may make inquiries about an applicant's ability to perform a job safely. Thus, an employer may not ask if an applicant is an epileptic but may ask whether the person can perform a particular job without endangering other employees.

Section 104.14(b) allows preemployment inquiries only if they are made in conjunction with required remedial action to correct past discrimination, with voluntary action to overcome past conditions that have limited the participation of handicapped persons, or with obligations under section 503 of the Rehabilitation Act of 1973. In these instances, paragraph (b) specifies certain safeguards that must be followed by the employer.

Finally, the revised provision allows an employer to condition offers of employment to handicapped persons on the results of medical examinations, so long as the examinations are administered to all employees in a nondiscriminatory manner and the results are treated on a confidential basis.

19. Specific acts of Discrimination. Sections 104.15 (recruitment), 104.16 (compensation), 104.17 (job classification and structure) and 104.18 (fringe benefits) have been deleted from the regulation as unnecessarily duplicative of § 104.11 (discrimination prohibited). The deletion of these sections in no way changes the substantive obligations of employers subject to this regulation from those set forth in the July 16 proposed regulation. These deletions bring the regulation closer in form to the Department of Labor's section 503 regulation.

A proposed section, concerning fringe benefits, had allowed for differences in benefits or contributions between handicapped and nonhandicapped persons in situations only where such differences could be justified on an actuarial basis. Section 104.11 simply bars discrimination in providing fringe benefits and does not address the issue of actuarial differences. The Department believes that currently available data and experience do not demonstrate a basis for promulgating a regulation specifically allowing for differences in benefits or contributions.

SUBPART C — PROGRAM ACCESSIBILITY

In general, Subpart C prohibits the exclusion of qualified handicapped persons from federally assisted programs or activities because a recipient's facilities are inaccessible or unusable.

20. Existing facilities. Section 104.22 maintains the same standard for nondiscrimination in regard to existing facilities as was included in the proposed regulation. The section states that a recipients program or activity, when viewed in its entirety, must be readily accessible to and usable by handicapped persons. Paragraphs (a) and (b) make clear that a recipient is not required to make each of its existing facilities accessible to handicapped persons if its program as a whole is accessible. Accessibility to the recipient's program or activity may be achieved by a number of means, including redesign of equipment, reassignment of classes or other services to accessible buildings, and making aides available to beneficiaries. In choosing among methods of compliance, recipients are required to give priority consideration to methods that will be consistent with provision of services in the most appropriate integrated setting. Structural changes in existing facilities are required only where there is no other feasible way to make the recipient's program accessible.

Under § 104.22, a university does not have to make all of its existing classroom buildings accessible to handicapped students if some of its buildings are already accessible and if it is possible to reschedule or relocate enough classes so as to offer all required courses and a reasonable selection of elective courses in accessible facilities. If sufficient relocation of classes is not possible using existing facilities, enough alterations to ensure program accessibility are required. A university may not exclude a handicapped student from a specifically requested course offering because it is not offered in an accessible location, but it need not make every section of that course accessible.

Commenters representing several institutions of higher education have suggested that it would be appropriate for one postsecondary institution in a geographical area to be made accessible to handicapped persons and for other colleges and universities in that area to participate in that school's program, thereby developing an educational consortium for the postsecondary education of handicapped students. The Department believes that such a consortium, when developed and applied only to handicapped persons, would not constitute compliance with § 104.22, but would discriminate against qualified handicapped persons by restricting their choice in selecting institutions of higher education and would, therefore, be inconsistent with the basic objectives of the statute.

Nothing in this regulation, however, should be read as prohibiting institutions from forming consortia for the benefit of all students. Thus, if three colleges decide that it would be cost-efficient for one college to offer biology, the second physics, and the third chemistry to all students at the three colleges, the arrangement would not violate section 504. On the other hand, it would violate the regulation if the same institutions set up a consortium under which one college undertook to make its biology lab accessible, another its physics lab, and a third its chemistry lab, and under which mobility-impaired handicapped students (but not other students) were required to attend the particular college that is accessible for the desired courses.

Similarly, while a public school district need not make each of its buildings completely accessible, it may not make only one facility or part of a facility accessible if the result is to segregate handicapped students in a single setting.

All recipients that provide health, welfare, or other social services may also comply with § 104.22 by delivering services at alternate accessible sites or making home visits. Thus, for example, a pharmacist might arrange to make home deliveries of drugs. Under revised § 104.22(c), small providers of health, welfare, and social services (those with fewer than fifteen employees) may refer a beneficiary to an accessible provider of the desired service, but only if no means of meeting the program accessibility requirement other than a significant alteration in existing facilities is available. The referring recipient has the responsibility of determining that the other provider is in fact accessible and willing to provide the service.

A recent change in the tax law may assist some recipients in meeting their obligations under this section. Under section 2122 of the Tax Reform Act of 1976, recipients that pay federal income tax are eligible to claim a tax deduction of up to $25,000 for architectural and transportation modifications made to improve accessibility for handicapped persons. See 42 FR 17870 (April 4, 1977), adopting 26 CFR 7.190.

Several commenters expressed concern about the feasibility of compliance with the program accessibility standard. The Secretary believes that the standard is flexible enough to permit recipients to devise ways to make their programs accessible short of extremely expensive or impractical physical changes in facilities. Accordingly, the section does not allow for waivers. The Department is ready at all times to provide technical assistance to recipients in meeting their program accessibility responsibilities. For this purpose, the Department is establishing a special technical assistance unit. Recipients are encouraged to call upon the unit staff for advice and guidance both on structural modifications and on other ways of meeting the program accessibility requirement.

Paragraph (d) has been amended to require recipients to make all nonstructural adjustments necessary for meeting the program accessibility standard within sixty days. Only where structural changes in facilities are necessary will a recipient be permitted up to three years to accomplish program accessibility. It should be emphasized that the three-year time period is not a waiting period and that all changes must be accomplished as expeditiously as possible. Further, it is the Department's belief, after consultation with experts in the field, that outside ramps to buildings can be constructed quickly and at relatively low cost. Therefore, it will be expected that such structural additions will be made promptly to comply with § 104.22(d).

The regulation continues to provide, as did the proposed version, that a recipient planning to achieve program accessibility by making structural changes must develop a transition plan for such changes within six months of the offective date of the regulation. A number of commenters suggested extending that period to one year. The secretary believes that such an extension is unnecessary and unwise. Planning for any necessary structural changes should be undertaken promptly to ensure that they can be completed within the three-year period. The elements of the transition plan as required by the regulation remain virtually unchanged from the proposal but § 104.22(d) now includes a requirement that the recipient make the plan available for public inspection.

Several commenters expressed concern that the program accessibility standard would result in the segregation of handicapped persons in educational institutions. The regulation will not be applied to permit such a result. See § 104.4(c)(2)(iv), prohibiting unnecessarily separate treatment; § 104.35, requiring that students in elementary and secondary schools be educated in the most integrated setting appropriate to their needs; and new § 104.43(d), applying the same standard to postsecondary education.

We have received some comments from organizations of handicapped persons on the subject of requiring, over an extended period of time, a barrier-free environment — that is, requiring the removal of all architectural barriers in existing facilities. The Department has considered these comments but has decided to take no further action at this time concerning these suggestions, believing that such action should only be considered in light of experence in implementing the program accessibility standard.

21. New construction. Section 104.23 requires that all new facilities, as well as alterations that could affect access to and use of existing facilities, be designed and constructed in a manner so an to make the facility accessible to and usable by handicapped persons. Section 104.23(a) has been amended so that it applies to each newly constructed facility if the construction was commenced after the effective date of the regulation. The words "if construction has commenced" will be considered to mean "if groundbreaking has taken place." Thus, a recipient will not be required to alter the design of a facility that has prograssed beyond ground-

breaking prior to the effective date of the regulation.

Paragraph (b) requires certain alterations to conform to the requirement of physical accessibility in paragraph (a). If an alteration is undertaken to a portion of a building the accessibility of which could be improved by the manner in which the alteration is carried out, the alteration must be made in that manner. thus, if a doorway or wall is being altered, the door or other wall opening must be made wide enough to accommodate wheelchairs. On the other hand, if the alteration consists of altering ceilings, the provisions of this section are not applicable bacause this alteration cannot be done in a way that affects the accessibility of that portion of the building. The phrase "to the maximum extent feasible" has been added to allow for the occasional case in which the nature of an existing facility is such as to make it impractical or prohibitively expensive to renovate the building in a manner that results in its being entirely barrier-free. In all such cases, however, the alteration should provide the maximum amount of physical accessibility feasible.

Section 104.23(d) of the proposed regulation, providing for a limited deferral of action concerning facilities that are subject to section 502 as well as section 504 of the Act, has been deleted. The Secretary believes that the provision is unnecessary and inappropriate to this regulation. The Department will, however, seek to coordinate enforcement activities under this regulation with those of the Architectural and Transportation Barriers Compliance Board.

SUBPART D — PRESCHOOL, ELEMENTARY, AND SECONDARY EDUCATION

Subpart D sets forth requirements for nondiscrimination in preschool, elementary, secondary, and adult education programs and activities, including secondary vocational education programs. In this context, the term "adult education" refers only to those educational programs and activities for adults that are operated by elementary and secondary schools.

The provisions of Subpart D apply to state and local educational agencies. Although the subpart applies, in general, to both public and private education programs and activities that are federally assisted, §§ 104.32 and 104.33 apply only to public programs and § 104.39 applies only to private programs; §§ 104.35 and 104.36 apply both to public programs and to those private programs that include special services for handicapped students.

Subpart B generally conforms to the standards established for the education of handicapped persons in Mills v. Board of Education of the District of Columbia, 348 F. Supp. 866 (D.D.C. 1972), Pennsylvania Association for Retarded Children v. Commonwealth of Pennsylvania, 344 F. Supp. 1257 (E.D. 1971), 343 F. Supp. 279 (E.D. Pa. 1972), and Lebanks v. Speares, 60, F.R.D. 135 (E.D. La. 1973), as well as in the Education of the Handicapped Act, as amended by Pub. L. 94-142 (the EHA).

The basic requirement common to those cases, to the EHA, and to this regulation are (1) that handicapped persons, regardless of the nature or severity of their handicap, be provided a free appropriate public education, (2) that handicapped students be educated with nonhandicapped students to the maximum extent appropriate to their needs, (3) that educational agencies undertake to identify and locate all unserved handicapped children, (4) that evaluation procedures be improved in order to avoid the inappropriate education that results from the misclassification of students, and (5) that procedural safeguard be established to enable parents and guardians to influence decisions regarding the evaluation and placement of their children. These requirements are designed to ensure that no handicapped child is excluded from school on the basis of handicap and, if a recipient demonstrates that placement in a regular educational setting cannot be achieved satisfactorily, that the student is provided with adequate alternative services suited to the student's needs without additional cost to the student's parents or guardian. Thus, a recipient that operates a public school system must either educate handicapped children in its regular program or provide such children with an appropriate alternative education at public expense.

It is not the intention of the Department, except in extraordinary circumstances, to review the result of individual placement and other educational decisions, so long as the school district complies with the "process" requirements of this subpart (concerning identification and location, evaluation, and due process procedures). However, the Department will place a high priority on investigating cases which may involve exclusion of a child from the education system or a pattern or practice of discriminatory placements or education.

22. Location and notification. Section 104.32 requires public schools to take steps annually to identify and locate handicapped children who are not receiving an education and to publicize to handicapped children and their parents the rights and duties established by section 504 and this regulation. This section has been shortened without substantive change.

23. Free appropriate public education. Under § 104.33(a), a recipient is responsible for providing a free appropriate public education to each qualified handicapped person who is in the recipient's jurisdiction. The word "in" encompasses the concepts of both domicile and actual residence. If a recipient places a child in a program other than its own, it remains financially responsible for the child, whether or not the other program is operated by another recipient or educational agency. Moreover, a recipient may not place a child in a program that is inappropriate or that otherwise violates the requirements of Subpart D. And in no case may a recipient refuse to provide services to a handicapped child in its jurisdiction because of another person's or entity's failure to assume financial responsibility.

Section 104.33(b) concerns the provision of appropriate educational services to handicapped children. To be appropriate, such services must be designed to meet handicapped children's individual educational needs to the same extent that those of nonhandicapped children are met. An appropriate education could consist of education in regular classes, education in regular classes with the use of supplementary services, or special education and related services. Special education may include specially designed instruction in classrooms, at home, or in private or public institutions and may be accompanied by such related services as developmental, corrective, and other supportive services (including psychological, counseling, and medical diagnostic services). The placement of the child must however, be consistent with the requirements of § 104.34 and be suited to his or her educational needs.

The quality of the educational services provided to handicapped students must equal that of the services provided to nonhandicapped students; thus, handicapped student's teachers must be trained in the instruction of persons with the handicap in question and appropriate materials and equipment must be available. The Department is aware that the supply of adequately trained teachers may, at least at the outset of the imposition of this requirement, be insufficient to meet the demand of all recipients. This factor will be considered in determining the appropriateness of the remedy for noncompliance with this section. A new § 104.33(b)(2) has been added, which allows this requirement to be met through the full implementation of an individualized education program developed in accordance with the standards of the EHA.

Paragraph (c) of § 104.33 sets forth the specific financial obligations of a recipient. If a recipient does not itself provide handicapped persons with the requisite services, it must assume the cost of any alternate placement. If, however, a recipient offers adequate services and if alternate placement is chosen by a student's parent or guardian, the recipient need not assume the cost of the outside services. (If the parent or guardian believes that his or her child cannot be suitably educated in the recipient's program, he or she may make use of the procedures established in § 104.36.) Under this paragraph, a recipient's obligation extends beyond the provision of tuition payments in the case of placement outside the regular program. Adequate transportation must also be provided. Recipients must also pay for psychological services and those medical services necessary for diagnostic and evaluative purposes.

If the recipient places a student, because of his or her handicap, in a program that necessitates his or her being away from home, the payments must also cover room and board and nonmedical care (including custodial and supervisory care). When residential care is necessitated not by the student's handicap but by factors such as the student's home conditions, the recipient is not required to pay the cost of room and board.

Two new sentences have been added to paragraph (c)(1) to make clear that a recipient's financial obligations need not be met solely through its own funds. Recipients may rely on funds from any public or private source including insurers and similar third parties.

The EHA requires a free appropriate education to be provided to handicapped children "no later than September 1, 1978," but section 504 contains no authority for delaying enforcement. To resolve this problem, a new paragraph (d) has been added to § 104.33. Section 104.33(d) requires recipients to achieve full compliance with the free appropriate public education requirements of § 104.33 as expeditiously as possible, but in no event later than September 1, 1978. The provision also makes clear that, as of the effective date of this regulation, no recipient may exclude a qualified handicapped child from its educational program. This provision against exclusion is consistent with the order of providing services set forth in section 612(3) of the EHA, which places the highest priority on providing services to handicapped children who are not receiving an education.

24. Educational setting. Section 104.34 prescribes standards for educating handicapped persons with nonhandicapped persons to the maximum extent appropriate to the needs of the handicapped person in question. A handicapped student may be removed from the regular educational setting only where the recipient can

show that the needs of the student would, on balance, be served by placement in another setting.

Although under § 104.34, the needs of the handicapped person are determinative as to proper placement, it should be stressed that, where a handicapped student is so disruptive in a regular classroom that the education of other students is significantly impaired, the needs of the handicapped child cannot be met in that environment. Therefore, regular placement would not be appropriate to his or her needs and would not be required by § 104.34.

Among the factors to be considered in placing a child is the need to place the child as close to home as possible. A new sentence has been added to paragraph (a) requiring recipients to take this factor into account. As pointed out in several comments, the parents' right under § 104.36 to challenge the placement of their child extends not only to placement in special classes or separate schools but also to placement in a distant school and, in particular, to residential placement. An equally appropriate educational program may exist closer to home; this issue may be raised by the parent or guardian under §§ 104.34 and 104.36.

New paragraph (b) specified that handicapped children must also be provided nonacademic services in as integrated a setting as possible. This requirement is especially important for children whose educational needs necessitate their being solely with other handicapped children during most of each day. To the maximum extent appropriate, children in residential settings are also to be provided opportunities for participation with other children.

Section 104.34(c) requires that any facilities that are identifiable as being for handicapped students be comparable in quality to other facilities of the recipient. A number of comments objected to this section on the basis that it encourages the creation and maintenance of such facilities. This is not the intent of the provision. A separate facility violates section 504 unless it is indeed necessary to the provision of an appropriate education to certain handicapped students. In those instances in which such facilities are necessary (as might be the case, for example, for severely retarded persons), this provision requires that the educational services provided be comparable to those provided in the facilities of the recipient that are not identifiable as being for handicapped persons.

25. Evaluation and placement. Because the failure to provide handicapped persons with an appropriate education is so frequently the result of misclassification or misplacement, § 104.33(b)(1) makes compliance with its provisions contingent upon adherence to certain procedures designed to ensure appropriate classification and placement. These procedures, delineated in §§ 104.35 and 104.36, are concerned with testing and other evaluation methods and with procedural due process rights.

Section 104.35(a) requires that an individual evaluation be conducted before any action is taken with respect either to the initial placement of a handicapped child in a regular or special education program or to any subsequent significant change in that placement. Thus, a full reevaluation is not required every time an adjustment in placement is made. "Any action" includes denials of placement.

Paragraph (b) and (c) of § 104.35 establishes procedures designed to ensure that children are not misclassified, unnecessarily labeled as being handicapped, or incorrectly placed because of inappropriate selection, administration, or interpretation of evaluation materials. This problem has been extensively documented in "Issues in the Classification of Children," a report by the Project on Classification of Exceptional Children, in which the HEW Interagency Task Force participated. The provisions of these paragraphs are aimed primarily at abuses in the placement process that result from misuse of, or undue or misplaced reliance on, standardized scholastic aptitude tests.

Paragraph (b) has been shortened but not substantively changed. The requirement in former subparagraph (1) that recipients provide and administer evaluation materials in the native language of the student has been deleted as unnecessary, since the same requirement already exists under title VI and is more appropriately covered under that statute. Paragraph (1) and (2) are, in general, intended to prevent misinterpretation and similar misuse of test scores and, in particular, to avoid undue reliance on general intelligence tests. Subparagraph (3) requires a recipient to administer tests to a student with impaired sensory, manual, or speaking skills in whatever manner is necessary to avoid distortion of the test results by the impairment. Former subparagraph (4) has been deleted as unnecessarily repetitive of the other provisions of this paragraph.

Paragraph (c) requires a recipient to draw upon a variety of sources in the evaluation process so that the possibility of error in classification is minimized. In particular, it requires that all significant factors relating to the learning process, including adaptive behavior, be considered.(Adaptive behavior is the effectiveness with which the individual meets the standards of personal independence and social responsibility expected of his or her age and cultural group.) Information from all sources must be documented and considered by a group of persons, and the procedure must ensure that the child is placed in the most integrated setting appropriate.

The proposed regulation would have required a complete individual reevaluation of the student each year. The Department has concluded that it is inappropriate in the section 504 regulation to require full reevaluations on such a rigid schedule. Accordingly, § 104.35(c) requires periodic reevaluations and specifies that reevaluations in accordance with the EHA will constitute compliance. The proposed regulation implementing the EHA allows reevaluation at three-year intervals except under certain specified circumstances.

Under § 104.36, a recipient must establish a system of due process procedures to be afforded to parents or guardians before the recipient takes any action regarding the identification, evaluation, or educational placement of a person who, because of handicap, needs or is believed to need special education or related services. This section has been revised. Because the due process procedures of the EHA, incorporated by reference in the proposed section 504 regulation, are inappropriate for some recipients not subject to that Act, the section now specifies minimum necessary procedures: notice, a right to inspect records, an impartial hearing with a right to representation by counsel, and a review procedure.The EHA procedures remain one means of meeting the regulation's due process requirements, however, and are recommended to recipients as a model.

26. Nonacademic services. Section 104.37 requires a recipient to provide nonacademic and extracurricular services and activities in such manner as is necessary to afford handicapped students an equal opportunity for participation. Because these

services and activities are part of a recipient's education program, they must, in accordance with the provisions of § 104.34, be provided in the most integrated setting appropriate.

Revised paragraph (c)(2) does permit separation or differentiation with respect to the provision of physical education and athletics activities, but only if qualified handicapped students are also allowed the opportunity to compete for regular teams or participate in regular activities. Most handicapped students are able to participate in one or more regular physical education and athletics activities. For example, a student in a wheelchair can participate in regular archery course, as can a deaf student in a wrestling course.

Finally, the one-year transition period provided in a proposed section was deleted in response to the almost unanimous objection of commenters to that provision.

27. Preschool and adult education. Section 104.38 prohibits discrimination on the basis of handicap in preschool and adult education programs. Former paragraph (b), which emphasized that compensatory programs for disadvantaged children are subject to section 504, has been deleted as unnecessary, since it is comprehended by paragraph (a).

28. Private education. Section 104.39 sets forth the requirements applicable to recipients that operate private education programs and activities. The obligations of these recipients have been changed in two significant respects: first, private schools are subject to the evaluation and due process provisions of the subpart only if they operate special education programs; second, under § 104.39(b), they may charge more for providing services to handicapped students than to nonhandicapped students to the extent that additional charges can be justified by increased costs.

Paragraph (a) of § 104.39 is intended to make clear that recipients that operate private education programs and activities are not required to provide an appropriate education to handicapped students with special educational needs if the recipient does not offer programs designed to meet those needs. Thus, a private school that has no program for mentally retarded persons is neither required to admit such a person into its program nor to arrange or pay for the provision of the person's education in another program. A private recipient without a special program for blind students, however, would not be permitted to exclude, on the basis of blindness, a blind applicant who is able to participate in the regular program with minor adjustments in the manner in which the program is normally offered.

SUBPART E — POSTSECONDARY EDUCATION

Subpart E prescribes requirements for nondiscrimination in recruitment, admission, and treatment of students in postsecondary education programs and activities, including vocational education.

29. Admission and recruitment. In addition to a general prohibition of discrimination on the basis of handicap in § 104.42(a), the regulation delineates, in § 104.42(b), specific prohibitions concerning the establishment of limitations on admission of handicapped students, the use of tests or selection criteria, and preadmission inquiry. Several changes have been made in this provision.

Section 104.42(b) provides that postsecondary educational institutions may not use any test or criterion for admission that has a disproportionate, adverse effect on handicapped persons unless it has been validated as a predictor of academic success and alternate tests or criteria with a less disproportionate, adverse effect are shown by the Department to be available. There are two significant changes in this approach from the July 16 proposed regulation.

First, many commenters expressed concern that § 104.42(b)(2)(ii) could be interpreted to required a "global search" for alternate tests that do not have a disproportionate, adverse impact on handicapped persons. This was not the intent of the provision and, therefore, it has been amended to place the burden on the Assistant Secretary for Civil Rights, rather than on the recipient, to identify alternate tests.

Second, a new paragraph (d), concerning validity studies, has been added. Under the proposed regulation, overall success in an education program, not just first-year grades, was the criterion against which admissions tests were to be validated. This approach has been changed to reflect the comment of professional testing services that use of first year grades would be less disruptive of present practice and that periodic validity studies against overall success in the education program would be sufficient check on the reliability of first-year grades.

Section 104.42(b)(3) also requires a recipient to assure itself that admissions tests are selected and administered to applicants with impaired sensory, manual, or speaking skills in such manner as is necessary to avoid unfair distortion of test results. Methods have been developed for testing the aptitude and achievement of persons who are not able to take written tests or even to make the marks required for mechanically scored objective tests; in addition, methods for testing persons with visual or hearing impairments are available. A recipient, under this paragraph, must assure itself that such methods are used with respect to the selection and administration of any admissions tests that it uses.

Section 104.42(b)(3)(iii) has been amended to require that admissions test be administered in facilities that, on the whole, are accessible. In this context, "on the whole" means that not all of the facilities need be accessibile so long as a sufficient number of facilities are available to handicapped persons.

Revised § 104.42(b)(4) generally prohibits preadmission inquiries as to whether an applicant has a handicap. The considerations that led to this revision are similar to those underlying the comparable revision of § 104.14 on preemployment inquiries. The regulation does, however, allow inquiries to be made, after admission but before enrollment, as to handicaps that may require accommodation.

New paragraph (c) parallels the section on preemployment inquiries and allows postsecondary institutions to inquire about applicants' handicaps before admission, subject to certain safeguards, if the purpose of the inquiry is to take remedial action to correct past discrimination or to take voluntary action to overcome the limited participation of handicapped persons in postsecondary educational institutions.

Proposed § 104.42(c), which would have allowed different admissions criteria in certain cases for handicapped persons, was widely misinterpreted in comments from both handicapped persons and recipients. We have concluded that the section is unnecessary, and it has been deleted.

30. Treatment of students. Section 104.43 contains general provisions prohibiting the discriminatory treatment of qualified handicapped applicants. Paragraph (b) requires recipients to ensure that equal opportunities are provided to its handicapped students in education programs and activities that are not operated by the recipient. The recipient must be satisfied that the outside education program or activity as a whole is nondiscriminatory. For example, a college must ensure that discrimination on the basis of handicap does not occur in connection with teaching assignments of student teachers in elementary or secondary schools not operated by the college. Under the "as a whole" wording, the college could continue to use elementary or secondary school systems that discriminate if, and only if, the college's student teaching program, when viewed in its entirety, offered handicapped student teachers the same range and quality of choice in student teaching assignments afforded nonhandicapped students.

Paragraph (c) of this section prohibits a recipient from excluding qualified handicapped students from any course, course of study, or other part of its education program or activity. This paragraph is designed to eliminate the practice of excluding handicapped persons from specific courses and from areas of concentration because of factors such as ambulatory difficulties of the student or assumptions by the recipient that no job would be available in the area in question for a person with that handicap.

New paragraph (d) requires postsecondary institutions to operate their programs and activities so that handicapped students are provided services in the most integrated setting appropriate. Thus, if a college had several elementary physics classes and had moved one such class to the first floor of the science building to accommodate students in wheelchairs, it would be a violation of this paragraph for the college to concentrate handicapped students with no mobility impairments in the same class.

31. Academic adjustments. Paragraph (a) of § 104.44 requires that a recipient make certain adjustments to academic requirements and practices that discriminate or have the effect of discriminating on the basis of handicap. This requirement, like its predecessor in the proposed regulation, does not obligate an institution to waive course or other academic requirements. But such institutions must accommodate those requirements to the needs of individual handicapped students. For example, an institution might permit an otherwise qualified handicapped student who is deaf to substitute an art appreciation or music history course for a required course in music appreciation or could modify the manner in which the music appreciation course is conducted for the deaf student. It should be stressed that academic requirements that can be demonstrated by the recipient to be essential to its program of instruction or to particular degrees need not be changed.

Paragraph (b) provides that postsecondary institutions may not impose rules that have the effect of limiting the participation of handicapped students in the education program. Such rules include prohibition of tape recorders or braillers in classrooms and dog guides in campus buildings. Several recipients expressed concern about allowing students to tape record lectures because the professor may later want to copyright the lectures. This problem may be solved by requiring students to sign agreements that they will not release the tape recording or transcription or otherwise hinder the professor's ability to obtain a copyright.

Paragraph (c) of this section, concerning the administration of course examinations to students with impaired sensory, manual, or speaking skills, parallels the regulation's provisions on admissions testing (§ 104.42(b)) and will be similarly interpreted.

Under § 104.44(d), a recipient must ensure that no handicapped student is subject to discrimination in the recipient's program because of the absence of necessary auxiliary educational aids. Colleges and universities expressed concern about the costs of compliance with this provision.

The Department emphasizes that recipients can usually meet this obligation by assisting students in using existing resources for auxiliary aids such as state vocational rehabilitation agencies and private charitable organizations. Indeed, the Department anticipates that the bulk of auxiliary aids will be paid for by state and private agencies, not by colleges or universities. In those circumstances where the recipient institution must provide the educational auxiliary aid, the institution has flexibility in choosing the methods by which the aids will be supplied. For example, some universities have used students to work with the institution's handicapped students. Other institutions have used existing private agencies that tape texts for handicapped students free of charge in order to reduce the number of readers needed for visually impaired students.

As long as no handicapped person is excluded from a program because of the lack of an appropriate aid, the recipient need not have all such aids on hand at all times. Thus, readers need not be available in the recipient's library at all times so long as the schedule of times when a reader is available is established, is adhered to, and is sufficient. Of course, recipients are not required to maintain a complete braille library.

32. Housing. Section 104.45(a) requires postsecondary institutions to provide housing to handicapped students at the same cost as they provide it to other students and in a convenient, accessible, and comparable manner. Commenters, particularly blind persons pointed out that some handicapped persons can live in any college housing and need not wait to the end of the transition period in Subpart C to be offered the same variety and scope of housing accommodations given to nonhandicapped persons. The Department concurs with this position and will interpret this section accordingly.

A number of colleges and universities reacted negatively to paragraph (b) of this section. It provides that, if a recipient assists in making off-campus housing available to its students, it should develop and implement procedures to assure itself that off-campus housing, as a whole, is available to handicapped students. Since postsecondary institutions are presently required to assure themselves that off-campus housing is provided in a manner that does not discriminate on the basis of sex (§ 106.32 of the title IX regulation), they may use the procedures developed under title IX in order to comply with § 104.45(b). It should be emphasized that not every off-campus living accommodation need be made accessible to handicapped persons.

33. Health and insurance. A proposed section, providing that recipients may not discriminate on the basis of handicap in the provision of health related services, has been deleted as duplicative of the general provisions of $ 104.43. This deletion

represents no change in the obligation of recipients to provide nondiscriminatory health and insurance plans. The Department will continue to require that nondiscriminatory health services be provided to handicapped students. Recipients are not required, however, to provide specialized services and aids to handicapped persons in health programs. If, for example, a college infirmary treats only simple disorders such as cuts, bruises, and colds, its obligation to handicapped persons is to treat such disorders for them.

34. Financial assistance. Section 104.46(a), prohibiting discrimination in providing financial assistance, remains substantively the same. It provides that recipients may not provide less assistance to or limit the eligibility of qualified handicapped persons for such assistance, whether the assistance is provided directly by the recipient or by another entity through the recipient's sponsorship. Awards that are made under wills, trusts, or similar legal instruments in a discriminatory manner are permissible, but only if the overall effect of the recipient's provision of financial assistance is not discriminatory on the basis of handicap.

It will not be considered discriminatory to deny, on the basis of handicap, an athletic scholarship to a handicapped person if the handicap renders the person unable to qualify for the award. For example, a student who hsa a neurological disorder might be denied a varsity football scholarship on the basis of his inability to play football, but a deaf person could not, on the basis of handicap, be denied a scholarship for the school's diving team. The deaf person could, however, be denied a scholarship on the basis of comparative diving ability.

Commenters on § 104.46(b), which applies to assistance in obtaining outside employment for students, expressed similar concerns to those raised under § 104.43(b), concerning cooperatove programs. This paragraph has been changed in the same manner as § 104.43(b) to include the "as a whole" concept and will be interpreted in the same manner as § 104.43(b).

35. Nonacademic services. Section 104.47 establishes nondiscrimination standards for physical education and athletics counseling and placement services, and social organizations. This section sets the same standards as does § 104.38 of Subpart D, discussed above, and will be interpreted in a similar fashion.

SUBPART F — HEALTH, WELFARE, AND SOCIAL SERVICES

Subpart F applies to recipients that operate health, welfare, and social service programs. The Department received fewer comments on this subpart than on others.

Although many commented that Subpart F lacked specificity, these commenters provided neither concrete suggestions nor additions. Nevertheless, some changes have been made, pursuant to comment, to clarify the obligations of recipients in specific areas. In addition, in an effort to reduce duplication in the regulation, the section governing recipients providing health services has been consolidated with the section regulating providers of welfare and social services. Since the separate provisions that appeared in the proposed regulation were almost identical, no substantive change should be inferred from their consolidation.

Several commenters asked whether Subpart F applies to vocational rehabilitation agencies whose purpose is to assist in the rehabilitation of handicapped persons. To the extent that such agencies receive financial assistance from the Department, they are covered by Subpart F and all other relevant subparts of the regulation. Nothing in this regulation, however, precludes sich agencies from servicing only handicapped persons. Indeed, § 104.4(c) permits recipients to offer services or benefits that are limited by federal law to handicapped persons or classes of handicapped persons.

Many comments suggested requiring state social service agencies to take an active role in the enforcement of section 504 with regard to local social service providers. The Department believes that the possibility for federal-state cooperation in the administration and enforcement of section 504 warrants further consideration.

A number of comments also discussed whether section 504 should be read to require payment of compensation to institutionalized handicapped patients who perform services for the institution in which they reside. The Department of Labor has recently issued a proposed regulation under the Fair Labor Standards Act (FLSA) that covers the question of compensation for institutionalized persons. 42 FR 15224 (March 18, 1977). This Department will seek information and comment from the Department of Labor concerning that agency's experience administering the FLSA regulation.

36. Health, welfare, and other social service providers. Section 104.52(a) has been expanded in several respects. The addition of new paragraph (a)(2) is intended to make clear the basic requirement of equal opportunity to receive benefits or services in the health, welfare, and social service areas. The paragraph parallels §§ 104.4(b)(ii) and 104.43(b). New paragraph (a)(3) requires the provision of effective benefits or services, as defined in § 104.4(b)(2) (i.e., benefits or services which "afford handicapped persons equal opportunity to obtain the same result (or) to gain the same benefit * * *").

Section 104.52(a) also includes provisions concerning the limitation of benefits or services to handicapped persons and the subjection of handicapped persons to different eligibility standards. One common misconception about the regulation is that it would require specialized hospitals and other health care providers to treat all handicapped persons. The regulation makes no such requirement. Thus, a burn treatment center need not provide other types of medical treatment to handicapped persons unless it provides such medical services to nonhandicapped persons. It could not, however, refuse to treat the burns of a deaf person because of his or her deafness.

Commenters had raised the question of whether the prohibition against different standards of eligibility might preclude recipients from providing special services to handicapped persons or classes of handicapped persons. The regulation will not be so interpreted, and the specific section in question has been eliminated. Section 104.4(c) makes clear that special programs for handicapped persons are permitted.

A new paragraph (a)(5) concerning the provision of different or separate services or benefits has been added. This provision prohibits such treatment unless necessary to provide qualified handicapped persons with benefits and services that are as effective as those provided to others.

Section 104.52(b) has been amended to cover written material concerning waivers of rights or consent to treatment as well as general notices concerning health benefits or services. The section requires the recipient to ensure that qualified handicapped persons are not denied effective notice because of their handicap. For example, recipients could use several different types of notice in order to reach persons with impaired vision or hearing, such as brailled messages, radio spots, and tacticle devices on cards or envelopes to inform blind persons of the need to call the recipient for further information.

Section 104.52(c) is a new section requiring recipient hospitals to establish a procedure for effective communication with persons with impaired hearing for the purpose of providing emergency health care. Although it would be appropriate for a hospital to fulfill its responsibilities under this section by having a full-time interpreter for the deaf on staff, there may be other means of accomplishing the desired result of assuring that some means of communication is immediately available for deaf persons needing emergency treatment.

Section 104.52(c), also a new provision, requires recipients with fifteen or more employees to provide appropriate auxiliary aids for persons with impaired sensory, manual, or speaking skills. Further, the Assistant Secretary may require a small provider to furnish auxiliary aids where the provision of aids would not adversely affect the ability of the recipient to provide its health benefits or service.

37. Treatment of Drug Addicts and Alcoholics. Section 104.53 is a new section that prohibits discrimination in the treatment and admission of drug and alcohol addicts to hospitals and outpatient facilities. Section 104.53 prohibits discrimination against drug abusers by operators of outpatient facilities, despite the fact that section 407 pertains only to hospitals, because of the broader application of section 504. This provision does not mean that all hospitals and outpatient facilities must treat drug addiction and alcoholism. It simply means, for example, that a cancer clinic may not refuse to treat cancer patients simply because they are also alcoholics.

38. Education of institutionalized persons. The regulation retains § 104.54 of the proposed regulation that requires that an appropriate education be provided to qualified handicapped persons who are confined to residential institutions or day care centers.

SUBPART G — PROCEDURES

In § 104.61, the Secretary has adopted the title VI complaint and enforcement procedures for use in implementing section 504 until such time as they are superseded by the issuance of a consolidated procedureal regulation applicable to all of the civil rights statutes and executive orders administered by the Department.

Chapter 11
FAIR HOUSING ACT AMENDMENTS OF 1988

FAIR HOUSING ACT AMENDMENTS OF 1988

§ 3601. Declaration of policy

It is the policy of the United States to provide, within constitutional limitations, for fair housing throughout the United States.

§ 3602. Definitions

As used in this subchapter —

(a) "Secretary" means the Secretary of Housing and Urban Development.

(b) "Dwelling" means any building, structure, or portion thereof which is occupied as, or designed or intended for occupancy as, a residence by one or more families, and any vacant land which is offered for sale or lease for the construction or location thereon of any such building, structure, or portion thereof.

(c) "Family" includes a single individual.

(d) "Person" includes one or more individuals, corporations, partnerships, associations, labor organizations, legal representatives, mutual companies, joint-stock companies, trusts, unincorporated organizations, trustees, trustees in cases under Title 11, receivers, and fiduciaries.

(e) "To rent" includes to lease, to sublease, to let and otherwise to grant for a consideration the right to occupy premises not owned by the occupant.

(f) "Discriminatory housing practice" means an act that is unlawful under section 3604, 3605, 3606, or 3617 of this title.

(g) "State" means any of the several States, the District of Columbia, the Commonwealth of Puerto Rico, or any of the territories and possessions of the United States.

(h) "Handicap" means, with respect to a person —

(1) a physical or mental impairment which substantially limits one or more of such person's major life activities,

(2) a record of having such an impairment, or

(3) being regarded as having such an impairment,

but such term does not include current, illegal use of or addiction to a controlled substance as defined in section 802 of Title 21.

(i) "Aggrieved person" includes any person who —

(1) claims to have been injured by a discriminatory housing practice; or

(2) believes that such person will be injured by a discriminatory housing practice that is about to occur.

(j) "Complainant" means the person (including the Secretary) who files a complaint under section 3610 of this title.

(k) "Familial status" means one or more individuals (who have not attained the age of 18 years) being domiciled with —

(1) a parent or another person having legal custody of such individual or individuals; or

(2) the designee of such parent or other person having such custody, with the written permission of such parent or other person.

The protections afforded against discrimination on the basis of familial status shall apply to any person who is pregnant or is in the process of securing legal custody of any individual who has not attained the age of 18 years.

(l) "Conciliation" means the attempted resolution of issues raised by a complaint, or by the investigation of such complaint, through informal negotiations involving the aggrieved person, the respondent, and the Secretary.

(m) "Conciliation agreement" means a written agreement setting forth the resolution of the issues in conciliation.

(n) "Respondent" means —

(1) the person or other entity accused in a complaint of an unfair housing practice; and

(2) any other person or entity identified in the course of investigation and notified as required with respect to respondents so identified under section 3610(a) of this title.

(o) "Prevailing party" has the same meaning as such term has in section 1988 of this title.

§ 3603. Effective dates of certain prohibitions

(a) Application to certain described dwellings

Subject to the provisions of subsection (b) of this section and section 3607 of this title, the prohibitions against discrimination in the sale or rental of housing set forth in section 3604 of this title shall apply:

(1) Upon enactment of this subchapter, to —

(A) dwellings owned or operated by the Federal Government;

(B) dwellings provided in whole or in part with the aid of loans, advances, grants, or contributions made by the Federal Government, under agreements entered into after November 20, 1962, unless payment due thereon has been made in full prior to April 11, 1968;

(C) dwellings provided in whole or in part by loans insured, guaranteed, or otherwise secured by the credit of the Federal Government, under agreements entered into after November 20, 1962, unless payment thereon has been made in full prior to April 11, 1968: Provided, That nothing contained in subparagraphs (B) and (C) of this subsection shall be applicable to dwellings solely by virtue of the fact that they are subject to mortgages held by an FDIC or FSLIC institution; and

(D) dwellings provided by the development or the redevelopment of real property purchased, rented, or otherwise obtained from a State or local public agency receiving Federal financial assistance for slum clearance or urban renewal with respect to such real property under loan or grant contracts entered into after November 20, 1962.

(2) After December 31, 1968, to all dwellings covered by paragraph (1) and to all other dwellings except as exempted by subsection (b) of this section.

(b)   Exemptions

Nothing in section 3604 of this title (other than subsection (c)) shall apply to —

(1) any single-family house sold or rented by an owner: Provided, That such private individual owner does not own more than three such single-family houses at any one time: Provided further, That in the case of the sale of any such single-family house by a private individual owner not residing in such house at the time of such sale or who was not the most recent resident of such house prior to such sale, the exemption granted by this subsection shall apply only with respect to one such sale within any twenty-four month period: Provided further, That such bona fide private individual owner does not own any interest in, nor is there owned or reserved on his behalf, under any express or voluntary agreement, title to or any right to all or a portion of the proceeds from the sale or rental of, more than three such single-family houses at any one time: Provided further, That after December 31, 1969, the sale or rental of any such single-family house shall be excepted from the application of this subchapter only if such house is sold or rented (A) without the use in any manner of the sales or rental facilities or the sales or rental services of any real estate broker, agent, or salesman, or of such facilities or services of any person in the business of selling or renting dwellings, or of any employee or agent of any such broker, agent, salesman, or person and (B) without the publication, posting or mailing, after notice, of any advertisement or written notice in violation of section 3604(c) of this title; but nothing in this proviso shall prohibit the use of attorneys, escrow agents, abstractors, title companies, and other such professional assistance as necessary to perfect or transfer the title, or

(2) rooms or units in dwellings containing living quarters occupied or intended to be occupied by no more than four families living independently of each other, if the owner actually maintains and occupies one of such living quarters as his

residence.

(c) Business of selling or renting dwellings defined

For the purposes of subsection (b) of this section, a person shall be deemed to be in the business of selling or renting dwellings if —

(1) he has, within the preceding twelve months, participated as principal in three or more transactions involving the sale or rental of any dwelling or any interest therein, or

(2) he has, within the preceding twelve months, participated as agent, other than in the sale of his own personal residence in providing sales or rental facilities or sales or rental services in two or more transactions involving the sale or rental of any dwelling or any interest therein, or

(3) he is the owner of any dwelling designed or intended for occupancy by, or occupied by, five or more families.

§ 3604. Discrimination in the sale or rental of housing and other prohibited practices

As made applicable by section 3603 of this title and except as exempted by sections 3603(b) and 3607 of this title, it shall be unlawful —

(a) To refuse to sell or rent after the making of a bona fide offer, or to refuse to negotiate for the sale or rental of, or otherwise make unavailable or deny, a dwelling to any person because of race, color, religion, sex, familial status, or national origin.

(b) To discriminate against any person in the terms, conditions, or privileges of sale or rental of a dwelling, or in the provision of services or facilities in connection therewith, because of race, color, religion, sex, familial status, or national origin.

(c) To make, print, or publish, or cause to be made, printed, or published any notice, statement, or advertisement, with respect to the sale or rental of a dwelling that indicates any preference, limitation, or discrimination based on race, color, religion, sex, handicap, familial status, or national origin, or an intention to make any such preference, limitation, or discrimination.

(d) To represent to any person because of race, color, religion, sex, handicap, familial status, or national origin that any dwelling is not available for inspection, sale, or rental when such dwelling is in fact so available.

(e) For profit, to induce or attempt to induce any person to sell or rent any dwelling by representations regarding the entry or prospective entry into the neighborhood of a person or persons of a particular race, color, religion, sex, handicap, familial status, or national origin.

(f) (1) To discriminate in the sale or rental, or to otherwise make unavailable or deny, a dwelling to any buyer or renter because of a handicap of —

(A) that buyer or renter;

(B) a person residing in or intending to reside in that dwelling after it is so sold, rented, or made available; or

(C) any person associated with that buyer or renter.

(2) To discriminate against any person in the terms, conditions, or privileges of sale or rental of a dwelling, or in the provision of services or facilities in connection with such dwelling, because of a handicap of —

(A) that person; or

(B) a person residing in or intending to reside in that dwelling after it is so sold, rented, or made available; or

(C) any person associated with that person.

(3) For purposes of this subsection, discrimination includes —

(A) a refusal to permit, at the expense of the handicapped person, reasonable modifications of existing premises occupied or to be occupied by such person if such modifications may be necessary to afford such person full enjoyment of the premises except that, in the case of a rental, the landlord may where it is reasonable to do so condition permission for a modification on the renter agreeing to restore the interior of the premises to the condition that existed before the modification, reasonable wear and tear excepted;

(B) a refusal to make reasonable accommodations in rules, policies, practices, or services, when such accommodations may be necessary to afford such person equal opportunity to use and enjoy a dwelling; or

(C) in connection with the design and construction of covered multifamily dwellings for first occupancy after the date that is 30 months after September 13, 1988, a failure to design and construct those dwellings in such a manner that —

(i) the public use and common use portions of such dwellings are readily accessible to and usable by handicapped persons;

(ii) all the doors designed to allow passage into and within all premises within such dwellings are sufficiently wide to allow passage by handicapped persons in wheelchairs; and

(iii) all premises within such dwellings contain the following features of adaptive design:

(I) an accessible route into and through the dwelling;

(II) light switches, electrical outlets, thermostats, and other environmental controls in accessible locations;

(III) reinforcements in bathroom walls to allow later installation of grab bars; and

(IV) usable kitchens and bathrooms such that an individual in a wheelchair can maneuver about the space.

(4) Compliance with the appropriate requirements of the American National

Standard for buildings and facilities providing accessibility and usability for physically handicapped people (commonly cited as "ANSI A117.1") suffices to satisfy the requirements of paragraph (3)(C)(iii).

(5) (A) If a State or unit of general local government has incorporated into its laws the requirements set forth in paragraph (3)(C), compliance with such laws shall be deemed to satisfy the requirements of that paragraph.

(B) A State or unit of general local government may review and approve newly constructed covered multifamily dwellings for the purpose of making determinations as to whether the design and construction requirements of paragraph (3)(C) are met.

(C) The Secretary shall encourage, but may not require, States and units of local government to include in their existing procedures for the review and approval of newly constructed covered multifamily dwellings, determinations as to whether the design and construction of such dwellings are consistent with paragraph (3)(C), and shall provide technical assistance to States and units of local government and other persons to implement the requirements of paragraph (3)(C).

(D) Nothing in this subchapter shall be construed to require the Secretary to review or approve the plans, designs or construction of all covered multifamily dwellings, to determine whether the design and construction of such dwellings are consistent with the requirements of paragraph 3(C).

(6) (A) Nothing in paragraph (5) shall be construed to affect the authority and responsibility of the Secretary or a State or local public agency certified pursuant to section 3610(f)(3) of this title to receive and process complaints or otherwise engage in enforcement activities under this subchapter.

(B) Determinations by a State or a unit of general local government under paragraphs (5)(A) and (B) shall not be conclusive in enforcement proceedings under this subchapter.

(7) As used in this subsection, the term "covered multifamily dwellings" means —

(A) buildings consisting of 4 or more units if such buildings have one or more elevators; and

(B) ground floor units in other buildings consisting of 4 or more units.

(8) Nothing in this subchapter shall be construed to invalidate or limit any law of a State or political subdivision of a State, or other jurisdiction in which this subchapter shall be effective, that requires dwellings to be designed and constructed in a manner that affords handicapped persons greater access than is required by this subchapter.

(9) Nothing in this subsection requires that a dwelling be made available to an individual whose tenancy would constitute a direct threat to the health or safety of other individuals or whose tenancy would result in substantial physical damage to the property of others.

§ 3605. Discrimination in residential real estate-related transactions

(a) In general

It shall be unlawful for any person or other entity whose business includes engaging in residential real estate-related transactions to discriminate against any person in making available such a transaction, or in the terms or conditions of such a transaction, because of race, color, religion, sex, handicap, familial status, or national origin.

(b) Definition

As used in this section, the term "residential real estate-related transaction" means any of the following:

(1) The making or purchasing of loans or providing other financial assistance —

(A) for purchasing, constructing, improving, repairing, or maintaining a dwelling; or

(B) secured by residential real estate.

(2) The selling, brokering, or appraising of residential real property.

(c) Appraisal exemption

Nothing in this subchapter prohibits a person engaged in the business of furnishing appraisals of real property to take into consideration factors other than race, color, religion, national origin, sex, handicap, or familial status.

§ 3606. Discrimination in provision of brokerage services

After December 31, 1968, it shall be unlawful to deny any person access to or membership or participation in any multiple-listing service, real estate brokers' organization or other service, organization, or facility relating to the business of selling or renting dwellings, or to discriminate against him in the terms or conditions of such access, membership, or participation, on account of race, color, religion, sex, handicap, familial status, or national origin.

§ 3607. Exemption

(a) Religious organizations and private clubs

Nothing in this subchapter shall prohibit a religious organization, association, or society, or any nonprofit institution or organization operated, supervised or controlled by or in conjunction with a religious organization, association, or society, from limiting the sale, rental or occupancy of dwellings which it owns or operates for other than a commercial purpose to persons of the same religion, or from giving preference to such persons, unless membership in such religion is restricted on account of race, color, or national origin. Nor shall anything in this subchapter prohibit a private club not in fact open to the public, which as an incident to its primary purpose or purposes provides lodgings which it owns or operates for other than a commercial purpose, from limiting the rental or occupancy of such lodgings to its members or from giving preference to its members.

(b) Numbers of occupants; housing for older persons; persons convicted of making or distributing controlled substances

(1) Nothing in this subchapter limits the applicability of any reasonable local, State, or Federal restrictions regarding the maximum number of occupants permitted to occupy a dwelling. Nor does any provision in this subchapter regarding familial status apply with respect to housing for older persons.

(2) As used in this section, "housing for older persons" means housing —

(A) provided under any State or Federal program that the Secretary determines is specifically designed and operated to assist elderly persons (as defined in the State or Federal program); or

(B) intended for, and solely occupied by, persons 62 years of age or older; or

(C) intended and operated for occupancy by persons 55 years of age or older, and —

(i) at least 80 percent of the occupied units are occupied by at least one person who is 55 years of age or older;

(ii) the housing facility or community publishes and adheres to policies and procedures that demonstrate the intent required under this subparagraph; and

(iii) the housing facility or community complies with rules issued by the Secretary for verification of occupancy, which shall —

(I) provide for verification by reliable surveys and affidavits; and

(II) include examples of the types of policies and procedures relevant to a determination of compliance with the requirement of clause (ii). Such surveys and affidavits shall be admissible in administrative and judicial proceedings for the purposes of such verification.

(3) Housing shall not fail to meet the requirements for housing for older persons by reason of:

(A) persons residing in such housing as of September 13, 1988, who do not meet the age requirements of subsections (2)(B) or (C): Provided, That new occupants of such housing meet the age requirements of subsection (2)(B) or (C); or

(B) unoccupied units: Provided, That such units are reserved for occupancy by persons who meet the age requirements of subsection (2)(B) or (C).

(4) Nothing in this subchapter prohibits conduct against a person because such person has been convicted by any court of competent jurisdiction of the illegal manufacture or distribution of a controlled substance as defined in section 802 of Title 21.

(5) (A) A person shall not be held personally liable for monetary damages for a violation of this subchapter if such person reasonably relied, in good faith, on the application of the exemption under this subsection relating to housing for older persons.

(B) For the purposes of this paragraph, a person may only show good faith reliance on the application of the exemption by showing that —

(i) such person has no actual knowledge that the facility or community is not, or will not be, eligible for such exemption; and

(ii) the facility or community has stated formally, in writing, that the facility or community complies with the requirements for such exemption.

Chapter 12
HUD FAIR HOUSING ACT AMENDMENTS REGULATIONS

FAIR HOUSING ACT AMENDMENTS
HUD REGULATIONS
Subpart A   General

§ 100.1   Authority.

This regulation is issued under the authority of the Secretary of Housing and Urban Development to administer and enforce Title VIII of the Civil Rights Act of 1968, as amended by the Fair Housing Amendments Act of 1988 (the Fair Housing Act).

§ 100.5   Scope.

(a) It is the policy of the United States to provide, within constitutional limitations, for fair housing throughout the United States. No person shall be subjected to discrimination because of race, color, religion, sex, handicap, familial status, or national origin in the sale, rental, or advertising of dwellings, in the provision of brokerage services, or in the availability of residential real estate-related transactions.

(b) This part provides the Department's interpretation of the coverage of the Fair Housing Act regarding discrimination related to the sale or rental of dwellings, the provision of services in connection therewith, and the availability of residential real estate-related transactions.

(c) Nothing in this part relieves persons participating in a Federal or Federally-assisted program or activity from other requirements applicable to buildings and dwellings.

§ 100.10   Exemptions.

(a) This part does not:

(1) Prohibit a religious organization, association, or society, or any nonprofit institution or organization operated, supervised or controlled by or in conjunction with a religious organization, association, or society, from limiting the sale, rental or occupancy of dwellings which it owns or operates for other than a commercial purpose to persons of the same religion, or from giving preference to such persons, unless membership in such religion is restricted because of race, color, or national origin;

(2) Prohibit a private club, not in fact open to the public, which, incident to its primary purpose or purposes, provides lodgings which it owns or operates for other than a commercial purpose, from limiting the rental or occupancy of such lodgings to its members or from giving preference to its members;

(3) Limit the applicability of any reasonable local, State or Federal restrictions regarding the maximum number of occupants permitted to occupy a dwelling; or

(4) Prohibit conduct against a person because such person has been convicted by any court of competent jurisdiction of the illegal manufacture or distribution of a controlled substance as defined in Section 102 of the Controlled Substances Act (21 U.S.C. 802).

(b) Nothing in this part regarding discrimination based on familial status applies with respect to housing for older persons as defined in Subpart E of this part.

(c) Nothing in this part, other than the prohibitions against discriminatory advertising, applies to:

(1) The sale or rental of any single family house by an owner, provided the following conditions are met:

(i) The owner does not own or have any interest in more than three single family houses at any one time.

(ii) The house is sold or rented without the use of a real estate broker, agent or salesperson or the facilities of any person in the business of selling or renting dwellings. If the owner selling the house does not reside in it at the time of the sale or was not the most recent resident of the house prior to such sale, the exemption in this paragraph (c)(1) of this section applies to only one such sale in any 24-month period.

(2) Rooms or units in dwellings containing living quarters occupied or intended to be occupied by no more than four families living independently of each other, if the owner actually maintains and occupies one of such living quarters as his or her residence.

§ 100.20 Definitions.

The terms "Department," "Fair Housing Act," and "Secretary" are defined in 24 CFR part 5. As used in this part:

"Aggrieved person" includes any person who —

(a) Claims to have been injured by a discriminatory housing practice; or

(b) Believes that such person will be injured by a discriminatory housing practice that is about to occur.

"Broker" or "Agent" includes any person authorized to perform an action on behalf of another person regarding any matter related to the sale or rental of dwellings, including offers, solicitations or contracts and the administration of matters regarding such offers, solicitations or contracts or any residential real estate-related transactions.

"Discriminatory housing practice" means an act that is unlawful under section 804, 805, 806, or 818 of the Fair Housing Act.

"Dwelling" means any building, structure or portion thereof which is occupied as, or designed or intended for occupancy as, a residence by one or more families, and any vacant land which is offered for sale or lease for the construction or location thereon of any such building, structure or portion thereof.

"Familial status" means one or more individuals (who have not attained the age of 18 years) being domiciled with —

(a) A parent or another person having legal custody of such individual or individuals; or

(b) The designee of such parent or other person having such custody, with the written permission of such parent or other person.

The protections afforded against discrimination on the basis of familial status shall apply to any person who is pregnant or is in the process of securing legal custody of any individual who has not attained the age of 18 years.

"Handicap" is defined in § 100.201.

"Person" includes one or more individuals, corporations, partnerships, associations, labor organizations, legal representatives, mutual companies, joint-stock companies, trusts, unincorporated organizations, trustees, trustees in cases under Title 11 of the United States Code, receivers, and fiduciaries.

"Person in the business of selling or renting dwellings" means any person who:

(a) Within the preceding twelve months, has participated as principal in three or more transactions involving the sale or rental of any dwelling or any interest therein;

(b) Within the preceding twelve months, has participated as agent, other than in the sale of his or her own personal residence, in providing sales or rental facilities or sales or rental services in two or more transactions involving the sale or rental of any dwelling or any interest therein; or

(c) Is the owner of any dwelling designed or intended for occupancy by, or occupied by, five or more families.

"State" means any of the several states, the District of Columbia, the Commonwealth of Puerto Rico, or any of the territories and possessions of the United States.

Subpart B   Discriminatory Housing Practices

§ 100.50   Real estate practices prohibited.

(a) This subpart provides the Department's interpretation of conduct that is unlawful housing discrimination under section 804 and section 806 of the Fair Housing Act. In general the prohibited actions are set forth under sections of this subpart which are most applicable to the discriminatory conduct described. However, an action illustrated in one section can constitute a violation under sections in the subpart. For example, the conduct described in § 100.60(b)(3) and (4) would constitute a violation of § 100.65(a) as well as § 100.60(a).

(b) It shall be unlawful to:

(1) Refuse to sell or rent a dwelling after a bona fide offer has been made, or to refuse to negotiate for the sale or rental of a dwelling because of race, color, religion, sex, familial status, or national origin, or to discriminate in the sale or rental of a dwelling because of handicap.

(2) Discriminate in the terms, conditions or privileges of sale or rental of a dwelling, or in the provision of services or facilities in connection with sales or rentals, because of race, color, religion, sex, handicap, familial status, or national origin.

(3) Engage in any conduct relating to the provision of housing which otherwise makes unavailable or denies dwellings to persons because of race, color, religion, sex, handicap, familial status, or national origin.

(4) Make, print or publish, or cause to be made, printed or published, any notice, statement or advertisement with respect to the sale or rental of a dwelling that indicates any preference, limitation or discrimination because of race, color, religion, sex, handicap, familial status, or national origin, or an intention to make any such preference, limitation or discrimination.

(5) Represent to any person because of race, color, religion, sex, handicap, familial status, or national origin that a dwelling is not available for sale or rental when such dwelling is in fact available.

(6) Engage in blockbusting practices in connection with the sale or rental of dwellings because of race, color, religion, sex, handicap, familial status, or national origin.

(7) Deny access to or membership or participation in, or to discriminate against any person in his or her access to or membership or participation in, any multiple-listing service, real estate brokers' association, or other service organization or facility relating to the business of selling or renting a dwelling or in the terms or conditions or membership or participation, because of race, color, religion, sex, handicap, familial status, or national origin.

(c) The application of the Fair Housing Act with respect to persons with handicaps is discussed in Subpart D of this part.

§ 100.60   Unlawful refusal to sell or rent or to negotiate for the sale or rental.

(a) It shall be unlawful for a person to refuse to sell or rent a dwelling to a person who has made a bona fide offer, because of race, color, religion, sex, familial status, or national origin or to refuse to negotiate with a person for the sale or rental of a dwelling because of race, color, religion, sex, familial status, or national origin, or to discriminate against any person in the sale or rental of a dwelling because of handicap.

(b) Prohibited actions under this section include, but are not limited to:

(1) Failing to accept or consider a bona fide offer because of race, color, religion, sex, handicap, familial status, or national origin.

(2) Refusing to sell or rent a dwelling to, or to negotiate for the sale or rental of a dwelling with, any person because of race, color, religion, sex, handicap, familial status, or national origin.

(3) Imposing different sales prices or rental charges for the sale or rental of a dwelling upon any person because of race, color, religion, sex, handicap, familial status, or national origin.

(4) Using different qualification criteria or applications, or sale or rental standards or procedures, such as income standards, application requirements, application fees, credit analysis or sale or rental approval procedures or other requirements, because of race, color, religion, sex, handicap, familial status, or national origin.

(5) Evicting tenants because of their race, color, religion, sex, handicap, familial status, or national origin or because of the race, color, religion, sex, handicap,

familial status, or national origin of a tenant's guest.

§ 100.65 Discrimination in terms, conditions and privileges and in services and facilities.

(a) It shall be unlawful, because of race, color, religion, sex, handicap, familial status, or national origin, to impose different terms, conditions or privileges relating to the sale or rental of a dwelling or to deny or limit services or facilities in connection with the sale or rental of a dwelling.

(b) Prohibited actions under this section include, but are not limited to:

(1) Using different provisions in leases or contracts of sale, such as those relating to rental charges, security deposits and the terms of a lease and those relating to down payment and closing requirements, because of race, color, religion, sex, handicap, familial status, or national origin.

(2) Failing or delaying maintenance or repairs of sale or rental dwellings because of race, color, religion, sex, handicap, familial status, or national origin.

(3) Failing to process an offer for the sale or rental of a dwelling or to communicate an offer accurately because of race, color, religion, sex, handicap, familial status, or national origin.

(4) Limiting the use of privileges, services or facilities associated with a dwelling because of race, color, religion, sex, handicap, familial status, or national origin of an owner, tenant or a person associated with him or her.

(5) Denying or limiting services or facilities in connection with the sale or rental of a dwelling, because a person failed or refused to provide sexual favors.

§ 100.70 Other prohibited sale and rental conduct.

(a) It shall be unlawful, because of race, color, religion, sex, handicap, familial status, or national origin, to restrict or attempt to restrict the choices of a person by word or conduct in connection with seeking, negotiating for, buying or renting a dwelling so as to perpetuate, or tend to perpetuate, segregated housing patterns, or to discourage or obstruct choices in a community, neighborhood or development.

(b) It shall be unlawful, because of race, color, religion, sex, handicap, familial status, or national origin, to engage in any conduct relating to the provision of housing or of services and facilities in connection therewith that otherwise makes unavailable or denies dwellings to persons.

(c) Prohibited actions under paragraph (a) of this section, which are generally referred to as unlawful steering practices, include, but are not limited to:

(1) Discouraging any person from inspecting, purchasing or renting a dwelling because of race, color, religion, sex, handicap, familial status, or national origin, or because of the race, color, religion, sex, handicap, familial status, or national origin of persons in a community, neighborhood or development.

(2) Discouraging the purchase or rental of a dwelling because of race, color, religion, sex, handicap, familial status, or national origin, by exaggerating drawbacks or failing to inform any person of desirable fea-tures of a dwelling or

of a community, neighborhood, or development.

(3) Communicating to any prospective purchaser that he or she would not be comfortable or compatible with existing residents of a community, neighborhood or development because of race, color, religion, sex, handicap, familial status, or national origin.

(4) Assigning any person to a particular section of a community, neighborhood or development, or to a particular floor of a building, because of race, color, religion, sex, handicap, familial status, or national origin.

(d) Prohibited activities relating to dwellings under paragraph (b) of this section include, but are not limited to:

(1) Discharging or taking other adverse action against an employee, broker or agent because he or she refused to participate in a discriminatory housing practice.

(2) Employing codes or other devices to segregate or reject applicants, purchasers or renters, refusing to take or to show listings of dwellings in certain areas because of race, color, religion, sex, handicap, familial status, or national origin, or refusing to deal with certain brokers or agents because they or one or more of their clients are of a particular race, color, religion, sex, handicap, familial status, or national origin.

(3) Denying or delaying the processing of an application made by a purchaser or renter or refusing to approve such a person for occupancy in a cooperative or condominium dwelling because of race, color, religion, sex, handicap, familial status, or national origin.

(4) Refusing to provide municipal services or property or hazard insurance for dwellings or providing such services or insurance differently because of race, color, religion, sex, handicap, familial status, or national origin.

§ 100.75   Discriminatory advertisements, statements and notices.

(a) It shall be unlawful to make, print or publish, or cause to be made, printed or published, any notice, statement or advertisement with respect to the sale or rental of a dwelling which indicates any preference, limitation or discrimination because of race, color, religion, sex, handicap, familial status, or national origin, or an intention to make any such preference, limitation or discrimination.

(b) The prohibitions in this section shall apply to all written or oral notices or statements by a person engaged in the sale or rental of a dwelling. Written notices and statements include any applications, flyers, brochures, deeds, signs, banners, posters, billboards or any documents used with respect to the sale or rental of a dwelling.

(c) Discriminatory notices, statements and advertisements include, but are not limited to:

(1) Using words, phrases, photographs, illustrations, symbols or forms which convey that dwellings are available or not available to a particular group of persons because of race, color, religion, sex, handicap, familial status, or national

origin.

(2) Expressing to agents, brokers, employees, prospective sellers or renters or any other persons a preference for or limitation on any purchaser or renter because of race, color, religion, sex, handicap, familial status, or national origin of such persons.

(3) Selecting media or locations for advertising the sale or rental of dwellings which deny particular segments of the housing market information about housing opportunities because of race, color, religion, sex, handicap, familial status, or national origin.

(4) Refusing to publish advertising for the sale or rental of dwellings or requiring different charges or terms for such advertising because of race, color, religion, sex, handicap, familial status, or national origin.

(d) 24 CFR Part 109 provides information to assist persons to advertise dwellings in a nondiscriminatory manner and describes the matters the Department will review in evaluating compliance with the Fair Housing Act and in investigating complaints alleging discriminatory housing practices involving advertising.

§ 100.80 Discriminatory representations on the availability of dwellings.

(a) It shall be unlawful, because of race, color, religion, sex, handicap, familial status, or national origin, to provide inaccurate or untrue information about the availability of dwellings for sale or rental.

(b) Prohibited actions under this section include, but are not limited to:

(1) Indicating through words or conduct that a dwelling which is available for inspection, sale, or rental has been sold or rented, because of race, color, religion, sex, handicap, familial status, or national origin.

(2) Representing that covenants or other deed, trust or lease provisions which purport to restrict the sale or rental of dwellings because of race, color, religion, sex, handicap, familial status, or national origin preclude the sale of rental of a dwelling to a person.

(3) Enforcing covenants or other deed, trust, or lease provisions which preclude the sale or rental of a dwelling to any person because of race, color, religion, sex, handicap, familial status, or national origin.

(4) Limiting information, by word or conduct, regarding suitably priced dwellings available for inspection, sale or rental, because of race, color, religion, sex, handicap, familial status, or national origin.

(5) Providing false or inaccurate information regarding the availability of a dwelling for sale or rental to any person, including testers, regardless of whether such person is actually seeking housing, because of race, color, religion, sex, handicap, familial status, or national origin.

§ 100.85 Blockbusting.

(a) It shall be unlawful, for profit, to induce or attempt to induce a person to sell or rent a dwelling by representations regarding the entry or prospective entry into the neighborhood of a person or persons of a particular race, color, religion, sex, familial status, or national origin or with a handicap.

(b) In establishing a discriminatory housing practice under this section it is not necessary that there was in fact profit as long as profit was a factor for engaging in the blockbusting activity.

(c) Prohibited actions under this section include, but are not limited to:

(1) Engaging, for profit, in conduct (including uninvited solicitations for listings) which conveys to a person that a neighborhood is undergoing or is about to undergo a change in the race, color, religion, sex, handicap, familial status, or national origin of persons residing in it, in order to encourage the person to offer a dwelling for sale or rental.

(2) Encouraging, for profit, any person to sell or rent a dwelling through assertions that the entry or prospective entry of persons of a particular race, color, religion, sex, familial status, or national origin, or with handicaps, can or will result in undesirable consequences for the project, neighborhood or community, such as a lowering of property values, an increase in criminal or antisocial behavior, or a decline in the quality of schools or other services or facilities.

§ 100.90   Discrimination in the provision of brokerage services.

(a) It shall be unlawful to deny any person access to or membership or participation in any multiple listing service, real estate brokers' organization or other service, organization, or facility relating to the business of selling or renting dwellings, or to discriminate against any person in the terms or conditions of such access, membership or participation, because of race, color, religion, sex, handicap, familial status, or national origin.

(b) Prohibited actions under this section include, but are not limited to:

(1) Setting different fees for access to or membership in a multiple listing service because of race, color, religion, sex, handicap, familial status, or national origin.

(2) Denying or limiting benefits accruing to members in a real estate brokers' organization because of race, color, religion, sex, handicap, familial status, or national origin.

(3) Imposing different standards or criteria for membership in a real estate sales or rental organization because of race, color, religion, sex, handicap, familial status, or national origin.

(4) Establishing geographic boundaries or office location or residence requirements for access to or membership or participation in any multiple listing service, real estate brokers' organization or other service, organization or facility relating to the business of selling or renting dwellings, because of race, color, religion, sex, handicap, familial status, or national origin.

Subpart C Discrimination in Residential Real Estate-Related Transactions

§ 100.110 Discriminatory practices in residential real estate-related transactions.

(a) This subpart provides the Department's interpretation of the conduct that is unlawful housing discrimination under section 805 of the Fair Housing Act.

(b) It shall be unlawful for any person or other entity whose business includes engaging in residential real estate-related transactions to discriminate against any person in making available such a transaction, or in the terms or conditions of such a transaction, because of race, color, religion, sex, handicap, familial status, or national origin.

§ 100.115 Residential real estate-related transactions.

The term residential "real estate-related transactions" means:

(a) The making or purchasing of loans or providing other financial assistance—

(1) For purchasing, constructing, improving, repairing or maintaining a dwelling; or

(2) Secured by residential real estate; or

(b) The selling, brokering or appraising of residential real property.

§ 100.120 Discrimination in the making of loans and in the provision of other financial assistance.

(a) It shall be unlawful for any person or entity whose business includes engaging in residential real estate-related transactions to discriminate against any person in making available loans or other financial assistance for a dwelling, or which is or is to be secured by a dwelling, because of race, color, religion, sex, handicap, familial status, or national origin.

(b) Prohibited practices under this section include, but are not limited to, failing or refusing to provide to any person, in connection with a residential real estate-related transaction, information regarding the availability of loans or other financial assistance, application requirements, procedures or standards for the review and approval of loans or financial assistance, or providing information which is inaccurate or different from that provided others, because of race, color, religion, sex, handicap, familial status, or national origin.

§ 100.125 Discrimination in the purchasing of loans.

(a) It shall be unlawful for any person or entity engaged in the purchasing of loans or other debts or securities which support the purchase, construction, improvement, repair or maintenance of a dwelling, or which are secured by residential real estate, to refuse to purchase such loans, debts, or securities, or to impose different terms or conditions for such purchases, because of race, color, religion, sex, handicap, familial status, or national origin.

(b) Unlawful conduct under this section includes, but is not limited to:

(1) Purchasing loans or other debts or securities which relate to, or which are secured by dwellings in certain communities or neighborhoods but not in others because of the race, color, religion, sex, handicap, familial status, or national origin of persons in such neighborhoods or communities.

(2) Pooling or packaging loans or other debts or securities which relate to, or which are secured by, dwellings differently because of race, color, religion, sex, handicap, familial status, or national origin.

(3) Imposing or using different terms or conditions on the marketing or sale of securities issued on the basis of loans or other debts or securities which relate to, or which are secured by, dwellings because of race, color, religion, sex, handicap, familial status, or national origin.

(c) This section does not prevent consideration, in the purchasing of loans, of factors justified by business necessity, including requirements of Federal law, relating to a transaction's financial security or to protection against default or reduction of the value of the security. Thus, this provision would not preclude considerations employed in normal and prudent transactions, provided that no such factor may in any way relate to race, color, religion, sex, handicap, familial status or national origin.

§ 100.130 Discrimination in the terms and conditions for making available loans or other financial assistance.

(a) It shall be unlawful for any person or entity engaged in the making of loans or in the provision of other financial assistance relating to the purchase, construction, improvement, repair or maintenance of dwellings or which are secured by residential real estate to impose different terms or conditions for the availability of such loans or other financial assistance because of race, color, religion, sex, handicap, familial status, or national origin.

(b) Unlawful conduct under this section includes, but is not limited to:

(1) Using different policies, practices or procedures in evaluating or in determining credit-worthiness of any person in connection with the provision of any loan or other financial assistance for a dwelling or for any loan or other financial assistance which is secured by residential real estate because of race, color, religion, sex, handicap, familial status, or national origin.

(2) Determining the type of loan or other financial assistance to be provided with respect to a dwelling, or fixing the amount, interest rate, duration or other terms for a loan or other financial assistance for a dwelling or which is secured by residential real estate, because of race, color, religion, sex, handicap, familial status, or national origin.

§ 100.135 Unlawful practices in the selling, brokering, or appraising of residential real property.

(a) It shall be unlawful for any person or other entity whose business includes engaging in the selling, brokering or appraising of residential real property to discriminate against any person in making available such services, or in the performance of such services, because of race, color, religion, sex, handicap, familial status, or national origin.

(b) For the purposes of this section, the term appraisal means an estimate or opinion of the value of a specified residential real property made in a business context in connection with the sale, rental, financing or refinancing of a dwelling or in connection with any activity that otherwise affects the availability of a residential real estate-related transaction, whether the appraisal is oral or written, or transmitted formally or informally. The appraisal includes all written comments and other documents submitted as support for the estimate or opinion of value.

(c) Nothing in this section prohibits a person engaged in the business of making or furnishing appraisals of residential real property from taking into consideration factors other than race, color, religion, sex, handicap, familial status, or national origin.

(d) Practices which are unlawful under this section include, but are not limited to, using an appraisal of residential real property in connection with the sale, rental, or financing of any dwelling where the person knows or reasonably should know that the appraisal improperly takes into consideration race, color, religion, sex, handicap, familial status or national origin.

Subpart D   Prohibition Against Discrimination Because of Handicap

§ 100.200   Purpose.

The purpose of this subpart is to effectuate sections 6 (a) and (b) and 15 of the Fair Housing Amendments Act of 1988.

§ 100.201   Definitions.

As used in this subpart:

"Accessible", when used with respect to the public and common use areas of a building containing covered multifamily dwellings, means that the public or common use areas of the building can be approached, entered, and used by individuals with physical handicaps. The phrase "readily accessible to and usable by" is synonymous with accessible. A public or common use area that complies with the appropriate requirements of ANSI A117.1-1986 or a comparable standard is "accessible" within the meaning of this paragraph.

"Accessible route" means a continuous unobstructed path connecting accessible elements and spaces in a building or within a site that can be negotiated by a person with a severe disability using a wheelchair and that is also safe for and usable by people with other disabilities. Interior accessible routes may include corridors, floors, ramps, elevators and lifts. Exterior accessible routes may include parking access aisles, curb ramps, walks, ramps and lifts. A route that complies with the appropriate requirements of ANSI A117.1-1986 or a comparable standard is an "accessible route".

"ANSI A117.1-1986" means the 1986 edition of the American National Standard for buildings and facilities providing accessibility and usability for physically handicapped people. This incorporation by reference was approved by the Director of the Federal Register in accordance with 5 U.S.C. 552(a) and 1 CFR Part 51. Copies may be obtained from American National Standards Institute, Inc., 1430

Broadway, New York, New York 10018. Copies may be inspected at the Department of Housing and Urban Development, 451 Seventh Street, S.W., Room 10276, Washington, D.C., or at the Office of the Federal Register, 1100 L Street, N.W., Room 8401, Washington, D.C.

"Building" means a structure, facility or portion thereof that contains or serves one or more dwelling units.

"Building entrance on an accessible route" means an accessible entrance to a building that is connected by an accessible route to public transportation stops, to accessible parking and passenger loading zones, or to public streets or sidewalks, if available. A building entrance that complies with ANSI A117.1-1986 or a comparable standard complies with the requirements of this paragraph.

"Common use areas" means rooms, spaces or elements inside or outside of a building that are made available for the use of residents of a building or the guests thereof. These areas include hallways, lounges, lobbies, laundry rooms, refuse rooms, mail rooms, recreational areas and passageways among and between buildings.

"Controlled substance" means any drug or other substance, or immediate precursor included in the definition in section 102 of the Controlled Substances Act (21 U.S.C. 802).

"Covered multifamily dwellings" means buildings consisting of 4 or more dwelling units if such buildings have one or more elevators; and ground floor dwelling units in other buildings consisting of 4 or more dwelling units.

"Dwelling unit" means a single unit of residence for a family or one or more persons. Examples of dwelling units include: a single family home; an apartment unit within an apartment building; and in other types of dwellings in which sleeping accommodations are provided but toileting or cooking facilities are shared by occupants of more than one room or portion of the dwelling, rooms in which people sleep. Examples of the latter include dormitory rooms and sleeping accommodations in shelters intended for occupancy as a residence for homeless persons.

"Entrance" means any access point to a building or portion of a building used by residents for the purpose of entering.

"Exterior" means all areas of the premises outside of an individual dwelling unit.

"First occupancy" means a building that has never before been used for any purpose.

"Ground floor" means a floor of a building with a building entrance on an accessible route. A building may have more than one ground floor.

"Handicap" means, with respect to a person, a physical or mental impairment which substantially limits one or more major life activities; a record of such an impairment; or being regarded as having such an impairment. This term does not include current, illegal use of or addiction to a controlled substance. For purposes of this part, an individual shall not be considered to have a handicap solely because that individual is a transvestite. As used in this definition:

(a) "Physical or mental impairment" includes:

(1) Any physiological disorder or condition, cosmetic disfigurement, or

anatomical loss affecting one or more of the following body systems: Neurological; musculoskeletal; special sense organs; respiratory, including speech organs; cardiovascular; reproductive; digestive; genito-urinary; hemic and lymphatic; skin; and endocrine; or

(2) Any mental or psychological disorder, such as mental retardation, organic brain syndrome, emotional or mental illness, and specific learning disabilities. The term "physical or mental impairment" includes, but is not limited to, such diseases and conditions as orthopedic, visual, speech and hearing impairments, cerebral palsy, autism, epilepsy, muscular dystrophy, multiple sclerosis, cancer, heart disease, diabetes, Human Immunodeficiency Virus infection, mental retardation, emotional illness, drug addiction (other than addiction caused by current, illegal use of a controlled substance) and alcoholism.

(b) "Major life activities" means functions such as caring for one's self, performing manual tasks, walking, seeing, hearing, speaking, breathing, learning and working.

(c) "Has a record of such an impairment" means has a history of, or has been misclassified as having, a mental or physical impairment that substantially limits one or more major life activities.

(d) "Is regarded as having an impairment" means:

(1) Has a physical or mental impairment that does not substantially limit one or more major life activities but that is treated by another person as constituting such a limitation;

(2) Has a physical or mental impairment that substantially limits one or more major life activities only as a result of the attitudes of other toward such impairment; or

(3) Has none of the impairments defined in paragraph (a) of this definition but is treated by another person as having such an impairment.

"Interior" means the spaces, parts, components or elements of an individual dwelling unit.

"Modification" means any change to the public or common use areas of a building or any change to a dwelling unit.

"Premises" means the interior or exterior spaces, parts, components or elements of a building, including individual dwelling units and the public and common use areas of a building.

"Public use areas" means interior or exterior rooms or spaces of a building that are made available to the general public. Public use may be provided at a building that is privately or publicly owned.

"Site" means a parcel of land bounded by a property line or a designated portion of a public right or way.

§ 100.202 General prohibitions against discrimination because of handicap.

(a) It shall be unlawful to discriminate in the sale or rental, or to otherwise make unavailable or deny, a dwelling to any buyer or renter because of a handicap of —

(1) That buyer or renter;

(2) A person residing in or intending to reside in that dwelling after it is so sold, rented, or made available; or

(3) Any person associated with that person.

(b) It shall be unlawful to discriminate against any person in the terms, conditions, or privileges of the sale or rental of a dwelling, or in the provision of services or facilities in connection with such dwelling, because of a handicap of —

(1) That buyer or renter;

(2) A person residing in or intending to reside in that dwelling after it is so sold, rented, or made available; or

(3) Any person associated with that person.

(c) It shall be unlawful to make an inquiry to determine whether an applicant for a dwelling, a person intending to reside in that dwelling after it is so sold, rented or made available, or any person associated with that person, has a handicap or to make inquiry as to the nature or severity of a handicap of such a person. However, this paragraph does not prohibit the following inquiries, provided these inquiries are made of all applicants, whether or not they have handicaps:

(1) Inquiry into an applicant's ability to meet the requirements of ownership or tenancy;

(2) Inquiry to determine whether an applicant is qualified for a dwelling available only to persons with handicaps or to persons with a particular type of handicap;

(3) Inquiry to determine whether an applicant for a dwelling is qualified for a priority available to persons with handicaps or to persons with a particular type of handicap;

(4) Inquiring whether an applicant for a dwelling is a current illegal abuser or addict of a controlled substance;

(5) Inquiring whether an applicant has been convicted of the illegal manufacture or distribution of a controlled substance.

(d) Nothing in this subpart requires that a dwelling be made available to an individual whose tenancy would constitute a direct threat to the health or safety of other individuals or whose tenancy would result in substantial physical damage to the property of others.

§ 100.203 Reasonable modifications of existing premises.

(a) It shall be unlawful for any person to refuse to permit, at the expense of a handicapped person, reasonable modifications of existing premises, occupied or to be occupied by a handicapped person, if the proposed modifications may be necessary to afford the handicapped person full enjoyment of the premises of a dwelling. In the case of a rental, the landlord may, where it is reasonable to do so, condition permission for a modification on the renter agreeing to restore the interior of the premises to the condition that existed before the modification, reasonable wear and tear excepted. The landlord may not increase for handicapped persons any customarily required security deposit. However, where it is necessary in order to ensure with reasonable certainty that funds will be available to pay for the restorations at the end of the tenancy, the landlord may negotiate as part of such a restoration agreement a provision requiring that the tenant pay into an interest bearing escrow account, over a reasonable period, a reasonable amount of money not to exceed the cost of the restorations. The interest in any such account shall accrue to the benefit of the tenant.

(b) A landlord may condition permission for a modification on the renter providing a reasonable description of the proposed modifications as well as reasonable assurances that the work will be done in a workmanlike manner and that any required building permits will be obtained.

(c) The application of paragraph (a) of this section may be illustrated by the following examples:

Example (1): A tenant with a handicap asks his or her landlord for permission to install grab bars in the bathroom at his or her own expense. It is necessary to reinforce the walls with blocking between studs in order to affix the grab bars. It is unlawful for the landlord to refuse to permit the tenant, at the tenant's own expense, from making the modifications necessary to add the grab bars. However, the landlord may condition permission for the modification on the tenant agreeing to restore the bathroom to the condition that existed before the modification, reasonable wear and tear excepted. It would be reasonable for the landlord to require the tenant to remove the grab bars at the end of the tenancy. The landlord may also reasonably require that the wall to which the grab bars are to be attached be repaired and restored to its original condition, reasonable wear and tear excepted. However, it would be unreasonable for the landlord to require the tenant to remove the blocking, since the reinforced walls will not interfere in any way with the landlord's or the next tenant's use and enjoyment of the premises and may be needed by some future tenant.

Example (2): An applicant for rental housing has a child who uses a wheelchair. The bathroom door in the dwelling unit is too narrow to permit the wheelchair to pass. The applicant asks the landlord for permission to widen the doorway at the applicant's own expense. It is unlawful for the landlord to refuse to permit the applicant to make the modification. Further, the landlord may not, in usual circumstances, condition permission for the modification on the applicant paying for the doorway to be narrowed at the end of the lease because a wider doorway will not interfere with the landlord's or the next tenant's use and enjoyment of the premises.

§ 100.204 Reasonable accommodations.

(a) It shall be unlawful for any person to refuse to make reasonable accommodations in rules, policies, practices, or services, when such accommodations may be necessary to afford a handicapped person equal opportunity to use and enjoy a dwelling unit, including public and common use areas.

(b) The application of this section may be illustrated by the following examples:

Example (1): A blind applicant for rental housing wants live in a dwelling unit with a seeing eye dog. The building has a "no pets" policy. It is a violation of § 100.204 for the owner or manager of the apartment complex to refuse to permit the applicant to live in the apartment with a seeing eye dog because, without the seeing eye dog, the blind person will not have an equal opportunity to use and enjoy a dwelling.

Example (2): Progress Gardens is a 300 unit apartment complex with 450 parking spaces which are available to tenants and guests of Progress Gardens on a "first come first served" basis. John applies for housing in Progress Gardens. John is mobility impaired and is unable to walk more than a short distance and therefore requests that a parking space near his unit be reserved for him so he will not have to walk very far to get to his apartment. It is a violation of § 100.204 for the owner or manager of Progress Gardens to refuse to make this accommodation. Without a reserved space, John might be unable to live in Progress Gardens at all or, when he has to park in a space far from his unit, might have great difficulty getting from his car to his apartment unit. The accommodation therefore is necessary to afford John an equal opportunity to use and enjoy a dwelling. The accommodation is reasonable because it is feasible and practical under the circumstances.

§ 100.205   Design and construction requirements.

(a) Covered multifamily dwellings for first occupancy after March 13, 1991 shall be designed and constructed to have at least one building entrance on an accessible route unless it is impractical to do so because of the terrain or unusual characteristics of the site. For purposes of this section, a covered multifamily dwelling shall be deemed to be designed and constructed for first occupancy on or before March 13, 1991, if the dwelling is occupied by that date, or if the last building permit or renewal thereof for the dwelling is issued by a State, County or local government on or before June 15, 1990. The burden of establishing impracticality because of terrain or unusual site characteristics is on the person or persons who designed or constructed the housing facility.

(b) The application of paragraph (a) of this section may be illustrated by the following examples:

Example (1): A real estate developer plans to construct six covered multifamily dwelling units on a site with a hilly terrain. Because of the terrain, it will be necessary to climb a long and steep stairway in order to enter the dwellings. Since there is no practical way to provide an accessible route to any of the dwellings, one need not be provided.

Example (2): A real estate developer plans to construct a building consisting of 10 units of multifamily housing on a waterfront site that floods frequently. Because of this unusual characteristic of the site, the builder plans to construct the building on stilts. It is customary for housing in the geographic area where the site is located to be built on stilts. The housing may lawfully be constructed on the proposed site on stilts even though this means that there will be no practical way to provide an accessible route to the building entrance.

Example (3): A real estate developer plans to construct a multifamily housing facility on a particular site. The developer would like the facility to be built on the site to contain as many units as possible. Because of the configuration and terrain of the site, it is possible to construct a building with 105 units on the site provided the site does not have an accessible route leading to the building entrance. It is also possible to construct a building on the site with an accessible route leading to the building entrance. However, such a building would have no more than 100 dwelling units. The building to be constructed on the site must have a building entrance on an accessible route because it is not impractical to provide such an entrance because of the terrain or unusual characteristics of the site.

(c) All covered multifamily dwellings for first occupancy after March 13, 1991 with a building entrance on an accessible route shall be designed and constructed in such a manner that —

(1) The public and common use areas are readily accessible to and usable by handicapped persons;

(2) All the doors designed to allow passage into and within all premises are sufficiently wide to allow passage by handicapped persons in wheelchairs; and

(3) All premises within covered multifamily dwelling units contain the following features of adaptable design:

(i) An accessible route into and through the covered dwelling unit;

(ii) Light switches, electrical outlets, thermostats, and other environmental controls in accessible locations;

(iii) Reinforcements in bathroom walls to allow later installation of grab bars around the toilet, tub, shower, stall and shower seat, where such facilities are provided; and

(iv) Usable kitchens and bathrooms such that an individual in a wheelchair can maneuver about the space.

(d) The application of paragraph (c) of this section may be illustrated by the following examples:

Example (1): A developer plans to construct a 100 unit condominium apartment building with one elevator. In accordance with paragraph (a), the building has at least one accessible route leading to an accessible entrance. All 100 units are covered multifamily dwelling units and they all must be designed and constructed so that they comply with the accessibility requirements of paragraph (c) of this section.

Example (2): A developer plans to construct 30 garden apartments in a three story building. The building will not have an elevator. The building will have one accessible entrance which will be on the first floor. Since the building does not have an elevator, only the "ground floor" units are covered multifamily units. The "ground floor" is the first floor because that is the floor that has an accessible entrance. All of the dwelling units on the first floor must meet the accessibility requirements of paragraph (c) of this section and must have access to at least one of each type of public or common use area available for residents in the building.

(e) Compliance with the appropriate requirements of ANSI A117.1-1986 suffices to satisfy the requirements of paragraph (c)(3) of this section.

(f) Compliance with a duly enacted law of a State or unit of general local government that includes the requirements of paragraphs (a) and (c) of this section satisfies the requirements of paragraphs (a) and (c) of this section.

(g) (1) It is the policy of HUD to encourage States and units of general local government to include, in their existing procedures for the review and approval of newly constructed covered multifamily dwellings, determinations as to whether the design and construction of such dwellings are consistent with paragraphs (a) and (c) of this section.

(2) A State or unit of general local government may review and approve newly constructed multifamily dwellings for the purpose of making determinations as to whether the requirements of paragraphs (a) and (c) of this section are met.

(h) Determinations of compliance or noncompliance by a State or a unit of general local government under paragraph (f) or (g) of this section are not conclusive in enforcement proceedings under the Fair Housing Amendments Act.

(i) This subpart does not invalidate or limit any law of a State or political subdivision of a State that requires dwellings to be designed and constructed in a manner that affords handicapped persons greater access than is required by this subpart.

Chapter 13
DAMAGES

CIVIL RIGHTS ACT OF 1991	
42 U.S.C. §	
1981a	**Damages in cases of intentional discrimination in employment**

§ 1981a. Damages in cases of intentional discrimination in employment

(a) Right of recovery

(1) Civil rights

In an action brought by a complaining party under section 706 or 717 of the Civil Rights Act of 1964 (42 U.S.C. 2000e-5) [42 U.S.C.A. § 2000e-5 or 42 U.S.C.A. § 2000e-16] against a respondent who engaged in unlawful intentional discrimination (not an employment practice that is unlawful because of its disparate impact) prohibited under section 703, 704, or 717 of the Act (42 U.S.C. 2000e-2 or 2000e-3) [42 U.S.C.A. § 2000e-2, 42 U.S.C.A. § 2000e-3, or 42 U.S.C.A. § 2000e-16], and provided that the complaining party cannot recover under section 1981 of this title, the complaining party may recover compensatory and punitive damages as allowed in subsection (b) of this section, in addition to any relief authorized by section 706(g) of the Civil Rights Act of 1964 [42 U.S.C.A. § 2000e-5(g)], from the respondent.

(2) Disability

In an action brought by a complaining party under the powers, remedies, and procedures set forth in section 706 or 717 of the Civil Rights Act of 1964 [42 U.S.C.A. § 2000e-5 or 42 U.S.C.A. § 2000e-16] (as provided in section 107(a) of the Americans with Disabilities Act of 1990 (42 U.S.C. 12117(a)), and section 794a(a)(1) of Title 29, respectively) against a respondent who engaged in unlawful intentional discrimination (not an employment practice that is unlawful because of its disparate impact) under section 791 of Title 29 and the regulations implementing section 791 of Title 29, or who violated the requirements of section 791 of Title 29 or the regulations implementing section 791 of Title 29 concerning the provision of a reasonable accommodation, or section 102 of the Americans with Disabilities Act of 1990 (42 U.S.C. 12112), or committed a violation of section 102(b)(5) of the Act [42 U.S.C.A. § 12112(b)(5)], against an individual, the complaining party may recover compensatory and punitive damages as allowed in subsection (b) of this section, in addition to any relief authorized by section 706(g) of the Civil Rights Act of 1964 [42 U.S.C.A. § 2000e-5(g)], from the respondent.

(3) Reasonable accommodation and good faith effort

In cases where a discriminatory practice involves the provision of a reasonable accommodation pursuant to section 102(b)(5) of the Americans with Disabilities Act of 1990 [42 U.S.C.A. § 12112(b)(5)] or regulations implementing section 791 of Title 29, damages may not be awarded under this section where the covered entity demonstrates good faith efforts, in consultation with the person with the disability who has informed the covered entity that accommodation is needed, to identify and make a reasonable accommodation that would provide such individual with an equally effective opportunity and would not cause an undue hardship on the operation of the business.

(b) Compensatory and punitive damages

(1) Determination of punitive damages

A complaining party may recover punitive damages under this section against a respondent (other than a government, government agency or political subdivision) if the complaining party demonstrates that the respondent engaged in a discriminatory practice or discriminatory practices with malice or with reckless indifference to the federally protected rights of an aggrieved individual.

(2) Exclusions from compensatory damages

Compensatory damages awarded under this section shall not include backpay, interest on backpay, or any other type of relief authorized under section 706(g) of the Civil Rights Act of 1964 [42 U.S.C.A. § 2000e-5(g)].

(3) Limitations

The sum of the amount of compensatory damages awarded under this section for future pecuniary losses, emotional pain, suffering, inconvenience, mental anguish, loss of enjoyment of life, and other nonpecuniary losses, and the amount of punitive damages awarded under this section, shall not exceed, for each complaining party —

(A) in the case of a respondent who has more than 14 and fewer than 101 employees in each of 20 or more calendar weeks in the current or preceding calendar year, $50,000;

(B) in the case of a respondent who has more than 100 and fewer than 201 employees in each of 20 or more calendar weeks in the current or preceding calendar year, $100,000; and

(C) in the case of a respondent who has more than 200 and fewer than 501 employees in each of 20 or more calendar weeks in the current or preceding calendar year, $200,000; and

(D) in the case of a respondent who has more than 500 employees in each of 20 or more calendar weeks in the current or preceding calendar year, $300,000.

(4) Construction

Nothing in this section shall be construed to limit the scope of, or the relief available under, section 1981 of this title.

(c) Jury trial

If a complaining party seeks compensatory or punitive damages under this section —

(1) any party may demand a trial by jury; and

(2) the court shall not inform the jury of the limitations described in subsection (b)(3) of this section.

(d) Definitions

As used in this section:

(1)   Complaining party

The term "complaining party" means —

(A) in the case of a person seeking to bring an action under subsection (a)(1) of this section, the Equal Employment Opportunity Commission, the Attorney General, or a person who may bring an action or proceeding under title VII of the Civil Rights Act of 1964 (42 U.S.C. 2000e et seq.); or

(B) in the case of a person seeking to bring an action under subsection (a)(2) of this section, the Equal Employment Opportunity Commission, the Attorney General, a person who may bring an action or proceeding under section 794a(a)(1) of Title 29, or a person who may bring an action or proceeding under title I of the Americans with Disabilities Act of 1990 (42 U.S.C. 12101 et seq.).

(2)   Discriminatory practice

The term "discriminatory practice" means the discrimination described in paragraph (1), or the discrimination or the violation described in paragraph (2), of subsection (a) of this section.

Chapter 14
INDIVIDUALS WITH DISABILITIES EDUCATION ACT[1]

Part A

§ 1400. Short title; findings; purposes

(a) Short title

This chapter may be cited as the "Individuals with Disabilities Education Act".

(b) Omitted

(c) Findings

Congress finds the following:

(1) Disability is a natural part of the human experience and in no way diminishes the right of individuals to participate in or contribute to society. Improving educational results for children with disabilities is an essential element of our national policy of ensuring equality of opportunity, full participation, independent living, and economic self-sufficiency for individuals with disabilities.

(2) Before the date of enactment of the Education for All Handicapped Children Act of 1975 (Public Law 94-142), the educational needs of millions of children with disabilities were not being fully met because —

(A) the children did not receive appropriate educational services;

(B) the children were excluded entirely from the public school system and from being educated with their peers;

(C) undiagnosed disabilities prevented the children from having a successful educational experience; or

(D) a lack of adequate resources within the public school system forced families to find services outside the public school system.

(3) Since the enactment and implementation of the Education for All Handicapped Children Act of 1975, this chapter has been successful in ensuring children with disabilities and the families of such children access to a free appropriate public education and in improving educational results for children with disabilities.

(4) However, the implementation of this chapter has been impeded by low expectations, and an insufficient focus on applying replicable research on proven methods of teaching and learning for children with disabilities.

(5) Almost 30 years of research and experience has demonstrated that the education of children with disabilities can be made more effective by —

(A) having high expectations for such children and ensuring their access to

---

[1] This is an edited version of the IDEA that emphasizes its substantive and procedural requirements. The funding formulas have been omitted.

the general education curriculum in the regular classroom, to the maximum extent possible, in order to —

(i) meet developmental goals and, to the maximum extent possible, the challenging expectations that have been established for all children; and

(ii) be prepared to lead productive and independent adult lives, to the maximum extent possible;

(B) strengthening the role and responsibility of parents and ensuring that families of such children have meaningful opportunities to participate in the education of their children at school and at home;

(C) coordinating this chapter with other local, educational service agency, State, and Federal school improvement efforts, including improvement efforts under the Elementary and Secondary Education Act of 1965 [20 U.S.C.A. § 6301 et seq.], in order to ensure that such children benefit from such efforts and that special education can become a service for such children rather than a place where such children are sent;

(D) providing appropriate special education and related services, and aids and supports in the regular classroom, to such children, whenever appropriate;

(E) supporting high-quality, intensive preservice preparation and professional development for all personnel who work with children with disabilities in order to ensure that such personnel have the skills and knowledge necessary to improve the academic achievement and functional performance of children with disabilities, including the use of scientifically based instructional practices, to the maximum extent possible;

(F) providing incentives for whole-school approaches, scientifically based early reading programs, positive behavioral interventions and supports, and early intervening services to reduce the need to label children as disabled in order to address the learning and behavioral needs of such children;

(G) focusing resources on teaching and learning while reducing paperwork and requirements that do not assist in improving educational results; and

(H) supporting the development and use of technology, including assistive technology devices and assistive technology services, to maximize accessibility for children with disabilities.

(6) While States, local educational agencies, and educational service agencies are primarily responsible for providing an education for all children with disabilities, it is in the national interest that the Federal Government have a supporting role in assisting State and local efforts to educate children with disabilities in order to improve results for such children and to ensure equal protection of the law.

(7) A more equitable allocation of resources is essential for the Federal Government to meet its responsibility to provide an equal educational opportunity for all individuals.

(8) Parents and schools should be given expanded opportunities to resolve their

disagreements in positive and constructive ways.

(9) Teachers, schools, local educational agencies, and States should be relieved of irrelevant and unnecessary paperwork burdens that do not lead to improved educational outcomes.

(10) (A) The Federal Government must be responsive to the growing needs of an increasingly diverse society.

(B) America's ethnic profile is rapidly changing. In 2000, 1 of every 3 persons in the United States was a member of a minority group or was limited English proficient.

(C) Minority children comprise an increasing percentage of public school students.

(D) With such changing demographics, recruitment efforts for special education personnel should focus on increasing the participation of minorities in the teaching profession in order to provide appropriate role models with sufficient knowledge to address the special education needs of these students.

(11) (A) The limited English proficient population is the fastest growing in our Nation, and the growth is occurring in many parts of our Nation.

(B) Studies have documented apparent discrepancies in the levels of referral and placement of limited English proficient children in special education.

(C) Such discrepancies pose a special challenge for special education in the referral of, assessment of, and provision of services for, our Nation's students from non-English language backgrounds.

(12) (A) Greater efforts are needed to prevent the intensification of problems connected with mislabeling and high dropout rates among minority children with disabilities.

(B) More minority children continue to be served in special education than would be expected from the percentage of minority students in the general school population.

(C) African-American children are identified as having mental retardation and emotional disturbance at rates greater than their White counterparts.

(D) In the 1998-1999 school year, African-American children represented just 14.8 percent of the population aged 6 through 21, but comprised 20.2 percent of all children with disabilities.

(E) Studies have found that schools with predominately White students and teachers have placed disproportionately high numbers of their minority students into special education.

(13) (A) As the number of minority students in special education increases, the number of minority teachers and related services personnel produced in colleges and universities continues to decrease.

(B) The opportunity for full participation by minority individuals, minority organizations, and Historically Black Colleges and Universities in awards for grants and contracts, boards of organizations receiving assistance under this chapter, peer review panels, and training of professionals in the area of special education is essential to obtain greater success in the education of minority children with disabilities.

(14) As the graduation rates for children with disabilities continue to climb, providing effective transition services to promote successful post-school employment or education is an important measure of accountability for children with disabilities.

(d)   Purposes

The purposes of this chapter are —

(1) (A) to ensure that all children with disabilities have available to them a free appropriate public education that emphasizes special education and related services designed to meet their unique needs and prepare them for further education, employment, and independent living;

(B) to ensure that the rights of children with disabilities and parents of such children are protected; and

(C) to assist States, localities, educational service agencies, and Federal agencies to provide for the education of all children with disabilities;

(2) to assist States in the implementation of a statewide, comprehensive, coordinated, multidisciplinary, interagency system of early intervention services for infants and toddlers with disabilities and their families;

(3) to ensure that educators and parents have the necessary tools to improve educational results for children with disabilities by supporting system improvement activities; coordinated research and personnel preparation; coordinated technical assistance, dissemination, and support; and technology development and media services; and

(4) to assess, and ensure the effectiveness of, efforts to educate children with disabilities.

§ 1401.   Definitions

Except as otherwise provided, in this chapter:

(1)   Assistive technology device

(A)   In general

The term "assistive technology device" means any item, piece of equipment, or product system, whether acquired commercially off the shelf, modified, or customized, that is used to increase, maintain, or improve functional capabilities of a child with a disability.

(B)   Exception

The term does not include a medical device that is surgically implanted, or the replacement o such device.

(2)   Assistive technology service

The term "assistive technology service" means any service that directly assists a child with a disability in the selection, acquisition, or use of an assistive technology device. Such term includes —

(A) the evaluation of the needs of such child, including a functional evaluation of the child in the child's customary environment;

(B) purchasing, leasing, or otherwise providing for the acquisition of assistive technology devices by such child;

(C) selecting, designing, fitting, customizing, adapting, applying, maintaining, repairing, or replacing assistive technology devices;

(D) coordinating and using other therapies, interventions, or services with assistive technology devices, such as those associated with existing education and rehabilitation plans and programs;

(E) training or technical assistance for such child, or, where appropriate, the family of such child; and

(F) training or technical assistance for professionals (including individuals providing education and rehabilitation services), employers, or other individuals who provide services to, employ, or are otherwise substantially involved in the major life functions of such child.

(3)   Child with a disability

(A)   In general

The term "child with a disability" means a child —

(i) with mental retardation, hearing impairments (including deafness), speech or language impairments, visual impairments (including blindness), serious emotional disturbance (referred to in this chapter as "emotional disturbance"), orthopedic impairments, autism, traumatic brain injury, other health impairments, or specific learning disabilities; and

(ii) who, by reason thereof, needs special education and related services.

(B)   Child aged 3 through 9

The term "child with a disability" for a child aged 3 through 9 (or any subset of that age range, including ages 3 through 5), may, at the discretion of the State and the local educational agency, include a child —

(i) experiencing developmental delays, as defined by the State and as measured by appropriate diagnostic instruments and procedures, in 1 or more of the following areas: physical development; cognitive development; communication development; social or emotional development; or adaptive development; and

(ii) who, by reason thereof, needs special education and related services.

* * *

(9)   Free appropriate public education

The term "free appropriate public education" means special education and related services that-

(A) have been provided at public expense, under public supervision and direction, and without charge;

(B) meet the standards of the State educational agency;

(C) include an appropriate preschool, elementary school, or secondary school education in the State involved; and

(D) are provided in conformity with the individualized education program required under section 1414(d) of this title.

* * *

(11) Homeless children

The term "homeless children" has the meaning given the term "homeless children and youths" in section 11434a of Title 42.

* * *

(14) Individualized education program; IEP

The term "individualized education program" or "IEP" means a written statement for each child with a disability that is developed, reviewed, and revised in accordance with section 1414(d) of this title.

(15) Individualized family service plan

The term "individualized family service plan" has the meaning given the term in section 1436 of this title.

(16) Infant or toddler with a disability

The term "infant or toddler with a disability" has the meaning given the term in section 1432 of this title.

* * *

(18) Limited English proficient

The term "limited English proficient" has the meaning given the term in section 9101 of the Elementary and Secondary Education Act of 1965 [20 U.S.C.A. § 7801].

(19) Local educational agency

(A) In general

The term "local educational agency" means a public board of education or other public authority legally constituted within a State for either administrative control or direction of, or to perform a service function for, public elementary schools or secondary schools in a city, county, township, school district, or other political subdivision of a State, or for such combination of school districts or counties as are recognized in a State as an administrative agency for its public elementary schools or secondary schools.

(B) Educational service agencies and other public institutions or agencies

The term includes —

    (i) an educational service agency; and

    (ii) any other public institution or agency having administrative control and direction of a public elementary school or secondary school.

* * *

(20)   Native language

The term "native language", when used with respect to an individual who is limited English proficient, means the language normally used by the individual or, in the case of a child, the language normally used by the parents of the child.

* * *

(23)   Parent

The term "parent" means —

    (A) a natural, adoptive, or foster parent of a child (unless a foster parent is prohibited by State law from serving as a parent);

    (B) a guardian (but not the State if the child is a ward of the State);

    (C) an individual acting in the place of a natural or adoptive parent (including a grandparent, stepparent, or other relative) with whom the child lives, or an individual who is legally responsible for the child's welfare; or

    (D) except as used in sections 1415(b)(2) and 1439(a)(5) of this title, an individual assigned under either of those sections to be a surrogate parent.

* * *

(26)   Related services

    (A) In general

The term "related services" means transportation, and such developmental, corrective, and other supportive services (including speech-language pathology and audiology services, interpreting services, psychological services, physical and occupational therapy, recreation, including therapeutic recreation, social work services, school nurse services designed to enable a child with a disability to receive a free appropriate public education as described in the individualized education program of the child, counseling services, including rehabilitation counseling, orientation and mobility services, and medical services, except that such medical services shall be for diagnostic and evaluation purposes only) as may be required to assist a child with a disability to benefit from special education, and includes the early identification and assessment of disabling conditions in children.

    (B) Exception

The term does not include a medical device that is surgically implanted, or the replacement of such device.

* * *

(29)   Special education

The term "special education" means specially designed instruction, at no cost to parents, to meet the unique needs of a child with a disability, including —

(A) instruction conducted in the classroom, in the home, in hospitals and institutions, and in other settings; and

(B) instruction in physical education.

(30)   Specific learning disability

(A)   In general

The term "specific learning disability" means a disorder in 1 or more of the basic psychological processes involved in understanding or in using language, spoken or written, which disorder may manifest itself in the imperfect ability to listen, think, speak, read, write, spell, or do mathematical calculations.

(B)   Disorders included

Such term includes such conditions as perceptual disabilities, brain injury, minimal brain dysfunction, dyslexia, and developmental aphasia.

(C)   Disorders not included

Such term does not include a learning problem that is primarily the result of visual, hearing, or motor disabilities, of mental retardation, of emotional disturbance, or of environmental, cultural, or economic disadvantage.

(31)   State

The term "State" means each of the 50 States, the District of Columbia, the Commonwealth of Puerto Rico, and each of the outlying areas.

(32)   State educational agency

The term "State educational agency" means the State board of education or other agency or officer primarily responsible for the State supervision of public elementary schools and secondary schools, or, if there is no such officer or agency, an officer or agency designated by the Governor or by State law.

(33)   Supplementary aids and services

The term "supplementary aids and services" means aids, services, and other supports that are provided in regular education classes or other education-related settings to enable children with disabilities to be educated with nondisabled children to the maximum extent appropriate in accordance with section 1412(a)(5) of this title.

(34)   Transition services

The term "transition services" means a coordinated set of activities for a child with a disability that —

(A) is designed to be within a results-oriented process, that is focused on improving the academic and functional achievement of the child with a disability to facilitate the child's movement from school to post-school activities, including post-secondary education, vocational education, integrated employment (including supported employment), continuing and adult education, adult services, independent living, or community participation;

(B) is based on the individual child's needs, taking into account the child's strengths, preferences, and interests; and

(C) includes instruction, related services, community experiences, the development of employment and other post-school adult living objectives, and, when appropriate, acquisition of daily living skills and functional vocational evaluation.

(35)   Universal design

The term "universal design" has the meaning given the term in section 3002 of Title 29.

(36)   Ward of the State

(A)   In general

The term "ward of the State" means a child who, as determined by the State where the child resides, is a foster child, is a ward of the State, or is in the custody of a public child welfare agency.

(B)   Exception

The term does not include a foster child who has a foster parent who meets the definition of a parent in paragraph (23).

* * *

§ 1403.   Abrogation of State sovereign immunity

(a)   In general

A State shall not be immune under the 11th amendment to the Constitution of the United States from suit in Federal court for a violation of this chapter.

(b)   Remedies

In a suit against a State for a violation of this chapter, remedies (including remedies both at law and in equity) are available for such a violation to the same extent as those remedies are available for such a violation in the suit against any public entity other than a State.

(c)   Effective date

Subsections (a) and (b) apply with respect to violations that occur in whole or part after October 30, 1990.

* * *

Part B

§ 1412. State eligibility

(a) In general

A State is eligible for assistance under this subchapter for a fiscal year if the State submits a plan that provides assurances to the Secretary that the State has in effect policies and procedures to ensure that the State meets each of the following conditions:

(1) Free appropriate public education

(A) In general

A free appropriate public education is available to all children with disabilities residing in the State between the ages of 3 and 21, inclusive, including children with disabilities who have been suspended or expelled from school.

(B) Limitation

The obligation to make a free appropriate public education available to all children with disabilities does not apply with respect to children —

(i) aged 3 through 5 and 18 through 21 in a State to the extent that its application to those children would be inconsistent with State law or practice, or the order of any court, respecting the provision of public education to children in those age ranges; and

(ii) aged 18 through 21 to the extent that State law does not require that special education and related services under this subchapter be provided to children with disabilities who, in the educational placement prior to their incarceration in an adult correctional facility —

(I) were not actually identified as being a child with a disability under section 1401 of this title; or

(II) did not have an individualized education program under this subchapter.

(C) State flexibility

A State that provides early intervention services in accordance with subchapter III to a child who is eligible for services under section 1419 of this title, is not required to provide such child with a free appropriate public education.

(2) Full educational opportunity goal

The State has established a goal of providing full educational opportunity to all children with disabilities and a detailed timetable for accomplishing that goal.

(3) Child find

(A) In general

All children with disabilities residing in the State, including children with disabilities who are homeless children or are wards of the State and children with disabilities attending private schools, regardless of the severity of their disabilities, and who are in need of special education and related services, are identified, located, and evaluated and a practical method is developed and implemented to determine which children with disabilities are currently receiving needed special education and related services.

(B)   Construction

Nothing in this chapter requires that children be classified by their disability so long as each child who has a disability listed in section 1401 of this title and who, by reason of that disability, needs special education and related services is regarded as a child with a disability under this subchapter.

(4)   Individualized education program

An individualized education program, or an individualized family service plan that meets the requirements of section 1436(d) of this title, is developed, reviewed, and revised for each child with a disability in accordance with section 1414(d) of this title.

(5)   Least restrictive environment

(A)   In general

To the maximum extent appropriate, children with disabilities, including children in public or private institutions or other care facilities, are educated with children who are not disabled, and special classes, separate schooling, or other removal of children with disabilities from the regular educational environment occurs only when the nature or severity of the disability of a child is such that education in regular classes with the use of supplementary aids and services cannot be achieved satisfactorily.

(B)   Additional requirement

(i)   In general

A State funding mechanism shall not result in placements that violate the requirements of subparagraph (A), and a State shall not use a funding mechanism by which the State distributes funds on the basis of the type of setting in which a child is served that will result in the failure to provide a child with a disability a free appropriate public education according to the unique needs of the child as described in the child's IEP.

(ii)   Assurance

If the State does not have policies and procedures to ensure compliance with clause (i), the State shall provide the Secretary an assurance that the State will revise the funding mechanism as soon as feasible to ensure that such mechanism does not result in such placements.

(6)   Procedural safeguards

(A)   In general

Children with disabilities and their parents are afforded the procedural safeguards required by section 1415 of this title.

(B) Additional procedural safeguards

Procedures to ensure that testing and evaluation materials and procedures utilized for the purposes of evaluation and placement of children with disabilities for services under this chapter will be selected and administered so as not to be racially or culturally discriminatory. Such materials or procedures shall be provided and administered in the child's native language or mode of communication, unless it clearly is not feasible to do so, and no single procedure shall be the sole criterion for determining an appropriate educational program for a child.

(7) Evaluation

Children with disabilities are evaluated in accordance with subsections (a) through (c) of section 1414 of this title.

(8) Confidentiality

Agencies in the State comply with section 1417(c) of this title (relating to the confidentiality of records and information).

(9) Transition from subchapter III to preschool programs

Children participating in early intervention programs assisted under subchapter III, and who will participate in preschool programs assisted under this subchapter, experience a smooth and effective transition to those preschool programs in a manner consistent with section 1437(a)(9) of this title. By the third birthday of such a child, an individualized education program or, if consistent with sections 1414(d)(2)(B) and 1436(d) of this title, an individualized family service plan, has been developed and is being implemented for the child. The local educational agency will participate in transition planning conferences arranged by the designated lead agency under section 1435(a)(10) of this title.

(10) Children in private schools

(A) Children enrolled in private schools by their parents (omitted)

(B) Children placed in, or referred to, private schools by public agencies

(i) In general

Children with disabilities in private schools and facilities are provided special education and related services, in accordance with an individualized education program, at no cost to their parents, if such children are placed in, or referred to, such schools or facilities by the State or appropriate local educational agency as the means of carrying out the requirements of this subchapter or any other applicable law requiring the provision of special education and related services to all children with disabilities within such State.

(ii) Standards

In all cases described in clause (i), the State educational agency shall determine whether such schools and facilities meet standards that apply to State educational agencies and local educational agencies and that children so served have all the rights the children would have if served by such agencies.

(C) Payment for education of children enrolled in private schools without consent of or referral by the public agency

(i)   In general

Subject to subparagraph (A), this subchapter does not require a local educational agency to pay for the cost of education, including special education and related services, of a child with a disability at a private school or facility if that agency made a free appropriate public education available to the child and the parents elected to place the child in such private school or facility.

(ii)   Reimbursement for private school placement

If the parents of a child with a disability, who previously received special education and related services under the authority of a public agency, enroll the child in a private elementary school or secondary school without the consent of or referral by the public agency, a court or a hearing officer may require the agency to reimburse the parents for the cost of that enrollment if the court or hearing officer finds that the agency had not made a free appropriate public education available to the child in a timely manner prior to that enrollment.

(iii)   Limitation on reimbursement

The cost of reimbursement described in clause (ii) may be reduced or denied —

(I) if —

(aa) at the most recent IEP meeting that the parents attended prior to removal of the child from the public school, the parents did not inform the IEP Team that they were rejecting the placement proposed by the public agency to provide a free appropriate public education to their child, including stating their concerns and their intent to enroll their child in a private school at public expense; or

(bb) 10 business days (including any holidays that occur on a business day) prior to the removal of the child from the public school, the parents did not give written notice to the public agency of the information described in item (aa);

(II) if, prior to the parents' removal of the child from the public school, the public agency informed the parents, through the notice requirements described in section 1415(b)(3) of this title, of its intent to evaluate the child (including a statement of the purpose of the evaluation that was appropriate and reasonable), but the parents did not make the child available for such evaluation; or

(III) upon a judicial finding of unreasonableness with respect to actions taken by the parents.

(iv)   Exception

Notwithstanding the notice requirement in clause (iii)(I), the cost of reimbursement —

(I) shall not be reduced or denied for failure to provide such notice if —

(aa) the school prevented the parent from providing such notice;

(bb) the parents had not received notice, pursuant to section 1415 of this title, of the notice requirement in clause (iii)(I); or

(cc) compliance with clause (iii)(I) would likely result in physical harm to the child; and

(II) may, in the discretion of a court or a hearing officer, not be reduced or denied for failure to provide such notice if —

(aa) the parent is illiterate or cannot write in English; or

(bb) compliance with clause (iii)(I) would likely result in serious emotional harm to the child.

(16) Participation in assessments

(A) In general

All children with disabilities are included in all general State and districtwide assessment programs, including assessments described under section 6311 of this title, with appropriate accommodations and alternate assessments where necessary and as indicated in their respective individualized education programs.

(B) Accommodation guidelines

The State (or, in the case of a districtwide assessment, the local educational agency) has developed guidelines for the provision of appropriate accommodations.

(C) Alternate assessments

(i) In general

The State (or, in the case of a districtwide assessment, the local educational agency) has developed and implemented guidelines for the participation of children with disabilities in alternate assessments for those children who cannot participate in regular assessments under subparagraph (A) with accommodations as indicated in their respective individualized education programs.

(ii) Requirements for alternate assessments

The guidelines under clause (i) shall provide for alternate assessments that —

(I) are aligned with the State's challenging academic content standards and challenging student academic achievement standards; and

(II) if the State has adopted alternate academic achievement standards permitted under the regulations promulgated to carry out section 6311(b)(1) of this title, measure the achievement of children with disabilities against those standards.

(iii) Conduct of alternate assessments

The State conducts the alternate assessments described in this subparagraph.

* * *

(22)   Suspension and expulsion rates

(A)   In general

The State educational agency examines data, including data disaggregated by race and ethnicity, to determine if significant discrepancies are occurring in the rate of long-term suspensions and expulsions of children with disabilities —

(i) among local educational agencies in the State; or

(ii) compared to such rates for nondisabled children within such agencies.

(B)   Review and revision of policies

If such discrepancies are occurring, the State educational agency reviews and, if appropriate, revises (or requires the affected State or local educational agency to revise) its policies, procedures, and practices relating to the development and implementation of IEPs, the use of positive behavioral interventions and supports, and procedural safeguards, to ensure that such policies, procedures, and practices comply with this chapter.

(23) Access to instructional materials (omitted)

(24)   Overidentification and disproportionality

The State has in effect, consistent with the purposes of this chapter and with section 1418(d) of this title, policies and procedures designed to prevent the inappropriate overidentification or disproportionate representation by race and ethnicity of children as children with disabilities, including children with disabilities with a particular impairment described in section 1401 of this title.

(25)   Prohibition on mandatory medication

(A)   In general

The State educational agency shall prohibit State and local educational agency personnel from requiring a child to obtain a prescription for a substance covered by the Controlled Substances Act (21 U.S.C. 801 et seq.) as a condition of attending school, receiving an evaluation under subsection (a) or (c) of section 1414 of this title, or receiving services under this chapter.

(B)   Rule of construction

Nothing in subparagraph (A) shall be construed to create a Federal prohibition against teachers and other school personnel consulting or sharing classroom-based observations with parents or guardians regarding a student's academic and functional performance, or behavior in the classroom or school, or regarding the need for evaluation for special education or related services under paragraph (3).

* * *

§ 1413. Local educational agency eligibility (omitted)

§ 1414. Evaluations, eligibility determinations, individualized education programs, and educational placements

(a) Evaluations, parental consent, and reevaluations

(1) Initial evaluations

(A) In general

A State educational agency, other State agency, or local educational agency shall conduct a full and individual initial evaluation in accordance with this paragraph and subsection (b), before the initial provision of special education and related services to a child with a disability under this subchapter.

(B) Request for initial evaluation

Consistent with subparagraph (D), either a parent of a child, or a State educational agency, other State agency, or local educational agency may initiate a request for an initial evaluation to determine if the child is a child with a disability.

(C) Procedures

(i) In general

Such initial evaluation shall consist of procedures —

(I) to determine whether a child is a child with a disability (as defined in section 1401 of this title) within 60 days of receiving parental consent for the evaluation, or, if the State establishes a timeframe within which the evaluation must be conducted, within such timeframe; and

(II) to determine the educational needs of such child.

(ii) Exception

The relevant timeframe in clause (i)(I) shall not apply to a local educational agency if —

(I) a child enrolls in a school served by the local educational agency after the relevant timeframe in clause (i)(I) has begun and prior to a determination by the child's previous local educational agency as to whether the child is a child with a disability (as defined in section 1401 of this title), but only if the subsequent local educational agency is making sufficient progress to ensure a prompt completion of the evaluation, and the parent and subsequent local educational agency agree to a specific time when the evaluation will be completed; or

(II) the parent of a child repeatedly fails or refuses to produce the child for the evaluation.

(D) Parental consent

(i) In general

(I)   Consent for initial evaluation

The agency proposing to conduct an initial evaluation to determine if the child qualifies as a child with a disability as defined in section 1401 of this title shall obtain informed consent from the parent of such child before conducting the evaluation. Parental consent for evaluation shall not be construed as consent for placement for receipt of special education and related services.

(II)   Consent for services

An agency that is responsible for making a free appropriate public education available to a child with a disability under this subchapter shall seek to obtain informed consent from the parent of such child before providing special education and related services to the child.

(ii)   Absence of consent

(I)   For initial evaluation

If the parent of such child does not provide consent for an initial evaluation under clause (i)(I), or the parent fails to respond to a request to provide the consent, the local educational agency may pursue the initial evaluation of the child by utilizing the procedures described in section 1415 of this title, except to the extent inconsistent with State law relating to such parental consent.

(II)   For services

If the parent of such child refuses to consent to services under clause (i)(II), the local educational agency shall not provide special education and related services to the child by utilizing the procedures described in section 1415 of this title.

(III)   Effect on agency obligations

If the parent of such child refuses to consent to the receipt of special education and related services, or the parent fails to respond to a request to provide such consent —

   (aa) the local educational agency shall not be considered to be in violation of the requirement to make available a free appropriate public education to the child for the failure to provide such child with the special education and related services for which the local educational agency requests such consent; and

   (bb) the local educational agency shall not be required to convene an IEP meeting or develop an IEP under this section for the child for the special education and related services for which the local educational agency requests such consent.

(iii)   Consent for wards of the State

(I)   In general

If the child is a ward of the State and is not residing with the child's parent, the agency shall make reasonable efforts to obtain the informed consent from the parent (as defined in section 1401 of this title) of the child for an initial evaluation to determine whether the child is a child with a disability.

(II) Exception

The agency shall not be required to obtain informed consent from the parent of a child for an initial evaluation to determine whether the child is a child with a disability if —

(aa) despite reasonable efforts to do so, the agency cannot discover the whereabouts of the parent of the child;

(bb) the rights of the parents of the child have been terminated in accordance with State law; or

(cc) the rights of the parent to make educational decisions have been subrogated by a judge in accordance with State law and consent for an initial evaluation has been given by an individual appointed by the judge to represent the child.

(E) Rule of construction

The screening of a student by a teacher or specialist to determine appropriate instructional strategies for curriculum implementation shall not be considered to be an evaluation for eligibility for special education and related services.

(2) Reevaluations

(A) In general

A local educational agency shall ensure that a reevaluation of each child with a disability is conducted in accordance with subsections (b) and (c) —

(i) if the local educational agency determines that the educational or related services needs, including improved academic achievement and functional performance, of the child warrant a reevaluation; or

(ii) if the child's parents or teacher requests a reevaluation.

(B) Limitation

A reevaluation conducted under subparagraph (A) shall occur —

(i) not more frequently than once a year, unless the parent and the local educational agency agree otherwise; and

(ii) at least once every 3 years, unless the parent and the local educational agency agree that a reevaluation is unnecessary.

(b) Evaluation procedures

(1) Notice

The local educational agency shall provide notice to the parents of a child with a disability, in accordance with subsections (b)(3), (b)(4), and (c) of section 1415 of this title, that describes any evaluation procedures such agency proposes to conduct.

(2)   Conduct of evaluation

In conducting the evaluation, the local educational agency shall —

(A) use a variety of assessment tools and strategies to gather relevant functional, developmental, and academic information, including information provided by the parent, that may assist in determining —

(i) whether the child is a child with a disability; and

(ii) the content of the child's individualized education program, including information related to enabling the child to be involved in and progress in the general education curriculum, or, for preschool children, to participate in appropriate activities;

(B) not use any single measure or assessment as the sole criterion for determining whether a child is a child with a disability or determining an appropriate educational program for the child; and

(C) use technically sound instruments that may assess the relative contribution of cognitive and behavioral factors, in addition to physical or developmental factors.

(3)   Additional requirements

Each local educational agency shall ensure that —

(A) assessments and other evaluation materials used to assess a child under this section —

(i) are selected and administered so as not to be discriminatory on a racial or cultural basis;

(ii) are provided and administered in the language and form most likely to yield accurate information on what the child knows and can do academically, developmentally, and functionally, unless it is not feasible to so provide or administer;

(iii) are used for purposes for which the assessments or measures are valid and reliable;

(iv) are administered by trained and knowledgeable personnel; and

(v) are administered in accordance with any instructions provided by the producer of such assessments;

(B) the child is assessed in all areas of suspected disability;

(C) assessment tools and strategies that provide relevant information that directly assists persons in determining the educational needs of the child are provided; and

(D) assessments of children with disabilities who transfer from 1 school district to another school district in the same academic year are coordinated with such children's prior and subsequent schools, as necessary and as expeditiously as possible, to ensure prompt completion of full evaluations.

(4)   Determination of eligibility and educational need

Upon completion of the administration of assessments and other evaluation measures —

(A) the determination of whether the child is a child with a disability as defined in section 1401(3) of this title and the educational needs of the child shall be made by a team of qualified professionals and the parent of the child in accordance with paragraph (5); and

(B) a copy of the evaluation report and the documentation of determination of eligibility shall be given to the parent.

(5)   Special rule for eligibility determination

In making a determination of eligibility under paragraph (4)(A), a child shall not be determined to be a child with a disability if the determinant factor for such determination is —

(A) lack of appropriate instruction in reading, including in the essential components of reading instruction (as defined in section 6368(3) of this title);

(B) lack of instruction in math; or

(C) limited English proficiency.

(6)   Specific learning disabilities

(A)   In general

Notwithstanding section 1406(b) of this title, when determining whether a child has a specific learning disability as defined in section 1401 of this title, a local educational agency shall not be required to take into consideration whether a child has a severe discrepancy between achievement and intellectual ability in oral expression, listening comprehension, written expression, basic reading skill, reading comprehension, mathematical calculation, or mathematical reasoning.

(B)   Additional authority

In determining whether a child has a specific learning disability, a local educational agency may use a process that determines if the child responds to scientific, research-based intervention as a part of the evaluation procedures described in paragraphs (2) and (3).

(c)   Additional requirements for evaluation and reevaluations

(1)   Review of existing evaluation data

As part of an initial evaluation (if appropriate) and as part of any reevaluation under this section, the IEP Team and other qualified professionals, as appropriate, shall —

(A) review existing evaluation data on the child, including —

(i) evaluations and information provided by the parents of the child;

(ii) current classroom-based, local, or State assessments, and classroom-based observations; and

(iii) observations by teachers and related services providers; and

(B) on the basis of that review, and input from the child's parents, identify what additional data, if any, are needed to determine —

(i) whether the child is a child with a disability as defined in section 1401(3) of this title, and the educational needs of the child, or, in case of a reevaluation of a child, whether the child continues to have such a disability and such educational needs;

(ii) the present levels of academic achievement and related developmental needs of the child;

(iii) whether the child needs special education and related services, or in the case of a reevaluation of a child, whether the child continues to need special education and related services; and

(iv) whether any additions or modifications to the special education and related services are needed to enable the child to meet the measurable annual goals set out in the individualized education program of the child and to participate, as appropriate, in the general education curriculum.

(2)   Source of data

The local educational agency shall administer such assessments and other evaluation measures as may be needed to produce the data identified by the IEP Team under paragraph (1)(B).

(3)   Parental consent

Each local educational agency shall obtain informed parental consent, in accordance with subsection (a)(1)(D), prior to conducting any reevaluation of a child with a disability, except that such informed parental consent need not be obtained if the local educational agency can demonstrate that it had taken reasonable measures to obtain such consent and the child's parent has failed to respond.

(4)   Requirements if additional data are not needed

If the IEP Team and other qualified professionals, as appropriate, determine that no additional data are needed to determine whether the child continues to be a child with a disability and to determine the child's educational needs, the local educational agency —

(A) shall notify the child's parents of —

(i) that determination and the reasons for the determination; and

(ii) the right of such parents to request an assessment to determine whether the child continues to be a child with a disability and to determine the child's educational needs; and

(B) shall not be required to conduct such an assessment unless requested to by the child's parents.

(5)   Evaluations before change in eligibility

(A)   In general

Except as provided in subparagraph (B), a local educational agency shall evaluate a child with a disability in accordance with this section before determining that the child is no longer a child with a disability.

(B) Exception

(i) In general

The evaluation described in subparagraph (A) shall not be required before the termination of a child's eligibility under this subchapter due to graduation from secondary school with a regular diploma, or due to exceeding the age eligibility for a free appropriate public education under State law.

(ii) Summary of performance

For a child whose eligibility under this subchapter terminates under circumstances described in clause (i), a local educational agency shall provide the child with a summary of the child's academic achievement and functional performance, which shall include recommendations on how to assist the child in meeting the child's postsecondary goals.

(d) Individualized education programs

(1) Definitions

In this chapter:

(A) Individualized education program

(i) In general

The term "individualized education program" or "IEP" means a written statement for each child with a disability that is developed, reviewed, and revised in accordance with this section and that includes —

(I) a statement of the child's present levels of academic achievement and functional performance, including —

(aa) how the child's disability affects the child's involvement and progress in the general education curriculum;

(bb) for preschool children, as appropriate, how the disability affects the child's participation in appropriate activities; and

(cc) for children with disabilities who take alternate assessments aligned to alternate achievement standards, a description of benchmarks or short-term objectives;

(II) a statement of measurable annual goals, including academic and functional goals, designed to —

(aa) meet the child's needs that result from the child's disability to enable the child to be involved in and make progress in the general education curriculum; and

(bb) meet each of the child's other educational needs that result from the child's disability;

(III) a description of how the child's progress toward meeting the annual goals described in subclause (II) will be measured and when periodic reports on the progress the child is making toward meeting the annual goals (such as through the use of quarterly or other periodic reports, concurrent with the issuance of report cards) will be provided;

(IV) a statement of the special education and related services and supplementary aids and services, based on peer-reviewed research to the extent practicable, to be provided to the child, or on behalf of the child, and a statement of the program modifications or supports for school personnel that will be provided for the child —

(aa) to advance appropriately toward attaining the annual goals;

(bb) to be involved in and make progress in the general education curriculum in accordance with subclause (I) and to participate in extracurricular and other nonacademic activities; and

(cc) to be educated and participate with other children with disabilities and nondisabled children in the activities described in this subparagraph;

(V) an explanation of the extent, if any, to which the child will not participate with nondisabled children in the regular class and in the activities described in subclause (IV)(cc);

(VI) (aa) a statement of any individual appropriate accommodations that are necessary to measure the academic achievement and functional performance of the child on State and districtwide assessments consistent with section 1412(a)(16)(A) of this title; and

(bb) if the IEP Team determines that the child shall take an alternate assessment on a particular State or districtwide assessment of student achievement, a statement of why —

(AA) the child cannot participate in the regular assessment; and

(BB) the particular alternate assessment selected is appropriate for the child;

(VII) the projected date for the beginning of the services and modifications described in subclause (IV), and the anticipated frequency, location, and duration of those services and modifications; and

(VIII) beginning not later than the first IEP to be in effect when the child is 16, and updated annually thereafter —

(aa) appropriate measurable postsecondary goals based upon age appropriate transition assessments related to training, education, employment, and, where appropriate, independent living skills;

(bb) the transition services (including courses of study) needed to assist the child in reaching those goals; and

(cc) beginning not later than 1 year before the child reaches the age of majority under State law, a statement that the child has been informed of the child's rights under this chapter, if any, that will transfer to the child on reaching the age of majority under section 1415(m) of this title.

(ii)   Rule of construction

Nothing in this section shall be construed to require —

(I) that additional information be included in a child's IEP beyond what is explicitly required in this section; and

(II) the IEP Team to include information under 1 component of a child's IEP that is already contained under another component of such IEP.

(B)   Individualized education program team

The term "individualized education program team" or "IEP Team" means a group of individuals composed of —

(i) the parents of a child with a disability;

(ii) not less than 1 regular education teacher of such child (if the child is, or may be, participating in the regular education environment);

(iii) not less than 1 special education teacher, or where appropriate, not less than 1 special education provider of such child;

(iv) a representative of the local educational agency who —

(I) is qualified to provide, or supervise the provision of, specially designed instruction to meet the unique needs of children with disabilities;

(II) is knowledgeable about the general education curriculum; and

(III) is knowledgeable about the availability of resources of the local educational agency;

(v) an individual who can interpret the instructional implications of evaluation results, who may be a member of the team described in clauses (ii) through (vi);

(vi) at the discretion of the parent or the agency, other individuals who have knowledge or special expertise regarding the child, including related services personnel as appropriate; and

(vii) whenever appropriate, the child with a disability.

(C)   IEP Team attendance

(i)   Attendance not necessary

A member of the IEP Team shall not be required to attend an IEP meeting, in whole or in part, if the parent of a child with a disability and the local educational agency agree that the attendance of such member is not necessary because the member's area of the curriculum or related services is not being modified or discussed in the meeting.

(ii)   Excusal

A member of the IEP Team may be excused from attending an IEP meeting, in whole or in part, when the meeting involves a modification to or discussion of the member's area of the curriculum or related services, if —

(I) the parent and the local educational agency consent to the excusal; and

(II) the member submits, in writing to the parent and the IEP Team, input into the development of the IEP prior to the meeting.

(iii)   Written agreement and consent required

A parent's agreement under clause (i) and consent under clause (ii) shall be in writing.

(D)   IEP Team transition

In the case of a child who was previously served under subchapter III, an invitation to the initial IEP meeting shall, at the request of the parent, be sent to the subchapter III service coordinator or other representatives of the subchapter III system to assist with the smooth transition of services.

(2)   Requirement that program be in effect

(A)   In general

At the beginning of each school year, each local educational agency, State educational agency, or other State agency, as the case may be, shall have in effect, for each child with a disability in the agency's jurisdiction, an individualized education program, as defined in paragraph (1)(A).

(B)   Program for child aged 3 through 5

In the case of a child with a disability aged 3 through 5 (or, at the discretion of the State educational agency, a 2-year-old child with a disability who will turn age 3 during the school year), the IEP Team shall consider the individualized family service plan that contains the material described in section 1436 of this title, and that is developed in accordance with this section, and the individualized family service plan may serve as the IEP of the child if using that plan as the IEP is —

(i) consistent with State policy; and

(ii) agreed to by the agency and the child's parents.

(C)   Program for children who transfer school districts

(i)   In general

(I)   Transfer within the same State

In the case of a child with a disability who transfers school districts within the same academic year, who enrolls in a new school, and who had an IEP that was in effect in the same State, the local educational agency shall provide such child with a free appropriate public education, including services comparable to those described in the previously held IEP, in consultation with the parents until such time as the local educational agency adopts the previously held IEP or develops, adopts, and implements a new IEP that is consistent with Federal and State law.

(II) Transfer outside State

In the case of a child with a disability who transfers school districts within the same academic year, who enrolls in a new school, and who had an IEP that was in effect in another State, the local educational agency shall provide such child with a free appropriate public education, including services comparable to those described in the previously held IEP, in consultation with the parents until such time as the local educational agency conducts an evaluation pursuant to subsection (a)(1), if determined to be necessary by such agency, and develops a new IEP, if appropriate, that is consistent with Federal and State law.

(ii) Transmittal of records

To facilitate the transition for a child described in clause (i) —

(I) the new school in which the child enrolls shall take reasonable steps to promptly obtain the child's records, including the IEP and supporting documents and any other records relating to the provision of special education or related services to the child, from the previous school in which the child was enrolled, pursuant to section 99.31(a)(2) of title 34, Code of Federal Regulations; and

(II) the previous school in which the child was enrolled shall take reasonable steps to promptly respond to such request from the new school.

(3) Development of IEP

(A) In general

In developing each child's IEP, the IEP Team, subject to subparagraph (C), shall consider —

(i) the strengths of the child;

(ii) the concerns of the parents for enhancing the education of their child;

(iii) the results of the initial evaluation or most recent evaluation of the child; and

(iv) the academic, developmental, and functional needs of the child.

(B) Consideration of special factors

The IEP Team shall —

(i) in the case of a child whose behavior impedes the child's learning or that of others, consider the use of positive behavioral interventions and supports, and other strategies, to address that behavior;

(ii) in the case of a child with limited English proficiency, consider the language needs of the child as such needs relate to the child's IEP;

(iii) in the case of a child who is blind or visually impaired, provide for instruction in Braille and the use of Braille unless the IEP Team determines, after an evaluation of the child's reading and writing skills, needs, and appropriate reading and writing media (including an evaluation of the child's future needs for instruction in Braille or the use of Braille), that instruction in Braille or the use of Braille is not appropriate for the child;

(iv) consider the communication needs of the child, and in the case of a child who is deaf or hard of hearing, consider the child's language and communication needs, opportunities for direct communications with peers and professional personnel in the child's language and communication mode, academic level, and full range of needs, including opportunities for direct instruction in the child's language and communication mode; and

(v) consider whether the child needs assistive technology devices and services.

(C) Requirement with respect to regular education teacher

A regular education teacher of the child, as a member of the IEP Team, shall, to the extent appropriate, participate in the development of the IEP of the child, including the determination of appropriate positive behavioral interventions and supports, and other strategies, and the determination of supplementary aids and services, program modifications, and support for school personnel consistent with paragraph (1)(A)(i)(IV).

(D) Agreement

In making changes to a child's IEP after the annual IEP meeting for a school year, the parent of a child with a disability and the local educational agency may agree not to convene an IEP meeting for the purposes of making such changes, and instead may develop a written document to amend or modify the child's current IEP.

(E) Consolidation of IEP Team meetings

To the extent possible, the local educational agency shall encourage the consolidation of reevaluation meetings for the child and other IEP Team meetings for the child.

(F) Amendments

Changes to the IEP may be made either by the entire IEP Team or, as provided in subparagraph (D), by amending the IEP rather than by redrafting the entire IEP. Upon request, a parent shall be provided with a revised copy of the IEP with the amendments incorporated.

(4) Review and revision of IEP

(A) In general

The local educational agency shall ensure that, subject to subparagraph (B), the IEP Team —

(i) reviews the child's IEP periodically, but not less frequently than annually, to determine whether the annual goals for the child are being achieved; and

(ii) revises the IEP as appropriate to address —

(I) any lack of expected progress toward the annual goals and in the general education curriculum, where appropriate;

(II) the results of any reevaluation conducted under this section;

(III) information about the child provided to, or by, the parents, as described in subsection (c)(1)(B);

(IV) the child's anticipated needs; or

(V) other matters.

(B) Requirement with respect to regular education teacher

A regular education teacher of the child, as a member of the IEP Team, shall, consistent with paragraph (1)(C), participate in the review and revision of the IEP of the child.

(5) Multi-year IEP demonstration

(A) Pilot program

(i) Purpose

The purpose of this paragraph is to provide an opportunity for States to allow parents and local educational agencies the opportunity for long-term planning by offering the option of developing a comprehensive multi-year IEP, not to exceed 3 years, that is designed to coincide with the natural transition points for the child.

(ii) Authorization

In order to carry out the purpose of this paragraph, the Secretary is authorized to approve not more than 15 proposals from States to carry out the activity described in clause (i).

(iii) Proposal

(I) In general

A State desiring to participate in the program under this paragraph shall submit a proposal to the Secretary at such time and in such manner as the Secretary may reasonably require.

(II) Content

The proposal shall include —

(aa) assurances that the development of a multi-year IEP under this paragraph is optional for parents;

(bb) assurances that the parent is required to provide informed consent before a comprehensive multi-year IEP is developed;

(cc) a list of required elements for each multi-year IEP, including —

(AA) measurable goals pursuant to paragraph (1)(A)(i)(II), coinciding with natural transition points for the child, that will enable the child to be involved in and make progress in the general education curriculum and that will meet the child's other needs that result from the child's disability; and

(BB) measurable annual goals for determining progress toward meeting the goals described in subitem (AA); and

(dd) a description of the process for the review and revision of each multi-year IEP, including —

(AA) a review by the IEP Team of the child's multi-year IEP at each of the child's natural transition points;

(BB) in years other than a child's natural transition points, an annual review of the child's IEP to determine the child's current levels of progress and whether the annual goals for the child are being achieved, and a requirement to amend the IEP, as appropriate, to enable the child to continue to meet the measurable goals set out in the IEP;

(CC) if the IEP Team determines on the basis of a review that the child is not making sufficient progress toward the goals described in the multi-year IEP, a requirement that the local educational agency shall ensure that the IEP Team carries out a more thorough review of the IEP in accordance with paragraph (4) within 30 calendar days; and

(DD) at the request of the parent, a requirement that the IEP Team shall conduct a review of the child's multi-year IEP rather than or subsequent to an annual review.

* * *

(7)   Children with disabilities in adult prisons

(A)   In general

The following requirements shall not apply to children with disabilities who are convicted as adults under State law and incarcerated in adult prisons:

(i) The requirements contained in section 1412(a)(16) of this title and paragraph (1)(A)(i)(VI) (relating to participation of children with disabilities in general assessments).

(ii) The requirements of items (aa) and (bb) of paragraph (1)(A)(i)(VIII) (relating to transition planning and transition services), do not apply with respect to such children whose eligibility under this subchapter will end, because of such children's age, before such children will be released from prison.

(B)   Additional requirement

If a child with a disability is convicted as an adult under State law and incarcerated in an adult prison, the child's IEP Team may modify the child's IEP or placement notwithstanding the requirements of sections 1412(a)(5)(A) of this title and paragraph (1)(A) if the State has demonstrated a bona fide security or compelling penological interest that cannot otherwise be accommodated.

(e)   Educational placements

Each local educational agency or State educational agency shall ensure that the parents of each child with a disability are members of any group that makes decisions on the educational placement of their child.

(f)   Alternative means of meeting participation

When conducting IEP team meetings and placement meetings pursuant to this section, section 1415(e) of this title, and section 1415(f)(1)(B) of this title, and carrying out administrative matters under section 1415 of this title (such as scheduling, exchange of witness lists, and status conferences), the parent of a child with a disability and a local educational agency may agree to use alternative means of meeting participation, such as video conferences and conference calls.

§ 1414a.   Omitted

§ 1415.   Procedural safeguards

(a)   Establishment of procedures

Any State educational agency, State agency, or local educational agency that receives assistance under this subchapter shall establish and maintain procedures in accordance with this section to ensure that children with disabilities and their parents are guaranteed procedural safeguards with respect to the provision of a free appropriate public education by such agencies.

(b)   Types of procedures

The procedures required by this section shall include the following:

(1) An opportunity for the parents of a child with a disability to examine all records relating to such child and to participate in meetings with respect to the identification, evaluation, and educational placement of the child, and the provision of a free appropriate public education to such child, and to obtain an independent educational evaluation of the child.

(2) (A) Procedures to protect the rights of the child whenever the parents of the child are not known, the agency cannot, after reasonable efforts, locate the parents, or the child is a ward of the State, including the assignment of an individual to act as a surrogate for the parents, which surrogate shall not be an employee of the State educational agency, the local educational agency, or any other agency that is involved in the education or care of the child. In the case of —

(i) a child who is a ward of the State, such surrogate may alternatively be appointed by the judge overseeing the child's care provided that the surrogate meets the requirements of this paragraph; and

(ii) an unaccompanied homeless youth as defined in section 11434a(6) of Title 42, the local educational agency shall appoint a surrogate in accordance with this paragraph.

(B) The State shall make reasonable efforts to ensure the assignment of a surrogate not more than 30 days after there is a determination by the agency that the child needs a surrogate.

(3) Written prior notice to the parents of the child, in accordance with subsection (c)(1), whenever the local educational agency —

(A) proposes to initiate or change; or

(B) refuses to initiate or change, the identification, evaluation, or educational placement of the child, or the provision of a free appropriate public education to the child.

(4) Procedures designed to ensure that the notice required by paragraph (3) is in the native language of the parents, unless it clearly is not feasible to do so.

(5) An opportunity for mediation, in accordance with subsection (e).

(6) An opportunity for any party to present a complaint —

(A) with respect to any matter relating to the identification, evaluation, or educational placement of the child, or the provision of a free appropriate public education to such child; and

(B) which sets forth an alleged violation that occurred not more than 2 years before the date the parent or public agency knew or should have known about the alleged action that forms the basis of the complaint, or, if the State has an explicit time limitation for presenting such a complaint under this subchapter, in such time as the State law allows, except that the exceptions to the timeline described in subsection (f)(3)(D) shall apply to the timeline described in this subparagraph.

(7) (A) Procedures that require either party, or the attorney representing a party, to provide due process complaint notice in accordance with subsection (c)(2) (which shall remain confidential) —

(i) to the other party, in the complaint filed under paragraph (6), and forward a copy of such notice to the State educational agency; and

(ii) that shall include —

(I) the name of the child, the address of the residence of the child (or available contact information in the case of a homeless child), and the name of the school the child is attending;

(II) in the case of a homeless child or youth (within the meaning of section 11434a(2) of Title 42, available contact information for the child and the name of the school the child is attending;

(III) a description of the nature of the problem of the child relating to such proposed initiation or change, including facts relating to such problem; and

(IV) a proposed resolution of the problem to the extent known and available to the party at the time.

(B) A requirement that a party may not have a due process hearing until the party, or the attorney representing the party, files a notice that meets the requirements of subparagraph (A)(ii).

(8) Procedures that require the State educational agency to develop a model form to assist parents in filing a complaint and due process complaint notice in accordance with paragraphs (6) and (7), respectively.

(c)   Notification requirements

(1)   Content of prior written notice

The notice required by subsection (b)(3) shall include —

(A) a description of the action proposed or refused by the agency;

(B) an explanation of why the agency proposes or refuses to take the action and a description of each evaluation procedure, assessment, record, or report the agency used as a basis for the proposed or refused action;

(C) a statement that the parents of a child with a disability have protection under the procedural safeguards of this subchapter and, if this notice is not an initial referral for evaluation, the means by which a copy of a description of the procedural safeguards can be obtained;

(D) sources for parents to contact to obtain assistance in understanding the provisions of this subchapter;

(E) a description of other options considered by the IEP Team and the reason why those options were rejected; and

(F) a description of the factors that are relevant to the agency's proposal or refusal.

(2)   Due process complaint notice

(A)   Complaint

The due process complaint notice required under subsection (b)(7)(A) shall be deemed to be sufficient unless the party receiving the notice notifies the hearing officer and the other party in writing that the receiving party believes the notice has not met the requirements of subsection (b)(7)(A).

(B)   Response to complaint

(i)   Local educational agency response

(I)   In general

If the local educational agency has not sent a prior written notice to the parent regarding the subject matter contained in the parent's due process complaint notice, such local educational agency shall, within 10 days of receiving the complaint, send to the parent a response that shall include —

(aa) an explanation of why the agency proposed or refused to take the action raised in the complaint;

(bb) a description of other options that the IEP Team considered and the reasons why those options were rejected;

(cc) a description of each evaluation procedure, assessment, record, or report the agency used as the basis for the proposed or refused action; and

(dd) a description of the factors that are relevant to the agency's proposal or refusal.

(II) Sufficiency

A response filed by a local educational agency pursuant to subclause (I) shall not be construed to preclude such local educational agency from asserting that the parent's due process complaint notice was insufficient where appropriate.

(ii) Other party response

Except as provided in clause (i), the non- complaining party shall, within 10 days of receiving the complaint, send to the complaint a response that specifically addresses the issues raised in the complaint.

(C) Timing

The party providing a hearing officer notification under subparagraph (A) shall provide the notification within 15 days of receiving the complaint.

(D) Determination

Within 5 days of receipt of the notification provided under subparagraph (C), the hearing officer shall make a determination on the face of the notice of whether the notification meets the requirements of subsection (b)(7)(A), and shall immediately notify the parties in writing of such determination.

(E) Amended complaint notice

(i) In general

A party may amend its due process complaint notice only if —

(I) the other party consents in writing to such amendment and is given the opportunity to resolve the complaint through a meeting held pursuant to subsection (f)(1)(B); or

(II) the hearing officer grants permission, except that the hearing officer may only grant such permission at any time not later than 5 days before a due process hearing occurs.

(ii) Applicable timeline

The applicable timeline for a due process hearing under this subchapter shall recommence at the time the party files an amended notice, including the timeline under subsection (f)(1)(B).

(d) Procedural safeguards notice

(1) In general

(A) Copy to parents

A copy of the procedural safeguards available to the parents of a child with a disability shall be given to the parents only 1 time a year, except that a copy also shall be given to the parents —

(i) upon initial referral or parental request for evaluation;

(ii) upon the first occurrence of the filing of a complaint under subsection (b)(6); and

(iii) upon request by a parent.

(B) Internet website

A local educational agency may place a current copy of the procedural safeguards notice on its Internet website if such website exists.

(2) Contents

The procedural safeguards notice shall include a full explanation of the procedural safeguards, written in the native language of the parents (unless it clearly is not feasible to do so) and written in an easily understandable manner, available under this section and under regulations promulgated by the Secretary relating to —

(A) independent educational evaluation;

(B) prior written notice;

(C) parental consent;

(D) access to educational records;

(E) the opportunity to present and resolve complaints, including —

(i) the time period in which to make a complaint;

(ii) the opportunity for the agency to resolve the complaint; and

(iii) the availability of mediation;

(F) the child's placement during pendency of due process proceedings;

(G) procedures for students who are subject to placement in an interim alternative educational setting;

(H) requirements for unilateral placement by parents of children in private schools at public expense;

(I) due process hearings, including requirements for disclosure of evaluation results and recommendations;

(J) State-level appeals (if applicable in that State);

(K) civil actions, including the time period in which to file such actions; and

(L) attorneys' fees.

(e) Mediation

(1) In general

Any State educational agency or local educational agency that receives assistance under this subchapter shall ensure that procedures are established and implemented to allow parties to disputes involving any matter, including matters arising prior to the filing of a complaint pursuant to subsection (b)(6), to resolve such disputes through a mediation process.

(2)   Requirements

Such procedures shall meet the following requirements:

(A) The procedures shall ensure that the mediation process —

(i) is voluntary on the part of the parties;

(ii) is not used to deny or delay a parent's right to a due process hearing under subsection (f), or to deny any other rights afforded under this subchapter; and

(iii) is conducted by a qualified and impartial mediator who is trained in effective mediation techniques.

(B)   Opportunity to meet with a disinterested party

A local educational agency or a State agency may establish procedures to offer to parents and schools that choose not to use the mediation process, an opportunity to meet, at a time and location convenient to the parents, with a disinterested party who is under contract with —

(i) a parent training and information center or community parent resource center in the State established under section 1471 or 1472 of this title; or

(ii) an appropriate alternative dispute resolution entity, to encourage the use, and explain the benefits, of the mediation process to the parents.

(C)   List of qualified mediators

The State shall maintain a list of individuals who are qualified mediators and knowledgeable in laws and regulations relating to the provision of special education and related services.

(D)   Costs

The State shall bear the cost of the mediation process, including the costs of meetings described in subparagraph (B).

(E)   Scheduling and location

Each session in the mediation process shall be scheduled in a timely manner and shall be held in a location that is convenient to the parties to the dispute.

(F)   Written agreement

In the case that a resolution is reached to resolve the complaint through the mediation process, the parties shall execute a legally binding agreement that sets forth such resolution and that —

(i) states that all discussions that occurred during the mediation process shall be confidential and may not be used as evidence in any subsequent due process hearing or civil proceeding;

(ii) is signed by both the parent and a representative of the agency who has the authority to bind such agency; and

(iii) is enforceable in any State court of competent jurisdiction or in a district court of the United States.

(G) Mediation discussions

Discussions that occur during the mediation process shall be confidential and may not be used as evidence in any subsequent due process hearing or civil proceeding.

(f) Impartial due process hearing

(1) In general

(A) Hearing

Whenever a complaint has been received under subsection (b)(6) or (k), the parents or the local educational agency involved in such complaint shall have an opportunity for an impartial due process hearing, which shall be conducted by the State educational agency or by the local educational agency, as determined by State law or by the State educational agency.

(B) Resolution session

(i) Preliminary meeting

Prior to the opportunity for an impartial due process hearing under subparagraph (A), the local educational agency shall convene a meeting with the parents and the relevant member or members of the IEP Team who have specific knowledge of the facts identified in the complaint —

(I) within 15 days of receiving notice of the parents' complaint;

(II) which shall include a representative of the agency who has decisionmaking authority on behalf of such agency;

(III) which may not include an attorney of the local educational agency unless the parent is accompanied by an attorney; and

(IV) where the parents of the child discuss their complaint, and the facts that form the basis of the complaint, and the local educational agency is provided the opportunity to resolve the complaint, unless the parents and the local educational agency agree in writing to waive such meeting, or agree to use the mediation process described in subsection (e).

(ii) Hearing

If the local educational agency has not resolved the complaint to the satisfaction of the parents within 30 days of the receipt of the complaint, the due process hearing may occur, and all of the applicable timelines for a due process hearing under this subchapter shall commence.

(iii) Written settlement agreement

In the case that a resolution is reached to resolve the complaint at a meeting described in clause (i), the parties shall execute a legally binding agreement that is —

(I) signed by both the parent and a representative of the agency who has the authority to bind such agency; and

(II) enforceable in any State court of competent jurisdiction or in a district court of the United States.

(iv)   Review period

If the parties execute an agreement pursuant to clause (iii), a party may void such agreement within 3 business days of the agreement's execution.

(2)   Disclosure of evaluations and recommendations

(A)   In general

Not less than 5 business days prior to a hearing conducted pursuant to paragraph (1), each party shall disclose to all other parties all evaluations completed by that date, and recommendations based on the offering party's evaluations, that the party intends to use at the hearing.

(B)   Failure to disclose

A hearing officer may bar any party that fails to comply with subparagraph (A) from introducing the relevant evaluation or recommendation at the hearing without the consent of the other party.

(3)   Limitations on hearing

(A)   Person conducting hearing

A hearing officer conducting a hearing pursuant to paragraph (1)(A) shall, at a minimum —

(i) not be —

(I) an employee of the State educational agency or the local educational agency involved in the education or care of the child; or

(II) a person having a personal or professional interest that conflicts with the person's objectivity in the hearing;

(ii) possess knowledge of, and the ability to understand, the provisions of this chapter, Federal and State regulations pertaining to this chapter, and legal interpretations of this chapter by Federal and State courts;

(iii) possess the knowledge and ability to conduct hearings in accordance with appropriate, standard legal practice; and

(iv) possess the knowledge and ability to render and write decisions in accordance with appropriate, standard legal practice.

(B)   Subject matter of hearing

The party requesting the due process hearing shall not be allowed to raise issues at the due process hearing that were not raised in the notice filed under subsection (b)(7), unless the other party agrees otherwise.

(C)   Timeline for requesting hearing

A parent or agency shall request an impartial due process hearing within 2 years of the date the parent or agency knew or should have known about the alleged action that forms the basis of the complaint, or, if the State has an explicit time limitation for requesting such a hearing under this subchapter, in such time as the State law allows.

(D)   Exceptions to the timeline

The timeline described in subparagraph (C) shall not apply to a parent if the parent was prevented from requesting the hearing due to —

(i) specific misrepresentations by the local educational agency that it had resolved the problem forming the basis of the complaint; or

(ii) the local educational agency's withholding of information from the parent that was required under this subchapter to be provided to the parent.

(E)   Decision of hearing officer

(i)   In general

Subject to clause (ii), a decision made by a hearing officer shall be made on substantive grounds based on a determination of whether the child received a free appropriate public education.

(ii)   Procedural issues

In matters alleging a procedural violation, a hearing officer may find that a child did not receive a free appropriate public education only if the procedural inadequacies —

(I) impeded the child's right to a free appropriate public education;

(II) significantly impeded the parents' opportunity to participate in the decisionmaking process regarding the provision of a free appropriate public education to the parents' child; or

(III) caused a deprivation of educational benefits.

(iii)   Rule of construction

Nothing in this subparagraph shall be construed to preclude a hearing officer from ordering a local educational agency to comply with procedural requirements under this section.

(F)   Rule of construction

Nothing in this paragraph shall be construed to affect the right of a parent to file a complaint with the State educational agency.

(g)   Appeal

(1)   In general

If the hearing required by subsection (f) is conducted by a local educational agency, any party aggrieved by the findings and decision rendered in such a hearing may appeal such findings and decision to the State educational agency.

(2)   Impartial review and independent decision

The State educational agency shall conduct an impartial review of the findings and decision appealed under paragraph (1). The officer conducting such review shall make an independent decision upon completion of such review.

(h)   Safeguards

Any party to a hearing conducted pursuant to subsection (f) or (k), or an appeal conducted pursuant to subsection (g), shall be accorded —

(1) the right to be accompanied and advised by counsel and by individuals with special knowledge or training with respect to the problems of children with disabilities;

(2) the right to present evidence and confront, cross-examine, and compel the attendance of witnesses;

(3) the right to a written, or, at the option of the parents, electronic verbatim record of such hearing; and

(4) the right to written, or, at the option of the parents, electronic findings of fact and decisions, which findings and decisions —

(A) shall be made available to the public consistent with the requirements of section 1417(b) of this title (relating to the confidentiality of data, information, and records); and

(B) shall be transmitted to the advisory panel established pursuant to section 1412(a)(21) of this title.

(i)   Administrative procedures

(1)   In general

(A)   Decision made in hearing

A decision made in a hearing conducted pursuant to subsection (f) or (k) shall be final, except that any party involved in such hearing may appeal such decision under the provisions of subsection (g) and paragraph (2).

(B)   Decision made at appeal

A decision made under subsection (g) shall be final, except that any party may bring an action under paragraph (2).

(2)   Right to bring civil action

(A)   In general

Any party aggrieved by the findings and decision made under subsection (f) or (k) who does not have the right to an appeal under subsection (g), and any party aggrieved by the findings and decision made under this subsection, shall have the right to bring a civil action with respect to the complaint presented pursuant to this section, which action may be brought in any State court of competent jurisdiction or in a district court of the United States, without regard to the amount in controversy.

(B)   Limitation

The party bringing the action shall have 90 days from the date of the decision of the hearing officer to bring such an action, or, if the State has an explicit time limitation for bringing such action under this subchapter, in such time as the State law allows.

(C)   Additional requirements

In any action brought under this paragraph, the court —

(i) shall receive the records of the administrative proceedings;

(ii) shall hear additional evidence at the request of a party; and

(iii) basing its decision on the preponderance of the evidence, shall grant such relief as the court determines is appropriate.

(3)   Jurisdiction of district courts; attorneys' fees

(A)   In general

The district courts of the United States shall have jurisdiction of actions brought under this section without regard to the amount in controversy.

(B)   Award of attorneys' fees

(i)   In general

In any action or proceeding brought under this section, the court, in its discretion, may award reasonable attorneys' fees as part of the costs —

(I) to a prevailing party who is the parent of a child with a disability;

(II) to a prevailing party who is a State educational agency or local educational agency against the attorney of a parent who files a complaint or subsequent cause of action that is frivolous, unreasonable, or without foundation, or against the attorney of a parent who continued to litigate after the litigation clearly became frivolous, unreasonable, or without foundation; or

(III) to a prevailing State educational agency or local educational agency against the attorney of a parent, or against the parent, if the parent's complaint or subsequent cause of action was presented for any improper purpose, such as to harass, to cause unnecessary delay, or to needlessly increase the cost of litigation.

(ii)   Rule of construction

Nothing in this subparagraph shall be construed to affect section 327 of the District of Columbia Appropriations Act, 2005.

(C)   Determination of amount of attorneys' fees

Fees awarded under this paragraph shall be based on rates prevailing in the community in which the action or proceeding arose for the kind and quality of services furnished. No bonus or multiplier may be used in calculating the fees awarded under this subsection.

(D) Prohibition of attorneys' fees and related costs for certain services

(i)   In general

Attorneys' fees may not be awarded and related costs may not be reimbursed in any action or proceeding under this section for services performed subsequent to the time of a written offer of settlement to a parent if —

(I) the offer is made within the time prescribed by Rule 68 of the Federal Rules of Civil Procedure or, in the case of an administrative proceeding, at any time more than 10 days before the proceeding begins;

(II) the offer is not accepted within 10 days; and

(III) the court or administrative hearing officer finds that the relief finally obtained by the parents is not more favorable to the parents than the offer of settlement.

(ii)   IEP Team meetings

Attorneys' fees may not be awarded relating to any meeting of the IEP Team unless such meeting is convened as a result of an administrative proceeding or judicial action, or, at the discretion of the State, for a mediation described in subsection (e).

(iii)   Opportunity to resolve complaints

A meeting conducted pursuant to subsection (f)(1)(B)(i) shall not be considered —

(I) a meeting convened as a result of an administrative hearing or judicial action; or

(II) an administrative hearing or judicial action for purposes of this paragraph.

(E) Exception to prohibition on attorneys' fees and related costs

Notwithstanding subparagraph (D), an award of attorneys' fees and related costs may be made to a parent who is the prevailing party and who was substantially justified in rejecting the settlement offer.

(F)   Reduction in amount of attorneys' fees

Except as provided in subparagraph (G), whenever the court finds that —

(i) the parent, or the parent's attorney, during the course of the action or proceeding, unreasonably protracted the final resolution of the controversy;

(ii) the amount of the attorneys' fees otherwise authorized to be awarded unreasonably exceeds the hourly rate prevailing in the community for similar services by attorneys of reasonably comparable skill, reputation, and experience;

(iii) the time spent and legal services furnished were excessive considering the nature of the action or proceeding; or

(iv) the attorney representing the parent did not provide to the local educational agency the appropriate information in the notice of the complaint described in subsection (b)(7)(A), the court shall reduce, accordingly, the amount of the attorneys' fees awarded under this section.

(G)   Exception to reduction in amount of attorneys' fees

The provisions of subparagraph (F) shall not apply in any action or proceeding if the court finds that the State or local educational agency unreasonably protracted the final resolution of the action or proceeding or there was a violation of this section.

(j)   Maintenance of current educational placement

Except as provided in subsection (k)(4), during the pendency of any proceedings conducted pursuant to this section, unless the State or local educational agency and the parents otherwise agree, the child shall remain in the then-current educational placement of the child, or, if applying for initial admission to a public school, shall, with the consent of the parents, be placed in the public school program until all such proceedings have been completed.

(k)   Placement in alternative educational setting

(1)   Authority of school personnel

(A)   Case-by-case determination

School personnel may consider any unique circumstances on a case-by-case basis when determining whether to order a change in placement for a child with a disability who violates a code of student conduct.

(B)   Authority

School personnel under this subsection may remove a child with a disability who violates a code of student conduct from their current placement to an appropriate interim alternative educational setting, another setting, or suspension, for not more than 10 school days (to the extent such alternatives are applied to children without disabilities).

(C)   Additional authority

If school personnel seek to order a change in placement that would exceed 10 school days and the behavior that gave rise to the violation of the school code is determined not to be a manifestation of the child's disability pursuant to subparagraph (E), the relevant disciplinary procedures applicable to children without disabilities may be applied to the child in the same manner and for the same duration in which the procedures would be applied to children without disabilities, except as provided in section 1412(a)(1) of this title although it may be provided in an interim alternative educational setting.

(D)   Services

A child with a disability who is removed from the child's current placement under subparagraph (G) (irrespective of whether the behavior is determined to be a manifestation of the child's disability) or subparagraph (C) shall —

(i) continue to receive educational services, as provided in section 1412(a)(1) of this title, so as to enable the child to continue to participate in the general education curriculum, although in another setting, and to progress toward meeting the goals set out in the child's IEP; and

(ii) receive, as appropriate, a functional behavioral assessment, behavioral intervention services and modifications, that are designed to address the behavior violation so that it does not recur.

(E)   Manifestation determination

(i)   In general

Except as provided in subparagraph (B), within 10 school days of any decision to change the placement of a child with a disability because of a violation of a code of student conduct, the local educational agency, the parent, and relevant members of the IEP Team (as determined by the parent and the local educational agency) shall review all relevant information in the student's file, including the child's IEP, any teacher observations, and any relevant information provided by the parents to determine —

(I) if the conduct in question was caused by, or had a direct and substantial relationship to, the child's disability; or

(II) if the conduct in question was the direct result of the local educational agency's failure to implement the IEP.

(ii)   Manifestation

If the local educational agency, the parent, and relevant members of the IEP Team determine that either subclause (I) or (II) of clause (i) is applicable for the child, the conduct shall be determined to be a manifestation of the child's disability.

(F)   Determination that behavior was a manifestation

If the local educational agency, the parent, and relevant members of the IEP Team make the determination that the conduct was a manifestation of the child's disability, the IEP Team shall —

(i) conduct a functional behavioral assessment, and implement a behavioral intervention plan for such child, provided that the local educational agency had not conducted such assessment prior to such determination before the behavior that resulted in a change in placement described in subparagraph (C) or (G);

(ii) in the situation where a behavioral intervention plan has been developed, review the behavioral intervention plan if the child already has such a behavioral intervention plan, and modify it, as necessary, to address the behavior; and

(iii) except as provided in subparagraph (G), return the child to the placement from which the child was removed, unless the parent and the local educational agency agree to a change of placement as part of the modification of the behavioral intervention plan.

(G)   Special circumstances

School personnel may remove a student to an interim alternative educational setting for not more than 45 school days without regard to whether the behavior is determined to be a manifestation of the child's disability, in cases where a child —

(i) carries or possesses a weapon to or at school, on school premises, or to or at a school function under the jurisdiction of a State or local educational agency;

(ii) knowingly possesses or uses illegal drugs, or sells or solicits the sale of a controlled substance, while at school, on school premises, or at a school function under the jurisdiction of a State or local educational agency; or

(iii) has inflicted serious bodily injury upon another person while at school, on school premises, or at a school function under the jurisdiction of a State or local educational agency.

(H)　Notification

Not later than the date on which the decision to take disciplinary action is made, the local educational agency shall notify the parents of that decision, and of all procedural safeguards accorded under this section.

(2)　Determination of setting

The interim alternative educational setting in subparagraphs (C) and (G) of paragraph (1) shall be determined by the IEP Team.

(3)　Appeal

(A)　In general

The parent of a child with a disability who disagrees with any decision regarding placement, or the manifestation determination under this subsection, or a local educational agency that believes that maintaining the current placement of the child is substantially likely to result in injury to the child or to others, may request a hearing.

(B)　Authority of hearing officer

(i)　In general

A hearing officer shall hear, and make a determination regarding, an appeal requested under subparagraph (A).

(ii)　Change of placement order

In making the determination under clause (i), the hearing officer may order a change in placement of a child with a disability. In such situations, the hearing officer may —

(I) return a child with a disability to the placement from which the child was removed; or

(II) order a change in placement of a child with a disability to an appropriate interim alternative educational setting for not more than 45 school days if the hearing officer determines that maintaining the current placement of such child is substantially likely to result in injury to the child or to others.

(4)　Placement during appeals

When an appeal under paragraph (3) has been requested by either the parent or the local educational agency —

(A) the child shall remain in the interim alternative educational setting pending the decision of the hearing officer or until the expiration of the time period provided for in paragraph (1)(C), whichever occurs first, unless the parent and the State or local educational agency agree otherwise; and

(B) the State or local educational agency shall arrange for an expedited hearing, which shall occur within 20 school days of the date the hearing is requested and shall result in a determination within 10 school days after the hearing.

(5)   Protections for children not yet eligible for special education and related services

(A)   In general

A child who has not been determined to be eligible for special education and related services under this subchapter and who has engaged in behavior that violates a code of student conduct, may assert any of the protections provided for in this subchapter if the local educational agency had knowledge (as determined in accordance with this paragraph) that the child was a child with a disability before the behavior that precipitated the disciplinary action occurred.

(B)   Basis of knowledge

A local educational agency shall be deemed to have knowledge that a child is a child with a disability if, before the behavior that precipitated the disciplinary action occurred —

(i) the parent of the child has expressed concern in writing to supervisory or administrative personnel of the appropriate educational agency, or a teacher of the child, that the child is in need of special education and related services;

(ii) the parent of the child has requested an evaluation of the child pursuant to section 1414(a)(1)(B) of this title; or

(iii) the teacher of the child, or other personnel of the local educational agency, has expressed specific concerns about a pattern of behavior demonstrated by the child, directly to the director of special education of such agency or to other supervisory personnel of the agency.

(C)   Exception

A local educational agency shall not be deemed to have knowledge that the child is a child with a disability if the parent of the child has not allowed an evaluation of the child pursuant to section 1414 of this title or has refused services under this subchapter or the child has been evaluated and it was determined that the child was not a child with a disability under this subchapter.

(D)   Conditions that apply if no basis of knowledge

(i)   In general

If a local educational agency does not have knowledge that a child is a child with a disability (in accordance with subparagraph (B) or (C)) prior to taking disciplinary measures against the child, the child may be subjected to disciplinary measures applied to children without disabilities who engaged in comparable behaviors consistent with clause (ii).

(ii) Limitations

If a request is made for an evaluation of a child during the time period in which the child is subjected to disciplinary measures under this subsection, the evaluation shall be conducted in an expedited manner. If the child is determined to be a child with a disability, taking into consideration information from the evaluation conducted by the agency and information provided by the parents, the agency shall provide special education and related services in accordance with this subchapter, except that, pending the results of the evaluation, the child shall remain in the educational placement determined by school authorities.

(6) Referral to and action by law enforcement and judicial authorities

(A) Rule of construction

Nothing in this subchapter shall be construed to prohibit an agency from reporting a crime committed by a child with a disability to appropriate authorities or to prevent State law enforcement and judicial authorities from exercising their responsibilities with regard to the application of Federal and State law to crimes committed by a child with a disability.

(B) Transmittal of records

An agency reporting a crime committed by a child with a disability shall ensure that copies of the special education and disciplinary records of the child are transmitted for consideration by the appropriate authorities to whom the agency reports the crime.

(7) Definitions

In this subsection:

(A) Controlled substance

The term "controlled substance" means a drug or other substance identified under schedule I, II, III, IV, or V in section 202(c) of the Controlled Substances Act (21 U.S.C. 812(c)).

(B) Illegal drug

The term "illegal drug" means a controlled substance but does not include a controlled substance that is legally possessed or used under the supervision of a licensed health-care professional or that is legally possessed or used under any other authority under that Act [21 U.S.C.A. § 801 et seq.] or under any other provision of Federal law.

(C) Weapon

The term "weapon" has the meaning given the term "dangerous weapon" under section 930(g)(2) of Title 18.

(D) Serious bodily injury

The term "serious bodily injury" has the meaning given the term "serious bodily injury" under paragraph (3) of subsection (h) of section 1365 of Title 18.

(l)   Rule of construction

Nothing in this chapter shall be construed to restrict or limit the rights, procedures, and remedies available under the Constitution, the Americans with Disabilities Act of 1990 [42 U.S.C.A. § 12101 et seq.], title V of the Rehabilitation Act of 1973 [29 U.S.C.A. § 791 et seq.], or other Federal laws protecting the rights of children with disabilities, except that before the filing of a civil action under such laws seeking relief that is also available under this subchapter, the procedures under subsections (f) and (g) shall be exhausted to the same extent as would be required had the action been brought under this subchapter.

(m)   Transfer of parental rights at age of majority

(1)   In general

A State that receives amounts from a grant under this subchapter may provide that, when a child with a disability reaches the age of majority under State law (except for a child with a disability who has been determined to be incompetent under State law) —

(A) the agency shall provide any notice required by this section to both the individual and the parents;

(B) all other rights accorded to parents under this subchapter transfer to the child;

(C) the agency shall notify the individual and the parents of the transfer of rights; and

(D) all rights accorded to parents under this subchapter transfer to children who are incarcerated in an adult or juvenile Federal, State, or local correctional institution.

(2)   Special rule

If, under State law, a child with a disability who has reached the age of majority under State law, who has not been determined to be incompetent, but who is determined not to have the ability to provide informed consent with respect to the educational program of the child, the State shall establish procedures for appointing the parent of the child, or if the parent is not available, another appropriate individual, to represent the educational interests of the child throughout the period of eligibility of the child under this subchapter.

(n)   Electronic mail

A parent of a child with a disability may elect to receive notices required under this section by an electronic mail (e-mail) communication, if the agency makes such option available.

(o)   Separate complaint

Nothing in this section shall be construed to preclude a parent from filing a separate due process complaint on an issue separate from a due process complaint already filed.

* * *

Part C

§ 1431. Findings and policy

(a) Findings

Congress finds that there is an urgent and substantial need —

(1) to enhance the development of infants and toddlers with disabilities, to minimize their potential for developmental delay, and to recognize the significant brain development that occurs during a child's first 3 years of life;

(2) to reduce the educational costs to our society, including our Nation's schools, by minimizing the need for special education and related services after infants and toddlers with disabilities reach school age;

(3) to maximize the potential for individuals with disabilities to live independently in society;

(4) to enhance the capacity of families to meet the special needs of their infants and toddlers with disabilities; and

(5) to enhance the capacity of State and local agencies and service providers to identify, evaluate, and meet the needs of all children, particularly minority, low-income, inner city, and rural children, and infants and toddlers in foster care.

(b) Policy

It is the policy of the United States to provide financial assistance to States —

(1) to develop and implement a statewide, comprehensive, coordinated, multidisciplinary, interagency system that provides early intervention services for infants and toddlers with disabilities and their families;

(2) to facilitate the coordination of payment for early intervention services from Federal, State, local, and private sources (including public and private insurance coverage);

(3) to enhance State capacity to provide quality early intervention services and expand and improve existing early intervention services being provided to infants and toddlers with disabilities and their families; and

(4) to encourage States to expand opportunities for children under 3 years of age who would be at risk of having substantial developmental delay if they did not receive early intervention services.

§ 1432. Definitions

In this subchapter:

(1) At-risk infant or toddler

The term "at-risk infant or toddler" means an individual under 3 years of age who would be at risk of experiencing a substantial developmental delay if early intervention services were not provided to the individual.

(3) Developmental delay

The term "developmental delay", when used with respect to an individual residing in a State, has the meaning given such term by the State under section 1435(a)(1) of this title.

(4)   Early intervention services

The term "early intervention services" means developmental services that —

(A) are provided under public supervision;

(B) are provided at no cost except where Federal or State law provides for a system of payments by families, including a schedule of sliding fees;

(C) are designed to meet the developmental needs of an infant or toddler with a disability, as identified by the individualized family service plan team, in any 1 or more of the following areas:

(i) physical development;

(ii) cognitive development;

(iii) communication development;

(iv) social or emotional development; or

(v) adaptive development;

(D) meet the standards of the State in which the services are provided, including the requirements of this subchapter;

(E) include —

(i) family training, counseling, and home visits;

(ii) special instruction;

(iii) speech-language pathology and audiology services, and sign language and cued language services;

(iv) occupational therapy;

(v) physical therapy;

(vi) psychological services;

(vii) service coordination services;

(viii) medical services only for diagnostic or evaluation purposes;

(ix) early identification, screening, and assessment services;

(x) health services necessary to enable the infant or toddler to benefit from the other early intervention services;

(xi) social work services;

(xii) vision services;

(xiii) assistive technology devices and assistive technology services; and

(xiv) transportation and related costs that are necessary to enable an infant or toddler and the infant's or toddler's family to receive another service described in this paragraph;

(F) are provided by qualified personnel, including —

(i) special educators;

(ii) speech-language pathologists and audiologists;

(iii) occupational therapists;

(iv) physical therapists;

(v) psychologists;

(vi) social workers;

(vii) nurses;

(viii) registered dietitians;

(ix) family therapists;

(x) vision specialists, including ophthalmologists and optometrists;

(xi) orientation and mobility specialists; and

(xii) pediatricians and other physicians;

(G) to the maximum extent appropriate, are provided in natural environments, including the home, and community settings in which children without disabilities participate; and

(H) are provided in conformity with an individualized family service plan adopted in accordance with section 1436 of this title.

(5) Infant or toddler with a disability

The term "infant or toddler with a disability" —

(A) means an individual under 3 years of age who needs early intervention services because the individual —

(i) is experiencing developmental delays, as measured by appropriate diagnostic instruments and procedures in 1 or more of the areas of cognitive development, physical development, communication development, social or emotional development, and adaptive development; or

(ii) has a diagnosed physical or mental condition that has a high probability of resulting in developmental delay; and

(B) may also include, at a State's discretion —

(i) at-risk infants and toddlers; and

(ii) children with disabilities who are eligible for services under section 1419 of this title and who previously received services under this subchapter until such children enter, or are eligible under State law to enter, kindergarten or elementary school, as appropriate, provided that any programs under this subchapter serving such children shall include —

(I) an educational component that promotes school readiness and incorporates pre-literacy, language, and numeracy skills; and

(II) a written notification to parents of their rights and responsibilities in determining whether their child will continue to receive services under this subchapter or participate in preschool programs under section 1419 of this title.

§ 1435.   Requirements for statewide system

(a)   In general

A statewide system described in section 1433 of this title shall include, at a minimum, the following components:

(1) A rigorous definition of the term "developmental delay" that will be used by the State in carrying out programs under this subchapter in order to appropriately identify infants and toddlers with disabilities that are in need of services under this subchapter.

(2) A State policy that is in effect and that ensures that appropriate early intervention services based on scientifically based research, to the extent practicable, are available to all infants and toddlers with disabilities and their families, including Indian infants and toddlers with disabilities and their families residing on a reservation geographically located in the State and infants and toddlers with disabilities who are homeless children and their families.

(3) A timely, comprehensive, multidisciplinary evaluation of the functioning of each infant or toddler with a disability in the State, and a family-directed identification of the needs of each family of such an infant or toddler, to assist appropriately in the development of the infant or toddler.

(4) For each infant or toddler with a disability in the State, an individualized family service plan in accordance with section 1436 of this title, including service coordination services in accordance with such service plan.

(5) A comprehensive child find system, consistent with subchapter II, including a system for making referrals to service providers that includes timelines and provides for participation by primary referral sources and that ensures rigorous standards for appropriately identifying infants and toddlers with disabilities for services under this subchapter that will reduce the need for future services.

(6) A public awareness program focusing on early identification of infants and toddlers with disabilities, including the preparation and dissemination by the lead agency designated or established under paragraph (10) to all primary referral sources, especially hospitals and physicians, of information to be given to parents, especially to inform parents with premature infants, or infants with other physical risk factors associated with learning or developmental complications, on the availability of early intervention services under this subchapter and of services under section 1419 of this title, and procedures for assisting such sources in disseminating such information to parents of infants and toddlers with disabilities.

(7) A central directory that includes information on early intervention services, resources, and experts available in the State and research and demonstration

projects being conducted in the State.

(8) A comprehensive system of personnel development, including the training of paraprofessionals and the training of primary referral sources with respect to the basic components of early intervention services available in the State that —

(A) shall include —

(i) implementing innovative strategies and activities for the recruitment and retention of early education service providers;

(ii) promoting the preparation of early intervention providers who are fully and appropriately qualified to provide early intervention services under this subchapter; and

(iii) training personnel to coordinate transition services for infants and toddlers served under this subchapter from a program providing early intervention services under this subchapter and under subchapter II (other than section 1419 of this title), to a preschool program receiving funds under section 1419 of this title, or another appropriate program; and

(B) may include —

(i) training personnel to work in rural and inner-city areas; and

(ii) training personnel in the emotional and social development of young children.

(9) Policies and procedures relating to the establishment and maintenance of qualifications to ensure that personnel necessary to carry out this subchapter are appropriately and adequately prepared and trained, including the establishment and maintenance of qualifications that are consistent with any State-approved or recognized certification, licensing, registration, or other comparable requirements that apply to the area in which such personnel are providing early intervention services, except that nothing in this subchapter (including this paragraph) shall be construed to prohibit the use of paraprofessionals and assistants who are appropriately trained and supervised in accordance with State law, regulation, or written policy, to assist in the provision of early intervention services under this subchapter to infants and toddlers with disabilities.

(10) A single line of responsibility in a lead agency designated or established by the Governor for carrying out —

(A) the general administration and supervision of programs and activities receiving assistance under section 1433 of this title, and the monitoring of programs and activities used by the State to carry out this subchapter, whether or not such programs or activities are receiving assistance made available under section 1433 of this title, to ensure that the State complies with this subchapter;

(B) the identification and coordination of all available resources within the State from Federal, State, local, and private sources;

(C) the assignment of financial responsibility in accordance with section 1437(a)(2) of this title to the appropriate agencies;

(D) the development of procedures to ensure that services are provided to infants and toddlers with disabilities and their families under this subchapter in a timely manner pending the resolution of any disputes among public agencies or service providers;

(E) the resolution of intra- and interagency disputes; and

(F) the entry into formal interagency agreements that define the financial responsibility of each agency for paying for early intervention services (consistent with State law) and procedures for resolving disputes and that include all additional components necessary to ensure meaningful cooperation and coordination.

(11) A policy pertaining to the contracting or making of other arrangements with service providers to provide early intervention services in the State, consistent with the provisions of this subchapter, including the contents of the application used and the conditions of the contract or other arrangements.

(12) A procedure for securing timely reimbursements of funds used under this subchapter in accordance with section 1440(a) of this title.

(13) Procedural safeguards with respect to programs under this subchapter, as required by section 1439 of this title.

(14) A system for compiling data requested by the Secretary under section 1418 of this title that relates to this subchapter.

(15) A State interagency coordinating council that meets the requirements of section 1441 of this title.

(16) Policies and procedures to ensure that, consistent with section 1436(d)(5) of this title —

(A) to the maximum extent appropriate, early intervention services are provided in natural environments; and

(B) the provision of early intervention services for any infant or toddler with a disability occurs in a setting other than a natural environment that is most appropriate, as determined by the parent and the individualized family service plan team, only when early intervention cannot be achieved satisfactorily for the infant or toddler in a natural environment.

(b)   Policy

In implementing subsection (a)(9), a State may adopt a policy that includes making ongoing good-faith efforts to recruit and hire appropriately and adequately trained personnel to provide early intervention services to infants and toddlers with disabilities, including, in a geographic area of the State where there is a shortage of such personnel, the most qualified individuals available who are making satisfactory progress toward completing applicable course work necessary to meet the standards described in subsection (a)(9).

(c)   Flexibility to serve children 3 years of age until entrance into elementary school

(1)   In general

A statewide system described in section 1433 of this title may include a State policy, developed and implemented jointly by the lead agency and the State educational agency, under which parents of children with disabilities who are eligible for services under section 1419 of this title and previously received services under this subchapter, may choose the continuation of early intervention services (which shall include an educational component that promotes school readiness and incorporates preliteracy, language, and numeracy skills) for such children under this subchapter until such children enter, or are eligible under State law to enter, kindergarten.

(2)   Requirements

If a statewide system includes a State policy described in paragraph (1), the statewide system shall ensure that —

(A) parents of children with disabilities served pursuant to this subsection are provided annual notice that contains —

(i) a description of the rights of such parents to elect to receive services pursuant to this subsection or under subchapter II; and

(ii) an explanation of the differences between services provided pursuant to this subsection and services provided under subchapter II, including —

(I) types of services and the locations at which the services are provided;

(II) applicable procedural safeguards; and

(III) possible costs (including any fees to be charged to families as described in section 1432(4)(B) of this title), if any, to parents of infants or toddlers with disabilities;

(B) services provided pursuant to this subsection include an educational component that promotes school readiness and incorporates preliteracy, language, and numeracy skills;

(C) the State policy will not affect the right of any child served pursuant to this subsection to instead receive a free appropriate public education under subchapter II;

(D) all early intervention services outlined in the child's individualized family service plan under section 1436 of this title are continued while any eligibility determination is being made for services under this subsection;

(E) the parents of infants or toddlers with disabilities (as defined in section 1432(5)(A) of this title) provide informed written consent to the State, before such infants or toddlers reach 3 years of age, as to whether such parents intend to choose the continuation of early intervention services pursuant to this subsection for such infants or toddlers;

(F) the requirements under section 1437(a)(9) of this title shall not apply with respect to a child who is receiving services in accordance with this subsection until not less than 90 days (and at the discretion of the parties to the conference, not more than 9 months) before the time the child will no longer receive those services; and

(G) there will be a referral for evaluation for early intervention services of a child who experiences a substantiated case of trauma due to exposure to family violence (as defined in section 10421 of Title 42).

(5)   Rules of construction

(A)   Services under subchapter II

If a statewide system includes a State policy described in paragraph (1), a State that provides services in accordance with this subsection to a child with a disability who is eligible for services under section 1419 of this title shall not be required to provide the child with a free appropriate public education under subchapter II for the period of time in which the child is receiving services under this subchapter.

(B) Services under this subchapter

Nothing in this subsection shall be construed to require a provider of services under this subchapter to provide a child served under this subchapter with a free appropriate public education.

§ 1436.   Individualized family service plan

(a)   Assessment and program development

A statewide system described in section 1433 of this title shall provide, at a minimum, for each infant or toddler with a disability, and the infant's or toddler's family, to receive —

(1) a multidisciplinary assessment of the unique strengths and needs of the infant or toddler and the identification of services appropriate to meet such needs;

(2) a family-directed assessment of the resources, priorities, and concerns of the family and the identification of the supports and services necessary to enhance the family's capacity to meet the developmental needs of the infant or toddler; and

(3) a written individualized family service plan developed by a multidisciplinary team, including the parents, as required by subsection (e), including a description of the appropriate transition services for the infant or toddler.

(b)   Periodic review

The individualized family service plan shall be evaluated once a year and the family shall be provided a review of the plan at 6-month intervals (or more often where appropriate based on infant or toddler and family needs).

(c)   Promptness after assessment

The individualized family service plan shall be developed within a reasonable time after the assessment required by subsection (a)(1) is completed. With the parents' consent, early intervention services may commence prior to the completion of the assessment.

(d)   Content of plan

The individualized family service plan shall be in writing and contain —

(1) a statement of the infant's or toddler's present levels of physical development, cognitive development, communication development, social or emotional development, and adaptive development, based on objective criteria;

(2) a statement of the family's resources, priorities, and concerns relating to enhancing the development of the family's infant or toddler with a disability;

(3) a statement of the measurable results or outcomes expected to be achieved for the infant or toddler and the family, including pre-literacy and language skills, as developmentally appropriate for the child, and the criteria, procedures, and timelines used to determine the degree to which progress toward achieving the results or outcomes is being made and whether modifications or revisions of the results or outcomes or services are necessary;

(4) a statement of specific early intervention services based on peer-reviewed research, to the extent practicable, necessary to meet the unique needs of the infant or toddler and the family, including the frequency, intensity, and method of delivering services;

(5) a statement of the natural environments in which early intervention services will appropriately be provided, including a justification of the extent, if any, to which the services will not be provided in a natural environment;

(6) the projected dates for initiation of services and the anticipated length, duration, and frequency of the services;

(7) the identification of the service coordinator from the profession most immediately relevant to the infant's or toddler's or family's needs (or who is otherwise qualified to carry out all applicable responsibilities under this subchapter) who will be responsible for the implementation of the plan and coordination with other agencies and persons, including transition services; and

(8) the steps to be taken to support the transition of the toddler with a disability to preschool or other appropriate services.

(e) Parental consent

The contents of the individualized family service plan shall be fully explained to the parents and informed written consent from the parents shall be obtained prior to the provision of early intervention services described in such plan. If the parents do not provide consent with respect to a particular early intervention service, then only the early intervention services to which consent is obtained shall be provided.

* * *

§ 1439. Procedural safeguards

(a) Minimum procedures

The procedural safeguards required to be included in a statewide system under section 1435(a)(13) of this title shall provide, at a minimum, the following:

(1) The timely administrative resolution of complaints by parents. Any party aggrieved by the findings and decision regarding an administrative complaint

shall have the right to bring a civil action with respect to the complaint in any State court of competent jurisdiction or in a district court of the United States without regard to the amount in controversy. In any action brought under this paragraph, the court shall receive the records of the administrative proceedings, shall hear additional evidence at the request of a party, and, basing its decision on the preponderance of the evidence, shall grant such relief as the court determines is appropriate.

(2) The right to confidentiality of personally identifiable information, including the right of parents to written notice of and written consent to the exchange of such information among agencies consistent with Federal and State law.

(3) The right of the parents to determine whether they, their infant or toddler, or other family members will accept or decline any early intervention service under this subchapter in accordance with State law without jeopardizing other early intervention services under this subchapter.

(4) The opportunity for parents to examine records relating to assessment, screening, eligibility determinations, and the development and implementation of the individualized family service plan.

(5) Procedures to protect the rights of the infant or toddler whenever the parents of the infant or toddler are not known or cannot be found or the infant or toddler is a ward of the State, including the assignment of an individual (who shall not be an employee of the State lead agency, or other State agency, and who shall not be any person, or any employee of a person, providing early intervention services to the infant or toddler or any family member of the infant or toddler) to act as a surrogate for the parents.

(6) Written prior notice to the parents of the infant or toddler with a disability whenever the State agency or service provider proposes to initiate or change, or refuses to initiate or change, the identification, evaluation, or placement of the infant or toddler with a disability, or the provision of appropriate early intervention services to the infant or toddler.

(7) Procedures designed to ensure that the notice required by paragraph (6) fully informs the parents, in the parents' native language, unless it clearly is not feasible to do so, of all procedures available pursuant to this section.

(8) The right of parents to use mediation in accordance with section 1415 of this title, except that —

(A) any reference in the section to a State educational agency shall be considered to be a reference to a State's lead agency established or designated under section 1435(a)(10) of this title;

(B) any reference in the section to a local educational agency shall be considered to be a reference to a local service provider or the State's lead agency under this subchapter, as the case may be; and

(C) any reference in the section to the provision of a free appropriate public education to children with disabilities shall be considered to be a reference to the provision of appropriate early intervention services to infants and toddlers with disabilities.

(b)   Services during pendency of proceedings

During the pendency of any proceeding or action involving a complaint by the parents of an infant or toddler with a disability, unless the State agency and the parents otherwise agree, the infant or toddler shall continue to receive the appropriate early intervention services currently being provided or, if applying for initial services, shall receive the services not in dispute.

* * *

§ 1450.   Findings

Congress finds the following:

(1) The Federal Government has an ongoing obligation to support activities that contribute to positive results for children with disabilities, enabling those children to lead productive and independent adult lives.

(2) Systemic change benefiting all students, including children with disabilities, requires the involvement of States, local educational agencies, parents, individuals with disabilities and their families, teachers and other service providers, and other interested individuals and organizations to develop and implement comprehensive strategies that improve educational results for children with disabilities.

(3) State educational agencies, in partnership with local educational agencies, parents of children with disabilities, and other individuals and organizations, are in the best position to improve education for children with disabilities and to address their special needs.

(4) An effective educational system serving students with disabilities should —

(A) maintain high academic achievement standards and clear performance goals for children with disabilities, consistent with the standards and expectations for all students in the educational system, and provide for appropriate and effective strategies and methods to ensure that all children with disabilities have the opportunity to achieve those standards and goals;

(B) clearly define, in objective, measurable terms, the school and post-school results that children with disabilities are expected to achieve; and

(C) promote transition services and coordinate State and local education, social, health, mental health, and other services, in addressing the full range of student needs, particularly the needs of children with disabilities who need significant levels of support to participate and learn in school and the community.

(5) The availability of an adequate number of qualified personnel is critical —

(A) to serve effectively children with disabilities;

(B) to assume leadership positions in administration and direct services;

(C) to provide teacher training; and

(D) to conduct high quality research to improve special education.

(6) High quality, comprehensive professional development programs are essential to ensure that the persons responsible for the education or transition of children with disabilities possess the skills and knowledge necessary to address the educational and related needs of those children.

(7) Models of professional development should be scientifically based and reflect successful practices, including strategies for recruiting, preparing, and retaining personnel.

(8) Continued support is essential for the development and maintenance of a coordinated and high quality program of research to inform successful teaching practices and model curricula for educating children with disabilities.

(9) Training, technical assistance, support, and dissemination activities are necessary to ensure that subchapters II and III are fully implemented and achieve high quality early intervention, educational, and transitional results for children with disabilities and their families.

(10) Parents, teachers, administrators, and related services personnel need technical assistance and information in a timely, coordinated, and accessible manner in order to improve early intervention, educational, and transitional services and results at the State and local levels for children with disabilities and their families.

(11) Parent training and information activities assist parents of a child with a disability in dealing with the multiple pressures of parenting such a child and are of particular importance in —

(A) playing a vital role in creating and preserving constructive relationships between parents of children with disabilities and schools by facilitating open communication between the parents and schools; encouraging dispute resolution at the earliest possible point in time; and discouraging the escalation of an adversarial process between the parents and schools;

(B) ensuring the involvement of parents in planning and decisionmaking with respect to early intervention, educational, and transitional services;

(C) achieving high quality early intervention, educational, and transitional results for children with disabilities;

(D) providing such parents information on their rights, protections, and responsibilities under this chapter to ensure improved early intervention, educational, and transitional results for children with disabilities;

(E) assisting such parents in the development of skills to participate effectively in the education and development of their children and in the transitions described in section 1473(b)(6) of this title;

(F) supporting the roles of such parents as participants within partnerships seeking to improve early intervention, educational, and transitional services and results for children with disabilities and their families; and

(G) supporting such parents who may have limited access to services and supports, due to economic, cultural, or linguistic barriers.

(12) Support is needed to improve technological resources and integrate technology, including universally designed technologies, into the lives of children with disabilities, parents of children with disabilities, school personnel, and others through curricula, services, and assistive technologies.

* * *

§ 1461. Purpose; definition of eligible entity

(a) Purpose

The purpose of this part is —

(1) to provide Federal funding for personnel preparation, technical assistance, model demonstration projects, information dissemination, and studies and evaluations, in order to improve early intervention, educational, and transitional results for children with disabilities; and

(2) to assist State educational agencies and local educational agencies in improving their education systems for children with disabilities.

(b) Definition of eligible entity

(1) In general

In this part, the term "eligible entity" means —

(A) a State educational agency;

(B) a local educational agency;

(C) a public charter school that is a local educational agency under State law;

(D) an institution of higher education;

(E) a public agency not described in subparagraphs (A) through (D);

(F) a private nonprofit organization;

(G) an outlying area;

(H) an Indian tribe or a tribal organization (as defined under section 450b of Title 25); or

(I) a for-profit organization, if the Secretary finds it appropriate in light of the purposes of a particular competition for a grant, contract, or cooperative agreement under this part.

(2) Special rule

The Secretary may limit which eligible entities described in paragraph (1) are eligible for a grant, contract, or cooperative agreement under this part to 1 or more of the categories of eligible entities described in paragraph (1).

* * *

§ 1470.   Purposes

The purposes of this part are to ensure that —

(1) children with disabilities and their parents receive training and information designed to assist the children in meeting developmental and functional goals and challenging academic achievement goals, and in preparing to lead productive independent adult lives;

(2) children with disabilities and their parents receive training and information on their rights, responsibilities, and protections under this chapter, in order to develop the skills necessary to cooperatively and effectively participate in planning and decision making relating to early intervention, educational, and transitional services;

(3) parents, teachers, administrators, early intervention personnel, related services personnel, and transition personnel receive coordinated and accessible technical assistance and information to assist such personnel in improving early intervention, educational, and transitional services and results for children with disabilities and their families; and

(4) appropriate technology and media are researched, developed, and demonstrated, to improve and implement early intervention, educational, and transitional services and results for children with disabilities and their families.

Chapter 15
DEPARTMENT OF EDUCATION IDEA REGULATIONS

United States Department of Education
Individuals with Disabilities Education Act Regulations (Selected Provisions)
Subpart A   General
Purposes and Applicability

34 C.F.R. Sec. 300.1   Purposes.

The purposes of this part are —

(a) To ensure that all children with disabilities have available to them a free appropriate public education that emphasizes special education and related services designed to meet their unique needs and prepare them for further education, employment, and independent living;

(b) To ensure that the rights of children with disabilities and their parents are protected;

(c) To assist States, localities, educational service agencies, and Federal agencies to provide for the education of all children with disabilities; and

(d) To assess and ensure the effectiveness of efforts to educate children with disabilities.

Definitions Used in This Part

Sec. 300.4   Act.

Act means the Individuals with Disabilities Education Act, as amended.

Sec. 300.5   Assistive technology device.

Assistive technology device means any item, piece of equipment, or product system, whether acquired commercially off the shelf, modified, or customized, that is used to increase, maintain, or improve the functional capabilities of a child with a disability. The term does not include a medical device that is surgically implanted, or the replacement of such device.

Sec. 300.6   Assistive technology service.

Assistive technology service means any service that directly assists a child with a disability in the selection, acquisition, or use of an assistive technology device. The term includes —

(a) The evaluation of the needs of a child with a disability, including a functional evaluation of the child in the child's customary environment;

(b) Purchasing, leasing, or otherwise providing for the acquisition of assistive technology devices by children with disabilities;

(c) Selecting, designing, fitting, customizing, adapting, applying, maintaining, repairing, or replacing assistive technology devices;

(d) Coordinating and using other therapies, interventions, or services with assistive technology devices, such as those associated with existing education and rehabilitation plans and programs;

(e) Training or technical assistance for a child with a disability or, if appropriate, that child's family; and

(f) Training or technical assistance for professionals (including individuals providing education or rehabilitation services), employers, or other individuals who provide services to, employ, or are otherwise substantially involved in the major life functions of that child.

Sec. 300.8 Child with a disability.

(a) General.

(1) Child with a disability means a child evaluated in accordance with Sec. Sec. 300.304 through 300.311 as having mental retardation, a hearing impairment (including deafness), a speech or language impairment, a visual impairment (including blindness), a serious emotional disturbance (referred to in this part as "emotional disturbance"), an orthopedic impairment, autism, traumatic brain injury, an other health impairment, a specific learning disability, deaf-blindness, or multiple disabilities, and who, by reason thereof, needs special education and related services.

(2) (i) Subject to paragraph (a)(2)(ii) of this section, if it is determined, through an appropriate evaluation under Sec. Sec. 300.304 through 300.311, that a child has one of the disabilities identified in paragraph (a)(1) of this section, but only needs a related service and not special education, the child is not a child with a disability under this part.

(ii) If, consistent with Sec. 300.39(a)(2), the related service required by the child is considered special education rather than a related service under State standards, the child would be determined to be a child with a disability under paragraph (a)(1) of this section.

(b) Children aged three through nine experiencing developmental delays. Child with a disability for children aged three through nine (or any subset of that age range, including ages three through five), may, subject to the conditions described in Sec. 300.111(b), include a child —

(1) Who is experiencing developmental delays, as defined by the State and as measured by appropriate diagnostic instruments and procedures, in one or more of the following areas: Physical development, cognitive development, communication development, social or emotional development, or adaptive development; and

(2) Who, by reason thereof, needs special education and related services.

(c) Definitions of disability terms. The terms used in this definition of a child with a disability are defined as follows:

(1) (i) Autism means a developmental disability significantly affecting verbal and nonverbal communication and social interaction, generally evident before age three, that adversely affects a child's educational performance. Other

characteristics often associated with autism are engagement in repetitive activities and stereotyped movements, resistance to environmental change or change in daily routines, and unusual responses to sensory experiences.

(ii) Autism does not apply if a child's educational performance is adversely affected primarily because the child has an emotional disturbance, as defined in paragraph (c)(4) of this section.

(iii) A child who manifests the characteristics of autism after age three could be identified as having autism if the criteria in paragraph (c)(1)(i) of this section are satisfied.

(2) Deaf-blindness means concomitant hearing and visual impairments, the combination of which causes such severe communication and other developmental and educational needs that they cannot be accommodated in special education programs solely for children with deafness or children with blindness.

(3) Deafness means a hearing impairment that is so severe that the child is impaired in processing linguistic information through hearing, with or without amplification, that adversely affects a child's educational performance.

(4) (i) Emotional disturbance means a condition exhibiting one or more of the following characteristics over a long period of time and to a marked degree that adversely affects a child's educational performance:

(A) An inability to learn that cannot be explained by intellectual, sensory, or health factors.

(B) An inability to build or maintain satisfactory interpersonal relationships with peers and teachers.

(C) Inappropriate types of behavior or feelings under normal circumstances.

(D) A general pervasive mood of unhappiness or depression.

(E) A tendency to develop physical symptoms or fears associated with personal or school problems.

(ii) Emotional disturbance includes schizophrenia. The term does not apply to children who are socially maladjusted, unless it is determined that they have an emotional disturbance under paragraph (c)(4)(i) of this section.

(5) Hearing impairment means an impairment in hearing, whether permanent or fluctuating, that adversely affects a child's educational performance but that is not included under the definition of deafness in this section.

(6) Mental retardation means significantly subaverage general intellectual functioning, existing concurrently with deficits in adaptive behavior and manifested during the developmental period, that adversely affects a child's educational performance.

(7) Multiple disabilities means concomitant impairments (such as mental retardation-blindness or mental retardation-orthopedic impairment), the combination of which causes such severe educational needs that they cannot be

accommodated in special education programs solely for one of the impairments. Multiple disabilities does not include deaf-blindness.

(8) Orthopedic impairment means a severe orthopedic impairment that adversely affects a child's educational performance. The term includes impairments caused by a congenital anomaly, impairments caused by disease (e.g., poliomyelitis, bone tuberculosis), and impairments from other causes (e.g., cerebral palsy, amputations, and fractures or burns that cause contractures).

(9) Other health impairment means having limited strength, vitality, or alertness, including a heightened alertness to environmental stimuli, that results in limited alertness with respect to the educational environment, that —

(i) Is due to chronic or acute health problems such as asthma, attention deficit disorder or attention deficit hyperactivity disorder, diabetes, epilepsy, a heart condition, hemophilia, lead poisoning, leukemia, nephritis, rheumatic fever, sickle cell anemia, and Tourette syndrome; and

(ii) Adversely affects a child's educational performance.

(10) Specific learning disability —

(i) General. Specific learning disability means a disorder in one or more of the basic psychological processes involved in understanding or in using language, spoken or written, that may manifest itself in the imperfect ability to listen, think, speak, read, write, spell, or to do mathematical calculations, including conditions such as perceptual disabilities, brain injury, minimal brain dysfunction, dyslexia, and developmental aphasia.

(ii) Disorders not included. Specific learning disability does not include learning problems that are primarily the result of visual, hearing, or motor disabilities, of mental retardation, of emotional disturbance, or of environmental, cultural, or economic disadvantage.

(11) Speech or language impairment means a communication disorder, such as stuttering, impaired articulation, a language impairment, or a voice impairment, that adversely affects a child's educational performance.

(12) Traumatic brain injury means an acquired injury to the brain caused by an external physical force, resulting in total or partial functional disability or psychosocial impairment, or both, that adversely affects a child's educational performance. Traumatic brain injury applies to open or closed head injuries resulting in impairments in one or more areas, such as cognition; language; memory; attention; reasoning; abstract thinking; judgment; problem-solving; sensory, perceptual, and motor abilities; psychosocial behavior; physical functions; information processing; and speech. Traumatic brain injury does not apply to brain injuries that are congenital or degenerative, or to brain injuries induced by birth trauma.

(13) Visual impairment including blindness means an impairment in vision that, even with correction, adversely affects a child's educational performance. The term includes both partial sight and blindness.

Sec. 300.9 Consent.

Consent means that —

(a) The parent has been fully informed of all information relevant to the activity for which consent is sought, in his or her native language, or through another mode of communication;

(b) The parent understands and agrees in writing to the carrying out of the activity for which his or her consent is sought, and the consent describes that activity and lists the records (if any) that will be released and to whom; and

(c) (1) The parent understands that the granting of consent is voluntary on the part of the parent and may be revoked at any time.

(2) If a parent revokes consent, that revocation is not retroactive (i.e., it does not negate an action that has occurred after the consent was given and before the consent was revoked).

(3) If the parent revokes consent in writing for their child's receipt of special education services after the child is initially provided special education and related services, the public agency is not required to amend the child's education records to remove any references to the child's receipt of special education and related services because of the revocation of consent.

Sec. 300.17 Free appropriate public education.

Free appropriate public education or FAPE means special education and related services that —

(a) Are provided at public expense, under public supervision and direction, and without charge;

(b) Meet the standards of the SEA, including the requirements of this part;

(c) Include an appropriate preschool, elementary school, or secondary school education in the State involved; and

(d) Are provided in conformity with an individualized education §§ 300.320 through 300.324.

Sec. 300.19 Homeless children.

Homeless children has the meaning given the term homeless children and youths in section 725 (42 U.S.C. 11434a) of the McKinney-Vento Homeless Assistance Act, as amended, 42 U.S.C. 11431 et seq.

Sec. 300.22 Individualized education program.

Individualized education program or IEP means a written statement for a child with a disability that is developed, reviewed, and revised in accordance with §§ 300.320 through 300.324.

Sec. 300.24 Individualized family service plan.

Individualized family service plan or IFSP has the meaning given the term in section 636 of the Act.

Sec. 300.25 Infant or toddler with a disability.

Infant or toddler with a disability —

(a) Means an individual under three years of age who needs early intervention services because the individual —

(1) Is experiencing developmental delays, as measured by appropriate diagnostic instruments and procedures in one or more of the areas of cognitive development, physical development, communication development, social or emotional development, and adaptive development; or

(2) Has a diagnosed physical or mental condition that has a high probability of resulting in developmental delay; and

(b) May also include, at a State's discretion —

(1) At-risk infants and toddlers; and

(2) Children with disabilities who are eligible for services under section 619 and who previously received services under Part C of the Act until such children enter, or are eligible under State law to enter, kindergarten or elementary school, as appropriate, provided that any programs under Part C of the Act serving such children shall include —

(i) An educational component that promotes school readiness and incorporates pre-literacy, language, and numeracy skills; and

(ii) A written notification to parents of their rights and responsibilities in determining whether their child will continue to receive services under Part C of the Act or participate in preschool programs under section 619.

Sec. 300.27 Limited English proficient.

Limited English proficient has the meaning given the term in section 9101(25) of the ESEA.

Sec. 300.28 Local educational agency.

(a) General. Local educational agency or LEA means a public board of education or other public authority legally constituted within a State for either administrative control or direction of, or to perform a service function for, public elementary or secondary schools in a city, county, township, school district, or other political subdivision of a State, or for a combination of school districts or counties as are recognized in a State as an administrative agency for its public elementary schools or secondary schools.

(b) Educational service agencies and other public institutions or agencies. The term includes —

(1) An educational service agency, as defined in § 300.12; and

(2) Any other public institution or agency having administrative control and direction of a public elementary school or secondary school, including a public nonprofit charter school that is established as an LEA under State law.

(c) BIA funded schools. The term includes an elementary school or secondary school funded by the Bureau of Indian Affairs, and not subject to the jurisdiction of any SEA other than the Bureau of Indian Affairs, but only to the extent that the inclusion makes the school eligible for programs for which specific eligibility is not provided to the school in another provision of law and the school does not have a student population that is smaller than the student population of the LEA receiving assistance under the Act with the smallest student population.

Sec. 300.29   Native language.

(a) Native language, when used with respect to an individual who is limited English proficient, means the following:

(1) The language normally used by that individual, or, in the case of a child, the language normally used by the parents of the child, except as provided in paragraph (a)(2) of this section.

(2) In all direct contact with a child (including evaluation of the child), the language normally used by the child in the home or learning environment.

(b) For an individual with deafness or blindness, or for an individual with no written language, the mode of communication is that normally used by the individual (such as sign language, Braille, or oral communication).

Sec. 300.30   Parent.

(a) Parent means —

(1) A biological or adoptive parent of a child;

(2) A foster parent, unless State law, regulations, or contractual obligations with a State or local entity prohibit a foster parent from acting as a parent;

(3) A guardian generally authorized to act as the child's parent, or authorized to make educational decisions for the child (but not the State if the child is a ward of the State);

(4) An individual acting in the place of a biological or adoptive parent (including a grandparent, stepparent, or other relative) with whom the child lives, or an individual who is legally responsible for the child's welfare; or

(5) A surrogate parent who has been appointed in accordance with § 300.519 or section 639(a)(5) of the Act.

(b) (1) Except as provided in paragraph (b)(2) of this section, the biological or adoptive parent, when attempting to act as the parent under this part and when more than one party is qualified under paragraph (a) of this section to act as a parent, must be presumed to be the parent for purposes of this section unless the biological or adoptive parent does not have legal authority to make educational decisions for the child.

(2) If a judicial decree or order identifies a specific person or persons under paragraphs (a)(1) through (4) of this section to act as the "parent" of a child or to make educational decisions on behalf of a child, then such person or persons shall be determined to be the "parent" for purposes of this section.

Sec. 300.32 Personally identifiable.

Personally identifiable means information that contains —

(a) The name of the child, the child's parent, or other family member;

(b) The address of the child;

(c) A personal identifier, such as the child's social security number or student number; or

(d) A list of personal characteristics or other information that would make it possible to identify the child with reasonable certainty.

Sec. 300.33 Public agency.

Public agency includes the SEA, LEAs, ESAs, nonprofit public charter schools that are not otherwise included as LEAs or ESAs and are not a school of an LEA or ESA, and any other political subdivisions of the State that are responsible for providing education to children with disabilities.

Sec. 300.34 Related services.

(a) General. Related services means transportation and such developmental, corrective, and other supportive services as are required to assist a child with a disability to benefit from special education, and includes speech-language pathology and audiology services, interpreting services, psychological services, physical and occupational therapy, recreation, including therapeutic recreation, early identification and assessment of disabilities in children, counseling services, including rehabilitation counseling, orientation and mobility services, and medical services for diagnostic or evaluation purposes. Related services also include school health services and school nurse services, social work services in schools, and parent counseling and training.

(b) Exception; services that apply to children with surgically implanted devices, including cochlear implants.

(1) Related services do not include a medical device that is surgically implanted, the optimization of that device's functioning (e.g., mapping), maintenance of that device, or the replacement of that device.

(2) Nothing in paragraph (b)(1) of this section —

(i) Limits the right of a child with a surgically implanted device (e.g., cochlear implant) to receive related services (as listed in paragraph (a) of this section) that are determined by the IEP Team to be necessary for the child to receive FAPE.

(ii) Limits the responsibility of a public agency to appropriately monitor and maintain medical devices that are needed to maintain the health and safety of the child, including breathing, nutrition, or operation of other bodily functions, while the child is transported to and from school or is at school; or

(iii) Prevents the routine checking of an external component of a surgically implanted device to make sure it is functioning properly, as required in § 300.113(b).

(c) Individual related services terms defined. The terms used in this definition are defined as follows:

(1) Audiology includes —

(i) Identification of children with hearing loss;

(ii) Determination of the range, nature, and degree of hearing loss, including referral for medical or other professional attention for the habilitation of hearing;

(iii) Provision of habilitative activities, such as language habilitation, auditory training, speech reading (lip-reading), hearing evaluation, and speech conservation;

(iv) Creation and administration of programs for prevention of hearing loss;

(v) Counseling and guidance of children, parents, and teachers regarding hearing loss; and

(vi) Determination of children's needs for group and individual amplification, selecting and fitting an appropriate aid, and evaluating the effectiveness of amplification.

(2) Counseling services means services provided by qualified social workers, psychologists, guidance counselors, or other qualified personnel.

(3) Early identification and assessment of disabilities in children means the implementation of a formal plan for identifying a disability as early as possible in a child's life.

(4) Interpreting services includes —

(i) The following, when used with respect to children who are deaf or hard of hearing: Oral transliteration services, cued language transliteration services, sign language transliteration and interpreting services, and transcription services, such as communication access real-time translation (CART), C-Print, and TypeWell; and

(ii) Special interpreting services for children who are deaf-blind.

(5) Medical services means services provided by a licensed physician to determine a child's medically related disability that results in the child's need for special education and related services.

(6) Occupational therapy —

(i) Means services provided by a qualified occupational therapist; and

(ii) Includes —

(A) Improving, developing, or restoring functions impaired or lost through illness, injury, or deprivation;

(B) Improving ability to perform tasks for independent functioning if functions are impaired or lost; and

(C) Preventing, through early intervention, initial or further impairment or loss of function.

(7) Orientation and mobility services —

(i) Means services provided to blind or visually impaired children by qualified personnel to enable those students to attain systematic orientation to and safe movement within their environments in school, home, and community; and

(ii) Includes teaching children the following, as appropriate:

(A) Spatial and environmental concepts and use of information received by the senses (such as sound, temperature and vibrations) to establish, maintain, or regain orientation and line of travel (e.g., using sound at a traffic light to cross the street);

(B) To use the long cane or a service animal to supplement visual travel skills or as a tool for safely negotiating the environment for children with no available travel vision;

(C) To understand and use remaining vision and distance low vision aids; and

(D) Other concepts, techniques, and tools.

(8) (i) Parent counseling and training means assisting parents in understanding the special needs of their child;

(ii) Providing parents with information about child development; and

(iii) Helping parents to acquire the necessary skills that will allow them to support the implementation of their child's IEP or IFSP.

(9) Physical therapy means services provided by a qualified physical therapist.

(10) Psychological services includes —

(i) Administering psychological and educational tests, and other assessment procedures;

(ii) Interpreting assessment results;

(iii) Obtaining, integrating, and interpreting information about child behavior and conditions relating to learning;

(iv) Consulting with other staff members in planning school programs to meet the special educational needs of children as indicated by psychological tests, interviews, direct observation, and behavioral evaluations;

(v) Planning and managing a program of psychological services, including psychological counseling for children and parents; and

(vi) Assisting in developing positive behavioral intervention strategies.

(11) Recreation includes —

(i) Assessment of leisure function;

(ii) Therapeutic recreation services;

(iii) Recreation programs in schools and community agencies; and

(iv) Leisure education.

(12) Rehabilitation counseling services means services provided by qualified personnel in individual or group sessions that focus specifically on career development, employment preparation, achieving independence, and integration in the workplace and community of a student with a disability. The term also includes vocational rehabilitation services provided to a student with a disability by vocational rehabilitation programs funded under the Rehabilitation Act of 1973, as amended, 29 U.S.C. 701 et seq.

(13) School health services and school nurse services means health services that are designed to enable a child with a disability to receive FAPE as described in the child's IEP. School nurse services are services provided by a qualified school nurse. School health services are services that may be provided by either a qualified school nurse or other qualified person.

(14) Social work services in schools includes —

(i) Preparing a social or developmental history on a child with a disability;

(ii) Group and individual counseling with the child and family;

(iii) Working in partnership with parents and others on those problems in a child's living situation (home, school, and community) that affect the child's adjustment in school;

(iv) Mobilizing school and community resources to enable the child to learn as effectively as possible in his or her educational program; and

(v) Assisting in developing positive behavioral intervention strategies.

(15) Speech-language pathology services includes —

(i) Identification of children with speech or language impairments;

(ii) Diagnosis and appraisal of specific speech or language impairments;

(iii) Referral for medical or other professional attention necessary for the habilitation of speech or language impairments;

(iv) Provision of speech and language services for the habilitation or prevention of communicative impairments; and

(v) Counseling and guidance of parents, children, and teachers regarding speech and language impairments.

(16) Transportation includes —

(i) Travel to and from school and between schools;

(ii) Travel in and around school buildings; and

(iii) Specialized equipment (such as special or adapted buses, lifts, and ramps), if required to provide special transportation for a child with a disability.

Sec. 300.35 Scientifically based research.

Scientifically based research has the meaning given the term in section 9101(37) of the ESEA.

Sec. 300.37 Services plan.

Services plan means a written statement that describes the special education and related services the LEA will provide to a parentally-placed child with a disability enrolled in a private school who has been designated to receive services, including the location of the services and any transportation necessary, consistent with § 300.132, and is developed and implemented in accordance with §§ 300.137 through 300.139.

Sec. 300.39 Special education.

(a) General.

(1) Special education means specially designed instruction, at no cost to the parents, to meet the unique needs of a child with a disability, including —

(i) Instruction conducted in the classroom, in the home, in hospitals and institutions, and in other settings; and

(ii) Instruction in physical education.

(2) Special education includes each of the following, if the services otherwise meet the requirements of paragraph (a)(1) of this section —

(i) Speech-language pathology services, or any other related service, if the service is considered special education rather than a related service under State standards;

(ii) Travel training; and

(iii) Vocational education.

(b) Individual special education terms defined. The terms in this definition are defined as follows:

(1) At no cost means that all specially-designed instruction is provided without charge, but does not preclude incidental fees that are normally charged to nondisabled students or their parents as a part of the regular education program.

(2) Physical education means —

(i) The development of —

(A) Physical and motor fitness;

(B) Fundamental motor skills and patterns; and

(C) Skills in aquatics, dance, and individual and group games and sports (including intramural and lifetime sports); and

(ii) Includes special physical education, adapted physical education, movement education, and motor development.

(3) Specially designed instruction means adapting, as appropriate to the needs of an eligible child under this part, the content, methodology, or delivery of instruction —

(i) To address the unique needs of the child that result from the child's disability; and

(ii) To ensure access of the child to the general curriculum, so that the child can meet the educational standards within the jurisdiction of the public agency that apply to all children.

(4) Travel training means providing instruction, as appropriate, to children with significant cognitive disabilities, and any other children with disabilities who require this instruction, to enable them to —

(i) Develop an awareness of the environment in which they live; and

(ii) Learn the skills necessary to move effectively and safely from place to place within that environment (e.g., in school, in the home, at work, and in the community).

(5) Vocational education means organized educational programs that are directly related to the preparation of individuals for paid or unpaid employment, or for additional preparation for a career not requiring a baccalaureate or advanced degree.

Sec. 300.41   State educational agency.

State educational agency or SEA means the State board of education or other agency or officer primarily responsible for the State supervision of public elementary schools and secondary schools, or, if there is no such officer or agency, an officer or agency designated by the Governor or by State law.

Sec. 300.42   Supplementary aids and services.

Supplementary aids and services means aids, services, and other supports that are provided in regular education classes, other education-related settings, and in extracurricular and nonacademic settings, to enable children with disabilities to be educated with nondisabled children to the maximum extent appropriate in accordance with §§ 300.114 through 300.116.

Sec. 300.43   Transition services.

(a) Transition services means a coordinated set of activities for a child with a disability that —

(1) Is designed to be within a results-oriented process, that is focused on improving the academic and functional achievement of the child with a disability to facilitate the child's movement from school to post-school activities, including postsecondary education, vocational education, integrated employment (including supported employment), continuing and adult education, adult services, independent living, or community participation;

(2) Is based on the individual child's needs, taking into account the child's strengths, preferences, and interests; and includes —

(i) Instruction;

(ii) Related services;

(iii) Community experiences;

(iv) The development of employment and other post-school adult living objectives; and

(v) If appropriate, acquisition of daily living skills and provision of a functional vocational evaluation.

(b) Transition services for children with disabilities may be special education, if provided as specially designed instruction, or a related service, if required to assist a child with a disability to benefit from special education.

Sec. 300.45 Ward of the State.

(a) General. Subject to paragraph (b) of this section, ward of the State means a child who, as determined by the State where the child resides, is —

(1) A foster child;

(2) A ward of the State; or

(3) In the custody of a public child welfare agency.

(b) Exception. Ward of the State does not include a foster child who has a foster parent who meets the definition of a parent in § 300.30.

Subpart B State Eligibility
General

Sec. 300.100 Eligibility for assistance.

A State is eligible for assistance under Part B of the Act for a fiscal year if the State submits a plan that provides assurances to the Secretary that the State has in effect policies and procedures to ensure that the State meets the conditions in §§ 300.101 through 300.176.

FAPE Requirements

Sec. 300.101 Free appropriate public education (FAPE).

(a) General. A free appropriate public education must be available to all children residing in the State between the ages of 3 and 21, inclusive, including children with disabilities who have been suspended or expelled from school, as provided for in § 300.530(d).

(b) FAPE for children beginning at age 3.

(1) Each State must ensure that —

(i) The obligation to make FAPE available to each eligible child residing in the State begins no later than the child's third birthday; and

(ii) An IEP or an IFSP is in effect for the child by that date, in accordance with § 300.323(b).

(2) If a child's third birthday occurs during the summer, the child's IEP Team shall determine the date when services under the IEP or IFSP will begin.

(c) Children advancing from grade to grade.

(1) Each State must ensure that FAPE is available to any individual child with a disability who needs special education and related services, even though the child has not failed or been retained in a course or grade, and is advancing from grade to grade.

(2) The determination that a child described in paragraph (a) of this section is eligible under this part, must be made on an individual basis by the group responsible within the child's LEA for making eligibility determinations.

Sec. 300.102   Limitation — exception to FAPE for certain ages.

(a) General. The obligation to make FAPE available to all children with disabilities does not apply with respect to the following:

(1) Children aged 3, 4, 5, 18, 19, 20, or 21 in a State to the extent that its application to those children would be inconsistent with State law or practice, or the order of any court, respecting the provision of public education to children of those ages.

(2) (i) Children aged 18 through 21 to the extent that State law does not require that special education and related services under Part B of the Act be provided to students with disabilities who, in the last educational placement prior to their incarceration in an adult correctional facility —

(A) Were not actually identified as being a child with a disability under § 300.8; and

(B) Did not have an IEP under Part B of the Act.

(ii) The exception in paragraph (a)(2)(i) of this section does not apply to children with disabilities, aged 18 through 21, who —

(A) Had been identified as a child with a disability under § 300.8 and had received services in accordance with an IEP, but who left school prior to their incarceration; or

(B) Did not have an IEP in their last educational setting, but who had actually been identified as a child with a disability under § 300.8.

(3) (i) Children with disabilities who have graduated from high school with a regular high school diploma.

(ii) The exception in paragraph (a)(3)(i) of this section does not apply to children who have graduated from high school but have not been awarded a regular high school diploma.

(iii) Graduation from high school with a regular high school diploma constitutes a change in placement, requiring written prior notice in accordance with § 300.503.

(iv) As used in paragraphs (a)(3)(i) through (a)(3)(iii) of this section, the term regular high school diploma does not include an alternative degree that is not fully aligned with the State's academic standards, such as a certificate or a general educational development credential (GED).

(4) Children with disabilities who are eligible under subpart H of this part, but who receive early intervention services under Part C of the Act.

(b) Documents relating to exceptions. The State must assure that the information it has provided to the Secretary regarding the exceptions in paragraph (a) of this section, as required by § 300.700 (for purposes of making grants to States under this part), is current and accurate.

Other FAPE Requirements

Sec. 300.103　FAPE — methods and payments.

(a) Each State may use whatever State, local, Federal, and private sources of support that are available in the State to meet the requirements of this part. For example, if it is necessary to place a child with a disability in a residential facility, a State could use joint agreements between the agencies involved for sharing the cost of that placement.

(b) Nothing in this part relieves an insurer or similar third party from an otherwise valid obligation to provide or to pay for services provided to a child with a disability.

(c) Consistent with § 300.323(c), the State must ensure that there is no delay in implementing a child's IEP, including any case in which the payment source for providing or paying for special education and related services to the child is being determined.

Sec. 300.104　Residential placement

If placement in a public or private residential program is necessary to provide special education and related services to a child with a disability, the program, including non-medical care and room and board, must be at no cost to the parents of the child.

Sec. 300.105　Assistive technology.

(a) Each public agency must ensure that assistive technology devices or assistive technology services, or both, as those terms are defined in §§ 300.5 and 300.6, respectively, are made available to a child with a disability if required as a part of the child's —

(1) Special education under § 300.36;

(2) Related services under § 300.34; or

(3) Supplementary aids and services under §§ 300.38 and 300.114(a)(2)(ii).

(b) On a case-by-case basis, the use of school-purchased assistive technology devices in a child's home or in other settings is required if the child's IEP Team determines that the child needs access to those devices in order to receive FAPE.

Sec. 300.106 Extended school year services.

(a) General.

(1) Each public agency must ensure that extended school year services are available as necessary to provide FAPE, consistent with paragraph (a)(2) of this section.

(2) Extended school year services must be provided only if a child's IEP Team determines, on an individual basis, in accordance with §§ 300.320 through 300.324, that the services are necessary for the provision of FAPE to the child.

(3) In implementing the requirements of this section, a public agency may not —

(i) Limit extended school year services to particular categories of disability; or

(ii) Unilaterally limit the type, amount, or duration of those services.

(b) Definition. As used in this section, the term extended school year services means special education and related services that —

(1) Are provided to a child with a disability —

(i) Beyond the normal school year of the public agency;

(ii) In accordance with the child's IEP; and

(iii) At no cost to the parents of the child; and

(2) Meet the standards of the SEA.

Sec. 300.107 Nonacademic services.

The State must ensure the following:

(a) Each public agency must take steps, including the provision of supplementary aids and services determined appropriate and necessary by the child's IEP Team, to provide nonacademic and extracurricular services and activities in the manner necessary to afford children with disabilities an equal opportunity for participation in those services and activities.

(b) Nonacademic and extracurricular services and activities may include counseling services, athletics, transportation, health services, recreational activities, special interest groups or clubs sponsored by the public agency, referrals to agencies that provide assistance to individuals with disabilities, and employment of students, including both employment by the public agency and assistance in making outside employment available.

Sec. 300.108 Physical education.

The State must ensure that public agencies in the State comply with the following:

(a) General. Physical education services, specially designed if necessary, must be made available to every child with a disability receiving FAPE, unless the public agency enrolls children without disabilities and does not provide physical education to children without disabilities in the same grades.

(b) Regular physical education. Each child with a disability must be afforded the opportunity to participate in the regular physical education program available to nondisabled children unless —

(1) The child is enrolled full time in a separate facility; or

(2) The child needs specially designed physical education, as prescribed in the child's IEP.

(c) Special physical education. If specially designed physical education is prescribed in a child's IEP, the public agency responsible for the education of that child must provide the services directly or make arrangements for those services to be provided through other public or private programs.

(d) Education in separate facilities. The public agency responsible for the education of a child with a disability who is enrolled in a separate facility must ensure that the child receives appropriate physical education services in compliance with this section.

Sec. 300.109 Full educational opportunity goal (FEOG).

The State must have in effect policies and procedures to demonstrate that the State has established a goal of providing full educational opportunity to all children with disabilities, aged birth through 21, and a detailed timetable for accomplishing that goal.

Sec. 300.110 Program options.

The State must ensure that each public agency takes steps to ensure that its children with disabilities have available to them the variety of educational programs and services available to nondisabled children in the area served by the agency, including art, music, industrial arts, consumer and homemaking education, and vocational education.

Sec. 300.111 Child find.

(a) General.

(1) The State must have in effect policies and procedures to ensure that —

(i) All children with disabilities residing in the State, including children with disabilities who are homeless children or are wards of the State, and children with disabilities attending private schools, regardless of the severity of their disability, and who are in need of special education and related services, are identified, located, and evaluated; and

(ii) A practical method is developed and implemented to determine which children are currently receiving needed special education and related services.

(b) Use of term developmental delay. The following provisions apply with respect to implementing the child find requirements of this section:

(1) A State that adopts a definition of developmental delay under § 300.8(b) determines whether the term applies to children aged three through nine, or to a subset of that age range (e.g., ages three through five).

(2) A State may not require an LEA to adopt and use the term developmental delay for any children within its jurisdiction.

(3) If an LEA uses the term developmental delay for children described in § 300.8(b), the LEA must conform to both the State's definition of that term and to the age range that has been adopted by the State.

(4) If a State does not adopt the term developmental delay, an LEA may not independently use that term as a basis for establishing a child's eligibility under this part.

(c)   Other children in child find. Child find also must include —

(1) Children who are suspected of being a child with a disability under § 300.8 and in need of special education, even though they are advancing from grade to grade; and

(2) Highly mobile children, including migrant children.

(d)   Construction. Nothing in the Act requires that children be classified by their disability so long as each child who has a disability that is listed in § 300.8 and who, by reason of that disability, needs special education and related services is regarded as a child with a disability under Part B of the Act.

Sec. 300.112   Individualized education programs (IEP).

The State must ensure that an IEP, or an IFSP that meets the requirements of section 636(d) of the Act, is developed, reviewed, and revised for each child with a disability in accordance with §§ 300.320 through 300.324, except as provided in § 300.300(b)(3)(ii).

Sec. 300.113   Routine checking of hearing aids and external components of surgically implanted medical devices.

(a)   Hearing aids. Each public agency must ensure that hearing aids worn in school by children with hearing impairments, including deafness, are functioning properly.

(b) External components of surgically implanted medical devices.

(1) Subject to paragraph (b)(2) of this section, each public agency must ensure that the external components of surgically implanted medical devices are functioning properly.

(2) For a child with a surgically implanted medical device who is receiving special education and related services under this part, a public agency is not responsible for the post-surgical maintenance, programming, or replacement of the medical device that has been surgically implanted (or of an external component of the surgically implanted medical device).

Least Restrictive Environment (LRE)

Sec. 300.114   LRE requirements.

(a)   General.

(1) Except as provided in § 300.324(d)(2) (regarding children with disabilities in adult prisons), the State must have in effect policies and procedures to ensure that public agencies in the State meet the LRE requirements of this section and §§ 300.115 through 300.120.

(2) Each public agency must ensure that —

(i) To the maximum extent appropriate, children with disabilities, including children in public or private institutions or other care facilities, are educated with children who are nondisabled; and

(ii) Special classes, separate schooling, or other removal of children with disabilities from the regular educational environment occurs only if the nature or severity of the disability is such that education in regular classes with the use of supplementary aids and services cannot be achieved satisfactorily.

(b) Additional requirement — State funding mechanism —

(1)   General.

(i) A State funding mechanism must not result in placements that violate the requirements of paragraph (a) of this section; and

(ii) A State must not use a funding mechanism by which the State distributes funds on the basis of the type of setting in which a child is served that will result in the failure to provide a child with a disability FAPE according to the unique needs of the child, as described in the child's IEP.

(2)   Assurance. If the State does not have policies and procedures to ensure compliance with paragraph (b)(1) of this section, the State must provide the Secretary an assurance that the State will revise the funding mechanism as soon as feasible to ensure that the mechanism does not result in placements that violate that paragraph.

Sec. 300.115   Continuum of alternative placements.

(a) Each public agency must ensure that a continuum of alternative placements is available to meet the needs of children with disabilities for special education and related services.

(b) The continuum required in paragraph (a) of this section must —

(1) Include the alternative placements listed in the definition of special education under § 300.38 (instruction in regular classes, special classes, special schools, home instruction, and instruction in hospitals and institutions); and

(2) Make provision for supplementary services (such as resource room or itinerant instruction) to be provided in conjunction with regular class placement.

Sec. 300.116   Placements.

In determining the educational placement of a child with a disability, including a preschool child with a disability, each public agency must ensure that —

(a) The placement decision —

(1) Is made by a group of persons, including the parents, and other persons knowledgeable about the child, the meaning of the evaluation data, and the placement options; and

(2) Is made in conformity with the LRE provisions of this subpart, including §§ 300.114 through 300.118;

(b) The child's placement —

(1) Is determined at least annually;

(2) Is based on the child's IEP; and

(3) Is as close as possible to the child's home;

(c) Unless the IEP of a child with a disability requires some other arrangement, the child is educated in the school that he or she would attend if nondisabled;

(d) In selecting the LRE, consideration is given to any potential harmful effect on the child or on the quality of services that he or she needs; and

(e) A child with a disability is not removed from education in age-appropriate regular classrooms solely because of needed modifications in the general education curriculum.

Sec. 300.117   Nonacademic settings.

In providing or arranging for the provision of nonacademic and extracurricular services and activities, including meals, recess periods, and the services and activities set forth in § 300.107, each public agency must ensure that each child with a disability participates with nondisabled children in the extracurricular services and activities to the maximum extent appropriate to the needs of that child. The public agency must ensure that each child with a disability has the supplementary aids and services determined by the child's IEP Team to be appropriate and necessary for the child to participate in nonacademic settings.

Sec. 300.118   Children in public or private institutions.

Except as provided in § 300.149(d) (regarding agency responsibility for general supervision of some individuals in adult prisons), an SEA must ensure that § 300.114 is effectively implemented, including, if necessary, making arrangements with public and private institutions (such as a memorandum of agreement or special implementation procedures).

Additional Eligibility Requirements

Sec. 300.121   Procedural safeguards.

(a)   General. The State must have procedural safeguards in effect to ensure that each public agency in the State meets the requirements of §§ 300.500 through 300.536.

(b) Procedural safeguards identified. Children with disabilities and their parents must be afforded the procedural safeguards identified in paragraph (a) of this section.

Sec. 300.123 Confidentiality of personally identifiable information.

The State must have policies and procedures in effect to ensure that public agencies in the State comply with §§ 300.610 through 300.626 related to protecting the confidentiality of any personally identifiable information collected, used, or maintained under Part B of the Act.

Sec. 300.124 Transition of children from the Part C program to preschool programs.

The State must have in effect policies and procedures to ensure that —

(a) Children participating in early intervention programs assisted under Part C of the Act, and who will participate in preschool programs assisted under Part B of the Act, experience a smooth and effective transition to those preschool programs in a manner consistent with section 637(a)(9) of the Act;

(b) By the third birthday of a child described in paragraph (a) of this section, an IEP or, if consistent with § 300.323(b) and section 636(d) of the Act, an IFSP, has been developed and is being implemented for the child consistent with Sec. 300.101(b); and

(c) Each affected LEA will participate in transition planning conferences arranged by the designated lead agency under section 635(a)(10) of the Act.

Children With Disabilities Enrolled by Their Parents in Private Schools

Sec. 300.130 Definition of parentally-placed private school children with disabilities.

Parentally-placed private school children with disabilities means children with disabilities enrolled by their parents in private, including religious, schools or facilities that meet the definition of elementary school in § 300.13 or secondary school in § 300.36, other than children with disabilities covered under §§ 300.145 through 300.147.

Sec. 300.131 Child find for parentally-placed private school children with disabilities.

(a) General. Each LEA must locate, identify, and evaluate all children with disabilities who are enrolled by their parents in private, including religious, elementary schools and secondary schools located in the school district served by the LEA, in accordance with paragraphs (b) through (e) of this section, and §§ 300.111 and 300.201.

(b) Child find design. The child find process must be designed to ensure —

(1) The equitable participation of parentally-placed private school children; and

(2) An accurate count of those children.

(c) Activities. In carrying out the requirements of this section, the LEA, or, if applicable, the SEA, must undertake activities similar to the activities undertaken for the agency's public school children.

(d)   Cost. The cost of carrying out the child find requirements in this section, including individual evaluations, may not be considered in determining if an LEA has met its obligation under § 300.133.

(e)   Completion period. The child find process must be completed in a time period comparable to that for students attending public schools in the LEA consistent with § 300.301.

(f)   Out-of-State children. Each LEA in which private, including religious, elementary schools and secondary schools are located must, in carrying out the child find requirements in this section, include parentally-placed private school children who reside in a State other than the State in which the private schools that they attend are located.

Sec. 300.132   Provision of services for parentally-placed private school children with disabilities — basic requirement.

(a)   General. To the extent consistent with the number and location of children with disabilities who are enrolled by their parents in private, including religious, elementary schools and secondary schools located in the school district served by the LEA, provision is made for the participation of those children in the program assisted or carried out under Part B of the Act by providing them with special education and related services, including direct services determined in accordance with § 300.137, unless the Secretary has arranged for services to those children under the by-pass provisions in §§ 300.190 through 300.198.

(b) Services plan for parentally-placed private school children with disabilities. In accordance with paragraph (a) of this section and §§ 300.137 through 300.139, a services plan must be developed and implemented for each private school child with a disability who has been designated by the LEA in which the private school is located to receive special education and related services under this part.

(c)   Record keeping. Each LEA must maintain in its records, and provide to the SEA, the following information related to parentally-placed private school children covered under §§ 300.130 through 300.144:

(1) The number of children evaluated;

(2) The number of children determined to be children with disabilities; and

(3) The number of children served.

Sec. 300.137   Equitable services determined.

(a)   No individual right to special education and related services. No parentally-placed private school child with a disability has an individual right to receive some or all of the special education and related services that the child would receive if enrolled in a public school.

(b)   Decisions.

(1) Decisions about the services that will be provided to parentally-placed

private school children with disabilities under §§ 300.130 through 300.144 must be made in accordance with paragraph (c) of this section and § 300.134(d).

(2) The LEA must make the final decisions with respect to the services to be provided to eligible parentally-placed private school children with disabilities.

(c) Services plan for each child served under §§ 300.130 through 300.144. If a child with a disability is enrolled in a religious or other private school by the child's parents and will receive special education or related services from an LEA, the LEA must —

(1) Initiate and conduct meetings to develop, review, and revise a services plan for the child, in accordance with § 300.138(b); and

(2) Ensure that a representative of the religious or other private school attends each meeting. If the representative cannot attend, the LEA shall use other methods to ensure participation by the religious or other private school, including individual or conference telephone calls.

Sec. 300.138 Equitable services provided.

(a) General.

(1) The services provided to parentally-placed private school children with disabilities must be provided by personnel meeting the same standards as personnel providing services in the public schools, except that private elementary school and secondary school teachers who are providing equitable services to parentally-placed private school children with disabilities do not have to meet the highly qualified special education teacher requirements of § 300.18.

(2) Parentally-placed private school children with disabilities may receive a different amount of services than children with disabilities in public schools.

(b) Services provided in accordance with a services plan.

(1) Each parentally-placed private school child with a disability who has been designated to receive services under § 300.132 must have a services plan that describes the specific special education and related services that the LEA will provide to the child in light of the services that the LEA has determined, through the process described in §§ 300.134 and 300.137, it will make available to parentally-placed private school children with disabilities.

(2) The services plan must, to the extent appropriate —

(i) Meet the requirements of § 300.320, or for a child ages three through five, meet the requirements of § 300.323(b) with respect to the services provided; and

(ii) Be developed, reviewed, and revised consistent with §§ 300.321 through 300.324.

(c) Provision of equitable services.

(1) The provision of services pursuant to this section and §§ 300.139 through 300.143 must be provided:

(i) By employees of a public agency; or

(ii) Through contract by the public agency with an individual, association, agency, organization, or other entity.

(2) Special education and related services provided to parentally-placed private school children with disabilities, including materials and equipment, must be secular, neutral, and nonideological.

Sec. 300.139   Location of services and transportation.

(a)   Services on private school premises. Services to parentally-placed private school children with disabilities may be provided on the premises of private, including religious, schools, to the extent consistent with law.

(b)   Transportation —

(1)   General.

(i) If necessary for the child to benefit from or participate in the services provided under this part, a parentally-placed private school child with a disability must be provided transportation —

(A) From the child's school or the child's home to a site other than the private school; and

(B) From the service site to the private school, or to the child's home, depending on the timing of the services.

(ii) LEAs are not required to provide transportation from the child's home to the private school.

(2)   Cost of transportation. The cost of the transportation described in paragraph (b)(1)(i) of this section may be included in calculating whether the LEA has met the requirement of § 300.133.

Sec. 300.140   Due process complaints and State complaints.

(a)   Due process not applicable, except for child find.

(1) Except as provided in paragraph (b) of this section, the procedures in §§ 300.504 through 300.519 do not apply to complaints that an LEA has failed to meet the requirements of §§ 300.132 through 300.139, including the provision of services indicated on the child's services plan.

(b) Child find complaints — to be filed with the LEA in which the private school is located.

(1) The procedures in §§ 300.504 through 300.519 apply to complaints that an LEA has failed to meet the child find requirements in §§ 300.131, including the requirements in §§ 300.300 through 300.311.

(2) Any due process complaint regarding the child find requirements (as described in paragraph (b)(1) of this section) must be filed with the LEA in which the private school is located and a copy must be forwarded to the SEA.

(c)   State complaints.

(1) Any complaint that an SEA or LEA has failed to meet the requirements in §§ 300.132 through 300.135 and 300.137 through 300.144 must be filed in accordance with the procedures described in §§ 300.151 through 300.153.

(2) A complaint filed by a private school official under § 300.136(a) must be filed with the SEA in accordance with the procedures in § 300.136(b).

Sec. 300.141 Requirement that funds not benefit a private school.

(a) An LEA may not use funds provided under section 611 or 619 of the Act to finance the existing level of instruction in a private school or to otherwise benefit the private school.

(b) The LEA must use funds provided under Part B of the Act to meet the special education and related services needs of parentally-placed private school children with disabilities, but not for meeting —

(1) The needs of a private school; or

(2) The general needs of the students enrolled in the private school.

Sec. 300.142 Use of personnel.

(a) Use of public school personnel. An LEA may use funds available under sections 611 and 619 of the Act to make public school personnel available in other than public facilities —

(1) To the extent necessary to provide services under §§ 300.130 through 300.144 for parentally-placed private school children with disabilities; and

(2) If those services are not normally provided by the private school.

(b) Use of private school personnel. An LEA may use funds available under sections 611 and 619 of the Act to pay for the services of an employee of a private school to provide services under §§ 300.130 through 300.144 if —

(1) The employee performs the services outside of his or her regular hours of duty; and

(2) The employee performs the services under public supervision and control.

Sec. 300.143 Separate classes prohibited.

An LEA may not use funds available under section 611 or 619 of the Act for classes that are organized separately on the basis of school enrollment or religion of the children if —

(a) The classes are at the same site; and

(b) The classes include children enrolled in public schools and children enrolled in private schools.

Sec. 300.144 Property, equipment, and supplies.

(a) A public agency must control and administer the funds used to provide special education and related services under §§ 300.137 through 300.139, and hold title to and administer materials, equipment, and property purchased with those funds for the uses and purposes provided in the Act.

(b) The public agency may place equipment and supplies in a private school for the period of time needed for the Part B program.

(c) The public agency must ensure that the equipment and supplies placed in a private school —

(1) Are used only for Part B purposes; and

(2) Can be removed from the private school without remodeling the private school facility.

(d) The public agency must remove equipment and supplies from a private school if

(1) The equipment and supplies are no longer needed for Part B purposes; or

(2) Removal is necessary to avoid unauthorized use of the equipment and supplies for other than Part B purposes.

(e) No funds under Part B of the Act may be used for repairs, minor remodeling, or construction of private school facilities.

Children With Disabilities in Private Schools Placed or Referred by Public Agencies

Sec. 300.145   Applicability of §§ 300.146 through 300.147.

Sections 300.146 through 300.147 apply only to children with disabilities who are or have been placed in or referred to a private school or facility by a public agency as a means of providing special education and related services.

Sec. 300.146   Responsibility of SEA.

Each SEA must ensure that a child with a disability who is placed in or referred to a private school or facility by a public agency —

(a) Is provided special education and related services —

(1) In conformance with an IEP that meets the requirements of §§ 300.320 through 300.325; and

(2) At no cost to the parents;

(b) Is provided an education that meets the standards that apply to education provided by the SEA and LEAs including the requirements of this part, except for § 300.18 and § 300.156(c); and

(c) Has all of the rights of a child with a disability who is served by a public agency.

Sec. 300.147   Implementation by SEA.

In implementing § 300.146, the SEA must —

(a) Monitor compliance through procedures such as written reports, on-site visits, and parent questionnaires;

(b) Disseminate copies of applicable standards to each private school and facility to which a public agency has referred or placed a child with a disability; and

(c) Provide an opportunity for those private schools and facilities to participate in the development and revision of State standards that apply to them.

Children With Disabilities Enrolled by Their Parents in Private Schools When FAPE Is at Issue

Sec. 300.148   Placement of children by parents when FAPE is at issue.

(a)   General. This part does not require an LEA to pay for the cost of education, including special education and related services, of a child with a disability at a private school or facility if that agency made FAPE available to the child and the parents elected to place the child in a private school or facility. However, the public agency must include that child in the population whose needs are addressed consistent with §§ 300.131 through 300.144.

(b)   Disagreements about FAPE. Disagreements between the parents and a public agency regarding the availability of a program appropriate for the child, and the question of financial reimbursement, are subject to the due process procedures in §§ 300.504 through 300.520.

(c)   Reimbursement for private school placement. If the parents of a child with a disability, who previously received special education and related services under the authority of a public agency, enroll the child in a private preschool, elementary school, or secondary school without the consent of or referral by the public agency, a court or a hearing officer may require the agency to reimburse the parents for the cost of that enrollment if the court or hearing officer finds that the agency had not made FAPE available to the child in a timely manner prior to that enrollment and that the private placement is appropriate. A parental placement may be found to be appropriate by a hearing officer or a court even if it does not meet the State standards that apply to education provided by the SEA and LEAs.

(d)   Limitation on reimbursement. The cost of reimbursement described in paragraph (c) of this section may be reduced or denied —

(1) If —

(i) At the most recent IEP Team meeting that the parents attended prior to removal of the child from the public school, the parents did not inform the IEP Team that they were rejecting the placement proposed by the public agency to provide FAPE to their child, including stating their concerns and their intent to enroll their child in a private school at public expense; or

(ii) At least ten (10) business days (including any holidays that occur on a business day) prior to the removal of the child from the public school, the parents did not give written notice to the public agency of the information described in paragraph (d)(1)(i) of this section;

(2) If, prior to the parents' removal of the child from the public school, the public agency informed the parents, through the notice requirements described in § 300.503(a)(1), of its intent to evaluate the child (including a statement of the

purpose of the evaluation that was appropriate and reasonable), but the parents did not make the child available for the evaluation; or

(3) Upon a judicial finding of unreasonableness with respect to actions taken by the parents.

(e)   Exception. Notwithstanding the notice requirement in paragraph (d)(1) of this section, the cost of reimbursement —

(1) Must not be reduced or denied for failure to provide the notice if —

(i) The school prevented the parents from providing the notice;

(ii) The parents had not received notice, pursuant to § 300.504, of the notice requirement in paragraph (d)(1) of this section; or

(iii) Compliance with paragraph (d)(1) of this section would likely result in physical harm to the child; and

(2) May, in the discretion of the court or a hearing officer, not be reduced or denied for failure to provide this notice if —

(i) The parents are not literate or cannot write in English; or

(ii) Compliance with paragraph (d)(1) of this section would likely result in serious emotional harm to the child.

SEA Responsibility for General Supervision and Implementation of Procedural Safeguards

Sec. 300.149   SEA responsibility for general supervision.

(a) The SEA is responsible for ensuring —

(1) That the requirements of this part are carried out; and

(2) That each educational program for children with disabilities administered within the State, including each program administered by any other State or local agency (but not including elementary schools and secondary schools for Indian children operated or funded by the Secretary of the Interior) —

(i) Is under the general supervision of the persons responsible for educational programs for children with disabilities in the SEA; and

(ii) Meets the educational standards of the SEA (including the requirements of this part).

(3) In carrying out this part with respect to homeless children, the requirements of subtitle B of title VII of the McKinney-Vento Homeless Assistance Act (42 U.S.C. 11431 et seq.) are met.

(b) The State must have in effect policies and procedures to ensure that it complies with the monitoring and enforcement requirements in §§ 300.600 through 300.602 and §§ 300.606 through 300.608.

(c) Part B of the Act does not limit the responsibility of agencies other than educational agencies for providing or paying some or all of the costs of FAPE to children with disabilities in the State.

(d) Notwithstanding paragraph (a) of this section, the Governor (or another individual pursuant to State law) may assign to any public agency in the State the responsibility of ensuring that the requirements of Part B of the Act are met with respect to students with disabilities who are convicted as adults under State law and incarcerated in adult prisons.

Sec. 300.150   SEA implementation of procedural safeguards.

The SEA (and any agency assigned responsibility pursuant to § 300.149(d)) must have in effect procedures to inform each public agency of its responsibility for ensuring effective implementation of procedural safeguards for the children with disabilities served by that public agency.

State Complaint Procedures

Sec. 300.151   Adoption of State complaint procedures.

(a)   General. Each SEA must adopt written procedures for —

(1) Resolving any complaint, including a complaint filed by an organization or individual from another State, that meets the requirements of § 300.153 by —

(i) Providing for the filing of a complaint with the SEA; and

(ii) At the SEA's discretion, providing for the filing of a complaint with a public agency and the right to have the SEA review the public agency's decision on the complaint; and

(2) Widely disseminating to parents and other interested individuals, including parent training and information centers, protection and advocacy agencies, independent living centers, and other appropriate entities, the State procedures under §§ 300.151 through 300.153.

(b)   Remedies for denial of appropriate services. In resolving a complaint in which the SEA has found a failure to provide appropriate services, an SEA, pursuant to its general supervisory authority under Part B of the Act, must address —

(1) The failure to provide appropriate services, including corrective action appropriate to address the needs of the child (such as compensatory services or monetary reimbursement); and

(2) Appropriate future provision of services for all children with disabilities.

Sec. 300.152   Minimum State complaint procedures.

(a)   Time limit; minimum procedures. Each SEA must include in its complaint procedures a time limit of 60 days after a complaint is filed under § 300.153 to —

(1) Carry out an independent on-site investigation, if the SEA determines that an investigation is necessary;

(2) Give the complainant the opportunity to submit additional information, either orally or in writing, about the allegations in the complaint;

(3) Provide the public agency with the opportunity to respond to the complaint,

including, at a minimum —

(i) At the discretion of the public agency, a proposal to resolve the complaint; and

(ii) An opportunity for a parent who has filed a complaint and the public agency to voluntarily engage in mediation consistent with § 300.506;

(4) Review all relevant information and make an independent determination as to whether the public agency is violating a requirement of Part B of the Act or of this part; and

(5) Issue a written decision to the complainant that addresses each allegation in the complaint and contains —

(i) Findings of fact and conclusions; and

(ii) The reasons for the SEA's final decision.

(b)   Time extension; final decision; implementation. The SEA's procedures described in paragraph (a) of this section also must —

(1) Permit an extension of the time limit under paragraph (a) of this section only if —

(i) Exceptional circumstances exist with respect to a particular complaint; or

(ii) The parent (or individual or organization, if mediation or other alternative means of dispute resolution is available to the individual or organization under State procedures) and the public agency involved agree to extend the time to engage in mediation pursuant to paragraph (a)(3)(ii) of this section, or to engage in other alternative means of dispute resolution, if available in the State; and

(2) Include procedures for effective implementation of the SEA's final decision, if needed, including —

(i) Technical assistance activities;

(ii) Negotiations; and

(iii) Corrective actions to achieve compliance.

(c) Complaints filed under this section and due process hearings under § 300.507 and §§ 300.530 through 300.532.

(1) If a written complaint is received that is also the subject of a due process hearing under § 300.507 or §§ 300.530 through 300.532, or contains multiple issues of which one or more are part of that hearing, the State must set aside any part of the complaint that is being addressed in the due process hearing until the conclusion of the hearing. However, any issue in the complaint that is not a part of the due process action must be resolved using the time limit and procedures described in paragraphs (a) and (b) of this section.

(2) If an issue raised in a complaint filed under this section has previously been decided in a due process hearing involving the same parties —

(i) The due process hearing decision is binding on that issue; and

(ii) The SEA must inform the complainant to that effect.

(3) A complaint alleging a public agency's failure to implement a due process hearing decision must be resolved by the SEA.

Sec. 300.153 Filing a complaint.

(a) An organization or individual may file a signed written complaint under the procedures described in §§ 300.151 through 300.152.

(b) The complaint must include —

(1) A statement that a public agency has violated a requirement of Part B of the Act or of this part;

(2) The facts on which the statement is based;

(3) The signature and contact information for the complainant; and

(4) If alleging violations with respect to a specific child —

(i) The name and address of the residence of the child;

(ii) The name of the school the child is attending;

(iii) In the case of a homeless child or youth (within the meaning of section 725(2) of the McKinney-Vento Homeless Assistance Act (42 U.S.C. 11434a(2)), available contact information for the child, and the name of the school the child is attending;

(iv) A description of the nature of the problem of the child, including facts relating to the problem; and

(v) A proposed resolution of the problem to the extent known and available to the party at the time the complaint is filed.

(c) The complaint must allege a violation that occurred not more than one year prior to the date that the complaint is received in accordance with § 300.151.

(d) The party filing the complaint must forward a copy of the complaint to the LEA or public agency serving the child at the same time the party files the complaint with the SEA.

Methods of Ensuring Services

Sec. 300.154 Methods of ensuring services.

(a) Establishing responsibility for services. The Chief Executive Officer of a State or designee of that officer must ensure that an interagency agreement or other mechanism for interagency coordination is in effect between each noneducational public agency described in paragraph (b) of this section and the SEA, in order to ensure that all services described in paragraph (b)(1) of this section that are needed to ensure FAPE are provided, including the provision of these services during the pendency of any dispute under paragraph (a)(3) of this section. The agreement or mechanism must include the following:

(1) An identification of, or a method for defining, the financial responsibility of each agency for providing services described in paragraph (b)(1) of this section to ensure FAPE to children with disabilities. The financial responsibility of each noneducational public agency described in paragraph (b) of this section, including the State Medicaid agency and other public insurers of children with disabilities, must precede the financial responsibility of the LEA (or the State agency responsible for developing the child's IEP).

(2) The conditions, terms, and procedures under which an LEA must be reimbursed by other agencies.

(3) Procedures for resolving interagency disputes (including procedures under which LEAs may initiate proceedings) under the agreement or other mechanism to secure reimbursement from other agencies or otherwise implement the provisions of the agreement or mechanism.

(4) Policies and procedures for agencies to determine and identify the interagency coordination responsibilities of each agency to promote the coordination and timely and appropriate delivery of services described in paragraph (b)(1) of this section.

(b)   Obligation of noneducational public agencies.

(1) (i) If any public agency other than an educational agency is otherwise obligated under Federal or State law, or assigned responsibility under State policy or pursuant to paragraph (a) of this section, to provide or pay for any services that are also considered special education or related services (such as, but not limited to, services described in § 300.5 relating to assistive technology devices, § 300.6 relating to assistive technology services, § 300.34 relating to related services, § 300.41 relating to supplementary aids and services, and § 300.42 relating to transition services) that are necessary for ensuring FAPE to children with disabilities within the State, the public agency must fulfill that obligation or responsibility, either directly or through contract or other arrangement pursuant to paragraph (a) of this section or an agreement pursuant to paragraph (c) of this section.

(ii) A noneducational public agency described in paragraph (b)(1)(i) of this section may not disqualify an eligible service for Medicaid reimbursement because that service is provided in a school context.

(2) If a public agency other than an educational agency fails to provide or pay for the special education and related services described in paragraph (b)(1) of this section, the LEA (or State agency responsible for developing the child's IEP) must provide or pay for these services to the child in a timely manner. The LEA or State agency is authorized to claim reimbursement for the services from the noneducational public agency that failed to provide or pay for these services and that agency must reimburse the LEA or State agency in accordance with the terms of the interagency agreement or other mechanism described in paragraph (a) of this section.

(c)   Special rule. The requirements of paragraph (a) of this section may be met through —

(1) State statute or regulation;

(2) Signed agreements between respective agency officials that clearly identify the responsibilities of each agency relating to the provision of services; or

(3) Other appropriate written methods as determined by the Chief Executive Officer of the State or designee of that officer and approved by the Secretary.

(d)   Children with disabilities who are covered by public benefits or insurance.

(1) A public agency may use the Medicaid or other public benefits or insurance programs in which a child participates to provide or pay for services required under this part, as permitted under the public benefits or insurance program, except as provided in paragraph (d)(2) of this section.

(2) With regard to services required to provide FAPE to an eligible child under this part, the public agency —

(i) May not require parents to sign up for or enroll in public benefits or insurance programs in order for their child to receive FAPE under Part B of the Act;

(ii) May not require parents to incur an out-of-pocket expense such as the payment of a deductible or co-pay amount incurred in filing a claim for services provided pursuant to this part, but pursuant to paragraph (g)(2) of this section, may pay the cost that the parents otherwise would be required to pay;

(iii) May not use a child's benefits under a public benefits or insurance program if that use would —

(A) Decrease available lifetime coverage or any other insured benefit;

(B) Result in the family paying for services that would otherwise be covered by the public benefits or insurance program and that are required for the child outside of the time the child is in school;

(C) Increase premiums or lead to the discontinuation of benefits or insurance; or

(D) Risk loss of eligibility for home and community-based waivers, based on aggregate health-related expenditures; and

(iv) (A) Must obtain parental consent, consistent with § 300.9, each time that access to public benefits or insurance is sought; and

(B) Notify parents that the parents' refusal to allow access to their public benefits or insurance does not relieve the public agency of its responsibility to ensure that all required services are provided at no cost to the parents.

(e)   Children with disabilities who are covered by private insurance.

(1) With regard to services required to provide FAPE to an eligible child under this part, a public agency may access the parents' private insurance proceeds only if the parents provide consent consistent with § 300.9.

(2) Each time the public agency proposes to access the parents' private insurance proceeds, the agency must —

(i) Obtain parental consent in accordance with paragraph (e)(1) of this section; and

(ii) Inform the parents that their refusal to permit the public agency to access their private insurance does not relieve the public agency of its responsibility to ensure that all required services are provided at no cost to the parents.

(f) Use of Part B funds.

(1) If a public agency is unable to obtain parental consent to use the parents' private insurance, or public benefits or insurance when the parents would incur a cost for a specified service required under this part, to ensure FAPE the public agency may use its Part B funds to pay for the service.

(2) To avoid financial cost to parents who otherwise would consent to use private insurance, or public benefits or insurance if the parents would incur a cost, the public agency may use its Part B funds to pay the cost that the parents otherwise would have to pay to use the parents' benefits or insurance (e.g., the deductible or co-pay amounts).

(g) Proceeds from public benefits or insurance or private insurance.

(1) Proceeds from public benefits or insurance or private insurance will not be treated as program income for purposes of 34 CFR 80.25.

(2) If a public agency spends reimbursements from Federal funds (e.g., Medicaid) for services under this part, those funds will not be considered "State or local" funds for purposes of the maintenance of effort provisions in §§ 300.163 and 300.203.

(h) Construction. Nothing in this part should be construed to alter the requirements imposed on a State Medicaid agency, or any other agency administering a public benefits or insurance program by Federal statute, regulations or policy under title XIX, or title XXI of the Social Security Act, 42 U.S.C. 1396 through 1396v and 42 U.S.C. 1397aa through 1397jj, or any other public benefits or insurance program.

Additional Eligibility Requirements

Sec. 300.155 Hearings relating to LEA eligibility.

The SEA must not make any final determination that an LEA is not eligible for assistance under Part B of the Act without first giving the LEA reasonable notice and an opportunity for a hearing under 34 CFR 76.401(d).

Sec. 300.157 Performance goals and indicators.

The State must —

(a) Have in effect established goals for the performance of children with disabilities in the State that —

(1) Promote the purposes of this part, as stated in § 300.1;

(2) Are the same as the State's objectives for progress by children in its

definition of adequate yearly progress, including the State's objectives for progress by children with disabilities, under section 1111(b)(2)(C) of the ESEA, 20 U.S.C. 6311;

(3) Address graduation rates and dropout rates, as well as such other factors as the State may determine; and

(4) Are consistent, to the extent appropriate, with any other goals and academic standards for children established by the State;

(b) Have in effect established performance indicators the State will use to assess progress toward achieving the goals described in paragraph (a) of this section, including measurable annual objectives for progress by children with disabilities under section 1111(b)(2)(C)(v)(II)(cc) of the ESEA, 20 U.S.C. 6311; and

(c) Annually report to the Secretary and the public on the progress of the State, and of children with disabilities in the State, toward meeting the goals established under paragraph (a) of this section, which may include elements of the reports required under section 1111(h) of the ESEA.

Sec. 300.160 Participation in assessments.

(a) General. A State must ensure that all children with disabilities are included in all general State and district-wide assessment programs, including assessments described under section 1111 of the ESEA, 20 U.S.C. 6311, with appropriate accommodations and alternate assessments, if necessary, as indicated in their respective IEPs.

(b) Accommodation guidelines.

(1) A State (or, in the case of a district-wide assessment, an LEA) must develop guidelines for the provision of appropriate accommodations.

(2) The State's (or, in the case of a district-wide assessment, the LEA's) guidelines must —

(i) Identify only those accommodations for each assessment that do not invalidate the score; and

(ii) Instruct IEP Teams to select, for each assessment, only those accommodations that do not invalidate the score.

(c) Alternate assessments.

(1) A State (or, in the case of a district-wide assessment, an LEA) must develop and implement alternate assessments and guidelines for the participation of children with disabilities in alternate assessments for those children who cannot participate in regular assessments, even with accommodations, as indicated in their respective IEPs, as provided in paragraph (a) of this section.

(2) For assessing the academic progress of students with disabilities under Title I of the ESEA, the alternate assessments and guidelines in paragraph (c)(1) of this section must provide for alternate assessments that —

(i) Are aligned with the State's challenging academic content standards and challenging student academic achievement standards;

(ii) If the State has adopted modified academic achievement standards permitted in 34 CFR 200.1(e), measure the achievement of children with disabilities meeting the State's criteria under Sec. 200.1(e)(2) against those standards; and

(iii) If the State has adopted alternate academic achievement standards permitted in 34 CFR 200.1(d), measure the achievement of children with the most significant cognitive disabilities against those standards.

(d)　Explanation to IEP Teams. A State (or in the case of a district-wide assessment, an LEA) must provide IEP Teams with a clear explanation of the differences between assessments based on grade-level academic achievement standards and those based on modified or alternate academic achievement standards, including any effects of State or local policies on the student's education resulting from taking an alternate assessment based on alternate or modified academic achievement standards (such as whether only satisfactory performance on a regular assessment would qualify a student for a regular high school diploma).

(e)　Inform parents. A State (or in the case of a district-wide assessment, an LEA) must ensure that parents of students selected to be assessed based on alternate or modified academic achievement standards are informed that their child's achievement will be measured based on alternate or modified academic achievement standards.

(f)　Reports. An SEA (or, in the case of a district-wide assessment, an LEA) must make available to the public, and report to the public with the same frequency and in the same detail as it reports on the assessment of nondisabled children, the following:

(1) The number of children with disabilities participating in regular assessments, and the number of those children who were provided accommodations (that did not result in an invalid score) in order to participate in those assessments.

(2) The number of children with disabilities, if any, participating in alternate assessments based on grade-level academic achievement standards.

(3) The number of children with disabilities, if any, participating in alternate assessments based on modified academic achievement standards.

(4) The number of children with disabilities, if any, participating in alternate assessments based on alternate academic achievement standards.

(5) Compared with the achievement of all children, including children with disabilities, the performance results of children with disabilities on regular assessments, alternate assessments based on grade-level academic achievement standards, alternate assessments based on modified academic achievement standards, and alternate assessments based on alternate academic achievement standards if —

(i) The number of children participating in those assessments is sufficient to yield statistically reliable information; and

(ii) Reporting that information will not reveal personally identifiable information about an individual student on those assessments.

(g)   Universal design. An SEA (or, in the case of a district-wide assessment, an LEA) must, to the extent possible, use universal design principles in developing and administering any assessments under this section.

Other Provisions Required for State Eligibility

Sec. 300.170   Suspension and expulsion rates.

(a)   General. The SEA must examine data, including data disaggregated by race and ethnicity, to determine if significant discrepancies are occurring in the rate of long-term suspensions and expulsions of children with disabilities —

(1) Among LEAs in the State; or

(2) Compared to the rates for nondisabled children within those agencies.

(b)   Review and revision of policies. If the discrepancies described in paragraph (a) of this section are occurring, the SEA must review and, if appropriate, revise (or require the affected State agency or LEA to revise) its policies, procedures, and practices relating to the development and implementation of IEPs, the use of positive behavioral interventions and supports, and procedural safeguards, to ensure that these policies, procedures, and practices comply with the Act.

Sec. 300.172   Access to instructional materials.

(a)   General. The State must —

(1) Adopt the National Instructional Materials Accessibility Standard (NIMAS), published as appendix C to part 300, for the purposes of providing instructional materials to blind persons or other persons with print disabilities, in a timely manner after publication of the NIMAS in the Federal Register on July 19, 2006 (71 FR 41084); and

(2) Establish a State definition of "timely manner" for purposes of paragraphs (b)(2) and (b)(3) of this section if the State is not coordinating with the National Instructional Materials Access Center (NIMAC) or (b)(3) and (c)(2) of this section if the State is coordinating with the NIMAC.

(b)   Rights and responsibilities of SEA.

(1) Nothing in this section shall be construed to require any SEA to coordinate with the NIMAC.

(2) If an SEA chooses not to coordinate with the NIMAC, the SEA must provide an assurance to the Secretary that it will provide instructional materials to blind persons or other persons with print disabilities in a timely manner.

(3) Nothing in this section relieves an SEA of its responsibility to ensure that children with disabilities who need instructional materials in accessible formats, but are not included under the definition of blind or other persons with print disabilities in § 300.172(e)(1)(i) or who need materials that cannot be produced from NIMAS files, receive those instructional materials in a timely manner.

(4) In order to meet its responsibility under paragraphs (b)(2), (b)(3), and (c) of this section to ensure that children with disabilities who need instructional materials in accessible formats are provided those materials in a timely manner, the SEA must ensure that all public agencies take all reasonable steps to provide instructional materials in accessible formats to children with disabilities who need those instructional materials at the same time as other children receive instructional materials.

(c) Preparation and delivery of files. If an SEA chooses to coordinate with the NIMAC, as of December 3, 2006, the SEA must —

(1) As part of any print instructional materials adoption process, procurement contract, or other practice or instrument used for purchase of print instructional materials, enter into a written contract with the publisher of the print instructional materials to —

(i) Require the publisher to prepare and, on or before delivery of the print instructional materials, provide to NIMAC electronic files containing the contents of the print instructional materials using the NIMAS; or

(ii) Purchase instructional materials from the publisher that are produced in, or may be rendered in, specialized formats.

(2) Provide instructional materials to blind persons or other persons with print disabilities in a timely manner.

(d) Assistive technology. In carrying out this section, the SEA, to the maximum extent possible, must work collaboratively with the State agency responsible for assistive technology programs.

(e) Definitions.

(1) In this section and § 300.210 —

(i) Blind persons or other persons with print disabilities means children served under this part who may qualify to receive books and other publications produced in specialized formats in accordance with the Act entitled "An Act to provide books for adult blind," approved March 3, 1931, 2 U.S.C. 135a;

(ii) National Instructional Materials Access Center or NIMAC means the center established pursuant to section 674(e) of the Act;

(iii) National Instructional Materials Accessibility Standard or NIMAS has the meaning given the term in section 674(e)(3)(B) of the Act;

(iv) Specialized formats has the meaning given the term in section 674(e)(3)(D) of the Act.

(2) The definitions in paragraph (e)(1) of this section apply to each State and LEA, whether or not the State or LEA chooses to coordinate with the NIMAC.

Sec. 300.173 Overidentification and disproportionality.

The State must have in effect, consistent with the purposes of this part and with section 618(d) of the Act, policies and procedures designed to prevent the inappropriate overidentification or disproportionate representation by race and ethnicity of children as children with disabilities, including children with disabilities with a particular impairment described in § 300.8.

Sec. 300.174 Prohibition on mandatory medication.

(a) General. The SEA must prohibit State and LEA personnel from requiring parents to obtain a prescription for substances identified under schedules I, II, III, IV, or V in section 202(c) of the Controlled Substances Act (21 U.S.C. 812(c)) for a child as a condition of attending school, receiving an evaluation under §§ 300.300 through 300.311, or receiving services under this part.

(b) Rule of construction. Nothing in paragraph (a) of this section shall be construed to create a Federal prohibition against teachers and other school personnel consulting or sharing classroom-based observations with parents or guardians regarding a student's academic and functional performance, or behavior in the classroom or school, or regarding the need for evaluation for special education or related services under § 300.111 (related to child find).

Sec. 300.177 States' sovereign immunity and positive efforts to employ and advance qualified individuals with disabilities.

(a) States' sovereign immunity.

(1) A State that accepts funds under this part waives its immunity under the 11th amendment of the Constitution of the United States from suit in Federal court for a violation of this part.

(2) In a suit against a State for a violation of this part, remedies (including remedies both at law and in equity) are available for such a violation in the suit against any public entity other than a State.

(3) Paragraphs (a)(1) and (a)(2) of this section apply with respect to violations that occur in whole or part after the date of enactment of the Education of the Handicapped Act Amendments of 1990.

Sec. 300.209 Treatment of charter schools and their students.

(a) Rights of children with disabilities. Children with disabilities who attend public charter schools and their parents retain all rights under this part.

(b) Charter schools that are public schools of the LEA.

(1) In carrying out Part B of the Act and these regulations with respect to charter schools that are public schools of the LEA, the LEA must —

(i) Serve children with disabilities attending those charter schools in the same manner as the LEA serves children with disabilities in its other schools, including providing supplementary and related services on site at the charter school to the same extent to which the LEA has a policy or practice of providing such services on the site to its other public schools; and

(ii) Provide funds under Part B of the Act to those charter schools —

(A) On the same basis as the LEA provides funds to the LEA's other public schools, including proportional distribution based on relative enrollment of children with disabilities; and

(B) At the same time as the LEA distributes other Federal funds to the LEA's other public schools, consistent with the State's charter school law.

(2) If the public charter school is a school of an LEA that receives funding under § 300.705 and includes other public schools —

(i) The LEA is responsible for ensuring that the requirements of this part are met, unless State law assigns that responsibility to some other entity; and

(ii) The LEA must meet the requirements of paragraph (b)(1) of this section.

(c)   Public charter schools that are LEAs. If the public charter school is an LEA, consistent with § 300.28, that receives funding under § 300.705, that charter school is responsible for ensuring that the requirements of this part are met, unless State law assigns that responsibility to some other entity.

(d) Public charter schools that are not an LEA or a school that is part of an LEA.

(1) If the public charter school is not an LEA receiving funding under § 300.705, or a school that is part of an LEA receiving funding under § 300.705, the SEA is responsible for ensuring that the requirements of this part are met.

(2) Paragraph (d)(1) of this section does not preclude a State from assigning initial responsibility for ensuring the requirements of this part are met to another entity. However, the SEA must maintain the ultimate responsibility for ensuring compliance with this part, consistent with § 300.149.

Subpart D   Evaluations, Eligibility Determinations, Individualized Education Programs, and Educational Placements

Parental Consent

Sec. 300.300   Parental consent.

(a)   Parental consent for initial evaluation.

(1) (i) The public agency proposing to conduct an initial evaluation to determine if a child qualifies as a child with a disability under § 300.8 must, after providing notice consistent with §§ 300.503 and 300.504, obtain informed consent, consistent with § 300.9, from the parent of the child before conducting the evaluation.

(ii) Parental consent for initial evaluation must not be construed as consent for initial provision of special education and related services.

(iii) The public agency must make reasonable efforts to obtain the informed consent from the parent for an initial evaluation to determine whether the child is a child with a disability.

(2) For initial evaluations only, if the child is a ward of the State and is not residing with the child's parent, the public agency is not required to obtain informed consent from the parent for an initial evaluation to determine whether the child is a child with a disability if —

(i) Despite reasonable efforts to do so, the public agency cannot discover the whereabouts of the parent of the child;

(ii) The rights of the parents of the child have been terminated in accordance with State law; or

(iii) The rights of the parent to make educational decisions have been subrogated by a judge in accordance with State law and consent for an initial evaluation has been given by an individual appointed by the judge to represent the child.

(3) (i) If the parent of a child enrolled in public school or seeking to be enrolled in public school does not provide consent for initial evaluation under paragraph (a)(1) of this section, or the parent fails to respond to a request to provide consent, the public agency may, but is not required to, pursue the initial evaluation of the child by utilizing the procedural safeguards in subpart E of this part (including the mediation procedures under § 300.506 or the due process procedures under §§ 300.507 through 300.516), if appropriate, except to the extent inconsistent with State law relating to such parental consent.

(ii) The public agency does not violate its obligation under § 300.111 and §§ 300.301 through 300.311 if it declines to pursue the evaluation.

(b)   Parental consent for services.

(1) A public agency that is responsible for making FAPE available to a child with a disability must obtain informed consent from the parent of the child before the initial provision of special education and related services to the child.

(2) The public agency must make reasonable efforts to obtain informed consent from the parent for the initial provision of special education and related services to the child.

(3) If the parent of a child fails to respond to a request for, or refuses to consent to, the initial provision of special education and related services, the public agency —

(i) May not use the procedures in subpart E of this part (including the mediation procedures under § 300.506 or the due process procedures under §§ 300.507 through 300.516) in order to obtain agreement or a ruling that the services may be provided to the child;

(ii) Will not be considered to be in violation of the requirement to make FAPE available to the child because of the failure to provide the child with the special education and related services for which the parent refuses to or fails to provide consent; and

(iii) Is not required to convene an IEP Team meeting or develop an IEP under §§ 300.320 and 300.324 for the child.

(4) If, at any time subsequent to the initial provision of special education and related services, the parent of a child revokes consent in writing for the continued provision of special education and related services, the public agency —

(i) May not continue to provide special education and related services to the child, but must provide prior written notice in accordance with § 300.503 before ceasing the provision of special education and related services;

(ii) May not use the procedures in subpart E of this part (including the mediation procedures under § 300.506 or the due process procedures under §§ 300.507 through 300.516) in order to obtain agreement or a ruling that the services may be provided to the child;

(iii) Will not be considered to be in violation of the requirement to make FAPE available to the child because of the failure to provide the child with further special education and related services; and

(iv) Is not required to convene an IEP Team meeting or develop an IEP under §§ 300.320 and 300.324 for the child for further provision of special education and related services.

(c)   Parental consent for reevaluations.

(1) Subject to paragraph (c)(2) of this section, each public agency —

(i) Must obtain informed parental consent, in accordance with § 300.300(a)(1), prior to conducting any reevaluation of a child with a disability.

(ii) If the parent refuses to consent to the reevaluation, the public agency may, but is not required to, pursue the reevaluation by using the consent override procedures described in paragraph (a)(3) of this section.

(iii) The public agency does not violate its obligation under § 300.111 and §§ 300.301 through 300.311 if it declines to pursue the evaluation or reevaluation.

(2) The informed parental consent described in paragraph (c)(1) of this section need not be obtained if the public agency can demonstrate that —

(i) It made reasonable efforts to obtain such consent; and

(ii) The child's parent has failed to respond.

(d)   Other consent requirements.

(1) Parental consent is not required before —

(i) Reviewing existing data as part of an evaluation or a reevaluation; or

(ii) Administering a test or other evaluation that is administered to all children unless, before administration of that test or evaluation, consent is required of parents of all children.

(2) In addition to the parental consent requirements described in paragraphs (a), (b), and (c) of this section, a State may require parental consent for other services and activities under this part if it ensures that each public agency in the State establishes and implements effective procedures to ensure that a parent's refusal to consent does not result in a failure to provide the child with FAPE.

(3) A public agency may not use a parent's refusal to consent to one service or activity under paragraphs (a), (b), (c), or (d)(2) of this section to deny the parent or child any other service, benefit, or activity of the public agency, except as required by this part.

(4) (i) If a parent of a child who is home schooled or placed in a private school by the parents at their own expense does not provide consent for the initial evaluation or the reevaluation, or the parent fails to respond to a request to provide consent, the public agency may not use the consent override procedures (described in paragraphs (a)(3) and (c)(1) of this section); and

(ii) The public agency is not required to consider the child as eligible for services under §§ 300.132 through 300.144.

(5) To meet the reasonable efforts requirement in paragraphs (a)(1)(iii), (a)(2)(i), (b)(2), and (c)(2)(i) of this section, the public agency must document its attempts to obtain parental consent using the procedures in § 300.322(d).

Evaluations and Reevaluations

Sec. 300.301 Initial evaluations.

(a) General. Each public agency must conduct a full and individual initial evaluation, in accordance with §§ 300.304 through 300.306, before the initial provision of special education and related services to a child with a disability under this part.

(b) Request for initial evaluation. Consistent with the consent requirements in § 300.300, either a parent of a child or a public agency may initiate a request for an initial evaluation to determine if the child is a child with a disability.

(c) Procedures for initial evaluation. The initial evaluation —

(1) (i) Must be conducted within 60 days of receiving parental consent for the evaluation; or

(ii) If the State establishes a timeframe within which the evaluation must be conducted, within that timeframe; and

(2) Must consist of procedures —

(i) To determine if the child is a child with a disability under § 300.8; and

(ii) To determine the educational needs of the child.

(d) Exception. The timeframe described in paragraph (c)(1) of this section does not apply to a public agency if —

(1) The parent of a child repeatedly fails or refuses to produce the child for the evaluation; or

(2) A child enrolls in a school of another public agency after the relevant timeframe in paragraph (c)(1) of this section has begun, and prior to a determination by the child's previous public agency as to whether the child is a child with a disability under § 300.8.

(e) The exception in paragraph (d)(2) of this section applies only if the subsequent public agency is making sufficient progress to ensure a prompt completion of the evaluation, and the parent and subsequent public agency agree to a specific time when the evaluation will be completed.

Sec. 300.302 Screening for instructional purposes is not evaluation.

The screening of a student by a teacher or specialist to determine appropriate instructional strategies for curriculum implementation shall not be considered to be an evaluation for eligibility for special education and related services.

Sec. 300.303 Reevaluations.

(a) General. A public agency must ensure that a reevaluation of each child with a disability is conducted in accordance with §§ 300.304 through 300.311 —

(1) If the public agency determines that the educational or related services needs, including improved academic achievement and functional performance, of the child warrant a reevaluation; or

(2) If the child's parent or teacher requests a reevaluation.

(b) Limitation. A reevaluation conducted under paragraph (a) of this section —

(1) May occur not more than once a year, unless the parent and the public agency agree otherwise; and

(2) Must occur at least once every 3 years, unless the parent and the public agency agree that a reevaluation is unnecessary.

Sec. 300.304 Evaluation procedures.

(a) Notice. The public agency must provide notice to the parents of a child with a disability, in accordance with § 300.503, that describes any evaluation procedures the agency proposes to conduct.

(b) Conduct of evaluation. In conducting the evaluation, the public agency must —

(1) Use a variety of assessment tools and strategies to gather relevant functional, developmental, and academic information about the child, including information provided by the parent, that may assist in determining —

(i) Whether the child is a child with a disability under § 300.8; and

(ii) The content of the child's IEP, including information related to enabling the child to be involved in and progress in the general education curriculum (or for a preschool child, to participate in appropriate activities);

(2) Not use any single measure or assessment as the sole criterion for determining whether a child is a child with a disability and for determining an appropriate educational program for the child; and

(3) Use technically sound instruments that may assess the relative contribution of cognitive and behavioral factors, in addition to physical or developmental factors.

(c) Other evaluation procedures. Each public agency must ensure that —

(1) Assessments and other evaluation materials used to assess a child under this part —

(i) Are selected and administered so as not to be discriminatory on a racial or cultural basis;

(ii) Are provided and administered in the child's native language or other mode of communication and in the form most likely to yield accurate information on what the child knows and can do academically, developmentally, and functionally, unless it is clearly not feasible to so provide or administer;

(iii) Are used for the purposes for which the assessments or measures are valid and reliable;

(iv) Are administered by trained and knowledgeable personnel; and

(v) Are administered in accordance with any instructions provided by the producer of the assessments.

(2) Assessments and other evaluation materials include those tailored to assess specific areas of educational need and not merely those that are designed to provide a single general intelligence quotient.

(3) Assessments are selected and administered so as best to ensure that if an assessment is administered to a child with impaired sensory, manual, or speaking skills, the assessment results accurately reflect the child's aptitude or achievement level or whatever other factors the test purports to measure, rather than reflecting the child's impaired sensory, manual, or speaking skills (unless those skills are the factors that the test purports to measure).

(4) The child is assessed in all areas related to the suspected disability, including, if appropriate, health, vision, hearing, social and emotional status, general intelligence, academic performance, communicative status, and motor abilities;

(5) Assessments of children with disabilities who transfer from one public agency to another public agency in the same school year are coordinated with those children's prior and subsequent schools, as necessary and as expeditiously as possible, consistent with § 300.301(d)(2) and (e), to ensure prompt completion of full evaluations.

(6) In evaluating each child with a disability under §§ 300.304 through 300.306, the evaluation is sufficiently comprehensive to identify all of the child's special education and related services needs, whether or not commonly linked to the disability category in which the child has been classified.

(7) Assessment tools and strategies that provide relevant information that directly assists persons in determining the educational needs of the child are provided.

Sec. 300.305 Additional requirements for evaluations and reevaluations.

(a) Review of existing evaluation data. As part of an initial evaluation (if appropriate) and as part of any reevaluation under this part, the IEP Team and other qualified professionals, as appropriate, must —

(1) Review existing evaluation data on the child, including —

(i) Evaluations and information provided by the parents of the child;

(ii) Current classroom-based, local, or State assessments, and classroom-based observations; and

(iii) Observations by teachers and related services providers; and

(2) On the basis of that review, and input from the child's parents, identify what additional data, if any, are needed to determine —

(i) (A) Whether the child is a child with a disability, as defined in § 300.8, and the educational needs of the child; or

(B) In case of a reevaluation of a child, whether the child continues to have such a disability, and the educational needs of the child;

(ii) The present levels of academic achievement and related developmental needs of the child;

(iii) (A) Whether the child needs special education and related services; or

(B) In the case of a reevaluation of a child, whether the child continues to need special education and related services; and

(iv) Whether any additions or modifications to the special education and related services are needed to enable the child to meet the measurable annual goals set out in the IEP of the child and to participate, as appropriate, in the general education curriculum.

(b)　Conduct of review. The group described in paragraph (a) of this section may conduct its review without a meeting.

(c)　Source of data. The public agency must administer such assessments and other evaluation measures as may be needed to produce the data identified under paragraph (a) of this section.

(d)　Requirements if additional data are not needed.

(1) If the IEP Team and other qualified professionals, as appropriate, determine that no additional data are needed to determine whether the child continues to be a child with a disability, and to determine the child's educational needs, the public agency must notify the child's parents of —

(i) That determination and the reasons for the determination; and

(ii) The right of the parents to request an assessment to determine whether the child continues to be a child with a disability, and to determine the child's educational needs.

(2) The public agency is not required to conduct the assessment described in paragraph (d)(1)(ii) of this section unless requested to do so by the child's parents.

(e)　Evaluations before change in eligibility.

(1) Except as provided in paragraph (e)(2) of this section, a public agency must evaluate a child with a disability in accordance with §§ 300.304 through 300.311 before determining that the child is no longer a child with a disability.

(2) The evaluation described in paragraph (e)(1) of this section is not required

before the termination of a child's eligibility under this part due to graduation from secondary school with a regular diploma, or due to exceeding the age eligibility for FAPE under State law.

(3) For a child whose eligibility terminates under circumstances described in paragraph (e)(2) of this section, a public agency must provide the child with a summary of the child's academic achievement and functional performance, which shall include recommendations on how to assist the child in meeting the child's postsecondary goals.

Sec. 300.306   Determination of eligibility.

(a)   General. Upon completion of the administration of assessments and other evaluation measures —

(1) A group of qualified professionals and the parent of the child determines whether the child is a child with a disability, as defined in § 300.8, in accordance with paragraph (c) of this section and the educational needs of the child; and

(2) The public agency provides a copy of the evaluation report and the documentation of determination of eligibility at no cost to the parent.

(b)   Special rule for eligibility determination. A child must not be determined to be a child with a disability under this part —

(1) If the determinant factor for that determination is —

(i) Lack of appropriate instruction in reading, including the essential components of reading instruction (as defined in section 1208(3) of the ESEA);

(ii) Lack of appropriate instruction in math; or

(iii) Limited English proficiency; and

(2) If the child does not otherwise meet the eligibility criteria under § 300.8(a).

(c)   Procedures for determining eligibility and educational need.

(1) In interpreting evaluation data for the purpose of determining if a child is a child with a disability under § 300.8, and the educational needs of the child, each public agency must —

(i) Draw upon information from a variety of sources, including aptitude and achievement tests, parent input, and teacher recommendations, as well as information about the child's physical condition, social or cultural background, and adaptive behavior; and

(ii) Ensure that information obtained from all of these sources is documented and carefully considered.

(2) If a determination is made that a child has a disability and needs special education and related services, an IEP must be developed for the child in accordance with §§ 300.320 through 300.324.

Additional Procedures for Identifying Children With Specific Learning Disabilities

Sec. 300.307   Specific learning disabilities.

(a)   General. A State must adopt, consistent with § 300.309, criteria for determining whether a child has a specific learning disability as defined in § 300.8(c)(10). In addition, the criteria adopted by the State —

(1) Must not require the use of a severe discrepancy between intellectual ability and achievement for determining whether a child has a specific learning disability, as defined in § 300.8(c)(10);

(2) Must permit the use of a process based on the child's response to scientific, research-based intervention; and

(3) May permit the use of other alternative research-based procedures for determining whether a child has a specific learning disability, as defined in § 300.8(c)(10).

(b)   Consistency with State criteria. A public agency must use the State criteria adopted pursuant to paragraph (a) of this section in determining whether a child has a specific learning disability.

Sec. 300.308   Additional group members.

The determination of whether a child suspected of having a specific learning disability is a child with a disability as defined in § 300.8, must be made by the child's parents and a team of qualified professionals, which must include —

(a) (1) The child's regular teacher; or

(2) If the child does not have a regular teacher, a regular classroom teacher qualified to teach a child of his or her age; or

(3) For a child of less than school age, an individual qualified by the SEA to teach a child of his or her age; and

(b) At least one person qualified to conduct individual diagnostic examinations of children, such as a school psychologist, speech-language pathologist, or remedial reading teacher.

Sec. 300.309   Determining the existence of a specific learning disability.

(a) The group described in § 300.306 may determine that a child has a specific learning disability, as defined in § 300.8(c)(10), if —

(1) The child does not achieve adequately for the child's age or to meet State-approved grade-level standards in one or more of the following areas, when provided with learning experiences and instruction appropriate for the child's age or State-approved grade-level standards:

(i) Oral expression.

(ii) Listening comprehension.

(iii) Written expression.

(iv) Basic reading skill.

(v) Reading fluency skills.

(vi) Reading comprehension.

(vii) Mathematics calculation.

(viii) Mathematics problem solving.

(2) (i) The child does not make sufficient progress to meet age or State-approved grade-level standards in one or more of the areas identified in paragraph (a)(1) of this section when using a process based on the child's response to scientific, research-based intervention; or

(ii) The child exhibits a pattern of strengths and weaknesses in performance, achievement, or both, relative to age, State-approved grade-level standards, or intellectual development, that is determined by the group to be relevant to the identification of a specific learning disability, using appropriate assessments, consistent with §§ 300.304 and 300.305; and

(3) The group determines that its findings under paragraphs (a)(1) and (2) of this section are not primarily the result of —

(i) A visual, hearing, or motor disability;

(ii) Mental retardation;

(iii) Emotional disturbance;

(iv) Cultural factors;

(v) Environmental or economic disadvantage; or

(vi) Limited English proficiency.

(b) To ensure that underachievement in a child suspected of having a specific learning disability is not due to lack of appropriate instruction in reading or math, the group must consider, as part of the evaluation described in §§ 300.304 through 300.306 —

(1) Data that demonstrate that prior to, or as a part of, the referral process, the child was provided appropriate instruction in regular education settings, delivered by qualified personnel; and

(2) Data-based documentation of repeated assessments of achievement at reasonable intervals, reflecting formal assessment of student progress during instruction, which was provided to the child's parents.

(c) The public agency must promptly request parental consent to evaluate the child to determine if the child needs special education and related services, and must adhere to the timeframes described in §§ 300.301 and 300.303, unless extended by mutual written agreement of the child's parents and a group of qualified professionals, as described in § 300.306(a)(1) —

(1) If, prior to a referral, a child has not made adequate progress after an appropriate period of time when provided instruction, as described in paragraphs

(b)(1) and (b)(2) of this section; and

(2) Whenever a child is referred for an evaluation.

Sec. 300.310 Observation.

(a) The public agency must ensure that the child is observed in the child's learning environment (including the regular classroom setting) to document the child's academic performance and behavior in the areas of difficulty.

(b) The group described in § 300.306(a)(1), in determining whether a child has a specific learning disability, must decide to —

(1) Use information from an observation in routine classroom instruction and monitoring of the child's performance that was done before the child was referred for an evaluation; or

(2) Have at least one member of the group described in § 300.306(a)(1) conduct an observation of the child's academic performance in the regular classroom after the child has been referred for an evaluation and parental consent, consistent with § 300.300(a), is obtained.

(c) In the case of a child of less than school age or out of school, a group member must observe the child in an environment appropriate for a child of that age.

Sec. 300.311 Specific documentation for the eligibility determination.

(a) For a child suspected of having a specific learning disability, the documentation of the determination of eligibility, as required in § 300.306(a)(2), must contain a statement of —

(1) Whether the child has a specific learning disability;

(2) The basis for making the determination, including an assurance that the determination has been made in accordance with § 300.306(c)(1);

(3) The relevant behavior, if any, noted during the observation of the child and the relationship of that behavior to the child's academic functioning;

(4) The educationally relevant medical findings, if any;

(5) Whether —

(i) The child does not achieve adequately for the child's age or to meet State-approved grade-level standards consistent with § 300.309(a)(1); and

(ii) (A) The child does not make sufficient progress to meet age or State-approved grade-level standards consistent with § 300.309(a)(2)(i); or

(B) The child exhibits a pattern of strengths and weaknesses in performance, achievement, or both, relative to age, State-approved grade level standards or intellectual development consistent with § 300.309(a)(2)(ii);

(6) The determination of the group concerning the effects of a visual, hearing, or motor disability; mental retardation; emotional disturbance; cultural factors; environmental or economic disadvantage; or limited English proficiency on the child's achievement level; and

(7) If the child has participated in a process that assesses the child's response to scientific, research-based intervention —

(i) The instructional strategies used and the student-centered data collected; and

(ii) The documentation that the child's parents were notified about —

(A) The State's policies regarding the amount and nature of student performance data that would be collected and the general education services that would be provided;

(B) Strategies for increasing the child's rate of learning; and

(C) The parents' right to request an evaluation.

(b) Each group member must certify in writing whether the report reflects the member's conclusion. If it does not reflect the member's conclusion, the group member must submit a separate statement presenting the member's conclusions.

Individualized Education Programs

Sec. 300.320   Definition of individualized education program.

(a)   General. As used in this part, the term individualized education program or IEP means a written statement for each child with a disability that is developed, reviewed, and revised in a meeting in accordance with §§ 300.320 through 300.324, and that must include —

(1) A statement of the child's present levels of academic achievement and functional performance, including —

(i) How the child's disability affects the child's involvement and progress in the general education curriculum (i.e., the same curriculum as for nondisabled children); or

(ii) For preschool children, as appropriate, how the disability affects the child's participation in appropriate activities;

(2) (i) A statement of measurable annual goals, including academic and functional goals designed to —

(A) Meet the child's needs that result from the child's disability to enable the child to be involved in and make progress in the general education curriculum; and

(B) Meet each of the child's other educational needs that result from the child's disability;

(ii) For children with disabilities who take alternate assessments aligned to alternate academic achievement standards, a description of benchmarks or short-term objectives;

(3) A description of —

(i) How the child's progress toward meeting the annual goals described in paragraph (2) of this section will be measured; and

(ii) When periodic reports on the progress the child is making toward meeting the annual goals (such as through the use of quarterly or other periodic reports, concurrent with the issuance of report cards) will be provided;

(4) A statement of the special education and related services and supplementary aids and services, based on peer-reviewed research to the extent practicable, to be provided to the child, or on behalf of the child, and a statement of the program modifications or supports for school personnel that will be provided to enable the child —

(i) To advance appropriately toward attaining the annual goals;

(ii) To be involved in and make progress in the general education curriculum in accordance with paragraph (a)(1) of this section, and to participate in extracurricular and other nonacademic activities; and

(iii) To be educated and participate with other children with disabilities and nondisabled children in the activities described in this section;

(5) An explanation of the extent, if any, to which the child will not participate with nondisabled children in the regular class and in the activities described in paragraph (a)(4) of this section;

(6) (i) A statement of any individual appropriate accommodations that are necessary to measure the academic achievement and functional performance of the child on State and districtwide assessments consistent with section 612(a)(16) of the Act; and

(ii) If the IEP Team determines that the child must take an alternate assessment instead of a particular regular State or districtwide assessment of student achievement, a statement of why —

(A) The child cannot participate in the regular assessment; and

(B) The particular alternate assessment selected is appropriate for the child; and

(7) The projected date for the beginning of the services and modifications described in paragraph (a)(4) of this section, and the anticipated frequency, location, and duration of those services and modifications.

(b)   Transition services. Beginning not later than the first IEP to be in effect when the child turns 16, or younger if determined appropriate by the IEP Team, and updated annually, thereafter, the IEP must include —

(1) Appropriate measurable postsecondary goals based upon age appropriate transition assessments related to training, education, employment, and, where appropriate, independent living skills; and

(2) The transition services (including courses of study) needed to assist the child in reaching those goals.

(c)   Transfer of rights at age of majority. Beginning not later than one year before the child reaches the age of majority under State law, the IEP must include a statement that the child has been informed of the child's rights under Part B of the Act, if any, that will transfer to the child on reaching the age of majority under § 300.520.

(d) Construction. Nothing in this section shall be construed to require —

(1) That additional information be included in a child's IEP beyond what is explicitly required in section 614 of the Act; or

(2) The IEP Team to include information under one component of a child's IEP that is already contained under another component of the child's IEP.

Sec. 300.321 IEP Team.

(a) General. The public agency must ensure that the IEP Team for each child with a disability includes —

(1) The parents of the child;

(2) Not less than one regular education teacher of the child (if the child is, or may be, participating in the regular education environment);

(3) Not less than one special education teacher of the child, or where appropriate, not less than one special education provider of the child;

(4) A representative of the public agency who —

(i) Is qualified to provide, or supervise the provision of, specially designed instruction to meet the unique needs of children with disabilities;

(ii) Is knowledgeable about the general education curriculum; and

(iii) Is knowledgeable about the availability of resources of the public agency.

(5) An individual who can interpret the instructional implications of evaluation results, who may be a member of the team described in paragraphs (a)(2) through (a)(6) of this section;

(6) At the discretion of the parent or the agency, other individuals who have knowledge or special expertise regarding the child, including related services personnel as appropriate; and

(7) Whenever appropriate, the child with a disability.

(b) Transition services participants.

(1) In accordance with paragraph (a)(7) of this section, the public agency must invite a child with a disability to attend the child's IEP Team meeting if a purpose of the meeting will be the consideration of the postsecondary goals for the child and the transition services needed to assist the child in reaching those goals under § 300.320(b).

(2) If the child does not attend the IEP Team meeting, the public agency must take other steps to ensure that the child's preferences and interests are considered.

(3) To the extent appropriate, with the consent of the parents or a child who has reached the age of majority, in implementing the requirements of paragraph

(b)(1) of this section, the public agency must invite a representative of any participating agency that is likely to be responsible for providing or paying for transition services.

(c)　Determination of knowledge and special expertise. The determination of the knowledge or special expertise of any individual described in paragraph (a)(6) of this section must be made by the party (parents or public agency) who invited the individual to be a member of the IEP Team.

(d)　Designating a public agency representative. A public agency may designate a public agency member of the IEP Team to also serve as the agency representative, if the criteria in paragraph (a)(4) of this section are satisfied.

(e)　IEP Team attendance.

(1) A member of the IEP Team described in paragraphs (a)(2) through (a)(5) of this section is not required to attend an IEP Team meeting, in whole or in part, if the parent of a child with a disability and the public agency agree, in writing, that the attendance of the member is not necessary because the member's area of the curriculum or related services is not being modified or discussed in the meeting.

(2) A member of the IEP Team described in paragraph (e)(1) of this section may be excused from attending an IEP Team meeting, in whole or in part, when the meeting involves a modification to or discussion of the member's area of the curriculum or related services, if —

(i) The parent, in writing, and the public agency consent to the excusal; and

(ii) The member submits, in writing to the parent and the IEP Team, input into the development of the IEP prior to the meeting.

(f)　Initial IEP Team meeting for child under Part C. In the case of a child who was previously served under Part C of the Act, an invitation to the initial IEP Team meeting must, at the request of the parent, be sent to the Part C service coordinator or other representatives of the Part C system to assist with the smooth transition of services.

Sec. 300.322　Parent participation.

(a)　Public agency responsibility — general. Each public agency must take steps to ensure that one or both of the parents of a child with a disability are present at each IEP Team meeting or are afforded the opportunity to participate, including —

(1) Notifying parents of the meeting early enough to ensure that they will have an opportunity to attend; and

(2) Scheduling the meeting at a mutually agreed on time and place.

(b)　Information provided to parents.

(1) The notice required under paragraph (a)(1) of this section must —

(i) Indicate the purpose, time, and location of the meeting and who will be in attendance; and

(ii) Inform the parents of the provisions in § 300.321(a)(6) and (c) (relating to the participation of other individuals on the IEP Team who have knowledge or special expertise about the child), and Sec. 300.321(f) (relating to the participation of the Part C service coordinator or other representatives of the Part C system at the initial IEP Team meeting for a child previously served under Part C of the Act).

(2) For a child with a disability beginning not later than the first IEP to be in effect when the child turns 16, or younger if determined appropriate by the IEP Team, the notice also must —

(i) Indicate —

(A) That a purpose of the meeting will be the consideration of the postsecondary goals and transition services for the child, in accordance with § 300.320(b); and

(B) That the agency will invite the student; and

(ii) Identify any other agency that will be invited to send a representative.

(c)   Other methods to ensure parent participation. If neither parent can attend an IEP Team meeting, the public agency must use other methods to ensure parent participation, including individual or conference telephone calls, consistent with § 300.328 (related to alternative means of meeting participation).

(d)   Conducting an IEP Team meeting without a parent in attendance. A meeting may be conducted without a parent in attendance if the public agency is unable to convince the parents that they should attend. In this case, the public agency must keep a record of its attempts to arrange a mutually agreed on time and place, such as —

(1) Detailed records of telephone calls made or attempted and the results of those calls;

(2) Copies of correspondence sent to the parents and any responses received; and

(3) Detailed records of visits made to the parent's home or place of employment and the results of those visits.

(e)   Use of interpreters or other action, as appropriate. The public agency must take whatever action is necessary to ensure that the parent understands the proceedings of the IEP Team meeting, including arranging for an interpreter for parents with deafness or whose native language is other than English.

(f)   Parent copy of child's IEP. The public agency must give the parent a copy of the child's IEP at no cost to the parent.

Sec. 300.323   When IEPs must be in effect.

(a)   General. At the beginning of each school year, each public agency must have in effect, for each child with a disability within its jurisdiction, an IEP, as defined in § 300.320.

(b)   IEP or IFSP for children aged three through five.

(1) In the case of a child with a disability aged three through five (or, at the discretion of the SEA, a two-year-old child with a disability who will turn age three during the school year), the IEP Team must consider an IFSP that contains the IFSP content (including the natural environments statement) described in section 636(d) of the Act and its implementing regulations (including an educational component that promotes school readiness and incorporates pre-literacy, language, and numeracy skills for children with IFSPs under this section who are at least three years of age), and that is developed in accordance with the IEP procedures under this part. The IFSP may serve as the IEP of the child, if using the IFSP as the IEP is —

(i) Consistent with State policy; and

(ii) Agreed to by the agency and the child's parents.

(2) In implementing the requirements of paragraph (b)(1) of this section, the public agency must —

(i) Provide to the child's parents a detailed explanation of the differences between an IFSP and an IEP; and

(ii) If the parents choose an IFSP, obtain written informed consent from the parents.

(c)   Initial IEPs; provision of services. Each public agency must ensure that —

(1) A meeting to develop an IEP for a child is conducted within 30 days of a determination that the child needs special education and related services; and

(2) As soon as possible following development of the IEP, special education and related services are made available to the child in accordance with the child's IEP.

(d)   Accessibility of child's IEP to teachers and others. Each public agency must ensure that —

(1) The child's IEP is accessible to each regular education teacher, special education teacher, related services provider, and any other service provider who is responsible for its implementation; and

(2) Each teacher and provider described in paragraph (d)(1) of this section is informed of —

(i) His or her specific responsibilities related to implementing the child's IEP; and

(ii) The specific accommodations, modifications, and supports that must be provided for the child in accordance with the IEP.

(e)   IEPs for children who transfer public agencies in the same State. If a child with a disability (who had an IEP that was in effect in a previous public agency in the same State) transfers to a new public agency in the same State, and enrolls in a new school within the same school year, the new public agency (in consultation with the parents) must provide FAPE to the child (including services comparable to those described in the child's IEP from the previous public agency), until the new public agency either —

(1) Adopts the child's IEP from the previous public agency; or

(2) Develops, adopts, and implements a new IEP that meets the applicable requirements in §§ 300.320 through 300.324.

(f) IEPs for children who transfer from another State. If a child with a disability (who had an IEP that was in effect in a previous public agency in another State) transfers to a public agency in a new State, and enrolls in a new school within the same school year, the new public agency (in consultation with the parents) must provide the child with FAPE (including services comparable to those described in the child's IEP from the previous public agency), until the new public agency —

(1) Conducts an evaluation pursuant to §§ 300.304 through 300.306 (if determined to be necessary by the new public agency); and

(2) Develops, adopts, and implements a new IEP, if appropriate, that meets the applicable requirements in §§ 300.320 through 300.324.

(g) Transmittal of records. To facilitate the transition for a child described in paragraphs (e) and (f) of this section —

(1) The new public agency in which the child enrolls must take reasonable steps to promptly obtain the child's records, including the IEP and supporting documents and any other records relating to the provision of special education or related services to the child, from the previous public agency in which the child was enrolled, pursuant to 34 CFR 99.31(a)(2); and

(2) The previous public agency in which the child was enrolled must take reasonable steps to promptly respond to the request from the new public agency.

Development of IEP

Sec. 300.324 Development, review, and revision of IEP.

(a) Development of IEP —

(1) General. In developing each child's IEP, the IEP Team must consider —

(i) The strengths of the child;

(ii) The concerns of the parents for enhancing the education of their child;

(iii) The results of the initial or most recent evaluation of the child; and

(iv) The academic, developmental, and functional needs of the child.

(2) Consideration of special factors. The IEP Team must —

(i) In the case of a child whose behavior impedes the child's learning or that of others, consider the use of positive behavioral interventions and supports, and other strategies, to address that behavior;

(ii) In the case of a child with limited English proficiency, consider the language needs of the child as those needs relate to the child's IEP;

(iii) In the case of a child who is blind or visually impaired, provide for instruction in Braille and the use of Braille unless the IEP Team determines, after an evaluation of the child's reading and writing skills, needs, and appropriate reading and writing media (including an evaluation of the child's future needs for instruction in Braille or the use of Braille), that instruction in Braille or the use of Braille is not appropriate for the child;

(iv) Consider the communication needs of the child, and in the case of a child who is deaf or hard of hearing, consider the child's language and communication needs, opportunities for direct communications with peers and professional personnel in the child's language and communication mode, academic level, and full range of needs, including opportunities for direct instruction in the child's language and communication mode; and

(v) Consider whether the child needs assistive technology devices and services.

(3)   Requirement with respect to regular education teacher. A regular education teacher of a child with a disability, as a member of the IEP Team, must, to the extent appropriate, participate in the development of the IEP of the child, including the determination of —

(i) Appropriate positive behavioral interventions and supports and other strategies for the child; and

(ii) Supplementary aids and services, program modifications, and support for school personnel consistent with § 300.320(a)(4).

(4)   Agreement.

(i) In making changes to a child's IEP after the annual IEP Team meeting for a school year, the parent of a child with a disability and the public agency may agree not to convene an IEP Team meeting for the purposes of making those changes, and instead may develop a written document to amend or modify the child's current IEP.

(ii) If changes are made to the child's IEP in accordance with paragraph (a)(4)(i) of this section, the public agency must ensure that the child's IEP Team is informed of those changes.

(5)   Consolidation of IEP Team meetings. To the extent possible, the public agency must encourage the consolidation of reevaluation meetings for the child and other IEP Team meetings for the child.

(6)   Amendments. Changes to the IEP may be made either by the entire IEP Team at an IEP Team meeting, or as provided in paragraph (a)(4) of this section, by amending the IEP rather than by redrafting the entire IEP. Upon request, a parent must be provided with a revised copy of the IEP with the amendments incorporated.

(b) Review and revision of IEPs —

(1)   General. Each public agency must ensure that, subject to paragraphs (b)(2) and (b)(3) of this section, the IEP Team —

(i) Reviews the child's IEP periodically, but not less than annually, to determine whether the annual goals for the child are being achieved; and

(ii) Revises the IEP, as appropriate, to address —

(A) Any lack of expected progress toward the annual goals described in § 300.320(a)(2), and in the general education curriculum, if appropriate;

(B) The results of any reevaluation conducted under § 300.303;

(C) Information about the child provided to, or by, the parents, as described under § 300.305(a)(2);

(D) The child's anticipated needs; or

(E) Other matters.

(2) Consideration of special factors. In conducting a review of the child's IEP, the IEP Team must consider the special factors described in paragraph (a)(2) of this section.

(3) Requirement with respect to regular education teacher. A regular education teacher of the child, as a member of the IEP Team, must, consistent with paragraph (a)(3) of this section, participate in the review and revision of the IEP of the child.

(c) Failure to meet transition objectives —

(1) Participating agency failure. If a participating agency, other than the public agency, fails to provide the transition services described in the IEP in accordance with § 300.320(b), the public agency must reconvene the IEP Team to identify alternative strategies to meet the transition objectives for the child set out in the IEP.

(2) Construction. Nothing in this part relieves any participating agency, including a State vocational rehabilitation agency, of the responsibility to provide or pay for any transition service that the agency would otherwise provide to children with disabilities who meet the eligibility criteria of that agency.

(d) Children with disabilities in adult prisons —

(1) Requirements that do not apply. The following requirements do not apply to children with disabilities who are convicted as adults under State law and incarcerated in adult prisons:

(i) The requirements contained in section 612(a)(16) of the Act and § 300.320(a)(6) (relating to participation of children with disabilities in general assessments).

(ii) The requirements in § 300.320(b) (relating to transition planning and transition services) do not apply with respect to the children whose eligibility under Part B of the Act will end, because of their age, before they will be eligible to be released from prison based on consideration of their sentence and eligibility for early release.

(2) Modifications of IEP or placement.

(i) Subject to paragraph (d)(2)(ii) of this section, the IEP Team of a child with a disability who is convicted as an adult under State law and incarcerated in an adult prison may modify the child's IEP or placement if the State has demonstrated a bona fide security or compelling penological interest that cannot otherwise be accommodated.

(ii) The requirements of §§ 300.320 (relating to IEPs), and 300.112 (relating to LRE), do not apply with respect to the modifications described in paragraph (d)(2)(i) of this section.

Sec. 300.325 Private school placements by public agencies.

(a) Developing IEPs.

(1) Before a public agency places a child with a disability in, or refers a child to, a private school or facility, the agency must initiate and conduct a meeting to develop an IEP for the child in accordance with §§ 300.320 and 300.324.

(2) The agency must ensure that a representative of the private school or facility attends the meeting. If the representative cannot attend, the agency must use other methods to ensure participation by the private school or facility, including individual or conference telephone calls.

(b) Reviewing and revising IEPs.

(1) After a child with a disability enters a private school or facility, any meetings to review and revise the child's IEP may be initiated and conducted by the private school or facility at the discretion of the public agency.

(2) If the private school or facility initiates and conducts these meetings, the public agency must ensure that the parents and an agency representative —

(i) Are involved in any decision about the child's IEP; and

(ii) Agree to any proposed changes in the IEP before those changes are implemented.

(c) Responsibility. Even if a private school or facility implements a child's IEP, responsibility for compliance with this part remains with the public agency and the SEA.

Sec. 300.327 Educational placements.

Consistent with § 300.501(c), each public agency must ensure that the parents of each child with a disability are members of any group that makes decisions on the educational placement of their child.

Sec. 300.328 Alternative means of meeting participation.

When conducting IEP Team meetings and placement meetings pursuant to this subpart, and subpart E of this part, and carrying out administrative matters under section 615 of the Act (such as scheduling, exchange of witness lists, and status conferences), the parent of a child with a disability and a public agency may agree to use alternative means of meeting participation, such as video conferences and conference calls.

Subpart E Procedural Safeguards Due Process Procedures for Parents and Children

Sec. 300.500 Responsibility of SEA and other public agencies.

Each SEA must ensure that each public agency establishes, maintains, and implements procedural safeguards that meet the requirements of §§ 300.500 through 300.536.

Sec. 300.501 Opportunity to examine records; parent participation in meetings.

(a) Opportunity to examine records. The parents of a child with a disability must be afforded, in accordance with the procedures of §§ 300.613 through 300.621, an opportunity to inspect and review all education records with respect to —

(1) The identification, evaluation, and educational placement of the child; and

(2) The provision of FAPE to the child.

(b) Parent participation in meetings.

(1) The parents of a child with a disability must be afforded an opportunity to participate in meetings with respect to —

(i) The identification, evaluation, and educational placement of the child; and

(ii) The provision of FAPE to the child.

(2) Each public agency must provide notice consistent with § 300.322(a)(1) and (b)(1) to ensure that parents of children with disabilities have the opportunity to participate in meetings described in paragraph (b)(1) of this section.

(3) A meeting does not include informal or unscheduled conversations involving public agency personnel and conversations on issues such as teaching methodology, lesson plans, or coordination of service provision. A meeting also does not include preparatory activities that public agency personnel engage in to develop a proposal or response to a parent proposal that will be discussed at a later meeting.

(c) Parent involvement in placement decisions.

(1) Each public agency must ensure that a parent of each child with a disability is a member of any group that makes decisions on the educational placement of the parent's child.

(2) In implementing the requirements of paragraph (c)(1) of this section, the public agency must use procedures consistent with the procedures described in § 300.322(a) through (b)(1).

(3) If neither parent can participate in a meeting in which a decision is to be made relating to the educational placement of their child, the public agency must use other methods to ensure their participation, including individual or conference telephone calls, or video conferencing.

(4) A placement decision may be made by a group without the involvement of a parent, if the public agency is unable to obtain the parent's participation in the decision. In this case, the public agency must have a record of its attempt to ensure their involvement.

Sec. 300.502　Independent educational evaluation.

(a)　General.

(1) The parents of a child with a disability have the right under this part to obtain an independent educational evaluation of the child, subject to paragraphs (b) through (e) of this section.

(2) Each public agency must provide to parents, upon request for an independent educational evaluation, information about where an independent educational evaluation may be obtained, and the agency criteria applicable for independent educational evaluations as set forth in paragraph (e) of this section.

(3) For the purposes of this subpart —

(i) Independent educational evaluation means an evaluation conducted by a qualified examiner who is not employed by the public agency responsible for the education of the child in question; and

(ii) Public expense means that the public agency either pays for the full cost of the evaluation or ensures that the evaluation is otherwise provided at no cost to the parent, consistent with § 300.103.

(b)　Parent right to evaluation at public expense.

(1) A parent has the right to an independent educational evaluation at public expense if the parent disagrees with an evaluation obtained by the public agency, subject to the conditions in paragraphs (b)(2) through (4) of this section.

(2) If a parent requests an independent educational evaluation at public expense, the public agency must, without unnecessary delay, either —

(i) File a due process complaint to request a hearing to show that its evaluation is appropriate; or

(ii) Ensure that an independent educational evaluation is provided at public expense, unless the agency demonstrates in a hearing pursuant to §§ 300.507 through 300.513 that the evaluation obtained by the parent did not meet agency criteria.

(3) If the public agency files a due process complaint notice to request a hearing and the final decision is that the agency's evaluation is appropriate, the parent still has the right to an independent educational evaluation, but not at public expense.

(4) If a parent requests an independent educational evaluation, the public agency may ask for the parent's reason why he or she objects to the public evaluation. However, the public agency may not require the parent to provide an explanation and may not unreasonably delay either providing the independent educational evaluation at public expense or filing a due process complaint to request a due process hearing to defend the public evaluation.

(5) A parent is entitled to only one independent educational evaluation at public expense each time the public agency conducts an evaluation with which the parent disagrees.

(c) Parent-initiated evaluations. If the parent obtains an independent educational evaluation at public expense or shares with the public agency an evaluation obtained at private expense, the results of the evaluation —

(1) Must be considered by the public agency, if it meets agency criteria, in any decision made with respect to the provision of FAPE to the child; and

(2) May be presented by any party as evidence at a hearing on a due process complaint under subpart E of this part regarding that child.

(d) Requests for evaluations by hearing officers. If a hearing officer requests an independent educational evaluation as part of a hearing on a due process complaint, the cost of the evaluation must be at public expense.

(e) Agency criteria.

(1) If an independent educational evaluation is at public expense, the criteria under which the evaluation is obtained, including the location of the evaluation and the qualifications of the examiner, must be the same as the criteria that the public agency uses when it initiates an evaluation, to the extent those criteria are consistent with the parent's right to an independent educational evaluation.

(2) Except for the criteria described in paragraph (e)(1) of this section, a public agency may not impose conditions or timelines related to obtaining an independent educational evaluation at public expense.

Sec. 300.503 Prior notice by the public agency; content of notice.

(a) Notice. Written notice that meets the requirements of paragraph (b) of this section must be given to the parents of a child with a disability a reasonable time before the public agency —

(1) Proposes to initiate or change the identification, evaluation, or educational placement of the child or the provision of FAPE to the child; or

(2) Refuses to initiate or change the identification, evaluation, or educational placement of the child or the provision of FAPE to the child.

(b) Content of notice. The notice required under paragraph (a) of this section must include —

(1) A description of the action proposed or refused by the agency;

(2) An explanation of why the agency proposes or refuses to take the action;

(3) A description of each evaluation procedure, assessment, record, or report the agency used as a basis for the proposed or refused action;

(4) A statement that the parents of a child with a disability have protection under the procedural safeguards of this part and, if this notice is not an initial referral for evaluation, the means by which a copy of a description of the procedural safeguards can be obtained;

(5) Sources for parents to contact to obtain assistance in understanding the provisions of this part;

(6) A description of other options that the IEP Team considered and the

reasons why those options were rejected; and

(7) A description of other factors that are relevant to the agency's proposal or refusal.

(c) Notice in understandable language.

(1) The notice required under paragraph (a) of this section must be —

(i) Written in language understandable to the general public; and

(ii) Provided in the native language of the parent or other mode of communication used by the parent, unless it is clearly not feasible to do so.

(2) If the native language or other mode of communication of the parent is not a written language, the public agency must take steps to ensure —

(i) That the notice is translated orally or by other means to the parent in his or her native language or other mode of communication;

(ii) That the parent understands the content of the notice; and

(iii) That there is written evidence that the requirements in paragraphs (c)(2)(i) and (ii) of this section have been met.

Sec. 300.504 Procedural safeguards notice.

(a) General. A copy of the procedural safeguards available to the parents of a child with a disability must be given to the parents only one time a school year, except that a copy also must be given to the parents —

(1) Upon initial referral or parent request for evaluation;

(2) Upon receipt of the first State complaint under §§ 300.151 through 300.153 and upon receipt of the first due process complaint under § 300.507 in a school year;

(3) In accordance with the discipline procedures in § 300.530(h); and

(4) Upon request by a parent.

(b) Internet Web site. A public agency may place a current copy of the procedural safeguards notice on its Internet Web site if a Web site exists.

(c) Contents. The procedural safeguards notice must include a full explanation of all of the procedural safeguards available under § 300.148, §§ 300.151 through 300.153, § 300.300, §§ 300.502 through 300.503, §§ 300.505 through 300.518, §§ 300.530 through 300.536 and §§ 300.610 through 300.625 relating to —

(1) Independent educational evaluations;

(2) Prior written notice;

(3) Parental consent;

(4) Access to education records;

(5) Opportunity to present and resolve complaints through the due process complaint and State complaint procedures, including —

(i) The time period in which to file a complaint;

(ii) The opportunity for the agency to resolve the complaint; and

(iii) The difference between the due process complaint and the State complaint procedures, including the jurisdiction of each procedure, what issues may be raised, filing and decisional timelines, and relevant procedures;

(6) The availability of mediation;

(7) The child's placement during the pendency of any due process complaint;

(8) Procedures for students who are subject to placement in an interim alternative educational setting;

(9) Requirements for unilateral placement by parents of children in private schools at public expense;

(10) Hearings on due process complaints, including requirements for disclosure of evaluation results and recommendations;

(11) State-level appeals (if applicable in the State);

(12) Civil actions, including the time period in which to file those actions; and

(13) Attorneys' fees.

(d)   Notice in understandable language. The notice required under paragraph (a) of this section must meet the requirements of § 300.503(c).

Sec. 300.505   Electronic mail.

A parent of a child with a disability may elect to receive notices required by §§ 300.503, 300.504, and 300.508 by an electronic mail communication, if the public agency makes that option available.

Sec. 300.506   Mediation.

(a)   General. Each public agency must ensure that procedures are established and implemented to allow parties to disputes involving any matter under this part, including matters arising prior to the filing of a due process complaint, to resolve disputes through a mediation process.

(b)   Requirements. The procedures must meet the following requirements:

(1) The procedures must ensure that the mediation process —

(i) Is voluntary on the part of the parties;

(ii) Is not used to deny or delay a parent's right to a hearing on the parent's due process complaint, or to deny any other rights afforded under Part B of the Act; and

(iii) Is conducted by a qualified and impartial mediator who is trained in effective mediation techniques.

(2) A public agency may establish procedures to offer to parents and schools that choose not to use the mediation process, an opportunity to meet, at a time

and location convenient to the parents, with a disinterested party —

(i) Who is under contract with an appropriate alternative dispute resolution entity, or a parent training and information center or community parent resource center in the State established under section 671 or 672 of the Act; and

(ii) Who would explain the benefits of, and encourage the use of, the mediation process to the parents.

(3) (i) The State must maintain a list of individuals who are qualified mediators and knowledgeable in laws and regulations relating to the provision of special education and related services.

(ii) The SEA must select mediators on a random, rotational, or other impartial basis.

(4) The State must bear the cost of the mediation process, including the costs of meetings described in paragraph (b)(2) of this section.

(5) Each session in the mediation process must be scheduled in a timely manner and must be held in a location that is convenient to the parties to the dispute.

(6) If the parties resolve a dispute through the mediation process, the parties must execute a legally binding agreement that sets forth that resolution and that —

(i) States that all discussions that occurred during the mediation process will remain confidential and may not be used as evidence in any subsequent due process hearing or civil proceeding; and

(ii) Is signed by both the parent and a representative of the agency who has the authority to bind such agency.

(7) A written, signed mediation agreement under this paragraph is enforceable in any State court of competent jurisdiction or in a district court of the United States.

(8) Discussions that occur during the mediation process must be confidential and may not be used as evidence in any subsequent due process hearing or civil proceeding of any Federal court or State court of a State receiving assistance under this part.

(c)   Impartiality of mediator.

(1) An individual who serves as a mediator under this part —

(i) May not be an employee of the SEA or the LEA that is involved in the education or care of the child; and

(ii) Must not have a personal or professional interest that conflicts with the person's objectivity.

(2) A person who otherwise qualifies as a mediator is not an employee of an LEA or State agency described under § 300.228 solely because he or she is paid

by the agency to serve as a mediator.

Sec. 300.507 Filing a due process complaint.

(a) General.

(1) A parent or a public agency may file a due process complaint on any of the matters described in § 300.503(a)(1) and (2) (relating to the identification, evaluation or educational placement of a child with a disability, or the provision of FAPE to the child).

(2) The due process complaint must allege a violation that occurred not more than two years before the date the parent or public agency knew or should have known about the alleged action that forms the basis of the due process complaint, or, if the State has an explicit time limitation for filing a due process complaint under this part, in the time allowed by that State law, except that the exceptions to the timeline described in § 300.511(f) apply to the timeline in this section.

(b) Information for parents. The public agency must inform the parent of any free or low-cost legal and other relevant services available in the area if —

(1) The parent requests the information; or

(2) The parent or the agency files a due process complaint under this section.

Sec. 300.508 Due process complaint.

(a) General.

(1) The public agency must have procedures that require either party, or the attorney representing a party, to provide to the other party a due process complaint (which must remain confidential).

(2) The party filing a due process complaint must forward a copy of the due process complaint to the SEA.

(b) Content of complaint. The due process complaint required in paragraph (a)(1) of this section must include —

(1) The name of the child;

(2) The address of the residence of the child;

(3) The name of the school the child is attending;

(4) In the case of a homeless child or youth (within the meaning of section 725(2) of the McKinney-Vento Homeless Assistance Act (42 U.S.C. 11434a(2)), available contact information for the child, and the name of the school the child is attending;

(5) A description of the nature of the problem of the child relating to the proposed or refused initiation or change, including facts relating to the problem; and

(6) A proposed resolution of the problem to the extent known and available to the party at the time.

(c)   Notice required before a hearing on a due process complaint. A party may not have a hearing on a due process complaint until the party, or the attorney representing the party, files a due process complaint that meets the requirements of paragraph (b) of this section.

(d)   Sufficiency of complaint.

(1) The due process complaint required by this section must be deemed sufficient unless the party receiving the due process complaint notifies the hearing officer and the other party in writing, within 15 days of receipt of the due process complaint, that the receiving party believes the due process complaint does not meet the requirements in paragraph (b) of this section.

(2) Within five days of receipt of notification under paragraph (d)(1) of this section, the hearing officer must make a determination on the face of the due process complaint of whether the due process complaint meets the requirements of paragraph (b) of this section, and must immediately notify the parties in writing of that determination.

(3) A party may amend its due process complaint only if —

(i) The other party consents in writing to the amendment and is given the opportunity to resolve the due process complaint through a meeting held pursuant to § 300.510; or

(ii) The hearing officer grants permission, except that the hearing officer may only grant permission to amend at any time not later than five days before the due process hearing begins.

(4) If a party files an amended due process complaint, the timelines for the resolution meeting in § 300.510(a) and the time period to resolve in § 300.510(b) begin again with the filing of the amended due process complaint.

(e)   LEA response to a due process complaint.

(1) If the LEA has not sent a prior written notice under § 300.503 to the parent regarding the subject matter contained in the parent's due process complaint, the LEA must, within 10 days of receiving the due process complaint, send to the parent a response that includes —

(i) An explanation of why the agency proposed or refused to take the action raised in the due process complaint;

(ii) A description of other options that the IEP Team considered and the reasons why those options were rejected;

(iii) A description of each evaluation procedure, assessment, record, or report the agency used as the basis for the proposed or refused action; and

(iv) A description of the other factors that are relevant to the agency's proposed or refused action.

(2) A response by an LEA under paragraph (e)(1) of this section shall not be construed to preclude the LEA from asserting that the parent's due process complaint was insufficient, where appropriate.

(f)   Other party response to a due process complaint. Except as provided in paragraph (e) of this section, the party receiving a due process complaint must, within 10 days of receiving the due process complaint, send to the other party a response that specifically addresses the issues raised in the due process complaint.

Sec. 300.509   Model forms.

(a) Each SEA must develop model forms to assist parents and public agencies in filing a due process complaint in accordance with §§ 300.507(a) and 300.508(a) through (c) and to assist parents and other parties in filing a State complaint under §§ 300.151 through 300.153. However, the SEA or LEA may not require the use of the model forms.

(b) Parents, public agencies, and other parties may use the appropriate model form described in paragraph (a) of this section, or another form or other document, so long as the form or document that is used meets, as appropriate, the content requirements in § 300.508(b) for filing a due process complaint, or the requirements in § 300.153(b) for filing a State complaint.

Sec. 300.510   Resolution process.

(a)   Resolution meeting.

(1) Within 15 days of receiving notice of the parent's due process complaint, and prior to the initiation of a due process hearing under § 300.511, the LEA must convene a meeting with the parent and the relevant member or members of the IEP Team who have specific knowledge of the facts identified in the due process complaint that —

(i) Includes a representative of the public agency who has decision-making authority on behalf of that agency; and

(ii) May not include an attorney of the LEA unless the parent is accompanied by an attorney.

(2) The purpose of the meeting is for the parent of the child to discuss the due process complaint, and the facts that form the basis of the due process complaint, so that the LEA has the opportunity to resolve the dispute that is the basis for the due process complaint.

(3) The meeting described in paragraph (a)(1) and (2) of this section need not be held if —

(i) The parent and the LEA agree in writing to waive the meeting; or

(ii) The parent and the LEA agree to use the mediation process described in Sec. 300.506.

(4) The parent and the LEA determine the relevant members of the IEP Team to attend the meeting.

(b)   Resolution period.

(1) If the LEA has not resolved the due process complaint to the satisfaction of the parent within 30 days of the receipt of the due process complaint, the due

process hearing may occur.

(2) Except as provided in paragraph (c) of this section, the timeline for issuing a final decision under § 300.515 begins at the expiration of this 30-day period.

(3) Except where the parties have jointly agreed to waive the resolution process or to use mediation, notwithstanding paragraphs (b)(1) and (2) of this section, the failure of the parent filing a due process complaint to participate in the resolution meeting will delay the timelines for the resolution process and due process hearing until the meeting is held.

(4) If the LEA is unable to obtain the participation of the parent in the resolution meeting after reasonable efforts have been made (and documented using the procedures in § 300.322(d)), the LEA may, at the conclusion of the 30-day period, request that a hearing officer dismiss the parent's due process complaint.

(5) If the LEA fails to hold the resolution meeting specified in paragraph (a) of this section within 15 days of receiving notice of a parent's due process complaint or fails to participate in the resolution meeting, the parent may seek the intervention of a hearing officer to begin the due process hearing timeline.

(c) Adjustments to 30-day resolution period. The 45-day timeline for the due process hearing in § 300.515(a) starts the day after one of the following events:

(1) Both parties agree in writing to waive the resolution meeting;

(2) After either the mediation or resolution meeting starts but before the end of the 30-day period, the parties agree in writing that no agreement is possible;

(3) If both parties agree in writing to continue the mediation at the end of the 30-day resolution period, but later, the parent or public agency withdraws from the mediation process.

(d) Written settlement agreement. If a resolution to the dispute is reached at the meeting described in paragraphs (a)(1) and (2) of this section, the parties must execute a legally binding agreement that is —

(1) Signed by both the parent and a representative of the agency who has the authority to bind the agency; and

(2) Enforceable in any State court of competent jurisdiction or in a district court of the United States, or, by the SEA, if the State has other mechanisms or procedures that permit parties to seek enforcement of resolution agreements, pursuant to § 300.537.

(e) Agreement review period. If the parties execute an agreement pursuant to paragraph (d) of this section, a party may void the agreement within 3 business days of the agreement's execution.

Sec. 300.511   Impartial due process hearing.

(a) General. Whenever a due process complaint is received under § 300.507 or § 300.532, the parents or the LEA involved in the dispute must have an opportunity for an impartial due process hearing, consistent with the procedures in §§ 300.507,

300.508, and 300.510.

(b) *Agency responsible for conducting the due process hearing.* The hearing described in paragraph (a) of this section must be conducted by the SEA or the public agency directly responsible for the education of the child, as determined under State statute, State regulation, or a written policy of the SEA.

(c) *Impartial hearing officer.*

(1) At a minimum, a hearing officer —

(i) Must not be —

(A) An employee of the SEA or the LEA that is involved in the education or care of the child; or

(B) A person having a personal or professional interest that conflicts with the person's objectivity in the hearing;

(ii) Must possess knowledge of, and the ability to understand, the provisions of the Act, Federal and State regulations pertaining to the Act, and legal interpretations of the Act by Federal and State courts;

(iii) Must possess the knowledge and ability to conduct hearings in accordance with appropriate, standard legal practice; and

(iv) Must possess the knowledge and ability to render and write decisions in accordance with appropriate, standard legal practice.

(2) A person who otherwise qualifies to conduct a hearing under paragraph (c)(1) of this section is not an employee of the agency solely because he or she is paid by the agency to serve as a hearing officer.

(3) Each public agency must keep a list of the persons who serve as hearing officers. The list must include a statement of the qualifications of each of those persons.

(d) *Subject matter of due process hearings.* The party requesting the due process hearing may not raise issues at the due process hearing that were not raised in the due process complaint filed under § 300.508(b), unless the other party agrees otherwise.

(e) *Timeline for requesting a hearing.* A parent or agency must request an impartial hearing on their due process complaint within two years of the date the parent or agency knew or should have known about the alleged action that forms the basis of the due process complaint, or if the State has an explicit time limitation for requesting such a due process hearing under this part, in the time allowed by that State law.

(f) *Exceptions to the timeline.* The timeline described in paragraph (e) of this section does not apply to a parent if the parent was prevented from filing a due process complaint due to —

(1) Specific misrepresentations by the LEA that it had resolved the problem forming the basis of the due process complaint; or

(2) The LEA's withholding of information from the parent that was required under this part to be provided to the parent.

Sec. 300.512　Hearing rights.

(a)　General. Any party to a hearing conducted pursuant to §§ 300.507 through 300.513 or §§ 300.530 through 300.534, or an appeal conducted pursuant to § 300.514, has the right to —

(1) Be accompanied and advised by counsel and by individuals with special knowledge or training with respect to the problems of children with disabilities, except that whether parties have the right to be represented by non-attorneys at due process hearings is determined under State law.

(2) Present evidence and confront, cross-examine, and compel the attendance of witnesses;

(3) Prohibit the introduction of any evidence at the hearing that has not been disclosed to that party at least five business days before the hearing;

(4) Obtain a written, or, at the option of the parents, electronic, verbatim record of the hearing; and

(5) Obtain written, or, at the option of the parents, electronic findings of fact and decisions.

(b)　Additional disclosure of information.

(1) At least five business days prior to a hearing conducted pursuant to § 300.511(a), each party must disclose to all other parties all evaluations completed by that date and recommendations based on the offering party's evaluations that the party intends to use at the hearing.

(2) A hearing officer may bar any party that fails to comply with paragraph (b)(1) of this section from introducing the relevant evaluation or recommendation at the hearing without the consent of the other party.

(c)　Parental rights at hearings. Parents involved in hearings must be given the right to

(1) Have the child who is the subject of the hearing present;

(2) Open the hearing to the public; and

(3) Have the record of the hearing and the findings of fact and decisions described in paragraphs (a)(4) and (a)(5) of this section provided at no cost to parents.

Sec. 300.513　Hearing decisions.

(a)　Decision of hearing officer on the provision of FAPE.

(1) Subject to paragraph (a)(2) of this section, a hearing officer's determination of whether a child received FAPE must be based on substantive grounds.

(2) In matters alleging a procedural violation, a hearing officer may find that a child did not receive a FAPE only if the procedural inadequacies —

(i) Impeded the child's right to a FAPE;

(ii) Significantly impeded the parent's opportunity to participate in the decision-making process regarding the provision of a FAPE to the parent's child; or

(iii) Caused a deprivation of educational benefit.

(3) Nothing in paragraph (a) of this section shall be construed to preclude a hearing officer from ordering an LEA to comply with procedural requirements under §§ 300.500 through 300.536.

(b) Construction clause. Nothing in §§ 300.507 through 300.513 shall be construed to affect the right of a parent to file an appeal of the due process hearing decision with the SEA under § 300.514(b), if a State level appeal is available.

(c) Separate request for a due process hearing. Nothing in §§ 300.500 through 300.536 shall be construed to preclude a parent from filing a separate due process complaint on an issue separate from a due process complaint already filed.

(d) Findings and decision to advisory panel and general public. The public agency, after deleting any personally identifiable information, must —

(1) Transmit the findings and decisions referred to in § 300.512(a)(5) to the State advisory panel established under § 300.167; and

(2) Make those findings and decisions available to the public.

Sec. 300.514 Finality of decision; appeal; impartial review.

(a) Finality of hearing decision. A decision made in a hearing conducted pursuant to §§ 300.507 through 300.513 or §§ 300.530 through 300.534 is final, except that any party involved in the hearing may appeal the decision under the provisions of paragraph (b) of this section and § 300.516.

(b) Appeal of decisions; impartial review.

(1) If the hearing required by § 300.511 is conducted by a public agency other than the SEA, any party aggrieved by the findings and decision in the hearing may appeal to the SEA.

(2) If there is an appeal, the SEA must conduct an impartial review of the findings and decision appealed. The official conducting the review must —

(i) Examine the entire hearing record.

(ii) Ensure that the procedures at the hearing were consistent with the requirements of due process;

(iii) Seek additional evidence if necessary. If a hearing is held to receive additional evidence, the rights in § 300.512 apply;

(iv) Afford the parties an opportunity for oral or written argument, or both, at the discretion of the reviewing official;

(v) Make an independent decision on completion of the review; and

(vi) Give a copy of the written, or, at the option of the parents, electronic findings of fact and decisions to the parties.

(c)   Findings and decision to advisory panel and general public. The SEA, after deleting any personally identifiable information, must —

(1) Transmit the findings and decisions referred to in paragraph (b)(2)(vi) of this section to the State advisory panel established under § 300.167; and

(2) Make those findings and decisions available to the public.

(d)   Finality of review decision. The decision made by the reviewing official is final unless a party brings a civil action under § 300.516.

Sec. 300.515   Timelines and convenience of hearings and reviews.

(a) The public agency must ensure that not later than 45 days after the expiration of the 30 day period under § 300.510(b), or the adjusted time periods described in § 300.510(c) —

(1) A final decision is reached in the hearing; and

(2) A copy of the decision is mailed to each of the parties.

(b) The SEA must ensure that not later than 30 days after the receipt of a request for a review —

(1) A final decision is reached in the review; and

(2) A copy of the decision is mailed to each of the parties.

(c) A hearing or reviewing officer may grant specific extensions of time beyond the periods set out in paragraphs (a) and (b) of this section at the request of either party.

(d) Each hearing and each review involving oral arguments must be conducted at a time and place that is reasonably convenient to the parents and child involved.

Sec. 300.516   Civil action.

(a)   General. Any party aggrieved by the findings and decision made under §§ 300.507 through 300.513 or §§ 300.530 through 300.534 who does not have the right to an appeal under § 300.514(b), and any party aggrieved by the findings and decision under § 300.514(b), has the right to bring a civil action with respect to the due process complaint notice requesting a due process hearing under § 300.507 or §§ 300.530 through 300.532. The action may be brought in any State court of competent jurisdiction or in a district court of the United States without regard to the amount in controversy.

(b)   Time limitation. The party bringing the action shall have 90 days from the date of the decision of the hearing officer or, if applicable, the decision of the State review official, to file a civil action, or, if the State has an explicit time limitation for bringing civil actions under Part B of the Act, in the time allowed by that State law.

(c)   Additional requirements. In any action brought under paragraph (a) of this section, the court —

(1) Receives the records of the administrative proceedings;

(2) Hears additional evidence at the request of a party; and

(3) Basing its decision on the preponderance of the evidence, grants the relief that the court determines to be appropriate.

(d) Jurisdiction of district courts. The district courts of the United States have jurisdiction of actions brought under section 615 of the Act without regard to the amount in controversy.

(e) Rule of construction. Nothing in this part restricts or limits the rights, procedures, and remedies available under the Constitution, the Americans with Disabilities Act of 1990, title V of the Rehabilitation Act of 1973, or other Federal laws protecting the rights of children with disabilities, except that before the filing of a civil action under these laws seeking relief that is also available under section 615 of the Act, the procedures under §§ 300.507 and 300.514 must be exhausted to the same extent as would be required had the action been brought under section 615 of the Act.

Sec. 300.517 Attorneys' fees.

(a) In general.

(1) In any action or proceeding brought under section 615 of the Act, the court, in its discretion, may award reasonable attorneys' fees as part of the costs to —

(i) The prevailing party who is the parent of a child with a disability;

(ii) To a prevailing party who is an SEA or LEA against the attorney of a parent who files a complaint or subsequent cause of action that is frivolous, unreasonable, or without foundation, or against the attorney of a parent who continued to litigate after the litigation clearly became frivolous, unreasonable, or without foundation; or

(iii) To a prevailing SEA or LEA against the attorney of a parent, or against the parent, if the parent's request for a due process hearing or subsequent cause of action was presented for any improper purpose, such as to harass, to cause unnecessary delay, or to needlessly increase the cost of litigation.

(2) Nothing in this subsection shall be construed to affect section 327 of the District of Columbia Appropriations Act, 2005.

(b) Prohibition on use of funds.

(1) Funds under Part B of the Act may not be used to pay attorneys' fees or costs of a party related to any action or proceeding under section 615 of the Act and subpart E of this part.

(2) Paragraph (b)(1) of this section does not preclude a public agency from using funds under Part B of the Act for conducting an action or proceeding under section 615 of the Act.

(c) Award of fees. A court awards reasonable attorneys' fees under section 615(i)(3) of the Act consistent with the following:

(1) Fees awarded under section 615(i)(3) of the Act must be based on rates prevailing in the community in which the action or proceeding arose for the kind

and quality of services furnished. No bonus or multiplier may be used in calculating the fees awarded under this paragraph.

(2) (i) Attorneys' fees may not be awarded and related costs may not be reimbursed in any action or proceeding under section 615 of the Act for services performed subsequent to the time of a written offer of settlement to a parent if —

(A) The offer is made within the time prescribed by Rule 68 of the Federal Rules of Civil Procedure or, in the case of an administrative proceeding, at any time more than 10 days before the proceeding begins;

(B) The offer is not accepted within 10 days; and

(C) The court or administrative hearing officer finds that the relief finally obtained by the parents is not more favorable to the parents than the offer of settlement.

(ii) Attorneys' fees may not be awarded relating to any meeting of the IEP Team unless the meeting is convened as a result of an administrative proceeding or judicial action, or at the discretion of the State, for a mediation described in § 300.506.

(iii) A meeting conducted pursuant to § 300.510 shall not be considered —

(A) A meeting convened as a result of an administrative hearing or judicial action; or

(B) An administrative hearing or judicial action for purposes of this section.

(3) Notwithstanding paragraph (c)(2) of this section, an award of attorneys' fees and related costs may be made to a parent who is the prevailing party and who was substantially justified in rejecting the settlement offer.

(4) Except as provided in paragraph (c)(5) of this section, the court reduces, accordingly, the amount of the attorneys' fees awarded under section 615 of the Act, if the court finds that —

(i) The parent, or the parent's attorney, during the course of the action or proceeding, unreasonably protracted the final resolution of the controversy;

(ii) The amount of the attorneys' fees otherwise authorized to be awarded unreasonably exceeds the hourly rate prevailing in the community for similar services by attorneys of reasonably comparable skill, reputation, and experience;

(iii) The time spent and legal services furnished were excessive considering the nature of the action or proceeding; or

(iv) The attorney representing the parent did not provide to the LEA the appropriate information in the due process request notice in accordance with § 300.508.

(5) The provisions of paragraph (c)(4) of this section do not apply in any action or proceeding if the court finds that the State or local agency unreasonably

protracted the final resolution of the action or proceeding or there was a violation of section 615 of the Act.

Sec. 300.518 Child's status during proceedings.

(a) Except as provided in § 300.533, during the pendency of any administrative or judicial proceeding regarding a due process complaint notice requesting a due process hearing under § 300.507, unless the State or local agency and the parents of the child agree otherwise, the child involved in the complaint must remain in his or her current educational placement.

(b) If the complaint involves an application for initial admission to public school, the child, with the consent of the parents, must be placed in the public school until the completion of all the proceedings.

(c) If the complaint involves an application for initial services under this part from a child who is transitioning from Part C of the Act to Part B and is no longer eligible for Part C services because the child has turned three, the public agency is not required to provide the Part C services that the child had been receiving. If the child is found eligible for special education and related services under Part B and the parent consents to the initial provision of special education and related services under § 300.300(b), then the public agency must provide those special education and related services that are not in dispute between the parent and the public agency.

(d) If the hearing officer in a due process hearing conducted by the SEA or a State review official in an administrative appeal agrees with the child's parents that a change of placement is appropriate, that placement must be treated as an agreement between the State and the parents for purposes of paragraph (a) of this section.

Sec. 300.519 Surrogate parents.

(a) General. Each public agency must ensure that the rights of a child are protected when —

(1) No parent (as defined in § 300.30) can be identified;

(2) The public agency, after reasonable efforts, cannot locate a parent;

(3) The child is a ward of the State under the laws of that State; or

(4) The child is an unaccompanied homeless youth as defined in section 725(6) of the McKinney-Vento Homeless Assistance Act (42 U.S.C. 11434a(6)).

(b) Duties of public agency. The duties of a public agency under paragraph (a) of this section include the assignment of an individual to act as a surrogate for the parents. This must include a method —

(1) For determining whether a child needs a surrogate parent; and

(2) For assigning a surrogate parent to the child.

(c) Wards of the State. In the case of a child who is a ward of the State, the surrogate parent alternatively may be appointed by the judge overseeing the child's case, provided that the surrogate meets the requirements in paragraphs (d)(2)(i) and (e) of this section.

(d) Criteria for selection of surrogate parents.

(1) The public agency may select a surrogate parent in any way permitted under State law.

(2) Public agencies must ensure that a person selected as a surrogate parent —

(i) Is not an employee of the SEA, the LEA, or any other agency that is involved in the education or care of the child;

(ii) Has no personal or professional interest that conflicts with the interest of the child the surrogate parent represents; and

(iii) Has knowledge and skills that ensure adequate representation of the child.

(e) Non-employee requirement; compensation. A person otherwise qualified to be a surrogate parent under paragraph (d) of this section is not an employee of the agency solely because he or she is paid by the agency to serve as a surrogate parent.

(f) Unaccompanied homeless youth. In the case of a child who is an unaccompanied homeless youth, appropriate staff of emergency shelters, transitional shelters, independent living programs, and street outreach programs may be appointed as temporary surrogate parents without regard to paragraph (d)(2)(i) of this section, until a surrogate parent can be appointed that meets all of the requirements of paragraph (d) of this section.

(g) Surrogate parent responsibilities. The surrogate parent may represent the child in all matters relating to —

(1) The identification, evaluation, and educational placement of the child; and

(2) The provision of FAPE to the child.

(h) SEA responsibility. The SEA must make reasonable efforts to ensure the assignment of a surrogate parent not more than 30 days after a public agency determines that the child needs a surrogate parent.

Sec. 300.520 Transfer of parental rights at age of majority.

(a) General. A State may provide that, when a child with a disability reaches the age of majority under State law that applies to all children (except for a child with a disability who has been determined to be incompetent under State law) —

(1) (i) The public agency must provide any notice required by this part to both the child and the parents; and

(ii) All rights accorded to parents under Part B of the Act transfer to the child;

(2) All rights accorded to parents under Part B of the Act transfer to children who are incarcerated in an adult or juvenile, State or local correctional institution; and

(3) Whenever a State provides for the transfer of rights under this part pursuant to paragraph (a)(1) or (a)(2) of this section, the agency must notify the child and the parents of the transfer of rights.

(b) Special rule. A State must establish procedures for appointing the parent of a child with a disability, or, if the parent is not available, another appropriate individual, to represent the educational interests of the child throughout the period of the child's eligibility under Part B of the Act if, under State law, a child who has reached the age of majority, but has not been determined to be incompetent, can be determined not to have the ability to provide informed consent with respect to the child's educational program.

Discipline Procedures

Sec. 300.530 Authority of school personnel.

(a) Case-by-case determination. School personnel may consider any unique circumstances on a case-by-case basis when determining whether a change in placement, consistent with the other requirements of this section, is appropriate for a child with a disability who violates a code of student conduct.

(b) General.

(1) School personnel under this section may remove a child with a disability who violates a code of student conduct from his or her current placement to an appropriate interim alternative educational setting, another setting, or suspension, for not more than 10 consecutive school days (to the extent those alternatives are applied to children without disabilities), and for additional removals of not more than 10 consecutive school days in that same school year for separate incidents of misconduct (as long as those removals do not constitute a change of placement under § 300.536).

(2) After a child with a disability has been removed from his or her current placement for 10 school days in the same school year, during any subsequent days of removal the public agency must provide services to the extent required under paragraph (d) of this section.

(c) Additional authority. For disciplinary changes in placement that would exceed 10 consecutive school days, if the behavior that gave rise to the violation of the school code is determined not to be a manifestation of the child's disability pursuant to paragraph (e) of this section, school personnel may apply the relevant disciplinary procedures to children with disabilities in the same manner and for the same duration as the procedures would be applied to children without disabilities, except as provided in paragraph (d) of this section.

(d) Services.

(1) A child with a disability who is removed from the child's current placement pursuant to paragraphs (c), or (g) of this section must —

(i) Continue to receive educational services, as provided in § 300.101(a), so as to enable the child to continue to participate in the general education curriculum, although in another setting, and to progress toward meeting the goals set out in the child's IEP; and

(ii) Receive, as appropriate, a functional behavioral assessment, and behavioral intervention services and modifications, that are designed to address the behavior violation so that it does not recur.

(2) The services required by paragraph (d)(1), (d)(3), (d)(4), and (d)(5) of this section may be provided in an interim alternative educational setting.

(3) A public agency is only required to provide services during periods of removal to a child with a disability who has been removed from his or her current placement for 10 school days or less in that school year, if it provides services to a child without disabilities who is similarly removed.

(4) After a child with a disability has been removed from his or her current placement for 10 school days in the same school year, if the current removal is for not more than 10 consecutive school days and is not a change of placement under § 300.536, school personnel, in consultation with at least one of the child's teachers, determine the extent to which services are needed, as provided in § 300.101(a), so as to enable the child to continue to participate in the general education curriculum, although in another setting, and to progress toward meeting the goals set out in the child's IEP.

(5) If the removal is a change of placement under § 300.536, the child's IEP Team determines appropriate services under paragraph (d)(1) of this section.

(e)   Manifestation determination.

(1) Within 10 school days of any decision to change the placement of a child with a disability because of a violation of a code of student conduct, the LEA, the parent, and relevant members of the child's IEP Team (as determined by the parent and the LEA) must review all relevant information in the student's file, including the child's IEP, any teacher observations, and any relevant information provided by the parents to determine —

(i) If the conduct in question was caused by, or had a direct and substantial relationship to, the child's disability; or

(ii) If the conduct in question was the direct result of the LEA's failure to implement the IEP.

(2) The conduct must be determined to be a manifestation of the child's disability if the LEA, the parent, and relevant members of the child's IEP Team determine that a condition in either paragraph (e)(1)(i) or (1)(ii) of this section was met.

(3) If the LEA, the parent, and relevant members of the child's IEP Team determine the condition described in paragraph (e)(1)(ii) of this section was met, the LEA must take immediate steps to remedy those deficiencies.

(f)   Determination that behavior was a manifestation. If the LEA, the parent, and relevant members of the IEP Team make the determination that the conduct was a manifestation of the child's disability, the IEP Team must —

(1) Either —

(i) Conduct a functional behavioral assessment, unless the LEA had conducted a functional behavioral assessment before the behavior that resulted in the change of placement occurred, and implement a behavioral intervention plan for the child; or

(ii) If a behavioral intervention plan already has been developed, review the behavioral intervention plan, and modify it, as necessary, to address the behavior; and

(2) Except as provided in paragraph (g) of this section, return the child to the placement from which the child was removed, unless the parent and the LEA agree to a change of placement as part of the modification of the behavioral intervention plan.

(g)   Special circumstances. School personnel may remove a student to an interim alternative educational setting for not more than 45 school days without regard to whether the behavior is determined to be a manifestation of the child's disability, if the child —

(1) Carries a weapon to or possesses a weapon at school, on school premises, or to or at a school function under the jurisdiction of an SEA or an LEA;

(2) Knowingly possesses or uses illegal drugs, or sells or solicits the sale of a controlled substance, while at school, on school premises, or at a school function under the jurisdiction of an SEA or an LEA; or

(3) Has inflicted serious bodily injury upon another person while at school, on school premises, or at a school function under the jurisdiction of an SEA or an LEA.

(h)   Notification. On the date on which the decision is made to make a removal that constitutes a change of placement of a child with a disability because of a violation of a code of student conduct, the LEA must notify the parents of that decision, and provide the parents the procedural safeguards notice described in § 300.504.

(i)   Definitions. For purposes of this section, the following definitions apply:

(1) Controlled substance means a drug or other substance identified under schedules I, II, III, IV, or V in section 202(c) of the Controlled Substances Act (21 U.S.C. 812(c)).

(2) Illegal drug means a controlled substance; but does not include a controlled substance that is legally possessed or used under the supervision of a licensed health-care professional or that is legally possessed or used under any other authority under that Act or under any other provision of Federal law.

(3) Serious bodily injury has the meaning given the term "serious bodily injury" under paragraph (3) of subsection (h) of section 1365 of title 18, United States Code.

(4) Weapon has the meaning given the term "dangerous weapon" under paragraph (2) of the first subsection (g) of section 930 of title 18, United States Code.

Sec. 300.531   Determination of setting.

The child's IEP Team determines the interim alternative educational setting for services under § 300.530(c), (d)(5), and (g).

Sec. 300.532 Appeal.

(a) General. The parent of a child with a disability who disagrees with any decision regarding placement under §§ 300.530 and 300.531, or the manifestation determination under § 300.530(e), or an LEA that believes that maintaining the current placement of the child is substantially likely to result in injury to the child or others, may appeal the decision by requesting a hearing. The hearing is requested by filing a complaint pursuant to §§ 300.507 and 300.508(a) and (b).

(b) Authority of hearing officer.

(1) A hearing officer under § 300.511 hears, and makes a determination regarding an appeal under paragraph (a) of this section.

(2) In making the determination under paragraph (b)(1) of this section, the hearing officer may —

(i) Return the child with a disability to the placement from which the child was removed if the hearing officer determines that the removal was a violation of § 300.530 or that the child's behavior was a manifestation of the child's disability; or

(ii) Order a change of placement of the child with a disability to an appropriate interim alternative educational setting for not more than 45 school days if the hearing officer determines that maintaining the current placement of the child is substantially likely to result in injury to the child or to others.

(3) The procedures under paragraphs (a) and (b)(1) and (2) of this section may be repeated, if the LEA believes that returning the child to the original placement is substantially likely to result in injury to the child or to others.

(c) Expedited due process hearing.

(1) Whenever a hearing is requested under paragraph (a) of this section, the parents or the LEA involved in the dispute must have an opportunity for an impartial due process hearing consistent with the requirements of §§ 300.507 and 300.508(a) through (c) and §§ 300.510 through 300.514, except as provided in paragraph (c)(2) through (4) of this section.

(2) The SEA or LEA is responsible for arranging the expedited due process hearing, which must occur within 20 school days of the date the complaint requesting the hearing is filed. The hearing officer must make a determination within 10 school days after the hearing.

(3) Unless the parents and LEA agree in writing to waive the resolution meeting described in paragraph (c)(3)(i) of this section, or agree to use the mediation process described in § 300.506 —

(i) A resolution meeting must occur within seven days of receiving notice of the due process complaint; and

(ii) The due process hearing may proceed unless the matter has been resolved to the satisfaction of both parties within 15 days of the receipt of the due process complaint.

(4) A State may establish different State-imposed procedural rules for expedited due process hearings conducted under this section than it has established for other due process hearings, but, except for the timelines as modified in paragraph (c)(3) of this section, the State must ensure that the requirements in §§ 300.510 through 300.514 are met.

(5) The decisions on expedited due process hearings are appealable consistent with § 300.514.

Sec. 300.533 Placement during appeals.

When an appeal under § 300.532 has been made by either the parent or the LEA, the child must remain in the interim alternative educational setting pending the decision of the hearing officer or until the expiration of the time period specified in § 300.530(c) or (g), whichever occurs first, unless the parent and the SEA or LEA agree otherwise.

Sec. 300.534 Protections for children not determined eligible for special education and related services.

(a) General. A child who has not been determined to be eligible for special education and related services under this part and who has engaged in behavior that violated a code of student conduct, may assert any of the protections provided for in this part if the public agency had knowledge (as determined in accordance with paragraph (b) of this section) that the child was a child with a disability before the behavior that precipitated the disciplinary action occurred.

(b) Basis of knowledge. A public agency must be deemed to have knowledge that a child is a child with a disability if before the behavior that precipitated the disciplinary action occurred —

(1) The parent of the child expressed concern in writing to supervisory or administrative personnel of the appropriate educational agency, or a teacher of the child, that the child is in need of special education and related services;

(2) The parent of the child requested an evaluation of the child pursuant to §§ 300.300 through 300.311; or

(3) The teacher of the child, or other personnel of the LEA, expressed specific concerns about a pattern of behavior demonstrated by the child directly to the director of special education of the agency or to other supervisory personnel of the agency.

(c) Exception. A public agency would not be deemed to have knowledge under paragraph (b) of this section if —

(1) The parent of the child —

(i) Has not allowed an evaluation of the child pursuant to §§ 300.300 through 300.311; or

(ii) Has refused services under this part; or

(2) The child has been evaluated in accordance with §§ 300.300 through 300.311 and determined to not be a child with a disability under this part.

(d) Conditions that apply if no basis of knowledge.

(1) If a public agency does not have knowledge that a child is a child with a disability (in accordance with paragraphs (b) and (c) of this section) prior to taking disciplinary measures against the child, the child may be subjected to the disciplinary measures applied to children without disabilities who engage in comparable behaviors consistent with paragraph (d)(2) of this section.

(2) (i) If a request is made for an evaluation of a child during the time period in which the child is subjected to disciplinary measures under § 300.530, the evaluation must be conducted in an expedited manner.

(ii) Until the evaluation is completed, the child remains in the educational placement determined by school authorities, which can include suspension or expulsion without educational services.

(iii) If the child is determined to be a child with a disability, taking into consideration information from the evaluation conducted by the agency and information provided by the parents, the agency must provide special education and related services in accordance with this part, including the requirements of §§ 300.530 through 300.536 and section 612(a)(1)(A) of the Act.

Sec. 300.535 Referral to and action by law enforcement and judicial authorities.

(a) Rule of construction. Nothing in this part prohibits an agency from reporting a crime committed by a child with a disability to appropriate authorities or prevents State law enforcement and judicial authorities from exercising their responsibilities with regard to the application of Federal and State law to crimes committed by a child with a disability.

(b) Transmittal of records.

(1) An agency reporting a crime committed by a child with a disability must ensure that copies of the special education and disciplinary records of the child are transmitted for consideration by the appropriate authorities to whom the agency reports the crime.

(2) An agency reporting a crime under this section may transmit copies of the child's special education and disciplinary records only to the extent that the transmission is permitted by the Family Educational Rights and Privacy Act.

Sec. 300.536 Change of placement because of disciplinary removals.

(a) For purposes of removals of a child with a disability from the child's current educational placement under §§ 300.530 through 300.535, a change of placement occurs if —

(1) The removal is for more than 10 consecutive school days; or

(2) The child has been subjected to a series of removals that constitute a pattern —

(i) Because the series of removals total more than 10 school days in a school year;

(ii) Because the child's behavior is substantially similar to the child's behavior in previous incidents that resulted in the series of removals; and

(iii) Because of such additional factors as the length of each removal, the total amount of time the child has been removed, and the proximity of the removals to one another.

(b) (1) The public agency determines on a case-by-case basis whether a pattern of removals constitutes a change of placement.

(2) This determination is subject to review through due process and judicial proceedings.

Confidentiality of Information

Sec. 300.610　Confidentiality.

The Secretary takes appropriate action, in accordance with section 444 of GEPA, to ensure the protection of the confidentiality of any personally identifiable data, information, and records collected or maintained by the Secretary and by SEAs and LEAs pursuant to Part B of the Act, and consistent with §§ 300.611 through 300.627.

Sec. 300.611　Definitions.

As used in §§ 300.611 through 300.625 —

(a) Destruction means physical destruction or removal of personal identifiers from information so that the information is no longer personally identifiable.

(b) Education records means the type of records covered under the definition of "education records" in 34 CFR part 99 (the regulations implementing the Family Educational Rights and Privacy Act of 1974, 20 U.S.C. 1232g (FERPA)).

(c) Participating agency means any agency or institution that collects, maintains, or uses personally identifiable information, or from which information is obtained, under Part B of the Act.

Sec. 300.612　Notice to parents.

(a) The SEA must give notice that is adequate to fully inform parents about the requirements of § 300.123, including —

(1) A description of the extent that the notice is given in the native languages of the various population groups in the State;

(2) A description of the children on whom personally identifiable information is maintained, the types of information sought, the methods the State intends to use in gathering the information (including the sources from whom information is gathered), and the uses to be made of the information;

(3) A summary of the policies and procedures that participating agencies must follow regarding storage, disclosure to third parties, retention, and destruction of personally identifiable information; and

(4) A description of all of the rights of parents and children regarding this information, including the rights under FERPA and implementing regulations in 34 CFR part 99.

(b) Before any major identification, location, or evaluation activity, the notice must be published or announced in newspapers or other media, or both, with circulation adequate to notify parents throughout the State of the activity.

Sec. 300.613   Access rights.

(a) Each participating agency must permit parents to inspect and review any education records relating to their children that are collected, maintained, or used by the agency under this part. The agency must comply with a request without unnecessary delay and before any meeting regarding an IEP, or any hearing pursuant to § 300.507 or §§ 300.530 through 300.532, or resolution session pursuant to § 300.510, and in no case more than 45 days after the request has been made.

(b) The right to inspect and review education records under this section includes

—

(1) The right to a response from the participating agency to reasonable requests for explanations and interpretations of the records;

(2) The right to request that the agency provide copies of the records containing the information if failure to provide those copies would effectively prevent the parent from exercising the right to inspect and review the records; and

(3) The right to have a representative of the parent inspect and review the records.

(c) An agency may presume that the parent has authority to inspect and review records relating to his or her child unless the agency has been advised that the parent does not have the authority under applicable State law governing such matters as guardianship, separation, and divorce.

Sec. 300.614   Record of access.

Each participating agency must keep a record of parties obtaining access to education records collected, maintained, or used under Part B of the Act (except access by parents and authorized employees of the participating agency), including the name of the party, the date access was given, and the purpose for which the party is authorized to use the records.

Sec. 300.615   Records on more than one child.

If any education record includes information on more than one child, the parents of those children have the right to inspect and review only the information relating to their child or to be informed of that specific information.

Sec. 300.616   List of types and locations of information.

Each participating agency must provide parents on request a list of the types and locations of education records collected, maintained, or used by the agency.

Sec. 300.617 Fees.

(a) Each participating agency may charge a fee for copies of records that are made for parents under this part if the fee does not effectively prevent the parents from exercising their right to inspect and review those records.

(b) A participating agency may not charge a fee to search for or to retrieve information under this part.

Sec. 300.618 Amendment of records at parent's request.

(a) A parent who believes that information in the education records collected, maintained, or used under this part is inaccurate or misleading or violates the privacy or other rights of the child may request the participating agency that maintains the information to amend the information.

(b) The agency must decide whether to amend the information in accordance with the request within a reasonable period of time of receipt of the request.

(c) If the agency decides to refuse to amend the information in accordance with the request, it must inform the parent of the refusal and advise the parent of the right to a hearing under § 300.619.

Sec. 300.619 Opportunity for a hearing.

The agency must, on request, provide an opportunity for a hearing to challenge information in education records to ensure that it is not inaccurate, misleading, or otherwise in violation of the privacy or other rights of the child.

Sec. 300.620 Result of hearing.

(a) If, as a result of the hearing, the agency decides that the information is inaccurate, misleading or otherwise in violation of the privacy or other rights of the child, it must amend the information accordingly and so inform the parent in writing.

(b) If, as a result of the hearing, the agency decides that the information is not inaccurate, misleading, or otherwise in violation of the privacy or other rights of the child, it must inform the parent of the parent's right to place in the records the agency maintains on the child a statement commenting on the information or setting forth any reasons for disagreeing with the decision of the agency.

(c) Any explanation placed in the records of the child under this section must —

(1) Be maintained by the agency as part of the records of the child as long as the record or contested portion is maintained by the agency; and

(2) If the records of the child or the contested portion is disclosed by the agency to any party, the explanation must also be disclosed to the party.

Sec. 300.621 Hearing procedures.

A hearing held under § 300.619 must be conducted according to the procedures in 34 CFR 99.22.

Sec. 300.622 Consent.

(a) Parental consent must be obtained before personally identifiable information is disclosed to parties, other than officials of participating agencies in accordance with paragraph (b)(1) of this section, unless the information is contained in education records, and the disclosure is authorized without parental consent under 34 CFR part 99.

(b) (1) Except as provided in paragraphs (b)(2) and (b)(3) of this section, parental consent is not required before personally identifiable information is released to officials of participating agencies for purposes of meeting a requirement of this part.

(2) Parental consent, or the consent of an eligible child who has reached the age of majority under State law, must be obtained before personally identifiable information is released to officials of participating agencies providing or paying for transition services in accordance with § 300.321(b)(3).

(3) If a child is enrolled, or is going to enroll in a private school that is not located in the LEA of the parent's residence, parental consent must be obtained before any personally identifiable information about the child is released between officials in the LEA where the private school is located and officials in the LEA of the parent's residence.

Sec. 300.623   Safeguards.

(a) Each participating agency must protect the confidentiality of personally identifiable information at collection, storage, disclosure, and destruction stages.

(b) One official at each participating agency must assume responsibility for ensuring the confidentiality of any personally identifiable information.

(c) All persons collecting or using personally identifiable information must receive training or instruction regarding the State's policies and procedures under § 300.123 and 34 CFR part 99.

(d) Each participating agency must maintain, for public inspection, a current listing of the names and positions of those employees within the agency who may have access to personally identifiable information.

Sec. 300.624   Destruction of information.

(a) The public agency must inform parents when personally identifiable information collected, maintained, or used under this part is no longer needed to provide educational services to the child.

(b) The information must be destroyed at the request of the parents. However, a permanent record of a student's name, address, and phone number, his or her grades, attendance record, classes attended, grade level completed, and year completed may be maintained without time limitation.

Sec. 300.625   Children's rights.

(a) The SEA must have in effect policies and procedures regarding the extent to which children are afforded rights of privacy similar to those afforded to parents, taking into consideration the age of the child and type or severity of disability.

(b) Under the regulations for FERPA in 34 CFR 99.5(a), the rights of parents regarding education records are transferred to the student at age 18.

(c) If the rights accorded to parents under Part B of the Act are transferred to a student who reaches the age of majority, consistent with § 300.520, the rights regarding educational records in §§ 300.613 through 300.624 must also be transferred to the student. However, the public agency must provide any notice required under section 615 of the Act to the student and the parents.

PART 303   EARLY INTERVENTION PROGRAM FOR INFANTS AND TODDLERS WITH DISABILITIES

Subpart A   General

Purpose, Eligibility, and Other General Provision

Sec. 303.1   Purpose of the early intervention program for infants and toddlers with disabilities.

The purpose of this part is to provide financial assistance to States to —

(a) Maintain and implement a statewide, comprehensive, coordinated, multidisciplinary, interagency system of early intervention services for infants and toddlers with disabilities and their families;

(b) Facilitate the coordination of payment for early intervention services from Federal, State, local, and private sources (including public and private insurance coverage);

(c) Enhance the States' capacity to provide quality early intervention services and expand and improve existing early intervention services being provided to infants and toddlers with disabilities and their families; and

(d) Enhance the capacity of State and local agencies and service providers to identify, evaluate, and meet the needs of historically underrepresented populations, particularly minority, low-income, inner-city, and rural populations.

Sec. 303.10   Developmental delay.

As used in this part, "developmental delay," when used with respect to an individual residing in a State, has the meaning given to that term under § 303.300.

Sec. 303.11   Early intervention program.

As used in this part, early intervention program means the total effort in a State that is directed at meeting the needs of children eligible under this part and their families.

Sec. 303.12   Early intervention services.

(a)   General. As used in this part, early intervention services means services that —

(1) Are designed to meet the developmental needs of each child eligible under this part and the needs of the family related to enhancing the child's development;

(2) Are selected in collaboration with the parents;

(3) Are provided —

(i) Under public supervision;

(ii) By qualified personnel, as defined in § 303.21, including the types of personnel listed in paragraph (e) of this section;

(iii) In conformity with an individualized family service plan; and

(iv) At no cost, unless, subject to § 303.520(b)(3), Federal or State law provides for a system of payments by families, including a schedule of sliding fees; and

(4) Meet the standards of the State, including the requirements of this part.

(b)   Natural environments. To the maximum extent appropriate to the needs of the child, early intervention services must be provided in natural environments, including the home and community settings in which children without disabilities participate.

(c)   General role of service providers. To the extent appropriate, service providers in each area of early intervention services included in paragraph (d) of this section are responsible for —

(1) Consulting with parents, other service providers, and representatives of appropriate community agencies to ensure the effective provision of services in that area;

(2) Training parents and others regarding the provision of those services; and

(3) Participating in the multidisciplinary team's assessment of a child and the child's family, and in the development of integrated goals and outcomes for the individualized family service plan.

(d)   Types of services; definitions. Following are types of services included under "early intervention services," and, if appropriate, definitions of those services:

(1) Assistive technology device means any item, piece of equipment, or product system, whether acquired commercially off the shelf, modified, or customized, that is used to increase, maintain, or improve the functional capabilities of children with disabilities. Assistive technology service means a service that directly assists a child with a disability in the selection, acquisition, or use of an assistive technology device. Assistive technology services include —

(i) The evaluation of the needs of a child with a disability, including a functional evaluation of the child in the child's customary environment;

(ii) Purchasing, leasing, or otherwise providing for the acquisition of assistive technology devices by children with disabilities;

(iii) Selecting, designing, fitting, customizing, adapting, applying, maintaining, repairing, or replacing assistive technology devices;

(iv) Coordinating and using other therapies, interventions, or services with assistive technology devices, such as those associated with existing education and rehabilitation plans and programs;

(v) Training or technical assistance for a child with disabilities or, if appropriate, that child's family; and

(vi) Training or technical assistance for professionals (including individuals providing early intervention services) or other individuals who provide services to or are otherwise substantially involved in the major life functions of individuals with disabilities.

(2) Audiology includes —

(i) Identification of children with auditory impairment, using at risk criteria and appropriate audiologic screening techniques;

(ii) Determination of the range, nature, and degree of hearing loss and communication functions, by use of audiological evaluation procedures;

(iii) Referral for medical and other services necessary for the habilitation or rehabilitation of children with auditory impairment;

(iv) Provision of auditory training, aural rehabilitation, speech reading and listening device orientation and training, and other services;

(v) Provision of services for prevention of hearing loss; and

(vi) Determination of the child's need for individual amplification, including selecting, fitting, and dispensing appropriate listening and vibrotactile devices, and evaluating the effectiveness of those devices.

(3) Family training, counseling, and home visits means services provided, as appropriate, by social workers, psychologists, and other qualified personnel to assist the family of a child eligible under this part in understanding the special needs of the child and enhancing the child's development.

(4) Health services (See § 303.13).

(5) Medical services only for diagnostic or evaluation purposes means services provided by a licensed physician to determine a child's developmental status and need for early intervention services.

(6) Nursing services includes —

(i) The assessment of health status for the purpose of providing nursing care, including the identification of patterns of human response to actual or potential health problems;

(ii) Provision of nursing care to prevent health problems, restore or improve functioning, and promote optimal health and development; and

(iii) Administration of medications, treatments, and regimens prescribed by a licensed physician.

(7) Nutrition services includes —

(i) Conducting individual assessments in —

(A) Nutritional history and dietary intake;

(B) Anthropometric, biochemical, and clinical variables;

(C) Feeding skills and feeding problems; and

(D) Food habits and food preferences;

(ii) Developing and monitoring appropriate plans to address the nutritional needs of children eligible under this part, based on the findings in paragraph (d)(7)(i) of this section; and

(iii) Making referrals to appropriate community resources to carry out nutrition goals.

(8) Occupational therapy includes services to address the functional needs of a child related to adaptive development, adaptive behavior and play, and sensory, motor, and postural development. These services are designed to improve the child's functional ability to perform tasks in home, school, and community settings, and include —

(i) Identification, assessment, and intervention;

(ii) Adaptation of the environment, and selection, design, and fabrication of assistive and orthotic devices to facilitate development and promote the acquisition of functional skills; and

(iii) Prevention or minimization of the impact of initial or future impairment, delay in development, or loss of functional ability.

(9) Physical therapy includes services to address the promotion of sensorimotor function through enhancement of musculoskeletal status, neurobehavioral organization, perceptual and motor development, cardiopulmonary status, and effective environmental adaptation. These services include —

(i) Screening, evaluation, and assessment of infants and toddlers to identify movement dysfunction;

(ii) Obtaining, interpreting, and integrating information appropriate to program planning to prevent, alleviate, or compensate for movement dysfunction and related functional problems; and

(iii) Providing individual and group services or treatment to prevent, alleviate, or compensate for movement dysfunction and related functional problems.

(10) Psychological services includes —

(i) Administering psychological and developmental tests and other assessment procedures;

(ii) Interpreting assessment results;

(iii) Obtaining, integrating, and interpreting information about child behavior, and child and family conditions related to learning, mental health, and development; and

(iv) Planning and managing a program of psychological services, including psychological counseling for children and parents, family counseling, consultation on child development, parent training, and education programs.

(11) Service coordination services means assistance and services provided by a service coordinator to a child eligible under this part and the child's family that are in addition to the functions and activities included under § 303.23.

(12) Social work services includes —

(i) Making home visits to evaluate a child's living conditions and patterns of parent-child interaction;

(ii) Preparing a social or emotional developmental assessment of the child within the family context;

(iii) Providing individual and family-group counseling with parents and other family members, and appropriate social skill-building activities with the child and parents;

(iv) Working with those problems in a child's and family's living situation (home, community, and any center where early intervention services are provided) that affect the child's maximum utilization of early intervention services; and

(v) Identifying, mobilizing, and coordinating community resources and services to enable the child and family to receive maximum benefit from early intervention services.

(13) Special instruction includes —

(i) The design of learning environments and activities that promote the child's acquisition of skills in a variety of developmental areas, including cognitive processes and social interaction;

(ii) Curriculum planning, including the planned interaction of personnel, materials, and time and space, that leads to achieving the outcomes in the child's individualized family service plan;

(iii) Providing families with information, skills, and support related to enhancing the skill development of the child; and

(iv) Working with the child to enhance the child's development.

(14) Speech-language pathology includes —

(i) Identification of children with communicative or oropharyngeal disorders and delays in development of communication skills, including the diagnosis and appraisal of specific disorders and delays in those skills;

(ii) Referral for medical or other professional services necessary for the habilitation or rehabilitation of children with communicative or oropharyngeal disorders and delays in development of communication skills; and

(iii) Provision of services for the habilitation, rehabilitation, or prevention of communicative or oropharyngeal disorders and delays in development of communication skills.

(15) Transportation and related costs includes the cost of travel (e.g., mileage, or travel by taxi, common carrier, or other means) and other costs (e.g., tolls and

parking expenses) that are necessary to enable a child eligible under this part and the child's family to receive early intervention services.

(16) Vision services means —

(i) Evaluation and assessment of visual functioning, including the diagnosis and appraisal of specific visual disorders, delays, and abilities;

(ii) Referral for medical or other professional services necessary for the habilitation or rehabilitation of visual functioning disorders, or both; and

(iii) Communication skills training, orientation and mobility training for all environments, visual training, independent living skills training, and additional training necessary to activate visual motor abilities.

(e) Qualified personnel. Early intervention services must be provided by qualified personnel, including —

(1) Audiologists;

(2) Family therapists;

(3) Nurses;

(4) Nutritionists;

(5) Occupational therapists;

(6) Orientation and mobility specialists;

(7) Pediatricians and other physicians;

(8) Physical therapists;

(9) Psychologists;

(10) Social workers;

(11) Special educators; and

(12) Speech and language pathologists.

Sec. 303.13   Health services.

(a) As used in this part, health services means services necessary to enable a child to benefit from the other early intervention services under this part during the time that the child is receiving the other early intervention services.

(b) The term includes —

(1) Such services as clean intermittent catheterization, tracheostomy care, tube feeding, the changing of dressings or colostomy collection bags, and other health services; and

(2) Consultation by physicians with other service providers concerning the special health care needs of eligible children that will need to be addressed in the course of providing other early intervention services.

(c) The term does not include the following:

(1) Services that are —

(i) Surgical in nature (such as cleft palate surgery, surgery for club foot, or the shunting of hydrocephalus); or

(ii) Purely medical in nature (such as hospitalization for management of congenital heart ailments, or the prescribing of medicine or drugs for any purpose).

(2) Devices necessary to control or treat a medical condition.

(3) Medical-health services (such as immunizations and regular "well-baby" care) that are routinely recommended for all children.

Sec. 303.16   Infants and toddlers with disabilities.

(a) As used in this part, infants and toddlers with disabilities means individuals from birth through age two who need early intervention services because they —

(1) Are experiencing developmental delays, as measured by appropriate diagnostic instruments and procedures, in one or more of the following areas:

(i) Cognitive development.

(ii) Physical development, including vision and hearing.

(iii) Communication development.

(iv) Social or emotional development.

(v) Adaptive development; or

(2) Have a diagnosed physical or mental condition that has a high probability of resulting in developmental delay.

(b) The term may also include, at a State's discretion, children from birth through age two who are at risk of having substantial developmental delays if early intervention services are not provided.

Sec. 303.18   Natural environments.

As used in this part, natural environments means settings that are natural or normal for the child's age peers who have no disabilities.

Sec. 303.19   Parent.

(a)   General. As used in this part, "parent" means —

(1) A natural or adoptive parent of a child;

(2) A guardian;

(3) A person acting in the place of a parent (such as a grandparent or stepparent with whom the child lives, or a person who is legally responsible for the child's welfare); or

(4) A surrogate parent who has been assigned in accordance with § 303.406.

(b)   Foster parent. Unless State law prohibits a foster parent from acting as a parent, a State may allow a foster parent to act as a parent under Part C of the Act if —

(1) The natural parents' authority to make the decisions required of parents under the Act has been extinguished under State law; and

(2) The foster parent —

(i) Has an ongoing, long-term parental relationship with the child;

(ii) Is willing to make the decisions required of parents under the Act; and

(iii) Has no interest that would conflict with the interests of the child.

Sec. 303.23   Service coordination (case management).

(a)   General.

(1) As used in this part, except in § 303.12(d)(11), service coordination means the activities carried out by a service coordinator to assist and enable a child eligible under this part and the child's family to receive the rights, procedural safeguards, and services that are authorized to be provided under the State's early intervention program.

(2) Each child eligible under this part and the child's family must be provided with one service coordinator who is responsible for —

(i) Coordinating all services across agency lines; and

(ii) Serving as the single point of contact in helping parents to obtain the services and assistance they need.

(3) Service coordination is an active, ongoing process that involves —

(i) Assisting parents of eligible children in gaining access to the early intervention services and other services identified in the individualized family service plan;

(ii) Coordinating the provision of early intervention services and other services (such as medical services for other than diagnostic and evaluation purposes) that the child needs or is being provided;

(iii) Facilitating the timely delivery of available services; and

(iv) Continuously seeking the appropriate services and situations necessary to benefit the development of each child being served for the duration of the child's eligibility.

(b)   Specific service coordination activities. Service coordination activities include —

(1) Coordinating the performance of evaluations and assessments;

(2) Facilitating and participating in the development, review, and evaluation of individualized family service plans;

(3) Assisting families in identifying available service providers;

(4) Coordinating and monitoring the delivery of available services;

(5) Informing families of the availability of advocacy services;

(6) Coordinating with medical and health providers; and

(7) Facilitating the development of a transition plan to preschool services, if appropriate.

(c)   Employment and assignment of service coordinators.

(1) Service coordinators may be employed or assigned in any way that is permitted under State law, so long as it is consistent with the requirements of this part.

(2) A State's policies and procedures for implementing the statewide system of early intervention services must be designed and implemented to ensure that service coordinators are able to effectively carry out on an interagency basis the functions and services listed under paragraphs (a) and (b) of this section.

(d)   Qualifications of service coordinators. Service coordinators must be persons who, consistent with § 303.344(g), have demonstrated knowledge and understanding about —

(1) Infants and toddlers who are eligible under this part;

(2) Part C of the Act and the regulations in this part; and

(3) The nature and scope of services available under the State's early intervention program, the system of payments for services in the State, and other pertinent information.

Sec. 303.322   Evaluation and assessment.

(a)   General.

(1) Each system must include the performance of a timely, comprehensive, multidisciplinary evaluation of each child, birth through age two, referred for evaluation, and a family-directed identification of the needs of each child's family to appropriately assist in the development of the child.

(2) The lead agency shall be responsible for ensuring that the requirements of this section are implemented by all affected public agencies and service providers in the State.

(b)   Definitions of evaluation and assessment. As used in this part —

(1) Evaluation means the procedures used by appropriate qualified personnel to determine a child's initial and continuing eligibility under this part, consistent with the definition of "infants and toddlers with disabilities" in § 303.16, including determining the status of the child in each of the developmental areas in paragraph (c)(3)(ii) of this section.

(2) Assessment means the ongoing procedures used by appropriate qualified personnel throughout the period of a child's eligibility under this part to identify —

(i) The child's unique strengths and needs and the services appropriate to meet those needs; and

(ii) The resources, priorities, and concerns of the family and the supports and services necessary to enhance the family's capacity to meet the developmental needs of their infant or toddler with a disability.

(c)   Evaluation and assessment of the child. The evaluation and assessment of each child must —

(1) Be conducted by personnel trained to utilize appropriate methods and procedures;

(2) Be based on informed clinical opinion; and

(3) Include the following:

(i) A review of pertinent records related to the child's current health status and medical history.

(ii) An evaluation of the child's level of functioning in each of the following developmental areas:

(A) Cognitive development.

(B) Physical development, including vision and hearing.

(C) Communication development.

(D) Social or emotional development.

(E) Adaptive development.

(iii) An assessment of the unique needs of the child in terms of each of the developmental areas in paragraph (c)(3)(ii) of this section, including the identification of services appropriate to meet those needs.

(d)   Family assessment.

(1) Family assessments under this part must be family-directed and designed to determine the resources, priorities, and concerns of the family and the identification of the supports and services necessary to enhance the family's capacity to meet the developmental needs of the child.

(2) Any assessment that is conducted must be voluntary on the part of the family.

(3) If an assessment of the family is carried out, the assessment must —

(i) Be conducted by personnel trained to utilize appropriate methods and procedures;

(ii) Be based on information provided by the family through a personal interview; and

(iii) Incorporate the family's description of its resources, priorities, and concerns related to enhancing the child's development.

(e)   Timelines.

(1) Except as provided in paragraph (e)(2) of this section, the evaluation and initial assessment of each child (including the family assessment) must be

completed within the 45-day time period required in § 303.321(e).

(2) The lead agency shall develop procedures to ensure that in the event of exceptional circumstances that make it impossible to complete the evaluation and assessment within 45 days (e.g., if a child is ill), public agencies will —

(i) Document those circumstances; and

(ii) Develop and implement an interim IFSP, to the extent appropriate and consistent with § 303.345 (b)(1) and (b)(2).

Sec. 303.323 Nondiscriminatory procedures.

Each lead agency shall adopt nondiscriminatory evaluation and assessment procedures. The procedures must provide that public agencies responsible for the evaluation and assessment of children and families under this part shall ensure, at a minimum, that —

(a) Tests and other evaluation materials and procedures are administered in the native language of the parents or other mode of communication, unless it is clearly not feasible to do so;

(b) Any assessment and evaluation procedures and materials that are used are selected and administered so as not to be racially or culturally discriminatory;

(c) No single procedure is used as the sole criterion for determining a child's eligibility under this part; and

(d) Evaluations and assessments are conducted by qualified personnel.

Individualized Family Service Plans (IFSPs)

Sec. 303.340 General.

(a) Each system must include policies and procedures regarding individualized family service plans (IFSPs) that meet the requirements of this section and §§ 303.341 through 303.346.

(b) As used in this part, individualized family service plan and IFSP mean a written plan for providing early intervention services to a child eligible under this part and the child's family. The plan must —

(1) Be developed in accordance with §§ 303.342 and 303.343;

(2) Be based on the evaluation and assessment described in § 303.322; and

(3) Include the matters specified in § 303.344.

(c) Lead agency responsibility. The lead agency shall ensure that an IFSP is developed and implemented for each eligible child, in accordance with the requirements of this part. If there is a dispute between agencies as to who has responsibility for developing or implementing an IFSP, the lead agency shall resolve the dispute or assign responsibility.

Sec. 303.342 Procedures for IFSP development, review, and evaluation.

(a) Meeting to develop initial IFSP — timelines. For a child who has been evaluated for the first time and determined to be eligible, a meeting to develop the initial IFSP must be conducted within the 45-day time period in § 303.321(e).

(b)   Periodic review.

(1) A review of the IFSP for a child and the child's family must be conducted every six months, or more frequently if conditions warrant, or if the family requests such a review. The purpose of the periodic review is to determine —

(i) The degree to which progress toward achieving the outcomes is being made; and

(ii) Whether modification or revision of the outcomes or services is necessary.

(2) The review may be carried out by a meeting or by another means that is acceptable to the parents and other participants.

(c)   Annual meeting to evaluate the IFSP. A meeting must be conducted on at least an annual basis to evaluate the IFSP for a child and the child's family, and, as appropriate, to revise its provisions. The results of any current evaluations conducted under § 303.322(c), and other information available from the ongoing assessment of the child and family, must be used in determining what services are needed and will be provided.

(d)   Accessibility and convenience of meetings.

(1) IFSP meetings must be conducted —

(i) In settings and at times that are convenient to families; and

(ii) In the native language of the family or other mode of communication used by the family, unless it is clearly not feasible to do so.

(2) Meeting arrangements must be made with, and written notice provided to, the family and other participants early enough before the meeting date to ensure that they will be able to attend.

(e)   Parental consent. The contents of the IFSP must be fully explained to the parents and informed written consent from the parents must be obtained prior to the provision of early intervention services described in the plan. If the parents do not provide consent with respect to a particular early intervention service or withdraw consent after first providing it, that service may not be provided. The early intervention services to which parental consent is obtained must be provided.

Sec. 303.343   Participants in IFSP meetings and periodic reviews.

(a)   Initial and annual IFSP meetings.

(1) Each initial meeting and each annual meeting to evaluate the IFSP must include the following participants:

(i) The parent or parents of the child.

(ii) Other family members, as requested by the parent, if feasible to do so;

(iii) An advocate or person outside of the family, if the parent requests that the person participate.

(iv) The service coordinator who has been working with the family since the initial referral of the child for evaluation, or who has been designated by the public agency to be responsible for implementation of the IFSP.

(v) A person or persons directly involved in conducting the evaluations and assessments in § 303.322.

(vi) As appropriate, persons who will be providing services to the child or family.

(2) If a person listed in paragraph (a)(1)(v) of this section is unable to attend a meeting, arrangements must be made for the person's involvement through other means, including —

(i) Participating in a telephone conference call;

(ii) Having a knowledgeable authorized representative attend the meeting; or

(iii) Making pertinent records available at the meeting.

(b) Periodic review. Each periodic review must provide for the participation of persons in paragraphs (a)(1)(i) through (a)(1)(iv) of this section. If conditions warrant, provisions must be made for the participation of other representatives identified in paragraph (a) of this section.

Sec. 303.344 Content of an IFSP.

(a) Information about the child's status.

(1) The IFSP must include a statement of the child's present levels of physical development (including vision, hearing, and health status), cognitive development, communication development, social or emotional development, and adaptive development.

(2) The statement in paragraph (a)(1) of this section must be based on professionally acceptable objective criteria.

(b) Family information. With the concurrence of the family, the IFS must include a statement of the family's resources, priorities, and concerns related to enhancing the development of the child.

(c) Outcomes. The IFSP must include a statement of the major outcomes expected to be achieved for the child and family, and the criteria, procedures, and timeliness used to determine —

(1) The degree to which progress toward achieving the outcomes is being made; and

(2) Whether modifications or revisions of the outcomes or services are necessary.

(d) Early intervention services.

(1) The IFSP must include a statement of the specific early intervention

services necessary to meet the unique needs of the child and the family to achieve the outcomes identified in paragraph (c) of this section, including —

(i) The frequency, intensity, and method of delivering the services;

(ii) The natural environments, as described in § 303.12(b), and § 303.18 in which early intervention services will be provided, and a justification of the extent, if any, to which the services will not be provided in a natural environment;

(iii) The location of the services; and

(iv) The payment arrangements, if any.

(2) As used in paragraph (d)(1)(i) of this section —

(i) Frequency and intensity mean the number of days or sessions that a service will be provided, the length of time the service is provided during each session, and whether the service is provided on an individual or group basis; and

(ii) Method means how a service is provided.

(3) As used in paragraph (d)(1)(iii) of this section, location means the actual place or places where a service will be provided.

(e)   Other services.

(1) To the extent appropriate, the IFSP must include —

(i) Medical and other services that the child needs, but that are not required under this part; and

(ii) The funding sources to be used in paying for those services or the steps that will be taken to secure those services through public or private sources.

(2) The requirement in paragraph (e)(1) of this section does not apply to routine medical services (e.g., immunizations and "well-baby" care), unless a child needs those services and the services are not otherwise available or being provided.

(f)   Dates; duration of services. The IFSP must include —

(1) The projected dates for initiation of the services in paragraph (d)(1) of this section as soon as possible after the IFSP meetings described in § 303.342; and

(2) The anticipated duration of those services.

(g)   Service coordinator.

(1) The IFSP must include the name of the service coordinator from the profession most immediately relevant to the child's or family's needs (or who is otherwise qualified to carry out all applicable responsibilities under this part), who will be responsible for the implementation of the IFSP and coordination with other agencies and persons.

(2) In meeting the requirements in paragraph (g)(1) of this section, the public agency may —

(i) Assign the same service coordinator who was appointed at the time that the child was initially referred for evaluation to be responsible for implementing a child's and family's IFSP; or

(ii) Appoint a new service coordinator.

(3) As used in paragraph (g)(1) of this section, the term profession includes "service coordination."

(h) Transition from Part C services.

(1) The IFSP must include the steps to be taken to support the transition of the child, in accordance with § 303.148, to —

(i) Preschool services under Part B of the Act, to the extent that those services are appropriate; or

(ii) Other services that may be available, if appropriate.

(2) The steps required in paragraph (h)(1) of this section include —

(i) Discussions with, and training of, parents regarding future placements and other matters related to the child's transition;

(ii) Procedures to prepare the child for changes in service delivery, including steps to help the child adjust to, and function in, a new setting; and

(iii) With parental consent, the transmission of information about the child to the local educational agency, to ensure continuity of services, including evaluation and assessment information required in § 303.322, and copies of IFSPs that have been developed and implemented in accordance with §§ 303.340 through 303.346.

Sec. 303.345 Provision of services before evaluation and assessment are completed.

Early intervention services for an eligible child and the child's family may commence before the completion of the evaluation and assessment in § 303.322, if the following conditions are met:

(a) Parental consent is obtained.

(b) An interim IFSP is developed that includes —

(1) The name of the service coordinator who will be responsible, consistent with § 303.344(g), for implementation of the interim IFSP and coordination with other agencies and persons; and

(2) The early intervention services that have been determined to be needed immediately by the child and the child's family.

(c) The evaluation and assessment are completed within the time period required in § 303.322(e).

Sec. 303.346 Responsibility and accountability.

Each agency or person who has a direct role in the provision of early intervention services is responsible for making a good faith effort to assist each eligible child in achieving the outcomes in the child's IFSP. However, part C of the Act does not require that any agency or person be held accountable if an eligible child does not achieve the growth projected in the child's IFSP.

Subpart E   Procedural Safeguards

General

Sec. 303.400   General responsibility of lead agency for procedural safeguards.

Each lead agency shall be responsible for —

(a) Establishing or adopting procedural safeguards that meet the requirements of this subpart; and

(b) Ensuring effective implementation of the safeguards by each public agency in the State that is involved in the provision of early intervention services under this part.

Sec. 303.401   Definitions of consent, native language, and personally identifiable information.

As used in this subpart —

(a) Consent means that —

(1) The parent has been fully informed of all information relevant to the activity for which consent is sought, in the parent's native language or other mode of communication;

(2) The parent understands and agrees in writing to the carrying out of the activity for which consent is sought, and the consent describes that activity and lists the records (if any) that will be released and to whom; and

(3) The parent understands that the granting of consent is voluntary on the part of the parent and may be revoked at any time;

(b) Native language, where used with reference to persons of limited English proficiency, means the language or mode of communication normally used by the parent of a child eligible under this part;

(c) Personally identifiable means that information includes —

(1) The name of the child, the child's parent, or other family member;

(2) The address of the child;

(3) A personal identifier, such as the child's or parent's social security number; or

(4) A list of personal characteristics or other information that would make it possible to identify the child with reasonable certainty.

Sec. 303.402   Opportunity to examine records.

In accordance with the confidentiality procedures in the regulations under part B of the Act (34 CFR 300.560 through 300.576), the parents of a child eligible under this part must be afforded the opportunity to inspect and review records relating to evaluations and assessments, eligibility determinations, development and imple-

mentation of IFSPs, individual complaints dealing with the child, and any other area under this part involving records about the child and the child's family.

Sec. 303.403 Prior notice; native language.

(a) General. Written prior notice must be given to the parents of a child eligible under this part a reasonable time before a public agency or service provider proposes, or refuses, to initiate or change the identification, evaluation, or placement of the child, or the provision of appropriate early intervention services to the child and the child's family.

(b) Content of notice. The notice must be in sufficient detail to inform the parents about —

(1) The action that is being proposed or refused;

(2) The reasons for taking the action;

(3) All procedural safeguards that are available under §§ 303.401-303.460 of this part; and

(4) The State complaint procedures under §§ 303.510-303.512, including a description of how to file a complaint and the timelines under those procedures.

(c) Native language.

(1) The notice must be —

(i) Written in language understandable to the general public; and

(ii) Provided in the native language of the parents, unless it is clearly not feasible to do so.

(2) If the native language or other mode of communication of the parent is not a written language, the public agency, or designated service provider, shall take steps to ensure that —

(i) The notice is translated orally or by other means to the parent in the parent's native language or other mode of communication;

(ii) The parent understands the notice; and

(iii) There is written evidence that the requirements of this paragraph have been met.

(3) If a parent is deaf or blind, or has no written language, the mode of communication must be that normally used by the parent (such as sign language, braille, or oral communication).

Sec. 303.404 Parent consent.

(a) Written parental consent must be obtained before —

(1) Conducting the initial evaluation and assessment of a child under § 303.322; and

(2) Initiating the provision of early intervention services (see § 303.342(e)).

(b) If consent is not given, the public agency shall make reasonable efforts to ensure that the parent —

(1) Is fully aware of the nature of the evaluation and assessment or the services that would be available; and

(2) Understands that the child will not be able to receive the evaluation and assessment or services unless consent is given.

Sec. 303.405   Parent right to decline service.

The parents of a child eligible under this part may determine whether they, their child, or other family members will accept or decline any early intervention service under this part in accordance with State law, and may decline such a service after first accepting it, without jeopardizing other early intervention services under this part.

Sec. 303.406   Surrogate parents.

(a)   General. Each lead agency shall ensure that the rights of children eligible under this part are protected if —

(1) No parent (as defined in § 303.18) can be identified;

(2) The public agency, after reasonable efforts, cannot discover the whereabouts of a parent; or

(3) The child is a ward of the State under the laws of that State.

(b)   Duty of lead agency and other public agencies. The duty of the lead agency, or other public agency under paragraph (a) of this section, includes the assignment of an individual to act as a surrogate for the parent. This must include a method for —

(1) Determining whether a child needs a surrogate parent; and

(2) Assigning a surrogate parent to the child.

(c)   Criteria for selecting surrogates.

(1) The lead agency or other public agency may select a surrogate parent in any way permitted under State law.

(2) Public agencies shall ensure that a person selected as a surrogate parent —

(i) Has no interest that conflicts with the interests of the child he or she represents; and

(ii) Has knowledge and skills that ensure adequate representation of the child.

(d)   Non-employee requirement; compensation.

(1) A person assigned as a surrogate parent may not be —

(i) An employee of any State agency; or

(ii) A person or an employee of a person providing early intervention services to the child or to any family member of the child.

(2) A person who otherwise qualifies to be a surrogate parent under paragraph (d)(1) of this section is not an employee solely because he or she is paid by a public agency to serve as a surrogate parent.

(e) Responsibilities. A surrogate parent may represent a child in all matters related to —

(1) The evaluation and assessment of the child;

(2) Development and implementation of the child's IFSPs, including annual evaluations and periodic reviews;

(3) The ongoing provision of early intervention services to the child; and

(4) Any other rights established under this part.

Mediation and Due Process Procedures for Parents and Children

Sec. 303.419 Mediation.

(a) General. Each State shall ensure that procedures are established and implemented to allow parties to disputes involving any matter described in § 303.403(a) to resolve the disputes through a mediation process which, at a minimum, must be available whenever a hearing is requested under § 303.420. The lead agency may either use the mediation system established under Part B of the Act or establish its own system.

(b) Requirements. The procedures must meet the following requirements:

(1) The procedures must ensure that the mediation process —

(i) Is voluntary on the part of the parties;

(ii) Is not used to deny or delay a parent's right to a due process hearing under § 303.420, or to deny any other rights afforded under Part C of the Act; and

(iii) Is conducted by a qualified and impartial mediator who is trained in effective mediation techniques.

(2) The State shall maintain a list of individuals who are qualified mediators and knowledgeable in laws and regulations relating to the provision of special education and related services.

(3) The State shall bear the cost of the mediation process, including the costs of meetings described in paragraph (c) of this section.

(4) Each session in the mediation process must be scheduled in a timely manner and must be held in a location that is convenient to the parties to the dispute.

(5) An agreement reached by the parties to the dispute in the mediation process must be set forth in a written mediation agreement.

(6) Discussions that occur during the mediation process must be confidential and may not be used as evidence in any subsequent due process hearings or civil

proceedings, and the parties to the mediation process may be required to sign a confidentiality pledge prior to the commencement of the process.

(c)   Meeting to encourage mediation. A State may establish procedures to require parents who elect not to use the mediation process to meet, at a time and location convenient to the parents, with a disinterested party —

(1) Who is under contract with a parent training and information center or community parent resource center in the State established under sections 682 or 683 of the Act, or an appropriate alternative dispute resolution entity; and

(2) Who would explain the benefits of the mediation process and encourage the parents to use the process.

Sec. 303.420   Due process procedures.

Each system must include written procedures including procedures for mediation as described in § 303.419, for the timely administrative resolution of individual child complaints by parents concerning any of the matters in § 303.403(a). A State may meet this requirement by —

(a) Adopting the mediation and due process procedures in 34 CFR 300.506 through 300.512 and developing procedures that meet the requirements of § 303.425; or

(b) Developing procedures that —

(1) Meet the requirements in § 303.419 and §§ 303.421 through 303.425; and

(2) Provide parents a means of filing a complaint.

Sec. 303.421   Appointment of an impartial person.

(a)   Qualifications and duties. An impartial person must be appointed to implement the complaint resolution process in this subpart. The person must —

(1) Have knowledge about the provisions of this part and the needs of, and services available for, eligible children and their families; and

(2) Perform the following duties:

(i) Listen to the presentation of relevant viewpoints about the complaint, examine all information relevant to the issues, and seek to reach a timely resolution of the complaint.

(ii) Provide a record of the proceedings, including a written decision.

(b)   Definition of impartial.

(1) As used in this section, impartial means that the person appointed to implement the complaint resolution process —

(i) Is not an employee of any agency or other entity involved in the provision of early intervention services or care of the child; and

(ii) Does not have a personal or professional interest that would conflict with his or her objectivity in implementing the process.

(2) A person who otherwise qualifies under paragraph (b)(1) of this section is not an employee of an agency solely because the person is paid by the agency to implement the complaint resolution process.

Sec. 303.422 Parent rights in administrative proceedings.

(a) General. Each lead agency shall ensure that the parents of children eligible under this part are afforded the rights in paragraph (b) of this section in any administrative proceedings carried out under § 303.420.

(b) Rights. Any parent involved in an administrative proceeding has the right to —

(1) Be accompanied and advised by counsel and by individuals with special knowledge or training with respect to early intervention services for children eligible under this part;

(2) Present evidence and confront, cross-examine, and compel the attendance of witnesses;

(3) Prohibit the introduction of any evidence at the proceeding that has not been disclosed to the parent at least five days before the proceeding;

(4) Obtain a written or electronic verbatim transcription of the proceeding; and

(5) Obtain written findings of fact and decisions.

Sec. 303.423 Convenience of proceedings; timelines.

(a) Any proceeding for implementing the complaint resolution process in this subpart must be carried out at a time and place that is reasonably convenient to the parents.

(b) Each lead agency shall ensure that, not later than 30 days after the receipt of a parent's complaint, the impartial proceeding required under this subpart is completed and a written decision mailed to each of the parties.

Sec. 303.424 Civil action.

Any party aggrieved by the findings and decision regarding an administrative complaint has the right to bring a civil action in State or Federal court under section 639(a)(1) of the Act.

Sec. 303.425 Status of a child during proceedings.

(a) During the pendency of any proceeding involving a complaint under this subpart, unless the public agency and parents of a child otherwise agree, the child must continue to receive the appropriate early intervention services currently being provided.

(b) If the complaint involves an application for initial services under this part, the child must receive those services that are not in dispute.

Chapter 16

UNITED NATIONS CONVENTION ON THE RIGHTS OF PERSONS WITH DISABILITIES RESOLUTION ADOPTED BY THE GENERAL ASSEMBLY

[without reference to a Main Committee (A/61/611)]

61/106. Convention on the Rights of Persons with Disabilities

The General Assembly,

Recalling its resolution 56/168 of 19 December 2001, by which it decided to establish an Ad Hoc Committee, open to the participation of all Member States and observers to the United Nations, to consider proposals for a comprehensive and integral international convention to promote and protect the rights and dignity of persons with disabilities, based on a holistic approach in the work done in the fields of social development, human rights and non-discrimination and taking into account the recommendations of the Commission on Human Rights and the Commission for Social Development,

Recalling also its previous relevant resolutions, the most recent of which was resolution 60/232 of 23 December 2005, as well as relevant resolutions of the Commission for Social Development and the Commission on Human Rights,

Welcoming the valuable contributions made by intergovernmental and non-governmental organizations and national human rights institutions to the work of the Ad Hoc Committee,

1. *Expresses its appreciation* to the Ad Hoc Committee for having concluded the elaboration of the draft Convention on the Rights of Persons with Disabilities and the draft Optional Protocol to the Convention;

2. *Adopts* the Convention on the Rights of Persons with Disabilities and the Optional Protocol to the Convention annexed to the present resolution, which shall be open for signature at United Nations Headquarters in New York as of 30 March 2007;

3. *Calls upon* States to consider signing and ratifying the Convention and the Optional Protocol as a matter of priority, and expresses the hope that they will enter into force at an early date;

4. *Requests* the Secretary-General to provide the staff and facilities necessary for the effective performance of the functions of the Conference of States Parties and the Committee under the Convention and the Optional Protocol after the entry into force of the Convention, as well as for the dissemination of information on the Convention and the Optional Protocol;

5. *Also requests* the Secretary-General to implement progressively standards and guidelines for the accessibility of facilities and services of the United Nations system, taking into account relevant provisions of the Convention, in particular when undertaking renovations;

6. *Requests* United Nations agencies and organizations, and invites intergovernmental and non-governmental organizations, to undertake efforts to disseminate information on the Convention and the Optional Protocol and to promote their understanding;

7. *Requests* the Secretary-General to submit to the General Assembly at its sixty-second session a report on the status of the Convention and the Optional Protocol and the implementation of the present resolution, under a sub-item entitled "Convention on the Rights of Persons with Disabilities".

76th plenary meeting
13 December 2006

Annex I
Convention on the Rights of Persons with Disabilities
Preamble

The States Parties to the present Convention,

(a) *Recalling* the principles proclaimed in the Charter of the United Nations which recognize the inherent dignity and worth and the equal and inalienable rights of all members of the human family as the foundation of freedom, justice and peace in the world,

(b) *Recognizing* that the United Nations, in the Universal Declaration of Human Rights and in the International Covenants on Human Rights, has proclaimed and agreed that everyone is entitled to all the rights and freedoms set forth therein, without distinction of any kind,

(c) *Reaffirming* the universality, indivisibility, interdependence and interrelatedness of all human rights and fundamental freedoms and the need for persons with disabilities to be guaranteed their full enjoyment without discrimination,

(d) *Recalling* the International Covenant on Economic, Social and Cultural Rights, the International Covenant on Civil and Political Rights, the International Convention on the Elimination of All Forms of Racial Discrimination, the Convention on the Elimination of All Forms of Discrimination against Women, the Convention against Torture and Other Cruel, Inhuman or Degrading Treatment or Punishment, the Convention on the Rights of the Child, and the International Convention on the Protection of the Rights of All Migrant Workers and Members of Their Families,

(e) *Recognizing* that disability is an evolving concept and that disability results from the interaction between persons with impairments and attitudinal and environmental barriers that hinders their full and effective participation in society on an equal basis with others,

(f) *Recognizing* the importance of the principles and policy guidelines contained in the World Programme of Action concerning Disabled Persons and in the Standard Rules on the Equalization of Opportunities for Persons with Disabilities in influencing the promotion, formulation and evaluation of the policies, plans, programmes and actions at the national, regional and international levels to further equalize opportunities for persons with disabilities,

(g) *Emphasizing* the importance of mainstreaming disability issues as an integral part of relevant strategies of sustainable development,

(h) *Recognizing also* that discrimination against any person on the basis of disability is a violation of the inherent dignity and worth of the human person, (*i*) *Recognizing further* the diversity of persons with disabilities,

(*j*) *Recognizing* the need to promote and protect the human rights of all persons with disabilities, including those who require more intensive support,

(*k*) *Concerned* that, despite these various instruments and undertakings, persons with disabilities continue to face barriers in their participation as equal members of society and violations of their human rights in all parts of the world,

(*l*) *Recognizing* the importance of international cooperation for improving the living conditions of persons with disabilities in every country, particularly in developing countries,

(*m*) *Recognizing* the valued existing and potential contributions made by persons with disabilities to the overall well-being and diversity of their communities, and that the promotion of the full enjoyment by persons with disabilities of their human rights and fundamental freedoms and of full participation by persons with disabilities will result in their enhanced sense of belonging and in significant advances in the human, social and economic development of society and the eradication of poverty,

(*n*) *Recognizing* the importance for persons with disabilities of their individual autonomy and independence, including the freedom to make their own choices,

(*o*) *Considering* that persons with disabilities should have the opportunity to be actively involved in decision-making processes about policies and programmes, including those directly concerning them,

(*p*) *Concerned* about the difficult conditions faced by persons with disabilities who are subject to multiple or aggravated forms of discrimination on the basis of race, colour, sex, language, religion, political or other opinion, national, ethnic, indigenous or social origin, property, birth, age or other status,

(*q*) *Recognizing* that women and girls with disabilities are often at greater risk, both within and outside the home, of violence, injury or abuse, neglect or negligent treatment, maltreatment or exploitation,

(*r*) *Recognizing* that children with disabilities should have full enjoyment of all human rights and fundamental freedoms on an equal basis with other children, and recalling obligations to that end undertaken by States Parties to the Convention on the Rights of the Child,

(*s*) *Emphasizing* the need to incorporate a gender perspective in all efforts to promote the full enjoyment of human rights and fundamental freedoms by persons with disabilities,

(*t*) *Highlighting* the fact that the majority of persons with disabilities live in conditions of poverty, and in this regard recognizing the critical need to address the negative impact of poverty on persons with disabilities,

(*u*) *Bearing in mind* that conditions of peace and security based on full respect for the purposes and principles contained in the Charter of the United Nations and observance of applicable human rights instruments are indispensable for the full protection of persons with disabilities, in particular during armed conflicts and foreign occupation,

(v) *Recognizing* the importance of accessibility to the physical, social, economic and cultural environment, to health and education and to information and communication, in enabling persons with disabilities to fully enjoy all human rights and fundamental freedoms,

(w) *Realizing* that the individual, having duties to other individuals and to the community to which he or she belongs, is under a responsibility to strive for the promotion and observance of the rights recognized in the International Bill of Human Rights,

(x) *Convinced* that the family is the natural and fundamental group unit of society and is entitled to protection by society and the State, and that persons with disabilities and their family members should receive the necessary protection and assistance to enable families to contribute towards the full and equal enjoyment of the rights of persons with disabilities,

(y) *Convinced* that a comprehensive and integral international convention to promote and protect the rights and dignity of persons with disabilities will make a significant contribution to redressing the profound social disadvantage of persons with disabilities and promote their participation in the civil, political, economic, social and cultural spheres with equal opportunities, in both developing and developed countries,

Have agreed as follows:

Article 1   Purpose

The purpose of the present Convention is to promote, protect and ensure the full and equal enjoyment of all human rights and fundamental freedoms by all persons with disabilities, and to promote respect for their inherent dignity.

Persons with disabilities include those who have long-term physical, mental, intellectual or sensory impairments which in interaction with various barriers may hinder their full and effective participation in society on an equal basis with others.

Article 2   Definitions

For the purposes of the present Convention:

"Communication" includes languages, display of text, Braille, tactile communication, large print, accessible multimedia as well as written, audio, plain-language, human-reader and augmentative and alternative modes, means and formats of communication, including accessible information and communication technology;

"Language" includes spoken and signed languages and other forms of non-spoken languages;

"Discrimination on the basis of disability" means any distinction, exclusion or restriction on the basis of disability which has the purpose or effect of impairing or nullifying the recognition, enjoyment or exercise, on an equal basis with others, of all human rights and fundamental freedoms in the political, economic, social, cultural, civil or any other field. It includes all forms of discrimination, including denial of reasonable accommodation;

"Reasonable accommodation" means necessary and appropriate modification and adjustments not imposing a disproportionate or undue burden, where needed in a particular case, to ensure to persons with disabilities the enjoyment or exercise on an equal basis with others of all human rights and fundamental freedoms;

"Universal design" means the design of products, environments, programmes and services to be usable by all people, to the greatest extent possible, without the need for adaptation or specialized design. "Universal design" shall not exclude assistive devices for particular groups of persons with disabilities where this is needed.

Article 3   General principles

The principles of the present Convention shall be:

(a) Respect for inherent dignity, individual autonomy including the freedom to make one's own choices, and independence of persons;

(b) Non-discrimination;

(c) Full and effective participation and inclusion in society;

(d) Respect for difference and acceptance of persons with disabilities as part of human diversity and humanity;

(e) Equality of opportunity;

(f) Accessibility;

(g) Equality between men and women;

(h) Respect for the evolving capacities of children with disabilities and respect for the right of children with disabilities to preserve their identities.

Article 4   General obligations

1. States Parties undertake to ensure and promote the full realization of all human rights and fundamental freedoms for all persons with disabilities without discrimination of any kind on the basis of disability. To this end, States Parties undertake:

(a) To adopt all appropriate legislative, administrative and other measures for the implementation of the rights recognized in the present Convention;

(b) To take all appropriate measures, including legislation, to modify or abolish existing laws, regulations, customs and practices that constitute discrimination against persons with disabilities;

(c) To take into account the protection and promotion of the human rights of persons with disabilities in all policies and programmes;

(d) To refrain from engaging in any act or practice that is inconsistent with the present Convention and to ensure that public authorities and institutions act in conformity with the present Convention;

(e) To take all appropriate measures to eliminate discrimination on the basis of disability by any person, organization or private enterprise;

(*f*) To undertake or promote research and development of universally designed goods, services, equipment and facilities, as defined in article 2 of the present Convention, which should require the minimum possible adaptation and the least cost to meet the specific needs of a person with disabilities, to promote their availability and use, and to promote universal design in the development of standards and guidelines;

(*g*) To undertake or promote research and development of, and to promote the availability and use of new technologies, including information and communications technologies, mobility aids, devices and assistive technologies, suitable for persons with disabilities, giving priority to technologies at an affordable cost;

(*h*) To provide accessible information to persons with disabilities about mobility aids, devices and assistive technologies, including new technologies, as well as other forms of assistance, support services and facilities;

(*i*) To promote the training of professionals and staff working with persons with disabilities in the rights recognized in the present Convention so as to better provide the assistance and services guaranteed by those rights.

2. With regard to economic, social and cultural rights, each State Party undertakes to take measures to the maximum of its available resources and, where needed, within the framework of international cooperation, with a view to achieving progressively the full realization of these rights, without prejudice to those obligations contained in the present Convention that are immediately applicable according to international law.

3. In the development and implementation of legislation and policies to implement the present Convention, and in other decision-making processes concerning issues relating to persons with disabilities, States Parties shall closely consult with and actively involve persons with disabilities, including children with disabilities, through their representative organizations.

4. Nothing in the present Convention shall affect any provisions which are more conducive to the realization of the rights of persons with disabilities and which may be contained in the law of a State Party or international law in force for that State. There shall be no restriction upon or derogation from any of the human rights and fundamental freedoms recognized or existing in any State Party to the present Convention pursuant to law, conventions, regulation or custom on the pretext that the present Convention does not recognize such rights or freedoms or that it recognizes them to a lesser extent.

5. The provisions of the present Convention shall extend to all parts of federal States without any limitations or exceptions.

Article 5   Equality and non-discrimination

1. States Parties recognize that all persons are equal before and under the law and are entitled without any discrimination to the equal protection and equal benefit of the law.

2. States Parties shall prohibit all discrimination on the basis of disability and guarantee to persons with disabilities equal and effective legal protection against

discrimination on all grounds.

3. In order to promote equality and eliminate discrimination, States Parties shall take all appropriate steps to ensure that reasonable accommodation is provided.

4. Specific measures which are necessary to accelerate or achieve de facto equality of persons with disabilities shall not be considered discrimination under the terms of the present Convention.

Article 6   Women with disabilities

1. States Parties recognize that women and girls with disabilities are subject to multiple discrimination, and in this regard shall take measures to ensure the full and equal enjoyment by them of all human rights and fundamental freedoms.

2. States Parties shall take all appropriate measures to ensure the full development, advancement and empowerment of women, for the purpose of guaranteeing them the exercise and enjoyment of the human rights and fundamental freedoms set out in the present Convention.

Article 7   Children with disabilities

1. States Parties shall take all necessary measures to ensure the full enjoyment by children with disabilities of all human rights and fundamental freedoms on an equal basis with other children.

2. In all actions concerning children with disabilities, the best interests of the child shall be a primary consideration.

3. States Parties shall ensure that children with disabilities have the right to express their views freely on all matters affecting them, their views being given due weight in accordance with their age and maturity, on an equal basis with other children, and to be provided with disability and age-appropriate assistance to realize that right.

Article 8   Awareness-raising

1. States Parties undertake to adopt immediate, effective and appropriate measures:

(a) To raise awareness throughout society, including at the family level, regarding persons with disabilities, and to foster respect for the rights and dignity of persons with disabilities;

(b) To combat stereotypes, prejudices and harmful practices relating to persons with disabilities, including those based on sex and age, in all areas of life;

(c) To promote awareness of the capabilities and contributions of persons with disabilities.

2. Measures to this end include:

(a) Initiating and maintaining effective public awareness campaigns designed:

(i) To nurture receptiveness to the rights of persons with disabilities;

(ii) To promote positive perceptions and greater social awareness towards persons with disabilities;

(iii) To promote recognition of the skills, merits and abilities of persons with disabilities, and of their contributions to the workplace and the labour market;

(b) Fostering at all levels of the education system, including in all children from an early age, an attitude of respect for the rights of persons with disabilities;

(c) Encouraging all organs of the media to portray persons with disabilities in a manner consistent with the purpose of the present Convention;

(d) Promoting awareness-training programmes regarding persons with disabilities and the rights of persons with disabilities.

Article 9   Accessibility

1. To enable persons with disabilities to live independently and participate fully in all aspects of life, States Parties shall take appropriate measures to ensure to persons with disabilities access, on an equal basis with others, to the physical environment, to transportation, to information and communications, including information and communications technologies and systems, and to other facilities and services open or provided to the public, both in urban and in rural areas. These measures, which shall include the identification and elimination of obstacles and barriers to accessibility, shall apply to, inter alia:

(a) Buildings, roads, transportation and other indoor and outdoor facilities, including schools, housing, medical facilities and workplaces;

(b) Information, communications and other services, including electronic services and emergency services.

2. States Parties shall also take appropriate measures:

(a) To develop, promulgate and monitor the implementation of minimum standards and guidelines for the accessibility of facilities and services open or provided to the public;

(b) To ensure that private entities that offer facilities and services which are open or provided to the public take into account all aspects of accessibility for persons with disabilities;

(c) To provide training for stakeholders on accessibility issues facing persons with disabilities;

(d) To provide in buildings and other facilities open to the public signage in Braille and in easy to read and understand forms;

(e) To provide forms of live assistance and intermediaries, including guides, readers and professional sign language interpreters, to facilitate accessibility to buildings and other facilities open to the public;

(f) To promote other appropriate forms of assistance and support to persons with disabilities to ensure their access to information;

(g) To promote access for persons with disabilities to new information and communications technologies and systems, including the Internet;

(*h*) To promote the design, development, production and distribution of accessible information and communications technologies and systems at an early stage, so that these technologies and systems become accessible at minimum cost.

Article 10   Right to life

States Parties reaffirm that every human being has the inherent right to life and shall take all necessary measures to ensure its effective enjoyment by persons with disabilities on an equal basis with others.

Article 11   Situations of risk and humanitarian emergencies

States Parties shall take, in accordance with their obligations under international law, including international humanitarian law and international human rights law, all necessary measures to ensure the protection and safety of persons with disabilities in situations of risk, including situations of armed conflict, humanitarian emergencies and the occurrence of natural disasters.

Article 12   Equal recognition before the law

1. States Parties reaffirm that persons with disabilities have the right to recognition everywhere as persons before the law.

2. States Parties shall recognize that persons with disabilities enjoy legal capacity on an equal basis with others in all aspects of life.

3. States Parties shall take appropriate measures to provide access by persons with disabilities to the support they may require in exercising their legal capacity.

4. States Parties shall ensure that all measures that relate to the exercise of legal capacity provide for appropriate and effective safeguards to prevent abuse in accordance with international human rights law. Such safeguards shall ensure that measures relating to the exercise of legal capacity respect the rights, will and preferences of the person, are free of conflict of interest and undue influence, are proportional and tailored to the person's circumstances, apply for the shortest time possible and are subject to regular review by a competent, independent and impartial authority or judicial body. The safeguards shall be proportional to the degree to which such measures affect the person's rights and interests.

5. Subject to the provisions of this article, States Parties shall take all appropriate and effective measures to ensure the equal right of persons with disabilities to own or inherit property, to control their own financial affairs and to have equal access to bank loans, mortgages and other forms of financial credit, and shall ensure that persons with disabilities are not arbitrarily deprived of their property.

Article 13   Access to justice

1. States Parties shall ensure effective access to justice for persons with disabilities on an equal basis with others, including through the provision of procedural and age-appropriate accommodations, in order to facilitate their effective role as direct and indirect participants, including as witnesses, in all legal proceedings, including at investigative and other preliminary stages.

2. In order to help to ensure effective access to justice for persons with disabilities, States Parties shall promote appropriate training for those working in the field of administration of justice, including police and prison staff.

Article 14   Liberty and security of person

1. States Parties shall ensure that persons with disabilities, on an equal basis with others:

(*a*) Enjoy the right to liberty and security of person;

(*b*) Are not deprived of their liberty unlawfully or arbitrarily, and that any deprivation of liberty is in conformity with the law, and that the existence of a disability shall in no case justify a deprivation of liberty.

2. States Parties shall ensure that if persons with disabilities are deprived of their liberty through any process, they are, on an equal basis with others, entitled to guarantees in accordance with international human rights law and shall be treated in compliance with the objectives and principles of the present Convention, including by provision of reasonable accommodation.

Article 15   Freedom from torture or cruel, inhuman or degrading treatment or punishment

1. No one shall be subjected to torture or to cruel, inhuman or degrading treatment or punishment. In particular, no one shall be subjected without his or her free consent to medical or scientific experimentation.

2. States Parties shall take all effective legislative, administrative, judicial or other measures to prevent persons with disabilities, on an equal basis with others, from being subjected to torture or cruel, inhuman or degrading treatment or punishment.

Article 16   Freedom from exploitation, violence and abuse

1. States Parties shall take all appropriate legislative, administrative, social, educational and other measures to protect persons with disabilities, both within and outside the home, from all forms of exploitation, violence and abuse, including their gender-based aspects.

2. States Parties shall also take all appropriate measures to prevent all forms of exploitation, violence and abuse by ensuring, inter alia, appropriate forms of gender- and age-sensitive assistance and support for persons with disabilities and their families and caregivers, including through the provision of information and education on how to avoid, recognize and report instances of exploitation, violence and abuse. States Parties shall ensure that protection services are age-, gender- and disability-sensitive.

3. In order to prevent the occurrence of all forms of exploitation, violence and abuse, States Parties shall ensure that all facilities and programmes designed to serve persons with disabilities are effectively monitored by independent authorities.

4. States Parties shall take all appropriate measures to promote the physical, cognitive and psychological recovery, rehabilitation and social reintegration of

persons with disabilities who become victims of any form of exploitation, violence or abuse, including through the provision of protection services. Such recovery and reintegration shall take place in an environment that fosters the health, welfare, self-respect, dignity and autonomy of the person and takes into account gender- and age-specific needs.

5. States Parties shall put in place effective legislation and policies, including women- and child-focused legislation and policies, to ensure that instances of exploitation, violence and abuse against persons with disabilities are identified, investigated and, where appropriate, prosecuted.

Article 17   Protecting the integrity of the person

Every person with disabilities has a right to respect for his or her physical and mental integrity on an equal basis with others.

Article 18   Liberty of movement and nationality

1. States Parties shall recognize the rights of persons with disabilities to liberty of movement, to freedom to choose their residence and to a nationality, on an equal basis with others, including by ensuring that persons with disabilities:

(a) Have the right to acquire and change a nationality and are not deprived of their nationality arbitrarily or on the basis of disability;

(b) Are not deprived, on the basis of disability, of their ability to obtain, possess and utilize documentation of their nationality or other documentation of identification, or to utilize relevant processes such as immigration proceedings, that may be needed to facilitate exercise of the right to liberty of movement;

(c) Are free to leave any country, including their own;

(d) Are not deprived, arbitrarily or on the basis of disability, of the right to enter their own country.

2. Children with disabilities shall be registered immediately after birth and shall have the right from birth to a name, the right to acquire a nationality and, as far as possible, the right to know and be cared for by their parents.

Article 19   Living independently and being included in the community

States Parties to the present Convention recognize the equal right of all persons with disabilities to live in the community, with choices equal to others, and shall take effective and appropriate measures to facilitate full enjoyment by persons with disabilities of this right and their full inclusion and participation in the community, including by ensuring that:

(a) Persons with disabilities have the opportunity to choose their place of residence and where and with whom they live on an equal basis with others and are not obliged to live in a particular living arrangement;

(b) Persons with disabilities have access to a range of in-home, residential and other community support services, including personal assistance necessary to support living and inclusion in the community, and to prevent isolation or segregation from the community;

(*c*) Community services and facilities for the general population are available on an equal basis to persons with disabilities and are responsive to their needs.

Article 20   Personal mobility

States Parties shall take effective measures to ensure personal mobility with the greatest possible independence for persons with disabilities, including by:

(*a*) Facilitating the personal mobility of persons with disabilities in the manner and at the time of their choice, and at affordable cost;

(*b*) Facilitating access by persons with disabilities to quality mobility aids, devices, assistive technologies and forms of live assistance and intermediaries, including by making them available at affordable cost;

(*c*) Providing training in mobility skills to persons with disabilities and to specialist staff working with persons with disabilities;

(*d*) Encouraging entities that produce mobility aids, devices and assistive technologies to take into account all aspects of mobility for persons with disabilities.

Article 21   Freedom of expression and opinion, and access to information

States Parties shall take all appropriate measures to ensure that persons with disabilities can exercise the right to freedom of expression and opinion, including the freedom to seek, receive and impart information and ideas on an equal basis with others and through all forms of communication of their choice, as defined in article 2 of the present Convention, including by:

(*a*) Providing information intended for the general public to persons with disabilities in accessible formats and technologies appropriate to different kinds of disabilities in a timely manner and without additional cost;

(*b*) Accepting and facilitating the use of sign languages, Braille, augmentative and alternative communication, and all other accessible means, modes and formats of communication of their choice by persons with disabilities in official interactions;

(*c*) Urging private entities that provide services to the general public, including through the Internet, to provide information and services in accessible and usable formats for persons with disabilities;

(*d*) Encouraging the mass media, including providers of information through the Internet, to make their services accessible to persons with disabilities;

(*e*) Recognizing and promoting the use of sign languages.

Article 22   Respect for privacy

1. No person with disabilities, regardless of place of residence or living arrangements, shall be subjected to arbitrary or unlawful interference with his or her privacy, family, home or correspondence or other types of communication or to unlawful attacks on his or her honour and reputation. Persons with disabilities have the right to the protection of the law against such interference or attacks.

2. States Parties shall protect the privacy of personal, health and rehabilitation information of persons with disabilities on an equal basis with others.

Article 23   Respect for home and the family

1. States Parties shall take effective and appropriate measures to eliminate discrimination against persons with disabilities in all matters relating to marriage, family, parenthood and relationships, on an equal basis with others, so as to ensure that:

(a) The right of all persons with disabilities who are of marriageable age to marry and to found a family on the basis of free and full consent of the intending spouses is recognized;

(b) The rights of persons with disabilities to decide freely and responsibly on the number and spacing of their children and to have access to age-appropriate information, reproductive and family planning education are recognized, and the means necessary to enable them to exercise these rights are provided;

(c) Persons with disabilities, including children, retain their fertility on an equal basis with others.

2. States Parties shall ensure the rights and responsibilities of persons with disabilities, with regard to guardianship, wardship, trusteeship, adoption of children or similar institutions, where these concepts exist in national legislation; in all cases the best interests of the child shall be paramount. States Parties shall render appropriate assistance to persons with disabilities in the performance of their child-rearing responsibilities.

3. States Parties shall ensure that children with disabilities have equal rights with respect to family life. With a view to realizing these rights, and to prevent concealment, abandonment, neglect and segregation of children with disabilities, States Parties shall undertake to provide early and comprehensive information, services and support to children with disabilities and their families.

4. States Parties shall ensure that a child shall not be separated from his or her parents against their will, except when competent authorities subject to judicial review determine, in accordance with applicable law and procedures, that such separation is necessary for the best interests of the child. In no case shall a child be separated from parents on the basis of a disability of either the child or one or both of the parents.

5. States Parties shall, where the immediate family is unable to care for a child with disabilities, undertake every effort to provide alternative care within the wider family, and failing that, within the community in a family setting.

Article 24   Education

1. States Parties recognize the right of persons with disabilities to education. With a view to realizing this right without discrimination and on the basis of equal opportunity, States Parties shall ensure an inclusive education system at all levels and lifelong learning directed to:

(a) The full development of human potential and sense of dignity and self-worth, and the strengthening of respect for human rights, fundamental freedoms and human diversity;

(b) The development by persons with disabilities of their personality, talents and creativity, as well as their mental and physical abilities, to their fullest potential;

(c) Enabling persons with disabilities to participate effectively in a free society.

2. In realizing this right, States Parties shall ensure that:

(a) Persons with disabilities are not excluded from the general education system on the basis of disability, and that children with disabilities are not excluded from free and compulsory primary education, or from secondary education, on the basis of disability;

(b) Persons with disabilities can access an inclusive, quality and free primary education and secondary education on an equal basis with others in the communities in which they live;

(c) Reasonable accommodation of the individual's requirements is provided;

(d) Persons with disabilities receive the support required, within the general education system, to facilitate their effective education;

(e) Effective individualized support measures are provided in environments that maximize academic and social development, consistent with the goal of full inclusion.

3. States Parties shall enable persons with disabilities to learn life and social development skills to facilitate their full and equal participation in education and as members of the community. To this end, States Parties shall take appropriate measures, including:

(a) Facilitating the learning of Braille, alternative script, augmentative and alternative modes, means and formats of communication and orientation and mobility skills, and facilitating peer support and mentoring;

(b) Facilitating the learning of sign language and the promotion of the linguistic identity of the deaf community;

(c) Ensuring that the education of persons, and in particular children, who are blind, deaf or deafblind, is delivered in the most appropriate languages and modes and means of communication for the individual, and in environments which maximize academic and social development.

4. In order to help ensure the realization of this right, States Parties shall take appropriate measures to employ teachers, including teachers with disabilities, who are qualified in sign language and/or Braille, and to train professionals and staff who work at all levels of education. Such training shall incorporate disability awareness and the use of appropriate augmentative and alternative modes, means and formats of communication, educational techniques and materials to support persons with disabilities.

5. States Parties shall ensure that persons with disabilities are able to access

general tertiary education, vocational training, adult education and lifelong learning without discrimination and on an equal basis with others. To this end, States Parties shall ensure that reasonable accommodation is provided to persons with disabilities.

Article 25   Health

States Parties recognize that persons with disabilities have the right to the enjoyment of the highest attainable standard of health without discrimination on the basis of disability. States Parties shall take all appropriate measures to ensure access for persons with disabilities to health services that are gender-sensitive, including health-related rehabilitation. In particular, States Parties shall:

(*a*) Provide persons with disabilities with the same range, quality and standard of free or affordable health care and programmes as provided to other persons, including in the area of sexual and reproductive health and population-based public health programmes;

(*b*) Provide those health services needed by persons with disabilities specifically because of their disabilities, including early identification and intervention as appropriate, and services designed to minimize and prevent further disabilities, including among children and older persons;

(*c*) Provide these health services as close as possible to people's own communities, including in rural areas;

(*d*) Require health professionals to provide care of the same quality to persons with disabilities as to others, including on the basis of free and informed consent by, inter alia, raising awareness of the human rights, dignity, autonomy and needs of persons with disabilities through training and the promulgation of ethical standards for public and private health care;

(*e*) Prohibit discrimination against persons with disabilities in the provision of health insurance, and life insurance where such insurance is permitted by national law, which shall be provided in a fair and reasonable manner;

(*f*) Prevent discriminatory denial of health care or health services or food and fluids on the basis of disability.

Article 26   Habilitation and rehabilitation

1. States Parties shall take effective and appropriate measures, including through peer support, to enable persons with disabilities to attain and maintain maximum independence, full physical, mental, social and vocational ability, and full inclusion and participation in all aspects of life. To that end, States Parties shall organize, strengthen and extend comprehensive habilitation and rehabilitation services and programmes, particularly in the areas of health, employment, education and social services, in such a way that these services and programmes:

(*a*) Begin at the earliest possible stage, and are based on the multidisciplinary assessment of individual needs and strengths;

(*b*) Support participation and inclusion in the community and all aspects of society, are voluntary, and are available to persons with disabilities as close as possible to their own communities, including in rural areas.

2. States Parties shall promote the development of initial and continuing training for professionals and staff working in habilitation and rehabilitation services.

3. States Parties shall promote the availability, knowledge and use of assistive devices and technologies, designed for persons with disabilities, as they relate to habilitation and rehabilitation.

Article 27   Work and employment

1. States Parties recognize the right of persons with disabilities to work, on an equal basis with others; this includes the right to the opportunity to gain a living by work freely chosen or accepted in a labour market and work environment that is open, inclusive and accessible to persons with disabilities. States Parties shall safeguard and promote the realization of the right to work, including for those who acquire a disability during the course of employment, by taking appropriate steps, including through legislation, to, inter alia:

(a) Prohibit discrimination on the basis of disability with regard to all matters concerning all forms of employment, including conditions of recruitment, hiring and employment, continuance of employment, career advancement and safe and healthy working conditions;

(b) Protect the rights of persons with disabilities, on an equal basis with others, to just and favourable conditions of work, including equal opportunities and equal remuneration for work of equal value, safe and healthy working conditions, including protection from harassment, and the redress of grievances;

(c) Ensure that persons with disabilities are able to exercise their labour and trade union rights on an equal basis with others;

(d) Enable persons with disabilities to have effective access to general technical and vocational guidance programmes, placement services and vocational and continuing training;

(e) Promote employment opportunities and career advancement for persons with disabilities in the labour market, as well as assistance in finding, obtaining, maintaining and returning to employment;

(f) Promote opportunities for self-employment, entrepreneurship, the development of cooperatives and starting one's own business;

(g) Employ persons with disabilities in the public sector;

(h) Promote the employment of persons with disabilities in the private sector through appropriate policies and measures, which may include affirmative action programmes, incentives and other measures;

(i) Ensure that reasonable accommodation is provided to persons with disabilities in the workplace;

(j) Promote the acquisition by persons with disabilities of work experience in the open labour market;

(k) Promote vocational and professional rehabilitation, job retention and return-to-work programmes for persons with disabilities.

2. States Parties shall ensure that persons with disabilities are not held in slavery or in servitude, and are protected, on an equal basis with others, from forced or compulsory labour.

Article 28   Adequate standard of living and social protection

1. States Parties recognize the right of persons with disabilities to an adequate standard of living for themselves and their families, including adequate food, clothing and housing, and to the continuous improvement of living conditions, and shall take appropriate steps to safeguard and promote the realization of this right without discrimination on the basis of disability.

2. States Parties recognize the right of persons with disabilities to social protection and to the enjoyment of that right without discrimination on the basis of disability, and shall take appropriate steps to safeguard and promote the realization of this right, including measures:

(a) To ensure equal access by persons with disabilities to clean water services, and to ensure access to appropriate and affordable services, devices and other assistance for disability-related needs;

(b) To ensure access by persons with disabilities, in particular women and girls with disabilities and older persons with disabilities, to social protection programmes and poverty reduction programmes;

(c) To ensure access by persons with disabilities and their families living in situations of poverty to assistance from the State with disability-related expenses, including adequate training, counselling, financial assistance and respite care;

(d) To ensure access by persons with disabilities to public housing programmes;

(e) To ensure equal access by persons with disabilities to retirement benefits and programmes.

Article 29   Participation in political and public life

States Parties shall guarantee to persons with disabilities political rights and the opportunity to enjoy them on an equal basis with others, and shall undertake:

(a) To ensure that persons with disabilities can effectively and fully participate in political and public life on an equal basis with others, directly or through freely chosen representatives, including the right and opportunity for persons with disabilities to vote and be elected, inter alia, by:

(i) Ensuring that voting procedures, facilities and materials are appropriate, accessible and easy to understand and use;

(ii) Protecting the right of persons with disabilities to vote by secret ballot in elections and public referendums without intimidation, and to stand for elections, to effectively hold office and perform all public functions at all levels of government, facilitating the use of assistive and new technologies where appropriate;

(iii) Guaranteeing the free expression of the will of persons with disabilities as electors and to this end, where necessary, at their request, allowing assistance in voting by a person of their own choice;

(b) To promote actively an environment in which persons with disabilities can effectively and fully participate in the conduct of public affairs, without discrimination and on an equal basis with others, and encourage their participation in public affairs, including:

(i) Participation in non-governmental organizations and associations concerned with the public and political life of the country, and in the activities and administration of political parties;

(ii) Forming and joining organizations of persons with disabilities to represent persons with disabilities at international, national, regional and local levels.

Article 30 Participation in cultural life, recreation, leisure and sport

1. States Parties recognize the right of persons with disabilities to take part on an equal basis with others in cultural life, and shall take all appropriate measures to ensure that persons with disabilities:

(a) Enjoy access to cultural materials in accessible formats;

(b) Enjoy access to television programmes, films, theatre and other cultural activities, in accessible formats;

(c) Enjoy access to places for cultural performances or services, such as theatres, museums, cinemas, libraries and tourism services, and, as far as possible, enjoy access to monuments and sites of national cultural importance.

2. States Parties shall take appropriate measures to enable persons with disabilities to have the opportunity to develop and utilize their creative, artistic and intellectual potential, not only for their own benefit, but also for the enrichment of society.

3. States Parties shall take all appropriate steps, in accordance with international law, to ensure that laws protecting intellectual property rights do not constitute an unreasonable or discriminatory barrier to access by persons with disabilities to cultural materials.

4. Persons with disabilities shall be entitled, on an equal basis with others, to recognition and support of their specific cultural and linguistic identity, including sign languages and deaf culture.

5. With a view to enabling persons with disabilities to participate on an equal basis with others in recreational, leisure and sporting activities, States Parties shall take appropriate measures:

(a) To encourage and promote the participation, to the fullest extent possible, of persons with disabilities in mainstream sporting activities at all levels;

(b) To ensure that persons with disabilities have an opportunity to organize, develop and participate in disability-specific sporting and recreational activities and, to this end, encourage the provision, on an equal basis with others, of appropriate instruction, training and resources;

(c) To ensure that persons with disabilities have access to sporting, recreational and tourism venues;

(d) To ensure that children with disabilities have equal access with other children to participation in play, recreation and leisure and sporting activities, including those activities in the school system;

(e) To ensure that persons with disabilities have access to services from those involved in the organization of recreational, tourism, leisure and sporting activities.

Article 31   Statistics and data collection

1. States Parties undertake to collect appropriate information, including statistical and research data, to enable them to formulate and implement policies to give effect to the present Convention. The process of collecting and maintaining this information shall:

(a) Comply with legally established safeguards, including legislation on data protection, to ensure confidentiality and respect for the privacy of persons with disabilities;

(b) Comply with internationally accepted norms to protect human rights and fundamental freedoms and ethical principles in the collection and use of statistics.

2. The information collected in accordance with this article shall be disaggregated, as appropriate, and used to help assess the implementation of States Parties' obligations under the present Convention and to identify and address the barriers faced by persons with disabilities in exercising their rights.

3. States Parties shall assume responsibility for the dissemination of these statistics and ensure their accessibility to persons with disabilities and others.

Article 32   International cooperation

1. States Parties recognize the importance of international cooperation and its promotion, in support of national efforts for the realization of the purpose and objectives of the present Convention, and will undertake appropriate and effective measures in this regard, between and among States and, as appropriate, in partnership with relevant international and regional organizations and civil society, in particular organizations of persons with disabilities. Such measures could include, inter alia:

(a) Ensuring that international cooperation, including international development programmes, is inclusive of and accessible to persons with disabilities;

(b) Facilitating and supporting capacity-building, including through the exchange and sharing of information, experiences, training programmes and best practices;

(c) Facilitating cooperation in research and access to scientific and technical knowledge;

(*d*) Providing, as appropriate, technical and economic assistance, including by facilitating access to and sharing of accessible and assistive technologies, and through the transfer of technologies.

2. The provisions of this article are without prejudice to the obligations of each State Party to fulfil its obligations under the present Convention.

Article 33 National implementation and monitoring

1. States Parties, in accordance with their system of organization, shall designate one or more focal points within government for matters relating to the implementation of the present Convention, and shall give due consideration to the establishment or designation of a coordination mechanism within government to facilitate related action in different sectors and at different levels.

2. States Parties shall, in accordance with their legal and administrative systems, maintain, strengthen, designate or establish within the State Party, a framework, including one or more independent mechanisms, as appropriate, to promote, protect and monitor implementation of the present Convention. When designating or establishing such a mechanism, States Parties shall take into account the principles relating to the status and functioning of national institutions for protection and promotion of human rights.

3. Civil society, in particular persons with disabilities and their representative organizations, shall be involved and participate fully in the monitoring process.

Article 34 Committee on the Rights of Persons with Disabilities

1. There shall be established a Committee on the Rights of Persons with Disabilities (hereafter referred to as "the Committee"), which shall carry out the functions hereinafter provided.

2. The Committee shall consist, at the time of entry into force of the present Convention, of twelve experts. After an additional sixty ratifications or accessions to the Convention, the membership of the Committee shall increase by six members, attaining a maximum number of eighteen members.

3. The members of the Committee shall serve in their personal capacity and shall be of high moral standing and recognized competence and experience in the field covered by the present Convention. When nominating their candidates, States Parties are invited to give due consideration to the provision set out in article 4, paragraph 3, of the present Convention.

4. The members of the Committee shall be elected by States Parties, consideration being given to equitable geographical distribution, representation of the different forms of civilization and of the principal legal systems, balanced gender representation and participation of experts with disabilities.

5. The members of the Committee shall be elected by secret ballot from a list of persons nominated by the States Parties from among their nationals at meetings of the Conference of States Parties. At those meetings, for which two thirds of States Parties shall constitute a quorum, the persons elected to the Committee shall be those who obtain the largest number of votes and an absolute majority of the votes

of the representatives of States Parties present and voting.

6. The initial election shall be held no later than six months after the date of entry into force of the present Convention. At least four months before the date of each election, the Secretary-General of the United Nations shall address a letter to the States Parties inviting them to submit the nominations within two months. The Secretary-General shall subsequently prepare a list in alphabetical order of all persons thus nominated, indicating the State Parties which have nominated them, and shall submit it to the States Parties to the present Convention.

7. The members of the Committee shall be elected for a term of four years. They shall be eligible for re-election once. However, the term of six of the members elected at the first election shall expire at the end of two years; immediately after the first election, the names of these six members shall be chosen by lot by the chairperson of the meeting referred to in paragraph 5 of this article.

8. The election of the six additional members of the Committee shall be held on the occasion of regular elections, in accordance with the relevant provisions of this article.

9. If a member of the Committee dies or resigns or declares that for any other cause she or he can no longer perform her or his duties, the State Party which nominated the member shall appoint another expert possessing the qualifications and meeting the requirements set out in the relevant provisions of this article, to serve for the remainder of the term.

10. The Committee shall establish its own rules of procedure.

11. The Secretary-General of the United Nations shall provide the necessary staff and facilities for the effective performance of the functions of the Committee under the present Convention, and shall convene its initial meeting.

12. With the approval of the General Assembly of the United Nations, the members of the Committee established under the present Convention shall receive emoluments from United Nations resources on such terms and conditions as the Assembly may decide, having regard to the importance of the Committee's responsibilities.

13. The members of the Committee shall be entitled to the facilities, privileges and immunities of experts on mission for the United Nations as laid down in the relevant sections of the Convention on the Privileges and Immunities of the United Nations.

Article 35   Reports by States Parties

1. Each State Party shall submit to the Committee, through the Secretary-General of the United Nations, a comprehensive report on measures taken to give effect to its obligations under the present Convention and on the progress made in that regard, within two years after the entry into force of the present Convention for the State Party concerned.

2. Thereafter, States Parties shall submit subsequent reports at least every four years and further whenever the Committee so requests.

3. The Committee shall decide any guidelines applicable to the content of the reports.

4. A State Party which has submitted a comprehensive initial report to the Committee need not, in its subsequent reports, repeat information previously provided. When preparing reports to the Committee, States Parties are invited to consider doing so in an open and transparent process and to give due consideration to the provision set out in article 4, paragraph 3, of the present Convention.

5. Reports may indicate factors and difficulties affecting the degree of fulfilment of obligations under the present Convention.

Article 36 Consideration of reports

1. Each report shall be considered by the Committee, which shall make such suggestions and general recommendations on the report as it may consider appropriate and shall forward these to the State Party concerned. The State Party may respond with any information it chooses to the Committee. The Committee may request further information from States Parties relevant to the implementation of the present Convention.

2. If a State Party is significantly overdue in the submission of a report, the Committee may notify the State Party concerned of the need to examine the implementation of the present Convention in that State Party, on the basis of reliable information available to the Committee, if the relevant report is not submitted within three months following the notification. The Committee shall invite the State Party concerned to participate in such examination. Should the State Party respond by submitting the relevant report, the provisions of paragraph 1 of this article will apply.

3. The Secretary-General of the United Nations shall make available the reports to all States Parties.

4. States Parties shall make their reports widely available to the public in their own countries and facilitate access to the suggestions and general recommendations relating to these reports.

5. The Committee shall transmit, as it may consider appropriate, to the specialized agencies, funds and programmes of the United Nations, and other competent bodies, reports from States Parties in order to address a request or indication of a need for technical advice or assistance contained therein, along with the Committee's observations and recommendations, if any, on these requests or indications.

Article 37 Cooperation between States Parties and the Committee

1. Each State Party shall cooperate with the Committee and assist its members in the fulfilment of their mandate.

2. In its relationship with States Parties, the Committee shall give due consideration to ways and means of enhancing national capacities for the implementation of the present Convention, including through international cooperation.

Article 38   Relationship of the Committee with other bodies

In order to foster the effective implementation of the present Convention and to encourage international cooperation in the field covered by the present Convention:

(*a*) The specialized agencies and other United Nations organs shall be entitled to be represented at the consideration of the implementation of such provisions of the present Convention as fall within the scope of their mandate. The Committee may invite the specialized agencies and other competent bodies as it may consider appropriate to provide expert advice on the implementation of the Convention in areas falling within the scope of their respective mandates. The Committee may invite specialized agencies and other United Nations organs to submit reports on the implementation of the Convention in areas falling within the scope of their activities;

(*b*) The Committee, as it discharges its mandate, shall consult, as appropriate, other relevant bodies instituted by international human rights treaties, with a view to ensuring the consistency of their respective reporting guidelines, suggestions and general recommendations, and avoiding duplication and overlap in the performance of their functions.

Article 39   Report of the Committee

The Committee shall report every two years to the General Assembly and to the Economic and Social Council on its activities, and may make suggestions and general recommendations based on the examination of reports and information received from the States Parties. Such suggestions and general recommendations shall be included in the report of the Committee together with comments, if any, from States Parties.

Article 40   Conference of States Parties

1. The States Parties shall meet regularly in a Conference of States Parties in order to consider any matter with regard to the implementation of the present Convention.

2. No later than six months after the entry into force of the present Convention, the Conference of States Parties shall be convened by the Secretary-General of the United Nations. The subsequent meetings shall be convened by the Secretary-General biennially or upon the decision of the Conference of States Parties.

Article 41   Depositary

The Secretary-General of the United Nations shall be the depositary of the present Convention.

Article 42   Signature

The present Convention shall be open for signature by all States and by regional integration organizations at United Nations Headquarters in New York as of 30 March 2007.

Article 43   Consent to be bound

The present Convention shall be subject to ratification by signatory States and to formal confirmation by signatory regional integration organizations. It shall be open for accession by any State or regional integration organization which has not signed the Convention.

Article 44 Regional integration organizations

1. "Regional integration organization" shall mean an organization constituted by sovereign States of a given region, to which its member States have transferred competence in respect of matters governed by the present Convention. Such organizations shall declare, in their instruments of formal confirmation or accession, the extent of their competence with respect to matters governed by the present Convention. Subsequently, they shall inform the depositary of any substantial modification in the extent of their competence.

2. References to "States Parties" in the present Convention shall apply to such organizations within the limits of their competence.

3. For the purposes of article 45, paragraph 1, and article 47, paragraphs 2 and 3, of the present Convention, any instrument deposited by a regional integration organization shall not be counted.

4. Regional integration organizations, in matters within their competence, may exercise their right to vote in the Conference of States Parties, with a number of votes equal to the number of their member States that are Parties to the present Convention. Such an organization shall not exercise its right to vote if any of its member States exercises its right, and vice versa.

Article 45 Entry into force

1. The present Convention shall enter into force on the thirtieth day after the deposit of the twentieth instrument of ratification or accession.

2. For each State or regional integration organization ratifying, formally confirming or acceding to the present Convention after the deposit of the twentieth such instrument, the Convention shall enter into force on the thirtieth day after the deposit of its own such instrument.

Article 46 Reservations

1. Reservations incompatible with the object and purpose of the present Convention shall not be permitted.

2. Reservations may be withdrawn at any time.

Article 47 Amendments

1. Any State Party may propose an amendment to the present Convention and submit it to the Secretary-General of the United Nations. The Secretary-General shall communicate any proposed amendments to States Parties, with a request to be notified whether they favour a conference of States Parties for the purpose of considering and deciding upon the proposals. In the event that, within four months from the date of such communication, at least one third of the States Parties favour such a conference, the Secretary-General shall convene the conference under the auspices of the United Nations. Any amendment adopted by a majority of two thirds

of the States Parties present and voting shall be submitted by the Secretary-General to the General Assembly of the United Nations for approval and thereafter to all States Parties for acceptance.

2. An amendment adopted and approved in accordance with paragraph 1 of this article shall enter into force on the thirtieth day after the number of instruments of acceptance deposited reaches two thirds of the number of States Parties at the date of adoption of the amendment. Thereafter, the amendment shall enter into force for any State Party on the thirtieth day following the deposit of its own instrument of acceptance. An amendment shall be binding only on those States Parties which have accepted it.

3. If so decided by the Conference of States Parties by consensus, an amendment adopted and approved in accordance with paragraph 1 of this article which relates exclusively to articles 34, 38, 39 and 40 shall enter into force for all States Parties on the thirtieth day after the number of instruments of acceptance deposited reaches two thirds of the number of States Parties at the date of adoption of the amendment.

Article 48   Denunciation

A State Party may denounce the present Convention by written notification to the Secretary-General of the United Nations. The denunciation shall become effective one year after the date of receipt of the notification by the Secretary-General.

Article 49   Accessible format

The text of the present Convention shall be made available in accessible formats.

Article 50   Authentic texts

The Arabic, Chinese, English, French, Russian and Spanish texts of the present Convention shall be equally authentic.

IN WITNESS THEREOF the undersigned plenipotentiaries, being duly authorized thereto by their respective Governments, have signed the present Convention.

ANNEX II
Optional Protocol to the Convention on the Rights of Persons with Disabilities

The States Parties to the present Protocol have agreed as follows:

Article 1

1. A State Party to the present Protocol ("State Party") recognizes the competence of the Committee on the Rights of Persons with Disabilities ("the Committee") to receive and consider communications from or on behalf of individuals or groups of individuals subject to its jurisdiction who claim to be victims of a violation by that State Party of the provisions of the Convention.

2. No communication shall be received by the Committee if it concerns a State Party to the Convention that is not a party to the present Protocol.

Article 2

The Committee shall consider a communication inadmissible when:

(*a*) The communication is anonymous;

(*b*) The communication constitutes an abuse of the right of submission of such communications or is incompatible with the provisions of the Convention;

(*c*) The same matter has already been examined by the Committee or has been or is being examined under another procedure of international investigation or settlement;

(*d*) All available domestic remedies have not been exhausted. This shall not be the rule where the application of the remedies is unreasonably prolonged or unlikely to bring effective relief;

(*e*) It is manifestly ill-founded or not sufficiently substantiated; or when

(*f*) The facts that are the subject of the communication occurred prior to the entry into force of the present Protocol for the State Party concerned unless those facts continued after that date.

Article 3

Subject to the provisions of article 2 of the present Protocol, the Committee shall bring any communications submitted to it confidentially to the attention of the State Party. Within six months, the receiving State shall submit to the Committee written explanations or statements clarifying the matter and the remedy, if any, that may have been taken by that State.

Article 4

1. At any time after the receipt of a communication and before a determination on the merits has been reached, the Committee may transmit to the State Party concerned for its urgent consideration a request that the State Party take such interim measures as may be necessary to avoid possible irreparable damage to the victim or victims of the alleged violation.

2. Where the Committee exercises its discretion under paragraph 1 of this article, this does not imply a determination on admissibility or on the merits of the communication.

Article 5

The Committee shall hold closed meetings when examining communications under the present Protocol. After examining a communication, the Committee shall forward its suggestions and recommendations, if any, to the State Party concerned and to the petitioner.

Article 6

1. If the Committee receives reliable information indicating grave or systematic violations by a State Party of rights set forth in the Convention, the Committee shall invite that State Party to cooperate in the examination of the information and to this end submit observations with regard to the information concerned.

2. Taking into account any observations that may have been submitted by the State Party concerned as well as any other reliable information available to it, the Committee may designate one or more of its members to conduct an inquiry and to report urgently to the Committee. Where warranted and with the consent of the State Party, the inquiry may include a visit to its territory.

3. After examining the findings of such an inquiry, the Committee shall transmit these findings to the State Party concerned together with any comments and recommendations.

4. The State Party concerned shall, within six months of receiving the findings, comments and recommendations transmitted by the Committee, submit its observations to the Committee.

5. Such an inquiry shall be conducted confidentially and the cooperation of the State Party shall be sought at all stages of the proceedings.

Article 7

1. The Committee may invite the State Party concerned to include in its report under article 35 of the Convention details of any measures taken in response to an inquiry conducted under article 6 of the present Protocol.

2. The Committee may, if necessary, after the end of the period of six months referred to in article 6, paragraph 4, invite the State Party concerned to inform it of the measures taken in response to such an inquiry.

Article 8

Each State Party may, at the time of signature or ratification of the present Protocol or accession thereto, declare that it does not recognize the competence of the Committee provided for in articles 6 and 7.

Article 9

The Secretary-General of the United Nations shall be the depositary of the present Protocol.

Article 10

The present Protocol shall be open for signature by signatory States and regional integration organizations of the Convention at United Nations Headquarters in New York as of 30 March 2007.

Article 11

The present Protocol shall be subject to ratification by signatory States of the present Protocol which have ratified or acceded to the Convention. It shall be subject to formal confirmation by signatory regional integration organizations of the present Protocol which have formally confirmed or acceded to the Convention. It shall be open for accession by any State or regional integration organization which has ratified, formally confirmed or acceded to the Convention and which has not signed the Protocol.

Article 12

1. "Regional integration organization" shall mean an organization constituted by sovereign States of a given region, to which its member States have transferred competence in respect of matters governed by the Convention and the present Protocol. Such organizations shall declare, in their instruments of formal confirmation or accession, the extent of their competence with respect to matters governed by the Convention and the present Protocol. Subsequently, they shall inform the depositary of any substantial modification in the extent of their competence.

2. References to "States Parties" in the present Protocol shall apply to such organizations within the limits of their competence.

3. For the purposes of article 13, paragraph 1, and article 15, paragraph 2, of the present Protocol, any instrument deposited by a regional integration organization shall not be counted.

4. Regional integration organizations, in matters within their competence, may exercise their right to vote in the meeting of States Parties, with a number of votes equal to the number of their member States that are Parties to the present Protocol. Such an organization shall not exercise its right to vote if any of its member States exercises its right, and vice versa.

Article 13

1. Subject to the entry into force of the Convention, the present Protocol shall enter into force on the thirtieth day after the deposit of the tenth instrument of ratification or accession.

2. For each State or regional integration organization ratifying, formally confirming or acceding to the present Protocol after the deposit of the tenth such instrument, the Protocol shall enter into force on the thirtieth day after the deposit of its own such instrument.

Article 14

1. Reservations incompatible with the object and purpose of the present Protocol shall not be permitted.

2. Reservations may be withdrawn at any time.

Article 15

1. Any State Party may propose an amendment to the present Protocol and submit it to the Secretary-General of the United Nations. The Secretary-General shall communicate any proposed amendments to States Parties, with a request to be notified whether they favour a meeting of States Parties for the purpose of considering and deciding upon the proposals. In the event that, within four months from the date of such communication, at least one third of the States Parties favour such a meeting, the Secretary-General shall convene the meeting under the auspices of the United Nations. Any amendment adopted by a majority of two thirds of the States Parties present and voting shall be submitted by the Secretary-General to the General Assembly of the United Nations for approval and thereafter to all States Parties for acceptance.

2. An amendment adopted and approved in accordance with paragraph 1 of this

article shall enter into force on the thirtieth day after the number of instruments of acceptance deposited reaches two thirds of the number of States Parties at the date of adoption of the amendment. Thereafter, the amendment shall enter into force for any State Party on the thirtieth day following the deposit of its own instrument of acceptance. An amendment shall be binding only on those States Parties which have accepted it.

Article 16

A State Party may denounce the present Protocol by written notification to the Secretary-General of the United Nations. The denunciation shall become effective one year after the date of receipt of the notification by the Secretary-General.

Article 17

The text of the present Protocol shall be made available in accessible formats.

Article 18

The Arabic, Chinese, English, French, Russian and Spanish texts of the present Protocol shall be equally authentic.

IN WITNESS THEREOF the undersigned plenipotentiaries, being duly authorized thereto by their respective Governments, have signed the present Protocol.